The Boeing KC-135 Stratotanker

To
Lieutenant Colonel Robert S 'Hop' Hopkins,
USAF, Retired

The Boeing KC-135 Stratotanker
More than a Tanker

Robert S Hopkins III

www.crecy.co.uk

Crécy Publishing Ltd

www.crecy.co.uk

First published in 1997 by Midland Publishing Ltd
Fully revised and updated in 2017
by Crécy Publishing Ltd
Copyright © Robert S Hopkins III 1997 and 2017

Layout by Russell Strong

A CIP record for this book is available from the British Library

ISBN 9781910 809013

Printed in Slovenia by GPS Print

Crécy Publishing Limited
1a Ringway Trading Estate, Shadowmoss Road, Manchester
M22 5LH

www.crecy.co.uk

Front cover: After more than 60 years of operations, the KC-135 is finally
entering the sunset of its career, with final retirement slated for 2040.
Photo by Nigel Blake

Rear cover, top: Reconnaissance '135s collect a wide variety of intelligence
in support of national policies, such as this RC-135S after a mission to
assess foreign missile capabilities. *Photo by the author*

Rear cover, middle: The SR-71 pilot was almost certainly farther forward
beneath the KC-135 than any other receiver, and every mission depended
on the fleet of KC-135Qs. *Photo by Dave Brown*

Rear cover, bottom: This KC-135R from Malmstrom AFB, MT, shows the
high visibility scheme which was soon replaced with the 'Shamu' dark grey
and later overall grey. *Photo by Brian Rogers*

Front flap, top: Although orange conspicuity markings added a splash of
color to an all-silver airplane, they quickly faded and proved difficult to
maintain. *Photo by Stephen Miller*

Rear flap, bottom: The author encountered his first '135 in April 1968, in
this case KC-135Q 58-0103. *Photo by Major Robert 'Hop' Hopkins*

Half title page: Alert always seemed synonymous with cold, northern tier
bases. AMC inherited these bases, alert went away, but the snow and cold
did not. *Photo by Jim Benson*

Title page: KC-135s have been based at RAF Mildenhall for more than
40 years, an association slated to end as they relocate to Germany.
Photo by Richard Vandervord

Contents

Foreword

On the morning of 17th December 1903 at Kitty Hawk, NC, Orville Wright conducted the first pilot-controlled take-off, flight and landing of a heavier-than-air flying machine. That historic flight, today's high performance aircraft, and, yes, the super flight vehicles of the future, was and will continue to be the product of man's infinite desires and technical achievements.

In May 1941, the whine of English engineer Sir Frank Whittle's gas turbine engine served as the *coup de grâce* for internal combustion engines in high performance aircraft. Shortly thereafter, under a Top Secret government contract, Bell Aircraft Corporation built and flight tested the first jet propelled aircraft in the US. The XP-59 Airacomet was a twin-jet, straight wing, single-seat fighter operational to 43,000ft (13,106m) altitude. The handling characteristics of the aircraft were satisfactory and the high altitude performance was phenomenal, introducing the industry to heretofore unknown high altitude and high speed problems. Due to the high operating temperatures and the absence of heat resistant materials, for example, the total engine life expectancy was a mere five hours.

The National Advisory Council for Aeronautics (NACA, later NASA) possessed captured German high-speed wind tunnel data which showed that a 35° swept wing provided superior high speed performance but had unacceptable low speed stall characteristics. Bell negotiated a contract with NACA to modify a conventional fighter, a P-63 Kingcobra, into the 35° swept wing configuration Model L-39 and conduct low speed and stall investigation. A series of flight tests utilizing various wing leading edge slat configurations and positions produced a configuration which solved the low speed problem, allowing the industry to utilize the benefits of the 35° swept wing.

With the increasing jet fighter and B-47 Stratojet inventory, the military identified a need for in-flight refueling. Early in-flight refueling utilized a 'probe and drogue' system, requiring the fighter to overtake the drogue receptacle with the refueling probe of the fighter, a difficult procedure, particularly in rough air. Recognizing this increasing requirement for stable and reliable in-flight refueling, Boeing designed, built, and perfected a 'flying boom' refueling system on the tail section of a KC-97 Stratofreighter. Refueling with the boom system proved superior to the drogue system and was much preferred by receiver pilots.

The growing number of fighters and B-47 bombers plus the rapidly approaching arrival of the eight-engine high altitude B-52 emphasized the requirement for tanker aircraft with jet-compatible speed and high altitude performance, as the low speed and low altitude refueling dictated by the KC-97 were both extremely inconvenient and costly.

The B-47 and B-52 prototype flight experience and performance numbers (plus the British decision to proceed with the DH Comet jet transport) convinced Boeing management that the future lay with military and commercial jet aircraft. In mid April 1952, the Board of Directors allocated $16 million to develop, construct, test, and demonstrate a prototype Boeing Model 707 jet transport, drawing number 367-80. The Dash 80's initial flight on 15th July 1954 demonstrated satisfactory flight characteristics and equipment operation. Previous technical experience with the design and development of the B-47 and B-52 was a significant factor in the design and success of the Dash 80.

The test program involving stability and control, performance, flutter and structural testing proceeded on schedule, and flight demonstrations to military and airline officials were frequent. On 16th October 1955, with Mr William Allen, Boeing President, and prominent industry officials aboard, we departed Seattle in the Dash 80 and landed at Andrews AFB, MD, three hours, 48 minutes later for an average speed of 595mph (957km/h). Following a briefing of the assembled dignitaries and press we returned to Seattle in four hours, eight minutes. The record speed, absence of cabin noise and vibration plus passenger comfort demonstrated the utility of the jet transport.

Numerous Dash 80 simulated refueling flights with B-47s and B-52s at mission altitude proved the KC-135 concept and mission capability. The KC-135 aircraft is a prime example of the advancing technical state of the art of aircraft propulsion units, lightweight materials, structural design and aerodynamic improvement. It is also an example of the technical foresight and financial commitment by Corporate America, in this case the Boeing Company. The Dash 80 prototype jet tanker and commercial transport provided the military with no-cost flight test performance data, flight crew familiarization and in-flight refueling simulation and mission validation at operational altitudes.

The coordinated efforts of the United States government, technical consultants, industry manufacturing and testing organizations, institutions of higher learning and the respective military organizations have produced the most advanced aircraft in speed, range, altitude, mission capability, and reliability, in the 51 years of powered flight since that historical day at Kitty Hawk.

A M 'Tex' Johnston
former Chief Test Pilot, Boeing
Seattle, Washington

No one did more to sell KC-135s and 707s than 'Tex' Johnston (l), seen here with fellow Boeing test pilot Elliott Merrill (r). From the 'Gold Cup Roll' in the Dash 80, to the KC-135 first flight, to flight tests and demonstration flights, to the final flight of the Dash 80, 'Tex' is synonymous with the KC-135. *Photo B10956 courtesy Boeing*

Preface

As a former Commander-in-Chief of Strategic Air Command, I appreciate a good book about a warplane that has been vital to SAC's mission for over 30 years. On 28th June 1957, SAC took delivery of its first KC-135 all-jet tanker. On 12th January 1965, the last KC-135 was delivered, giving SAC a total of 641, the largest tanker fleet in the world.

This book is about that warplane. The Boeing KC-135 and its variants have been workhorses of the jet age. Over the years our KC-135 tankers have amassed in excess of 4.5 million hours of flying time. They undertook continuous support of operations in Vietnam from June 1964 to August 1973, flying 195,000 sorties, providing over 800,000 aerial refuelings, and transferring a total of nine billion pounds of fuel. As many as 172 KC-135s were committed to operations in Southeast Asia.

The KC-135 is still going strong. With ongoing modernization programs such as re-engining with quiet, fuel efficient, and powerful engines, airframe reskinning, and new fuel management systems, the KC-135 will be flying well into the 21st century.

This book is also about the concept of aerial refueling – the mating and transfer of fuel between two aircraft, in flight, and at all altitudes. The concept had a 'daredevil' beginning in 1921, when an American, with a five-gallon can of aviation gasoline strapped to his back, climbed from the wing of one biplane to the wing of another and poured the gasoline into the fuel tank. But it was the KC-135 with its speed, endurance, and high volume fuel transfer methods which gave our bomber, fighter, reconnaissance, and airlift aircraft their truly global capabilities.

Recently, for example, tankers were indispensable in the support of US air strikes against Libya. Strike aircraft flying from England were denied overflight rights by France, Spain, and Portugal. This forced a 2,800nm (5,188km) circuitous route south from England along the European Atlantic coast and through the Strait of Gibraltar to the Libyan coast. Strike aircraft received eight refuelings – four pre-strike and four post-strike. The composite force of 19 McDonnell Douglas KC-10 Extenders and ten KC-135s made this successful mission possible.

Finally, this book is about those unsung heroes, the men (and now the women) who crew SAC's tanker force and contribute daily to the success of SAC's mission – deterrence. One of my predecessors as CINCSAC, General Curtis LeMay, said it best: 'Tanker guys have not received the great credit they deserve; they are always there when you need them.'

During the war in Southeast Asia, KC-135 crews accomplished many remarkable feats of airmanship. For example, on 3rd May 1967 two Republic F-105 Thunderchiefs, returning from a mission over

CINCSAC General John T 'Jack' Chain serves as the AEAO on LOOKING GLASS EC-135C 63-8054. Chain was the AEAO on the final continuously airborne 'Glass' mission on 24th July 1990 in EC-135C 63-8046. *Photo via Joe Bruch (l)*

North Vietnam and flying protective cover for a downed airman found themselves without enough fuel to land in friendly territory. With stormy weather in the refueling area and an unusual number of airborne emergencies preventing them from reaching standby tankers, they radioed for any tanker assistance they could get. Major Alvin L Lewis and his KC-135 crew, monitoring the situation while in another refueling area, managed to keep track of the F-105s and arrived just as one fighter pilot was about to eject. To effect a hook-up, Major Lewis had to maneuver the KC-135 into a dive while turning in front of the F-105 just as it was about to flame out for the lack of fuel. His actions saved two pilots and their airplanes.

Bob Hopkins provides valuable insight into the history of aerial refueling, the KC-135, and the people who made it so effective. The book also provides an in-depth look at a number of tanker variants, such as the RC-135 reconnaissance versions and the EC-135 airborne command and control airplanes, like the famous LOOKING GLASS that has maintained continuous airborne alert in protection of the United States since 1961.

I've flown tankers; I know and understand their mission and I'm proud to have been the Commander of the warplanes and warriors of our KC/EC/RC and C-135 fleet.

General John T Chain, Jr,
former Commander-in-Chief, Strategic Air Command
Offutt AFB, Nebraska

Author's Notes

'Writing a book was an adventure.
To begin with it was a toy, an amusement;
then it became a mistress, and then a master, and then a tyrant.'
– *Sir Winston S Churchill*

I first flew a KC-135 in 1985, about the same time I began collecting material on the airplane and its many variants. Over the next six years, I added a long list of different types of KCs, ECs, TCs, and RCs to my pilot's logbook. I also added a long list of material to this manuscript. Just as I have closed out my flying career in this timeless airplane, it now seems appropriate to finish this endless book. As Thomas Jefferson wrote upon the release in 1787 of his only book, six years after 'finishing' it:

'To apologize for this by developing the circumstances of the time and place of [its] composition, would be to open wounds which have already bled enough. To these circumstances some of [the book's] imperfections may with truth be ascribed; the great mass to the want of information and want of talents in the writer. (*Notes on the State of Virginia*, London, Stockdale, 1787), in the reprint ed. Merrill D Peterson, *The Portable Thomas Jefferson* (New York, Penguin Books, 1977.)

There has been much to include, and, sadly, much to exclude from these pages. Limited by space, I found it necessary to omit events, programs, descriptions, photographs, and details desired by a variety of audiences ranging from aviation historians to KC-135 crewmembers to model builders. Although the material included here does much to fill the considerable void in references on the KC-135, it still leaves many questions unanswered and many paths of inquiry unfollowed. Perhaps as more information is declassified or otherwise becomes available, other historians will take up the challenge.

As this book was first readied, Iraq invaded Kuwait. The months that followed validated the essential nature of the KC-135 and its variants in the projection and prosecution of US and Allied military power. Since then the US Air Force has undertaken sweeping organizational changes and force structure alterations that have drastically altered the number and type of KC-135s, who operates them, and the conduct of their missions. A large number of KC-135As and other variants have been retired. Most importantly, the end of the Cold War has compelled a substantial reconsideration of the future of KC-135s in particular and strategic airpower in general.

Acknowledgements

I am indebted to the army of historians and photographers who made this book possible. In many cases, these people participated in the KC-135 epic. Karl Johnson spoke with fondness as one of the first KC-135 boom operators. Alton E Chamberlin, was 'present at the creation' of the RC-135A and opened the floodgates on the history of the photo–mapping program. William Gibbons also shared his considerable experiences with the RC-135A. Together their records and first-hand accounts represent the most accurate history to date of this little-known program. Oscar E Niebes recounted his 20 years of experience with test-bed KC-135s at Wright-Patterson AFB. This is, in part, their story, and they are best qualified to tell it.

I received countless photographs and material from Joe Algranti, Robert D Archer, Robert J Archer, Russ Barber, Dana Bell, Jim Benson, Patrick Bigel, Steve Bond, Oscar Bonnefoy, John Bowdler, Paul Brown, Bill Burr, Mark Cain, Tony Cassanova, John Coon, Steve Edwards, René Francillon, Mike Franczek, Jerry Fugere, John Gaffney, John Gourley, Mike Habermehl, Dick Hallion, Chuck Hansen, Jeff Harper, Paul Hart, Tom Hildreth, Terry Horstead, Pete Hurd, Marty Isham, Christian Jacquet, Tom Kaminski, Dave Lavery, Robert Lawson, Don Logan, Eric Le Gendre, Jim Oberg, Dave Menard, Paul Minert, Robert Moitessier, Walton Moody, Rick Morgan, William Norton, Terry Panopalis, John Phaler, Jay Porter, Dana Potts, Mike Quan, Fred Quinn, Jeff Rankin-Lowe, Yves Richard, Arnold Swanberg, Martyn Swann, Norm Taylor, the late Jon Von Gohren, Dominique Vivier, and Nate Wilds.

Archivists who worked 'above and beyond' include Stephen Allard of the *Omaha World-Herald*, Tom Brewer at the Air Force Museum, Andrew S Burrows, formerly of the Natural Resources Defense Council, Dr Robert Duffner of the Air Force Special Weapons Center, Wanda Odom of the National Aeronautics Association, Anne Rutledge of the Museum of Flight, Lee Saegesser and Marty Curry of NASA, and Larry Wiggins of the *South Dade News Leader*.

Thanks to William L Ochsenwald, who first taught me how to write good history despite my stubborn efforts. Thanks also to Mel Leffler, Maria Morrison, Peter Onuf, Mark Smith, David Snead, Ilicia Sprey, and my colleagues at the University of Virginia. I doubt if the Cold War and Thomas Jefferson will ever be the same. Harold Carr, Boeing's Director of Public Affairs, introduced me to David Olson and Marilyn Phipps of Boeing's Historical Archives, who put me in touch with the people who designed, built, and tested the KC-135. George Schairer, Boeing's KC-135 Technology Director, and Joseph Sutter, Chief of Boeing's Transport Division Aerodynamics Unit during the development of the Boeing 367-80 Dash 80, 707, and KC-135, offered a paternal perspective on the origins of the KC-135. Richard L Rouzie, the KC-135 Chief Engineer, and George C Martin, former Vice President of Engineering, added their recollections on the birth and adolescence of the KC-135. Vaughn Blumenthal, B-52 Senior Aerodynamicist, discussed the B-52 bomber and the need for a jet tanker. John E Steiner, former Vice President for Corporate Development, provided memories and memorabilia, and guided me through existing 'official' histories with an open mind.

I owe this book to the persistence of Bill Peake and his original serial number list. He provided photographs, read manuscripts, sent clippings, and proofed every page of every document and chart produced for this book. Special thanks are in order to Brian Gardner for his superb research on the history of aerial refueling, which forms the body and soul of the second chapter of this book, with which I no doubt tampered too much. Dave Brown lent a critical editorial eye to the entire manuscript, and it is solely due to his efforts that the chapter on testbeds exists today. George Cockle's photographs, long distance calls to Alaska, and bottomless address book were equally helpful.

Jim Moseley argued ceaselessly (and victoriously) for the exclusion of the Boeing 707 and its derivatives from this work, rightly insisting that they are not KC-135s and, though related, should not be considered here. Jim's letters, 'phone calls, and packages of rare source materials have made this book complete. Without them this work could not stand up to any historical test.

I am especially indebted to General John T Chain, Jr, one of SAC's most notable Commanders-in-Chief for his preface to this book, and to Lieutenant Colonel George Peck, formerly of SAC Public Affairs, for his guidance and encouragement. I owe the deepest personal thanks to 'Tex' Johnston for his foreword, his contributions to this book, and most of all, for The Barrel Roll.

Readers will share in my indebtedness to those who reviewed manuscripts and opened doors long sealed in the history of reconnaissance platforms, particularly Brigadier General Regis Urschler. He championed the need for security with a tempered appreciation to tell an untold story. I am equally grateful to those who reviewed the manuscript at General Urschler's request and who shall remain nameless but not unremembered. Ted Boydston, Bill Strandberg, and Bruce Bailey contributed both photos and recollections of years of flying RC-135s, and Mike Ginn, the 6th SRW historian, helped with the early history of the recon KC-135s.

Lieutenant Colonel Brian 'Buck' Rogers offered his entire KC-135 photograph collection, as well as valuable data on the history of individual airplanes and unit updates through the end of SAC. It is an equal honor to have flown combat missions alongside this distinguished fellow officer and pilot. Joe Bruch has lent his unwavering support for this project, provided photographs and contacts, and, when appropriate, delivered a well needed head shot to bring me back to my senses.

I must thank Flight Lieutenant Phil Thomas, Royal Australian Air Force, who taught me how to fly the KC-135, and for his many post-flight briefings at the Castle AFB Officer's Club. Major Steve Clark taught me a great deal about the KC-135 that I shall never forget, as did Captain Jim Kilty, Majors Ward Anderson, Mike Frye, and Kent Lund, and Lieutenant Colonel Dave Yates. Thanks to Captain Dave Peck for being the 'best first co-pilot'. Major 'Mad Jack' Elliott deserves a medal for having to fly 20 hours with an *artiste*. Major Bill Zehner taught me all about the RC-135, and, most importantly, about being the best. Thanks for the greatest TDY ever to RODN (with Tim and Roger) and flying the 'Ball' up initial!

I owe a deep personal debt to Jay Miller, who took a big chance in helping this project get started, and after my long, prodigal wanderings, in bringing it to an end. Were it not for his photos, his files, his library, his time, his home, his hospitality, his patience, and most of all his confidence, this book would never have come to fruition. Special thanks go to Ken Ellis and all at Aerofax/Midland Publishing who enthusiastically embraced the challenge of breathing life into this monster beneath the sheets.

I must also thank those people closest to me, who, during the years of researching and preparing this manuscript seemed to be kept the farthest away. Robin's continued acceptance made this all possible, Sarah's giggles and grins got me through the darkest of times, and Michael's arrival during the Gulf War reminded me that there are things more important than 'Rivet Joint' and 'Cobra Ball'.

It is traditional in these paragraphs to pay homage to the person who spent countless hours revising the manuscript in trivial and meaningless ways. Amy has done this and more. At times her enthusiasm to finish this book has been motivated by her commitment to see it published. At other times, it has been driven by her desire to be rid of it and the grief it brings. Either way, it is done, thanks to Amy. I hope she will be as patient and understanding with me in the years to come.

I lovingly dedicate this book to a man who spent far too many hours behind KC-135s, taking on millions of pounds of fuel all over the world, often in combat. He has forgotten more about flying than I could ever hope to learn, and what he has taught me along the way has given me the strength and understanding to accept his absence during those many, many years.

Robert S Hopkins, III
Omaha, Nebraska
September 1997

Using this Book

An early goal of this book was to provide a complete and concise history of each KC-135 by tail number from delivery to current assignment or final attrition or retirement. This strictly chronological exercise proved both cumbersome and confusing given the KC-135's lengthy operational history and the multiple designations often applied to individual airplanes. Conversely, organizing this book by mission offered a more coherent overall history, with individual airframe types and tail numbers included within each mission section. The book may be read sequentially to appreciate the natural evolution of the KC-135 and its many variants and their relation to the many problems confronting the planners of strategic airpower doctrine in the Cold War years. Nonetheless, the chapters can be read in any order, although references to material from earlier chapters may be helpful.

Readers interested in the chronological history of a specific airplane need only refer to Appendix I, the KC-135 Mission-Design-Series (MDS) List, which delineates by tail number an airplane's complete mission evolution. Each MDS listed for a specific tail number may then be reviewed fully in the appropriate mission section throughout the chapters. Airplane attrition and retirement are treated in a similar manner, annotated in both the appropriate chapters and appendices. Appendix II provides a detailed summary of each loss, and Appendix III lists aircraft placed into storage or assigned to ground instructional use, museums and static displays, or scrapped. While this arrangement may require extra effort on the part of the reader seeking a complete chronological history of one particular airframe, it offers a more systematic and less redundant system of cross-referencing the Byzantine evolution of the KC-135.

The first edition of this book included detailed endnotes, omitted here to save space. Researchers may still find these in library copies or via interlibrary loan. Quoted material in this edition reflects attribution of content or ideas by other writers or sources.

The military lexicon thrives on acronyms and code names ranging from programs to operations to procedures. It is neither possible nor desirable to divorce this book completely from such usage. Readers unfamiliar with the many acronyms can find them defined in the Glossary, which follows.

Finally, unless otherwise specified, the statements and opinions in this book are exclusively those of the author and should not be construed in any fashion to represent any official opinion or policy of the United States Air Force, any agency of the government of the United States of America, or any other government or agency.

Notes to the Revised Edition

I write these notes as a passenger aboard British Airways 747-436 G-BNLN *en route* from London to Dallas some 25 years after following nearly the same course from RAF Mildenhall to Offutt AFB as the Aircraft Commander of RC-135W 62-4131 on my final flight as a '135 crewdog. Despite being a quarter century apart, these two airplanes share a similar legacy. Both were classic Boeing designs that defined a generation of air travel and air power. Both were approaching what seemed to be the end of their operational life, with expectations that in just a few years' time they would be baking in the Arizona sun while awaiting the scrapper's torch or in storage at 'the Boneyard.' Both were pressed to remain in service, however, beyond their expected lifetimes. Few imagined in 1991 that the KC-135 and its variants would not only be in front-line service today but would be programmed to fly for yet another 25 years – through 2040 – some *80 years* of operational flying.

It will fall to a future generation of aviation historians to record the final years of the KC-135 fleet. Until then this revised edition seeks to cover the many events and missions undertaken since the book's initial publication in 1997 as well as expand and revise its earlier operational history. Indeed, the declassification of large numbers of SAC histories provides a more robust story of refueling airborne nuclear alert missions as part of CHROME DOME, for example, as well as a more nuanced understanding of KC-135 operations in Southeast Asia, or a more detailed history of the evolution and operation of the Post Attack Command and Control System, particularly the airborne portion, including (but not limited to) the LOOKING GLASS. Personal recollections and the publication of the BIG SAFARI history have corrected and expanded the secret role of the many different reconnaissance and testbed variants.

Readers of the previous edition will notice similarities and differences. I have chosen to include the original Author's Notes to acknowledge the helpful efforts of the many contributors to the first edition. Moreover, 'Tex' Johnston's Foreword and General 'Jack' Chain's Preface remain. Other than editorial revisions and minor inclusions, the chapters on early air refueling and developmental history are largely unchanged. The chapter on aircraft systems has been updated to incorporate the most recent alterations to the airplane and cockpit, including the Block 45 revision. The appendices have all been updated to reflect the many changes to the fleet. Changes in

security in the post-9/11 world, however, mean that detailed information about specific fleet changes is no longer available. Whereas declassification efforts of material 50 years old are now increasingly possible, determining the date when a specific KC-135R was re-engined is now nearly impossible. Hardly a military secret, it is usually classified as 'FOUO' – For Official Use Only – rendering it well beyond reasonable access. Consequently, some recent dates are at best only approximations. Several of the images used in this edition have appeared on the World Wide Web or in dedicated aviation journals, but not all readers will have seen them in those sources.

Notable differences begin with the book's style. Enhanced readability, more color images, and additional diagrams and maps make for a richer and more accessible reference, all the result of Russell Strong's superb layout work. Each of the main chapters has been expanded to include new material without compromising earlier content. I have chosen not to explore current classified capabilities and missions, however, given their relation to ongoing combat operations. The bibliographic essay and footnotes have been removed; discursive content has been moved to the relevant chapter or appendix. The original color separations as well as black-and-white images used in the first edition have been lost in the transition from traditional to digital publishing and the sale of the original publisher to an intermediary and finally to Crécy. Many of the original prints are no longer available as several of the expansive collections (notably those of Joe Bruch and Jay Miller) have been sold to scattered buyers or become inaccessible for reasons that need not be considered here.

Since the first edition was released, several original contributors have 'Gone West'. 'Tex' Johnston, George Schairer, Vaughn Blumenthal, John Steiner, Dick Whitcomb, Doyle Larson, Robb Hoover, Peter Hurd, Chuck Hansen, Jim Moseley, Bill Peake, Robert D Archer, Bob Dorr, Al Lloyd, Norman Graebner, Kenneth Thompson, and Dick Smith were good friends. They will be missed.

Fortunately, new friends and enthusiasts have added their expertise to this revised edition. Mike Lombardi, Boeing's Corporate Historian, facilitated my research efforts in Boeing's magnificent archives (and anointed me with Ed Wells's slide rule). George Cully, Maranda Gilmore and Archie DiFante found diamonds among the coal in my

Left: As with thousands of other KC-135 crewdogs, the author's first flight in the Stratotanker was at Castle AFB, CA, in this case KC-135A 57-1432 on 4th June 1985. It became a KC-135R on 9th February 1993, and remains in service. *Photo by the author*

Opposite: For years RC-135s were regular visitors to RAF Mildenhall, where they attracted the attention of spotters and photographers throughout East Anglia. The author's final flight as an aircraft commander was in RC-135W 62-4131 on 21st March 1991 from EGUN to KOFF following DESERT STORM. *Photo by Bob Archer*

inquiries at the Air Force Historical Research Agency. Gregory Graves provided FOIA documents from the National Security Archives at George Washington University. Doug Keeney graciously shared his collection of declassified materials on SAC and nuclear history. Thanks as well to Geoff Hays at the National Museum of the US Air Force, and to Matthew Aid for his declassified sources.

Access to new material has derived not only from archives but from the kind and helpful efforts of the US Air Force Office of Public Affairs. Lieutenant Colonel Elizabeth Ortiz and Captain Son Lee at SAF/PA oversaw the initial approval to work with a variety of units. Daryl Mayer at AFMC/PA facilitated interviews with Colonel Christopher Coombs (KC-46A Program Manager) and Lynn Duncan (BIG SAFARI Program Manager and fellow Shemya alumnus). Marlin Zimmerman with the 72nd ABW/PA at Tinker AFB put together an extraordinary interview with the Legacy Tanker Team that leads thousands of passionate experts in the successful effort to keep the KC-135 flying through 2040, including Colonel Martin O'Grady (KC-135 Program Manager), William Barnes, Charles Darnell, Mahlon Smith, Theresa Farris, Mark Estorga, and Jerold Smith.

Technical Sergeant Roberto Velez of the 97th AMW pioneered the effort to retrain an old '135 pilot with a visit to the 'School House' at Altus AFB, including a flight aboard KC-135R 62-3502 and a successful session in the simulator. Thanks to Colonel Todd Hohn (97th AMW Wing Commander), Lieutenant Colonel Tharon Sperry (54th AREFS Commander), Major Colin Henderson, and the crew of Oiler 48 – Lieutenant Colonel Brent Toth, Captain Jason Lunger, Captain Peter Robinson, and Staff Sergeant Bryan Lee.

Delanie Stafford with the 55th Wing was a patient 'minder' for my interviews with the RC-135 operational squadron commanders at Offutt AFB, including Lieutenant Colonel Brian Thomas (45th RS), Lieutenant Colonel Matthew Waszak (38th RS), and Lieutenant Colonel David Murphy (343rd RS). I appreciate their sensitivity in discussing current reconnaissance operations, as well as the anonymous reviewers of the reconnaissance chapter. Thanks also to Todd Clark for his explication of the RC-135 cockpit and simulator.

General Jorge Robles, Commander-in-Chief of the Chilean Air Force, graciously oversaw my inquiries. Colonel Ronald Lüttecke and Lieutenant Celeste Aller provided images and information. Mariela Gómez Cortés kindly served as intermediary. Patrick Laureau facilitated contacts within the FACh, shared background material, photographs, and friendship.

I cannot thank Colonel Bill Grimes enough for his patient replies to my many inquiries about early reconnaissance operations. Anyone interested in the extraordinary history of the modifications and operations undertaken as part of the BIG SAFARI program should purchase his magnum opus History of Big Safari. Similarly, Senior Master Sergeant Larry Tart has thankfully opened a long-sealed window on the critical role of the Air Force Security Service (and its successors). These dedicated men and women have flown in reconnaissance KC-135s for years in near total obscurity due to excessive secrecy and security requirements. Learn more in his superb multi-volume history Freedom Through Vigilance.

Allen Johnson graciously shared his 50 years and 7,000 hours of flying experience developing airborne satellite communication systems, beginning with Curtis LeMay's Project STEER in 1959, most of which were tested and validated in C-135s 55-3129, 60-0372, and 61-2662. Major General Doug Raaberg recounted flying B-1B Bat 01 in the 1995 Mackay Trophy round-the-world mission (a 'hat tip' to Colonel Mike Frye for making the introductions). John Casteel and Mike Clover provided updates to their Mackay Trophy KC-135 flights. Dave Wilson described his many sampling flights in WC-135Bs. Greg Ogletree, Hank Carriger, and Wilton Curtis all shared their experience and knowledge of airborne command post operations. Lieutenant Colonel Kevin Sweeney recounted his crew's outstanding handling of the loss of two engines on one side during DESERT STORM.

As he did with the original edition, Dave Brown lent a sharp reader's eye to the revised chapters. His years of experience flying in the KC-135 and the many testbed EC-135s are reflected in his thoughtful comments and suggestions. No doubt he should be acknowledged in the Records section after spending his SAC career as a KC-135 navigator without ever sitting alert! Paul and Ali Crickmore were gracious hosts as I learned more about the role of '135s in the SR-71 and F-117 programs. Once again Bob Archer kindly shared his photo collection and encyclopedic knowledge of KC-135 history. Brian 'Buck' Rogers updated the unit and aircraft histories, clarified hundreds of individual airplane histories, and shared an equal number of interesting and important images. Martyn Swann provided an update on AMARG issues. Christopher J B Hoctor compared notes on aircraft attrition. David Carter clarified the tragic crash in Wichita. Thanks also to Steve Liewer at the Omaha World-Herald for his enlightening discussions of all things RC-135. Any errors which appear in this book are my own.

Stephen Miller enthusiastically shared his vast collection of aircraft images, adding both depth and breadth to the quality of this edition. Other photo and material contributors include Toshi Aoki, Michael Baldock, Rainer Baxter, Nigel Blake, Bob Burns, Tony Buttler, Wayne Button, J-C Carbonel, Ryan Dorling, Glenn Downer,

As the KC-135 begins to approach the end of its operational life, the challenge at the 'Schoolhouse' is how to combine 'glass cockpit' capability with 60-year-old airframe technology. The instructors on 54th AREFS KC-135R 62-3502 *Oiler 48* on 3rd December 2015 include IBO Staff Sergeant Bryan Lee (l), IP Lieutenant Colonel Brent Toth (c), IP Captain Jason Lunger (r) and IP Captain Peter Robinson (not pictured). *Photo by the author*

David Eyre, Manfred Faber, George Flynn, Dave Forster, Barry Fryer, Mikhail Glazyrin, Jakub Gornicki, Yongkiat Goh, Yefim Gordon, Pierre-Clément Got, Ferenc Hamori, Steve Hill/EMCS, Ken Hopkins, Paul Jeanes, Phil Jones, Josh Kaiser, Andras Kisgergely, Mark Kwiatkowski, Dave Lavery, Alan Lebeda, David Lednicer, Steve Link, Matthew Lyons, Ralf Mantueful, Ryo Matsuki, Ray McFadyen, Mark Morgan, Jacques Moulin, Wolfgang Muehlbauer, Andrey Nesvetaev, Greg Ogletree, Fernando Olivares, Terry Panopalis, Bob Parker, Bruce Radebaugh, Jim Rotramel, Ray Ruetsch, Charlie Simpson, Erez M Sirotkin, Bill Strandberg, Pieter Taris, Akira Uekawa, Luc Van Belleghem, Mark van Cuilenborg, Richard Vandervord, and Peter Vercruijsse.

I am indebted to Jeremy Pratt and Gill Richardson at Crécy for their enthusiastic support and commitment to this project. Chris Gibson converted my incoherent chicken scratchings into meaningful maps and drawings, tirelessly proofread the manuscript for errors and omissions, and provided pithy encouragement as deadlines scurried past. Despite his reticence to accept public acknowledgement of his efforts on my behalf, this revised edition would not have been possible without the support, encouragement, and hospitality of Neil Lewis. I also owe an impossible debt of gratitude to Jay Miller for a lifetime of mentoring and our Friday lunches.

Finally, thanks go to my friends, including Darrell, Scherry, and Emileigh Engelbrecht, and family for allowing me to devote time and resources to a subject which one child (who shall remain nameless) called 'almost interesting.' Robin provided a place to stay and moral support. Sarah and Mike were present at the creation of the first edition, and now Mike and Samantha share the release of this edition with the arrival of Olivia Rae. Robert, Emily, and Christopher competed for desk space, internet bandwidth, and a place to eat, play, and sleep amid the endless piles of books, manuscripts, and memorabilia stacked on the dinner table, on top of video games, and in bedrooms. Amy has my eternal gratitude for taking on the role of single parent during my absences to archives and bases around the world. Perhaps one day as 'empty nesters' I will be able to make it up to her. Until then, she has my thanks and my love. My parents – Lieutenant Colonel Robert 'Hop' and Eula Mae Hopkins – have stood behind me throughout my career as a '135 pilot and historian. Without their unstinting support none of this would have been possible. As with the first edition, this book remains dedicated to my father.

Robert S Hopkins, III
Dallas, Texas
February 2017

First Lieutenants Robert 'Hop' Hopkins (r) and Paul Benini (l) in front of F-89C 50-0782 at BW-1, Greenland, in 1956. A flying career that began with P-47s during the Second World War and ended with B-52s during the Cold War included many hours refueling behind KC-135s. *Photo courtesy Lieutenant Colonel Robert S Hopkins*

CHAPTER ONE

A Determinant of Strategy

'Thus far the chief purpose of our military establishment has been to win wars. From now on its chief purpose must be to avert them.' – *Bernard Brodie, 1945*

'The responsible military commanders are the ones remembered in disasters and defeats. Don't be remembered in history for a single mistake.' – *General Curtis LeMay, 1974*

The bomb bay doors on the B-29 snapped open. Major Harold Wood, the bombardier in the nose of *Dave's Dream,* pressed the button that released a bomb similar to the one dropped on Nagasaki. This was Operation CROSSROADS, and at one second past 9 AM and 518ft (158m) above the warm, placid waters of Bikini Atoll, *Gilda* detonated with the equivalence of 23 kilotons (kt) of TNT. It was 1st July 1946, and Strategic Air Command (SAC) just dropped its first atomic bomb, a weapon which – many argued – had just ended one war and which – many feared – would start the next war.

Throughout the first 15 years of the Cold War, SAC's thousands of heavy bombers each carrying a single atom bomb were the primary instruments of US national security strategy. In articulating what this strategic air force should look like, SAC planners identified three crucial issues: the need for overseas basing to resolve the problem of inadequate range of SAC's mainstay B-29s, B-50s, B-47s, and early

B-52s; the need for accurate intelligence to warn of an impending attack as well as identify suitable targets and their defenses; and the need to survive a surprise atomic attack and then execute and control a retaliatory strike. The range limit led to SAC's tanker force, the intelligence requirement led to SAC's reconnaissance fleet, and the surprise attack vulnerability led to SAC's airborne command post mission. In each case, the Boeing KC-135A Stratotanker became the cornerstone of SAC's strike, surveillance, and survival capabilities.

Traditional histories of the Boeing KC-135 focus upon the means and methods of aerial refueling, or upon the appearance and configuration of the dozens of unusual KC-135 variants. Similarly, existing studies of the evolution of Western defense policy since the Second World War are restricted to the political and economic factors which have directed its development. To segregate the means from the motive fails to recognize their complicated interrelationships and concurrent gestation. In fact weapons and weapon systems have become *determinants* of strategy instead of merely *implements* of strategists. The KC-135 and its variants have been more than simple

On 1st July 1946, the crew of B-29A 44-27354 *Dave's Dream* was the first SAC crew to drop an atomic bomb. It would still be several years before SAC had a meaningful intermediate-range, let alone intercontinental, atomic delivery capability. *Author's collection*

instruments of modern defense policy: for 60 years they have been crucial to its evolution. Their influence, direct or indirect, upon America's strategic deterrence, conventional force projection, research and development, and intelligence-gathering policies remains unequalled. The KC-135 jet tanker is the first weapons system of the Cold War and, arguably, has proven to be the most important. KC-135s and their variants have affected the development of almost every existing notion of land-based air power today.

Without the KC-135 tanker fleet, SAC bombers could not reach their strategic targets, effectively emasculating the national policy of Deterrence. Without tankers, tactical fighters and special operations aircraft could not engage in the conventional wars that punctuated and defined open conflict during the Cold War. Without tankers, heavy transports filled with troops and supplies could not fly across vast oceans to enable the rapid build-up of defenses to protect friendly nations under threat of imminent invasion. Without tankers, even advanced 'silver bullet' stealth aircraft like the Lockheed F-22 could not fly from their home bases in the United States to engage enemy forces on the other side of the world.

Reconnaissance variants of the KC-135 have gathered intelligence essential to the assessment of foreign nuclear weapons programs and evolving technologies, provided tactical and operational combat intelligence in multiple wars, and verified foreign compliance (or lack thereof) with international arms limitation or reduction treaties. Most, if not all of these sorties, required air refueling from KC-135 tankers.

Throughout the Cold War, airborne command posts and those of other nuclear-weapon-wielding commanders defined US (and Western) national security policy. SAC's EC-135s – one of which was until 1990 always airborne, further reducing US vulnerability to sneak attack – could direct nuclear-armed bombers and their supporting tankers, launch Intercontinental Ballistic Missiles (ICBM), and direct submarines to launch their Sea-Launched Ballistic Missiles (SLBM), effectively controlling all three 'legs' of America's strategic triad, dissuading potential adversaries from attempting such an attack. At first these aircraft were little more than a survivable means to *launch* America's retaliatory nuclear forces (including nuclear-tipped missiles) in the event of a surprise attack. As technology improved to enable more robust communication in a trans- and post-nuclear attack environment, KC-135 airborne command posts provided a genuine second strike capability, raising the possibility among some policy makers that a global thermonuclear war could be controlled and even won.

KC-135 variants defined modern jet travel, first by providing the Boeing Company with the economic and logistical means to build its iconic 707 through coproduction, and later as test aircraft that evaluated high-altitude jet routes around the world or in evolving avionics and technology. The C-135's shortcomings as a troop and cargo transport highlighted the crucial need for a dedicated jet transport. As the 1973 Arab-Israeli War demonstrated, even these capacious transports were effectively limited without the ability to refuel in flight.

Science and technology benefitted as well from the KC-135. From basic aerodynamic research into large, swept-wing jet aircraft to advanced research in solar physics, the Aurora Borealis, and sending man to the moon, KC-135 variants served as high-altitude, long-endurance platforms capable of carrying delicate scientific equipment and researchers anywhere in the world. These aircraft also supported military research – especially associated with nuclear weapons – that developed and defined multiple weapons, defense and satellite communications, and even stealth technology.

Above: RC-135s have acquired a certain mystique over 50 years. Originally secret from most US military commanders, they are now called upon first at trouble spots around the world. *Photo courtesy USAF*

Left: SAC's airborne command posts, most notably the LOOKING GLASS, have not received the credit they deserve in the evolution of US national security policy. *Photo by Joe Bruch*

To be sure, other airplanes throughout the Cold War undertook each of these roles. KC-97s and KC-10s share a portion of the credit for America's air refueling capability. The U-2 and SR-71, along with the rise of unmanned aerial vehicles (UAVs) were part of SAC's dedicated reconnaissance fleet. The US Navy's EC-130Qs, E-6As, and SAC's E-4Bs were all interconnected with EC-135 airborne command posts. C-141s, C-5s, and C-17s get all of the glory for moving men and materiel to hot spots and humanitarian crises around the world, but credit for pioneering international jet cargo goes to the largely forgotten C-135. A B-52 launched the X-15 and myriad research aircraft, and NASA's C-141 offered a glimpse into the heavens. None of these aircraft, however, did it all. Only the C-130 comes close, with tanker, transport, testbed, command post, and reconnaissance versions. The key difference is the level of significance, with the '135 variants broadly fulfilling a greater national and strategic mission, far more essential to American national security than the theater and tactical operations of the C-130.

Strategy By Default

The end of the Second World War brought with it the dissolution of the Grand Alliance between the United States, Great Britain, and the Soviet Union, and erstwhile allies resumed their pre-war animosity. By early 1946 American planners considered the USSR to be the only nation which could threaten the United States, but few political or military leaders believed that war between America and Russia was imminent or even inevitable. Most officials thought that the earliest such a war might erupt would be between 1953 and 1955, depending on the availability of Soviet atom bombs and a mature Soviet aerial refueling capability. Fears of an 'atomic Pearl Harbor', however, meant that America needed a powerful force-in-being, ready to preemptively attack the Soviet Union at the first sign of Russian preparations for an attack on the United States. Indeed, American officials and pundits debated the relative merits of retaliation versus pre-emption and even preventive war in the atomic age.

What such a war would look like, if and when it should come, was determined more by geography than by military strategy. US ground forces were no quantitative match for the residual Red Army, which had just repulsed the largest land invasion in history. With a fragile logistics trail originating in Western Europe, an attacking US Army would fare little better than Napoleon's *Grande Armée* or Hitler's *Wehrmacht*. Despite some 68,350nm (126,584km) of coastline, little of the Soviet Union was suitable for a US Marine Corps amphibious assault or US Navy shore bombardment due to year-round ice and lack of beaches.

The solution was obvious.

Fresh from the experience of World War II where strategic bombing of Germany and Japan was held to be a decisive determinant of Axis surrender, American officials opted to use strategic airpower as the cornerstone of US national security policy. As a 1956 SAC history recorded, 'The dropping of an atomic bomb … on Hiroshima … offered dramatic and undebatable proof of the capabilities of a strategic air arm. This one devastating strike brought about for the first time in the history of warfare the capitulation of a major enemy homeland without full-scale invasion by ground troops.' However accurate this contentious boast might be, strategic airpower was the only practical choice to be the cornerstone of post-war American security policy. In late 1945 under the direction of General of the Army Dwight D Eisenhower and in anticipation of an independent Air Force, the US Army Air Force (AAF) was reorganized into three major combat commands: Strategic Air Command, Tactical Air Command, and Air Defense Command. On 31st March 1946 SAC was established 'to conduct long range offensive operations in any part of the world … [by providing] units

Testbed KC-135s have been an integral part of evaluating new airplanes, weapons, and technologies, allowing each new design to be exploited to its fullest. *Author's collection*

capable of intense and sustained combat operations employing the latest and most advanced weapons.' Its mission was clear: *defeat* an enemy using atomic weapons. In SAC's formative years, deterrence was never an option. In addition to its strategic bombardment duties, SAC would 'conduct maximum range reconnaissance over land or sea either independently or in cooperation with land and naval forces.' The intelligence SAC was ordered to collect would benefit not only military and civilian policy makers, but would satisfy SAC's global targeting requirements as well. Most importantly, aerial intelligence would provide the margin needed for America to learn of an impending attack, no doubt with atomic weapons. With the creation of SAC in 1946, the seeds were planted for aerial refueling and strategic aerial reconnaissance as a matter of the highest US national security priority.

From Post War to Cold War: Origins of a Nuclear Armada

During the two years that followed the 1946 Bikini atomic test, disinterested and misguided leadership, unrealistic expectations of man and machine, a dysfunctional custodial arrangement of the tiny American nuclear arsenal, and post-war weariness all combined to impede SAC's development from inception into a mature fighting force. For many observers the development of nuclear weapons was the most significant event in the history of warfare. Although the influence of nuclear weapons cannot be minimized, in the grand scheme of global defense and security issues, *having* nuclear weapons is just as significant as having the *means* to employ them. Consequently, development programs following the Second World War focused upon both the production and stockpiling of nuclear weapons as well as the evolution of the means to deliver them to their targets. The AAF began an extensive analysis of its past operations with an eye toward planning its future role in supporting US defense policies. The atomic bomb complicated this study. Few senior military leaders were sufficiently knowledgeable about the bomb – how many, how effective, and how limited – to make intelligent recommendations, let alone define national defense and security policy.

Among those select few was Major General Curtis E LeMay, Chief of Staff of the US Army Strategic Air Forces in the Pacific. LeMay submitted a report to Lieutenant General Ira C Eaker, the AAF's Deputy Commanding General, on 30th August 1945 recommending the fullest possible expansion of the AAF's strategic bombing capability. LeMay argued that the AAF should develop a

'comprehensive plan for an atomic bombardment organisation, probably a wing... capable of immediate independent operation in any part of the world.' Two weeks later, on 14th September, Eaker appointed General Carl A 'Tooey' Spaatz as chairman of a committee 'to determine at the earliest date the effect of the atomic bomb on the size, organization, composition, and employment of the Air Forces'. The 'Spaatz Board', as it came to be known, submitted its findings to General Henry A 'Hap' Arnold, the AAF's Commanding General, on 23rd October 1945.

The Spaatz Board concluded that the two most important factors to be considered in any assessment of the atomic bomb and its future use by the AAF were the production and delivery of the bomb. 'The limited amounts of fissionable, weapons grade material likely to be available and the great costs associated with facilities and bomb production...indicated that the number of bombs on hand for any future conflict would be small. For some time to come, the bombs were expected to remain experimental "special weapons" of great cost and complexity, difficult to build and transport, and of limited availability'. At the end of the Second World War, only 46 SILVERPLATE (later SADDLETREE) Boeing B-29 Superfortresses had been modified with a special H-frame and hook to handle the atomic bomb, as well as special wiring in the bomb bay for weapon fuses and monitoring equipment. By the end of 1946, only 23 of these aircraft remained operational.

To carry the 10,000 lb (4,536kg) weapon meant that the SILVERPLATE B-29s had to be located at key overseas bases, otherwise they lacked the range to reach the intended targets of their 'special weapons'. Until the intercontinental Convair B-36 Peacemaker began operations from bases within the US, SAC needed overseas bases, and that meant SAC's vulnerability to any political or military restrictions placed upon the use of its bombers by the host nation's government. Such limitations became painfully clear in 1947 when SAC's Operation PARKWAY – the operational deployment of B-29s to Europe – 'ended prematurely when several European countries refused to permit American bombers to penetrate their airspace'. Plans for a second around-the-world flight in 1949 were thwarted for similar reasons. In addition, a shortage of high-grade aviation fuel at many forward operating locations in Europe and Asia severely restricted potential combat operations.

The Spaatz Board understood the limitations on production and delivery of the atomic bomb, and stressed a greater reliance upon conventional weapons and tactics. This decision may seem shortsighted and naive, but it has proven itself otherwise. Had the Board recommended the exclusive development of atomic bombs, their use in 'conventional scenarios' would have been neither militarily nor politically viable and American options would have been reduced considerably or eliminated altogether. Board members, most of them with considerable bomber experience, were also

Above: Throughout SAC's history, the success of its bomber fleet has been air refueling, whether by KB-29 or KC-135. Unlike 'cheaper' ICBMs, bombers can convey a warning to an adversary.
Photo by Brian Rogers

Left: SAC's modern fleet of B-29s could carry heavy bombs, but doing so limited their range. Overseas bases helped, but foreign governments were uneasy about the presence of such a lucrative target for Soviet attack.
Author's collection

painfully aware of the limitation on AAF bombers which lacked the unrefueled range with their heavy payloads – atomic or conventional – to reach targets in the USSR from bases in the USA. Among its final conclusions, the Board held that:

1. The atomic bomb does not at this time warrant a material change in our present conception of the employment, size, organization, and composition of the post-war Air Force.
2. The atomic bomb has not altered our basic concept of the strategic air offensive but has given us an additional weapon.
3. Forces using non-atomic bombs will be required for use against targets which cannot be effectively or economically attacked with atomic bombs.
4. An adequate system of outlying strategic bases must be established and maintained. …
6. An intelligence organization that will know at all times the strategic vulnerability, capabilities, and probable intentions of any potential enemy is essential. …

Arnold approved the recommendations of the Spaatz Board and appointed LeMay as the newly created Deputy Chief of the Air Staff for Research and Development to spearhead the build up of both conventional and nuclear forces.

The original build-up plan called for the number of atomic weapon capable groups to increase from the existing one (the 509th Composite Group) to four, each with one squadron of 12 atomic bombers. However, the Air Staff felt that creating a specialized strategic atomic bombing force would convey the false impression that only these few elite units would be required to defend the US given the bomb's potential destructive power. The solution to this dilemma proved to be the origin of the modern alert force.

Colonel William P Fisher, former secretary of the Spaatz Board, recommended that an atomic bomber force 'sufficient in size to fully exploit the expected availability and effectiveness of the atomic bomb' be outfitted with the most modern equipment and manned by only the most competent personnel. This unit would maintain a constant state of readiness to deploy worldwide to augment existing conventional strategic bombing forces. These atomic bombers could also carry the British developed 'Tall Boy' (12,000lb/5,443kg) and 'Grand Slam' (22,000 lb/9,979kg) high explosive conventional bombs for use 'if and when atomic bombs are not required or available'. Indeed, SAC war plans prior to 1950 such as PINCHER, FROLIC, and HALFMOON relied primarily on conventional bombing with only a few targets marked for atomic attack during a six-month campaign against the Soviet Union.

Fisher's plan suffered from several fundamental problems. It relied upon continuing access to the necessary overseas bases (with appropriate fighter defenses – after all, these bomber bases were themselves presumed targets for Soviet bombers) because of the extremely limited range of the B-29s when carrying an atomic bomb. In addition, the atomic bombs were of such complexity that moving them to these overseas bases was both a technical and logistical nightmare. These immediate issues were resolved by increasing the number and defensive capability of overseas bases, by increasing training, and by developing better operational and organizational plans for the atomic bomb deployment teams.

Capability Counts

In August 1946, Yugoslavian Yak-3s forced down one AAF C-47 transport and shot down another. SAC undertook its first 'show of force' atomic diplomacy mission when President Harry S Truman ordered six B-29s from the 43rd Bomb Group (BG) to deploy to Rhein-Main AB in Germany to conduct routine flights along the border. This was the '… first instance in which SAC bombers were

In 1946 a Yugoslav Yak-3 shot down a USAAF C-47, provoking President Truman to send SAC B-29s to Germany as a warning to the communists. Some 70 years later, B-52s convey a similar message. *Photo via Yefim Gordon*

used as instruments of international diplomacy … [and although not] regarded as a threat to Russia, the presence of the B-29s and their reputation as carriers of the A-bomb served notice … to the Communists'. On 24th June 1948 the Soviet Union blockaded Berlin. SAC B-29s from the 28th BG and the 307th BG headed to England to join 301st BG B-29s already in Germany as part of Truman's efforts to dissuade the Soviets from further aggression. Press releases described the B-29s as 'atomic capable', but none of those sent had the SILVERPLATE modification and no atomic weapons ever left US soil. The B-29s were little more than a bluff. R Gordon Arneson, the US Department of State's senior advisor on nuclear issues said that by '… sending the B-29s, we hoped to leave the impression that … they were armed with nuclear weapons, and that we were prepared to use them … [it was] psychological warfare'. Even had the aircraft been atomic capable and weapons deployed with them, their use would have been of questionable military value because '… it would still have required seven to nine days for the three existing US atomic bomb assembly teams to load 12 armed bombs into combat aircraft for launching at enemy targets. At that time, there were only … 12 fully qualified crews capable of making a combat drop with an atomic bomb … but their proficiency "was not as high as desirable … [because of the] non-availability of proper training equipment".' It may never be known if the presence of the B-29s indeed influenced Soviet actions in this Berlin crisis, but it is clear that American policy makers hoped they would.

Moreover, the total number of atomic bombs in the US inventory was insufficient to conduct any kind of sustained military operation. As late as October 1946 even President Truman believed that there were not more than 'a half dozen' atomic bombs in the US stockpile

Only the SILVERPLATE B-29s, like *Dave's Dream*, could carry atomic bombs. Moreover, the extremely limited number of bombs and qualified crews severely constrained SAC's early capabilities. *Author's collection*

but 'that was enough to win a war'. Once Truman became aware of the actual shortage of weapon components he authorized plans to correct these deficiencies (see Table 1.1). By October 1947 the Joint Chiefs of Staff (JCS) had established a vigorous atomic weapon production schedule through 1953. Each bomb was under the control of the US Atomic Energy Commission (AEC), and the transfer to SAC, shipment, and preparation took nearly a week, hardly suitable for a prompt retaliatory or timely pre-emptive attack. By 1947 there were only *two* qualified bomb assembly teams. Initially it required two days to assemble each bomb, meaning it would take 12-14 days to have the 13 weapons ready for SAC to use. After some nine days, however, the batteries in the bomb would begin to corrode, requiring disassembly of the bomb to replace them. After ten days, the plutonium pit had decayed sufficiently so that it, too, needed to be removed and replaced. The first few bombs put together were therefore useless. An even greater problem remained. As of December 1945 there were only 27 SILVERPLATE B-29s available, and these suffered a significant degrade in mission capability due to the poor reliability of their radar bombing systems. By the end of 1947, only 35 of 319 B-29s were configured to carry atomic weapons, nearly a third of all SAC B-29s were unusable due to lack of parts and mechanics, and there were only *six* crews in SAC qualified to drop an atom bomb.

However limited in number and readiness atomic bombs, planes, and crews might be, the ability to deliver them was equally circumscribed. US target intelligence in the early Cold War was nonexistent, relying on captured Nazi maps and Nineteenth Century travelogues gleaned from the Library of Congress. SAC target planners didn't even know what targets to attack, let alone details about them or their defenses. The service chiefs warned that the April 1946 PINCHER war plan, for example, was meaningless because 'the scarcity of reliable and detailed intelligence on the USSR precludes the determination at this time of specific target systems for air attack.'

Beyond insufficient target intelligence, SAC's B-29s and B-50s lacked the range to reach targets in the USSR unless launched from bases in England, North Africa, or Saudi Arabia, highlighting SAC's operational vulnerability to international political good will. Moreover, none of SAC's aircraft, including the B-36, could attack targets in the Soviet Union and expect to reach safe haven in friendly countries afterward. In short, SAC crews were assigned to one-way missions – and they knew it. Most importantly, they lacked the skill to conduct precision bombing.

Table 1-1. **US Post-War Atomic Arsenal, 1945-1949**

Year	Bombs	Year	Bombs	Year	Bombs
1945	2	1947	13	1949	159
1946	9	1948	56		

(Source: *Bulletin of the Atomic Scientists*, March 1993)

Table 1-2. **SAC Rated Officer Cross-Training Duty Positions**

Primary Duty Position	Cross-Trained Duty Positions
Pilot (Aircraft Commander or Copilot)	Navigators, Bombardiers, Flight Engineers, Radar Operators, and Gunner 'Familiarization'
Bombardiers	Navigators, Flight Engineers, and Radar Operators
Navigators	Bombardiers and Radar Operators
Radar Operators	Navigators and Bombardiers
Flight Engineers (Officers)	Bombardiers, Maintenance, and Engineering ground duties

(Source: *SAC History 1947*, Air Force Historical Research Center)

A Question of Leadership

Given SAC's newfound importance as America's atomic strike command, it was vital to select as its first commander someone of the appropriate rank and stature essential to guide SAC's operational preparedness and defining role in atomic national security policy. In 1946 there were only three four-star generals in the AAF. Carl Spaatz had just replaced General of the Army 'Hap' Arnold as the AAF commander. Spaatz commanded US strategic bombing operations in both Europe and the Pacific, and was a natural choice to lead a separate Air Force and its predominantly strategic bombardment mission. Joseph McNarney commanded US occupation forces in Europe and had little bomber experience, serving primarily in staff positions. George Kenney was recently the commander of Allied Air Forces in the Southwest Pacific Area on the staff of General of the Army Douglas MacArthur. Kenney, a reconnaissance pilot with two aerial kills during World War One, oversaw innovations in tactical airpower in support of ground and amphibious operations during the war in the Pacific, but viewed bombers only in a combat support role. He outranked Spaatz by four days and was deeply disappointed not to have been chosen as AAF commander. As a MacArthur protégé Kenney was politically a better choice than McNarney, and so became, almost by default, SAC's first Commanding General. Major General St Clair 'Bill' Streett served as his deputy.

Kenney, for all his success in World War Two, was ill suited to lead SAC. In addition to his duties as SAC's commander, he was also the airpower commander of the United Nations (UN) Military Staff Committee. In the post-war world hopes were high that UN forces would 'keep the peace', and Kenney viewed his duties there as a higher priority than organizing SAC. Consequently, Streett assumed responsibility for SAC's operational evolution. He frequently clashed with MacArthur (who controlled US bomber units in the Pacific sought by SAC) and openly contested hollow public relations claims echoed by Kenney that SAC was operationally ready to fulfill its mission. Not surprisingly, Streett's tenure ended after only eight months when Major General Clements McMullen – Kenney's logistics chief in the Pacific theater – replaced him in January 1947.

With his UN duties finally over, Kenney focused his attention on SAC, but even so his efforts were misguided. His early criticism of the new Convair B-36 Peacemaker as ineffective and plagued by development problems showed how little he understood about the procurement of new aircraft, and in so doing undermined the credibility of the nascent Air Force and SAC, which had staked their future on the B-36. He made alarmist speeches about the imminence of a Soviet atomic attack. 'When,' Kenney asked an anxious civilian audience in Bangor, ME, 'will the Communist crowd start "Operation America"?' Most egregiously, he completely abdicated SAC operations and training to McMullen.

In a scenario that would play out repeatedly over decades to come, post-war military budget austerity required that SAC 'do more with less.' McMullen, characterized in a 1948 SAC history as a 'fearless, and sometimes ruthless, taskmaster who boasted that "he had no cousins in SAC",' and was known pejoratively as 'Cement-head' and 'Concrete' for his stubbornness, believed that the only solution to the dwindling numbers of SAC crews, maintenance personnel, and staff was to have each person perform double duty. However well intentioned, this effort contradicted nearly two centuries of evidence supporting the division of labor and led to critical deficiencies in primary duty capability, substandard secondary duty skills, and deep resentment among SAC personnel.

McMullen's cross-training program showed little consideration for professional skill, rank, or job motivation (see Table 1.2). A command pilot with 4,000 hours, including combat time over Europe or Japan, could easily be assigned to fly as a tail gunner, affecting chain-of-command and rank issues as enlisted gunners oversaw the training and operational duties of officer gunners. A few SAC commanders astutely worried that plummeting morale of fliers and maintenance personnel would spread to their families: 'Dissatisfied wives of well-trained specialists…could easily drive such personnel out of Strategic Air Command.' With so few experienced fliers and 'wrench turners' remaining in the post-war AAF, McMullen's misuse of scarce resources led to widespread resignations, further exacerbating the manpower shortage.

On top of this discordant utilization of highly trained flight crews and maintenance personnel, SAC decreed that 'all combat crew members have an ability to speak Russian to improve their chances of survival should aircraft be forced down in Soviet territories.' Efforts began to institute Russian language training (ignoring the fact that many 'Soviets' didn't speak Russian at all), but fortunately were short lived. This absurd language requirement, however, epitomized the high priority given to ad hoc and operationally irrelevant programs at a time when basic mission skills were at their absolute worst.

Using circular error probable (CEP) as a metric, SAC B-29s and B-50s in 1949 were no better – and often worse – than AAF B-17s in 1942 despite improvements in bomb sights, aircraft performance, and wartime experience by navigators and bombardiers. During the 17th August 1942 B-17 raid on Rouen, France, for example, the CEP was in excess of 5,500ft (1,676m). On 31st March 1943, in a B-17 attack on Rotterdam, only 78 out of 383 bombs fell within 2,000ft (610m) of the target. By late 1944, 87 out of 100 bombs dropped on one oil facility missed completely, and a typical 'hit box' of a B-17 raid in good weather was 13,000 x 26,000ft (3,962 x 7,925m). SAC's post-war bombing accuracy was even more appalling. On 29th April 1949, six B-29s from the 43rd BG conducted a simulated attack on Denver, with CEPs of 15,480, 9,660, 14,970, 7,950, 10,140, and 6,690ft (4,718, 2,944, 4,563, 2,423, 3,091, and 2,039m). Only three of the Group's B-29s managed to reach Ft Worth, with CEPs of 5,580, 25,860, and 18,270ft (1,701, 7,882, and 5,569m). SAC's miss distances were measured in miles rather than feet.

Lack of proficiency in high-altitude bombing meant that B-29 crews flew at the suicidal-in-combat altitude of 15,000ft (4,572m) in order to meet bureaucratic mandatory minimal bombing scores reported daily to SAC Headquarters. Crews relied on daylight visual bombing. Cross-trained bombardiers were utterly ineffective at radar bombing, so huge radar reflectors were installed at bombing sites to improve target identification. Even the atom bomb failed to resolve the issue of missed targets. In Operation CROSSROADS, conducted under well-planned and optimal peacetime test conditions, *Dave's Dream* missed the USS *Nevada* aim point (painted bright red for easy identification) by almost half a mile. Out of some 50 ships in the target area, only five light ships were sunk. Even in the atomic age, precision still mattered.

Rumors of War

Escalating tensions in 1948 over the current and future status of Germany led to the Soviet closure of all ground access to Berlin and the Berlin Blockade. With the looming possibility of war with the USSR, American officials were understandably concerned about SAC's preparedness. Despite glowing reports from Kenney and his staff, the evidence suggested that America's bomber command was anything but ready. Turnover at one unit, for example, was so high that 25% of its personnel left within a two-month period. The new Air Force Chief of Staff, General Hoyt S Vandenberg, needed to know with confidence the true state of SAC's readiness. To find out he called on famed aviator Charles Lindbergh for on-site visits to six SAC bases to meet with personnel, fly with crews, and observe first-hand SAC's readiness. Concurrently, Vandenberg asked Colonel Paul

Left: General George C Kenney was SAC's first commander, but lacked the vision to see what SAC should become in the future. Instead he focused on alarmist speeches to civic groups, abdicating leadership of SAC to his deputy. *USAAF photo*

Right: No one did more to cripple SAC's operational capability than Major General Clements McMullen. His despised cross-training program made pilots into gunners, and his harsh attitude drove personnel out of SAC *en masse*. *USAAF photo*

Tibbets, pilot of the *Enola Gay* and now commander of SAC's 509th BG, to inspect SAC Headquarters at Andrews AFB to assess its effectiveness.

The results were a devastating indictment of SAC's preparedness, Kenney's absentee leadership, and McMullen's despised cross-training program. Lindbergh warned that SAC fliers were worse than airline pilots, couldn't hit a target under realistic combat conditions, and suffered from plummeting morale issues. Tibbets found that SAC was full of poorly trained crews and maintenance personnel, as well as staff officers who lacked guidance and purpose, telling Vandenberg, 'There isn't anyone out there who knows what the hell they are doing.' On 15th September Kenney briefed the JCS on SAC war plans. Kenney seemed 'ill-prepared and uninformed,' hardly the reassurance needed from America's atomic force commander with the prospect of war on the horizon. A week later, on 21st September, in arguably the most important decision of his career, Vandenberg relieved Kenney as SAC's Commanding General, replaced him with Lieutenant General Curtis LeMay, and terminated the cross-training program.

A Question of Priorities

No doubt many of SAC's early travails were the result of issues outside of its immediate control. The evolving strategy debate over roles and missions (especially between the newly constituted Air Force and the Navy), the rapid decrease in manpower associated with post-war demobilization, concurrent budget cuts, turf-battles over control of atomic weapons, and popular fatigue with wartime all contributed to SAC's inadequacies during its formative years. But SAC effectively was its own worst enemy, from the top down. Kenney failed to exercise the necessary leadership both within the command and the halls of Congress to get the resources essential to develop SAC into a capable long-range strike force. He lacked the strategic vision to see what SAC *ought to look like in 1955* when fears of a Soviet attack might be realized, and in so doing failed to take the appropriate steps to enable that vision. Most importantly, he did nothing to limit McMullen's damage to operational readiness and morale.

LeMay's decisive, no-nonsense leadership slowly reversed the damage to SAC's capability caused by Kenney and McMullen. LeMay understood the potential and limits of strategic bombing. Despite his gruff exterior he articulated this vision as well as a profound sense of urgency to American lawmakers and public alike, generating strong support for SAC and its mission. Between 1948 and 1957 he effectively and inextricably linked SAC and its atomic weapons to the Soviet threat. By 1960 SAC had evolved from an ineffective combat force under Kenney into a powerful force capable of deterring war with the Soviet Union under LeMay. Without LeMay's leadership, SAC likely would have remained a 'hollow threat.'

That America's atomic potential was militarily insignificant in the early years of the Cold War was either a closely guarded secret or one of the greatest examples of ignorance and naiveté in political and diplomatic history. Air Force scholar Harry Borowski succinctly summarized this paradox. 'Shortages in men, aircraft, and weapons hindered the development of a strong force. In coping with these problems, SAC's commanders [under Kenney] mishandled their crew resources, misdirected training, and the command suffered a decline in its capability to put the bombs on target. … The mere possession of atomic weapons and planes to deliver them was not enough; overseas bases, intelligence, aircrews with the ability to fly their bombers through air defenses and over the proper targets were also needed'.

LeMay and the SAC build up

Deeply disturbed by what he properly saw as SAC's inability to fulfil its mission, LeMay aggressively tackled the issue of training. He made Kenney's 1948 bombing competition an annual affair and incorporated 'spot promotions' to recognise outstanding performance and improve morale. Equally concerned about shortages in aircraft and personnel, LeMay demanded and got priority for SAC in the acrimonious budget battles going on in the Pentagon and in the halls of Congress. In just two years, the number of atomic capable bombers in his command increased from fewer than 36 B-29s in 1948 to over 250 B-29s, Boeing B-50s, and B-36s in 1950. Similarly, the number of atomic bomb trained crews and weapons assembly teams increased proportionately.

By 1950 the two major issues confronting nuclear planners had been resolved. There were now sufficient atomic bombs available (or in production) and an adequate number of bombers and properly trained crews to deliver them. Still, one considerable obstacle remained which seriously degraded the potential global striking capability of SAC's bomber force – range. The B-36 was unhindered by the range problem, but it suffered from operational limitations that seriously degraded its combat potential. In particular, it was still a piston-engined leviathan that faced nimble jet-powered Soviet MiG-15 *Fagots* and forthcoming MiG-17 *Frescos*. Although the looped-hose method of air refueling was in limited use by B-29s and B-50s at this time, it was an awkward procedure that demanded a level of crew proficiency higher than SAC felt could be maintained through normal training. Further, tankers still required forward basing in order to rendezvous with their mated bombers en route from the US. The best solution to SAC's range problem lay in an aggressive program to develop fully the means and methods of aerial refueling.

Top left: Curtis LeMay was the natural choice to lead SAC, and replaced Kenney at the height of the 1948 Berlin Crisis. LeMay was a powerful advocate of aerial refueling to achieve the bomber's fullest potential. No one in the Air Force did more to champion the KC-135 than LeMay. *Author's collection*

Top right: Jets like the B-47 had the speed to evade MiGs, but lacked intercontinental range. *Stephen Miller*

Left: The B-36 could deliver atom bombs to Soviet targets, but it was slow and highly vulnerable to MiG-15s. *Author's collection*

CHAPTER TWO

Birth of Aerial Refueling

'All of our medium bombers are now intercontinental bombers.'
– *Secretary of the Air Force Stuart Symington, 1949*

'We built, and are continuing to build, our strategy around refueling. As of today, the "tail is wagging the dog".'
– *Major General Frank A Armstrong, Jr, 18th July 1956*

Between 1917 and 1921 several aviators proposed schemes for picking up fuel from the ground or transferring it aloft from another airplane. Among the first was Alexander P de Seversky (then a pilot in the Imperial Russian Navy), who in 1917 proposed increasing the range of combat aircraft by refueling them in flight. De Seversky went to the United States that same year as part of a Russian naval mission and, following the Bolshevik Revolution, remained in the United States where he was appointed an aeronautical engineer in the War Department. Encouraged by General William E 'Billy' Mitchell, de Seversky applied for and received the first patent for air-to-air refueling. In the preamble to his patent, filed on 13th June 1921, he proposed 'large tankers to supply fuel to pursuit ships while in flight.' De Seversky moved on to other projects, including founding Seversky Aviation in 1931 (reorganized in 1938 into Republic Aviation), and it fell to others to continue the development of air refueling.

In 1918 Godfrey L Cabot, a US Navy Reservist, suggested (as did other aviators) that large aircraft might achieve non–stop trans-Atlantic flight by picking up fuel containers from surface vessels. The airplane would trail a weighted cable into a suitable guide on the surface vessel and engage a device on the container which would then be hoisted up and its contents dumped into the airplane's fuel tanks. This scheme was intended to facilitate rapid and safe air delivery of US-built airplanes to France, but was later suggested as a means to double the radius of action of combat aircraft and to make possible commercial non-stop trans-Atlantic services. After several years of trials, Cabot eventually managed to pick up a fuel container and replenish an airplane, but the scheme was far too clumsy and impracticable for large quantities of fuel. The procedure proved more useful as a means of mail pick-up, however, and was later demonstrated to the Post Office Department and eventually put into operation by All American Aviation in 1939.

The first air-to-air fuel transfer took place as a stunt on 12th November 1921 when wing-walker Wesley May climbed from a Lincoln Standard to a Curtiss JN-4 with a can of fuel strapped to his back. Others repeated the performance but no practical applications were attempted until 1923. Inspired by the endurance and distance records set by Lieutenants Fred W Kelly and John MacReady in a

SAC bomber pilots were emphatic in their preference for the flying boom over the probe-and-drogue. Flight tests favoring the latter were conducted with rested crews on short flights, not exhausted pilots on 20-hour missions across the globe to drop nuclear weapons. *Photo P10045 courtesy Boeing*

Left: The first recorded image of an air refueling on 27th June 1923. The receiver DH.4 stayed aloft for 6 hours, 38 minutes using two refuelings. This was also the first refueling using a hose to transfer the fuel rather than passing cans of gas between the airplanes. *Photo 130202B courtesy Boeing*

Below: The tanker crew for the June 1923 refueling was made up of pilot Lieutenant Virgil Hines (r) and 'hose operator' Lieutenant Frank Seifert (l). *Photo 130200B courtesy Boeing*

US Army Air Service Fokker T-2 while attempting a non-stop transcontinental flight (finally achieved in May 1923), pilots at Rockwell Field near San Diego, CA, suggested in-flight refueling as a means to extend endurance. Permission was granted to attempt a refueled endurance record, and trials began in April 1923 using de Havilland DH.4Bs.

On 20th April two DH.4Bs – captained by Rockwell Field commander Major Henry 'Hap' Arnold – completed the first successful in-flight contact using a hose. No fuel was transferred, but the test validated the concept. The first successful fuel transfer by hose took place on 27th June 1923 when a DH.4B piloted by Lieutenants Lowell H Smith and John P Richter stayed aloft for six hours, 38 minutes, refueled twice by a second DH.4B. The first 'tanker pilot' was Lieutenant Virgil Hines and the first 'boom operator' (actually hose operator) was Lieutenant Frank Seifert. Arnold expounded the potential military advantages of aerial refueling in a 1923 magazine article, suggesting that military aircraft be loaded with a full complement of crew and equipment but only a small amount of fuel. 'After… reaching an altitude of a few hundred feet, a refueling plane can service the heavily-loaded bombing or torpedo plane so that it will have its tanks full thereby permitting the plane to function to its extreme radius of action. … There are probably many more [examples] which will become apparent as the years go by.'

During 27-28th August, Lieutenants Smith and Richter established an endurance record of 37 hours, 15 minutes in a DH.4B, replenished with fuel, oil, and supplies from two DH.4B tankers. Another record setting flight took place on 25th October, when a DH.4B flew non-stop from Sumas, WA, on the US-Canadian border, to Tijuana, Mexico, on the US-Mexican border (landing in San Diego, CA), in 12 hours, refueled three times by two DH.4B tankers.

The first fatal air refueling accident occurred at Kelly Field, TX, on 18th November 1923 when the refueling hose became tangled in the wings of the receiver. The tanker pilot, Lieutenant P T Wagner, was killed in the ensuing crash. This accident and the subsequent dispersion of the participating pilots to other duties effectively ended further US air refueling trials for the next five years. Foreign interest

had been aroused by the US Army flights, however, and within months of the American accident refueling trials were underway in Europe. In June 1928, two pilots from Belgium's *Aéronautique Militaire* raised the refueled endurance record to 60 hours, seven minutes in a de Havilland DH.9.

Revival of Interest
US military interest in aerial refueling resurfaced late in 1928, when Major Carl Spaatz and Captain Ira Eaker discussed the feasibility of refueling a three-engined Atlantic C-2A from a single-engined Douglas C-1. Air Corps approval was given for trials to proceed with the intention of creating a new endurance record and determining the effect of prolonged flight on both men and machine. On 1st January 1929, the C-2A – dubbed simply '?' – took off from Los Angeles Metropolitan Airport with Spaatz and his crew of four. During the next seven days the crew of the *Question Mark* made some 50 exchanges with the C-1 for fuel, oil, food, and even a wash basin.

The flight time of 150 hours, 14 minutes not only set a new refueled endurance record but also captured the public's imagination around the world. Widely reported in the press, the flight encouraged optimistic forecasts of the future of aviation and instantly threw down the gauntlet. Even before the flight was over, several civilian pilots announced plans for endurance flights. Attracted by the fame and fortune associated with a new record, dozens of fliers made the attempt during 1929, with the highest time achieved being 420 hours aloft.

The Army planned to demonstrate a refueled bombing mission during maneuvers on 21st-22nd May 1929 when a Keystone LB-7 was to make a non-stop flight from Dayton, OH, to New York City and back, dropping parachute flares on its target. Fog prevented the tanker from taking off, however. The LB-7 reached its target unrefueled but landed to refuel before returning to Ohio. This ended official Army interest in air refueling until the Second World War, although Army officers unofficially participated in several subsequent record attempts.

As the effort and expense necessary to set new records grew, they became less frequent and the public tired of them. Occasional attempts continued until 1935 when, in a fitting climax to this era, Fred and Al Key remained airborne for 653 hours in a Curtiss Robin named *Ole Miss*. By this time the *Fédération Aéronautique Internationale* (FAI) had discontinued the record class of endurance with refueling. A new form of endurance flight continued in the US for many years, however. This was the refueling of light planes by means of passing cans of fuel from a speeding automobile. The unofficial record for this type of endurance flight reached 1,558 hours in 1959, remaining the longest time man had remained aloft until surpassed in 1974 by US astronauts aboard Skylab 4. While these flights proved that pilot and machine could remain airborne for weeks at a time, few flights were made for any purpose other than record chasing, and they demonstrated little technical innovation. In the years following 1929, inventors filed numerous refueling patents that showed originality and imagination, but little was done to translate these ideas into operable systems.

Early Foreign Developments
These American flights again stimulated interest abroad. Between 1929 and 1936, refueling trials were carried out in Germany, Great Britain, Japan, and the Soviet Union. In 1930 Britain embarked on an official research program, with the Royal Aircraft Establishment (RAE) at Farnborough directed to develop a practical means for refueling large aircraft in flight. During these trials, a variety of aircraft tested several refueling methods with varying degrees of success. The first Royal Air Force (RAF) bomber specification to include provision for in-flight refueling was issued as part of Project B1/35. This requirement for aerial refueling was soon dropped in favor of increased fuel capacity and more powerful engines, and the projected airplane eventually became the Vickers Warwick.

At the same time, British pioneer long-distance aviator Sir Alan J Cobham was planning a non-stop refueled flight from England to India in a single-engined Airspeed Courier monoplane. Cobham was a Royal Flying Corps pilot, barnstormer, and air taxi pilot during the 1920s, and had made survey flights to Africa and Australia. In 1926 he was knighted for services to aviation. Cobham conducted numerous experiments to find a safe and practical means of refueling during the flight. With preparations completed and tankers positioned, Cobham and RAF Squadron Leader William Helmore set out for India on 22nd September 1934. A throttle control problem resulted in a forced-landing at Malta, ending the record attempt. Determined not to waste the two years of research, effort, and expense, Cobham formed the company Flight Refuelling Limited (FRL) in October 1934 to develop in-flight refueling. (The company was renamed Cobham Ltd in 1996 in honor of the founder.) Trials were carried out by both the RAE and FRL until 1937, when the tests were taken over by FRL under government funded contracts.

While the RAE program focused on refueling military aircraft, Cobham pressed the case for refueled commercial services and obtained the backing of Imperial Airways. At this time, nonstop trans-Atlantic commercial services were in their infancy and little payload could be carried due to the weight of the necessary fuel. To overcome this

British aviation pioneer Sir Alan J Cobham led early efforts to master aerial refueling. His probe-and-drogue method eventually became standard for the Royal Air Force, the Royal Navy, and fighters around the world. *Author's collection*

disadvantage, the Germans developed a scheme of landing a flying-boat in the Atlantic for replenishment and then catapulting it into the air from a waiting surface vessel. The British also developed a composite flying-boat arrangement, with the upper component continuing on its own after being released at a suitable point on the journey. The lower half landed near a waiting ship, refueled, and returned home.

An alternative to these logistical nightmares was to refuel in flight, either after takeoff (to increase the airplane's payload) or during the journey (to increase the airplane's range). Imperial Airways introduced the latter scheme on 5th August 1939, with the maiden flight of weekly non-stop trans-Atlantic mail service between England and the United States. A modified Shorts Empire flying boat was refueled by modified Handley Page Harrow bomber-transports over Ireland and Newfoundland. The outbreak of war in Europe ended this service in late September, after 15 air-refueled crossings.

Early Methods
Two principle means of refueling were developed prior to the Second World War: the 'cross-over' method and the 'looped hose' or 'ejector' method. The cross-over method was conceived by Flight Lieutenant Richard Atcherley – an RAF officer involved in the early RAE trials – and was first accomplished in March 1935. Both the tanker and receiver trailed a line with a grapnel at the end. The receiver flew above and across the path of the tanker line and engaged it by means of the grapnels. The lines were then winched in to the tanker where the receiver's line was connected to the fuel hose. The two airplanes maneuvered so that fuel flowed by gravity to the receiver.

The looped hose (ejector) method was developed by FRL and used for the 1939 trans-Atlantic service and, with improvements in design and technique, in wartime and post-war trials. The receiver trailed a weighted line from the reception coupling in its tail, while the tanker flew alongside and fired a projectile that pulled a line that intercepted the receiver's line. Grapnels on each line ensured engagement. Both lines were then hauled into the tanker where the weight was removed from the receiver line. A bayonet fitting on this line was connected to the tanker's hose nozzle which was then winched back to the receiver. The nozzle was drawn into the reception coupling by a cable and held in place by locking the toggles. Fuel flowed by gravity due to the relative positions of the aircraft. The receiver disconnected by letting out the hose and line and then flying away from the tanker causing the weak link in the line to separate at a safe distance from both airplanes.

Air Refueling and the Second World War
The many refueled endurance flights demonstrated the advantages of aerial refueling, and US military leaders and politicians had acknowledged its military value. There was still little official interest, however, because of inter-service rivalry and nationalist isolationist policies, both of which severely affected the range and employment of bombers. In Britain, FRL proposed several schemes for using aerial refueling in wartime operations but the Air Ministry rejected them because of the anticipated difficulty of large scale operations, the cost and time involved in training crews and modifying the airplanes, and the promise of better airplanes which would make air refueling unnecessary.

Studies and trials nonetheless continued throughout the war years. In 1942, the US Army Air Force ordered a set of British equipment for installation in a Consolidated B-24D Liberator tanker and a Boeing B-17E Flying Fortress receiver. Flight trials were carried out the following year. Sample flight plans showed that, with refueling, the B-17s could fly from Alaska's Aleutian Islands to bomb Tokyo and then continue on to China. Although the scheme was feasible, the longer-ranged Boeing B-29 Superfortress would be available by the time the Liberators and Fortresses could be modified and crews trained, so the plan was dropped. Later studies considered refueling B-29s from B-24 tankers but this was not pursued, again because of the extensive modifications and training required.

The difficulty of bombing Japan with conventional bombers led the RAF to conclude in 1943 that aerial refueling was the only practical means to fly the distances from available bases in China, Burma, or the Philippines. Consequently, FRL was asked to develop equipment for use in Avro Lancasters. Plans for the proposed 'Tiger Force' – as the British contribution to Allied raids on Japan was known – called for 500 Lancaster and Lancaster Mk IV (eventually renamed the Lincoln) bombers supported by 500 Lancaster tankers. Refueling trials commenced in late 1944 but official opinion moved away from aerial refueling in favor of increasing the maximum gross weight (and hence fuel capacity) of the bombers. In April 1945 the air refueling requirement was canceled due to the greater potential range of the Lincoln with added fuel tanks as well as the anticipated availability of Pacific island bases as American forces advanced toward Japan.

Planning and development of 'Tiger Force' continued with every intention of deploying to the Far East. The use of the atomic bomb led to an immediate end of the war, however, and the production contract for aerial refueling equipment was canceled. FRL retained the partially completed components, and the small batch of development aircraft already equipped as tankers and receivers was used in post-war civil air refueling trials. Some of the unfinished equipment was later updated and delivered to the United States for use in Air Force and Navy programs.

Post-War Development
Strategic Air Command was established on 26th March 1946 with the mission 'to conduct long range offensive operations in any part of the world' and 'to conduct maximum range reconnaissance over land or sea.' To accomplish these missions, SAC's bomber inventory included 148 B-29s operated by six bomb groups, with additional B-29s assigned during 1947 and 1948, and B-50s and B-36s expected to enter service in 1948. Neither the B-29 nor the B-50 had intercontinental range, so forward basing in Allied nations was essential for coverage of all target areas. Although the B-36 did have intercontinental range, its operational future was then uncertain.

By late 1947 termination of the B-36 was a distinct possibility given its slow speed and recognized vulnerability to Soviet jet fighters. The B-36C – with variable discharge turbine engines intended to increase speed over target – suffered from developmental problems and delays, resulting in its cancelation in early 1948. SAC's commander, General George Kenney, initially opposed the B-36 program and favored converting existing B-36s into other roles, including tankers. In January 1948 SAC endorsed this conversion and urged that a formal air refueling research and development program begin. On 26th February 1948 the Air Force awarded Air Materiel Command (AMC) a contract for $1 million to study an air refueling system for bombardment aircraft, with SAC given the responsibility for all 'operational suitability tests.'

Almost immediately after the US Air Force became an independent service in September 1947, a dispute erupted with the Navy over which service could best carry out the strategic nuclear delivery mission. In December 1947, Rear Admiral Daniel Gallery, Assistant Chief of Naval Operations (Guided Missiles), urged the Navy to start an aggressive campaign showing that the Navy could deliver an atom bomb more effectively than could the Air Force. Citing the vulnerability of the B-36 and the limited combat radius of the B-29 and its need for politically sensitive forward basing, Gallery

argued that a carrier-based bomber with a radius of action of 1,500 miles (2,413km) could be launched on the high seas and be able to cover all targets in Europe and most of Asia. He proposed that the Navy be given the primary responsibility for nuclear attack, with the Air Force having this only as a secondary mission. To demonstrate the feasibility of operating nuclear-armed bombers from carriers, trials were carried out during 1948 in which Lockheed P2V-2 Neptunes were launched from the aircraft carrier USS *Coral Sea* and landed ashore.

Not surprisingly, this proposal fanned the conflict between the Air Force and the Navy, where the 'Gallery Memorandum' enjoyed strong and vocal support as part of what came to be known during 1949 as the 'Revolt of the Admirals'. In an early effort to end the vituperative and divisive bickering, Secretary of Defense James V Forrestal called the chiefs of staff together from 11-14th March 1948 for a meeting at Key West Naval Base. An agreement was reached recognizing the sole right of the Air Force to maintain a strategic air arm for nuclear weapons delivery, but permitted the Navy to use atomic weapons against naval targets. As part of the Navy effort to develop further tactics for delivering nuclear weapons from carrier-based heavy aircraft, Navy squadrons VC-5 and VC-6 operated 12 P2V-3Cs between 1949 and 1951 pending the introduction of the carrier-based North American AJ Savage.

Unresolved Problem of Range
The Key West agreement still did not settle the range issue. Air Force Secretary Stuart K Symington told the Senate Armed Services Committee on 25th March 1948 that in-flight refueling could 'broaden' the B-29's range. Although AMC had since 1947 informally studied refueling B-29s, this research had little urgency and no meaningful funding, and hence few results. In the wake of Symington's congressional testimony, senior Air Force officers levied considerable pressure on the Boeing Company to demonstrate – in only three days – aerial refueling with the B-29. Brigadier General Horace Shepard, chief of Air Force procurement, succinctly described the task by saying, 'We've got to transfer fuel in the air immediately. By this weekend. Even if we have to do it with a teaspoon.' A hastily installed unit consisting of 300ft (91.4m) of fire hose, reels, and cables transferred water instead of fuel from one B-29 to another, barely meeting the Easter deadline. Boeing's initial test – Operation DRIP – was completed at sundown on 28th March 1948.

This single successful flight was a long way from an operational capability with a large fleet of tankers and bombers operating world-wide on no-notice operations. The only equipment readily available in any quantity was that developed for the British 'Tiger Force' and then in use supporting civilian refueling trials. Following a series of trials carried out by FRL over the English Channel during 1946-47 (using the Lancasters modified for 'Tiger Force'), approval was given for a series of trials to assess the practicability of flight-refueled commercial services across the Atlantic. Between May and August 1947 FRL cooperated with British South American Airways (BSAA) in a non-stop service from the UK to Bermuda, with BSAA Lancasters refueled by Lancaster tankers based in the Azores. Between February and May 1948 British Overseas Airways Corporation (BOAC) carried out an experimental service across the Atlantic with a converted Liberator refueled by Avro Lancastrian tankers.

Officers from AMC and engineers such as Boeing's Cliff Leisy flew to England to negotiate with FRL for air refueling equipment to be installed in B-29s even while Operation DRIP was under way. Following trials with the FRL-equipped B-29, SAC adopted a version of the British looped hose system which remained in use through the mid-1950s.

Initial Operations

The US Air Force Chief of Staff's annual report, published in mid-1948 (when the future of the B-36 was still in doubt), stated, after considering several methods of bombing targets at extreme range, that 'an aircraft of acceptable size could not be built to perform its mission at the desired range unless air-to-air in-flight refueling were employed.' The report also noted that an extensive modification program was under way to provide tankers and receivers in the near future. One such future receiver was a Boeing design that would become the B-52 Stratofortress.

Until these new airplanes could be delivered, the Air Force requested that 92 B-29s be converted into KB-29M tankers (code-named SUPERMAN), and 74 B-29MRs, 57 B-50As, and 44 RB-50Bs converted into receivers (code-named RURALIST). The 43rd AREFS and 509th AREFS became the first air refueling units in the US Air Force when they were activated on 19th July 1948, and the first KB-29M was delivered to the 43rd AREFS late the same year. SAC demonstrated its new air refueling capability in December 1948 when a B-50A made a 9,870 mile (15,883km) flight in 41 hours, 40 minutes, refueled three times by KB-29M tankers. From 26th February through 2nd March 1949 B-50A *Lucky Lady II* completed the first non-stop around-the-world flight, covering 23,452 miles (37,741km) in 94 hours, one minute with four in-flight refuelings by 43rd AREFS KB-29M tankers prepositioned along the way. Despite the eventual success of the *Lucky Lady II*, SAC planners estimated the chances for completing the flight at no better than 1 in 4. The first aircraft in the flight, the *Global Queen*, was forced to land at Lajes Field in the Azores due to technical problems. Further, the 43rd AREFS tanker crews had among them only one previous successful air refueling contact prior to the global mission! Nonetheless, the successful flight proved the feasibility of long range bombing and provided a dramatic indication of SAC's operational readiness. General LeMay explained the flight's significance in less elegant terms: 'We can now deliver an atomic bomb to any place in the world that requires an atomic bomb.' SAC had finally acquired global status with its air-refueled B-29 and B-50 bombers, continued forward basing in Europe, and improved performance from the B-36.

Need for Improvement

Although SAC now had an operational air refueling capability, it suffered from fundamental inadequacies that hindered its operational value. While the looped hose system achieved the object of range extension, its use of contacting cables, hoses strung between aircraft, and manual connection of cable to hose within an unpressurized compartment in the tanker seriously limited the speed and altitude at which refueling could be conducted. These lower altitudes and speeds largely negated the benefits of air refueling.

Recognizing this, FRL considered ways of adapting the looped hose system for semi-automatic operation under the control of an operator in a pressurized compartment, primarily for use in civil aircraft. The looped hose system itself was, however, part of the problem. Operation DRIP had shown that air refueling with the looped hose was feasible but not completely satisfactory. The gravity-fed fuel flow rate was only 200 gallons per minute (gpm – 757 liters per minute) instead of the desired 600gpm (2,271 liters pm). Operations in the frigid Arctic were not possible because the coiled hose would freeze on the reel while the airplane was still on the ground and could not be trailed out in flight. Air Force planners were sufficiently concerned about this cold weather limitation that they sought to 'winterize' the tankers for Arctic duty. Operational plans would then be predicated on the proportional availability of winterized and non-winterized tankers.

The SUPERMAN and RURALIST tanker-receiver combination used the looped-hose method. Developed before World War Two, it appeared to be the natural choice for post-war aerial refueling. It was cumbersome, risky, and unreliable, prompting other initiatives. *Photo BW38524 courtesy Boeing*

In addition, the awkward position required to maintain contact during air refueling posed considerable problems. 'Wingtip to wingtip position got [the receiver] free of propeller downwash, but side visibility was poor [in the B-29 and B-50]. Pilots got stiff necks. Direct nose-to-tail was good for vision, but the crew couldn't stand the buffeting. A close staggered position worked best…with the tanker 10ft (3m) behind and 25ft (7.6m) below the receiver. The tanker would have the more experienced crew so it should have the [more difficult to maintain] rear position.' Refueling was itself more an acquired art than a basic flying skill. By March 1949 only the few SAC crews that had completed SAC's Transition Training School at MacDill AFB, FL, were qualified to perform aerial refueling.

The introduction of jet powered bombers into SAC's inventory added another problem as the jet engines demanded a much higher fuel consumption rate than their piston counterparts. For the new jets to reach their targets, forward basing of bombers and tankers was still necessary, even with in-flight refueling. SAC was equally unhappy about relying on a small foreign company – FRL – as the sole source of equipment and training for the critically important air refueling program. This dependency on foreign equipment was as distasteful to SAC's commanders as the dependency on foreign bases and their host nation's political goodwill. All of SAC's tankers were equipped with refueling gear supplied by FRL, and in 1949 both the 43rd AREFS and the 509th AREFS 'lacked the equipment and crews to conduct much [air refueling] training.' At the time, FRL was struggling to survive. With little interest shown by the RAF or civil operators in adopting in-flight refueling and only a limited contract for further development, the company relied on contracts for maintenance conversion and training. SAC's order for B-29 air refueling equipment virtually rescued the company from oblivion.

Concerned about these inadequacies, SAC began its own investigations into improved air refueling systems. Boeing was also deeply interested in air refueling to improve the ranges of the B-47 then undergoing flight tests and the larger B-52 under development, as well as improving the company's conversion work already under way on piston powered tankers and receivers. In April 1948 Boeing began a study of improved methods of refueling in an effort to (1) reduce the performance penalty; (2) achieve a satisfactory position for contact and refueling; (3) increase the fuel flow rate; and (4) develop visual and electronic means to facilitate the rendezvous. They also endorsed an AMC proposal for a conference between AMC and '… all interested aircraft manufacturers to discuss the in-flight refueling methods currently being used and developed by Boeing …

YKB-29T 45-21734 demonstrated triple-point probe-and-drogue refueling ('triple nipple'). For fighters this was an efficient solution to air refueling. Fuel delivery rate to a bomber, however, proved to be inadequate and excessively tiresome for bomber pilots. *Photo P30077 courtesy Boeing*

[as well as] to acquaint other aircraft manufacturers with the history and background of in-flight refueling methods and to discuss the theory and background of the flying boom method.' By late 1948, when Boeing began considering turbojets instead of propeller turbines for the B-52, the new boom system was being tested and promised a practical means for refueling.

The British Solution

In 1948 FRL created a US subsidiary (Flight Refueling Inc – FRI) to serve the North American market. Cobham visited the US that year to explore other applications, meeting with Navy and Air Force officers to discuss refueling single-seat fighters. He promised a demonstration in early 1949 to coincide with the visit of a US Air Force technical mission to England. After considering several methods derived from the existing looped hose system to satisfy this new mission, Cobham's engineers produced the 'probe and drogue'.

In the probe and drogue system, the tanker carries a hose drum reel that holds the air refueling hose. At the free end of this hose is a coupling and drogue – popularly referred to as the 'basket'. The receiver has a forward-projecting probe that is fitted with a nozzle. During refueling, the tanker trails the hose which takes up a natural trail angle due to drogue drag, and the receiver maneuvers to insert the probe into the drogue. Once the nozzle engages the coupling it is held in place by spring-loaded toggles. The movement of the hose drum actuates switches which open and close valves that allow fuel to flow, and illuminate indicator lights showing the appropriate drum position. Only a small force is required to engage the coupling, but a much greater force is required to disengage, enabling contact to be maintained throughout a normal range of maneuvers. To prevent 'hose whip' when the receiver makes contact, a constant retraction torque is applied to the hose drum. Although insufficient to retract the hose during normal trail, it is sufficient to take up slack when the forward motion of the receiver relieves tension on the drogue.

There was little official British interest in this scheme, and FRL was forced to use company money for its initial development. Cobham did manage to obtain an elderly Gloster Meteor III with which to carry out initial trials. Tests began with the Meteor and a Lancaster III tanker originally modified for 'Tiger Force' and that had remained in use with FRL for further tests. The first probe and

drogue contact was made on 24th April 1949, and the US mission had its promised demonstration a few days later. Subsequent demonstrations to manufacturers, the British armed services, civil servants, and politicians did much to convince them that FRL had indeed produced a practical method of refueling single-seat jet fighters. A 12-hour endurance flight in August was widely publicized and helped FRL acquire official support. Only then did the Air Ministry place a contract with FRL for continued development, although it emphasized that there was no current military requirement for air refueling.

The US Air Force was sufficiently impressed with the FRL system to order, on 22nd August 1949, an applicability study of the probe and drogue on US jet fighters. On 7th December 1949 the Air Force approved the installation of the probe and drogue in six planes as part of Project OUTING. The Project OUTING airplanes included two Republic F-84 Thunderjet receivers, two B-29 probe receivers (one equipped for a high fuel-transfer rate, the other equipped for a low fuel-transfer rate), a single-point B-29 tanker, and a three-point YKB-29T tanker (45-21734). Following initial tests in England, the two F-84s were flown non-stop to the United States on 22nd September 1950 in Operation FOX ABLE FOUR, ('fighter/Atlantic/four') refueling from Lincoln and B-29 tankers. One F-84 was unable to complete its second refueling and the pilot bailed out over Newfoundland. Earlier fighter deployments across the Atlantic had been in stages with refueling stops in Scotland, Iceland, Greenland and Labrador. In July 1951 the three-point YKB-29T was the first to demonstrate simultaneous refueling with the assistance of three borrowed RAF Meteor F.8s (16 RAF Meteor F.8s had been fitted with probes for trials during 1951, and two of these – together with a Meteor F.4 used by FRL – were used for this demonstration). The first combat air refueling took place on 6th July 1951 when a KB-29M refueled four Lockheed RF-80 Shooting Stars over Korea, using the FRL probe and drogue.

Birth of the 'Flying Boom'

While FRL was busy trying to overcome the mechanical and operational inadequacies associated with the looped hose arrangement, Boeing was equally busy with its own replacement. Boeing's solution was to use a telescoping pipe that was not vulnerable to freezing and allowed a greater fuel flow rate than the hose. The proposed pipe was 28ft (8.5m) long when retracted and 48ft (14.6m) long when extended, and protruded forward from above the tanker's cockpit. Recognizing the potential for catastrophic failure, Air Force project officer Captain Mack Elliott suggested putting the tanker above the receiver and lowering the pipe out the back of the tanker, or as Leisy described it, 'lowering the boom'. Small aerodynamic surfaces called 'ruddervators' were installed on the boom for aerodynamic control, allowing the operator to 'fly' the boom into position and help the receiver maintain contact during the off–load. The result was the Boeing Flying Boom. Lieutenant Colonel Tom Gerrity, in charge of the B-50 program, quickly approved its development – particularly with the B-50 in mind. The Boeing design would not only surmount the problems associated with the looped hose system, it would also rid the Air Force of its dependence on British equipment. However, Gerrity directed Boeing to continue work on the FRL system in B-29 tankers and receivers until its flying boom was operable.

The flying boom was a universally mounted telescopic device fitted in the tail of the tanker, and was controlled by the boom operator from the tail compartment. The boom was extended and retracted by hydraulic power which drove an endless chain loop. The boom nozzle mated with a receptacle in the top of the receiver and was held in place by hydraulically powered toggles. Signal coils in the nozzle and receptacle activated relays that controlled boom functions. Pilot director indicator (PDI) lights mounted beneath the tanker assisted the receiver pilot in maintaining correct air refueling position. Excessive movement or exceeding the limits of the refueling envelope caused an automatic disconnect. When not in use the boom was hoisted up by a steel cable and stowed beneath and behind the fuselage. The flying boom in use today on KC-135s, KC-10s, and KC-46s differs little in principle from this prototype.

Flight trials of a 'dry' boom installed on two modified RB-29Js, redesignated as YKB-29J tankers, together with a B-29 boom receiver commenced in October 1948, and quickly proved the feasibility of the concept. To validate the fuel transfer capability and increase the transfer rate up to the desired 600gpm (2,271 liters pm), Boeing constructed a 'boom tower' at Wichita, KS, where a full-size boom was lowered into an actual receiver airplane to check flow

rates, pressures, and distribution to the receiver's fuel tanks. Together with a 'tank farm' set up at the Boeing power plant laboratory to simulate a tanker aircraft fuel system, these facilities enabled many of the initial problems to be easily overcome.

The flying boom was quickly recognized as a success, and total of 116 B-29s were converted to boom tankers and designated KB-29Ps. The first KB-29P (44-86427) was delivered to the 97th AREFS at Biggs AFB, TX, on 1st September 1950. Boeing instructors trained two 97th AREFS crews initially, which then returned to Biggs AFB to serve as instructors for the rest of the unit. The first two Air Force boom operators were Master Sergeants Curtis W Compton and Frank L Hobart.

The first boom receivers were B-50Ds (also from Biggs AFB), and were originally intended to have the FRL hose refueling system installed. SAC's insistence that they have the boom receptacle rather than the hose system delayed their initial delivery. The flying boom was used to refuel a jet bomber for the first time on 2nd February 1951 when a KB-29P refueled a North American RB-45C Tornado over Edwards AFB, CA. On 14th July the first combat refueling using the flying boom took place with an RB-45C receiver over Korea. An RB-45C made the first non-stop trans-Pacific flight – from Elmendorf AFB, AK, to Yokota AB, Japan – on 29th July 1951, with two refuelings from KB-29Ps.

Above: Boeing built a number of test rigs to evaluate the flying boom. By the time the KC-135 arrived, they had become simple devices to confirm proper contact and operation. *Photo A119459 courtesy Boeing*

Right: The first jet refueling using the flying boom took place on 2nd February 1951, recorded here. KB-29Ps were soon refueling RB-45Cs in combat over North Korea, and secret reconnaissance overflights of the Soviet Union and Red China. *Photo HS5411 courtesy Boeing*

Parallel and Conflicting Systems

The US Air Force now had at its disposal two operating but incompatible air refueling systems: the British probe and drogue and the US flying boom. In an especially fateful decision, the Air Force decided to continue acquisition of both systems. The result would foster years of infighting within the Air Force, create artificial operational limitations for every air refuelable airplane in the Air Force (and the US Navy and Marine Corps) inventory, and undermine the desire to have a system compatible with the North Atlantic Treaty Organization (NATO).

The primary motivation for the development of an Air Force air refueling system was to extend the range of SAC's nuclear armed strategic bombers sufficiently to allow them to operate from bases in the US, free from the restrictions attendant with overseas basing in foreign nations as well as their risk of being destroyed in a pre-emptive or surprise attack. Bombers based in the US required large fuel transfers necessitating lengthy contacts with the tanker, a process that could quickly fatigue a pilot, particularly one who had already flown halfway around the world from America en route to his target in the Soviet Union. The Boeing Flying Boom offered a stable transfer system capable of offloading large quantities of fuel in a short period. This meant that even a tired bomber pilot could get 'on the boom' and stay there with assistance from the boom operator and quickly get all the gas required to complete the mission. Although the flying boom easily satisfied SAC's need for air refueling, it did not necessarily satisfy other existing and potential commands or services which required air refueling.

Growth of Fighter Refueling

The original tests of the probe and drogue system in Project OUTING sufficiently validated the concept to allow its immediate introduction into combat operations. The single-point B-29 tanker was assigned to the Far East Air Force (FEAF) to support fighter combat operations in Korea. Additionally, eight KB-29M tankers had their looped hose system replaced with the FRL probe and drogue. Nicknamed 'Quickie' tankers, these too were deployed to the FEAF and pressed into immediate combat support as part of Project HIGHTIDE.

HIGHTIDE was a three-phase program to evaluate the probe and drogue system in combat operations in Korea. Lockheed F-80 and RF-80s, as well as additional F-84s, had a refueling probe and relief valve installed on their wingtip fuel tanks. The wingtip-mounted probe made it difficult for the receiver pilot to judge the final closure rate to contact and usually required several contacts for a complete fill up. Nonetheless, the wingtip probes provided a rapid means to convert a large number of fighters without considerable and time-consuming modifications.

Following the initial training phase, Phase 2 involved refueled combat missions. Notable among these was one involving an F-80C flown by Lieutenant Colonel H W Dorris who remained airborne for 14 hours, 15 minutes on 28th September 1951. Dorris made five attacks on various targets in North Korea and was refueled eight times by two KB-29M 'Quickie' tankers. Although the F-80 was refueled in flight, one is hard-pressed to believe that it could have delivered more than a token weapon load on each target without landing and being rearmed.

Phase 3 was the deployment of an entire wing of fighters equipped with the probe and drogue system. Forty-eight F-84Es of the 116th Fighter Bomber Wing (FBW) completed the first air refueled deployment to the Far East in May 1951. The next HIGHTIDE deployment took place in August 1951, with F-84Gs of the 31st Fighter Escort Wing (FEW) from Turner AFB, GA. This unit flew its first refueled combat mission on 27th August. An operational phase was to have followed, with other fighter groups being trained in aerial refueling and additional aircraft being fitted with probed tanks. SAC, however, was unwilling

to release further B-29s for conversion into tankers and Project HIGHTIDE ended. On 17th January 1952 USAF Headquarters directed SAC to send additional tankers to Korea, and six KB-29Ms were deployed to Japan to support increasing fighter refueling operations.

The Boom and Fighter Refueling

SAC also operated several FEWs to protect bombers from enemy interceptors. These escort fighters suffered even greater range limitations than their bomber counterparts, and several innovative techniques were tested to extend their range. These included cable towing, wingtip towing, and 'parasiting', but were all abandoned in favor of aerial refueling. Provision was made in the original design of both the boom and the probe/drogue to tow small receiver aircraft by increasing the pressure on the locking toggles once in contact. This has been used in emergencies and has saved several fighters and their crews (see Appendix V)

The first jet fighter equipped for boom refueling was the F-84G Thunderjet. The first delivery was in 1951, but problems with refueling equipment and the higher priority given to bomber and tanker training delayed F-84G refueling training until early 1952. The first mass fighter deployment to demonstrate this new long range capability was carried out in July 1952 as part of Operation FOX PETER ONE – 'fighter/Pacific/one', the first fighter transit of the Pacific Ocean. During this exercise, 58 F-84Gs of the 31st FEW flew from Turner AFB to Misawa AB and Chitose AB, Japan. (These were the same F-84Gs that later flew to the Far East as part of Phase 3 of Project HIGHTIDE, refueling with the probe and drogue system. They were therefore the first dual-system receivers. The North American F-86 Sabre was tested with both twin underwing probed tanks and a boom receptacle installed above the engine intake. Neither was adopted, although the US Navy North American FJ-3/4 Fury derivatives were fitted with an air refueling probe.) The F-84Gs made en route stops for fuel and crew rest but were refueled by KB-29P tankers on the over-water legs. Although the deployment took ten days, it was still several days quicker than weather proofing the fighters for surface shipment, transporting them by aircraft carrier, and then preparing them on arrival.

An Unclear Decision

In early February 1952 SAC conducted a series of demonstration flights at its Offutt AFB, NE, headquarters to evaluate and recommend a single air refueling system. Test results showed that each system was best suited to a particular receiver. From the fighter pilot's perspective 'the drogue system is quite adaptable to fighter aircraft... Once contact has been made the problem of maintaining position is considerably more simpler than in the case of the boom system. It should be possible to refuel two or three aircraft at a time with the present drogue arrangement although the rate of flow is not as high as the boom system, the time differential realized between refueling of three fighters at once and one at a time in the boom system would most likely show to the advantage of the drogue system. Once contact has been made, probably the effect of turbulence would be less in the drogue operation than it would be in the boom system. The boom system offers no particular problem with respect to a fighter pilot maintaining his position, however, some consideration should be given to the expense of the equipment, the necessity of training the boom operators and the ever present possibility of damaging the boom mechanism or the nozzle itself to the extent that that particular tanker would be inoperative. In the case of the drogue, if one drogue is damaged two alternates still remain for utilization by other fighters. ... Generally, it would appear that the boom system is technically more complicated than is the probe and drogue system. In summation, it is my opinion that the test has been inadequate to conclusively determine the relative desirability of one system to the absolute exclusion of the other system.'

Strategic Air Commands's bomber pilots clearly held a different set of priorities:

'…5. Pilot fatigue should be considered in the evaluation of the two systems. The boom system requires a high level of proficiency in close-in formation. The probe-drogue system requires the same level of proficiency in formation flying plus the responsibility of guiding the receiver probe into contact with the drogue. When a pilot is making the contact, it is necessary to hold the receiver aircraft within 30in (76.2cm) limits in both altitude and direction. This requires an extreme amount of concentration and abnormal technique in the use of the controls. After a pilot has flown for eight to ten hours in any type bomber, his efficiency is lowered considerably; thus, I doubt if he could ever establish contact a second time with probe-drogue equipment, if an unintentional disconnect occurred at heavy gross weights (140,000 lb/63,503kg). The boom receiver pilot has only to obtain and maintain position while the boom operator establishes contact and transfers fuel.

'6 …The probe installation in the bomber receiver and the 30in (76.2cm) drogue, when in contact, seriously restricts the area of visibility which must be utilized in flying close-in formation. … In certain allowable positions of the probe receiver, the entire fuselage is blocked out of view. … I attempted to maintain position with radio silence using only my reference to the tanker. I estimate an average time in contact to be approximately one minute before either an inner or outer limit disconnect occurred. …There is no assistance available for the pilot of a probe receiver in stopping the rate of closure after contact is made or in maintaining position during a rapid increase in gross weight while onloading fuel.'

These tests showed what SAC's bomber pilots wanted, and in the absence of measurable opposition from the probe and drogue evaluators, Major General John B Montgomery Jr, SAC's Deputy Commander for Operations, concluded that the flying boom represented 'the best solution to the in-flight refueling problems for the present time.' Despite Montgomery's self-interested endorsement of the flying boom, Air Research and Development Command (ARDC) held the opposite view and planned to recommend the probe and drogue system as the standard for future aircraft.

In an effort to change or at least defer this decision, Montgomery appealed directly to old friends in the Pentagon. '… I found B-29 probe hook-up much more difficult to execute than the B-50 boom receiver. In fact, for that particular airplane, I believe only our best pilots, with lots of practice, could maintain proficiency. If you don't believe me, ask anyone [sic] of about ten other pilots out here who tried it.' Montgomery acknowledged the fighter pilots' preference for the probe and drogue but dismissed it, saying 'as for the probe fighter, I found it easier to handle than the boom job although neither one presented any real pilot problem.' Montgomery offered to repeat the tests previously conducted at Offutt AFB, this time to be impartially conducted by the Air Force's test unit at Eglin AFB, FL: '… my entire investigation of the refueling problem convinces me that Eglin is the outfit to come up with the answer and not people who take one or two flights (like me and that FEAF fellow). …You must admit that acceptance of the fact at this time that the probe-drogue system is superior (across the board) to the boom system is in fact admitting that the USAF made an erroneous decision on the boom. If we are that stupid, we are equally capable of making another bad decision on the Probe and Drogue. We should give Eglin ample time and opportunity to analyze this problem and make recommendations. There are apparently both good and bad features in each system.'

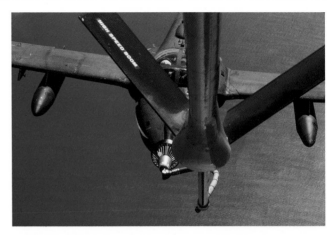

The author (white helmet) 'on the basket' in OA-37B *Hammer 71*. On a clear day with no turbulence this was a simple process. At night, in bad weather, and especially with a basket on a long drogue (rather than the BDA), probe-and-drogue refueling is very demanding. *Photo by Jeffrey Harper*

Montgomery's vague *mea culpa* and appeals fell on deaf ears. On 11th July 1952 ARDC recommended the probe and drogue as the standard Air Force air refueling system. At LeMay's insistence, ARDC did not require that the probe and drogue be retrofitted to existing airplanes since this would hamper SAC's combat capability during the conversion program.

ARDC's decision was based upon five considerations: (1) price – the probe and drogue cost was half that of the flying boom; (2) shorter training time for probe and drogue tanker crew members; (3) reduced accident hazard – 'the probe and drogue unit has a larger formating envelope and is therefore easier to fly and less fatiguing to the receiver pilot,' – clearly favoring the fighter pilot; (4) growth potential – the flying boom was limited to speeds of '300mph IAS', the perceived 'practical limit for boom maneuverability' – whereas proposed modifications to the drogue would allow refueling at speeds in excess of 300mph (482km/h); and (5) rate of flow – although the boom could achieve the desired 600gpm (2,271 liters pm) and the probe and drogue could only reach 250gpm (946 liters pm), proposals had been received for 'flow rates up to 1,200 gpm' (4,542 liters pm) for the probe and drogue.

Although the flying boom was superior to the probe and drogue in several areas, particularly its proven ability to satisfy SAC's refueling needs, the probe and drogue was endorsed based on unproven engineering proposals which had yet to be thoroughly tested. Nonetheless, on 13th August 1952 the Undersecretary of the Air Force approved ARDC's recommendation and the probe and drogue became the Air Force's single standard air refueling system.

Need for a Better Tanker

Although the KB-29Ps were satisfactory when used with other B-29s and B-50s, SAC recognized that they would be inadequate to refuel the jet powered B-47 and B-52. In mid-1950 SAC therefore requested an 'improved aerial refueling platform able to match the minimum speed of the B-47.' After considering several available alternatives, in December 1950 SAC selected a tanker version of the Boeing C-97 Stratofreighter transport. The piston-engined KC-97A was capable of carrying a greater quantity of fuel for offload but its performance was barely sufficient to accommodate the B-47. The KC-97 still had notable limits. Because the maximum speed of the KC-97 was below the minimum speed of the B-47 at high gross weights, it was necessary to perform a 'toboggan' maneuver in which both tanker and receiver descended while in contact to increase speed as the B-47 became heavier.

In 1951 three C-97As had an improved flying boom installed in place of the existing clamshell cargo doors in the aft lower fuselage. Initial tests validated the design and orders were ultimately placed for more than 800 KC-97 tankers. The first KC-97E (51-0183) was delivered on 14th July 1951 to the 306th AREFS at MacDill AFB. Deliveries of the B-47B began in late 1951, but due to crew training requirements and an initial lack of operational refueling equipment in the KC-97s, it was not possible to start training B-47 crews in air refueling until April 1952. This delayed training was further hampered by constant equipment failure and operational problems. Despite these difficulties, the combat radius of the B-47 increased threefold with two or more refuelings.

Overseas deployment of B-47 bomb wings together with their KC-97 tanker squadrons began in June 1953 when the 306th BW deployed from MacDill AFB to RAF Fairford, England. The B-47s and KC-97s all landed at Limestone AFB, ME, staying overnight. The B-47s then deployed nonstop to RAF Fairford, while the KC-97s again spent the night at Harmon AFB, Newfoundland. The B-47s returned to MacDill AFB nonstop. In August 1954 B-47s from Hunter AFB, GA, flew a simulated bombing mission as part of Operation LEAP FROG, landing in North Africa after air refueling. LEAP FROG showed that SAC's jet bombers no longer required forward basing but could be stationed in the US and still satisfy their strike commitment. Nonetheless, their tankers still had to be based overseas.

A Major Reversal

It was, no doubt, the large number of tankers (by the end of 1952 SAC had 20 refueling squadrons and 318 KB-29 and KC-97 tankers) and LeMay's influence that reversed the Air Force's decision on the probe and drogue system. Although the actual motivation for this change has not been confirmed, LeMay certainly would have argued that because (1) the ARDC recommendation did not require retrofitting the probe and drogue system to existing tankers; (2) SAC had so many tankers with the flying boom already installed (less than a third were looped-hose equipped, and there were only nine KB-29Ms); (3) the primary mission of SAC's tankers was to refuel SAC's bombers; (4) the Korean war had ended and the number of fighter refuelings was dramatically reduced; and (5) Boeing had announced the development of a jet powered tanker designed specifically to refuel the B-47 and B-52, that any future air refueling system should perforce be a flying boom system. The flying boom was the Air Force's de facto air refueling system, and LeMay and SAC wanted to keep it that way.

On 14th July 1958 the Air Force formalized what already existed, announcing that '... the flying boom would be the standard for its aircraft. The KC-97 and then the KC-135, both with flying booms, had already created a de facto standard. Combat aircraft without boom-refuelable capabilities that were already in service or in production were to retain their installed or programmed refueling systems, and boom-to-drogue adapters would be employed by SAC tankers to fuel probe-equipped aircraft on an interim basis.'

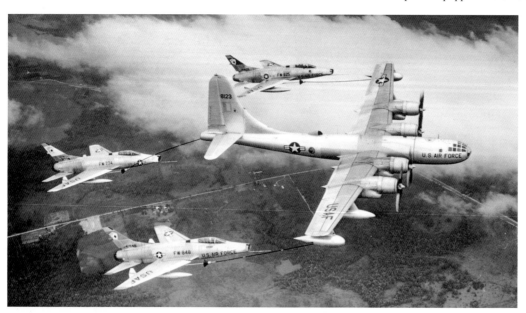

Above: KC-97E 51-0214 refuels B-47B 49-2642. Although an improvement over the KB-29, the KC-97's performance was a poor match for B-47s, which often flew at the edge of a stall during air refueling – spins were common after falling off the boom. *Photo BW60093 courtesy Boeing*

Left: TAC acquired drogue-equipped KB-50s for its fighters and medium bombers. By 1965 the KB-50s were all withdrawn from service due to corrosion. What followed was a bureaucratic battle between SAC and TAC over ownership of 70 KC-135s. *Author's collection*

TAC and Air Refueling

Tactical Air Command (TAC), which controlled the majority of the Air Force's fighters, remained adamant in its support for the probe and drogue method of air refueling and quickly recognized the need to acquire its own tankers. The first of two TAC refueling squadrons was activated in March 1954 and was equipped with KB-29Ps. SAC KB-29Ps and KC-97s continued to provide supplementary air refueling. Concerned that large, slow, piston powered tankers would be vulnerable in a jet dominated combat area, TAC also evaluated fighter-to-fighter refueling. During the late 1950s several types (including the Republic F-84F Thunderstreak, North American F-100 Super Sabre, McDonnell F-101 Voodoo and Republic F-105 Thunderchief) were tested in the 'buddy' tanker role. Although the buddy tanker entered service with the US Navy in 1957, it was not adopted by the Air Force.

In addition to the buddy tanker, TAC sought a newer, more suitable heavy tanker, preferably with multiple-point refueling. Several bombers and transports were considered, including in 1955 a two-point Lockheed C-130 Hercules tanker. In spite of performance limitations, however, only a three-point B-29 tanker similar to that modified by FRL in Project OUTING appeared to offer any immediate and realistic multi-point capability. Hayes Aircraft Corporation modified one B-29 into a KB-29 before the Air Force canceled this program. During 1955 the B-50 was withdrawn from bomber duties, and Hayes converted the first of an eventual total of 136 B-50As, RB-50Bs, and TB-50Hs to the three-point tanker role which were assigned to TAC pending further studies of its air refueling requirements.

At approximately the same time, TAC developed the Composite Air Strike Force (CASF), whose bombers, fighters, transports, and reconnaissance aircraft could deploy worldwide and operate independently for up to 30 days. This global mobility required both an uninterrupted and rapid deployment capability. Previous deployments proved this an unrealistic expectation, particularly given complications such as bad weather or political and diplomatic interference from other nations. Air refueling appeared as the only viable solution to the rapid deployment requirement, and the June 1956 debut of the three-point KB-50 offered the means to achieve this goal.

Operation MOBILE BAKER demonstrated this new capability a few months later when a strike force – including 16 F-84Fs, 16 F-100Cs, four RF-84Fs, and four Douglas B-66s – flew to Europe to participate in a NATO exercise. The deployment was complicated by the need for both probe and drogue and boom tankers, as the F-100Cs and B-66s were probe-equipped and the F-84Fs and RF-84Fs were boom receivers. Subsequent CASF exercises validated the ability of the KB-50 fleet to support tactical combat aircraft deployments over long distances on short notice. The KB-50's limited performance became a hindrance, however, during refueling operations with newer receivers such as the F-101, Lockheed F-104C Starfighter, and the F-105. The tanker was often forced to descend to a lower altitude or carry out a toboggan maneuver in order for the receiver to stay in contact. To improve the KB-50's performance, J47 turbojets were fitted in place of the underwing tanks. In testimony to the House Defense Appropriations Subcommittee in 1959, TAC Commander General Otto P Weyland expressed his concern about the obsolete equipment with which TAC was forced to carry out its mission. Specifically, he argued that the existing KB-50 fleet could not guarantee timely deployment of US tactical aircraft. 'TAC needed a jet tanker and [Weyland] would give its acquisition top priority even though it was not a combat airplane. Such a tanker was needed to provide the mobility to get tactical forces to the right place at the right time.' TAC had looked enviously at SAC's KC-135 for some time, and although concerned about its runway requirements, felt it would nonetheless satisfy the command's tanker needs.

SAC as Single Manager

TAC's plan to acquire KC-135s met with immediate and formidable resistance from General LeMay, now the Air Force Vice Chief of Staff. He saw two tanker programs as redundant and unnecessary, and, as the original purpose of the tanker was to extend the range of SAC's bombers, any use of these tankers for other than bomber support undermined (in LeMay's view) the ability of the US to project its nuclear armada. In the age of the bomber and missile gap (and a finite defense budget), support for tactical projects at the expense of strategic projects was perceived as counterproductive to US national security policy. He called for 'a single tanker force equipped to provide support to all combat operations requiring air refueling.'

SAC was not insensitive to TAC's refueling needs, however, and in January 1959 initiated plans to adapt a KC-135 boom for drogue refueling. Actual testing began on 10th February 1959. Additional testing resumed on 26th August 1959 with Operation STAY ON II, which 'showed the need for an improved boom-to-drogue adapter, increased rendezvous capability, modification to the fuel capacity of fighter aircraft, and standardized training requirements for aircrews.' Nonetheless, on 3rd May 1960 LeMay announced the approval of 'a single tanker force, SAC managed and KC-135 equipped' in support of both SAC and TAC training and combat needs. The single-manager program – with SAC in total control – was scheduled for full implementation by the end of FY63.

Operation STAY ON III, conducted from February through March 1961, successfully demonstrated the KC-135's drogue adapter, by transferring 844,440 lb (383,037kg) of fuel to probe-equipped F-100 Super Sabres, F-101 Voodoos, F-105 Thunderchiefs, and RB-66 Destroyers. With a viable system to satisfy TAC requirements at hand, the Air Force designated SAC as the single manager for all KC-135 refueling operations. On 17th November 1961 Secretary of Defense Robert S McNamara approved the program, which dedicated 70 KC-135s in support of TAC requirements when needed, but were flown and managed by SAC crews and commanders. SAC's reticence to support routine TAC operations at the expense of bomber support is underscored in a TAC history. 'The stage was being set for the incorporating of the KC-135 into [TAC] employment plans, but it was obvious that SAC was not enthusiastic.'

A conference held in December published directives for joint SAC-TAC refueling operations. SAC's first major support of TAC requirements came during Operation BIG LIFT in October 1963. In all, 115 KC-135s provided air refueling for 71 TAC fighters staging to Europe in support of BIG LIFT troop movements. TAC's hopes for an independent jet tanker force were effectively ended. KB-50 operations, especially in Southeast Asia, continued until late 1964 when the fleet was finally grounded due to structural problems and corrosion.

US Naval and Marine Air Refueling

Concerned about the limited endurance of carrier-borne jet fighters, the US Navy saw the probe and drogue as a relatively simple means to increase endurance and provide several operational benefits. North American Aviation modified its XAJ-1 Savage into a tanker in 1952, and refueling trials commenced with a Grumman F9F-5 Panther and a McDonnell F2H Banshee. Beginning in 1953 AJ-1 and AJ-2 Savages assigned to Heavy Attack Squadrons were fitted with a removable tanker kit and were used as carrier-borne tankers. Navy fighters had been fitted with probes from 1953 onward, and in 1955 the Navy announced that all new fighters would be so equipped for air refueling. Few of the large Savages could fit on board a carrier, however, and in an effort to increase the availability of air refueling without sacrificing limited deck space, the Navy began exploring the use of external refueling stores carried on single-seat attack types.

These buddy tankers, initially Douglas AD-6 Skyraiders and A4D-2 Skyhawks, entered service in 1957. The first external refueling store in wide use was the Douglas D-704, and many units were still in use 30 years later.

Flying-boat tankers were also planned, and a few Convair R3Y-2 Tradewinds were fitted with four underwing refueling pods before the type was withdrawn from service because of engine problems. In August 1956 one of these tankers simultaneously refueled four Grumman F9F-8 Cougars.

The US Marine Corps introduced air refueling during the mid 1950s, initially on the F9F-8 and the North American FJ-3 Fury. In 1957 the Marines acquired A4D-2 buddy tankers. Seeking their own independent assault transport/ tanker force, the Corps ordered the Lockheed GV-1 (KC-130F), giving Marine fighter units the ability to deploy rapidly over long distances.

Continued British Developments

Although the probe and drogue was a British invention, the RAF was slow to adopt it. Following squadron evaluation trials carried out in 1951, the Air Staff acknowledged the operational advantages of air refueling, but turned down any acquisition because of a concern

that buying tankers would limit purchases of front-line fighters.

A review in the early 1950s of operational requirements for the V-bomber force (Vickers Valiant, Avro Vulcan and the Handley Page Victor) showed that coverage of potential targets in the Soviet Union required a radius of action greater than that available with the basic aircraft. Various means to extend the V-bombers' range were considered, including exceeding the maximum gross take-off weight which would necessitate rocket-assisted take-offs. Before any of the V-bombers flew, FRL showed that the range and bomb load of each could be significantly increased by single or multiple refueling. FRL's development of self-contained tanker kits (primarily for US Air Force and Navy operations), which could be quickly installed or removed in the bombers once the fixed piping had been incorporated, provided an immediate solution to refueling the 'V-force'. Finally, the success of air refueling in the United States, coupled with intensive lobbying by FRL, prompted the Air Staff to decide in late 1952 to adopt the probe and drogue system for the V-force.

The Mk.16 Hose Drum Unit was installed in a Valiant, and trials of Valiant-to-Valiant refueling commenced in 1957. Squadron trials began the following year, and in 1962 two Valiant squadrons became dedicated tanker units. Vulcan and Victor squadrons began air refueling training in the early 1960s and in June 1961, a Vulcan B.1A of 617 Squadron flew non-stop from England to Australia with air refueling from Valiant tankers. RAF fighter squadrons also began air refueling training in the early 1960s, and the Royal Navy introduced air refueling in 1961.

Limits and Implications

Although the usefulness of aerial refueling was apparent through tests and operations in air forces and by companies around the world, the availability of a suitable tanker for the new B-52 was another matter entirely. Despite the obvious operational limitations of piston tankers such as the KB-29 or the KC-97, government sponsorship and funding in the US and abroad of a jet tanker was not forthcoming. It remained for the aerospace industry to take the initiative, a bold move that had little obvious chance for success.

Above: The US Navy opted for the probe-and-drogue system, which allowed for a common method to refuel from BDA-equipped KC-135s as well as drogue-configured Navy tankers and fighters carrying a buddy refueling pack. *Photo by Rick Morgan*

Left: The KC-97 was ill suited to refuel the B-52. Large fuel offloads added to the weight of the new bomber, requiring higher speeds to maintain controlled flight. To allow for higher power settings without overrunning the tanker, B-52 refuelings were tested with the gear down adding drag, hardly a suitable choice. A jet tanker was the obvious solution. *Photo HS666 courtesy Boeing*

CHAPTER THREE

Bill Allen's Vision

'Talent hits a target no one else can hit; genius hits a target no one else can see.' – *German Philosopher Arthur Schopenhauer, 1859*

'Lots of power and lots of tail, I believe, make for a successful airplane and a happy pilot.' – *Joseph Sutter, Boeing Transport chief aerodynamicist, 1988*

The origin and development of the KC-135 were inextricably interwoven with that of the Boeing 707 jet airliner, as both tanker and airliner were the progeny of a single unsolicited company funded jet transport prototype first envisaged by Boeing Company President William M 'Bill' Allen. From this common ancestry, no doubt, derives the erroneous notion that the KC-135 is a military version of the 707. At best, the Air Force saw the KC-135 as only an interim solution to its air refueling needs, and the purchase of large quantities of these tankers took place under unusual circumstances. Further, KC-135 and 707 production was inseparably linked and the subject of considerable controversy between Boeing and the Air Force. As with any new weapons system, the KC-135 was beset with technical problems, some of which continue six decades later, still affecting its performance and capability.

Following the Second World War, considerable efforts were made in Britain, North America, France, and the Soviet Union to develop a jet transport. The British pioneered the field with the Rolls-Royce Nene-powered Avro Lancastrian I, which first flew on 14th August 1946, and on 19th September 1946 – flying on the Nenes only –

became the 'world's first jet airliner by making three passenger flights carrying [non-fare-paying] representatives of the Press as well as Ministry officials and other passengers.' Britain's de Havilland Comet 1, which first flew on 27th July 1949, became the world's first turbojet airliner to enter service, beginning commercial operations on 2nd May 1952. The Soviet Union's Tupolev Tu-104 *Camel* was the world's second jet airliner, entering commercial service on 15th September 1956.

North American efforts to develop a jet transport were not as visible as those in Britain but were by no means insignificant. The Avro Canada C-102 Jetliner was the first turbojet commercial aircraft designed as such *ab initio*. Its maiden flight was on 10th August 1949, but no orders were forthcoming and the program was discontinued in 1951. The first jet transport developed in the US was a four-engined variant of the Chase XCG-20 glider. It first flew on 21st April 1951, becoming the first jet transport to fly in the US and the first transport in the world to fly with pod-mounted engines. It was not until 26th October 1958 that the US had a commercial jet – the Boeing 707 – in service, and France followed by introducing Sud Caravelle service on 6th May 1959.

Blue skies for Boeing. In May 1959, the test ramp shows B-52D 56-0591 *The Tigator*, KC-135A 55-3118, four Boeing 707s, and a VC-137A. Bill Allen's vision for a jet tanker allowed Boeing to transition from a bomber manufacturer to the world's leading commercial jet airliner builder. Sadly, the B-52D crashed on 23rd June 1959, weeks after this image was taken. *Photo courtesy Boeing*

Development at Boeing

Boeing started jet transport feasibility studies as early as 1946, undergoing as many as 150 'paper airplane' iterations before choosing its final design. In the late 1940s airline officials were highly sceptical of the economic viability of operating jet transports. Boeing responded to these concerns with volumes of test data and detailed studies of military heavy jet operations, in particular those of the company's widely produced B-47 Stratojet.

The greatest concern of potential airline customers was the perception that jet engines were inefficient and that the design compromises necessary in order to achieve high speed were such that this type of power was useful only for military combat aircraft, where tactical considerations justified the 'luxury' of very high speeds. Boeing showed that although jet engines consumed approximately 20% more fuel per thrust horsepower than existing reciprocating engines, they resulted in reduced drag due to the engine's small size and eliminated the airflow disturbances created by the propeller slipstream. Since a jet transport could travel at speeds nearly twice those of existing piston-powered transports and carry more while en route, a jet could, according to Boeing, have a 'work capacity … three to four times that of the larger present-day transports,' earning considerably more revenue than its conventionally-powered predecessor.

Boeing's experience with military jet aircraft showed that jet maintenance was no greater than that for non-jet aircraft. In fact, airframe complexity actually decreased with jets. For example, a four-engine piston-powered airplane has – in addition to its four throttles – four mixture controls, four propeller pitch controls, four cowl flap controls, four oil cooler controls, and in some cases four supercharger and four intercooler controls. Turbojet engines have only four throttles. This reduction in complexity contributed to increased operational safety as jets benefitted from a sizeable increase in performance. Their increased takeoff, climb, and cruise capability easily allowed them to exceed minimum safety regulations for reciprocating engine aircraft. Overall, Boeing was convinced that a jet transport would be successful not only with the military but the airlines as well. It remained only to convince both parties…

Genesis

The company's first proposal, dating to 1947, was based upon the B-47. Designated the Model 473-1, it was powered by two Rolls-Royce Nenes and could carry 27 passengers. This design evolved into the Model 473-28, which closely resembled its bomber predecessor, including its large underwing fuel tanks. It was further developed into the 473-30, which lacked the external tanks but had a longer fuselage. One interesting Boeing proposal was the 1949 473-19A, a delta-shaped flying wing with a passenger capacity of 60 persons. By late 1949 this design had matured into the Model 473-30 and wind tunnel testing began, but Boeing engineers were dissatisfied with the design's narrow tricycle landing gear arrangement. Although this limitation is usually given as the primary reason for the design's discontinuation, John E Steiner, former Vice President for Corporate Product Development at Boeing, offered a different reason for the termination of the 473-60 project: 'we were unable to seriously interest the major airlines in starting the program.' Most likely both of these issues conspired to doom the 473-60 project.

It was yet another Boeing airplane that had the best potential for the demanding metamorphosis into the company's new jet transport. Boeing suggested that its Model 367, known in the military as the C-97 Stratofreighter (and later as the KC-97) and to the airlines as the Boeing 377 Stratocruiser, have its four piston engines replaced with turboprop engines. Still, this was not the jet transport Boeing envisaged. By the end of 1950 Boeing proposed further changes to the 367, incorporating a thin swept wing and empennage, and four jet engines mounted in pairs in a single pod beneath each wing. Designated the Model 367-64, little serious consideration was given to this proposal as it lacked the fuel capacity necessary for its voracious jet engines on long distance flights. A new wing with a thicker chord and greater fuel capacity was designed to replace the thin wing; this proposal was designated the Model 367-70-5.

During 1951 Boeing proposed a tanker variant of the jet-powered Model 367 to the Air Force. This offer was tied closely to SAC's precious B-52 Stratofortress strategic bomber. As Vaughn Blumenthal, Senior Aerodynamicist for the B-52 program remembered: 'In October 1948, emphasis on the B-52 design was changed from a propellered airplane to a pure jet which required double refueling. In late 1949, the gross weight of the B-52 was increased so that only outbound refueling was needed. A tanker, however, was a basic requirement for the B-52 from late 1948 onward.' This contrasts sharply with Air Force records that suggest the B-52 was initially designed to operate without aerial refueling because at the time no practical means existed to refuel the airplane. According to one Air Force source, it was not until 1953 that plans were even developed to conduct air refueling tests between the B-52 and the KC-97.

Despite official interest, SAC's heavy financial commitment to an operational fleet of B-47s and KC-97s and its projected acquisition

Boeing's jet tanker was the missing link between its piston-powered KC-97 and its new jet-powered B-52. The 367-80 was a derivative of the KC-97, and filled the niche perfectly. *Photo P15904 courtesy Boeing*

of a fleet of B-52s precluded any commitment to this new tanker effort: 'Boeing already has too many Air Force projects.' 'The money's needed for bombers.' 'B-47s can be made into jet tankers at less cost.' Further, the Air Force was not interested in the Boeing proposal as a jet transport because it lacked the 'new look' in cargo planes – a truckbed-high cargo floor, a high wing, and body-mounted gear. On 17th August 1951 the Air Force officially rejected Boeing's jet tanker/transport. Steiner recalls that 'by about the end of 1951, we became convinced that we could not sell a new tanker for the reasons [noted above]. It was this realization that propelled us to consider a company-financed prototype. Most of these designs had lower sweep wings than the B-47 and B-52, and we offered both turbo-prop and turbo-jet designs. We did a lot of wind tunnel work on a 25° swept wing (not 35°, as in the B-47 and B-52)'. Boeing was undaunted, going on to produce an entirely new airplane – the Model 367-80 (also dubbed 'Project X'). This design retained the overall appearance of its predecessors, had a slimmer fuselage and, most notably, had each of its four Pratt & Whitney J57-P-1 jet engines located in separate pods, two beneath each wing.

One advantage of the separate jet engine pod configuration was the protection gained against an engine fire burning into the wing or fuselage. Should fire engulf the pod, the supporting pylon could burn through and the entire flaming structure could then drop from the airplane. If both engines on one wing were in a single pod and were lost in this fashion, adequate control of the airplane during a go-around or missed approach could not be guaranteed. Placing each engine pod on a separate pylon on the Model 367-80 provided an added measure of safety. There is an adage among KC-135 crewmembers attesting to their confidence in the design: 'If Boeing had meant the KC-135 to fly with four engines they would have built it with five'. However amusing this anecdote, the primary reason for the pylon mounting was in fact primarily aerodynamic. Embedding the engine in the wing required an air intake that disrupted the leading edge of the wing, drastically reducing its lift efficiency, particularly on a swept wing. Boeing applied this lesson to its B-47 as compared to other early jet designs such as the North American B-45, Martin B-48, as well as the British Comet and the V-bomber force, all of which had the engines mounted embedded within the wing.

On 26th March 1952 Boeing President Bill Allen distributed a memorandum to his division heads asking if they felt that Boeing could fly a prototype jet transport within two years. Allen stipulated that the design and construction of this private venture must not impede existing or potential military contracts. Within a week of the first flight of the XB-52 on 15th April 1952, senior Boeing officials met to summarize their findings: 'Jim Barton of Cost Accounting said the prototype could be built for $13 million to $15 million. Maynard Pennell said the plane would meet the range requirements of a military tanker and would have three times the work capacity of the C-97 [Stratofreighter]. As a commercial airplane its… operating costs would be competitive. [George] Schairer said the same prototype could be used to demonstrate both a military and a commercial transport and could provide the performance data needed for production airplanes. Chief engineer Lysle Wood said engineering manpower was available. Experimental manager Al Jacobson said manufacturing manpower and floor space would be available. [Wellwood] Beall said Pratt & Whitney would have engines. John Yeasting said the prototype would provide the cost figures needed for pricing production models.'

Less than a month later, on 22nd April 1952, Boeing's board of directors unanimously approved $15 million (and later added another $1 million) of company funds, more than twice the company's 1951 net profits, for further development and construction of a prototype airplane. The new airplane was now designated the Model 707, but

Engines embedded in the wing or fuselage were not only a fire risk, they degraded the aerodynamics on the wing leading edge, significantly hurting aircraft performance. Martin's XB-48 was a good example of this design limit. *Author's collection*

Boeing chose to keep its new prototype under wraps and referred to it simply as the Boeing 367-80. Boeing had run out of its then-current 400-series designations, and the 500- and 600-series were reserved for 'pilotless aircraft' – missiles. It merits reemphasizing that the 367-80 was neither a 707 nor a 717 (KC-135) prototype, but a proof-of-concept prototype for a multi-engine jet aircraft from which both the 707 and KC-135 evolved along separate paths. Subsequent airliners would be designated as Model 707s, tankers as Model 717s.

In August 1952 Allen announced that Boeing '[had] for some time been engaged in a company-funded project which will enable it to demonstrate a prototype jet airplane of new design to the armed services and the commercial airlines in the summer of 1954.' As a military venture, the as-yet unidentified airplane would function as a jet transport and tanker, and as a commercial venture the new airplane would fill the jet transport production void on the west side of the Atlantic Ocean. Beyond that, a heavy veil of secrecy enveloped this novel design.

Construction of the Model 367-80 prototype began in October 1952 as work continued on a dedicated tanker variant. On 4th April 1953 Boeing completed the design of the Model 367-80-111 equipped with a British FRL Mk.14 hose drum in place of the standard air refueling boom. SAC rejected this design, insisting instead on the boom. In March 1954 Boeing revealed that the Model 367-80 would be 'ideally suited for high speed, high altitude tanker-transport duties,' and would be capable of refueling existing and future jet bombers, fighters, and reconnaissance aircraft 'at or near their operational altitudes.' As the roll-out neared for Boeing's new airplane, Allen elaborated his company's motivation for building the 367-80: 'Boeing's first consideration…was the nation's security. [Allen] made it clear that Boeing's principal aim was to fill what it considered a military need. That need,' he explained, 'was a jet tanker for aerial refueling. At the same time, and in the commercial interest, we believed America should no longer delay getting into the jet field. We only regret that economic considerations forced us to wait as long as we did.'

The 'economic considerations' Allen described were the pervasive fears in parts of the company about the lack of Boeing's financial success in the commercial market. He never let the commercial transport staff forget that the company's primary objective was to build a jet tanker for the Air Force, and that a commercial jet transport was of lesser (but nonetheless significant) importance. Allen insisted that the prototype be renamed the 367-80, so that the commercial airliner staff 'would not forget about' the tanker requirement, a decision that did not sit well with Boeing's commercial airline division. By emphasizing the 367-80's tanker/transport role, the Air Force would become the launch customer not only for the KC-135 but provide the kernel for 707 production. This strategy required suborning Boeing's commercial jet airliner priorities to those of the military tanker/transport. Arguably, without the considerable support within the company for the jet tanker program, there might never have been sufficient confidence to build the highly successful 707 jet airliner or its equally successful offspring. To many, the KC-135 is seen as the military version of the 707. Given Allen's priorities, it may be more appropriate to say that the 707 is the derivative of the KC-135.

The new airplane, known informally as the Dash 80, was rolled-out on 15th May 1954, two months ahead of schedule, and was christened by Bertha M Boeing, wife of company founder William E Boeing, with two bottles of champagne, one for each of the two names the airplane bore: Stratoliner for its commercial uses and Stratotanker for its military operations. The Dash 80 first flew on 15th July 1954.

Air Force Tanker Requirements

Although the Air Force chose not to fund early research and development of the 'Dash 80', it was not uninterested in Boeing's proposed jet tanker. At the SAC Requirements Conference held from 18-19th November 1953, General LeMay, SAC's commander, called for 200 jet tankers to be procured with fiscal year (FY) 1954 funds, clearly with the Boeing proposal in mind. On 30th November 1953, the Air Force Air Research and Development Command (ARDC) directed the Wright Air Development Center (WADC) at Wright-Patterson AFB, OH, beginning 14th December 1953, to evaluate the Air Force requirement for a jet tanker, finally acknowledging Boeing's foresight of just such an airplane.

SAC was not the only Air Force command interested in this airplane. Tactical Air Command was originally interested in the KC-135 during its development, but the runway it required and its lack of a three-point refueling capability were unsuitable for TAC's needs, primarily the support of the command's worldwide jet fighter deployments and operations. LeMay, however, wanted the new jet tanker to refuel nuclear-laden SAC B-47s and B-52s en route to their communist targets. Any diversion of airplanes to TAC would, SAC leaders argued, seriously undermine SAC's ability to carry out its nuclear strike mission, the Air Force's highest priority. (The same year that SAC accepted its first KC-135A [1957], TAC introduced the first of 136 Boeing KB-50J and KB-50K tankers into service.)

The Air Force considered a number of tanker proposals: two from Boeing (one for a 'lightweight' version of the KC-135 with a 261,000 lb [118,388kg] gross weight and another for a 'heavyweight' with a 295,000 lb [133,810kg] gross weight), a tanker version of the Douglas DC-8 jet airliner proposal (with a gross weight of 330,000 lb [149,685kg] and powered by J67 engines), the proposed Douglas XC-132 turboprop, and WADC's 'Design 1018.' Little is known of these proposals. Douglas' XC-132 was a swept-wing turboprop transport. Why this was included in the jet tanker competition is unclear, but it may have been considered only as an interim tanker pending a more complete evaluation and testing of the proposed jet tankers.

The Air Force tanker program, however, was subject to considerable internal confusion and lack of direction despite the immediate and pressing need for a jet tanker. One officer called the tanker program 'neither well planned nor cohesive.' Although SAC did not want the turboprop-powered C-132, an Air Force Air Council memo of 5th November 1953 recommended 'immediate programming for C-132 aircraft...toward support of B-52 and [Convair] B-58 [Hustler] bombers.' The Air Council reversed itself by 12th February 1954, insisting instead on obtaining 'a jet tanker inventory in consonance with operational needs as soon as feasible, considering both engineering and budget aspects...' It was not until 5th May 1954 that the Air Force officially announced both the requirement for a jet tanker and that a design competition would begin. ARDC invited Boeing, Convair, Douglas, Fairchild, Lockheed, and Martin to participate in the Jet Tanker/Transport Design Parameter Study that started on 18th June 1954. Martin declined to participate. Interestingly, Convair's proposal was for a tanker approximately the same size as the KC-135 but with a delta wing and conventional empennage.

Despite official existence of the procurement competition, four of the five competitors held few illusions that they might win. Rumors from both the Pentagon and ARDC headquarters intimated that Boeing's heavyweight proposal enjoyed the influential support of General LeMay and General Thomas Power. Such rumors were not without some basis. LeMay's official journal shows on 3rd May 1954 that although the competition 'killed' the KB-36 and KB-52 proposals, it did not 'close the field on the Boeing tanker', and that LeMay wanted 'no delay' in procuring a jet tanker, clearly revealing his preferences. In a 12th May 1954 'phone conversation between Allen and Major Gen John P McConnell, SAC's Deputy Chief of Staff for Plans, McConnell told Allen that LeMay was 'concerned' that SAC was 'already too late in getting a jet tanker'. Aware that a shorter competition favored the Boeing design, McConnell added that he 'did not know whether or not [LeMay] could effect any shortening of the time period' involved. There is no evidence that LeMay did unfairly influence the competition, but the impression was there that he had the power to do so. These rumors induced the Air Force to announce in late June 1954 that it had not already surreptitiously selected the Boeing tanker and would indeed honor ARDC's recommendation.

The 22nd July 1954 rendezvous flight between the Dash 80 and B-52 did not include refueling. Boeing subsequently installed a flying boom on the Dash 80 to demonstrate full operational capability. *Photo A87821 courtesy Boeing*

Boeing was not about to lose whatever initiative it might have had. On the Dash 80's seventh flight it practiced rendezvous and air refueling procedures with a B-52, although it lacked an air refueling boom and any means by which to transfer fuel (these were later installed). The message of the 22nd July 1954 demonstration flight was clear: while the other competitors were *talking* about building a tanker, Boeing was *flying* one. Boeing took the competition very seriously, however, and feared that the winner would undoubtedly be from southern California due to immense political pressure being exerted.

On 30th July 1954, with the tanker competition well under way, ARDC recommended (with LeMay's concurrence) purchasing 70 to 100 'interim' tankers, specifically the Boeing 367-80 tanker proposal, which Boeing now called the 367-138B and would later redesignate as the Model 717. These airplanes would provide SAC with an immediate source of jet tankers 'pending availability of the aircraft selected as a result of the current competition.' With the full support of LeMay and Power, the Air Force decided on 3rd August 1954 to buy the interim tankers. Two days later, Air Force Secretary Harold E Talbott announced that the service would procure 29 jet tankers from Boeing. On 6th August 1954, Procurement Authorization 55-27 provided $150 million for these 29 airplanes, fueling speculation that Boeing's proposal had already been chosen for the full tanker contract despite repeated Air Force denials. Less than two weeks later (and prior to the 27th August 1954 competition deadline), the Air Force announced the expenditure of $240 million for 88 additional Boeing interim tankers. By all appearances, Boeing had won; what remained seemed academic.

Competition Results

The outcome was not altogether as predicted. During October 1954 Air Materiel Command (AMC) recommended that from a production standpoint, Boeing should produce only the interim tanker and that either Douglas or Lockheed should build the full production tanker. Further, Secretary of Defense Charles E Wilson was reconsidering the 27th August purchase of the 88 additional KC-135As that Charles Anderson, Deputy Secretary of Defense, had approved and announced without his consent while Wilson was out of Washington, DC. Much to the relief of Boeing executives and SAC commanders, Wilson reaffirmed this purchase. Boeing's tanker was still known as the 'ultimate configuration', underscoring the Air Force's confidence in its selection. During December 1954 Major General Patrick W Timberlake, Commander of the USAF Air Proving Grounds at Eglin AFB, Florida, and Brigadier General J Stanley Holtoner, Commander of the Air Force Flight Test Center (AFFTC) at Edwards AFB, CA, flew the Dash 80. These officers would direct the operational test and evaluation of whatever tanker was selected, and their first-hand observations of the Dash 80's performance unquestionably influenced the eventual outcome.

That decision came in February 1955, although according to an official Air Force history the selection was reached on 10th October 1954. If so, it is surprising that this information was kept secret until four months later when Talbott announced that Lockheed's proposal had won the tanker design competition on the basis of its technical potential, and that at least one Lockheed prototype would be purchased and built immediately. This airplane, similar to Lockheed's proposed L-193 jet airliner, was about the same size as the KC-135A

AND THE WINNER IS...

It should not be surprising that even though Lockheed won the jet tanker competition it never built a prototype, let alone sold any airplanes. The distinguished company had no track record of designing and building large jet airplanes, although it did build a tranche of B-47s for Boeing. Nonetheless there has to be a first time for everything, and Lockheed was not entirely unprepared to go head-to-head against the world's largest jet bomber manufacturer.

The Lockheed L-193 design was the company's most significant effort to build a commercial jet airliner. First proposed in 1949, it underwent multiple configurations to accommodate loads from 48 to 125 passengers. Its performance was on par with the Boeing 707 and Douglas DC-8: cruise speed in excess of 520 KIAS at 40,000ft (12,192m), and a range of more than 3,000nm (5,556km). Gross weights varied from 150,000-225,000 lb (68,309-102,058kg) with takeoff and landing distances of approximately 6,000ft (1,829m). The L-193-55's appearance was similar to the Vickers VC10 and Ilyushin IL-62 *Classic* with two engines (with or without afterburners!) mounted on each side of the lower aft fuselage but without the 'T' tail. A fifth-engine version was also considered.

Lockheed was equally interested in the dedicated jet tanker market, and designed the CL-291-1 to meet the basic requirements to transfer 60,000 lb (27,216kg) of fuel to a B-52 during a rendezvous at a 2,500nm (4,630km) radius, but specific performance numbers have not been identified. The CL-291-1 looked much like a Lockheed C-141 but without the 'T' tail. Its four engines were mounted in two pods,

one under each wing. Interestingly, they were swept backward. Lockheed considered several variants (including the CL-291-3 with a low-versus shoulder-mounted wings) but each suffered substantial degrades in fuel capacity over the -1 version.

Which design won the jet tanker competition? Official Air Force records and contemporary news reports cite the L-193 airliner – not the CL-291 tanker – as the winner,

going so far as to include a summary of the L-193's appearance with aft-mounted engines similar to the VC10. Perhaps one day Lockheed will clarify the issue, but in any case none were ever built. Some 30 years later Lockheed could finally claim a large jet tanker among its aircraft, although the RAF TriStar K1s and KC1s were conversions of its L-1011-500 wide-body airliner undertaken by Marshall Aerospace, rather than a dedicated new-build airframe.

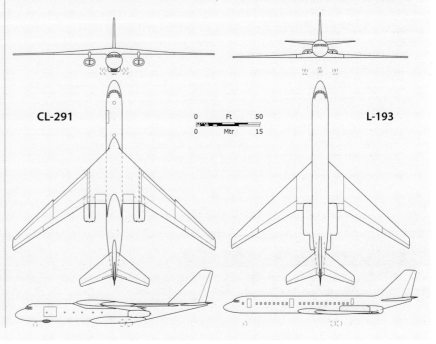

but with its engines mounted at the rear of the fuselage much like the Vickers VC10. There was more to Talbott's announcement, however, as he directed that KC-135A orders with Boeing would increase to $700 million, sufficient to purchase 169 new planes in addition to the 117 already ordered. Paradoxically, the winner of the tanker competition was funded to build only a prototype whereas one of the losers was funded to build a sizeable fleet of airplanes.

The motivation for this irregular selection may never be known. Both the Air Force and the Department of Defense (DoD) made it clear that a second source tanker would be both prohibitively expensive (in excess of $100 million) and a logistics nightmare. ARDC and AMC agreed that two competing designs would unnecessarily complicate SAC's logistics support and recommended selection of only one: Boeing's 'ultimate configuration'. SAC concurred, arguing that two tankers would require duplicate logistics systems, and SAC's desired tanker crew interchangeability program would require training in both systems, again needlessly duplicating costs. There was little doubt SAC supported the Boeing tanker. Satisfied for over a decade with Boeing products in the form of B-29s, B-50s, KC-97s, B-47s (and soon B-52s), it seemed natural 'not to switch horses in midstream'. In addition, the US was locked in a fevered strategic weapons build-up with the Soviet Union, and the KC-135A's imminent availability was a significant factor in its selection. Clearly, the Boeing tanker enjoyed considerable advantages in the competition, and it is not altogether unreasonable that it should have been chosen as the single source tanker.

Speculatively, Lockheed's selection as the winner was more an act of face than of pragmatism, particularly in view of the considerable pressure applied by California politicians to have the contract awarded to Lockheed. By announcing that Lockheed had won the competition, the Air Force could claim impartiality in selecting the tanker, thus defusing the many charges that Boeing had won the competition even before it had begun. The Air Force would buy additional Boeing tankers as a stop-gap measure until the Lockheed tanker was ready. The Air Force could then declare that it was neither possible nor preferable to buy two tankers, and, unfortunately for Lockheed, the credible availability of the Boeing KC-135A made it the only realistic choice.

Regardless of the means of its selection, the KC-135 had become the de facto Air Force jet tanker. Despite its merit, it still faced at least one final attempt to end its acquisition. As part of an effort throughout the DoD to decrease the number of airplanes in the inventories of its constituent services, one study recommended that the KC-135A be canceled. Testifying before the House Appropriations Committee, Assistant Secretary of Defense for Applications Engineering Frank Newbury described his office's goal of reducing the number of different types of aircraft in service to a minimum. 'Based on a technical review', he stated '… it was recommended that the KC-135 be discontinued and replaced by converted B-36 or B-52 aircraft, until such time as the characteristics of a special jet tanker can be more permanently delineated.' Despite the recommendations of this review, the KC-135 by this time enjoyed the fullest support of Defense Secretary Wilson, who overruled Newbury's recommended cancelation.

The selection of the Boeing KC-135 as the new jet tanker attracted the critical congressional attention of the Surveys and Investigations Staff of the House Appropriations Committee. As part of their overall investigation of irregularities in DoD weapons system procurement, the staff sought relevant 'documents, files or records' associated with the 'J57 engine program and the Boeing KC-135 jet tanker program'. Air Force Headquarters responded grudgingly to these requests, creating what the congressional staff called 'serious delays' in producing the requested material. As a result of its inquiry, the staff

criticized Air Force tanker procurement policies in three areas: '(a) Boeing's apparent anticipation of Air Force need for a jet tanker prior to the Air Force's decision and the resulting directed procurement from Boeing, (b) lack of knowledge by the Air Force that Boeing was working in an Air Force facility on the 707 project from June 1952 to August 1952, and (c) lack of knowledge by the Air Force and the Navy of diversion of four J-57 engines from Pratt & Whitney, in November and December 1953, to Boeing for commercial purposes. The clear inference is something was wrong in the way Boeing got the jump on its competitors.'

The Air Force responded to these criticisms first by defending its purchase of Boeing tankers despite Lockheed's selection as the winner of the jet tanker program: 'the desire to produce an optimum tanker conflicted with the operational urgency for a weapons system at an earlier date'. Consequently, Air Force Headquarters decided that 'Lockheed had won the design competition but that earlier availability and the less expensive Boeing proposal offset the optimum tanker proposed by Lockheed.' As to any benefits accrued by Boeing as a result of the availability of its military jet tanker prior to any Air Force request for such an airplane, the Air Force challenged the investigators' judgement. An Air Force representative wished that 'more contractors had the courage of their convictions to carry on development at their own expense in anticipation of military requirements.' The Air Force further dismissed Boeing's use of Air Force facilities at Renton for the 707 project, saying that the company had already reimbursed the Air Force for use of its facilities and had been warned against allowing the 707 project to interfere with existing Air Force programs underway at Boeing.

In true parochial fashion, the Air Force passed the blame to the Navy over the diversion of J57 engines to Boeing for use in the Dash 80. According to the Air Force, the Navy had control of the Pratt & Whitney program. Acknowledging its responsibility, the Navy said that the engines 'were shipped without the [Navy's] knowledge…,' but 'did not result in any diversion of Government-owned engines, did not delay delivery of engines to the Government, did not result in any increased cost to the Government, and did not result in any breach of security.'

With this congressional catharsis, questions over irregularities in the KC-135 purchase came to an end. For Lockheed, the results did not mean vindication or additional sales. For Boeing, it validated its multi-million dollar gamble in building the tanker prototype. For the Air Force, particularly SAC, it meant more tankers sooner than later, with a commensurate increase in strategic capability. This was not, however, the end of procurement problems for the KC-135.

Contract Difficulties
Following the procurement announcement, negotiations started on the production contract. At the first meeting on 13th December 1954 Boeing presented three KC-135 production schemes. The first would produce 13 airplanes per month and required no additions to the production facility at Boeing's Renton, WA, plant. New facilities would, however, be required at Larson AFB, WA, where acceptance flight tests would be undertaken. The second proposal provided for 21 airplanes per month but required additional assembly jigs for the Renton plant, as well as the previously mentioned increase in testing facilities at Larson AFB. In this proposal, some 40% of the work would be subcontracted. The third proposal would generate 44 airplanes per month and, like the previous proposal, required expansion of both the Renton facilities and Larson AFB. AMC selected the first plan, arguing that any greater production would exceed the 'present requirements that exist for the KC-135A airplane.'

The use of the Dash 80 in the flight test program was the focus of a second negotiating conference held on 15th December. Boeing

Boeing's ability to build KC-135s was limited only by how much the Air Force was willing to spend. Additional wing assembly jigs, for example, allowed more jets to be built each month but added to the overall cost of production. *Photo A91677 courtesy Boeing*

requested indemnification amounting to $13,500,000 should the prototype be destroyed or damaged beyond repair during the flight test program. The Air Force rejected this figure, considering it more than the fair value of the airplane. Instead, the Air Force reminded Boeing that the company would benefit in its commercial efforts, particularly the 707 program, thanks to the KC-135 flight test program. AMC recommended that the Air Force pay for 95% of the flight test program while Boeing pay the remaining 5%. Not surprisingly, Boeing rejected this offer.

The two parties met again on 6th January 1955, with the Air Force now agreeing to indemnify Boeing for use of the company's airplane, albeit with certain restrictions. The Air Force would not be liable if the damage or loss occurred during a flight not considered part of the KC-135 flight test program or if the damage was covered by existing insurance. In addition, the Air Force could use government facilities to repair any damage. Finally, if the Dash 80 was damaged beyond repair or otherwise lost, Boeing could choose to (a) receive, at no cost, one of the first seven KC-135As, (b) build a new 707 or KC-135

Table 3-1. **Contract AF 33(600)-28410 Authorizations**

Item	Purpose	Amount
1	Design and fabrication of 29 KC-135As	$197,899,072.26
2	Spare parts for Item 1, above	$15,664,495.00
3	Ground support equipment	$1,674,750.00
4	Training parts, tools, and equipment	$1,000,000.00
5	Handbooks and publications	$1,159,451.00
6	Static test article	unknown
7	Mock up	unknown
8	Wind tunnel test models	unknown
9	Two copies of the summary bills of materials	unknown
10	Contractor's personnel training program	unknown
11	Engineering and specification changes	$2,233,000.00
12	Flight simulator	$51,265.33
13	Mobile training units and graphic aids	$700,000.00
14	Engineering changes required for Item 13, above	$73,000.00
15	Hydrostatic test article	$998,000.00

at government expense for company use, or (c) accept a cash settlement for the loss, not to exceed $7,500,000. The Air Force also agreed to pay all expenses of the test program, and the flight test contract was completed.

Negotiations then stalled on the production contract for Boeing's fee for each airplane. The Air Force first offered a fee of 6%, which Boeing rejected. The Air Force refused to process the completed flight test contract until the production contract was completed, despite Boeing's insistence that the two could be resolved as separate issues. At a 21st January meeting, the Air Force maintained its unwillingness to separate the flight test and production contracts. As the Dash 80 was already involved in flight tests, Boeing announced it would discontinue flying the airplane because of the contract difficulties. Another meeting on 15th February met with equal failure and 'no future plans to resume negotiations.' The KC-135 was now hostage to the inability of the Air Force and Boeing to agree upon a suitable price per airplane necessary to complete the production contract.

A final conference was held on 9th June 1955, with Boeing and the Air Force each tendering several proposals. After 'due consideration', Boeing accepted a modified version of one proposal. The agreement called for '(1) a fixed-price-incentive type contract without reset, (2) a target cost of $184,313,447, (3) a target fee of 8% of the target cost, (4) a Government-Boeing split of 75-25% of the overrun or underrun, and (5) a maximum 12% profit ceiling on the target cost.' This translated into a profit for Boeing of $15,200,000 for the first 29 airplanes, reflecting a full reimbursement of Bill Allen's corporate gamble on the Dash 80.

On 30th September 1955, over a year after announcing the procurement of the KC-135A, contracts finally authorized both flight testing and full scale production of the 29 'interim' tankers. Major General David H Baker, Director of Procurement and Production, Headquarters AMC, approved contract AF 33(600)-28410, for eleven items with four more added through subsequent negotiations, listed in Table 3-1.

Table 3-2. **KC-135A Contracts and Deliveries**

KC-135A Contract Number	Airplanes in Original Contract	Airplanes Delivered
AF 33(600)-28410	29	29
AF 33(600)-31525	88	68
AF 33(600)-33012	118	118
AF 33(600)-34694	157	130
AF 33(600)-37871	81	81
AF 33(600)-40063	86	56
AF 33(600)-41979	65	65
AF 33(600)-43416	84	84
AF 33(657)-9694	88	88
AF 33(657)-12292	13	13
Total	**810**	**732**

In January 1956 Boeing and AMC met to negotiate an incentive contract for 68 additional KC-135s, 20 fewer than originally approved in August 1954. AMC proposed that the cost be negotiated in February 1957, as by then three KC-135s would be built and realistic figures upon which to base future costs would be available. Boeing rejected this offer, fearing that an increase in labor rates in California aircraft companies would spread to Seattle and thereby increase KC-135 manufacturing costs. The recommended AMC price would not allow Boeing to pass on labor costs and maintain its profit margin by increasing the KC-135's price to the Air Force. Without an agreement, negotiations continued.

By the end of February 1956 Boeing finally agreed to $145,800,024 for the 68 airplanes as proposed by the Air Force, with a billing price of $2,144,118 per KC-135. Both the Air Force and Boeing agreed to reset this figure after the third airplane (from the original 29) was completed. On 5th June 1956 contract AF 33(600)-31525 was finally sealed. Additional Air Force requirements for tankers resulted in further orders. Procurement Authorization 57-81 (dated 22nd August 1956) provided for 118 additional KC-135s. On 4th April 1957 Procurement Authorization 58-1 funded 157 new KC-135s, although this figure was eventually reduced to 130 airplanes. Finally, on 15th April 1958, Procurement Authorization 59-3 provided for 81 tankers, resulting in a total of 426 KC-135s ordered, with an eventual total of 810 tankers ordered and 732 delivered through the contracts listed in Table 3-2.

Both Boeing and the Air Force were quick to recognize the KC-135's potential for uses other than aerial refueling. SAC identified the Stratotanker as the basis for its future airborne command post as well as the replacement for the RB-47 in the strategic reconnaissance role. In addition, SAC wanted six C-135 transports for use as administrative aircraft. The Military Air Transport Service (MATS) saw the C-135 as an ideal airplane to expedite high priority passengers and cargo. It would also be the first global-capable jet airplane for MATS, the only major command in the Air Force still relying exclusively on propeller driven aircraft in a burgeoning age of jet airplanes. Other organizations which ordered and received the KC-135 included the Air Force Logistics Command (AFLC) and the Federal Aviation Administration (FAA). Several were also loaned to the National Advisory Committee on Aeronautics' (NACA, the precursor to the National Aeronautics and Space Administration – NASA) Dryden High Speed Flight Research Center at Edwards AFB. Specific KC-135 variant contracts are shown in Table 3-3.

Problem of Co-production

The Air Force was quick to remind Boeing that its commercial projects, notably the 707 airliner, would benefit from the testing and development of the KC-135. In addition, both Boeing and the Air Force recognized that many 707 parts could be produced on equipment designed to fabricate KC-135 parts, construction equipment paid for by the government as part of the KC-135 contract. The Air Force addressed this potential problem when it announced that Boeing had won the 'interim' tanker contract. Secretary Talbott and General LeMay insisted that as part of this contract, Boeing was obligated to complete and deliver all KC-135s to the Air Force prior to beginning any commercial production using this equipment. Concern about the effect this restriction might have on as-yet non-existent commercial sales prompted Boeing officials to declare that they could produce the 707 without delaying or interrupting the agreed upon KC-135 delivery schedule.

Roger E Lewis, Assistant Secretary of the Air Force for Materiel, responded firmly to Boeing's claim by saying that the Air Force 'bought that airplane to meet a military requirement and until we are satisfied that the military requirement is going to be met, we are not going to talk about anything else … There is no authority given [Boeing] to use any of the work we are doing for purposes other than meeting our requirements for tanker airplanes.'

Discussions between the Air Force and Boeing ensued, resolving the existing differences and concerns over coproduction. Talbott issued a press release on 13th July 1955 stating that there was 'no objection to Boeing building commercial jet aircraft concurrent with its production of military jet tanker transports'. Lewis added that he had no objections to Boeing building 'commercial aircraft on Air Force tooling procured for the KC-135 tanker, provided the Government's interests were protected.' Despite these pronouncements, problems did arise from coproduction, specifically the use of facilities, special tools, and sharing of benefits. The first two problems were resolved with a minimum of difficulty, but the sharing of benefits produced a major stumbling block in the production pathway.

The first 707 was scheduled for completion concurrently with the 100th KC-135. This meant that as a result of the KC-135 'learning curve', 707 labor costs would be significantly lower than those for the KC-135. Boeing argued that if the company shared the 'learning curve' benefits, then the Air Force should share in the cost of developing the 707 and in its Phase I flight test program. Boeing's actual commercial benefits from the KC-135 'learning curve' were not as great as anticipated. On 13th October 1955 Pan American World Airways ordered 25 as-yet unflown DC-8s and only 20 707s. Pan Am chose the DC-8 because of its larger wing and higher gross weight than that of the 707, and purchased only a token number of 707s because of their earlier delivery date, considering them only interim equipment. On 25th October 1955 United Airlines also ordered the DC-8, selecting it over the 707 because of its wider fuselage cross section. Boeing responded by increasing the 707

Table 3-3. **KC-135 Variant Contracts and Deliveries**

Model Type	Contract Number	Number Ordered	Number Delivered	Type Total
KC-135B	AF 33(600)-43416	5	5	
	AF 33(657)-9694	12	12	17
RC-135A	AF 33(657)-9694	9	4	4
RC-135B	AF 33(657)-9694	1	1	
	AF 33(657)-12292	9	9	10
C-135A	AF 33(600)-40063	10	10	
	AF 33(600)-41979	5	5	15
C-135B	AF 33(600)-41979	15	15	
	AF 33(600)-43416	15	15	30
C-135F	AF 33(657)-9694	12	12	12
Total		**93**	**88**	

The Air Force's ultimate nightmare. Expertise gleaned from building KC-135s meant that the 'learning curve' for building 707s would be smoother. In effect, this proved to be an indirect government subsidy for Boeing commercial airline production. *Photo courtesy Boeing*

fuselage diameter beyond that of the DC-8, and was rewarded on 8th November 1955 with an order for 30 707-100s from American Airlines. Boeing offered this new wider fuselage to Pan American, which promptly accepted the change for its 20 airplanes.

Despite the fuselage improvements, the 707-100 still could not compete with the DC-8 on international routes. The DC-8's larger wing could carry more fuel and allow a higher take-off gross weight, both crucial selling points in the jet airliner competition. Boeing responded by increasing the 707's overall span by 10ft (3.0m) with a new wing planform from midway between the inboard and outboard engines to the wing root. The fuselage diameter remained unchanged, but its length was increased. This new airliner was designated the 707-300. As a result of these design changes, the 707 grew less and less similar to the KC-135, and two separate production lines developed. 'Some common production space and joint overhead allowed for some cost saving, but only 22% of parts remained common between the two programs.' The problems of coproduction became less complicated logistically, but remained economically troublesome.

In a special report presented during October 1955 by Nate Silverston of AMC's Cargo and Special Aircraft Branch to General William T Thurman, AMC's Deputy Director of Procurement, the Air Force stated that Boeing was asking the Air Force 'to recognize costs incurred … in the development of the 707 which the contractor had publicly announced would not be shared by the [Air Force] in the event of any procurement of KC-135s.' Boeing agreed not to amortize the 707 prototype development costs in the KC-135, but now the company had changed its position. The report further stated that regardless of any Air Force contribution to the 707's development costs, Boeing would still be able to sell the 707 for from 15-18% cheaper than could its competitors in the jet airliner market, in part because of experience gained from KC-135 production. Consequently, the Air Force insisted that as a quid pro quo for joint production there would be a sharing of the KC-135 'learning curve'

but no Air Force participation in 707 development and flight test costs. On 14th May 1956 the Air Force and Boeing agreed in principle to Boeing's use of KC-135 tooling to produce the 707 provided it did not interfere with or delay Stratotanker production. By July the Air Force authorized joint use of the KC-135 assembly process, and by 16th October procedures to accomplish this were completed and in place. Specifically, 80% of all nonrecurring costs common to both programs would be charged to the KC-135 program and the remainder to the 707 program.

Although the logistics and finances of coproduction now seemed resolved, the Air Force was still dissatisfied with several legal issues stemming from the coproduction arrangements. On 15th February 1956 Assistant Air Force General Counsel William Munves stated that the Secretary of the Air Force must first get the approval of the Senate Armed Services Committee before allowing Boeing to use the KC-135 facilities for 707 production if the company's annual rent exceeded $25,000. What followed became an extensive if not tedious legal exercise in property taxes.

A new agreement between the Air Force and Boeing was signed on 6th March 1958, providing for the joint use of government special tooling and equipment. The company's production of 707s could not interfere with KC-135 production and Boeing would reimburse the government $110,000 per airplane for the first 100 707s produced with KC-135 tooling and $60,000 per airplane for the second 100 707s so produced. The Air Force and Boeing agreed to negotiate further reimbursements should 707 production exceed 200 units. At the time, neither Boeing nor the Air Force would have dared predict that the 707 production line would remain open for nearly 35 years and produce over 900 airplanes. Finally, during October 1958, the definitive agreement was settled for the initial KC-135 contract, signed four years earlier. Price for the first 29 airplanes was $216,877,318, an increase of almost 10% (or some $9 million), with a cost per airplane of $7,478,528 – over $650,000 more per airplane than originally agreed.

Specially trained divers made adjustments to the HST before and after each testing spectrum. Despite the appearance of an engineer in the cockpit area, the HST was unoccupied during the tests. *Photo P18587 courtesy Boeing*

An unserialled airframe was tested to destruction in the static rig. These tests in 1955 validated the KC-135's maximum gross weight of 325,000 lb, far in excess of a J57-equipped airplane. They also foreshadowed the limits of the KC-135R 25 years later. *Photo P19033 courtesy Boeing*

Initial Testing

Before the first KC-135A ever flew it had already benefitted from an extensive test program designed to protect it from a fatal problem which had beset its European counterpart. During its early months of operations, the Comet 1 suffered several catastrophic failures while climbing to high altitude. Tests at the Royal Aircraft Establishment (RAE) at Farnborough revealed that these were caused by fuselage failure at the corners of square apertures resulting from cyclic cabin pressurization. AMC was concerned that similar problems might befall America's fledgling high altitude jet transport program, especially the KC-135. The Comet 1's troubles would 'affect not only British aviation, but jet developments … the world over, including the Boeing 707 and the wide range of military aircraft now in operation and on the drawing boards.'

In October 1955 AMC directed that a hydrostatic test program be undertaken to study the KC-135's vulnerability to these pressurization problems and to determine the type, location, and intensity of pressure stresses the KC-135 could endure over its normal lifetime before suffering structural failure. These underwater tests were similar to those the British conducted as part of their efforts to identify the Comet's structural problems. Specific conditions to be tested included cabin pressures, fin loads, wind gusts of up to 50ft (15.2m) per second, and landing loads. These tests required that a KC-135 fuselage, a complete center wing section, and the front and rear wing spar fittings (all of which weighed some 50,000 lb – 22,680kg) be submerged in a water tank and then be subjected to varying pressurization schedules and 'gust' loads. No Air Force serial number or Boeing construction number was allocated to the hydrostatic test article, although it was built between the seventh and eighth KC-135s on the assembly line. The tank, located at Boeing's Seattle plant, was 130ft (39.6m) long, 20ft (6.0m) wide and deep, had a capacity of 423,000 gallons (1,601,224 liters), and weighed 3,600,000 lb (1,632,923kg). Draining and refilling the tank took approximately six hours.

Water was pumped into the tank and the fuselage pressurization cycle started. After the cabin reached the maximum differential pressure level for high-altitude cruise, the cabin pressure was decreased over a span of four minutes. Once fully depressurized, the cycle was then repeated. During the four minute depressurization, 14 hydraulic jacks applied pressures on the outside of the fuselage at predetermined places, simulating gust or maneuver load pressures which the airplane might encounter in flight. Five jacks were located forward of the wing, nine were located aft of the wing, and two jacks applied torsion loads to the tail. In all 25 gust simulations composed a complete testing spectrum, equating to a six-hour mission.

Boeing Project engineer A I Ostlund reported in October 1957 that after completing 3,650 test spectra (91,250 gusts), results showed convincingly that the KC-135 fuselage structure was sound. The tests represented approximately ten years of use (about 21,000 flying hours) without 'significant structural failure'. The fate of the hydrostatic test article is not known, but was almost certainly disassembled and scrapped. In addition to verifying the structural integrity of the KC-135, the hydrostatic test article produced several engineering changes, such as improvements to the fuel bulkhead shear ties and clips, as well as the fuel bulkhead webs in the upper and side walls of the nose wheel well. After 12,155 test spectra (303,875 gusts simulating some 72,930 flying hours), engineers intentionally damaged the test article. A 12in (30cm) crack appeared in the fuselage skin between sections FS1248 and FS1260, and a 4in (10cm) crack was detected in the lower aft corner of one of the overwing escape hatches. These were repaired and crack propagation and repair data were obtained. By December 1957 Colonel A G Leslie, Chief of the Tanker Weapons System Project Office, concluded that the structural failures found during the hydrostatic testing could 'reasonably be expected to occur during [the KC-135's] service life', and recommended incorporating the identified engineering changes into the entire fleet.

Additional testing was undertaken during October 1957 with an unserialled static test airframe complete except for engines, electrical equipment, and other non-structural systems. Major wing failure occurred at 110% of the design ultimate load, after deflecting through an arc of approximately 12ft 6in (3.8m) upward and 4ft (1.2m) downward. Over 100 different tests were conducted on the fuselage, wings, flaps, engine mounts, doors, and many smaller components. Boeing concluded that KC-135s could operate at gross weights as high as 325,000 lb (147,420kg), well above the 295,000 lb (133,812kg) required, but the airplane was power limited at these high weights by its inadequate engines.

Roll-out and Early Flights
The first KC-135A Stratotanker 55-3118 rolled out of Boeing's Renton facility on 18th July 1956 right behind the 888th and final KC-97. With considerable fanfare, the first jet tanker was named *City of Renton*, and Mrs Sarah Baxter, wife of Renton's mayor, christened it with a bottle of water from the nearby river. The *City of Renton*, along with several of her sister ships, would spend its next few years participating in acceptance flight tests conducted by Boeing and the Air Force. The new airplane, unlike the B-47 and B-52 before it, did not have either an 'X' or 'Y' prefix as prototype flight test work for the KC-135A had been undertaken by the Dash 80, including initial air refueling tests; there was no need for a prototype KC-135A. Following nearly a month and a half of ground tests, the KC-135A first flew on 31st August 1956, eleven days ahead of the first flight date Boeing promised when the production papers were signed almost two years earlier. The flight lasted one hour and 19 minutes, with Richard L 'Dix' Loesch in the left seat and A M 'Tex' Johnston in the right seat, flying from Renton to Boeing Field in Seattle.

Although the Dash 80 had pioneered much of the KC-135A's test program, there were some surprises with the KC-135A. During a Phase I test flight on 18th October 1956, while attempting to determine the amount of pressure required to control the KC-135's rudder, it began to flutter violently. Before the plane's airspeed could

Mrs Sarah Baxter, wife of Renton mayor Joseph Baxter, christens 55-3118 at the rollout ceremony on 18th July 1956. The airplane remained in service for 40 years – until 15th October 1996, when it was put on display at McConnell AFB. *Author's collection*

be reduced sufficiently, oscillations ripped some of the metal skin from the vertical fin. Following considerable wind tunnel testing, Boeing attempted to correct the flutter by installing a hydraulic rudder damper at the top of the vertical fin. A flight test on 27th November 1956 showed this damper to be ineffective, with the flutter consistently recurring above Mach 0.8. The Air Force representative at Boeing reported that 'until this flutter problem is fully resolved, full impact on testing schedules, production, and scheduled deliveries cannot be determined'. Despite these 'teething problems', confidence remained high among SAC's leaders. A little over a week before the initial roll-out ceremony, LeMay told a SAC commander's conference that there was 'no major problem in the KC-135 program'.

On 30th December 1955 the Deputy Chief of Staff for Operations at the AFFTC at Edwards AFB directed that the first KC-135A would participate in Phase II flight tests. The initial portion took place at Boeing Field with Air Force crews flying the airplane and support provided by Boeing personnel. The Air Force accepted KC-135A 55-3118 from Boeing on 24th January 1957 and flew it to Edwards AFB for continuation of Phase II operational acceptance testing. The

The rollout of the first KC-135 in 1956 was more than just a new airplane meeting the public. Local news channel KOMO covered the event. White-shirted engineers and journeymen would be employed for decades to come building tankers and airliners for Seattle's largest employer. *Photo A104716 courtesy Boeing*

Wearing a new pair of cowboy boots made for the occasion, A M 'Tex' Johnston watches Richard L 'Dix' Loesch board 55-3118 for its maiden flight on 31st August 1956. Ladder placement was eventually moved to the aft wall of the entry chute to allow more room to climb in while wearing a parachute. *Photo P17342 courtesy Boeing*

The $16 million gamble that paid off. Boeing President William 'Bill' Allen (l) is all smiles along with 'Tex' Johnston (c) and 'Dix' Loesch (r) following a successful first flight of the KC-135. *Photo P17340 courtesy Boeing*

airplane still lacked a remedy for its rudder flutter problem. Boeing recommended that until this was corrected all KC-135s would be limited to speeds below that which induced the flutter, and ARDC approved a limiting airspeed of 0.9 Mach. How this would affect the KC-135A's testing program was a source of some concern: '... while this flutter problem has not caused any major program revisions up to this time, it has certainly reduced [Boeing's] capability to incorporate any additional changes early in production that may be desired as a result of Phase I and Phase II flight test experience.'

From 25th January through 27th February 1957, the first KC-135A conducted 12 test flights totaling 55 hours, 35 minutes to check Boeing's 'estimated performance and stability data ... to determine if the [specified] stability and control requirements ... were met'. Captain Charles L Gandy served as project pilot, with B Lyle Schofield as project engineer. Results of the Phase II tests were mixed. The airplane was described as 'a great improvement over previous tanker aircraft in speed, altitude, and fuel off-load capabilities. The flight characteristics generally are good'. An offload of 26,650 gallons (100,880 liters) of fuel could be achieved by the KC-135 versus only 14,980 gallons (56,705 liters) from the KC-97F. Air refueling altitudes were now compatible with the operational altitudes of existing bombers and fighters, increasing from 18,000ft (5,485m) with the KC-97F to a maximum of 35,000ft (10,668m) with the Stratotanker, significantly enhancing the range of the B-47 and B-52. The test KC-135A was now limited to Mach 0.87 or 350 knots indicated airspeed (KIAS) because of the rudder flutter, although test crews felt that this speed could be easily exceeded. Service ceiling at military power with a take-off gross weight of 242,500 lb (109,998kg) was 39,500ft (12,039m), with a sea level rate of climb of 2,200ft (670.5m) per minute. The KC-135A's performance in the approach and landing modes was far superior to any existing large transports. A self-contained fuel-air starter in the KC-135's No.4 engine allowed engine starts without the aid of ground equipment, a definite advantage for alert responses, although this was not without its own developmental difficulties.

Despite these advantages, the KC-135A was beset by three critical deficiencies which seriously compromised its refueling mission: '(1) poor dynamic lateral direction stability, (2) high boom maneuvering stick forces and inadequate control of the flying boom, and (3) unsafe heavy weight take-off and initial climb performance under engine out conditions.' At extremely low speeds the airplane was especially susceptible to high sink rates, abrupt pitch-up tendencies, and an excessive stall buffet range. Further, under asymmetric power conditions, full rudder deflection could not be obtained below 140 KIAS without placing the airplane in a dangerous flight attitude.

Initial KC-135 flight tests took place in Seattle before relocating to Edwards AFB. Almost immediately, flutter problems arose in the rudder and vertical stabilizer, issues which would affect KC-135 operations for years to come. *Photo P17334 courtesy Boeing*

Tests at Edwards revealed problems with Dutch Roll, inadequate control of the flying boom, and unsafe operations at heavy weights or engine-out conditions. Corrections to the boom were quickly forthcoming, but inherent lateral control issues and poor engine performance lasted for decades. *Author's collection*

The poor dynamic lateral directional instability (also known as 'Dutch Roll' – so named because of its resemblance to the rhythmic rocking and rolling motion of an ice skater) was, in part, inherent in the KC-135A's swept-wing design. In the clean configuration the oscillations were poorly damped but could be controlled, while at low speeds in the approach configuration the oscillations were divergent and could lead to loss of airplane control. Boeing was well aware of this problem, and intended to use a yaw damper to alleviate it. Unfortunately, the yaw damper was part of the yet-to-be-installed and untested Lear MC-1 autopilot, which itself was the subject of considerable developmental problems. Until the autopilot with yaw damper could be installed, Dutch Roll remained a serious problem, especially during air refueling and landing.

Air refueling operations 'were not completely satisfactory', and were difficult to accomplish even in lightly turbulent air. Other deficiencies included unsatisfactory crew escape provisions, particularly at high speed or other than normal g-loading conditions, i.e., no ejection seats, and there was no oxygen source for use by passengers carried in the cargo compartment. 'Extreme forces' were required to maneuver the aerial refueling boom and the available control envelope of the boom was 'unacceptable'. The boom operator's prone couch was inadequate, the boom pod was bitterly cold and lacked any means of emergency egress, and there was insufficient visibility of the receiver during aerial refueling.

Of major concern was the unsatisfactory take-off and initial climb performance due to 'insufficient power' under engine-out conditions. The first airplane was equipped with non-production Pratt & Whitney J57-P-29A engines rated at 10,500 lb (46.7kN) of thrust (dry) and 12,100 lb (53.8kN) of thrust with water injection. Although the more powerful J57-P-43Ws (rated at 13,750 lb [61.6kN] of static thrust with water injection) were installed on the other test airplanes (and throughout the KC-135A fleet), the 'insufficient power' problem remained. For example, at a gross weight of 262,000 lb (118,843kg), landing gear down, and the flaps set at the prescribed 40° take-off position (this was later changed to a maximum of 30°), the KC-135A had a zero rate of climb with only three engines operating. Because SAC planned to operate the type with a gross take-off weight of 297,000 lb (134,719kg), this meant that an engine-out airplane could neither climb nor maintain altitude and would most likely crash after take-off.

Solutions to these problems were immediately forthcoming, but not necessarily immediately implemented. These included '(1)

improvements to make the KC-135A fully capable of performing its design mission, (2) improvements to eliminate annoying and distracting factors in aircraft operation, (3) items of major importance which required further study and development, and (4) deficiencies of a secondary importance but which should be corrected in production aircraft.'

The Lear MC-1 autopilot and yaw damper were installed on most subsequent test airplanes, and AFFTC undertook a re-evaluation of the KC-135A's lateral instability problem. Reliability of the autopilot, however, was 'poor', and the yaw damper was considered 'unsatisfactory' at its existing stage of development; the lateral instability remained. Despite the increased thrust available with the production J57-P-43Ws, the KC-135A's engine-out performance remained unsatisfactory, particularly under high gross weight operating conditions.

Unorthodox Proposals

In January 1958 the All American engineering firm offered a unique solution to resolve two of the most significant problems with the KC-135: its poor take-off performance when fully loaded for wartime conditions (as when it was on alert); and its inability to disperse to small airports (and their short runways) in an effort to reduce the tanker's vulnerability to a pre-emptive or sneak attack. Using two Turbo-Cat launchers and four arresting gear units (each valued at $2.6 million), All American claimed that it could launch five fully loaded B-52s and four KC-135As in less than 15 minutes, with the first launch in less than seven minutes and using less than 5,000ft (1,524m) of runway. The Turbo-Cat launchers were powered by six Allison J33-A-16A jet engines, generating some 50,000hp (37,300kW) for launch with an unspecified number of gs. The arresting cables were attached to large plungers which would distribute the landing airplane's energy through huge cylinders of water alongside and beneath the runway. The company promised to stop KC-135s (at up to 350,000 lb [158,760kg] gross weight) in less than 2,000ft (609m) of runway under 1.5g conditions at two-minute intervals. This radical program found favor among few of SAC's leaders. While it offered an unusual solution to a major problem, SAC commanders felt that it smacked too much of naval carrier operations. Having just endured a major inter-service budget and policy battle over the merits of new Air Force strategic bombers versus additional Navy carriers, it is not surprising that despite initial funding, the Air

BAIL OUT, BAIL OUT, BAIL OUT!

As jet aircraft entered the military inventory throughout the 1950s, technology had yet to mature sufficiently to ensure a high degree of safety and reliability. B-47s were delivered without ejection seats, for example, leading to needless fatalities during the operational adolescence of jet engines that failed at critical times or took too long to produce power. Even ejection seats were suspect, as early examples failed to work consistently and correctly. SAC and ARDC planners were deeply concerned about the safety of the new jet tanker. In a summary of critical deficiencies of the initial design (which a later generation would call 'show stoppers'), ARDC commander Major General Thomas S Power warned that 'there's no means of escape under uncontrolled flight conditions in the present configuration.' Power insisted upon the procurement and installation of ejection seats in the KC-135 on a 'No Delay Basis.' Doing so would add 1,200 lb (544kg) of weight to the forward compartment. The navigator, who sat sideways at his station, would turn his seat to face forward prior to ejecting, much like the B-47 copilot whose seat could turn around completely to operate the tail guns.

Installation of these seats quickly became tied with development and testing schedules as the initial aircraft were built without ejection seats entirely. Waiting for the ejection seats would delay production of the KC-135 and allow Lockheed more time to build and test its own tanker (which would go on to win the competition), substantially weakening Boeing's tenuous position in the tanker sales game and critically delaying the operational availability of SAC's new jet tanker. Brigadier General Howell M Estes, Jr, wrote to the Air Force liaison to Boeing saying that 'it is our plan to ask Boeing to study a proposal for modification of one of the test vehicles to include ejection seats. This would provide maximum safety for an aircraft performance test crew and not delay production of the Model 717.' Power added that the 'seats could be provided in the twenty-fifth (25th) airplane on the production line [55-3142] without affecting current delivery schedules.'

The ejection seat discussion proved to be a fruitless exercise. From Boeing's perspective, putting ejection seats in the military cousin of its planned 707 commercial airliner drastically undermined its image of safety for a traveling public already leery of jet travel thanks to the de Havilland Comet accidents, and would effectively kill any sales to airlines such as Pan American or TWA. Despite Power's insistence on ejection seats, SAC's priority was to have airplanes in service as soon as possible. Any delays, even in the name of safety, would prove disastrous to SAC's timetable. Moreover, SAC recognized the implications of providing the flight crew with ejection seats whereas any personnel riding in the back of the airplane were expected to fend for themselves without parachutes, much less ejection seats.

Despite cancelation of the ejection seats for the KC-135, the issue of emergency egress for the crew remained an important issue. Bail out tests determined that using the overwing hatch to jump out of the airplane was safe as low as 150 KIAS and as fast as 345 KIAS. 'Around 200 KIAS', however, there was a high likelihood of the person striking the horizontal stabilizer. Given the opportunity, the recommendation was to bail out using the forward crew entrance hatch. A crewmember would pull down a handle bar to actuate a gas cylinder that blew off the hatch and extended a spoiler into the airstream. The crewmember would then grab the bar and drop out of the airplane. Tests showed that this procedure allowed sufficient clearance beneath the airplane. There is a joke in the RC-135 community, however, that the lowest ranking person on the airplane would go first to clear off all the antennas under the fuselage to ensure that everyone else would make it out safely!

KC-135s were never meant to operate in a combat zone at direct risk, where a surface-to-air missile (SAM) or a MiG attack would likely result in a total in-flight failure. Originally KC-135 crewmembers wore helmets and parachutes throughout each flight as a precaution for the early vagaries of jet operations, not out of concern for combat. This was later amended to just critical phases of flight such as takeoff, landing, and air refueling, and – given the absence of any attacks on KC-135s during the war in Southeast Asia – even this requirement was eventually eliminated. By the late 1980s crewmembers simply carried their helmets on board, and many never wore a helmet throughout their entire career except in the altitude chamber for recertification. A number of early KC-135 alumni felt that parachutes were there only for bailout during the SIOP after emptying their tanks to refuel B-52s en route to the Soviet Union (despite this popular belief, SAC planned for KC-135s to land at remote recovery bases, eventually to be refueled and then conduct post SIOP missions – they were hardly one-shot disposable tankers). By 2008 parachutes had been removed entirely from the KC-135 fleet and the spoiler system deactivated.

During the 60-year history of the KC-135 and variants, there have only been six known bailouts. The first is believed to be the unsuccessful attempt by the boom operator from KC-135A 57-1442 which crashed on 16th January 1965. The second bailout is unidentified, but may well have been from the 28th August 1963 mid-air collision of KC-135As 61-0319 and 61-0322.

The last four bailouts are the stuff of legend. During August 1969 an instructor pilot (IP) allowed KC-135A 61-0313 to run out of fuel while on approach to KI Sawyer AFB, MI. The regular crew of four parachuted to safety. Thanks to sheer dumb luck, the IP – who remained on board – completed a dead-stick landing in the overrun.

Four of the five crewmembers on KC-135A 61-0313 reportedly bailed out prior to a 'dead-stick' landing at K I Sawyer AFB in 1969. It is seen here 20 years later as a KC-135R at Castle AFB on 9th April 1989. *Author photo*

Force allowed this proposal to die a quiet death. Congressman Everett P Scrivener of Kansas raised the question of barrier arrested landings as early as 1948, but, as he recalled in 1955, Air Force officers 'just looked at me and I heard nothing more about it'. Donald A Quarles, the Assistant Secretary of Defense for Research and Development, responded to Scrivener's remarks by saying 'The Air Force still feels that the installation of equipment of that kind on fields or airports would not be a preferred solution to the problem...'

Large jet arrested landings were not so easily ignored. The FAA actually tested its Boeing 720 (N113) complete with tailhook at NAS Lakehurst, NJ, in 1962. The $966,000 contract with All American was part of a competition with the E W Bliss Company's Launch and Recovery Equipment Division for an airliner launch and arresting system. Airline interest in this effort, not surprisingly, also failed to materialize. Additionally, Boeing proposed a carrier on-board delivery (COD) variant of its 727 tri-jet airliner, going so far as demonstrating the airplane's capabilities on the simulated carrier deck at NAS Patuxent River, MD

A 1970 proposal suggested that either two or four Rolls Royce-Allison XJ99 booster engines be added to the KC-135's existing four

Pratt & Whitney turbojets. Studies with Boeing indicated that two booster engines installed at each wingtip was the most suitable arrangement, with alternate locations including the lower rear fuselage (similar to the Boeing 727) or in Whitcomb fairings on top of each wing. The wingtip pod had the advantage of being removable when not required and could be transported easily inside the KC-135 when deploying to a short field where the pods would then be installed. The pods had aerodynamic intake covers which closed following take-off to reduce drag during cruise, offered good slow speed performance, and reduced foreign object damage (FOD) during ground operations.

The booster engines offered a considerable increase in performance. With four wingtip XJ99s, the KC-135's take-off ground roll decreased from the existing 10,900ft (3,322m) to 5,700ft (1,737m). When operating from short runways, the airplane was normally limited to a gross weight at takeoff of 228,000 lb (103,420kg), a figure which increased to 296,000 lb (134,265kg) with the addition of the four boosters, allowing the airplane to double its fuel offload available from 41,000 to 82,000 lb (18,591 to 37,195kg). The first flight test was projected to take place 28 months after program approval and Allison promised initial delivery ten months after that. By 1970, however, sufficient research had been undertaken on re-engining the KC-135 to eliminate the need for these boosters.

Following Phase II testing, 55-3118 returned to Boeing. By late February 1957 Boeing had stiffened the vertical fin by overlapping additional skin on the top portion of the fin and by installing dual rudder tab dampers to provide more constant control over existing rudder oscillations. These modifications were sufficient to correct the rudder flutter problem. As they were considered the result of a design flaw, Boeing paid for the modification.

In an effort to rectify the poor air refueling boom control, Boeing tested a hydraulically powered boom on 55-3118. A single six-hour, 20-minute flight from Seattle on 28th May 1958 defined the new boom envelope for three Mach numbers at 35,000ft (10,668m) during repeated contacts with a B-52. AFFTC personnel found that boom control was improved although some aspects were still unsatisfactory (such as poor control of the boom through the automatic disconnect envelope).

Boeing used the second KC-135A (55-3119) for static air load survey tests, and five others were used for other phase testing. KC-135A 55-3122 participated in the Phase IV performance evaluation, 55-3124 took part in the Phase IV Stability tests, 55-3121 was destined for Phase V adverse weather tests, and KC-135As 55-3125 and 55-3126 conducted Phase VI functional development tests. The Air Force bailed 56-3591 back to Boeing for high gross weight and air refueling compatibility testing.

Performance Tests
From 1st June 1957 through 17th February 1958, AFFTC evaluated KC-135A 55-3122 as part of Phase IV performance testing, involving 34 flights totaling 77 hours, 55 minutes. The project pilot was Major Reese S Martin, with Marion H Yancey as project engineer. Specific test goals were the acquisition of performance data to revise the KC-135A's flight handbook and Standard Aircraft Characteristics Charts. This airplane had production J57-P-43Ws and had a basic weight of 97,000 lb (43,999kg) plus 1,000 lb (453kg) of test equipment. It could offload 26,300 gallons (99,556 liters) of fuel at a rate of 900 gallons (3,406 liters) per minute, with a nontransferable reserve of 1,200 gallons (4,542 liters).

Phase IV Performance test results confirmed the problems identified by KC-135A 55-3118 during Phase II tests, finding that 'the capability of the KC-135A to accomplish its design mission is seriously compromised by the following problem areas: (1) Reduced take-off gross weights required by critical field length based on a 10,000ft [3,048m] runway being available to using commands; (2) High boom maneuvering stick forces and inadequate control of the boom throughout its automatic disconnect envelope; (3) Lateral-direction oscillations occurring at refueling speeds and altitudes make off-loading almost impossible in heavy turbulence without stability augmentation. Refueling under these conditions may be marginal even with stability augmentation.'

Estimated take-off performance data were too optimistic as the airplane's gross weight increased. At the maximum gross takeoff weight of 297,000 lb (134,719kg), the KC-135A required a ground roll of 9,250ft (2,828m) on a standard day [59° Fahrenheit (F) and sea level pressure]. On a hot, high-pressure altitude day, ground roll increased requiring the KC-135A to download fuel or it could not take off, both undesirable wartime alternatives. Maximum level flight speed was Mach 0.882 at 30,000ft (9,144m) at 148,500 lb (67,359kg), and Mach 0.842 at 35,000ft (10,668m) at 252,000 lb (114,307kg). Mission range was 2,932 nautical miles (nm) (5,432km) with a transfer of 94,800 lb (43,001kg) of fuel.

Another shortcoming was the KC-135A's inability to 'buddy' refuel the Convair B-58 Hustler. This involved flying in formation with the B-58 from takeoff to the refueling. As the Hustler flew at supersonic speeds, the KC-135A could not maintain formation with it. Two solutions were forwarded. The first required the B-58 to fly at subsonic speed to the air refueling point with the KC-135A, on-load fuel, and then accelerate to supersonic speed for the remainder of its flight. This profile so seriously degraded the B-58's range and performance that it required more fuel to accomplish the mission with the tanker than without any 'buddy' air refueling at all. The other solution involved the installation of afterburners on the KC-135A's engines. Realistically, the KC-135A was simply not suited for supersonic flight, and both ideas were dismissed. The boom was also limited to 288 KIAS, forcing the B-58 to refuel in a region where it suffered from excessive drag and required more fuel. Efforts were made to correct this deficiency and the boom placard speed was increased to 330 KIAS. The method eventually used to refuel B-58s was the same as that used to refuel B-47s from KC-97s. By prepositioning the tanker at forward operating locations, the B-58 and KC-135 could take off at the same time and, with the B-58 at supersonic speed, the two would reach the air refueling point simultaneously, alleviating the need for 'buddy' refueling. (This is not to say that the KC-135A is incapable of supersonic flight. On 2nd November 1982 KC-135A 57-1476 suffered an autopilot malfunction and rolled inverted to 210° of bank and 70° nose low. It descended from FL330 to approximately 7,600ft [2,316m] in just under 30 seconds, with an average descent rate of over 50,000fpm [15,240m/min], briefly exceeding the speed of sound. The pilot recovered the airplane without further mishap, and it remained in service until retired to AMARC on 13th August 1992. Another reported supersonic flight was that of C-135B 61-2662 during an inadvertent 455 KIAS dive from FL310 to 16,000ft [4,876m] over the North Atlantic in 1977.)

In order to obtain complete handling, stability, and control data, and to verify Boeing's compliance with military design specifications, KC-135A 55-3124 participated in Phase IV stability tests from 15th June 1957 through 11th February 1958 (although one such flight was undertaken by KC-135A 55-3122). Project pilot was Major Jones P Siegler and Charles C Crawford served as the project engineer. The program involved 22 flights totaling 112 hours. 55-3124 lacked several systems installed on other airplanes, including water injection and a brake anti-skid system. A complete autopilot was not installed until half way through the test program. The airplane was equipped with a 170in (4.3m) long nose boom

55-3124 was the lead aircraft in the Phase IV stability tests at Edwards AFB. These reaffirmed the dangerous limits of engine-out capability on takeoff, a problem caused by the inadequacies of jet engine technology rather than an inherent design flaw. *Author's collection*

containing airspeed systems and test vanes designed to measure angle of attack and sideslip forces.

Phase IV tests involved flights in a variety of configurations ranging from takeoff through approach and landing. Test results were no different than those obtained previously: 'Excessive stick lightening and force gradient reversal with increasing load factors reduce safe maneuvering capabilities. With an outboard engine failure, there is insufficient rudder power for adequate control during take-off at calibrated speeds less than 136 knots… This deficiency will be more critical on aircraft equipped with water injection.' Problems with the air refueling boom and the boom compartment environment remained. Test personnel were, however, favorably impressed with the KC-135A's altitude, range, speed, and fuel off-load capabilities, and recommended 27 improvements which they felt would alleviate the serious inadequacies in the KC-135A's development.

Adverse Weather Testing

In order to verify the all-weather capability of the KC-135, Phase V Adverse Weather tests were conducted to '(a) determine instrument condition and night flying characteristics of the KC-135; (b) establish pilot procedures and techniques for use during these conditions; (c) obtain preliminary icing data to determine the adequacy of the existing anti-ice equipment; and (d) recommend corrections for identified discrepancies.'

The icing tests would be conducted under artificial conditions, i.e., produced by a water spray tanker in front of the test airplane. Actual icing conditions would be evaluated in the Arctic portion of the Phase V tests. 55-3121 was selected for all of these tests, having been previously fitted by Boeing with a complete test instrumentation suite measuring 342 parameters (including 141 temperature, 95 pressure, and 61 electrical power readings). The test airplane also incorporated the latest engineering change proposals (ECPs) installed on production airplanes and retrofitted to those already in the fleet. The airplane lacked an autopilot, brake anti-skid system, and carried test equipment in the aft portion of the cargo compartment. Although it was equipped with J57-P-43Ws, it lacked the necessary internal plumbing to use water injection.

The airplane was delivered for testing to Wright-Patterson AFB on 30th April 1957, with the first adverse weather test flight on 2nd May 1957. This was also the first KC-135 delivered directly to a 'user agency' rather than undergoing testing conducted by Boeing. The Air Force accepted it from Boeing on 30th April 1957. Project pilots were Major Lewis E Kesterson and Captain Frank L Wright, with Captain

Frank J Passarello as project engineer. The airplane flew 22 flights, accumulating 78 hours, 40 minutes of flying time. Of that, 20 hours, five minutes were in actual instrument flying conditions. The last test flight was on 22nd June 1957, after which the airplane began Arctic testing.

Test results were favorable, with no significant increase in pilot workload during instrument flying conditions. The pilots' instrument panels were found to be poorly arranged, and were tested in several configurations prior to choosing an acceptable final layout. Handling in turbulence was notably less successful. The KC-135 suffered excessive roll and yaw in conditions of light to moderate turbulence due to the lack of a yaw damper. During an inadvertent thunderstorm penetration by another test KC-135, the airplane experienced heavy turbulence and yawed some 25° either side of center, an excessive rate for a large airplane.

Artificial icing tests were accomplished in conjunction with a KB-29 tanker and included three icing runs totaling approximately one hour, 15 minutes. At this stage of development, early KC-135As incorporated a wing and empennage surface anti-icing system which removed over 1in (2.5cm) of ice on the leading edge of the wings and stabilizers within one minute of activation. Despite this impressive capability, this equipment was deleted on production airplanes because it required extensive regular maintenance. Further, the engine bleed air ducts along the leading edge of the wing adequately heated the wing leading edge to prevent icing, while ice build-up on the empennage was not considered sufficient to require a special anti-icing system. The pitot system was particularly vulnerable to icing. The unheated pitot mast was replaced during the tests with a heated mast from a B-52. The KC-135 windshield heating system was also inadequate and identified for improvement.

Overall, the Phase V tests showed that the KC-135 had 'satisfactory handling qualities for instrument flight if flown according to the procedures recommended' by the test report. The report emphasized the poor handling of the airplane in turbulence due to the lack of a yaw damper, and otherwise identified nine unsatisfactory areas in the airplane's adverse weather capabilities. The same KC-135 was then subjected to extreme cold conditions to '(a) determine the adequacy of the airplane's systems while operating in very cold weather; (b) identify and correct any design deficiencies which would detract from cold weather operations; (c) determine changes or additions to the KC-135A flight handbook; and (d) compile environmental data for design purposes.'

Static ground tests were undertaken at the Air Force's Climatic Projects Laboratory at Eglin AFB with the Arctic tests conducted at

Eielson AFB, AK. Results of these tests were of particular interest to SAC, as KC-135s had already been delivered to (or were scheduled for) locations noted for their extreme winters (such as Minot AFB, ND, or Loring AFB, ME). On 24th June 1957 55-3121 arrived at Eglin AFB for static tests with a total flying time of 137 hours, five minutes. Project pilot was again Major Kesterson, with project engineers Captain William C Dale and Second Lieutenant Reed S Nelson of WADC's Directorate of Flight and All-Weather Testing. The airplane was positioned in the laboratory on 9th July 1957, and configured for testing. Exhaust ducts were attached to engines Nos. 2 and 4, and the airplane was moored to the hangar floor and the landing gear restrained with cables. A fuel trailer was positioned behind the KC-135 and a standard air refueling receptacle was fitted to a makeshift stand for boom and refueling tests. Approximately 30,000 lb (13,608kg) of fuel were transferred to this 'receiver' at each temperature tested.

On 13th July the temperature in the laboratory hangar was lowered from a hot Florida summer's day to a balmy 70°F (21°C) and allowed to stabilize. Following a cold-soak period of 48 hours, testing began on 15th July 1957. On 20th July the temperature was further lowered to 0°F (-17°C), and, following the requisite 48 hour cold-soak period, the tests were repeated. A week later the temperature was lowered to -30°F (-34°C) and the process repeated. The temperature was reset to -65°F (-54°C) on 3rd August and the final series of tests completed. On 22nd August, the temperature was raised to +70°F (21°C) prior to

removing the airplane from the test hangar. Static testing ended on 26th August 1957, and after a complete inspection, the airplane returned to Wright-Patterson AFB on 16th September 1957.

Following routine modification and the incorporation of additional ECPs, 55-3121 departed Wright-Patterson AFB on 14th November 1957 for Eielson AFB. While in Alaska the airplane did not receive any special cold-protective measures, although it was placed in a hangar for 16 days while undergoing repair of the left hydraulic system. The airplane made 16 flights totaling 75 hours, ten minutes, with takeoffs made in temperatures ranging from +22°F (-6°C) to -36°F (-38°C). Testing was completed and the airplane returned to Wright-Patterson AFB on 24th February 1958.

Arctic test results were disappointing but useful. A number of weaknesses were identified which compromised the airplane's Arctic mission capability, and 69 Unsatisfactory Reports were submitted for review as a result of the tests. Most notable among these were inadequate directional control on takeoff and continued poor reliability of the engine starter system. The time required to repair cold-induced deficiencies further degraded the cold weather capability. After more than 60 years, many of the problems identified in these tests remain uncorrected; for example, the need to preheat engines and fuel control units still exists. Although this requirement might only hamper routine operations, it potentially nullified the KC-135's quick reaction start and launch capability. Rudder authority for directional control in engine-out takeoffs remains likewise

Wearing a conspicuous 'Phase V' marking, 55-3121 sits inside the Air Force Climatic Projects Laboratory at Eglin AFB, with temperatures reaching as low as -65°F (-54°C) on 3rd August 1957. *Photo 6B2701 courtesy Boeing*

Maintenance personnel attempt to work on the No.2 engine on 55-3121 in severe conditions. Attempting to engage a cold-soaked starter shaft, for example, might well cause it to shear, a critical failure on an alert aircraft. *Photo 6B2708 courtesy Boeing*

Phase V operational testing in 55-3121 at Eielson AFB from November 1957 through February 1958 included 16 flights. Ironically, 55-3121 would be lost in a blizzard at Valdez, AK, some 27 years later. *Photo 6B2705 courtesy Boeing*

KC-135A 55-3126 *City of Moses Lake* took part in logistics evaluations to develop the supply pipeline from Boeing to Castle AFB, where the airplanes would be deployed. *Photo P18516 courtesy Boeing*

degraded without adequate hydraulic warmup time prior to flight.

Phase V adverse weather testing concluded with hot weather evaluations at MCAS Yuma, AZ. Dates and results of these tests have not been made available for this history.

KC-135As 55-3125 and 55-3126 participated in tests designed 'to provide an engineering evaluation of the functional characteristics, durability and maintainability of the aircraft, the individual components and systems, and the complete support system'. These tests were conducted from 4th June 1957 through 8th November 1957, and required 577 hours, 20 minutes of flying time. Additional data were acquired from the other test aircraft also located at Edwards AFB. Project officer was Lieutenant Colonel George A Kirsch, project pilot was Captain Charles Gandy Jr, and project engineer was First Lieutenant Douglas Nielsen. Phase VI Functional Development Testing focused upon three main areas: pilot familiarization, systems evaluation, and functional reliability. Half of the flying time was dedicated to systems evaluation with the remainder of flying hours divided between pilot familiarization and functional reliability tests. Five pilots from the 93rd AREFS, 93rd BW, Castle AFB, CA, were qualified during Phase VI testing. These pilots would serve as the initial cadre of instructors at Castle AFB when that base began operational conversion and training of SAC flight crews. Over 1,000 SAC maintenance personnel received on-the-job training as well.

Systems evaluations included rigorous and exhaustive operation of hydraulic, pneumatic, engine, fuel, and other component systems, usually at their operating limits. Based on a two-shift, six-day work week during the first three months of the program (and a two-shift, five-day work week during the final two months), the KC-135A demonstrated an out-of-commission time of 2.4 hours for every hour of in-commission time, with an overall in-commission rate of 57.2%. KC-135A 55-3125 was fitted with special equipment for a landing gear load survey. In September 1957 it flew to Seattle where it was taxied over a variety of surfaces. These landing gear load tests would help to validate Boeing's 'heavyweight' tanker, now the de facto winner in the Air Force's tanker competition.

The Phase VI final report identified numerous areas of concern for KC-135A maintenance and logistics personnel, specifying 98 deficiencies which required correction. For example, the airplane suffered from excessive fuel tank contamination as well as a high malfunction rate of the electronic navigation equipment. In general, however, the report was favorable. 'Overall aircraft maintenance required a total of 35 direct man-hours/flying for hour [*sic*] during the Phase VI test which was very favorable for an aircraft this size. Accessibility for maintenance and the general maintenance environment, with minor exceptions, are considered excellent.'

Accelerated Production Problems

Although the one-of-a-kind Dash 80 had adequately demonstrated the concept and feasibility of a jet transport and tanker, it could not inherently validate the individual components and production methods involved in the mass assembly of the KC-135. As with many new weapon systems, problems with a few components degraded the overall success of the Stratotanker. Part of this derived from the KC-135's expedited procurement schedule. Boeing had little more than two years to deliver the first example, dramatically reducing the amount of time available to design and develop many of the subsystems intended for the new airplane.

In December 1954 Boeing engineer A I Ostlund expressed concern that the accelerated delivery schedule failed to allow sufficient time to develop and flight test the KC-135's autopilot system. Instead he recommended the selection of an 'off-the-shelf' autopilot. Several new systems were considered but not chosen as they had yet to complete testing, while the Sperry A-12D autopilot (used on the B-47) was available but deemed 'somewhat obsolete' and 'should not be considered for the tanker airplanes.' Of the two remaining autopilot candidates, Boeing preferred the Minneapolis-Honeywell

MH-43 over the Lear L-10. The former would be easier to incorporate, had a proven operational record in the North American F-89D Scorpion, had effectively eliminated existing problems with the autopilot vertical gyro unit, was more advanced than the Lear product, and the engineering staff at Honeywell enjoyed the fullest confidence of the Boeing engineers.

The Air Force, however, proved unresponsive to Boeing's request for the necessary engineering specifications needed to select an autopilot. Specifically, WADC could not agree upon a satisfactory interpretation of purchasing regulations to allow the release of the requisite data. It was not until 4th March 1955, after five months of bureaucratic wrangling, that bids were finally mailed to autopilot manufacturers. During June 1955, ten months after the need for an autopilot was established, AMC selected the unproven Lear autopilot for the KC-135. Why Lear was selected over the recommended Honeywell system is not known.

The KC-135's autopilot was now designated as government-furnished aircraft equipment (GFAE). As Boeing predicted, Lear failed to deliver the prototype autopilots on schedule. By October 1955 this delay was seen to 'critically affect the reliability of production autopilots in the KC-135A'. A strike at the Lear plant and engineering problems further compromised production. It was not until 9th July 1956, some 13 months after Lear was contracted to deliver an *off-the-shelf* autopilot, that the first MC-1 system (formerly designated the L-10) was test flown in the Dash 80. By September 1956 the autopilot had demonstrated a consistent track record of failures. Continued engineering problems and a shortage of usable autopilot components further aggravated the situation. Boeing was forced to deliver the first tankers without autopilots and a major retrofit program seemed inevitable. (Why the B-52 autopilot was not adapted for use in the KC-135 was never addressed.)

By January 1958, a year and a half after the KC-135's first flight, the autopilot problem was still unresolved. Boeing was pressed to deliver KC-135s to the Air Force without operable autopilots as those units delivered by Lear were found to be riddled with discrepancies and even unsafe. AMC intervened directly with Lear and instituted strict production control measures that it hoped would rectify the disappointing situation; these were marginally successful. Autopilot problems were to plague the KC-135 fleet for the next four decades.

Engine Selection

The KC-135 was designed from the outset with Pratt & Whitney J57 turbojets. The first three airplanes had J57-P-29Ws, although these were eventually replaced with the same J57-P-31Ws installed on the other 26 interim tankers. AMC's goal was to use the J57-P-43W engine in both fleets of KC-135s and B-52s, enabling the Air Force to reduce its engine inventory. Since the tankers and bombers were usually co-located, the common engine would reduce maintenance and logistics problems, and allow for 'out-of-the-can' engine interchangeability. However, AMC planners were pessimistic that the engine production rate required to achieve this goal could not be attained until the 80th tanker was ready for engine installation.

By May 1956 sufficient J57-P-43Ws had been produced to install them instead of the J57-P-31Ws on the first 29 airplanes. SAC argued, however, that these interim tankers would be used only for training and should not receive the costly modifications necessary to alter the existing water injection system. The J57-P-31W used a lower water injection flow rate than did the J57-P-43W which required a more extensive water injection system. Further, the more powerful water injection pumps in the newer engines were still unproven. As of April 1957 some KC-135s were moving along the assembly line with concrete blocks suspended from the engine pylons simulating the weight and moment of the absent engines.

Using subcontractors such as Ryan in San Diego, CA, which built the aft fuselage section, created a new set of production problems for Boeing. Something as simple as a delay in shipping could result in a missed delivery deadline with financial penalties for Boeing and lack of aircraft for SAC. *Photo P28877 courtesy Boeing*

AMC recommended that the J57-P-31Ws be uprated, that Boeing intensify its efforts to develop the high capacity water pump, and that the J57-P-43W engine be installed on the fourth and subsequent examples. Should Boeing's pump improvement efforts fail, Pratt & Whitney was instructed to make a 'derating' kit designed to make it possible to use J57-P-43Ws on the first 29 airplanes but with a decreased water injection rate. These efforts were successful and Boeing installed the J57-P-43Ws on the remaining undelivered airplanes. Accelerated development of the J57-P-43W engine was not without its side effects. A procedure for the rapid spot welding of the first four stages of the engine's aluminum stator vanes resulted in flaws in 68 engines delivered to the Air Force, necessitating considerable repair work.

On 16th October 1956 AMC directed that the steel J57-P/F-59W engine replace the titanium J57-P-43W engine in the KC-135. The steel engine weighed 400 lb (181kg) more than the titanium version but cost $100,000 less per engine. Tankers already delivered with the titanium J57-P-43W engines would be retrofitted under Project QUICK SWITCH, and the lighter engines installed on the B-52. Although this would result in significant savings it effectively negated the out-of-the-can interchangeability for the KC-135 and B-52, which was always more illusory than practical. For example, in addition to the basic engine, a Quick Engine Change (QEC) kit included a nose ring cowl, nose dome, starter and associated ducting, water tubing and pumps, tail cone, exhaust duct, plus other associated parts, all necessary to adapt a bare engine to the KC-135 or B-52. Once

The constant need to repair or tune J57s meant a lot of engine noise. This 13th November 1958 picture shows the Koppers Sound Suppression system designed to reduce the noise levels at SAC bases. It was never adopted. *Photo P21459 courtesy Boeing*

configured with its appropriate QEC kit, the engine then had to be installed in a specific position (Nos. 1, 2 or 3, or 4 on the KC-135, or inboard or outboard in each pylon on the B-52), further reducing simple engine interchangeability.

The J57-P/F-59W was not without its own developmental problems. Repeated instances of icing in the engine fuel controls resulted in mission aborts and engine flame-outs. Although icing was not a new phenomenon, the need to resolve this problem became acute because of the routine high altitude operations of the KC-135 and B-52. As the airplanes climbed to high altitude water droplets in the fuel froze and blocked fuel lines and control units, starving the engine of fuel. The fix involved stricter attention to avoiding fuel tank contamination (in the form of a fungus that thrived in the tanks) and the installation of fuel system heaters in the KC-135. These fuel heaters were eventually removed from J57-P/ F-43W and J57-P/F-59W engines and either removed or deactivated in TF33-P-5, TF33-P-9, and TF33-PW-102s. A more recent solution to the fuel icing problem has been the addition to the fuel of an anti-icing mixture, as well as changing the fuel itself.

The No.4 engine Hamilton-Standard fuel air starter, used to ground start that engine (the others were then started pneumatically by bleed air from the No.4 engine), was yet another source of unsatisfactory performance. Since the first airplane had been delivered, the fuel air starters had a dismal 50% failure rate, usually requiring four or five attempts per successful start. Redesign of the combustion chamber, among other engineering changes, corrected this problem. A later solution involved the installation of a 3,000 lb per square inch (psi) metal air bottle in the No.4 engine strut. The bottle was 35in (89cm) long, had a 13½in (34cm) diameter, and added 84 lb (38kg) to the airplane's basic weight. Compressed air was piped from this bottle to the starter for engine start, after which a small electrically operated compressor recharged the bottle for the next start. This system was subject to considerable maintenance and was eventually replaced beginning in November 1962 with more capable starters and ground start carts (and explosive cartridge starters for alert starts).

By December 1957 continued overheating of the KC-135's hydraulic system reached near-epidemic proportions. Designed to operate at temperatures from -65°C to +160°C, the actual pump, reservoir, and return line temperature ranged between +400°C and +450°C. Filters and cooling loops were installed to increase both the air flow over and surface area of the hydraulic system. Filters also removed foreign particles which clogged pumps and caused them to run hotter..

These many engine problems led to Boeing's recommendation that the KC-135A's J57 turbojet engines be replaced with TF33 turbofan engines, increasing thrust by over 6,800 lb (30.2kN) per engine. MAC accepted this recommendation for its 30 new C-135Bs, a wise move considering the same engine core was installed in their new Lockheed C-141A Starlifters. SAC was not impressed and installed the turbofan only on its new fleet of 17 KC-135B airborne command posts and ten RC-135B reconnaissance platforms. Boeing next proposed to deliver future KC-135As with TF33s along with a re-engining program for those already delivered (well over 400 airplanes), but again SAC demurred. The reason for this has never been made clear. Unconfirmed reports suggest that SAC did not want to complicate its logistics system with two sets of engines. Another report claims that SAC could not afford the re-engining without sacrificing undelivered airplanes. Yet another report, however apocryphal, contends that LeMay, when told of the fuel savings offered by the new turbofan, responded that 'gas is cheap, engines aren't'. Twenty years later, SAC found that gas was no longer cheap, and the same engines it bought for the KC-135E were by then far more expensive (even with used commercial engines) than they were when Boeing first offered the conversion.

The turbofan engines also eliminated the turbojets' need for demineralized water to increase take-off thrust. Each full load of water weighed 5,500 lb (2,495kg), weight not available as extra fuel or cargo, and demineralized water cost nearly the same as jet fuel. When water was unavailable takeoff loads were decreased, hence requiring more than one airplane to do the job of a single tanker. When the water injection system failed, the water was dumped overboard to decrease weight further for a 'dry' take-off. SAC could have saved millions of dollars by eliminating the need for demineralized water, more than enough to re-engine the entire fleet several times over.

The turbojet engines used on the KC-135 – particularly when augmented with water injection – produced a deafening noise. This caused considerable sonic damage to the aft fuselage, an area especially vulnerable to dynamic stresses in turns and maneuvering flight. To strengthen the aft fuselage, 25 circumferential bands 2in (5cm) wide were bonded onto the exterior of the airplane aft of the wing root and forward of the horizontal stabilizer. These bands are on all variants of the KC-135, regardless of engine type.

Wet versus Dry
The adverse effects resulting from the short time available to Boeing to produce the first Stratotanker affected not only the subsystems installed on the airplane but its overall design as well. To increase engine thrust, demineralized water could be injected into each engine for nearly two minutes beginning at takeoff and continuing through initial climbout, adding approximately 2,250 lb (10.0kN) of thrust per engine. Boeing engineers felt that four separate water injection control systems would be needlessly repetitive and instead settled on two systems. The left system provided water for the two left engines and the right system provided water for the two right engines. This arrangement ignored the disastrous potential given the loss of one system during the critical takeoff phase, particularly when the airplane was extremely heavy with fuel or under strong or gusty crosswind conditions. Should water injection be lost on one side, the extra 4,500 lb (20.1kN) of thrust on the opposite side would provide greater lift and raise that wing, leading to a low altitude stall or cartwheel and crash. Moreover, the water injection system left a great deal to be desired in terms of operational restrictions, temperature constraints, maintenance and logistics, and safety.

After more than a decade of operations with the original left-right water injection system, Oklahoma City Air Materiel Area (OCAMA) at Tinker AFB, Oklahoma, finally undertook efforts to eliminate the potential for loss of control due to asymmetric thrust in the event of one system failing. This significant difference in thrust had implications far beyond the critical issue of aircraft control as the need for large rudder deflections to maintain directional authority placed high side loads on the vertical fin. In its October 1968 proposal to resolve these issues, OCAMA noted that no KC-135As had yet been lost to asymmetric water injection issues. The report did note, however, that the loss of KC-135A 56-3655 near Mt Lassen, CA, on 30th July 1968 due to separation of the vertical stabilizer represented the potential outcome of loss of water on one side with subsequent high side loads on the fin needed to maintain directional control. In short, the 'boot full of rudder' needed to keep the airplane going straight was enough to shear off the vertical stabilizer.

During November 1968 OCAMA proposed the 'Class IV Modification to Provide Symmetrical Water Injection System, EC/KC/RC-135 Aircraft,' calling for 70 modification kits per month to be installed beginning June 1969, although this would be too late for the pilot of KC-135A 56-3602 who aborted takeoff at Loring AFB on 25th March 1969 due to loss of left-side water injection and ran

Crucial problems related to wing fatigue, inadequate vertical stabilizer area, and rudder issues remained uncorrected through the production of the first 200 airframes, necessitating fleet-wide repair and replacement programs. *Photo P21752 courtesy Boeing*

off the runway, destroying the aircraft. Manufacturing delays and shortage of components led to the reduction in monthly modification kits to just 50, earning the personal (and unwanted) attention of CINCSAC General Bruce Holloway. By the end of 1969, thanks to 'four-star' leverage, all KC-135A, C-135F, and C-135A airframes and their derivatives had the newer and safer system. The first conversion was the CINCSAC's own airplane 57-2589.

Near the end of 1958, when the 200th KC-135 took off on its maiden flight, the fleet was already showing signs of structural weakness such as cracks in the wing splice plates. By 1961 fractures appeared in wing leading edge panels and in the wing skin, a problem that had not only structural implications but, since the KC-135 has a 'wet' wing, meant dangerous fuel leak problems. Changes were made to production airplanes, but those in service continued operations without a fix pending approval by Boeing and Air Force engineers. This decision was reached on 10th July 1961 with the beginning of Project WING FIX at OCAMA. The airplanes most in need of repair (32 were considered 'critical') were fixed first, followed by the balance of the KC-135 fleet. The urgency of this problem was considerable, as nearly two months later an unmodified aircraft landed with a 27in (68.5cm) crack in the wing, caused by an overstressed wing fastener. This occurred after only 970 total flight hours, a problem which static testing did not predict to occur until 7,640 flight hours, a miscalculation of some 800%! Over the next two years, these structural problems were eventually minimized, if not fully resolved.

A crucial problem remained, however, which SAC considered 'the most significant KC-135 concern in 1962': inadequate rudder directional stability and control characteristics. The KC-135A, like the Dash 80 prototype, was designed and built with the so-called 'short' vertical stabilizer. The rudder was manually operated, meaning that rudder displacement was contingent upon the strength in the pilot's leg. Flight tests found that the amount of rudder available to the pilot in an asymmetric engine situation (especially following the loss of an outboard engine at full takeoff thrust with water injection operating) was inadequate, and the pilot could not control the airplane within safe design parameters. In addition, training on the 707 required that pilots be able to maintain aircraft control following the rapid cut-off of an outboard engine with the other three engines at full takeoff power and at takeoff airspeed. If the pilot failed to react immediately and allowed excessive yaw to build up, there was insufficient rudder authority to control the airplane and it would roll and yaw rapidly. If still close to the ground, the airplane could drag a wingtip and cartwheel. Even if the pilot intervened early, the initial

abrupt yaw is said to have on at least one occasion created enough transverse g-forces to throw off an outboard engine.

OCAMA proposed installing a hydraulically powered rudder boost and an extended vertical fin on the KC-135 as early as 1st November 1962. Boeing engineers redesigned the vertical stabilizer, increasing its height by 40in (101cm) and increasing the surface area of the rudder. Beginning with the 583rd KC-135A (62-3532), a powered rudder boost system was installed which used hydraulic pressure to move the rudder, dramatically reducing the pilot's workload in engine-out conditions. Airplanes not yet delivered had the new tail installed while still on the assembly line, while field modification kits for those already in service were installed at OCAMA. Collateral work included elevator control modification, corrosion control, lower wing reskin, and landing gear enhancement. The first KC-135 retrofitted under this program was from the 34th AREFS at Offutt AFB. The 'tall tail' greatly improved the KC-135's handling, especially under extreme engine-out conditions. In the words of Joseph Sutter, Chief of Boeing Transport Division's aerodynamics unit during the development of the 367-80, KC-135, and 707, 'lots of power and lots of tail, I believe, make for a successful airplane and a happy pilot'.

The rudder problems identified during initial flight tests came back to haunt the KC-135. Unscheduled rudder deflection caused or was a significant contributing factor in two KC-135 accidents in 1965 – KC-135A 61-0265 at Loring AFB, ME, and KC-135A 57-1442 at McConnell, KS. Between March 1967 and May 1968 there were four rudder-related mishaps. KC-135A 57-2591 experienced full left rudder deflection during takeoff at Columbus AFB, MS, on 15th March 1967. A month later – 27th April – KC-135A 63-7985 suffered uncommanded right roll and yaw during autopilot cruise on a flight from Lockbourne AFB, OH. Immediately after takeoff from Andersen AB, Guam, on 31st May 1967, KC-135A 62-3550 yawed abruptly to the right. Finally, on 9th May 1968 KC-135A 58-0060 experienced a left hard-over rudder two minutes (concurrent with the end of water injection) after takeoff from Hickam AFB, HI. Turning off the rudder power allowed the crew to regain control during this critical phase, preventing loss of an airplane. Flight tests, design analysis, and careful study of the aircraft components by OCAMA and Boeing failed to reveal any cause for these rudder problems. Additional reports of rudder issues were traced to improper flight control rigging, hydraulic malfunctions, and autopilot discrepancies which were readily corrected. OCAMA implemented TCTO-749 to 'limit rudder travel in the event of a hard-over rudder occurrence during the critical flight segment between flaps up and IAS of 250 knots.' Despite spending $1.5 million over 16 months, OCAMA, Boeing, the FAA, and even American Airlines failed to duplicate the problem or find any cause.

By 1966 Project WING FIX was drawing to a close and the extended vertical stabilizer and rudder power boost modification had been installed on all previously unequipped aircraft. Unfortunately, another structural problem began to appear: fatigue cracks in the vertical stabilizer attachment points. Although these were first noted during an accident investigation of a Boeing 707, the similarity in structure between the 707 and KC-135 at the vertical stabilizer attachment points made this a serious concern for the Air Force as well as airlines. Once again, the loss of KC-135A 56-3655 on 30th July 1968 due to the separation of the vertical stabilizer cast serious doubts on the safety of the KC-135 tail. Within a week of the crash, OCAMA had identified a fix for the problem and presented a plan to modify all KC-135s.

PACER FIN was implemented on 1st July 1968, and involved the inspection and repair of cracked vertical fin aft attachment points on all '135 model aircraft. Beginning 5th August 1968 16 airplanes per day underwent the 24-hour inspection. By 27th September, when PACER FIN ended, 761 aircraft had been inspected and modified as required, with six additional aircraft remaining for examination. Of these, 693 were undertaken at Tinker AFB and 74 at Kadena AB. Each aircraft required 152 man-hours of effort by two mechanics, a sheet metal worker, a crew leader, and a quality control inspector with a cost per airplane of $1,845, for a total manpower cost of $1,414,863. Not surprisingly, the parts required cost only $187,061, a situation familiar to any person seeking a car repair. Crews worked in two 12-hour shifts, seven days a week, although beginning 1st September this was reduced to two 10-hour shifts, six days a week. Because the work was done on an outside ramp at Tinker AFB, there were inadequate 'latrine facilities for work crews,' and the government footed the bill of $608 for nine portable toilets.

Production Increases

The KC-135A production rate itself was subject to external influences, typically in the form of DoD and Air Force reactions to budget requirements and a growing Soviet build-up of strategic bombers. The original contract specified a production rate of 13 KC-135As per month, although this was eventually increased once production began. The appearance of the Soviet Union's Tupolev Tu-16 *Badger* intermediate-range and Tu-20 *Bear* and Myasishchev Mya-4 *Bison* strategic bombers fueled Air Force fears over the perceived erosion of American strategic superiority over its communist adversary. Consequently, the Air Force asked to increase the production rate of the B-52 and KC-135, the two key elements in its own strategic modernization program. Before the first KC-135A flew, over $150 million had been requested and approved to increase the KC-135A production rate. SAC's position on production numbers was unequivocal. 'In order to realize a truly intercontinental capability, SAC must promote the procurement of tankers on a 1.1 [*sic*] ratio with B-52 aircraft'. By 1st July 1958 SAC asked Boeing to deliver 20 airplanes per month (as well as necessary spare parts and equipment).

Despite this initial increase in the tanker production rate (which actually peaked at 15 airplanes per month), money was not available in FY58 to sustain this accelerated level. A 'fund expenditure limitation' was imposed on all Boeing contracts as of 27th September 1957, and by 7th November 1957 Boeing, AMC, and the Air Force had agreed upon a reduced production rate and 27 tankers (58-0131 through 58-0157) were canceled. Overall, the delivery rate dropped dramatically from 15 airplanes per month to an average of six tankers per month until KC-135 production ended. An additional 30 KC-135As were canceled (60-0379 through 60-0408). These 30 airplanes were never given Boeing construction numbers.

Above: The 'Pacer Fin' equivalent of 'Kilroy was here' appeared on many of the airplanes examined at Tinker AFB. *Author's collection*

Below: The 100th KC-135A leaves the assembly line. *Photo P20276 courtesy Boeing*

Above: The crew of KC-135A 57-2594 *Stephen F Austin*, the 200th KC-135 delivered, demonstrates some close-order formation reminiscent of SAC in its early years. *Photo courtesy Boeing*

Below: KC-135A 59-1947 *County of Marquette* delivered on 4th August 1960 as the 400th KC-135. *Photo P25385 courtesy Boeing*

Above: KC-135A 58-0085 *Paso Del Norte* was the 300th KC-135 delivered. *Photo FA56719 courtesy Boeing*

Bottom: Although KC-135A 61-0278 *Miss Ak-Sar-Ben* was the 500th KC-135 delivered, Boeing soon converted it into a KC-135A airborne command post. *Photo P28746 courtesy Boeing*

These cancelations did not affect Boeing's willingness to improve the airplane. For example, at the slow speeds flown during takeoff and approach and landing, airflow separation causing a wing stall begins on the wing leading edge inboard of the outboard pylon. To increase the stall margin for the KC-135 in this slow speed regime, Boeing installed leading edge flaps beginning in March 1959 to all production-line aircraft, as well as retrofitting them to extant airframes. These flaps are located from midway between the wing

pylons to the outer pylon, and lower the stall speed by six knots. They extend approximately 100° when the flaps are lowered, and retract fully when the flaps are raised or when (on airplanes so equipped) the No.1 engine thrust reverser is actuated, thus preventing damage to the leading edge flaps due to jet blast.

Lessons learned from these flaps were applied to the remainder of Boeing's jet fleet, all of which now use full-span leading edge flaps and/or slats.

Flying the KC-135: Early Impressions

Despite the many apparent problems and deficiencies inherent in the KC-135, the airplane proved immensely popular with its crews, long accustomed to flying the tedious KC-97. The following report by Boeing's Senior Experimental Test Pilot 'Dix' Loesch, written in October 1957, is representative of the enthusiasm and general pilot acceptance of the KC-135, and merits repeating in full. Although in some places it appears to contradict some flight test results, the report was written before these tests were reported or even undertaken. KC-135 crewmembers will quickly recognize many familiar features described in this report (such as the nose wheel rotation technique and the approach to initial buffet in stalls).

'The advent of the Boeing KC-135 jet tanker-transport as an operational airplane in the Strategic Air Command is sure to arouse questions from aircrews on the flight characteristics of this newest addition to our air power inventory.

'As project pilot for the KC-135 and as one of the pilots who conducted the maiden flight and a large share of the flight testing on the prototype, a brief description from my personal experiences regarding the handling and performance characteristics we have in the new airplane may be beneficial to crewmen who will be flying the KC-135s.

'The Boeing 707 prototype, from which the KC-135 was developed, has been flying for more than three years. Early in this airplane's test program we proved the feasibility of jet-to-jet refueling by means of the new high speed Boeing Flying Boom developed from the system on the KC-97 Stratofreighter. The characteristics of the prototype, with improvements in some areas, are found in the KC-135s.

'Pilots who have been handling transports should find it simple to convert to the KC-135. The jet tanker-transports are similar to present-day transports and tankers in handling, with the new airplane having the advantages. It has excellent stability and control, and

generally speaking, control response is better than you have with today's transports.

'The primary controls are manually operated, internally balanced and tab-controlled. The pilot can check the ailerons, elevators and rudder on the ground for freedom of movement of both the tab and control surface because additional control column or rudder movement at the end of the tab travel moves the entire surface. Also, it's nice to know that there are no gust locks to worry about on this airplane. In place of gust locks there are built-in gust dampers.

'The lateral control is a little unusual in comparison with present transports. There are two sets of ailerons: an outboard set which only operates when flaps are down and an inboard set which operates at all speeds. The ailerons are assisted by wing spoilers on the upper surface which are activated by hydraulic pressure and which are very effective at high speeds and Mach numbers where a wing with ailerons only tends to lose control. These spoilers retain their effectiveness right down to the stalling speed of the aircraft. The spoilers are also effective speed brakes. Using spoilers as speed brakes in conjunction with the landing gear, which can be used at up to 320 knots, provide[s] possible descent rates as high as 18,000ft [5,486m] per minute.

'Pilots will find the cockpit well laid out. It is much simpler than that of the usual four-engine transport of today, due to the jet engines. They don't require propeller pitch controls, feathering buttons, manifold pressure gauges and other instruments and controls peculiar to piston-engines. Visibility from the cockpit is excellent.

'As with other jet aircraft, the KC-135 can be almost entirely checked for flight before starting engines, and takeoff can be made immediately after a power check on the runway.

'The airplane has conventional tricycle gear, with the main gear made up of four-wheel bogies. The turning radius is a little greater than with airplanes which have dual-wheel gear because excessive scrubbing and high torque loads would occur on the inside gear if it was used as a pivot. The main gear is a little closer to the center of gravity than most transports, and the nose can be lifted off at a speed considerably under normal takeoff speed. The best and safest technique is to leave the nose wheel on the runway until about five knots below takeoff speed, otherwise the airplane will take longer to get airborne.

'The fore-and-aft trimming on the KC-135 is done by varying the angle of incidence of the horizontal stabilizer, just as on the prototype. The stabilizer is trimmed by means of and 'up' or 'down' button on the control wheel. A manual trim wheel on the pedestal can be used to manually drive the stabilizer in the event the motor system fails. Before takeoff, the stabilizer should be set so that only a small pull force is needed to lift off at takeoff speed. Elevator effectiveness is high enough and forces are low enough such that the airplane can be flown off with almost any setting of the stabilizer. Once you are off and climbing, or cruising, the pitch trim by the adjustable stabilizer is highly effective at all speeds and the control column is in the same position with the center of gravity at any point. At high Mach numbers, trim remains effective.

'Most transport pilots are flying airplanes which do not have the capability of exceeding IAS limits. This is not true of a jet transport which can easily exceed placard speeds at low altitudes. Pilots will need to be alert regarding this until they have acquired a feel for power settings and for the sound and vibration build-up which occurs at higher speeds.

'The KC-135 has nearly two and a half times as good lateral control as the KC-97. Its directional control is effective enough to handle an outboard engine failure at speeds below takeoff speed except at very light weights. In normal flight the KC-135 is a 'one-hand' airplane. Yet stick force per 'g' is high enough to prevent the pilot from accidentally loading the airplane beyond its limits.

'Although higher fuel consumption rates are apparent, the attention required to the ground miles versus fuel consumed does not increase since cruising speeds are so much higher and consequently tend to minimize variables such as wind, temperature, etc.

'We have done complete stalls in the KC-135 with the airplane in all configurations and with the stick all the way back. The airplane has nearly perfect stalling characteristics. There is a small tendency to roll, and any roll can be counteracted by the lateral control which remains effective throughout the stall. As you approach the stall, buffeting begins 12% to 16% above the stall speed and increases as the stall is approached. You can't mistake it. At the stall, the nose falls straight through the horizon. Absence of propeller slipstream cause power-off and power-on stalling speeds to be virtually the same.

'Let down can be controlled by means of the spoilers, used as speedbrakes. On the approach, if you are above the ILS glidepath or desired approach path, you can apply speedbrakes to descend to it. In the pattern, and on the approach, the KC-135 is able to stay behind today's airplanes. Its speed, while about 600mph [956km/h] for high cruising speed, is only 125 knots [143mph – 231km/h] during final at normal landing weights.

'Approach is a little more nose high than in present-day transport and tanker aircraft, but visibility is excellent and there is no difficulty in judging clearance over obstacles or height above the runway. It's a good idea to keep the airplane trimmed hands-off during final approach, rather than with the slight nose down trim used in some airplanes. Once on the ground, getting the nose wheel down early and raising the speedbrakes will greatly aid in minimizing ground roll. Ninety per cent of the weight of the airplane is on the main gear at landing speeds after the nose gear is on and the speedbrakes raised.

'More than 100 pilots have already flown the prototype. Even those without any previous knowledge of the airplane, or of jet airplanes of any kind, have experienced no difficulty in making successful takeoffs and landings. None of the differences between the KC-135 and present-day transports should be of any real concern. The general simplicity of operation will, by far, be the biggest difference encountered and bears out the old maxim that progress marches from the complex to the simple.

'If pilot enthusiasm, as far as the prototype is concerned, is a guide for acceptance of the KC-135, then the KC-135s should be one of the best liked airplanes in the Air Force. I would predict that any difficulty that arises will not be in getting pilots in the KC-135s, but in keeping them out.'

Opposite: The Dash 80 served not only as the prototype for the KC-135 fleet, but as the primary testbed for the flying boom. Bill Allen never let his engineers and staff forget that the Dash 80 was first and foremost designed to garner the jet tanker business for Boeing. *Author's collection*

Right: The real legacy of the KC-135 derives from its crew. Words like 'flexibility,' 'adaptability,' 'resourcefulness,' and 'determination' have meant the difference between a successful air refueling and an aborted mission – or worse. *Photo P17864 courtesy Boeing*

CHAPTER FOUR

Schoolhouse

'The instructions in this manual are designed to provide for the needs of a crew inexperienced in the operation of these airplanes. This book provides the best possible operating instructions under most circumstances, but it is a poor substitute for sound judgment.'
– *(K)C-135A-1 Flight Manual*

'To err is human. To forgive is not SAC policy.'
– *Attributed to General Curtis LeMay*

When KC-135 crewdogs need to review how a piece of equipment on board their airplane works, where it gets its power and how much it uses, or what to do when it breaks and goes 'Tango Uniform', they turn to the ubiquitous 'Dash One', the KC-135 flight manual. Within minutes, their eyes begin to glaze over and they are overwhelmed with the uncontrollable urge to take a 'combat nap'. The Dash One has struck again.

It would be easy to describe the KC-135 and its variants simply by transferring huge blocks of text from the Dash One to these pages. However, in addition to running the serious risk of putting readers to sleep or at least inducing a strong soporific effect, this tedious approach misses the essential flavor of how the KC-135's components shape the airplane's day-to-day use. For example, as the Dash One dryly records: 'The KC-135R is a four-engine swept-wing jet tanker capable of sustained high-altitude cruise and high-speed flight. The fuselage is divided into a pressurized compartment which includes the cockpit, the cargo compartment, the lower nose compartment, and the boom operator's compartment. The unpressurized lower deck beneath the cargo compartment houses fuel tanks, the landing gear, and other equipment.' Hardly the stuff to inspire any budding young Curt LeMays or Chuck Yeagers!

What is not recorded in these terse sentences is that the cargo compartment, in reality a dark, hot and stuffy steam tunnel in warm weather and an icebox in cold weather, can induce even the strongest-stomached flier to lose more than his lunch during a two-hour traffic pattern only flight consisting of dozens of takeoffs, landings, and missed approaches, not all of them planned. What is not written on page 1-1 is that the lower nose compartment, popularly known as the 'hell hole', was the place that navigators were loath to go during flight to replace burned-out radar components. Although the material covered in this chapter is presented in the same general sequence as in the Dash One, it has the added perspective of a long-suffering crewdog who knows that what the Dash One *says* and what it *really means* are often two distinctly different things.

ENGINES

J57 Turbojets

The Pratt & Whitney J57-P-29A was installed only on a few of the initial Stratotankers, and was quickly replaced by later J57 versions. The first J57 variant to enter operational service was the J57-P/F-43W. The 'P' in the designation indicates that the engine was built by Pratt & Whitney and the 'F' indicates that the engine was built by Ford Aerospace, being respectively designated J57-P-43 or J57-F-43. They are otherwise identical, and for ease of reference are commonly referred to with the 'P/F' designation. The 'W' suffix indicates the capability of water injection for thrust augmentation, earning these engines the ignominious nickname of 'Steamjets' (with the airplanes called 'Water Wagons'). The J57-P/F-43Ws were made of titanium as a weight saving measure, a benefit offset by a commensurate increase in cost. To reduce engine costs as the fleet size grew, the titanium items were replaced with steel parts. The result was the J57-P/F-59W, by far the most numerous engine type used on the Stratotanker. Although the steel -59W weighed approximately 400 lb (181kg) more than the titanium -43Ws, it cost $100,000 less per engine (when purchased in the 1950s).

The J57 was an axial-flow engine with two compressor sections. Low-pressure bleed air was used for pneumatic starting and air conditioning, stabilizer trim pressurization, and defrosting the celestial sighting and boom operator's sighting window, as well as cockpit and boom pod heat. High-pressure bleed air was used for, among other things, engine anti-icing, hydraulic reservoir pressurization, and engine water injection pumps. The engines could be started pneumatically by high-pressure air from a ground cart or bleed air from another engine, or by an explosive cartridge in each engine (some early models were equipped for cartridge starts in the No.4 engine only). All engines could be started simultaneously with the cartridges. There were two engine cartridge configurations when on alert, with carts installed in the No.1 and No.4 engine, or the 'Quick Start' mode, with carts in all four engines, ensuring minimum time required to launch. Alert starts were fairly dramatic events, as black smoke engulfed the airplane and the crew chief that monitored the engine start, prompting the occasional use of gas masks when the airplane was in the Quick Start configuration.

Above 20°F (-6.7°C), demineralized water could be injected into the air inlet and diffuser section of each engine. This increased the density of inlet and combustion air, resulting in increased thrust (and the characteristic dense black smoke and noise). Water injection was intended for takeoff use only, and the 670-gallon (2,536 liters) tank provided the airplane with sufficient water (5,580 lb/2,531kg) for about two minutes of added thrust. Indeed, many navigators would hack their stopwatch when the water started and announce '110 water' at the 110-second mark to warn the pilots that water injection was due to end in approximately 10 seconds. Unused water (if any) was drained before the airplane passed 10,000ft (3,048m) altitude. The water tank was located between the main landing gear wells, and the water drain mast was underneath the fuselage just aft of the main gear wells.

Using the water injection system could be a nightmare, especially for an inexperienced copilot. First, two sets of takeoff data were computed, one for the planned 'wet' takeoff and one for a 'dry' takeoff in the event the water is not used due to temperature changes or mechanical failure of the water injection system. (Computing takeoff data manually was often treated as the arithmetic equivalent of proving Einstein's equations!) Starting the water system required flipping a switch on the copilot's front instrument panel. Unfortunately for many an embarrassed copilot, the switch to *start* the water injection was next to the switch to *drain* the water tank… There was no guarantee that starting the water injection system would necessarily mean that each engine would 'take' the water – which could be determined only by watching the Exhaust Pressure Ratio (EPR) gauge jump to 2.83. Pilots learned a number of tricks to force-start the water, ranging from banging a fist on the throttle quadrant (where additional activation switches were located) to setting the delinquent engine's revolutions per minute (rpm) above 80% and then starting the water, the reverse of the normal procedure. In addition, water injection could fail after the takeoff started, and at times could be tantamount to losing an engine during takeoff. Water injection and alert operations were a constant source of problems,

particularly in cold weather climates. A water heater kept the water from freezing between 20°-40°F (-6.7°C - 4.4°C), but the water had to be removed when the ambient temperature dropped below 20°F (-6.7°C). This often meant downloading water in the evening as temperatures slowly decreased, and then uploading water during the day, a sizeable headache for any crew chief.

Water augmentation originally may have been an effective means of improving engine thrust at takeoff, but in the long run was more trouble and more costly than re-engining the fleet. Demineralized water was very expensive, and at remote airfields was often impossible to come by. Nonetheless, the black smoke and thundering roar of a 'Steam Jet' trundling down a long runway, clawing for airspeed, barely getting airborne before the end of the runway, all the while converting jet fuel to noise and smoke, made for an impressive sight. It was not so impressive, however, for any following aircraft, such as those that might be in a minimum interval takeoff (MITO) 12 seconds behind the preceding airplane, obscured in black smoke that also hid the runway. To many KC-135 crew dogs, however, the black smoke and roar were an integral part of the 'Sound of Freedom'.

TF33 Turbofans

Three types of TF33s are in use on different versions of the Stratotanker: TF33-P-5, -P-9, and, -PW-102. The following description applies to the TF33-P-5, with variations noted below.

The TF33-P-5 is a twin-spool axial-flow turbofan engine producing approximately 16,050 lb (71.9kN) of thrust. Eight blow-in doors on the nose cowl open to provide additional air to the engine during high power settings, such as during takeoff. The doors are spring loaded to the closed position and open by means of differential pressure. The engine has low- and high-pressure compressor sections. Low-pressure compressor bleed air is used for pneumatic starting, air conditioning, and window defrosting. High-pressure bleed air is used for engine anti-ice, hydraulic pressurization, the fuel heater, and thrust reverser actuation.

The TF33-P-5 and -PW-102 have fan and core thrust reversers. The fan section reverser consists of a cowl ring, 12 blocker doors, and pneumatic actuators. A lever on each throttle manually activates the reversers. The lever can only be moved to the 'interlock' position when the throttle is in idle and the aircraft weight is on the landing gear, preventing reverse thrust in flight. When actuated, the blocker doors deflect fan exhaust air forward to produce reverse thrust. The core reverser consists of a sliding reverser sleeve, pneumatic actuators, and clamshell reversers and circumferential cascade vane openings. The sleeve moves aft to expose the cascade vane openings and the clamshells close, forcing thrust forward out through the cascade vanes. To prevent damage to the leading edge flap due to reverse thrust, the leading edge flaps retract when the number one reverse thrust lever is actuated.

Interestingly, availability of thrust reversers is not a normal consideration in planning takeoffs (in the case of an abort) or landings (to decrease stopping distance). As there is always the possibility of thrust reverser failure or asymmetric actuation, crews do not routinely plan takeoff data under the assumption that thrust reversers will be available in the event of an abort. Using thrust reversers means a greater stopping capacity, hence a higher decision speed at which to initiate an abort, thus allowing takeoffs at higher gross weights or on shorter runways. Similarly, use of thrust reversers upon landing is not a standard part of landing data computation. This is not to suggest that thrust reversers are never or seldom used, or that in some special situations (as in operational reconnaissance missions launched from Shemya AFB, AK) are not taken into consideration in takeoff planning. As with all things mechanical, thrust reversers on the TF33s do not always work as advertised, and current operational doctrine

Opposite: Thick black smoke and thundering noise accompany a 'wet' takeoff for 7th BW KC-135A 60-0328 at Carswell AFB. Not everyone appreciated the 'sound of freedom', especially during late night or early morning departures. *Photo by Brian Rogers*

Table 4-1. **Engine Summary**

USAF Designation	Turbojet	Turbofan	Water Injection	Thrust Reversers	Max Thrust (lb/kN static)		Max Continuous EGT
					Wet	Dry	
J57-P-29A	X	-	X	-	12,100/54.2	10,500/47.0	560°C
J57-P/F-43W	X	-	X	-	12,925/57.9	11,200/50.1	
J57-P/F-59W	X	-	X	-	12,925/57.9	11,200/50.1	
TF33-P-5	-	X	-	X	-	16,050/71.9	490°C
TF33-P-9	-	X	-	-	-	16,050/71.9	
TF33-PW-102	-	X	-	-	-	16,050/71.9	
F108-CF-100	-	X	-	-	-	22,000/98.5	855°C

Thrust is Military Rated Thrust (MRT) in pounds with the engine mounted on the airplane during a standard day (sea level, 29.92 in/Hg, 59°F/15°C). Wet thrust is Takeoff Rated Thrust (TRT). EGT is Exhaust Gas Temperature

emphasizes a conservative approach to their use for planning purposes.

None of the TF33s use water injection. They are markedly quieter and produce less smoke than do the J57s, but still leave quite an audible impression during full-power takeoffs. By 2016 only eight airplanes equipped with TF33s remain in service – the three Chilean Air Force KC-135Es, the NC-135W, the two OC-135Bs, the WC-135C, and the WC-135W.

F108 Turbofans

The military designation of the CFM International CFM-56 high-bypass turbofan engine is F108-CF-100; the 'CF' is the builder designation. The engine develops 22,000 lb (98.5kN) of thrust from –62° to +86°F (-52° to 30°C), with thrust decreasing at ambient temperatures above +86°F (30°C).

The engine is divided into five major sections: a four-stage low-pressure high-bypass fan section, a nine-stage high-pressure compressor section, a combustion section, the turbine or core section, and engine accessories. A redundant detection system warns of engine fire and engine compartment overheat, and two fire extinguisher bottles are installed in each wing for use in either engine, a feature not found on other engines used on KC-135s. The KC-135R's pneumatic system uses fifth-stage bleed air from the compressor section for engine start, anti-ice, and environmental regulation. The engines can be started via the auxiliary power unit (APU), an operating engine, or by ground cart. A power management control automatically maintains the desired thrust rating regardless of changes in altitude or Mach number. A turbine engine monitoring system provides a record of engine operation for post-flight analysis, increasing engine life and facilitating maintenance.

Along with reinforcing the vertical stabilizer, reskinning the lower wing, and installing a 'glass cockpit', replacing the J57 engines with F108s enabled the KC-135 fleet to fly until 2040. 'Butterfly' cowlings facilitate maintenance. *Photo by the author*

Currently, none of the F108s are equipped with thrust reversers. Widely considered a needlessly expensive luxury, this omission was dictated as much by operational doctrine as by simple economics. Thrust reversers are primarily intended for use during landing to stop a heavy airplane. Since the intended mission of the KC-135R was to offload all available fuel to nuclear-armed bombers, it would land at extremely light weight nearly devoid of fuel. By improving the KC-135R's braking system, there would be no need to install expensive (and heavy) thrust reversers.

The lack of reversers has been a central issue in the re-engining of RC-135s, which have high landing weights and must often operate from short or icy runways. Still, as an economy measure the re-engined RC-135s did not receive F108s equipped with thrust reversers. Another consideration in the F108 thrust reverser controversy has been in the assignment of KC-135Rs without reversers to Air National Guard (ANG) and Air Force Reserve (AFRES) units that previously operated KC-135Es equipped with them. Using thrust reversers, KC-135Es were able to slow down after landing to exit the runway at the high-speed taxiway, as do reverser-equipped airliners. Despite their improved braking potential, KC-135Rs are not always able to slow to a safe exit speed until after passing the high speed taxiway, forcing the airplane to taxi to the end in order to exit, thus tying up the active runway. This increased congestion at busy civil airports such as Chicago's O'Hare IAP, especially in bad weather. Reservations notwithstanding, during 1991 Wisconsin became the first ANG unit to convert from the KC-135E to KC-135R – without thrust reversers – with a number of other Guard and Reserve units following suit. The ANG and AFRES resolved the airport congestion issue (notably at O'Hare) by relocating several units entirely.

Table 4-2. **Production Engine Installation**

Engine Type	Airframes
J57-P-29A	KC-135A, JKC-135A
J57-P/F-43W	EC-135K, JKC-135A, KC-135A, KC-135A (recon), KC-135R (recon), NKC-135A, RC-135T
J57-P/F-59W	C-135A, C-135F, EC-135A, EC-135G, EC-135H, EC-135K, EC-135L, EC-135N, EC-135P, JC-135A, JKC-135A, KC-135A, KC-135A-II, KC-135A (recon), KC-135A-VIII, KC-135D, KC-135Q, KC-135R (recon), KC-135T (recon), NC-135A, NKC-135A, RC-135A, RC-135D, C-135A
TF33-P-5 *	C-135B, C-135C, EC-135B, NC-135W, OC-135B, RC-135E, RC-135M, RC-135S, RC-135W, RC-135X, TC-135B, TC-135S, TC-135W, VC-135B, WC-135B, WC-135W
TF33-P-9	EC-135C, EC-135J, KC-135B, NKC-135B, RC-135B, RC-135C, RC-135U, RC-135V
TF33-PW-102 *	C-135E, EC-135E, EC-135H, EC-135K, EC-135N, EC-135Y, KC-135D, KC-135E, NKC-135E, RC-135T
F108-CF-100	C-135FR, KC-135R, KC-135RG, KC-135T, NKC-135R, RC-135S, RC-135U, RC-135V, RC-135W, TC-135S, TC-135W

* indicates engines equipped with thrust reversers

SYSTEMS

Hydraulics

Two independent hydraulic systems supply fluid to operate the hydraulically actuated components. The left hydraulic system is pressurized by two pumps driven by the numbers one and two engines, and provides hydraulic power for the inboard spoilers, forward air refueling pumps, landing gear, and pilot's brakes. The right hydraulic system supplies the outboard spoilers, the aft air refueling pumps, copilot's brakes, copilot's instrument power system (on airplanes so equipped), nose wheel steering, boom controls, flaps, leading edge flaps, and the powered rudder. On airplanes with an inflight refueling (IFR) system, the slipway doors are powered by the right hydraulic system, with backup from the left. On the KC-135R, the right system also provides hydraulic pressure for the auxiliary power unit (APU) start system. Although the two systems are independent, there is a crossover capability, enabling crucial components such as the landing gear, main flaps, air refueling boom, and powered rudder to be powered by the opposite system should their primary hydraulic source fail.

Fuel

The KC-135 has six integral wing tanks in a 'wet' wing and a combination bladder and integral center wing tank, a forward and aft fuselage body tank. Beginning with KC-135A 55-3127 an upper deck tank could also be fitted. The body tanks are located in the lower fuselage beneath the main deck floor beams. The forward tank consists of four bladder cells (only three if the upper deck tank is not installed), and the aft tank has five bladder cells. The upper deck tank is in the cargo compartment between the boom operator's compartment and the aft pressure bulkhead. Two hydraulically powered air refueling pumps (one forward, one aft) are located in each body tank. The upper deck tank operates via gravity feed, emptying into the aft body tank. Each wing houses a reserve tank near the wingtip and two main wing fuel tanks. Two boost pumps are in each main wing tank, and two override pumps are located in the center wing tank. The reserve tanks feed through gravity flow into the outboard main tanks. Main wing tank fuel also can be fed by gravity to the aft body fuel tank. Center wing fuel can be gravity fed to the forward body tank.

Fuel in all tanks can be used by the KC-135 or offloaded to a receiver, although approximately 300 gallons (1,135 liters) per main wing tank (known as 'standpipe fuel') is retained for tanker use only. On the KC-135A, total usable fuel (with upper deck installed) was 30,000 gallons (113,562 liters – 195,000 lb/88,452kg). On the KC-135R, total usable fuel (with upper deck installed) is 31,275 gallons (118,388 liters – 203,288 lb/92,211kg). Total fuel capacity is lower on airplanes with fuel tanks removed, or on airplanes that are weight limited due to the addition of mission equipment or cargo.

An engine fuel manifold in the wing provides fuel to each engine from any main wing tank or the center wing tank. An air refueling manifold carries fuel from both body tanks to the air refueling boom. This manifold can also be used to feed the tanker's engines via the wing manifold. Fuel may be dumped through the air refueling boom when required. On airplanes without an air refueling boom, fuel dump capability is provided by a fuel dump tube beneath the aft fuselage. On airplanes equipped with an IFR system, an IFR manifold allows fuel to be onloaded into any tank.

The airplane is equipped for ground single point refueling (SPR) through a receptacle in the right main gear well (the KC-135Q had an SPR receptacle in each main gear well for JP-7 – see Chapter 5). Primary fuel was JP-4 (NATO F40), since replaced by JP-8. Acceptable alternates include JP-5 and commercial grade Jet A, A-1, and B.

Fuel Tank Location

Air Refueling

The boom operator lies prone on a couch in the boom operator's compartment. A mirror enables the boom operator to see receivers aft of the airplane from 0° to 15° below the horizon, an area otherwise obscured by the empennage. Normal vision extends downward to 48° below the horizon.

The air refueling boom is manually controlled by means of a side-stick controller on the right hand side for boom control, and a lever on the left hand side for boom extension. Boom movement is by hydraulics and control is through the boom's ruddervators. A hydraulically powered reversible motor provides extension and retraction. The boom may be manually stowed via a hoist in the event of hydraulic failure. By moving the side-stick controller, the boom operator literally flies the boom to the desired position. Movement of the boom behind and below the aircraft can also steer the airplane. As the boom moves to one side it induces drag sufficient to turn the KC-135 in that direction. As the boom is raised or lowered, the drag affects the tanker's airspeed.

By the time the flying boom was in use on the KC-135 it had matured into an effective means of transferring large volumes of fuel. Its secret was its simplicity, a lesson seemingly lost in the latest software-driven booms plagued by production delays and operational limits. *Photo courtesy Boeing*

There are two types of air refueling booms: a standard-speed boom and a high-speed boom. The standard speed boom was installed on the first 345 airplanes. The high-speed boom has a 5in (12.7cm) extension to the boom latching fairing where it retracts to join the fuselage. With few exceptions, all of the high-speed booms have a boundary layer control feature that improves boom stability at high speeds. Located around the boom latching fairing, this consists of thin secondary skins coated with coarse aluminum oxide grit. The boom itself consists of two concentric tubular sections, and is 28ft (8.5m) long fully retracted and 47ft (14.3m) long fully extended. The boom can move through an envelope 30° to either side of centerline, plus 12.5° above the horizon, and minus 50° below the horizon. Normal boom position for air refueling is 30° below the horizon, 12ft (3.6m) extension (40ft [12.1m] total), and along the tanker's centerline.

After contact is made, the boom electrical system sends a signal enabling automatic fuel transfer to the receiver provided at least one air refueling pump is operating and fuel is available through the air refueling manifold. The receiver pilot director indicator lights (PDIs) are also activated. In addition, automatic boom limit switches are activated to effect a disconnect if the boom reaches an envelope limit. Some tankers have a boom interphone system, enabling the boom operator to talk with the receiver crew (if also equipped with the system) in a radio-silent environment.

The KC-135 has a number of high-intensity lights for night operation. Underbody illumination lights are installed on the inside of the inboard engine pylons and shine on the underside of the fuselage. Underwing illumination lights are installed in the fuselage fairing aft of the wing and illuminate the underside of the wing and engines. Engine nacelle and leading edge lights are installed in the forward fuselage above and forward of the wing leading edge. Two small boom nozzle lights are located in the upper portion of the boom nozzle fairing. These emit a near ultra-violet light that causes the luminous colored boom markings to fluoresce during night operations. An air refueling floodlight has been installed retroactively at the top of the vertical stabilizer, providing the boom operator with additional illumination of the receiver envelope to aid in night refueling, particularly with darkly camouflaged receivers. KC-135Qs and KC-135Ts have a special receiver envelope illumination light that is fully described in the KC-135Q/T section. The boom operator can control the intensity of all of the air refueling illumination lights.

PDIs are located beneath the forward fuselage between the nose gear and the main gear. These consist of two rows of lights: the left row (facing forward from the receiver position) is for height and the

right row is for extension. Azimuth guidance is provided by a broad yellow stripe painted along the length of the KC-135 centerline. Additional elevation guidance is available in the form of a small white line which, when visually placed by the receiver pilot in a position where it seems to touch the tip of one of the tanker's lower UHF radio antennas, shows the 30° elevation position. The PDIs have green lights that indicate relative position of the receiver by means of electrical relays from the boom. The extension PDI has a centered light, an intermediate light, and a full extension light in each direction, with the letter 'A' for aft and 'F' for forward (indicating the desired direction to move). The elevation PDI has a centered light, an intermediate light, and full elevation light in each direction, with the letter 'U' for up and 'D' for down. With the receiver in the center of the envelope, the two centered PDIs are illuminated, producing what is known as 'Captain's Bars', resembling the shoulder rank worn by US captains. As the receiver moves throughout the envelope, the PDIs reflect that position. For example, if an intermediate aft light is illuminated, the receiver has backed to 14ft (4.2m) extension. If the red full extension light is illuminated, the receiver has reached the aft limit of 16ft (4.8m). Combinations of lights indicate in-between positions (ie an intermediate aft light and a red full extension light mean approximately 15ft [4.5m] aft extension.)

A boom drogue adapter (BDA) can be installed prior to flight to refuel probe-equipped receivers. This weighs an additional 143 lb (64.8kg) including trapped fuel. On airplanes equipped with an ARR system, slipway doors cover the receptacle above the navigator's station on top of the forward fuselage.

Electrical

The KC-135A had a 3-phase, 115/200 volt, 400-cycle AC system, and a 28-volt DC system, with a battery as a secondary source of DC power. Electrical power was provided to a bus which then powered the appropriate equipment. The generators needed to operate in parallel prior to bringing them on line, an automatic feature in the KC-135R, KC-135T, and some TF33-equipped airplanes. Should one or more generator fail, a bus allowed the remaining generator(s) to pick up the load, although some equipment (eg the water injection system) required power from all three generators.

Prior to the installation of the 'glass cockpit', a hydraulically powered generator provided 115/200 volt AC power to the copilot's instrument power system as an emergency backup in the event of total electrical failure. When connected to a transformer rectifier, it provided 28-volt DC power. Two transformer-rectifiers converted 115/200 volt AC power into 28-volt DC power. DC battery power is provided by a 24-volt, 22-amp nickel cadmium (Nicad) battery located in the toilet compartment. The battery has a separate transformer rectifier.

Flight Controls

The KC-135 is equipped with conventional ailerons, elevators, and rudder. These are actuated by cables from the pilot's and copilot's control columns which move 'flying tabs' in the appropriate control surface. Little effort is required to displace these tabs, and the resultant aerodynamic pressures move the larger control surface. Although pilots like to joke that the airplane is a 'true fly-by-wire' jet – using wire cables to move the control surfaces – there are no plans to replace this with either hydraulically actuated or digital flight controls.

Two sets of ailerons and two sets of hydraulically powered spoilers on each wing provide lateral control. The inboard ailerons (commonly referred to as 'high speed ailerons') are used throughout the entire speed range, and the outboard ailerons (commonly referred to as 'low speed ailerons') are locked out unless the outboard flaps are extended, with full effectiveness achieved at 23° or more of flap

Luminescent color markings on the inner portion of the boom show extension – in this case it indicates approximately 15ft (4.6m), nearing the aft limit. In contact, pilots seldom see the boom unless the receptacle is in front of the cockpit, as in the A-10 or B-1. *Photo by Robert D Archer*

Flaps are normally positioned at 20° or 30° for takeoff, depending on aircraft weight and field conditions. Some pilots feel that using 40° flaps makes for a smoother landing, but 50° flaps (seen here) allow for lower landing speeds and shorter stopping distance. *Photo by the author*

extension. At high speeds the outboard ailerons are extremely effective and would otherwise induce abrupt and possibly extreme rolling motions. Using the less effective inboard spoilers at high speed ensures smooth aircraft control. The ailerons move by an innovative system. Movement of the control column actuates a cable which displaces the flying tab in the trailing edge of the aileron. Deflection of this tab causes an air load on the tab which moves the control surface. A balance bay cavity is located forward of the aileron. Pressure changes on the control surface of the aileron are transmitted to this balance chamber. As deflection increases and aerodynamic loads are the greatest, the balance forces are also at a maximum. This reduces the amount of force and effort the pilot must use to move the control surface. Although not as effective as modern hydraulically boosted flight controls, it was a notable improvement over contemporary control designs where pilots simply ran out of strength to control the airplane at high speeds. Since the KC-135 was designed as a 'high speed jet tanker', solving this problem was a major design consideration.

Elevators provide pitch control. Inputs from the control columns are transmitted via cables to the elevator control tabs which then aerodynamically position the elevators. Varying the angle of incidence of the entire horizontal stabilizer by means of a jackscrew provides pitch trim. The pilot or copilot may electrically trim the aircraft, the pilot may manually trim the aircraft, and the autopilot can electrically trim the aircraft.

The KC-135 rudder is capable of both manual and hydraulically powered operations, with the boosted mode used in all normal operations. Powered rudder deflection is by a hydraulic control unit. In the powered mode, the rudder tab moves opposite the rudder through 17° of deflection. At greater deflections, the tab reverses and acts as a rudder antibalance tab, and a 'Q-spring' system provides the pilot with an artificial sense of rudder feel. Ram air from the Q-inlet on the leading edge of the vertical stabilizer produces a mechanically transmitted force to the rudder pedals. As airspeed increases, rudder deflection has a greater effect on the longitudinal axis of the airplane. Conversely, as the airplane slows, more rudder travel is needed to account for asymmetric forces or yaw. To ensure that the airplane is not overstressed at high speeds and that the pilot has sufficient controllability at low speeds, there are two rudder power pressure ranges. As the airplane slows and the inboard flaps are extended

beyond 5°, the rudder power moves into the high range (2,800-3,050 psi), maximizing rudder deflection potential. As the airplane's speed increases and the flaps are retracted, the rudder power moves into the low range (800-1,175psi). Manual operation of the rudder without hydraulic power is via a control tab on the trailing edge of the rudder which operates the same as the aileron system. Maximum deflection in the manual mode is approximately 12°.

Each wing has an outboard flap, an inboard flap, two leading edge Krueger-style flaps, and a fillet flap. The main flaps each have a fore flap. Normal takeoff setting is 20° or 30°, depending upon gross weight, runway available, desired engine thrust and other considerations. Originally, there was a 40° setting for takeoff, but in the aftermath of the first KC-135 accident, this was deleted. Landing settings range from 30° (used in some emergency and abnormal situations) to 50°, the full flap position. Some pilots feel that 'flap 40' landings are smoother than 'flap 50' landings, but to a good pilot the flap setting is irrelevant. Two connected hydraulically powered drive motors move the flaps, one for the inboard flaps and one for the outboard flaps. In the event of right side hydraulic failure, the left system can be crossed over to provide sufficient hydraulic pressure to operate the flaps. In addition, the flaps can be operated manually by turning a pair of bypass handles in the cargo compartment floor. In some airplanes that have equipment or cargo that would cover these access ports, the flaps can be operated by a secondary electrical drive. The leading edge flaps extend when the outboard flaps are extended beyond 9.5° and retract when the flaps are retracted above 6°. Leading edge flaps improve the low-speed performance of the aircraft, and reduce the stall speed by approximately 6kts (11.1km/h). On airplanes so equipped, the leading edge flaps retract when the No.1 engine thrust reverser is actuated, thus preventing blast damage to the leading edge flap.

Four spoilers, two on each wing, augment lateral control of the airplane. Spoiler deflection limits are 60° and are usable throughout the entire speed range, but at higher speeds the deflection is decreased due to spoiler blowdown. Maximum roll rate can be achieved at approximately 30°. Deflection is based on control wheel displacement and is automatic unless disabled by the spoiler cutout switches. The spoilers can be used as speed brakes by moving the speed brake handle. In this case, all four spoilers extend simultaneously.

Landing Gear and Brakes

The KC-135 has a tricycle landing gear arrangement. The nose gear has two tires on a steerable strut, and each main gear has four tires each on a single truck.

The nose gear is steerable through approximately 55° either side of centerline, but is normally limited to 45° deflection. Steering is by means of a small wheel on the pilot's left forward side panel. In the KC-135R the primary means of steering is the rudder pedals, although the steering wheel must still be used for acute turns. The landing gear is extended and retracted hydraulically using left side hydraulics. The nose gear retracts forward into the nose gear well in the fuselage and the main gear retracts into gear wells in the fuselage wing root. Normal gear retraction and extension takes ten seconds, although this can increase in extremely cold weather or when hydraulic pressure is reduced. The gear is both hydraulically and mechanically locked in the up or down position. They may be manually extended from within the cockpit (nose gear) and in the floor of the cargo compartment (main gear).

The KC-135 has segmented rotor brakes. These were originally four-rotor brakes, although some aircraft (especially those that land at high gross weights such as the cargo and reconnaissance variants) had more powerful five-rotor brakes, since installed across the fleet. Braking may be accomplished from either the pilot's or the copilot's position. Only the pilot's side provides anti-skid capability which removes braking from a skidding wheel and allows the wheel to spin up to speed. The pilot then reapplies brakes to slow the airplane further. Some aircraft have an improved modulated anti-skid system that anticipates a skid by monitoring rate of change of wheel speed and immediately reduces braking force just enough to allow the wheel to resume speed. Braking force is then automatically reapplied, giving the best possible stopping capability, especially on wet or icy runways. A reserve brake hydraulic accumulator provides for at least one emergency brake actuation in the event of loss of left side hydraulics (and hence pilot's brakes).

The KC-135R has a beefier landing gear to support the increase in gross weight. It also has five-rotor brakes and Mk. III modulating anti-skid system, as do a number of special use airplanes such as EC-135s and RC-135s.

Pressurization and Air Conditioning

Low-pressure bleed air from each engine provides air for pneumatic starting, window defrosting, stabilizer trim actuator pressurization and the cabin air conditioning and pressurization system. The KC-135 has a single air conditioning pack with a ram air intake located at the underside of the leading edge of the right wing root, while other variants such as RC-135s have an additional air conditioning system installed to accommodate the increased cooling demands of their special equipment. Airplanes equipped with this extra air conditioning system have an additional ram air intake on the underside of the leading edge of the left wing.

All of the air conditioning and cabin pressurization systems are automated with manual backup provided. Ordinarily, the airplane was unpressurized (and without air conditioning or heating) on initial takeoff to prevent a decrease of engine thrust due to loss of the bleed air. The KC-135R, however, normally takes off fully pressurized (and somewhat more temperate inside) because of its increase in thrust (and hence excess bleed air), providing for a more pleasant cockpit environment. Because of extreme heat in the cockpit, it has been reported that KC-135A pattern training sorties at bases in Thailand sometimes were flown with the pilots' windows open!

Above: Original KC-135As were equipped with 4-rotor brakes. The key assumption was that a KC-135A would land at low weight (120,000 lb/ 54,431kg) after offloading all its fuel, eliminating the need for high braking capacity. KC-135Rs and special-mission aircraft that land at higher weights (185,000 lb/83,915kg) have 5-rotor brakes. *Photo P27863 courtesy Boeing*

Left: Passenger seats in the KC-135R cargo compartment are less luxurious than low-cost airlines. During flight the cargo area is dark and temperatures vary from freezing to stifling. APU in the back right provides bleed air for engine starting. *Author photo*

Communications, Navigation, and Surveillance Equipment

Aside from the KC-135E and KC-135R re-engining program, the greatest single improvements to the KC-135 fleet have been to its Communications, Navigation, and Surveillance (CNS) capabilities. This is hardly surprising, as this equipment has evolved considerably over the first 60 years of the airplane's operational lifetime. KC-135s were initially delivered with the horribly flawed Lear autopilot that never fully achieved expectations or reliability. Radios had an excessive failure rate, parts were in short supply, and the lack of qualified personnel created a repair backlog in maintenance shops everywhere. Basic navigation instruments changed from World War II era NDB to TACAN and ILS to INS and GPS, acronyms that reflect the increasing sophistication of aviation electronics. The introduction of computerized flight management systems in the 1980s eventually led to improvements in safety and operational flexibility, ultimately resulting in the elimination of the navigator as a regular member of the crew.

The first major fleet-wide cockpit enhancement took place following the losses of KC-135R 59-1465 on 17th July 1967 and KC-135A 58-0026 on 17th January 1968 due to overrotation on takeoff. OCAMA began the study of a new flight director on 21st November 1968, leading to the FD-109 flight director and rotation/go-around (RGA) system. The proposal sought an off-the-shelf flight director and related instruments, with particular emphasis on those in current use by aircraft type and total number installed, total hours of use, common commercial and military components, compatibility with existing KC-135 flight instrumentation, mean time between failure (MTBF), and user reaction and satisfaction. By 3rd December 1968 the Collins proposal appeared to be the optimum choice, but, in typical bureaucratic fashion, OCAMA and AFLC staff officers were reluctant to make a formal endorsement and procurement recommendation. Eventually CINCSAC General Bruce K Holloway intervened and approved the acquisition of the FD-109 for all US '135s. French tankers did not have the FD-109 system.

The FD-109 attitude direction indicator (ADI) incorporated two yellow command bars that provided steering guidance for selected headings, pitch guidance for altitude changes, and a safe takeoff or go-around pitch attitude (which automatically compensated for engine out conditions). The airplane symbol on the ADI was an orange 'wedge', prompting pilots to put 'Howard Johnson's inside the Golden Arches', a reference to 'HoJo's' orange-roofed hotels and the McDonald's fast-food chain. Each ADI was connected to a horizontal situation indicator (HSI) to display navigational information. The autopilot could be coupled to the instrument landing system (ILS), but lacked an autoland feature.

By 1979-80 a number of new navigation and communications initiatives were under way. These included upgrade of the solid state AN/APN-59E radar, installation of the AN/ARN-118 tactical aerial navigation system (TACAN – which doubled the number of channels available from 126 to 252), replacing the unsupportable AN/ARC-65 HF radio with a new radio with 'nuclear hardening, instant frequency lock-up, reduced cooling requirements, and modular circuit construction,' and a Delco Carousel IVE Inertial Navigation System (INS) / Doppler Navigation System (DNS). The INS continuously computed navigation information over a Great Circle route using the shortest course, and could be coupled to the pilot's flight director and the autopilot. The DNS performed a similar function and was coupled to the copilot's flight director. Some specialized variants (notably the

Clockwise from top left: Pilots' station on C-135B 61-0331 shows basic navigation aids, many of which were in use during the Second World War. TF33-P-5 turbofan engines had start levers and thrust reversers, accounting for the 'extra' throttle levers not found on all other KC-135s. *Photo P28569 courtesy Boeing*

Pilots' station in KC-135R prototype 61-0293 shows Delco INS/DNS control (right of throttles). Box above fire handles is F108 fire suppression activation system; three vertical lights to the right are receiver air refueling ready, contact, and disconnect lights. *Photo 682-690 courtesy Boeing*

C-135FR pilots' station differ considerably from all other KC-135Rs, both in choice of instruments and placement. France briefly operated loaned USAF KC-135Rs with US instruments, including the FD-109 flight director. *Photo courtesy Mark van Cuilenborg*

Table 4-3. **KC-135 CNS Upgrades**

Block	Content	Block	Content
20	PACER CRAG	40	CNS/ATWM (GATM)
30	RVSM	45	Digital Instrument & Display

(See text for full description)

RC-135s) have been equipped with a stellar-inertial system, which updates the INS with an astro-tracker. A global positioning satellite (GPS) system provides additional navigational data for extremely precise positioning. Special variant airplanes (such as RC-135s, airborne command posts, some KC-135Q/Ts, and refuelable KC-135s) have a satellite communications (SATCOM) capability, both for voice and teletype. The SATCOM antenna is a white flat disc mounted atop a small pylon on the upper fuselage. Some airplanes have more than one SATCOM antenna.

The energy crisis of the late 1970s – rather than a conscious program of enhanced flight safety and crew ease of use – led to the development of the Fuel Savings Advisory System (FSAS). This was a 'bare bones' flight management system (FMS), designed to calculate critical flight data (e.g., takeoff and landing data) and

determine optimal fuel-consumption altitudes. A Simmons Precision system was selected and installed on an RC-135V for flight tests from March through June 1979. Results were impressive with savings ranging from 3.5-5%, about the same as the proposed winglets tested on NKC-135A 55-3129 (see Chapter 8). Two KC-135As were equipped with the FSAS and delivered to SAC on 15th November 1979 for 120 days of flight tests. Located on the lower center instrument panel, the FSAS also included a smaller, digital fuel panel.

The FSAS was incorporated fleet wide but suffered from significant limits. SAC refused to pay Boeing to validate the takeoff data which the FSAS calculated, rendering it unusable. Copilots continued the unnecessary and tedious process to calculate takeoff data, and boom operators were still required to use their 'slip stick' load adjusters to determine the center of gravity (cg) rather than accept the figure shown on the digital fuel panel. (In both cases, the data were accurate, just 'unapproved' by SAC) In addition, the FSAS would inexplicably enter 'Hold' mode rather than display altitude and navigation guidance, and could not be released. For many pilots, the solution was to turn the brightness switch to Full Dim and ignore the FSAS entirely.

In addition to the standard ultra-high frequency (UHF) and high frequency (HF) radios in all '135s, several of specialized KC-135s

Clockwise from top:

Block 40 pilots' station on KC-135R 62-3502 shows glass displays and navigation control panels on the glare shield, facilitating pilot operations. For older pilots the result is 'information overload,' but for a generation of pilots who grew up with iPads and smart phones it is rudimentary.
Photo by the author

A copilot's dream. Center color display automatically calculates takeoff data and shows departure route of flight. Small white Plexiglas panel above the display was used for years for takeoff data written in grease pencil, subject to change at the end of the runway with the dreaded 'winds calm, cleared for takeoff' radio call from the tower. *Photo by the author*

Block 45 instrument panel with single MFD for engine instruments. Electrical redundancies ensure that all digital instruments are usable even in the case of power failure – 'Battery Switch: Emergency' will keep the crew informed should all generators drop off line. *Author's collection*

used very-high frequency (VHF) radios. These were first prevalent among KC-135s assigned to the ANG and AFRES as they operated from civilian fields that prefer VHF. Since Operation DESERT STORM, however, most KC-135Rs and KC-135Ts have acquired a VHF radio.

Glass Cockpits

By the late 1990s, nearly all newly built aircraft were delivered with 'glass cockpits,' a digital display of navigation and performance data. Early efforts to install a glass cockpit in KC-135s had been evaluated in the C-135C SPECKLED TROUT (see Chapter 8), but this was purely a low budget research program and was not undertaken. Changes in global airspace requirements, driven by the explosive growth in international commercial air travel and advances in navigation technology, finally compelled fleet managers to develop and install a glass cockpit in the '135 fleet.

First among these changes was PACER CRAG (Compass Radar And GPS). Known as the 'Block 20' avionics upgrade, this included a Collins FMS-800 Flight Management System (FMS), FMR-200X color multi-mode weather radar, INS/GPS, and FDS-255 color flat panel flight displays. In addition, 'Block 30' upgrades were undertaken at the same time, which installed an enhanced ground proximity warning system (EGPWS), a flight data recorder (FDR) and cockpit voice recorder (CVR), an improved emergency locator transmitter (ELT), and additional flight instruments to satisfy international reduced vertical separation minima (RVSM) requirements (a digital air data computer, new digital altimeters, and digital airspeed indicators). This enabled aircraft flying internationally at altitudes between flight level FL290 and FL410 to use 1,000ft (305m) vertical separation instead of 2,000ft (610m), allowing for double the traffic to use the airways.

By 2005 Air Mobility Command approved full-scale testing of 'Block 40' avionics as part of the Global Air Traffic Management (GATM) program [renamed the Department of Defense (DoD) Communications, Navigation, and Surveillance for Air Traffic Management (CNS/ATM)]. This provided a highly accurate aircraft position, as well as the capability to transmit both that position and the airplane's next intended position to ground Air Traffic Control (ATC) via a data link, allowing '135s to operate on all global air routes and to airfields that would otherwise be inaccessible due to outdated navigation systems on the '135s. Block 40 tests included 153 hours of ground evaluation and 44.5 flight hours, including a 13-day trip in Pacific Ocean civil airspace. Results were mixed due to 'information assurance limitations.' By 2011 these issues were eventually resolved.

The 'Block 45' upgrade followed, with the first flight on 22nd July 2013. This $910 million program removes 21 analog instruments and adds an additional liquid crystal display (LCD) for engine instrumentation, a radar altimeter, an advanced autopilot, and a new flight director to replace obsolescent systems. Block 45 improves international navigation compliance and reduces the 'logistics footprint' for the 60-year old aircraft, as many parts are no longer available for existing analog instruments.

Training

For decades, learning the systems and how to fly the KC-135 has been synonymous with Castle AFB. Although this belief overlooks additional training operations at Walker AFB, the point is well taken. Multiple generations of pilots, navigators, and boom operators came to know Atwater, Merced, and the vagaries of the San Joaquin Valley's summer heat and winter fog. Castle's closure in 1995 and the transfer of KC-135 training to Altus AFB (in keeping with Air Mobility Command's single training base concept for C-141s, C-5s, and its newly acquired KC-135s) not only changed where KC-135 crews would learn their duties but how that training would be conducted.

As with many new aircraft, the initial crew cadres came from other platforms, particularly KC-97s – given their air refueling experience – and B-47s – given their jet experience. Initially the KC-135 was a highly desirable assignment, especially for B-47 copilots for whom

The view from the tower at Castle AFB in 1957, familiar to anyone who qualified on the KC-135 during the nearly 40 years it was the primary training base. Within a decade, two of these jets, 55-3138 and 55-3140, would be lost in Southeast Asia. *Photo courtesy Boeing*

upgrade to Aircraft Commander seemed to be too far in the future. Once KC-135 deliveries were complete and it was a mature weapon system, however, a tanker became arguably the second-worst assignment, better only than a B-52. This opprobrium was less a matter of flying a KC-135 *per se* than being part of SAC and what that ultimately entailed for fliers. An assignment to SAC meant endless alert, rigid and uninspiring mission flight profiles, dogmatic rules and regulations, repeated temporary duty (TDY) to Southeast Asia (over nearly a decade), and crews with two (sometimes even three) copilots and navigators due to pipeline and manning requirements driven by the theoretical numbers of the SIOP rather than reality of training and currency. Although tanker crews at a SAC base were lower in the pecking order than B-52 crews, at least they had the occasional luxury of deploying to a tanker task force in England, Spain, or Alaska, affording a six-week break to the monotony of alert and exposure to receivers other than B-52s.

During the heyday of SAC operations, initial qualification training at Castle AFB for copilots, navigators, and boom operators typically began with four to six weeks of classroom instruction with the 4017th Combat Crew Training Squadron (CCTS), 93rd Bombardment Wing, better known as the 'Schoolhouse', to learn systems and procedures. Students were then assigned to an instructor crew on the flight line made up of an instructor pilot (IP), instructor navigation (IN), and instructor boom operator (IBO) from the 93rd AREFS. Depending on the number of students in the pipeline, actual student crew makeup could vary, notably with two student copilots or the addition of a pilot upgrade (PUP) to aircraft commander (AC). The PUP process evolved considerably throughout the KC-135's operational lifetime, with some upgrades conducted at the unit level and others at Castle AFB. Training inconsistencies across the command, operational exigencies, and the absence of common standards in local PUP programs meant that SAC preferred having the PUPs train at Castle AFB. This provided the added benefit of the PUP serving as a teacher to the new copilots, as well as a model for 'crew coordination' among student navigators and boom operators as well.

Days on the flight line were long, and tended to run in threes. The first day of the cycle began with mission planning and briefings which often took the entire morning, sometimes lasting into the afternoon. A trip to the simulator often finished the day to ensure appropriate crew rest prior to the flight the next day. For pilots the simulators were hardly more than instrumented procedural trainers. They lacked visual cues and motion but were ideal for training, especially in recognizing and resolving emergencies such as loss of electrics or hydraulics, as well as basic instrument procedures.

Training flights were generally split into two waves – an early morning launch that would later turn into the evening's sorties. Given that each flight lasted some eight hours and required crews report to the bus three hours before the scheduled takeoff time, this typically translated to a 4:00 AM show time. Air Force regulations required that fliers be accorded eight hours of uninterrupted sleep prior to a mission, resulting in a 7:00 PM bed time. Crew members with families (especially children) found it difficult to get to sleep, often leaving them with only three to four hours of rest prior to a long and stressful day of flying. Night sorties were equally difficult, especially as SAC did little to recognize and accommodate sleep cycle disruption, either in training or operations. It is a real testimony to the instructor crews who worked under such harsh conditions that they suffered so few mishaps due to fatigue. Still, duty as an instructor was a highly desirable assignment – no alert, no TDY, improved family time (especially on weekends), and choice follow-on assignments – making for a steady stream of volunteer instructors. Indeed, a number of foreign instructors were also seconded for duty, including Royal Air Force Squadron Leader Bob Tuxford, who would

later fly Handley Page Victor K.2 XL189 on the final refueling of Avro Vulcan XM607 during the first Operation BLACK BUCK mission in the 1982 Falklands/Malvinas War [the IP for the author's initial qualification was a Royal Australian Air Force 707 pilot].

Training flights all followed a standard syllabus that mirrored most flights across the command. Air refueling took place right after takeoff and typically lasted some 45 minutes to an hour or more, and usually involved a B-52 flown by a student crew from Castle AFB. At least one mission was dedicated to refueling fighters, and eventually other airplanes such as the Lockheed C-5 with its unique aerodynamic effects during closure and breakaway. A two-hour navigation leg followed the air refueling, and was often done in 'grid' mode, the method used in polar navigation where SIOP missions would be flown. In addition to air refueling duties, boom operators learned to 'shoot the stars' for celestial navigation. Additional flight time was allocated for the navigator and boom operator to practice emergency landing gear and flap extension procedures. A training mission ended with at least two hours of 'transition', a euphemism for pilot and copilot touch-and-go landings. Summer heat at Castle AFB and other local airfields such as Beale AFB and Mather AFB, unstable approaches by fledgling copilots, and landings that registered on the Richter scale made for an unpleasant experience for student and instructor navigators and boom operators alike. After landing the crew would meet for the maintenance debrief, a short mission recap, and then head home.

The third day began with a full debrief of the preceding day's flight. Each procedure was reviewed and critiqued with an emphasis on safety and crew coordination, and students given a grade for the mission ranging from Excellent to Satisfactory to Unsatisfactory. Additional simulator time or remedial academics were undertaken to correct any deficiencies. Despite the grind, student crews frequently bonded together. Trips to the gym, weekend outings to local lakes and nearby Yosemite National Park, or longer drives to enjoy the sights and nightlife of San Francisco or Sacramento punctuated the long training hours.

After nine training missions (sometimes more when crews were not yet fully proficient), the student crew would repeat their three-day routine with an evaluator crew for their initial qualification check ride. Although the profile would remain the same as training flights, the check ride invariably never went as planned. The jet might break prior to engine start, shifting the whole schedule accordingly. The receiver might 'crump' forcing a reversal of the flight plan to do the navigation leg first then the air refueling. Weather was always a factor, especially for transition. Assuming the student crew demonstrated not only procedural proficiency but the situational awareness to overcome these adversities, they learned during the next day's debrief that they had passed their check ride. During several periods throughout training at Castle AFB, SAC 'rewarded' new graduates with a solo ride, although these were frequently curtailed or halted due to mission requirements, fuel limitations, or other austerity measures.

Current KC-135R initial qualification training with the 54th AREFS, 97th AMW, at Altus AFB, OK, is far more…enlightened. Academic content remains largely the same, although computerized instruction allows students to move through training at their own pace, a definite plus for a generation that grew up with home computers and laptops. Airplane manuals (including the Dash One) and flight publications, which once weighed some 30 lb (14kg) and filled a huge satchel, are now contained on a 1 lb (469g) iPad. The majority of training is undertaken through full-motion, full-visual level D simulators in four-hour sessions. Actual flight hours are significantly curtailed. Compared to the 70-80 hours across nine flights at Castle AFB, pilots accrue typically 13 hours in just three flights in an airplane prior to their check ride, while boom operators

usually log 21.5 hours in five flights before a check. Additional specialized mission training and certification takes place at their follow-on assignment.

Despite the truncation of active training and flying time, the results are familiar to any KC-135 crewmember across the generations. The Interior Inspection checklist remains the longest in the Air Force, and the mantra recited by the crew chief during rudder, elevator, aileron, and spoiler checks is unchanged after nearly a half century. The use of a flight management system (FMS), beginning with PACER CRAG and additional improvements with the Block 40 FMS, have eliminated the need for time-consuming takeoff data calculations and navigation/fuel log computations, eliminating errors as well as facilitating in-flight procedures.

New pilots are dual-seat qualified, attenuating the earlier two- to three-year wait for upgrade to aircraft commander, although pilots typically accrue some 300 additional hours before being mission certified as ACs. Contrary to widespread belief, the removal of navigators from a standard KC-135R crew did not eliminate the position entirely. A modest number of navigators complete initial training at Altus AFB. As with pilots and boom operators, the navigators then complete their mission certification at their assigned bases. Navigators are typically used on unique missions such as Special Operations Aerial Refueling (SOAR) or classified combat

missions. Boom operators leave Altus AFB qualified in day and night heavy aircraft refueling, as well as daytime fighter refueling. Once they reach their final assignment they are further certified in refueling using the boom-drogue adapter (BDA), the multipoint refueling system (MPRS), and nighttime fighter refueling.

Clockwise from top left: Early KC-135 simulators lacked motion and visual displays and were little more than procedural trainers capable of simulating basic instrument flight and most emergency situations. *Author's collection*

The C-135B simulators for MATS were the first to incorporate motion, but tended to be exaggerated and occasionally made the occupants sick. SAC crews flying the RC-135E RIVET AMBER qualified with MATS as SAC lacked thrust-reverser equipped C-135Bs. *Photo P35927 courtesy Boeing*

Once many pilots got to their operational units they remained current in emergency and instrument procedures thanks to a KC-135 simulator in a railcar that shuttled between bases. The simulator was in the large silver section which expanded once on site. *Author's collection*

54th AREFS Boss Bird 62-3549 on the ramp at Altus AFB. Changes in crew manning coupled with technological improvements in the airplane have made initial and upgrade training in the KC-135R far less brutal than when SAC ran the program. *Photo by the author*

CHAPTER FIVE

'Without Us, the War Stops'*

'Tanker guys have not received the great credit they deserve; they are always there when you need them.' – *General Curtis E LeMay*

* – *LtCol Brent Toth, Instructor Pilot, 54th AREFS, 2015*

The summer of '57 was a time of innocence. We still liked Ike. Parents were reading the new book *Cat in the Hat* to their toddlers, glad to be rid of 'dreary' primers like *Dick and Jane*. The Wham-O Company had just released the Frisbee, which quickly occupied youngsters on summer vacation. Thanks to Elvis Presley, Americans were *All Shook Up*. Long before the term 'RomCom' became shorthand for romantic comedy, Cary Grant and Deborah Kerr charmed moviegoers in *An Affair to Remember*. Action enthusiasts watched Glenn Ford and Van Heflin battle each other and bad guys in *3:10 to Yuma*. Television had yet to eclipse reading as America's pastime, and *Peyton Place* by Grace Metalious topped the bestseller lists, titillating readers with its lurid appeal.

It was hot in California's San Joaquin Valley. Temperatures topped 100°F (38°C) every day. In fact, on 28th June 1957, it was 101°F at Castle AFB, just outside Atwater, where it hadn't rained all month. Acres and acres of concrete baked everything and everyone who stood on it. Military and civilian officials, fliers, 'wrench turners', a few families, and a handful of newsmen stood sweltering in the heat, which did little to disrupt the festive atmosphere. By 3:30PM, however, excitement began to build. The small crowd surged forward to the restraining line, eager for a better view.

Few people noticed as it turned onto final approach to Runway 31 following its flight from Larson AFB, WA, where it was a balmy

72°F (22°C). Fewer still saw it land, their view blocked by the tails of B-52s cluttering the ramp. The crowd could not fail to hear it, however, as it taxied to the empty space in front of base operations, its four J57s delivering an ear-splitting scream painful to dogs and humans. It turned, came to a stop facing north, and, once the engines had shut down, there was an eerie moment of silence. It was 3:45PM, and the first KC-135A, 55-3127, was now in the SAC inventory. An hour later 55-3128 landed, and, at 5:50PM, 55-3129 touched down. All three were assigned to the 93rd AREFS, 93rd BW at Castle AFB, the new tanker's training and replacement squadron. More would follow, and for decades Castle AFB would be synonymous with KC-135 training.

By year's end the first Stratotankers had been delivered to SAC operational units. KC-135A 55-3140, nicknamed *Aroostook Queen*, arrived on 16th October 1957 at the 42nd AREFS, 42nd BW at Loring AFB, ME, while KC-135A 56-3592 landed on 6th December 1957 at Westover AFB, MA, assigned to the 99th AREFS, 4050th AREFW. These units had also received the first B-52s Stratofortresses, emphasizing the closely integrated role of the new jet tanker with SAC's premier bomber. Sadly, both of these KC-135s were lost in crashes in 1967 and 1989, respectively (see Appendix II).

Fliers greeted the arrival of the jet-powered KC-135 with enthusiasm. It was an exciting improvement over the KC-97 and raised the status of the tanker crew to near equals of SAC's 'glamor

The arrival of 55-3127 on 28th June 1957 at Castle AFB inaugurated 60 years of operational service of the KC-135. The airplane's simplicity has kept it capable all these years. *Photo courtesy Boeing*

boy' jet bomber crew. Crewmembers accustomed to the sheer physical effort needed to fly the KC-97 were thrilled with the KC-135. No longer did the boom operator have to turn the heavy four-bladed propellers through two complete revolutions prior to flight. The 'boomer', who also served as the loadmaster, found the KC-135 significantly easier to load with cargo and passengers than the KC-97 with its two decks and ladders and its four cargo bay fuel tanks. The KC-135 required less ground support and servicing when away from its home base. The boom operator could act as the crew chief and had only to supervise ground refueling via the airplane's single point refueling system, check the oil in the four engines, and monitor the hydraulic fluid level in each wing, tasks that normally took many hours with the KC-97. This ease of servicing was particularly useful when KC-135s deployed to civilian or remote airfields, away from the normal support equipment and personnel that the KC-97 required.

The KC-135 was not without peculiarities, however, most of which were common to large swept-wing jet aircraft like the B-47 and the B-52. As Master Sergeant Karl Johnson, one of the original KC-135A boom operators recalled, 'though the KC-135 was a beauty, it had its teething problems. Hydraulics overheated (no coolers), the engine fuel control units froze up (no heaters), it wouldn't take off on three engines, no matter how far down the runway you were (killed many refueling crews those first years), air engine starter failure blew a lot of ORIs (Operational Readiness Inspections), and [the KC-135] didn't often forgive a pilot boo-boo. Still, when the KC-135 was churning just right, your blood was up and you both were a thing of beauty – we were a proud and happy gang of fly boys in those days. I suspect the crews flying today feel pretty much the same as we did – darn proud to be on such a fine team and a grand ride to boot.'

Crewmembers were not the only ones impressed with the new jet tanker. On 12th September 1957, the entire Joint Chiefs of Staff (JCS) was treated to a flight in a KC-135A. Following a briefing by General LeMay at SAC headquarters at Offutt AFB, the JCS flew 55-3127 to Peterson Field, CO. The primary purpose of this flight was to familiarize the Chiefs with the Air Force's newest weapon. On board the one hour, 55 minute flight commanded by Major Salvador Felices, 93rd AREFS operations officer, were Air Force General Nathan F Twining, chairman of the JCS, General Thomas D White, Air Force Chief of Staff, Admiral Arleigh A Burke, Chief of Naval Operations, General Maxwell D Taylor, Army Chief of Staff, and General Randolph McC Pate, Marine Corps Commandant. The chiefs observed an aerial refueling of a B-47 from Lincoln AFB, NE. They each briefly flew the KC-135 and were 'very impressed' by its performance and its 'triple-purpose capabilities – refueling, troop carrying and cargo hauling.'

Above: The first SAC KC-135 crew moments after arriving at Castle AFB. Colonel Winton R Close (far left) was the Aircraft Commander. *Photo courtesy Bobby McCasland (believed to be third from right)*

The closing months of 1957 marked the beginning of the end for the KC-135's predecessors. On 1st November 1957 the last squadron equipped with KB-29s was deactivated and its airplanes relegated to the Military Aircraft Storage and Disposition Center (MASDC) at Davis-Monthan AFB, AZ. That same month a KC-135A set the first of a series of world records. On 11-12th November 1957 Air Force Vice Chief of Staff General LeMay flew KC-135A 55-3126 to and from Buenos Aires, Argentina, as part of Operation LONG LEGS, earning the Harmon Trophy. The following year saw even more

Above: Wing Commander Colonel Donald E Hillman (c) welcomes the first KC-135 to Loring AFB. Hillman flew the first B-47 reconnaissance overflight of the USSR. Lieutenant Colonel George M Broutsas, (back to camera) the tanker squadron commander, flew RB-47s. *Photo courtesy Boeing*

Left: The KC-97 was a beast compared to the KC-135, which was designed with ground crews in mind. *Photo by Tom Hildreth*

records fall to the KC-135, as well as the first loss of one of the new jet tankers, a tragic event that took place during one record-setting flight. Other SAC airplanes such as the B-52 and the B-58 Hustler set records requiring air refueling, demonstrating the value of the KC-135's superior speed and range over the piston-powered KB-50 and KC-97 (see Appendix V). That this translated into increased striking power for SAC's bomber force was certainly not lost on the Soviet Union. At a time when the US and the USSR were claiming military superiority over each other, these record-setting flights forcefully demonstrated to the Soviets and the world that SAC bombers, refueled en route by jet tankers, could strike their targets anywhere in the world from bases in the United States. LONG LEGS in particular underscored the continuing value of the manned bomber, soon to be pronounced dead by American and Soviet champions of ballistic missiles. A *New York Times* editorial hailed LeMay's flight, saying it '... demonstrated that manned aircraft are still far from being ready for the antiquated role assigned to them in some quarters as the result of the advent of the guided missile. This flight gives an effective answer to those who would sing a swan song for the manned intercontinental air force, and for this reassuring demonstration General LeMay deserves the plaudits of the nation and of the free world.' Soviet Premier Nikita Khrushchev had challenged the US to an accuracy 'duel' designed to 'prove the superiority of [Soviet] missiles and rockets'. As the result of its performance in Operation LONG LEGS, Defense Secretary Neil H McElroy chose the KC-135 to represent the United States. McElroy said that with LeMay at the controls of the KC-135, '... there would be no question about who would win. ...' Not surprisingly, Khrushchev's duel never took place.

A Change in Strategy
The jet-powered KC-135 changed the way military planners viewed strategic bombing operations. Beginning in 1954 SAC was committed to the FULLHOUSE concept based on the modernization of the medium bomber force from piston-powered B-29s and B-50s to jet-powered B-47s and the projected B-52. SAC's new jet bombers would be able to strike Soviet targets directly from bases within the continental United States, bypassing vulnerable and politically delicate overseas forward bases. To do so meant using bases such as Goose AB, Labrador, Thule AB, Greenland, and Ernest Harmon AB in Newfoundland as pre- and post-strike staging bases, as well as hosting KC-97s ready to refuel B-47s and B-52s.

With the arrival of the KC-135, however, SAC planners argued that it was no longer necessary for tankers to be deployed to forward bases in order to rendezvous with a jet bomber *en route* to its targets. Instead, KC-135s could be co-located at B-52 bases, launch with them, fly at the same speed and altitude with them to the refueling point, offload the required fuel, and then land at these forward recovery bases. Once there, the KC-135s would refuel and await the next bomber stream. Because the KC-135 had only a short distance to fly for this second refueling, it could offload more fuel, land, and repeat the process (known as YO YO refueling). The numbers were compelling. A co-located KC-135 could offload only 96,000 lb (43,545kg) of fuel to its mated B-52. A YO YO KC-135 operating from Churchill AP, Canada, however, could offload 136,000 lb (61,689kg) of fuel to a passing bomber. This additional gas greatly expanded the target list. According to a 1962 declassified SAC study, a B-52 from Ellsworth AFB, SD, could reach its target at 'Archangel and return [to its recovery base] without [additional] refueling.' Using YO YO KC-135 refueling, however, it could 'reach a target like Gorki (east of Moscow on the Volga River) approximately 600nm (1,111km) deeper inside the Soviet Union.' Similarly, a B-47 from Whiteman AFB, MO, 'could reach a target like Murmansk and post-strike at Lakenheath, United Kingdom,' but with YO YO refueling 'could attack

a target in the Ivanovo area (northeast of Moscow), over 900nm (1,667km) deeper.' Through 1974 the YO YO tasking fell to KC-135s from SAC bases in the 'Northeast Complex', including Loring AFB, Pease AFB, Plattsburgh AFB, Griffiss AFB, and Westover AFB deployed to Goose AB. To test this new approach, the KC-135 fleet flexed its operational muscle from 13-15th October 1959 in Operation FAST MOVE. This was the first major exercise involving the new tanker, and 70 KC-135s and 86 KC-97s deployed to forward bases in the northeast US and Canada to refuel 29 B-52s and 164 B-47s, simulating the dispersal of the alert force and its improved survivability, as well as verifying the fuel offload numbers projected by YO YO refueling.

By July 1958, SAC planned to have 29 KC-135 squadrons in service by the end of FY63. General Power considered this inadequate, however, arguing that 'more tankers than programmed were needed to assure [B-52] range extension for target coverage, tactics, and intercontinental capability.' Problems with the KC-97 accentuated this shortfall, as the KC-97 offload dropped from 55,000 lb (24,948kg) to only 40,000 lb (18,144kg) due to propeller difficulties. Even after resolving the propeller issue, it took 'three KC-97 squadrons to do the work of one KC-135 squadron.' Headquarters USAF was not only disinclined to purchase new tankers, it proposed stretching out the acquisition of budgeted KC-135s from eight to six per month. Power was incensed, telling his superiors that if SAC bombers needed to use low-level tactics to evade Soviet defenses (not to mention any airborne alert initiative) they would need more fuel, requiring more KC-135s, not fewer. He urged that production should be increased to 15 per month, saying 'on a dollar-for-dollar basis, the KC-135 provides the maximum payoff in terms of improved capability for effective bombs-on-target.' Despite Power's opposition, production of KC-135s slowed from eight to seven airplanes per month in March 1960, dropping to six per month in December 1960, and remaining there through the 'buy out' point in December 1964. No new purchases were approved.

By November 1959 the KC-135 was already beginning to show its first signs of wear-and-tear. A spate of cracks in the main landing gear trunnion appeared on a KC-135A assigned to the 41st AREFS at Griffiss AFB, NY. Boeing and USAF engineers were initially unable to determine the cause of the cracks, and directed that heavy weight ground operations be curtailed. Alert tankers had to be swapped out after seven days, and were prohibited from performing 'free flow' takeoffs. By April 1960 some 15 aircraft had been affected, including one gear collapse. Subsequent investigation revealed that the metal used in forging the trunnion box and aft support fitting had become brittle, weakening the structure. In mid-May 1960 AMC began Project ROLL ON at OCAMA to retrofit the current fleet of 248 aircraft with new forgings. The remaining 107 aircraft would be modified during IRAN either at OCAMA or the Boeing facility at Moses Lake, WA, by 30th June 1961. Other wheel related problems remained. By September 1961 the KC-135 had experienced excessive main landing gear wheel failures, and inspections revealed a high number of unsatisfactory wheels in service. SAC completed a one-and-a-half year fleetwide study on 6th May 1963, and directed that the original magnesium wheels be replaced with stronger aluminum ones.

'For Alert Force, for Alert Force...'
In an age of 'think tanks' and 'blue ribbon panels' dedicated to strategic nuclear issues, Albert Wohlstetter of the RAND Corporation upset SAC's apple cart in 1958 by publishing his seminal report 'The Delicate Balance of Terror' on the susceptibility of SAC bases and bombers – and hence America's deterrent force – to Soviet surprise attack. Vulnerability quickly became a critical issue in SAC planning.

The B-47's inadequate range made REFLEX alert missions in England mandatory. Still, SAC wanted non-stop range from the United States, and KC-135s were part of that solution. *Steve Hill/EMCS*

A 1959 SAC study revealed that out of 174 KC-135s, only 18 could survive a 1961 surprise attack of Soviet ICBMs and SLBMs, too few to refuel even a meaningful number of the 139 surviving 'heavy bombers'. The heart of this problem was the amount of time it took for SAC's bomber force to become airborne. This was the hardly the practical issue of running to an airplane, starting engines, and then taking off. Rather, it was linked to the nationally mandated procedures for launching SAC's nuclear forces.

During SAC's early years all US atomic weapons were under the exclusive control of the Atomic Energy Commission (AEC) and stored at central facilities in New Mexico and Texas. Should the president direct the launch of SAC forces, for example, it was necessary for SAC Douglas C-124s to fly at 200KIAS (370kph) the 1,676nm (3,104km) from Limestone AFB (later Loring AFB) in Maine to the storage facility at Amarillo, TX, a flight of more than nine hours. After collecting the weapons the C-124s returned to Limestone AFB, arriving after a total transit time of nearly 24 hours. By this time the bombers and crews were ready, but the bombs still had to be loaded into the bombers one at a time given the complexities of the weapons and the special facilities required. The bombs then had to be armed, starting a clock on how long they were usable (see Chapter 1). Ultimately, from the time of the presidential decision to retaliate with nuclear weapons until the first bombers were ready to leave SAC readiness times ranged from 72-96 hours, hardly a quick response. Under LeMay, SAC became the custodian for atomic weapons, allowing them to be stored at SAC bases to eliminate the wasteful transit time. Although the bombs were then maintained in guarded bunkers on base, they still required the same time-intensive loading and arming process, and SAC's reaction time was still no better than 24-48 hours from notification to launch.

On 3rd October 1955 LeMay requested authority to place a portion of SAC's combat force on ground alert. In doing so, LeMay sought permission to place atomic bombs in its B-47s instead of the bunkers. Flight crews would arm the 'open pit' bombs once airborne, and the arming mechanism would be stored in the alert airplane (later weapons were 'sealed pit' and did not required this 'bird cage' device). This was a radical idea. Not only would it allow SAC to launch an attack in less than an hour, it gave the military uncontested control over nuclear weapons and the means to deploy them. LeMay's alert force proposal challenged the fundamental American belief in civilian control of nuclear weapons. Air Force Chief of Staff General Nathan F Twining endorsed the proposal 'in principle' in December 1955, but sought further guidance from civilian defense officials. The Air Staff concurred with LeMay's proposal in March 1956, but debate within the DoD, AEC, and other agencies meant that no further action was taken until December 1957, more than two years after LeMay's initial request. LeMay was not idle, however, and beginning in November 1956 conducted a four-month trial of ground alert at Hunter AFB, GA. Key lessons included the need to have the airplanes parked at the end of the primary runway to ensure their ability to take off in less than 15 minutes, and that an alert force of no more than 25% of a wing's total aircraft could sustain alert operations without serious disruption to overall effectiveness. Further tests at Little Rock AFB, AR, and Mountain Home AFB, ID, validated these initial findings.

One critical weakness to SAC's proposed ground alert was the range of the B-47, which required at least one air refueling to reach its targets in the USSR. Moreover, the distance involved required considerable flying time, which SAC commanders argued was wasteful – strikes needed to happen quickly to be effective, not after 12-14 hours of flying. With this in mind, SAC B-47s began REFLEX ground alert in England on 1st July 1957. The program expanded to include deployments to Eielson AFB in Alaska, and Andersen AFB on Guam (the latter were known as AIRMAIL ground alert). Another crucial issue was the ability to get all of the airplanes off the ground within a 15-minute launch window, first introduced in SAC EWO 50-61, effective 15th July 1960 (discussed in full in Chapter 9). This time was based on 30-minute warning from the Ballistic Missile Early Warning System (BMEWS) radars, of which 15 minutes were allocated for presidential decision making to retaliate, leaving only 15 minutes for SAC's bombers to become airborne prior to impact of the first incoming warhead. Existing plans called for the bombers and tankers to 'become airborne as soon as possible after receipt of the execution message consistent with EWO directives', but this led to considerable congestion as B-47s might end up queued behind slower KC-97s. The solution was Project HURRY HURRY, a study of the minimum time and physical separation required between large aircraft. In December 1959 KC-135s from the 42nd and 72nd BWs took part in an interesting series of tests. According to the HURRY HURRY final report, there were two options – sharing a 300ft (91m) wide runway in formation takeoffs allowed six airplanes per minute to become airborne, day or night; or they could launch in 15-second intervals at the rate of four per minute. Formation takeoffs were far too risky and restricted the departure sequence to two B-52s or KC-135s at a time (rather than 'free flow'), and SAC wisely chose the 15-second solution. By January 1960, all SAC crews had been trained and qualified in Minimum Interval Take Offs (MITOs), and demonstrated the ability to have all alert aircraft airborne within 15 minutes of notification, with the first airborne within eight minutes. Under DEFCON 1, however, with crews in their aircraft at the end of the runway, the first aircraft could be airborne within three minutes (a time later crucial to surviving an SLBM attack). Within a year, this proved essential as SAC moved to a 50% alert posture, increasing the number of aircraft on alert. As of 30th June 1960, SAC had nearly 700 aircraft on ground alert, including 113 B-52s, 346 B-47s, 85 KC-135s, and 152 KC-97s. Notably, KC-135 alert aircraft rose from the previous year from 37 to 85, reflecting both an increase in deliveries of airplanes from Boeing and full operational readiness of squadrons newly equipped with KC-135s.

Additional measures to ensure survival of the ground alert force included a novel dispersion effort. Beginning in September 1961, SAC evaluated unprepared areas for 'recovery and reconstitution' of combat forces. This program, known as DRY STONE, identified 201 dry lake beds suitable for use as natural alternative landing sites (NALS). SAC officials quickly realized that these dry lakes could be used not only for landing after execution of the SIOP, but for dispersal of the peacetime alert force to locations considered unimaginable to Soviet target planners. The initial operational feasibility test, nicknamed DUSTY BEARD I, took place on 6-7th March 1962, when a B-47 and a KC-135 landed at Bicycle Lake, near Edwards AFB. The airplanes and crews spent the night while on simulated alert, and were in constant contact with the SAC command post at Offutt AFB or an airborne command post.

A follow-on evaluation, DUSTY BEARD II, validated dry lake bed dispersal procedures, as well as determined their suitability for the forthcoming RS-70 (B-70). Between 10-26th April 1962, bomber and tanker strike teams rotated every two days to one of four dry lakes (Hidden Hills, Silver Lake, and Three Sisters West in California, and Mudd Lake in Nevada). For the first week teams included B-47s and KC-135s, and B-52s and KC-135s for the second week. A total of 26 KC-135s took part. Takeoffs and landings were all conducted under day VFR conditions, with only minor difficulties. Within an hour of landing, all airplanes were on simulated alert. Over the course of two weeks, crews responded to 26 Bravo alerts (reporting to the airplane, starting engines, and declaring ready). The maximum reaction time was just eight minutes. Overall DUSTY BEARD II demonstrated that EWO operations from dry lakes were feasible, but would 'probably be utilized as a "last resort" recovery area.' Beginning 1st July 1963, DRY STONE locations were included in the SIOP. Returning B-47s and B-52s would be directed to specific lake beds, where 'sufficient KC-135 tankers would have a primary or secondary EWO assignment to support these bombers.'

Other ground alert measures during the mid-1960s included dispersal of the alert force, where bombers and tankers relocated to other USAF bases to increase their likelihood of survival under surprise attack conditions. This was driven by the increased number of SAC B-52s and KC-135s in SEA, decreasing the number available for alert and reducing the number of potential target bases for Soviet ICBMs. With fewer airplanes available to execute the SIOP, SAC needed some means to improve their survivability in the event of a surprise attack. The success of the dispersal program used during the 1962 Cuban Missile Crisis provided the answer, and B-52s and KC-135s were deployed to military and civilian airfields around the United States. Not only did this increase the number of targets necessary for the Soviet Union to attack to ensure the destruction of SAC's nuclear deterrent force, it allowed more airplanes to become airborne in the event of a surprise attack. As there were fewer airplanes at each site, they could all become airborne in the short amount of time available, unlike the longer time needed to launch a large number of airplanes, something which could not be guaranteed under surprise attack conditions. The dispersal program evolved

further into satellite basing which was designed to protect SAC alert aircraft from the increasing threat of SLBMs. For example, B-52s and KC-135s from the 72nd BW, Ramey AFB, PR, were placed on alert at Homestead AFB, Florida, on 20th February 1969 (this test only demonstrated the logistical feasibility of satellite basing, and was not intended to enhance their survivability by relocating from their home base on an island to a base just a few miles from the ocean). With the test successfully completed on 20th May, the satellite basing program went into effect on 1st July 1969. Although KC-135As had used explosive cartridges to start a single engine while on alert, satellite basing, decreased warning time, and other operational considerations led to the 1974 introduction of the QUICK START program. For the KC-135, cartridges were placed in all four engines, and tests on 16th May 1974 resulted in a 100% success rate. Average 'engine start time (timed from start initiation to idle power on all four engines) was 27.1 seconds, compared to' 90 seconds in existing alert starts. By the end of 1974 Boeing had modified all J57-equipped KC-135As for QUICK START, although the procedure was not implemented across all SAC bases.

Actual details varied over time, but the ground alert program remained fairly consistent. Starting in October 1961, SAC implemented a 74-hour work week for all crews taking part in the 50% ground alert. Duty time included 60 consecutive hours on alert followed by six hours of flying, ending with eight hours of duty that could not be undertaken while on alert. Moreover, units sustained this alert manning for only four months, at which time they stood down to 'recover', and the cycle then repeated itself. Ground alert remained in place until it was finally deactivated on 27th September 1991.

As more and more bombers and their tankers were placed on alert (with some crewmembers on alert for up to three weeks out of every four), the need to maintain proficiency of their crews increased dramatically. Every three KC-135 bases shared a single flight simulator, but crews on alert at two of the three bases could not train in the simulator with any degree of regularity. According to one early KC-135 flier, 'alert was the dog days to all crew members. ... [it] started out as three-day tours but soon blossomed to seven days with a mission flown immediately after. We got 3½ days off, but most times you were faced with that seven day tour two or three times a month. Flying became almost a new experience each time. They brought the train simulator in often to keep the pilots proficient.' Rather than buy additional fixed-base simulators, Power recommended the purchase of mobile simulators on railcars. He wrote to Air Force Vice Chief of Staff General LeMay on 29th June 1961, urging LeMay's support: 'I consider this action essential to support the increased alert posture, as well as for flying safety, and solicit your support in obtaining expeditious approval of this project'. Power got LeMay's support. The Air Force accepted the first of nine mobile KC-135 flight simulators on 1st December 1961. Each simulator, mounted in a Pullman railroad car, served four different bases. For example, one simulator shuttled between Barksdale AFB, LA, Dyess AFB, TX, Columbus AFB, MS, and Carswell AFB, TX. Once deployed to a base, all pilots, even those on alert, were able to use it to practice routine instrument flying and emergency procedures (see Chapter 4).

One significant effect of ground alert was the co-location of mated bombers and tankers. KC-97 crews seldom sat alert with the bomber crews they were scheduled to refuel, and would deploy to Goose AB, for example, to await their mated bombers. Now KC-135s sat alert at the same base (usually in the same building) with their mated bombers. They participated in ground training and mission study together, flew training sorties together, and while on alert ate, slept and waited together. The KC-135 can be argued to have been the catalyst that forged the team upon which SAC (and ultimately the United States) would base its aerial nuclear deterrent capability.

As US forces were increasingly assigned to operations in Southeast Asia, there were substantial changes to the alert force. On 31st December 1965, all B-47 REFLEX and AIRMAIL deployments were terminated, all B-47s and KC-97 ground alert came to an end, and, with the exception of 30 B-52s on Guam, all SAC alert aircraft were based in the United States. At the end of 1966 Secretary McNamara directed that bomber and tanker alert be reduced from 50 to 40% by July 1967. One other event in 1966 highlighted a controversial portion of SAC's alert force, the mid-air collision of a KC-135 and a B-52 laden with nuclear weapons flying a CHROME DOME airborne alert indoctrination mission.

CHROME DOME

SAC's ground alert force did much to alleviate concerns about vulnerability to an surprise Soviet ICBM strike, but the implications of an attack by Soviet SLBMs from submarines off the American coast were far more troublesome. A Soviet SLBM could destroy bases such Loring AFB in less than the vaunted 15 minutes needed to get SAC's bombers airborne, emasculating the alert force and its deterrent effect. To counteract this threat, SAC proposed an alert force of B-52s continuously airborne at their 'fail safe' orbits. Should the USSR attack the United States with SLBMs, these few surviving B-52s would retaliate quickly against the highest priority targets. SAC leaders believed that this airborne force would dissuade Kremlin leaders from initiating any attacks.

Initial tests of an airborne alert program began in January 1959 with B-36s from Ramey AFB in Operation CURTAIN RAISER. They flew 278 sorties from 1st January to 30th June. General Power planned to have a fully operational airborne alert capability on 1st July 1961, although the number of B-52s airborne at any time had yet to be determined. LeMay, now Air Force Vice Chief of Staff, surprisingly opposed a large continuous airborne alert force, arguing that 'it should be an emergency posture assumed only at times of international crisis,' and bluntly told Power to 'stop beating the drum so loudly for airborne alert.' Power, long considered a LeMay 'yes man,' refused to back down, arguing that 'airborne alert represented the only efficient safeguard against surprise attack,' especially during peacetime when there was no crisis. Moreover, Power advocated that one fourth of the B-52 fleet should be airborne as SAC's initial goal for 1960, and, as he told reporters, the B-52s would be 'bombed up and they don't carry bows and arrows'. Power seemed oblivious to the cost and political implications (both domestic and foreign) of having 150 nuclear-laden B-52s circling the globe without absolute command and control links (see Chapter 9).

While the Air Staff debated, Power implemented Operation HEAD START I. Beginning in 1959, B-52s and KC-135s from the 42nd BW at Loring AFB launched a B-52 every six hours. During the three-month test, KC-135s flew 200 sorties per month. The 92nd BW at Fairchild AFB and the 28th BW at Ellsworth AFB took part in Operation HEAD START II beginning in March 1959. KC-135s completed 2,133 refueling missions over the following three months. Operation HEAD START II proved to SAC officials that airborne alert was a viable operation, and they began training other SAC wings in earnest. Four indoctrination programs, known as STEEL TRAP I and II and HIGH TRIP I and II, trained nine wings (including eight KC-135 squadrons). Despite the apparent success of these programs, the Air Force refused to pay for more of them. By 1961 airborne alert would add $800 million per year to SAC's budget, nearly 4% of the total US defense budget, a figure which President Dwight D Eisenhower would surely reject. Nonetheless, indoctrination flights continued through November 1961 along 'ladder type' routes 'stretching from the United States north into the Canadian Arctic.' These routes were 'largely determined' by the availability and 'proximity of supporting KC-135 tankers.'

On 6th November 1961, the Air Force finally approved SAC's airborne alert program, but with significant restrictions. Known as CHROME DOME, these were *only* indoctrination flights, would be limited to only one bomber per day from each wing on alert, and would avoid overflying Canada or any other nation while carrying nuclear weapons. Tanker support for CHROME DOME missions came from KC-135s at Griffiss AFB, NY, Loring AFB, and Westover AFB in the northeastern United States, Eielson AFB in Alaska, and Torrejon AB in Spain. CHROME DOME represented a significant potential, both retaliatory and first strike. Once executed, the airborne B-52s were only short distances from Soviet territory and, until the advent of operational ICBMs, were the fastest means to strike targets in the USSR. Alert missions called for 12 B-52s flying 24–26-hour missions, and another B-52 had already launched to replace the alert B-52 before it could return to land.

Between 1962 and 1968 the airborne alert program increasingly became the subject of considerable controversy. Secretary of Defense McNamara saw the program as wasteful spending, and instead championed 'more cost effective ICBMs' in lieu of manned bombers. CHROME DOME also acquired an ignominious reputation on 17th January 1966 when B-52G 58-0256 on airborne alert collided with KC-135A 61-0273 while refueling over Palomares, Spain (see Appendix II). Two of the four nuclear bombs onboard the B-52 released radioactive material, and one bomb required a significant multi-national effort to recover. The Palomares incident earned the program international condemnation and added vigor to McNamara's crusade to eliminate it entirely and reduce the bomber force. On 1st July 1966 CHROME DOME was renamed GIANT WHEEL to mitigate this adverse publicity, but the name change hardly helped. Two years and four days later B-52G 58-0188 flying a GIANT WHEEL mission crashed near Thule AB, Greenland, again releasing radioactive residue from its nuclear weapons. McNamara canceled SAC's full-time airborne alert indoctrination program a week later on 22nd January. These two accidents surely contributed to the termination of the airborne alert

Airborne alert missions included all operational variants of B-52s carrying both internal weapons and, eventually GAM-77 HOUND DOG missiles.
Author's collection

Beginning in 1969 B-52Gs from the 744th BS at Beale AFB flew GIANT LANCE missions as part of SAC's 'visual deterrence' effort. *Photo by the author*

program in 1968, but were not solely responsible for its demise. B-52s and KC-135s were in increasing demand for combat operations in Southeast Asia. In addition, rising operating costs (for both bombers and tankers), the demands these missions placed on the aircrews that flew and units that supported them, and the increasing maturity of SAC's ICBM force all combined to end routine airborne nuclear alert. Further, improvements to US early warning systems, especially platforms such as the Defense Support Program (DSP) satellite, offered increased warning time of an impending attack and hence reduced the need for airborne alert as a means of strike force survivability.

The end of the continuous airborne alert force did not invalidate its need or desirability. Indeed, the 1st July 1968 Selective Employment of Air and Ground Alert (SEAGA) program effectively duplicated the CHROME DOME mission and routes, although SEAGA missions were not flown continuously. Instead, these GIANT LANCE sorties were flown using a number of aircraft directed by CINCSAC in response to increased levels of international tension as a 'visual deterrence' component of SAC's retaliatory capability. As an

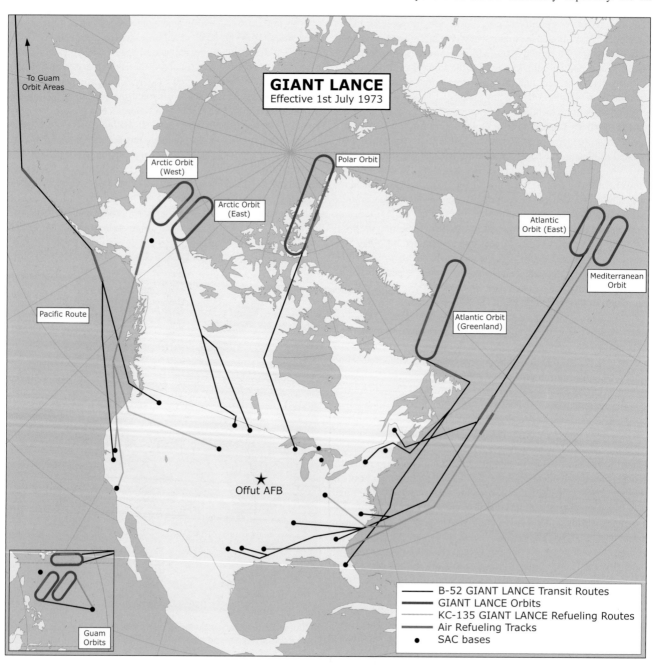

example, in 1969 a B-52G would conspicuously depart Beale AFB on a GIANT LANCE sortie (closely monitored by Soviet agents who tracked SAC's alert force status, not to mention SR-71 operations at Beale AFB) and fly to Alaska for refueling by KC-135s from Eielson AFB. It would continue to a point south of Japan, orbit, and then return to Beale AFB. This route was especially sensitive to fuel consumption during the westbound portion of the flight. High-altitude jet streams meant that engine settings had to be higher than normal to maintain speed and timing, increasing fuel burn rates. As such the two outbound refuelings were critical to the success of the mission. Conversely, the eastbound flight was often completed with two or more throttles at idle to avoid arriving at timing gates early.

For many years SAC personnel who flew and supported GIANT LANCE missions, as well as scholars and the public, believed they were part of superpower politics. Sino-Soviet tensions reached a peak in October 1969, and SAC B-52 and KC-135 crews were told that GIANT LANCE missions were a signal to the USSR not to attack Red China with nuclear weapons. As historians Bill Burr and Jeffrey Kimball have shown, however, this was a smoke screen. In an effort to compel Soviet leaders to pressure the North Vietnamese into an agreement ending the war in Southeast Asia, President Richard Nixon decided to invoke his 'Madman' persona. Nixon believed that GIANT LANCE would show Kremlin officials that he was just crazy enough to use nuclear weapons, and it was in Soviet interests to help bring the war to an end. Needless to say, this proved unsuccessful, and subsequent GIANT LANCE sorties were far less psychotic in purpose.

Tankers, Bombers, and Missiles
The 1960s saw the expansion of the ICBM program to such a degree that the future of the manned bomber force (and the tanker fleet required to support it) appeared to be in jeopardy. On 11th December 1961 Secretary of Defense McNamara said that '… the introduction of ballistic missiles is already exerting a major impact on the size, composition, and deployment of the manned bomber force, and this impact will become greater in the years ahead. As the number of … ballistic missiles increases, requirements for strategic aircraft will be gradually reduced. Simultaneously, the growing enemy missile capability will make grounded aircraft more vulnerable to sudden attack, and further readiness measures will have to be taken to increase the survivability rate of the strategic bomber force.'

The implications were myopic and chilling. As McNamara pressed the US toward a strategic weapon system which, once launched, could never be recalled, the flexibility of American defense decreased drastically. Because bombers (and their tankers) could be recalled after launch, a bomber launch might serve as sufficient warning to the USSR that the US was serious about its national security interests. The bombers' long flight times from the US to Soviet airspace (eight hours or more) allowed for a final measure of negotiations in this time of crisis. Should the Soviets and the United States reach an agreement, the bombers (and their tankers) could be recalled before any nuclear weapons were employed. ICBMs, however, cannot be recalled once launched, and the flight time to their targets is on the order of 30 minutes. Sea-launched missiles take even less time, as little as five to ten minutes. Once launched, there is no other recourse but for the other side to launch its ICBMs lest they be destroyed by the opponent's first-strike missiles. With a strategic deterrent force composed of only ICBMs, once the first missile is launched, there would be no outcomes other than the cataclysmic nuclear exchange that everyone feared was both imminent and inevitable, or immediate surrender and devastation by the nation under attack.

Despite the flexibility that encouraged the continued development and operation of manned strategic bombers (and their tankers),

McNamara chose instead to view the price of deterrence with his economist's eye. ICBMs were cheaper to produce, required significantly less maintenance and training, had no need for a fleet of support tankers, needed only a token crew to launch dozens of missiles, and seemed an overall cost-effective approach to defense procurement. By eliminating the manned bomber (or at a minimum emasculating it) as McNamara envisaged, the only major options open to the US were holocaust or surrender; there was no 'in-between'. Given the fears of what a post-nuclear world might be like, the likelihood of an American president 'pushing the button' for anything other than a direct attack on American soil was next to nothing. This particularly worried America's European allies who feared that the US pledge to consider an attack by the USSR on Europe as an attack on the US was little more than political hyperbole. Would the US launch its ICBMs against Russia if Soviet tanks invaded the Federal Republic of Germany? European leaders were unconvinced. The United States could, however, increase the number of bombers on alert or launch them to their 'fail safe' points, sending a strong message to the Soviets to withdraw before escalation into a global thermonuclear exchange.

There were still, however, a number of 'old bomber pilots' in the Air Force command structure who were firmly convinced of the value of strategic bombing and who distrusted the 'whiz-kid newness' of the ICBM or their value 'as an independent strike force sufficiently reliable in themselves'. LeMay especially was concerned about the operational reliability of the missiles: 'We have never fired a missile with an atomic warhead on it. … So there is always some question: will they work? …To this day I think everybody has one reservation: we never shot a missile under war conditions' [the 1962 FRIGATE BIRD Polaris SLBM launch from the USS *Ethan Allen* was the only test firing of a live nuclear warhead on a ballistic missile]. LeMay needed proven – not promising – weapons, telling Air Force Chief of Staff General Twining on 26th November 1955 that until the ICBM's 'capabilities are proven, we must establish initial [strategic] objectives and utilize demonstrably effective weapons systems', which he unequivocally identified as SAC's proposed fleet of 1,900 'B-52 aircraft, the only proven delivery system' coupled with 'some 1,300 KC-135 tankers in support'. LeMay was equally worried about the ability of the new ICBMs to hit their targets. 'The accuracy of the first missiles was nothing to jump up and down about, either'. General Jack J Catton echoed this concern, saying 'There you are, shooting a rocket like a cannon, and it is going to go 5,000 miles and be within a mile of the aiming point. That was just hard for me to comprehend. That makes you apprehensive.'

Resistance to McNamara's policy ensured that the bomber force stayed firmly entrenched as one-third of America's nuclear deterrent triad, maintaining US strategic flexibility. Events in October 1962 proved the merit of the manned bomber over the ICBM. Among SAC's responses to the Cuban missile crisis were an increase in the number of airborne alert B-52s and the dispersal of B-47 and B-52 bombers to civilian airfields across the nation, presenting Soviet missiles and bombers with an overwhelming number of targets. B-52s on airborne alert briefly increased from 12 to 65, for example, and KC-135 numbers rose accordingly, with the Spanish Tanker Task Force jumping from six to 28 tankers. Had the USSR launched an attack, there were too many bomber dispersal bases to ensure that all would be targeted and destroyed (in addition to the missile silos and airborne alert), leaving the Soviet Union vulnerable to an unacceptably devastating nuclear retaliatory attack. Without this bomber option in McNamara's utopian ICBM-only force, America could have only acquiesced to the Soviet action in Cuba or 'pushed the button'. Instead, the flexibility with which President John F Kennedy could employ his strategic nuclear forces helped to convince Khrushchev of US resolve to use those forces, resulting, in part, in the withdrawal of Soviet missiles from Cuba.

A hidden implication of the strategic bomber issue was its demand upon SAC's tanker force. If the bombers were phased out there would be little need for tankers to support them. Those already built could support TAC's fighter commitment, and the cancelation of existing and future orders would result in significant defense budget savings. What Kennedy's 'best and brightest' could not do was predict the future, particularly the exponential growth in demand for air refueling by airplanes, commands, services, and nations other than SAC's bombers and TAC's fighters. Had the tanker fleet been cut or production terminated in 1961 or 1962, the availability of tankers in the late 1960s and throughout the 1990s and 2000s would be less than half of the existing level, already inadequate in the event of a major sustained combat operation. The implication for KC-135 variants (such as reconnaissance platforms and airborne command posts) would have been even more disturbing. These special airframes were built or converted to satisfy specific needs, and their construction or modification would have been impossible given a shortage of tankers. The value of these variants and their influence on the evolution of US national security policy is profound, and their absence cannot be minimized.

End of the Line

KC-135 production continued through the acquisition of FY64 aircraft, and included both KC-135As and RC-135Bs. As the debate raged over the bomber versus ICBM issue, SAC officials realized that with the end of procurement of FY61 B-52Hs terminating the B-52 production line there was little value in claiming that SAC needed more KC-135s to refuel future B-52 deliveries. If there were to be any more KC-135s built after FY64, SAC planners recognized they would be needed to refuel the yet-to-be approved Advanced Manned Strategic Aircraft (AMSA) and would have to justify their acquisition on that basis. McNamara, however, argued that 'the numbers' showed there was no need for any more KC-135s at all. According to his figures, retirement of the B-52C through B-52F models would reduce the number of existing tankers assigned to SIOP commitments, more than enough to fulfill any future requirements that the AMSA might generate. Even more damaging to SAC's hope to keep the KC-135 production line open was McNamara's assertion that the B-52H and the AMSA could reach their targets *without any* refueling; there was no need for any more KC-135s. Tankers obligated to those sorties could then be used to refuel the planned FB-111A and proposed FB-111H. McNamara also inflated the ability of the FB-111A to reach its target using a high-altitude subsonic cruise, low-altitude supersonic

penetration (Hi-Lo) profile as part of his commitment to justify the troubled TFX. In fact, once it entered service, the FB-111A could not reach its target even with a single refueling, and had to rely completely on its standoff SRAMs to hit the target. Moreover, based on his figures, the B-58 could not reach its target at all using a Hi-Lo profile with a single refueling (it lacked any standoff weapons), justifying his intent to withdraw it from service at the earliest opportunity. In any case, McNamara used these spurious figures to block any SAC requests for more KC-135s to meet its SIOP requirements. KC-135 production had come to an end.

European Tanker Task Force

During early 1960s strike aircraft assigned to USAFE and based in Germany or elsewhere on the European continent were viewed as having only a 'one-shot' mission from those bases. Assuming sufficient warning of a Warsaw Pact invasion of Western Europe, aircraft including F-84s and North American F-100s would be able to execute their initial strikes to blunt the advancing forces, but their bases in West Germany, for example, would be destroyed by Warsaw Pact aircraft or overrun by ground units. As such, these USAFE aircraft would have to recover at bases in England. To do so would require post-strike aerial refueling. Moreover, USAFE aircraft based in (or deployed to) English bases would equally require pre- and post-strike aerial refueling to reach targets in the Fulda Gap or other crucial routes of advance. USAFE had largely resolved this by means of TAC KB-50Js based at RAF Sculthorpe, England. Nonetheless, USAFE's priorities understandably included deploying additional F-100s at English bases, increasing strike capacity by adding the new Republic F-105s, and having an in-theater KC-135 base which would 'lengthen the reach of the England-based force.'

Although McNamara had pledged some 70 KC-135s to meet TAC's refueling needs, it remained for SAC to make them available and to provide crews and maintenance. SAC viewed this obligation merely as providing air refueling on an 'as needed, if available' basis (i.e., emergency air refueling), leading to growing tension between the commands. For CINCSAC, permanently allocating KC-135s to Europe was not a prudent decision. Doing so removed tankers from the SIOP force, compelling a reduction in mated bombers. In addition, KC-135s on the ground in Europe were lucrative targets for Warsaw Pact pre-emptive air strikes. A small number of SAC KC-135s had been regularly deployed since the late 1950s to the 3970th SW at Torrejon AB in Spain (the foundation of the Spanish Tanker Task Force – STTF), a location considered 'safe' from hostile air attack. This was as much as General Power was willing to concede. USAFE would have to make do with its KB-50s.

Table 5-1. **SAC Bomber Planning Ranges, FY64**

	B-52C	B-52H	B-58A	FB-111A	FB-111H	AMSA
Ferry Range (subsonic, unrefueled, no weapons)	7,450nm 13,797km	9,454nm 17,509km	4,250nm 7,871km	5,320nm 9,853km	5,960nm 11,038km	8,880nm 16,298km
Combat Range (all subsonic, 1 refueling, SIOP SRAM load)	7,400nm 13,705km	9,500nm 17,594km	6,602nm 12,227km	7,450nm 13,797km	8,150nm 15095km	9,150nm 16,946km
Combat Range (subsonic cruise, supersonic penetration, 1 refueling, SIOP SRAM load)	n/a	n/a	4,567nm 8,458km	5,400nm 10,001km	7,500nm 13,890km	8,100nm 15,001km
No.of SRAMS	0	18	0	5	5	18
Launch Base	Westover AFB	Carswell AFB	Bunker Hill AFB	Pease AFB	Bunker Hill AFB	Minot AFB
Range to Target (follow-on strike of Moscow hardened command post)	4,545nm 8,417km	5,761nm 10,855km	5,022nm 9,301km	4,442nm 8,227km	5,022nm 9,301km	4,865nm 9,010km
Shortfall (if any)	n/a	n/a	-455nm -843km (supersonic)	n/a*	n/a	n/a

* The actual figure is 3,210nm/5,950km, resulting in a shortfall of -1,132nm/-2,227km

As with the sale of KC-135s to France (see Chapter 6) and the basing issue for RC-135Ms (see Chapter 10), in the early 1960s the presence of US forces in Europe was tied in large measure to the 'gold flow' problem, the transfer of US gold to European nations in payment for US basing and operational costs. On 16th July 1963, in an effort to reduce the gold flow out of the United States, McNamara implemented the CLEARWATER program, which reduced SAC REFLEX alert bombers (primarily B-47s) and eliminated TAC's KB-50J tanker squadron at RAF Sculthorpe but retained the STTF. Losing the KB-50s was a mixed blessing. The airplanes were old and needed to be retired, but in doing so USAFE was now without a dedicated tanker force in Europe and had to rely on SAC as the single manager for KC-135s. The CINCSAC was not inclined to release any KC-135s to another command, however, and without aerial refueling USAFE aircraft in England could barely reach their targets in the event of a Warsaw Pact invasion, if at all.

The solution to USAFE's fighter refueling needs bypassed SAC's new jet tanker entirely and relied instead on Air National Guard's KC-97s. In August 1964 some 28 KC-97Gs refuelled 19 F-100s and 12 RF-84Fs as they 'crossed the Pond' in Operation READY GO. Although the transit was successful, it highlighted the KC-97's weaknesses of slow speed and limited altitude. By the end of 1964 these had been mitigated by the installation of surplus J47 engines, and the newly converted ANG KC-97Ls proved satisfactory in the 'fighter drag' role. By June 1965 they were regular visitors to Rhein-Main AB in West Germany. Beginning 1st May 1967 these were known as CREEK PARTY deployments, and the ANG assumed primary responsibility for getting TAC fighters to and from Europe. Once there, both KC-97s from Rhein-Main AB and KC-135s from the STTF (by now under control of the 98th SW) at Torrejon AB, would provide aerial refueling.

The 98th SW did not have any KC-135s or crews of its own, and all aircraft were deployed on a rotational temporary duty (TDY) basis for approximately 28 days. In addition to air refueling training for USAFE F-4s, F-101s, and F-100s, the STTF supported USAFE deployments to and from forward bases in Turkey and Libya. Normally four KC-135s were assigned, but a fifth tanker was added in March 1968 because of emergency standby requirements for KC-135R BRIAR PATCH missions. In addition, Det 1, 98th SW, located at RAF Upper Heyford, coordinated air refueling operations for SAC reconnaissance missions including BURNING CANDY, BURNING PIPE, and GARLIC SALT (see Chapter 10). The STTF KC-135s also supported B-58 GLASS ROAD SIOP training missions flown from the US.

Most notably, KC-135s from the STTF refueled CHROME DOME airborne alert missions beginning in the early 1960s, including the mid-air collision on 17th January 1966 between a B-52G and KC-135A 61-0273 operating out of Morón AB. When these were canceled in 1968, the STTF was tasked to refuel sorties taking part in GIANT LANCE missions. STTF KC-135As refueled a B-52 west of Portugal (Atlantic Orbit) and a B-52 east of Spain (Mediterranean Orbit) but this required an increase to seven KC-135s, which still proved insufficient. Any KC-135s at Det 1 at RAF Upper Heyford supporting SAC recon missions would not be able to offload more than 114,200 lb (51,800kg) of fuel, but the Atlantic Orbit B-52 required 132,000 lb (59,874kg) and the Mediterranean Orbit B-52 needed 136,000 lb (61,689kg). Consequently, the STTF was forced to reduce air refueling support for USAFE to a maximum of 40 sorties per month to ensure tanker availability for the GIANT LANCE B-52s.

By 1974 the Spanish government sought to relocate the Spanish Tanker Task Force from Torrejon AB, claiming that excessive operations there caused havoc with the airspace around Madrid. An unspoken issue was Spain's unwillingness to risk an oil embargo by Arab nations for any overt support of the United States in the wake

of the 1973 Arab-Israeli War (see below). USAFE strongly objected to relocating the STTF to England, and wanted the new base to remain in Spain, preferably at either Zaragoza AB or Morón AB. The final agreement, however, signed on 24th January 1976, allowed only a small detachment to remain at Zaragoza AB while the remaining KC-135s would have to relocate to RAF Mildenhall (Det 1, 98th SW had previously moved from RAF Upper Heyford to RAF Mildenhall on 1st April 1970). In addition, on 1st July 1976 SAC assumed control of the CREEK PARTY KC-97 mission, completing its integration of ANG and AFRES tanker units into SAC concurrent with their transition to KC-135s.

Control of the newly renamed European Tanker Task Force (ETTF) was passed on 15th August 1976 to the 306th SW at Ramstein AB, West Germany, which assumed control of all SAC tanker and reconnaissance operations in Europe. CREEK PARTY closed in 1977, with the last two KC-97Ls departing Rhein-Main AB on 29th April. Henceforth, all future ANG and AFRES KC-135 deployments to Europe on behalf of SAC would be to RAF Mildenhall. On 1st July 1978, the 306th relocated to RAF Mildenhall, where it remained until it was inactivated on 31st March 1992 and replaced by the 100th ARW.

The Southeast Asia Years

SAC tanker operations in Southeast Asia (SEA) and the Pacific did not begin in mid-1964 with what is traditionally considered the onset of hostilities in Vietnam. Early KC-135 refueling operations in SEA included support for McDonnell RF-101C Voodoos flying PIPE STEM reconnaissance missions over the Republic of Vietnam from 20th October to 21st November 1961. Trans-Pacific fighter deployments to and from bases in the Far East required KC-135 support, often operating under the nickname LIMA MIKE. From July 1962 through June 1963, SAC allocated 200 KC-135s in support of 18 major TAC overseas movements. By the end of 1963, SAC tankers supported eleven more such movements. Additional refueling capability for early operations in SEA was available with TAC's few KB-50s and the handful of remaining SAC KC-97s. SAC tankers also provided air refueling and airlift support for B-47s deployed to Andersen AFB, Guam, as part of the AIRMAIL mission, the Pacific equivalent of REFLEX, as well as refueling for RB-47, KC-135A-II and KC-135A reconnaissance operations throughout the Western Pacific.

Formal SAC operations in SEA began in February 1964 when SAC Lockheed U-2s conducted photographic reconnaissance of South Vietnam's borders. Increasing hostilities over Laos (including the loss of two Vought F-8 Crusaders on reconnaissance missions) elicited a more militant US response. On 7th June 1964 the JCS directed SAC to move four (later six) KC-135s from Andersen AFB to Clark AB, Republic of the Philippines, to support planned strikes in Laos by US Air Force tactical bombers. This tanker deployment – part of LIMA MIKE X – became known as the YANKEE TEAM Tanker Task Force (TTF), acquiring its name from the reconnaissance missions then being flown over Laos. All six YANKEE TEAM tankers were placed on 30-minute strip alert, ready to refuel as directed by the JCS. The first KC-135 missions in support of combat operations took place on 9th June 1964, when four YANKEE TEAM KC-135s refueled eight North American F-100 Super Sabres over Da Nang, Republic of Vietnam, en route to targets on the Plaines des Jarres in Laos. Post-strike refueling occurred over southern Laos. The YANKEE TEAM tankers were immediately prepared for another mission on 13th June, but this did not take place. On 15th June the YANKEE TEAM KC-135s returned to Andersen AFB but were still susceptible to short notice demands for tanker support. They also resumed participation in the TAC deployments. Major air refueling programs throughout the war in Southeast Asia are listed in Table 5-2 (see overleaf).

Table 5-2. **Major Air Refueling Programs in Southeast Asia**
(excludes missions in support of the *USS Pueblo*)

Name	Primary Base	Mission
LIMA MIKE	US and overseas	Trans-Pacific fighter deployments, 1962+
YANKEE TEAM	Clark AB, Philippines	Support tactical strikes in Laos, early 1964 to 3rd Sept 1964, to FOREIGN LEGION
FOREIGN LEGION	Clark AB	Renamed from YANKEE TEAM to support tactical strikes in Laos, 3rd September 1964-1965. Became TIGER CUB.
TAMALE PETE	Kadena AB, Okinawa, Japan	Planning name for Okinawa TTF, became YOUNG TIGER
YOUNG TIGER	Kadena AB	Refuel tactical air ops in SEA, 1965+
TIGER CUB	Don Muang IAP, Thailand	Relocation of FOREIGN LEGION TTF to support tactical strikes in Laos, 1965+
ARC LIGHT	*	Refuel B-52 operations in SEA
KING COBRA	Takhli RTAFB, Thailand	Supplement TIGER CUB TTF for tactical strikes in Laos, 1965+
GIANT COBRA	U-Tapao RTNAB, Thailand	Supplement TIGER CUB TTF for tactical strikes in Laos, 1966+
JUMPING JACK	†	Emergency post-mission B-52 refueling
BLACK SHIELD	Kadena AB	Refuel CIA A-12 missions, May 1967 to March 1968
GLASS KEY	Ching Chuan Kang AB, Taiwan	Supplement YOUNG TIGER and ARC LIGHT missions, 1968+
GIANT SCALE	Kadena AB,	Refuel SR-71 missions, March 1968-1973
BULLET SHOT I	US and overseas	Deployment of 29 B-52Ds to Andersen AFB, and 10 KC-135s to Kadena AB, 8th February 1972
BULLET SHOT II	US and overseas	Deployment of 6 more KC-135s to Kadena AB and 20 B-52Ds to Andersen AFB (and 3 more KC-135As and B-52Ds under BULLET SHOT II Extension) April 1972
BULLET SHOT III	US and overseas	Deployment of 3 KC-135 to Kadena AB and 7 KC-135 to U-Tapao RTNAB, April 1972, plus 28 B-52Gs to Andersen AFB on 10-16th April
BULLET SHOT IV	US and overseas	Deployment of 2 KC-135 to Kadena AB, May 1972, plus 7 B-52Gs to Andersen AFB on 21st May and 59 B-52Gs on 23rd May
CONSTANT GUARD I	US and overseas	Deployment of 12 F-105Gs to Korat RTAFB on 6th April 1972, 18 F-4E to Ubon RTAFB from 11th April 5th Aug 1972, 18 F-4E to Ubon RTAFB from 12th April - 30th September 1972, and 8 EB-66 to Korat RTAFB, 11th April 1972
CONSTANT GUARD IIA	US and overseas	Deployment of 12 KC-135 to Clark AB, 2nd May 1972, 18 F-4E Udorn RTAFB from 29th April - 18th October 1972, and 18 F-4E to Udorn RTAFB, 1st May - ca 29th July 1972
CONSTANT GUARD IIB	US and overseas	Deployment of 11 KC-135 to Clark AB, 10th May 1972
CONSTANT GUARD III	US and overseas	Deployment of 72 F-4Ds from Holloman AFB to Takhli RTAFB on 4th May - ca 1st October 1972
CONSTANT GUARD IV	US and overseas	Deployment of 36 C-130Es to CCK AB, 13th May 1972
CONSTANT GUARD V	US and overseas	Deployment of 48 F-111As to Takhli RTAFB, 27th September 1972
CONSTANT GUARD VI	US and overseas	Deployment of 72 A-7Ds to Korat RTAFB, November 1972

* ARC LIGHT tanker missions were flown initially from Kadena AB and later Ching Chuan Kang AB
† JUMPING JACK typically conducted from ARC LIGHT refueling bases as well as Andersen AB

Following the disclosure of the Gulf of Tonkin incident, on 5th August the JCS ordered the re-establishment of the YANKEE TEAM TTF at Clark AB with eight KC-135s. TAC deployed 84 fighters to the Western Pacific, requiring 172 air refueling sorties and 48 KC-135s, including those at Clark AB plus those at Andersen AFB and Hickam AFB, HI. On 3rd September 1964 the YANKEE TEAM TTF was renamed FOREIGN LEGION, with the next strike refueling mission on 28th September 1964. FOREIGN LEGION was purely an interim organization, little more than 'a mighty sparse ops room consisting primarily of a crew and aircraft roster and a phone to Saigon'. Plans were well under way to establish a tanker task force at Kadena AB, Okinawa, early in 1965. The TTF at Kadena AB would have as its primary mission the daily refueling operations throughout SEA, theater training, and preparation for the introduction of B-52s involved with conventional bombing in SEA. Specific refueling assignments included '(1) tactical aircraft, mainly those performing photographic and reconnaissance missions over North Vietnam; (2) PACAF aircraft operating out of Japan, South Korea, Okinawa, and the Philippines, including those on inter-theater missions; and (3) SAC aircraft which meant bombers on training missions in addition to reconnaissance aircraft.' Planning for the Okinawa TTF acquired the nickname TAMALE PETE. Operations at Kadena AB were scheduled to commence no later than 31st January 1965, although TAC preferred a December 1964 operational capability. A forward operating location (FOL) would also be established at Don Muang International Airport (IAP), Thailand.

The crash in late 1964 of one of TAC's elderly KB-50s and the subsequent grounding of the remaining fleet due to widespread airframe corrosion forced a reappraisal of the tanker task force deployment schedule. With the elimination of the KB-50, TAC was now completely without its own tanker fleet and was wholly dependent upon SAC for air refueling, creating an excessive demand for SAC tanker support. During 1964 SAC retired five KC-97 squadrons and discontinued KC-97 operations at Sondrestrom AB, Greenland, and Namao RCAF Station, Canada, leaving Harmon AB, Newfoundland, as the sole remaining full-time KC-97 overseas base. As more KC-97s retired, the burden on KC-135s to refuel alert B-47s and B-52s increased. KC-135s were also in increased demand for conventional support, as in May 1964 when 20 KC-135s participated in Operation DESERT STRIKE, a joint Army–Air Force exercise. Losing any KC-135s to the proposed TTF was not a prospect welcomed by SAC planners.

The final KC-135A (64-14840) was delivered to the 380th AREFS, 380th SAW at Plattsburgh AFB, NY, on 12th January 1965. On the same day, the 4252nd SW was activated at Kadena AB and tanker operations from there assigned the nickname YOUNG TIGER. These were dedicated exclusively to support of 7th AF tactical fighter and reconnaissance operations. The first YOUNG TIGER mission was flown on 25th January 1965. A force of 15 KC-135s was anticipated to be in place by 30th June 1965, with a portion of those airplanes on temporary duty (TDY) to Don Muang IAP. On 11th February, however, the 4252nd SW received notice of the impending arrival of additional KC-135s in support of ARC LIGHT B-52 conventional bombing operations conducted from Andersen AFB. On 12-13th February, 32 KC-135s arrived at Kadena AB, overwhelming the facilities there. SAC's plan to conduct B-52 operations in the Western Pacific had failed to account for adequate tanker support and the necessary organizational infrastructure. For the first time SAC tankers were involved in a conventional wartime situation, not a practice nuclear war generation or an alert dispersal, and the differences were quickly apparent. By mid-1965 there were 45 KC-135s in place at Kadena AB which had provisions for only 15. Only the 15 YOUNG TIGER KC-135s were available for fighter support while the remaining 30 ARC LIGHT KC-135s were held in reserve for operations with B-52s, a restriction that was soon removed.

The first ARC LIGHT B-52 mission took place on 18th June 1965, conducted by 27 B-52Fs from the 7th and 320th BWs. Two B-52s (57-0179 from the 7th BW and 57-0047 from the 320th BW) were lost in a mid-air collision in the refueling area, and the overall military effect of the mission was of questionable value. The limitations of the air refueling plan were corrected by an increase in the number of refueling tracks at different altitudes, increasing their lateral separation, instituting timing triangles to account for flight timing discrepancies, relocating some of the refueling tracks closer to the Philippine Islands, and eventually developing and implementing the en route refueling rendezvous procedure.

Although KC-135s based in Thailand flew only one-third the total sorties per day as those based in Okinawa, the Thailand-based tankers could offload nearly three times the fuel available from Kadena tankers given the shorter flying distances from Thailand to the air refueling areas. Despite this obvious benefit, Kadena AB enjoyed greater access to the source of jet fuel via a seaborne logistics pipeline. Still, tanker basing in Thailand was not immediately forthcoming. Considerable Thai diplomatic pressure sought to decrease or eliminate the tankers completely at the TIGER CUB TTF at Don Muang IAP, and limited basing facilities were to be found elsewhere in SEA. Don Muang IAP was the only port of entry to Thailand through which all visitors had to pass, and the conspicuous presence of US military forces was politically awkward for the Thais. KC-135 bases in South Vietnam were out of the question due to the demonstrated presence of hostile action. [KC-135s in Southeast Asia were not immune to battle damage. One KC-135 suffered a 3in (7.62cm) x 6in (15.24cm) hole in its wing skin from the explosion of a B-52 that crashed at Kadena AB. The KC-135 flew back to Tinker AFB for repair and, four days later, returned to Kadena AB.] In September 1965 KC-135s deployed to Takhli RTAFB to supplement the TIGER CUB TTF aircraft at Don Muang IAP, creating the KING COBRA TTF. The first KING COBRA refuelings took place on 15th September. The Thais finally granted approval for a permanent tanker base at Takhli RTAFB on 20th December 1965.

During the last six months of 1965, Kadena-based KC-135s flew over 4,000 sorties – some 65% of the 4252nd SW's refueling missions – in support of PACAF. At the end of 1965 there were 40 KC-135s at Kadena AB, ten at Takhli RTAFB, and five still at Don Muang IAP. The tankers flew more than 9,200 sorties, conducted 31,250 refuelings, and transferred 315 million pounds (142,881,597kg) of fuel.

The final KC-135A tanker delivered to the Air Force was 64-14840, which went to the 380th BW at Plattsburgh AFB. For such an auspicious occasion, the wing commander (on ladder to the right of sign) carried his trusty white plastic spoon in his shoulder pocket. *Photo P37290 courtesy Boeing*

Sustained Operations

On 10th November 1965 the last KC-97 in SAC was removed from ground alert at the 9th AREFS, 9th SAW, Mountain Home AFB, ID, The last two KC-97s were removed from SAC's inventory on 21st December 1965 when one airplane each from the 100th AREFS at Pease AFB, NH, and the 384th AREFS at Westover AFB were flown to MASDC. Although KC-97s would remain in ANG service for quite some time, there were no more piston-powered tankers in SAC.

By June 1966 B-52s in SEA dropped approximately 8,000 tons of bombs per month and at year's end had flown over 5,000 sorties. Because the B-52s flew great distances from Andersen AFB or Kadena AB, the need for air refueling en route to and from the target was absolute. Tactical fighter-bomber operations increased as well, placing a commensurate demand on the tanker fleet in SEA. To accommodate these new requirements, SAC established an additional tanker base at Sattahip, Thailand, and sent more tankers to SEA, usually from the same wing as the B-52s deployed to Andersen AFB.

The 4258th SW was activated at U-Tapao RTNAB (formerly Sattahip) on 2nd June 1966, with the first GIANT COBRA TTF sortie

18 KC-135s are visible in this image of U-Tapao RTNAB. Buddha Mountain is in the background. *Author's collection*

A 'Thud' pilot rolls off the boom following a pre-strike refueling en route to North Vietnam. KC-135 YOUNG TIGER missions enabled tactical fighters to reach their targets and return safely. *Author's collection*

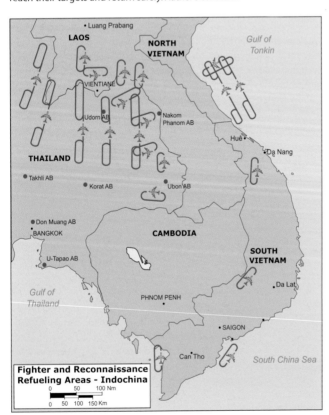

Fighter and Reconnaissance Refueling Areas - Indochina

from U-Tapao RTNAB on 11th August; 15 tankers had been assigned there by September, with a total of 35 in place by mid 1967. Takhli RTAFB remained an FOL for eight of the 35 YOUNG TIGER KC-135s. By October operations at Don Muang IAP had finally ground to a halt. During 1966 the 75 KC-135s in SEA had flown 18,203 sorties and transferred more than 850 million pounds (385,553,515kg) of fuel. The build-up of tanker forces in Thailand continued through 1967. Fuel requirements for PACAF fighters alone doubled from 1.8 million pounds per day to 3.7 million pounds (816,466kg to 1,678,292kg).

An additional issue facing tanker operations in SEA was which command – PACAF's 7th Air Force or SAC – controlled the tanker assets available. PACAF planners sought to increase the number of tankers available, especially over Laos and near North Vietnam for post-strike air refueling. SAC commanders argued that these plans placed the KC-135s in unnecessary high-risk situations. Because SAC still felt that the primary mission of the KC-135 fleet was support of the Single Integrated Operations Plan (SIOP) — the attack plan executed in the event of a nuclear war – anything that placed even a single tanker at risk was detrimental to SAC's mission of strategic deterrence. In addition, PACAF wanted the KC-135s moved out of Takhli RTAFB to allow increased fighter operations from there, a trade-off that would dramatically affect SAC's ability to satisfy PACAF's refueling needs.

Fighters, not Bombers
This increase in demand by PACAF fighters placed tanker planners and crews in a considerable predicament. Accustomed to supporting B-52s whose missions were planned in minute detail days in advance of the flight, the need for extremely flexible tanker crew responses to fighter missions and emergencies taxed the training of even the most experienced tanker crewmember. Instead of one or two scheduled bomber receivers, dozens of fighters – most of them unscheduled and in desperate need of the gas intended for other receivers – could show up for air refueling. The strain on the KC-135s themselves was considerable. Flights were typically at extremely high or maximum gross weights, the airplanes flew more sorties and accrued more flying hours than normal, air refueling altitudes were lowered, and the airplanes occasionally landed at their maximum gross landing weights to avoid dumping valuable fuel.

Boeing designed the KC-135 to refuel the B-52 at altitudes typically at FL250-FL270. Air refueling operations in Southeast Asia, especially of tactical aircraft, took place much lower at 12,000-14,000ft (3,658-4,267m) AGL, with proposals to reduce this even further to 10,000ft (3,048m) AGL to reduce the need for wasted time and fuel required to climb to an arbitrarily higher refueling level. The consequence of these lower altitudes was an adverse impact on structural integrity of the KC-135 fleet due to increased turbulence. KC-135A 57-2608 was equipped with test instruments to measure these effects, which would be analyzed following its 28th November 1968 return to the United States. This issue raised concern among SAC officials leading to the KC-135 Structural Integrity Program, which SAC's commanders felt did not 'adequately consider the fact that the various age/usage/environmental combinations produce different fatigue deterioration rates.' SAC urged that AFLC and OCAMA should undertake a 'Lead-the-Force program and cyclic tests' to prevent catastrophic failures such as the loss of KC-135A 56-3655 near Mt Lassen, CA.

Despite these significant airframe problems, compromises satisfied most of the contentious issues between SAC and 7th AF. PACAF commander Lieutenant General William W Momyer, wrote to thank CINCSAC General John D Ryan, saying, 'I would like to extend my personal appreciation for the increased KC-135 tanker support now being provided to my Tactical Forces in Southeast Asia … The professionalism and "Can Do" attitude of your KC-135 tanker crews … in meeting my complex operational requirements, have given me the flexibility to make adjustments to a daily changing tactical situation. My employment of forces has been materially improved by their sustained high level of performance.' An excerpt from another letter of appreciation from an F-4 crew epitomized the more personal thanks PACAF owed the KC-135 crews: 'This [fuel] emergency … could have ended in the loss of an F-4 and the loss or imprisonment of the crew had it not been for the immediate and professional assistance rendered by the crew of [the KC-135]. Our heartiest thanks.' Nonetheless, there would be more demands to expand tanker operations in support of both ARC LIGHT and YOUNG TIGER missions. By the end of 1967, KC-135s had flown nearly 23,000 sorties and dispensed over 1.1 billion pounds (499 billion kilograms) of fuel in support of ARC LIGHT B-52s and YOUNG TIGER tactical fight operations. Monthly sortie rate had increased from 40 to 71, with PACAF projections reaching nearly 100.

The sustained tanker operations in SEA significantly affected SAC's strategic deterrent operations and plans. The increase in conventional combat operations in SEA did not alter the need to maintain the alert force, nominally about 40% of SAC's fleet. At the end of 1966 there were 75 KC-135s in SEA: the 40 ARC LIGHT tankers at Kadena AB and the 35 YOUNG TIGER tankers in Thailand. In order to fulfill its Emergency War Order (EWO) mission, 100% of SAC's KC-135 fleet could refuel only 75% of SAC's B-52 fleet. The current SIOP called for 255 generated B-52 sorties, requiring 433 tankers. If the projected 230 generated sorties for the new FB-111 were factored in, this would require 297 tankers. In short, the 484 generated bomber sorties dictated 730 KC-135s. With 75 tankers in SEA, plus a dozen or so in PDM, the shortfall would gut the SIOP.

The constant deployments were surely a hardship for tanker and bomber crews who were scheduled for a deployment to SEA for up to six months only to return home and spend at least half (and usually more) of the remaining time on alert, away from their families and homes. Operations in SEA also emphasized the KC-135's inadequacies. The need for long runways, for example, underscored the airplane's limited dispersal field capability while on alert. The poor performance of the KC-135's engines under high pressure altitude or high temperature conditions and their need for demineralized water for augmented thrust takeoffs all dictated a replacement, or at least an improvement, to the basic KC-135 airframe. Consequently, in June 1967 SAC requested a new 'advanced capability tanker', based on an entirely new airframe with TF39 high-bypass turbofan engines, or at a minimum, a significantly improved version of the KC-135. This 'KC-X' proposal would lead to the KC-135R and the KC-10 (and, indirectly, the KC-135E), but still would not fully satisfy SAC's long-term tanker inadequacies.

By mid December 1967 plans to increase B-52 sorties in Southeast Asia required the movement of 10 KC-135As and five 'EC-135s' – COMBAT LIGHTNINGS – from U-Tapao RTNAB and Kadena AB to CCK AB in Taiwan to make room for additional B-52s as part of the COMMANDO WALLOP program. On 23rd January North Korea seized the USS *Pueblo*, a US naval intelligence-gathering ship. As part of Operation PORT BOW, 26 B-52s and nine KC-135s deployed to Southeast Asia. These bombers were operationally separate from the ARC LIGHT B-52s and were committed to possible conventional (and nuclear) strikes against North Korea known as FRESH STORM. The tankers stopped briefly at Kadena AB prior to continuing to the newly completed airbase at Ching Chuan Kang, Taiwan (known simply as 'CCK'). A tenth KC-135 was added to the PORT BOW group while at Kadena AB. All PORT BOW tankers were in place on Taiwan by 7th

February, as were five COMBAT LIGHTNING radio relay airplanes. During COMBAT FOX, four task forces of 20, 16, 12, and nine KC-135s refueled additional tactical aircraft deployed in response to the *Pueblo* seizure. Once these tactical assets were in position, KC-135s refueled them on a daily basis as part of COMMANDO ROYAL.

The PORT BOW deployment in response to the seizure of the USS *Pueblo* further complicated the basing of KC-135s, as SAC forces at Kadena AB reached the daunting level of 15 PORT BOW B-52s, 45 KC-135As in support of both PORT BOW and ARC LIGHT, 10 KC-135Qs to meet SR-71 SENIOR CROWN operations, plus the six COMBAT APPLE RC-135Ms for a total of 76 airplanes. Refuelings nearly doubled – from 6,864 to 12,725. These demands placed considerable strain on the KC-135 logistics supply line. Repairing or replacing parts for SIOP-dedicated tankers in the continental United States was relatively straightforward. Stockpiles were small and replenished as needed. Given the heavy operational requirements on the other side of the world, however, this was hardly efficient or effective, especially for certain high priority items such as the AN/ARC-89 radio, J57 engines, and, interestingly enough, tires (at one point there were only 20 spare nose wheels in SEA!). Maintenance problems included the premature failure of air cycle machines due to turbine icing, for example, with the mean time between failure (MTBF) plummeting from 1,275 hours to only 160 hours. Modification costs to rectify the problem reached $2 million, but OCAMA developed a temporary field repair pending PDM for a total of $73,000. Problems with the air refueling boom led to the 1st July 1968 effort to inspect and repair all KC-135 booms, with half of the fleet equipped with overhauled booms by December 1968. Additional programs included SEEK SILENCE, the conversion of AN/ARC-34 UHF radios to AN/ARC-133V secure voice radios on 648 KC-135s.

On 30th January 1968 North Vietnamese, Viet Cong, and People's Republic of China (PRC) ground combat forces launched the Tet Offensive. The US response to this series of major assaults was Operation NIAGARA, an air offensive that necessitated a considerable increase in tanker support for the rise in both tactical fighter and B-52 operations. At the beginning of February there were 94 KC-135s in-theater, with over two thirds of the airplanes based at U-Tapao RTNAB and Kadena AB. B-52 sorties, for example, rose from 800 per month to 1,200 per month as of 1st February. By 15th February the number increased again to 1,800 per month. Tanker missions were divided among YOUNG TIGER, ARC LIGHT, COMMANDO ROYAL, reconnaissance, PORT BOW, and JUMPING JACK emergency post-mission B-52 refuelings. An increase in YOUNG TIGER tanker sorties from 53 to 66 sorties per day placed an even greater demand on the tanker assets in theater. On 29th February the eight KC-135s at Takhli RTAFB relocated to U-Tapao RTNAB, making the YOUNG TIGER TTF the largest in SEA with 40 airplanes. Additional KC-135s needed to support this increase in operations over Vietnam and Korea would be based at the new facility on Taiwan.

Taiwan is nearly as close to the Gulf of Tonkin as the bases in Thailand and typically an hour's flight closer than Kadena AB (given variations in winds aloft and weather conditions). As early as 1966 plans were under consideration for the basing of up to 15 KC-135s on Taiwan but political obstructions and lack of a base large enough and with adequate support facilities delayed these plans. Nonetheless, construction began in 1966 for a 'multi-role base', originally known as Kung Kuan AB, to accommodate 15 KC-135s, plus 30 B-52s, and a wing of C-130s. Political sensitivities (i.e., the base's proximity to the PRC) eventually precluded B-52 operations. By the end of 1966 the Nationalist Chinese government renamed the base Ching Chuan Kang AB. With construction well under way, preparations were made to activate the 4220th AREFS (which reported to the 4252nd SW) on 2nd January 1967. However, Air Force Headquarters notified SAC on 18th November 1966 that due to heightened political pressures deriving from the association of SAC with the B-52 and nuclear weapons, Ching Chuan Kang AB would be unavailable for SAC's potential use, although it could divert airplanes there in the event of bad weather at its other Pacific bases. Interestingly, Nationalist Chinese officials were kept in the dark about SAC's use of the base 'until such time as the US Departments of State and Defense were ready to advise them'.

By mid-1967 Ching Chuan Kang AB (popularly referred to as 'CCK') was nearly completed with one exception. The base had grossly inadequate access to the fuel distribution system on Taiwan, certainly unacceptable for a tanker base. The *Pueblo* seizure and the Tet Offensive provided the needed pressure to activate CCK as a SAC tanker base. Still, the fuel shortage there remained while other major problems such as inadequate air traffic control, hazardous terrain, and inadequate manning all complicated initial operations from the new base. In addition, Japanese political pressure to remove combat airplanes from Kadena AB forced the based B-52s to move to U-Tapao RTNAB and the KC-135s at U-Tapao to redeploy to CCK. As part of this redeployment, CCK took over ARC LIGHT and YOUNG TIGER refuelings as well as all COMBAT LIGHTNING operations, while Kadena AB took over the entire COMMANDO ROYAL mission. KC-135 operations from CCK were known by the operational nickname of GLASS KEY.

On 1st April 1968 President Lyndon B Johnson ordered a halt to all bombing sorties north of 19° North latitude. Seven months later he extended this prohibition to all bombing of North Vietnam and the Demilitarized Zone. These halts decreased the overall demand on KC-135 operations, although this was gradual and took place over the ensuing six months. By the end of 1968 SAC tanker operations in SEA exceeded all previous levels, with some 32,000 sorties completing more than 129,000 refuelings (of which 114,744 involved tactical aircraft) and transferring 1.6 billion pounds (726 billion kilograms) of fuel. With the advent of President Johnson's November bombing halt, tanker sortie numbers decreased through 1969. ARC LIGHT sorties dropped from 1,800 to 1,400 by 6th October with a commensurate decrease in air refuelings. YOUNG TIGER refueling sorties also decreased, although the total number of air refuelings increased to a record level (i.e., each tanker refueled more airplanes per sortie). By year's end, KC-135s had conducted 138,164 refuelings over 28,000 sorties while transferring 1.4 billion pounds (635 billion kilograms) of fuel.

As part of a major organizational change within SAC, on 1st April 1970 the 4252nd SW at Kadena AB was replaced by the 376th SW, and the 4258th SW at U-Tapao RTNAB was replaced by the 307th

SW. Sortie numbers continued to wane, with ARC LIGHT missions dropping to the 1,000 level by late summer of 1970. Tanker missions from CCK fell to nearly zero, with COMBAT LIGHTNING continuing operations from there until 14th November 1970, when they moved to U-Tapao RTNAB. CCK tanker operations officially ended on 31st January 1971. Overall tanker numbers declined from 71 in mid-1970 to 48 in December 1970. During 1970, KC-135s flew 19,540 sorties and transferred 888.2 million pounds (403 billion kilograms) of fuel.

A brief surge in US tactical and B-52 missions in May 1971 temporarily increased the number of tankers in-theater to 51. On 1st July 1971 the 909th AREFS was assigned to the 376th SW at Kadena (where it joined the 82nd SRS which flew RC-135Ms), replacing two TDY tanker task forces. Equipped with ten KC-135As, the 909th also had five KC-135Qs, the latter for SR-71 support. Tanker sorties again increased at the end of 1971 with the beginning of the COMMANDO HUNT VII interdiction campaign against supplies from North Vietnam and PRC. Still, the total number of refuelings in 1971 decreased from previous years: 14,400 sorties with 62,200 refuelings which offloaded 618.5 million pounds (281 billion kilograms) of fuel.

Intelligence reports in early 1972 of increased communist activity in preparation for what was believed to be a major offensive against South Vietnam spurred an immense and rapid build-up of SAC forces in SEA. On 8th February 1972, 29 B-52s and ten KC-135s deployed to Andersen AFB and Kadena AB, respectively, as part of BULLET SHOT I. ARC LIGHT refuelings increased to 1,500 per month. Additional tactical aircraft were deployed to SEA as part of CONSTANT GUARD, with the first such deployment taking place between 6th and 12th April when three tanker task forces of 13 KC-135s each (all from bases in the US) escorted two squadrons of F-4Es and one squadron of F-105G 'Wild Weasel' Thunderchiefs to Korat RTAFB, Thailand. Six more KC-135s went to SEA under BULLET SHOT II in April, three more in BULLET SHOT II Extension later the same month, and three more KC-135s went to Kadena AB and seven went to U-Tapao RTNAB in mid-April under BULLET SHOT III. CONSTANT GUARD sorties continued and a CONSTANT GUARD IIA task force was established on 2nd May at Clark AB with 12 KC-135s but was almost immediately replaced on 10th May with eleven new KC-135s as part of CONSTANT GUARD IIB. This unit fell under the operational control of the 376th SW as Detachment 2, but was soon renamed Operating Location Clark Field (OL-CF). Four squadrons of F-4s deployed to SEA from Holloman AFB, NM, beginning on 3rd May as part of CONSTANT GUARD III. Two more KC-135s deployed to Kadena AB at the end of May as part of BULLET SHOT IV, bringing the total number of tankers at Kadena AB to 26 BULLET SHOT airplanes, six COMBAT LIGHTNING airplanes, and the existing 28 airplanes already in place in January.

KC-135Qs from the 456th BW not only refueled BLACK SHIELD A-12 and GIANT SCALE SR-71 missions, but provided relay for crews back to Beale AFB.
Photo by Frank MacSorely via Stephen Miller

Table 5-3. **KC-135A Activity During LINEBACKER II, 18-29th December 1972**

| Date | Kadena AB | | U-Tapao RTNAB | | Clark AB | | Takhli RTAFB | | Total | |
	Sorties	Air Refuelings	Sorties	Air Refuelings	Sorties	Air Refuelings	Sorties	Air Refuelings	Sorties	Air Refuelings
18-Dec	69	128	28	109	0	0	18	52	115	289
19-Dec	56	98	55	266	0	0	31	106	142	470
20-Dec	47	91	57	282	0	0	27	77	131	450
21-Dec	7	6	50	283	0	0	22	85	79	374
22-Dec	4	5	58	272	4	8	17	46	83	331
23-Dec	22	29	69	264	16	22	23	106	130	421
24-Dec	9	9	38	181	15	18	23	117	85	325
25-Dec	0	0	5	20	0	0	1	4	6	24
26-Dec	76	124	30	178	19	32	24	97	149	431
27-Dec	22	44	71	397	20	35	32	175	145	651
28-Dec	31	51	49	218	17	35	22	80	119	384
29-Dec	31	49	54	251	19	56	24	87	128	443
Total	374	634	564	2,721	110	206	264	1,032	1,312	4,593

By the middle of 1972, there were 172 KC-135s based in SEA and the Far East. The increase in SAC airplanes was so great that one runway at Andersen AB was briefly closed and used as a parking ramp.

The increase in tanker numbers necessitated a major organizational change. The 307th SW gave up control of its KC-135s to the 310th SW (P) [Provisional] on 1st June. On 5th June the 4101st AREFS (P) was activated at Takhli RTAFB and the 4102nd AREFS (P) was activated at Clark AB. The 4102nd AREFS (P) relocated to CCK in August 1972 as a consequence of severe rainstorms and an acute shortage of fuel at Clark AB. This unit did not return to Clark AB prior to deactivation on 8th November 1972, and was reactivated on 18th December 1972 at Clark AB as part of LINEBACKER II. In an effort to relieve the crowded basing conditions in SEA, 13 KC-135s deployed in June to Don Muang IAP in Thailand, with the 4103rd AREFS (P) activating there on 1st July. Seven KC-135s also deployed to Korat RTAFB in June, with the 4104th AREFS (P) activating there on 9th June. Two thirds of the KC-135s in SEA – 114 airplanes – were YOUNG TIGER aircraft refueling tactical combat aircraft while the remainder were Kadena AB aircraft supporting ARC LIGHT B-52 air refueling, COMBAT LIGHTNING radio relay, reconnaissance support, and other SAC and PACAF missions. ARC LIGHT missions increased to 2,250 per month by mid-April, rising to a record 3,150 per month by the end of June, a level sustained until the start of LINEBACKER II in December.

Tactical deployments continued as 48 General Dynamics F-111As moved in September to Takhli RTAFB under CONSTANT GUARD V and 72 Vought A-7D Corsair IIs deployed in October to Korat RTAFB under CONSTANT GUARD VI. Basing limitations forced the termination of KC-135 operations from Don Muang IAP and the 4103rd AREFS (P) was inactivated 8th October 1972, while the 4014th AREFS (P) was inactivated one month later. During September 1972 there were 164 KC-135As in WESTPAC, and they flew 2,661 YOUNG TIGER and 1,241 ARC LIGHT, COMBAT LIGHTNING and PACAF support missions, totalling 3,902 missions. This was the 'high water' mark for the entire nine-year refueling period.

Beginning on 18th December, B-52s and tactical combat aircraft commenced LINEBACKER II, a series of massive airstrikes against North Vietnam, particularly in the Hanoi-Haiphong area. KC-135s flew 1,312 sorties during this 'eleven day war,' providing 4,593 air refuelings (see Table 5-3). LINEBACKER II missions ended on 29th December. The next day North Vietnam announced its willingness to resume peace negotiations. At year's end, KC-135s had flown 34,700 sorties, conducted 115,272 refuelings, and transferred more than 1.4 billion pounds (635 billion kilograms) of fuel. Tanker sorties continued to support US bombing of Vietnam until 27th January 1973, when an agreement ending the war was signed in Paris. Combat operations did not cease entirely as strikes against Laotian and Cambodian targets continued until 15th August 1973 (a date mandated by Congress), when B-52s struck a target in Cambodia.

The number of B-52s and KC-135s participating in LINEBACKER II was certainly significant in contributing to its operational success. As SAC feared, however, their absence from SIOP duties was equally, if not more, dramatic. During the latter half of the war in SEA, SAC averaged approximately 100 B-52s and FB-111s (plus their mated tankers) on alert. During 1972, with the shift of forces to SEA in preparation for LINEBACKER II, that number dropped to 49 *total* bomber aircraft on alert, half of which were FB-111s (see Chart 5-1). Revision N of the SIOP alert requirement called for 216 KC-135s, but only 59 were actually on alert. Nearly all of this tanker shortfall – 147 sorties – was due to mated bomber degrades. Only 10 sorties were lost to tanker crew shortages. In either case, deployments to SEA were responsible. Tanker unit EWO mission readiness was abysmal. Of 38 KC-135 squadrons in service in December 1972, only 12 were considered 'mission ready', and 16 were considered 'fully unqualified'. By June 1973 this had improved somewhat, with 18 'mission ready' and eight 'fully unqualified'. B-52 squadrons were even worse. In December 1972 only five of 30 squadrons were EWO 'mission ready', and 18 were unqualified. By June 1973 this had deteriorated even further, with only four 'mission ready' and 17 unqualified. It was not until June 1974 that all KC-135 squadrons were again EWO 'mission ready', but only 30% of B-52 squadron were 'mission ready.' Alert sorties also improved. Following the return of B-52Gs from SEA during the Arab-Israeli War alert in October 1973 (see below), the number of KC-135s on alert increased from 59 to 82, although there were still 129 tanker sorties lost due to

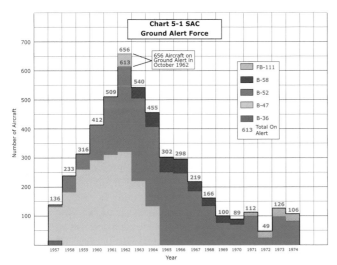

bomber degrades. By the end of June 1974, there were 163 KC-135s on alert out of the required 215.

Commitments to the war in Southeast Asia also dramatically undermined the sole remaining KC-135 REFLEX mission to the Goose Tanker Task Force (GTTF) at Goose Bay Airport in Labrador, Canada. SIOP-4 called for 12 KC-135s to deploy to the GTTF, four from each of three different wings on a rotational basis. Because of SEA tasking, there were only three KC-135s at the GTTF at any given time. By December 1973 this number increased to nine, including six KC-135As and three KC-135Qs. The following month the GTTF alert status peaked at 11 aircraft, with only one KC-135Q on alert.

In nearly a decade of combat operations in SEA, KC-135s flew 194,687 sorties, conducted 813,878 in-flight refuelings, and transferred 1.4 billion gallons (5.3 billion liters) totalling 8,963,700,000 lb (4,065,865,927kg) of fuel. Historians will long dispute the role and efficacy of airpower in the war in Southeast Asia. Critics claim that for nine years air strikes produced no measurable victory at the incredible expense of wasted fuel, money, airplanes, and the lives of hundreds of fliers and thousands of civilian casualties. Airpower apologists reply that political interference and meddling – from the White House to the Pentagon to the offices of admirals and generals far removed from the tactical situation – hindered air operations by forcing them to attack meaningless targets in a war of attrition driven by ill-defined political goals. Irrespective of these claims, the events of 1967, 1973, and 1991 have shown the effectiveness of an air force committed to a swift, decisive victory. The Israeli Air Force played the pivotal role in Israel's victory in two major wars, and the air campaign in Operation DESERT STORM again demonstrated the value of a well-orchestrated aerial assault with clearly defined military objectives designed to fulfill clearly defined political objectives.

Regardless of the view to which historians of the air war in Southeast Asia ascribe, the influence of the KC-135 was unequivocal. Without KC-135s strike aircraft could not reach or return from their targets. Without KC-135s combat air patrol fighters could not loiter long enough to protect strike and reconnaissance aircraft from enemy MiGs. Without KC-135s more airplanes and fliers would have been lost due to combat-intensive fuel starvation. Clearly, the operational effects and breadth of influence of the KC-135 equals or exceeds that of any other single airplane involved in the war in Southeast Asia.

A Change in the Cockpit

The greatest single challenge affecting SAC during the years after Vietnam was the profound drop in morale and retention in bomber and tanker crews, as well as the maintenance force and other mission-related specialties. Airmen who had flown extensively in combat in Southeast Asia were now once again idle on alert and flying perhaps three to four times a month instead of every day. Second Lieutenant intelligence officers with no 'real world' experience in SEA briefed alert crews on what to expect in a hypothetical war with the Soviet Union, leading to a decrease in crew confidence in the relevance of SAC and its ability to apply the lessons of Vietnam to its SIOP mission. Manpower issues were ill considered, as training pipelines continued to produce wartime numbers of pilots, navigators, and boom operators. Junior pilots were especially hard hit, with many assigned to SAC after a year of flying combat missions in Vietnam in airplanes like Fairchild AC-119s and F-4s. Now they found themselves on a KC-135 crew with two (or even three) copilots, and the lowest seniority to upgrade to aircraft commander. Despite having over 1,000 hours of combat time, they were forced to wait behind copilots with only 400 total hours but with more exposure to the 'SAC way of doing things'. With the decrease in available flying

hours, upgrade seemed an impossibility and morale suffered accordingly. Even more damning was the need to fill ICBM crew slots. A number of pilots and navigators were moved out of flying billets and assigned to Minuteman or Titan missiles. Moreover, SAC maintainers walked out the doors into civilian life in droves, and with them the experience needed to train the next generation of personnel who could 'keep 'em flying.'

Pilot retention became a major issue across the Air Force, particularly in the KC-135 community, where retention plummeted from 76% in FY83 to a dismal 36% in FY87, based on '…cumulative continuation rates (CCR) for USAF pilots with between six and 11 years of service.' According to USAF military personnel center calculations, 'the CCR percentage is regarded as the best index of retention. To maintain the pilot force, USAF needs a CCR of about 60%…' The issues that drove pilots from SAC seldom included the much-ballyhooed 'salary' concerns voiced by Air Force generals or the desire for a leather 'bomber jacket'. Instead, pilots left because they flew too little, spent too much time on alert, and were faced with administrative duties created as 'make work' jobs designed to give the appearance of productivity. During the last six months of 1975, for example, on average tanker pilots flew 21.1 hours per month, copilots flew 20.5, navigators logged 22.7, and boom operators flew 21.6. The average aircraft commander had only 900 hours KC-135 time. Promotions and commands, however, went to those who had 'punched the right tickets' (duties that seldom involved flying, emphasizing instead professional military education, the right staff positions, and first-name relationships with the right generals).

The post-war glut of copilots affected both B-52 and KC-135 crews, and SAC responded to it in traditional fashion by transferring the excess fliers to non-flying positions for 'one to two *years*' in a program known as Temporary Overmanning of the Operations Staff/Temporary Augmentee Support Program (TOOS/TASP). At Fairchild AFB, for example, seven KC-135 copilots and three B-52 copilots were assigned to 'Executive Support Officer' and 'Morale, Welfare, and Recreation Officer' billets. Senior SAC officials warned Wing Commanders that the TOOS/TASP program was 'not be used as dumping grounds for copilots whose records were below average,' which is what happened at many bases.

In an effort to address the inadequacies of copilot experience and upgrade, in September 1975 SAC began an assessment of the Accelerated Copilot Enrichment (ACE) program (later renamed Aviation Career Enhancement to avoid 'demeaning co-pilots'), ostensibly 'to increase [a copilot's] exposure to flying in order to improve basic flying skills, and where possible, reinforce and validate procedural proficiency gained through the use of advanced simulation.' In fact, the intent was clearly to address the declining morale and loss of core flight skills by copilots who had yet to master the necessary operational skill sets at a level that would allow them to retain those skills under SAC's severely reduced flying hours.

CINCSAC General Russell E Dougherty directed that Cessna T-37Bs from the 12th FTW at Columbus AFB, MS, participate in tests with B-52 and KC-135 copilots assigned to the 2nd BW at Barksdale AFB. The results were favorable, and SAC recommended expansion of the program to include Northrop T-38 Talons for bases that were not suitable for T-37 operations (e.g., long distances to nearby bases such as Grand Forks AFB, high-density jet operations such as March AFB, and eventually B-1 bases). During the initial phase which included eight wings, each copilot would log five ACE sorties per month in addition to any scheduled KC-135 or B-52 flights. ACE operations were quickly expanded to eight additional wings. Air Force Chief of Staff General David Jones approved the ACE program for full implementation across SAC on 1st October 1976.

ACE was generally a success for SAC copilots. It gave them a renewed sense of value as pilots, encouraging them to make piloting decisions that otherwise were made for them by their aircraft commander. Indeed, for decades SAC copilots were little more than checklist readers and fuel panel operators, and were seen by many (along with B-52 copilots) as the bottom of the barrel from undergraduate pilot training classes. ACE flights improved a copilot's judgement which served him or her well when upgraded to a KC-135 aircraft commander. ACE was also a lot of fun, as copilots flew into bases other than the 'home drome' for a weekend, leading to not wholly undeserved criticism that ACE was just a 'gentleman's flying club.' Nonetheless, ACE was well received and its benefits were substantial to both the pilots involved and SAC operations in the long term. On 1st October 1993 Beechcraft C-12Fs were added to Air Mobility Command (AMC) tanker bases and the entire ACE program renamed the Companion Trainer Program. This was short-lived, however, and ended in 1995. By this time the problem had become worse.

'Peace Dividend' force reductions in the early to mid-1990s led to a surplus of pilots but a shortage of navigators across Air Mobility Command. The immediate solution was to assign new graduates from Undergraduate Pilot Training (UPT) to a pilot 'bank'. These were non-flying assignments lasting up to three years, at which time the pilot became an actual copilot in a KC-135 (or other AMC aircraft). In 1994 alone there were 900 'banked' copilots in non-rated jobs. This proved utterly unworkable, and AMC officials subsequently introduced the inappropriately named 'Third Pilot' program. New UPT graduates assigned to KC-135s would instead attend KC-135 *navigator* training, eerily reminiscent of McMullen's abysmal cross training program that crippled SAC in the late 1940s. In true Orwellian double-speak, this would allow Third Pilots the opportunity 'to gain experience in the operational mission' while allowing existing KC-135 navigators the 'chance to broaden their careers.' In fact, this initiative took place as most navigators were being removed from the KC-135 following the PACER CRAG and other cockpit modification. Third Pilots were required to make two instrument approaches and landings per month in the KC-135, as well as monthly systems and emergency procedure training in the simulator, but had little to do while flying as a navigator. The program was extensive, with the 19th AREFW at Robins AFB, for example, having 15 Third Pilots in June 1995 alone. As with other quick-fix solutions, the long-term result of this ill-considered program was an increase in the number of applications to US commercial airlines from dissatisfied Air Force pilots.

Pilot retention and assignment policies continue to plague KC-135 operations. Despite the heavy demand for air refueling assets in combat theaters from Afghanistan to Iraq to Syria and for power projection missions in the Pacific Theater, KC-135 pilots are routinely pulled for 'career broadening' assignments such as Beechcraft MC-12 Liberty COMINT missions, which is at least a flying billet. Throughout the early 2000s, the Air Force has struggled with finding pilots to fly drones, and KC-135 pilots have not been immune to this mentally exhausting but unfulfilling assignment.

Navigator retention following the war in Southeast Asia and during the mid-1970s was equally troublesome for SAC, especially for the KC-135. On 1st July 1975 Headquarters USAF directed that SAC, AFSC, and AFLC determine the suitability of modernizing the KC-135's navigation system in light of the possible elimination of the navigator position. SAC recommended the installation of dual inertial navigation system (INS). Beginning in 1974 a palletized INS (PINS) was tested with excellent results, and it made sense to install the INS on a permanent basis in the airplane. SAC recommended adding the INS but retaining the navigator, in large measure because

of concerns that although the INS would be effective during peacetime operations, the risk of EMP during the SIOP could render the INS inoperable. The navigator could then guide the KC-135 on its route in polar regions through traditional methods, including grid navigation.

During November 1975 KC-135s from the 509th BW at Pease AFB participated in GIANT CHANGE, a 12-sortie test designed to measure workload impact on a three-man KC-135 crew (pilot, copilot, and boom operator). The copilot served as the navigator as well as fulfilled existing copilot duties. Results of the test were clear: navigators made a positive difference in crew coordination, mission effectiveness, and safety of flight. There were in-flight emergencies on several of the test sorties, and the copilot focused on resolving them rather than safe operation of the airplane. SAC strongly recommended retaining the navigator, but reaffirmed the need for improved avionics in the form of the dual INS.

Debate continued, however, as budget cuts limited spending on crews plus new avionics, and other commands such as MAC pointed out that navigators were not needed on many of their flights nor were they used any longer on jet airliners circling the globe. One solution was to retain a fourth cockpit crewmember akin to the MAC flight engineer, an enlisted position. SAC undertook GIANT BOOM, a test based on a flight crew of pilot, copilot, and two boom operators, one of whom would function as a flight systems operator (FSO). Seven test flights at Castle AFB proved successful, and SAC moved forward under the assumption that the budget would allow for the dual INS given the removal of the navigator (an officer), replaced by the enlisted FSO. By early 1977, however, other issues affecting SAC manning and budgeting allowed for the eventual acquisition of the dual INS while retaining the officer navigator force. It would be nearly 20 years before the introduction of the Block 20 PACER CRAG and subsequent Blocks 30 and 40 upgrades that KC-135 navigators were removed from the cockpit. This was not an absolute exclusion, as a small number of navigators are assigned to the special mission KC-135Rs at McConnell AFB as well as other bases (navigators are also still active on crews with the 55th Wing RC-135s, OC-135s, and WC-135s).

Another major personnel issue was not unique to SAC or even the Air Force, but was an issue facing American society as a whole. By congressional edict, women were barred from any military position considered to be a combat role. Since, by definition, the tanker role is combat support, women could be and were assigned to the KC-135. On 23rd March 1978 Captain Sandra M Scott – the first female pilot in SAC – was assigned to the 904th AREFS at Mather AFB, CA. Two female KC-135 navigators at Mather AFB became the first women in SAC to perform alert duties beginning 27th April 1978 (the first woman to perform Titan missile alert duty was A1C Tina M Ponzer, on 18th August 1978).

The existence of women in SAC's crew force was of no little concern to the crewmembers themselves. Issues ranging from billeting to fraternization to the emotional fears of spouses were soon resolved with the results showing a workable solution. Still sensitive was the issue of discrimination, both positive and negative, affecting women crewmembers. Exceptional women fliers – pilots, navigators, and boom operators – had to prove their skills and establish their *bona fides* at levels far beyond their male cohort to avoid the appearance of favoritism. Marginal women pilots were continued long after their male equivalents had been dismissed or assigned to desk jobs, both to maintain appearances and to avoid the sensitive accusation of sexual discrimination. By the 1990s the issue had been resolved not by any institutional regulation but by the crewmembers themselves, as women gained acceptance as fliers always have over the years, by virtue of their flying skills and commitment to 'the team' rather than by virtue of their chromosomes. Moreover, four women have paid the ultimate price for admission to the KC-135 community, as two female pilots and two boom operators have perished in aircraft crashes.

These assignments, however, begged the issue of women's involvement in combat. As part of the SIOP, for example, tankers crewed by women were just as likely to be targets for hostile long range fighters, surface-to-air missiles (SAMs), and anti-aircraft artillery (AAA) fired by enemy naval pickets as were the B-52s, FB-111s, B-1s, and Northrop Grumman B-2s crewed by men. In fact, tankers are easier targets because they lacked the extensive electronic countermeasures and infrared defensive systems installed in bombers to protect them. Tankers are also more lucrative targets. If the tanker is shot down before it refuels its mated bomber, then that bomber's effectiveness is notably reduced and it might well be unable to strike its primary target(s). The same argument may be applied to tanker missions in support of fighters and ground attack aircraft during conventional warfare. During DESERT STORM, administrative battles raged at SAC headquarters over whether RC-135s and KC-135s with female crewmembers that overflew Iraq and Kuwait could log 'O-1A' combat time (as required by Air Force Regulation 60-1), or should instead log combat support time, as women were not allowed in combat. Beginning in 1993 the US allowed women to become fighter pilots and serve in other combat aircraft, including B-52s. By 2016, with KC-135 refueling operations taking place directly above the battlefield in Afghanistan, *every* KC-135 sortie had become, by definition, a combat mission flown by dedicated men and women equally capable of and committed to flying the mission.

The 1973 Arab-Israeli War

Just as it failed to do so at the onset of the 1956 Operation KADESH – the Israeli attack on Sinai in conjunction with the Franco-British Operation MUSKETEER to reclaim the Suez Canal – the CIA did not correctly predict the 6th October 1973 Arab attack on Israel. Similarly, Israeli intelligence and military planners did not respond with sufficient urgency to ensure that Israeli forces were suitably prepared to resist and then defeat Arab forces. Consequently, Egyptian and Syrian ground forces – under cover of mobile SA-6 *Gainful* SAMs – made significant territorial gains, especially at the expense of the vaunted Israeli Air Force (IAF). Fearing a possible defeat as its forces expended weapons with no replacements in sight, on the evening of the 8th October Israel reportedly prepared its unconfirmed atomic weapon stockpile for use, perhaps signaling its American ally that the situation was now desperate. On the following day, US President Richard Nixon recognized this extreme situation and ordered Operation NICKEL GRASS, the US resupply of Israeli materiel, to begin. As events over the next three weeks would show, KC-135s were significantly involved in NICKEL GRASS, US intelligence collection, and the SAC alert that followed the outbreak of yet another war in the Middle East.

Rapidly moving vast amounts of materiel from the United States to Israel represented a profound logistical challenge. Most traditional US and Israeli allies refused basing and overflight rights to avoid the wrath of an Arab oil embargo. US leverage on Portugal, however, ensured that Lajes Field in the Azores remained available as an American operating location and transit point. The impressive air bridge between the United States and Israel over the ensuing weeks utilized IAF and El Al Airlines Boeing 707s, a smattering of charter cargo aircraft, and USAF C-141s and C-5s. From 13th October through 13th November, MAC aircraft flew 567 sorties from the United States and carried 44,636,000 lb (20,246,549kg) of supplies and equipment.

Although the C-5s were configured for in-flight refueling, none of the MAC crews were qualified in air refueling, forcing the C-5s to make an intermediate fuel stop at Lajes before proceeding to Tel Aviv, just like the 707s and C-141s. This shortcoming in MAC airlift capability led to a substantial high-priority training program for C-5 crews in the months ahead, and it was not until 1st May 1974 that a SAC KC-135A refueled a C-5A. The first operational C-5A air refueling took place as part of COLD JUICE I during a 30th August 1974 non-stop flight from Dover AFB, DE, to Clark AB in the Philippines. The 9,211nm (17,059km) flight lasted 21 hours and 30 minutes and involved two air refuelings which transferred a total of 282,880 lb (128,312kg) of fuel. Similarly, the lessons of the October War compelled the modification of C-141s for in-flight refueling. The first C-141B operational refueling occurred on 6th April 1980 when a KC-135A refueled a modified Starlifter on a flight from Beale AFB to RAF Mildenhall.

KC-135As had little to do, then, with the traditional resupply effort. They did, however, play a crucial role in providing replacement F-4 Phantoms and A-4 Skyhawks to the IAF under the overall NICKEL GRASS resupply effort. Two KC-135As from the 509th BW at Pease AFB provided refueling for the first two F-4Es en route from Seymour Johnson AFB, NC, to Lajes on 12th October as part of CORONET EAST 35. The following day Pease AFB transitioned to Tanker Task Force status for all air refueling sorties across the North Atlantic, ultimately receiving 20 KC-135As from multiple Second Air Force bases. On 14th October seven 301st AREFW KC-135As from Lockbourne AFB 'dragged' eight F-4Es to Lajes for CORONET EAST 53. These tankers remained at Lajes to serve as the core of a task force on the European side of the Atlantic, along with KC-135As already in place at the Spanish Tanker Task Force. Operations at Lajes proved challenging. Poor communications, limited demineralized water service (for water-injected takeoffs), not enough electrical power, a deficiency in MC-1A air compressors, a limited number of aerospace ground equipment (AGE) technicians, no capability to reproduce classified papers for mission packages, and some aircraft were either approaching or had exceeded phase inspection time. By 19th October these issues were largely overcome.

Transferring the A-4s required the additional step of refresher training in air refueling for the deployment pilots. From 17th to 21st October, 911th AREFS drogue-equipped KC-135As from Seymour Johnson AFB served in this capacity. The first 10 A-4s deployed on 19th October under CORONET EAST 59, and 12 more followed the next day as CORONET EAST 61. Interestingly, following their stop at Lajes, all A-4s flew to the USS *Franklin D Roosevelt* in the Mediterranean Sea prior to final delivery to Israel. Additional A-4 'drags' took place over the next four days. With the trans-Atlantic portion of CORONET EAST completed, SAC terminated the Lajes and Pease TTFs on 23rd October, following the successful transfer of 40 F-4Es and 38 A-4s. The last four KC-135As left Lajes on 25th October, two bound for Pease AFB, one to Loring AFB, and one to Lockbourne. In total, KC-135As flew 122 sorties and offloaded 2,882,000 lb (1,307,000kg) of fuel during the crisis.

SAC's SR-71A proved ideal for the timely acquisition of battlefield intelligence, although the issue of overseas basing and overflight rights was equally problematic. Existing plans called for SR-71As to launch from Beale AFB and recover at RAF Mildenhall, but the British excluded this option for political reasons. Consequently, on 11th October the JCS directed two SR-71As to deploy instead to Griffiss AFB in preparation for GIANT REACH missions over the Middle East. These 'round-robin' missions doubled the required KC-135Q refueling force needed for each sortie. Ten KC-135Qs deployed from Beale AFB to three locations. Three went to Griffiss AFB, four went to Goose AB, Canada, and five to Torrejon AB, Spain. Eventually Torrejon AB hosted at least 16 KC-135Qs

Table 5-4. GIANT REACH **Refueling Summary**

Mission	SR-71 OL	SR-71	Takeoff	Landing	Total Time	Total Mileage
13 Oct 73	KRME	61-7979	0600Z	1713Z	11+13	11,879nm
A/R Track	Old Barge East	Rota East	Crete East	Crete West	Rota West	Old Barge West
No.of Tankers	1	2	2	2	2	1
25 Oct 73	KRME	61-7979	0600Z	1713Z	11+13	11,859nm
A/R Track	Busy Ralph East	Lajes East	Crete East	Crete West	Lajes West	Busy Ralph West
No.of Tankers	1	2	2	2	2	1
4 Nov 73	KRME	61-7979	0600Z	1722Z	11+22	11,973nm
A/R Track	Busy Ralph East	Lajes East	Crete East	Crete West	Lajes West	Busy Ralph West
No.of Tankers	1	2	2	2	2	1
11 Nov 73	KRME/KGSB	61-7964	0600Z	1649Z	10+49	12,181nm
A/R Track	Busy Ralph East	Lajes East	Crete East	Crete West	Atlantis West	
No.of Tankers	1	2	2	2	2	
2 Dec 73	KGSB	61-7964	0500Z	1456Z	9+56	12,320nm
A/R Track	Busy Chip East	Atlantis East	Crete East	Crete West	Atlantis West	
No.of Tankers	1	2	2	2	2	
10 Dec 73	KGSB	61-7979	0430Z	1432Z	10+02	12,320nm
A/R Track	Busy Chip East	Atlantis East	Crete East	Crete West	Atlantis West	
No.of Tankers	1	2	2	2	2	
25 Jan 74	KGSB	61-7979	0430Z	1434Z	10+04	12,147
A/R Track	Busy Chip East	Atlantis East	Crete East	Crete West	Atlantis West	
No.of Tankers	1	2	2	2	2	

* Two BUSY PILOT sorties were flown from KGSB on 7 Mar 74 and 6 Apr 74; KRME - Griffiss AFB; KGSB - Seymour Johnson AFB

The first SR-71A GIANT REACH sortie was on 13th October, flown by Lieutenant Colonel James Shelton and Major Gary Coleman with inbound refuelings over the Gulf of St Lawrence using Beale AFB tankers, west of Portugal prior to passing through the Straits of Gibraltar, and south of Crete (which was protected by US Navy fighters due to the proximity of the war zone and to Libya). European refuelings were provided by KC-135Qs from the Spanish Tanker Task Force. SR-71A 61-7979 refueled at the same locations on the return trip. Total flight time was 11 hours and 21 minutes and involved 14 KC-135Qs, plus those required to shuttle JP-7 fuel from storage facilities at Little Rock AFB and Incirlik AB to the deployed tankers. The second GIANT REACH sortie took place on 25th October using the same air refueling tracks as before. Seven additional flights took place (the last six exclusively via Seymour Johnson AFB) through 6th April 1974. The missions from Seymour Johnson AFB required only five air refueling rather than the six needed from Griffiss AFB, and the refueling tracks were adjusted accordingly. On 5th February 1974 the GIANT REACH missions concluded and all the KC-135Qs returned to Beale AFB, although five remained at Torrejon AB in the event subsequent overflights were required.

The 1973 October War erupted at the height of the Watergate political crisis. Preoccupied with the scandal, President Nixon deferred the general handling of foreign affairs to Secretary of State Henry Kissinger. By 24th October, the US resupply effort had enabled an Israeli reversal of fortune. The Egyptian Third Army was in danger of destruction, and Israeli forces were in 'Africa' on the west side of the Suez Canal. Unwilling to see its Egyptian client state humiliated yet again by an Israeli victory, the USSR proposed joint US-Soviet military intervention to end the fighting. In a startling démarche, the Soviets declared that if the United States was unwilling to intervene jointly, then the USSR would do so unilaterally. To signal America's grave disapproval of any unilateral Soviet action, Kissinger and other senior US officials declared a nuclear alert, reflecting the extreme seriousness of the matter.

Just before midnight on 24th October, the JCS directed the change from DEFCON 4 to DEFCON 3. Alert aircraft at SAC bases were repositioned to facilitate a rapid launch as well as reveal to Soviet satellites that the United States was taking this extraordinary action as a show of resolve. CINCSAC General John C Meyer ordered 71 BULLET SHOT/CONSTANT GUARD B-52Gs deployed to the Western Pacific to return immediately to their CONUS bases, along with seven KC-135As to join the remainder of SAC B-52s and KC-135As on SIOP alert. Crew tensions were high, and an inadvertent klaxon at Kincheloe AFB, MI, on 25th October (caused by klaxon maintenance at the base softball field) added to the sense of unease. SAC's increased alert status made its point, however, and the Soviets backed down. By midday on 26th October the JCS ended the alert, and SAC returned to its normal DEFCON 4 state.

Post-War Years
With the end of direct American combat operations in Southeast Asia, SAC focused its attention once again on its primary mission – preparing to execute the SIOP. One of the major problems confronting SAC was the selection of the advanced tanker – now known as the Advanced Tanker/Cargo Aircraft (ATCA) – as well as the necessary improvements to the KC-135 fleet. Ongoing demands to test modifications to the KC-135 fleet as well as the need to provide timely movement of parts and personnel to facilities around the world had prompted OCAM to request its own KC-135A. The 12th April 1968 proposal articulated the need for a 'Depot Prototype' for 'flight testing of modifications peculiar to the KC-135A', and cited 16 Engineering Change Proposals (ECPs) which were hostage to insufficient flight test capability, including critical issues such as ECP 342 'Wing Lower Surface Skin Rework' and ECP 345 'Install Modified Fin-Body Aft Terminal Fitting'. Unsurprisingly, SAC declined, saying that 'heavy operational demands' and 'conversion of tankers to special mission' platforms precluded the transfer of a KC-135A from SAC to OCAMA.

Efforts to upgrade the fleet in general were already accelerating, reflecting the increasing age and obsolescence of many components. Between 1958 and 1977, there were 11 major modifications to the fleet, totaling $326 million, or roughly $400,000 per aircraft. For example, skin corrosion on the KC-135 was eliminated by painting the fuselage and tail surfaces with an anticorrosion finish called Coroguard. The first airplane was repainted beginning 7th October

1964, with another 17 by the end of the year. Boeing and OCAMA painted another 200 by June 1965, with an equal number slated for completion by the end of 1965. In 1977 alone there were 13 major modifications amounting to $790 million, or approximately $1 million per jet. These modifications would 'extend the structural life of the aircraft and update the various systems on board in order to maintain the fleet at least until the year 2000.' These included $485 million – nearly half a billion dollars – to reskin the lower wing involving 6,700 man-hours per airplane, multiple fatigue mitigation packages, and ongoing navigation instrument upgrades. With no real replacement in sight, SAC and OCAMA proposed 15 additional modifications – such as global positioning satellite, the Advanced Air Refueling Boom (AARB), and winglets (see Chapter 8) for FY79 to keep the fleet serviceable beyond 2000, including new engines, at a cost of $15 million for each of 615 airplanes and a total of $9.225 billion. One might argue that the money was indeed well spent considering the airplanes are now slated to operate 40 years past 2000; conversely, the money could have been better spent on a new replacement aircraft. In the post-Vietnam era of budget austerity and emphasis on tactical aircraft, there was simply no support for new a fleet-wide replacement aircraft.

The need for an advanced multi-purpose tanker derived from a combination of lessons learned from operations in Southeast Asia, SAC's continuing commitment to its SIOP bomber force, and a growing need to support the aircraft of US Navy and Marine Corps, as well as those of allied nations. Improvements to Soviet defenses projected to be operational by 1980 would require extensive use of low level penetration tactics. The KC-135's fuel offload would be insufficient to exploit the bomber's low altitude range potential. Either SAC needed more tankers to make up this inadequate fuel capacity or it needed new tankers capable of carrying more fuel (see Table 5-5). Given that SAC was unlikely to get new KC-135s to raise its total inventory to over 1,000, a new tanker seemed to be the practical option.

By the end of 1973 no official decision had been made concerning selection of the advanced tanker, so on 15th December 1973 SAC submitted revised requirements for its advanced tanker, stressing the existing tanker fleet's inability to support SAC's current and projected bomber refueling requirements, as well as Military Airlift Command's (MAC's) airlift and fuel needs. SAC reiterated its desire that the proposed ATCA should be a derivative of an existing commercial civilian transport aircraft rather than a new design. As early as 12th December 1969 AFSC recommended the purchase of either the Lockheed C-5 or Boeing 747 for the advanced tanker, arguing that 'when modified for aerial refueling, either plane would provide at least four times the transfer capability of the KC-135'. Air Force Headquarters felt otherwise, and recommended only a modified version of the KC-135. The wide-body tanker was still not

a dead issue, and Boeing demonstrated a 747 configured as a tanker in mid-1972. In January 1974 AFSC accelerated the advanced tanker program and allocated $20 million for its development. By the end of the year efforts to procure the new tanker were proceeding with great urgency (in the face of a prospective $18 million budget cut), including plans to purchase a fleet of up to 150 new aircraft the following year. Secretary of Defense James Schlesinger recommended on 22nd November 1974 the immediate purchase of a half dozen 747s for conversion to the advanced tanker-cargo configuration. These would assess and demonstrate the performance of the proposed airplane, scheduled for full-scale production in 1976.

Improvements to the KC-135 were also forthcoming. The KC-135's ASN-6/7 navigation computer and associated APN-81 Doppler radar had been plagued by a high failure rate. This poor reliability meant that the KC-135's navigation system could not meet international navigation accuracy standards, which limited the KC-135 to altitudes below 29,000ft (8,839m) during transoceanic operations, wasting a considerable amount of fuel. In late 1973, SAC recommended installation of the Palletized Inertial Navigation System (PINS). The first trans-Atlantic PINS mission was flown on 4th March 1974, and test flights eventually achieved 96.7% reliability. Higher altitude flights resulted in considerable fuel savings, some 128,000 lb (58,060kg) per week on flights across the Atlantic. On 22nd March 1974 SAC approved replacing the existing navigation system on the entire fleet with the new PINS.

Plans to acquire large numbers of the ATCA halted in early 1975 after a DoD study concluded that 'the current tanker force can adequately support the SIOP and contingencies both today and in the future'. Funding for the ATCA was completely cut except for a token to study the 'modifications necessary to make wide-body aircraft capable of carrying outsize cargo'. By August 1975 the ATCA's cargo mission was emphasized over its tanker role, as Air Force Chief of Staff General David C Jones informed CINCSAC General Dougherty that the Air Force needed a new wide-body cargo aircraft, not increased capacity tanker, and that development of the ATCA – primarily as a cargo plane – would resume. Simultaneously, the Secretary of Defense increased the levy on SAC's refueling assets by directing it to provide the peacetime training and transoceanic movements of US Navy and Marine Corps tactical aircraft. Paradoxically, SAC's tanker force was being asked to do more with less. For example, KC-135s continued to provide air refueling to tactical aircraft in Southeast Asia as well as to B-52s during early- to mid-1975. In April KC-135s supported Operations EAGLE PULL and FREQUENT WIND, the evacuations of Phnom Penh, Cambodia, and Saigon, respectively. On 12th May, KC-135s refueled combat aircraft participating in the rescue of crewmen on board the SS *Mayaguez*, a freighter captured by Cambodian pirates. Some 20 YOUNG TIGER aircrews provided nearly 24 hours of continuous refueling coverage for the operation. The end of 1975 also brought the end of a major KC-135 presence in Southeast Asia as 17 KC-135s from U-Tapao RTNAB escorted 36 A-7s from Korat RTAFB back to Hill AFB, UT. YOUNG TIGER had finally come to an end.

The ATCA issue did not end, however, and remained controversial. SAC was adamant that it needed a new tanker to satisfy its existing (let alone future) needs, and that the ATCA could satisfy both SAC's tanker requirement and MAC's wide-body transport requirement. On 6th November 1976, Secretary of Defense Donald Rumsfeld approved production of two McDonnell Douglas KC-10 ATCA prototypes. Outgoing President Gerald R Ford increased the ATCA development purchase to six KC-10s, and increased the overall purchase to 91 airplanes. Incoming President Jimmy Carter halted procurement of the ATCA on 19th February 1977 as too expensive and a financial threat to the rewinging program for the Lockheed C-5

Table 5-5. **KC-135 Requirements for Low Level Bomber Tactics, 1980**
(ie, the total number of KC-135s required for each bomber mix and profile)

Bomber Profile	Bomber Mix		
	255 B-52G/H 80 B-52D 66 FB-111A	255 B-52G/H 230 B-1A 58 FB-111A	255 B-52G/H 230 B-1
Profile #1 Low Altitude to Target	655	669	630
Profile #2 Low Altitude to Exit from USSR	878	870	831
Profile #3 Low Altitude to Post-Strike Base 500nm (926km) after Exit from USSR	1,063	1,080	1,041

(being undertaken in Carter's home state of Georgia). Carter also canceled SAC's Rockwell B-1 bomber (later to be resurrected and named the Lancer) in favor of the air launched cruise missile (ALCM). SAC was now without replacement aircraft for its two primary aircraft, the B-52 and the KC-135, both of which were already between 20 and 30 years old.

In an effort to salvage some kind of improved tanker, DoD requested an evaluation of the benefits of re-engining the KC-135. The Air Force took the study a step farther, requesting information on the benefits of rewinging the KC-135 as well as adding new engines. Both of these proposals were ostensibly offered as complementary measures to the ATCA rather than as outright replacements for what seemed an otherwise dead program. SAC released a study on 24th March 1977 touting the improved flexibility and capability of a re-engined KC-135. The study showed that modern engines would allow KC-135s to operate from shorter runways, allow takeoffs at a heavier gross weight, reduce fuel consumption and environmental pollutants, and lower maintenance and operating costs. In August SAC followed this recommendation with a modification program to reskin the lower wing of the fleet. The current KC-135 wing skin was prone to cracking and had a life expectancy of 10,000 flying hours. By reskinning the wings with the same material used on commercial 707s, the life expectancy of the KC-135 would increase to 27,000 flying hours, providing air refueling for SAC well into the 21st century. The wing reskin program, known as TCTO 989, involved six aircraft per month at a total cost of $400 million. Each year 13 KC-135As and KC-135Qs underwent PDM on a 48-month basis at Hayes International, Birmingham, AL, with 18 BIG SAFARI special mission aircraft undergoing PDM every 36 months at E-Systems in Greenville, TX, and took place at the 8,500-hour mark rather than the 11,500-hour point as originally planned in 1972 when the program was first proposed. The reskin extended the life of more than 640 KC-135s, EC-135s and RC-135s beyond 13,000 hours by replacing the original aluminum skin with a more fatigue-resistant aluminum alloy. Other changes included the installation of fuel supply system with fully submerged booster pumps, a feature first used on the B-52Gs. By 27th September 1979 BMAC had modified 166 aircraft. TCTO 989 extended the life of the KC-135 by only 1,500 hours – roughly five years per airplane – at a total cost of nearly a half-billion dollars. Pending completion of the wing reskin, an Acoustic Crack Detection System (ACDS) was installed to identify cracks before they reached critical length. It remains as an exercise for a newly minted MBA to determine if that money, plus all the dollars spent afterward to sustain the KC-135 fleet, could have been better spent on an entirely new airframe.

The re-engining plans, however, were fraught with controversy. Despite claims by Boeing engineers that the first airplane could be re-engined by 1981, Representative Les Aspin (and later Secretary of Defense under President Bill Clinton) announced with pontifical accuracy 'there is just no way that the Air Force could re-engine a single active KC-135 airplane by 1981'. Instead, Aspin asserted that 'the first re-engined KC-135 … could not go into service until at least 1985'. Aspin would no doubt rue this wild prognostication (tipped by 'unnamed Air Force officials') when by mid-1982 nearly two dozen KC-135 variants re-engined with TF33-PW-102s were in operational service. The Air Force Chief of Staff likewise opposed the re-engining program, primarily because of its financial threat to the ATCA. General Jones warned Congress early in 1978 that 'it would cost more to modify KC-135s than to buy DC-10 airliners for conversion into tanker aircraft', a disingenuous claim as Jones wanted the ATCA not for aerial refueling but for cargo and troop transport.

Proposed Variants

Baseline performance for both the re-engined and rewinged proposals required that the new airplane launch under EWO conditions, fly 2,000nm (3,706km) to rendezvous with its bomber receiver, offload 91,000 lb (41,277kg) of fuel, and then continue an additional 1,000nm (1,853km) to the tanker recovery base. Five major proposals survived the initial evaluation phase. Two were based on simply re-engining the KC-135, and the other three assumed a change both of wing and engine.

KC-135P-7: Installation of TF33-P-7 engines on existing KC-135s would increase its overall fuel capacity to 202,800 lb (91,990kg) with a maximum gross weight of 315,400 lb (143,065kg). Maximum engine thrust would increase from 13,000 lb (5,896kg) per engine to 21,000 lb (9,525kg) per engine. The fuel offload to a receiver would increase by 23,000 lb (10,432kg) or the total range flown increased by 900nm (1,667km). A new horizontal stabilizer (enlarged from 500 to 545ft^2 [46.4 to 50.6m^2] at the outboard tips as on the 707) and new landing gear struts comprised the other major structural modifications for this proposal.

KC-135ME: This idea was perhaps the most radical solution to the KC-135 problem and certainly one of the most unusual proposals of the jet age. The KC-135ME – 'Mixed Engine' – incorporated two different engine types on the same airplane. The inboard engines would be in the 'ten-ton class', specifically the SNECMA/ General Electric CFM-56 turbofan, while the outboard engine would remain the existing J57 turbojet. Fuel capacity on the KC-135ME would increase to 202,800 lb (91,990kg) and the airplane would have a maximum gross weight of 317,800 lb (144,154kg). New landing gear struts would allow the airplane to operate at these higher gross weights, and the increased span horizontal stabilizer (as on the KC-135P-7) would improve pitch authority. The 'mixed engine' version would increase offload by 26,000 lb (11,793kg) or range by 1,100nm (2,038km). Boeing's estimated cost for conversion of a portion of the KC-135 fleet into 'MEs was the lowest of all the proposals, with a cost projection of $3.7 million per airplane. Boeing projected a first flight for the new configuration in 1979 with production aircraft delivered in 1982.

KC-135H: To satisfy the Air Force's request for a proposal which included the benefits of an improved wing, Boeing resorted to an accessible and proven solution. The engines would be TF33-P-7s and the wing would be the same as on the 707-300 series of airliners. The KC-135's wing span would increase from 130ft 10in (39.65m) to 142ft 5in (43.44m) with an increase in total wing area from 2,433ft^2 (226.0m^2) to 3,101ft^2 (288.8m^2). Maximum gross weight would rise to 374,400 lb (169,827kg) and fuel offload would increase by 55,000 lb (24,948kg) or range would go up by 2,000nm (3,707km).

The proposed KC-135ME combined CFM-56 turbofans with existing J57 turbojets, but it was not clear if they retained the water injection system. *Photo C1005-3 courtesy Boeing*

The KC-135Y proposal included a newly designed supercritical wing comparable to the 707-300 series plus CFM-56 engines. Not surprisingly, it was the most expensive proposal. *Photo C1005-5 courtesy Boeing*

KC-135X: This variant was a KC-135A with a 707-300 wing and four CFM-56 or JT10D engines installed. The KC-135X maximum gross weight increased to 376,400 lb (170,735kg) while offload rose 61,000 lb (27,669kg) or range improved by 2,600nm (4,817km). As with the KC-135H, the landing gear would be improved and an increased-span horizontal stabilizer installed.

KC-135Y: The most expensive Boeing proposal was the KC-135Y. Costing some $10.6 million per airplane, this variant would use CFM-56 or JT10D engines and a new supercritical wing incorporating the latest technology in aerodynamic design. It would have the same airframe improvements as the KC-135X but have an increased maximum gross weight of 424,000 lb (192,326kg). This variant could offload an additional 69,000 lb (31,298kg) of fuel or extend its range by 3,200nm (5,929km).

As it did over 25 years earlier with the 367-80, Boeing felt that a flying demonstrator was a far more effective evaluation tool (and salesman) than any number of paper proposals. Boeing converted the last commercial 707 built into a demonstrator by installing four CFM-56s on a 707-3W6C, which made its first flight on 27th November 1979. The airplane – redesignated a 707-700 – was registered N707QT and made a grand tour of 15 SAC, ANG, AFRES, and AFLC bases to allow as many pilots and senior officers as possible to fly the airplane and experience the improved performance first hand. The quieter engines were also a major selling point to the surrounding civilian communities, as the roar of jet engines is not always interpreted as the 'Sound of Freedom' at 4:30am. The

demonstrator easily confirmed the value of the improved engines, using 'less runway, left a cleaner exhaust and was considerably quieter than the [existing] KC-135s'.

Funding restricted the total amount of modifications that could be undertaken, and the Air Force opted for the new engines but not the new wing, the opinion being that the improved performance from the engines was sufficient and the extra funds necessary to buy the improved wing were not offset by sufficiently significant performance improvements. Subsequently, the demonstrator was demodified, had JT3D engines re-installed, and delivered to the Royal Moroccan Air Force where it served as a tanker. The 707 Series 700 demonstrations validated the re-engining proposals, and orders for KC-135Rs followed. The ATCA acquisition imbroglio continued, however, until Secretary of Defense Harold Brown announced the acquisition of a 'small number' – 12 to 20 ATCAs. On 19th December 1977, Brown approved production of the KC-10, with SAC eventually receiving 60.

While it may never be possible to confirm, SAC's re-engining, rewinging, and reskinning proposals may well have been *quid pro quos* for the purchase of any new tankers, ATCAs, or improved KC-135s. SAC was desperate to increase its number of tankers and by requesting a smaller number of the expensive ATCA, coupled with an increase in the operational performance of existing KC-135s, SAC could finally circumvent the political infighting and satisfy its current and projected tanker requirements. In short, ATCA could *never* replace the KC-135 in SAC. Numbers alone precluded a one-for-one replacement, and the fact that each ATCA was 'equivalent' to several KC-135s was meaningless when that ATCA needed to be at more than one place at one time to refuel multiple receivers. Still, the ATCA fulfilled an important need in the air refueling community. The KC-10 became an integral part of fighter deployments and other collateral air refueling missions, while the improved KC-135s remained the essential tanker component of the SIOP, SAC's primary mission. The KC-10 had no effective SIOP role in a 'bolt from the blue' scenario. No KC-10s were maintained on alert and SIOP sortie generation times were in excess of the 15-20 minutes expected to be available to launch the tanker fleet prior to the arrival of enemy nuclear weapons. In a generated scenario, KC-10s did play an important role in the SIOP, particularly in trans- and post-SIOP operations.

(Almost) A New Airplane
Eleven months ahead of schedule and under budget, BMAC rolled out the first KC-135R from its Wichita facility on 22nd June 1982, revealing a new airplane with a service life expectancy through the year 2050, an operational life of nearly 100 years per airplane. Although the original intent was to re-engine 642 KC-135Rs by 1993, budget limitations kept that number to nearly 250 by the end of 1990. Unit cost was estimated at approximately $16.3 million per airplane given a 300-airplane buy. By 1995 nearly 400 KC-135Rs had been converted. In addition to the improved performance gained by the new engines, BMAC estimated a fuel savings of 2.3-3.2 million barrels of fuel annually, saving $1.1 billion in 15 years of operations.

First flight of the KC-135R was scheduled for 13th August 1982, but, as with its roll-out, the airplane flew ahead of schedule on 4th August with BMAC pilot Charles Gebhardt in command. Flight test results were both immediate and dramatic. Given a flight profile of a 2,000nm (3,706km) cruise to refuel followed by another 2,000 nm return to base, a KC-135A could only offload 40,000 lb (18,144kg) of fuel. By contrast, a KC-135R can offload 70,000 lb (31,752kg) of fuel under the same conditions. The testing pace was accelerated by using a refuelable KC-135 (61-0293) as the prototype, which allowed

CFM56-1B1

The Air Force ultimately chose to buy the KC-135R with CFM-56 engines but without a new wing to minimize costs. *Photo TW578-97C-4 courtesy Boeing*

Nearly a year ahead of schedule, the first KC-135R 61-0293 rolls out of modification on 22nd June 1982. *Photo 682-694 courtesy Boeing*

Still configured for flight tests, prototype KC-135R 61-0293 visits Offutt AFB for a demonstration flight for CINCSAC General Bennie Davis. *Photo by George Cockle*

the accomplishment of three heavyweight flutter tests on one flight instead of the normal three flights.

Obvious changes to the KC-135R were the new F108 engines, but the differences are far more extensive than a simple re-engining might suggest. The water injection system was removed completely. The old APU was taken out and replaced with a dual APU system. Under normal conditions, one APU provides ground power and starting capability, eliminating the need for ground power equipment such as electrical and air pressure carts. Under EWO conditions, both APUs are used to allow for a quick start. As crews climb the crew entry chute they press the APU EWO start button, ensuring that sufficient air pressure to start two engines simultaneously is available within eleven seconds. Two engine and cowl fire extinguishers are installed in each wing. The two extinguishers may be used individually on two different engines or both on one engine.

The horizontal stabilizers are increased in surface area as they are on the KC-135E and C-135B derivatives. A series yaw damper (SYD) is installed to replace the autopilot rudder axis as the primary means of damping Dutch Roll. Under asymmetric high power conditions, pilot response time to engine failure on the runway is typically too slow to avoid running off the side of the runway. An engine failure assist system (EFAS) is installed which helps alleviate (but does not eliminate) this problem. When the EFAS senses an rpm difference between the outboard engines it automatically initiates a 26° per second rudder input and increases available rudder authority. Under light gross weights the asymmetric yaw is created so fast, however, that the EFAS cannot respond quickly enough. Consequently, KC-135Rs typically use reduced thrust takeoffs at light to medium gross weights which not only provides a significant safety factor but decreases engine wear as well.

Engine maintenance and reliability are improved by the addition of the Turbofan Engine Monitoring System (TEMS), an electronic device which records a snapshot of actual engine parameters during flight. TEMS also records any out-of-limits parameters to help identify the appropriate post-flight corrective maintenance. TEMS means better maintenance, fewer in-flight shutdowns, and improved engine reliability. The electrical system on the KC-135R is nearly identical to that on the KC-135A with the exception new integrated drive generators (IDGs). These generators automatically come on line (and, if required, trip external electrical power) without the need for manual paralleling or balancing.

Strength of the landing gear has been improved significantly to allow for operations at higher gross weights. The KC-135R has 5-rotor brakes with the new Mk.III anti-skid system. Both pilots can now steer the airplane using the foot pedals, while the tiller on the pilot's side (previously the means used to steer) is still available for sharp turns or improved nose wheel steering authority. Use of rudder pedal steering is particularly useful in crosswind conditions.

Fundamentally the KC-135R is a different airplane when compared with its J57-equipped predecessors. Nonetheless, its mission remains the same. Two KC-135Rs can do the same mission as three KC-135As, a lesson borne out during DESERT STORM. One KC-135R, for example, can offload more fuel after flying extreme distances than can a KC-10, since it burns less than the KC-10 to get to the offload point. For KC-135 pilots the KC-135R is the sports car of the tanker community – light weight, plenty of excess power, and few handling abnormalities.

ANG and AFRES

The exodus of KC-135 fliers and maintenance personnel after the war in Southeast Asia created a dilemma for SAC's commanders. The need to utilize all the KC-135s in service to meet SIOP requirements as well as training, deployments, and other missions remained unchanged, but manning had dropped to the point where there were more airplanes that crews to operate them. A sizeable portion of departing KC-135 crewmembers and 'wrenchturners' opted to join Air National Guard (ANG) and Air Force Reserve (AFRES) units, a number of which had an existing air refueling

Table 5-6. **Planned Initial ANG/AFRES KC-135 Activation**

Base	Component	Operational Quarter
Rickenbacker AFB	Ohio ANG	FY76/1
Pease AFB	New Hampshire ANG	FY76/2
Little Rock AFB	Arkansas ANG	FY76/3
Bangor IAP	Maine ANG	FY76/4
Fairchild AFB	Washington ANG	FY77
March AFB	AFRES	FY77/1
McGhee-Tyson AP	Tennessee ANG	FY77/1
Mather AFB	AFRES	FY77/2
O'Hare IAP	Illinois ANG	FY77/2
McGuire AFB	New Jersey ANG	FY77/3
Pittsburgh IAP	Pennsylvania ANG	FY77/4
Phoenix IAP	Arizona ANG	FY77/4
Milwaukee IAP	Wisconsin ANG	FY78/1
Salt Lake City IAP	Utah ANG	FY78/1
Forbes ANGB	Kansas ANG	FY78/2
Grissom AFB	AFRES	FY78/2

mission using KC-97s (both the ANG and AFRES were part of the military's reserve component, as opposed to active duty component). What seemed to be an obvious choice – incorporate reserve units into SAC's overall mission and equip them with KC-135s – proved to be both complicated and contentious.

On 1st July 1961 the 126th AREFW of the Illinois ANG was equipped with the KC-97 to become the first ANG tanker wing. In May 1964 the jet-augmented KC-97L entered service with the 126th AREFW, enhancing the older tanker's lagging ability to operate with existing jet airplanes. These KC-97Ls were particularly valuable in supporting active duty, ANG, and AFRES jet fighter deployments and operations, filling in the tanker shortfall caused by TAC's increasing demands. With the 1965 retirement of TAC's KB-50s and the onset of steady tanker operations in SEA, Guard KC-97s assumed the primary mantle for fighter deployments to Europe under CREEK PARTY.

As far as SAC was concerned, however, the ANG KC-97s were of limited value to the SIOP. With the removal of all B-47s from alert in 1965, SAC's bomber force was exclusively B-52s and B-58s, neither of which was well suited for refueling by KC-97s. Consequently, SAC planned to use KC-97s after the initial SIOP strike as last-ditch Strategic Reserve Force (SRF) assets, believing that marginal tanker capability for second and third strikes was better than none. This was as far as incoming CINCSAC General Dougherty was willing to go to incorporate reserve units into the SIOP. A number of SAC's senior leaders endorsed this limited role, arguing that the SIOP required crews who were always combat ready and on alert. Perceptions at that time of guardsmen as 'weekend warriors', whose military service was always secondary to their 'real jobs', colored SAC's belief that any reserve unit could ever reliably fill an alert sortie. In July 1974, however, Secretary of Defense Schlesinger overruled Dougherty, and directed SAC to transfer 104 KC-135As to the ANG and 24 to the AFRES by December 1978 under the PACER ANGLER program.

Although reserve units would have KC-135s, the CINCSAC was in no hurry to incorporate them into the SIOP, even after they were declared operational and mission ready. Aside from any negative attitudes toward reserve crews, there were other practical factors which limited their ability to meet SIOP requirements. As these new KC-135 units were often located at major airports, launching within the specified 15-minute might prove troublesome. A KC-135 at Chicago's O'Hare IAP, for example, would not be able to participate in some ground exercises, including a simulated launch where the airplane is timed to cross the runway hold line, then taxis down the runway. Unless it was really war, a 'mover' would cost airlines a lot of money and unhappy passengers. In other cases, an alert aircraft

might be at a reserve base with activity limited to drill weekends. To ensure a KC-135 at a reserve base could launch on its EWO mission even in bad weather, snow removal would be required even if the airport or base were closed to civilian traffic. Many of these reserve units operated from civilian airports where 'the sound of freedom' was little different from the never-ending cacophony of jet airliners flying over adjacent neighborhoods. Local communities filed legal injunctions preventing all flying on Sundays (a prime day during weekend drill), prohibiting any noisy water-injected takeoffs, eliminating all operations between 10PM and 6AM, and prohibiting touch-and-go landings. SAC even considered giving a portion of the PACCS airborne command post mission to the Guard, but rejected this on similar grounds (see Chapter 9). Ultimately, these issues were resolved or mitigated and ANG and AFRES units acquired alert lines, but typically only with a single airplane for each unit.

Over the next three years, a total of 16 units each received eight airplanes (see Table 5-6). Although these KC-135s would be under the control of reserve units in peacetime, SAC would regain operational control of the aircraft in the event of war, but the airplanes would still be flown and maintained by ANG and AFRES crews. On 18th April 1975 the 301st AREFS at Rickenbacker AFB, OH, transferred KC-135A 57-1507 to the 145th AREFS (ANG), also at Rickenbacker AFB. The 133rd AREFS at Pease AFB, NH, was the second ANG unit to receive KC-135s. The ANG and AFRES conversion to KC-135As proved to be particularly challenging given the initial plan to transfer some 46 active-duty KC-135As from Kincheloe AFB, MI, and Loring AFB (slated for closure and realignment, respectively). While schedule delays, environmental impact studies, and political second thoughts slowed aircraft availability to a trickle, Guard and Reserve units desperately needed airplanes for training crews and maintenance personnel. The Illinois ANG's 126th AREFW at O'Hare IAP, for example, was authorized to have eight jets but had received just two by 1st January 1977, borrowed from the 91st and 380th AREFS. In addition, SAC loaned the O'Hare unit five COMBAT LIGHTNING jets from 'nonoperating active status' at Ellsworth AFB.

By 1980 the initial 16 reserve KC-135 units were operational and integrated into the SIOP. Mission readiness and capabilities were better than expected, and units acquitted themselves on par with active duty units. That year, the 336th AREFS from March AFB, an AFRES squadron, won the Spaatz Trophy for the best air refueling unit in SAC. In 1983 the 336th was awarded the Holloway Trophy for the best navigation phase during 'Bomb Comp' (a feat which they repeated in 1985). The Kansas ANG's 117th AREFS won the Saunders Trophy for the best air refueling squadron during PROUD SHIELD. The 336th AREFS once again took home honors in 1987 when Crew R-015 was selected the best KC-135 crew at 'Bomb Comp' (see Appendix V).

In the rich tradition of CREEK PARTY, ANG and AFRC KC-135s routinely 'drag' fighters across the pond, including these Illinois ANG Wild Weasel F-4Cs. *Photo by the author*

New Engines for the Reserves

Plans during the late 1970s to re-engine SAC's KC-135s with the CFM-56 engine were originally limited to those assigned to active duty units and was not intended for those assigned to ANG or AFRES units. These units had equal requirements for new engines, however, as well as several obligations not levied against the active duty units. ANG and AFRES units are typically located at civilian airfields surrounded by residential areas highly sensitive to jet airplane noise. A KC-135 water-injected takeoff is louder than many fighter afterburner takeoffs and proved to be of special concern to the community surrounding the airport. Further, ANG units at locations such as Salt Lake City IAP, UT, and Sky Harbor IAP at Phoenix, AZ, suffer from high temperatures and high pressure altitudes that decrease the maximum allowable gross takeoff weight (and hence fuel on board). In addition to noise reduction, benefits of the new engines (based on the proposed JT3D, redesignated by the Air Force as TF33-PW-102s) over the J57 engines included an increase in takeoff thrust from 13,750 to 18,000 lb (61.6 to 80.6kN), meaning that TF33-PW-102 equipped airplanes required 2,000ft (609m) less runway for takeoff than J57-equipped airplanes. Compared with the J57, the new engines offered 12% less fuel consumption, 60% noise reduction, 90% reduction in pollution, reverse thrust, and up to 400% improved reliability.

By September 1978 a selection board had narrowed the choices to three candidates: a refanned Pratt & Whitney JT8D-209 used on the Boeing 727 with 18,000 lb (80.1kN) of thrust, the absolute minimum required by SAC (Boeing referred to this variant as the KC-135RF); the Pratt & Whitney TF33-P-7 with 21,000 lb (97.9kN) of thrust, and the General Electric/SNECMA engine based on the B-1/F101 engine, a six-foot diameter fan with 22,000 lb (97.9kN) of thrust (Boeing proposal KC-135TT). In true bureaucratic fashion, the decision was delayed as AFLC and AFSC argued over who should manage the re-engining program: was it a new acquisition under AFR 800-4 and the domain of AFSC or a 'Class V modification to a mature weapon system under AFM 57-4', appropriately assigned to AFLC. AFLC won the argument, and the program began in earnest. On 4th September 1979 the program management directive (PMD) to re-engine the KC-135E was extended from a single prototype to the full production of 100 aircraft conversions, with the first planned for November 1980 and the last due to roll out in FY85, although this was overly optimistic. Replacing the engines was not simply a matter of swapping a new engine for an old, but involved completely redesigned wing mountings and struts, nacelles, horizontal stabilizers, yaw controls, pneumatic and electrical systems, cockpit controls and displays, new brakes, and deletion of the water injection system. Congress appropriated $37.3 million in June 1981 for the re-engining of ANG and AFRES KC-135s with JT3D engines, and Boeing received the contract for the conversion on 18th September 1981 with a scheduled delivery on 30th January 1982.

Modifications and Differences

The Air Force delivered KC-135A (ARR) 59-1514 to the Boeing Military Airplane Company (BMAC) on 30th September 1981, and the newly re-engined airplane first flew on 19th January 1982. Four days ahead of schedule, on 26th January 1982, Boeing returned the first KC-135E to the Air Force. The first 18 airplanes converted with the new engines were all special purpose KC-135s variants (see Table 5-7). Parts common to the KC-135E and its donor 707 included the engines (including struts, cowls, and thrust reversers), cockpit displays and controls, series yaw damper (SYD), and horizontal stabilizers. Originally the KC-135E was to have the 707's vertical stabilizer installed, but this was not undertaken. The first 18 707 donors came from American Airlines while the next 16 were former Trans World Airlines airplanes. Donor 707s were stripped at MASDC

JT8D-209B

ANG and AFRES requirements to re-engine the KC-135 included one proposal to use surplus Boeing 727 engines. *Photo TW578-97C-3 courtesy Boeing*

and the parts then shipped to BMAC at Wichita, Kansas. The engines were overhauled and other components were refurbished before installation on the KC-135E (see Appendix I, Table A1-2)

The most visible difference between the KC-135A and the KC-135E was the new engines on the KC-135E. Prior to installation on the KC-135E, the 707 engines were modified to incorporate hydraulic pumps on all four engines (707s lacked these on the Nos. 1 and 4 engines). The engine bleed air system was also changed. KC-135E cabin pressurization was bleed air from the ninth-stage compressors on all four engines (707s had air-driven turbo-compressors installed in engine strut forward fairings on two and later three engines) and the 707 turbo-compressors were removed from the strut, although the fairings remain. The intake and exhaust ducts for this vestigial system were sealed shut. The KC-135E retained the 707 nose cowl and engine anti-ice system. The TF33-PW-102 engine included a forward fan and aft core thrust reverser (whose structure and function are described in Chapter 4). The water injection system was removed on the KC-135E. Modifications to the brakes on the KC-135E included Mk. II antiskid system and five-rotor brakes. ANG KC-135Es have been modified to carry an Air Combat Maneuvering and Instrumentation (ACMI) pod, allowing the airplane to be more fully integrated into fighter exercises.

Cockpit changes in the KC-135E included changing the pilot's aisle stand to accommodate the new throttles with thrust reverser

Table 5-7. **Original TF33-PW-102 Conversions**

MDS	Serial No.	Re-engined	New MDS
KC-135A	59-1514	30 Jan 82	KC-135E
RC-135T	55-3121	1 Mar 82	RC-135T
EC-135K	55-3118	9 Mar 82	EC-135K
EC-135H	61-0274	27 Feb 82	EC-135H
EC-135N	61-0330	20 Mar 82	EC-135E
NKC-135A	55-3135	27 Mar 82	NKC-135E
EC-135H	61-0285	6 Apr 82	EC-135H
EC-135N	60-0374	10 Apr 82	EC-135E
C-135A	60-0376	17 Apr 82	C-135E
EC-135K	59-1518	24 Apr 82	EC-135K
EC-135H	61-0286	10 May 82	EC-135H
C-135N	60-0375	3 May 82	C-135E
EC-135P	58-0022	17 May 82	EC-135P
C-135N	60-0372	24 May 82	C-135E
EC-135H	61-0282	15 Jun 82	EC-135H
EC-135H	61-0291	8 Jun 82	EC-135H
EC-135P	58-0019	23 Jun 82	EC-135P
NKC-135A	55-3129	28 Jun 82	NKC-135E

actuators and the new start levers. KC-135E tankers had cartridge start capability on all four engines, but this feature was retained only on the No.3 engine on special purpose KC-135Es (such as the EC-135H and EC-135K). Engine start was otherwise similar to those of the C-135B. Engine instruments from the 707 installed in the KC-135E were the engine pressure ratio (EPR), fuel flow, and oil pressure indicators. Exhaust gas temperature (EGT) and tachometer (RPM) indicators from the KC-135A were retained. An oil temperature gauge similar to that fitted on the C-135B was also installed. One proposal suggested a new nacelle for the TF33-PW-102, enabling the engine to meet FAA Stage 3 noise regulations, but this was not taken up.

The ANG and AFRES were the first users of the KC-135E. Not surprisingly, crew reception to the KC-135E was extremely positive. 'The performance capabilities of the KC-135E are very impressive when compared with the KC-135A. It gives pilots a much more comfortable feeling knowing that at our normal training takeoff gross weights of 180,000 lb [81,647kg], we have ground rolls of about 3,000ft [914m], initial climb rates at four-engine climbout speeds of 3,500fpm [1,066m/min], and available climb gradients of 22%. It is not unusual to see a 15° nose high pitch attitude [compared to 8.5° on the KC-135A] and 250 KIAS and then have to reduce power to avoid exceeding pitch and airspeed restrictions while all the time showing a 5,000+ fpm rate of climb. On the other end of a flying mission the KC-135E again excels compared with the A model. No more Dutch Roll on final approach on bumpy and turbulent days thanks to the yaw damper that replaces the autopilot rudder axis. The most important change, though, as far as safety and operating capability compared with the KC-135A, is having reverse thrust and five-rotor brakes with the modulating antiskid system. They take away virtually all of our stopping problems on landing. Even with a delayed braking [factor] of 0.80 it is possible to stop a 185,000 lb [83,916kg] KC-135E in 3,800ft [1,158m] using full reverse. Where reverse thrust really becomes a big safety factor is on wet or icy runways... you just can't beat our JT3D-3B-powered Air National Guard KC-135Es.'

By 1991 some 167 KC-135As had been modified into KC-135Es, including the four KC-135Ds (which remained so designated), along with 20 special purpose KC-135s. Beginning in 1994 at least ten KC-135Es had been identified for re-engining with F108s, converting them into KC-135Rs. Plans were underway to convert the entire fleet of KC-135Es into KC-135Rs by 1998, but budget cuts, a proposed new tanker deal, and structural wear curtailed this. Between April 1996 and June 2005, 30 KC-135Es were converted into KC-135Rs.

Given extensive problems with the engine struts on the KC-135E, coupled with other maintenance reliability issues, the Air Force retired 12 KC-135Es to AMARG, with the intention of retiring the whole fleet by 2007. Nearly 30 others were grounded, and all were subject to an Expanded Interim (strut) Repair (EIR) program to resolve safety of flight issues with thermal heating and corrosion damage to the engine struts. Repair costs to keep the KC-135Es flying reached $17.3 million per airplane, totaling $1.4 billion for the remaining 85 airplanes. Retiring the KC-135E fleet *en masse* would save the Air Force $6.1 billion. By late 2006, some 51 KC-135Es were grounded for safety reasons, resulting in an annual fleet availability of only 45%, compared to 65% for the KC-135R/T. Congressional politics interfered, however, restricting the actual retirement to just 29 KC-135Es, and these reached AMARG beginning in January 2007. Replacing the KC-135E entirely became embroiled in the politically charged issue of replacing all KC-135s (see below), and by 2009 all but three KC-135Es (delivered to the Chilean Air Force – see Chapter 6) had been retired.

With the retirement en masse between 2007 and 2009 of the KC-135E fleet, all Guard and Reserve units converted to KC-135Rs (the first reserve units to operate KC-135Rs did so in 1991), and they were finally using the same aircraft as their active duty counterparts. By this time reserve units were also engaged in other initiatives designed to improve their performance and survivability. Following their successful combat support roles beginning with Operation DESERT STORM, reserve commanders identified the need for some kind of protection capability from infrared man-portable air defense missiles (MANPADs). Other Air Mobility Command (AMC)

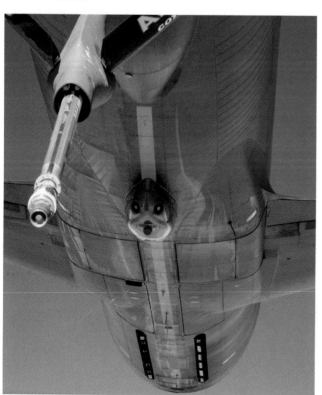

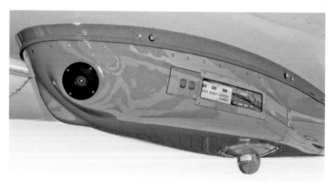

Left image shows mounting location of the LAIRCM pod on the centerline aft of the main gear doors. Upper image (looking aft) shows front and left side of the pod. Bottom image (looking port) shows the right side of the pod. Four sensors detect MANPADs and the laser on the bottom fires, disabling the warhead. *USAF photos*

aircraft such as the C-5, C-17, and C-130 had been configured with the Large Aircraft Infrared Countermeasures (LAIRCM) pod. Initial testing on large transports began in 2006, with full operational evaluation underway in 2008. By 2011 Kansas ANG volunteered one of its airplanes to test the LAIRCM on KC-135Rs, assessing the impact (if any) of the pod on air refueling. The LAIRCM uses a laser beam that can be aimed anywhere in a 360° arc around the pod, disabling the MANPAD's warhead. The pod can be moved from one aircraft to another, providing operational flexibility while reducing total cost of acquisition. Results from flight tests at Edwards AFB showed no adverse effects on either the tanker or receiver. As a result, the Air National Guard and the Air Force Reserve Command (AFRC – previously AFRES), ordered the Block 30 LAIRCM. Any purchases of the LAIRCM pod by active duty units remains to be determined.

Early on the morning of 11th September 2001, terrorists hijacked four airliners and flew them into the World Trade Center in New York City and the Pentagon in Washington DC (the fourth crashed in a field in Pennsylvania). Immediately F-15s from the Massachusetts ANG launched to provide a combat air patrol over New York City, as a Maine ANG KC-135E set up an orbit over John F Kennedy IAP to refuel the Eagles when needed. Operation NOBLE EAGLE had begun. ANG and AFRC aircraft and crews flew some 95 to 98% of NOBLE EAGLE missions. During the first year, KC-135s flew 6,175 NOBLE EAGLE sorties. By 2002 constant airborne surveillance shifted to different ground based alert levels. At a minimum, 35 fighters and eight tankers (KC-135s and KC-10s) were on alert, with more at higher threat levels, including airborne assets. By 2007 NOBLE EAGLE aircraft had flown 44,000 sorties and responded 2,200 times to threatening activities, at a cost of $27 billion.

Despite their inauspicious start, Air National Guard and Air Force Reserve units have acquitted themselves with distinction. They have since gained an additional 18 squadrons and, by 2010, ANG and AFRES units 'owned' 58% of the KC-135 force.

A Shift in Priorities

The November 1980 election of Ronald Reagan as president had significant effects on the KC-135 fleet. Unlike his predecessor, Reagan believed that negotiations with adversaries should be based on American strength, not concessions. He added new stridency to the conversation about America's role in the world and relations with the 'Evil Empire' – the Soviet Union. During the 1980s SAC, like much of the US military, benefitted from deeper budgetary pockets, acquired or started new weapon systems, and enjoyed a resurgence of the prestige it held under Eisenhower. But Reagan was committed to eliminating all nuclear weapons, and in doing so he set in motion the demise of SAC, the end of the Cold War, and the start of ongoing regional conflicts lasting decades.

Prior to the 1980 election, SAC was essentially a bargaining chip in superpower relations. The arcane calculus of détente and efforts to maintain nuclear parity with the Soviet Union as a means to prevent a first strike further contributed to SAC's stagnation. Domestic discord, a lengthy economic downturn during the 1970s, and three presidents in four years (each with a different strategic vision) significantly weakened SAC's combat preparedness and capability. Terms like 'window of vulnerability' became commonplace in discussions about the lack of America's military preparedness, and cancelation of the B-1A and additional E-4 airborne command posts, along with the emphasis on human rights as the basis for negotiation with the USSR and other nations flipped traditional national security strategies on their head. During the early years of the Cold War, SAC crews believed that sitting alert made a difference, that Soviet leaders like Nikita Khrushchev would look at the alert force – poised and ready – and say 'not today.' They believed

that US leaders like Dwight Eisenhower, John Kennedy, and Richard Nixon would, if the situation was desperate, 'push the button' to retaliate to a Soviet attack on America's freedom and way of life. Alert mattered, and the personal sacrifices they made were worth it. Following in the footsteps of Lyndon Johnson, however, SAC crews saw Jimmy Carter as unwilling to stand up to aggression for fear of offending Soviet leaders. Both Johnson and Carter saw 'victory' in the Cold War as a 'win-win' situation for both sides, an outcome that military personnel saw as wholly incompatible. For one side to win, the other side had to lose, and SAC crews felt that Carter, as with Johnson before him, would be unwilling to retaliate should the USSR launch a first strike against the United States. Alert suddenly became irrelevant, and the personal sacrifices not worth it.

This perception of Carter's inaction was clearly his own doing. On 27th December 1979, for example, the Soviet Union invaded Afghanistan. Carter responded by leading a boycott of the 1980 Moscow Olympic Games. On 4th November 1979, Iranian students, acting with the support of the new clerical government, seized the US Embassy in Teheran, taking hostages and beginning a 444-day siege. Carter did nothing. On 24th April 1980, a rescue attempt known as Operation EAGLE CLAW, failed. The abortive mission resulted in eight dead Americans and the hulks of airplanes and helicopters in the Iranian desert. For SAC and KC-135 crews, these signal events could hardly have been more telling. The United States was unwilling to use its military might to confront aggression and protect American sovereignty. SAC, however, responded to the Iran Hostage Crisis on 12-14th March 1980 by flying two B-52Hs nonstop around the world. KC-135s provided each B-52 with over 500,000 lb (226,796kg) of fuel during the 42.5-hour flight. CINCSAC General Richard H Ellis praised the flight, which won the Mackay Trophy, for showing SAC's 'ability to rapidly project US military power to any point in the world in a matter of hours' (The next nonstop aerial global circumnavigation was unrefueled in the Rutan *Voyager*, see Appendix V). Although this flight clearly demonstrated American military capability, Carter failed to demonstrate America resolve to use that capability, and American adversaries around the world understood this.

The same year the JCS created the Rapid Deployment Joint Task Force (RDJTF) that would respond on short notice with conventional weapons to any location worldwide. SAC's contribution to the Strategic Projection Force (SPF) consisted of B-52s, KC-135s, SR-71s, U-2s, RC-135s, and EC-135s. SAC tested the SPF on 22–25th September 1980 at Whiteman AFB, MO, as part of BUSY PRAIRIE. KC-135As also deployed to Saudi Arabia in October to refuel TAC Boeing E-3A Sentry Airborne Warning and Control System (AWACS) missions. One year later B-52Hs flew non-stop from Minot AFB, ND, to simulated targets in Egypt and back as part of Operation BRIGHT STAR 82.

Reagan's election in November 1980 changed this. For some he was the 'new sheriff in town,' bringing order and dignity back to US policy. For others he was a dangerous ideologue, willing to sacrifice social and economic progress at home and good will abroad on the altar of traditional Cold War rhetoric. He restored the B-1, liberated Grenada in Operation URGENT FURY, and, in time, established the Strategic Defense Initiative – derogatorily known as 'Star Wars' – to end the threat of ICBMs and nuclear war. In 1982 Argentina seized the Falklands Islands (the Malvinas), prompting an unexpected British response. To refuel RAF Vulcan strikes on Argentine targets at Port Stanley, on 10th May the RAF requested a KC-135 to be flown by an RAF crew, but this was declined. US KC-135s did supplant the RAF Victor tanker force in European operations, allowing them to deploy to Wideawake AP on Ascension Island to support Vulcan and Nimrod missions. A single event during his second term, however, had the greatest effect on SAC, the KC-135, and the ability of the United States to project power abroad over the next four decades.

A terrorist's bomb exploded on 5th April 1986 at the 'La Belle' discotheque in West Berlin, killing three (including an American serviceman) and injuring 229 others. The bomb was quickly linked to Libyan terrorists operating with the full knowledge and support of Libyan dictator Muammar Gaddafi. On 14th April, Reagan ordered a retaliatory strike, Operation EL DORADO CANYON, using F-111Fs based in England and US Navy carrier-borne assets in the Mediterranean Sea. SAC KC-10s provided refueling for the USAFE F-111s. For incoming CINCSAC General John T 'Jack' Chain, however, EL DORADO CANYON should have been an exclusively SAC mission using B-52s based in the United States. Keenly aware that Pentagon planners viewed SAC as purely a Cold War anachronism dedicated to global thermonuclear war, Chain initiated a series of initiatives that gave SAC a highly capable conventional warfare capability.

In the wake of EL DORADO CANYON, SAC embarked on two highly secret programs – the conventional air launched cruise missile (CALCM) and integration of the Israeli AGM-142 Popeye precision standoff missile as part of the HAVE NAP program. Chain increased emphasis on training for conventional/contingency operations and warfare, and advocated auxiliary missions such as maritime operations (prior to Chain's arrival, SAC had partnered with the US Navy to equip Atlantic- and Pacific-oriented B-52G squadrons with antiship missiles and developed joint tactics to counter Soviet battle groups on the high seas anywhere in the world). The new CINCSAC oversaw expansion of the Strategic Training Range Complex (STRC) with its array of several range sites providing radar bomb scoring and robust threat arrays. Following on the heels of the STRC came the Strategic Warfare Center (SWC) at Ellsworth AFB, a multipurpose organization encompassing intense training programs for line crews, tactics development and evaluation, and, eventually, the Strategic Weapons School. SAC also increased its participation in TAC's RED FLAG and GREEN FLAG exercises. KC-135s were heavily invested in these many initiatives, not simply to 'pass gas' but in the development of tanker tactics in a conventional combat arena, lessons which had been forgotten by all but the oldest tanker crewmembers that had flown these types of missions in Southeast Asia. Although SAC crews still sat alert, they planned and flew missions that had 'real world' relevance, not some hypothetical end-of-the-world nuclear conflagration.

One such program was Low Altitude Air Refueling (LAAR), better known as 'gas in the grass.' Although early results suggested that low-altitude turbulence would prevent successful contacts, SAC eventually endorsed the program. Training flights took place as low as 3,000ft (914m) AGL. Crews wore their helmets with visors down to protect against bird strikes, and were flown in daylight VFR conditions for hazard avoidance. The maximum gross weight of the tanker was 220,000 lb (99,790kg), and the mission would terminate if the airplane exceeded g limits of 0.6-1.4.

For many KC-135 crews, Chain's agenda was seen as an effort to make SAC into the likeness of TAC. The loss of the 'Thunderhawks' KC-135 (see Appendix II), colorful cloth nametags, and calling SAC crewdogs 'Warriors' flew in the face of everything that SAC had become under LeMay and his successors: deadly serious custodians of nuclear weapons and the secure future of global peace. Despite these criticisms, Chain's conventional training programs proved invaluable during Operations DESERT SHIELD and DESERT STORM. Indeed, the commander of strategic air forces during DESERT STORM, Brigadier General Pat Caruana, said that KC-135 fleet modernization, release of strategic assets to theater commanders, global 'bare bones' exercises, and conventional combat training during the 1980s were directly responsible for the success of air refueling assets during the 1990-91 Gulf War.

DESERT STORM

In mid July 1990 Iraqi forces began massing opposite the border with Kuwait, and Iraqi President Saddam Hussein warned April Glaspie, the US Ambassador to Iraq, that he would not accept any compromises on Iraqi demands for Kuwaiti oil and debt repayments. Unaware that this was an implicit declaration of war, the United States responded timidly by deploying two KC-135Rs to the United Arab Emirates as part of IVORY JUSTICE, an exercise intended to 'improve UAE pilot readiness and overall security in the face of potential Iraqi aggression against Emirati oil fields.' Days later, Iraqi troops invaded Kuwait and appeared to be ready to invade Saudi Arabia. The First Gulf War had begun.

KC-135s were quickly pressed into service beginning 9th August to establish both Atlantic and Pacific 'Air Bridges' between the United States and the Persian Gulf. For the 7,000nm (11,265km) flight (taking 16 hours flying time), McDonnell Douglas F-15E Eagles required seven refuelings each, and F-4Gs required more than double that at 15 refuelings per airplane. Nearly 100 tankers, many of them from ANG and AFRES units, refueled fighters en route to the Gulf. This represented a major effort by Guard and Reserve tanker units, with all 13 ANG and three Reserve KC-135E units activated for full-time duty. Some 80 Guard and Reserve tankers and 5,000 personnel were mobilized throughout the Gulf Crisis. Guard and Reserve KC-135Es and active duty KC-135As, along with a number of KC-10s, represented the majority of the tanker types used in these air bridges, freeing the KC-135Rs for duty in the Saudi peninsula.

During DESERT SHIELD, pilots from all US services, as well as those from other Coalition air forces, were able to hone their refueling skills (developed under Chain's leadership) in a 'peacetime training environment', skills which would become crucial during DESERT STORM. As with YOUNG TIGER operations in Southeast Asia, KC-135s also served in a transport capacity during the Gulf Crisis. Although SAC resisted efforts to use its tankers (especially KC-10s) in a purely cargo role, KC-135s nonetheless were a small but integral part of the supply lines to the Gulf. During January 1991, SAC began MIGHTY EXPRESS, a KC-135 operation in support of deployed B-52 operations in the Gulf. Over a four-month period, these six KC-135s ferried 680 personnel and nearly 200 tons of cargo.

Throughout the course of the war, more than 275 tanker sorties per day refueled strike, fighter, reconnaissance, surveillance, transport, special mission, and airborne command and control aircraft in the 60-plus air refueling tracks, several of which extended into Iraqi airspaces. Without these 'deep' tracks, for example, Lockheed F-117 Nighthawks would have been unable to fly from their base at Khamis Mushayt AB, Saudi Arabia, to their targets in Baghdad and return, a distance more than double the F-117's operational range. Most of the air refuelings during the initial phase of DESERT STORM were conducted in radio silence. In addition, encrypted radio transmissions were used with reduced communication procedures to facilitate some rendezvous and refueling efforts. Most KC-135s lacked the necessary radios to communicate with many Allied aircraft, but these were

installed throughout the course of the war. Communications were vital to both mission effectiveness and safety, as the primary limitation on tanker operations was airspace congestion.

Over the course of the Gulf Crisis, KC-135s deployed to and operated from nearly two dozen bases in France, Greece, Spain, Egypt, Oman, Saudi Arabia, the UAE and the UK. KC-135s also deployed to Incirlik AB, Turkey, in support of Joint Task Force PROVEN FORCE. Just as they had been during the war in SEA, so too were basing rights during DESERT SHIELD and DESERT STORM an issue of considerable diplomatic delicacy. For example, the US presence at Hellenikon AB, Athens, Greece, was due to conclude on 1st February 1991, two weeks after the projected start of the war, and efforts had long been underway to reduce the American operations there. Consequently, SAC ordered that the base remain in operation despite being in a nearly 'bare-bones' status. Further diplomatic efforts enabled KC-135A basing at Morón AB in Spain. Most notable among European tanker bases was the American KC-135R detachment at Mont-de-Marsan, France, an *Armée de l'Air* C-135FR base. This was the first time since 1966, when French President Charles de Gaulle withdrew France from NATO unified military command and expelled US forces from French soil, that US aircraft had been deployed to France.

During the 22 weeks of Operation DESERT SHIELD, KC-135s flew 11,500 refueling sorties while logging nearly 75,000 flying hours. They refueled more than 33,000 receivers and transferred 455 million pounds (206 million kilograms) of fuel. During the six weeks of Operation DESERT STORM, a force of 262 KC-135s flew an impressive 17,000 sorties over 66,000 flying hours. KC-135s refueled almost 52,000 receivers and offloaded 812 million pounds (368 million kilograms) of fuel, numbers equivalent to a year's worth of operations in Southeast Asia. Even more impressive was the 30-year old Stratotanker's operational record: not one air refueling was missed for reasons other than weather. If a KC-135 'broke', there was another to take its place; KC-135 mission capable rates exceeded 90%.

The Gulf War offered substantial lessons for the future of aerial refueling. As the official *Gulf War Air Power Survey* recounts, 'the success of the aerial attacks also depended on the ability to mass formations of aircraft, made possible by an extensive network of aerial refueling KC-135 aircraft. High technology played a crucial role, but just as crucial was the ability to employ nearly 200 tankers at a time, organize and maneuver large attack formations, stage large airlifts routinely, and conduct continuous aircraft carrier operations …'. All of these efforts were heavily dependent upon the availability of air refueling, which, by virtue of sheer numbers, meant mostly KC-135s (US Navy, Marine, and Coalition forces tankers flew more than 4,000 sorties, while USAF KC-135s, KC-10s and HC-130s flew more than 15,000 air refueling sorties). The *Survey* continued: 'The … KC-135R made disproportionate contributions to the refueling effort … because of the increased tactical flexibility bestowed by its highly fuel-efficient turbofan engines.'

The Gulf War also highlighted a number of shortcomings and inadequacies within the fleet of KC-135s. These included the need for basket adapters (BDAs) for KC-135s to refuel probe-equipped aircraft, and a keen awareness that KC-135A and KC-135Q performance was 'marginal' and wholly dependent upon the availability of demineralized water for wet takeoffs necessary at high gross weights in hot temperatures. Further, in terms of mission capability, it took two KC-135As or KC-135Qs to replace a single KC-135R, and operating locations for these 'Steam Jets' were limited to bases without noise or pollution restrictions.

End of the Cold War

On 27th September 1991, along with guests from the UK, I joined an old friend and EC-135 'back-ender' on a visit to the SAC underground command post. Our private tour started late that evening, ironically, as every television in the facility was tuned to President George H W Bush's historic address directing that all US strategic bombers immediately stand down from their alert posture. ICBMs, airborne command posts, and tankers would likewise come off alert. The following day US Secretary of Defense Dick Cheney signed the order implementing Bush's directive. By 3pm on 28th September, SAC's bombers, tankers, and ICBMs were off alert. In his address President Bush also announced the end of SAC and the formation of a new command, designated the United States Strategic Command (STRATCOM). This new command would have no assets of its own, but, in the event of increasing tensions, would assume operational control over all US nuclear offensive alert systems, including ballistic missile submarines. Founded on 21st March 1946 with General George Kenney as its first commander, Strategic Air Command was inactivated 1st June 1992. General George L 'Lee' Butler, the last CINCSAC, became STRATCOM's first commander.

On Christmas Day 1991, Mikhail Gorbachev resigned as President of the USSR, and in compliance with the 8th December Belavezha Accord, the Soviet Union ceased to exist. The Cold War was over.

Fifty years of Cold War conflicts using conventional weapons demonstrated that nuclear weapons were militarily irrelevant except in the ultimate nuclear holocaust. With the dissolution of the Soviet Union the nuclear deadlock evaporated, and without an equivalent nuclear threat to replace the USSR, the need for Strategic Air Command disappeared as well.

The ensuing years would see changes to the KC-135 fleet as radical as those nearly 40 years earlier when the jet-powered KC-135 replaced the piston-powered KC-97 and KB-50. Terms like 'tanker shortfall', 'third pilot', 'Composite Wing', 'privatization', and 'multi-point tanker' entered the military lexicon. Broadly speaking, the mission of the KC-135 – aerial refueling – remained the same. What changed was how the tankers and their crews were expected to accomplish this mission. Base closures coupled with force reductions in manpower and spending spelled the end for the KC-135A. KC-135As not scheduled for conversion to KC-135Rs or KC-135Es were retired to AMARG, some were converted to KC-135Rs and transferred to foreign countries, and the remainder stripped for parts and scrapped.

With the end of SAC, KC-135s were assigned primarily to Air Mobility Command (AMC), a decision which Air Force Chief of Staff General Merrill A 'Tony' McPeak later regretted. 'It was a mistake not to put all tankers at Langley' under the control of Air Combat Command (ACC) he said in an interview after he retired, 'there is no capability more critical to theater air warfare than air refueling.' A few KC-135s were assigned to ACC as part of the new Composite Wing (CW) strategy. Either way, this represented a material change not only in the way things were done but in the way the new commands took care of their people. Tanker crews assigned to AMC found themselves immersed in a 'laid-back transport' culture, and their mission changed accordingly. Modifications to KC-135s included rollers to allow easier loading of palletized container cargo. As Lockheed C-141s were grounded for wing cracks due to the stressful conditions inherent in heavyweight cargo flights, KC-135s were pressed into service to supplant the Starlifter's decreased capacity. The KC-135 has never been well suited for use as a cargo transport and its use as a transport reduced its useful life as a tanker (see Chapter 7). There was a significant cultural shift, and SAC personnel found it difficult to assimilate to the AMC way of doing things after decades of operations infused with a sense of urgency and commitment 'to be there.'

KC-135 crews assigned to ACC's composite wings faced equal challenges. Although co-located with the fighters and strike aircraft they would refuel during a crisis, a benefit which resulted in improved training, tanker crews were typically the 'low men on the totem pole' in terms of promotions, job recommendations, and other personnel benefits. With the demise of SAC, the Air Force had become a 'fighter pilot's world', and tanker crews were clearly on the margins. Navigators, in particular, were 'chased out' of the Air Force through myopic involuntary reductions in force. Changes within the cockpit were equally dramatic. Force reductions lowered the demand for pilots, creating a glut of new pilots who were still in training during the early 1990s. With fewer cockpits available, these flight training graduates were assigned as 'banked' pilots to non-flying jobs, sometimes for up to three years, before getting a flying assignment (see pages 86-87).

Operations and Relief

If KC-135 crews expected the end of the Cold War to reduce tanker workload and deployments, they were sadly mistaken. The disintegration of the Cold War world order and the rise of terrorism has led to a seemingly never ending list of 'Operations' ranging from short-lived efforts to quell ethnic cleansing in the Balkans to a quarter of a century of continuous warfare in Southwest Asia. KC-135 crews are constantly deployed, spending on average two months in theater at which point they have reached their limit on flying hours. Crews return home for routine training and other duties over the next two months, and the cycle repeats itself with a TDY average of 180-200 days each year. Much like operations in SEA, fliers can accrue anywhere from 600-1,000 hours in a year, hardly the 300 typical in the dog days of SAC alert. Tactics, too, mirror those first used in SEA and honed in DESERT STORM. In areas where there is a threat to tankers from hostile SAMs or aircraft, as in the Balkans, KC-135s fly traditional orbits, well back from the battle area.

In other regions, where the United States has total aerial dominance and there is little to no threat to the KC-135s, such as Afghanistan, tankers operate directly over the battlefield at low altitudes to reduce the need for fighters to waste time away from their mission to climb needlessly to a high altitude for refueling. In addition to traditional deployment locations such as NATO bases and those in the Middle East such as Prince Sultan AB in Saudi Arabia and al Udeid AB in Qatar, KC-135s deployed to Manas IAP at Bishkek, the capital of Kyrgyzstan, a location once part of the Soviet Union. The operational pace is high, with an average over the past 25 years of 45-50 KC-135s refueling 250 receivers *every day*. The impact of these constant operations has been tremendous, burning through the KC-135's lifespan at a pace that concerns even the most optimistic tanker force planner. At the height of these operations, the Air Force retired its fleet of KC-135Es due to structural deficiencies, reducing the total available tanker force. The addition of wingtip refueling pods, known as Multipoint Refueling System (MPRS), mitigated some of this loss by doubling the capability to refuel probe-and-drogue receivers. Two KC-135Rs have been lost in Kyrgyzstan, underscoring the recognition that increased operations carry an increased risk. A brief summary of key operations highlights this demand.

In its first air campaign, the North Atlantic Treaty Organization (NATO) provided aerial support for NATO ground forces during Bosnian Civil War from 1st April 1992 and continued through 14th December 1995. Operation DELIBERATE FORCE began on 30th August 1992 and ended on 20th September 1995. It also included Operation DENY FLIGHT, from 12 April 1993 through 20th December 1995. DELIBERATE FORCE provided ground units to prevent massacres by Bosnian Serbs of Bosnian Muslims and Croats, and DENY FLIGHT enforced the United Nations no-fly zone over Bosnia and Herzegovina. A dozen KC-135s operated primarily from Pisa, Italy, flying 265 air refueling sorties, some 69.2% of all tanker missions. KC-135s also operated from NAS Sigonella, Sicily, and Istres, France. KC-135s from RAF Mildenhall flew 108 sorties pending the arrival of a KC-10 contingent. On 28th February 1994, KC-135s refueled NATO's first aerial combat mission, when a NATO E-3 vectored two US F-16s to attack a flight of five Soko J-21 Jastrebs (one F-16 shot down three of the J-21s and the other F-16 accounted for one other, the first triple kill since 10th May 1972 by US Navy aces Randy Cunningham and Willie Driscoll).

When it appeared in 1998 that the Iraqis were not cooperating with UN-approved weapons inspectors, US President Bill Clinton ordered strikes against key Iraqi facilities. B-52s based at Diego Garcia launched CALCMs on missions from 16-19th December 1998. B-1s

MPRS eliminated the need for the BDA to refuel probe-and-drogue receivers while retaining the ability to refuel boom receivers on the same sortie. Only 20 KC-135Rs are so configured. *Top photo courtesy Boeing, middle and bottom photo Josh Kaiser*

flew non-stop missions from Ellsworth AFB. Critics charged that the attacks were unnecessary and were a distraction from Clinton's domestic scandal – he was impeached on 19th December for lying under oath.

In an effort to remove Serbian forces from Kosovo, where they had been conducting attacks against ethnic Albanians, NATO authorized military action. US air operations took place as part of

Operation ALLIED FORCE, lasting from 24th March 1999 through 10th June 1999.

The terrorist attacks on New York City and Washington, DC, on 11th September 2001 resulted in two major efforts – Operation NOBLE EAGLE which provided aerial protection for US territory, and Operation ENDURING FREEDOM which launched the Global War on Terrorism (GWOT) and a decade-long hunt for the mastermind of the attacks, Osama bin Laden. ANG and AFRC KC-135s covered nearly all the refueling requirements of NOBLE EAGLE (see above). Active duty and reserve component KC-135s refueled US and allied aircraft on GWOT missions not only over Afghanistan but the Philippines, the Horn of Africa, and even Central America. Operation ENDURING FREEDOM began on 7th October 2001 and lasted through 28th December 2014. At its peak phase between October 2001 and February 2002, tankers flew more than 5,000 sorties. Offload numbers were comparable to those from Southeast Asia. In 2006, for example, KC-135s refueled 42,083 receivers with 871 million pounds (395 million kilograms). By 2008 this reached a high point of 86,288 receivers and 1.1 billion pounds (499 million kilograms). Over the last six years of Operation ENDURING FREEDOM, KC-135s refueled 441,070 receivers and delivered 5.9 billion pounds (2.68 billion kilograms) of fuel.

In addition to US military operations in Afghanistan in response to the 11th September 2001 attacks, President George W Bush directed military action against Iraq, ostensibly because of links between Saddam Hussein and the al Qaeda terrorists who executed the attacks. Moreover, the Bush administration argued that Hussein had a mature weapons of mass destruction (WMD) program which needed to be destroyed. On 19th March 2003, Operation IRAQI FREEDOM began with its 'shock and awe' assault. IRAQI FREEDOM continued until 1st September 2010, when it was renamed Operation NEW DAWN. During the seven years, no WMDs were found, Hussein was captured and executed, and the country left in political turmoil. A total of 149 KC-135s and 33 KC-10s completed 6,193 sorties during the main phase of IRAQI FREEDOM and off-loaded 376.4 million pounds (170.7 million kilograms) of fuel.

Civil war in Libya in early 2011 prompted NATO and European nations to intervene on behalf of forces in opposition to Muammar Gaddafi. The US portion of the mission was Operation ODYSSEY DAWN, and lasted from 19-31st March 2011, at which time it was subsumed under Operation UNIFIED PROTECTOR, ending 11th October 2011. Coalition airpower enforced a no fly zone, and KC-135s refueled combat aircraft, including B-1s which flew non-stop from Ellsworth AFB, SD. Air refueling was critical to the success of each mission. Fighter sorties flown from Europe 'averaged eight hours and required five air refuelings to generate just one hour on station.' Some 34 Active duty, ANG, and AFRC KC-135Rs took part in what became known as the Calico Wing, and delivered more than 17 million pounds (7.7 million kilograms) of fuel. Total cost of ODYSSEY DAWN was $1.2 billion, and, despite jingoistic claims of 'victory' that appeared in some aviation magazines, by 2016 Libya remains embroiled in civil war and a fight against forces loyal to the militant group Islamic State in Iraq and the Levant (ISIL).

The onset of civil war in Syria in 2011 led to the collapse of effective control over large regions of Syria. Over the ensuing three years, forces loyal to Syrian President Bashir al-Assad fought to preserve his authority, aided indirectly by Russian support and later direct Russian military intervention. The concurrent rise of the ISIL sought to establish an Islamic caliphate in territory encompassing portions of both Iraq and Syria. They exploited sectarian unrest and the absence of any effective state control to impose a fundamentalist Islamic regime based on strict Sunni interpretation of Sharia law,

provoking a huge humanitarian crisis and a massive efflux of refugees to Europe. In response and in conjunction with a multinational coalition, the United States initiated Operation INHERENT RESOLVE to destroy ISIL forces. Beginning in June 2014 in Iraq and in September 2014 in Syria, coalition aircraft conducted some 11,000 air strikes by 2016, nearly 80% of these by the United States, nearly all of which required aerial refueling. As of 1st August 2015, USAF KC-135Rs had offloaded 557 million pounds (253 million kilograms) over 8,900 sorties.

A Troubled Replacement

Retiring the KC-135E portended a bright future for the KC-135 replacement. In a novel 2003 approach, Boeing offered the Air Force a 'lease-to-buy' option on 100 KC-767s. Each new airplane would cost $138.7 million, with a buyout fee of an additional $40 million per jet. Air Force Secretary Edward C Aldridge and Defense Secretary Donald Rumsfeld approved the deal, with the intent to purchase even more airplanes beyond the first 100. Senator John McCain objected, however, arguing that the proposed agreement was little more than 'corporate welfare' to sustain Boeing following its slump in sales in the wake of the 9/11 attacks. Instead, McCain wanted more funding to repair the KC-135E fleet, which suffered from engine strut and other safety of flight issues. The KC-767's superior performance, however, plus the capability to carry refueling pods for probe-and-drogue receivers, swayed the decision in favor of the new airplane.

The deal, however, quickly fell apart in scandal. Boeing fired its chief financial officer and a vice president – Darlene A 'Ann' Druyun – amid evidence that Druyun have inappropriately influenced the KC-767 acquisition decision while she was still employed by the Pentagon. A new tanker competition followed, with Boeing and the European Aeronautic Defense and Space Company (EADS) and its North American partner Northrop-Grumman as the primary contenders. After a bitter and protracted competition, the Air Force selected the EADS design based on the A330 MRTT. Boeing immediately contested the decision, claiming that the A330, which was larger than the 767, was designed to replace the smaller KC-135E and was instead suited as a KC-10 replacement. Had Boeing known this, they would have included a 777 proposal. Pentagon officials replied that EADS simply exceeded the minimum specifications, which Boeing's proposal did not, but that EADS received no special credit for this extra size and capability. Air Force officials, however, privately favored the smaller 767 because they needed more airplanes in theater, and that meant the A330 was constrained by limited ramp space. Both companies emphasized that the airplanes would be built in the United States, defusing criticism that the EADS choice favored European workers at the expense of American security. In an 18th June 2008 report, the Government Accounting Office (GAO) overturned the tanker competition, saying that it found 'a number of significant errors' that 'could have affected the outcome of what was a close competition,' but denied a number of Boeing's other claims of unfair treatment in the KC-X contest. A new competition began on 24th September 2009, and on 24th February 2011 the Air Force selected Boeing's KC-767, now redesignated as KC-46.

Pending the KC-46's operational readiness, KC-135Rs have continued in service, although the total number of KC-135Rs available decreased. On 20th June 2012, the first KC-135R – 61-0319 – was retired to AMARG, and subsequently underwent disassembly to determine the structural status of the KC-135R fleet. Beginning with KC-135R 61-0312 on 21st February 2013, an additional 12 KC-135Rs have been retired, leaving some 415 KC-135Rs and KC-135Ts in service until 2040.

OTHER KC-135 VARIANTS

KC-135A/E/R (ARR)

SAC's tanker capability reached its maturity during the era of the B-47/KC-97 duo, and the core assumption was that after refueling a B-47 that the KC-97 would either land somewhere to be refuelled and regenerated for a subsequent sortie, or, most likely, would crash somewhere in the ocean or the Arctic. At no time was there any serious discussion about equipping a tanker – especially the new jet KC-135A – with an in-flight refueling capability. After all, SAC officials argued, there was no point in sending a tanker to refuel another tanker which would then refuel a bomber. It was far easier to send two tankers to refuel the bomber, which likely needed the extra gas anyway. As former special-mission '135s were demodified into tankers they retained their in-flight refueling (IFR) capability, but SAC planners simply didn't know what to do with them; there was no need for these special tankers in the SIOP. As the USAF single manager for air refueling, however, not all of SAC's receivers were bombers, and the value of a refuelable tanker became readily apparent (but not always fully appreciated).

Between 1973 and 1976 one EC-135A, two EC-135Ps, three RC-135Ds, one KC-135A and two KC-135R reconnaissance airplanes were demodified into KC-135A tankers but retained the IFR system installed when they were converted into air refueling receiver (ARR) special purpose airplanes. The official designation for these airplanes remained KC-135A (and later KC-135E and KC-135R), but they were colloquially distinguished from standard KC-135As by several unofficial designations such as 'KC-135A(RT)' which stood for 'refuelable tanker' – or the popular but equally unofficial 'RT-135'. They were also known as 'Christine' tankers, after Christine Jorgensen, the world's first successful sex-change patient, a reference to the airplanes' 'AC-DC' ability to switch roles and receive as well as give fuel. As far as SAC was concerned, however, the airplanes were simply 'KC-135As' and had no special designation to denote their ARR capability. They are referred to in this book as 'KC-135A (ARR)', 'KC-135E (ARR)', and 'KC-135R (ARR)'.

E-Systems converted special-mission airplanes into refuelable tankers by 'removing the special mission equipment and avionics modifications associated with the [existing] configuration and performing the airframe modifications and equipment installations required for the KC-135 tanker/ cargo mission.' Modifications to the former RC-135Ds, for example, included:

a. Converting the navigator station from the special mission dual station configuration to the tanker/cargo mission configuration,

b. Converting the HF and UHF communication from special purpose configuration to the more general purpose tanker/cargo configuration,

c. Converting the special purpose navigation systems configurations to the more general purpose AN/APN-99 configuration,

d. Modifying the search radar systems from the special purpose configurations now installed to the more general purpose AN/APN-59 configuration required for the tanker/cargo mission,

e. Modifying the interior of the aircraft to conform to the general arrangement and structural requirements of the KC-135 tanker/cargo mission.

f. Removing the existing special purpose radomes and antennas associated with the RC-135 missions and modifying the exterior arrangement to general KC-135 configuration.

The first full demonstration of the KC-135A (ARR)'s potential came soon after the delivery in 1979 of the first KC-135A (ARR) to the 305th AREFW at Grissom AFB. Three KC-135As and 'two modified KC-135 Air Refuelable Tankers [ARTs]' were used to deploy four McDonnell Douglas RF-4C Phantom IIs from Shaw AFB, SC, to Spain. Benefits of the 'ART' were obvious: ' ... one advantage of the ART is the availability of greater fuel offloads with the use of fewer tanker aircraft. Also, the ART will play a key role in conserving resources. Because of the ART's dual capability, this [deployment to Spain] saved the use of one airframe, seven-and-a-half hours flying time and approximately 15,000 gallons of fuel'. In another operation in 1974, SAC tankers on temporary duty with the BURNING LIGHT task force at Hickam AFB refuelled both mission aircraft NC-135A 60-0369 and KC-135A (ARR) 58-0124 en route to the mission area near French Polynesia. Once there, 58-0124 then refuelled the NC-135A as it reached the orbit area. Now fully replenished, 60-0369 extended its orbit duration by several hours, allowing the collection of intelligence related to a delayed French nuclear test.

Despite this novel capability, USAF and SAC officials viewed the KC-135A (ARR)s much as they did the Air Force Special Operations Forces – a throwback to seemingly discredited Army special operations in Southeast Asia – and of little value as 'force multipliers' in an Air Force increasingly influenced by pilots with tactical fighter

'RT-135s' offered a mission capability that few SAC and TAC planners respected. Both the KC-10 and the KC-46 have an IFR, thanks in some measure to the refuelable KC-135s. *Photo by George Cockle*

Former KC-135R 59-1514 was a good choice for the prototype KC-135E, as it could refuel in flight to test maximum weight performance. It is seen here slowing after its first flight. *Photo courtesy Boeing*

experience over Vietnam. KC-135A (ARR)s saw their first operational use in support of Operation EAGLE CLAW, the 24th April 1980 failed attempt to rescue US embassy officials held hostage by the government of Iran through its student proxies. According to at least one source, a KC-135A (ARR) refueled the MC-130s en route to 'Desert One', the landing site at which the mission was eventually aborted. Although unconfirmed, other sources, including a KC-135A (ARR) pilot who participated in this operation, suggest that the 'ARTs' refueled 'unidentified' assets, although what these might be is purely speculative. These same sources also hinted that for these missions the KC-135A (ARR) deployed to a 'highly sensitive' location, 'from which US aircraft [let alone KC-135s] had never before operated.'

During 1981 KC-135A (ARR) 59-1514, formerly a reconnaissance KC-135R, received TF33-PW-102 engines and became the prototype KC-135E. This choice was not without good reason. It retained the IFR system installed when the airplane was converted into a reconnaissance platform, allowing the prototype KC-135E to be refueled to its maximum in-flight gross weight, which exceeded the take-off maximum gross weight. On 31st August 1982, 59-1514 became an air refueling trainer for 55th SRW flight crews at Offutt AFB who operated turbofan-equipped EC-135s and RC-135s, replacing turbojet-equipped KC-135A (ARR) 58-0124. Using only 58-0124, crews were forced to acquire their initial proficiency in a turbojet, acquire and maintain operational proficiency in a turbofan airplane, and then continue to train in the turbojet. The differences in engine performance (such as spool-up time, fan lapse, thrust

available, and need for water injection) all made this a needlessly complicated training program. Initially crews from both the 2nd ACCS and the 38th SRS flew '514' for pilot proficiency, and the 38th SRS used it for occasional deployment flights to operating locations or to carry replacement parts or maintenance crews. The 22nd April 1988 arrival of TC-135W 62-4129 eliminated the general need for crews from the 38th SRS to use 59-1514, although they continued to fly the airplane on an infrequent basis. In 1997 it was sent to PDM at Hayes in Birmingham, AL, and determined to be suffering from irreparable corrosion and written off on 6th November 1997 and subsequently scrapped.

As with the first KC-135E conversion, the first KC-135A to be converted into a KC-135R was KC-135A (ARR) 61-0293 represents perhaps the ultimate evolution of the KC-135 airframe and powerplant especially with ongoing avionics upgrades. The increased performance, range, and fuel capacity of the KC-135R (ARR) can, under most conditions, surpass that of the KC-10, especially on long-range missions. All of the KC-135R (ARR)s were originally assigned to the 305th AREFW at Grissom AFB except 61-0293 which remained with the 22nd AREFW at McConnell AFB as it became the inaugural KC-135R wing. With the closure of Grissom AFB in 1993, the KC-135R (ARR)s were transferred to the 19th ARW at Robins AFB, GA, where they were also used as air refueling proficiency trainers for the EC-135N and EC-135Y Central Command (CENTCOM) airborne command posts. The airplanes were again transferred in 1994 to the 22nd ARW at McConnell AFB, where they remain.

All eight refuelable KC-135Rs are currently assigned to the 22nd ARW at McConnell AFB. *Photo by Brian Rogers*

Table 5-8. **Special Capability KC-135R/Ts**

Special Operations Aircraft (SOAR)

58-0011	58-0065	59-1511	60-0356	61-0293	62-3554	63-7995
58-0018	58-0124	60-0313	60-0357	62-3534	62-3569	63-8002
58-0042	58-0126	60-0343	60-0362	62-3545		

MPRS Configured Aircraft

57-1440	58-0035	59-1486	59-1515	61-0267	62-3541	63-8025
57-1483	58-0118	59-1508	60-0333	61-0311	62-3551	63-8871
58-0016	59-1476	59-1511	60-0355	62-3499	63-8008	

With the rise in US and allied special operations missions, the KC-135R (ARR)s finally found their calling. They are among the 22 KC-135s configured for Special Operations Aerial Refueling (SOAR). Moreover, KC-135R (ARR) pilots master receiver air refueling, facilitating cross-training opportunities into C-17s, for example, much like their earlier counterparts learned receiver refueling before transferring to RC-135s or EC-135s. As with all of the SOAR KC-135s, the KC-135R (ARR)s carry a navigator on operational missions (all KC-135 navigator operational training is conducted at the 22nd ARW).

Special operation missions remain highly classified, both in terms of mission objectives as well as procedures and capabilities. One example that reflects the extraordinary value of the air refuelable tankers took place over Afghanistan as part of Operation ENDURING FREEDOM. When A-10s conducting close air support of US and allied troops in contact with Taliban forces ran low on fuel, they normally had to leave the area, climb to air refueling altitudes (say, FL240B260) and proceed to the refueling anchor area, refuel, and then return, losing valuable 'in contact' time and putting friendly ground forces at risk. KC-135R (ARR)s radically changed this operational equation. They fly closer to the areas where the A-10s operate and at substantially lower altitudes [say 8,000ft (2,438m) AGL]. This allows the A-10s to cycle quickly one at a time to the tanker, flying only a short distance with minimal time wasted climbing to a higher altitude. The presence of the navigator ensures precision route planning while flying among the mountainous terrain in Afghanistan, as well as enhancing crew coordination and mission situational awareness. Although any KC-135R could do this, the advantage of the KC-135R (ARR) is that once it has depleted its on-board fuel load, it need not return the 1,074nm (1,989km) to its home base at al-Udeid AB, Qatar, for ground refueling and then return. Instead, it can quickly refuel in flight from any of the aerial stand-by tankers and then return to a closer location and lower altitude where it can be ready to support ground attack aircraft or special mission C-130s.

In retrospect it would be easy to argue that the failure of Air Force planners to anticipate the value of an IFR-capable tanker was an egregious error. The KC-10 and KC-46 were both designed *ab initio* as air refuelable, and other nations were equally prescient with airplanes like the RAF Victor K2. When asked during a 2015 interview with the KC-135 Legacy Tanker Team at Tinker AFB if there was any interest in installing an IFR system in the balance of the KC-135R fleet, the planners indicated that there was not, nor had there been, any interest at the highest levels of the Air Force to do so. Arguably without anyone to champion such a program (not to mention find the money to pay for it), the modification would never get off the drawing board. Surprisingly, this missed a golden opportunity to double the size of the IFR-capable KC-135 fleet. With the 1992 retirement of the PACCS EC-135As, EC-135Gs, and EC-135Ls, 14 ARR airframes were available for conversion for a total of 23 KC-135R (ARR)s. All of these EC-135s were relatively low flight time aircraft, required minimal effort to remove the airborne command post gear, and could have been easily docked into the queue to replace their J57 engines with F108 engines. Converted ARR tankers, however, competed with long-term plans for an entirely new tanker fleet based on the Boeing 767. They also had to compete for scarce funds in a post-Cold War budget and command environment that gave absolute preference to advanced fighters and stealth technology (i.e., the F-22). In the mid 1990s no one had the foresight to anticipate the value of a larger KC-135R (ARR) fleet.

KC-135A/E/R INDIVIDUAL AIRCRAFT

58-0011 E-Systems converted this EC-135P to KC-135A (ARR) status by 28th July 1976 when it was assigned to the 93rd BW at Castle AFB. By 1979 it had been assigned to the 305th AREFW at Grissom AFB. On 27th April 1989 it returned to the 305th AREFW after conversion into a KC-135R (ARR). Transferred to the 19th ARW during August 1993. Reassigned during 1994 to the 22nd ARW.

58-0018 E-Systems converted this EC-135P into a KC-135A (ARR) by 31st March 1976, when it was assigned to the 2nd BW at Barksdale AFB. By 1979 it had been assigned to the 305th AREFW at Grissom AFB. On 17th February 1989 it returned to the 305th AREFW after conversion to a KC-135R (ARR). Transferred to the 19th ARW during August 1993. Reassigned during 1994 to the 22nd ARW.

58-0124 E-Systems converted this KC-135A into a KC-135A (ARR) for use as a refueling trainer. Initially assigned to the 93rd BW at Castle AFB, it was reassigned to the 55th SRW at Offutt AFB for initial and recurring air refueling training by EC-135 and RC-135 flight crews. By 1979 it had been transferred to the 305th AREFW at Grissom AFB. On 12th May 1989 it returned to the 305th AREFW after conversion into a KC-135R (ARR). Transferred to the 19th ARW during August 1993. Reassigned during 1994 to the 22nd ARW.

58-0126 E-Systems demodified this recce KC-135R into a KC-135A (ARR) during 1976. By 1979 it had been assigned to the 305th AREFW at Grissom AFB. On 13th January 1989, it returned to the 305th AREFW after conversion into a KC-135R (ARR). Reassigned during 1994 to the 22nd ARW.

59-1514 E-Systems demodified this recce KC-135R into a KC-135A (ARR) beginning in January 1973. In September 1981 this airplane received TF33-PW-102s and became the prototype KC-135E. On 31st August 1982 the sole KC-135E (ARR) was assigned to the 55th SRW at Offutt AFB for use as an air refueling trainer. On 9th November 1997 it was written off due to corrosion and scrapped. (see Appendix III)

58-0124 is the only refuelable KC-135R that was not previously a reconnaissance or ABNCP aircraft. *Photo by Brian Rogers*

60-0356 This RC-135D was delivered to E-Systems for conversion into a KC-135A (ARR) on 4th January 1978. By 1979 it had been assigned to the 305th AREFW at Grissom AFB. On 5th January 1989 it returned to the 305th AREFW after conversion into a KC-135R (ARR). Transferred to the 19th ARW during August 1993. Reassigned during 1994 to the 22nd ARW.

60-0357 This RC-135D was delivered to E-Systems for conversion into a KC-135A (ARR) during 1976. By 1979 it had been assigned to the 305th AREFW at Grissom AFB. On 5th July 1988 it returned to the 305th AREFW after conversion into a KC-135R (ARR). Transferred to the 19th ARW during August 1993. Reassigned during 1994 to the 22nd ARW.

60-0362 This RC-135D was delivered to E-Systems for conversion to a KC-135A (ARR) in 1976. By 1979 it had been assigned to the 305th AREFW at Grissom AFB. On 27th May 1988 it returned to the 305th AREFW after KC-135 (ARR) conversion. Transferred to the 19th ARW during August 1993. Reassigned during 1994 to the 22nd ARW.

61-0293 This EC-135A was delivered to E-Systems for conversion into a KC-135A (ARR). It was assigned to the 305th AREFW at Grissom AFB. In August 1982 it received F108-CF-100 engines and became the prototype KC-135R and was used by Boeing and AFSC for testing. On 29th June 1984 it was returned to operational use and assigned to the 384th AREFW at McConnell AFB. In 1987 it was transferred to the 19th AREFW at Robins AFB. It moved again in 1988 to the 305th AREFW although it returned to the 19th ARW during August 1993. Reassigned during 1994 to the 22nd ARW.

KC-135D

After the termination of the RC-135A photo-mapping program, SAC acquired the airplanes as Command Support Aircraft (CSAs) – 'demodified tanker/logistics support, cargo carrier, and troop transport aircraft', although MAC had daily control of their operations. With some 128 KC-135As moving from SAC to Guard and Reserve units as part of the PACER ANGLER program, SAC argued that using the RC-135As as 'trash haulers' or trainers was an inefficient use of a scarce resource. SAC wanted four more KC-135s, and in 1978 received funding to convert the four RC-135As into fully capable tankers. At least two of the airplanes were later used as flight-deck trainers for ANG pilots and navigators.

Beginning in 1979 E-Systems received all four RC-135As for conversion under program R-Q6076. It was not practical to modify them into KC-135As given the extensive airframe differences (over 70 major engineering changes) between the KC-135A (Boeing Models 717-100 and 717-148) and the RC-135A (Boeing Model 739-700). Notable among these differences were the RC-135A's electrically-powered secondary wing-flap drive mechanism (the KC-135A has a manually-powered secondary wing-flap drive mechanism) and the RC-135A's second air conditioning system needed to cool the on-board photo-mapping equipment. The RC-135As had VHF radios in addition to KC-135A standard complement of UHF radios. As a result, the four converted airplanes were redesignated KC-135Ds.

Following conversion the KC-135Ds were delivered to the 305th AREFW at Grissom AFB, IN. From 1989-91 all four KC-135Ds had their J57-P/F-59W engines replaced with TF33-PW-102s and were transferred to the Alaska ANG's 168th AREFS, 176th CompG at Eielson AFB. As all four had received the new engines, they remained as KC-135Ds rather than be redesignated as KC-135Es. By mid-1995, after the Alaska ANG unit converted to KC-135Rs, their KC-135Ds were transferred to other ANG units, including Arizona's 197th AREFS, 161st AREFG at Sky Harbor IAP and California's 196th AREFS, 163rd ARW at March AFB. They were then transferred to Forbes Field in Topeka, KS, with the 117th AREFS, 190th ARW of the Kansas ANG. During 2007 they were retired to AMARC.

KC-135D INDIVIDUAL AIRCRAFT

63-8058 In 1979 E-Systems converted 63-8058 into a KC-135D, after which it was assigned to the 305th AREFW at Grissom AFB. In 1990 it was re-engined with TF33-PW-102 turbofans and assigned to the 168th AREFS, 176th COMPG, Alaska ANG, at Eielson AFB. In 1995 it was reassigned to the 190th ARG, Kansas ANG, at Forbes ANGB. Retired to AMARC on 19th March 2007 as AACA0152 (see Appendix III).

63-8059 E-Systems converted this RC-135A into a KC-135D in 1979, after which it was assigned to the 305th AREFW at Grissom AFB. In 1990 it was re-engined with TF33-PW-102 turbofans and assigned to the 168th AREFS, 176th COMPG, Alaska ANG, at Eielson AFB. In 1995 it was reassigned to the 190th ARG, Kansas ANG, at Forbes ANGB. Retired to AMARC on 14th March 2007 as AACA0151 (see Appendix III).

63-8060 E-Systems converted this airplane into a KC-135D in 1979, after which it was assigned to the 305th AREFW at Grissom AFB. In 1990 it was re-engined with TF33-PW-102 turbofans and assigned to the 168th AREFS, 176th COMPG, Alaska ANG, at Eielson AFB. In 1995 it was reassigned to the 190th ARG, Kansas ANG, at Forbes ANGB. Retired to AMARC on 28th March 2007 as AACA0153 (see Appendix III).

63-8061 In 1979 E-Systems converted this RC-135A into a KC-135D, after which it was assigned to the 305th AREFW at Grissom AFB. In 1990 it was re-engined with TF33-PW-102 turbofans and assigned to the 168th AREFS, 176th COMPG, Alaska ANG, at Eielson AFB. In 1995 it was reassigned to the 190th ARG, Kansas ANG, at Forbes ANGB. Retired to AMARC on 4th April 2007 as AACA0154 (see Appendix III).

KC-135Q/T

On 4th July 1956, Central Intelligence Agency (CIA) pilot Hervey Stockman took off in Article 347 from Wiesbaden AB in West Germany on Mission #2013. His U-2 climbed to 70,000ft (21,336m) before turning east to overfly East Germany, Poland, Minsk, Leningrad, Estonia, Latvia, and back over Poland. Stockman landed after eight hours and 45 minutes, bringing the first U-2 overflight of the Soviet Union to a successful end. Much to the surprise of CIA planners and Lockheed designers, however, Soviet radar tracked Stockman's U-2 the entire time it was over Soviet territory. The U-2's absolute advantage in altitude had meant that it remained beyond the reach of Soviet interceptors, but US officials were concerned that high-flying MiGs and nascent surface-to-air missiles (SAM) would eventually render this moot. Indeed, on 7th October 1959, a Red Chinese SA-2 *Guideline* SAM (bought from the USSR) claimed the first SAM kill when it shot down Republic of China Air Force (RoCAF) RB-57D 53-3978. Although the RB-57D flew some 10,000ft (3,048m) lower than the U-2, it was just a matter of time before a lucky shot would claim a U-2. After 23 unsuccessful attempts and seven months after the RoCAF RB-57D loss, a Soviet

Opposite, top to bottom:
The prototype KC-135R was refuelable 61-0293, previously an ABNCP. It is now one of the SOAR KC-135s. *Brian Rogers*

Kansas ANG took great pride in airplanes, including KC-135D 63-8059 as a heritage bird. *Richard Vandervord*

The KC-135Ds tended to be 'Alert Queens', but occasionally visited other bases. They were not suitable for Tanker Task Forces as not all crews were qualified to fly them. *Brian Rogers*

Right: A comparison of KC-135Q 59-1504 in Coroguard with tail band from Beale AFB (most had been painted light grey before acquiring the band) and as a KC-135T in the medium grey scheme at Fairchild AFB. *Brian Rogers*

SA-2 finally managed to shoot down a CIA U-2 on 1st May 1960 during a deep overflight of the USSR.

Aside from the political fallout of the 'U-2 Incident,' plans were already underway to replace the U-2 with a more capable platform for future overflights. As part of project GUSTO, the CIA had previously accepted Clarence 'Kelly' Johnson's 1958 'Archangel' design for a new strategic reconnaissance airplane. The newest product of Lockheed's 'Skunk Works' – the OXCART A-12 – would fly in excess of three times the speed of sound and at altitudes above 80,000ft (24,384m), far beyond the reach of the SAMs that claimed Frank Powers' U-2. The A-12 was originally intended to operate unrefueled but the installation of additional sensors increased its gross weight and reduced its available fuel capacity, limiting it to less than an hour of useful flight time. The solution to this shortcoming lay in aerial refueling, but selecting the KC-135 was not without significant challenges. The A-12's PF-1 fuel was extremely caustic and eroded existing fuel bladders and fuel lines. Any tanker that would carry PF-1 required special fuel tanks and lines separate from those needed to haul the tanker's own regular JP-4 jet fuel. To accommodate the A-12's special fuel, the liners in the KC-135's forward body, center wing, aft body, and upper deck fuel tanks, along with the air refueling manifold would need to be replaced with a special ceramic material impervious to PF-1, adding considerable weight (and cost) to the airplane. The actual rendezvous and refueling

procedures would also differ dramatically for the Mach 3+ A-12, requiring additional navigation and communication equipment. During 1961-62 the CIA funded the modification of the initial cadre of KC-135s (determined by the minimum number needed to sustain maximum flight operations for 10 A-12s). SAC identified 21 KC-135As for modification, all low-time airframes with good maintenance records.

The first A-12 air refueling took place on 11th July 1962 during the 24th flight of Article 121 (60-0924). A-12s were still equipped with two Pratt & Whitney J75 engines (pending delivery of the production Pratt & Whitney J58s) so air refueling tests used JP-4. Crew for this first refueling was from the 924th AREFS, 93rd BW at Castle AFB. Originally the A-12 refueling mission was to be assigned the 924th AREFS which was closer to the desert home of the A-12s at Groom Lake, NV. The subsequent development of the SENIOR CROWN SR-71 altered this plan. Since the SR-71 would be an Air Force asset (versus the A-12 which was a CIA asset), SAC argued that the SR-71s and their dedicated KC-135s should be co-located at Beale AFB, CA, so the refueling mission went to the 903rd AREFS, 4126th SAW rather than the 924th AREFS. SAC SR-71 operations were known as GIANT ELK. Combat reconnaissance missions over Southeast Asia and North Korea beginning in 1968 were known as GIANT SCALE, and the program name for KC-135 refueling support for operational reconnaissance missions was GIANT BEAR.

In an effort to eliminate the caustic PF-1 fuel for the A-12, Shell Oil Company, Ashland Oil Company, and Monsanto Chemical Company developed JP-7, a hydrocarbon fuel of low vapor pressure for the SR-71 and the YF-12 interceptor. The eventual use of JP-7 eliminated the need for the expensive and heavy ceramic linings, which were removed and replaced by the standard rubber liners. The KC-135 tankers could burn JP-7, although not as a primary fuel (much as B-47s could burn AvGas from KC-97s). Following an 'air flush' of the JP-7, the KC-135 could then carry JP-4 in all of its tanks, as well as offload it to any receiver.

Throughout the first four years of operations, A-12 and SR-71 tankers were designated simply as KC-135As. On 16th June 1966 Aeronautical Systems Division (ASD) specified the redesignation *en masse* of the dedicated KC-135As as KC-135Qs, although the actual MDS change did not take place until the latter half of 1967, and then in several tranches. Why the series suffix 'Q' was selected is unknown. Using normal designation procedures, the KC-135Q should have been called the KC-135C as the MDS 'KC-135B' had already been allocated to the airborne command post then under development. Given the extremely secretive development of the A-12, this out-of-sequence designation might best be explained by security concerns, or perhaps the motivation for this unusual

KC-135Q UNIT EVOLUTION

The A-12 and SR-71 tanker fleet underwent major organizational changes throughout its lifetime. The tankers were initially assigned to the 903rd AREFS, 4126th SAW at Beale AFB, CA. On 1st February 1963 the 4126th SAW was inactivated and replaced by the 456th SAW, which later became the 456th BW. A second tanker squadron, the 9th AREFS, was activated as part of the 456th BW on 1st January 1970. The 456th BW was inactivated on 30th September 1975 and replaced by the 17th BW, which itself was inactivated on 30th September 1976. The 903rd AREFS was likewise inactivated, and the remaining 9th AREFS reassigned to the 100th AREFW, newly relocated to Beale AFB. The 349th AREFS joined the 9th AREFS on 30th March 1976, but the 9th AREFS was replaced by the 350th AREFS on 28th January 1982. The 100th AREFW was inactivated on 15th March 1983, and the 349th AREFS and 350th AREFS absorbed *in situ* by the 9th SRW.

In 1967 crews from the 70th AREFS, 43rd BW at Little Rock AFB, AR, and the 306th AREFS, 306th BW at McCoy AFB, FL, completed training in SR-71 refueling procedures and operated 'Partial Qs'. These were later reassigned to the 380th BW at Plattsburgh AFB and the 376th SW at Kadena AB. Eventually Beale AFB had both partial 'Qs and fully-equipped KC-135Qs.

designation was recorded but not forwarded to the ASD history office. Still, official Air Force documents record no 'special reason for giving it the Q designation.'

By the end of 1966 21 KC-135Qs had been modified and were in service with the 903rd AREFS – by now part of the 456th SAW – at Beale AFB. In addition to their support of SR-71 and A-12 operations, KC-135Qs and their crews shared operational commitments with B-52Gs assigned to the 744th BS, also stationed at Beale AFB. As the demands on the KC-135Qs grew, it became clear that the fleet would have to grow to accommodate these increasing requirements due to the need for a large number of ready-to-go spare aircraft. Since A-12 and SR-71 missions were critically dependent upon receipt of their scheduled fuel at each refueling point, a ground or air abort by a KC-135Q effectively scrubbed the entire reconnaissance mission. This was especially frustrating if the affected tanker was scheduled for the initial air refueling. Standard procedures called for the SR-71 to take off with 55 to 60% full fuel load to ensure that the pilot could maintain lateral maximum control in the event of an engine failure on takeoff, with the first air refueling scheduled some 15-20 minutes after takeoff. This also filled the tanks to allow purging of air by nitrogen gas as they emptied during the course of the flight to prevent cavitation or other problems. As each A-12 and SR-71 mission cost several hundred thousand dollars, it was absurd to cancel it because of a problem with a single tanker. Consequently, both air and ground spares were required for many operational sorties. The A-12s and SR-71s had to get their fuel, regardless of how many tankers were needed to get it there.

In 1967 OCAMA converted 35 additional airplanes into KC-135Qs, with 20 KC-135As from the 70th AREFS, 43rd BW at Little Rock AFB, AR, and 15 from the 306th AREFS, 306th BW at McCoy AFB, FL. Because of the expense involved, SAC elected not to convert these airplanes into 'full' KC-135Qs, and they were known informally as 'partial Qs'. They lacked a full avionics suite – especially the AN/ARN-90 TACAN and the LORAN A – although the intention was that it could be installed with sufficient notice prior to a mission. Realistically, however this proved difficult to undertake,

Table 5-9. **KC-135Q Initial Distribution**

903rd AREFS, 456th SAW, Beale AFB, California (all 'full' Qs)

58-0054	58-0084	58-0089	58-0099	58-0117	59-1490	59-1513
58-0071	58-0086	58-0094	58-0103	58-0125	59-1504	59-1520
58-0074	58-0088	58-0095	58-0112	58-0129	59-1512	59-1523

70th AREFS, 43rd BW, Little Rock AFB, Arkansas (all 'partial' Qs)

59-1460	59-1467	59-1471	59-1510	60-0337	60-0342	60-0345
59-1462	59-1468	59-1474	60-0335	60-0338	60-0343	60-0346
59-1464	59-1470	59-1480	60-0336	60-0339	60-0344	

306th AREFS, 306th BW, McCoy AFB, Florida (all 'partial' Qs)

58-0039	58-0046	58-0049	58-0055	58-0061	58-0065	58-0072
58-0042	58-0047	58-0050	58-0060	58-0062	58-0069	58-0077
58-0045						

if ever. Of the 56 KC-135Q conversions, 21 were full modifications based at Beale AFB and 35 were partial Qs at McCoy AFB and Little Rock AFB.

The major differences between the KC-135Q and other KC-135s were primarily related to the fuel system and rendezvous and communications equipment. The KC-135Q utilized two single-point ground refueling receptacles – one in each main landing gear wheel well. Other KC-135s have only one located in the right main gear well. On the KC-135Q, the left system services the airplane's JP-4 in the wing tanks and the right system fills the JP-7 normally carried in the body fuel tanks (the forward body, center wing, and aft body tanks plus the upper deck tank). The KC-135Q could simultaneously carry a maximum of 74,490 lb (33,788kg) of JP-7 and 110,000 lb (49,896kg) of JP-4. To account for changes in the airplane's center-of-gravity (cg) during SR-71 refueling operations, 850 lb (385kg) of ballast was added to the lower nose compartment.

Rendezvous and communications equipment differences in a 'full Q' included the addition of a third UHF radio and an AN/ARN-90 TACAN, both located at the navigator's station. The third UHF radio – an AN/ARC-50 known as 'Comm 3' – also provided distance

Opposite page:

KC-135A 58-0054 refuels A-12 60-0924 on 11th June 1962. The tankers had yet to be redesignated as KC-135Qs and were from Castle AFB rather than Beale AFB.
Author's collection

This page:

54 KC-135Ts are in service, 3 of which are configured for SOAR missions and 16 to carry ROBE. 58-0061 is not among either of these special configurations.
Photo by Brian Rogers

'Partial Q' 58-0062 from Dyess AFB visits the 1993 Andrews AFB Open House in the new light grey color scheme.
Photo by Stephen Miller

measurement between the KC-135Q and A-12/SR-71. In the partial Q, Comm 3 was the sole source of air-to-air distance measurement for the rendezvous with an A-12 or SR-71. The power of the Comm 3 was considerable, with two KC-135Qs reported to have maintained ranging out to a distance of 700 miles (1,126km). The TACAN provided the SR-71 with range and bearing data for a head-on rendezvous, but in early use was notoriously unreliable in the air-to-air mode. KC-135Qs were at one time equipped with LORAN-A for precise maintenance of their orbit at air refueling control points (ARCPs) beyond the range of existing navigational aids such as TACANs. This equipment was eventually removed. In the late 1980s a satellite communications (SATCOM) antenna was installed on the upper forward fuselage. Strobe lights were installed on the upper and lower fuselage and tail, although similar strobes mounted on the wingtips were deactivated after several wing fires and explosions were attributed to them. On some KC-135Qs the boom operator had a boom interphone system installed which allowed radio silent communication with the receiver once boom contact is made. A searchlight was mounted in bottom of the tail cone of the KC-135Q to illuminate the air refueling envelope. This feature was installed as part of the KC-135Q modification and was different from the tail-mounted floodlight (TMF) later installed on all KC-135s and KC-135Qs. All KC-135Qs had high-speed air refueling booms.

Refueling operations with the A-12 and SR-71 were unique and demanding. As the receivers were on classified reconnaissance missions, operational and communications security were much more stringent than in routine tanker operations. The dependency of the receiver on the tanker, especially at times when divert bases were closed due to bad weather or were unavailable due to political considerations, made the rendezvous and refueling critical both to the success of the mission and the safety of the receiver and crew. The aerodynamic dissimilarity of the subsonic KC-135Q and its triple-sonic receiver dictated a precise rendezvous, and the actual air refueling was conducted at the limits of each airplane's operational envelope.

There were two types of rendezvous used by KC-135Qs during missions in support of A-12s and SR-71s. Other than differences in timing, these two procedures were identical. The first of these, known as the 'cold' rendezvous, was used when the receiver was subsonic prior to the air refueling, such as for the initial onload after takeoff or during pilot qualification training. The 'hot' rendezvous was used when the receiver was supersonic prior to the air refueling, such as during an operational mission or ferry flight. Under extreme or degraded conditions such as poor visibility or radio silent operations,

KC-135Qs dumped a small amount of fuel, leaving a visible trail for the receiver crew to follow to find the tanker (a practice not limited to A-12 or SR-71 operations but used as needed by all tankers). The KC-135Q's strobe lights helped the receiver pilot spot the tanker in the final stages of the rendezvous, reducing unnecessary delays and radio transmissions during the closure to contact.

SR-71 refueling was particularly delicate and required considerable skill by the receiver pilot to maintain visual and physical contact during refueling. On 17th June 1970, for example, SR-71A 61-7970 collided with the horizontal stabilizer of KC-135Q 59-1474 during air refueling over Texas, probably the result of passing through jetwash or clear air turbulence. The SR-71 lost its nose and became uncontrollable; the crew ejected safely. Although one of the tanker's horizontal stabilizers was almost completely separated from the aircraft, the tanker crew was able to maintain control, pinpoint the downed SR-71 crew, and return safely to Beale AFB for recovery. Normal refueling for the SR-71 was conducted at 355 KIAS – red-line speed for the KC-135Q – and at block altitude of FL260–FL270, an altitude lower than SR-71 crews preferred but as high as a KC-135Q 'fat with gas' could go while maintaining 355 KIAS. Near the end of the air refueling, the SR-71 was at the limits of its subsonic heavy weight performance capability, and often used one afterburner in order to stay in contact with the tanker. Tests with KC-135Rs showed a 20 KIAS increase in the tanker's maximum speed, allowing the SR-71 to refuel at 375 KIAS, a considerable improvement, especially during heavy weight operations. Refueling operations with KC-10s increased the base refueling block up to 33,000ft (10,058m) and the speed to Mach 0.88.

According to an unclassified SAC history, the first KC-135Q deployment to Southeast Asia involved ten KC-135Qs relocating from Beale AFB to Kadena AB between 27th September-30th October 1967. As each KC-135Q arrived at Kadena AB, a local KC-135A would depart for the 4258th SW at U-Tapao RTNAB. These first KC-135Q missions from Kadena AB were reportedly 'bomber refueling missions'. In fact, KC-135Qs were quite active throughout 1967 in the trans-Pacific deployment of the A-12s to Kadena AB. The first A-12 overflight mission of North Vietnam – Operation BLACK SHIELD – took place on 31st May 1967. CIA pilot Mele 'Mel' Vojvodich flew A-12 Article 131 (60-6937) over Hanoi, Haiphong, and Dien Bien Phu (Mel had previously flown RF-86F HAYMAKER overflights of the USSR and PRC). The mission required a pre- and post-overflight refueling with KC-135Qs. Given that this was four months *before* the first SAC-acknowledged deployment of KC-135Qs to Southeast Asia, it is clear that either SAC historians

After hitting wake turbulence during refueling on 17th June 1970, SR-71A 61-7970 struck the horizontal stabilizer of KC-135Q 59-1474. The SR-71 was lost, but the KC-135Q landed safely. *Photo by Richard Vandervord*

KC-135Qs supported the YF-12 program before its military role was canceled, and afterward while in NASA research duty. *Author's collection*

were unaware of the CIA A-12 mission support or they were publishing disinformation. 'Bomber refueling missions' indeed! The final A-12 BLACK SHIELD mission was on 8th March 1968. A-12s had also overflown North Korea three times in 1968 during the USS *Pueblo* incident, all of which used KC-135Qs for air refueling.

Two weeks after the final BLACK SHIELD mission, its successor had its first overflight of North Vietnam, again with the assistance of KC-135Qs. USAF Major Jerome 'Jerry' O'Malley and Captain Ed Payne flew SR-71A 61-7976 on the initial GIANT SCALE mission from Kadena AB in a classic reconnaissance sortie, including a 'goat rope' finale. Following refueling immediately after takeoff, the SR-71 overflew Hanoi and Haiphong before refueling from two KC-135Qs (plus an airborne spare) over Thailand prior to again overflying North Vietnam, this time close to the DMZ to identify supply efforts related to the siege of Khe Sanh. Approaching Kadena AB, the weather deteriorated and, despite a low visual approach, O'Malley had to divert to Ching Chuan Kang AB (CCK) on Taiwan. Escorted and refueled by two air spare KC-135Qs, the SR-71 landed and then 'hid' between the two tankers on the ramp while waiting for a hangar to be vacated in which the SR-71 could be parked.

The intensity of the December 1972 LINEBACKER II aerial campaign meant that current Battle Damage Assessment (BDA) and targeting intelligence acquired by GIANT SCALE SR-71 missions be made available quickly to senior planners in Washington DC. In the absence of real-time satellite data links, this required a dedicated courier system known as GIANT CIRCLE, and involved four KC-135s, including KC-135Qs, when available. The first of these carried SR-71 imagery from Kadena AB to MACV at Tan Son Nhut AB, South Vietnam. Additional intelligence acquired from US Navy BLUE TREE tactical reconnaissance flights and SAC drones would be uploaded to this KC-135 which then returned to Kadena AB. A second KC-135 would then take this consolidated material (and any new SR-71 imagery) and fly direct to Eielson AFB. A third KC-135 then carried this material to Washington DC, landing at Andrews AFB. It took 12 hours from the time the SR-71 landed at Kadena AB until its imagery was in the hands of theater planners in Saigon, and 24 hours until it reached the Pentagon. GIANT CIRCLE began on 19th December 1972, although operational demand for KC-135s meant that the inaugural flight from Kadena AB to Eielson AFB was aboard a BURNING PIPE RC-135C. On 27th December, the fourth KC-135 was added to transfer duplicate intelligence from Eielson AFB direct to Offutt AFB.

For all the seeming emphasis on A-12 and SR-71 operations in Southeast Asia, SAC had similar plans for SR-71 missions on the other side of the world. By April 1970 SAC planned GIANT REACH missions to provide ELINT and PHOTINT coverage of the Middle East and peripheral ELINT missions to cover Eastern Europe. An SR-71 and three KC-135Qs would deploy to Torrejon AB, Spain, with five additional KC-135Qs at Incirlik AB, Turkey. Spain rejected the proposal, however, and the SR-71 and the three KC-135Qs were instead slated for RAF Mildenhall, as were the Incirlik-based KC-135Qs. Despite these early plans, the first SR-71 visit to England did not take place until the 1974 record-setting flight to the Farnborough Air Show (supported by KC-135Qs), and the first operational evaluation sortie in April 1976. When SAC sought to use SR-71s to monitor the October 1973 Arab-Israeli war, Britain declined to allow the airplanes to operate from RAF Mildenhall out of concern that Arab oil producing nations would retaliate. Instead, GIANT REACH missions over the Middle East in 1973 and 1974 were flown from Griffiss AFB and later Seymour Johnson AFB, NC, making for 11-hour flights with six total refuelings (described in the general narrative above). Additional SR-71 missions over the Middle East included flights over Libya in 1986 after Operation EL DORADO CANYON. Four 'butt-buster' sorties from Kadena AB to the Persian Gulf in 1987 and 1988 demonstrated the continuing value of the SR-71 but could not have happened without aerial refueling. Peripheral missions continued from Kadena AB and RAF Mildenhall, especially over the Barents Sea and Baltic Sea.

For all its glamour, mystique, and operational capability, the days of the SR-71 were numbered. Its lack of digital sensors and real-time data downlink limited its effectiveness, and the cost to maintain and operate the airplane and its dedicated fleet of KC-135Qs grew commensurately. With national intelligence agencies relying increasingly on satellites and with senior USAF – especially SAC – commanders pursuing other budget priorities, there was little chance of a long-term reprieve. The program ended in 1990, and the SR-71s were placed in flyable storage or seconded to NASA. An effort to reinstate the SR-71 program came, surprisingly enough, from the US Navy, which sought to station two SR-71s at RAF Mildenhall to track Russian ballistic missile submarines ('boomers') in the Barents and their home port at Polyarny Naval Base. On 28th September 1994 the US Congress voted to restore funding to SR-71 operations. Relying upon NASA's operational research SR-71s for training, six former SR-71 crewmembers formed a new detachment in 1995 for an airplane without a mission but with $100 million in funding. Aerial refueling for the newly reactivated SR-71 fleet came primarily from KC-10s, however, not KC-135Qs or KC-135Ts. Interestingly enough, the SR-71 became embroiled in a 1998 US Supreme Court case when the court ruled that US President Bill Clinton had acted unconstitutionally in October 1997 when he used a line-item veto to eliminate all funding for the SR-71. Nonetheless, money for the SR-71 dried up and the program ended a second time in 1998.

KC-135Q 58-0129 slows after landing at Boeing Field. It is in the 'Shamu' scheme with BB tail code and full color tail band, an unusual combination.
Photo by Jim Morrow via Stephen Miller

The end of the SR-71 did not mean the end of the KC-135Q. In early 1990 there were indications that some of the KC-135Qs would be relegated to AMARG. The rest would lose their special electronic equipment and fuel tanks, be converted into KC-135Es or KC-135Rs, and be distributed to other SAC or ANG and AFRES refueling units, there to join KC-135As, KC-135Es, and other KC-135Rs in support of contingency and SIOP commitments. None of the KC-135Qs were stored at the Boneyard, but beginning in 1993 the 54 remaining KC-135Qs received CFM56 engines and were redesignated KC-135Ts. The last to be converted was 58-0099, which departed Fairchild AFB, Washington on 29th September 1995. Two KC-135Qs have been lost (see Appendix II).

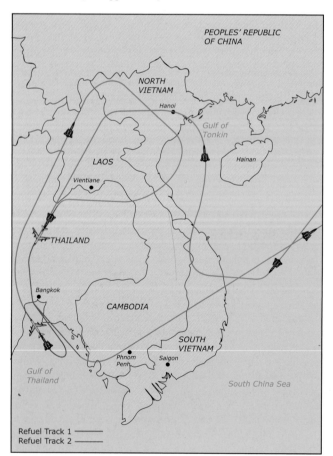

PEOPLES' REPUBLIC OF CHINA

NORTH VIETNAM

Hanoi

Gulf of Tonkin

LAOS

Hainan

Vientiane

THAILAND

Bangkok

CAMBODIA

SOUTH VIETNAM

Phnom Penh

Saigon

Gulf of Thailand

South China Sea

Refuel Track 1 ————
Refuel Track 2 ————

Known KC-135Q missions after the demise of the SR-71 were varied and interesting. One was as dedicated transports for JP-7 fuel. Like the SR-71, the U-2 also used JP-7, and the need to carry this exotic fuel to remote locations in support of U-2R operations made the KC-135Q well suited as a highly mobile ground-based fuel storage tank. It was widely believed that KC-135Qs were the primary source of JP-7 for U-2R operations from Saudi Arabia during the Gulf War, although official reports showed this was undertaken by KC-10s and C-141s, not KC-135Qs.

Refueling the Lockheed F-117 also become a duty for the KC-135Q, although this is not believed to be due to any special air refueling requirement on the part of the F-117. Rather, KC-135Q crews were familiar with the many sensitive refueling procedures required in the type of operations the F-117 undertook. Like its SR-71 stablemate from Lockheed, the F-117 retired while the KC-135Ts continued flying. Perhaps the most intriguing role for the KC-135Q was a repeated, but never verified, 1990 association with an unidentified and highly classified 'black' aircraft. Reports of KC-135Qs flying with diamond-shaped airplanes from Beale AFB, occasionally in conjunction with two F-117s, continued to surface. The KC-135Q has also been associated with the 1990 BLACK HORSE program, a single-stage to orbit research effort that never left the drawing board. This tangential association with reconnaissance – real or hypothetical – is typical of previous KC-135Q operations. 'Q-crews' have always worked in an undefined world. An integral part of the reconnaissance mission, their shoulder patch boasted of being part of 'Team Recce', along with the SR-71 and the U-2. Still, they were not part of the reconnaissance community, particularly as viewed by some of their RC-135 counterparts who, on a shoulder patch, provided a stinging and impromptu spelling lesson with the reminder that 'There are no 'Qs' in 'Reconnaissance'.

Former SR-71 pilot Rich Graham and aviation historian Paul Crickmore have ably recounted the storied history of the A-12 and SR-71. Suffice to say that for all the tests and evaluation flights, the overflight missions of North Vietnam, North Korea, the Middle East, Nicaragua, the peripheral sorties over the Barents and Baltic Seas, the many record-setting flights, and the final days with NASA, the role of the KC-135Q was absolutely essential to the capability and legacy of the Lockheed 'Blackbird'.

Map of GIANT SCALE mission 310 on 20th November 1970. Tony Bevacqua and Jim Kogler flew SR-71A 61-9792 on a 5.5-hour mission from Kadena AB. The overflights required two air refuelings over Thailand and Laos, as well as the initial refueling after departing Kadena AB.

CHAPTER SIX

Foreign Tankers

'Any assistance to the French nuclear capability, including selling them KC-135s, is a dead issue.' – *John F Kennedy, 1962*

At least three countries – Australia, Canada, and France – expressed interest in acquiring the KC-135 while it was still in production. The extent to which the Royal Australian Air Force (RAAF) was genuinely committed to buying the KC-135 is unclear, but Boeing conducted orientation flights in the late 1950s for senior RAAF officials. Given that the RAAF did not have any refuelable aircraft until the 1970 arrival of two dozen F-4Es (pending delivery of their F-111Cs), one is hard-pressed to take seriously any plans to purchase the KC-135. It is not known if there was any effort by Boeing in 1958 or 1959 to press the RAAF into being a launch customer for the C-135 transport. In 1978 the RAAF purchased two ex-QANTAS 707s for VIP and strategic transport. Two more were added in 1983, and three more in 1988. Four of these were converted through 1992 to accommodate wingtip probe-and-drogue refueling. All were retired by 2011. Similarly, Canada considered adding KC-135s to the Royal Canadian Air Force (RCAF) fleet during the mid-1960s. As with Australia, the RCAF did not have an immediate need for air refueling at the time (assuming the CF-104s were not configured for probe-and-drogue refueling). By the time the RCAF had decided to move forward with a possible C-135 acquisition, the production line had closed. In 1970 Canada selected the Boeing 707-347C (CC-137) as its strategic jet transport, and these were equipped in 1972 with wingtip refueling pods for the RCAF F/A-18s (CF-5As). All were retired by 1997. French *Armée de l'Air* interest in acquiring KC-135s was both timely and more successful, as it became the first foreign customer in 1962. More than three decades later, Turkey, Singapore, and Chile would follow suit.

Chile

As with many nations, the geography of the Republic of Chile defines its national security. Bounded on three sides by Bolivia, Peru, and Argentina, and by the Pacific Ocean to the west, Chile runs 2,322nm (4,300km) north-to-south but only some 189nm (350km) east-to-west. Consequently, Chilean defense forces must either be numerous and based throughout its extraordinary length or be more concentrated but highly mobile. In addition, Chile has a large oceanic area of responsibility, including economic exclusion zones rich with fishing. In both cases, Chilean defense policy has been centered on a few bases and flexible response. Traditional national security issues include protection of sovereignty and resources, and newer threats include arms and drug trafficking, and piracy.

The initial requirement for an aerial refueling capability for the Chilean Air Force (*Fuerza Aérea de Chile* – FACh) derived from its probe-equipped fighters and attack aircraft, including the Cessna A-37, Northrop F-5E Tiger IIs, and Mirage 50s upgraded as Panteras. The FACh had four 707s (901-904) acquired from LAN Airlines for strategic transport, and in April 1995 ENAER converted 903 into a KC-707 *Águila* (Eagle). Using Sargent-Fletcher wingtip pods, it could refuel a Pantera in five minutes and an A-37 in three minutes.

The 2006 arrival of the first PEACE PUMA Block 50 F-16s, plus surplus Dutch F-16As, changed the FACh air refueling dynamic, as the F-16s could only be refueled by the flying boom. Moreover, the two new F-16 squadrons would be based in the north of Chile, with the F-5Es (by now upgraded to 'Tiger III' standards) in the far south, requiring more than a single tanker. To meet these new air refueling demands, as well as strategic transport and humanitarian requirements, the FACh approved a $40 million agreement for three former USAF Air National Guard KC-135Es on 8th July 2009.

The PEACE PUMA F-16 sale compelled the FACh to acquire a boom-capable tanker, leading to the sale of 3 KC-135Es. *Photo courtesy FACh*

It is not clear why the FACh chose KC-135Es over AMARG KC-135Rs. Both would incur similar costs prior to entry into service. 981 is towed at Santiago-Pudahel. *Photo by Andras Kisgergely*

Without wingtip refueling pods, the FACh KC-135Es are still limited to single-receiver type missions. Having three tankers available helps to mitigate this problem. *Photo by Patrick Laureau*

Following routine PDM, the first of these was delivered on 18th February 2010, and the final jet arrived on 9th March 2012. All three are assigned to *Grupo de Aviación* No.10 at Santiago-Pudahel AB. The 151st ARW, Utah ANG, provided initial operational and maintenance training for *Grupo* No.10.

The airplanes retain the TF33-PW-102 engines, with no plans to upgrade them. No replacement has been identified (nor has a need to do so been articulated).

KC-135E INDIVIDUAL AIRCRAFT

981 Previously 57-1501, this KC-135E underwent PDM prior to delivery on 18th February 2010. Shortly after its delivery KC-135E 981 took part in a humanitarian deployment to Haiti in the wake of the January 2010 earthquake.

982 Previously 57-2594, this KC-135E underwent PDM prior to delivery on 30th August 201.

983 Previously 58-0014, this KC-135E underwent PDM prior to delivery on 9th March 2012.

And then there were eight. As of 2016 the three FACh KC-135Es are the only remaining '135s using TF33s, along with the four OC-135s and WC-135s at Offutt AFB and the single NC-135 at Majors Field. *Photo by Patrick Laureau*

France – *Les Ravitailleurs*

The sale of KC-135s to France remains a paradox. For the French, the purchase was tied to the nascent French nuclear strike force, an issue of critical political, diplomatic, and military importance, and of considerable prestige to the Fifth Republic. For the US, the sale was opposed by senior administration officials (including President Kennedy) because of its intimate association with an autonomous French nuclear strike force, a capability beyond American control that raised serious objections among American policy planners concerned with the heady issues of nuclear nonproliferation, cohesion among the European allies, and changes in US nuclear policy.

On 13th February 1960 France exploded a 60kt atomic bomb over the Algerian Sahara Desert near Reggane. Operation *Gerboise Bleue* (Blue Jerboa) inducted France as the fourth member of the world's most exclusive club – the wielders of nuclear weapons. President Charles de Gaulle formally announced on 6th December 1960 his intention to establish an autonomous French nuclear strike force independent of US authority. The key to this independent nuclear force was French reliance upon its fledgling strategic bomber force to deliver these nuclear weapons to targets in the Soviet Union. In 1956 French Prime Minister Guy Mollet endorsed the construction of a supersonic bomber designed to cruise at low level and high subsonic speed, climb to altitude for a Mach 1.7 dash over the target, drop its atomic bomb, and then recover with its fuel tanks nearly empty at the nearest NATO air base. This interim bomber lacked the range to strike targets other than those on the westernmost fringe of the USSR, so French designers planned a follow-on bomber three times as large with a significantly greater radius of action. The cost of this newly proposed replacement proved prohibitive, leaving France without a long-range strategic bomber to carry its as yet untested atomic bombs. France resolved the range problem by slightly enlarging the interim bomber, now known as the Dassault *Mirage* IVA, and giving it aerial refueling capability. Without refueling, the *Mirage* IV had a range of 1,550nm (2,872km), which could be extended to 2,975nm (5,512km) with a single air refueling.

To refuel this high speed jet on its nuclear strike mission required a tanker capable of launching at a moment's notice, refueling at high speeds and altitudes, and quickly offloading a large quantity of jet fuel. The *Armée de l'Air* (French Air Force) briefly considered the Franco-German Transall C.160, a twin-engine turboprop transport, as the tanker for the Mirage IV, but rejected it because it did not satisfy these minimum operational requirements. Only the KC-135 would do. Each *ravitailleur* (tanker) was intended to service four *Mirage* IVs, requiring a fleet of nine KC-135s plus one spare to support the projected 36-bomber fleet, popularly known as the *Force de Frappe* (Strike Force). In early 1960 France began discussions with Boeing, the US Department of State, and the DoD to buy 10 KC-135s. No agreement was forthcoming, and further negotiations coincided with the presidential election of John Kennedy.

With the new administration came a shift from the existing US nuclear policy of 'massive retaliation' to one of 'flexible response'. To Kennedy, Secretary of Defense McNamara, and Secretary of State Dean Rusk, the French nuclear force would both undermine flexible response and increase the likelihood of premature use of nuclear weapons in any superpower crisis, especially if those nuclear weapons were in the hands of a nation – like France – that refused any American influence over their use. As the French nuclear bomber force depended solely upon jet tankers for its credibility, these tankers soon achieved a level of importance equal to nuclear weapons themselves.

Despite the apparent American reluctance to sell KC-135s, the French pressed forward with negotiations after a year's hiatus. In January 1962 *Armée de l'Air* Chief of Staff General Paul Stehlin announced that by 1965 France would have its own 'first-generation' strategic strike force composed of some 50 nuclear-equipped *Mirage* IVBs, boosting speculation that the sale of the necessary KC-135s would be approved. US presidential advisor Army General Maxwell D Taylor, after a March 1962 meeting with de Gaulle, recommended that the US embargo on France's nuclear weapons program be lifted and that the US invite a French military mission to Washington with a 'shopping list' including the previously unavailable KC-135s.

Contradictions and Decisions

President Kennedy rejected the recommendations of his military and economic advisors, however, and disapproved the sale of nuclear weapons technology and support equipment (ie KC-135s for the *Force de Frappe*) on the grounds of standard State Department dogma which held that such a sale would be contrary to established US policy of not contributing to the proliferation and development of nuclear weapons capabilities and delivery systems among the NATO countries. He announced in a news conference held on 7th June 1962 that assistance to the French nuclear program and autonomous nuclear deterrent – the latter epitomized by the KC-135 – was a 'dead issue'. On the same day as President Kennedy publicly rejected the sale, Deputy Secretary of Defense Roswell L Gilpatric quietly approved the sale of a dozen KC-135s to France.

This discreet *volte face* represented active assistance to the development of a French independent nuclear capability, something Kennedy and McNamara had so strongly and publicly opposed. Less than two weeks later, Secretary McNamara maintained the public facade of opposing any aid to the French nuclear force, including the sale of the KC-135s. As part of his famous 16th June commencement address at the University of Michigan at Ann Arbor, McNamara attacked the French nuclear program as 'not likely to be sufficient to perform even the function of deterrence … [and called it] dangerous, expensive, prone to obsolescence and lacking in credibility'. A month later, however, he and Rusk publicly approved the sale of KC-135s to France in a deal worth $50 million, 'reflecting improved relations between the two countries.' [In a 1991 letter to the author McNamara denied recalling these events or the decision]. Paradoxically, the US sold France the very weapon system – jet tankers, support equipment, and initial training – that would firmly establish a French autonomous nuclear strike capability at a time and in an American political climate committed to inhibiting nuclear proliferation and what some Americans such as Henry Kissinger perceived as Gaullist adventurism in superpower politics.

The original explanation for this turnabout is that the tanker sale helped offset American gold losses to France, at the time estimated to be some $250–275 million per annum. President Kennedy was concerned — perhaps too worried — over foreign accumulation of US gold and may have viewed the tanker sale as one way to reduce this outflow, an opinion shared by US Secretary of the Treasury

From the outset French C-135Fs were intended to refuel *Mirage* IVs on nuclear strikes, a capability which the US strongly opposed. *Photo via Tony Buttler*

C Douglas Dillon. There is little doubt that the balance of payments issue was an important consideration in approving the sale, but it seems unlikely that the US would have reversed a major strategic security policy on nonproliferation and French nuclear autonomy simply to save $50 million in gold, a skeptical view shared by then-Assistant Secretary of Defense for International Security Affairs Paul H Nitze. Declassified documents suggest a more compelling reason for the sale, one not incompatible with the issue of gold losses to France. According to the primary DoD memorandum recommending the transfer, the sale of KC-135s to France was undertaken 'in order to improve the strained relations between France and the US and to possibly set the stage for future negotiations for increased purchases [of other items] from the US'.

It would be easy to conclude that the sale took place amid considerable bureaucratic confusion, and that it contradicted presidential policy forbidding nuclear transfers to France. It also made President Kennedy and Secretary McNamara appear to be out of control of the Department of Defense by publicly opposing the tanker sale while at the same time their subordinates were expeditiously approving it in private. The embarrassing contradictions between Kennedy's press conference remarks, Secretary McNamara's Ann Arbor address opposing nuclear aid to France, and the Department of Defense's concerted efforts to sell the tankers are good examples of the bureaucratic confusion that exists in any government. None of the documents associated with the sale reflect any coordination with the Secretary of Defense or the Oval Office. Kennedy's National Security Advisor McGeorge Bundy confided in the author that the sale epitomized 'the way the Kennedy administration did business', and that the sale likely happened 'short of White House approval'. Bundy said that he had 'no clear recollection of the sale of jet tankers to France', adding 'I know it happened, but I do not at all remember how or why'.

It may be tempting to assert that this lack of coordination suggests a sinister effort on the part of one segment of the Department of Defense to advance its policy views without the knowledge or approval of the Secretary of Defense and the president. Far from dishonest, these failures most likely represent sincere efforts of the Department of Defense to satisfy the president's desire to improve Franco-American relations. In the course of its efforts, this group failed to confirm that what it was doing was indeed what the president wanted. It also failed to coordinate its efforts with the president and Secretary of Defense to prevent any embarrassing public contradictions. The sale of KC-135s to France is a good example of how governments work despite the best intentions of those who run them.

Les Sous-Marines

French tankers differed from their American counterparts both on the drawing board and in actual operations. Originally France requested KC-135s with turbofan engines, but settled for the J57 turbojet version because of its lower initial costs. France planned to use the airplanes in a dual tanker-transport role, so they were designated as C-135Fs, eventually garnering the nickname 'Sous-Marine' (Submarine) because of their lack of windows. They also had the heavier steel floor from the C-135 transport, increasing their basic weight over the wooden-floored KC-135s. French C-135s were assigned pseudo-national registrations in addition to their military serial numbers, with usually only the last two letters represented on the airplane (ie F-UKCA as 'CA, 'Charlie Alpha'). These registrations were used as call signs and identifiers for flight planning purposes and clearance requests for non-military flights abroad, especially when the airplanes were flown in a pure transport role.

Perhaps the most important difference between American and French tankers was that the C-135Fs were originally configured only with the BDA attached to the air refueling boom. Until the French accepted delivery of their first Boeing E-3F Sentry AWACS, France used probe-and-drogue refueling exclusively. The arrival of the E-3F (which can be refueled by both boom or probe-and-drogue) complicated this because with the BDA attached to the air refueling boom, the C-135F could not supply fuel fast enough to the E-3F, prompting a 1990 proposal to install two Flight Refuelling (later Cobham) Mk.32B wingtip probe-and-drogue refueling pods on the French tankers. This allowed the boom to refuel the E-3F through the standard IFR receptacle, and the wingtip pods could refuel French probe-and-drogue equipped aircraft on the same tanker mission without the need to land and install the BDA. Boeing began this conversion in May 1993, with the first modified airplane completed

This page: France has always preferred the probe-and-drogue method given the limited offloads to nimble receivers. The planned A330 *Phénix* will retain the boom to refuel aircraft built in the United States. *Author's collection*

Opposite page: Boeing installed the Flight Refueling Mk.32B wingtip refueling pod on C-135FR 63-12736 in 1993. The remaining aircraft were modified in France. *Photo courtesy Boeing*

Inaugural flight of the first C-135FR at BMAC's Wichita, KS, facility on 3rd August 1985, in the same airplane (63-12736) that would be the first to carry wingtip refueling pods. *Photo courtesy Boeing*

by September 1993 and, following flight testing, delivered to the French in February 1994. Air France completed the modification of the remaining ten airplanes.

Compatibility with the E-3F was not the only problem solved by installing the wingtip refueling system. The pods also effectively doubled the number of French tankers by allowing simultaneous refueling of two probe-equipped aircraft. According to one French Defense Ministry official, 'We found that with a crisis on our hands in one part of the world, we didn't have enough tanker refueling capacity to cover all our needs ... If we had to launch our *Mirage* IV fleet in anger during the Chad crisis, we would have had only the minimal support capability required by the nuclear force. Providing KC-135s with a three-point refueling system would be a significant improvement and would allow us to operate the aircraft with maximum efficiency.'

The French C-135Fs were beneficiaries of ongoing improvement to the US KC-135 fleet. BMAC began wing reskin modifications to the C-135Fs during 1977 to extend their service life through the year 2005, a prudent decision considering they are now a decade past that with perhaps another decade to come. France was also quick to re-engine its fleet, no doubt happy to get rid of the troublesome water injection system responsible for the loss of one C-135F in 1972 (see Appendix II). In January 1980 France signed an agreement with BMAC to

modify its C-135s with CFM-56-2B-1s [three French *Commandement du Transport Aérien Militaire* (CoTAM) DC-8s were also modified to Series 70 standard]. The first modified tanker (63-12736), redesignated C-135FR, made its inaugural flight on 3rd August 1985. On 14th August 1985 it completed the ten-hour non-stop delivery flight from Wichita, KS, to Istres-Le Tubé. The French officially accepted the airplane on 26th August 1985. Two more (63-12735 and 63-12739) were re-engined in 1985, four more (63-8471, 63-8470, 63-8472, and 63-8474) in 1986, two (63-8475 and 63-12740) were re-engined in 1987, and the remaining two completed in 1988.

In mid-1986 C-135FR 63-12736 was repainted in two shades of blue and grey (the same scheme applied to French Dassault *Mirage* F1s), becoming the first of any type of KC-135 to be camouflaged. Just as the French pioneered the use of camouflage on their C-135FRs, so too were they first to install a defensive electronic countermeasures (ECM) suite, as well as chaff and flare dispensers on their tankers. At least one of the C-135FRs deployed to Riyadh during the 1991 Gulf War was equipped with Dassault Avionique ADÈLE 'Sherlock' radar warning receivers. The receiver antennae were mounted facing aft above the rudder on the vertical stabilizer and facing forward above the pilot's windows. This fairing over the cockpit produced excessive airflow noise, and the system was removed after Operation *Daguet* ended.

In late 1989 a C-135FR participated in joint Anglo-French air refueling compatibility tests in the UK, including the Panavia Tornado F.3, Phantom FGR.2, and Jaguar GR.1. As the French and British refueling hardware and procedures differ significantly (the French drogue is solid metal whereas the British drogue is a collapsible 'basket' and the British system does not require the receiver to maintain pressure on the hose connection to sustain fuel flow like the French – and American – system), these tests enabled pilots from either country to refuel from tankers of either country, especially as both nations have acquired E-3 variants.

Organization

The delivery of the first *ravitailleur* to the *Armée de l'Air* on 3rd February 1964 steadied French progress toward a fully capable *Forces Aériennes Stratégiques* (FAS), culminating in her nuclear strike force, the *Force de Frappe*. The C-135F assignment history and lineage is somewhat complicated and difficult to follow. The 90e *Escadre de Ravitaillement en Vol* (ERV – Air Refueling Wing) was established on 1st August 1963 at *Base Aérienne* (BA) 125, Istres - Le Tubé (Bouches-du-Rhône), France. The first C-135F arrived there on 3rd February 1964 following initial crew training at Castle AFB. In addition, Detachment 1/90 '*Landes*' was established at BA 118, Mont-de-Marsan, where, on 1st October 1964, the first French nuclear alert sortie became operational. This was a *Mirage IVA* from the 91e *Escadre de Bombardment* (EB), loaded with an AN11 nuclear device and to be refueled en route to its target by a 90e ERV C-135F. The last C-135F was delivered on 10th October 1964.

On 30th May 1965 the 90e ERV was disbanded and its airplanes and crews redistributed, primarily an organizational change rather than a physical reshuffling. The FAS was divided into three bombardment wings each with three bomb squadrons and a single tanker squadron. On 1st June 1965 *Escadron de Ravitaillement en Vol* (Air Refueling Squadron) ERV 1/90 '*Landes*' at Mont-de-Marsan was redesignated 4/91, part of the 91e EB. On the same day ERV 90 became 4/93 '*Aunis*' at Istres - Le Tubé as part of 93e EB. Finally, on 1st December 1965, ERV 4/94 '*Sologne*' was formed at BA702, Avord (Cher) as part of 94e EB. Each squadron was assigned four C-135Fs. As part of the Bastille Day parade on 14th July 1965, a dozen *Mirage IVA* bombers made their public debut, emphasizing France's nuclear strike potential. On 9th March 1966 France announced its withdrawal from NATO's military command structure, saying that the conditions in 1966 were 'fundamentally different than those of 1949', the year in which NATO was created with France a founding member.

Following the introduction of French S-3 surface-to-surface intermediate range ballistic missiles (IRBMs) on the Albion plateau,

three *Mirage* IV squadrons were dissolved and six others regrouped into two wings – the 91e at Mont-de-Marsan and the 94e at Avord. This regrouping took place on 1st July 1976. The tankers were reorganized into the 93e *Escadre de Ravitaillement en Vol* at Istres - Le Tubé, with each *Escadron de Ravitaillement en Vol* reporting to this wing. ERV 4/93 at Istres - Le Tubé was redesignated 1/93 '*Aunis*', ERV 4/94 at Avord was redesignated 2/93 '*Sologne*', and ERV 4/91 at Mont-de-Marsan was redesignated 3/93 '*Landes*'.

A number of reorganizations and consolidations followed. ERV 2/93 moved from Avord to Istres in July 1993. In August 1996 ERV 1/93 and ERV 3/93 were disestablished and all C-135FR operations grouped together at Istres - Le Tubé simply as ERV 93 *Bretagne*. This changed on 1st September 2004 from *Escadre* to *Groupe* as GRV 93, and again in August 2009 to GRV 2/91 *Bretagne*. On 29th June 2012, GRV 2/91 incorporated four flights made up of C-135FR crewmembers: BR108 *Le Pégase* (Pegasus – pilots); VB25 *Étoile Américaine* (American Star – navigators); BR129 *Lapin Trimardeur* (Vagabond rabbits – boom operators); and SAL22 *Louve Romaine* (Roman Wolves – training). Beginning 27th August 2014, GRV 2/91 *Bretagne* and the *Escadron des Soutiens Techniques Spécialisés* (ESTS – Special Technical Support Squadron) 15/93 were assigned to the 31st *Escadre Aérienne de Ravitaillement et de Transport Stratégiques* (Strategic Transport and Air Refueling Wing) at Istres - Le Tubé AB.

Operations

As with the American CHROME DOME airborne nuclear alert, initial *Mirage IVA* operations included a dozen airplanes airborne at all times, a dozen more at five-minute ground alert, and a further dozen at 45-minute ground alert. This proved expensive and demanding for the *Armée de l'Air*. In 1967 the first full year of these sustained aerial alert operations, *Mirage* IVAs and C-135Fs flew a total of 52,000 hours, with some missions as long as 14 hours. Not surprisingly, these draining operations were halted and the *Mirage* IVAs and their tankers maintained strictly on ground alert.

In addition to this strategic support role, C-135Fs and C-135FRs also have a notable legacy in conventional combat operations. Among these were Operation *Lamantin* in 1977, refueling SEPECAT Jaguars against Polisario rebels in Mauritania, Operations *Murène* throughout 1981-84, *Manta* in 1983 and *Chevesne* in 1984 involving Jaguars and Dassault *Mirage* F1C-200s in Chad against Libyan-backed anti-government forces, and Operation *Épervier* in 1986 as part of Jaguar and *Mirage* F1C-200 and F1CR missions against Libyan forces in northern Chad. At least one C-135FR was based full time at N'Djamena, Chad, throughout the conflict there.

Although France sent helicopters and transports to Saudi Arabia following the August 1990 Iraqi invasion of Kuwait, it was not until the violation of sovereignty of the French embassy in Kuwait City by Iraqi troops that French President François Mitterand authorized on 15th September a large-scale deployment of aircraft as part of Operation *Daguet*. Among the forces deployed to the Gulf on 2nd October were at least two 93e ERV C-135FRs, although more may have been involved in the transit of the *Mirage* F1s, *Mirage* 2000s, and Jaguars to the Gulf. The C-135FRs were based at King Khalid IAP near Riyadh and used the static call sign *Bellay*. Follow-on missions over Iraq took place as part of Operation *Alysse*, as well as in 1992-1996 from Turkey under Operation *Aconit*.

C-135FR missions in support of NATO over Bosnia in 1993 included Operations *Crécerelle* and *Salamandre*, and Operation *Trident* over Kosovo in 1999. Following the October 2001 start of the American Operation ENDURING FREEDOM, C-135FRs flew air refueling missions over Afghanistan in Operation *Héraclès*. Additional demands on the C-135FRs included Operation *Licorne* beginning in 2002 in Côte d'Ivoire and in 2003 in the Democratic Republic of the Congo.

French commitments in North Africa increased substantially beginning with the 2011 Libyan Civil War. In conjunction with the US Operation ODYSSEY DAWN, Operation *Harmattan* supported a 'no-fly zone' over Libya for some seven months to ensure that air forces loyal to Libyan leader Muammar al-Gaddafi could not attack ground forces seeking to oust the dictator. Six French C-135s provided air refueling support, including 'flights of up to 12 hours in duration…from Istres-Le Tubé in southern France.' In response to UN Security Council Resolution 2085 in December 2012, the French began Operation *Serval* to oust Islamic militants from their enclaves in Northern Mali. C-135FRs refueled strike aircraft and provided strategic transport until its termination on 15th July 2014. French forces at N'Djamena began Operation *Barkhane* on 1st August 2014

as the successor to Operation *Serval*, although over a much broader area of sub-Saharan Africa from the Atlantic Ocean to the Red Sea. The ongoing mission is designed to destroy Islamic extremist groups in the Sahel Region, as well as the former French colonies of Burkina Faso, Chad, Mali, Mauritania, and Niger.

New Demands and the Future

Far from being a mere laundry list of C-135FR accomplishments, these deployments reflect the considerable demand placed not only on French aerial refueling capacity, but on the airplanes themselves. For example, while a 'majority' of C-135FRs participated in the deployment to Chad in 1984 and 1986, only the absolute minimum remained to support FAS *Mirage* IVs on nuclear alert, an operational shortcoming of serious potential. This shortfall due to combat commitments in Chad prompted increased French interest in replacing, or at least augmenting, their C-135 fleet. Possible successors included the Airbus Industrie A300B4 (or its stablemate the A310) incorporating probe and drogue refueling equipment, Transall C.160s, and Lockheed C-130s. *Armée de l'Air* officials had an understandable preference, however, for jet-powered tankers to escort French combat aircraft on their long-distance deployments, a capability not available in the slower turboprop C-130 and C.160. Nonetheless, ten C.160 Transall *Nouvelle Générations* (NG – new generation) were equipped with a Sargent-Fletcher hose drum refueling unit in an extended port landing gear fairing. These tanker-configured Transall NGs were used for intra-African operations by Jaguars and *Mirage* F1s, while C-135FRs remained dedicated to *Mirage* IVP strategic bombers and overseas deployments by tactical aircraft (such as ferry flights to and from Nellis AFB, NV, for RED FLAG). Pending a decision on replacing the C-135FR fleet, the *Armée de l'Air* leased three US Air Force KC-135Rs (57-1439, 62-3516, and

Opposite, left: The 'Sherlock' radar warning receiver above the cockpit reportedly produced so much noise from turbulent air flow that it adversely affected the ability of the crew to communicate with each other and over the radio. *Photo by Jacques Moulin via Tony Buttler*

Opposite, right: Over 40 years the French C-135s have been assigned to a variety of units and bases, as the special markings on C-135FR 63-8471 attest. *Photo by Pierre-Clément Got*

Above: With the onset of Operation *Barkhane* in 2014, French C-135s have been supporting combat missions over the past 30 years, with no end in sight. *Photo by Alan Lebeda*

Right: 62-3516 was a standard USAF KC-135R loaned to France pending conversion of five (eventually three) KC-135Rs modified to *Armée de l'Air* standards. *Photo by Jacques Moulin via Tony Buttler*

63-8033). The last of these (62-3516) returned to the USAF on 28th July 1997. These 'loaner' airplanes were painted in the French scheme and had French markings, but were not redesignated as C-135FRs because of their internal differences from the French version.

Despite the retirement of the *Mirage* IV fleet, the demand for C-135FRs did not decrease. The French strategic nuclear deterrence mission remained, although now with Dassault *Mirage* 2000N and Dassault *Rafale* fighters equipped with the ASMP-A missile. Tactical operations and peacekeeping exercises around the globe actually increased French tanker requirements. By 1995 the need for additional KC-135s by the French had become compelling. Although the *Armée de l'Air* had the three 'loaner' KC-135Rs from the USAF inventory, in 1996 it asked for five AMARG KC-135As to be converted to C-135FR standards and delivered over the course of the following year. The first such aircraft transferred was 62-3525, which departed AMARG on 19th September 1995 for PDM at Tinker AFB prior to installation of CFM56 engines. KC-135A 62-3497 followed on 19th January 1996, and 62-3574 on 18th August 1997. The final two KC-135s (62-3555 and 63-8009 – the latter was transferred to Singapore) were not taken up. The three new airplanes were designated simply as KC-135Rs.

On 14th January 2009 the *Armée de l'Air* directed that the 11 original C-135FRs undergo an avionics upgrade to the International Civil Aviation Organization (ICAO) 'Reno 2' standard. This would ensure compliance for operations in civilian airspace, similar to the Block 40 GATM upgrade for USAF KC-135Rs. Delivery of the first C-135FR 'Reno 2' was slated for early 2011, with the final modification completed by 2013. Delays in the acquisition of A330 MRTTs, however, meant that the three French KC-135Rs would also require upgrade beginning in June 2013. The first of these, 62-3574, was delivered on 21st August 2014. Interestingly, the three are identified as KC-135RGs (G for GATM).

By November 2010 France was in discussions with the UK about supplementing French aerial refueling and strategic transport capacity through joint participation in the Future Strategic Tanker Aircraft (FSTA) program. A year later France was still interested in FSTA collaboration, but was committed to acquiring its own fleet of Airbus A330 MRTT. As of November 2014, the *Armée de l'Air* planned to replace its C-135FRs with 12 A330 *Phénix* (Pheonix) MRTTs, with delivery of the initial eight aircraft beginning in 2018 and continuing through 2025. By the time all of the *Phénix* MRTTs are in service, the C-135FRs will have been in use for some 60 years.

C-135F/FR INDIVIDUAL AIRCRAFT

63-8470 Delivered on 12th December 1964 as C-135F F-UKCA. Re-engined from 10th June 1986 through 13th August 1986 and redesignated as a C-135FR.

63-8471 Delivered on 3rd February 1964 as C-135F F-UKCB. Re-engined from 21st November 1985 through 1st January 1986 and redesignated as a C-135FR.

63-8472 Delivered on 4th March 1964 as C-135F F-UKCC. Re-engined from 17th July 1987 through 18th September 1987 and redesignated as a C-135FR.

63-8473 Delivered on 8th April 1964 as C-135F F-UKCD. It crashed after takeoff on 1st July 1972 (see Appendix II).

63-8474 Delivered on 6th May 1964 as C-135F F-UKCE. Re-engined from 13th August 1986 through 16th October 1986 and redesignated as a C-135FR.

63-8475 Delivered on 3rd June 1964 as C-135F F-UKCF. Re-engined from 22nd October 1986 through 13th January 1987 and redesignated as a C-135FR.

63-12735 Delivered on 8th July 1964 as C-135F F-UKCG. Re-engined from 2nd August 1985 through 22nd September 1985 and redesignated as a C-135FR.

63-12736 Delivered on 22nd July 1964 as C-135F F-UKCH. Re-engined from 1st June 1985 through 6th August 1985 and redesignated as a the first C-135FR.

63-12737 Delivered on 5th August 1964 as C-135F F-UKCI. Re-engined from 27th January 1988 through 4th April 1988 and redesignated as a C-135FR.

63-12738 Delivered on 19th August 1964 as C-135F F-UKCJ. Re-engined from 16th November 1987 through 30th January 1988 and redesignated as a C-135FR.

63-12739 Delivered on 9th September 1964 as C-135F F-UKCK. Re-engined from 24th September 1985 through 20th November 1985 and redesignated as a C-135FR.

63-12740 Delivered on 28th September 1964 as C-135F F-UKCL. Re-engined from 10th June 1986 through 18th November 1987 and redesignated as a C-135FR.

KC-135R/RG INDIVIDUAL AIRCRAFT

57-1439 Loaned to the *Armée de l'Air* as KC-135R F-UKAE and returned to US service.

62-3497 Withdrawn from AMARG as AACA0071 on 19th January 1996 for PDM and returned on 19th September 1996 as AACA0108. Withdrawn from AMARG on 21st May 1997 and re-engined from 23rd May through 10th October 1997 and delivered to France as a KC-135R. Following the GATM upgrade in 2014 it became a KC-135RG.

62-3516 Loaned to the *Armée de l'Air* as KC-135R F-UKAS and returned to US service on 28th July 1997.

62-3525 Withdrawn from AMARG as AACA0081 on 19th September 1995 for PDM and returned on 15th May 1996 as AACA0105. Withdrawn from AMARG on 19th February 1997 and re-engined from 20th February through 2nd June 1997 and delivered to France as a KC-135R. Following the GATM upgrade in 2014 it became a KC-135RG.

62-3574 Withdrawn from AMARG as AACA0074 on 1st July 1996 for PDM and returned on 5th May 1997 as AACA0112. Withdrawn from AMARG on 15th August 1997 and re-engined from 18th August through 5th December 1997 and delivered to France as a KC-135R. Following the GATM upgrade in 2014 it became a KC-135RG.

63-8033 Loaned to the *Armée de l'Air* as KC-135R F-UKAA and returned to US service.

It is ironic that the airplane wearing 50th anniversary markings is KC-135RG 62-3497 and not one of the original C-135Fs. (Not to mention the nose is a bit low for a good flare.) *Photo by Luc Van Belleghem*

Above: RAF receivers are accustomed to a flexible basket but the French C-135FRs use the hard BDA. 63-8472 visits Prestwick following interoperability training. *Photo by Ray McFadyen*

Left and below: An amazing difference as C-135F 63-12735 appears at an Open House with its primary mission to refuel Mirage IVs destined to strike the USSR and its allies (upper). As a C-135FR some 40 years later, it sits on the snowy ramp at Tallinn, Estonia, once a target for NATO aircraft. *Photos by Peter Vercruijsse (upper) and Andrey Nesvetaev (lower)*

Bottom left: 63-12739 visits the Wright-Patterson AFB transient ramp. Although the C-135Fs were used for strategic transport, this jet has the BDA installed, suggesting it may have diverted during a fighter drag. *Author's collection*

Bottom right: In addition to ongoing military action in Africa and the Middle East, the *Armée de l'Air* still maintained a nuclear deterrent force, requiring temporary aircraft such as 57-1439 until newly modified KC-135Rs arrived. *Author's collection*

Israel

The United States rebuffed Israeli requests in the 1970s to acquire KC-135As to replace its small fleet of KC-97 tankers, especially as it planned to purchase F-15s and F-16s. American military officials argued that as the KC-135 production line was closed, SAC needed all the tankers in its fleet to support its SIOP commitments and could ill afford to transfer any to Israel. Moreover, US politicians were deeply concerned that Israel would use any new jet tankers to refuel pre-emptive Israeli strikes on hostile Arab nations. At a time when the United States was working to improve relations with Egypt and establish a more stable Arab-Israeli peace framework, allowing Israel to project airpower by means of aerial refueling was highly counterproductive. Consequently, Israel developed an indigenous air refueling capability by reverse engineering the KC-97 air refueling boom and installing it on modified Boeing 707s. Some five or six KC-707s entered service with the Israeli Air Force (IAF – *Hey'l Ha'avir*) by 1981, and saw their combat debut during Operation WOODEN LEG, the 1st October 1985 attack on the headquarters of the Palestine Liberation Organization (PLO) in Tunis, Tunisia. Total flight distance for the four F-15s was 2,225nm (4,120km), and required one air refueling in each direction.

By 2005, two decades after the Tunis attack, it was clear that a replacement was needed for the KC-707s, and the IAF asked the United States for five KC-135Rs. Although the two airframes were approximately the same age, the 707s had accrued far more flying hours and had a shorter projected remaining lifespan than the KC-135s. At the time of the Israeli request, the KC-135R conversion program had ended, and it was prohibitively expensive to restart for just five airplanes. Instead, US officials suggested, the Israelis could have five KC-135Es (57-1482, 57-1511, 58-0053, 58-0064, and 58-0096) recently stored in AMARG. In addition to their prompt availability, they had the added advantage of using TF33-PW-102 engines which were in use on some IAF 707s. The Israelis balked at this offer, however, acutely aware that part of the reason the KC-135Es were retired en masse was a fleet-wide problem with the engine struts. Repairing or replacing these struts was a costly proposition. According to Israeli sources, however, rejection of the KC-135Es was less about repairing engine struts than about conflicting control over their use, an issue that affected future efforts to complete the transfer.

In 2013, Israel and the United States announced that the sale was on again as part of a larger package involving Bell/Boeing MV-22 Ospreys. A *New York Times* report on 18th April 2013 noted that the 'new generation of KC-135 refueling tanker planes would let Israel's warplanes stay in the air longer, an ability essential for any long-range mission – like a strike on Iran. The tankers would also be useful for air patrols protecting Israeli borders.' Aharon Lapidot, an Israeli military analyst, said the KC-135 was 'of the utmost tactical importance,' allowing Israeli fighters 'to partake in operations far from the country's borders.... There is no doubt this is a force multiplier for the IAF.' US Secretary of Defense Charles 'Chuck' Hagel said the sale will 'ensure Israel's air superiority in the future and allow the Israeli Air Force long-range capabilities,' and was consistent with American policy to guarantee Israel's 'qualitative military edge' while not recklessly emboldening Israeli hawks – a presumed reference to any possible Israeli military intervention in Iran.

As before, nothing happened. The Israelis didn't want KC-135Es, and instead asked for up to 12 of the KC-135Rs that had been relegated to AMARG. Two of these would be used as VIP transports. Moreover, the Israelis insisted that the airplanes be transferred at little or no cost. Part of this was linked to the planned Israeli purchase of Lockheed F-35s, which required boom air refueling. The KC-135Rs

would serve as financial offsets to the expense of the MV-22s and F-35s, making their sale more appealing. IAF commanders noted their boom-equipped 707s were approaching the end of their useful (and safe) operational lives, and the KC-135Rs were essential to future support of the F-35. America, however, still refused to sell (or donate) the KC-135Rs.

With the April 2015 understanding between the Islamic Republic of Iran and the permanent members of the UN Security Council on Iran's nuclear capability, in July 2015 US Secretary of Defense Ashton 'Ash' Carter went to Tel Aviv to 'sell the agreement' to the Israelis. The KC-135s, Carter reassured the Israelis, would allow the IAF to strike Iran, a powerful deterrent. The Israelis, however, reserved the right to use the KC-135s without prior US approval. This would allow a pre-emptive Israeli strike on Iran in spite of any US objections, much like the 1981 Israeli attack on the Iraqi Osirak reactor. Carter refused to yield this authority given that it was intended precisely to prevent such a pre-emptive attack. Carter did say that if Iran attacked first, then there would be no US constraints on the use of the KC-135s for any Israeli retaliatory attack. Israeli Prime Minister Benjamin Netanyahu scoffed that was a hollow promise: if the Iranian attack used nuclear weapons it would be too late for Israel to 'pre-empt'. Without an agreement on pre-emptive use of the KC-135s, the tanker deal stalled.

Whether or not Israel will be content to use its 707s until such time as the US changes its position on pre-emptive use, the IAF may expand its tanker search to include the Airbus A330 MRTT (which ironically are in use in Saudi Arabia) or indigenously modified KC-767s. Ultimately, however, the issue may well hinge on the relation of any tanker to refuel a pre-emptive strike on Iran by stealthy F-35s and the willingness of Israel to give the United States a veto over any such mission.

Saudi Arabia

Within weeks of taking office, the Reagan administration announced on 2nd February 1981 the agreement in principle of a $5 billion deal with Saudi Arabia for F-15s with conformal fuel tanks, E-3 AWACs, and 'six or eight KC-135 tankers'. The proposed sale had strong support within the DoD, especially among military leaders, who saw it as an opportunity to expand US influence in the Gulf. The 'loss' of Iran as an ally and the growing Soviet presence in the Gulf made Saudi Arabia the natural benefactor of American arms sales that would counterbalance any Soviet or radical Iranian capability that might threaten Western interests (specifically oil) in the region. The E-3s would provide a real-time image of aerial threats, and F-15s could target any hostile aircraft or be configured with bomb racks to strike appropriate ground targets. KC-135s would refuel both, extending their time on station as well as the strike range of the F-15s. For a Cold Warrior like Reagan, the sale was a reasonable effort to deter Soviet encroachment in the Middle East.

The proposal sparked immediate controversy. Not only was Saudi Arabia seen as an unsuitable ally, it was intractably hostile to America's most-favored client state Israel. Critics charged that giving E-3s to the Saudis would allow them to 'track every move' of the Israeli Air Force in preparations for a surprise attack, the 'basis for Israeli defense doctrine.' Opponents of the sale argued that the F-15s with conformal tanks could reach 'deep into Israel'. The KC-135s would, as Reagan officials intended, allow the E-3s and F-15s to remain airborne longer or extend their range, although toward Israel rather than Iran.

The debate devolved into acrimony and fallacious arguments, especially by Congressional opposition. The same critics who now opposed the sale of the E-3 because of its 'sophisticated capabilities that directly threaten Israel' had, only five years earlier, tried to cancel

The Royal Saudi Air Force originally wanted 6-8 KC-135s, but these were replaced by KE-3As. 1817, seen here transiting RAF Mildenhall on initial delivery, later became an RE-3A. *Photo by Bob Archer*

Even a small city state such as Singapore requires an air refueling capability to project power. Three of the four RSAF KC-135Rs (751-3) refuel RSAF F-15SGs. *Photo via Yongkiat Goh*

the procurement of the E-3 because it was 'flawed' and 'incapable of performing its mission.' Detection of a pre-emptive Israeli strike was a legitimate Saudi defense concern. Indeed, on 7th June 1981 four Israeli F-16s struck the Iraqi Osirak nuclear reactor in a surprise attack. Claims that refueling from KC-135s would allow strikes 'deep' into Israel stupidly ignore geography. The distance from King Faisal AB at Tabuk, Saudi Arabia, to Tel Aviv, Israel, is only 242nm (448km), a flight of some 32 minutes at 460 KIAS (852km/h). Israel is only 229nm (424km) long and 99nm (183km) at its widest. The combat radius of the F-15 is on the order of 1,000nm (1,852km), so there was absolutely no need for air refueling to strike Israel from Saudi Arabia. The KC-135s were clearly oriented toward the Gulf of Arabia.

Congressional histrionics aside, the Reagan administration pressed hard for the sale. On 8th April 1981 US Secretary of State Alexander Haig officially informed the Saudis of the intent to sell them five E-3s and seven KC-135s. By the end of the year Congress approved the sale, including a final number of eight KC-135s. Where these airplanes would come from, however, had not been well thought out. CINCSAC General Bennie L Davis opposed transferring any of SAC's active duty tankers, as well as any from ANG or AFRES units.

As the United States placed a renewed emphasis on the SIOP, senior defense officials agreed with Davis, fearing any decrease in KC-135 numbers would adversely affect bomber readiness. In lieu of KC-135s, however, Boeing successfully recommended its proposed 707 tanker equipped with CFM-56 engines, the same airframe for the planned Saudi E-3s. Eight of these were delivered, with serials 1811-1818.

By 2016 the Saudi KE-3 fleet had dwindled from eight to five with the acquisition of six Airbus A330 Multirole Tanker Transports (MRTTs). Three former KE-3s have reportedly been converted into RE-3As, including 1817 reserialled as 1901, as well as former YE-8B 88-0322 as 1902.

Singapore
Aerial refueling achieves two goals – it extends the range of an airplane (power projection) or it extends its endurance (a benefit for defense). For the Republic of Singapore, acquiring an air refueling capability combined both of these goals. The tiny city state on the southern tip of Malaysia is only 31 miles (50km) by 17 miles (27km). To be meaningful any aerial defense of Singapore must be forward based, so its F-16s need to operate well out over international waters

Flight and ground crews from Singapore trained at McConnell AFB using 'local' jets, but by late 1999 were using RSAF 750. *Photo by Brian Rogers*

far enough from the city to prevent any attacker from delivering its weapons. That requires fuel to get there, fuel to orbit, and fuel to return home. Moreover, Singapore abuts the crucially important Malacca Strait. Each year nearly 100,000 ships transit this narrow passage between the Malay Peninsula and the Indonesian island of Sumatra as they move between the Indian Ocean and the South China Sea and into the Pacific Ocean. Some 25% of all oil transported by sea passes through the Strait before reaching Japan, the Philippines, Taiwan, and China. Its economic value is incalculable, and it falls, in part, to Singapore to protect it from everything from piracy to blockade to terrorism. In addition, Singapore is a member of the Association of

Southeast Asian Nations (ASEAN) and has mutual defensive agreements with the other members. Although Singapore makes no claim on the Paracels or Spratly Islands, for example, other ASEAN members do, leading to a strong potential for conflict. The distance from Singapore to the Paracels is 1,037nm (1,920km), requiring two or more air refuelings for its F-15SGs or F-16Cs. Given these demands, Singapore, a city state of no more than 278 square miles (719 square km), has a genuine requirement for air refueling tankers.

With the acquisition in 1988 of F-16s, the existing Republic of Singapore Air Force (RSAF) tanker fleet of drogue-equipped KC-130Bs was unusable to refuel the boom-only F-16s. Although

KC-135Rs gave the RSAF the opportunity to participate in exercises abroad, such as PITCH BLACK with Australia. 751 refuels RAAF F-111Cs. *Photo via Yongkiat Goh*

RSAF overseas deployments could occasionally rely on USAF KC-135s, there was a clear need for an autonomous aerial refueling capability. During 1995 the RSAF solicited proposals for a tanker, prompting Airbus to offer a tanker version of its A310, Boeing to offer a KC-767, McDonnell Douglas to offer a KDC-10, and Bedek from Israel to offer converted KC-707s. None of these appealed to the Singaporean officials, who were skeptical about acquiring a conversion with a trans-oceanic logistics pipeline. By April 1996 the RSAF had reassessed its requirements, and on 2nd September 1996 the RSAF announced the foreign military sales (FMS) purchase of four KC-135As stored in AMARG with the intent to convert them to KC-135Rs. In addition to the F108 engines, the airplanes would receive the PACER CRAG cockpit upgrade and the multi-point refueling system (MPRS) to provide both flying boom refueling for RSAF's F-15s and F-16s, and drogue refueling for its A-4s and F-5s.

Beginning 27th July 1998, the airplanes, flight and ground crews and their families were based at McConnell AFB for training with the 22nd ARW as part of the PEACE GUARDIAN program. Initially the RSAF personnel trained on USAF KC-135Rs, but following the roll-out of the first RSAF KC-135R 750 (63-8009) on 9th September 1999 RSAF crews used their own airplanes. The PEACE GUARDIAN detachment closed on 25th September 2003.

The first RSAF KC-135R arrived at Changi AB (West) on 7th September 2000, with the three remaining jets in place by the end of the year. They were assigned to 112 Squadron, which officially activated on 12th December 2000.

Operations include the June 2003 deployment of four RSAF F-16s from Luke AFB to Singapore. The F-16s were stationed in Arizona as part of the PEACE CARVIN III detachment, responsible for initial training of RSAF F-16 pilots. The flight covered some 9,179nm (17,000km). On 9th June 2004 an RSAF KC-135R flew to al Udeid AB, Qatar, for a three-month deployment in support of multinational efforts for Iraqi reconstruction. Other deployments included F-16s as part of WESTERN ARC with France in September 2004, including stops in India, the United Arab Emirates, and Greece en route to Dijon AB. A similar deployment took place in June 2010 as Exercise GARUDA. Ongoing operations include joint exercises with Australia such as PITCH BLACK and WALLABY, both of which require air refueling to travel to the 3,808nm (6,128km) between Singapore and RAAF Base Amberley. The July 2004 visit of RAF Eurofighter Typhoons to Paya Lebar AB in Singapore allowed 112 Sqd KC-135Rs to conduct initial operational refueling trials using the MPRS.

By 2014 the RSAF sought to replace its KC-135Rs, and selected six Airbus A330MRTTs, with a planned service introduction of 2017.

KC-135R INDIVIDUAL AIRCRAFT

750 Former USAF KC-135A 63-8009 stored in AMARG as AACA0073 from 26th July 1993 through 24th July 1997. Converted to KC-135R from 9th October 1998 through 25th May 1999 and delivered to the PEACE GUARDIAN detachment at McConnell AFB following further conversion with PACER CRAG and MPRS on 9th September 1999.

751 Former USAF KC-135A 61-0325 stored in AMARG as AACA0091 from 29th September 1993 through 12th December 1997. Converted to KC-135R from 19th April 1998 through 20th December 1999, and delivered. Reportedly used on 5th November 2000 as an airborne intensive care unit to transport three Singaporean survivors from the crash of Singapore Airlines flight SQ006 in Taiwan.

752 Former USAF KC-135A 59-1454 stored in AMARG as AACA0088 from 1st September 1993 through 19th June 1998. Converted to KC-135R from 23rd November 1999 through 9th June 2000 (as the 420th and final KC-135R conversion) and delivered.

753 Former USAF KC-135A 63-8066 stored in AMARG as AACA0099 from 12th May 1994 through 6th November 1998. Converted to KC-135R beginning 22nd March 2000 (finished prior to 9th June 2000, but the date has not been verified) and delivered.

Above: Although 750 had Singaporean markings throughout training at McConnell AFB, it also carried the 22nd ARW tail band. *Photo by Brian Rogers*

Right: The ability to refuel both receiver types on a single mission has been a requirement for every new tanker since the end of the Cold War, leading to wingtip pods and a central boom. *Photo by Yongkiat Goh*

Turkey

The end of the Cold War changed the global military dynamic. There was suddenly little chance of a conflict between East and West as the Soviet Union collapsed into Russia, China discovered capitalism, and Western nations began to reap the 'peace dividend.' The abrupt elimination of superpower domination over former client states, however, spawned sectarian conflict in places like Bosnia and Iraq, prompting NATO intervention. As part of its membership obligation, Turkey provided F-4Es, RF-4Es, and F-16s to support NATO air strikes in Operation ALLIED FORCE, as well as supporting the no-fly zone over Iraq and Operation PROVIDE COMFORT, the relief effort for Kurds in Northern Iraq. The distances involved meant that Turkish fighters required air refueling for sustained operations. Rather than rely exclusively on US KC-135 support, the Turkish Air Force (*Türk Hava Kuvvetleri* – THK) submitted a request for proposals for a boom-equipped jet tanker in what one Turkish official called 'first on our agenda' for modernization. After ruling out used 707s converted by Israel because the United States refused to allow third-party export of its flying boom technology, the two final choices were the KC-10 and the KC-135.

Financing the sale proved the decisive factor. US legislation passed in 1986 known as the 'Modernization of Defense Capabilities of Countries of NATO's Southern Flank' allowed for the transfer of Excess Defense Articles (EDA) provided the transfer incurred no cost to the United States. As former SAC KC-135As were already in storage at AMARG, in November 1992 the THK requested three KC-135s (as well as 50 Republic A-10s). The US disingenuously rejected this request, however, saying that 'no KC-135s were available.' The THK appropriately issued a reclama, pointing out that there were nearly 50 KC-135As in AMARG. Moreover, they raised the number requested from three to 10, at a cost of $560 million for PDM, conversion from KC-135A to KC-135R standards, and spare parts.

By September 1994 the sale very nearly fell apart, however, due to program costs. Turkey complained about the high cost of the conversion, and warned that it could consequently afford only three KC-135Rs and would look elsewhere for tankers. THK commanders were also squeamish about US restrictions placed on the use of the KC-135s, requiring prior American approval for any operational use outside of NATO or UN-mandated missions. In addition, Turkish

politicians wanted the reconditioning and conversion to take place at the Turkish Aerospace Industries' plant at Murted, Turkey, which was building F-16s under license.

Despite these obstacles, the deal finally moved forward in January 1995. Only seven KC-135Rs would be acquired and converted, and the total cost was reduced to $315 million. Ground and flight crews would go to the United States for training, and 'two or three KC-135As' would 'be leased for early operations.' In fact, two KC-135Rs (62-3512 and 62-3568) arrived at Incirlik AB on 22nd July 1995 for familiarization training with 101 Filo (squadron). These 'loaners' remained in use until 11th December 1997 when they returned to the US, with the first three Turkish KC-135Rs delivered on 19th December 1997. The four remaining aircraft arrived over the course of the first six months in 1998. All seven of the Turkish KC-135s were previously stored in AMARG, were removed for PDM or re-engining, and returned to AMARG (with different PCN codes) prior to final delivery to Turkey.

Operations over the past two decades have focused primarily on NATO missions and regional conflicts. Ongoing conflicts with domestic terrorist groups, civil war in Iraq between Kurdish factions in 1997, Operation ALLIED FORCE in the former Yugoslavia in 1999, International Security Assistance Force (ISAF) operations in Afghanistan, and NATO duty during the Libyan Civil War in 2011 all kept Turkish air forces in combat requiring air refueling. Beginning in 2015 Turkish F-16s have been active defending the Turkish border from incursions by Syrian aircraft and Russian aircraft supporting the beleaguered Syrian president Bahsar al-Assad in the Syrian Civil War, as well as conducting airstrikes against Islamic State in Iraq and the Levant (ISIL) fighters in Syria and Iraq. In each case the availability of air refueling from THK KC-135s has allowed longer endurance defensive patrols and strikes deeper into hostile territory.

Although surprising, KC-135s have been involved in an attempt to overthrow their own government. During the night of 15th July 2016, a small number of Turkish military forces attempted a coup d'état against the government of President Recep Tayyip Erdoğan. Several Turkish F-16s took part in the coup, and refueled from a Turkish KC-135R, call sign *Asena 02*. Throughout the course of the evening, at least four KC-135s (*Asena 01* through *Asena 04*) established orbits to refuel anti-government F-16s. Two loyalist F-16s were ordered to shoot down *Asena 02* but did not, ostensibly because

it was orbiting over a residential area and any crash damage would have caused considerable civilian casualties. The coup attempt ended quickly, and THK officers were among those arrested. Given the number of THK KC-135s involved, the arrest of any crewmembers and maintenance personnel supporting the coup would no doubt have a significant, if not critical, adverse impact of Turkish air refueling capability.

KC-135R INDIVIDUAL AIRCRAFT

57-2609 Withdrawn from AMARG as AACA0057 on 27th March 1997 for PDM. Underwent re-engining from 21st January 1998 through 21st May 1998, and returned to AMARG as AACA0121 on 21st May 1998. Withdrawn from AMARG on 17th July 1998 and delivered to the THK as a KC-135R.

58-0110 Withdrawn from AMARG as AACA0089 on 28th February 1996 for PDM and returned on 28th October 1996 as AACA0109. Withdrawn from AMARG on 18th March 1997 and re-engined from 20th March through 1st July 1997 and delivered to the THK on 19th December 1997 as a KC-135R.

60-0325 Withdrawn from AMARG as AACA0088 on 7th August 1996 for PDM. Underwent re-engining from 8th December 1997 through 19th April 1998, and returned to AMARG as AACA0120 on 20th April 1998. Withdrawn from AMARG on 20th June 1998 and delivered to the THK on 21st June 1998 as a KC-135R.

60-0326 Withdrawn from AMARG as AACA0084 on 17th May 1996 for PDM. Underwent re-engining from 15th July 1997 through 1st November 1997, and returned to AMARG as AACA0116 on 3rd November 1997. Withdrawn from AMARG on 17th December 1997 and delivered to the THK on 19th December 1997 as a KC-135R.

62-3512 This USAF KC-135R was loaned to the THK for initial training and operations from 22nd July 1995 through 19th December 1997.

62-3539 Withdrawn from AMARG as AACA0098 on 13th June 1996 for PDM. Underwent re-engining from 4th September 1997 through 27th January 1998, and returned to AMARG as AACA0118 on 27th January 1998. Withdrawn from AMARG on 15th March and delivered to the THK on 16th March 1998 as a KC-135R.

62-3563 Withdrawn from AMARG as AACA0097 on 26th March 1996 for PDM and returned on 8th November 1996 as AACA0110. Removed from AMARG on 22nd April 1997 for re-engining through 19th August 1997 and returned on 1st July 1997 as AACA0113. Removed from AMARG on 11th December 1997 and delivered to the THK on 19th December 1997.

62-3567 Withdrawn from AMARG as AACA0085 on 9th August 1996 for PDM and returned on 29th April 1997 as AACA0111. Removed from AMARG on 22nd October 1997 for re-engining and returned on 25th February 1998 as AACA0119. Removed from AMARG on 12th April 1998 and delivered to the THK on 24th April 1998.

62-3568 This USAF KC-135R was loaned to the THK for initial training and operations from 22nd July 1995 through 19th December 1997.

Opposite: 58-0110 was one of the first three KC-135Rs delivered to the THK on 19th December 1997. Modelers should enjoy weathering this airplane. *Photo by Rainer Baxter*

This page: THK tankers including 62-3563 support strike operations against ISIL in Syria and Iraq, but also separatist forces such as the PKK. *Photo by Richard Vandervord*

The THK celebrated its 100th anniversary in 2011, and 60-0326 carried special markings forward of the cargo door. *Photo by Richard Vandervord*

Turkish KC-135Rs also serve in the long-range transport role, supporting troop and fighter deployments along with A400Ms and C-130s. *Photo by Kenneth Hare via Stephen Miller*

CHAPTER SEVEN

A False Start

'Obtaining additional air transport mobility – and obtaining it now – will better assure the ability of our conventional forces to respond, with discrimination and speed, to any problem at any spot on the globe at any moment's notice.' – *John F Kennedy, 1961*

'These significant limitations in range, capacity, and accessibility make it unwise to attempt further interim modernization of the C-135.' – *Robert S McNamara, US Secretary of Defense, 1963*

In 1960 the Military Air Transport Service (MATS) had but three jet transports. These were Boeing C-137As (707-153s) assigned to Detachment 1, 1254th ATW, Andrews AFB, MD, the Special Air Mission (SAM) unit that provided transport service for senior government officials, most notably the President of the United States. Who would fly these new jets was the subject of considerable controversy. Air Force Vice Chief of Staff General LeMay felt that since MATS had no highly experienced jet pilots, the C-137A pilots should come from the bomber and tanker crews in SAC. MATS' commander, Lieutenant General William H Tunner, felt otherwise, confident that his pilots were as capable of flying heavy jets as were LeMay's pilots. Air Force Chief of Staff General Thomas D White sided with Tunner, arguing that MATS pilots, although not skilled in jet operations, were better trained for the 'delicate mission' of dealing with government VIP passengers. Further, MATS had no more than 50 Douglas C-133 Cargomaster turboprop transports. The remainder of its fleet was piston-powered – transports designed to standards in use during the Second World War. Indeed, MATS was the only major command in the US Air Force that did not have any jet-powered primary aircraft. With these limits in mind, the US Congress passed Public Law 86-601 which allocated $311 million to airlift modernization, including preliminary funding for a jet transport.

In his 30th January 1961 State of the Union address, President Kennedy announced that modernization of America's strategic airlift capability was among his administration's highest priorities, saying 'I have directed prompt attention to increase our airlift capacity. … In particular it will enable us to meet any deliberate effort to avoid or divert our forces by starting limited wars in widely scattered parts of the globe.' Under Kennedy, US defense policy emphasized NATO commitments and 'brush-fire' crisis management around the world rather than his predecessor's emphasis on strategic airpower. Kennedy's policy made it clear that it was neither feasible nor economical to station large numbers of troops and equipment at dozens of potential 'hot spots' around the world. Instead they would remain in the United States ready for immediate deployment when needed. The problem was getting them there in time and ready to make a difference.

The answer lay in a massive quick-response capability. Transports would fly troops and their equipment from bases in the US to the crisis location, ideally arriving in such force as to dissuade an opponent from initiating hostilities, or failing this, to defeat the enemy quickly and restore the *status quo ante*. Unfortunately MATS' piston and turboprop airplanes (such as the C-124 and the C-133) could neither do this expeditiously nor carry the quantity required. A C-124, for example, could take as many as 95 flying hours over 13 days to fly from Travis AFB, CA, to Saigon, South Vietnam, hardly a fast response.

Time was not only significant in getting the troops to the battle, but in the adverse effects of travel on the troops themselves. According to one first-hand account of a deployment, 'jet equipment can deliver rested men ready to fight while piston-powered aircraft,

Other than turboprop C-133s, the United States Air Force had only piston-powered cargo and passenger aircraft in 1960.
Photo by Stephen Miller

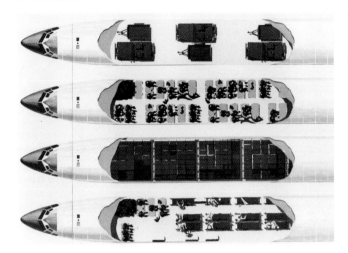

Left: Boeing's proposed C-135 was designed around its limitations. It could carry passengers, litters, pallets, and small vehicles, but not outsize cargo such as tanks, artillery, or paratroopers. *Photo P28054 courtesy Boeing*

Right: To make the C-135 (or a C-137) compatible with Air Force requirements to load cargo without a 90° turn (which limited the length of cargo), Boeing offered a swing tail configuration which required special loading equipment and which the Air Force did not want. *Photo A23588 courtesy Boeing*

especially convertible cargo-transports, exhausted the men during long flights and refueling stops. The men who travelled in non-soundproofed aircraft [like the C-124] were noticeably below par physically and psychologically when they debarked.'

Low maintenance reliability of the piston and turboprop transports equally affected US plans to deploy troops abroad. These transports required several refueling stops along the way, where even a small problem might ground the airplane until it was fixed, stranding the troops in places such as Goose Bay, Labrador, or Wake Island. Such maintenance problems might not be of sufficient nature to force the airplane to land prematurely but could prevent it from taking off again until corrected. A non-stop jet flight would allow the troops and cargo to be delivered and necessary maintenance accomplished while the airplane was readied for its return flight to pick up more troops or cargo. Because propeller-equipped engines were of greater complexity than jet engines, the potential effect of engine-related maintenance delays on a major airlift was disastrous. The need for a fleet of heavy jet transports was clear.

Even before Kennedy took office, congressional and DoD interest in a jet transport was considerable. As early as 1958, efforts to improve the US strategic airlift fleet included the development and acquisition of a jet transport. The Reed Report, delivered to Secretary of the Air Force Dudley C Sharp on 4th April 1960, stressed the need for a new cargo and troop carrier. 'Modernization of MATS is essential through procurement of an off-the-shelf turbine powered cargo aircraft and the immediate approval of a development program to modernize the remainder of the MATS fleet with a cargo aircraft meeting the specific future operating requirements of the military.' An Air Force Program of Implementation wholeheartedly endorsed this recommendation.

Solutions were proposed from both the aviation industry and the military. Douglas offered a freighter version of its DC-8 (equipped with turbofan engines) that could carry 30 tons of cargo over 4,000nm (7,412km). Boeing proposed its Model 735, a KC-135 variant with JT3D turbofan engines, capable of carrying a payload of 100,000 lb (45,360kg) with a maximum gross take-off weight of 316,000 lb (143,337kg). Like the proposed DC-8 cargo transport, the Model 735 had a 'swing tail' to load outsized cargo. The appeal of a jet transport was compelling, and MATS commander Lieutenant General Tunner 'recommended the immediate purchase of 45 converted Boeing KC-135 tankers for "fast reaction" cargo service.'

Deep concerns within Congress and the Air Force stalled any hasty purchases. House Armed Services Subcommittee Chairman L Mendel Rivers recommended that MATS 'be permitted to purchase cargo versions of the Boeing 707 or Douglas DC-8 turbojet transport as an interim aircraft, pending development of the [proposed turbofan

workhorse transport]'. MATS was torn between the long-term need for a new long-range turbofan jet transport and the short-term desire to have any jet transport capacity sooner rather than later. Lieutenant General Mark E Bradley, Jr, Air Force Deputy Chief of Staff for Materiel, said that it 'has not been decided whether MATS should have a new cargo aircraft or modernized, cargo version of a design already in existence. We may go into a fairly short range development program that would actually get some hardware for this money.'

Resistance was heavy to an off-the-shelf purchase or the modernization of an existing design that would undermine the development a true cargo jet. Aerospace companies argued that 'the ideal cargo jet should be designed from the wheels up for cargo services rather than converted from a passenger design,' and that the Air Force 'should be willing to accept a time penalty of at least one year to gain a more advanced freighter'. Crucial design capabilities of the proposed turbofan cargo plane included a truck-bed height cargo floor, straight-in cargo loading, and the ability to drop cargo and paratroopers. Neither the Douglas nor the Boeing design had any of these features.

FAA chief Elwood R Quesada (one of the crew aboard the famed *Question Mark* aerial refueling flight) offered prescient comments that were representative of arguments against the interim purchase of KC-135s converted to transports. 'Another proposal has received some attention, which is to buy KC-135 tanker aircraft for MATS and remove the tanker equipment; allegedly such a program purports to be economical. It would be difficult to imagine a more illogical thing to do. A series of lash-up modifications would follow, such as swing-the-tail to correct loading problems. Then, later, the installation of turbofan engines would become a critical need to reduce runway requirements and so on. All this would not only be time consuming and a waste of money but, what is more important, the end product would be far from what is needed. Buying anything other than an uncompromised cargo aircraft runs counter to the objective of equipping MATS with the proper equipment for its wartime job. If we compromise the military fleet now, it will have been compromised for the next decade at least.'

Which is precisely what happened.

In May 1960 Congress approved the purchase of 50 C-135 jet cargo transports for a total cost of $169 million, at a cost per airplane of $3.39 million. To save $1.4 million per airplane, the C-135s would not have the swing tail modification nor would they have turbofans. The unsuccessful DC-8 proposal, which incorporated turbofan engines and had the swing tail, offered better performance than the C-135 but would not be available until approximately eleven months after the first C-135 transport squadron would be operational. Further, senior Air Force leaders worried that if the DC-8 was selected then the 'new uncompromised strategic cargo aircraft would die right where it is'. Douglas did not give up trying to sell the DC-8F freighter to the Air Force, however. In late 1962 a DC-8F conducted cargo loading demonstrations and VIP flights for senior USAF and DoD officials. Three one-hour flights took place at Andrews AFB on 15th November 1962, and guests were treated to a sumptuous luncheon. Nonetheless, Congress issued a Specific Operational Requirement (SOR) for the cargo C-135, with 'complete support from every branch of the government concerned' and given 'top priority'. Just as with Boeing's 'victory' over Lockheed in the jet tanker competition, Boeing had 'defeated' Douglas in the jet transport competition.

Interestingly, the C-135s destined to modernize MATS were purchased with SAC in mind, according to Earl J Morgan, the chief investigator for the House Military Operations Subcommittee: 'These aircraft will be in MATS, but they are being procured solely for the SAC mission, SAC support mission, the deployment of SAC and the post-strike recovery mission'. Despite this obligation to SAC, their contribution to MATS was inestimable.

An Interim Solution

The C-135A (Boeing Model 717-157) was a derivative of the Model 738-13J Military Cargo Airplane, a 'minimum change J57-P-59W powered KC-135 modified to a cargo airplane configuration by the removal of the air refueling system, addition of strengthened floor, and fuel dumping provisions'. The C-135A had a maximum design take-off weight of 272,000 lb (123,379kg), and could carry a 90,620 lb (41,105kg) payload 2,350nm (4,354km). The cargo area was approximately 81ft (24.6m) long, had a constant width of 10ft 9in (3.27m), and a useful height of 6ft 11in (2.12m), providing a stowage space of greater than 6,000ft³ (169.9m³). Passenger capability was similar to that of the KC-135A, with 80 personnel seated in opposing rows of troop seats, with up to 160 troops if another double row was installed. Conspicuously missing from the C-135A were additional toilet facilities, a significant issue for 80 or more personnel over the course of an eight- to ten-hour flight.

An F71230 overhead cargo loader was also installed to 'facilitate cargo handling at advance bases'. Beginning in 1956 this loader was incorporated into the KC-135A (starting with 56-3607) as part of ECP 23 'Installation of Cargo Loading and Handling Provision'. The F71230 cargo loader included a framework installed in the cargo door to support two overhead rails. A carriage assembly attached to these rails could lift up to 6,000 lb (2,721kg) of cargo to the airplane's deck level and then move it inside the airplane. The F71231 traverser included a set of overhead rails running lengthwise in the cargo compartment. An electrically powered carriage mounted on the traverser then moved cargo from the loader back into the cargo compartment. With the cargo loader and traverser installed in the C-135A the cargo compartment's useful height decreased to 5ft 8in (1.72m).

The C-135A was also designed to take advantage of the soon-to-be delivered 463L Cargo Handling System, and could carry eight 108 x 88in (2.74 x 2.23m) pallets and one 54 x 88in (1.37 x 2.23m) pallet in the cargo compartment with a 20in (0.50m) aisle on each side. The 463L system was intended primarily for the forthcoming Lockheed C-141 but was tested with success on C-135s and other MATS transports during 1962. Still, cargo-loading operations required high-lift cargo trucks or forklifts capable of raising cargo to the 10ft (3.0m) high cargo deck, considerably reducing the effectiveness of the self-contained loader-transverser system.

Delivery ceremonies for the new jet transport were held at Boeing Field, where the new MATS commander Lieutenant General Joe Kelly hailed the C-135 as 'the first concrete step in a long range airlift modernization program'. He called the new jet 'a significant milestone along the route to strategic mobility for all the dynamic fighting forces of the United States'. The first C-135A Stratolifter delivered to an operational unit (60-0369) arrived on 12th August 1961, at the 18th ATS, 1611th ATW, McGuire AFB, NJ. MATS had also directed that three KC-135As already on the assembly line be

The rudimentary F71230 cargo loading device could be fitted to both KC-135As and C-135s, but this proved to be both cumbersome and reduced the airplane's cargo capacity. *Photo 6A6765 courtesy Boeing*

The first C-135A delivered was 60-0369 on 12th August 1961. Interestingly, it and all the C-135As and C-135Bs had the additional 40in (1.02m) extension to the vertical stabilizer, unlike KC-135As which were still being produced with the shorter tail. *Photo P27437 courtesy Boeing*

modified into C-135A transports. The first of these (60-0356) had arrived at McGuire AFB on 9th June 1961. Although Congress originally approved the purchase of 50 C-135 transports, only 15 turbojet C-135As (plus the three KC-135As converted into C-135As) were delivered. The balance of the order was filled during 1962 by 30 turbofan-powered C-135Bs (Model 717-158s) which were still viewed as interim airplanes. The first of these (61-2662) was handed over to the Air Force on 27th February 1962, and arrived at the 44th ATS, 1501st ATW at Travis AFB on 1st March 1962.

In response to the May 1960 SOR for a dedicated heavy jet cargo transport, the Air Force requested proposals on 20th December 1961, for Logistics Transport System SS476-L. Boeing, Convair, Douglas, and Lockheed quickly submitted proposals as all four companies had been working on such a design. Lockheed, for example, began its project in 1957. It took the Air Force only three months (until 13th March 1961, six weeks earlier than the projected deadline), to select the Lockheed C-141 Starlifter design as the winner. MATS had clearly placed its future operational capability and success on the C-141, and there was consequently little doubt that the usefulness of the C-135 as a transport was limited and that its lifetime in MATS would be short. On 5th February 1963, well before the delivery of the first C-141A, Secretary of Defense McNamara, citing the C-135's decreasing worth and increasing disadvantages when compared with the C-141, directed the Secretary of the Air Force to consider using the MATS C-135s in other roles. The first C-141 was delivered to Tinker AFB for training on 19th October 1964, and the Starlifter's first operational mission was on 23rd April 1965, flown by the 1501st ATW at Travis AFB, a unit which also operated C-135Bs. That same year the Air Force let a contract for its next generation of heavy jet transports which Lockheed won with its C-5 Galaxy, beating out proposals by Boeing and Douglas. Boeing's luck in acquiring large orders of aircraft despite losing a competition did not hold up, and additional purchases of transport C-135s with either engine type were not forthcoming.

On 1st January 1966 MATS was reorganized into the Military Airlift Command (MAC). As deliveries of C-141s increased and the number of operational units grew in number and strength, C-135As and C-135Bs were relegated to other missions and commands in accordance with the 1963 instructions from Secretary McNamara. These secondary missions included test-beds, special air mission transports, aeromedical evacuation, reconnaissance platforms, and airborne command and control.

A Host of Limitations

Although Boeing's 707 and 720 jetliners established an unbeatable reputation as passenger and commercial cargo transports, and the speed, range, and maintenance reliability of the C-135 were significantly better than its piston and turboprop predecessors, passenger and cargo versions of the KC-135 never satisfied the Air Force's requirements to the degree necessary to substantiate the purchase and continued use of a large fleet of airplanes. For example, the 117 x 78in (2.97 x 1.98m) cargo door in the fuselage side could admit most desired cargo but was over 10ft (3.0m) from the ground, requiring special loading equipment that could be stationed at major cargo destinations such as New York and London but was unavailable at many of the worldwide (if not remote) locations to which the C-135 might deploy. The side-loading cargo door necessitated an immediate 90° turn of the cargo in order to advance it along the airplane's interior, a cargo-handler's nightmare. The 463L cargo loading handler elevated the cargo but was costly and not widely available. The ECP 23 loading system was cumbersome to operate and, like the 463L, did not eliminate the awkward maneuvering required to load oversize cargo.

Boeing stressed the ability of the C-135 to carry pallets that would become standard in the air cargo industry. These required special loading vehicles located at dedicated air terminals, however, and were unlikely to be found at C-135 military destinations. *Photo P28039 courtesy Boeing*

The Air Force acknowledged that the C-135's cargo 'load capacity was insufficient, particularly for outsized cargo'. Once filled to this inadequate capacity, the C-135A suffered from the same long take-off roll common to all turbojet versions of the KC-135. The need for long paved runways and for demineralized water to increase take-off thrust severely limited its global operability. The C-135A also required a sizeable piece of concrete on which to land when fully loaded. In 1961, runways around the world usable by cargo-laden C-135As were typically found only at major civil airports and were seldom near military installations or perceived combat zones. Consequently, troops would have to be trucked from the airfield over considerable distances to reach their ultimate destination. As one airlift exercise showed, 'there was so much congestion in the [assembly] areas that [troops] were delayed from proceeding immediately to their deployment areas'. Troops flown directly to their destination by propeller-powered airplanes often arrived at approximately the same time as did those who were flown on C-135s and then trucked great distances from the airfield to the combat zone.

At heavy cargo weights the C-135A could carry only 90,000 lb (40,824kg) of fuel, limiting the airplane to five or six hours of flying time (with the necessary fuel reserves at landing). This barely provided sufficient unrefueled range from the east coast of the US to Europe, but not from the US to Pacific Ocean destinations such as Okinawa or the Republic of Korea. After the 1962 Operation LONG THRUST global transport exercise, one MATS official expressed concern over the airplane's range: '[The C-135] has its limits. It's not an ideal vehicle. It's an aircraft with a 6,000 mile [9,655km] range and we're using it for a 6,000 mile mission. We don't have the cushion we would like to have. It's a pretty raw, basic, austere aircraft.' Secretary McNamara was also keenly aware of the C-135's

limitations and wisely resisted efforts to improve them for a short-term gain in the face of long-term demands. He told the House Armed Services Committee that 'The C-135 has a relatively long take-off and landing distance, it has no airdrop capability, and does not have truck-bed height loading. Moreover, its restricted cargo cross section limits severely the size of the vehicles it can carry.' In the early 1960s the 'economics' of a weapons system often overrode its tactical and strategic value. The C-135A's ability to arrive sooner and make more trips in a given time and its improved maintenance reliability over its piston or turboprop counterparts was seen as sufficient justification for the airplane's initial acquisition despite its considerable deficiencies. These few advantages were not, however, sufficient for the Air Force to spend more money on the C-135 to improve or eliminate these shortcomings. Until the C-141's arrival, the C-135 would have to do.

Top: Airports with the long runways needed for C-135 operations were limited in number and location, requiring troops to be trucked to or from congested transit facilities. It was not until the C-17 that a cargo jet with intercontinental range could land at austere fields near the battlefront. *Photo P28613 courtesy Boeing*

Above: In November 1962 C-135Bs flew missions every three hours from Rhein-Main AB to Calcutta IAP during the Sino-Indian War. Range limits meant a fuel stop at Incirlik AB, Turkey, in each direction. *Photo courtesy Boeing*

Opposite page: An honor guard awaits the departure of Secretary Dulles from Taiwan in October 1958. Despite its speed and prestige, the accommodations in KC-135A 55-3126 were designed for military personnel accustomed to basic amenities. Diplomats and VIPs were hardly impressed. *Photo P21231 courtesy Boeing*

Despite its fundamental shortcomings, the C-135 compiled a credible record of global transport achievements ranging from cargo operations to medical evacuations. The first operational use of the new C-135A came in September 1961 as part of Operation CHECK MATE, the deployment of US troops to and from Adana, Turkey. In February 1962 C-135As flew 2,300 troops and 285 tons of cargo to the Arctic during GREAT BEAR, the annual Army/Air Force cold weather combat training exercise. Later that year, 14 C-135s carried 1,517 troops and 29 tons of cargo from Fort Riley, KS, to Rhein-Main AB, West Germany, on 9th July, during LONG THRUST IV, an exercise in support of the US Strike Command.

From 10-16th October 1962 four C-135s airlifted 16.6 tons of cargo and 1,232 Swedish peacekeeping troops over 4,258nm (7,885km) from Stockholm, Sweden, to Leopoldville, the Congo. Operation NEW TAPE was the first all-jet airlift; each non-stop flight lasted ten hours. On one return flight, a C-135B set a world record for its non-stop flight from Leopoldville to McGuire AFB (see Appendix V). C-135s returned to the Congo during November 1962 with food and medical supplies for relief efforts to aid refugees and victims of the civil war. Beginning 2nd November 1962, C-135s transported weapons to the Indian Army during the 1962 invasion of India by the People's Republic of China (PRC). This airlift over 12,000nm (19,311km) was completed over eight days. Two weeks later, the same airplanes were used to evacuate residents from Guam as it prepared for a major typhoon.

MATS C-135s also have been used during times of domestic disturbance. In early October 1962 C-135s took part in Project RAPID ROAD, the airlift of 12,500 US troops to Columbus AFB, MS, to quell violence during the racial integration of the University of Mississippi. In October 1962 MATS C-135s provided troop and cargo support for the US military build-up in Cuba and throughout the southern United States during the 1962 missile crisis. During this airlift MATS lost its first C-135B (62-4136), which crashed while landing at NAS Leeward Point, Guantànamo Bay, Cuba (see Appendix II).

Exactly one year after the Cuban Missile Crisis, the US sent a strong message to its NATO Allies and to the Soviet Union: American commitment to Europe remained resolute and the US had the means and will to support it. Operation BIG LIFT deployed the US Army's 2nd Armored Division from Texas to Europe. During this project, 23 C-135s each made two round-trip flights of the 5,600nm (9,000km) trip between Texas airfields and Rhein-Main AB. The airlift was preceded by seven advance deployment flights. Each of the C-135s typically carried 73 troops plus their duffel bags, and the non-stop flights averaged ten hours, 25 minutes. The airplanes were refueled while unloading, limiting their ground time to under three hours. BIG LIFT demonstrated the reliability of jet transports over their piston counterparts. None of the C-135s were grounded for maintenance while a considerable number of C-124s, C-130s, and C-133s were delayed for engine and propeller changes. Further, the C-135s flew nonstop to Europe whereas the propeller-driven airplanes required time-consuming fuel stops to complete the flight.

Symbols of Power
Originally jet airliners were novelties in the air transport world, designed, built, owned, and operated by the great industrial nations of the world. Leaders who arrived and departed in these jets when attending international conferences achieved a significant level of diplomatic 'one-upmanship' over their colleagues who arrived by propeller-powered airplane or by train. John Foster Dulles, the first American Secretary of State under President Dwight D Eisenhower, emphasized the need to portray the US as a nation of power and leadership through its use of the jet transport. In 1952 Britain had inaugurated international jet airliner service. In 1956 the Soviet Union did the same, and a year later orbited the world's first artificial satellite. Dulles told Eisenhower that the prestige of the US suffered every time he arrived at an international conference aboard a propeller-driven airplane while Russian diplomats were coming in aboard Soviet turbojets. In the global tug-of-war for the hearts and minds of other nations, Dulles argued, it was essential to establish in every way possible that America was technologically superior to the Soviet Union.

Just as the jet transport meant prestige, it also meant speed. Diplomatic negotiations were often protracted because of the distances between the participants. The jet age shrunk those distances, and a negotiator could work out a proposal with one nation, fly immediately to another nation to discuss it, and then return to the first nation with the revised proposal all in the same day. Beginning in 1973 US Secretary of State Henry A Kissinger exploited this capability to its fullest, introducing 'Shuttle Diplomacy' into the lexicon of international relations.

Until the VC-137A (the military designation of the 707) entered VIP service, the KC-135A was the only jet capable of carrying important passengers over long distances and at high speeds. Despite these clear advantages over existing piston-powered VIP transports such as the Lockheed C-121 Constellation or the Douglas C-118 Liftmaster, KC-135s were designed for military operations with few frills appropriate to the comfort of senior American diplomats. Consequently, not all early VIP jet operations were luxurious experiences.

On 17th October 1958, for example, Foster Dulles flew to the Vatican in KC-135A 55-3126 to attend the funeral of Pope Pius XII. While sleeping during the nine-hour overnight flight, Dulles's bunk collapsed, dropping him to the floor and badly wrenching his back.

No one knew that Dulles had fallen and he lay on the cold, hard floor in great pain until the flight reached Rome. On 19th October, Dulles and his delegation flew to RAF Brize Norton, England, to meet with British Foreign Secretary Selwyn Lloyd, who pitied Dulles and his wife, calling them a 'gallant couple' for their discomfort from flying in the military airplane. The KC-135A then flew to Eielson AFB for refueling before continuing to Taiwan, where Dulles would negotiate with Nationalist Chinese leader Jiang Jieshi (Chiang Kai Shek) in an effort to defuse the 1958 Quemoy-Matsu Crisis with the PRC.

Writing about a flight a few years later on board a KC-135 (believed to be 55-3126) known among the power brokers of the Kennedy administration as the 'McNamara Special', Paul H Nitze recalls that it was '...unbelievably uncomfortable, with portable bunks and seats arranged in the windowless plane. There was no inner shell in the dimly lighted cabin area and the noise level prohibited normal conversation, much less the ability to discuss complex issues. The extremes of heat and cold added to our misery. Eighteen hours after leaving Andrews we landed in New Delhi [India]. We emerged from the open hatch, blinking in the sunlight, like moles emerging from their dark underground tunnels on a sunny day.' The return trip was no better, as Nitze recalled arriving back at Andrews AFB 'suffering from a good deal more than jet lag'.

VIP C-135s were similarly embroiled in petty politics. At the onset of the 1982 Falklands War, US Secretary of State Alexander Haig reportedly refused to fly from Andrews AFB to London in the C-135 allocated for his flight because it did not have any windows. After a lengthy delay he agreed to fly to London in the C-135 but only if a VC-137 planned for a Congressional junket be reassigned to Haig for his flight to Buenos Aires. Haig's staff denied the issue was the lack of windows, however, claiming instead that Reagan administration officials critical of Haig planted the story. Besides, Haig's aide noted, 'the C-135 lacked a copying machine.'

Despite lacking creature comforts, the C-135 reflected American power in other ways, especially by establishing a number of speed, distance, and payload records (see Appendix V). For example, on 20th-21st February 1963, a C-135B flew unrefueled from Clark AB to McGuire AFB, a distance of 9,868nm (15,880km), setting an unofficial record for the longest non-stop flight ever made by a transport aircraft. Hardly mere grandstanding displays, these flights emphasized the decreased flying time needed to cross oceans and continents. On 1st May 1962 a C-135B carried 38 military medical evacuees from Yokota AB, Japan, to Travis AFB in nine hours, seven minutes, compared with the 42 hours required for the same trip in a piston-powered airplane which included refueling and crew rest stops.

VIP transport roles assigned to C-135s have not been limited to operations on behalf of the president and senior diplomatic officials. Air Force commands such as Air Force Systems Command (AFSC) and SAC typically have had or use a C-135 or KC-135 for the commander when traveling on official business. These VIP C-135s and KC-135s have earned a measure of fame as their radio call signs, including *Trout 99* and *Casey 01*, have been heard around the world. VIP C-135s have also acquired a degree of notoriety, as critics have charged (in some cases rightly so) that the costly modifications and operations are for the personal use of the commanding general.

Still, the movement of senior military officials was a legitimate and urgent priority. In an interesting and previously unpublicized recommendation made in 1962, MATS proposed the establishment of a Command and Control Squadron in 1964. This unit would receive newly acquired C-135s, and a portion of the existing MATS C-135 and SAC KC-135 fleets would be diverted to the new squadron, providing '... top level commanders a means of rapidly reaching trouble areas while maintaining constant airborne communication with higher headquarters, en route task forces, and

adjacent commands.' This was a particularly attractive idea for the senior commanders in the Pacific Command who had to travel across the Pacific Ocean, particularly to Viet Nam. The aircraft would be under the operational control of MATS but was scheduled by the borrowing organization (e.g., PACAF or CINCPAC). The squadron would operate 8-12 airplanes (another staff summary recommended 14), preferably C-135Bs with turbofans. Each airplane would have a palletized staff suite which could be removed so the airplane could be used for purely cargo missions. A third HF radio would be available as a spare. At the same time Pentagon planners submitted a similar proposal to establish a 'Command Air Transport Unit with 10 C-135s, to provide transportation for key DoD officials, members of the JCS, and Commanders of Unified/Specified Commands.' The JCS approved these and forwarded both to Secretary McNamara

Not surprisingly, SAC was hostile to this idea, fearing that any KC-135As withdrawn from its tanker force for conversion into staff transports for other Air Force branches or the other services would adversely affect SAC's ability to carry out the SIOP. Moreover, SAC worried that its own staff transport and airborne command post requirements would suffer. As far as is known, these proposals died without implementation. Nonetheless, their intent was satisfied eventually through airborne command post units assigned directly to major commands, airborne deployment squadrons, and the use of command support aircraft.

Other C-135s have been used as command support aircraft (CSA – known derogatorily as 'Chicken Shit Airlines'). As early as 1956 SAC wanted to buy six C-135s for administrative duties such as carrying command evaluation teams around the world to inspect operational units. SAC operational readiness inspections (ORIs) were conducted without any advance warning. The CSAs were painted white on top of the fuselage; the announcement of an 'unexpected white-top on final approach' meant the arrival of the ORI and the careers of the wing's senior staff hung in the balance. Although the CSA C-135s were assigned to SAC, their missions were assigned and directed by MAC, and after 31st May 1992 by Air Mobility Command (AMC), and funding was terminated for the CSA program in 1993.

With the drawdown in the US military during the 1990s, several proposals addressed the retirement of all transport C-135s (except for the SPECKLED TROUT C-135C 61-2669). One recommendation was the conversion of five KC-135As from AMARG into C-135Rs with the air refueling boom removed and the installation of an IFR receptacle. Another suggestion called for a one-for-one substitution of Boeing VC-32As (757s) for VIP C-135s, already slated to replace ageing and noisy VC-137s. Irrespective of the overall requirement and acquisition process of the USAF VIP transport fleet, the goal was straightforward: replace the C-135 fleet as quickly as possible with airframes that were more fuel efficient, had a quieter footprint, were more easily maintained, and were more cost effective. As such, subsequent VIP duties have been assigned to C-32As, Boeing C-40B/Cs, and Gulfstream C-37As, among others.

SAC KC-135 tankers also had a secondary transport role. They frequently carried military passengers and dependents on a 'space available' basis, as well as those traveling on official business. During fighter deployments, support elements of the fighter unit were carried by the KC-135s which refueled the fighters en route to their forward bases, although this capability was somewhat limited by runway and parking availability at the destination air base. Although the primary mission of YOUNG TIGER was the aerial refueling of combat aircraft used in the war in Southeast Asia, the constant tanker deployments and redeployments served unquestionably as invaluable transport flights. Once AMC acquired primary responsibility for the former SAC tanker fleet, KC-135s added 'channel missions' – dedicated cargo and passenger flights – to their list of primary duties. A pallet

and roller system has been installed in KC-135Rs and KC-135Ts, enhancing their cargo loading capability and mission flexibility. In this sense, the KC-135 tanker has been a more effective transport than either the dedicated C-135A and C-135B.

Most ironical, however, was the 2006 retirement of the C-141 – designed to replace the C-135 in cargo and transport duties – and the assumption by AMC KC-135Rs of some former MAC C-141 roles. These additional missions had the potential to be highly significant and not altogether conducive to the KC-135R's lifespan. Every sortie that did not support the air refueling mission burned total flying hours that were otherwise irreplaceable in the absence of a follow-on tanker. The near-term savings incurred by retiring the C-141 fleet, for example, which was replaced in large measure by C-17As and to a lesser degree by KC-135Rs, was modestly offset by the long-term costs incurred in keeping KC-135Rs flying longer to meet both the transport and refueling mission. Since the end of the Cold War, KC-135Rs have seen an increase in annual flying time of approximately 150 hours per year, nearly all of which is attributable to increases in operational tempo associated with missions around the world. Fortunately, processes are in place at the PDM facility at Tinker AFB to mitigate these effects, ensuring that non-refueling transport missions do not adversely affect the KC-135R's dwindling lifetime.

The number of units that operated transport C-135s was fairly small. The first was the 18th ATS, 1611th ATW at McGuire AFB, beginning on 9th June 1961. This was joined on 8th January 1962 by the 40th ATS, also at McGuire AFB. The 44th ATS, 1501st ATW at Travis AFB was the only west coast unit to operate C-135s, beginning 1st March 1962. Operations within Europe were first undertaken by the 7407th CSW at Rhein-Main AB, then the 7111th SS (later the 7111th OS) at Rhein-Main AB, and finally by the 58th MAS (later the 58th ALS) at Ramstein AB. Those in the Pacific were first conducted by airplanes assigned to the 6486th ABW (later the 15th ABW), then by Det. 1, 89th MAW, and finally by the 65th ALS, 15th ABW at Hickam AFB. SAC CSAs were part of the 55th SRW, later the 55th Wing, at Offutt AFB. Space Command's C-135E was part of the 552nd ACW, previously assigned to the 28th AD, at Tinker AFB. Special Air Mission C-135s were originally assigned to the 1st MAS, 89th MAW, later the 1st ALS, 89th AW at Andrews AFB. In 1993 C-135B 62-4126 was assigned to the 21st Air Force and based at McGuire AFB. By 1997 three C-135Bs were converted to RC-135Ws and a TC-135W

Designations applied to transport C-135s include C-135A, C-135B, C-135C, C-135E and C-135K. Tankers dedicated to VIP or transport roles retained their 'KC' designation. One converted testbed served as a transport with the designation NKC-135A. Beginning in 1968 the prefix 'V' was added to the designation of C-135B transports assigned to the 89th MAW, but on 1st December 1977 this was discontinued and they once again became C-135Bs as part of President Jimmy Carter's government 'low profile' program.

C-135s transports were originally natural metal and carried MATS markings, which were replaced with MAC markings in 1966. Later color schemes varied from grey with a white fuselage top to white and highly polished silver to a darker variation of the scheme applied to C-137Cs, popularly known as the 'Air Force One scheme', created by noted industrial designer Raymond Loewy. (This scheme is often and incorrectly attributed to President Kennedy's wife, *viz:* 'Jacqueline Kennedy designed the exterior markings, the interior appointments, and color scheme', or the C-135B's 'distinctive blue-and-white colour scheme [is] based on that designed by Jacqueline Kennedy for the first VC-137C'.)

SPECKLED TROUT C-135C 61-2669 *Trout 99* prepares to depart Berlin-Tempelhof AP. In addition to its testbed role, it was also used to transport senior AF and DoD officials on business around the world.
Photo by Ralf Manteufel

'Left over' C-135As were used as Command Support Aircraft, essentially on-demand airliners for military personnel. They were retired by 1992.
Photo by the author

Two of the three C-135A 'falsies' (60-0356 and 60-0357) share the delivery line with two KC-135As (60-0359 and 60-0360), with which they had more in common than any of the MATS C-135As. *Photo P27213 courtesy Boeing*

Although C-135As gave MATS intercontinental jet capability, they were limited in useful payload and range. As such, C-135As were better suited to trans-Atlantic missions than longer flights over the Pacific. *Photo by Stephen Miller*

Although C-135A 60-0376 'bounced' between units at Andrews AFB and Hickam AFB, it spent most of its time at Offutt AFB. A year later it would be re-engined and reassigned to Tinker AFB. *Photo by Brian Rogers*

After conversion to a C-135E, 60-0376 acquired a paint scheme similar to its 'bicentennial' scheme, although in light grey instead of light blue. *Photo by Peter Zastrow via Stephen Miller*

Opposite: While assigned to the 89th MAW, C-135A 60-0378 acquired the distinctive 'Air Force One' color scheme. It retained this after being reassigned to the 55th SRW in 1977, but it was removed during its next PDM. *Photo by Brian Rogers*

C-135A/E INDIVIDUAL AIRCRAFT

MATS initially ordered ten C-135A Stratolifters in February 1961 to serve as interim jet transports pending the development and delivery of what would become the C-141 Starlifter. In addition, MATS directed the conversion of three KC-135As already on the assembly line (60-0356, 60-0357, and 60-0362) into C-135As. The first of these three — referred to as 'falsies' – was delivered to the 1611th ATW at McGuire AFB on 9th June 1961. C-135A deliveries to McGuire AFB began on 12th August 1961, although two airplanes (60-0376 and 60-0377) were assigned to the 1501st ATW at Travis AFB in support of the Los Alamos Laboratory while retaining MATS markings (these two jets had both a transport and an observational/testbed mission). A follow-on order for five more C-135As brought the total to 15 airplanes, plus the three 'falsies', which were counted as part of KC-135A production figures. These three were delivered without the 40in (1.0m) extension to the vertical stabilizer, a modification present in all the other MATS C-135As. All 15 of the C-135As and the three 'falsies' had J57-P/F-43 turbojets.

As with any new weapon system, the C-135A's first few years of operation were fraught with numerous but common problems. A shortage of qualified loadmasters and navigators, for example, seriously affected the ability to fly a large number of C-135As over extended periods. Similarly, a shortage of J57 engines grounded some aircraft. MATS utilized the SAC KC-135A training program at Castle AFB for pilot qualification. After the initial cadre of MATS navigators was trained at Castle AFB, this task was assumed by the 1611th ATW at McGuire AFB. Moreover, new facilities unique to jet airplanes such as a jet engine test cell (which was eventually disapproved), blast deflectors, and enlargements to existing hangars had to be built at McGuire AFB to accommodate the new airplanes.

C-135As flew their first major operational transport mission as part of Operation CHECK MATE from 15-25th September 1961, transporting troops and equipment of the US Army's 101st Airborne Infantry Division to and from Adana, Turkey. During these ten missions, the C-135As achieved a dismal controllable delay rate of 8.1% (the percentage of delays which could be prevented by better maintenance and improved operational factors, excluding weather and air traffic control delays), nearly double that for the C-118, a fault easily attributable to problems associated with any new weapon system. This rate dropped to approximately 5% for the rest of 1961.

Beginning in 1962 Ling-TEMCO-Vought (LTV) converted the three 'falsies' into KC-135A-II OFFICE BOY reconnaissance platforms. During January and February 1965, ten C-135As were placed in flyable storage at Hunter AFB, GA, to make room at McGuire AFB for the 16 C-135Bs used in Operation BEST BALL, which determined 'the optimum wartime flying hour utilization of military aircraft'. After the test the ten C-135As returned to McGuire AFB. Despite appearing in VIP paint schemes and assignment to units responsible for high-priority transport, there is no documentary evidence that any C-135As – especially 60-0376 and 60-0378 – were ever designated as VC-135As. Of the eighteen C-135As, all were ultimately converted into a variety of subsequent configurations including tankers, test-beds, and trainers. They have all since been stored or scrapped.

60-0356 One of three KC-135As converted on the production line into a C-135A. First flew 19th May 1961. Delivered to the Air Force on 2nd June 1961 and arrived at McGuire AFB on 9th June. Departed McGuire AFB on 31st October 1961 for conversion into a KC-135A-II.

60-0357 One of three KC-135As converted on the production line into a C-135A. First flew 24th May 1961. Delivered to the Air Force on 6th June 1961 and arrived at McGuire AFB on 9th June. Departed McGuire AFB on 6th October 1961 for conversion into a KC-135A-II.

60-0362 One of three KC-135As converted on the production line into a C-135A. First flew on 14th June 1961. Delivered to McGuire AFB on 5th July 1961. Departed McGuire AFB on 6th September 1961 for conversion into a KC-135A-II.

60-0369 First flew on 23rd June 1961. Delivered on 6th October 1961. Transferred to AFSC in 1964 for conversion into an NC-135A.

60-0370 First flew on 20th July 1961. Delivered on 12th August 1961. Transferred to AFSC in 1964 for conversion into an NC-135A.

60-0371 First flew on 9th August 1961. Delivered on 23rd August 1961. Transferred to AFSC in 1964 for conversion into an NC-135A.

60-0372 First flew on 24th August 1961. Delivered on 31st August 1961. Douglas converted it into the first EC-135N Apollo Range Instrumented Aircraft (ARIA) in 1966.

60-0373 First flew on 5th September 1961. Delivered 15th September 1961. Crashed on 25th June 1965 (see Appendix II).

60-0374 First flew on 15th September 1961. Delivered to the Air Force on 25th September 1961. Converted into an EC-135N ARIA in 1966.

60-0375 First flew on 22nd September 1961. Delivered to MATS on 28th September 1961. Converted to an EC-135N ARIA in 1966.

60-0376 First flew on 11th October 1961. Delivered on 30th October 1961. Reassigned in September 1963 to the 1501st ATW at Travis AFB for support of the Los Alamos Laboratory. Assigned by 23rd June 1965 to AFSC as a JC-135A and transferred to Los Alamos for use as a dedicated test-bed involving 'nuclear readiness testing' (see Chapter 8). It was redesignated as a C-135A on 31st October 1967.

From 7th September 1972 through 17th May 1973, 60-0376 was converted into a staff transport under PACER JOURNEY, an episode that earned the airplane the unwanted attention of Senator William Proxmire, famous for his 'Golden Fleece' award given to government agencies that 'squander' taxpayer dollars. The senator claimed that the airplane was being converted into a 'flying playboy penthouse at the taxpayers' expense' for the 'personal use of logistics commander Gen Jack Catton'. The airplane required considerable labor and expense to demodify and then cover the nearly 100 residual small windows acquired as a test-bed. A congressional team went to Tinker AFB to investigate Proxmire's claims. What followed was classic Keystone Kops. One flight-line worker recalled: 'I can assure you that we heard that the plane was indeed for Gen Catton's use, as well as other VIP transport. We were told to "get rid of" and "hide" everything connected with that plane, i.e., blue carpet (by the roll!), Sears range and built-in ovens (2), already upholstered blue and white seats, etc., etc. We carted off several trailer loads of goodies. When the congressional team came to "investigate," there was very little to see! That's why that very team gave us advance notice that they were going to show up – they didn't want to report that it was all true! We did bring it all back and install it!' Despite Proxmire's protests and the investigation, the luxury modification was nonetheless completed with the rationalization that the airplane would be used as a command support aircraft to 'haul AFLC repair crews around the world'.

On 21st March 1975 the airplane was loaned to the 15th ABW at Hickam AFB and on 10th November to the 89th MAW at Andrews AFB for use as a VIP transport. In January 1977 it was reassigned to the 55th SRW at Offutt AFB as a CSA. Through 1979, 60-0376 was regularly transferred between the 552nd AWACW at Tinker AFB, the 15th ABW at Hickam AFB, and the 55th SRW at Offutt AFB. In December 1979 this 'rotation' stopped and 60-0376 was assigned to the 55th SRW at Offutt AFB.

The airplane was converted into a C-135E from 27th March 1982 through 17th April 1982. It was loaned to the 58th MAS at Ramstein AB from June to October 1983 while C-135B 62-4125 underwent programmed depot maintenance (PDM). From Ramstein AB, 60-0376 was transferred on 26th October 1983, to the 8th TDCS, 552nd AWACW at Tinker AFB.

From February to May 1984 it received an interior upgrade, converting the airplane to support the Commander, USAF Space Command. In March 1986 the 8th TDCS, which operated 60-0376, was reassigned to the 28th AD, and on 29th May 1992, was again reassigned to the 552nd ACW, still at Tinker AFB. There was an effort to retire 60-0376 in October 1993, but this did not happen. On 1st July 1994, the 8th ADCS was redesignated the 8th ACCS and 60-0376 was transferred. With the 15th May 1996 inactivation of the 8th ACCS, 60-0376 was reassigned to the 552nd ACW. 60-0376 ended its transport duties with the 65th AS at Hickam AFB. Relegated to AMARG on 21st November 2001 as AACA0130 (see Appendix III).

60-0377 First flew on 12th October 1961. Delivered on 1st November 1961. Assigned to the 1501st ATW at Travis AFB in 1963 for support of the Los Alamos Laboratory (see Chapter 8).

60-0378 First flew on 17th October 1961. Delivered on 3rd November 1961. Assigned to AFSC at Wright-Patterson AFB on 17th January 1968. Modified under Project 97309(635) into a weightlessness trainer effective 24th July 1968. Demodified from this configuration beginning 23rd May 1973 and assigned on 17th August 1973 to the 1866th Flight Check Squadron, Air Force Communications Service (AFCS), at Richards-Gebaur AFB, MO, (which moved to Tinker AFB on 7th September 1973). It served both as a VIP transport and as a communications check platform. Reassigned to the 89th MAW by 30th June 1975, and in December 1975 received a VIP interior. Reassigned to the 55th SRW at Offutt AFB on 31st August 1977 as a C-135A CSA. At one time there were efforts to re-engine the airplane with TF33-PW-102s, converting it into a C-135E, but budget limitations prevented this. On 23rd July 1993, it was written off as a battle damage repair (BDR) trainer at Tinker AFB (see Appendix III).

61-0326 First flew on 3rd November 1961. Delivered on 17th November 1961. Converted into an EC-135N ARIA in 1967.

61-0327 First flew on 13th November 1961. Delivered on 29th November 1961. Converted into an EC-135N ARIA in 1966.

61-0328 First flew on 14th November 1961. Delivered on 6th December 1961. Converted into an EC-135N ARIA in 1967.

61-0329 First flew on 1st December 1961. Delivered on 12th December 1961. Converted into an EC-135N ARIA in 1967.

61-0330 First flew on 14th December 1961. Final C-135A delivered to the Air Force on 3rd January 1962, and arrived at McGuire AFB the following day. Converted to an EC-135N ARIA in 1966.

V/C-135B INDIVIDUAL AIRCRAFT

In addition to the 15 C-135As ordered while awaiting the delivery of the C-141, MATS ordered 30 C-135Bs. The first C-135B flew on 15th February 1962, and differed considerably from the C-135A. The most obvious change was the use of TF33-P-5 turbofans instead of the J57 turbojets on the C-135A. The 40% increase in thrust (over 5,000 lb – 22.4kN) per engine improved the C-135B's take-off performance enabling it to use shorter runways or, when using longer runways, carry more troops or cargo. The TF33-P-5 has thrust reversers, improving the airplane's short field landing capability. The C-135B's horizontal stabilizers were increased in span to that of later 707 stabilizers to improve pitch control, affected by the increase in thrust available.

Capacity was 89,000 lb (40,370kg) of cargo, 126 fully equipped combat troops, or 44 litters and 54 seats in the medevac role. Range in the latter two configurations was over 4,500nm (8,338km). Additional cargo compartment soundproofing was added, as were improved galley and latrine facilities. A second air conditioning pack was installed to regulate the cargo compartment temperature, but this proved to be less than adequate. Airliner windows were originally proposed for the C-135B but were not adopted as a cost savings measure. A fuel dump tube was substituted for the air refueling boom. The C-135B transports were not equipped with an IFR system for in-flight refueling. These improvements were not without a price. Each C-135B cost $3,320,000 as compared with $2,620,000 per C-135A. A proposal to retrofit the 15 C-135As with TF33-P-5s was rejected because of the cost coupled with a shortage of engines.

In a rainy ceremony held at Travis AFB on 1st March 1962, WESTAF Commander Major General Glen R Birchard delivered the first C-135B to the Air Force. Accompanying Birchard were Boeing Vice President John O Yeasting (who a decade earlier participated in the momentous decision to build the Dash 80), and Lieutenant Colonel William L Brinson, commander of the 44th ATS, the first C-135B squadron. Mrs Lenore Anderson, wife of California's Lieutenant Governor, christened C-135B 61-2662 *The Golden State* in honor of the airplane's new home state of California.

The airplanes were assigned to the 18th and 41st ATS, 1611th ATW at McGuire AFB, and the 44th ATS, 1501st ATW at Travis AFB. They were routinely transferred between the two bases, as photographs show most of the airplanes in the markings of either wing. Travis AFB had only C-135Bs assigned as the C-135As lacked the necessary range and payload capacity for non-stop Pacific operations, although C-135As flew a variety of missions throughout the Pacific region but using shorter hops.

The C-135B demonstrated an immediate and notable improvement in performance and operations over the C-135A. By June 1962, Birchard described the reliability of the C-135B as 'phenomenal'. Of 78 scheduled flights during June, there were only six maintenance delays, reflecting a 93% reliability rate. Still, there were a few issues to be resolved before the C-135 fleet was considered fully operational. Some communication and navigation equipment was in extremely short supply (airplanes were frequently dispatched without primary radios or TACANs), as were turbofan engines and components. MATS restricted to 72 the number of troops or passengers in its C-135s, only 90% of its capacity, due to the shortage of emergency exits in the airplane. Bureaucratic wrangling over who would modify the

In addition to building new C-135Bs, Boeing proposed re-engining all the C-135As with TF33-P-5s. The Air Force declined, knowing full well that future jet cargo aircraft would look like the C-141, not the C-135. *Photo P28794 courtesy Boeing*

The C-135B provided austere toilet facilities, and even this had to be retrofitted to C-135As. Two restrooms, each with 5gals (18.9ls) of potable water, one small chemical toilet, and three 'white rocket' urinals, barely met the needs of 80 passengers and 6-8 coffee-fueled crewmembers on a 10-hour flight. A proper galley would have taken up cargo space, so box lunches were provided, if at all. *Photo P28571 courtesy Boeing*

President Jimmy Carter's 'low profile' scheme on the US fleet of VIP aircraft was synonymous with the loss of prestige abroad. The subdued colors for C-135B 62-4125 did little to improve relations with Iran, Salvadoran rebels, or prevent the USSR from invading Afghanistan. *Photo by Stephen Miller*

Six consecutively serialled C-135Bs prior to final painting. All would become WC-135Bs, and two would later become C-135Cs, most notably 61-2669 as the second SPECKLED TROUT. *Photo P29074 courtesy Boeing*

airplanes – Boeing or OCAMA – delayed the installation of additional doors and emergency egress slides. A shortage of galleys adversely affected C-135 operations, with each airplane initially equipped with a partial galley, hardly suitable to feed 70 passengers and a crew of 11. Finally, SAC and MATS quibbled over aircrew training. SAC training at Castle AFB emphasized air refueling operations, and MATS requested an abbreviated course which did not include this unnecessary training for MATS transport pilots and navigators. At first SAC balked but eventually relented. MATS crews learned to fly the KC-135 at Castle AFB, then transitioned to the C-135, especially the B-model, at their home bases.

Following the 1965 delivery of the first C-141s, C-135Bs were slowly transferred to other transport units or converted for other missions such as Telemetry Range Instrumented Aircraft (TRIA) C-135Bs or WC-135B weather reconnaissance airplanes. Beginning 5th April 1966, five C-135Bs – 62-4125, 62-4126, 62-4127, 62-4129, and 62-4130 – were transferred to the 89th MAW at Andrews AFB as SAM aircraft. From 1967-68 Lockheed Aircraft Systems (LAS) at Jamaica, NY, configured them VIP airliner interiors and they were designated VC-135Bs, possibly as part of the RIVET KING program. The 89th MAW's inventory of C-135Bs changed little for the next two decades, although 61-2663 was briefly assigned to the 89th MAW prior to its transfer to ASD on 22nd December 1967.

With the 1st December 1977 directive as part of the Carter 'Low Profile' program for VIP operations, the five VC-135Bs were repainted from the famous and popular 'Air Force One scheme' to a bland overall white and gold motif. The airplanes were also redesignated C-135Bs, de-emphasizing their VIP role. Following the 1981 inauguration of Ronald Reagan, the airplanes were again painted in the blue and silver scheme, although they remained designated C-135Bs. In February 1987 62-4129 departed the 89th MAW for conversion into the initial TC-135W, and the four remaining C-135Bs were given wide-body interiors gleaned from former airline 707s. This effort emphasized the differences between the 707 and KC-135, as the 707 interiors required considerable modification to fit inside the C-135Bs. By October 1992 the remaining C-135Bs were transferred to the 55th Wing at Offutt AFB for use as CSAs, replacing the C-135A and NKC-135A. Other C-135Bs were transferred to or remained assigned to Det 1, 89th AW (later the 65th ALS, 15th ABW) at Hickam AFB. Ultimately three of these C-135Bs (62-4125, 62-4127 and 62-4130) were converted into RC-135Ws and another TC-135W from 1997 onwards.

61-0331 First flew on 20th December 1961. Delivered to the Air Force on 31st January 1962, for initial flight test and certification. Assigned to the 1611th ATW at McGuire AFB on 9th October 1962. Transferred during July 1963 to the 1501st ATW at Travis AFB, returning to the 1611th ATW at McGuire AFB in April 1965. Converted in 1967 into a TRIA C-135B.

61-0332 First flew on 2nd February 1962. Delivered to the Air Force the same day for flight testing and certification. Delivered to the 1501st ATW at Travis AFB on 27th April 1962. Crashed on 11th May 1964 (see Appendix II).

61-2662 First flew on 15th February 1962. Delivered to the Air Force on 28th February, and on the following day became the first C-135B handed over to MATS. Transferred to AFSC on 11th December 1967, for use as a test-bed.

61-2663 First flew on 26th February 1962. Delivered on 24th March 1962. Some records show that it was transferred on 12th May 1966 to the 1st MAS, 89th MAW at Andrews AFB, but there is nothing to indicate that it was redesignated a VC-135B. Transferred to AFSC on 22nd December 1967, for testbed duties.

61-2664 First flew on 9th March 1962. Delivered to the Air Force on 28th March 1962. Transferred to the 55th WRS, 9th WRW at McClellan AFB on 17th October 1967 for use as a 'hack' and flight-deck trainer. Reassigned to AFSC on 15th February 1968 and converted into a TRIA C-135B.

61-2665 First flown 16th March 1962. Delivered to the 1501st ATW at Travis AFB on 29th March 1962. Converted 30th March 1968 into a WC-135B.

61-2666 First flew on 27th March 1962. Delivered to MATS on 30th March 1962. This C-135B set several world-class cargo lift and speed records in April 1962 (see Appendix V). Converted in 29th September 1965 into a WC-135B.

61-2667 First flew on 3rd April 1962. Delivered on 20th April 1962, to the 1501st ATW at Travis AFB. Converted to a WC-135B 16th March 1966.

61-2668 First flew on 4th April 1962. Delivered 20th April 1962. Converted into a WC-135B on 7th September 1965. Demodified to C-135B in 1971 and stored at MASDC from 20th July 1972 through 1st November 1972, with the PCN code CA002. It received a staff interior and returned to service as a C-135B on 3rd April 1973. Modified into a C-135C on 6th September 1973. By 1996 it had been scrapped at Tinker AFB (see Appendix III).

61-2669 First flew on 11th April 1962. Accepted by the Air Force on 25th April 1962. Converted into a WC-135B on 7th September 1965. Placed in storage at MASDC from 20th July 1972 through 8th November 1972, and given the PCN code CA003. It was then demodified and relegated to MASDC on 20th July 1972, and given the PCN code CA003. Beginning 8th November 1972 it was modified into staff configuration and reactivated as a C-135B on 21st April 1973. On 11th October 1973 it was redesignated a C-135C. It then became the second SPECKLED TROUT aircraft on 8th February 1975. On 13th January 2006 it was retired and placed on static display at the Air Force Flight Test Center Museum at Edwards AFB.

61-2670 First flew on 18th April 1962. The Air Force received this C-135B on 26th April 1962. Converted into a WC-135B on 1st September 1965.

61-2671 First flew on 25th April 1962. Assigned to the 1501st ATW at Travis AFB from 28th April 1962 until 21st September 1965 when it was converted into a WC-135B. Demodified in March 1973 back into C-135B status, and on 5th April 1974 was further converted into a C-135C. Placed on static display at Tinker AFB 30th October 1991 (see Appendix III).

61-2672 First flew on 27th April 1962. Arrived at the 1501st ATW at Travis AFB on 30th April 1962. Converted on 30th March 1965 into a WC-135B.

61-2673 First flew on 7th May 1962. Assigned to the 1501st ATW at Travis AFB on 16th May 1962. Converted to a WC-135B on 17th March 1965.

61-2674 First flew on 11th May 1962. Delivered on 18th May 1962. Converted into a WC-135B on 1st September 1965.

62-4125 First flew on 30th April 1962. Assigned to the 1611th ATW at McGuire AFB on 28th May 1962. Reassigned on 5th April 1966, to the 1st MAS, 89th MAW at Andrews AFB, as the first SAM C-135. By 15th December 1968 LAS had installed a VIP interior and redesignated it as a VC-135B. Redesignated a C-135B on 27th March 1977, and transferred to Det. 2, 435th TAW (later the 58th MAS) at Ramstein AB, as the second CREEK FALCON aircraft providing VIP and high priority passenger transport throughout Europe and western Asia, replacing KC-135A 63-8020. By September 1991 it was reassigned to the 55th Wing at Offutt AFB as a CSA. It was reassigned to the 65th ALS, 15th ABW at Hickam AFB. Converted into an RC-135W RIVET JOINT 15 by 15th October 1999.

62-4126 First flew on 18th May 1962. Delivered on 29th May 1962. Assigned on 15th December 1967 to the 1st MAS, 89th MAW at Andrews AFB. Configured with a VIP interior and redesignated a VC-135B on 15th December 1968. Redesignated C-135B on 28th July 1978, under the Carter Administration's 'low-profile' effort. Transferred in September 1991 to the 55th Wing at Offutt AFB as a CSA. Since transferred to the 21st AF at McGuire AFB for an unidentified transport mission, possibly with the On-Site Inspection Agency (OSIA) or for discreet VIP operations, with crews from the 141st AREFS, 108th AREFW, New Jersey ANG. Converted into an RC-135W RIVET JOINT 17 on 15th November 2006.

62-4127 First flew on 25th May 1962. Delivered on 31st May 1962. Transferred to the 89th MAW at Andrews AFB on 8th October 1967. LAS configured it with a VIP interior, and it was redesignated a VC-135B on 15th December 1968. Redesignated a C-135B on 28th July 1978. Transferred in September 1991 to the 55th Wing at Offutt AFB as a CSA. It was then reassigned to the 65th ALS, 15th ABW at Hickam AFB. Converted into a TC-135W on 30th August 2005.

62-4128 First flew on 25th May 1962. Assigned to MATS on 1st June 1962. Served briefly in November 1967 with the 55th WRS, 9th WRW at McClellan AFB and then from 10th November 1967 through 25th January 1968 with the 56th WRS at Yokota AB, when it departed to AFETR at Patrick AFB.

62-4129 First flew on 4th June 1962. Delivered on 9th June 1962. Became the second SAM C-135 assigned to the 1st MAS, 89th MAW at Andrews AFB on 6th April 1966. Received a VIP interior in 1967 and was redesignated a VC-135B on 15th December 1968. Redesignated a C-135B on 1st July 1977. Assigned in 1978 to the 55th SRW at Offutt AFB as a CSA. Returned to the 89th MAW in the early 1980s. Following the purchase of two ex-airline Boeing 707s for the 89th MAW, 62-4129 returned to SAC in February 1987 for conversion into the TC-135W and was delivered on 22nd April 1988.

62-4130 First flew on 6th June 1962. Assigned to MATS on 15th June 1962. This was the third SAM C-135 assigned to the 1st MAS, 89th MAW at Andrews AFB on 22nd April 1966. Received a VIP interior in 1967 and redesignated a VC-135B on 8th December 1968. Redesignated a C-135B on 20th July 1977 and assigned to the 55th SRW at Offutt AFB as a CSA until April 1979, when it returned to the 89th MAW. Loaned to the 552nd AW&CW at Tinker AFB during September 1985 for command support duties, thereafter returning to the 89th MAW. Transferred by July 1991 to the 55th SRW (the 55th Wing after 1st September 1991) at Offutt AFB as a CSA. Loaned to 65th ALS, 15th ABW, in October 1991. Converted into an RC-135W RIVET JOINT 16 on 30th March 2000.

62-4131 First flew on 9th June 1962. Delivered to the 438th MAW on 22nd June 1962. Handed over to LTV on 15th June 1966, for conversion into an RC-135M.

62-4132 First flew on 12th June 1962. Delivered on 27th June 1962. LTV began converting it to RC-135M on 14th November 1966.

62-4133 First flew on 14th June 1962. Assigned to the 1611th ATW at McGuire AFB on 29th June 1962. Converted in 1967 into a C-135B TRIA.

62-4134 First flew on 19th June 1962. MATS received this airplane on 29th June 1962. LTV began converting this airplane into an RC-135M on 11th September 1967.

62-4135 First flew on 21st June 1962. Delivered on 3rd July 1962. This was the first C-135B converted into an RC-135M; LTV started the conversion during 1966.

62-4136 First flew on 3rd July 1962. Delivered to the Air Force on 16th July 1962. Crashed on 23rd October 1962 (see Appendix II).

62-4137 First flew on 18th July 1962. Assigned to the 1611th ATW at McGuire AFB from 27th July 1962 through 30th September 1963, when LTV converted it into the sole RC-135E.

62-4138 First flew on 1st August 1962. Delivered on 15th August 1962. LTV began converting it to an RC-135M on 27th October 1967.

62-4139 First flew on 7th August 1962. Assigned to the 1611th ATW at McGuire AFB on 29th August 1962. It was the last C-135B converted into an RC-135M, with work commencing on 14th December 1967.

Opposite, top: C-135Bs were assigned to both Travis AFB and McGuire AFB, so were routine visitors around the world. C-135As, which lacked the extra range, were assigned only to McGuire AFB and tended to be used in European operations.

Opposite, bottom: On 1st January 1966 MATS became MAC, and the fleet of C-135s were repainted accordingly. Some of the airplanes had a white background behind the 'Military Airlift Command' on the fuselage, as on C-135 62-4126.
Both: Author's collection

This page, top to bottom: VC-135B 62-4126 visits Heathrow. C-135s of all variants regularly came to London carrying diplomats and military officials on visits to the UK. *Photo by Richard Vandervord*

New Jersey ANG crews flew C-135B 62-4126 on discreet missions abroad, typically from Andrews AFB. *Photo by Stephen Miller*

The 'Air Force One' scheme was created by industrial designer Raymond Loewy, but is widely attributed to Jackie Kennedy. By mid-1978 the scheme disappeared and VC-135Bs, such as 62-4127 at Heathrow, were redesignated as C-135Bs.
Photo by Richard Vandervord

C-135B 62-4127 served as a CSA at both Offutt AFB and Hickam AFB before being converted into the third TC-135W.
Photo by Joe Bruch

In May 1967 the United States was deeply embroiled in war in Southeast Asia. Although most of the heavy lifting was done by C-141s and later C-5s, MAC C-135Bs routinely flew to bases like Cam Ranh Bay AB, Clark AB, and Kadena AB. *Photo by Richard Sullivan via Stephen Miller*

C-135B 62-4129 visits Davis-Monthan AFB on 17th May 1980 while assigned to the 15th ABW at Hickam AFB. The PACAF emblem is visible on the weather door, and four stars are discernable in the pilot's aft window, attesting to the rank of the flight's passenger. *Photo by Brian Rogers*

C-135B 62-4131 taxis at SeaTac IAP in June 1962. In the background is Boeing 720-047B N93144 with Western Airlines, delivered a year earlier. Boeing was quick to take advantage of the KC-135 'learning curve' and get 707s into service. *Photo P30054 courtesy Boeing*

C-135C INDIVIDUAL AIRCRAFT

Three former WC-135Bs were converted into C-135Bs transports following their decommissioning from use as weather reconnaissance platforms. Two were temporarily stored at MASDC. From 1974 to 1975, the Oklahoma City Air Logistics Center (OCALC) at Tinker AFB converted the three airplanes into C-135Cs. Modifications include the addition of a staff interior. The airplanes retained the IFR system installed as WC-135Bs.

All three airplanes served as VIP transports. Two (61-2668 and 61-2671) were assigned to Det 1, 89th MAW at Hickam AFB serving, among others, the Commander-in-Chief, Pacific Air Forces (CINCPACAF). On 10th March 1992 this unit was replaced by the 65th ALS, 15th ABW. The other C-135C (61-2669) was assigned for use by the Air Force Chief of Staff (but was also available to a variety of high-ranking military officials), and was also used as the SPECKLED TROUT avionics testbed. It was on board 61-2669 that new USAF Chief of Staff Michael T Dugan reportedly revealed classified information during an interview about the imminent launch of combat operations during DESERT STORM, for which he was relieved of command and replaced by General Merrill A 'Tony' McPeak.

Perhaps the most significant mission flown by 61-2669 took place on 11th September 2001. The SPECKLED TROUT was en route to London with the JCS Chairman, US Army General H Hugh Shelton, when hijacked airplanes struck the World Trade Center and the Pentagon. Despite being a US military aircraft with the top US military officer on board, it took at least three hours for the SPECKLED TROUT to get a clearance back to the United States as it orbited over Greenland. Even then, 61-2669 was delayed at Canadian airspace, and then again at Andrews AFB as US Secretary of State Colin Powell was also trying to land. Over the ensuing week, the SPECKLED TROUT remained on alert at Andrews AFB for any potential VIP mission.

61-2668 Following this WC-135B's removal from MASDC on 1st November 1972, E-Systems reconfigured it for use as a C-135B VIP transport. OCALC converted it into a C-135C on 6th September 1973, and it assigned to the 15th ABW at Hickam AFB. It was reassigned on 1st October 1975 to Det 1, 89th MAW at Hickam AFB, which on 10th March 1992, was replaced by the 65th ALS, 15th ABW. Withdrawn from use in 1996 at Tinker AFB (see Appendix III).

61-2669 This WC-135B was removed from MASDC on 8th November 1972, and E-Systems removed the weather gear and installed a staff interior. Following PDM it was delivered on 8th March 1972, to the 7111th SS (later the 7111th OS), 322nd TAW at Rhein-Main AB. Interestingly, its WC-135B MDS did not change to C-135B until 21st April 1973, and then to C-135C until 11th October 1973. It was delivered on 8th February 1975 to Det 1, 1st ACCS, 1st CW at Andrews AFB where it replaced the SPECKLED TROUT KC-135A 55-3126 (which then retired to MASDC). Following the 1st November 1975, departure of the 1st ACCS from Andrews AFB, 61-2669 came under the operational control of Det 1, 4950th TW, also located at Andrews AFB. From June 1980 through October 1981, 61-2669 was reportedly stationed at Offutt AFB, but this has not been independently verified. During October 1985, it set two world speed records on flights between Japan and the PRC (see Appendix V). The airplane was assigned to HQ, US Air Force, and located at Andrews AFB until all AFSC heavy testbed assets, including the SPECKLED TROUT, were reassigned to Edwards AFB during 1994. Retired on 13th January 2006 to the AFFTC Museum.

61-2671 Demodified from a WC-135B into a C-135B VIP transport in March 1973. On 5th April 1974 it was converted to a C-135C and assigned to the 15th ABW at Hickam AFB, later to Det 1, 89th MAW at Hickam AFB. Withdrawn from use during PDM on 30th October 1991, and placed on display at Tinker AFB (see Appendix III).

Initially two of the three C-135Cs were assigned to Det 1, 89th MAW at Hickam AFB to provide global transport for CINCPAC and CINCPACAF and their staffs. C-135C 61-2668 was one of these. *Photo by George Cockle*

Arguably the most visually impressive of the VIP schemes to appear on any '135 were those applied at the end of their operational lives. C-135C 61-2668, visiting Andrews AFB on 27th January 1995, would be withdrawn from use in 1996. *Photo by Stephen Miller*

By the time C-135C 61-2669 visited Heathrow for the final time, it had been reassigned to Edwards AFB, acquired a variety of new avionics and antennae, and received a new paint scheme. *Photo by Richard Vandervord*

C-135K INDIVIDUAL AIRCRAFT

Former HEAD DANCER EC-135K 59-1518 was redesignated as a C-135K in late 1996 and reassigned to the 65th ALS, 15th ABW at Hickam AFB. On 10th March 2003 it was relegated to AMARG as AACA0131, and placed on the 'Celebrity Row'. It was scrapped on 21st September 2016 (See Appendix III).

KC-135A/D/E/R INDIVIDUAL AIRCRAFT

KC-135 tankers have served and continue to serve as dedicated transports, mostly in a VIP role for major commands, particularly SAC. All retained the air refueling boom and were capable of offloading fuel. The interiors were often quite nicely appointed and were highly modified to include a communications suite or other command and control elements. The aviation press has occasionally referred to some of these airplanes as 'VKC-135s', although this MDS is completely unofficial.

Several EC-135s have also served as VIP transports, but they remained fully functional as airborne command posts although they were often used as transports. Among these have been EC-135P 58-0007 for CINCPAC and CINCPACAF, EC-135A 61-0282 for the Commander-in-Chief, Europe (CINCEUR), as well as EC-135Ks 55-3118 and 59-1518, and 62-3536 for CINCTAC and later the Commander, Air Combat Command (COMACC).

55-3126 This was the first KC-135 of any MDS to serve as a VIP transport. How this airplane was chosen for this mission is the stuff of a classic flier's tale. In the late 1950s, jet transports were a novelty usually reserved for heads of state. Eisenhower was due to receive three new 707s, and his counterpart in the Soviet Union, Nikita Khrushchev, had his Tu-104. Just as the jet transport meant prestige, it also meant speed. Curtis LeMay, now Air Force Vice Chief of Staff, and other US Department of Defense officials believed they should similarly enjoy the benefits of jet travel, and he knew just where to look. The KC-135A had just entered the Air Force inventory on 28th June 1957 as SAC's new jet tanker, and several of the first airplanes off the assembly line were undergoing Phase VI functional development tests at Wright-Patterson AFB, Ohio. He figured they could do with one less testbed and asked that one be sent to Washington, but the folks at 'Wright-Pat' politely declined. Unaccustomed to hearing the word 'no,' LeMay wielded the full weight of his four stars and soon had his airplane when KC-135A 55-3126 arrived at Andrews AFB, Maryland.

In 1938 LeMay led a flight of Boeing B-17s to Argentina, using, among other things, a *National Geographic* map for navigation. On 11-13th November 1957, LeMay established two world records while flying 55-3126 on a similar mission between the United States and Argentina, as well as other records (official or otherwise – see Appendix V). The airplane was converted into the SPECKLED TROUT avionics test-bed, although it continued to serve as a VIP transport, primarily for the Air Force Chief of Staff and the AFSC Commander. In 1975 C-135C 61-2669 became the new SPECKLED TROUT and 55-3126 was retired to MASDC on 31st July 1975. It was written off on 5th January 1978 (see Appendix III).

57-2589 Configured for use by SAC's Commander-in-Chief (CINCSAC), this airplane (call sign *Casey 01*), was initially assigned to the 3902nd ABW, and in 1967 to the 55th SRW (55th Wing after 31st August 1991) at Offutt AFB. When delivered from Boeing in 1959 it was natural metal, but from 1961-1964 it was painted silver, white, and red the same as KC-135A 55-3126. Beginning in 1964 is acquired the basic white over silver scheme, with minor variations to follow. The airplane always had a dedicated crew (see Table 7-1). Among these were IP Major John H Casteel (May 72-May 74), aircraft commander of the 1967 Mackay Trophy flight in SEA, Captain (later Brigadier General) Lawrence A Mitchell (Feb 67-Jan 69), the first assigned co-pilot (previously the CINCSAC's aides served as co-pilot), as well as co-

Table 7-1. *Casey 01's* **First Crew, Feb 1959-Dec 1964**

Position	Name
Instructor Pilot	Maj Thomas J Sims
Navigator	Capt George R Henriet
Boom Operator	MSgt William H Marchman
Radio Operator	MSgt Albert S Hurst
Flight Steward	TSgt Joseph D Carrig / TSgt Robert D Roggentine
Crew Chief	TSgt Darwin J Summerton
Maintenance Officer	CWO-4 Harold F Foster

The two C-135Cs based at Hickam AFB suffered from considerable corrosion due to the salty sea air of Hawai'i. During a PDM in October 1991, 61-2671 was deemed too expensive to repair and it was put on display at Tinker AFB. Sadly, its vertical stabilizer was replaced with one from a Boeing 707; the difference is obvious. *Photo by Stephen Miller*

pilot Captain Diane Reynolds (Feb 88-Feb 91) and Flight Steward Technical Sergeant Stephanie A Danner (Feb 88-Jan 91) the first female crewmembers on *Casey 01*. During 1969 it was the lead aircraft for the conversion of the water injection system from left/right to inboard/outboard. In 1983 Boeing Military Airplane Company (BMAC) converted it to a KC-135E, returning it to the SAC on 11th October 1983. Along with other officials and dignitaries, President Gerald R Ford flew aboard this airplane, as did country singer 'Tennessee' Ernie Ford, Generals Ira C Eaker and 'Jimmy' Doolittle, and a 'rogue's gallery' of Nixon administration officials – John D Ehrlichman, H R 'Bob' Haldeman, and John Dean. With the demise of SAC on 1st June 1992, the airplane briefly served its new owner, US Strategic Command at Offutt AFB. It was subsequently assigned to the 65th AS at Hickam AFB, and ultimately headed for Edwards AFB. On 15th March 2003 it began flight operations with the 412th TS, and in April underwent conversion into the third SPECKLED TROUT platform. It was declared 'excess' on 22nd July 2007, and by 29th July 2008 had become a ground trainer at Lackland AFB, TX (see Appendix III).

61-0300 Dedicated to the support of the 15th Air Force commander, this airplane was assigned to the 22nd AREFW (previously the 22nd BW until 1982), March AFB, CA.

61-0310 Used from the late 1960s through October 1973 by CINCPACAF. Assigned to the 6486th ABW (later the 15th ABW) at Hickam AFB. In 1973 it returned to a purely tanker role.

61-0316 Following its demodification in 1975 from the airborne command post for the Commander-in-Chief, Strike Command, this airplane was assigned to the 71st AREFS, 2nd BW, Barksdale AFB, LA. By 1979 it was in use by the 8th Air Force commander, replacing KC-135A 63-7992. KC-135A 61-0316 burned on the ramp at Cairo IAP, Arab Republic of Egypt, on 19th March 1985 (see Appendix II).

61-0317 This airplane was unofficially referred to as a 'VKC-135A' and was used as a Commander-in-Chief, Pacific (CINCPAC) transport based at Hickam AFB. It returned to SAC as a tanker in the second half of 1973.

63-7992 Used by the 8th Air Force commander from 1971-79, when replaced by KC-135A 61-0316. Transferred to the 909th AREFS, 376th SW at Kadena AB, and may have been used there to support VIP and passenger transport in the Pacific region.

63-7980 During 2008 this KC-135R replaced KC-135 57-2589 as the SPECKLED TROUT. Assigned to the 412th TS at Edwards AFB, it served both as a testbed and a VIP transport. The 412th TS was inactivated on 15th May 2015, and the airplane was reassigned to the 418th TS (also at Edwards AFB), but its SPECKLED TROUT VIP transport role was eliminated.

63-8020 The early years of the CREEK FALCON program have not been well documented. By April 1968, 63-8020 was assigned to the 7101st ABW at Rhein-Main AB. From 1969 through 1972, it was assigned to the 7402nd CSW, still at Rhein-Main AB. It was reassigned on 1st February 1972 to the 7111th OS, 322nd TAW at Rhein-Main AB. The airplane operated through 1973, providing intra-European passenger service for US military and allied-nation personnel. In 1977 this mission was undertaken by C-135B 62-4125 at the 58th MAS at Ramstein AB. What airplane was used between 1973 and 1977, if any, has not been identified. KC-135A 63-8020 has since returned to tanker duties as a KC-135R.

NKC-135A INDIVIDUAL AIRCRAFT

55-3119 On 13th September 1983 this AFSC test-bed was transferred to SAC for use as a CSA, retaining the NKC-135A designation, while assigned to the 55th SRW (later 55th Wing) at Offutt AFB. The airplane was scheduled to receive TF33-PW-102s by 28th February 1988 and be redesignated an NKC-135E, but this did not take place. The airplane was stored in AMARC on 6th July 1993, as AACA067 (see Appendix III).

RC-135A INDIVIDUAL AIRCRAFT

From 1971 through 1979, the four RC-135As (63-8058, 63-8059, 63-8060, 63-8061) served as CSA jets with the 55th SRW at Offutt AFB. The photomapping gear was removed. Beginning 19th July 1978, 63-8058 was loaned to the Maine ANG. During 1979 all the RC-135As were converted into KC-135D tankers, which were assigned to tanker units.

This page, top to bottom:
KC-135A 55-3126 appeared in four basic color schemes, beginning with natural metal. In 1961 it was repainted white over silver with red conspicuity markings (KC-135A 57-2589 *Casey 01* was also painted in this scheme at the time). By 1964 55-3126 had been repainted in a silver, insignia blue, and white scheme, although this did not last long due to its similarity to the 'Air Force One' scheme. Although appropriate for military VIP transports, it was not acceptable on an airplane associated with the Air Force Chief of Staff. This led to the final scheme of white over silver with blue trim, as seen at the 'Boneyard.'
Photo HS6049 courtesy Boeing; Author's collection; Richard Sullivan via Stephen Miller; and Brian Rogers

The basic radio communications gear in KC-135A 55-3126 coupled with its location at Andrews AFB led to claims it was an airborne command post. Over time the equipment became lighter and could be contained in a smaller compartment opposite the main cargo door, and included a Telex machine at one station. By the early 1960s the airplane had a complete galley, including a grill (movie actor and Air Force Brigadier General Jimmy Stewart always liked the steaks on board). Although most people associate Curtis LeMay with bombers and SAC, his link with 55-3126 was deeply personal. He set records while flying it and used it extensively while Vice and then later as Chief of Staff. LeMay hand-picked the flight crew, radio operators, stewards, and the maintenance personnel.
All photos author's collection

Unlike many of the other C-135s in use by CINCs or other senior officers, KC-135A 57-2589 was delivered directly to Offutt AFB for CINCSAC General Thomas S Power. Ground crews took great pride in its shiny appearance. *Photo by Brian Rogers*

Still painted as a VIP transport with the 65th AS at Hickam AFB, KC-135E 57-2589 had become the third SPECKLED TROUT assigned to the 412th TS at Edwards AFB. *Photo by Paul Minert via Stephen Miller*

A dedicated KC-135 transport for CINCPACAF from the mid 1960s through 1973 made sense. Given the growing US involvement in Southeast Asia and the vast distances across the Pacific Ocean, a long-range VIP aircraft such as 61-0310 was a practical choice. *Author's collection*

In 1979 KC-135A 61-0316 replaced KC-135A 63-7992 as the 8th AF Commander's airplane. Less than three years after it was pictured at Barksdale AFB on 14th October 1982, it caught fire and was destroyed at Cairo IAP on 19th March 1985. *Photo by Brian Rogers*

KC-135R 63-7980 departs Tel Aviv for the trip to Ramstein AB on 8th August 2013. The final SPECKLED TROUT, it ended its transport duties with the 2015 inactivation of the 412th TS, but it retains its testbed role.
Photo by Erez M Sirotkin

KC-135A 63-8020 was the original CREEK FALCON transport for USAFE, but was replaced by VC-135B 62-4125. All markings were light blue, including the falcon on each engine nacelle. *Author's collection*

For 25 years NKC-135A 55-3119 served as a testbed before being transferred to SAC as a CSA transport. The expense of converting it to an NKC-135E and increasing maintenance costs outweighed any fuel savings as C-20s and C-32s assumed VIP transport duties.
Photo by Brian Rogers

The cancelation of the RC-135A photomapping program released four '135s for transport duties, among other missions. RC-135A 63-8058 on 21st September 1975.
Photo by Don McGarry via Stephen Miller

CHAPTER EIGHT

Discovering the Future

Testbed C-135s such as the 'big nose ARIAs' and NASA's 'Vomit Comets' are understandably associated with the birth and development of the American manned space program. As with many other events in the KC-135's history, the lineage of dedicated C-135 testbeds began, paradoxically, with the origins of the *Soviet* space program. On 4th October 1957 people around the world listened with rapt attention to the sound of electronic beeps emanating from a 184 lb (83.4kg) metal sphere whirring around the Earth every 96 minutes. This was *Sputnik*, the world's first man-made satellite, and it portended both great and ominous things. For the Soviet Union, the nation that had won the opening round in the space race by building and launching *Sputnik* (ironically meaning 'fellow traveller'), scientific socialism had triumphed over the decadent bourgeois capitalism of the West. It also meant that American military superiority in manned strategic bombers was effectively negated by the new Soviet monopoly on the nascent field of intercontinental ballistic missiles. For the United States, a nation that was unable to coordinate its fledgling civilian and military missile and rocket programs, let alone successfully launch anything, *Sputnik* sounded a tocsin that pealed throughout every level of American government and society. Aside from the immediately apparent implications of a Soviet military challenge to American strategic superiority, *Sputnik* struck at the very core of what many Americans believed made America great – their educational system. In a flurry of well-intentioned activities ranging from federal budget increases for education to the establishment of physics and slide-rule clubs at thousands of high schools across the nation, Americans rushed to reestablish their traditional educational advantage over *homo sovieticus*. Just as Americans had worried about a 'Bomber Gap' with the Soviets in the mid-1950s, they now worried about a 'Knowledge Gap'. This anxiety blended seamlessly with the existing post-war belief in science as the ultimate panacea. Manhattan Project physicists achieved near rock-star status as arbiters not only of scientific knowledge but also in matters of policy. In popular culture and film, scientists were seen as the experts who would advise the 'One World Government' on how to eliminate the specter of atomic warfare, who would champion peaceful uses of atomic energy to cure disease and tame nature, who would lead Earthlings into utopian dwellings in interplanetary space, and, most importantly, who would finally defeat Godzilla and Ghidora in their endless attacks on Tokyo.

These efforts translated, in part, into an expansive increase in scientific testing and research, especially in the physical sciences associated with atmospheric and astronomic studies, initiatives that were poorly suited to many existing ground-based research facilities. In addition to 'pure' and 'applied' scientific research, this was also an era of increased research into the development, use, and effects of high-technology weapons, particularly atomic and hydrogen bombs, as well as ballistic missiles (and defenses against them). Indeed, the two were often one in the same.

The RIVET DIGGER NC-135As reflect the breadth of testbed '135 operations ranging from nuclear weapons development to pure and applied science. *Photo P38194 courtesy Boeing*

For example, the effects of the *Aurora Borealis* on radio wave propagation in the northern polar region affected not only commercial radio broadcasts and international civilian air traffic but the ability of military units to communicate over long distances or detect Soviet Tu-95 *Bear* bombers flying 'over the top' to attack the United States. Not only could an aurora induce passive constraints to American defenses, it could actively endanger global security. In 1963, for example, four of the seven false alarms of a Soviet ICBM launch reported by the BMEWS radar were caused by the aurora. In a worst-case scenario, a freak auroral event could inadvertently trigger global thermonuclear war. Far fetched, perhaps, but in a science-obsessed world understanding the aurora was seen as a critical step in controlling another of nature's phenomena – the atom.

Scientific examination of the aurora was best undertaken at extreme altitudes well above clouds and atmospheric pollution, and over long periods of time. Building dozens of observatories across vast, uninhabited expanses of Canada or Alaska was both impractical and costly, so aerial research platforms were clearly preferable choices. Existing airframes such as Boeing B-50s and C-97s, however, which had proved suitable in the similar mission of aerial reconnaissance, lacked the ability to reach the necessary altitudes while carrying heavy payloads of scientific equipment and large numbers of researchers. Airplanes that could 'go high', including the Lockheed U-2 and Martin RB-57F, had no room for scientists and the research equipment had to fit in cramped quarters and meet stringent weight limits, severely constraining its capability.

The Perfect Choice

Just as with the need for an airborne command post, a strategic reconnaissance platform, and a new jet transport, the KC-135 was the logical choice as a testbed platform due to its size, capacity, speed, endurance, high altitude capability, and suitability for extensive modification. With a dozen early production KC-135s serving in a temporary test and evaluation role at Wright-Patterson AFB, the nexus of Air Force research, their jump from basic flight test airplanes to research platforms was simple and immediate. The KC-135 could carry more and larger equipment than smaller aircraft, as well as seat a larger crew complement to operate the equipment or act as mission observers. Its large fuel capacity enabled it to fly long distances and remain on station for extended durations, and the installation of an IFR system gave it a range and duration limited primarily by crew endurance. Testbed KC-135s could fly long distances quickly, loiter at slow speeds for maximum orbit duration at medium to high altitudes, and then recover at high speed to allow for immediate analysis of newly collected data.

The KC-135 was also easily adaptable as a testbed because of its structural design characteristics. High fuselage ground clearance enabled the placement of downward-looking antennae and fairings beneath the fuselage. Four engine-driven electrical generators provided considerable power to operate the electronic suite or test system on board the airplane. If needed, the generators could be enhanced or replaced with more capable units. Although other cargo airplanes have been used as testbeds, they were constrained by limits not applicable to KC-135s. C-130s, for example, suffered from slow speed, a low operational ceiling, and propeller vibrations and harmonics. Their low fuselage ground clearance further degraded their potential for external, downward-looking modifications. C-141 Starlifters enjoyed the benefits of jet transports, but the placement of flight control cables and their high wing root made upper fuselage modifications (such as those for the Airborne Laser Lab, radiation optics programs like RAMP and TRAP, and satellite communications systems) impractical. In addition, the C-141's 'T'-tail obstructed upward aft sensor operation and range of vision. As with the C-130

Hercules, the Starlifter suffered from low ground clearance. To be sure, both the C-130 and C-141 have been modified as testbeds, but nowhere near as prolifically as the KC-135.

From their arrival in 1957 at Wright-Patterson AFB for operational test and evaluation until their transfer in 1994 to Edwards AFB as part of the sweeping reorganization of the Air Force, testbed KC-135s have long been synonymous with 'Wright-Pat'. These early airplanes were assigned to the Flight and All-Weather Test Division at WADC. In 1959 the WADC was redesignated the Wright Air Development Division (WADD) and the Flight and All-Weather Test Division reassigned to WADD. In a major reorganization during 1961, ARDC was redesignated Air Force Systems Command (AFSC) and WADD changed to Aeronautical Systems Division (ASD). At the same time, flight test operations were transferred to the newly established Deputy for Test and Support, which combined flight operations with maintenance and modification. This meant that a single organization could propose, install, flight test, and reevaluate modifications, dramatically accelerating the research process.

Additional organizational changes, some minor and some substantial, followed during the 1960s and early 1970s. In the first of these, the Deputy for Test and Support was renamed in 1963 as the Deputy for Flight Test, and included five directorates, including Flight Test Operations (to which testbed KC-135 operations were assigned), Test Data, Aircraft Maintenance, Test and Integration Analysis, and Supply Services. During 1968 the Deputy for Flight Test became the Directorate of Flight Test. After nearly 25 years, the all-weather flight tests at Wright-Patterson AFB were transferred in June 1970 to the AFFTC at Edwards AFB. The following year the Directorate of Flight Test – still at Wright-Patterson AFB – became a wing. Initially known as the 4950th Test Wing (Technical), it quickly became just the 4950th Test Wing (TW). Just as 'Wright-Pat' was known as the home of testbed C-135s, so too was the 4950th TW the most widely known testbed C-135 unit.

As US forces withdrew from the war in Southeast Asia, the Air Force underwent another major reorganization as overall force numbers decreased dramatically. First known as Project REALIGN, the consolidation of AFSC heavy aircraft assets is best known by its final name HAVE CAR. On 24th April 1975 HAVE CAR Implementation Program 75 – 6 directed that all heavy cargo-designated test aircraft be assigned to the 4950th TW at Wright-Patterson AFB or to Detachment 1 of the 4950th TW located at Andrews AFB (for the SPECKLED TROUT airplane). The 4950th TW acquired ten EC-135s from the 6549th Test Squadron (TS), 6550th ABW, Air Force Eastern Test Range (AFETR) at Patrick AFB, FL. These were used in support of America's burgeoning space program, as well as its ballistic missile tests. The airplanes often deployed to the Air Force Western Test Range (AFWTR) at Vandenberg AFB, CA, for missile shots originating there. Two NKC-135As from the Rome Air Development Centre (RADC) at Griffiss AFB, NY, were also transferred to the 4950th TW as part of HAVE CAR. These had been involved in electronic warfare testing, and continued these missions after moving to Wright-Patterson AFB (RADC still uses the burned-out shell of

Table 8-1. **Testbed Static Call-signs**

55-3119 *Agar 16*	55-3134 *Nucar 01*	60-0372 *Agar 26*
55-3120 *Agar 17*	55-3135 *Agar 20*	60-0374 *Agar 27*
55-3122 *Agar 03*	56-3596 *Nucar 02*	60-0375 *Agar 28*
55-3123 *Agar 33*	57-2589 *Trout 99*	60-0377 *Agar 09*
55-3124 *Agar 08*	60-0326 *Agar 21*	61-2669 *Trout 99*
55-3125 *Agar 15*	60-0327 *Agar 22*	62-4128 *Agar 06*
55-3127 *Agar 31*	60-0328 *Agar 23*	62-4133 *Agar 07*
55-3128 *Agar 34*	60-0329 *Agar 24*	63-7980 *Trout 99*
55-3131 *Agar 18*	60-0330 *Agar 25*	
55-3132 *Agar 30*	60-0371 *Agar 35*	

Hardly glamorous or mysterious, NKC-135A 55-3135 is arguably the most significant testbed '135, supporting hundreds of other programs and training test pilots and engineers. *Photo by Gerald Markgraf via Stephen Miller*

When once there were more than a dozen testbed KC-135s, by 2016 there were only two, including the 'TT' (test tanker) KC-135R 61-0320. *Photo by Toshi Aoki*

KC-135Q 60-0338 for electromagnetic tests) In addition to the two RADC aircraft, NKC-135As and JKC-135As from the Air Force Geophysics Laboratory (AFGL) – previously the Air Force Cambridge Research Laboratory (AFCRL) – at Hanscom Field, MA, moved from the 6520th ABG (previously the 3245th ABW) to the 4950th TW under the HAVE CAR reorganization.

Additional heavy cargo-designated test aircraft were consolidated at the Air Force Special Weapons Center (AFSWC) at Kirtland AFB, NM, and with AFFTC at Edwards AFB. These relocations eliminated needless duplication of training, maintenance, and support. Two NKC-135As from the 6512th TS, 6510th TW, AFFTC, seconded to the US Air Force Test Pilot School (USAFTPS) at Edwards AFB were transferred to the 4950th TW, as were seven testbed KC-135 variants from the 4949th TW (previously the 4900th TG) at the AFSWC at Kirtland AFB. The KC-135As, NC-135As, and NKC-135As were part of several major projects associated with nuclear weapons research, electronic warfare testing and training (such as BIG CROW), and unconventional weapons research (such as the Airborne Laser Lab – ALL). Not all of these airplanes physically relocated to Wright-Patterson AFB, as the BIG CROW and the ALL NKC-135As remained instead at Kirtland AFB or Edwards AFB but were under the administrative control of the 4950th TW.

Yet another reorganization within the Air Force, this time spread throughout the early 1990s, meant further changes to the testbed KC-135 community. During 1992 AFSC and AFLC combined to become Air Force Materiel Command (AFMC), reminiscent of the earlier Air Materiel Command. Similarly, ASD became the Aeronautical Systems Center (ASC). The 6512th TS, 6510th TW was inactivated on 1st October 1992 and the testbed KC-135 variants were consolidated into the 445th Test Squadron – now abbreviated as TESTS – 412th TW at Edwards AFB. This squadron was

inactivated on 30th September 1993 and replaced by the 452nd Test Squadron (TESTS), still part of the 412th TW. The 452nd TESTS was again redesignated on 1st March 1994, this time as the 452nd Flight Test Squadron (FTS). By mid-1994 all heavy cargo-designated testbed aircraft had departed Wright-Patterson AFB for Edwards AFB and been consolidated into the 452nd FLTS. Without its airplanes, the 4950th TW lost its primary mission, and it was inactivated on 30th June 1994. On 1st October 2000 the 418th FTS assumed control of KC-135R 61-0320, one of the few remaining testbed '135s. The 412th FTS retained control of KC-135R 63-7980 through 15th May 2015, when SPECKLED TROUT transport duties were eliminated (see Chapter 7). The squadron was inactivated and the airplane reassigned to the 418th FTS.

The designations applied to the variety of testbed KC-135s are often a source of confusion. Some testbeds retained their original delivery MDS designations, whereas others received an entirely new MDS from which a few aviation historians have improperly inferred an electronic warfare or command post mission. The 'EC-' prefix assigned to some modified C-135As, C-135Bs, and C-135Es reflects the 'electronic' operations and test nature of their mission. The airplanes were never members of the Post Attack Command and Control PACCS airborne command post system or collateral platforms such as SILK PURSE or BLUE EAGLE (see Chapter 9). Some of the airplanes described in this chapter (such as the EC-135 ARIAs) were not truly *testbeds* but were operational airplanes. They are considered here because of their association and colocation with the testbed KC-135As.

Testbed KC-135s were typically given a 'J' or 'N' prefix to their existing MDS. The 'J' indicated temporary test and usually reflected minor modifications to the airframe; this designation is seldom used anymore. By 1969 all JKC-135s had been redesignated NKC-135s.

Table 8-2. **Some Common Testbed Programs**

AACS		ARIA		FAA		IFF		RAMP		TRAP	
NKC-135A	55-3135	EC-135N	60-0372	KC-135A	59-1481	NKC-135A	55-3127	J/NKC-135A	55-3127	JKC-135A	55-3127
C-135A	60-0376	EC-135N/E	60-0374	(N98)		C-135A/N/E	60-0375			JKC-135A	55-3134
ADC 'Blink Jammer'		EC-135N	60-0375	KC-135A	59-1518	C-135B	62-4128	**RECCE STRIKE**		JKC-135A	59-1491
NKC-135A	55-3124	EC-135N/E	61-0326	(N96)				NKC-135A	55-3132		
C-135N	60-0375	EC-135N	61-0327			**METEOR BURST**		NKC-135A	56-3596	**TRIA**	
Airborne Laser		EC-135N	61-0328	**FEWSG**		NKC-135A	55-3124			C-135B	60-0331
Lab/HEL/ABL		EC-135N/E	61-0329	NKC-135A	553134	C-135N	60-0375	**SATCOM**		C-135B	61-2664
NKC-135A	55-3123	EC-135N/E	61-0330	NKC-135A	563596			NKC-135A	55-3129	C-135B	62-4128
NC-135A	60-0371	EC-135B	62-4128			**MILSTAR**		C-135N/E	60-0372	C-135B	62-4133
EC-135C	63-8050	EC-135B	62-4133	**FISTA**		NC-135A	60-0371	C-135B	61-2662		
NKC-135B	63-8050			NKC-135A	55-3120	C-135N/E	60-0372	C-135B	61-2663	**Zero-G/Weightless**	
		BIG CROW		NKC-135E	55-3135	NKC-135A	55-3122			JKC-135A	55-3129
ALOTS		NKC-135A/E	55-3132					**SKYSCRAPER**		KC-135A	59-1481
NKC-135A	55-3123	NKC-135B	63-8050	**HAVE LACE**		**NNTRP/RIVET**		JKC-135A	55-3124	C-135A	60-0378
NKC-135A	56-3596			NC-135A	60-0371	**DIGGER/EARLY DAY**		JKC-135A	55-3127	KC-135A	62-3536
		ARGUS		C-135E	60-0372	NC-135A	60-0369			KC-135A	63-7998
AMSA		NC-135A	60-0371			NC-135A	60-0370	**SPECKLED TROUT**			
C-135A	60-0376	C-135E	60-0375	**Icing/Water Spray**		NC-135A	60-0371	KC-135A	55-3126		
C-135A	60-0377			KC-135A	55-3121			C-135C	61-2669		
NKC-135A	55-3128	**CRRES**		NKC-135A	55-3125	**ORSEP**		KC-135E	57-2589		
		NKC-135A	55-3127	NKC-135A	55-3128	NKC-135A	55-3135	KC-135R	63-7980		
		NKC-135A	55-3131			C-135A	60-0376				

The 'N' prefix was assigned to those aircraft given a permanent test role, as the test modifications to the airframe was so significant or extensive that it was not economically feasible (read 'cost effective') to reconfigure the aircraft to its original or standard configuration.

Because individual airplanes have not always maintained a permanent association with one specific long-term program, there has often been confusion over what airplane participated in what program (particularly classified programs), especially as one airplane was actively involved with multiple projects simultaneously. In addition, most testbed '135s had a static radio call sign irrespective of mission (see Tables 8.1 and 8.2).

STRUCTURAL AND AERODYNAMIC TESTING

A handful of the earliest KC-135s were involved in flight tests related to the aerodynamics and overall improvement to the '135 airframe, and are discussed in Chapter 3. These tests also demonstrated the value of the KC-135 as a testbed for a better understanding of high-altitude, high-speed flight properties so crucial to the nascent civilian jet airliner market and the development of new large military jets, including the generalized benefits of winglets and the development of improved air refueling systems. Moreover, the KC-135's air refueling boom and high capacity body fuel tanks were excellent resources in assessing the adverse effects of icing on other aircraft. Even at the end of their operational lives, a number of KC-135s proved useful in calibrating fatigue estimates and the tolerance of the airframe to explosive damage.

Icing Tests

The presence of ice – particularly on wings and empennage, propellers, engine intakes, and pylons – significantly alters the surface's aerodynamic shape and degrades its lifting potential. Control surfaces covered with ice become sluggish or even immobile. The added weight of ice adversely affects the airplane's performance. Ice-covered pylons alter the releasability and drop characteristics of weapons, especially missiles, rendering them unreliable. Icing tests evaluate these effects as well as the effectiveness of anti-ice systems to prevent icing, and of de-icing systems to eliminate any ice once formed. They also determine the effects of ice shed from an aircraft's structure (such as its nose radome or wing leading edge). Could the test aircraft's engines ingest this ice, causing engine damage or failure? Could the ice strike and damage other components such as

antennae or pylons? Although icing is more likely to occur at low altitude, the margin for error during low altitude test flights is virtually non-existent. Consequently, tests conducted at higher altitudes allowed for a greater safety margin, and icing conditions could be better controlled. Icing testbed KC-135s were ideally suited for high-altitude tests in the 200-300 KIAS (370-555km/h) range, with low-speed icing tests left to a modified C-130 or Boeing/Vertol CH-47C Chinook.

During the late 1950s and early 1960s, JKC-135A 55-3121 was used as an icing testbed as a temporary replacement for the existing KB-29P Superfortress icing testbed (44-83951). Two of the aft fuel cells from 55-3121 were filled with water that was dispensed through the air refueling boom, producing droplets of crude size and unknown shape. Inconsistent test results emphasized the need for a dedicated icing testbed capable of more precise control over droplet parameters. Additionally, these water tests were highly detrimental to the service life of the airplane's fuel valves and fuel sensors.

In early 1964, NKC-135A 55-3128 became the second KC-135 converted into a water spray/aerial icing test platform. These water spray tests were conducted at AFFTC at Edwards AFB and provided 'all-weather development and certification flight testing of military and civilian aircraft under simulated rain and icing conditions'. Structural modifications to 55-3128 included the installation of a water spray system designed to spray the 4,000 gallons (15,141 liters) of water carried in the fuselage fuel tanks through a spray ring or bar attached to the end of the extended air refueling boom. The subject aircraft flew in the path of this spray, evaluating whatever icing conditions were encountered. Precise boom control allowed the spray and ice to build up on a specific location on the subject aircraft without affecting other locations. The water spray NKC-135 participated in airframe and external stores icing tests for a variety of aircraft including the General Dynamics F-111, the AGM-109 cruise missile, and civilian aircraft such as the Boeing 757.

In 1983, 55-3128's water spray system was upgraded, improving its ability to simulate a natural cloud versus simple water spray. At altitudes above 15,000ft (4,572m) and relative humidities above 70%, natural cloud droplets are on the order of 20 microns in diameter. With this modification, the tanker droplets approached 30 microns in size, a considerable improvement over the grossly larger sizes previously attainable. The actual droplets (and hence cloud size) were controlled by mixing water with high-pressure air from the NKC-135's engines or the APU bleed-air system. This mixture was then sprayed through a variety of nozzles arranged in the desired

During its career 55-3128 was best known as the water spray tanker, conducting icing test flights from Edwards AFB for nearly every military and civilian prototype from 1964 through 1996. *Photo by Stephen Miller*

pattern. Colored dye could be added to enhance observation of the icing phenomenon. Outside air temperatures above freezing supercooled the water droplets, which then solidified the instant they contacted the subject aircraft. An axially scattering spectrometer used a laser to determine droplet size by measuring the forward diffraction of light from the water droplet. A computer then calculated droplet size and water content based on the test aircraft's true airspeed, pressure altitude, outside air temperature, and the light diffraction pattern created by the water droplets.

At least one other '135 is known to have served as an icing and water spray platform. KC-135A 58-0027 was used temporarily when NKC-135A 55-3128 was undergoing PDM. During 1977 55-3125 was reportedly used as an 'icing dispenser' although without special water tanks. This claim remains the subject of some controversy. At least one photograph of 55-3125 taken during 1977 shows an attachment at the end of the air refueling boom similar to a water spray device. In keeping with the airplane's 'electronic' background, however, this was almost certainly a special antenna rather than water spray equipment.

The icing testbed NKC-135A was scheduled for retirement during 1994 as a means to reduce operational costs. The 31st October 1994 crash of American Eagle Aérospatiale ATR 72 flight 4184 due to excessive icing, however, offered a reprieve for 55-3128. Supported by the FAA – and in strong opposition to Air Force desires – the icing testbed remained in service. Air Force opposition stemmed from a lack of funding for a mission to support civilian aircraft at a time of post Cold War budget cuts and emphasis on combat-related aircraft and missions. As the *New York Times* reported on 9th May 1995, 55-3128, 'which requires a staff of more than 20 to support it, was scheduled for a comprehensive maintenance check in October that would have cost about $2.3 million. The Air Force also saw few sure outside customers in the near future for its icing tanker program.' Not surprisingly, the Air Force won, and 55-3128 was retired to AMARG.

J/NKC-135A INDIVIDUAL AIRCRAFT

55-3121 This JKC-135A was the first '135 used as an icing tanker prior to 1964 while it was assigned to WADC at Wright-Patterson AFB.

55-3128 From 1964 until its retirement in 1996, 55-3128 was the primary US Air Force icing tanker, and was stationed at Edwards AFB. By 1965 it had been redesignated as an NKC-135A. It was retired to AMARG as AACA0106 on 20th May 1996 (see Appendix III).

Ice Runways

During the 1930s the Soviet Union established a significant presence in the northern polar region, and eventually developed the capability to fly large aircraft from ice islands floating in the Arctic Ocean. By the late 1940s and early 1950s, Soviet Tu-4 *Bull* and Tu-16 *Badger* bombers were operating from these ice bases, which were equipped with hangars, barracks, trucks, and fuel supplies. A *Badger* flying to its target in the United States would land on an ice island, refuel, and then resume its flight with extended range to reach more targets in the United States.

Aware of the benefits of these Soviet ice islands, in January 1961 AFCRL geophysicists began Project ICE WAY near Thule AB to test the feasibility of landing heavy aircraft such as the B-52 and KC-135 on ice runways. Project ICE WAY concluded on 31st May 1961, and demonstrated the ability of ice runways wholly constructed of natural seawater and reinforced with strands of fiberglass to support aircraft operations. The final project report does not specify which, if any, lucky KC-135 and crew successfully landed on a giant ice cube floating in the Arctic Ocean.

General Flight Characteristics

KC-135A 55-3121 was the first '135 given directly to the Air Force rather than subjected to testing by Boeing, which delivered it with a complete test instrumentation suite measuring 342 flight and system parameters. The airplane arrived at WADC at Wright-Patterson AFB on 30th April 1957 and was redesignated as a JKC-135A on 7th May 1957. It began adverse weather, arctic, and desert testing for the KC-135. Following these tests 55-3121 remained at Wright-Patterson AFB through 19th April 1962 where it continued to serve as an instrumented testbed for both the KC-135 weapon system and for other aerodynamic projects.

In addition to Boeing and the Air Force, the National Advisory Committee for Aeronautics (NACA) conducted other tests related to large-aircraft flight dynamics. NACA test pilot Stan Buchart first flew 55-3125 on 30th August 1957 on a handling and evaluation flight while it was participating in Phase VI developmental testing. Buchart again flew the airplane in September 1957 en route to Seattle. Following completion of Phase VI testing on 8th November 1957, 55-3125 was redesignated a JKC-135A and loaned to the NACA High Speed Flight Station (HSFS) at the Dryden Flight Research Center (DFRC) for flight tests of heavy jet transports and high speed flight studies. During its first NACA research flight on 12th November 1957, however, 55-3125 collided in mid-air with

Lockheed NT-33A 53-5540A. The NT-33A was lost, killing its USAFTPS pilot Daniel J Veronica. Buchart was able to land the KC-135 safely on Rogers Dry Lake. As a result of damage incurred, 55-3125 was withdrawn from NACA flight tests.

KC-135A 55-3124 was released from Air Force Phase IV flight testing on 12th February 1958, and then loaned from 6th March through May 1958 to NACA as the replacement for KC-135A 55-3125. While at DFRC 55-3124 flew 14 test flights as part of heavy jet approach and landing research, as well as high-altitude high-speed cruise research. These tests, requested by the NACA Subcommittee on Flight Safety on behalf of the Civil Aeronautics Administration (CAA), helped define and establish safe jet airliner operating procedures to be used with the imminent delivery of the 707 and the DC-8. In May 1958 it was redesignated a JKC-135.

NKC-135A 55-3128 was also used by the USAFTPS where it was noted for its heavy controls and 'cantankerous' Dutch Roll characteristics. The airplane provided a stable platform for engine-out studies, structural strain research, and the performance, stability, and control research of heavy aircraft as part of TPS student training.

Structural Fatigue and Destructive Testing

KC-135A 55-3126 participated (along with KC-135A 55-3125) in KC-135A Phase VI Functional Development Testing, and was assigned to FTD at Wright-Patterson AFB. In October 1957 it was transferred to Headquarters Air Force at Andrews AFB for use as a VIP transport, and by 1966 had become the first SPECKLED TROUT (see the section below on Communications and Navigation). On 8th February 1975, C-135C 61-2669 became the new SPECKLED TROUT and 55-3126 was slated for retirement. It flew for the last time on 31st July 1975, landing at the Military Aerospace Storage and Disposition Center (MASDC) at Davis-Monthan AFB, AZ, with a total of 9,057.0 flying hours. It was given a temporary reprieve when considered for one final project. The Department of Energy (DoE) evaluated the airplane on 4th May 1979 for use as an expendable remotely piloted test platform. In order to test the integrity of radioactive material shipping casks carried by air, the airplane would be outfitted for remote control, loaded with several casks containing simulated spent nuclear fuels, and then crashed into a mountainside. Unfortunately, the airplane could not be configured for the flight following its cannibalization for 61-2669, so the plan was dropped and the airplane further dismantled. This nuclear waste test was later suggested as part of the 1981 NASA/FAA controlled impact demonstration (CID) test crash using a Boeing 720, although this add-on proposal did not come to fruition.

As early as 1968 the Air Force and Boeing recognized that the projected service life requirements for some KC-135s would exceed their design lifetime. This estimate was based on early fatigue testing and the expected structural failure of key airframe components: 'The presence of 7178 aluminum alloy in the primary wing structure of the -135 airplanes (with its low fracture toughness and relatively high operating stress levels) makes it imperative that service life estimates be continuously updated using the latest data on airplane usage, load history and fleet fatigue experience, plus verification by additional testing as necessary. Based on the foregoing considerations ... OCAMA embarked upon a "Fatigue Life Extension Program". This program consisted of both analysis and testing with a major part being the cyclic testing of a complete -135 airframe.' The technical proposal for the cyclic test was submitted on 13th March 1969, and program authorization was officially received on 17th February 1970. KC-135A 62-3535 was selected as the cyclic test article, arriving at BMAC on 6th April 1970 with 2,975 flight hours. The test was conducted in the old B-47 Experimental Flight Hangar at the Boeing-operated facility (Air Force Plant 13) at Wichita.

The cyclic test loads applied to the airplane simulated actual flight conditions experienced by fleet tankers. Each spectrum of 40 load cycles represented one 5.1-hour flight, with the first portion of each test simulating the heavyweight condition of the tanker prior to air refueling and the second half of each test representative of the lower gross weight cruise and landing portion of flight. The test article was 'free floating' with no rigid ties to the floor, instead being suspended at points on each wing and along the fuselage. Actual test procedures and equipment were identical to those used in 1957 and 1962 in similar tests on a KC-135 and 707, respectively, allowing a direct comparison and validation of test data.

Results confirmed the anticipated design limits of the KC-135, particularly those associated with the wing structure, which were considered to be the most critical. The brittle nature of the aluminum alloy used in the lower wing skin made it especially vulnerable to cracking, which not only affected the strength of the wing but allowed fuel leaks from the 'wet' wing fuel tank arrangement. As a result, Boeing and the Air Force began what would become the lower wing reskin program (TCTO 989) and the Aircraft Structural Integrity Program (ASIP), extending the service life of the KC-135 fleet well into the next century (see Chapter 5).

Beginning in 1993 four surplus KC-135As (56-3616, 56-3617, 56-3632, and 56-3656) were delivered to NATC Patuxent River, MD, for destructive testing. The purpose of these tests was to evaluate methods of improving civilian airliner survivability from on-board explosions, especially those from terrorist bombs located in the baggage compartments.

Four aircraft were removed from AMARG following their retirement and disassembled to determine their degree of structural fatigue. These included KC-135Es 57-1465 and 57-1505, EC-135H 61-0291, and KC-135R 60-0319, the latter for the 'CAStLE' Program. The US Air Force Academy (AFA) at Colorado Springs, CO, conducts materials research at its Center for Aircraft Structural Life Extension (CAStLE). During 2005-2006, AFA cadets were part of a successful project that allowed the KC-135 Program Office to save nearly $1.3 billion annually on its fleet of 535 KC-135 Stratotankers, approximately $2.4 million per aircraft. The cadets showed 'that a significant amount of costs and resources [could] be avoided by confining repairs to situations where the damage actually affects an aircraft's structural performance.'

Air Refueling Improvements

Beginning in November 1977, NKC-135A 55-3124 flight-tested the advanced aerial refueling boom (AARB) for the Advanced Tanker and Cargo Aircraft (ATCA) competition, eventually won by the KC-10A. This fly-by-wire AARB was 10ft (3.0m) longer (56ft 7in – 17.2m) than the existing KC-135 boom, allowing a 25% increase in the vertical separation between tanker and receiver. A larger fuel line and more efficient nozzle allowed an increase in the fuel transfer rate. The test program lasted just over six months and involved nearly 1,400 test hook-ups in 47 flights totaling 184 flying hours.

In 1979 the Air Force Flight Dynamics Laboratory (AFFDL) developed equipment that 'display[ed] critical information within the boom operator's field of vision, enabling the crewmember to see the data and receiver aircraft simultaneously... the first time a head-up display has been designed for an aircrew member other than a pilot'. Flight tests were conducted in an unspecified KC-135A assigned to the 307th AREFG at Travis AFB. Program results are not available, and the modification was not adopted. This did not necessarily dissuade boom operators from developing their own improvements. A long-term issue for instructor boom operators (IBO) is significant neck and back pain caused by instructing students in flight (no pun intended). The student BO occupies the center couch, and the IBO lies

Right: A gloomy end for four KC-135As, including 56-3656, at NAS Patuxent River, where they were used in explosive testing.
Photo by Tom Kaminski

Below: Flight tests of the AARB for the KC-10 were conducted on NKC-135A 55-3124. Interestingly, there were no efforts to replace the boom on the KC-135A fleet with the AARB.
Photo via Brian Rogers

on the adjacent couch but must do so in a very awkward position to ensure clear visibility of the receiver and immediate access to the boom retraction handle in case of emergency. In 2015, one innovative 54th AREFS IBO at Altus AFB designed a new cushion for the instructor's couch that better supports the IBO and eliminates the physical discomfort and long-term disability. It remains to be seen if the Air Force will adopt this improvement for entire the KC-135R fleet.

As part of the Air Force's efforts to improve the KC-135's air refueling capabilities, NKC-135A 55-3127 participated in a number of tests under the 1980 Improved Aerial Refueling Systems (IARS) program. Specific IARS subprograms included the MA-4 air refueling boom coupling, the tail-mounted floodlight (TMF), high flow-rate pumps, various boom station modifications, air refueling basket modifications, and a fuselage-mounted drogue refueling system known as HOSE REEL.

In Project HOSE REEL – conducted from 1982 through 1983 – the Air Force sought to provide the KC-135 with the ability to air refuel boom-capable aircraft and probe-equipped aircraft in a single sortie. This modification was designed to avoid degrading tanker performance, avoid taking up space in the cargo compartment (as the stored basket did), and avoid removing any fuselage fuel cells. The right keel bay aft of the right main landing gear well was selected as the best site for the installation of a Sargent-Fletcher hose reel with 110ft (33.5m) of standard 4in (10cm) diameter air refueling hose. Installation and initial testing was done by the 4950th TW, with further testing undertaken by the 6520th TG at Edwards AFB.

Program results were highly controversial. Although the tests themselves were successful, the modification was not undertaken. Reasons given for the rejection of HOSE REEL ranged from the degradation of airframe structural integrity in the fuselage to

Above: 55-3127 was the IARS testbed, evaluating the tail-mounted floodlight and improved fuel pumps. Black and white bands on ventral fuselage were for the HOSE REEL drogue evaluation. *Photo by Bob Shane via Stephen Miller*

excessive instability of the hose and basket. Although the structural concerns associated with HOSE REEL were genuine they were not insurmountable, representing basic engineering problems rather than major design flaws. Further, the hose and basket flutter were deficiencies inherent in any probe-and-drogue system rather than unique to the HOSE REEL modification. The most probable causes for the rejection of HOSE REEL were financial and political. Air Force probe-and-drogue refueling is used almost exclusively in collateral operations which support US Navy, Marine, and Allied nation operations, a role which was seen at the time as the nearly exclusive domain of the KC-10. Because the HOSE REEL system could be installed on over 600 KC-135s, it had a greater potential impact on Air Force tanker capability than could the total purchase of only 60 KC-10s. Consequently, HOSE REEL was seen as a threat to the requirement for and hence the continued funding of the KC-10 program (in its heyday at the time), and the proposed modification was therefore canceled because of unidentified 'technical problems'. The need for single-mission, dual capability was eventually resolved with the Multi-Point Refueling System (MPRS – see Chapter 5).

As more and more military aircraft were painted in low-visibility schemes, it became increasingly difficult for KC-135 boom operators to assess accurately the depth and perspective of the air refueling envelope. Airplanes such as the General Dynamics F-16 were highly vulnerable to having a TACAN antenna – mounted near the air refueling receptacle – knocked off by the air refueling boom during night and bad weather operations. In 1983 the 4950th TW successfully developed the tail-mounted floodlight (TMF) for the KC-135. Flight tests were conducted on 55-3127, with the floodlight – nicknamed 'the streetlight' – mounted at the top trailing edge of the vertical stabilizer. The boom operator controls the intensity of the floodlight to avoid blinding the receiver pilot during the closure to contact, after which the intensity may be increased to illuminate the refueling envelope while the receiver is in the contact position. This modification has since been retrofitted to the entire KC-135 fleet and other MDS's with the air refueling boom installed (examples, EC-135C, EC-135G, EC-135P, etc), and has been incorporated on Boeing KE-3s for Saudi Arabia (on these airplanes the TMF is mounted just above the rudder rather than at the top of the vertical stabilizer). KC-135Qs had a fuselage-mounted spotlight intended to illuminate the SR-71's refueling receptacle. The TMF proved far superior and was retrofitted to the KC-135Q (see Chapter 5).

Additional KC-135 IARS modifications included the installation of high flow-rate fuel pumps that increased offload rates by 25%, thereby decreasing the refueling time required for such 'heavy' aircraft as the B-52, C-5, KC-10, and McDonnell Douglas C-17 Globemaster III. A new boom nozzle and independent disconnect system were tested, enhancing the boom operator's ability to recognize and correct dangerous boom loads generated by the receiver while in contact. A new boom control stick with vernier control was also evaluated. None of these were adopted.

Winglets

As a wing produces lift it also generates induced drag, especially at the wingtip, in the form of a vortex. This reduces the wing's efficiency and increases drag with a consequent penalty in fuel consumption and aircraft performance. A small winglet on each wingtip reduces turbulent airflow separation and drag, thereby saving fuel. Dr Richard T Whitcomb developed the winglet concept in NASA's Langley Research Center (LRC) wind tunnels. Whitcomb, a brilliant and prolific aerodynamicist, can certainly be said to have left his mark on aviation. In the 1950s he demonstrated and developed the 'area rule' or 'Coke bottle' theory of fuselage shape which facilitated supersonic flight. In the 1960s he theorized, designed, and developed the 'supercritical wing', now standard on advanced jetliners around the world. In the 1970s he produced the winglets, effectively converting unwanted drag into lift.

Although winglets slightly reduce the hazardous wingtip vortices, they are not intended primarily as a safety feature. Winglets may extend upward or downward (or both). Ground clearance of some low-wing jet transports restricts the span of downward winglets while interference with the upper winglet's separation airflow restricts the chord of a lower winglet. These considerations actively influenced the winglet test program on the KC-135. 'From a practical standpoint for low-wing aircraft, the lower winglet must be relatively small. As a result, for the jet transports being discussed herein [KC-135 and C-141], the contributions of the lower winglet to the reduction of drag were relatively small'. Given these assumptions, the KC-135 winglet test program only considered upper winglets.

Based on research conducted by NASA/LRC wind tunnel teams, a memorandum of understanding was issued in 1976 for a joint NASA/USAF development program. On 10th June 1977 Boeing received a $3 million contract to design, install, and test winglets for the KC-135. Tests at Langley on a half-span KC-135 model provided a theoretical baseline for the eventual flight tests and the program entered full-scale wind tunnel testing prior to flight verification. Wind tunnel testing predicted an 8% total drag reduction under cruise flight conditions. Non-optimum conditions were also evaluated and shown to have a 6% total drag reduction. These figures translated to a 37 million gallon per year (140 million liters per year) fuel savings for the KC-135 fleet worldwide. Given the high priority of fuel conservation (just four years earlier the 1973 Arab oil embargo dramatically increased the cost of jet fuel and reduced both military and civil flying), the Air Force undertook full scale operational flight testing. NASA joined as a partner to validate wind tunnel data with operational results.

Left: Outboard view of the winglet during a test flight on NKC-135A 55-3129. The winglet could be adjusted between flights to test different airflow results. *NASA Photo*

Opposite: The winglet test NKC-135A carried an extended nose boom which provided accurate airspeed, attitude, angle of attack, and sideslip data for each winglet configuration. *Photo by Mick Roth via Stephen Miller*

The winglets were designed from February to June 1978. NKC-135A 55-3129 was transferred from the Air Force to NASA in December 1978 and delivered to NASA's DFRC at Edwards AFB in February 1979. While on loan to NASA, the airplane was given the NASA registration N837NA. The winglets (modified from the wingtips of former SPECKLED TROUT KC-135A 55-3126) were delivered in May 1979 and installed in July 1979. Each light alloy winglet weighed approximately 150 lb (68kg) and measured 2ft (0.6m) wide at the top, 6ft (1.8m) wide at the base, and 9ft (2.7m) high. The angle of incidence could be changed to allow for a variety of settings. Because 55-3129 had not yet received the lower wing reskin (TCTO 989), it was restricted to normal flight operations and excluded those at the extremes of the flight envelope. Large wing splices were added as a safety measure pending this reskin. A lengthy research boom was added to the nose to support a pitot-static probe, an angle of attack vane, and a side slip indicator. A variety of instrumentation and a PDP-11 computer were also installed in the aircraft. This computer conducted real-time analysis of the airplane's performance and environment, which were displayed on a CRT in the cockpit for optimum testing.

The first flight with the winglets in place occurred on 24th July 1979, and testing ended on 8th January 1981. A total of 55 flights took place, 39 of these with the winglets installed. Following one flight a winglet was bent 'in a half circle,' demonstrating the energy in the vortices that spiral outward from the wingtip. After the flight tests, the winglets were removed and stored at Davis-Monthan AFB. Test results based on nearly 173 hours of flight test showed that the winglets provided a 6.5% fuel savings over the baseline figures, saving close to 45 million gallons (170 million liters) of fuel annually. Further advantages included improved takeoff performance and fuel offload capability.

The winglet program was not adopted for the KC-135 as the Air Force instead selected a competing fuel-savings program – the Fuel Savings Advisory/Cockpit Avionics System (FSA/CAS) computer. The FSA/CAS offered a mere 2% fuel savings, and only if the airplane was flown on a strict flight profile optimized for airliner-like cruise performance, hardly the environment experienced on a typical KC-135 tanker sortie. The FSA/CAS did have the advantage of the MIL STD-1553 data bus which allowed for future cockpit avionics modernization and expansion, a program hostage to increasing budget cuts. Still, one is hard pressed to ignore the low cost and high value of winglets, which became standard equipment for fuel conservation on airplanes such as the Boeing 747-400, the Gulfstream C-20, and the C-17. In 1981, 55-3129 was demodified and returned to the 4950th TW for routine test duties.

BASIC AND APPLIED SCIENCE

As with many other testbed '135 programs, there is often a fine line between basic scientific research and potential military applications. Auroral research tells us as much about the Earth's magnetosphere as it does about communications in a post-EMP environment. Global mapping studies indicate not only variation in gravity around the Earth but its potential impact on the trajectory of ballistic missiles. Testbed KC-135s were involved in a number of research efforts on behalf of the AEC and AFSWC to establish baseline data in the study of both atmospheric science and ballistic reentry vehicles. Project TORDO, for example, was an AEC study of auroral phenomena and the Earth's magnetic field structures. Project PERQUITO served as a follow-on study.

The first known use of testbed KC-135s in basic scientific research took place during the 1957-1958 International Geophysical Year (IGY), when KC-135A 55-3136 participated in experiments to determine the effects of the Aurora Borealis on radio communications. During 1962 it was further modified as the DOMINIC U platform for the DOMINIC tests in the Pacific.

Conversions of other KC-135s followed during the early 1960s. In 1963, for example, JKC-135A 55-3120 underwent modification for airborne gravity research. The airplane was transferred to Edwards AFB in 1964 for flight testing, and operational flights resumed thereafter at Hanscom Field. The airplane carried LaCoste-Romberg and Askania-Graf stabilized gravity meters capable of detecting vertical deviations in gravity as small as one part per million. These were originally designed for shipboard use but were modified for aerial employment. Two notable projects involving this equipment were a precise study of the Earth's shape and the gravitational effects on ballistic missiles. In the former study, 55-3120 flew over as much of the Free World as possible recording gravitational variations and extrapolating figures for inaccessible areas such as Communist Bloc airspace. From these data the true shape of the Earth was determined. In the latter experiment, the airplane flew mission routes and profiles simulating ballistic missiles. Both programs identified and studied the significant effect of gravity on ICBM guidance systems.

By May 1967 55-3120 had been reconfigured as a flying infrared laboratory known as the 'Infrared Properties Airplane'. In March 1970 a solar eclipse, a solar flare, and polar cap electromagnetic absorption all occurred within a few days of each other. AFCRL used 55-3120 to measure and record the effects of these phenomena on the atmosphere and on communications. Subsequent projects included radiometric and spectral measurements of the plume of the Apollo 14 booster during launch on 31st January 1971, a process

THE ATOMIC KC-135

In October 1951, Gordon Dean, the Chairman of the Atomic Energy Commission (AEC), told a House committee that 'in the next decade you will probably have a plane in the air the power for which comes from [an atomic] reactor.' Far from a scientist's pipe dream, the goal of an atomic-powered bomber had incredible operational appeal. If a bomber's load of 75 or 100 tons of fuel could be replaced by 10 lb (4.5 kg) of uranium, then the bomber could carry more or bigger weapons, would not require air refueling to reach its target, and could travel at tremendous speed. Over time engineers might improve the design of the reactor and reduce the weight and amount of shielding required to run the reactor without harming the crew. (Later programs, like Project PLUTO – an atomic-powered cruise missile – dispensed with the crew hazard altogether but would have spewed lethal radiation along its course, even over friendly territory).

Over the next six years the AEC made considerable efforts to achieve this vision of an atomic-powered airplane, most notably through the Convair NB-36H and the Aircraft Nuclear Propulsion (ANP) program. Between July 1955 and March 1957, the NB-36H flew 215.75 hours over 47 flights, of which 89.0 hours during 21 flights were with the test reactor 'critical.' The flights demonstrated that an airborne nuclear reactor was feasible but the practicality was illusory, although both the Air Force and the Navy were committed to fielding an atom-powered bomber and seaplane by 1965. The Air Force went so far as to plan a huge runway adjacent to the Idaho Falls, ID, reactor site to facilitate flight testing.

The NB-36H showed that it was possible to operate an atomic reactor in flight, but the next step required testing an atomic engine in flight. The primary issue quickly became a choice between an existing airframe to serve as a testbed for the atomic engine or an entirely new design. The October 1957 launch of *Sputnik* rendered this question moot, as the Air Force immediately proposed a 'fly early' program utilizing a KC-135, while the Navy recommended the British Saunders-Roe SR.45 Princess flying boat. The atomic engine would be placed inside the KC-135's capacious cargo hold. Once airborne, the crew would turn off the four wing-mounted J57 engines and fly using only the atomic engine, which would produce thrust through an exhaust in the tail. The Air Force estimated the first flight of the atomic-powered KC-135 would take place within 30 months of approval.

Debate over the 'fly early' off-the-shelf KC-135 versus the dedicated atomic design grew heated and hysterical, dragging out the decision process. Program advocates warned that the three-month delay in selecting a testbed 'might well be the margin of Russia getting the first atomic plane in the air.' By March 1958 President Eisenhower weighed in, telling Representative Melvin Price that it was not possible to produce the first atomic-powered airplane in a race with the Soviet Union and at the same time produce a militarily relevant atomic airplane. However desirable both these objectives might be, there was only so much funding and so many engineers available for all defense programs. The atomic plane was an important, but not top, priority.

The ANP program was finally abandoned in March 1961 after the expenditure of $907 million since 1947. Representative Price remained a staunch advocate of the ANP program, however, charging that bureaucrats intentionally scuttled the project when it was on the 'brink of achieving its objectives' just as 'scientists had devised an atomic airplane engine that could eventually have been successful had the program been pursued.' He cited the example of US Navy Admiral Hyman Rickover and the nuclear submarine, saying that Rickover overcame these bureaucrats to build an atomic submarine fleet, but that the Air Force lacked a suitable champion. Perhaps that was a good thing, as 50 years later the technology and desire to build an atomic-powered airplane remains elusive and unrequited.

repeated for the 26th July 1971 launch of Apollo 15. The airplane was later used for weapons development using IR technology.

Other early basic science projects involved JKC-135A 55-3131 following its role in the 1962 DOMINIC nuclear tests. Much of the science equipment on 55-3131 was residual from those tests, including five blade antennae located circumferentially around the forward dorsal fuselage for use in HF radio wave propagation studies. A large loop antenna aft of these on the fuselage spine was for very low frequency (VLF) research. The airplane carried a five-channel photometer, a spectrograph, an infrared spectrograph, a neutron counter, and a gamma-ray spectrometer, all used in studying electromagnetic phenomena in the D, E, and F regions of the atmosphere. The airplane also studied the 80,000-ampere electro-jet current running from east to west in the ionosphere. During 1964, 55-3131 became involved with the Aerospace Radio Propagation (ASRP) tests. This program evaluated the effect of natural ionized environments on communications, surveillance, and navigation systems which required the propagation of radio waves. By the end of 1965 LAS had modified the airplane for 'upper atmospheric research'. It acquired two transparent domes on the dorsal fuselage. These domes housed 'a gyro-stabilized, 35mm, all-sky camera' and a photometer head 'to measure artificial and natural airglow'. Other new equipment included a gamma-ray monitor. Test missions involved study of 'aurora, ionospheric drift and irregularities, and [investigation of] electron dumping in the middle and North Atlantic'. The airplane also studied ionospheric physics, and was known as the Airborne Ionospheric Observatory (AIO). It participated in a program at the rocket launch facility at Fort Churchill, Manitoba, Canada, from July through November 1969, studying 'polar cap absorption (PCA) events [which] caus[ed] communications blackouts'. The highlight of this program was the 2nd November 1969 airborne observation of a giant solar proton burst. Results from this program were instrumental in the formation of existing models for D-region behavior. In May 1971 sensors on board 55-3131 [in conjunction with a Defense Meteorological Satellite Program (DMSP) satellite] provided the 'first simultaneous measurements of incoming particle fluxes… made by the ISIS-II satellite'. From 26–29th January 1974, 55-3131 participated in a coordinated experiment with the Thule, Greenland, ground station confirming 'that geomagnetic effects are not uniform over the polar cap region'.

The last project supported by 55-3131 (along with NKC-135A 55-3127) was the Combined Release and Radiation Effects Satellite (CRRES) program during 1990 and 1991. The satellite ejected different canisters, each filled with barium, strontium, or lithium into the earth's ionosphere. Once ionized, these produced an aurora that could be analyzed and data compared with similar natural phenomena. CRRES was discontinued on 3rd December 1991.

Other scientific research efforts involving KC-135s included the Leonid Meteor Showers, which occur every November. Beginning with the 1998 event, the National Center for Atmospheric Research (NCAR) Lockheed Electra (registration N308D) and the NKC-135E

Basic science missions conducted by '135 testbeds were often overshadowed by military applications. 55-3131 used its sensors to study the Aurora Borealis. *Photo by Jack Morris via Stephen Miller*

Flying Infrared Signature Technology Aircraft – II (FISTA II) 55-3135 deployed to Kadena AB and observed the meteor shower. In 1999, the FISTA II flew from Tel Aviv, Israel, to RAF Mildenhall, to McGuire AFB, NJ, and an unspecified EC-18B flew a more southerly variation of this track, transiting Lajes Field in the Azores. Poor observation conditions during 2000 prevented a dedicated mission, but in 2001 the FISTA II flew from Edwards AFB to the vicinity of Alabama and then returned, optimizing tracking and recording of the meteor event. In November 2002 55-3135 flew from Madrid, Spain, to Offutt AFB along with NASA DC-8-72 (N817NA). Flying approximately 100km (62nm) apart, they collected stereoscopic imagery of the meteors.

J/N/KC-135A INDIVIDUAL AIRCRAFT

55-3120 Delivered to the Air Force on 27th March 1958, it was redesignated a JKC-135A on 18th October, and conducted infrared research flights on behalf of the AFCRL. It was redesignated a KC-135A on 27th October 1967, but remained in service as a research platform. It was again redesignated on 22nd March 1969 as an NKC-135A assigned to weapons development.

55-3127 This airplane – named *Thunder Chicken* – was involved in a variety of weapons- and systems-related research until its CRRES role in 1990 as an NKC-135A. When CRRES ended, 55-3127 was declared excess and relegated to AMARC on 31st August 1992 as AACA0040 (see Appendix III).

55-3131 This airplane was delivered as a KC-135A to the 93rd BW at Castle AFB on 13th August 1957. Redesignated a JKC-135A on 1st February 1961 and assigned to the AFCRL. It was redesignated a KC-135A on 27th October 1967, but remained in service as a research platform. It was again redesignated on 22nd March 1969 as an NKC-135A. Under HAVE CAR, 55-3131 moved to Kirtland AFB during 1975. In 1976 it was reassigned to the 4950th TW at Wright-Patterson AFB. It was retired to AMARG on 19th October 1992 as AACA0053, and scrapped on 2nd September 2010 (see Appendix III).

55-3136 Originally assigned to the 93rd BW at Castle AFB on 18th September 1957, this airplane was seconded to the AFCRL at Hanscom Field later that year. It remained on loan to AFCRL for basic science initiatives through 30th January 1962 when BIG SAFARI modified it into the DOMINIC U platform for US atmospheric nuclear tests.

NKC-135E INDIVIDUAL AIRCRAFT

55-3135 During 1994 this NKC-135E instrumented tanker acquired the FISTA suite from NKC-135A 55-3120. It participated in several research projects until its retirement to AMARG on 28th September 2004 as AACA0144 (see Appendix III).

RIVET DIGGER

Although best remembered for their unique 'one-sided' paint schemes and nuclear readiness missions, the EARLY DAY/RIVET DIGGER NC-135As also supported considerable scientific research efforts in the form of solar eclipse studies, comet photography, and cosmic ray studies. The 'back-end' science crews argued that the infrequent weapons-simulations mission (such as ROUND UP, described below) did not maintain a suitable level of proficiency. Flying basic science missions would enhance their skills without the huge cost of a simulation mission and would provide valuable research data for the scientific community. The Air Force acquiesced, and an NC-135A flew the first of seven solar eclipse missions from Pago Pago in 1965. There were some lighter moments during this mission, as one researcher found that the only option to photograph the sun during totality was from the small window in the airplane's latrine. The following year an NC-135A joined AFCRL JKC-135A 55-3120 and a NASA Convair 990 in Brazil to study the eclipse, recording some 160 seconds of totality. An NC-135A and 55-3120 flew the next solar study mission in 1970 from San Antonio, TX.

On 10th July 1972, 60-0370 observed a total solar eclipse for a period of 224 seconds at an altitude of 39,400ft (12,009m) northwest of Hudson Bay, Canada. This marked the first use of an NC-135A in solar research, and the unique sensors onboard the airplane enabled collection of previously unattainable data. From 3rd-15th December 1972, 60-0369 participated in FALL AIRGLOW, a highly technical 'investigation of the features of northern and southern intertropical areas, relatively intense east-west airglow bands north and south of the geomagnetic equator [and to] learn more about the tropical

Details about the 'stability test' using this attachment to 60-0369 have not been uncovered, but reflect the extent to which '135s have been modified to serve as testbeds. *Photo via Jay Miller*

[ionospheric] F-layer variations in composition by monitoring the N_2/O_2 concentration ratio to determine diurnal, longitudinal, and northern hemisphere variations.' The airplane was also fitted with an ionosonde to map electron densities in the F-region for correlation with the airglow features. During the next solar eclipse flight known as SEX VI, 60-0371, operating in conjunction with a British Aerospace Concorde, was able to track a total eclipse on 30th June 1973 over North Africa for a remarkably long 12 minutes. (It is not clear if the acronym SEX derived from 'Solar EXpedition' or 'Solar Eclipse eXpedition', as both appear in official documents about the program.) A 1979 mission involving NC-135A 60-0371 with NKC-135A 55-3120, took place over North Dakota. The final NC-135A eclipse mission was over Africa in 1980.

Other NC-135A basic research programs included PICA POSTE, a joint NASA, LANL, and SNL project in 1972 which examined 'high-altitude ionospheric injections and rocketborne experiments'. Rockets were launched from Barking Sands, HI, and Poker Flats, AK, with the airplanes deployed to Eielson AFB, Christchurch, New Zealand, American Samoa, and Hawai'i. Despite three mission failures due to rocket malfunctions (and a fourth due to an engine failure on 60-0370), the program collected sufficient data over 184 flying hours and 42 sorties to term the program an overall success.

Along with its AEC nuclear readiness test duties, 60-0369 supported other test programs. In early 1972 this NC-135A participated in a 'stability control test', sporting a 10-15ft (3.0-4.5m) aerodynamic boom (with disc-shaped cap) protruding perpendicularly from the center of the right forward fuselage immediately aft of the copilot's No.3 window. The airplane retained the dorsal fairing and absence of markings, but no other information about this test is known. Given the airplane's extensive 'electromagnetic' background, this structure was likely related to 'field dynamics' of some sort surrounding the disc-shaped cap.

From 25th February through 10th March 1973, 60-0370 served as the test aircraft for a joint AEC, AFSWC, and Department of Transportation (DoT) dual tasking mission known as VELA/CIAP. The VELA portion 'studied visual auroral substorms by correlating data taken simultaneously by an NC-135 flying just under the tropopause with data taken from a VELA satellite in the Earth's magnetotail.' These substorms corresponded to changes in the plasma properties in the Earth's magnetotail, and the VELA satellite measured these changes in plasma particles. This research established baseline data used by VELA satellites to detect atmospheric nuclear detonations.

The Climatic Impact Assessment Program (CIAP) established a baseline for the DoT of the 'earth's present natural atmospheric composition from the Equator to the North Pole.' CIAP was a direct response to 'the requirement, by law, for an environmental impact determination to be made on all future weapon systems, such as the B-1.' VELA/CIAP missions operated from Goose AB, Canada, Eielson AFB, and Hickam AFB. Initial validation flights were conducted on 16th and 22nd February 1973, and the airplane departed Kirtland AFB on 25th February for Goose AB. For the VELA portion of the mission, the airplane (call sign *Mike 02*) was scheduled to fly from Goose AB to Eielson AFB any day between the 26th February and 1st March, depending on weather and auroral conditions. It then conducted four eight-hour 'round robin' data gathering missions (both VELA and CIAP) from Eielson AFB, and on 6th March proceeded to Hickam AFB. On 8th March the airplane flew a CIAP mission to the equator, and redeployed to Kirtland AFB on 9th March. The VELA missions could only be flown in the dark of the moon when the VELA satellite was in the proper position, severely limiting potential mission dates. Additional flights from 8-17th April 1973 validated the airplane's sensors against a known atmospheric pollution source, Icelandic volcanic eruptions.

From 1977, when it was demodified as a nuclear weapons studies testbed, until 1984, 60-0371 served as an airborne data recording and transmission platform and as a diagnostics airplane for the ALL NKC-135A 55-3123 located at Kirtland AFB. By this time the dorsal fairing was removed and a variety of theodolite markings and test patterns were painted on the starboard forward fuselage. When not supporting the ALL, 60-0371 'chased' solar eclipses (as it did in March 1979), photographed comets, and studied cosmic rays. The ALL was placed in flyable storage in 1984 and 60-0371 was relocated to Wright-Patterson AFB for use as a flight proficiency trainer and other test support.

NC-135A INDIVIDUAL AIRCRAFT

60-0369 Converted by BIG SAFARI and redesignated as an NC-135 on 3rd June 1964. Its duties after the RIVET DIGGER program are not known, and on 9th June 1976, 60-0369 (minus its dorsal fairing) was transferred to the Chanute Technical Training Center (CTTC) at Chanute AFB, IL, and redesignated a GNC-135A ground maintenance trainer. It was cut in half after October 1991 and scrapped (see Appendix III).

60-0370 Converted by BIG SAFARI and redesignated as an NC-135 on 3rd June 1964. Following its use as a nuclear weapons and electromagnetic testbed, 60-0370 was relegated to MASDC on 30th June 1976, and given the storage number CA005. It was officially written off on 6th September 1978 (see Appendix III).

60-0371 Converted by BIG SAFARI and redesignated as an NC-135 on 3rd June 1964. Following its RIVET DIGGER duties it supported the ALL program.

SPACE PROGRAMS

As Neil Armstrong stepped from the Lunar Excursion Module *Eagle* onto the Sea of Tranquility and became the first human to stand on the Moon, few people stopped to think of the important role of '135 variants in making that momentous event possible. Testbed '135s were an integral part of the burgeoning US missile and rocket program, and provided optical tracking and data telemetry for the many launch successes and failures that defined the early years at Cape Canaveral. Weightless trainers allowed astronauts to acquire their 'space legs' and determined how they would eat and live in zero gravity, as well as verified that equipment would work under conditions that could not be duplicated on Earth. The well-known 'big nose' ARIAs ensured that astronauts and ground controllers remained in radio contact with each other over the vast distances around the Earth and between the Earth and the Moon.

Optical Tracking of Rockets and Missiles

KC-135A 55-3127 was not only the very first KC-135A delivered to SAC, it was first '135 optical testbed. During 1959 BMAC modified it into a JKC-135A by adding a 'doghouse', a large fairing atop the forward fuselage and two 30in (76.2cm) optically ground windows (later increased to eleven windows) along the port side of the fuselage. The port wing and upper surfaces attached to it (such as the engines and pylons) were painted flat black to reduce glare. The airplane was assigned on 24th November 1959 to the AFCRL's Optical Physics Laboratory as part of the Advanced Research Projects Agency's (ARPA) Project SKYSCRAPER. Bendix's Systems Division then installed optical and microwave instrumentation into 55-3127. This suite was designed to detect and record ultraviolet, visible, and infrared radiation associated with the reentry performance and physics of missile and rocket payloads. The 'fingerprint' radiation signature of a reentry vehicle is the result of the body's interaction with the atmosphere, and the amount of radiation varies with the composition and configuration of the reentry vehicle and its angle of entry and attack. To accommodate this test, the airplane's cargo door was cut in half vertically and a gimballed tracking 'eye' was installed behind an opening approximately 2ft by 4ft (0.6 x 1.2m).

From the 22nd-27th October 1961, BIG SAFARI converted 55-3127 into the SPEED LIGHT-BRAVO aircraft to monitor the Soviet *Tsar Bomba* surface detonation on 30th October at the Novaya Zemlya test site (see Chapter 10). Following this and several other Soviet nuclear tests, the airplane returned to AFCRL in November 1961, and resumed its SKYSCRAPER duties.

In early 1962, JKC-135A 55-3124 replaced 55-3127 in Project SKYSCRAPER. JKC-135A 55-3127 then began flight tests on behalf of the Massachusetts Institute of Technology (MIT) Lincoln Laboratory as part of the Radiation Monitoring Program (RAMP) which observed radiation emitted during the launch phase of ballistic missiles and rockets. The operational goal of these tests was a fleet of airplanes patrolling outside the periphery of the Soviet Union. When the airplanes detected an ICBM or SLBM launch, a laser-equipped platform would shoot down the missile during its vulnerable boost phase, similar to the Lockheed U-2 LOW CARD program suggested by Clarence 'Kelly' Johnson. RAMP showed that such an operation was only marginally successful against ICBMs, but reasonably successful against SLBMs.

Mission equipment included a precision tracker and an optical radiation spectrometer. The optical system was maintained in a pressurized doghouse compartment on top of the fuselage above the leading edge of the wing root. Flush-mounted doors opened in flight to uncover a 20 x 30in (50 x 76.2cm) flat mirror that reflected incident radiation onto an optical telescope. Temperature and air density of this cavity were carefully regulated by forcing hot bleed air into the cavity, ensuring precise alignment of the optical system. The airplane had the short vertical stabilizer, acquired another dorsal radome aft of the doghouse, and retained the air refueling boom.

By 1963 Martin-Baltimore had modified 55-3127 and JKC-135A 55-3134 for the Terminal Radiation Program (TRAP), successor to the earlier RAMP tests undertaken by 55-3127. TRAP examined radiation patterns during a ballistic vehicle's terminal phase of flight. Although both airplanes participated in TRAP, their configurations differed significantly, as 55-3134 had a larger doghouse fairing atop the fuselage and the large fuselage optics windows were installed approximately 7in (17.7cm) higher to accommodate the greater elevation angles required for the internal research equipment.

TRAP met with mixed success. From 1st January through 30th June 1963, there were six successful collections out of 13 events. Nine sounding rockets were tracked during missions from Holloman

During 1963 Martin modified JKC-135A 55-3134 for the TRAP program, which met with mixed success. *Author's collection*

AFB, NM, and of these only two were successfully followed, two provided marginal data, and five provided no data, all ascribed to the loss of an ion generator on the reentry vehicle. Two later events at the Pacific Missile Range at Kwajalein were successful, however, as were two rockets fired from the Atlantic Missile Range and covered from Roberts IAP at Monrovia, Liberia. A third shot was canceled. The number of successful collections increased, with data recorded on 14 events, although no total number of missions is available for comparison.

From 1st January through 30th June 1965, JKC-135A 55-3127 was assigned to the Flight Test Division at Wright-Patterson AFB and participated in TRAP VII on behalf of the Naval Ordnance Laboratory, Raytheon, and the General Electric Company. JKC-135A 55-3134 continued to support TRAP I through at least late 1965. Subsequently, E-Systems updated it under a combined Air Force/Army contract. The company installed 'two open-port rotating drum assemblies and the necessary supporting structure in [the] existing fuselage canopy [the 'doghouse']. The drums [were] capable of being rotated to a closed position, sealed, and environmentally conditioned while the aircraft [was] on the ground or in transit to or

from its operational location and altitude. This modification also included the installation of gimbals, sensors, racks, displays, and a cryogenic cooling system'. In addition to the basic TRAP mission, 55-3134 also studied the radiation pattern of ballistic vehicles while at their apogee as part of the Midcourse Acquisition and Tracking System (TRAP-MATS), although to a significantly lesser degree of success than observations made during launch and reentry. These missions were euphemistically referred to as 'celestial navigation studies'.

Between 1965 and 1970, NKC-135A 55-3135 and JC-135A 60-0376 took part in the Airborne Astrographic Camera System (AACS). The two airplanes flew parallel tracks on either side of the trajectory of a reentry vehicle (RV) under study, triangulating and photographing the RV's actual position. In June 1969 60-0376 was reassigned to the AFETR and continued to use the AACS to track missiles and ballistic vehicles. The AACS program ended in 1970.

In 1969 NKC-135A 55-3124 was used by the MIT Lincoln Laboratory at Hanscom Field as part of ESD's Project PRESS, a program that studied ballistic vehicle reentry characteristics in the Kwajalein Islands area. The airplane frequently deployed to Hickam

By 1965 JKC-135A 55-3127 had the vertical stabilizer extension installed and had been modified for the TRAP-VII program. Red covers protected optically ground windows. *Photo by Richard Sullivan via Stephen Miller*

Top: Along with C-135A 60-0376, NKC-135A 55-3135 took part in the AACS program to track reentry vehicles. *Photo by Clyde Gerdes via Stephen Miller*

Middle: NKC-135A 55-3134 is easily distinguished from its cohort 55-3127, as the windows on '134 are higher on the fuselage and larger in diameter. The 'doghouse' differed in configuration on '134 as the sensors changed on both jets. *Photos (top) by Bill Sides via Stephen Miller and (bottom) by Jack Morris via Stephen Miller*

Bottom: The AACS program used multiple cameras and spectrometers to monitor launches from Cape Canaveral. *Photo by Stephen Miller*

AFB and was named *Liki Tiki*. Further modifications to the airplane for this program included the installation of nine large-diameter optically ground windows along the starboard side of the fuselage.

J/NKC-135A INDIVIDUAL AIRCRAFT

55-3124 From 1962 this airplane was assigned to the AFCRL and replaced 55-3127 as the primary SKYSCRAPER aircraft. By 1969 it was associated with ESD's Project PRESS.

55-3127 This airplane was assigned to the AFCRL from 1959 through the mid 1960s and took part in SKYSCRAPER, SPEED LIGHT-BRAVO, and the RAMP/TRAP programs.

55-3134 This airplane was assigned to the AFCRL from 1959 through the mid 1960s for the TRAP program. It was then reassigned to Patrick AFB as part of National Ranges support along with the EC-135N ARIAs. At one point 55-3134 was named *Big Daddy*. On 2nd July 1968 the airplane was redesignated an NKC-135A. In 1977 the doghouse was removed and the airplane transferred to the US Navy as NKC-135A BuNo 553134 as NAVY KING CROW I'.

55-3135 Part of the AACS program from 1965-70, redesignated a KC-135A on 17th November 1967, and then an NKC-135A on 10th March 1969, and reassigned to the AFETR. After AACS ended 55-3135 was reassigned to the AFFTC at Edwards AFB for use as an 'instrumented tanker'.

JC-135A INDIVIDUAL AIRCRAFT

60-0376 This C-135A was reassigned on 21st June 1965 to ASD at Wright-Patterson AFB. It was redesignated as a JC-135A from 23rd June 1965 through 31st October 1967, and was part of the AACS program until 1970.

ALOTS

In August 1962 the Air Photographic and Charting Service (APCS) recommended development of a 'specially equipped RC-135 with an improved optical system for better photographic and television recording of nuclear tests and missile launching and re-entry.' The proposal called for 'an improved optical stabilization system and 200 to 1,000in [5 to 25.3m] focal length lenses' installed in the RC-135, which would operate at altitudes up to 45,000ft [13,716m], above most haze and cloud cover. Although this particular project was not undertaken, it became the basis for the Airborne Lightweight Optical Tracking System (ALOTS) program.

Beginning in 1964, JKC-135As 55-3123 and 56-3596 served as the primary test platform for ALOTS. This system provided high quality optical tracking of rocket and missile launches, and is best known for its use on EC-135N ARIAs. ALOTS consisted of four main components – a control system and its computers, a timing section, a manual tracking station, and a removable, externally-mounted teardrop-shaped pod attached to the airplane's cargo door. The pod contained a 2¾in (70mm) high resolution camera with a 200in (508cm) focal length. Camera resolution was better than two seconds of an arc, and it could spot and track a 7in (17.7cm) target at 10 miles (16km) and a 12ft (3.6m) target at 200 miles (321km). At high altitude the camera filmed both stars and planets. The entire pod weighed in excess of 3,000 lb (1,360kg).

An operator at the manual tracking station (inside a small clear dome atop the fuselage) visually acquired the object using a gunsight from a B-50 (similar to the mechanism in the RIVET BALL). Once spotted, computers would automatically track and direct cameras to film the target. The camera image was both recorded on film and displayed on two monitoring screens inside the airplane. A timing section printed the exact time (with microsecond accuracy) on each frame of film.

Flight tests began in 1965 at the AFWTR, AFETR, and the Army's White Sands Missile Range, NM. The ALOTS platform orbited 40 miles (64km) from the launch site. The airplane flew in the opposite direction from the target's planned track until approximately two minutes prior to launch, at which time the airplane turned around and then paralleled the target's track; the entire flight pattern looked like a giant fishhook. During 1965 55-3123 and the ALOTS gear successfully located, tracked, and photographed the booster separation of an Air Force Titan 3C missile. The first operational use of ALOTS was for the launch of Gemini 8 on 16th March 1966. Once the ALOTS development and testing was completed, additional pods were then installed on selected EC-135Ns. Four ARIAs were configured to carry the ALOTS pod, including 61-0326, 61-0327, and 61-0329; the fourth ALOTS-capable airplane has not been conclusively identified.

Prototype test flights of the ALOTS pod focused both on aerodynamic suitability as well as optical resolution. *Author's collection*

Tests of the ALOTS pod on 56-3596 included flights over the White Sands Missile Range conducted from Kirtland AFB. *Photo by Mick Roth via Stephen Miller*

Top and above left: Following its participation in the ALOTS program and prior to its conversion into the ALL, NKC-135A 55-3123 was assigned to routine transport duties, as well as other test projects. One such project incorporated a variety of sensors in the tail. *Photos by Jack Morris via Stephen Miller*

Above: This view of EC-135N 61-0327 taken in June 1967 during a test flight shows the ALOTS pod and the observer's blister. *Photo by Bob Burns*

Upper left: The ARIAs were originally assigned to the AFETR at Patrick AFB (see nose emblem), but were reassigned to Wright-Patterson AFB as part of HAVE CAR. *Photo via René Francillon*

Left: In order to be in the optimal position for voice and telemetry relay, the ARIAs deployed globally. *Photo via René Francillon*

NKC-135A INDIVIDUAL AIRCRAFT

55-3123 From 1964 through 1967, 55-3123 was one of two ALOTS testbeds. It was subsequently transferred for use as the ALL platform.

56-3596 By mid-1966, 56-3596 had surrendered its radome, acquired an ALOTS pod, and was reassigned to the AFSWC at Kirtland AFB.

EC-135N INDIVIDUAL AIRCRAFT

61-0326 Converted into an EC-135N ARIA on 11th February 1967 as one of the four ALOTS-capable ARIAs. Converted in 1982 into an EC-135E.

61-0327 Converted into an EC-135N ARIA on 7th September 1966. Configured for ALOTS. Fully demodified to C-135N (the large nose was removed and installed on an unidentified EC-18B) and transferred to CENTCOM in July 1985 for use as an EC-135N airborne command post.

61-0329 Converted into an EC-135N ARIA on 1st September 1967. This ALOTS-configured EC-135N was converted into an EC-135E in 1982.

Telemetry and Communications Relay

The EC-135N/E Apollo Range Instrumented Aircraft (ARIA – and later Advanced Range Instrumented Aircraft) can trace their origins to a 1960 Boeing proposal to modify four KC-135s with tracking and data recording equipment. The tracking antennae would be located in a long fairing on top of the fuselage. The airplanes would deploy around the world and fly precise telemetry acquisition profiles to provide optimal monitoring of US civil and military space vehicles, especially over the vast expanses of ocean where no surface-based facilities were available. In addition, these aircraft could collect similar data on Soviet space activities, although this was not considered a primary mission role. None of these proposed tracking airplanes was built or converted from existing airframes.

In 1964 the Air Force estimated that 12 specially configured EC-135s could provide the global tracking coverage necessary for the Apollo lunar missions. NASA, however, argued that 35 C-121 Constellations and C-130 Hercules would be needed to provide the same coverage. Because each proposed ARIA airplane had a projected modification cost of $1.5 million, the selection became academic. The delivery of C-141s to MATS in 1965 meant that its surplus C-135As were available for immediate conversion into ARIAs, further simplifying the decision. NASA accepted the Air Force's recommendation to use the converted C-135s, and on 27th November 1964 the Air Force agreed to transfer eight C-135As to NASA for conversion into ARIAs. On 10th December 1964 NASA paid $600,000 to AFSC's Electronic Systems Division (ESD) for the definition phase of the C-135 Apollo program. Although only eight of the 12 had been identified for transfer, NASA was confident that the four additional airplanes would be forthcoming and the agency would 'continue planning on the basis of 12 C-135 aircraft for Apollo support'.

The actual conversion cost was significantly higher than predicted – approximately $4 - 4.5 million per airplane. Douglas was chosen as the primary airframe contractor with Bendix selected as the chief electronics contractor. Beginning in 1966 as part of the PACER LINER program, Douglas's Modification Division in Tulsa, OK, converted the first of eight C-135As into EC-135Ns, with the ARIA's first flight on 19th September 1966. In addition, four C-135Bs were delivered in 1967 to Douglas for conversion. These became Telemetry Range Instrumented Aircraft (TRIA) and remained designated as C-135Bs. The ARIAs were originally assigned to the AFETR at Patrick AFB, but were all reassigned in July 1975 to the 4950th TW at Wright-Patterson AFB under HAVE CAR.

The ARIA's primary Apollo support roles were vehicle tracking and two-way voice relay between the astronauts and the mission director at the Manned Spacecraft Center in Houston, TX. Secondary missions included data recording and retransmission, and assistance in locating the Apollo command module after splashdown. The airplanes normally deployed over the Atlantic Ocean and the Gulf of Mexico for mission launches and over the Pacific Ocean for reentry and splashdown. Two airplanes could provide coverage over some 5,000 square miles (12,949km²) of ocean, eliminating the need for the numerous and expensive surface vessels – known as Apollo Range Instrumented Ships (ARIS) – previously used to perform the same mission. Not only were the ARIS's more costly to operate than the ARIAs, they were extremely slow and required careful prepositioning to ensure maximum effectiveness. Any short-notice mission changes left NASA without coverage in the new area of interest. Beginning in 1968, the USNS *Watertown* was the first of the five Apollo support ships retired from service. All eight ARIAs were first used together during the Apollo 6 mission in 1968. Three EC-135Ns operated from Kindley AB, Bermuda, covering the Atlantic Ocean, while two EC-135Ns flew from Hickam AFB covering the Pacific Ocean, and the remaining three airplanes operated from Patrick AFB to cover the Gulf of Mexico.

A typical ARIA mission began with two to three days of equipment calibration at Patrick AFB. The airplanes would then deploy approximately one week prior to the Apollo launch, allowing the ARIAs and their crews to be fully mission capable and rested five days prior to launch. Aircraft maintenance discrepancies were corrected and crews adjusted their 'biological clocks' to their new location. These staging bases included Ascension Island, Pago Pago, Capetown, South Africa, and Buenos Aires, Argentina. The ARIAs were airborne and on station at least two to three hours prior to the Apollo's lift-off, flying precisely timed tracks to facilitate signal

During the heyday of the Apollo program, the ramp at Patrick AFB was full of ARIAs and other testbeds all monitoring launches and missions.
Photo by Stephen Miller

acquisition by the ARIA's on-board receivers. Average flights lasted nearly ten hours and were occasionally longer, limited only by available fuel on board (EC-135 ARIAs were not equipped for air refueling; Boeing EC-18B ARIAs were equipped with IFR receptacles during 1995, beginning with 81-0891). Following their missions, the ARIAs returned to Patrick AFB where the recorded data were processed and analyzed.

ARIA crewmembers included two pilots, a navigator, a flight engineer, the airborne mission controller, and a mission team of no fewer than eight technicians, with the actual number dependent upon mission duration and complexity. Total crew number was often as high as 23 persons.

ARIA Prime Mission Electronic Equipment (PMEE) was made up of three major subsystems – the voice and telemetry subsystem, the timing subsystem, and the HF communications subsystem – all contained in a 30,000 lb (13,608kg) modular package. Specific PMEE capabilities included:

a. Realtime retransmission of high speed digital spacecraft data … via DoD communications satellites and existing ground stations … allow[ing] the instantaneous analysis of critical events as they occur on-board the spacecraft.

b. Realtime retransmission of analog or low-speed digital data … via HF radio, also allowing continuous monitoring of selected spacecraft parameters.

c. On-board readout of selected spacecraft parameters for voice report … via HF radio.

d. Post-mission transfer of one or two tracks of recorded data to a ground station, within line of sight of the aircraft, via VHF and UHF transmitters. The ground station [could] then send the data … through existing channels, allowing … access to ARIA data several days in advance of the actual delivery [of the recorded data].

e. Post-mission reception and recording of an instrumented ship's data, thereby speeding up … delivery of its data.

The voice and telemetry subsystem incorporated an antenna group, a radio frequency (RF) group, and a record group. Heart of the antenna group was the 'world's largest airborne steerable antenna', a 7ft (2.13m) diameter two-axis steerable antenna weighing approximately 700 lb (317kg). Located in the ARIA's 10ft (3.0m) diameter nose, the antenna was used for telemetry and voice collection and transmission in the P-band (225-260 MHz) and S-band (2200-2300 MHz). The antenna could be steered either manually or automatically if the signal strength was adequate to maintain tracking lock. Once the signal was acquired, it was then routed to the telemetry receivers in the RF Group for processing.

The RF group included UHF and VHF receivers for spacecraft telemetry and tracking data, transmitters and receivers necessary for spacecraft communications during manned space flight missions, and test and calibration equipment. In addition, special equipment could be installed that allowed the airplane to receive and process Space Ground Link Subsystem (SGLS) signals, 'a standardized telemetry format used frequently in USAF missile operations'. Once processed, the data were then sent to the communications subsystem for retransmission. The data were also sent to the voice and telemetry subsystem record group for data storage, monitoring, and playback.

Primary components of the record group included two M-28 wideband magnetic tape recorders, each capable of recording 14 tracks of data on 9,200ft (2,804m) reels. Each reel provided 15 minutes of recording time, and all timing codes, telemetry data, receiver signal strengths, voice communications, and other low frequency signals were multiplexed prior to recording in order to conserve tape.

The timing subsystem generated time codes and precision pulse repetition rates which were recorded with the data for time correlations in interpreting spacecraft events when the tapes were processed. This subsystem utilized a rubidium clock as the primary signal source, capable of ± 5 milliseconds when crosschecked against National Bureau of Standards broadcasts on HF radio, or better than one microsecond when crosschecked with an external synchronization source.

The HF communications subsystem included three 1,000-watt single-sideband transmitters and receivers, operable over 280,000 discrete frequencies in simplex or full duplex configurations. If a satellite terminal was installed on the EC-135N, the telemetry received by the ARIA could be then be retransmitted via satellite to a waiting ground station. The ARIAs had a wingtip HF antenna on each wing and a trailing wire antenna (TWA) mounted in a fairing beneath the fuselage. Four of the ARIAs – including 61-0326, 61-0327, and 61-0329 – were configured to carry the Northrop ALOTS pod (see above).

After termination of the Apollo program, the airplanes were renamed *Advanced* Range Instrumented Aircraft and dedicated to a variety of space and atmospheric test operations. Missions included those for agencies such as NASA, DoD, and the defense and space agencies of several foreign countries. Specific missions include cruise missile development and operational test and evaluation (OT&E) flights, flights in support of the Space Shuttle and the Shuttle Inertial Upper Stage (IUS), tests of the US Army's Pershing I and II battlefield missile, the Poseidon and Trident SLBMs, the Peacekeeper (the MX) and Small ICBM (the 'Midgetman'), and a variety of DoD satellite operations.

Two of the ARIAs were demodified in 1980 for use in other test programs, one crashed in 1981, and one was transferred in July 1985 to Central Command (CENTCOM) for use as an airborne command post (see Chapter 9). The PMEE from the three demodified EC-135Ns was installed in C-135Bs 62-4133 and 62-4128 (converting them to EC-135B ARIAs, which were themselves later demodified) and into a C-18A, converting it to an EC-18B. Beginning in 1982 the EC-135Ns were converted into EC-135Es with TF33-PW-102 turbofans.

Initial plans for the second-generation of ARIA called for eight airplanes, including four EC-135Es (60-0374, 61-0326, 61-0329, and 61-0330) and, beginning in 1985, four EC-18Bs (81-0891, 81-0892, 81-0894, and 81-0896). Only seven PMEE suites were available, however, meaning that as one airplane underwent programmed depot maintenance (PDM) or other scheduled grounding, its PMEE suite would be installed on another ARIA. During the late 1980s EC-135E ARIAs 61-0329 and 61-0330 were identified for conversion to

Opposite page:

Diameter of the ARIA nose was 10ft (3.0m), and contained a 7.1ft (2.13m) steerable antenna. No doubt the ARIAs had one of the largest drag coefficients of all '135s. *Photo P40911 courtesy Boeing*

This page:

Four of the ARIAs were configured to carry the ALOTS pod, including 61-0326. *Photo by the author*

Only 61-0328 was lost as an ARIA. Former TRIAs 61-0331 and 61-2664 crashed after conversion to other variants. *Author's collection*

'EC-135s for SAC'. Details of this conversion are not known, and the modification was not undertaken.

The first four of six C-135Bs were delivered in 1967 and 1968 to AFSC for use as Apollo support aircraft. Douglas Aircraft Company's Modification Division in Tulsa, OK, converted four C-135Bs (61-0331, 61-2664, 62-4128, and 62-4133) into Apollo support airplanes, designated Telemetry Range Instrumented Aircraft (TRIA). Although similar in appearance to the EC-135N ARIAs, the TRIAs differed significantly in capability and mission. All of the TRIAs had the ARIA's large nose but could not carry the ALOTS pod. In addition, the TRIAs' mission equipment collected information in frequency ranges different from those of the ARIAs. The TRIAs were equipped with TF33-P-5 turbofans whereas the ARIAs initially used the J57-P/F-59W turbojets, and later TF33-PW-102s. Despite the designation change associated with the ARIAs (from C-135As to EC-135Ns), the four TRIAs remained designated only as C-135Bs and were never EC-135B TRIAs. After their acceptance from MAC but prior to their conversion the airplanes were temporarily assigned to the 4950th TW at Wright-Patterson AFB. After conversion each airplane was then assigned to the AFETR. In the middle of 1971 all four TRIAs were reassigned to the 4950th TW at Wright-Patterson AFB. One of these (60-0331) crashed in 1971 after demodification and two (62-4128 and 62-4133) were used for additional electronics testing until they were further converted into EC-135B ARIAs in 1980. The fourth TRIA (61-2664) was converted in 1969 directly into a reconnaissance platform.

From 1979 to 1980 62-4128 and 62-4133 were converted into EC-135B ARIAs following the installation of the PMEE from two EC-135N ARIAs which were demodified for other testbed missions. The EC-135Bs offered several advantages over their EC-135N counterparts. Because they had TF33-P-5 turbofans instead of the J57-P/F-59W turbojets, the EC-135Bs saved over $350 per flying hour in fuel alone ($1,500 per hour in 2015 dollars). The turbofans increased both range and endurance, and eliminated the need for demineralized water required for takeoff. Not all takeoffs required water injection, but when it was needed (as when operating

from short runways at high temperatures and pressure altitudes, or when fully loaded with fuel), the limited worldwide availability of pure demineralized water often degraded the ARIAs mission capability. Without the water, the ARIAs would have to takeoff with less fuel than desired, reducing their ability to loiter on station, meaning they might not be available to collect or retransmit essential voice or data communications (this problem also beset RC-135A operations in South America). The TF33-P-5 engines' thrust reversers enabled the airplane to operate from shorter runways, increasing its flexibility to deploy worldwide. The EC-135Bs retained the large nose acquired while TRIAs, thus eliminating the added conversion expense required to modify a basic airplane into the ARIA configuration.

EC-135N INDIVIDUAL AIRCRAFT

60-0372 Converted into an EC-135N ARIA on 29th April 1966 and delivered on 5th October 1967. Demodified in 1979 into a C-135N, and in 1980 its PMEE installed in C-135B 62-4128, converting it to an EC-135B ARIA.

60-0374 Converted into an EC-135N ARIA on 16th April 1966 and delivered on 26th May 1966. This EC-135N was modified into an EC-135E from 20th March through 10th April 1982.

60-0375 Converted into an EC-135N ARIA on 16th April 1966 and delivered on 23rd August 1967. Demodified in 1979 to a C-135N and used for other test operations, but retained the large nose. In 1980 its PMEE was donated to C-135B 62-4133, converting it to an EC-135B ARIA.

61-0326 Converted into an EC-135N ARIA on 11th February 1967 and delivered on 31st October 1967. One of four ALOTS-capable ARIAs. Converted in 1982 into an EC-135E.

61-0327 Converted into an EC-135N ARIA on 7th September 1966 and delivered on 28th October 1967. Configured for ALOTS. Fully demodified to C-135N (the large nose was removed and installed on an unidentified EC-18B) and transferred to CENTCOM in July 1985 for use as an EC-135N airborne command post.

61-0328 Converted into an EC-135N ARIA on 8th September 1967 and delivered on 28th December 1967. This was the final EC-135N ARIA. It was delivered to the Air Force on 27th December 1967. It crashed on 6th May 1981 during a spouse-orientation flight (see Appendix II).

61-0329 Converted into an EC-135N ARIA on 1st September 1967 and delivered on 1st December 1967. This ALOTS-configured EC-135N was converted into an EC-135E in 1982.

61-0330 Converted into an EC-135N ARIA on 9th September 1966 and delivered on 13th October 1967. Converted into an EC-135E in 1982. Scheduled for demodification in late 1987 from an ARIA. This plan was abandoned, however, and the airplane remained in use as an ARIA. Stored and believed scrapped at Kirtland AFB.

61-0331 was demodified from a TRIA for a special mission associated with the BURNING LIGHT task force, but disappeared over the Pacific Ocean following its first mission. *Author's collection*

During 1971 the TRIAs were relocated from Patrick AFB to Wright-Patterson AFB, and acquired the traditional red band on the vertical stabilizer. *Photo by Clyde Gerdes via Stephen Miller*

E/C-135B INDIVIDUAL AIRCRAFT

61-0331 This TRIA was part of the AFETR from late 1967 through 1971, when it was modified into a C-135B for 'Project III' as part of the BURNING LIGHT missions monitoring French nuclear tests in the Pacific.
61-2664 This C-135B operated as a TRIA from March 1968 through early 1970 when it was delivered to BIG SAFARI for conversion into the second COBRA BALL RC-135S.
62-4128 This TRIA operated as part of the AFETR from 1967 until its transfer in 1971 to the 4950th TW. Following the end of the TRIA program in 1973, 62-4128 participated in several other projects, retaining the large nose it acquired as a TRIA. In 1979 the PMEE from EC-135N 60-0372 was transferred to this C-135B, converting it to an ARIA. The modification was completed in 1980 and the airplane officially redesignated an EC-135B. On 29th July 1983, 62-4128 was delivered to E-Systems for conversion into the RC-135X. Its PMEE was then installed on Boeing C-18A 81-0891, making it the first EC-18B ARIA.
62-4133 This TRIA operated as part of the AFETR from 1967 until its transfer in 1971 to the 4950th TW. Following the end of the TRIA program in 1973, 62-4133 was active in several other projects, retaining its TRIA nose. In 1979 the PMEE from EC-135N 60-0375 was installed in 62-4133, converting it into an ARIA. In 1980 the modification was completed and the airplane redesignated as an EC-135B. In 1985 this airplane was demodified and delivered to SAC for conversion into the TC-135S. Its PMEE was then installed on C-18A 81-0896 as it was converted into the second EC-18B ARIA.

The 'Vomit Comets'

Initial US Air Force efforts to assess the effects of weightlessness on man and machine began in Convair C-131s assigned to WADC at Wright-Patterson AFB (including C-131B 53-7823, 53-7806, and 53-7791). These proved reasonably effective in training the Mercury astronauts and other early studies, but were limited by their inability to fly more weightless segments in a given flight. The availability of JKC-135A 55-3129 made it a good choice to replace the C-131s, allowing longer flights with a greater number of weightless segments. The willingness of the US Air Force to continue funding and operational support of NASA's zero-g C-135 training program at Wright-Patterson AFB, however, reached an end in April 1972. The first three airplanes involved in these duties (NKC-135A 55-3129, KC-135A 62-3536, and C-135A 60-0378 – see Table 8.3) had passed or were nearing their individual limits on weightless flight time or

parabolas and had since been returned or scheduled to return to SAC, TAC, and AFSC, respectively. Throughout their tenure as zero-g trainers, these airplanes flew 33,988 parabolic arcs, each including approximately 30 seconds of weightlessness for a total of some 346 hours of zero-g over 7,600 flights.

AFSC urged the transfer of the program to NASA by 1974 and identified KC-135A 59-1481 as a replacement weightlessness trainer for NASA. Estimated cost for converting this airplane was $1.3 million, which included reskinning the lower wing, major inspections, and 'zero-timing' the airframe and engines, but did not include an additional $50,000 for the necessary zero-g modifications. Although NASA wanted the airplane and was willing to accept full responsibility for the zero-g program, it had major reservations about accepting the AFSC proposal, saying that 'Funds for reconditioning the airframe will be very difficult to find. There is no NASA requirement for a zero-time airframe… It is recommended that the Air Force be requested to search for another C-135 model that requires less reconditioning, using more relaxed total accumulated flying hours criteria.' In view of 59-1481's abysmal maintenance record while it was in service with the FAA, NASA's concern was not surprising.

Unable to find a substitute, however, NASA finally acquiesced and accepted 59-1481 given Boeing's assurance that the airplane could safely attain the 14,000 zero-g parabolas (approximately four to five years of operations) deemed necessary to justify the expense of its update and modification. It completed PDM at OCAMA in March 1973. Following the lower wing reskin modification and the Aircraft Structural Integrity Program (ASIP) by BMAC, 59-1481 was delivered in August 1973 as N930NA to NASA's Johnson Space Center (JSC) at Ellington AFB, TX, with a total of 12,453 flight hours. [Only the US Air Force *Weightless Wonders* (55-3129,

60-0378, and 62-3536) were assigned to Wright-Patterson AFB. NASA's KC-135A zero-g trainers (59-1481 and 63-7998) were assigned to NASA's Ellington AFB.]

The airplane was extensively modified to allow for this testing. For example, the engine-driven electrical generators in an unmodified KC-135 would 'trip off' under zero-g conditions, causing the airplane to lose all electrical power. To prevent this an 'all-attitude' constant speed drive (CSD) oil tank was added to each engine-driven electrical generator. Both 110V AC and 28V DC power systems were available in the cargo compartment which was completely padded and fitted with flood lights. The air refueling boom was removed and the airplane's hydraulic system pumps were modified to prevent cavitation during low-g maneuvers. Cockpit changes included the addition of vertical accelerometer readouts on the pilot's instrument panel, and the pilot's control yoke was replaced with a Convair F-102A Delta Dagger control stick for more precise pitch control during zero-g maneuvering.

The weightless maneuver is a fairly simple one. From an entry altitude of 25,000ft (7,620m), the airplane entered a shallow dive to allow its airspeed to build to approximately 350 KIAS. It then

Table 8-3. *Weightless Wonders*

MDS	Serial	From	To	Total Hours*	Total Parabolas
C-131B	53-7823	1957	Aug-61	970	7,001
C-131B	53-7806	Oct-61	Nov-65	850	6,980
C-131B	53-7791	Apr-66	Jul-67	225	817
J/NKC-135A	55-3129	Jan 60	Jun 68	2,012	12,347
KC-135A	62-3536	Jan 67	May 70	1,069	9,846
C-135A	60-0378	Jul 69	May 73	1,120	11,795
KC-135A	59-1481 (N930NA)	Aug 73	Dec 95	5,296	57,667
KC-135A	63-7998 (N931NA)	Sep 95 †	Oct 04	n/a	34,757
			Total '135	9,497	126,412
			Grand Total	11542	141,210

* At gravities other than 1g; † Acquired Nov 94 but not operational until Sep 95; n/a – Not available

Top: The first Air Force '135 *Weightless Wonder* was 55-3129. It established the tradition of depicting the weightless parabola as nose art. *Photo by Jack Morris via Stephen Miller*

Above: NASA did not want 59-1481 given its poor maintenance record. After extensive repairs, however, it flew 57,667 parabolas over its 22-year career. *Photo by Bob Burns via Stephen Miller*

Right: Pilot's instrument panel in Weightless Wonder 62-3565. Top two instruments are accelerometer and g-meter to show the exact 'non-normal' g conditions desired. *Photo via Jim Moseley*

Top: The nose of KC-135A 59-1481 (N930NA) depicts the different steps of the weightless arc.
Photo by Bob Burns

Below: Astronaut Edwin 'Buzz' Aldrin practices for his space walk in NKC-135A 55-3129 prior to his November 1966 Gemini 12 mission. 'Weightless Wonders' proved crucial to preparing astronauts for zero-g conditions.
NASA Photo

Bottom: Along with its zero-g duties, N930NA served as the SCA Pathfinder, the STDN testbed, and in other roles.
Photo by Bob Burns via Stephen Miller

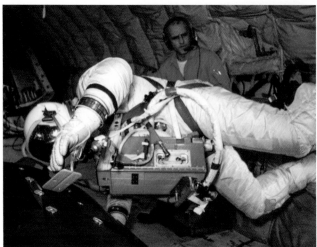

began a 2g-climb to a 45° angle, at which time the pilot pulled the throttles to idle and unloaded the airplane, topping out at approximately 37,000ft (11,277m), allowing for over 20-30 seconds of weightlessness across the top of the arc. Recovery was at 25,000ft (7,620m), and the airplane was ready for another parabola. This 'track' required an area nine miles long and two miles high (14.4 and 3.2km). A typical 2.5-hour mission included approximately 42 arcs, although one crew is reported to have flown 134 parabolas in a single sortie (see Tables 8-4 and 8-5).

While under weightless conditions, astronauts performed a variety of tasks ranging from donning space suits to emergency egress through spacecraft hatches. The lunar rover was tested aboard the weightlessness trainer, as were scooters and other extravehicular activity (EVA) equipment. Just as the airplane could simulate totally weightless conditions, the pilot could vary the trajectory of the parabolic arc to simulate other gravity conditions, duplicating the gravities of the moon, Mars, and spacecraft under a variety of flight

Table 8-4. **NASA Reduced Gravity Parabolas in 59-1481**

Pilot	FY73	FY74	FY75	FY76	FY77	FY78	FY79	FY80	FY81	FY82	FY83	FY84	FY85	FY86	FY87	FY88	FY89	FY90	FY91	FY92	FY93	FY94	FY95	Total
Algranti	0	0	0	0	0	835	1,057	1,385	815	730	710	750	623	456	953	746	654	509	87	0	0	0	0	10,310
Cobb	0	1,267	1,558	1,680	0	0	0	0	0	0	0	0	0	0	0	0	0	0	0	0	0	0	0	4,505
Fullerton	74	859	509	560	521	733	831	683	352	178	289	203	152	297	63	0	0	0	0	0	0	0	0	6,304
Haugen	0	0	0	0	0	0	0	0	0	0	0	102	394	248	539	644	636	0	0	0	0	0	0	2,563
Mumme	0	0	0	0	0	0	0	0	303	372	204	256	318	375	490	973	576	756	1,290	1,053	894	616	594	9,070
Roy	0	5	0	618	701	578	1,170	701	201	206	467	762	853	383	817	1,122	855	1,197	1,492	1,433	1,283	776	817	16,437
Beall	0	0	0	0	0	0	0	0	0	0	0	0	0	0	0	0	0	834	1,352	1,321	750	873	719	5,849
Feaster	0	0	0	0	0	0	0	0	0	0	0	0	0	0	0	0	0	0	0	742	566	731	543	2,582
Other	8	0	0	0	0	0	0	0	9	0	0	0	0	5	0	0	0	0	0	0	0	0	25	47
Year total	82	2,131	2,067	2,858	1,222	2,146	3,058	2,769	1,680	1,486	1,670	2,073	2,340	1,764	2,862	3,485	2,721	3,296	4,221	4,549	3,493	2,996	2,698	57,667

conditions. In addition to weightlessness training, N930NA supported low-g projects such as combustion in microgravity, flame-shape evolution, and the development of a zero-g shower, all projects that were crucial to the design of any future space station or long-duration missions. Perhaps one of the most unusual weightless missions undertaken by N930NA was the filming of the movie *Apollo 13*. An Apollo command module interior was installed in the 'Vomit Comet', and the relevant scenes were filmed in actual weightlessness. The film studio paid for the flights.

Budget cuts in 1977 and 1978 threatened continued zero-g operations. A lack of high-priority program commitments for the airplane prompted NASA's Associate Administrator for Operations to write 'I will take the necessary disposal action, as I cannot justify maintaining an institutional capability for unforeseeable programmatic requirements'. A meeting was held in October 1977 to determine the fate of the zero-g trainer, at which time sufficient justification and funding were ensured to continue NASA's use of N930NA.

Until the early 1980s N930NA was used almost exclusively for other-than-one-g indoctrination and training and for space flight hardware testing. By 1987 the airplane had been granted an indefinite safe operational life provided all routine inspections were complied with, and had accumulated some 16,000 flight hours and 30,000 weightless parabolas, far more than originally anticipated by NASA. The airplane's mission had also gradually changed, and by 1987 some 200 hours (out of the 300-plus yearly average) were dedicated to weightlessness training.

Since the beginning of Space Shuttle operations in 1981, N930NA flew 100-150 hours annually in Shuttle support programs. These included heavy aircraft training (HAT) to familiarize shuttle pilots with the peculiarities of heavy aircraft handling, similar to those of the Shuttle itself. The airplane also served as a 'pathfinder' for the Boeing 747 Shuttle Carrier Aircraft (SCA), supporting both its ground and flight operations. In this role, N930NA flew some 20-30 minutes ahead of the 747 SCA, carrying necessary ground crew and support equipment for use if and when the SCA should divert due to bad en route or destination weather (as it often does). Finally, N930NA flight checked the Shuttle Tracking Data Net (STDN). In one interesting 1987 proposal, should a hurricane threaten the JSC at Houston, the shuttle control team would board N930NA and fly to Holloman AFB, where they would travel by helicopter to White Sands Missile Range to resume connectivity with the shuttle.

Table 8-5. **Total NASA Reduced Gravity Parabolas**

Pilots				Test Directors	
Roy	16,437	Beall	5,849	Williams	55,623
Algranti	10,310	Feaster	2,582	Griggs	47,266
Mumme	9,070	Haugen	2,563	Billica	24,799
Fullerton	6,304	Other	47		

Despite the vote of confidence on an indefinite life extension for N930NA, NASA sought to replace N930NA with a 'younger' airframe. The retirement of a number of KC-135As to AMARC in the early 1990s made this an economical decision. By October 1995 N930NA was withdrawn from zero-g testing and replaced with the fifth and final KC-135 *Weightless Wonder*.

KC-135A 63-7998 entered service with NASA as N931NA during the summer of 1995 after undergoing the extensive modifications necessary for the zero-g mission. These included removal of the APU, the upper deck fuel tank, the air refueling boom and associated plumbing, and extensive electrical modifications. Unlike N930NA, the new airplane had a standard control yoke at both the pilot's and copilot's positions, rather than a fighter control stick. The airplane flew its first eight parabolas on 28th September 1995, and the next day logged 2.1 hours on its first reduced gravity mission, flying 50 parabolas. Additional tasks included alignment missions for the Microwave Scanning Beam Landing System (MSBLS) at the Kennedy Space Center, White Sands, NM, Edwards AFB, Zaragoza AB and Morón IAP, Spain.

The future of NASA's authority over the weightlessness program was soon in doubt. As a cost-cutting measure, one congressman proposed legislation that would privatize weightless operations, which is in fact what happened. KC-135A 63-7998 flew its final research mission – related to Shuttle tile repair – on 29th October 2004. It accrued 34,757 parabolas over its NASA career, and (according to NASA records) induced 285 gals (1,079 l) of vomit. On 10th December 2004 it made its final flight to the Pima Air Museum for display, accruing a final total of 13,605.0 hours (see Appendix III)

JKC-135A INDIVIDUAL AIRCRAFT

55-3129 This airplane was transferred on 28th January 1960 from the 93rd BW at Castle AFB to Wright-Patterson AFB where it was redesignated a JKC-135A. It became the first in the series of three AFSC *Weightless Wonders*. By 1965 it was redesignated as an NKC-135A. In 1968 KC-135A 62-3536 replaced 55-3129 as a zero-g trainer. Interestingly, 55-3129 retained a bulkhead autographed by the original seven *Mercury* astronauts (plus others who followed).

KC-135A INDIVIDUAL AIRCRAFT

59-1481 KC-135A 59-1481 was delivered in August 1973 as N930NA to Ellington AFB, TX, with a total of 12,453 flight hours. By October 1995 N930NA was withdrawn from zero-g testing, demodified, and placed on static display at JSC in Houston, TX (see Appendix III). It retired with a total of 5,296 hours of other-than-one-g flight time and 57,667 parabolas (see Tables 8-4 and 8-5).

62-3536 OCAMA converted this KC-135A into the second zero-g trainer and delivered it in March 1968 to AFSC at Wright-Patterson AFB. Following the completion in May 1970 of some 14,000 weightless parabolas, it was converted into an EC-135K.

63-7998 This KC-135A was withdrawn from AMARC on 30th June 1994, returned to flight status and departed AMARG on 4th November 1994 for modification as the replacement for NASA's N930NA KC-135A weightless trainer. It entered service as N931NA during the summer of 1995. On 10th December 2004 it made its final flight to the Pima Air Museum for display (see Appendix III).

C-135A INDIVIDUAL AIRCRAFT

60-0378 This C-135A was assigned to AFSC at Wright-Patterson AFB on 17th January 1968, performing unidentified test duties. It was converted by 24th July 1969, into a zero-g training platform named *Weightless Wonder III*. It ended its zero-g duties on 22nd May 1973.

COMMUNICATIONS, NAVIGATION AND AVIONICS

The evolution of technology during the Cold War, especially the exploitation of space, had a profound effect on communications and navigation. Satellites provided reliable improvements in worldwide radio transmissions, as well as innovations in global navigation. The birth of lasers in the 1960s created new ways to communicate and transmit data. The miniaturization of computers meant that increasingly sophisticated navigation systems could be installed on airplanes, improving their ability to reach targets while flying safely. Not surprisingly, testbed '135s were at the forefront of many of these research and development programs during the 1970s and 1980s. NC-135A 60-0371, for example, supported the Gimballed Electrostatic Aircraft [Navigation] System (GEANS) for AFAL from 1971 through 1973. This program, undertaken in conjunction with a McDonnell Douglas NRF-4C Phantom, examined compact inertial navigation systems (INS) and Doppler navigation systems (DNS), and evaluated their potential use in military cargo and fighter aircraft.

Navigation and Communications

One of the most significant early communication programs was the Joint Tactical Information Distribution System (JTIDS), a 'high-capacity, jam-resistant, secure digital information system that [would] permit the distribution of intelligence data among fighter aircraft, surveillance aircraft, ground air defense units, and naval vessels'. NKC-135A 55-3119 began JTIDS test missions in August 1975 that were applicable to the E-3 Airborne Warning And Control System (AWACS) program, and JTIDS quickly became a significant progenitor for all modern airpower data link capabilities. NKC-135A 55-3131 also participated in AWACS secure data compatibility tests from December 1979 until February 1981. In addition, 55-3131 was part of unidentified programs believed related to secure communications such as MERLA from June until September 1982, and START from October through December 1984. Other communications programs involving 55-3131 include testing of over-the-horizon backscatter (OTH-B) radar equipment and a project involving satellite phase scintillation measurements.

In one creative solution to secure communications, from December 1979 until April 1980, C-135N 60-0375 and NKC-135A 55-3124 participated in the METEOR BURST program. METEOR BURST was a precursor of current research involving the transmission of voice and data by bouncing radio signals off of meteor trails in the ionosphere. Already demonstrated as a reliable system by the US Department of Agriculture (DoA), METEOR BURST represented the ability to provide a quick-recovery post-nuclear attack-environment communication system. 'Since [atmospheric] ionization would increase in a nuclear war, and thus enhance MBC [meteor burst communications], MBC plays a prominent role in [potential] … post-attack communications'. Whereas normal HF communications could be disrupted for up to 24 hours following an atmospheric nuclear explosion, meteor burst communications could be recovered within 1.5 to 10 hours. The METEOR BURST signal was also highly resistant to jamming and interception.

Research projects in the late 1980s associated with improved voice and data transmission included C-135A 60-0372 and the Integrated Communication Navigation Identification Avionics (ICNIA) program. Flown in conjunction with Boeing C-18B 81-0898, this tri-service program was intended to reduce the size, weight, and cost of communications, navigation, and IFF systems in the 2MHz to 2,000 MHz range, especially in a jamming-intensive environment. Beginning in 1990 C-135E 60-0375 replaced NKC-135A 55-3122 (in conjunction with a EC-18B 81-0896), was part of the Airborne Imagery Transmission (ABIT) program, a 'modular, wideband,

multiple sensor, jam-resistant, air-to-air data link for transmission of reconnaissance imagery or digital data'. Flight testing took place between 1992 and 1993 with one aircraft over Wright-Patterson AFB and the other over the Gulf of Mexico. ABIT II was the successor program, installing the equipment in a U-2. Following its transfer from testbed duties to CSA operations for SAC, C-135A 60-0378 may have been the testbed in the late 1980s for the Mystic Star Console Evaluation, a secure high frequency communications system to and from the presidential aircraft.

NKC-135A INDIVIDUAL AIRCRAFT

55-3119 The airplane was assigned to the 4950th TW at Wright-Patterson AFB on 29th August 1975 as part of HAVE CAR, where it participated in JTIDS and E-3 AWACS development.

55-3122 The initial test aircraft for the DARPA ABIT project from 1984 through 1992, when it was replaced by C-135A 60-0375.

55-3124 In conjunction with C-135N 60-0372, this NKC-135A was part of the METEOR BURST program while assigned to the 4950th TW at Wright-Patterson AFB from 1979 through 1980.

55-3131 This 4950th TW NKC-135A took part in a variety of communications tests between 1979 and 1984 while at Wright-Patterson AFB. It was declared surplus and retired to AMARC on 19th October 1992 and given the PCN AACA0053 (see Appendix III).

NC-135A INDIVIDUAL AIRCRAFT

60-0371 Along with its nuclear detection mission while assigned to Kirtland AFB, this NC-135A evaluated the GEANS system from 1971 through 1973. In 1973, NC-135A 60-0371 flew test missions for the Integrated NAV/SAT Inertial (INI) Navigation System consisting 'of a time-shared navigation satellite receiver integrated with an inertial platform'.

C-135A/E INDIVIDUAL AIRCRAFT

60-0372 During the late 1980s, this 4950th TW C-135A worked in conjunction with C-18B 81-0898 at Wright-Patterson AFB on the ICNIA program.

60-0375 In conjunction with NKC-135A 55-3124, this C-135N was part of the METEOR BURST program while assigned to the 4950th TW at Wright-Patterson AFB from 1979 through 1980. It was subsequently used in the ABIT program beginning in 1992.

60-0378 While assigned to SAC as a CSA with the 55th SRW at Offutt AFB, this C-135A may have been the testbed in the late 1980s for the Mystic Star Console Evaluation.

SATCOM

With the 1957 launch of *Sputnik*, US military planners quickly recognized the value of a satellite to provide global communications. Although HF radios were in use to provide this global reach, they were unreliable in the polar region, and SAC especially required a more reliable system to send and receive EAMs to SAC bombers orbiting over Alaska, Canada, and Greenland. In early 1958 Air Force Vice Chief of Staff General LeMay expressed interest in a satellite communications (SATCOM) program, but was concerned that a single orbiting satellite would not provide the necessary 24-hour coverage of the extreme northern hemisphere. The solution was Project STEER, a constellation of six satellites in polar orbit. STEER would provide initial coverage until Project DECREE, a geosynchronous satellite, could be implemented. Additional satellites would follow as technology improved. Each satellite would use vacuum tubes and an AN/ARC-34 UHF radio operating in full duplex mode. WADC moved forward with the project, but in 1960 DoD elected to transfer the satellite communications program to the civilian sector.

Additional SATCOM research by the Air Force Avionics Laboratory (AFAL) began in 1965 with the Tactical Satellite Communications Project 591. A LOOP VEE antenna was installed on C-135A 60-0376 on the dorsal fuselage above the star-and-bar insignia, and connected to the Lincoln Laboratory LES-5 satellite. Despite its role in Project 591, 60-0376 had little else to do with the Air Force Satellite Communication (AFSATCOM) or other satellite evaluation programs. Beginning in the late 1960s, NKC-135A 55-3129, C-135B 61-2662, and C-135A 60-0372 were the primary research and development aircraft. C-135B 61-2663 served in a support role.

During 1968 testing began with the Hughes TacSat-1 and Lincoln Laboratory LES-6 satellites. A variety of terminals, including the AN/ARC-146, AN/ARC-151, and AN/ARC-152 proved successful. In one test, for example, NKC-135A 55-3129 and C-135B 61-2662 were able to establish and maintain a reliable satellite link while the two airplanes were some 5,000nm (9,260km) apart. The following year, 61-2662 tested the viability of installing a UHF satellite radio on helicopters, serving as the relay aircraft along with a Bell UH-1B. It also started the Airborne Strategic SATCOM System Project 698-AQ, using a super high frequency (SHF) terminal during some 300 hours of flight tests of the AN/ASC-18.

In 1972 C-135A 60-0372 began an evaluation that lasted through 2000 called Ionospheric Scintillation Fade Mitigation, which reduced the adverse impact of charged particles in the ionosphere on SATCOM transmissions. This was similar to a project undertaken by C-135B 61-2662 from 1975 through 1977 known as Fade-Resistant Modem. Flights took place along the equator near Lima, Peru, and proved highly successful in maintaining SATCOM signal strength. Nearly 1,000 operational units were placed in SAC aircraft.

During 1977, 55-3129 was reassigned to NASA for use in the winglet program, and 61-2662 assumed the primary SATCOM duties, beginning with the Lincoln Laboratory LES-8/9 satellites using an AN/ASC-22 extra-high frequency (EHF) airborne terminal, a system destined for the E-4B. This was coupled to 61-2662's inertial navigation system for precise alignment, and the AN/ASC-22's narrow bandwidth and frequency-hopping capability made it extremely jam- and interception-resistant.

The subsequent ASC-30 SATCOM testbed incorporated modular antennae, modems, and other related equipment allowing easy and rapid installation and replacement of developmental systems following tests and modification. Flight tests were often in conjunction with SAC tankers, bombers, and airborne command posts, as well as with ground relay stations around the world, with 61-2662 transmitting and receiving messages via orbiting satellites. These tests studied polar and equatorial effects on satellite communications, and involved deployments to the North Pole, around the equator, Ascension Island, Peru, Greenland, Hawai'i, and Australia. Among the other programs evaluated alongside SATCOM were the E-3 Sentry AWACS, and the E-4B AABNCP

Following the crash of the RIVET BALL RC-135S on 13th January 1969, C-135B 61-2663 was transferred to SAC for modification into a replacement RC-135S, leaving 61-2662 as the sole AFSATCOM testbed. The 15th March 1981 crash of COBRA BALL II RC-135S 61-2664 necessitated a speedy replacement with a similar airframe to maintain operational and maintenance commonality among the COBRA BALL fleet. C-135B 61-2662 was an ideal choice, but it was still serving as the primary AFSATCOM testbed. Despite considerable protests by AFSC, in 1982 BIG SAFARI transferred the SATCOM antenna fairing and gear from 61-2662 to C-135A 60-0372. The total project took only 90 days and $200,000, well under the pessimistic two years and $2 million forecast by AFSC.

Throughout the 1980s and 1990s 60-0372 was active in a variety of SATCOM programs, some of which were research oriented while others assessed the practical applicability of specific equipment. During September 1982 it participated in the Colored Bubbles Ionospheric Modification Project. This evaluated the effect of the earth's atmosphere on SATCOM transmissions. The airplane flew two missions off the coast of Natal, Brazil, on 17th and 18th September 1982. Each mission involved the sunset launch of a sounding rocket to a height of 173nm (320km), where it would inject two 88lb (40kg) packages of barium into the atmosphere. The airplane would then measure the impact of the resulting instability

Prior to its conversion into an RC-135S, C-135B 61-2662 was the second SATCOM testbed, replacing 55-3129 when it was transferred to the NASA winglets program. *Photo by Richard Vandervord*

C-135E 60-0372 was the final '135 SATCOM testbed, and evaluated a variety of antenna shapes and systems. *Photo by Robert Greby via Stephen Miller*

on a SATCOM connection with a US Navy satellite (the 'colored bubbles' appeared in one optical sensor).

The Military Strategic and Tactical Relay (MILSTAR) satellite is a 'reliable, jam-resistant, survivable extra high frequency (EHF) satellite communications' system designed for the transmission of EAMs from SAC (and later STRATCOM) commanders to aircraft under its operational control worldwide, the relay of warnings of SLBM launches, the relay of messages between the elements of Air Force's Satellite Control Facilities, and the relay of reconnaissance satellite imagery. Research and development began in 1985. C-135A was the back-up aircraft for these tests, and NKC-135A 55-3122 served as the initial testbed for the MILSTAR radome modification. These flights took place between November 1989 and March 1990. The radome showed few aerodynamic problems, and it was later transferred to C-135E 60-0372.

Perhaps the final use of 60-0372 in the SATCOM realm was the 1999-2001 Global Broadcast Satellite (GBS) Airborne Antenna program. This low-profile antenna was tested during flights from Edwards AFB to Bermuda and back.

NKC-135A INDIVIDUAL AIRCRAFT

55-3122 This NKC-135A served as the testbed for the MILSTAR antenna from November 1989 through March 1990 while assigned to the 4950th TW at Wright-Patterson AFB.

55-3129 From 1969 through 1977 this airplane was involved in testing as an airborne avionics lab, accumulating over 1,000 hours of flight testing. Originally 55-3129 lacked the large dorsal radome that would become the trademark of the SATCOM program. This radome was later installed for testing of the RCA AN/ASC-14 super-high frequency (SHF) X-band satellite terminal, which used a 33in (83.8cm) diameter antenna located underneath the radome. In 1977 it was transferred to NASA for use in the winglet research program.

NC-135A INDIVIDUAL AIRCRAFT

60-0371 In addition to supporting the ALL, beginning in 1973 this NC-135A also evaluated early satellite communications systems.

C-135A/B/E INDIVIDUAL AIRCRAFT

60-0372 Following its conversion into the SATCOM platform by April 1982, Boeing installed TF33-PW-102 engines on 60-0372, and it was redesignated a C-135E. It was also involved in other communications test programs such as HAVE LACE and ICNIA.

60-0376 Used for Project 591 from 1965 through 1968.

61-2662 This C-135B was delivered to the 4950th TW on 11th December 1967 for use in the AFSATCOM program. It assumed primary SATCOM duties in 1977 through its conversion into an RC-135S in 1982.

61-2663 Intended as a companion for AFSATCOM test-bed 61-2662, MAC delivered 61-2663 to the 4950th TW on 22nd December 1967. The airplane was never fully converted into an AFSATCOM platform, as on 29th April 1969 it was delivered to BIG SAFARI for conversion into the first COBRA BALL RC-135S.

Laser Communications

Prior to the development of laser communication technology, the Air Force sought to use infrared communications in a variety of programs. One such program, known as the Airborne Infrared Communications System, took place between 1960 and 1963. It was intended to provide secure, stealthy communications between the A-12 and SR-71 and their tanker. The Air Force Avionics Laboratory (AFAL) and Raytheon built a 'powerful broad-beam IR beacon to provide initial location detection and a separate narrow-band two-way IR communication system,' funded by the SENIOR CROWN program. Flight tests took place on C-131B 53-7823, with poor results, which halted the program before it would repeat the tests using a KC-135 and an A-12. Instead, the Air Force selected the AN/ARC-50 wideband UHF radio and the IR program was canceled.

From October 1979 through December 1980, C-135A 60-0377 participated in Airborne Laser Communications (LASERCOM) tests. Airframe modifications included the installation of a 30in (76.2cm) optically ground window in the cargo door. Using a neodymium-yttrium-aluminum garnet (Nd:YAG) laser, this program evaluated the secure transmission of large quantities of information in extremely short 'bursts'. Ground tests in September 1978 at the White Sands Missile Range validated the concept. Airborne performance was considered the most critical phase of the test as airframe vibration and effects of turbulence would jostle the laser beam, which had an extremely small 'signature' and was sensitive to misdirection. Flight tests involved orbits at altitudes of 33-37,000ft (10,058-11,277m) over ground test stations. Transmission rates of up to 20,000 bits per second were conducted with a loss rate of one bit per million. The program's success paved the way for future laser communications development, including the HAVE LACE program.

A crucial weakness of laser communication was the signal degradation by clouds. From 1984 through 1987, NKC-135A 55-3131 and a Flight Systems Saberliner took part in the Scattered-Light Test Airborne Receiver (STAR) program. The Saberliner flew at 25,000ft (7,620m), and sent a laser signal to 55-3131 which flew at 2,000ft (610m). Results of the tests were sufficiently encouraging to continue exploring laser communications.

In addition to its SATCOM duties, 60-0372 was the primary aerial platform (supported by NC-135A 60-0371) in the HAVE LACE (Laser Airborne Communications Equipment) program. HAVE LACE was designed as an 'air-to-air communications system that could provide secure, anti-jam, low probability of intercept communications for

The SATCOM aircraft did not always carry the large dorsal antenna, as they evaluated other shapes that induced less drag or were less conspicuous.
Photo by Stephen Miller

applications such as ELINT operations off Russia's Kamchatka Peninsula for passing large amounts of data as the aircraft leaving the orbit passed the aircraft taking up the patrol.' A 1986 contract provided $1.5 million for McDonnell Douglas Astronautics to begin a 42-month test program in 1989. The 4950th TW modified 60-0371 and 60-0372 for HAVE LACE by installing 'a large optical window in the cargo door, an optical radome atop the fuselage, and a microprocessor for the collection of data and analysis in flight'. The laser communications system includes a 'transmitter, a receiver, acquisition and tracking components and a video camera [designed to] track the laser beam and serve as the electronic eyes for project engineers and scientists'. C-135E 60-0372 had the window on the left side of the aircraft, and 60-0371 had the window in the right side of the aircraft. The two airplanes conducted some 40 hours of aerial tests, flying parallel tracks 100nm (185km) apart.

NKC-135A INDIVIDUAL AIRCRAFT

55-3131 From 1984 through 1987 this airplane took part in the STAR program.

N/C-135A/E INDIVIDUAL AIRCRAFT

60-0371 This NC-135A served as the 'diagnostic' support aircraft for the HAVE LACE program from 1985-86.
60-0372 Concurrent with its participation in SATCOM research and development, this C-135E was the primary testbed for the HAVE LACE program in the early 1990s, as well as ICNIA. On 16th May 2002, it caused quite a stir over Sydney, Australia, as it orbited above the famed Opera House and Sydney Harbour, escorted by a second airplane taking photographs. Local residents, fearful of a repeat of the infamous attacks on the World Trade Center in New York City only nine months earlier, called police to report a 'hijacked' airplane behaving in a threatening manner. Where once opportunities such as this were cause for considerable national pride or public enthusiasm, the events of 9/11 sadly changed the tolerance level of people and governments to the presence of aircraft around cities and major landmarks. The airplane was retired to AMARG on 28th September 2005 as AACA0145 and scrapped by 13th March 2013 (see Appendix III).
60-0377 This C-135A was the primary platform for the LASERCOM program in 1979-1980.

Approach and Landing

Efforts to reduce pilot workload during the critical phases of approach and landing – for both KC-135 pilots and those of other airplanes – have been under way since the mid 1960s. One of the earliest was a project sponsored by the Flight Dynamics Laboratory (FDL) at Wright-Patterson AFB entitled 'Pilot Control Factors' (PIFAX), of which little is known. This involved JKC-135A 55-3121 from 1st July through 31st December 1964. Beginning in late 1969, NKC-135A 55-3119 served as the testbed for the FD-109 flight director system (see Chapter 4). Program modifications were undertaken at Wright-Patterson AFB and testing completed at the RADC.

Laser-based communications were the subjects of both the LASERCOM and the HAVE LACE programs. 60-0377 only took part in LASERCOM, acquiring the black anti-glare paint aft of a transmitter. *Photo by Stephen Miller*

Arguably the most famous of all avionics testbeds was the SPECKLED TROUT. Beginning in 1966, KC-135A 55-3126, best known as General Curtis LeMay's record-setting transport during his years as Air Force Vice Chief and Chief of Staff from 1957 through 1965, was assigned to FDL at Wright-Patterson AFB (it remained based at Andrews AFB to fulfill its concurrent VIP transport role). It served as the testbed for advanced technology automatic landing systems and terminal area navigation projects, and evaluated other high-technology equipment in a variety of operational environments. While assigned to FDL, it earned the nickname SPECKLED TROUT in honor of Faye Trout, the civilian program monitor at the laboratory 'who had a lot of freckles'. One unique advantage derived from the SPECKLED TROUT was the ability of avionics developers and manufacturers to test new equipment in an operational venue, much as they did onboard scheduled airliners following the Second World War. The individual manufacturers provided most of the test equipment without charge, and much of the technology evaluated ending up in newer generation aircraft. At the time – the 1970s and 1980s – few of these projects were adopted for the KC-135 fleet. By the 1990s, however, the need to extend the fleet's longevity as well as make it more compatible with the evolving sophistication of international navigation and communications gear meant that many of the SPECKLED TROUT innovations found their way into PACER CRAG and subsequent KC-135 cockpit updates.

One program evaluated on 55-3126 was a fully automated landing system in which the pilot could land the airplane without removing his hands from the control column, even to adjust the throttles. A yoke-mounted button controlled the actual throttle setting. During a missed approach, following actuation of the desired yoke-mounted button, the throttles would automatically move to full power for go-around and the airplane would climb to and level off at the preselected altitude. In addition to allowing the pilot more precise control of the airplane, it allowed him to use both hands to fly the aircraft in difficult conditions such as extreme crosswind landings. The automatic landing system enhanced the airplane's ability to land in strong crosswinds without touching down in a crab. The Boeing design direct crosswind (90°) limit for the KC-135 is 40 knots (74km/h), but SAC placed a 25kt (46.3km) limit on crosswind operations. The automatic system was safely demonstrated with 37kt

(68.5km/h) direct crosswinds. In a 30kt (55.5km/h) direct crosswind, the system was able to land the airplane routinely within 9ft (2.74m) of the runway centerline. The system also provided a limited ability to react to wind shear.

This new rotate and go-around system was also used for fully automated 'hands off' takeoffs. The pilot preselected the desired rotation speed and, upon reaching this speed, the autopilot would automatically introduce the required pitch and climbout profile. Considering the critical nature of this phase of flight, this system

Above: C-135C 61-2669 was the second SPECKLED TROUT. It divided its missions between testbed duties and VIP transport. *Photo by Stephen Miller*

Below: Nose view of SPECKLED TROUT 63-7980 reveals both the IFR capability of the airplane as well as the LAIRCM 'chin' fairing. It was visiting Franz Liszt IAP in Budapest on 20th May 2011, and its VIP transport days ended in 2015. *Photo by Ferenc Hamori*

could prevent premature and/or excessive rotation, a situation from which the airplane might not be able to climb or accelerate (resulting in two KC-135 losses), but was ultimately mitigated by the FD-109 flight director. Other projects tested on the SPECKLED TROUT included autothrottles, an advanced autopilot, experimental inertial and Doppler navigational systems, 'glass' cockpit displays, and new radars. In a similar initiative, C-135A 60-0378 participated in the Traffic Control and Landing System (TRACALS) evaluation between 1973 and July 1975.

On 8th February 1975, C-135C 61-2669 replaced KC-135A 55-3126 as the SPECKLED TROUT, and it was joined by a smaller version known as the SPECKLED MINNOW, beginning with T-39A Sabreliner 62-4478 (from February 1974 until 24th October 1984), then a Gates C-21A Learjet 84-0098 (beginning December 1984 through August 1991, and eventually a Grumman C-20E 87-0139 (2008-2009). As with the SPECKLED TROUT these had several test items and systems on board.

The new SPECKLED TROUT's primary development and testing role remained advanced cockpit avionics. In conjunction with BMAC and avionics manufacturers such as Honeywell, Litton, and Collins, the airplane was part of the 'Transport Advanced Avionics and Cockpit Enhancement' (TRAACE) program designed to integrate updated flight-deck avionics and digital flight management systems to facilitate testing new subsystems such as a KC-135 'glass cockpit'. During 1988 these modifications – totaling some $42 million – incorporated a Boeing 757/767 glass cockpit and a fully integrated flight management system, all future components of the PACER CRAG KC-135 cockpit upgrade program.

From 23rd November through 2nd December 1989, 61-2669 completed a series of around-the-world flights 'as satellites continuously tracked it and maintained digital communications with engineers on the ground'. The airplane's position and velocity were taken from the airplane's inertial navigation system (INS) and

Table 8-6. **The SPECKLED Fleet**

SPECKLED TROUT

MDS	Serial	From	To
KC-135A	55-3126	1966	7 Feb 75
C-135C	61-2669	8 Feb 75	13 Jan 06
KC-135E	57-2589	April 03	22 Jul 07
KC-135R	63-7980	23 Jul 07	current

SPECKLED MINNOW

MDS	Serial	From	To
T-39A	62-4478	1974	24 Oct 84
C-21A	84-0098	Dec-84	Aug-91
C-20E	87-0139	2008	2009

transmitted every 15 seconds via the Geostar and Inmarsat satellites. This marked the first time that an aircraft used a satellite to report its position and velocity automatically to ground stations. Although previous experiments demonstrated the feasibility of satellite communications with aircraft, none had relied exclusively on a digital system. In addition to the obvious military applications, this satellite reporting system could 'offer significant enhancements in airspace capacity and reductions in operating costs, particularly for intercontinental [civil] air transport'. Implementing this type of satellite tracking capability could provide commanders with a near-instant global update on the location of each B-52 on a mission, for example, or airline officials with a similar status check on each of its hundreds of daily passenger flights around the world. This knowledge cost money, however, money that military commanders preferred to spend elsewhere or airline executives preferred to include as profits or pass on to investors as dividends. Interestingly, this capability existed some 25 years before the loss of Malaysian Airlines flight MH370, a Boeing 777-200ER which disappeared without a trace on 8th March 2014.

C-135C 61-2669 (call sign *Trout 99*) was replaced as the SPECKLED TROUT by another well-known airplane, the former CINCSAC aircraft KC-135E 57-2589 (call sign *Casey 01*), although the dates for this transfer are somewhat ambiguous. The KC-135E entered PDM and began modification to assume SPECKLED TROUT duties in April 2003, and C-135C 61-2669 was officially retired on 13th January 2006. It is not clear exactly when 57-2589 assumed the SPECKLED TROUT mantle or if 61-2669 was stored for an indefinite period before its retirement. KC-135R 63-7980 replaced 57-2589 on 22nd July 2007 as SPECKLED TROUT. On 15th May 2015 the VIP transport role for the SPECKLED TROUT came to an end, but the airplane remains in use as an advanced avionics testbed.

N/JKC-135A INDIVIDUAL AIRCRAFT

55-3119 Beginning on 9th December 1969, this NKC-135A was the testbed for the FD-109 flight director.

55-3121 From 1st July through 31st December 1964, this JKC-135A participated in the PIFAX Program.

KC-135A/E/R INDIVIDUAL AIRCRAFT

55-3126 From 1966 through 8th February 1975, this KC-135A served as the SPECKLED TROUT primary advanced avionics testbed while located at Andrews AFB. On 31st July 1975, KC-135A 55-3126 flew for the last time, landing at MASDC (AMARG) with a total of 9,057.0 flying hours. It was assigned the control number CA004, stripped of parts for use in its replacement (C-135C 61-2669), and officially written off on 5th January 1978 (see Appendix III).

57-2589 Previously used by the CINCSAC, this KC-135E replaced C-135C 61-2669 as the SPECKLED TROUT by 13th January 2006. It was subsequently replaced by KC-135R 63-7980 on 22nd July 2007, and by 29th July 2008 had become a ground trainer at Lackland AFB, TX (see Appendix III).

63-7980 This KC-135R replaced KC-135E 57-2589 as the SPECKLED TROUT on 22nd July 2007. Assigned to the 412th TS at Edwards AFB, it served both as a testbed and a VIP transport. The 412th TS was inactivated on 15th May 2015, and the airplane was reassigned to the 418th TS (also at Edwards AFB), but its SPECKLED TROUT VIP transport role was eliminated.

C-135A INDIVIDUAL AIRCRAFT

60-0378 Following its role as the third USAF weightless trainer, this C-135A began TRACALS tests in 1973 while assigned to the 4950th TW. After July 1975 it was handed over to the 89th MAW at Andrews AFB as a VIP transport.

C-135C INDIVIDUAL AIRCRAFT

61-2669 This C-135C was delivered to Det 1, 1st ACCS at Andrews AFB, on 8th February 1975, replacing KC-135A 55-3126 as the SPECKLED TROUT. The new SPECKLED TROUT retained the IFR system from its WC-135B days, and had TF33-P-5 turbofans. When the 1st ACCS moved to Offutt AFB on 1st November 1975, the new SPECKLED TROUT stayed at Andrews AFB, assigned to Det 1, 4950th TW. During March 1985 it was assigned directly to AFSC as a detachment at Andrews AFB. As more sophisticated and fuel efficient VIP transports such as Gulfstream C-20s entered service during the early 1990s, the SPECKLED TROUT lost a sizeable portion of its transport role. Consequently, it was reassigned to the 445th TESTS, 412th TW at Edwards AFB on 1st October 1992. That squadron was inactivated on 30th September 1993, and the airplane assigned to the 452nd TESTS (and later the 412th FLTS), 412th TW, still at Edwards AFB. C-135C 61-2669 was finally retired on 13th January 2006 – replaced by former CINCSAC aircraft KC-135E 57-2589 – and placed on display in the Air Force Flight Test Center Museum at Edwards AFB (see Appendix III).

Right: From one famous mission to another, KC-135E 57-2589 went from *Casey 01*, CINCSAC's transport, to *Trout 99*, the third SPECKLED TROUT.
Photo by Brian Rogers

Below: As part of its test duties, SPECKLED TROUT KC-135R 63-7980 departs Boeing Field, perhaps to participate in refueling tests of the KC-46.
Photo by Josh Kaiser

FAA Flight Check

The increasing numbers of jet airliners operating at high speed and high altitude during the early 1960s prompted the need to verify that high altitude jet routes and navigational aids met with requisite standards to ensure safe separation of aircraft and reliable equipment. To meet these requirements, the US Federal Aviation Administration (FAA) acquired two KC-135As (59-1481 and 59-1518) in 1960. OCAMA converted these into flight check aircraft as part of the PACER CLERK program, and delivered them to the FAA at Oklahoma City AP.

KC-135A INDIVIDUAL AIRCRAFT

59-1481 Following initial service at Oklahoma City, it was relocated to Hickam AFB in 1966 to certify Pacific Ocean routes and navigational aids. While with the FAA, 59-1481 was registered N98. It had a Long RAnge Navigation (LORAN) 'towel rack' antennae on the lower fuselage ahead of the main gear wells.

The airplane earned a 'nasty' reputation for maintenance discrepancies, but the FAA was loath to remove it from operation for PDM or other lengthy inspections. Finally, an Air Force inspector grounded the airplane for safety violations. It reportedly sat at Hickam AFB for a year or more before being granted a 'one-time only' flight to Tinker AFB for a complete and thorough overhaul. No date is known for termination of this airplane's duties with the FAA. SAC records list the airplane as 'NOA' – a non-operational aircraft from June 1972 through 1973. These same records show that 59-1481 was stored at MASDC, but no MASDC records support this. Most likely the SAC records incorrectly assumed that because the airplane was in storage it must have been at MASDC, not at Tinker AFB. In August 1973 it was transferred to NASA as N930NA for weightless training.

59-1518 This KC-135A was initially delivered to the FAA at Oklahoma City on 20th October 1960 under the PACER CLERK program. It was registered N96 and during a portion of its tenure with the FAA bore the nickname *Ol' Smoky*, ostensibly due to the smoke produced by its water-injection engines. The airplane had at least three electronics consoles for route data collection and verification, and conducted flight operations much like its sister ship 59-1481. The airplane was returned to the Air Force in 1975 and stored at Tinker AFB until 1979. In March 1979 the Air Force directed that the airplane be converted into an EC-135K to replace EC-135K 62-3536 lost during 1977. On 10th March 2003 it was retired to AMARG as AACA0131 and displayed on 'Celebrity Row'.

Less than two years after its delivery, N96 (59-1518) looks ratty. The FAA KC-135s earned a justified reputation for poor maintenance. *Photo by Jim Morrow via Stephen Miller*

FAA flight check KC-135A 59-1481 had pride of place at the Paris Air Salon, but soon acquired a terrible maintenance record. Still, NASA converted it into a 'Vomit Comet'. *Author's collection*

A fresh coat of paint and a new tail give N96 a more professional appearance. White cross on nose is target for ground cameras tracking aircraft on instrument approaches. *Photo by Jack Morris via Stephen Miller*

WEAPONS DEVELOPMENT

Long before a new weapon is dropped or a new combat airplane flies its first mission, it has undergone months, if not years, of testing. For nearly all of the weapons and airplanes built during the Cold War, that evaluation began in a KC-135 variant based at Wright-Patterson AFB, Kirtland AFB, or Edwards AFB. Testbed '135s were intimately involved in the development of specific weapons such as airborne lasers and cruise missiles, as well as work on the subsystems of advanced bombers or the infrared signatures of stealth aircraft. Only JKC-135A 55-3128 ever carried any 'weapons' for an unidentified project. The airplane had a pod carrying unguided rockets mounted beneath each wingtip. The rockets were fired during flight, exploded, and their effects recorded as baseline references for on-board systems calibration and studies, perhaps related to atmospheric research.

The Airborne Lasers

Initial concept demonstration of airborne laser weapon capability came in 1973 when a gas-dynamic laser destroyed a drone over the Sandia Optical Range at Kirtland AFB. That same year, the Air Force and the Defense Advanced Research Projects Agency's (DARPA) 'Agency O' awarded a $2.4 million contract to United Aircraft Corporation's Pratt & Whitney Aircraft Division's Florida Research and Development Center for the design and development of an airborne gas-dynamic laser. Funds were also awarded to General Dynamics to convert NKC-135A 55-3123 into the Airborne Laser Lab (ALL), a modification completed in 1977. DARPA's high-energy laser (HEL) program was intended to provide 'a new weapon that could revolutionize tactical and strategic attack, as well as defense against airborne targets, both in the atmosphere and in space'. The laser's intense beam would damage the target's guidance system or ignite its fuel or warhead and cause its destruction. Secretary of the Air Force John C Stetson described the ALL as just a 'proof of concept' testbed rather than a focal point in the development of any specific airborne laser weapon. Non-military research conducted by the ALL included laser propagation and air-to-air laser effects experiments.

Among the many modifications General Dynamics made to 55-3123 was the addition of a large dorsal 'turret' and posterior fairing (in several different configurations) above the cargo door. These covered the laser itself and the pointing and tracking telescope. To accommodate the increased electrical demands of the laser and its associated equipment, generators from a B-52 were installed on each of 55-3123's engines, resulting in a noticeable 'bulge' on each engine pod. The fuselage interior was divided into three sections. The forward section contained the cockpit and flight crew area. The center

section, isolated by securable bulkheads and inaccessible during flight, contained the laser and appropriate support equipment such as toxic asphyxiants and highly explosive cryogenically stored laser fuel. The aft section housed the technicians and operators, mission instrumentation and recording equipment, and the laser's controls. Mission support for the ALL was provided by NC-135A 60-0371, which served as an airborne data recording and transmission platform and as a diagnostic aircraft.

Key to the success of the airborne laser weapons program was the development of a system capable of identifying and tracking any target given extremely critical and demanding tolerances. The designator had to focus the laser's thin beam of high energy on a rapidly moving target hundreds of miles away in an environment littered by weather, debris, and deceptive atmospheric garbage. This task was particularly complicated because both the laser and its target were moving, and the laser was subject to turbulence that destabilized its references, diffused the intensity of the laser beam at the target, and degraded its accuracy.

The ALL program achieved 100% mission readiness and met with some success in a variety of technical and operational tests. The laser was first fired while airborne on 2nd May 1981, engaging a towed target. On 28th May 1981 the laser attempted to engage an AIM-9 Sidewinder air-to-air missile above the China Lake test range; results of this test have not been divulged. Although critics claimed that in initial tests the airborne laser failed to destroy ('blow up') its targets with the laser beam, it eventually did disable the guidance system of an AIM-9 launched from a Naval Weapons Center LTV A-7E Corsair II. As the 'learning curve' improved, so too did the laser's capability. On 26th July 1983 the ALL successfully 'engaged and defeated five AIM-9 Sidewinders aimed at the ALL', and on 26th September 1983 the laser actually destroyed a low-altitude subsonic BQM-34A drone simulating an anti-ship cruise missile attack profile off the California coast. The 'laser burned through the drone's skin and in the process destroyed critical components, causing a flight-control failure'. Flight testing was completed on 14th May 1984, and 55-3123 was placed in flyable storage at Kirtland AFB.

Although the NKC-135A ALL achieved its intended goal of demonstrating the feasibility of an airborne laser weapon platform, it also highlighted the considerable requirements needed to bring an operational system to fruition. Most notable among these limits for future development was the constant 'growth' of the laser and its associated equipment. By the time the ALL was placed in storage, it could no longer contain the laser and its systems. Studies were begun in the mid- to late-1980s to evaluate replacing the ALL with a wide-bodied aircraft capable of handling existing and projected

JKC-135A 55-3128 may well have been the only '135 to carry conventional armaments, as seen in the wingtip-mounted rocket pods. The purpose of these has not been determined. *Photo PM-6834 Seattle Museum of Flight (1997)*

configurations. A Boeing 767 was briefly considered for further airborne laser testing but the idea was dropped due to budget limitations.

The use of Iraqi *Scud* surface-to-surface tactical ballistic missiles during the 1991 Gulf War rekindled interest in high technology assets to locate and destroy ballistic missiles. Although the ALL proof-of-concept tests undertaken by NKC-135A 55-3123 were generally successful, development and production of an actual operational weapon during the mid-1980s were not considered feasible. Additional technology derived from the Strategic Defense Initiative (SDI), however, yielded a viable detection mechanism and made an airborne laser a more practical and attainable weapon system. Officials argued that it was at last possible to build an airborne laser that could defeat *Scuds* and other ballistic weapons. By 1996 funding was in place for what would eventually result in the AirBorne Laser (ABL) Boeing YAL-1A, a 747-400F (serial 00-0001), equipped with a Chemical Oxygen Iodine Laser (COIL) as the primary weapon. Initial projections called for a fleet of seven aircraft. Operationally, a pair of ABL aircraft would orbit continuously some 56nm (90km) from the nearest threat at altitudes between 40-50,000ft (12,192-

15,240m). Using passive infrared sensors, the laser platforms would detect, identify, target, and destroy missiles within 30 seconds (one can easily imagine the life expectancy of these two airplanes in the minutes prior to a massive launch of hostile ballistic missiles).

The 1993 consolidation of airborne research assets included the retirement of NC-135A 60-0371, which had long been used as the primary diagnostic aircraft for the ALL. Instead, former EC-135C 63-8050 joined NKC-135E 55-3132 as BIG CROW I and II. Among their missions was support of the YAL-1A ABL program, replicating many of the duties of 60-0371. Sometime after 2003, both BIG CROWS received a unique paint scheme for the ABL program. The forward fuselage and wings were painted black, and a white 'missile' painted on the port side of the fuselage. An array of lights (or perhaps heat-generating sources) was placed at the back of the 'missile,' simulating an exhaust plume. The YAL-1A successfully test fired its laser and 'hit' BIG CROW I (55-3132) on 15th March 2007.

By 2010 the Missile Defense Agency (MDA) budget no longer included funding for the ABL as a prototype weapon, and instead provided only minimal funds for the renamed Airborne Laser Test Bed (ALTB) for research purposes. After 16 years and some $5

The ALL appeared in several configurations, but this image best shows the laser turret. The fairing aft of the turret was aerodynamic rather than part of the laser itself. *Photo by Mick Roth via Stephen Miller*

NC-135A 60-0371 served as the diagnostic aircraft in support of the ALL. It also participated in basic science research. *Photo by Mick Roth via Stephen Miller*

Both BIG CROWS were painted with missile warheads and equipped with a heat/light source at the 'exhaust'. The YAL-1A airborne laser actually 'hit' the missile on 55-3132. *Photo by Paul Minert via Stephen Miller*

billion, however, the program was finally canceled on 16th February 2012. The physical limits of the laser, as well as the operational requirement to operate in an unacceptably dangerous proximity to the missile fields, and the limited number of 'shots' that could be fired before the need for ground refueling of the laser, all combined to shut down the program. A fully operational ABL program would require 10-20 747s, each costing $1 billion, plus an annual operating budget of $100 million. The on-board laser would need to be 20-30 times more powerful than the YAL-1A was able to achieve. Moreover, the airplanes would need to operate close to the combat theater in order to have the necessary power at impact. A hostile nation would be unlikely to allow huge targets such as the ABL to loiter near its borders, making the airplane a high-value platform requiring extensive fighter defenses. It was simply unrealistic. The YAL-1A was scrapped on 25th September 2014.

In the wake of the ABL cancelation, reports of advanced laser technology in significantly smaller sizes and with greater applicability to the air-to-air arena, especially in off-bore-sight aiming, suggest that the ALL and ABL were not wasted efforts.

NKC-135A/B/E INDIVIDUAL AIRCRAFT

55-3123 Following initial flight testing by Boeing, this airplane was delivered to the Air Force in 1958 for use as a dedicated testbed and designated a JKC-135A. Other than only brief associations with short-term programs (such as QRC-220A testing from 1st January through 30th June 1964), 55-3123 has participated in only two major projects in its lifetime – the Northrop ALOTS program and the DARPA/General Dynamics ALL. It was assigned to Kirtland AFB. The ALL program ended and the airplane placed in flyable storage on 14th May 1984. Nearly four years later (4th May 1988), NKC-135A 55-3123 was flown to Wright Field, and on 20th May 1988 presented to the National Museum of the US Air Force, the first KC-135 of any kind on permanent display (see Appendix III).

55-3132 The 1993 consolidation of test and research assets resulted in this airplane – BIG CROW I – serving as one of two support aircraft for the ABL program. Reassigned to the 412th TS at Edwards AFB. Retired to AMARG on 16th September 2008 as AACA0226 (see Appendix III).

63-8050 Between 1993 and October 1996, EC-135C 63-8050 was configured as BIG CROW II, and was redesignated as an NKC-135B in keeping with its testbed duties. Among other projects it was used in support of the HEL and ABL programs. It was assigned to the 412th TS at Edwards AFB. On 16th September 2008 it was retired to AMARG as AACA0225 (see Appendix III).

NC-135A INDIVIDUAL AIRCRAFT

60-0371 In addition to its basic science research tasking, this NC-135A served as the 'diagnostic' platform for the ALL beginning in 1977. It was painted with a variety of optical theodolite markings to evaluate the targeting accuracy of the laser. After the cessation of the ALL program in 1984, 60-0371 was assigned to other missions.

Air Launched Cruise Missiles

During 1979 the EC-135N ARIAs became an integral part of cruise missile test operations for the AGM-86 Air Launched Cruise Missile (ALCM) and later the AGM-129 Advanced Cruise Missile (ACM). Initially the airplanes were used to track and record telemetry data, but by 1984 they had become airborne control platforms for the entire cruise missile flight profile. EC-135E 60-0374 was converted into the first Cruise Missile Mission Control Aircraft (CMMCA) 'Phase Zero' (basic configuration) aircraft in 1984. EC-135E 61-0326 and 61-0329 were similarly modified during 1986. Two EC-18Ds (81-0893 and 81-0895) were also converted into CMMCAs.

A single CMMCA eliminated the need for seven support aircraft and the numerous ground stations normally required for each cruise missile test, saving over $250,000 per flight. Each CMMCA had a Hughes AN/APG-63 radar installed (the same as in the McDonnell Douglas F-15 Eagle) to track the cruise missile and look for other airplanes (eliminating the need for AWACS or ground radar tracking station). Should an emergency arise, the CMMCA could take control of and fly the cruise missile, or command an autodestruct if required. The CMMCAs (in particular 61-0326) also participated in AIM-120 Advanced Medium Range Air-to-Air Missile (AMRAAM) test operations.

EC-135N/E INDIVIDUAL AIRCRAFT

60-0374 The first ARIA CMMCA conversion in 1984. It was retired to the National Museum of the US Air Force on 3rd November 2000.

61-0326 It was converted into a CMMCA 'Phase Zero' aircraft in mid-1986. It was retired to AMARG on 1st June 1998 as AACA0122 (see Appendix III).

61-0329 It was converted into a CMMCA 'Phase Zero' aircraft in mid-1986. It was written off in June 1996 and sent to Tinker AFB, OK, as a BDR aircraft (see Appendix III).

ARGUS

Project ARGUS was designed to collect high-resolution imagery and spectroscopy on various targets on behalf of the AFWL and, beginning in 1986, the Strategic Defense Initiative Organization (SDIO). The program used two airplanes, NC-135A 60-0371 (*Argus 1*) and C-135E 60-0375 (*Argus 2*). The ability of the ARGUS platforms to be on-station, on-time with no deviation in desired track or bank angle was critical to the effective use of this mission. A sophisticated computer program combined the preplanned target data with existing conditions in the orbit and along the data track to provide accurate timing and positioning information to the flight crew. Data flights were typically from '36,000 to 41,000ft [10,972-12,496m] – where the airplane's performance and maneuvering margins [were] severely limited'. It bears comparing the ARGUS NC-135A and C-135E with the COBRA EYE RC-135X (see Chapter 10), both of which had similar mission goals.

Early ARGUS missions validated the sensors against baseline data. For example, on 5th October 1983, 60-0375 captured plume signature data on a Titan III launched from Vandenberg AFB. The C-135E, known as the Airborne Sensor and Atmospheric Research Aircraft (ASARA), was also involved with tests of an airborne light detection and ranging (LIDAR) system. In 1986 General Dynamics further modified NC-135A 60-0371 to support research specifically for SDIO. This provided, in part, 'high resolution optical documentation of reentry vehicles, rocket plumes and specific SDI test events at ranges of 100-500km [62-310 miles] …providing significant information to SDIO's data base on reentry vehicles and missile plume signatures for sensor system development'. NC-135A 60-0371 operated in conjunction with the High Altitude Learjet Observatory (HALO) operated by Aeromet, Inc, contracted to the Army Strategic Defense Command (ASDC). During 1987 ESI enhanced the sensor equipment in 60-0371 for Project ARGUS. Onboard equipment included 'five visible-band cameras, one infrared spectrometer and two imaging infrared cameras'. Other sensors on modular pallets (which could be installed as required) included 'low-power laser designators, star trackers and infrared imaging radiometers' and (in 1988) the US Navy's CAST GLANCE cargo door photodocumentation system.

Additional ARGUS missions included several to the UK (such as ROYAL SHIELD) to collect IR data on British aircraft. During 1990 the ARGUS aircraft supported both NASA and SDI programs. In 1991 the airplane conducted Defense Nuclear Agency (DNA) missions to verify arms limitation and reduction treaties. In one test, the ARGUS pointed its sensors at actual and simulated Soviet equipment to determine if US 'national technical means' could verify treaty compliance by visual and infrared means. The *Argus 1* (60-0371) flew its last operational sortie in September 1991 in support of one such DNA mission, leaving C-135E 60-0375 as the sole remaining ARGUS aircraft.

Argus 2 expanded its research portfolio to include laser studies, several of which contributed to the ongoing ABL program, but this was not the airplane's primary mission. The first of these began in July 1992, and they were conducted at night in conjunction with a contractor Learjet. Later flight tests of the *Argus 2* with a Grumman Gulfstream II evaluated the effects of the atmosphere on laser

propagation and precision. Additional modifications to 60-0375 included two special optical windows installed in the cargo door. Use of a laser as a detection or verification tool spawned the 1996 Non-Proliferation Airborne Laser Experiment (N-ABLE). The *Argus 2* flew the first N-ABLE mission on 9th October 1996, demonstrating a capability for the airborne detection of chemicals for counter proliferation. The *Argus 2* was retired in early 2001.

C-135E INDIVIDUAL AIRCRAFT

60-0375 By 1983 C-135N 60-0375 was assigned to the ARGUS Program undertaken by the Air Force Weapons Laboratory (AFWL) at Kirtland AFB. The airplane was retired to AMARG on 18th April 2001 as AACA0129 and scrapped by 12th September 2013 (see Appendix III).

NC-135A INDIVIDUAL AIRCRAFT

60-0371 Beginning in 1983, this NC-135A was assigned to and operated by crews from the 4950th TW at Wright-Patterson AFB but was based at Kirtland AFB on behalf of the ARGUS program. The airplane was retired to Kirtland AFB on 12th August 1994, although its activities between September 1991 and its retirement have not been confirmed. According to some sources, the airplane was used as a proficiency trainer for flight crews at the 4950th TW. Other sources suggest that the airplane was used as a trainer for firefighters and rescue personnel at Kirtland AFB. Other sources say it was placed on static display in the small Rescue Museum at Kirtland AFB (see Appendix III).

FISTA

Beginning in 1960, JKC-135A 55-3120 took part in studies that measured the infrared signature of airborne targets and their background as part of research conducted by AFCRL at Hanscom Field. The sensor equipment was capable of high-quality spectral resolution that allowed target discrimination techniques, ultimately permitting precise identification of airborne targets or distinguishing ballistic missile warheads from decoys. Because of its infrared research capabilities, the airplane was known as the 'IR Properties' aircraft. Basic science projects conducted by 55-3120 included IR aurora and airglow phenomena research.

From 16th July 1973 onward, the 3245th Materials Squadron at Hanscom Field reportedly installed equipment in 55-3120 from an unidentified HULA HOOP aircraft, a BURNING LIGHT mission (see below and Chapter 10). Later the same year the air refueling boom was removed and 55-3120 acquired an IFR system (the airplane was occasionally loaned to the AFFTC at Edwards AFB for heavy receiver air refueling practice).

By the early 1980s 55-3120 was modified into the Flying Infrared Signatures and Technology Aircraft (FISTA). There are some reports that claim it was in the FISTA configuration as early as 1961 for US nuclear tests. The airplane did indeed participate in the DOMINIC series of tests in 1962, but whether the airplane carried FISTA gear or was so designated remains unverified. FISTA projects included HI CAMP and TEAL RUBY. HI CAMP compared the IR signatures of a variety of aircraft and weapons acquired from 55-3120 at medium altitude with

The ARGUS I airplane is best known for its work in support of SDI programs, providing optical and spectroscopic recordings. *Photo by Robert Pickett via Stephen Miller*

those acquired from a U-2 flying at high altitude. TEAL RUBY was an AFGL program intended to locate and identify low-flying targets, such as cruise missiles and bombers, from space by detecting their IR signature. On 15th July 1982 the FISTA measured the IR signature of the Lockheed F-117A. Using the third Full Scale Development aircraft (FSD-3, serial 79-10782), the FISTA assessed the F-117 from a variety of angles to determine its heat radiation patterns due to exhaust, internal equipment, and aerodynamic friction. Each of these could compromise the airplane to IR detection systems or render it vulnerable to IR weapons. FISTA data resulted in efforts to mitigate these 'hot spots'. Additional programs for 55-3120 included HAVE SHAVER, designed to detect relocatable targets, and a 1993 program for additional reduction of the IR signature of the F-117A.

The FISTA gear was transferred from NKC-135A 55-3120 to NKC-135E 55-3135 as the FISTA II aircraft, with installation completed and flight testing during May 1995. Far beyond simply reducing the IR signature of an aircraft due to heat emissions, the FISTA II facilitated 'testing of new design techniques and low-observable coatings.' Upgraded FISTA II sensors include 'three imagers, three spectral sensors, and a dual channel radiometer' that cover all infrared wavelengths. 'Multiple video and film cameras suppl[ied] background, aspect, and ranging information and the documentation necessary to decipher and calibrate the data accurately. FISTA II [was] designed so that all of its windows [could] support the use of any of its sensors, allowing customized configuration' Additional changes to 55-3135 included a 'calibrated visible imager and digital recording systems with increased resolution and sensitivity.'

NKC-135E 55-3135 participated in basic science research missions as well, including those related to the Leonid Meteor Showers. The NKC-135E FISTA II program ended in 2004 with the retirement of 55-3135 to AMARG, and future IR evaluations were assigned to an unspecified replacement.

JKC-135A INDIVIDUAL AIRCRAFT

55-3120 On 22nd March 1969, this airplane was redesignated as an NKC-135A. HAVE CAR directed on 24th April 1975, that the AFGL's geophysics section move to Kirtland AFB, and 55-3120 moved along with it. The following year 55-3120 was transferred from Kirtland AFB to the 4950th TW at Wright-Patterson AFB. By the end of 1993 the airplane was declared 'excess' and retired to AMARC as AACA095 on 15th December 1993 (see Appendix III).

NKC-135E INDIVIDUAL AIRCRAFT

55-3135 The FISTA gear was removed from NKC-135A 55-3120 in 1993 and installed in 55-3135 by early 1995, and it became the FISTA II platform. Throughout this time it was assigned to the 412th TW at Edwards AFB. The airplane was retired to AMARG on 28th September 2004 as AACA0144 (see Appendix III).

Above: The Flying Infrared Signatures Technology Aircraft (FISTA I) utilized dozens on IR sensors mounted behind small windows for both weapons development and basic science research. *Photo by Ian Macpherson via Stephen Miller*

Above: The FISTA determined the IR signature of the third FSD F-117, seen here refueling from KC-135E 57-1512. *Photo via Paul Crickmore*

Right: Interior of the FISTA NKC-135A 55-3120 looks like the laboratory of any mad scientist. In the image on the right (looking forward), sensor technicians monitor IR sensor status. In the image on the far right (looking aft), an unidentified technician kills time en route to the orbit area. *Photos by Dave Brown*

Advanced Bomber Development

The 28th March 1961 cancelation of the North American B-70 Valkyrie left SAC without a replacement for the B-52 and B-58 strategic bombers. A crucial factor in the decision to end B-70 development was the growth in Soviet high-altitude defenses, particularly SAMs. Any follow-on bomber SAC required would be a low-altitude, high-speed penetrator. Several designs ensued, beginning with the Subsonic Low-Altitude Bomber (ingloriously known as the 'SLAB'), followed by the variable-geometry Extended Range Strike Aircraft (ERSA), and SAC's preferred choice, the Low-Altitude Manned Penetrator (LAMP). By 1963 this had evolved into the Advanced Manned Precision Strike System (AMPSS), culminating in the Advanced Manned Strategic Aircraft (AMSA – derogatorily known as 'America's Most Studied Aircraft'). Secretary of Defense McNamara strongly opposed any new strategic bomber, however, and limited AMSA funding to research studies. Following the 1968 presidential election, however, newly elected President Richard Nixon ordered that AMSA proceed to development. In April 1969 AMSA became the B-1A, and Rockwell (formerly North American) won the competition in June 1970.

Beginning in October 1970, three '135s participated in AMSA research along with NC-141A 61-2777 and C-141A 61-2779. NKC-135A 55-3128 acquired an enlarged nose radome to cover the Raytheon AN/APQ-140 Km-band radar under consideration for use on the AMSA. C-135A 60-0377 took part in AMSA ECM research and development. By 1973, C-135B 62-4133 was configured for the Standard Electronic Module Radar (SEMR) program, although it is not known if this airplane actually participated in this evaluation.

Whereas AMSA/B-1 bomber development and testing took place under considerable public scrutiny, the next generation bomber evolved in a comparable amount of secrecy. The rise of 'stealth' technology during the late 1970s offered a new approach to aircraft design, resulting in the 1979 Advanced Technology Bomber (ATB) program. On 20th October 1981 the Northrop design won the competition for the B-2 Spirit, and evaluation of new technologies began in three '135s.

In 1984 C-135E 60-0377 received a 'hog nose' such as those on the RC-135s and acquired two flat-plate fairings above and below the forward fuselage. The upper 40 x 40in (12.19 x 12.19m) openings housed the competing Hughes and Aerojet General infrared systems being tested as part of the Advanced Avionics System (AAS), a program later revealed to be part of the B-2A development. That same year NKC-135A 55-3122 started the Atmospheric Properties Study (APS) at Edwards AFB, a predecessor to a subsequent program known as the Contrail Suppression System (CSS). Chemicals were injected into an engine's exhaust to dissipate or prevent altogether its contrails. This program reached maturity during tests involving a B-2 General Electric F118-GE-100 engine mounted in lieu of the No.3 J57 engine on 55-3122, along with an additional pod containing

Below: For the AMSA program (which became the B-1A) 55-3128 acquired an enlarged nose and multiple ventral fairings on the aft fuselage. *Photo by Jack Morris via Stephen Miller*

Bottom: The black upper surfaces on 60-0377 were residue from the IWATCH program and were not part of the AMSA research under way in this 1972 image. *Photo by Jack Morris via Stephen Miller*

the suppressant. [This airplane continued involvement with engine testing through the early 1990s, carrying the General Electric F404-GE-100 engine used in the Advanced Technology Fighter (ATF), prototype for the Lockheed F-22A].

Beginning in November 1986, C-135A 60-0377 — known as the Avionics Flight Test Bed (AFTB) – 'conducted flight testing of the [B-2A] radar and navigation subsystems'. The Hughes radar began operating in 60-0377 in January 1987, and 'all active in-flight radar testing [was] on the C-135', totaling some 1,600 hours over 305 flights. The AFTB contributed 'significantly' to 'rapid progress [in] avionics development' for the B-2. Changes to software or technical modifications to equipment could be tested on the AFTB and validated without having to be tested in the B-2, thus minimizing costs. Further testing of B-2 software included Global Positioning Satellite (GPS) munitions delivery systems.

NKC-135A INDIVIDUAL AIRCRAFT

55-3122 Beginning in 1984 this NKC-135A was used in APS and CSS for advanced engine evaluations at Edwards AFB. By 1993 55-3122 was declared excess and retired to AMARC as CA094 on 19th October 1993 (see Appendix III).

55-3128 During 1971 this airplane acquired an enlarged nose for AMSA radar trials.

C-135A/B/E INDIVIDUAL AIRCRAFT

60-0376 During 1984-1986 this C-135A was part of the AAS program for the B-2.

60-0377 This C-135A took part in AMSA ECM testing (along with other ECM trials) from 1971 through 1975 while assigned to Wright-Patterson AFB. By November 1986 it acquired a hog nose and had been relocated to Edwards AFB as the AFTB, conducting radar tests for the B-2. By mid-1995, the hog nose was removed and 60-0377 identified for retirement to AMARC. Instead, 60-0377 was placed on static display at the Air Force Flight Test Center Museum at Edwards AFB on 15th December 1995 (see Appendix III).

62-4133 During the mid-1970s this C-135B was assigned to the 4950th TW at Wright-Patterson AFB for SEMR tests related to the AMSA radar program.

ELECTRONIC WARFARE AND RECONNAISSANCE

Following the Second World War, electronic warfare grew in importance both to detect hostile aircraft and to avoid detection by hostile radars. This was particularly significant for SAC bombers, which had originally planned to penetrate Soviet airspace at high altitude but were now increasingly vulnerable to detection by Soviet early warning radar. Even the shift to low-altitude operations required electronic countermeasures (ECM) to mask the bomber from ground-based and aerial tracking radars. Developing ECM equipment required considerable electrical power and a platform capable of long duration missions to evaluate the systems in multiple scenarios, configurations, and settings. Testbed KC-135s proved highly suitable for this mission. Moreover, their ability to carry both electronic warfare (EW) gear and a large crew made them ideal as airborne EW simulators.

Electronic Warfare and ECM

Beginning in 1958, JKC-135A 55-3128 conducted airborne ECM tests at Wright-Patterson AFB. External modifications included removing the air refueling boom and reshaping the boom pod, adding several small radomes along the fuselage spine, and attaching a small pod protruding from the right forward fuselage. Most of the fuselage fuel cells were removed to make room for the installation of ECM test equipment. JKC-135A 55-3119 followed suit with ECM testing while assigned to RADC at Griffiss AFB. For an unknown project, a forward-pointing cone-shaped cylinder was attached beneath the forward fuselage and a small square fairing installed beneath the fuselage aft of the main gear well. The airplane had no air refueling boom.

For many years 55-3122 was used as an ECM Quick Reaction Capability (QRC) testbed. The fuselage fuel cells were removed to accommodate ECM equipment and test gear, the air refueling boom was removed, and an ECM receiver was mounted atop the nose radome. A Westinghouse QRC-125 and a Hughes QRC-126 IR warning receiver were installed during 1961 in the tail cone. These were intended to detect a missile launch flash under operational conditions. The airplane was flown over the Eglin AFB, FL, ranges and more than 100 missiles were fired at it from fighters located just beyond the missiles' ranges. One crewmember involved in these tests no doubt justly claims that 55-3122 'is probably the most shot-at aircraft in the Air Force!' Neither system worked well and development was discontinued (it must have worked well enough to preclude any errant missile hits, even if out of range).

From 1st January through 30th June 1964, the airplane conducted aerial tests for an infrared search-while-tracking (IRST) system. Until 31st December 1964, 55-3122 was part of the 'Countdown Countermeasures' program. It carried ECM and 'radar deception' gear to jam missiles. It was tested against the F-106A MA-1 radar fire-control system, the HAWK (Homing All-the-Way Killer) missile system, and the Nike-Hercules tracking radar. During 1967 the airplane was noted with a square area above the left wing root that appeared to be highly polished and of unknown purpose. Later programs involving 55-3122 included Polarization ECM from October 1979 to May 1980.

Other JKC-135As (later NKC-135As) known to be associated with ECM and electronic-related projects include 55-3124 while assigned to RADC at Griffiss AFB, where it supported a variety of tests for ESD, and 55-3125, also assigned to RADC. From 1981 through September 1985, NKC-135A 55-3124 participated in Project CROSS TRAK, an AFWAL ECM test program at Eglin AFB. In addition to the nine large windows (residue from Project PRESS), the airplane had small fairings along each side of the nose and above the radome. In 1986 the airplane became involved with Advanced Systems Evaluation, and in 1987 had slender wingtip pods.

As part of the PAVE ONYX program in the early 1970s, NKC -135A 55-3125 had a bulge on the starboard side of the fuselage and a cylindrical fairing with a series of small antennae was attached to the end of the extendible portion of the boom. PAVE ONYX referred to all research programs that measured the time of arrival (ToA) of individual radar pulses. It included the Advanced Location Strike System (ALSS), a combined RADC/Armament Lab effort to suppress enemy surface-to-air missile (SAM) sites. Flight tests took place at Holloman AFB. PAVE ONYX was the highest-priority short-term project in the Air Force as SAM-related losses over Vietnam increased substantially, especially of B-52s during LINEBACKER II. After February 1974, however, the urgency associated with the program abated and PAVE ONYX continued as only a technical development program.

Beginning in 1968 C-135A 61-0377 was associated with a QRC project known as 'IWATCH'. The airplane had an overall natural metal finish with a flat black fuselage spine and vertical stabilizer (excluding the rudder). The black paint reduced surface glare, suggesting an optical or infrared-sensitive mission, possibly related to infrared countermeasures (IRCM). Following this enigmatic program, 60-0377 participated in a variety of ECM evaluations. The forward and aft body fuel tanks were removed to allow an increase in electronic and test equipment weight. In 1982 it was outfitted with a modified Boeing 707 passenger kit, providing AFSC personnel with a modicum of pleasant, comfortable transport en route to testing locations. From August 1982 until March 1983, following the partial removal of this passenger interior, 60-0377 participated in the Single Axis Jammer program.

185

Several '135s were involved in test projects related to Identification, Friend or Foe (IFF) systems. An IFF is an electronic signal interrogator which determines if an aircraft is friendly or not based on a pre-programmed code inserted into its IFF transmitter. The equipment had applications in air-to-air, surface-to-air, and surface-to-surface uses, and was compatible with air traffic control (both civil and military) equipment then in use and of future design. Some tests were in conjunction with other initiatives. From 1976 through 1980, for example, C-135B 62-4128 undertook initial Mark XII IFF tests while conducting RINT studies (see below). From December 1979 until April 1980, C-135N 60-0375 and NKC-135A 55-3124 participated in the 'ADC BLINK JAMMER' (or possibly 'Beacon Link' = 'BLINK' JAMMER) program, of which nothing is known, while 60-0375 replaced 62-4128 on Mark XII IFF testing from 1980 through 1983. In early 1986 NKC-135A 55-3127 acquired an RC-135 'hog nose' and began tests on the Mark XV IFF system, a program scheduled to end in the early 1990s. Mark XV IFF was intended to replace the Mark XII IFF and provide a secure and reliable jam-resistant IFF for US and NATO countries. NKC-135A 55-3127 served as the airborne interrogator testbed and an unidentified ASD T-39s flew as the transponder testbed. During 1986 and 1987 C-135E 60-0375 (along with NT-39A 59-2870 and T-39B 59-2874) was part of a highly classified proof-of-concept program known as HAVE DARK. Given the collaboration between the C-135E and two T-39s, it is possible that this was a communications system similar to the Mark XV IFF. Subsequent projects for 60-0375 included multiple QRC missions (those requiring completion in an extremely short period and with great urgency).

J/NKC-135A INDIVIDUAL AIRCRAFT

55-3119 This airplane was delivered to the Air Force on 19th March 1958, and redesignated a JKC-135A when it was transferred to AMC on 1st July 1958. It was redesignated an NKC-135A on 14th May 1962.

55-3122 This airplane was redesignated as a JKC-135A on 17th February 1958, and participated in ECM testing and evaluation at Griffiss AFB through at least 1980. By 1966 it had been redesignated as an NKC-135A.

55-3124 Following initial flight testing at Boeing and Edwards AFB, this airplane was assigned to a variety of ECM and EW programs at RADC at Griffiss AFB, and at Wright-Patterson AFB during the early 1980s. On 10th March 1969 it was redesignated as an NKC-135A.

55-3125 Assigned to ECM and EW evaluation at RADC in the late 1950s as a JKC-135A. The forward and aft body fuel tanks were removed to make room for additional electronic test equipment. It was redesignated an NKC-135A by 1964.

55-3127 During the mid 1980s this NKC-135A conducted Mark XV IFF tests.

55-3128 Beginning in 1958 this JKC-135A was part of ECM and EW evaluation at RADC and at Wright-Patterson AFB. It was redesignated as an NKC-135A by 1965.

C-135A/B/E/N INDIVIDUAL AIRCRAFT

60-0375 While a C-135N, this airplane was active in IFF and related programs while assigned to Wright-Patterson AFB beginning in 1980. It was converted into a C-135E on 3rd May 1982, and continued as a QRC testbed.

60-0377 This C-135A was transferred to multiple ECM and EW test roles with AFSC at Wright-Patterson AFB from 5th January 1968 through 1983.

62-4128 Between 1976 and 1980 this C-135B was the primary Mark XII IFF testbed at Wright-Patterson AFB.

BIG CROWS and LITTLE CROWS

In 1973, NKC-135A 55-3132 was modified for the Army Office of Missile Electronic Warfare (OMEW) of the Army Materiel and Laboratory Command. Nicknamed BIG CROW, the airplane was stationed at Kirtland AFB. There have also been several NT-39A LITTLE CROWS (59-2870, 59-2873, 60-3474, and 60-3476 – see Table 8.7). BIG CROW served as an airborne laboratory to probe weaknesses of US Air Force, Navy, Army, and Allied nations electronic systems to hostile electronic interference. Its mission equipment could duplicate the electronic signature of a variety of modern aircraft, simulating electronic threats for jamming practice and electronic signature calibration. It carried ECM pods on pylons inboard of the inner engines and on the wingtips, had chaff dispensers, and a significant decoy capability. Each flight's events were recorded for extensive ground analysis. It was arguably the most capable ECM test aircraft in existence at the time and its value was reflected in the increasing use of similar airborne ECM platforms used in both routine training and operational test and evaluation. Indeed, talks were under way during 1992 to consider loaning the BIG CROW to the UK.

The airplane flew some 250 hours per year for both military and commercial customers, including, for example, the ECM support branch of the Army's Vulnerability Assessment Laboratory as part of tests associated with the Patriot missile, the MIM-23 Improved HAWK (I-HAWK) SAM, and the Aquila remotely piloted vehicle. Other service's programs involving the BIG CROW include BMEWS, the OTH-B radar, and JTIDS. The airplane had a flight-deck crew including two pilots, a navigator, and a flight engineer, with a mission crew of five maintenance technicians and five electronic warfare crewmembers.

The BIG CROW has been noted in a variety of configurations, underscoring its flexibility to represent a wide variety of electronic systems. Large removable dorsal and ventral canoe-shaped radomes were added to the forward fuselage. A large nose radome replaced the standard nose. The airplane has also been seen with a long cylindrical tail extension, likely a platform for some energy radiation

The BIG CROW has appeared in multiple configurations, all of which are variations on a theme: a large 'canoe' fairing on the dorsal fuselage, with a ventral fairing added later. *Photo via Brian Rogers*

BIG CROW NKC-135E 55-3132 departs Souda Bay, Crete, in early 2003. Its mission there has not been identified, but was likely ECM training for naval units in the Mediterranean Sea. *USAF Photo*

test. The large dorsal radome created a certain delicacy in the event of engine-out operations. Given the yaw associated with an outboard engine failure, the radome blocked airflow around the vertical stabilizer and rudder, reducing their effectiveness in countering the yaw, a particularly challenging problem during landing. As most of its fuselage fuel tanks were removed to allow the installation of additional ECM equipment, the BIG CROW initially suffered from an extremely short radius of action. In 1986 the airplane acquired an IFR system, considerably enhancing the airplane's range and mission capability.

As part of a major consolidation of US test and evaluation assets during the early 1990s, the DoD agreed to retire the three NAVY KING CROW aircraft (see below), the ARGUS I C-135E 60-0371, three Cruise Missile Mission Control Aircraft (CMMCA – EC-135E 60-0374 and EC-18Ds 81-0893 and 81-0895), the C-135E 60-0372 SATCOM aircraft, and the Missile Defense Agency (MDA) DC-10 (N910SF). To replace these, the DoD transferred EC-135C 63-8050 to Kirtland AFB where it was reconfigured as the second BIG CROW. Moreover, the BIG CROW mission would expand from EW testing and training to include US Navy ship qualification trials, Air Force cruise missile testing, MDA support as the ABL 'target board' aircraft, general data link and communications tests, and 'downrange telemetry' for missile and rocket launches from Vandenberg AFB. Between 18th March and 26th April 2003, NKC-135E 55-3132 flew some 19 missions from Souda Bay, Crete. It is not known if these were related to Operation IRAQI FREEDOM or if the airplane was participating in tests in the Eastern Mediterranean.

Table 8-7. **The CROW Fleet**

MDS	Serial	From	To
BIG CROW			
NKC-135A/E	55-3132	1975	16 Sep 08
NKC-135B	63-8050	1996	16 Sep 08
NAVY KING CROW			
NKC-135A	55-3134	1978	20 Feb 96
NKC-135A	56-3596	1978	25 Jun 95
LITTLE CROWS			
NT-39A	59-2870	NT-39A	60-3474
NT-39A	59-2873	NT-39A	60-3476

Further Air Force budget cuts led to the 6th June 2006, decision to fund both BIG CROWS only until their next schedule PDM, at which point they would be retired to AMARG. Moreover, the planned mass retirement of the KC-135E fleet and elimination of TF33-PW-102 engines from the inventory added to the Air Force's commitment to cease funding for the BIG CROWS. In a last-ditch effort in 2008, the DoD's Office of the Undersecretary of Defense – Acquisitions, Technology & Logistics (OSD-AT&L) sought to shift responsibility for the BIG CROWS to NASA. Funding for the airplanes would come from OSD-AT&L, but NASA would operate them and give them NASA Airworthiness Certificates, eliminating the need for the Air Force to be involved while retaining the mission capability. Despite this appeal, both BIG CROWS were relegated to AMARG on 16th September 2008, ending 30+ years of BIG CROW operations.

NKC-135A/B/E INDIVIDUAL AIRCRAFT

55-3132 This airplane was converted into BIG CROW I during 1973. It received TF33-PW-102 engines from 4th October 1990 through 31st January 1991, and was redesignated an NKC-135E. Reassigned to the 412th TS at Edwards AFB. Retired to AMARG on 16th September 2008 as AACA0226 (see Appendix III).
63-8050 Converted from an EC-135C airborne command post into the BIG CROW II beginning in 1993, and it was redesignated an NKC-135B by 1996. It was assigned to the 412th TS at Edwards AFB. Initially the airplane retained its air refueling boom, but some images show this removed. Retired to AMARG on 16th September 2008 as AACA0225 (see Appendix III).

NAVY KING CROWS

During the 1960s and 1970s, Douglas-Tulsa operated three B-47s on behalf of the US Navy for ECM operations. The first of these, B-47B 51-2077, crashed at NAS Pt Mugu on 29th October 1965, and was eventually replaced by B-47Es 52-4100 (call sign *Nucar 03*) and 52-4120 (call sign *Nucar 04*). By 1975 the B-47s were becoming difficult to maintain and the Navy sought two KC-135s as replacements. Beginning in 1977 NKC-135As 55-3134 and 56-3596 were modified and delivered to the US Navy in late 1977. They were based at Tulsa IAP, OK, and were assigned administratively to the Combined Fleet Electronic Warfare Service Group (ComFltEW-ServGru) at NAS Norfolk, VA, and then as part of the Fleet Electronic Warfare Support Group (FEWSG). In 1986 Douglas EC-24A BuNO 163050 was added to the group. The airplanes were operated and maintained by McDonnell Douglas contract crews (how ironic!) until late 1989, when Chrysler Technologies Airborne

Wearing hastily applied markings, NAVY KING CROW 56-3596 visits NAS Miramar after delivery in December 1977. *Photo by Roy Lock via Stephen Miller*

Systems (CTAS) at Waco/TSTI AP in Waco, TX, acquired the contract.

Known as 'NAVY KING CROWS' for their 'NKC' mission prefix, the two NKC-135As and the EC-24A deployed around the world to conduct training and evaluation of the US Navy's fleet capability to identify, defend, and intercept simulated hostile electronic threats. As with the BIG CROW, the FEWSG platforms could simulate a wide variety of hostile and friendly electronic signatures against which realistic training could be undertaken. The value of this program was reflected in the 1986 acquisition of the EC-24A, the growth in contractor-operated electronic warfare SMART CROW trainers, and the plan to develop a Multi-Service Electronic Warfare Support Group (MSEWG) for NATO using 'three Boeing 707–class jamming aircraft'.

The FEWSG NKC-135As operated in a variety of external configurations, demonstrating their adaptability to specific requirements. They lacked an air refueling capability, either as a tanker or as a receiver, and the forward body and upper deck fuel tanks were removed to make room for the additional electronic equipment. The residual windows on 55-3134 were covered. Other modifications included replacement of the weather radar with a sea search unit. The airplanes had an enlarged nose radome, a number of antennae along the fuselage, and an underwing pylon for electronic warfare pods [such as the TREE SHARK and TREE HORN transmitters or the AN/ALQ-167(V)] on each side of the inboard engines. The engine-driven electrical system was modified by the addition of larger electrical generators necessary to satisfy the large power demands of the electrical equipment. These resulted in bulges along the engine pod.

Both NKC-135As were slated to receive TF33-PW-102 engines in 1990 and be redesignated an NKC-135E. However, funding for this modification was reportedly diverted to the Trident SLBM program. In 1992 FEWSG was redesignated the Fleet Tactical Readiness Group (FTRG). Budget cuts, plans to eliminate J57-equipped KC-135s from the USAF inventory, and the 'end' of the Cold War spelled the end for the NKC-135As, and they were retired to AMARG.

NKC-135A INDIVIDUAL AIRCRAFT

55-3134 On 15th May 1978, 55-3134 was transferred to the US Navy as NKC-135A BuNo 553134 and became known as NAVY KING CROW I. The airplane acquired the call sign Nucar 01, previously used on Douglas A3B BuNO 138968. It was retired to AMARC on 20th February 1996 as AN6G0002, but this changed to AACA0246 on 1st August 2009 (see Appendix III).

56-3596 During 1977 the airplane was modified for use by the US Navy's FEWSG, and given the BuNo 563596 and became known as NAVY KING CROW II. It acquired the call sign Nucar 02, previously used on Douglas A3B BuNO 138922. A shortage of funds in 1994 prevented 563596 from receiving scheduled PDM, and it sat unused at CTAS for nearly nine months before being retired to AMARC on 25th June 1995 as AN6G0001, which changed on 1st August 2009 to AACA0245 (see Appendix III).

Strategic Reconnaissance

As part of the development of the ASD-1 automated electronic intelligence (ELINT) system for the planned BIG TEAM RC-135C, LTV modified JKC-135A 55-3132 to carry the XH-1 Electronic Reconnaissance System, the prototype of the ASD-1 (see Chapter 10). The program, known as GOLDEN PHEASANT, began in 1962. Operational tests started in late 1963, as the airplane deployed to bases in Europe. The airplane was assigned to the 34th AREFS at Offutt AFB for these tests, which were conducted under 'real world' conditions along the periphery of the Soviet Union. The XH-1

performed well, and underwent a planned upgrade followed by additional operational flight tests performed by flight crews from the 4157th SW at Eielson AFB. Missions took place out of RAF Brize Norton, Incirlik AB, Turkey, and Eielson AFB during mid 1964. Once again, results were excellent and the ASD-1 integration into the RC-135C proceeded as planned.

A critical issue for SAC planners was bomb damage assessment (BDA) during the SIOP. There was no point in allowing additional bombers or ICBMs to strike targets already destroyed, nor was there any sense in leaving targets intact when weapons could be directed to attack them. Getting accurate and timely BDA during a nuclear conflagration was unrealistic using traditional reconnaissance methods, however, but by 1961 SAC was committed to acquiring a 'satellite-borne, post-strike, all weather' BDA capability 'in near real time'. The then-secret National Reconnaissance Office (NRO) sought to determine the feasibility of using existing side-looking radars (SLARs) to take post-strike images that were sufficiently detailed to determine if a target had been destroyed by a nuclear weapon. A Convair C-131 equipped with an AN/APS-55 SLAR flew 2,200ft (671m) above existing nuclear bomb craters at Frenchman's Flats, NV, and successfully took the necessary images.

Following this demonstration, a joint SAC-NRO planning group recommended that an AN/APS-73 SLAR 'be integrated with a Thor booster, an Agena-D orbiting vehicle, a CORONA recovery capsule,' and other components as the planned BDA satellite. The program, known as QUILL, proved nettlesome from the start. SAC required multiple launches over the course of the trans-SIOP period, each salvo would use five Minutemen to launch simultaneously and insert their satellites into orbits that passed over the maximum number of Soviet targets. It was then necessary to de-orbit the CORONA recovery capsule and have airplanes in place to 'catch' it as it descended in the lower atmosphere, then develop the film and relay it to SAC planners

The original RECCE STRIKE evaluation took place using 56-3596 from 1963 through 1966. *Photo by Stephen Miller*

RECCE STRIKE Step II in 55-3132 was the continuation of research begun with 56-3596 related to space-based battle-damage assessment. Later variants retained the large side lobe but not the dorsal intake. *Photo by Richard Sullivan via Stephen Millter*

for retargeting. A single QUILL test mission took place with a launch from Vandenberg AFB on 21st December 1964. The APS-73 radar took images which were recorded on film and de-orbited on 24th December, although the satellite continued in orbit until 26th December when it lost power and was intentionally destroyed. Results were very encouraging, leading to the development of a long history of radar imaging satellites.

Concurrent with the GOLDEN PHEASANT program, in mid-1963 JKC-135A 56-3596 participated in the Reconnaissance Strike Program, also known as RECCE STRIKE, which evaluated the AN/APS-73 SLAR for QUILL and other projects, including QUICK CHECK, a SLAR pod for the planned reconnaissance B-58B. The JKC-135A was modified by the addition of a large and deep radome on the right forward fuselage. This structure was flight checked on 15th July 1963, with no unusual flight characteristics noted. The radome covered the AN/APS-73 radar and its associated sensory equipment such as infrared and ELINT gear and a T-11 camera, its correlator and film developing equipment. By 1964 the program had been renamed RECCE STRIKE Step II and testing continued through at least the end of 1965, including modification of NKC-135A 55-3132 to a similar configuration as part of the Hi Resolution Radar program. By mid-1966, 56-3596 had surrendered its radome and was assigned to ALOTS program.

At least one other testbed is known to have conducted a reconnaissance-related initiative. Beginning in 1976, C-135B 62-4128 participated in the Radiation Intelligence (RINT) program.

J/NKC-135A INDIVIDUAL AIRCRAFT

55-3132 This KC-135 was delivered to Wright-Patterson AFB on 15th March 1960, and redesignated as a JKC-135A. By March 1964 it had been redesignated as an NKC-135A. Following its reconnaissance testbed duties, it saw service with other programs before becoming the first BIG CROW airplane.

56-3596 This airplane was first assigned to Wright-Patterson AFB on 7th December 1962, and by 1965 had been redesignated as a JKC-135A. Beginning in 1966 it was reassigned to the AFSWC at Kirtland AFB. Following its reconnaissance testbed duties, it saw service with other programs before becoming the second NAVY KING CROW airplane.

C-135B INDIVIDUAL AIRCRAFT

62-4128 After its RINT role from 1976 until 1980, this airplane was converted into an EC-135B ARIA.

NUCLEAR WEAPONS AND EFFECTS

Of all the '135 testbed programs, those associated with nuclear weapons and their effects are among the most significant in terms of investment of aircraft, funding, and implications. They are also blurred in their relation to strategic reconnaissance missions associated with nuclear weapons tests. It would be easy to assert that testbeds monitored US nuclear tests whereas SAC reconnaissance aircraft monitored those of foreign nations. This would be only partially true, as testbed '135s observed both Soviet and French atmospheric tests throughout the 1960s and early 1970s. SAC pilots and navigators, however, flew those aircraft, with the remainder of the crew from the Air Force Technical Applications Center (AFTAC) and the Air Force Security Service (AFSS), agencies responsible for monitoring foreign nuclear tests and foreign communications intelligence (COMINT), respectively. Many of the operations associated with nuclear weapons development or monitoring remain classified. For example, little is known of specific programs such AURORA, an atomic intelligence-gathering project in which unspecified testbed KC-135s participated. Testbed monitoring of atomic tests has also not been without risk. Between 1960 and the end of French atmospheric testing in 1974, one testbed C-135B was lost returning from an operational sortie, and one JKC-135A crashed during a flight at its home station (see Appendix II).

In the post-war rush to develop atomic (and later thermonuclear) weapons, the United States, Great Britain, and the Soviet Union established multiple test facilities. For the United States, these primarily included New Mexico and the Nevada Test Site as well as remote island territories in the South Pacific. For the USSR, the primary site was at Semipalatinsk in the Kazakh Soviet Socialist Republic (now Kazakhstan), and later three additional sites on Novaya Zemlya, the island dividing the Barents and Kara Seas. For Britain, tests took place at remote South Pacific islands as well as three sites in Australia.

On 31st October 1958 US President Dwight D Eisenhower proposed a global moratorium on all nuclear testing, contingent upon progress at the Geneva negotiations and other arms limitation efforts. The Soviets did not agree to these additional stipulations, but nonetheless joined the US and halted their own testing. On 30th August 1961, however, Soviet First Secretary Nikita Khrushchev announced that the USSR would end its voluntary suspension. Beginning the next day, the Soviets conducted 25 nuclear explosions through the end of 1961, including the notorious 50Mt 'Tsar Bomba'. President Kennedy responded by authorizing resumption of US atmospheric testing in the South Pacific as well as New Mexico and Nevada under a dormant program known as EVER READY. On 1st November 1961 EVER READY was renamed BLUE STRAW, which included all support for nuclear testing. In early January 1962, the Department of Defense (DoD) changed BLUE STRAW to DOMINIC. Some 31 American tests took place throughout 1962 as part of DOMINIC (which focused on weapons development and basic science), including five high-altitude detonations as part of Operation FISHBOWL, most notably the STARFISH-PRIME test.

Operation DOMINIC

Initial plans for the DOMINIC tests included only two C-130Bs (60-0298 and 60-0299) as diagnostic aircraft, but researchers were acutely aware that they were incapable of collection at high altitudes and had excessive vibrations that would invalidate high-speed photography (one post-test report noted that the C-130 fireball measurements 'were not worth the film they were printed on'). By 11th December 1961 planners had revised their requirements, specifying the need for 'approximately five C-135 aircraft for optical and photographic measurements.' Both Los Alamos Scientific Laboratory (LASL) and the Lawrence Radiation Laboratory (LRL) argued that they each required a dedicated aircraft for optical observations of the high-altitude shots, preferably a C-135. The Defense Atomic Support Agency (DASA) also wanted two C-135s 'in addition to the already modified AFCRL C-135' (actually JKC-135A 55-3144). At a January 1962 meeting, LRL withdrew their request for a C-135, but AFTAC's sudden interest in participating in the testing meant that a fifth airplane would once again be needed. Acquiring these five airplanes proved extremely troublesome.

In late January 1962 AFSC reluctantly agreed to provide the LASL KC-135 for modification by BIG SAFARI on 29th January. To LASL's surprise and disappointment, the KC-135 was not the 'recent model' they desired but a 'vintage 1955 aircraft [55-3136], which had not been maintained in accordance with USAF tech orders.' After multiple delays 55-3136 was finally modified as the DOMINIC U airplane, subsequently outfitted at Kirtland AFB (departing there on 21st April), and finally arrived at the primary base on Johnston Island on 23rd April 1962. DASA faced similar difficulties with its two requested KC-135s to be modified by the Air Force Office of Aerospace Research at Wright-Patterson AFB. AFSWC also struggled to acquire a C-135, and the requested fifth KC-135 for 'ionospheric observations' was simply unavailable.

At least 10 '135s were ultimately involved in all aspects of US testing throughout 1962 (the last year of US atmospheric tests). Two of these – 59-1514 and 55-3121 – had been seconded to BIG SAFARI under the SPEED LIGHT program for rapid conversion in support of the DOMINIC series of US tests as SPEED LIGHT-DELTA and -ECHO, respectively. (BIG SAFARI had previously modified JKC-135A 55-3127 into the SPEED LIGHT-BRAVO aircraft to monitor the Tsar Bomba and subsequent Soviet tests at Novaya Zemlya in 1961 – see Chapter 10). The two new SPEED LIGHT aircraft each had some 19 windows on both sides of the fuselage to allow collection from either side of the airplane. Test equipment included 'eight cameras, a photo-electric system, three panoramic electromagnetic systems, four bhangmeters, and data photo systems for recording the precise chronometer readings.' A closed circuit TV monitored various arrays. Both 59-1514 and 55-3121 were equipped with an IFR system. The airplanes operated from Hickam AFB, HI. KC-135A 55-3121 participated in each DOMINIC-series test beginning 25th April 1962, but 59-1514 was deployed initially to RAF Brize Norton to monitor expected Soviet tests at Novaya Zemlya, which did not take place. In late May it flew to Hickam AFB to join 55-3121, and both airplanes flew for each detonation starting with the 15th June RINCONADA test through the 11th July PAMLICO test. Neither participated in the FISHBOWL series of tests from 2nd-30th October onward as they relocated to RAF Brize Norton for the flurry of additional Soviet tests.

In addition to the SPEED LIGHT-DELTA and -ECHO, BIG SAFARI converted KC-135A 55-3136 into the DOMINIC U platform. This was a reference to Dominique You, a French privateer who fought with distinction under American general Andrew Jackson at the 8th January 1815 Battle of New Orleans, the last engagement of the War of 1812. The DOMINIC U mission established baseline data from

known US nuclear tests to calibrate photometric, spectroscopic, and photographic equipment that would be used to measure foreign tests. Using 'fireball cameras, bhangmeters, and time interval measuring equipment,' DOMINIC U would study the fireball from first light to decay. Sensors were placed on the right side of the aircraft, which had 38 windows. Of these 27 were glass, eight were quartz, and 3 were a special glass known as 'Vycor'. Additional generators provided power for the mission equipment as well as air conditioning to mitigate the heat generated by the additional gear. The airplane acquired so much test gear that once fueled it easily reached its maximum allowable weight, leading to some 'tense' departures from Hickam AFB. DOMINIC U (call sign *Kibosh 02*) flew its first operational mission for the ADOBE detonation on 25th April 1962.

The FISHBOWL series

In an effort to assess the impact of atomic detonations at heights in excess of 200 miles (322km), Operation DOMINIC included five tests where a Thor intermediate range ballistic missile (IRBM) would launch an atomic warhead to explode at high altitudes. Known as FISHBOWL, these tests would investigate electromagnetic pulse (EMP), the impact of radio blackout, and the basic science of auroral phenomena. Three tests (URRACA, BLUEGILL, and STARFISH) were canceled or failed. The first successful test, STARFISH PRIME, occurred on 9th July 1962, when a Thor lofted a W49 thermonuclear warhead, which detonated with a yield of 1.4Mt at an altitude of 248 miles (399km) and a distance of 19nm (30.5km) from the Johnston Islands southwest of Hawai'i. The fireball was visible 900 miles (1445km) away in Honolulu, where the electromagnetic pulse knocked out electricity and street lights. Radiation from the blast caused a number of satellites – including Telstar – to fail.

During the STARFISH series of nuclear tests, KC-135A 55-3136 supported LASL 'electromagnetic and photographic measurements data collection' (see Table 8-8). The airplane was required to be 'above all clouds in order to observe [the nuclear weapon re-entry] vehicle at time of detonation'. In August 1962 BIG SAFARI upgraded the mission equipment, and 55-3136 returned to the South Pacific. The airplane flew its final mission on 4th November, five days after the 30th October HOUSATONIC test, the final detonation in the DOMINIC series.

C-135A 60-0376, JKC-135A 55-3120, and JKC-135A 55-3144, (call signs *Kettle*) took part in Project 8A.2 'Optical Phenomenology of High-Altitude Nuclear Detonations' on behalf of US defense contractor Edgerton, Germeshausen, and Grier (EG&G) during the five planned STARFISH, BLUEGILL, KINGFISH, CHECKMATE, AND TIGHTROPE shots. JKC-135As 55-3120 and 55-3144 participated in Project 8A.1 'High Altitude Nuclear Detonation Optical-Infrared Effects' for AFCRL. In addition, JKC-135A 55-3134 (call sign *Grantham 01*) participated in the STARFISH test in support of Project 8C, Optical Tracking of Re-entry Vehicle. JKC-135A 55-3120 also

Table 8-8. **Joint Task Force 8.4 Starfish Prime KC-135s**

MDS	Serial No.	Call Sign	Sponsor	Altitude	Location
JKC-135A	55-3120	*Kettle 01*	AFSWC	above clouds	17 20 N 169 30 W
KC-135A	55-3121	*Kibosh 01*	AFTAC	FL350-FL400	20 20 N 168 W
JKC-135A	55-3131		WADC		
JKC-135A	55-3134	*Grantham 01*	WADC	FL350	17 19 N 170 41 W
KC-135A	55-3136	*Kibosh 02*	LASL	FL350	24 09 N 165 57 W
JKC-135A	55-3144	*Kettle 02*	AFSWC	above clouds	17 N 169 W
KC-135A	58-0011	*Cognac*	SAC	FL310	18 N 166 35 W
KC-135A	58-0022	*Fake 03*	SAC	FL310	19 N 163 W
KC-135A	59-1514	*Kibosh 05*	AFTAC	FL350-FL400	22 54 N 164 W
KC-135A	60-0341	*Cordova*	SAC	FL350	15 N 172 15 W
C-135A	60-0376	*Kettle 03*	AFSWC	above clouds	

conducted ionospheric scatter tests for VHF teletype transmissions, utilizing a small three-element antenna array on each wingtip and two transmitter fairings on each side of the vertical stabilizer and on the nose of the aircraft. The program was fairly successful, with adequate transmissions out to 1,500nm (2,413km).

JKC-135A 55-3131 took part in Operation FISHBOWL as part of Project 6.10 'Large Scale Ionization Effects From High Altitude Nuclear Detonations,' a program that examined the high altitude effects of atmospheric nuclear blasts, particularly upon ICBMs, early warning radars, and C3 systems. It measured 'atmospheric and ionospheric effects' while the other three '135s measured 'thermal and optical emissions'. This test also marked the first time that a Michelson interferometer was operated successfully on an aircraft. Follow-up tests occurred between 2nd October and 1st November, with submegaton warheads detonated at high altitudes. The 2nd October test (DOMINIC I – ANDROSCOGGIN) was the 'first US nuclear test in which all the diagnostic instrumentation was contained within airborne [Lockheed] RC-121, C-130, KC-135, and the AFSWC RB-52B drop aircraft'.

SAC provided two KC-135A LOOKING GLASS airborne command posts (58-0011 and 58-0022) to serve as 'sampler control aircraft' (call signs *Cognac* and *Fake 30*, respectively) to coordinate RB-57 aerial sampling of the atomic cloud. They also played an active test role, assessing the effect of a nuclear detonation on the ability of the communications suite to fulfil its wartime mission. As such, they served as the '…relay for the UHF multiplex link between Hickam and Johnston Island. …[and were] also instrumented to test UHF FM, UHF AM, HF, SSB, and low frequency air-to-air reception in an environment created by high altitude nuclear explosions'. Boeing configured the two airplanes with the appropriate test equipment. Scheduled orbit time during the atmospheric test was ten hours at an altitude of 31,000ft (9,448m).

During the 9th July STARFISH-PRIME test, 58-0011 took part in SAC Project 7.4 'Communications Propagation Investigation Equipment', which assessed 'high-altitude nuclear blast effects on a KC-135 ABNCP and UHF, HF, and LF propagation and communication systems performance.' This measured 'nuclear effects on (1) Ground/air/ground operation of 15-channel UHF FM multiplex system; (2) Ground and airborne operation of high-powered LF system; and (3) SAC HF command communications system.' KC-135A 58-0011 functioned in the ABNCP configuration and served as an air-to-air-to-ground relay between Hickam AFB and the task force's surface ships. KC-135A 60-0341 (call sign *Cordova*) from Larson AFB, WA, served as an 'airborne transmitting platform for LF propagation tests and as an airborne receiving platform for HF and UHF tests…' Boeing installed a special 'high power' LF transmitter and trailing wire antenna (TWA) in this standard KC-135A tanker, and provided technicians to operate them during the nuclear detonation. Two PIPECLEANER radio relay EB-47Ls (52-0292 and 53-2329, call signs *Baxter* and *Byron*, respectively) provided the communications link between Hickam AFB and KC-135A 58-0011.

Test results were ominous. Although UHF communications were restored fairly rapidly, they were limited by line-of-sight and had a marginal radius of 250nm (400km). Effects on HF and LF were far more serious. HF transmissions returned to normal after two hours, but LF communications – intended for use with underground and submarine launch facilities – were still not usable after 20 hours. Given that any potential nuclear exchange would involve dozens of high-altitude bursts designed to cripple SAC's command and control of the alert force and residual aircraft, HF, LF, and later VLF equipment would require significant hardening. Moreover, the initial broadcast of the emergency action message (EAM) launching the alert force would almost certainly have to be via SAC's ground-based UHF GREEN PINE alerting system, and the planned PACCS orbits would be designed to provide UHF overlap for full connectivity.

C-135 transports, including C-135B 61-2668, carried atmospheric samples collected during the tests – sealed inside lead 'pigs' – from NAS Barber's Point, HI, back to the United States for analysis.

Opposite page:

The SPEED LIGHT-ECHO JKC-135A 55-3121 participated in the 1962 DOMINIC nuclear tests, but for all practical purposes was still a joint SAC/AFTAC asset. *Photo by Richard Sullivan via Stephen Miller*

BIG SAFARI modified 55-3136 into the DOMINIC U platform. It also conducted AFCRL projects before conversion into a standard KC-135A. *Photo by Stephen Miller*

This page:

A variety of KC-135s took part in US nuclear tests, ranging from sensor-equipped testbeds to an operational LOOKING GLASS. Some were within 50nm of the blast, others more than 500nm away.

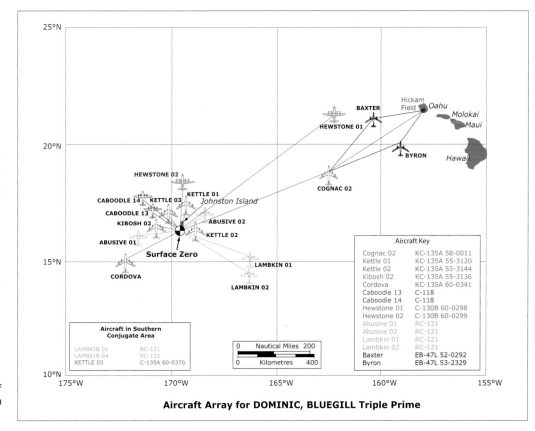

Aircraft Array for DOMINIC, BLUEGILL Triple Prime

C-135A INDIVIDUAL AIRCRAFT

60-0376 This airplane was initially delivered as a C-135A to the 1501st ATW at Travis AFB for support of the Los Alamos Laboratory, and retained MATS markings. As such, many press accounts noted that 60-0376 provided 'commuter' service for scientists and researchers traveling between Travis AFB (near the many nuclear research facilities located in Northern California) and Kirtland AFB, located near the nuclear research facilities at Los Alamos, NM. In fact, 60-0376 was actively involved in aerial research associated with nuclear weapons on behalf of the Atomic Energy Commission (AEC), and had been since at least early 1962. Along with JKC-135A 55-3135, this airplane participated in a program known only as ORSEP. The exact nature of this test, which lasted through at least June 1965, has not been identified, but it is likely associated with 'nuclear readiness testing'. The ORSEP airplanes were configured with 50-plus small windows along each side of the fuselage, earning the nickname 'piccolo tube'. C-135A 60-0376 was subsequently assigned to Wright-Patterson AFB for missions related to the US space program.

KC-135A INDIVIDUAL AIRCRAFT

55-3121 From 20th April through 9th May 1962, BIG SAFARI modified JKC-135A 55-3121 into the SPEED LIGHT-ECHO KC-135A. Following the DOMINIC series of tests, BIG SAFARI delivered it to SAC in early 1963 as a GARLIC SALT reconnaissance KC-135R, and it eventually participated in BURNING LIGHT missions.

55-3136 From 30th January through 4th April 1962, BIG SAFARI converted this KC-135A into the DOMINIC U platform. Following the DOMINIC series of tests, BIG SAFARI demodified the airplane into basic tanker configuration between 15th March and 20th May 1963. It retained enough of the wiring and other components to enable its reversion to a nuclear test role within 30 days.

58-0011 SAC KC-135A airborne command post on loan for the tests.

58-0022 SAC KC-135A airborne command post on loan as backup aircraft.

59-1514 From 6th February through 23rd March 1962, BIG SAFARI modified 59-1514 into the SPEED LIGHT-DELTA airplane. Following the DOMINIC series of tests, BIG SAFARI delivered it to SAC in early 1963 as a GARLIC SALT reconnaissance KC-135R, and it eventually participated in BURNING LIGHT missions.

60-0341 Boeing modified this KC-135A by installing electronics, communication gear, and a TWA. These were installed just for the DOMINIC series of tests and were removed thereafter.

JKC-135A INDIVIDUAL AIRCRAFT

55-3120 Modified by an unidentified agency for the 1962 FISH BOWL nuclear tests. The airplane received dozens of small windows throughout the fuselage for sensors that observed the atmospheric effects of nuclear explosions. The windows earned it the nicknames of 'piccolo tube' and 'the flying piccolo'. Antenna fairings were also added to the nose and vertical stabilizer. It retained the air refueling boom and differed little externally (other than the many small windows) from its tanker colleagues. After the DOMINIC tests, 55-3120 participated in basic science research projects.

55-3131 Originally delivered as a KC-135A tanker, this airplane was redesignated a JKC-135A on 1st February 1961 when it was reassigned to the AFCRL for ionospheric research. After the DOMINIC tests, 55-3131 participated in basic science research projects.

55-3134 In the early 1960s, this JKC-135A was assigned to the Terminal RAdiation Program (TRAP), a corollary mission to the RAdiation Monitoring Program (RAMP) conducted by JKC-135A 55-3127. It was later modified to the Midcourse Acquisition and Tracking System (TRAP-MATS) configuration, but this proved less than successful. This airplane participated in the STARFISH series of tests. By June 1963 55-3134 was fully devoted to TRAP-MATS missions.

55-3144 Originally assigned to the 93rd BW at Castle AFB, 55-3144 was transferred to ASD at Wright-Patterson AFB on 8th April 1959. It underwent conversion by an unidentified agency at MacArthur AP in Islip, NY, and was redesignated a JKC-135A on 14th June 1960. The airplane was frequently loaned to the AFCRL at Hanscom Field as a research platform supporting nuclear weapons tests, although full details of 55-3144's duties have not been declassified. It crashed on 8th August 1962, after returning from Hickam AFB following a portion of the DOMINIC series of nuclear tests (see Appendix II). This airplane appears as a standard KC-135A tanker in the refueling scene during the opening credits of Stanley Kubrick's film *Dr Strangelove: Or How I Learned to Love the Bomb and Stop Worrying*.

Believed to be part of the ORSEP project, C-135A 60-0376 was hardly a MATS transport. As early as 1962 it participated in the DOMINIC nuclear tests. *Photo by Paul Stephenson via Stephen Miller*

In this April 1962 image, JKC-135A 55-3134 is configured for the DOMINIC tests as part of JTF-8. *Photo by Jim Morrow via Steve Hill/EMCS*

The Partial Test Ban Treaty

On 7th October 1963 President Kennedy signed the Treaty Banning Nuclear Weapon Tests in the Atmosphere, in Outer Space and Under Water, known informally as the Limited Test Ban Treaty or the Partial Test Ban Treaty (PTBT). This prohibited the testing of nuclear weapons anywhere but in underground sites, and was agreed by the United States, Soviet Union, and Great Britain. France did not sign as it maintained its right to conduct atmospheric nuclear tests (at least until it detonated its first hydrogen bomb), first in French Algeria in North Africa through 1966 and subsequently in French Polynesia.

A crucial and controversial issue in the US Senate ratification of the Partial Test Ban Treaty was the ability of US assets to verify foreign compliance with the treaty and monitor any potential violation. Moreover, should the treaty be abrogated and atmospheric testing resume, treaty skeptics insisted on having a test and monitoring capability ready for immediate use. Another consideration was that of nuclear weapon burst effects on ICBMs and their warheads. During the second half of 1963, for example, AFSC informed SAC that ICBMs might be highly vulnerable to gamma ray effects from high altitude nuclear detonations. There were fears that gamma rays from a nuclear explosion might affect a missile's trajectory during the launch phase, and guidance system components might be damaged at distance up to thousands of miles when an ICBM was leaving the lower atmosphere. (A 1973 study revealed that a 5Mt high-altitude air burst would produce 25,000-50,000 volts per meter, which was sufficient to put a substantial number of unlaunched ICBMs into 'automatic restart', causing significant delays to their launch and rendering them vulnerable to destruction by inbound warheads.) SAC was equally worried about X-rays, neutron flux, and EMP. As a result of these and similar concerns, in 1964 Air Force Chief of Staff General Curtis LeMay directed AFSC to expand its nuclear studies to include all elements of ICBM vulnerability (especially the new Minuteman), with special attention given to hardened sites, launch, and flight phases. Answers to these questions would come from testbed KC-135s participating in US and monitoring foreign nuclear tests.

Consequently, the Air Force and the AEC agreed to fund three 'quick-response' airborne diagnostic airplanes as one *quid pro quo* for JCS endorsement of the PTBT. These were developed under the EARLY DAY (later RIVET DIGGER) program for the National Nuclear Test Readiness Program (NNTRP), and were maintained on constant alert, ready to deploy worldwide to analyze any actual or imminent atmospheric nuclear blast. All planning, coordination, provisioning and execution of USAF support of nuclear test operations fell under the SEEK STRAW program.

EARLY DAY/RIVET DIGGER

During early 1963 MATS transferred three C-135As to AFSC for conversion by General Dynamics into NC-135As, with a planned operational readiness date of June 1964. BIG SAFARI began the modification process in June 1963, and they were delivered in May, June, and July of 1964. Each airplane was dedicated to one of the AEC's three main laboratories: the Lawrence Livermore National Laboratory (LLNL – previously LRL), the Sandia National Laboratory (SNL), and the Los Alamos National Laboratory (LANL – previously LASL). The airplanes were part of Joint Task Force 8 (JTF-8), and assigned to the AFSWC at 'Sandia Base' at Kirtland AFB. All three airplanes were reassigned in 1969 from AFSWC to ASD, but remained based at Kirtland AFB. In 1973 they were reassigned to the 4900th TG, still at Kirtland AFB. Specific tasks included the measurement of any atomic fireball, optical and spectral data collection, and radiation analysis. Defense contractors EG&G

and the Denver Research Institute (DRI) designed much of the primary mission equipment.

NC-135As 60-0369 and 60-0370 each lacked starboard markings (such as stenciling and national insignia, although the white fuselage top remained) and would fly clockwise around the atomic blast site. This absence of markings prevented flash burns to the airplane's skin due to possible ignition of these markings as a result of the thermal flash from the detonation. NC-135A 60-0371 was devoid of markings on the port side and would fly counterclockwise around the blast site. All three had numerous windows throughout the fuselage and a four-by-four array of 16 large optically ground windows in the forward fuselage on the appropriate side in the vicinity of the cargo door. Each airplane also had a large dorsal fairing above the forward fuselage which housed a variety of electromagnetic sensors. Sensor spectra on the aircraft included infrared, ultra-violet, and optical. Three dipole antenna 'rails' ran circumferentially around a portion of the forward fuselage on the 'hot' side of the fuselage immediately aft of the cockpit.

Further modifications to the three airplanes, scheduled for completion in time for participation in Operation CROSSCHECK during late 1964, were undertaken at a cost of some $2.2 million, including a 440,000 BTU air conditioner system to cool the electronics. These addressed existing problems or shortcomings in the NC-135As such as an unreliable electrical system, weaknesses in the positional display system, addition of special telemetry equipment, and the redesign and modification of the space probe reel (which deployed a trailing package) after two probes were lost in flight. Other significant modifications were considered as well. Short runways, the NC-135's heavy operational weight, and the need for demineralized water for injected takeoffs hampered the diagnostic airplanes' operational flexibility. The 'Fan Jet Subcommittee of AEC's Aircraft Use Committee' recommended against replacing the NC-135's turbojets with turbofans despite the obvious benefits, arguing 'that fan-jet engines did not significantly improve the performance of the aircraft insofar as safety or radius of action were concerned in relation to the high cost of conversion'. The installation of a drag chute to decrease landing ground roll was considered in lieu of thrust reversers but rejected. Finally, inflight refueling was discussed. Although aware of the Air Force's 'excellent safety record during recent years in refueling aircraft in flight', the AEC was not convinced that air refueling was a viable choice because of what it perceived to be 'potential hazards to the radomes and degradation of safety during the refueling operation'. Photographs of the NC-135As, however, reveal an IFR receptacle, so this modification must have been adopted, although when remains unconfirmed.

The three newly converted EARLY DAY aircraft suffered from a crucial weakness: they were built *after* the cessation of atmospheric nuclear testing. There was no way to assess their effectiveness in collecting accurate nuclear detonation data. Baseline data collected during the DOMINIC tests, however, meant that AFSWC could create devices that simulated a nuclear flash and an EMP burst. During October 1964 AFSWC conducted Operation CROSSCHECK, a readiness test to ensure that the US could resume atmospheric nuclear testing on short notice. A 'mountain top' EMP and flash simulator, in conjunction with B-52s dropping simulated weapons, allowed AFSWC to calibrate the sensors aboard the NC-135As. Tests were conducted at Kirtland AFB, Eglin AFB, and at Johnston Island.

Results showed that the technical equipment worked as expected, but there were substantial operational problems to be overcome. For example, flight and mission crews would begin crew rest 12 hours prior to scheduled takeoff, but this meant 'that it was almost impossible to find a responsible individual with whom to discuss the flight' during the time prior to launch. Similarly, ground equipment

Right: The RIVET DIGGER airplanes were calibrated during Operation CROSSCHECK, using simulated nuclear detonations. 60-0371 suffered from multiple problems, but these were resolved and the airplane declared operational.

Below: Poor quality video screen grab of the trailing wire antenna installed on the three RIVET DIGGER aircraft, taken during an early test flight prior to the other conversions. *Both: Author's collection*

had to run continuously for days to provide electricity, hydraulics, and – most importantly – cooling for the myriad on-board systems. Existing power carts ran out of diesel fuel or overheated, and there were simply no air conditioners capable of cooling the equipment while the jets were on the ground in high-temperature, high-humidity environments. Aircraft security was equally inconsistent. Personnel with badges could board the airplane without being verified, but it was impossible to bring an urgently needed but uncleared technician onto the airplane. Detecting clouds during night operations proved troublesome, as the flares dropped from B-57 sampler aircraft were ineffective. A pulsed laser fired from the NC-135As replaced the flares with good results.

Flight operations identified other shortcomings. The B-52s drop point for the simulated weapons differed slightly from the planned drop point to be monitored by the NC-135As, resulting in the misalignment of sensors. The EMP transmitter was weaker than desired, which reduced the frequency range of the onboard sensors, and the 'Teller Light Source' generator (a Xenon candle) did not always produce the required flash. NC-135A 60-0371 seemed to have its own set of problems. It experienced considerable power spikes when turning on the EG&G cameras. The airplane could never be cooled properly. Temperature at the front of the cargo compartment was typically 40°F (4.4°C), but it was nearly 100°F (37.8°C) at the back, unsuitable for both man and machine. The communication link between NC-135A 60-0371 and the EC-121 command airplane dropped whenever the EARLY DAY airplane was in a bank away from the RC-121. Moving the antenna from the top to the bottom of 60-0371 solved this problem.

Given the results from Operation CROSSCHECK, the three laboratories (LLNL, SNL, and LANL) incorporated multiple technical changes into their respective airplanes for Operation ROUNDUP, held in the Pacific test area from 15th November through 17th December 1965. ROUNDUP was a joint DoD-AEC non-nuclear air drop exercise where B-52s dropped 'instrumented test-simulation objects while other aircraft in the drop areas simulated gathering nuclear effects data.' During the first event in this series, nicknamed CUTLASS, the NC-135As collected sample data to determine the best orbit patterns from which to gather optimum EMP signatures. CUTLASS was judged to be highly successful. The second event in the series, nicknamed SOMBRERO, sought to determine the ability of the NC-135As to collect optical and EMP data at the 'sporting' altitude of only 500ft (152m) only 12nm (22.2km) from the intended detonation point at Kingman Reef. The test was successfully completed on 2nd December. All of the NC-135As were within 2,000ft (609m) laterally of their planned range, and collected data within the prescribed stringent tracking limits.

Weather delayed the third event in the series, known as CATAPULT, which was superseded by the final event, BROADSWORD. This test was far more complicated than the previous two, and the first attempt on 9th December failed due to an equipment malfunction. BROADSWORD was finally completed on 11th December. One NC-135A flew perpendicular to the others to collect telemetry data from a companion device dropped from a B-52 9.9 seconds prior to the primary test device. Overall NC-135A systems performance was mixed: telemetry data were successfully recorded on all three NC-135As, fireball yield measurements were disappointing as cameras in only one of the three NC-135As functioned properly, and the bhangmeter tests failed completely. CATAPULT eventually took place on 16th December, reinforcing the need for improved NC-135A orbits and collection procedures. Overall, Operation ROUNDUP identified weaknesses in the ability of the NC-135As to provide accurate detonation diagnostic capability. Corrective measures were undertaken and the NC-135As operated successfully in future nuclear tests, most notably BURNING LIGHT.

NC-135A INDIVIDUAL AIRCRAFT

60-0369 This was the EARLY DAY/RIVET DIGGER 2 aircraft, and was 'sponsored' by the Los Alamos Diagnostic Laboratory. It was designed for right-hand orbits and had 33 windows along the right side of the fuselage. As with the RIVET DIGGER 1 (60-0370), it had a large dorsal fairing covering two tracking antennas, and a trailing tethered probe. This probe – like a trailing wire antenna – could be extended on Mylar line some 330ft (100m) behind the aircraft. Its duties after the RIVET DIGGER program are not known, and on 9th June 1976, 60-0369 (minus its dorsal fairing) was relegated to CTTC, and redesignated a GNC-135A ground maintenance trainer. It was cut in half after October 1991 and scrapped (see Appendix III).

60-0370 This was the EARLY DAY/RIVET DIGGER 1 aircraft, and was 'sponsored' by the Sandia National Laboratories. It was designed for right-hand orbits and had 30 windows along the right side of the fuselage. As with the RIVET DIGGER 2 (60-0369), it had the dorsal fairing that covered two tracking antennas and the trailing tethered probe. It was subsequently used for basic science research programs.

Censored photo of C-135B 61-0331 as it appeared for Project III related to French atmospheric nuclear tests. Its disappearance was likely related to the dorsal fairing. *Photo via Stephen Miller*

60-0371 This was the EARLY DAY/RIVET DIGGER 3 aircraft, and was 'sponsored' by the Lawrence Livermore Radiation Lab. It was designed for left-hand orbits and had 35 windows along the left side of the fuselage. The dorsal fairing was substantially longer, covering not only the two tracking antennas, but two SHORT TOM 'light pipes' through which LIDAR beams could be emitted. A 5ft (1.5m) parabolic reflector (known as 'Flying Bertha') was installed behind the 16 windows in the main cargo door. It was later used for a variety of basic science research, communications and navigation programs, and for research related to SDI.

BURNING LIGHT

During 1966 French atmospheric tests shifted from Algeria to the South Pacific. SAC reconnaissance KC-135Rs missions deployed to Hickam AFB monitored these tests through 1970 as part of the BURNING LIGHT program (see Chapter 10). Beginning with the 1971 NICE DOG 'season' of tests, a single AFSC C-135B (61-0331) joined the BURNING LIGHT task force as the 'Program III' aircraft. LTV converted the former TRIA C-135B by manufacturing and installing a large aluminum dorsal fairing which housed a radar antenna, inserted eleven optically ground observation windows along the starboard side of the aircraft, removed the distinctive TRIA nose radome (although it retained its distinctive theodolite markings on the forward fuselage), and installed the mission electronic and optical equipment supplied by the Air Force. LTV handed over the modified airplane to the 4950th TW on 21st May 1971. It then flew from Greenville, TX, where the modification work was undertaken, to McClellan AFB, CA, and arrived at the BURNING LIGHT task force at Hickam AFB on 3rd June. It flew a successful operational mission on 12th June, monitoring the French *Encelade* balloon burst test at Mururoa Atoll of a 440 kt MR41 thermonuclear warhead for *Redoubtable* class SLBMs. Crew for the 12th June mission comprised 12 military personnel, including the commander of the 2nd ACCS (which at the time oversaw the BURNING LIGHT task force) and, interestingly, a boom operator. There were 12 civilians on board (including four from AFCRL and three from LTV) as systems operators and manufacturer's technical representatives. Following the operational mission the crew landed at Pago Pago, American Samoa, and spent the night. The airplane departed on 13th June for Hickam AFB and disappeared en route after some five hours. The airplane had accrued only 38.2 total flight hours over the span of three flights since the LTV modification and delivery to the 4950th TW (See Appendix II).

After this tragic loss, AFSC did not return to the BURNING LIGHT Task Force until the 1973 HULA HOOP 'season.' Two NC-135As, one supporting the Defense Nuclear Agency (DNA) and one operating on behalf of the AEC, deployed to Hickam AFB from 12th-19th July, and flew operational sorties from 21st July through 28th August in conjunction with SAC KC-135Rs. Both NC-135As flew on each mission, and each was refueled by four KC-135As. The NC-135As collected information for all six of the French tests and the 1973 'season' came to a close on 16th September, and the NC-135As returned to Kirtland AFB.

The following year NC-135A 60-0369 deployed to Hickam AFB for the 1974 DICE GAME 'season', and was the only collection aircraft available for BURNING LIGHT missions. During each sortie, the NC-135A would launch in a cell with three KC-135As. Approximately 20 minutes later, KC-135A 59-1514 (now a 'Christine' refuelable tanker) would launch in a cell with two more KC-135As. In a procedure similar to what the RAF would use during the 1982 BLACK BUCK Vulcan raid on Port Stanley AP in the Falkland Islands, both 60-0369 and 59-1514 were each refueled three times en route to Mururoa Atoll. The Christine tanker then refueled the NC-135A just before it entered the collection area, providing 2.5 hours of orbit time. Overall the NC-135A flew 16.5-hour missions, and the tanker sorties were between 2 and 14 hours' duration.

However successful these missions proved to be, funding for the Task Force ran out. On 16th July 1974, the AEC and the DNA agreed to shut down BURNING LIGHT. The NC-135A returned to Kirtland AFB shortly thereafter, with six tests taking place without airborne coverage, including the final French atmospheric test – *Verseau* – taking place on 14th September 1974.

C-135B INDIVIDUAL AIRCRAFT

61-0331 Following its TRIA duties, LTV modified the airplane in 1971 to participate in monitoring atmospheric nuclear tests and the associated electromagnetic pulse as part of a classified program known as "Project III." It crashed on 13th June 1971 in the Pacific Ocean (see Appendix II).

OTHER NUCLEAR PROGRAMS

JKC-135A INDIVIDUAL AIRCRAFT

55-3135 Accepted into the test-bed program as a JKC-135A, this airplane was configured with 50-plus small windows along each side of the fuselage. It participated along with C-135A 60-0376 in the ORSEP program, likely associated with 'nuclear readiness testing'. These many windows earned these two airplanes the nickname 'piccolo tube'. While based at Kirtland AFB, 55-5135 participated in a program on behalf of the Air Force Missile Development Center known as SLEIGH RIDE, beginning 9th March 1964, an atmospheric nuclear weapons test program designed to assess ICBM vulnerability to nuclear detonations (a similar program – ARCTIC NIGHT – was previously discontinued). On 28th December 1964 the airplane was assigned to Wright-Patterson AFB, where it remained through at least late 1965.

CHAPTER NINE

Managing Nuclear War

'The President can make you a general, but only communications can make you a commander.' – *General Curtis E LeMay, 1954*

'…without communications, all I command is my desk, and that is not a very lethal weapon.' – *General Thomas S Power, 1959*

The early morning sun was low over the flat scrubland. Scudding clouds and light rain blew past the lone tower as scientists and military officials waited nervously. Careers – indeed *lives* – hinged on the successful test of a bomb that was a nearly identical copy of the one detonated in the New Mexico desert some four years earlier. This was Operation FIRST LIGHTNING, and at exactly 7 AM a 20 kt detonation illuminated the Kazakh steppe with an 'unbearably bright light'. It was 29th August 1949, and the Soviet Union just exploded its first atomic bomb. The nuclear arms race had begun.

It would be another two years before the Soviets detonated their second atom bomb, largely due to limits in their nuclear program infrastructure. During that time, Western reactions to the Soviet atomic bomb ranged from panic to paranoia, from aggression to avoidance. With the atomic genie out of the bottle on both sides of

the Iron Curtain, American military officials, policy makers, academics, and public figures debated the relative morals and merits of atomic warfare. Should Western atomic policy be defined by retaliatory use only in response to a Soviet attack on the United States? What about an attack on America's allies, particularly in Europe? If the Soviets succeeded in an atomic first strike, however, what US forces would remain for any retaliatory attack? Should Western policy be preemptive in nature, unleashed in the face of clear evidence of an imminent Soviet attack? Or if atomic warfare was inevitable, as some argued, should it not begin immediately in a preventive war, when the United States held a clear advantage over the Soviet Union in strategic forces and nuclear weapons?

These debates were also linked to the profound residual impact of 7th December 1941 on the American psyche, now made even more horrific by the fear of a 'nuclear Pearl Harbor'. After Joseph Stalin's

SAC's underground headquarters was not only vulnerable to SS-7 *Saddler* ICBMs but was outdated. Computers were as large as houses and proved cumbersome to display the limited answers they produced. It remained for humans to update huge charts, a process little different than that used by commanders for centuries. *Author's collection*

death in 1953, Soviet strategy changed under First Secretary Nikita Khrushchev from the traditional defense-in-depth strategy, so successful during the German invasion, to surprise, long-range air attacks using nuclear weapons. The 1957 launch of *Sputnik* meant that existing warning of a Soviet bomber attack – previously on the order of four to eight hours thanks to the Distant Early Warning (DEW) Line – would drop to 30 minutes in a Soviet ICBM attack. By 1960 Soviet military doctrine shifted even further away from traditional ground and air force superiority toward a nearly absolute reliance on strategic rocket forces. Soviet rhetoric added fuel to the fire. Air Marshal Konstantin A Vershinin, the Commander-in-Chief of the Soviet Air Force, boasted in 1957 that it was possible to deliver atomic weapons 'instantly to the remotest areas of any continent of the world by intercontinental ballistic missiles,' and that '[m]any of the major cities of the United States and some Western countries, may, in the event of war, be attacked by rockets and bombers as well as submarines.'

At the heart of this new direct threat to America was the degree of SAC's vulnerability to surprise attack. LeMay had little faith in the US intelligence community's ability to provide SAC with tactical warning of an imminent attack on the United States. By December 1957 the US Air Defense Command (ADC) warned the new CINCSAC General Thomas S Power that 'under many conditions no [tactical] warning could be guaranteed to any SAC base.' The immediate solution against a surprise attack was to establish a SAC ground alert force. Beginning in October 1957 SAC placed '130 aircraft on alert capable of reacting quickly to tactical warning,' which amounted to only two hours for US bases and 30 minutes for overseas bases. By December 1959 there were 519 SAC bombers and tankers on ground alert in the US and 17 foreign bases. Of these, SAC commanders believed that the 88 B-47s on overseas alert were its only 'potent early strike capability'. As such, they were initially assigned to the highest priority targets – long-range air bases and command-and-control centers believed responsible for coordinating the attack on the United States. SAC planners, however, quickly realized that by the time the B-47s reached the Russian bomber bases they would be empty. Consequently, the alert target system changed to 'government centers, heavily populated areas, and industrial complexes.'

In addition to the establishment of an alert force, SAC began a dispersal program designed to complicate Soviet targeting. This significantly improved the survivability of SAC bombers and tankers by forcing 'the enemy to increase the number of weapons he must

have to be successful, [and making] the chances of early warning greater.' Dispersal also 'reduced SAC's vulnerability to destruction by only a few weapons, [as] with only a few aircraft on a base there was less congestion and greater reaction capability.'

By 1960, as weapon technology improved and tactical warning time for ICBMs decreased to half an hour, the effectiveness of SAC's response dropped significantly. During those precious 30 minutes, the American president and his advisors had to understand that an actual attack was under way, debate the options available, reach a decision on whether or not to retaliate, and then communicate that decision to SAC forces at least 15 minutes prior to the first expected warhead impact in order to get the ground alert force of B-47s, B-52s, KC-135s, and KC-97s into the air. Once Soviet submarines equipped with sea-launched ballistic missiles or cruise missiles could target the United States, the time from first warning to initial impact dropped to as low as three minutes.

Protecting the American leadership, however, was an equally complex matter. The National Command Authority (NCA), including the President, Vice President, Secretary of Defense, and the Joint Chiefs of Staff, among others, as well as SAC's command-and-control centers, were highly vulnerable. A Soviet SS-N-6 *Serb* missile launched from a Yankee-class submarine could 'decapitate' the NCA in Washington DC as they slept. Despite being 50ft (15m) underground, SAC headquarters at Offutt AFB would almost assuredly be destroyed when the first handful of SS-7 *Saddler* ICBMs hit Nebraska. The unhardened back-up command posts for SAC's Second, Eighth, and Fifteenth Air Forces would fare even worse. Plans to improve the survivability of these Numbered Air Force (NAF) command posts found little budgetary support, however, as the primary purpose of these facilities in the event of war with the USSR was simply 'flashing the execution message to the force'; in effect, their value was limited to 'pulling the trigger' and little more.

The solutions to the dual threats of national decapitation and destruction of SAC's command facilities were the codification of a presidential succession and delegation program (begun under Eisenhower), and the implementation of a survivable airborne command post. These two efforts were closely linked. In the event of the death of the president, the only American official authorized to approve the use of nuclear weapons, someone else had to act in his stead. America's highly classified continuity of government program meant that authority to launch a retaliatory nuclear strike could eventually pass to a senior military official, quite possibly a SAC general in an airborne command post.

B-47Es such as 53-1884 from the 380th BW sat REFLEX alert in England to provide an 'early strike capability' should war erupt. They were also highly vulnerable to a sneak attack or sabotage. *Photo via Stephen Miller*

Presidential candidate John Kennedy (l) visits Offutt AFB on 21st August 1960 with Air Force Vice Chief of Staff General Curtis LeMay (c) and CINCSAC General Thomas Power (r). SAC's KC-135 LOOKING GLASS had been under evaluation since July 1960, so Kennedy's visit did not plant the seed for airborne command posts. *Author's collection*

The origin of the SAC airborne command post has become the stuff of legend. According to one version, John F Kennedy visited the SAC underground command post. Kennedy asked Power and LeMay if the underground facility was 'targetable and could it be neutralized by an enemy strategic force?' Both generals agreed that it could. Kennedy next asked how they proposed to continue positive command and control of SAC forces. Neither general offered a good answer. Apparently Kennedy then wondered aloud if SAC's 'command and control capability could be made more survivable by putting it in an aircraft.' With that suggestion, so the story goes, SAC's airborne command post was born. However quaint, this tale is simply not true. Kennedy visited Offutt AFB twice – once from 21st-22nd August 1960 as a presidential candidate, and again on 7th December 1962 as president. Serious proposals for SAC's KC-135 airborne command post were first articulated in 1959, so the Kennedy connection is just a myth. In fact, at the end of his first visit on 22nd August, he observed an alert response and, according to the Omaha *World-Herald*, 'a chartered plane carrying 30 newsmen was held up by one of SAC's new aerial command post jets which took off with General LeMay for Washington.' President Kennedy (and his successor Lyndon Johnson) would do much to expand SAC's airborne command post capability, but he certainly did not create it.

The Early Years
During a 1959 exercise SAC war gamers determined that a surprise Soviet attack on the US and its allies (e.g., UK-based B-47s and Thor IRBMs) in the early 1960s would 'decimate SAC's retaliatory capability.' Using ICBMs, IRBMs, and SLBMs in a 'bolt from the blue' scenario, Soviet forces would destroy 495 out of 521 alert bombers and all but 41 tankers and 19 ICBMs. Of the remaining 26 bombers, only 22 would reach the USSR to face some 9,000 Soviet interceptors, plus SAMs and AAA. However, given 15 minutes' warning time from the Ballistic Missile Early Warning System (BMEWS) expected to be fully operational in 1963, 196 SAC bombers (carrying 686 weapons) would survive to reach 268 targets in the Soviet Union, achieving an 81% mission effectiveness rate. This exercise also reaffirmed the fears of SAC's senior staff – not only would its strike force be crippled by an 'atomic Pearl Harbor' but SAC would be decapitated as well. SAC's command post at Offutt AFB was capable of withstanding only 25 pounds per square inch (psi) overpressure, a key measurement of survivability of an atomic blast. However, it required at least a 100psi capability to resist

a direct hit by Soviet megaton warheads. Not only was SAC's strike force at risk by a surprise attack, but the ability of SAC leaders to launch and execute the force was compromised as well.

SAC's commanders were fully aware of these vulnerabilities and began multiple initiatives to redress them well before this 1959 war game. On 14th December 1955 Air Force Chief of Staff General Nathan F Twining approved 'in principal' SAC's request for a ground alert program, including overseas alert basing for its B-36s and B-47s. Initial tests between November 1956 and December 1957 at Hunter AFB, GA, Little Rock AFB, AR, and Mountain Home AFB, ID, validated the concept of a 24-hour ground alert force. By May 1960 some 30% of SAC's strike force was on ground alert. Moreover, SAC had begun tests of an airborne alert initiative from January through June 1959 in CURTAIN RAISER (utilizing B-36s from Ramey AB, Puerto Rico), which would ultimately culminate in the CHROME DOME 'airborne alert indoctrination' program. With sufficient BMEWS warning time, SAC was confident that these measures would mitigate the vulnerability of the strike force to surprise attack.

Plans to address the exposure of the SAC Command Posts at Offutt AFB and the NAF Headquarters at Westover AFB, MA, Barksdale AFB, LA, and March AFB, CA, involved substantial 'hardening' of each facility. Funding for any such construction, however, died in Congress, leaving the existing command post structures at risk. Congress did fund an effort to duplicate the SAC Command Post at Offutt AFB with the proposed Deep Underground Support Center (DUSC), a 40,000ft^2 (3,716m^2) command post buried 3,500ft (1,067m) underground. Scheduled for completion in 1965, it would be located near Pawnee City, NE, and was designed to withstand a 100Mt hit within a 0.5nm (0.93km) circular error probable (CEP).

SAC was also committed to a fully automated command-and-control capability, which would provide real-time operational status for the entire command. Early efforts to use an IBM 704 computer had failed miserably. The proposed SAC Control System (SACCS) would be based on the System 465L, designed to provide 'information and data to aid in war planning, command post exercises, flight path planning, missile employment, trajectory computations, war gaming, strike and restrike planning, damage assessments, reporting of readiness, and logistics status of [SAC's] force.' Planned for an initial operational capability (IOC) of 1st April 1963 and fully operational by 1st January 1965, SACCS would provide a robust pre-attack ability to command SAC's forces.

All of these efforts, however, addressed only future operational capabilities, leaving a three- to four-year gap in SAC's ability to survive a surprise attack. Until then, SAC needed some mechanism to ensure that if a Soviet attack took place SAC's commanders could issue the presidential order to execute the Emergency War Plan (EWP – later the SIOP). This requirement led to System 481L, the Post Attack Command and Control System (PACCS), which included both ground-based and airborne components.

Along with other dedicated ground communications networks, the GREEN PINE System 488L provided direct links between Offutt AFB and 'remote UHF stations' at SAC and dispersal bases, as well as to airborne assets within UHF range. GREEN PINE functioned as an extension of SAC's Primary Alerting System (PAS). [In perhaps the ultimate 'cool' ground-based PACCS component, SAC Brigadier General Ken Keller announced on 27th February 1992 the existence of a classified fleet of truck convoys, called the Secure Enduring Command Center (SECC) system. These SAC '18-wheelers' were designed for communications, war planning, battle management, and intelligence analysis.]

The PACCS aerial component began with a 1959 study that assessed 'the feasibility of placing a command and control element in an airborne posture.' This led to the COVERALL airborne command post (ABNCP) program, which offered the immediate ability to issue the EWP execution order in the event SAC's ground-based command centers were incapacitated. In what would become SAC's 'number one' priority for survival, General Power ordered the establishment of an airplane 'on 15 minute [ground] alert by 1st July 1960,' and that it be fully integrated with plans for the airborne alert force then under consideration.

SAC selected five KC-135As (58-0007, 58-0011, 58-0018, 58-0019, and 58-0022) assigned to the 34th AREFS, 4321st SW at Offutt AFB to be modified, with three as 'command post vehicles' and two additional aircraft as backups. The first of these (58-0022) arrived at OCAMA on 15th April 1960. Modification began four days later and was finished on 26th May. The work consisted of installing the following:

- Dual radio operator positions on the right side of the cargo compartment approximately station 490 with equipment, console, work table, chairs, lights, oxygen and interphone facilities, including loudspeakers.
- Three sets of AN/ARC-58 radio equipment on the console with controls accessible to both operators and circuits designed to allow variations in control configuration.
- Two additional AN/ARC-34 controls on the console to allow radio operators to control the existing AN/ARC-34 command radio sets.
- A 7-channel recorder on the console [to] record all frequencies being monitored continuously for 13 hours.
- Two AN/ARC-58 antenna couplers and one antenna mast aft of the main cargo door at approximately station 580.
- A long wire antenna between the new antenna mast and the vertical stabilizer.
- A conference table on the right side of the cargo compartment at station 620 with four chairs, lights, oxygen, interphone facilities, including loudspeakers. Interphone systems [were] designed so that all six radio sets being monitored [could] be operated from the conference table.
- One each Univac coupler on vertical stabilizer and connect to existing probe antenna.

By 31st May two aircraft (58-0022 and 58-0019) had returned to Offutt AFB, and operational testing began on 1st July 1960 (nearly two months before Kennedy's visit!). One airborne command post was launched twice weekly on a no-notice basis for flights of approximately five hours. The initial command post team consisted only of a general officer, a senior controller (a Lieutenant Colonel or Major), a communications officer (a Captain), a duty controller (a Technical Sergeant or above), and two enlisted radio operators. Missions demonstrated connectivity with SAC's communications network and the JCS, as well as verified the reliability of existing and proposed command-and-control procedures codified in SAC LOOKING GLASS Operational Order (OpOrd) 33-61. From 5th-28th July 1960, the airplanes flew 13 alert missions, with nine more flown in August. In November 1960 the airplanes and crews started 48-hour ground alert tours with random launches. Orbits remained within the general vicinity of Offutt AFB, extending southward to Kansas City, MO. The tests proved quite successful, and KC-135A command posts began continuous 24-hour-a-day airborne missions on 3rd February 1961 with the first sortie flown by aircraft commander Major Richard M Snow, founding the LOOKING GLASS legacy. The 'Glass' flew two 12-hour 30-minute sorties a day, with takeoff times at 1000 and 2200 hrs. This changed on 10th May 1961 to three daily sorties lasting 8.5 hours with takeoff times at 0000, 0800, and 1600 hrs.

All of SAC's rated general officers (except the CINC and VCINC) were assigned to an airborne command post mission once every ten days as the 'Airborne Senior Emergency Action Officer', later renamed the Airborne Emergency Action Officer (AEAO). The AEAO was an integral part of SAC's continuity of command. In case of war, according to a 1962 SAC history, 'the CINCSAC could launch the SAC strike force under positive control and could execute, divert, or commit SAC forces upon direction of higher authority. Only the President could authorize the use of nuclear weapons.' This meant that the CINCSAC could order SAC aircraft to take off and proceed on their SIOP routes, but they could not pass their 'fail safe' points and execute their SIOP mission (positive control of the force). Upon the express order of the President or his successor under the national continuity of government plan, the CINCSAC would then direct the SAC force to execute their mission (drop bombs, launch ICBMs, etc). Given the tenuous survivability of SAC Headquarters in a nuclear attack, succession of the CINCSAC was a critical issue. The Vice CINCSAC was first in this chain, followed by the Lieutenant Generals commanding the three NAFs (precedence based on date of rank), and finally by the AEAO. Early on, each AEAO would be on 24-hour telephone alert at a facility near the aircraft, ready to launch as directed. Once the 'Glass' began continuous airborne operations, the AEAO flew on every mission.

Air Force policy required that an instructor pilot (IP) with access to the flight controls accompany all generals who were pilots and wished to fly the airplane during takeoff, landing, and air refueling. Consequently, beginning in November 1960 every LOOKING GLASS aircraft commander was also an IP. Typically the IP offered the AEAO the opportunity to make the takeoff or landing (and air refueling if there was one). If the AEAO accepted, he usually sat in the left seat with the IP in the right seat. If the AEAO declined, the IP sat in the left seat and the copilot took his normal place in the right seat. Not surprisingly, copilots spent most takeoffs, landings, and air refuelings watching from the jump seat. At least four LOOKING GLASS front-end crewmembers – Walt Ratliff, Gene Buzard, Larry Mitchell, and Lou Buckman – later became general officers and flew as the AEAO. There were also two 'father-son' AEAOs, including Lieutenant General James Keck and Brigadier General Tom Keck, and Brigadier Generals George Cole and George Cole, Jr. In 1995 Brigadier General Tiiu Kera, USSTRATCOM's Director of Intelligence, became the first female AEAO. General Jack Watkins reportedly flew the most AEAO sorties, logging more than 900 flights (totaling an amazing 7,650 hours of flying time).

PACCS provided SAC with the necessary 'command and control survivability under conditions of nuclear attack, and was the primary means of control in carrying out' the EWP. According to a 1962 SAC history, PACCS – primarily the ABNCP, the DUSC, and 'a multiplicity of survivable communications,' would 'enable the CINCSAC to (1) keep in contact with the President or national decision-making authority; (2) analyze enemy attacks; (3) assess results of US strikes; and (4) direct residual forces.' Pending completion of the DUSC, SAC requested a train to function as an 'interim mobile support center', although this proposal was shelved on 20th February 1962.

Beginning in April 1962 PACCS underwent the first of four major reorganizations, expanding to include three KC-135A auxiliary command post (AUXCP) units and four radio relay support squadrons. The AUXCPs were assigned to tanker squadrons based at NAF headquarters with the Eighth Air Force at Westover AFB (99th AREFS, 499th BW), the Second Air Force at Barksdale AFB (913th AREFS, 2nd BW), and the Fifteenth Air Force at March AFB (22nd AREFS, 22nd BW), where they assumed ground alert. They would launch upon declaration of DEFCON II (or higher) or as directed by the CINCSAC.

The Eighth Air Force aircraft served as the East Auxiliary Command Post (EASTAUX) with the static call sign *Achieve*. During alert launches the airplane would taxi to the end of the runway at Westover AFB and await the battle staff, which was located in the 'Notch', an adjacent secure facility in Bare Mountain. Once they were on board, the airplane would launch to its orbit over Wilkes-Barre, PA. The Second Air Force aircraft served as the Central Auxiliary Command Post (CENTAUX) with the static call sign *Grayson*. The Fifteenth Air Force aircraft was the West Auxiliary Command Post (WESTAUX) and used the static call sign *Stepmother* (one WESTAUX sortie claims the record for the shortest-duration alert flight of 18 minutes thanks to an in-flight fire. The crew landed safely and bag-dragged to the spare). The *Stepmother* orbit was northeast of Las Vegas, NV, generally over the Grand Canyon to the Nevada-Utah border. The vast distances between these NAF orbits and Offutt AFB prompted SAC on 20th July 1962 to organize four EB-47L support squadrons at Mountain Home AFB, ID, Lincoln AFB, NE, Lockbourne AFB, OH, and Plattsburgh AFB, NY. The copilot on these 36 PIPECLEANER aircraft served as the monitor/operator of the automated radio gear which provided a link between the primary and secondary airborne command posts as well as ground facilities.

The growth and success of the LOOKING GLASS airborne command post program created unexpected problems. Improvements to the ground alert force (including an increase to 50% alert) and the ongoing CHROME DOME airborne alert reassured SAC's leaders that the alert force would be ready to launch within the 15-minute window created by early warning from the BMEWS. SAC commanders were worried, however, about their ability to transmit the 'go code' to CHROME DOME aircraft in remote airspace such as crossing oceans or in the high Arctic where HF reception was unreliable and UHF reception of ground-based transmissions was non-existent. The solution was to transmit the message from SAC missiles carrying the Emergency Rocket Communications System (ERCS). Beginning two minutes after launch, an onboard UHF transmitter would send the Emergency Action Message (EAM) 'go code' which could be remotely updated prior to launch as required from SAC Headquarters (and eventually from the LOOKING GLASS). Transmission would continue for approximately 27 minutes. ERCS testing began at Vandenberg AFB, CA, in early 1962 as part of the BEANSTALK program, and achieved Initial Operational Capability (IOC) on 1st January 1963 using Blue Scout IRBMs launched from Wisner, West Point, and Tekamah (all sites in Nebraska), but their broadcast range was severely circumscribed. These launch sites were later moved to

Hastings, NE, Ft Riley, KS, and Ottumwa, IA, which increased the range somewhat. It was not until ERCS was installed on six Minutemen ICBMs based at Whiteman AFB, MO, and configured with two 1,000-watt UHF transmitters that EAM coverage included the Mediterranean Sea and Alaska where B-52s on CHROME DOME routes were least able to receive the UHF message.

Multiple early warning systems were designed to ensure that the alert force would not be caught on the ground, but these were subject to failure or were unreliable. The Bomb Alarm System (BAS), for example, was designed to detect atomic blasts at key locations. Unfortunately, it was plagued with false alarms (known as 'Triple Ambers' because the illumination of three amber lights on a central warning panel was considered a valid detection of an atomic blast) and eventually discontinued.

The critical 15 minutes of warning time needed to launch SAC's alert force required absolutely reliable communications between SAC and NORAD and the BMEWS sites at Thule AB, Clear AFS, AK, and RAF Fylingdales, England. A Soviet pre-emptive attack on the Thule facility, whether an overt military strike or a covert sabotage mission, would break this link and eliminate any advance warning. Soviet ICBMs would then catch SAC's alert force on the ground, all but guaranteeing a successful Soviet first strike without fear of any meaningful US retaliatory strike. This vulnerability created a significant dilemma for SAC commanders. If the Thule link disappeared, should SAC launch the bomber alert force under positive control to ensure its survival? This was certainly a prudent choice, but so too was it a provocative choice (not to mention expensive). The implication for the soon-to-be-operational US ICBM force was even more staggering. If the Thule link dropped out, should SAC and NORAD commanders advise the President to order the pre-emptive launch of the Atlas (and later Titan and Minuteman) fleet, an irreversible start to global thermonuclear war? In the illogic of nuclear war calculations, that might be the correct decision if Thule had been destroyed or disabled as part of an impending Soviet attack. But what if the link was broken because a circuit failed somewhere, or a powerful auroral storm disrupted atmospheric radio communications, or, just as likely, an airman spilled his coffee on a critical piece of equipment? SAC could ill afford any disruption in communication with Thule, whether by design or by accidental disruption.

The solution was simple: an airborne backup monitor of the Thule BMEWS station. A SAC airplane – normally a B-52 on airborne alert – would orbit above the station at Thule, where its crew would

The distance between the KC-135A airborne command post orbits over Pennsylvania and Utah and the LOOKING GLASS over Kansas required EB-47L PIPECLEANER radio relay aircraft. They served from 1962-1965 and were then replaced by EC-135As and EC-135Ls. *Photo by Stephen Miller*

B-52Cs from the 99th BW at Westover AFB flew CHROME DOME missions that included a THULE MONITOR orbit over Thule AB to verify that it was still operational in the event communication was broken with SAC and NORAD. *Photo by Thomas Cuddy II via Stephen Miller*

visually observe the radar antennae and supporting buildings. Should communications be lost between Thule and SAC Headquarters or NORAD, the orbiting B-52 would inform SAC by HF radio if the remote facility had been hit by a Soviet sneak attack or if the base was just experiencing a communications failure (no documents reveal what flight crews were to do in the event the BMEWS site was obscured by cloud cover or a blizzard). Confusion about the BMEWS observer – also known as the THULE MONITOR – led to the mistaken belief that that '… the Thule Monitor was an elaborately equipped KC-135 always flying above Thule, Greenland, as an alternate advance station should the ground radar center be wiped out'. THULE MONITOR was far from being an 'elaborately equipped KC-135' airborne command post, and was instead simply a SAC aircraft acting as an airborne observer.

SAC began non-continuous monitoring of Thule in August 1961 with two B-52 sorties per day as part of the CHROME DOME airborne alert indoctrination program. The bomber (initially a B-52C from the 99th BW at Westover AFB) would spend a portion of its mission orbiting above Thule. If the B-52 was delayed on the ground or unable to fulfill this duty, then the KC-135A mission from Eielson AFB scheduled to refuel the B-52 on the GHOST CABIN air refueling track would take over as monitor until the B-52 (or its replacement) was airborne. On 6th November 1961, B-52 coverage of Thule increased to 21 out of 24 hours.

The value of the THULE MONITOR was quickly realized. During the 'Black Forest' incident of 24th November 1961, SAC experienced simultaneous communication failures with both Thule BMEWS and NORAD due to a technical problem at the Colorado Springs, CO, switching station. SAC placed its alert force in a ready-to-launch posture (engines running at the runway hold line), pending receipt of a valid positive control launch message. A B-52C monitor from Westover AFB confirmed that Thule BMEWS was still there and operating normally. After a short time, the link was reestablished and the alert force returned to its normal DEFCON 4 posture. Additional THULE MONITOR 'saves' include one on 15th April 1964, also due to technical problems.

A modified route went into service on 15th January 1962, becoming the only CHROME DOME route over Canada. Three months later, on 1st April, B-52Gs from the 42nd BW at Loring AFB with longer endurance replaced the B-52Cs from Westover AFB to provide 24-hour Thule coverage. If a B-52G aborted, a designated ground alert KC-135A from SAC's 'Northeast complex' (Griffiss

AFB, Loring AFB, or Westover AFB, as well as the tanker task force at Goose AB, Canada) would launch to provide continuous BMEWS surveillance, eliminating the need for the Eielson AFB KC-135A to fulfill this duty. Effective 1st July 1966 SAC changed the name for the airborne alert indoctrination program from CHROME DOME to GIANT WHEEL, and created the separate name BUTTER KNIFE to refer to the continuous monitoring of Thule. Nonetheless, the oversight of Thule was primarily a B-52 rather than a KC-135 mission. By 1st April 1968, however, the 6th SW at Eielson AFB flew three daily eight-hour KC-135 missions (Sorties 81, 82, and 83), providing 24-hour visual coverage of the BMEWS site at Clear AFS, but this monitor mission ended in December 1968 when the entire SAC airborne alert program was terminated.

The DUSC was canceled on 4th April 1963, meaning that SAC would have to rely exclusively on its airborne command posts. Paradoxically, in Congressional testimony during early 1963, SAC emphasized the weakness of its ABNCPs to justify funding for the DUSC, contradicting its own glowing assessment of the PACCS program. 'The airborne command post is limited to alert execution of the force, primarily the airborne alert force. It has no planning or control capability; its prime purpose is to ensure that the execution message is issued. Strategic Air Command [cannot] plan on a future war being a one-shot effort. Basic to the command function [is] the capability to control forces prior to and after initiation of hostilities.'

PACCS was equally affected by substantial changes in US national security policy, first articulated in JCS Plan JCSP-63, which called for 'gradations of conflict below all-out nuclear war while stressing flexibility and selective, controlled nuclear response.' This was also the conceptual basis for the revised SIOP-63, which included both Major Attack Options (MAOs) and Selective Attack Options (SAOs), replacing the existing EWP's 'all-out, launch everything available' strategy referred to by physicist and nuclear pundit Herman Kahn as 'wargasm'. PACCS would now have to provide the necessary command and control capability to 'monitor [SIOP] forces during the initial strike, to analyze results of strikes, to direct recovery of aircraft, and to plan additional strikes.' In short, this would give the United States the ability to absorb a Soviet first strike and still retain a robust retaliatory command-and-control capability. To do so, however, the planned 'Phase IV' and 'Phase V' ABNCPs would need a miniaturized airborne duplicate of the 465L ground-based computer which filled a substantial portion of SAC Headquarters, an unrealistic requirement. Consequently, on 13th March 1964 SAC submitted its

Advanced ABNCP (AABNCP) proposal for an airplane large enough to carry a computer the size of a house, eventually leading to the Boeing E-4 program.

The success of SAC's ABNCP effort generated considerable envy among other senior military and civilian commanders. During 1961 and 1962 the VC-137As assigned to presidential support as 'Air Force One' provided swift and comfortable travel for the president and his entourage, but had no meaningful capability to function as an airborne command post in the event of a national emergency. The National Command Authority had no airborne platform comparable to SAC's commander. Consequently, Secretary of Defense McNamara directed that a National Emergency Airborne Command Post (NEACP) be evaluated during 1962. The first airplane (KC-135A 61-0274) was delivered as the NIGHT WATCH I to the 1000th ACCS, 1001st ABW at Andrews AFB on 19th February 1962, and assumed an alert posture on 1st March. Impressed with the NEACP, on 13th April the JCS specified that three modified KC-135As would be located at Andrews AFB under JCS – not SAC – control. Beginning in mid 1962, Boeing delivered three KC-135A Phase II NIGHT WATCH II NEACPs (61-0282, 61-0285, and 61-0291) under contract AF34(601)-12086 to the 1000th ACCS. On 1st July 1962 the first of these new airplanes went on 24-hour alert, and on 25th July NIGHT WATCH Phase II was declared operational. By the end of 1962 NIGHT WATCH airplanes had been on satellite alert and conducted routine training at Griffiss AFB, NY, and Blytheville AFB, AR, and demonstrated on overseas capability by deploying to Rabat IAP, Morocco, and Torrejon AB, Spain.

From 8th-17th May, SAC's LOOKING GLASS and the NEACP KC-135A participated in the WHIP LASH JCS command post exercise to 'test initiating and reporting procedures required for execution of contingency plans and the start of general war.' This led the other US theater CINCs with nuclear authority – the Atlantic Commander (CINCLANT), the European Commander (CINCEUR), and the Pacific Commander (CINCPAC) – to request their own KC-135A ABNCPs. CINCEUR had previously requested two additional C-118s to augment its five SILK PURSE airborne command posts, and that the airplanes be given an airborne alert role. The JCS denied this request, and recommended instead to the Secretary of Defense that CINCEUR replace its ageing C-118 ABNCPs with KC-135As. These external demands for KC-135s conflicted with General Power's goal to replace SAC's EB-47Ls with additional new-build KC-135Bs. Power wanted to retire the EB-47L fleet due to its limited endurance, lack of space for new equipment, and extensive transmitter failures (indeed, a radio maintenance technician routinely flew on PIPECLEANER missions to repair the radios). McNamara rejected Power's plan, and directed on 26th June 1964 that 10 KC-135A

Boeing delivered KC-135A 61-0285 as a Phase II NIGHT WATCH II NEACP. They were declared operational in July 1962, providing an airborne command post for the JCS. *Photo by Frank MacSorley via Stephen Miller*

ABNCPs be assigned to CINCEUR and CINCPAC (five each). SAC would keep five of its KC-135A ABNCPs and could modify an additional five KC-135A tankers into radio relay aircraft to be stationed at Ellsworth AFB, SD, and at Lockbourne AFB, leaving Power with a significant dilemma. Converting five KC-135As would indeed enhance the PACCS mission but would also eliminate an equal number of B-52 SIOP sorties due to the loss of their mated tanker. Power opted for PACCS.

To this end, by 1963 Boeing modified eight additional KC-135As (61-0262, 61-0278, 61-0287, 61-0289, 61-0293, 61-0297, 63-7994, and 63-8001) into airborne command posts. Two more (62-3570 and 62-3579) were so configured the next year, and the last KC-135A airborne command post was delivered to the 34th AREFS on 19th February 1964. The original LOOKING GLASS KC-135As remained operational at Offutt AFB throughout most of 1964 even as Boeing delivered the more advanced KC-135Bs to the 34th AREFS beginning 2nd July 1964. Flight crews quickly became qualified in the new airplanes and the new systems were accepted for operational use.

The new KC-135Bs offered considerable improvements in flight and mission capability. They were equipped with TF33-P-9s without thrust reversers, allowing for greater basic weight with a commensurate upgrade in takeoff performance. They also had an IFR system installed, which the initial KC-135A ABNCPs did not. Improvements to mission equipment included 'multiplex avionics enabling the handling of many transmissions simultaneously on a single carrier frequency'. Communications monitoring was improved to semi-automatic from the earlier manual monitoring system. The airplanes had a five-man flight crew of pilot, copilot, navigator, boom operator, and an in-flight passenger specialist, plus a back-end battle staff composed of a SAC general as the AEAO, an operations planner, an intelligence staff member, a material operations controller (with assistant), a teleprinter operator, a communication controller, and three radio engineers. Later crew makeup included an additional operations planner, intelligence officer, and logistics planner.

The last KC-135A LOOKING GLASS sortie was flown on 2nd September 1964. When the 34th AREFS finally transferred all LOOKING GLASS duties to Det 1, 55th SRW on 25th June 1966, it had flown 50,000 accident-free hours with 5,800 takeoffs and landings, and had a mission reliability rate of 99.99% (one 'Glass' landed briefly in 1963 to drop off a critically ill crewmember; another such landing took place in 1972).

KC-135A INDIVIDUAL AIRCRAFT

58-0007 Delivered to the Air Force on 20th February 1959 and assigned to the 34th AREFS at Offutt AFB on 26th February. During 1960 it became one of the five original LOOKING GLASS KC-135A airborne command posts. It was redesignated an EC-135A on 1st January 1965.

58-0011 Delivered to the Air Force on 27th February 1959 and arrived at the 34th AREFS at Offutt AFB on 3rd March. It was one of the five original KC-135As modified into an airborne command post. On 24th June 1960 it became the fourth original KC-135A modified into a LOOKING GLASS airborne command post. It received the enhanced LOOKING GLASS Phase IV modification on 15th April 1963. It was redesignated an EC-135A on 1st January 1965.

58-0018 Handed over to the Air Force on 4th March 1959 and delivered to the 34th AREFS at Offutt AFB on 11th March. It was one of the five original LOOKING GLASS KC-135As. The airborne command post suite was installed by 9th June 1960. On 1st January 1965 it was redesignated an EC-135A.

58-0019 Delivered to the Air Force on 5th March 1959 and assigned to the 34th AREFS at Offutt AFB on 10th March. It became one of the five original LOOKING GLASS KC-135A airborne command posts on 28th May 1960. From 22nd July through 11th September 1964, 58-0019 was loaned to the 1000th ACCS at Andrews AFB, thereafter returning to Offutt AFB. On 1st January 1965 it was redesignated an EC-135A.

58-0022 Handed over to the Air Force on 19th March 1959 and delivered to the 34th AREFS at Offutt AFB on 20th March. It became the first LOOKING GLASS KC-135A after installation of the airborne command post suite ending on 26th May 1960. It was redesignated an EC-135A on 1st January 1965.

61-0261 On 28th August 1967 this KC-135A was assigned to the 906th AREFS at Minot AFB as a KC-135A airborne command post. Following modification by Lockheed it was redesignated an as EC-135L on 25th September 1967.

61-0262 Delivered to the Air Force on 23rd January 1962 for installation of its airborne command post suite after 26th January. Assigned on 4th April 1962 to the 34th AREFS at Offutt AFB. From 9th October 1963 through 8th July 1964, it was assigned to the 22nd AREFS at March AFB, and until 2nd September 1964 with the 913th AREFS at Barksdale AFB. It was then transferred to the 99th AREFS at Westover AFB. On 1st January 1965 it was redesignated an EC-135A.

61-0263 On 10th August 1967 this KC-135A was assigned to the 906th AREFS at Minot AFB as an airborne command post. Following modification by Lockheed it was redesignated as an EC-135L on 16th October 1967.

61-0269 On 18th September 1967, this KC-135A was assigned to the 906th AREFS at Minot AFB as an airborne command post. Following modification by Lockheed it was redesignated an EC-135L on 30th October 1967.

61-0274 Boeing is believed to have converted this KC-135A into a NEACP during mid-1962. It was the first NEACP delivered to the 1000th ACCS, arriving there on 19th February 1962, assuming alert on 1st March 1962. On 6th September 1967 LTV began conversion of this airplane into an EC-135H.

61-0278 This KC-135A was delivered on 1st February 1962 and assigned to the 34th AREFS at Offutt AFB as an airborne command post the following day. On 9th October 1963 it was reassigned to the 22nd AREFS at March AFB. It was redesignated an EC-135A on 1st January 1965.

61-0279 On 9th July 1965 this KC-135A was assigned to the 28th AREFS, 28th BW at Ellsworth AFB as an airborne command post. From 2nd August through 27th October 1965 Lockheed converted it into an EC-135L.

61-0281 Boeing delivered this KC-135A ABNCP on 12th February 1962. On 30th June 1966 it was redesignated as an EC-135L.

61-0282 Boeing converted this tanker into a KC-135A NEACP by 11th June 1962 when it was assigned to the 1000th ACCS. Redesignated an EC-135A on 16th November 1964.

61-0283 On 7th July 1965 this KC-135A was assigned to the 28th AREFS, 28th BW at Ellsworth AFB as an airborne command post. Following modification by Lockheed it was redesignated an EC-135L on 16th August 1965.

61-0285 Boeing converted this tanker into a KC-135A NEACP prior to its delivery to the Air Force on 12th March 1962. It was redesignated EC-135A on 16th November 1964.

61-0286 Boeing converted this KC-135A into an ABNCP with delivery on 9th March 1962. From 20th March through 19th September 1967, E-Systems modified this into the SILK PURSE configuration, but its MDS was not changed. It was then stored at Martin-Marietta, in Baltimore, MD, until 23rd February 1968. On 2nd March 1968 its MDS was changed to EC-135H.

61-0287 This KC-135A was delivered to the Air Force on 12th March 1962 and assigned to the 34th AREFS at Offutt AFB on 28th March as an airborne command post. On 10th January 1964 it was reassigned to the 22nd AREFS at March AFB. It was transferred on 30th November 1964 to the 32nd AREFS at Lockbourne AFB. On 1st January 1965 it was redesignated an EC-135A.

61-0288 Boeing converted this KC-135A into an ABNCP with delivery on 4th April 1962. On 1st December 1967 it was delivered to Lockheed for modification, and on 9th January 1968 was redesignated an EC-135L.

61-0289 This KC-135A was delivered to the 34th AREFS at Offutt AFB on 11th April 1962 as an airborne command post. Transferred on 31st January 1964 to the 99th AREFS at Westover AFB. On 1st January 1965 it was redesignated as an EC-135A.

61-0291 Boeing delivered this KC-135A tanker to the Air Force on 13th April 1962, although it remained at Boeing's Moses Lake facility until 20th April. Boeing converted 61-0291 into a NEACP beginning 29th June 1962, and it served with the 1000th ACCS. On 15th August 1966 it was transferred to LTV Electrosystems for conversion to an EC-135H.

Delivery of KC-135B 62-3584 *Miss AKSARBEN* ('Nebraska' spelled backward; an Omaha philanthropic organization) on 29th June 1964. Its stay at Offutt AFB was brief as it was assigned to the 913th AREFS at Barksdale AFB three days later. *Photo P36108 courtesy Boeing*

Ask any pilot to explain something about flying and invariably he (or she) will use his hands. Other than the OFFICE BOY KC-135A-IIs, KC-135Bs equipped for receiver air refueling were still a novelty. 62-3581 prior to delivery. *Photo P35868 courtesy Boeing*

61-0293 Delivered to the Air Force on 4th May 1962 and assigned to the 34th AREFS at Offutt AFB on 31st July 1962 as an airborne command post. On 4th March 1964 it was transferred to the 99th AREFS at Westover AFB. It was redesignated an EC-135A on 1st January 1965.

61-0297 Delivered to the Air Force on 9th May 1962 and assigned to the 34th AREFS at Offutt AFB on 10th August 1962 as an airborne command post. Transferred on 21st July 1964 to the 913th AREFS at Barksdale AFB, and reassigned on 14th December 1964 to the 28th AREFS at Ellsworth AFB. On 1st January 1965 it was redesignated an EC-135A.

61-0302 Boeing converted this KC-135A into an ABNCP, with delivery on 14th June 1962. Lockheed modified it into an EC-135L by 11th December 1967.

62-3570 Delivered on 1st July 1963 and assigned to the 34th AREFS at Offutt AFB on 14th November 1963 as an airborne command post. On 5th August 1964 it was transferred to the 913th AREFS at Barksdale AFB. Reassigned on 30th November 1964 to the 28th AREFS at Ellsworth AFB. Subsequently converted and redesignated an EC-135G on 14th February 1966.

62-3579 Delivered on 2nd August 1963 and assigned to the 34th AREFS at Offutt AFB on 10th December as an airborne command post. Transferred on 2nd September 1964 to the 1000th ACCS at Andrews AFB. It was redesignated an EC-135A on 1st January 1965.

63-7994 Delivered to the Air Force on 17th October 1963 and assigned to the 34th AREFS at Offutt AFB on 17th January 1964 as an airborne command post. Transferred on 18th August 1964 to the 913th AREFS at Barksdale AFB, and reassigned on 30th November 1964 to the 28th AREFS, 28th BW at Ellsworth AFB. Subsequently converted and redesignated an EC-135G on 3rd May 1966.

63-8001 Delivered on 18th November 1963 and assigned to the 34th AREFS at Offutt AFB on 19th February 1964 as an airborne command post. Reassigned on 14th December 1964 to the 28th AREFS, 28th BW at Ellsworth AFB. Converted and redesignated an EC-135G on 3rd May 1966.

KC-135B INDIVIDUAL AIRCRAFT

(KC-135Bs delivered after 1st January 1965 were designated as EC-135Cs.)

62-3581 Delivered 'on paper' to SAC on 28th February 1964 but not handed over until 29th September 1964, and assigned to the 22nd AREFS at March AFB. Redesignated an EC-135C on 1st January 1965.

62-3582 Delivered 'on paper' to SAC on 5th June 1964, but not handed over until 16th September 1964, and assigned to the 22nd AREFS at March AFB. Redesignated an EC-135C on 1st January 1965.

62-3583 Delivered 21st July 1964 to the 22nd AREFS at March AFB. Redesignated an EC-135C on 1st January 1965.

62-3584 Delivered 29th June 1964 and arrived at the 913th AREFS at Barksdale AFB on 2nd July. Redesignated an EC-135C on 1st January 1965.

62-3585 Delivered 24th July 1964 to the 913th AREFS at Barksdale AFB. Redesignated an EC-135C on 1st January 1965.

63-8046 Delivered 13th August 1964 to the 913th AREFS at Barksdale AFB. Redesignated an EC-135C on 1st January 1965.

63-8047 Delivered 26th August 1964 to the 99th AREFS at Westover AFB. Redesignated an EC-135C on 1st January 1965.

63-8048 Delivered to SAC on 14th September 1964 and arrived at the 34th AREFS at Offutt AFB on 30th September. Redesignated an EC-135C on 1st January 1965.

63-8049 Delivered to SAC on 5th October 1964 and arrived at the 34th AREFS at Offutt AFB on 23rd October. Redesignated an EC-135C on 1st January 1965.

63-8050 Delivered to SAC on 23rd September 196, and arrived at the 34th AREFS at Offutt AFB on 30th September. Redesignated an EC-135C on 1st January 1965.

63-8051 Delivered to SAC on 12th November 1964 and arrived at the 34th AREFS at Offutt AFB on 13th November. Redesignated an EC-135C on 1st January 1965.

63-8052 Delivered on 30th October 1964 to the 34th AREFS at Offutt AFB. Redesignated an EC-135C on 1st January 1965.

63-8053 Delivered to SAC on 30th November 1964 and arrived on 8th December at the 34thAREFS at Offutt AFB. Redesignated an EC-135C on 1st January 1965.

63-8054 Delivered to SAC on 9th December 1964 and arrived on 29th December at the 34th AREFS at Offutt AFB. Redesignated an EC-135C on 1st January 1965.

63-8055 Handed over to the Air Force on 6th January 1965 as an EC-135C. Assigned on 20th January to the 1000th ACCS at Andrews AFB as a NEACP.

63-8056 Handed over to SAC on 25th February 1965 as an EC-135C and assigned on 2nd March to the 99th AREFS, 499th AREFW at Westover AFB.

63-8057 This KC-135B was handed over to the Air Force on 25th February 1965 as an EC-135C and assigned on 4th March to the 22nd AREFS at March AFB.

Above: KC-135A 61-0293 was among the second batch of eight KC-135 airborne command posts, although Boeing converted these rather than OCAMA at Tinker AFB. They were functionally equivalent to the five original LOOKING GLASS KC-135As, but were assigned as backups with the NAFs. *Author's collection*

Below: KC-135Bs such as 63-8047 had an HF antenna on each wingtip, additional long-wire HF antennae, and multiple UHF antennae on the dorsal and ventral fuselage, all designed to facilitate communication with SAC forces in a national emergency. This was illusory, however, as the 1962 DOMINIC tests showed. *Photo P36508 courtesy Boeing*

PACCS Matures

To reflect more properly the 'electronic' mission of the airborne command post and to distinguish them from KC-135A tankers, on 1st January 1965 all dedicated ABNCPs were redesignated with an 'EC' prefix – KC-135As became EC-135As while KC-135Bs became EC-135Cs. In addition, PACCS underwent its second major reorganization on 25th March 1965. The EB-47L units at Lockbourne AFB and Mountain Home AFB were inactivated (EB-47L units at Lincoln AFB and Plattsburgh AFB had previously been shut down) and their radio relay missions absorbed by EC-135As newly assigned to the 32nd AREFS, 301st AREFW at Lockbourne AFB and the 28th AREFS, 28th BW at Ellsworth AFB, SD, respectively. A further shuffling of assets and new conversions was undertaken to accommodate the wider control of nuclear forces by the NCA, SAC, and the other CINCs. Eleven EC-135As were added to SAC's roster. The five original SAC KC-135A airborne command posts (58-0007, 58-0011, 58-0018, 58-0019, and 58-0022) were redesignated as BLUE EAGLE EC-135As for CINCPAC, and assigned to the 6486th ACCS, 6486th ABW at Hickam AFB, HI. Four SAC KC-135A ABNCPs (61-0278, 61-0287, 61-0289, and 61-0297) were redesignated as EC-135As and remained with SAC; two others (61-0262 and 61-0293) briefly became SILK PURSE EC-135As loaned to CINCEUR and assigned to the 7120th ACCS, 7513th TG at RAF Mildenhall, pending delivery of the SILK PURSE EC-135Hs. All four KC-135A NEACPs (61-0274, 61-0282, 61-0285, and 61-0291) were redesignated as EC-135As on 1st January 1965, and were subsequently transferred to the CINCEUR SILK PURSE mission, eventually being converted into EC-135Hs, along with EC-135A 61-0286. Finally, a single KC-135A (62-3579) was loaned on 2nd September 1964 to the 1000th ACCS, 1001st ABW at Andrews AFB as a NIGHT WATCH NEACP before returning to SAC as an EC-135G. Three EC-135Cs (63-8055, 63-8056, and 63-8057) were converted into EC-135Js to replace the NCA's EC-135As as NIGHT WATCH III NEACPs.

The technological sophistication of long-range radio transmission and reception improved substantially during the 1960s, including initial efforts to reduce vulnerability to EMP from nuclear detonations (see Chapter 8). Coupled with the ERCS, this meant that the LOOKING GLASS or an AUXCP could reliably transmit an EAM to SAC bombers and tankers around the world. It remained for those crews to conduct their air refueling and then reach their targets to drop bombs or launch stand off missiles. By the end of 1964, however, the last full year with B-47s on ground alert, the makeup of SAC's alert force changed dramatically. There were 464 B-47s, B-52s and B-58s bombers, and 701 Atlas, Titan, and Minuteman ICBMs on alert. SAC was no longer a bomber command with missiles; it was a missile command with bombers. This new dynamic had clear implications for the LOOKING GLASS mission. Just as it could with the airborne force, the LOOKING GLASS now needed to communicate with the ICBM launch control centers (LCC). More importantly, as the solid-fueled Minuteman missiles were effectively automated and required a human only to 'turn the key' to launch them, it was now conceptually possible to duplicate the hundreds of underground LCCs on board the LOOKING GLASS. It was merely a technological problem to enable a single ABNCP to launch America's ICBM force.

By 1964 plans were already under way for the LOOKING GLASS to function as a substitute in the event that LCCs were destroyed or unable to receive the launch order. On 2nd February 1965 SAC announced that the Minuteman II (but not the liquid-fueled Atlas or Titan, which required manual pre-launch fueling) could be 'launched via radio signals from an airborne command post'. The challenge to launching the Minuteman (and later Peacekeeper) fleet from the LOOKING GLASS was the distance involved. The Minuteman ICBMs were located at widely dispersed silos from Montana to Missouri, from North Dakota to Kansas and Colorado. A single LOOKING GLASS could not hope to cover the tens of thousands of square miles of territory while simultaneously functioning in its primary ABNCP role near Offutt AFB. Consequently, plans were first developed in 1966 for an airborne launch control system (ALCS) to be installed not only in the LOOKING GLASS but in backup aircraft as well. One backup airplane would be based at Ellsworth AFB to cover the western Minuteman 'fields' and another would be based at Minot AFB, ND, to cover the northeastern fields. The LOOKING GLASS itself would cover the southern fields. Launch crews at Ellsworth AFB (initially assigned to the 67th Strategic Missile Squadron (SMS), later the 68th SMS) and Minot AFB [initially assigned to the 741st SMS, later the 91st Strategic Missile Wing (SMW)] would be highly experienced Missile Combat Crew Commanders (MCCC) and Deputy Missile Combat Crew Commanders (DMCCC). Personnel from Offutt AFB would be experienced operations and communications controllers from SAC missile units, and would serve in both battle staff duties and as launch crews. For missile combat crews, assignment as ACLS officers was a choice plum. For many years, only crews from the missile wing at Ellsworth AFB were selected, leading to grumblings among the rest of SAC's missileers about the 'EPA'– the 'Ellsworth Protection Agency'.

Other command posts such as SILK PURSE or BLUE EAGLE lacked the equipment and codes necessary to launch SAC's ICBMs. This

EC-135A 61-0262 briefly served with the 7120th ACCS at RAF Mildenhall as CINCEUR awaited delivery of the SILK PURSE EC-135Hs.
Photo by Denis Hughes via Stephen Miller

'Whatever you do, don't turn this key unless you *really, really* mean to.' ALCS allowed crews in the LOOKING GLASS or the ALCCs to launch Minuteman ICBMs. Although they had the capability to do so, they still required a valid launch order from the president or his pre-delegated successor. *Photo P40516 courtesy Boeing*

was intentional, as SAC viewed its Minutemen as private turf not to be trod upon by other commanders. Only SAC airborne launch platforms – LOOKING GLASS and AUXCP EC-135Cs, and the seven newly modified Airborne Launch Control Center (ALCC) EC-135As and EC-135Gs – had the ALCS installed under Program No.1858. Three KC-135A airborne command posts and one EC-135A were redesignated EC-135Gs. These were distinguished from their EC-135A counterparts by having automated on-board systems in place of the manual systems on the EC-135As. Although redesignated EC-135Gs in 1965 and 1966, it was not until 1967 that all four had been fully converted for use as backup airborne command posts. The following year, all four were fully modified into ALCCs under Program No.1129, a mission also supported by EC-135As.

SAC missile crews flying aboard the LOOKING GLASS and the ALCCs used the same safeguards against accidental or nefarious launch as in ground control centers. The LOOKING GLASS or ALCC could launch ICBMs only after it was determined that ground-based missile launch centers could no longer initiate the launch and that a valid EAM from the president via the NCA or its authorized representatives had been issued. The AEAO, the communications officer, the operations officer, and the aircraft commander all had to

validate the launch order. The aircraft commander then activated a switch on his left side panel enabling the ALCS equipment. The operations officer and the communications officer, separated by 'many feet', then had to turn their launch keys within two seconds of one another to launch ICBMs. Ground-based missile crews also require a second missile crew in a separate LCC to 'vote' that the launch code is valid before any missiles are fired. It is not clear (or perhaps remains classified) if the LOOKING GLASS and ALCCs had this same limitation. During the early 1970s the 'Phase II' ALCCs received additional unspecified safeguards to prevent unauthorized launch or the accidental compromise of launch codes. The LOOKING GLASS could also launch the ERCS Minutemen, as well as reprogram the EAM broadcast in the ERCS for evolving SIOP requirements.

The first attempt to launch an ICBM on 17th April 1967 met with success when an airborne battle staff 'turned the key' to launch a Minuteman II from Vandenberg AFB, CA. The ALCS achieved its initial operational capability on 31st May 1967, and reached full operational capability in February 1968. By June 1969 some 850 out of 1,000 Minuteman ICBMs were configured for ALCS operations, although there were still problems to be resolved. During the first six months of 1969, for example, there were three successful test launches on 18th April, 28th May, and 18th June. A 12th March launch – known as GIANT FIST 3 – failed due to a master tape error. Later that year, LOOKING GLASS crews failed on two consecutive launch attempts due to technical difficulties. By 27th January 1970 these issues had been largely resolved as an ALCS team completed the 24th successful Minuteman launch from Vandenberg AFB. Since that first airborne launch, SAC EC-135s repeatedly demonstrated this capability as part of missions known as GLORY TRIPS. Top crews flying EC-135C LOOKING GLASS and EC-135A and EC-135G ALCCs have launched operational Minuteman ICBMs (minus their nuclear payload) that were moved from an operational alert silo to one at Vandenberg AFB. After each ICBM launch, the airplane landed at Vandenberg AFB and the crew received a familiarization briefing on missile research, development, and operations – a real 'dog and pony show' according to the crewmembers. A GLORY TRIP was nonetheless an expensive and operationally complex endeavor, so SAC implemented a Simulated Electronic Launch-Minuteman (SELM) capability on 1st February 1974. During an initial test, 11 SELM-configured Minuteman IIs at Ellsworth AFB were successfully 'launched' on command from two underground launch centers and an ALCC. Minutemen have also been launched from Vandenberg AFB by EC-135s at the culmination of SAC's annual GLOBAL SHIELD exercise, including a dual launch on 9th February 1981.

4th ACCS EC-135A 61-0287 on alert at Minot AFB (note thermal curtains in hatch windows). In the event of a SIOP launch, *Axel 33* would cover the Minuteman fields in the Dakotas. *Photo by Stephen Miller*

EC-135A 61-0297 prepares to depart Ellsworth AFB. Although the ALCCs could launch ICBMs, the crews were subject to the same effective command and control procedures applicable to ground-based missile crews. *Photo by Brian Rogers*

EC-135A INDIVIDUAL AIRCRAFT

The EC-135As had an IFR system installed and HF aerials on each wing tip, retained the air refueling boom and complete tanker capability, although with a reduced maximum fuel load due to the battle staff suite and communications equipment installed in the cargo compartment and the additional crewmembers. Beginning in 1967 the seven remaining EC-135As were modified under Program No 1858 to become ALCCs.

58-0007 Assigned as a KC-135A ABNCP to the 913th AREFS, 2nd BW at Barksdale AFB when redesignated an EC-135A on 1st January 1965. Transferred on 27th August 1965 to the 6486th ACCS at Hickam AFB as a BLUE EAGLE airborne command post. Redesignated an EC-135P on 31st March 1967.

58-0011 Assigned as a KC-135A ABNCP to the 913th AREFS at Barksdale AFB when redesignated an EC-135A on 1st January 1965. Reassigned on 3rd March 1965 to the 34th AREFS, 818th Strategic Aerospace Division (SAD) at Offutt AFB. On 14th July 1966 it was transferred to the 6486th ACCS at Hickam AFB as a BLUE EAGLE airborne command post. It was redesignated as an EC-135P on 31st March 1967.

58-0018 Assigned as a KC-135A ABNCP to the 28th AREFS at Ellsworth AFB when redesignated an EC-135A on 1st January 1965. On 20th April 1965 it was transferred to the 6486th ACCS at Hickam AFB as a BLUE EAGLE airborne command post. Redesignated an as EC-135P on 31st March 1967.

58-0019 Assigned as a KC-135A ABNCP to the 99th AREFS, 499th AREFW at Westover AFB when redesignated an EC-135A on 1st January 1965. Boeing modified this beginning 25th May 1965 into the BLUE EAGLE configuration and delivered it to the 6486th ACCS at Hickam AFB on 23rd August 1965. It was redesignated an EC-135P on 31st March 1967.

58-0022 Assigned as a KC-135A ABNCP to the 99th AREFS at Westover AFB when redesignated an EC-135A on 1st January 1965. Modified beginning 2nd June 1965 and delivered on 27th August 1965 to the 6486th ACCS at Hickam AFB as a BLUE EAGLE airborne command post. Redesignated an EC-135P on 31st March 1967.

61-0262 Assigned as a KC-135A ABNCP to the 99th AREFS at Westover AFB when redesignated an EC-135A on 1st January 1965. Assigned on 23rd November 1965 to the 7120th ACCS, 7513th Tactical Group (TG) at RAF Mildenhall. On 23rd January 1967 it was assigned to the 28th AREFS at Ellsworth AFB, and received the ALCC modification by 26th July 1967. Transferred on 31st July 1968 to the 906th AREFS, 5th BW at Minot AFB, where it remained until 13th January 1969 when it returned to the 28th AREFS. On 1st March 1970 it was transferred to the 4th ACCS at Ellsworth AFB. Placed on static display at Ellsworth AFB on 30th March 1992 (see Appendix III).

61-0278 Assigned to the 22nd AREFS, 22nd BW at March AFB when redesignated an EC-135A on 1st January 1965. Transferred on 28th November 1965 to the 32nd AREFS at Lockbourne AFB, where it remained until 29th June 1966 when reassigned to the 305th AREFS, 305th BW at Bunker Hill AFB. It moved to the 28th AREFS at Ellsworth AFB on 14th July 1967, then to the 906th AREFS, 450th BW at Minot AFB on 28th January 1968. Returned to the 305th AREFS at Grissom AFB on 15th July 1968, and reassigned to the 906th AREFS (by now part of the 5th BW) at Minot AFB on 14th May 1969. On 31st December 1969 it moved to the 28th AREFS. Transferred on 1st March 1970 to the 4th ACCS at Ellsworth AFB. Stored in AMARC on 18th September 1992 as AACA0048, and finally scrapped on 22nd June 2016 (see Appendix III).

61-0282 Boeing converted this KC-135A into a NEACP during 1962. Delivered by 11th June 1962 to the 1000th ACCS at Andrews AFB. Redesignated an EC-135A on 16th November 1964. Transferred in November 1965 to the 7120th ACCS, 7513th TG at RAF Mildenhall. Converted into an EC-135H during 1967.

61-0285 Converted this KC-135A into a NEACP during 1962. It was delivered by 12th March 1962 to the 1000th ACCS at Andrews AFB. On 16th November 1964 it was redesignated an EC-135A. Transferred on 5th October 1966 to the 7120th ACCS, 7513th TG at RAF Mildenhall, after conversion by E-Systems into an EC-135H.

61-0287 Assigned to the 32nd AREFS at Lockbourne AFB when redesignated an EC-135A on 1st January 1965. Assigned to the 305th AREFS at Bunker Hill AFB on 29th June 1966. Transferred on 4th October 1967 to the 28th AREFS at Ellsworth AFB where it remained until 8th December 1967, when it moved to the 906th AREFS, 450th BW at Minot AFB. Reassigned to the 28th AREFS on 31st December 1969. Transferred on 1st March 1970 to the 4th ACCS at Ellsworth AFB. Placed on static display at Offutt AFB on 10th February 1992 (see Appendix III).

61-0289 Assigned to the 99th AREFS at Westover AFB when redesignated an EC-135A on 1st January 1965. Assigned on 22nd January 1965 to the 32nd AREFS at Lockbourne AFB where it remained until 30th June 1966, when it moved to the 305th AREFS at Bunker Hill AFB. Transferred to the 906th AREFS, 450th BW at Minot AFB on 16th January 1968. Again transferred on 31st December 1969, this time to the 28th AREFS. On 1st March 1970 it was transferred to the 4th ACCS at Ellsworth AFB. Stored in AMARC on 8th June 1992 as AACA0022 and scrapped on 21st June 2016 (see Appendix III).

61-0293 Assigned to the 99th AREFS at Westover AFB when redesignated an EC-135A on 1st January 1965. Sometime during early 1965 it was loaned or transferred to the 32nd AREFS, 301st AREFW at Lockbourne AFB. It was transferred on 9th November 1965 to the 7120th ACCS at RAF Mildenhall until reassigned on 23rd February 1968 to the 305th AREFS at Grissom AFB. Transferred on 31st May 1968 to the 28th AREFS. Reassigned on 1st March 1970 to the 4th ACCS at Ellsworth AFB. Demodified into a KC-135A (ARR).

61-0297 Assigned to the 28th AREFS at Ellsworth AFB when redesignated an EC-135A on 1st January 1965. On 6th June 1967 it was transferred to the 305th AREFS at Bunker Hill AFB and by 18th September 1967, received the ALCC modification. Transferred on 15th November 1967 to the 28th AREFS at Ellsworth AFB, and then on 15th February 1968 to the 906th AREFS, 5th BW at Minot AFB. Returned on 23rd December 1969 to the 28th AREFS. On 1st March 1970 it was transferred to the 4th ACCS at Ellsworth AFB. Stored in AMARC on 2nd June 1992, as AACA0021, and eventually scrapped on 16th June 2016 (see Appendix III).

62-3579 This airplane was transferred on 2nd September 1964 from the 34th AREFS at Offutt AFB to the 1000th ACCS, 1001st ABW at Andrews AFB. It was the first airplane to be designated as an EC-135A, effective the date of its transfer. Then assigned to the 28th AREFS at Ellsworth AFB on 21st December 1964. By 14th February 1966 it had been modified as an EC-135G.

EC-135C INDIVIDUAL AIRCRAFT

62-3581 Assigned to the 22nd AREFS, 22nd BW at March AFB on 1st January 1965 when redesignated an EC-135C. Reassigned on 5th May 1965 to the 34th AREFS, 810th SAD at Offutt AFB, where it remained until transferred to the 913th AREFS, 2nd BW at Barksdale AFB on 15th March 1966. Returned to Offutt AFB on 13th January 1967 where it was assigned to the 38th SRS at Offutt AFB on 9th April 1967. It has since alternated assignments between the 2nd ACCS at Offutt AFB and the 4th ACCS at Ellsworth AFB. In 1989 it was assigned to the 2nd ACCS. By early 1990 it had acquired the MILSTAR system. On 19th July 1994 the 2nd ACCS was disestablished and replaced by the 7th ACCS and the airplane reassigned accordingly. This EC-135C was placed in AMARG on 10th February 1999 as AACA0127, and scrapped on 8th August 2016 (see Appendix III).

62-3582 Assigned to the 22nd AREFS at March AFB on 1st January 1965 when redesignated an EC-135C. Reassigned on 14th July 1965 to the 34th AREFS at Offutt AFB and to the 38th SRS at Offutt AFB on 9th April 1967. Transferred to the 913th AREFS at Barksdale AFB on 29th January 1968. From 16th June 1970 through 6th July 1970 it served briefly with the 3rd ACCS, 305th AREFW at Grissom AFB before returning to the 2nd ACCS. It has since alternated assignments between there and the 4th ACCS at Ellsworth AFB. By 1992 it was reassigned to the 2nd ACCS. On 19th July 1994 the 2nd ACCS was disestablished and replaced by the 7th ACCS and the airplane reassigned accordingly. By 1999 it had been redesignated a WC-135C.

Traditionally associated with the 2nd ACCS at Offutt AFB, EC-135Cs such as 62-3581 were also assigned to NAF bases as well as Ellsworth AFB and Grissom AFB as fleet requirements dictated. *Photo by Charles Mayer via Stephen Miller*

Four EC-135Cs received the MILSTAR antenna modification under PACER LINK II, including 62-3585. *Photo by Joe Bruch*

7th ACCS crews occasionally flew EC-135s on overseas deployment flights, often to fulfil reconnaissance-related tasks for RC-135 missions abroad. *Photo by Richard Vandervord*

EC-135C 63-8050 was the first to be equipped with the AFSATCOM, indicated by the three small white fairings on the dorsal fuselage. *Photo by Charles Mayer via Stephen Miller*

PACCS jets appeared in several different color schemes, beginning with natural metal, then white over Coroguard (as with 4th ACCS EC-135C 63-8051), and then white over gloss grey. *Photo by Stephen Miller*

62-3583 Assigned to the 22nd AREFS at March AFB on 1st January 1965 when redesignated an EC-135C. On 5th October 1965 it was reassigned to the 34th AREFS at Offutt AFB. Reassigned on 29th April 1967 to the 38th SRS at Offutt AFB. Transferred to the 913th AREFS at Barksdale AFB on 10th July 1968. On 30th March 1970 it was reassigned to the newly formed 4th ACCS at Ellsworth AFB. It has since alternated assignments between there and the 2nd ACCS at Offutt AFB. Stored in AMARC on 26th May 1992 as AACA0019, and scrapped on 16th November 2013 (see Appendix III).

62-3584 Assigned to the 913th AREFS at Barksdale AFB on 1st January 1965 when redesignated an EC-135C. Reassigned on 17th June 1966 to the 34th AREFS at Offutt AFB, and transferred to the 38th SRS on 16th August 1966. During 1969 it served as the prototype for the ADA computer upgrade (see below). Assigned in late 1978 to the 9th ACCS, 15th ABW at Hickam AFB for use as a trainer by BLUE EAGLE EC-135J crews. From May 1979 through February 1980 E-Systems converted 62-3584 into an EC-135J.

62-3585 Assigned to the 913th AREFS at Barksdale AFB on 1st January 1965, when redesignated an EC-135C. Transferred on 7th March 1966 to the 34th AREFS at Offutt AFB and reassigned on 16th August 1966 to the 38th SRS. On 30th October 1969 it was transferred to the 913th AREFS at Barksdale AFB where it remained (except during a brief – 10th February through 6th March 1970 – temporary duty assignment with the 99th AREFS, 99th BW at Westover AFB) until 30th March 1970. Following a short assignment until 2nd June 1970 with the 3rd ACCS at Grissom AFB, it arrived at the 4th ACCS at Ellsworth AFB. It has since alternated assignments between there and the 2nd ACCS at Offutt AFB. Equipped with the MILSTAR modification. On 19th July 1994 the 2nd ACCS was disestablished and replaced by the 7th ACCS and the airplane reassigned accordingly. This EC-135C was placed in AMARG on 2 June 1998 as AACA0123, where it was placed on 'Celebrity Row'. It was scrapped on 21st September 2016 (see appendix III).

63-8046 Assigned to the 913th AREFS at Barksdale AFB on 1st January 1965 when redesignated an EC-135C. Reassigned on 11th October 1966 to the 38th SRS at Offutt AFB. During 1970 it was also briefly assigned to the 22md AREFS at March AFB, and the 4th ACCS at Ellsworth AFB. Transferred to the 4th ACCS on 7th December 1970, and loaned to the 3rd ACCS at Grissom AFB in December 1971. Returned to Ellsworth AFB, alternating assignments between there and the 2nd ACCS at Offutt AFB. This airplane flew the final continuous airborne alert LOOKING GLASS mission on 24th July 1990, although this honor was erroneously attributed to EC-135C 63-8049. Soon thereafter it was configured with the MILSTAR modification. On 19th July 1994, 63-8046 was reassigned to the 7th ACCS when the 2nd ACCS was inactivated. It was relegated to AMARG on 21st October 1998 as AACA0124, and scrapped on 1st August 2016 (see Appendix III).

63-8047 Assigned to the 99th AREFS at Westover AFB on 1st January 1965 when redesignated an EC-135C. On 8th August 1966 it was reassigned to the 38th SRS at Offutt AFB. Temporarily assigned to the 3rd ACCS at Grissom AFB on 2nd November 1971. It returned to the 2nd ACCS at Offutt AFB, alternating between there and the 4th ACCS at Ellsworth AFB. It transferred to the 2nd ACCS by September 1992. On 12th October 1993 it was relegated to AMARC as AACA0093, and scrapped on 1st August 2106 (see Appendix III).

63-8048 Assigned to the 34th AREFS at Offutt AFB on 1st January 1965 when redesignated an EC-135C. Reassigned on 1st January 1966 to the 99th AREFS at Westover AFB. Beginning on 27th February 1967 it alternated assignments between Offutt AFB, Westover AFB, and March AFB (as well as a brief stint with the 3rd ACCS at Grissom AFB) through 8th October 1970, when it was reassigned to the 2nd ACCS at Offutt AFB. It has since alternated assignments between there and the 4th ACCS at Ellsworth AFB. Following the 3rd January 1980 loss of 6th ACCS EC-135P 58-0007, this EC-135C was loaned from the 4th ACCS to the 6th ACCS as a replacement. In June 1984, following the conversion of NKC-135E 55-3129 into an EC-135P, 63-8048 was returned to the 4th ACCS. It was assigned to the 2nd ACCS in 1989. On 19th July 1994, it was reassigned to the 7th ACCS when the 2nd ACCS was inactivated. It was assigned to AMARG on 26th February 1999 as AACA0128, and scrapped on 4th August 2016 (see Appendix III).

63-8049 Assigned to the 34th AREFS at Offutt AFB on 1st January 1965 when redesignated an EC-135C. On 1st January 1966 it was reassigned to the 99th AREFS at Westover AFB. Transferred repeatedly between the 99th AREFS, the 38th SRS, the 22nd AREFS, and the 3rd ACCS until it returned to the 2nd

ACCS on 8th October 1970. It has since alternated assignments between there and the 4th ACCS at Ellsworth AFB. In 1989 it was assigned to the 2nd ACCS. This airplane was retired on 29th January 1992 and placed on static display at the SAC Museum (see Appendix III).

63-8050 Assigned to the 34th AREFS at Offutt AFB on 1st January 1965 when redesignated an EC-135C. On 16th July 1965 it was reassigned to the 22nd AREFS at March AFB. Transferred on 25th April 1970 to the 2nd ACCS at Offutt AFB. It has since alternated assignments between there and the 4th ACCS at Ellsworth AFB. In 1989 it was assigned to the 2nd ACCS. This was the first EC-135C to receive the AFSATCOM modification. By 1993 this airplane had been deconfigured as an airborne command post and assigned to testbed duties associated with a resurgent airborne laser program (see Chapter 8). In 1996 it was redesignated an NKC-135B.

63-8051 Assigned to the 34th AREFS at Offutt AFB on 1st January 1965 when redesignated an EC-135C. Transferred on 20th May 1965 to the 22nd AREFS at March AFB. On 18th January 1966 it returned to the 34th AREFS at Offutt AFB. Moved again on 14th October 1966 to the 913th AREFS at Barksdale AFB. It returned to Offutt AFB on 30th June 1968, this time to the 38th SRS. Transferred on 16th June 1969 to the 99th AREFS at Westover AFB. Returned to Offutt AFB on 20th February 1970 with the 2nd ACCS. It has since alternated assignments between there and the 4th ACCS, where it was assigned in 1989. Stored in AMARC on 10th July 1992 as AACA0027, and it was scrapped on 1st August 2016 (see Appendix III).

63-8052 Assigned to the 34th AREFS at Offutt AFB on 1st January 1965 when redesignated an EC-135C. On 10th May 1969 it was reassigned to the 22nd AREFS at March AFB. Transferred exactly a year later to the 4th ACCS at Ellsworth AFB. Moved to the 3rd ACCS at Grissom AFB on 2nd July 1970. It has since returned to the 2nd ACCS at Offutt AFB, and alternated assignments between there and the 4th ACCS at Ellsworth AFB. In 1989 it was assigned to the 2nd ACCS. On 19th July 1994 it was reassigned to the 7th ACCS when the 2nd ACCS was inactivated. It was assigned to AMARG on 16th January 1998 as AACA0117, and was scrapped on 1st August 2016 (see Appendix III).

63-8053 Assigned to the 34th AREFS at Offutt AFB on 1st January 1965 when redesignated an EC-135C. Transferred on 11th October 1965 to the 22nd AREFS at March AFB. Returned to the 38th SRS at Offutt AFB on 2nd January 1969. Handed over to the 2nd ACCS at Offutt AFB on 1st April 1970. It has since alternated assignments between there and the 4th ACCS at Ellsworth AFB. In 1989 it was assigned to the 2nd ACCS. On 19th July 1994 it was reassigned to the 7th ACCS when the 2nd ACCS was inactivated. It crashed at Pope AFB on 2nd September 1997 (see Appendix II).

63-8054 Assigned to the 34th AREFS at Offutt AFB on 1st January 1965 when redesignated an EC-135C. Interestingly, it had been delivered only two days before, making it the airplane with the shortest operational time under any MDS (KC-135B). Transferred on 28th February 1966 to the 22nd AREFS at March AFB. Returned to the 38th SRS at Offutt AFB on 14th August 1969, and handed over to the 2nd ACCS on 1st April 1970. It has since alternated assignments between there and the 4th ACCS at Ellsworth AFB. In 1989 it was assigned to the 2nd ACCS. Equipped with the MILSTAR modification. On 19th July 1994, it was reassigned to the 7th ACCS when the 2nd ACCS was inactivated. It was relegated to AMARG on 28th October 1998 as AACA0125, and was scrapped on 20th September 2016 (see Appendix III).

63-8055 This EC-135C was delivered to the Air Force on 6th January 1965, and arrived at the 1000th ACCS at Andrews AFB on 20th January for use by the NCA. By 21st September 1966, E-Systems had modified the airplane into the NIGHT WATCH III configuration and was it redesignated an EC-135J.

63-8056 Delivered to SAC on 25th February 1965, arriving at the 99th AREFS at Westover AFB on 2nd March 1965. Transferred on 3rd June 1965 to the 913th AREFS at Barksdale AFB. On 6th October 1965 it was reassigned to the 34th AREFS at Offutt AFB. Arrived at the E-Systems conversion facility at Greenville, TX, on 3rd January 1966 for modification into the NIGHT WATCH III configuration. Delivered to the 1000th ACCS at Andrews AFB on 20th June 1966. It was not redesignated an EC-135J until 31st May 1967.

63-8057 This EC-135C was handed over to SAC on 25th February 1965 and delivered to the 22nd AREFS at March AFB on 4th March 1965. Transferred to the 34th AREFS at Offutt AFB on 19th October 1965. Converted by E-Systems during 1966 and delivered to the 1000th ACCS at Andrews AFB as a NIGHT WATCH III EC-135C NEACP. Redesignated an EC-135J on 31st May 1967.

EC-135G INDIVIDUAL AIRCRAFT

EC-135Gs retained the air refueling boom and tanker capability, and had an IFR system installed. Numerous UHF antennae were attached along the fuselage spine, both top and bottom. An HF antenna was attached above each wingtip and two wire HF aerials run from the vertical stabilizer to the forward fuselage. A battle staff suite was installed in the cargo compartment, although this was removed on aircraft configured for radio relay, which carried a crew of two radio operators and a radio maintenance technician.

62-3570 On 14th February 1966 TEMCO completed modification of this EC-135G. The following day it was assigned to the 28th AREFS at Ellsworth AFB. On 1st March 1970, the PACCS mission at Ellsworth AFB was acquired by the 4th ACCS and the airplane and crews transferred accordingly. Reassigned on 14th August 1987 to the 70th AREFS, 305th AREFW at Grissom AFB. Stored in AMARC on 23rd June 1992 as AACA0024. It was scrapped on 3rd February 2010 (see Appendix III).

62-3579 Redesignated from KC-135A airborne command post to EC-135G on 31st December 1964. Assigned on 15th February 1966 to the 28th AREFS while at TEMCO, returning to Ellsworth AFB on 23rd

March 1966. Received the ALCC modification by 15th August 1967. Transferred on 1st March 1970 to the 4th ACCS. Stored in AMARC on 16th June 1992, as AACA0023, and scrapped on 31st October 2013 (see Appendix III).

63-7994 On 29th March 1966 this airborne command post was delivered to TEMCO for conversion into an EC-135G, which was completed on 3rd May 1966, when the airplane was redesignated and returned to the 28th AREFS at Ellsworth AFB. Transferred on 27th August 1970 to the 3rd ACCS at Grissom AFB. On 31st December 1975 the 3rd ACCS was deactivated and its airplanes and mission acquired by the 70th AREFS, also at Grissom AFB. Transferred on 21st May 1987 to the 4th ACCS at Ellsworth AFB. Stored in AMARC on 11th September 1992 as AACA0045, and scrapped on 29th October 2013 (see Appendix III).

63-8001 Delivered on 3rd May 1966 to TEMCO for conversion to EC-135G, which was completed on 6th June 1966, when the airplane was redesignated and returned to the 28th AREFS at Ellsworth AFB. On 1st March 1970 it was transferred to the 4th ACCS at Ellsworth AFB. Stored in AMARC on 18th May 1992, as AACA0017, and scrapped on 5th December 2013 (see Appendix III).

Radio Relay

The 1965 PACCS realignment replaced the PIPECLEANER EB-47Ls with EC-135As as the airborne link between the NAF Headquarters and their respective AUXCPs, the LOOKING GLASS, and SAC Headquarters at Offutt AFB. This change was only temporary, as SAC wanted to preserve its EC-135As for the planned installation of the ALCS to launch Minuteman ICBMs. In addition, the EC-135As would serve as backup AUXCPs, although with notable degrades in capability. To meet its long-term radio relay requirements, SAC directed the conversion of eight KC-135As into EC-135L airborne radio relay platforms under project modification Nos. 1674 and 1900. The EC-135Ls (as well as similarly capable EC-135As and EC-135Gs) provided a secure radio link between CINCSAC and the NCA as part of the PACCS structure. In the event of a national emergency or execution of the SIOP, two EC-135Ls (instead of four EB-47Ls) could establish and maintain links between the National Military Command Center (NMCC) at Washington, DC, the NIGHT WATCH National Emergency Airborne Command Post, the LOOKING GLASS, and the ALCS-configured EC-135A and EC-135G ALCC aircraft.

Lockheed Aerospace Corporation at New York City's Idlewild/John F Kennedy airport completed the EC-135L modification. The first two airplanes were converted in 1965, two more in 1966, and the remainder by 1967. Originally, four EC-135Ls were assigned to the 305th AREFS, 305th BW at Grissom AFB, two were assigned to the 32nd AREFS, 301st AREFW at Lockbourne AFB, and two were assigned to the 906th AREFS, 450th BW at Minot AFB. During 1970 three EC-135Ls (61-0281, 61-0288, and 61-0302) were demodified to KC-135As. Two of these (61-0281,

Opposite page, top to bottom: Despite flying three missions a day for nearly 30 years, no PACCS jets were lost, an extraordinary safety record. Under ACC, however, EC-135C 63-8053 was written off at Pope AFB on 2nd November 1997, as was EC-135J 62-3584 on 29th May 1992, also at Pope AFB. *Photo by George Cockle*

Throughout the 1980s, one of the four EC-135Gs was assigned to Grissom AFB where it was used as a radio relay platform lacking the ALCS. Its increased operational weight earned it the sobriquet 'Miss Piggy.' This applied to 62-3570 and 63-7994, both of which spent time with the 70th AREFS. *Photo by Brian Rogers*

All of the PACCS jets were also tankers, and crews maintained proficiency in both delivering and receiving fuel. Although the front-end crews were part of the PACCS mission, at heart they were still 'Tanker Toads.' *Photo by Brian Rogers*

This page: Eight EC-135Ls, including 61-0261 seen at Andrews AFB on 13th May 1983, replaced 36 PIPECLEANER EB-47Ls as PACCS radio relay jets. Three EC-135Ls were demodified into tankers. *Photo by Stephen Miller*

61-0288) were again redesignated EC-135Ls on 6th January 1971, but reverted back to KC-135As on 14th September 1971 – explanation unknown. These two KC-135As remained associated with the 55th SRW at Offutt AFB, although in what capacity is not clear. The remaining five airplanes were reassigned to the 70th AREFS, 305th AREFW at Grissom AFB.

PACCS was not just about air-to-air radio links. Multiple 'ground entry points' were strategically located around the Midwest and Plains states, allowing an airborne EC-135 to link directly via radio to hardened telephone land lines. These included North Bend, NE, Fairview, KS, Lamar, CO, Newbern IL, Tyler, TX, Turquoise Junction, CA, and Peru, MA.

COMBAT LIGHTNING

Beginning in 1966 the Lockheed EC-121T Airborne Surveillance and Control System (AS&CS) provided 'long-range air situation control' in Southeast Asia. E-Systems converted at least 27 Lockheed C-121s into EC-121Ts by installing an AN/ASQ-136 Airborne Detection and Processing System, special HF and UHF radios, computer analysis gear, and high-speed data link equipment. The EC-121T's on-board computer provided situational data such as a target aircraft's location, altitude, and speed. These data could then be stored or transmitted in an encrypted form at 1,200 or 2,400 baud. Data transmission beyond line-of-sight from the EC-121T to the ground-based AN/GYQ-14 Digital Data Processing Station, however, required some form of airborne radio relay platform. In June 1966 Air Force Headquarters notified SAC that two EC-135L were under consideration as the COMBAT LIGHTNING radio relay platforms to support the EC-121Ts, as well as for other high-priority communications such as those associated with RC-135M COMBAT APPLE sorties (see Chapter 10). The COMBAT LIGHTNINGs would also extend the range of ground communications stations in South Vietnam, 'mainly to pass warning information to aircraft operating over North Vietnam, a mission it performed while orbiting over the Gulf of Tonkin'. This ground facility, located at Monkey Mountain near Da Nang, transmitted warnings via the COMBAT LIGHTNING of MiGs, US aerial violations of the Chinese border, and SAM launch warnings to tactical aircraft operating over North Vietnam.

Not wishing to lose two PACCS airplanes to a mere contingency operation, SAC recommended instead using two KC-135As equipped with the AN/ARC-89 radio relay system. This alternate plan was adopted and E-Systems modified two KC-135As (61-0280 from the 916th AREFS, 5th BW at Travis AFB, CA, and 61-0271 from the 97th BW at Blytheville AFB, AR) by incorporating the KC-135 Signal Data Multiplexer/Transmitter System, which included automated high-speed HF and UHF communications relay equipment. Some 700 lb (318kg) of lead weight was installed in the

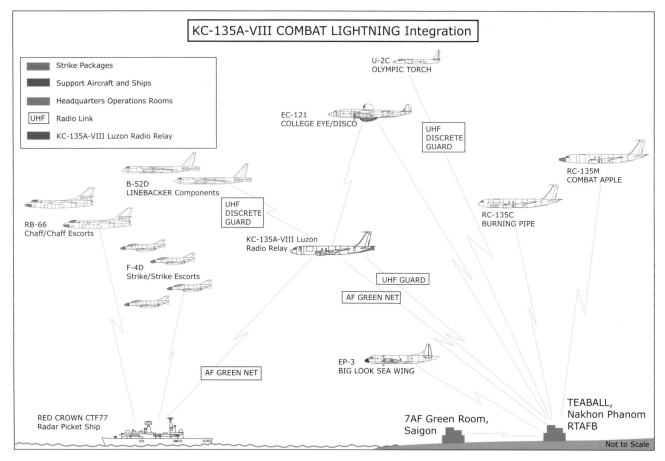

front of the airplane to counterbalance the added weight of the radio gear in the back. COMBAT LIGHTNINGS, redesignated as KC-135A-VIIIs, were easily identifiable by nine UHF radio antennae along their dorsal fuselage and four on the ventral fuselage, earning the airplanes the nickname 'Razorback.'

The first KC-135A-VIII COMBAT LIGHTNING arrived at Kadena AB on 14th September 1966 (the second arrived shortly thereafter). They deployed to U-Tapao RTNAB on 20th and 22nd September 1966, where one flew the first COMBAT LIGHTNING mission on 5th October 1966. It soon became apparent that the desired 24-hour coverage would require at least five airplanes. Modification of additional KC-135A-VIIIs was delayed, so SAC was finally compelled to send two EC-135Ls to U-Tapao RTNAB in mid-May 1967. Full 24-hour coverage with these four airplanes (two EC-135Ls and two KC-135A-VIIIs) began at the end of May. By October 1967 three additional KC-135As were delivered, incorporating a new secure voice capability and a scheduled wing fatigue retrofit. The two existing KC-135A-VIII COMBAT LIGHTNINGs were then so modified, delaying departure of the two EC-135Ls until December 1967.

COMBAT LIGHTNING operations began at U-Tapao RTNAB, but the demand for additional ramp space required by escalating B-52 operations in December 1967 meant that the five KC-135A-VIII COMBAT LIGHTNING jets (referred to as 'EC-135s') would have to relocate on 2nd February 1968 to Ching Chuan Kang AB as part of COMMANDO WALLOP. By the end of 1970, US tanker operations from Taiwan had ended, and COMBAT LIGHTNING operations returned to U-Tapao RTNAB. Further increases in B-52 numbers at U-Tapao RTNAB in the ensuing years dictated that COMBAT LIGHTNINGS deploy to Kadena AB from 23rd February through 8th June 1971, as well as briefly in April 1972 and February 1973. Routine depot-level maintenance of the KC-135A-VIIIs once again required SAC to deploy two of its EC-135Ls (61-0263 and 61-0281) to U-Tapao

RTNAB from 1971-73. A rumor exists among PACCS alumni that during 1972 a LOOKING GLASS EC-135C took part in LINEBACKER II. In what capacity has never been suggested nor has any evidence been uncovered to support this assertion.

COMBAT LIGHTNING missions – static call sign *Wager* (*Luzon* for the EC-135Ls in 1971-73) – were typically 8-12 hours long with six to eight hours on station in the Tan Anchor Orbit. It required four aircraft to enable 24-hour continuous coverage as they lacked an IFR for receiver air refueling. Transit time to and from Kadena AB was four hours each way, three hours each way to CCK, and two hours in each direction to U-Tapao RTNAB. Fighter escorts provided protection against the rare attempts by MiGs to attack the COMBAT LIGHTNING or the COMBAT APPLE aircraft over the Gulf of Tonkin. Front-end crews included a pilot, copilot, navigator, and boom operator. Back-end crews were two radio operators (ROs) and a Radio Maintenance Technician (RM). Although the COMBAT LIGHTNING's primary mission was radio relay, they were fitted with the boom-drogue adapter (BDA) in order to refuel drogue-equipped Air Force aircraft should they experience fuel emergencies. In this capacity, COMBAT LIGHTNINGS conducted 91 Emergency Air Refueling Tanker (EART) missions. Following a heavy fuel offload, the COMBAT LIGHTNING could divert to Da Nang AB where it would refuel and then return to its COMBAT LIGHTNING orbit. On 26th December 1972 a KC-135A-VIII escorted B-52D 56-0584 – call sign *Ash 01* – to U-Tapao RTNAB after it was

Table 9-1. COMBAT LIGHTNING **KC-135A-VIIIs**

Serial	Disposition	Date	Serial	Disposition	Date
61-0268	KC-135E, AMARG	18 Mar 08	61-0303	KC-135E, AMARG	13 May 08
61-0270	KC-135E, AMARG	17 Sep 08	61-0321	KC-135R	31 Jul 90
61-0271	KC-135E, AMARG	21 May 07	63-8881	KC-135R	27 Sep 93
61-0280	KC-135R	7 Aug 98			

badly damaged over North Vietnam and the gunner was wounded. Rather than bail out and risk fatal injuries to the gunner, the crew attempted to land but crashed. Only the copilot and gunner (Technical Sergeant Spencer Grippen) survived, and the same COMBAT LIGHTNING which escorted the B-52 then served as the MEDEVAC flight to transport the gunner to a hospital at Clark AB (the B-52D copilot, then-First Lieutenant Bob Hymel, was among those who perished in the Pentagon attack on 11th September 2001).

COMBAT LIGHTNING airplanes participated in Operation HOMECOMING, the return of American prisoners of war from Southeast Asia. In June 1973 COMBAT LIGHTNING began an evaluation to relay real-time target updates to bombers en route to their targets in Cambodia and Laos, but the termination of hostilities ended this program. By the end of the war, COMBAT LIGHTNING airplanes had flown 5,802 missions. Afterward, COMBAT LIGHTNING KC-135As were used only as tankers, with their fuel capacity reduced due to the weight of the residual radio relay equipment. In 1973 they were assigned to the 43rd SW at Andersen AFB, and subsequently returned to the KC-135 fleet, serving with both active duty and ANG units. In FY78 two COMBAT LIGHTNING were completely demodified into standard KC-135As. During 1990 four former COMBAT LIGHTNINGS

were converted into KC-135Es, and were eventually stored in AMARG in 2007 and 2008. The remaining three COMBAT LIGHTNINGS were converted into KC-135Rs (see Table 9-1, opposite).

Two EC-135Ls from the 70th AREFS, 305th AREFW saw combat duty yet again in 1991 as part of Operation DESERT STORM in a role similar to that of COMBAT LIGHTNING. EC-135Ls 61-0269 and 61-0283 were 'the critical communications lifeline between front-line troops, tactical air support, and their command and control agencies,' overcoming the line-of-sight limits to UHF radio traffic. The airplanes were assigned to the 1703rd AREFW(P) at King Khalid IAP, Saudi Arabia, although crews considered themselves part of the unofficial '1703rd ACCS'. The EC-135L static call sign was *Mirror*, echoing its 'Looking Glass' cousin. The two airplanes logged 319.2 mission hours. They reportedly assisted in eight search-and-rescue missions and air strikes that accounted for more than 150 Iraqi tanks and 'numerous' *Scud* launchers. EC-135L 61-0269 contributed to a MiG-25 *Foxbat* and a MiG-29 *Fulcrum* kill on 7th February. Despite the genuine efforts of the 70th AREFS, these specific claims are suspect. Post-war analysis revealed that no *Scud* launchers were destroyed by any Coalition airstrikes. Moreover, the last MiG-25 and MiG-29 kills were on 19th January. There were four kills on 7th

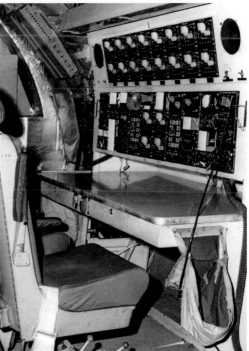

Above: The addition of multiple UHF antennae along the dorsal fuselage earned the nickname 'Razorback' for the COMBAT LIGHTNING KC-135A-VIIIs. The SAC 'Milky Way' band has been removed. *Author's collection*

Right: Interior views of the COMBAT LIGHTNING. Two radio operators (ROs) and a Radio Maintenance Technician (RMT) sat on the left side of the cargo compartment aft of the wing root. *Author's collection*

The KC-135A-VIIIs retained the UHF antennae well after their return from Southeast Asia, as this 17th October 1980 photo of 61-0268 shows. The internal radio gear, equipment racks, and counterweight were all removed. *Photo by Brian Rogers*

One of the first two COMBAT LIGHTNING modifications, 61-0280 remains in service in 2016 after conversion to a KC-135E and again to a KC-135R. It wears Bicentennial markings in this 15th July 1976 image. *Photo by Stephen Miller*

As with many of the short-lived special-mission '135s, COMBAT LIGHTNING jets were farmed out to units that used them as 'buck' tankers. 61-0303 sits next to another former COMBAT LIGHTNING aircraft. *Photo via Lionel Paul via Stephen Miller*

February – a Sukhoi Su-7 *Fitter A*, a 'double kill' of two Sukhoi Su-22 *Fitters*, and a Mil Mi-24 *Hind*. Perhaps two of these could be credited to 61-0269's efforts. During 1991 the remaining EC-135Ls were stored at AMARG or placed on static display (see Appendix III).

In a more modern, automated initiative similar in concept to the original COMBAT LIGHTNING program, the Air Force acquired the Northrop Grumman Roll-On Beyond-Line-of-Sight Enhancement (ROBE) system, developed in 2003. This is a roughly 2ft x 4ft (0.6m x 1.2m) palletized digital network router, and is strapped to the floor of any of the 40 KC-135Rs configured to carry the ROBE suite. The ROBE system automatically connects with local tactical data networks, extending their range considerably. It requires no crewmember intervention once installed. Given the constant presence of tankers in the air over Iraq, Afghanistan, or near other combat theaters, ROBE KC-135s can 'conduct air refueling, airlift, and be a link for command and control.'

KC-135A-VII INDIVIDUAL AIRCRAFT

61-0268 This airplane was selected from the 28th AREFS, 28th BW at Ellsworth AFB for conversion into a COMBAT LIGHTNING platform. Following the war in Southeast Asia it served as a tanker with a variety of active duty and ANG units. From 24th May through 4th September 1990 this airplane was converted into a KC-135E and assigned to the 940th AREFG at Mather AFB, CA.

61-0270 This KC-135A was converted into a COMBAT LIGHTNING aerial radio relay platform. Following the war in Southeast Asia it served as a tanker with a variety of active duty and ANG units. From 21st February through 12th June 1990 it was converted into a KC-135E and assigned to the 434th AREFW at Grissom AFB.

61-0271 This airplane was selected from the 97th AREFS at Blytheville AFB for conversion into one of the first two COMBAT LIGHTNING platforms. Following the war in Southeast Asia, it served as a tanker with a variety of active duty and ANG units. From 1st November through 26th April 1990 it was converted into a KC-135E and assigned to the 434th AREFW at Grissom AFB.

61-0280 This airplane was selected from the 916th AREFS at Travis AFB for conversion into one of the first two COMBAT LIGHTNING platforms. Following the war in Southeast Asia it served as a tanker with a variety of active duty and ANG units. From 1st December 1989 through 22nd May 1990 it was converted into a KC-135E and assigned to the 452nd AREFW at March AFB. By 7th August 1998 it had been further converted into a KC-135R.

61-0303 This airplane was selected from the 922nd AREFS, 17th BW at Wright-Patterson AFB for conversion into a COMBAT LIGHTNING platform. Following the war in Southeast Asia it served as a tanker with a variety of active duty and ANG units. From 4th January through 1st June 1990 it was converted into a KC-135E and assigned to the 452nd AREFW at March AFB. By 1st March 1997 it had been further converted to a KC-135R.

61-0321 This airplane was selected from the 99th AREFS, at Westover AFB for conversion into a COMBAT LIGHTNING platform. Following the war in Southeast Asia it served as a tanker with a variety of active duty and ANG units. During 1971 it supported LOOKING GLASS operations at Offutt AFB, although details of this are not known. By 30th July 1990 it had been further converted into a KC-135R.

63-8881 This airplane was selected from the 380th BW at Plattsburgh AFB for conversion into a COMBAT LIGHTNING platform. Following the war in Southeast Asia it served as a tanker with a variety of active duty and ANG units. By 27th September 1993 it had been further converted into a KC-135R.

EC-135L INDIVIDUAL AIRCRAFT

EC-135Ls had numerous radio antennae along both the dorsal and ventral fuselage. The airplanes retained the air refueling boom, and as part of normal training operations routinely offloaded fuel. They also had an IFR system. This modification was not incorporated in all eight airplanes as part of the initial conversion, and was apparently installed in the remaining five EC-135Ls after three of the eight airplanes were demodified in 1970. The EC-135L carried a normal flight crew of aircraft commander, co-pilot, navigator, and boom operator, as well as a 'back-end' crew of two radio operators and a radio maintenance technician.

61-0261 Following conversion by Lockheed, this KC-135A airborne command post was redesignated an EC-135L on 25th September 1967. It was assigned to the 305th AREFS, the 3rd ACCS, and finally the 70th AREFS, all at Grissom AFB. By 1989 it had been reassigned to the 4th ACCS at Ellsworth AFB. Stored in AMARC on 29th May 1992 as AACA0020 (see Appendix III). It was scrapped on 9th December 2013.

61-0263 This KC-135A airborne command post was delivered to Lockheed on 16th October 1967. Redesignated as an EC-135L on 13th December 1967 and delivered to the 305th AREFS at Grissom AFB on 15th December 1967. Transferred to the 3rd ACCS and later the 70th AREFS, both at Grissom AFB. Stored in AMARC on 5th May 1992 as AACA0015, and scrapped on 3rd December 2013 (see Appendix III).

61-0269 This KC-135A airborne command post was delivered to Lockheed on 30th October 1967. Redesignated as an EC-135L on 21st December 1967 and delivered to the 305th AREFS at Grissom AFB. It remained there until 19th November 1968 when it was reassigned to the 28th AREFS at Ellsworth AFB. Transferred on 9th January 1969 to the 906th AREFS at Minot AFB. Returned to the 305th AREFS at Grissom AFB on 20th January 1970. Reassigned to the 3rd ACCS and later the 70th AREFS, both at Grissom AFB. Placed on static display at Grissom AFB on 29th June 1992 (see Appendix III). It bears the mission marks earned supporting combat operations during Operation DESERT STORM, including two 'MiGs' shot down, and 27 mobile launchers and more than 100 tanks destroyed.

61-0279 Lockheed converted this KC-135A airborne command post into an EC-135L from 2nd August through 27th October 1965. Delivered on 3rd November 1965 to the 32nd AREFS at Lockbourne AFB. Transferred on 29th June 1966 to the 305th AREFS at Grissom AFB. Reported to have received the ALCC modification on 5th March 1968, a refit not known to be applied to EC-135Ls. Reassigned to the 3rd ACCS and later the 70th AREFS, both at Grissom AFB. Stored in AMARC on 22nd May 1992 as AACA0018, and scrapped on 16th June 2016 (see Appendix III).

61-0281 Redesignated an EC-135L on 30th June 1966 and assigned to the 305th AREFS at Grissom AFB. It remained there until 13th February 1968 when it was reassigned to the 906th AREFS, 450th BW at Minot AFB. On 25th July 1968 the 450th BW was inactivated and replaced by the 5th BW, and the airplane and crews appropriately reassigned. It returned to the 305th AREFS at Grissom AFB on 31st December 1969. Official Air Force records show that 61-0281 was redesignated as a KC-135A on 1st May 1970, but was redesignated an EC-135L on 6th January 1971 and assigned to the 3902nd ABW at Offutt AFB on 15th January. It was assigned to the 55th SRW at Offutt AFB on 14th September 1971 and had its designation changed back to KC-135A. It remained associated with the 55th SRW through 12th September 1972, and then underwent some undetermined modification by E-Systems, possibly to remove any existing or remaining communications equipment. By 1989 it was assigned to the 93rd BW at Castle AFB as a KC-135A. It became a KC-135E on 15th February 1991, and was retired to AMARG on 25th August 2009 at AACA0243 (see Appendix III).

61-0283 Lockheed modified this KC-135A airborne command post into an EC-135L on 16th August 1965. It was then assigned to the 32nd AREFS at Lockbourne AFB on 3rd January 1966. It was reassigned on 14th February 1966 to the 28th AREFS at Ellsworth AFB where it remained until 20th November 1967 when it was transferred to the 305th AREFS at Grissom AFB. The airplane was again transferred to the 906th AREFS at Minot AFB on 15th July 1968 and returned to the 305th AREFS at Grissom AFB on 17th February 1969. Reassigned to the 3rd ACCS and later the 70th AREFS, both at Grissom AFB. Stored in AMARC on 6th May 1992, as AACA0016, and scrapped on 20th November 2013 (see Appendix III).

The EC-135Ls have traditionally been associated with Grissom AFB, although they were also briefly based at Lockbourne AFB. 61-0261 visits Ellsworth AFB during runway maintenance at Grissom AFB. *Photo by Brian Rogers*

EC-135L 61-0269 was one of two radio relay jets that participated in Operation DESERT STORM, with impressive results. It is now on display at Grissom AFB.
Photo by William R Peake

Prior to the 1972 demodification of the three EC-135Ls into KC-135As, none of the EC-135Ls had IFR systems, which was later installed on the remaining five EC-135Ls. Hence, the three demodified jets were never KC-135A (ARRs) like 58-0011, 58-0018, and 61-0293.
Photo by Brian Rogers

USAF records show that EC-135L 61-0302 was converted into a KC-135A on 20th May 1970. This photo taken at Wright-Patterson AFB on 2nd June 1972 suggests that the 1970 demodification may not have been complete. The SAC emblem on the weather door indicates that it (and the other two EC-135Ls) were in use at Offutt AFB as CSAs.
Photo by Jack Morris via Stephen Miller

61-0288 This KC-135A airborne command post was delivered for modification to Lockheed on 1st December 1967. It was redesignated an EC-135L on 9th January 1968 and assigned to the 906th AREFS, 450th BW at Minot AFB on 4th February 1968. It remained there until 20th March 1968 when it was reassigned to the 305th AREFS at Grissom AFB. It returned to the 906th AREFS at Minot AFB (although the wing had changed from the 450th BW to the 5th BW) on 23rd August 1968. On 31st December 1969 the airplane was transferred to the 28th AREFS at Ellsworth AFB. On 1st May 1970 the airplane's MDS was changed to KC-135A, although nothing is known of any change in mission or configuration. The designation was changed back to EC-135L on 5th January 1971, and like EC-135L 61-0281, it was assigned to the 3902nd ABW at Offutt AFB on 12th January 1971. Its designation was changed back to KC-135A on 14th September 1971 and the airplane remained associated with the 55th SRW at Offutt

AFB. From 25th June through 1st September 1972, E-Systems demodified the airplane, after which it was assigned to the 28th AREFS at Ellsworth AFB. By 1989 it was in service with the 93rd BW at Castle AFB as a tanker. It also served from 1989 through early 1992 as a 'steam jet' proficiency trainer for the 4th ACCS, as the co-located 28th AREFS (from which the 4th ACCS had previously drawn its J57-equipped proficiency KC-135s) had converted to KC-135Rs. On 29th June 1992 61-0288 was modified into a KC-135R.
61-0302 This KC-135A airborne command post completed conversion into an EC-135L on 11th December 1967 when it was assigned to Grissom AFB. It was demodified to a KC-135A tanker on 20th May 1970. BMAC converted it into a KC-135R on 15th May 1990, and it was relegated to AMARG on 27th June 2013 as '7811' (see Appendix III).

Reorganization

The 1962 PACCS restructuring added to the overall survivability of SAC's airborne command post fleet by dispersing the aircraft from a single location at Offutt AFB to each of the three NAF headquarters at Westover AFB, Barksdale AFB, and March AFB. This ensured that all ABNCPs could launch simultaneously from four geographically separate bases rather than have them launch sequentially at Offutt AFB, where congestion might mean that only one or two could take off before the first Soviet ICBM arrived. Despite the apparent wisdom of dispersing the ABNCPs, the NAF locations proved highly vulnerable to Soviet SLBMs. By the mid to late 1960s, Russian submarines could destroy any of the NAF bases, as well as the NEACP at Andrews AFB, within three to five minutes, far less than the 15-minute minimum SAC required to launch its alert force on warning of an impending attack.

The solution was to relocate the PACCS fleet to interior bases not susceptible to inadequate warning time for SLBMs. This would also relieve tanker squadrons from operating PACCS assets and instead assign the airplanes and crews to newly formed Airborne Command and Control Squadrons (ACCS). Initial plans called for the establishment of a PACCS 'super wing' at Offutt AFB. Despite the logistical advantages in having all the aircraft and crews at a single base, doing so would render the entire PACCS force vulnerable to a surprise attack or sabotage. Instead, the 1st April 1970 reorganization redistributed the aircraft to three bases within the central United States. These geographic and administrative changes did not affect the PACCS mission: the LOOKING GLASS continued with 24-hour airborne alert and the AUXCPs, ALCCs, and radio relay airplanes remained on 15-minute ground alert (see Table 9-2).

The 2nd ACCS, 55th SRW at Offutt AFB took over the airplanes and crews assigned to the 38th SRS, and was responsible for EC-135C LOOKING GLASS primary airborne command post, and the EC-135C Central AUXCP (*Grayson*) from 913th AREFS at Barksdale AFB, now referred to as the MIDAUX. The airplane sat ground alert at Offutt AFB and, once launched, served as an airborne backup to the LOOKING GLASS. The 2nd ACCS also supported a dedicated ground alert EC-135C for the CINCSAC (provided there was sufficient warning time for him to arrive at the aircraft).

The 3rd ACCS, 305th AREFW at Grissom AFB took over the EC-135C EASTAUX (*Achieve*) from the 99th AREFS at Westover AFB, and the radio relay EC-135Ls from the 305th AREFS at Grissom AFB and the 32nd AREFS at Lockbourne AFB. The EASTAUX EC-135C and one radio relay EC-135L sat alert at Grissom AFB, and one EC-135L was on alert at Lockbourne AFB. The 3rd ACCS flew its first scheduled LOOKING GLASS sortie on 9th November 1970. A month later, a major blizzard hit the Midwest on 10th December 1970, effectively shutting down the 2nd ACCS and the 4th ACCS. A 3rd ACCS EC-135C flew to Blytheville AFB, AR, picked up Brigadier General James E Hill, the 42nd Air Division Commander, to serve as AEAO, and flew its first unscheduled LOOKING GLASS sortie. The final commander for the 3rd ACCS was Lieutenant Colonel James Spence, the first navigator to command a USAF operational flying squadron.

The 4th ACCS acquired the WESTAUX (*Stepmother*) from the 22nd AREFS at March AFB, as well as EC-135A/G ALCCs and a backup EC-135A ABNCP from the 906th AREFS at Minot AFB. The WESTAUX – typically an EC-135C, but occasionally an EC-135A/G with attendant mission degrade – provided a secure link between the LOOKING GLASS and the three ALCCs which orbited above the Minuteman missile fields in the Dakotas, Wyoming, Nebraska, Colorado, and Montana. One ALCC sat alert alongside the WESTAUX at Ellsworth AFB, and two ALCCs sat alert at Minot AFB. The 4th ACCS regularly flew the LOOKING GLASS mission on Thursdays, usually from Offutt AFB but occasionally from Ellsworth AFB.

Table 9-2. **1970 PACCS Reorganization**

From	To	From	To
SAC ABNCP	**SAC ABNCP**	**CentAUXCP**	**MidAUXCP**
Looking Glass	*Axel 11**	*Grayson*	*Axel 22**
38th SRS	2nd ACCS	913th AREFS	2nd ACCS
Offutt AFB	Offutt AFB	Barskdale AFB	Offutt AFB
WestAUXCP	**WestAUXCP**	**EastAuxCP**	**EastAUXCP**
Stepmother	*Axel 21**	*Achieve*	*Axel 23**
22nd AREFS	4th ACCS	99th AREFS	3rd ACCS
March AFB	Ellsworth AFB	Westover AFB	Grissom AFB
Radio Relay	**Radio Relay**	**Radio Relay**	**Radio Relay**
-	*Axel 41*	-	*Axel 42*
305th AREFS	3rd ACCS	32nd AREFS	3rd ACCS
Grissom AFB	Grissom AFB	Lockbourne AFB	Grissom AFB
ABNCP	**ALCC**	**ALCC**	**ALCC**
-	*Axel 32*	-	*Axel 33*
906th AREFS	4th ACCS	906th AREFS	4th ACCS
Minot AFB	Ellsworth AFB	Minot AFB	Ellsworth AFB
ALCC	**ALCC**	**CINCSAC**	**CINCSAC**
-	*Axel 31*	-	*Axel 88*
28th AREFS	4th ACCS	38th SRS	2nd ACCS
Ellsworth AFB	Ellsworth AFB	Offutt AFB	Offutt AFB

* Front-end call signs. Prior front-end call signs were randomly generated each day. Back-end call signs remained the same, i.e., *Stepmother, Grayson, Achieve,* and *Looking Glass.*

Changes to the other airborne command post units and aircraft followed the 1970 PACCS reorganization. Beginning in 1974, Boeing E-4A AABNCPs replaced the NIGHT WATCH III EC-135J NEACPs assigned to the 1st ACCS at Andrews AFB, which was transferred to Offutt AFB on 1st July 1977. The NIGHT WATCH EC-135Js were then reassigned to the 9th ACCS, 15th ABW at Hickam AFB, and reconfigured with the BLUE EAGLE battle staff suites taken from the EC-135Ps. These were then transferred to the 6th ACCS, 4500th ABW at Langley AFB. Along with an EC-135H (later converted into an EC-135P), the EC-135Ps formed the CINCLANT SCOPE LIGHT airborne command post system.

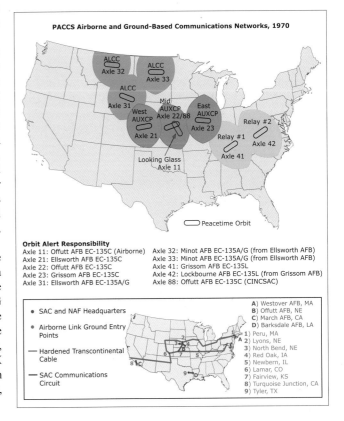

PACCS Airborne and Ground-Based Communications Networks, 1970

Orbit Alert Responsibility
Axle 11: Offutt AFB EC-135C (Airborne)
Axle 21: Ellsworth AFB EC-135C
Axle 22: Offutt AFB EC-135C
Axle 23: Grissom AFB EC-135C
Axle 31: Ellsworth AFB EC-135A/G
Axle 32: Minot AFB EC-135A/G (from Ellsworth AFB)
Axle 33: Minot AFB EC-135A/G (from Ellsworth AFB)
Axle 41: Grissom AFB EC-135C
Axle 42: Lockbourne AFB EC-135L (from Grissom AFB)
Axle 88: Offutt AFB EC-135C (CINCSAC)

- SAC and NAF Headquarters
- Airborne Link Ground Entry Points
- Hardened Transcontinental Cable
- SAC Communications Circuit

A) Westover AFB, MA
B) Offutt AFB, NE
C) March AFB, CA
D) Barksdale AFB, LA
1) Peru, MA
2) Lyons, NE
3) North Bend, NE
4) Red Oak, IA
5) Newbern, IL
6) Lamar, CO
7) Fairview, KS
8) Turquoise Junction, CA
9) Tyler, TX

Faced with post-Vietnam budget cuts, in January 1975 CINCSAC General Russell E Dougherty looked for ways to sustain the PACCS force while spending less on infrastructure and operations. In one proposal, Headquarters SAC Directorate of Operations examined the practicality of assigning a portion of the PACCS mission to the Air Force Reserve, specifically the radio relay EC-135Ls at Grissom AFB. Completed in early in December 1975, the study found that 'while it was theoretically possible for the reserves to undertake these

Table 9-3. **1975 PACCS Reorganization**

Base	Mission	Needed to Support Alert	
		Aircraft	Battle Staffs
Offutt AFB	Looking Glass	5	5
	CINCSAC	1	1
	EASTAUXCP	3	3
Grissom AFB	Radio Relay #1	1	0
	Radio Relay #2	1	0
Ellsworth AFB	WESTAUXCP	3	3
	ALCC #1	1	0
	ALCC #2	1	0
	ALCC #3	1	0

Table 9-4. **1975 PACCS Aircraft Distribution**

Base	Aircraft Type	Number Assigned		
		3 Jul 75	2 Oct 75	6 Nov 75
Offutt AFB	EC-135C	8	10	9
Grissom AFB	EC-135C	3	-	-
	EC-135G	1	1	1
	EC-135L	5	5	5
Ellsworth AFB	EC-135A	5	5	5
	EC-135C	3	4	5
	EC-135G	3	4	4

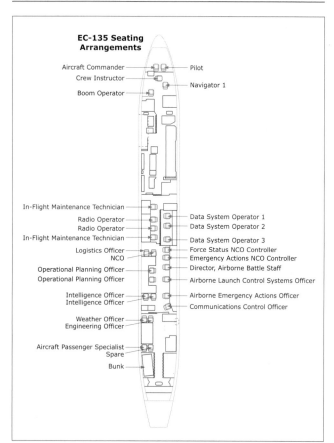

EC-135 Seating Arrangements

Aircraft Commander — Pilot
Crew Instructor
Boom Operator — Navigator 1

In-Flight Maintenance Technician
Radio Operator — Data System Operator 1
Radio Operator — Data System Operator 2
In-Flight Maintenance Technician — Data System Operator 3
Logistics Officer — Force Status NCO Controller
NCO — Emergency Actions NCO Controller
Operational Planning Officer — Director, Airborne Battle Staff
Operational Planning Officer — Airborne Launch Control Systems Officer
Intelligence Officer — Airborne Emergency Actions Officer
Intelligence Officer — Communications Control Officer
Weather Officer
Engineering Officer
Aircraft Passenger Specialist
Spare
Bunk

duties, it was neither practical nor cost effective to do so.' Despite the decision not to shift the radio relay mission to the Reserves, SAC nonetheless consolidated the PACCS force in a two-stage effort from October to December 1975.

Beginning on 1st October, the MIDAUX was abolished and its duties assumed by the LOOKING GLASS. At the same time, the EASTAUX was transferred from the 3rd ACCS at Grissom AFB to the 2nd ACCS at Offutt AFB, leaving the Radio Relay mission at Grissom AFB. The second and final part of the 1975 PACCS reorganization took place on 31 December, when the 3rd ACCS was inactivated and the Radio Relay mission was transferred to the 70th AREFS, 305th AREFW, still located at Grissom AFB. These actions reduced the number of PACCS aircraft on ground alert from eight to seven, with a similar reduction in the battle staff personnel assigned to the aircraft (see Tables 9-3 and 9-4).

For the next 16 years, SAC's airborne command post fleet remained constant in numbers, mission, and organization. Centered on an EC-135C LOOKING GLASS operated by the 2nd ACCS, the PACCS fleet included two AUXCPs (one from the 2nd ACCS – the EASTAUX – and one from the 4th ACCS – the WESTAUX) on 15-minute ground alert. The 4th ACCS provided ALCCs Nos. 1, 2 and 3, and the 70th AREFS supported Radio Relays Nos. 1 and 2.

Operations and Capabilities

Just as with SAC's bombers, tankers, and missiles, PACCS elements spent a good deal of time practicing simulated wartime conditions. A ground simulator allowed the Battle Staff crews to conduct a variety of scenarios ranging from routine message transmission to all-out nuclear war, including equipment failure or alternate continuity of government situations. Airborne exercises were commonplace, and served both to ensure crew familiarity and readiness as well as desensitize anyone 'listening in' to the radio traffic. These included GIANT DRILL, a battle staff Emergency War Order (EWO) exercise, and HIGH HEELS, a JCS SIOP management exercise. Some JCS exercises included other EC-135 operators. POLO HAT was a 'controlled timing exercise that measured the speed and accuracy of SIOP execution and termination messages transmitted to US nuclear delivery forces.' In POLO HAT 71-5, for example, which took place on 21st October 1971, a Minuteman launched from Vandenberg AFB used the ERCS to broadcast a simulated EAM. Purpose of this test was to determine if the CINCPAC BLUE EAGLE EC-135P orbiting 150nm (278km) south of Hickam AFB could receive the message. The airborne EC-135P did indeed receive the message on both test frequencies for a period of 13 minutes, but another EC-135P on ground alert at Hickam AFB heard the EAM for only five minutes on a single frequency. The exercise validated the importance of an airborne command post rather than one on ground alert in receiving critical SIOP-related communications.

An on-station LOOKING GLASS did not leave its orbit until the replacement EC-135C was airborne and had taken over the necessary command and communications links. If a replacement was unable to launch due to bad weather or mechanical trouble, the on-station airplane remained airborne (known as 'Doubles'), refueled in flight by a tanker conceivably launched from anywhere in the US. Even if the LOOKING GLASS should lose an engine while airborne it would still remain on station until replaced. LOOKING GLASS crews were very 'go' oriented – no one wanted to be the crew that couldn't get a jet airborne, let alone fail to complete the sortie and have to land early. On one mission the landing gear wouldn't retract after takeoff from Offutt AFB and the crew flew the entire mission with the gear down. The excess drag dictated four unplanned air refuelings, quite an accomplishment for both the successful pilot and the back-enders along for a very bumpy ride! By this time the LOOKING GLASS back-end crew included the AEAO, an operations controller, a communications officer, as well as plans, weather, and intelligence officers, a logistics officer, communications technicians, a force status non-commissioned officer (NCO) who briefed force and weapons status, and a passenger specialist (the 'stew').

Occasional claims appeared in print during the 1980s that the EC-135 airborne command posts could 'provide a measure of eavesdropping capability to augment strategic reconnaissance assets, although no details are available of this or any operation where this has been practised'. 'Details' of such operations were unavailable because this never happened. SAC EC-135s, other than an occasional 'good will' trip to the United Kingdom, did not operate close enough to any potential areas of interest to 'eavesdrop' on anyone other than Kansas City country-western radio stations.

The LOOKING GLASS acquired a modest degree of television fame when a four-part episode of *Lassie* titled 'Peace is Our Profession' aired in February 1972. Part One had the famous collie visit a Minuteman site, and in Part Four Lassie was at a B-52 base. In Parts Two and Three, a diabetic poodle named Sparky stows away with his master on the LOOKING GLASS. Without his insulin, the poodle becomes critically ill during the flight. Thanks to Lassie, Sparky is saved. The LOOKING GLASS appeared in apocalyptic movies such as the 1983 TV drama *The Day After*, the 1984 film *Countdown to Looking Glass*, and the 1990 movie *By Dawn's Early Light* (where actor James Earl Jones salutes patriotically as his EC-135 purposefully rams the acting president's E-4 to prevent nuclear escalation). The LOOKING GLASS also earned considerable notoriety when a multi-page letter to the editor appeared in *Penthouse* Magazine. Purportedly written by one of the female flight stewards, it was an explicit account of sexual hijinks with most of the crew, including the AEAO, during a single LOOKING GLASS mission. Subsequent investigation showed that the letter was a hoax.

Efforts to manage the vast amounts of incoming data for the battle staff led to the 1967 airborne data automation (ADA) initiative. In order to make space for the new Variable Instruction Computer (VIC) prototype, EC-135C 62-3584 went to OCAMA in September 1968. From 20th January through 7th March 1969, it was assigned to the 3245th ABG at Hanscom Field, where the VIC was installed. Ground tests began on 17th March. The airplane returned to Offutt AFB on 14th July 1969. The LOOKING GLASS finally had a rudimentary data management capability, but this would remain a crucial weakness for the remainder of its operational lifetime. In an age where a cell phone offers real-time video conferencing and can remotely control a drone around the world, it is difficult to appreciate that in 1967 a computer capable of tracking every SAC asset in the SIOP – gravity bombs, missile warheads, bombers, tankers, ICBMs – would fill a warehouse. Thirty years later computers were more capable and smaller, but the amount of data they would need to handle had grown exponentially. By that time, the LOOKING GLASS EC-135Cs had retired.

Other upgrades to the EC-135Cs included the installation in the mid 1960s of the High Altitude Radiation Detection System (HARDS), which was designed to 'detect nuclear explosions in the atmosphere that would affect missile guidance and control systems.' In 1969 the 487L Survivable Low Frequency Communications System (SLFCS) began operational testing on SAC's EC-135Cs at Offutt AFB, with the remaining EC-135H, EC-135J, and EC-135P airborne command posts to be configured in 1970. This was a low data rate teletype capable of 71 words per minute (wpm) under normal circumstances, but was expected to be as poor as 7 wpm under SIOP conditions. Heart of the SLFCS was the AN/ARC-96 radio and a trailing wire antenna (TWA), operating in the 3-30kc range. By June 1969 the first six EC-135Cs (62-3581, 62-3584, 63-8046, 63-8047, 63-8050, and 63-8054) had been configured with

The central communications suites on EC-135C 62-3581. Top image shows teletypes used to transmit orders to SAC command posts and other NCA agencies. Bottom image shows the many HF and UHF radios used to communicate with SAC aircraft and ground-based facilities. Red buttons on AUTOVON phone pad define the precedence over other callers using the system. **P**riority is the lowest level, followed by **I**mmediate, and then **F**lash. **F**lash **O**verride is usable only by the President, the Secretary of Defense, the JCS Chairman, and Unified commanders such as CINCSAC. *Author's collection*

the TWA and transceiver. Throughout initial tests of the TWA in 1968 the wire antenna experienced repeated failures. On 10 different flights, portions of the wire (which cost $35,000) broke off or were cut off because it failed to retract. On 16th December 1968, for example, 27,000ft (8,230m) of the stranded steel cable antenna had to be cut away over the Pacific Ocean. This remained an unresolved and perennial problem. TWA missions were nearly always flown over water in the event the wire did not retract fully and had to be severed in flight, thus generally avoiding people or structures on the ground.

The EC-135Cs were arguably only a second generation system, and increasingly came under sharp criticism for their vulnerability to EMP as well as their operational shortcomings such as limited crew space, relatively short endurance without the need for air refueling (usually by an EC-135 dedicated as a tanker sortie, further degrading the total PACCS force), limited computational and data storage facilities, and outdated communication suite technology. One pundit warned in 1971 that the United States had 'clearly staked its ability to control [American nuclear] retaliation on an airborne system, and the EC-135 was pitifully outmoded'. Plans for a replacement AABNCP began in the early 1960s, largely due to space limits on the EC-135s. In justifying the acquisition of the Boeing 747-based

E-4A, Secretary of Defense Melvin Laird argued during 1973 that the E-4 was '… an urgent program if we are to retain a credible and realistic deterrent in the future … Our current airborne command system is severely deficient in survivability and capacity and cannot fulfill our essential needs in the event of nuclear attack on our country. It lacks the survivable secure communications needed for control and execution of the [SIOP] forces.'

Original plans called for the E-4A to replace the entire LOOKING GLASS EC-135C and NIGHT WATCH EC-135J fleet in a one-to-one ratio. The first three E-4As replaced the EC-135Js prior to the 1st July 1977 relocation of the 1st ACCS from Andrews AFB to Offutt AFB, with subsequent deliveries of the more advanced E-4B slated to replace SAC's EC-135Cs. The fourth E-4 was used in the development and acquisition of the advanced equipment for the E-4B. Baseline evaluation involved the installation of specified command and control communications gear that would be removed from the LOOKING GLASS and installed in the E-4B. On 1st September 1976, EC-135C 62-3584 'donated' much of its back end gear to development E-4B 75-0125, with three flight tests completed on 28th

Top: EC-135C 62-3584 was the functional prototype for improvements to the airborne data automation initiative, and later served as the 'donor' aircraft for LOOKING GLASS E-4B evaluations. *Author's collection*

Above left: Control panel on EC-135C 62-3581 for the trailing wire antenna. The TWA always proved nettlesome, and on more than a few occasions the RO was compelled to pull the red handle to cut a TWA that would not retract. *Author's collection*

Above right: The trailing wire antenna fairing mounted on the right side of the fuselage forward of the main gear well was the heart of the 487L SLFCS using an AN/ARC-96 LF radio. *Photo by the author*

December. Soon-to-be inaugurated President Jimmy Carter was the first president to fly on an E-4A from Andrews AFB to Robins AFB, GA, on 11th January 1977. While en route, he participated in a simulated JCS exercise. Three days later, on 14th February, Carter directed Secretary of Defense Harold Brown to cancel all remaining E-4B orders. There would be no EC-135C replacement. For a brief period the E-4s had both NEACP and EC-135C capabilities, and the first E-4 LOOKING GLASS mission took place on 4th March 1980. The E-4 also carried the ALCS; the first launch of a Minuteman from an E-4 took place on 1st April 1981 using a 2nd ACCS launch crew. Soon thereafter the ALCS equipment was removed and the use of the E-4 in place of the LOOKING GLASS ended.

During June 1987 the first COMMON/PACER LINK I EC-135C went on alert. PACER LINK included a new interior with state-of-the-art equipment which allowed the battle staff to remotely retarget Peacekeeper ICBMs, as well as improved capabilities to connect with and manage both Minutemen and Peacekeepers, hence the name COMMON. The PACER LINK modifications were not without substantial problems. For the first six months of 1990, for example, the system suffered from 'serious wiring problems' that could neither be identified nor resolved. A year later, on 28th January 1991, a 2nd ACCS PACER LINK II EC-135C finally flew its first '100% effective sortie'.

Beginning in 1990 four EC-135Cs (62-3581, 62-3585, 63-8046, and 63-8054) were configured with a large fairing above the forward fuselage to cover the MILSTAR satellite antenna as part of the PACER LINK II communications suite upgrade. With the demise of the EC-135C fleet, the MILSTAR equipment already installed on such EC-135Cs was removed and placed on US Navy E-6As, which were then redesignated as E-6Bs.

THE *OTHER* CINCS

NIGHT WATCH

The first KC-135 airborne command posts assigned outside of SAC were the NIGHT WATCH NEACPs on behalf of the US National Command Authority. Deliveries to the 1000th ACCS, 1001st ABW at Andrews AFB began on 19th February 1962 with KC-135A 61-0274, followed by three additional KC-135As (KC-135As 61-0282, 61-0285, and 61-0291) by mid 1962. All four KC-135A NEACPs were redesignated as EC-135As on 1st January 1965 and were subsequently transferred to the CINCEUR SILK PURSE mission. Beginning in 1965 E-Systems modified the first of three SAC EC-135Cs (believed to be 63-8057) into EC-135Js as Class V modification No.1705 for the NIGHT WATCH III program. Two additional EC-135Cs (63-8055, 63-8056) were converted and redesignated as EC-135Js during 1966 and 1967. On 1st July 1969 the 1000th ACCS was redesignated as the 1st ACCS and the 1001st ABW redesignated as the 1st CW, with the airplanes and crews reassigned accordingly.

The EC-135J conversion included 'installation of two command compartments containing 15 operating stations and considerable expansion of the [EC-135C's] communication capability'. The battle staff included 14 senior personnel plus two radio operators, and a teletype operator. A special suite was installed for the 'National Authority Position', a euphemism for the President or his representative. NIGHT WATCH aircraft used the static call sign *Skytop*, with *Skytop 01* assigned to the primary NIGHT WATCH aircraft, *Skytop 02* assigned to the backup aircraft, and *Skytop 03* assigned to the secondary aircraft. These static call signs were not applied to specific serial numbers, but to whichever airplane was assigned to a specific mission. The NEACP battle staff and other 'backenders' used the static call sign *Silver Dollar*. As with the front-end *Skytop* call signs, these were enumerated by mission – *Silver Dollar 01*, etc. As the size of the NCA staff grew, so too did the need for a bigger platform. During early May 1969 President Richard Nixon flew aboard a NIGHT WATCH EC-135J.

Nixon publicly commented favorably about the experience afterward, but privately despised the airplane and its implications for post-SIOP command and control. As late as 19th April 1972 he told National Security Advisor Henry A Kissinger 'I don't like that goddamn command airplane.' Nixon's 1969 flight highlighted the EC-135J's cramped quarters and limited capabilities. If Pan Am could carry more passengers in a new Boeing 747s, then why couldn't one

be used to carry the president and his staff in time of national emergency? In 1974 E-Systems removed the NIGHT WATCH mission suite and trailing wire antenna equipment from one of the EC-135Js for installation in the first E-4A. The barren EC-135J was then reconfigured and delivered to the 9th ACCS, 15th ABW at Hickam AFB to replace the BLUE EAGLE EC-135Ps used by CINCPAC, then destined for the 6th ACCS, 1st TFW at Langley AFB as CINCLANT SCOPE LIGHT airborne command posts. The mission suites from the two remaining NIGHT WATCH EC-135Js were installed in two more E-4As by 1975, with the EC-135Js reconfigured as BLUE EAGLES and delivered to the 9th ACCS. In mid 1977, EC-135C (62-3584) was assigned to the 9th ACCS to supplement the three EC-135Js, and was itself converted into an EC-135J from May 1979 through January 1980.

SILK PURSE

During 1963 two EC-135As (61-0262 and 61-0293) briefly served as SILK PURSE EC-135As on temporary loan to CINCEUR pending delivery of the SILK PURSE EC-135Hs. Beginning in late 1964 LTV modified the first of four NEACP EC-135As (61-0274, 61-0282, 61-0285, and 61-0291) into EC-135Hs to 'incorporate the SILK PURSE Airborne Command Post for use as part of the [Worldwide] Airborne Command and Control Network', replacing the existing C-118 platforms. A fifth airplane, former NIGHT WATCH KC-135A 61-0274, was modified in 1968 into an EC-135H under Program No.1856. The EC-135Hs were first assigned to the 7120th ACCS, 7513th TG following its move in 1965 from Chateauroux AB, France, to RAF Mildenhall. During April 1966 the 7120th SG replaced the 7513th TG as the 7120th ACCS' parent unit. The 7120th ACCS was reassigned on 1st July 1966 to the 513th TAW, still at RAF Mildenhall. On 1st January 1970 the 7120th ACCS was inactivated and replaced by the 10th ACCS, again part of the 513th TAW, which was redesignated the 513th ACCW on 18th June 1987. As part of US budget cuts and the reduction in airborne command post assets, the 10th ACCS was inactivated on 31st December 1991. The EC-135Hs were relegated to AMARC for storage or scrapping, or to Sheppard AFB, TX, as ground instructional trainers and redesignated as GEC-135Hs.

The EC-135Hs provided CINCEUR with a survivable backup command, control, and communications facility for the direction of strategic assets and coordination with NCA directives. At least one SILK PURSE EC-135H was on continuous airborne alert until December 1969, when the operation was changed to a full-time ground alert. In addition to ground alert at RAF Mildenhall, a SILK

The English weather seems to suit EC-135H 61-0285 (minus an intake cover). As with the other SILK PURSE aircraft, this was previously a NIGHT WATCH EC-135A. *Photo by Richard Vandervord*

CINCPAC BLUE EAGLE aircraft included the five original EC-135As, later redesignated EC-135Ps, and finally the former NIGHT WATCH EC-135Js, including 63-8055. *Photo by John Gaffney*

CINCLANT was the last to acquire EC-135 ABNCPs. All were 'cast off' BLUE EAGLE EC-135Ps, former LOOKING GLASS KC-135As. EC-135H 61-0274 was the exception, finally converted into a SCOPE LIGHT EC-135P in 1988. *Photo by Stephen Miller*

The 7120th ACCS became the 10th ACCS on 1st January 1970, and EC-135H 61-0282 was photographed during a missed approach just five months later, still in overall natural metal. *Photo by Jack Friell via Stephen Miller*

PURSE sat ground alert at Lajes AB, Azores. In September 1974, one EC-135H (61-0274) was assigned to the 6th ACCS, 1st TFW at Langley AFB as a SCOPE LIGHT airborne command post for CINCLANT. It became an EC-135P on 23rd May 1988.

Interior modifications to the EC-135H included 'provisions for 16 battle staff personnel, 13 command staff personnel, two radio operators, two switchboard operators, and one secure communications/teletype operator'. Crew makeup later changed to nine CINCEUR and four Supreme Allied Commander, Europe (SACEUR) battle staff personnel. Electronic systems changes included the 'expansion of the AN/ARC-89 Radio System, modification of the multiplex system, [and] installation of a recording system' and improvement to the HF, VHF, and UHF communications equipment.

BLUE EAGLE

As SAC acquired new KC-135Bs for its LOOKING GLASS mission, the five original KC-135A ABNCPs (58-0007, 58-0011, 58-0018, 58-0019, and 58-0022), newly redesignated as EC-135As, were transferred to the 6486th ACCS, 6486th ABW at Hickam AFB. On 31st March 1967, the BLUE EAGLE EC-135As were redesignated as EC-135Ps. The 9th ACCS replaced the 6486th ACCS on 15th October 1969, and on 1st November 1971 the 9th ACCS was reassigned to the 15th ABW.

The CINCPAC BLUE EAGLE ABNCPs provided a secure command and control link between the CINCPAC Headquarters at Pearl Harbor, Hawai'i, and US naval forces throughout the Pacific. The airplanes typically sat remote alert at bases in Japan, Okinawa, Guam, and the Philippines, as well as three daily 8-hour missions providing full airborne coverage at Hickam AFB. During 1969 CINCPAC built a ground alert facility at Hickam AFB, ending the 24-hour airborne coverage. The EC-135Ps also provided VIP transport for CINCPACAF.

The crew included a front-end of pilot, copilot, navigator, and boom operator. Back-end crew was made up of two radio operators, a cryptographic teletype operator, a radio maintenance technician, and the CINCPAC battle staff, typically led by a Navy captain (equivalent to an Air Force colonel). The BLUE EAGLE back-end static call sign was *Upkeep*.

During 1972 three of the BLUE EAGLE EC-135Ps (58-0007, 58-0019, and 58-0022) were reassigned to the newly formed 6th ACCS, 4500th ABW at Langley AFB as the new CINCLANT SCOPE LIGHT ABNCPs, along with EC-135H 61-0274. The two remaining BLUE EAGLE EC-135Ps (58-0011 and 58-0018) were demodified into KC-135A (ARR)s and assigned to the 93rd BW at Castle AFB (former NIGHT WATCH EC-135Js replaced the CINCPAC EC-135Ps). When the 9th ACCS was inactivated on 31st March 1992, two of its EC-135Js were stored in AMARC and two were transferred to the 2nd ACCS, 55th Wing at Offutt AFB. One of these (62-3584) crashed shortly thereafter and the other (63-8055) was eventually stored in AMARC (see Appendices II and III).

An EC-135J BLUE EAGLE crew inadvertently demonstrated its quick response capability in June 1980, when a failed chip in a minicomputer issued an erroneous message that the US was under attack. The BLUE EAGLE airborne command post launched as required, then, after the error was identified and the situation confirmed as 'all clear', it recovered safely.

SCOPE LIGHT

The first of three 9th ACCS EC-135Ps was transferred during late 1972 to the 6th ACCS, 4500th ABW at Langley AFB for CINCLANT as SCOPE LIGHT airborne command posts. EC-135H 61-0274 joined them in September 1974; it was converted into an EC-135P on 23rd May 1988. The 6th ACCS, which was assigned administratively to TAC but was under the operational control of CINCLANT, became fully operational on 1st January 1974 when an EC-135P was first placed on ground alert. On 19th August 1976 the 6th ACCS was reassigned to the 1st TFW. EC-135P 58-0007 was destroyed in a ground fire on 3rd January 1980, and former NKC-135E 55-3129 was converted into an EC-135P as a replacement.

EC-135H INDIVIDUAL AIRCRAFT

EC-135H modifications included the addition of an IFR system (the air refueling boom was retained), wingtip HF antennae, and a trailing wire antenna forward of the starboard main gear well. The airplanes also had the 'saddleback' VLF antenna on the dorsal fuselage and accompanying side lobe fairings on either fuselage side aft of the wing trailing edge. All five airplanes had their J57s replaced with TF33-PW-102s with thrust reversers during 1982 with no change in MDS.

61-0274 This EC-135A airborne command post was converted into an EC-135H from 6th September 1967 through February 1968, when it was delivered to the 7120th ACCS. It was transferred in September 1974 to the 6th ACCS. From 17th February through 13th March 1982 it became the first EC-135H equipped with TF33-PW-102s. Redesignated an EC-135P on 23rd May 1988 following the PACER LINK modification.

61-0282 This EC-135A was converted into an EC-135H in 1967 while assigned to the 7120th ACCS. Modified from 8th – 29th May 1982 with TF33-PW-102s. In 1988 it was nicknamed *Burma Butch*. This airplane reportedly operated as a VIP-configured KC-135A and was known unofficially as a 'VKC-135A'. As it was assigned until November 1965 to the 1000th ACCS at Andrews AFB this appellation is understandable, if incorrect. It became a ground maintenance trainer and was redesignated a GEC-135H on 15th November 1991 (see Appendix III).

61-0285 LTV Electrosystems converted this EC-135A NEACP into an EC-135H, redesignating and delivering it on 5th October 1966 to the 7120th ACCS. From 13th March through 3rd April 1982 it received TF33-PW-102s. Nicknamed *Silver Dollar* by 1989. Stored in AMARC on 9th March 1992 as AACA0012, and scrapped on 5th November 2013 (see Appendix III).

61-0286 From 20th March through 19th September 1967, E-Systems modified this EC-135A into the SILK PURSE configuration, but its MDS was not changed. It was stored at Martin-Marietta, in Baltimore, MD, until 23rd February 1968. On 2nd March 1968 its MDS was changed to EC-135H and it was assigned on 7th March 1968 to the 7120th ACCS. Equipped from 10th April through 1st May 1982 with TF33-PW-102s. It was nicknamed *Dark Angel* in 1988. Stored at Sheppard AFB as a ground maintenance trainer and redesignated a GEC-135H on 22nd January 1992 (see Appendix III).

61-0291 From 15th August through 10th October 1966, LTV Electrosystems converted this EC-135A airborne command post into one of the three original SILK PURSE EC-135Hs assigned to the 7120th ACCS. From 15th May through 6th June 1982 it was equipped with TF33-PW-102s. It was flown to Langley AFB on 28th May 1991 where parts of its battle staff suite were removed for use on other airborne command posts. On 30th May 1991 it was delivered to AMARC and given the storage code AACA0007. The engines, horizontal stabilizers, and other relevant parts were scheduled for use in converting an unidentified KC-135A into a KC-135E, and it was eventually scrapped on 4th December 1995 (see Appendix III).

Few people can recall the high-pitched scream of J57 engines on an EC-135 during final approach. A good thing for local residents, a splash of nostalgia for enthusiasts and spotters. *Photo by Richard Vandervord*

A dark blue cheat line, double chevrons, and lightning bolts distinguish this NIGHT WATCH EC-135J. Emblem on the right side of the weather door is 1st ACCS patch. *Author's collection*

The SCOPE LIGHT EC-135Ps briefly acquired the FF tail code. Almost immediately thereafter 55-3129 was relegated to AMARG, with the rest of the EC-135Ps to follow. *Author's collection*

EC-135P 58-0007 assigned to the 6486th ACCS departs Hickam AFB on 23rd April 1969. At the height of both the war in Southeast Asia and the Cold War, BLUE EAGLE jets served double duty as VIP transports and SIOP-related ABNCPs. *Photo by Stephen Miller*

Boeing converted the EC-135As into EC-135Ps, beginning with 58-0011. The bottom left image shows the battle staff area; bottom right shows the communications center. *Photos P41787 and P41789 courtesy Boeing*

EC-135J INDIVIDUAL AIRCRAFT

EC-135Js had TF33-P-9s without thrust reversers, retained the air refueling boom, had an IFR capability, and had wingtip HF fence antennae, plus the characteristic VLF saddleback antenna on the fuselage spine.

62-3584 Assigned as an EC-135C to the 9th ACCS at Hickam AFB on 28th July 1977 for use as a trainer. Transferred to E-Systems for conversion into a BLUE EAGLE in May 1979. Returned to the 9th ACCS as an EC-135J in February 1980. Transferred to the 2nd ACCS in early 1992. It crashed at Pope AFB, NC, on 29th May 1992 (see Appendix II).

63-8055 Assigned to the 1000th ACCS at Andrews AFB as a NIGHT WATCH III NEACP when redesignated an EC-135J on 21st September 1966. Reassigned on 1st July 1969 to the 1st ACCS, still at Andrews AFB. By 1975 it had been demodified from its NIGHT WATCH mission, reconfigured for the BLUE EAGLE role, and transferred to the 9th ACCS. Transferred to the 2nd ACCS in early 1992. Stored at AMARC on 4th October 1993 as AACA0092, and scrapped on 17th October 2013 (see Appendix III).

63-8056 This EC-135C was delivered on 3rd January 1966, to LTV-Electrosystems for conversion into a NIGHT WATCH III NEACP. Handed over to the 1000th ACCS at Andrews AFB on 20th June 1966 and redesignated an EC-135J on 31st May 1967. Reassigned on 1st July 1969 to the 1st ACCS at Andrews AFB. By 1975 it had been demodified from its NIGHT WATCH role, configured for the BLUE EAGLE mission, and reassigned to the 9th ACCS. It was stored in AMARC on 23rd March 1992 as AACA0013, and scrapped on 14th November 2013 (see Appendix III).

63-8057 E-Systems converted this EC-135C into a NIGHT WATCH NEACP in 1966, when it was assigned to the 1000th ACCS at Andrews AFB. Redesignated an EC-135J on 31st May 1967. Reassigned to the 1st ACCS at Andrews AFB on 1st July 1969. By 1975 it had been demodified from its NIGHT WATCH role, converted to a BLUE EAGLE and reassigned to the 9th ACCS. Stored in AMARC on 31st March 1992 as AACA0014, and later transferred to the Pima Air Museum (see Appendix III).

EC-135P INDIVIDUAL AIRCRAFT

EC-135Ps retained the air refueling boom and had an IFR system installed, as well as a full battle staff suite installed in the cargo compartment. A TWA allowed the EC-135P battle staff to communicate with submerged submarines directly, or via Lockheed EC-130Q and Boeing E-6 TACAMOs

55-3129 From 7th April 1983 through June 1984, this NKC-135E was converted into an EC-135P and assigned to the 6th ACCS to replace EC-135P 58-0007, which was destroyed in 1980. Interestingly, 55-3129 retained a bulkhead autographed by the original seven Mercury astronauts (plus others who followed) while the airplane served as a weightlessness trainer. During 1989 the airplane was noted with the name *Drogue Dragon*. It was stored in AMARC on 31st January 1992 as CA008, and scrapped on 11th May 2016 (see Appendix III).

58-0007 This EC-135A was modified and redesignated an EC-135P on 31st March 1967 while assigned to the 6486th ACCS at Hickam AFB (later redesignated the 9th ACCS). Transferred to the 6th ACCS at Langley AFB after 1974. It was destroyed at Langley AFB on 3rd January 1980 as the result of a fuselage fire (see Appendix II).

58-0011 This EC-135A was converted and redesignated an EC-135P on 31st March 1967 while assigned to the 6486th ACCS at Hickam AFB (later redesignated the 9th ACCS). Demodified into a KC-135A (ARR) by 28th July 1976, when it was assigned to the 93rd BW at Castle AFB.

58-0018 This EC-135A was modified and redesignated an EC-135P on 31st March 1967 while assigned to the 6486th ACCS at Hickam AFB (later the 9th ACCS). Demodified into a KC-135A (ARR) by 31st March 1976, when it was assigned to the 2nd BW at Barksdale AFB.

58-0019 This EC-135A was modified and redesignated an EC-135P on 31st March 1967 while assigned to the 6486th ACCS at Hickam AFB (later the 9th ACCS). Transferred to the 6th ACCS at Langley AFB after 1974. From 24th May through 14th June 1982, 58-0019 received TF33-PW-102s. Stored in AMARC on 12th February 1992 as AACA0009, and scrapped on 25th November 2013 (see Appendix III).

58-0022 This EC-135A was modified and redesignated an EC-135P on 31st March 1967 while assigned to the 6486th ACCS at Hickam AFB (later the 9th ACCS). Transferred to the 6th ACCS at Langley AFB after 1974. From 24th April through 14th May 1982, 58-0022 received TF33-PW-102s. It was stored in AMARC on 5th March 1992 as AACA0011, and scrapped on 21st November 2013 (see Appendix III).

61-0274 This 6th ACCS EC-135H was converted into an EC-135P as part of the PACER LINK program, and was redesignated an EC-135P on 23rd May 1988. It was stored in AMARC on 27th February 1992 as AACA0010, and scrapped on 20th June 2016 (see Appendix III).

Tactical Deployment

Traditional notions of EC-135 airborne command posts focus on the LOOKING GLASS and the PACCS mission or theater CINCs and SCOPE LIGHT or BLUE EAGLE. Although a CINC headed the Tactical Air Command (TAC) and its aircraft were assigned missions with nuclear weapons, it did not have a Triad role that required a dedicated SIOP 'battle management' ABNCP. Indeed, TAC forces in combat were seconded to the theater commander, such as PACAF during the war in Southeast Asia or USAFE in the event of a NATO conflagration, each of whom reported in turn to CINCPAC or CINCEUR. As a result, any TAC airborne command post would have functioned primarily in a VIP transport role for the CINCTAC. This did not stop

TAC from acquiring a tiny number of EC-135K ABNCPs; rather, it changed the rationale. TAC's airborne command posts would provide '(1) CINCTAC with the capability to exercise command and control of Tactical Air Command, (2) conduct global employment and redeployment operations, and (3) oversee United States Air Forces Strike Command.'

To fulfill its 'command and control' duties, TAC's EC-135K ABNCPs offered a 'secure, survivable platform for CINCTAC' in the event of general war. Arguably this allowed for the CINCTAC to undertake his role in any continuity of command protocol, but was otherwise just a place for him to avoid incoming warheads. TACs EC-135Ks were best known, however, for their HEAD DANCER mission, an airborne command post used for fighter deployments to and from Europe and Asia, allowing a high degree of on-scene control during overwater movements. Initially TAC asked that 'several' SAC EC-135s be transferred to TAC (or at least made available to TAC on demand) for its own uses, especially 'fighter drags'. SAC successfully opposed this request, arguing that any reallocation of aircraft from the evolving PACCS mission would weaken the US nuclear deterrent force. Instead, TAC was allocated just one of the early flight test aircraft at Wright-Patterson AFB. As part of the OXEYE DAISY program, on 21st January 1961 ARDC reassigned the first KC-135A – 55-3118 – to TAC for conversion into an EC-135K. PACER DAISY modifications undertaken at OCAMA included installation of four HF transmitters and five HF receivers, four VHF/AM radios, two VHF/FM radios, eight UHF/AM radios, and a secure teletype [an ARC-146 super high frequency (SHF) SATCOM was added during the 1980s]. OCAMA also removed the air refueling boom, and none of the eventual three EC-135Ks was equipped with an IFR system. Nine bunks were installed, along with a galley, additional seats, and tables. One person who flew on 55-3118 described these accommodations as hardly Spartan. It was sumptuously outfitted with 'thick wall-to-wall carpeting from the cockpit to the rear of the airplane, had sound-proofing insulated padding on the walls of the communications section and battle staff area, very comfortable airline seats for the communications team and the battle staff area, a large galley that included a stove, refrigerator, microwave, and a sink with hot and cold running water, and two spacious, airline-type latrines with lighted mirrors and flush toilets.'

For aerial deployments, the 'battle staff' was a Mission Control Team (MCT) comprised of a Commander (Colonel), an MCT Ops Officer, and five or six Headquarters TAC command post officer and enlisted specialists. Eventually there were also three radio operators (RO) dedicated to a TGC-29 secure air/ground teletype, a SATCOM voice radio, and a TGC-14 teletype. Two of these ROs were responsible for acquiring en route and destination weather data, making over-water position reports and hourly situation reports (SITREPs) to the TAC command post at Langley AFB, VA, via HF or SATCOM, and coordinating assistance should one of the fighters develop an in-flight emergency and need to divert. The third RO was dedicated to secure communications.

By 1963 TAC identified the requirement for eight additional HEAD DANCER aircraft, and immediately sought to purchase five of these. Despite command-level emphasis, funds for additional aircraft were severely limited. It was not until May 1970 that a second EC-135K was converted from former KC-135A zero-g trainer 62-3536. This airplane crashed on 14th September 1977 and was replaced in November 1979 by former FAA KC-135A 59-1518 as the third and final EC-135K.

Operational highlights include the October 1962 Cuban Missile Crisis, the 1965 crisis in the Dominican Republic, and the US response to Sudan's request for assistance in 1984 during Libya's invasion of Chad. Major deployments include PORT BOW fighter

movements to the Republic of Korea in 1968 following the North Korean seizure of the USS *Pueblo*, F-4Es flown to Israel during the 1973 October War as the CORONET EAST component of Operation NICKEL GRASS (see Chapter 5), the first BRIGHT STAR exercise of the Rapid Deployment Joint Task Force (RDJTF) to Egypt in 1980, Operations DESERT SHIELD and DESERT STORM, and redeployments to the United States in the wake of post-Cold War unit realignments and base closures in Europe and Asia.

EC-135Ks also conducted numerous special air missions, including the transport of high-ranking government officials and Air Force personnel. Among its many notable achievements was the May 1971 around-the-world diplomatic mission for US Secretary of State Henry A Kissinger. Operation POLO was a particularly sensitive mission because Kissinger planned to fly secretly and incommunicado from Islamabad, Pakistan, into the People's Republic of China (PRC) to establish the groundwork for the opening of diplomatic relations between the US and the PRC. Kissinger actually made his historic flight into the PRC in a Pakistan International Airlines Boeing 707 while 55-3118 remained on the ground in Islamabad. Still, the EC-135K provided secure communications to handle the sensitive dispatches associated with the mission, and its presence aroused less attention than would have one of the VC-135s or VC-137s routinely used to transport Kissinger.

The unit lineage of the EC-135Ks has been circuitous and not completely confirmed by official histories. In 1961 the first EC-135K was assigned to the 19th AF at Seymour Johnson AFB, NC, instead of TAC Headquarters at Langley AFB. According to a former HEAD DANCER crewmember, this was so 'TAC could hide it from Congress, the general public, and the news media.' As the MCT crew was based at Langley AFB, before each overwater deployment the airplane

would go there first to pick them up or the MCT would fly to Seymour Johnson AFB the night prior.

In October 1963, 55-3118 was assigned to the 4th TFW, and in 1964 reassigned to Det 2, 4500th SS, both located at Seymour Johnson AFB. The airplane was reassigned in April 1969 to the 4500th ABW, and later to Det 1, 8th ACCS, 19th AF, still at Seymour Johnson AFB. In 1970 it was reassigned again to Det 2, 4500th SS at Seymour Johnson AFB. In 1972, 55-3118 was reassigned to the 8th ACCS, which was redesignated the 8th TDCS (Tactical Deployment and Control Squadron) on 30th April 1974, more accurately reflecting the unit's deployment mission instead of the airborne command post role associated with TAC's SCOPE LIGHT airborne command post for CINCLANT. In January 1978 the 8th TDCS became a 'geographically separate' unit of the 552nd AWACW based at Tinker AFB. The 8th TDCS moved to Tinker AFB on 26th June 1978, and in March 1986 was assigned directly to the 28th AD, also at Tinker AFB. The 8th TDCS was redesignated the 8th ADCS (Aerial Deployment and Control Squadron) on 1st November 1992 in keeping with Air Force Chief of Staff General 'Tony' McPeak's decree eliminating 'tactical' and 'strategic' from unit designations. With the inactivation of the Air Force's Air Divisions, the 8th ADCS was assigned on 29th May 1992 to the 552nd ACW, still at Tinker AFB.

After the 1992 inactivation of TAC and assumption of its mission by Air Combat Command (ACC), EC-135K 55-3118 continued its HEAD DANCER mission but also served the ACC Commander as a VIP transport (static call sign *Ace 01*) along with Learjet C-21A 84-1014. The 8th ADCS was redesignated as the 8th ACCS on 1st July 1994. The 8th ACCS was finally inactivated on 15th May 1996 and both EC-135Ks were relieved of their duties – 55-3118 was retired and 59-1518 relegated to the VIP transport role and redesignated as a C-135K.

EC-135K 55-3118 at Langley AFB on 1st May 1965. Although OCAMA converted it as part of the PACER DAISY program, it did not receive the extension to the vertical stabilizer until later. *Photo by Ken Hampton via Stephen Miller*

This photo of EC-135K 59-1518 was taken in December 1979, less than a month after it was converted to replace 62-3536. *Photo by Don Jay via Stephen Miller*

Contingency Operations

The proposed merger in 1961 of TAC and the US Army's strategic component resulted in the 1962 establishment of Strike Command (STRICOM), which, among its other duties, would undertake global contingency operations in the Middle East, Africa, Southwest Asia, and Southern Asia. Beginning in 1962 TAC's EC-135K – in addition to its HEAD DANCER mission – provided a ready made airborne command post capability for STRICOM to coordinate operations in what were seen as 'remote regions' without established command and control infrastructure. It was replaced in 1967 by a dedicated STRICOM airplane in the form of KC-135A 60-0316, assigned to MacDill AFB, FL. US Readiness Command replaced STRICOM in 1972, and in 1975 60-0316 was demodified and transferred to the 8th AF Commander at Barksdale AFB. TAC's EC-135Ks resumed support of Readiness Command deployments as part of the Rapid Deployment Joint Task Force (RDJTF). In 1983 US Central Command (CENTCOM) replaced the RDJTF, and operational requirements dictated a specialized aircraft for CENTCOM deployments, leading to the procurement of the EC-135N and EC-135Y ABNCPs.

During 1983 NKC-135A 55-3125 was converted into the EC-135Y, followed two years later by the demodification of ARIA 61-0327 into a C-135N and thence to an EC-135N. Although the back-end of these two airplanes was similar, the internal airframe peculiarities among the two were sufficient to retain the separate designations. Both were re-engined in 1986 with TF33-PW-102s, and acquired an IFR system (55-3125 retained its air refueling boom). Both airplanes were assigned to the 912th AREFS, 19th AREFW at Robins AFB. The 912th AREFS was reassigned on 1st April 1994 and the airplanes were reassigned to the 99th AREFS, 19th ARW. They were relocated to the 6th ARW at MacDill AFB by late 1997.

During Operations DESERT SHIELD and DESERT STORM, EC-135Y 55-3125 was assigned to the 1700th AREFS (P). In addition to support

for CINC CENTCOM General H Norman Schwarzkopf, the EC-135Y occasionally refueled other airplanes during the course of the war. By March 1991, 55-3125 required scheduled maintenance and was replaced by EC-135N 61-0327, also assigned to the 1700th AREFS (P).

Following DESERT STORM 55-3125 underwent regular upgrades, including real-time voice and data streaming via the civilian International Maritime Satellite (INMARSAT). This effort proved challenging given the increased relative motion of a jet at 300 KIAS versus a ship at 20 kts. Not all the problems were technical, however, as one amusing anecdote revealed. In the wake of what appeared to be a sudden and permanent inability to use the system, an investigation by the BIG SAFARI staff determined that the government had simply failed to pay its INMARSAT bill and the service was shut off.

Both aircraft were retired, with 55-3125 going to AMARG as AACA0126 on 4th February 1999 (it was scrapped by 12th September 2013. By February 2003, 61-0327 was displayed at the Museum of Aviation adjacent to Robins AFB, GA, although it may be scrapped due to insufficient funds for regular maintenance (see Appendix III).

KC-135A INDIVIDUAL AIRCRAFT

61-0316 This KC-135A was converted in 1967 into the airborne command post for the CINC, Strike Command, and stationed at MacDill AFB until 1972, when Readiness Command replaced STRICOM. It was then demodified into a KC-135A and assigned by 1979 to the 71st AREFS, 2nd BW at Barksdale AFB for use by the 8th AF Commander. It burned during ground refueling in Egypt on 19th March 1985 (see Appendix II).

EC-135K INDIVIDUAL AIRCRAFT

55-3118 This testbed KC-135A was transferred to TAC on 21st January 1961 for conversion into the first EC-135K. From 6th February to 6th March 1982, 55-3118 received TF33-PW-102s and remained designated an EC-135K. As the first KC-135A built, 55-3118 served as the flagship for the entire fleet. Special ceremonies held at Tinker AFB on 2nd September 1986 celebrated the 30th anniversary of its first flight on 31st August 1956. The airplane was retired on 15th October 1996 and placed on display at McConnell AFB (see Appendix III).

STRICOM KC-135A 60-0316 carried a dark 'Army' green cheat line, reflecting its direct support of ground forces around the world.

Although the HEAD DANCER EC-135Ks are associated with Langley AFB, VA, they were based at Seymour Johnson AFB, NC, ostensibly to remain out of sight of the press and public likely to 'misunderstand' their deployment mission as a VIP duty. *Both photos by Stephen Miller*

59-1518 OCALC converted this former FAA KC-135A into the third EC-135K from March through November 1979, when it was assigned to the 8th TDCS. The airplane received additional modifications from October 1981 to February 1982, revisions necessary to complete its full conversion into an EC-135K. From 3rd–24th April 1982, 59-1518 received TF33-PW-102s but retained its EC-135K designation. In 1996 it was redesignated a C-135K and assigned to VIP transport duties at Hickam AFB.

62-3536 This KC-135A (previously a zero-g weightlessness trainer) was converted into the second EC-135K after May 1970. Soon after takeoff during an exercise from Kirtland AFB on 14th September 1977, 62-3536 struck high terrain and was destroyed (see Appendix II).

EC-135N INDIVIDUAL AIRCRAFT

61-0327 During 1985 this former ARIA C-135N was converted into an EC-135N airborne command post. It was assigned to the 912th AREFS, 19th AREFW at Robins AFB. The 912th AREFS was reassigned on 1st April 1994, and 61-0327 were reassigned to the 99th AREFS, 19th ARW, finally relocating to the 6th ARW at MacDill AFB by late 1997. In March 1991 61-0327 replaced EC-135Y 55-3125 at Riyadh AB, assigned to the 1700th AREFS (P). By February 2003 the airplane had been relegated to display at the Georgia Museum of Flight adjacent to Robins AFB (see appendix III).

EC-135Y INDIVIDUAL AIRCRAFT

55-3125 During 1983 NKC-135A 55-3125 was converted into the EC-135Y, and was assigned to the 912th AREFS, 19th AREFW at Robins AFB. The 912th AREFS was reassigned on 1st April 1994, and 55-3125 was reassigned to the 99th AREFS, 19th ARW, finally relocating to the 6th ARW at MacDill AFB by late 1997. It served as the primary CENTCOM ABNCP during Operation DESERT STORM at Riyadh AB [assigned to the 1700th AREFS (P)] until March 1991, when it was replaced by EC-135N 61-0327. The EC-135Y was retired to AMARG on 4th February 1999, and scrapped by 12th September 2013 (see Appendix IV).

Endgame

On 3rd February 1976 the LOOKING GLASS flew its 15th anniversary mission, having compiled 16,078 sorties in 149,600 flying hours. Upon reaching its 25th anniversary on 3rd February 1986, the LOOKING GLASS had accrued a total of 240,900 hours of accident-free flying time. There would be no 35th anniversary on 3rd February 1996. As the front-end crew of EC-135C 63-8046 from the 2nd ACCS and back-end crew from the 4th ACCS awaited the arrival of Major General Howell M Estes, III, the scheduled AEAO for the 24th July 1990 morning departure, CINCSAC General John T 'Jack' Chain, Jr, arrived at the jet and assumed the AEAO duties. Following the 6:59 AM departure and without any fanfare, Chain informed the crew that the flight would be the last continuously airborne alert LOOKING GLASS mission. It landed 7.5 hours later at 2:32 PM CDT with no replacement airborne, an unanticipated but nonetheless fitting final flight with crews from both squadrons that conducted LOOKING GLASS missions.

Although many cite the decline in superpower tensions as justification for ending the continuous airborne sorties, the 'end' of the Cold War still lay ahead in 1991. Instead, budget cuts that offered a savings of approximately $23 million per year in maintenance and operating costs, and 'improved US intelligence capabilities and the resulting increased warning times also were factors in the decision…'

Clearly marked as the CINCTAC jet (note engine covers), 55-3118 was based at Tinker AFB. When it retired in 1996 after 40 years of service, it was placed on display at McConnell AFB, a location with which it had no prior connection.

61-0327 retained its EC-135N designation after its conversion from an ARIA to the CENTCOM airborne command post, and did not acquire the EC-135Y designation given to its sister jet 55-3125.

EC-135Y 55-3125 kept its air refueling boom (receiving maintenance here). Indeed, '125 refueled the author's RC-135 during Operation DESERT STORM.
All photos by Brian Rogers

In short, US officials believed that American vulnerability to surprise attack had decreased to the point where the expenditure was no longer justifiable. Critics of the decision to end the missions pointed out that $23 million – roughly 16% the cost of a single Lockheed F-22 – was trivial compared to the cost of a 'bolt from the blue' attack by Soviet or Chinese SLBMs, and that strategic security was being sacrificed in the name of politically compelling budget cuts and the purchase of 'silver bullet' stealth aircraft.

The end of 24-hour airborne alert did not mean the end of the LOOKING GLASS mission. Instead of three sorties each day for 'round the clock coverage, the LOOKING GLASS flew once a day with a classified takeoff time and mission duration. Other changes quickly followed suit. In 1991 the 4th ACCS discontinued its ALCC satellite alert mission at Minot AFB. The EC-135As, EC-135Gs, and EC-135Ls were retired. ERCS was discontinued at Whiteman AFB and the airborne components in the ALCS were permanently switched off. The number of ALCS-qualified crewmembers dropped by 85%. On 1st June 1992, just six months after the collapse of the Soviet Union, US Strategic Command (USSTRATCOM) replaced SAC.

In a process that was as rapid as it was sweeping, nearly all of the EC-135 airborne command posts were retired and placed in storage, on display, or scrapped. On 17th December 1992 Deputy Secretary of Defense Donald J Atwood, Jr, directed the Secretaries of the Navy and Air Force, as well as the Chairman of the JCS, to '(1) terminate modifications of the remaining EC-135 ABNCP fleet; (2) inactivate all but five of the remaining EC-135 ABNCP fleet effective immediately; [and to] (3) plan to operate five EC-135 ABNCPs through FY 1997 to support the CINCSTRAT ABNCP mission…' All uninstalled MILSTAR satellite communications terminals, scheduled for installation on the EC-135Cs as part of the PACER LINK II program, would be transferred to the US Navy for eventual installation on Boeing E-6A Mercury TACAMOs, which would then be redesignated as E-6Bs and take over the EC-135 airborne command post mission on behalf of the STRATCOM commander. The E-6Bs were assigned to Tinker AFB, but deployed to Offutt AFB for ground alert. The Strategic Command Airborne Control System (SCACS) replaced PACCS, further distancing the remaining EC-135Cs from their SAC legacy.

The 2nd ACCS was inactivated and replaced by the 7th ACCS on 19th July 1994, a unit with a C-130 Airborne Battlefield Command, Control and Communications (ABCCC) history in Southeast Asia. Although the EC-135Cs continued their ABNCP mission for STRATCOM, their primary role would be 'command, control, and communications' in support of contingency operations as E-6Bs assumed the main role of strategic ABNCP in conjunction with their TACAMO role. A single EC-135J (62-3584) had been transferred to the 2nd ACCS in early 1992. It crashed at Pope AFB, NC, on 29th May 1992 while landing during one such conventional operation, as did

The Navy's E-6B shows its direct descent from the PACER LINK II EC-135Cs with the MILSTAR antenna on the dorsal fuselage. Beginning in 1998, the E-6B replaced EC-135s on all STRATCOM ABNCP missions. *Photo by Brian Rogers*

EC-135C 63-8053 on 9th September 1997 (see Appendix II). On 25th September 1998, an EC-135C flew the final USAF LOOKING GLASS ABNCP mission from Offutt AFB, and the 7th ACCS was inactivated a week later on 1st October 1998. Subsequently, US Navy E-6Bs would fly all LOOKING GLASS missions. SAC's EC-135 legacy was at an end.

During his last year as CINCSAC, General Curtis LeMay sought to consolidate all of America's strategic nuclear forces under a single command which would include SAC's bombers, ICBMs, and tankers and the US Navy's forthcoming Polaris SLBM submarines. Even after leaving SAC in the summer of 1957 for duty as the Air Force Vice Chief of Staff, LeMay persisted. By 1960 efforts to create a new Strategic Command had come up empty, however, as inter-service rivalry and turf battles meant that neither SAC nor the Navy would cede control of its nuclear weapons to anyone else. For LeMay, SAC was the only logical choice to oversee the American nuclear armada. To prove his point, he reportedly kept a large model of a Polaris submarine in his office, emblazoned with the SAC emblem and Milky Way band around its hull. One wonders what LeMay would think if he knew that an Admiral occupied his former office in SAC Headquarters, and that a Navy plane would serve as the backbone of America's strategic airborne command and control system.

For nearly 40 years, SAC's airborne command post and ancillary aircraft were a critical part of US national security policy. As former CINCSAC General Bruce K Holloway told veterans of the Airborne Command and Control Association, PACCS was 'a principal element of [American] deterrent strategy success. Whether or not we would have preempted, in the face of unequivocal intelligence that the USSR was preparing an immediate attack, will never be known. But the threat of an airborne bomber alert backed by a secure airborne control system, must surely have discouraged any thoughts about a first strike by the Soviets.' Holloway's recollection of a threatening 'airborne bomber alert' certainly exaggerates the importance of CHROME DOME missions. He is right on target, however, with his assessment of the impact of PACCS on the Cold War. Once the Soviet Union had achieved nuclear parity with the United States, there was always the risk that one day a Soviet leader would be convinced that a Soviet first strike would cripple US retaliatory capability, and that a critically weakened America would surrender rather than attempt a feeble response. PACCS guaranteed the ability of US civilian leadership and military commanders to survive a Soviet first strike and then be able to launch and manage a retaliatory strike against the USSR. In the delicate nuclear balance of terror that defined the Cold War, PACCS ensured the odds were always even.

CHAPTER TEN

Videmus Omnia

'I believe the Air Force should press for a large-scale intelligence project to obtain the information necessary to destroy the enemy's long-range atomic forces. I believe you will agree this is important enough to warrant the formation of a project equal in nature and scope to the Manhattan Project.' – *General Curtis E LeMay, 1952*

'This is not your Cold War RIVET JOINT'
– *Captain Mark Cramer, RC-135 Navigator, 2014*

We sat at the end of the runway in near total darkness. The dim red glow of the instruments offered only the faintest light inside the airplane, preserving our night vision. The engines, set at idle power, were barely audible. The radios were silent. Beside me the copilot quietly reviewed the takeoff data and departure procedures. Farther back the two navigators spoke to one another in hushed tones, hunched over their charts depicting tonight's route and our orbit area. On the other side of the cockpit door – where the overhead lights were on full – the three Ravens sat anxiously, their sensors in stand-by mode until we were airborne, ready to locate and identify radar sites and any other electronic emissions. The inflight maintenance technician (IMT) monitored the banks of computers and gear that filled the cavernous fuselage save for the narrow path leading to the rear of the airplane. Should any ELINT equipment fail

during the 15-hour flight, he would fix it. Tonight's sortie was in RC-135V 63-9792, an airplane informally nicknamed *Damien* for its demonic tendencies to experience problems that could neither be duplicated nor repaired. No doubt the IMT hoped for boredom in the hours ahead. Behind him sat some 20 linguists and communications specialists, facing sideways and staring at huge computer screens and radio receivers. Good-naturedly referred to as 'SLEBs' – 'self-loading excess baggage' or 'BEEPs' – 'back-end enlisted pukes', many of these men were hardly out of their teens. Given their exceptional intelligence and aptitude, however, they were selected right out of basic training to learn languages far different from the English they grew up with in their hometowns – Mandarin, Russian, Czech, Polish, Vietnamese, Hebrew.

As I had so many times before on peripheral reconnaissance flights all over the world, I mentally walked through the mission ahead: the flight path to our orbit, where to turn, when to climb, and how to keep the airplane optimally positioned so that the sensors always pointed in the desired direction. I thought about both of tonight's planned aerial refuelings. Each time we hooked up with our tanker we would take on 120,000 lb (54,431 kg) of jet fuel – some 18,500 gallons (70,030 liters), enough to fill nearly 1,000 cars back home in Nebraska. I reviewed the procedures we would use if we were intercepted during our long flight. I even thought about food.

Opposite page: DREAM BOAT RB-50G 47-0136 operated primarily along the Pacific coast of the USSR on COMINT missions. The airplane was slow and had reached its operational limit, prompting calls for a replacement. *Photo FA-10318 courtesy Boeing*

Right: DESERT STORM proved to be the transition point for the RIVET JOINT from PARPRO to combat operations. The author flew RC-135V 63-9792 on his first combat sortie. *Photo by the author*

The radio crackled as the tower controller told us to pull onto the runway and 'line up and wait.' The airplane came alive as I pushed up the power enough to move us into position and steered us onto the runway centerline, just as I had on any of the RC-135 missions I'd flown from places like Shemya, Mildenhall, Kadena, Eielson, or Athens. Tonight, however, was different. Tonight, however, my destination was not Russia, China, or any of their communist client states, locked in the same grand Cold War superpower struggle over the past 45 years. Tonight my destination was Iraq. Tonight my airplane, my crew, and I were going to war.

'Rumor 3-1, winds 3-5-0 at 6, cleared for takeoff.' I set takeoff power and 140 tons of steel, jet fuel, electronics, and people accelerated to nearly 160 miles per hour before we climbed into the black Saudi sky.

The 1990 Iraqi invasion of Kuwait triggered an extraordinary American military build up in the Gulf and created the largest coalition of forces in a conflict since the Second World War. In the days immediately after the Iraqis captured Kuwait, American and Saudi leaders feared that Saddam Hussein would continue his drive southward and invade Saudi Arabia. The immediate American priority was the rapid deployment of defensive forces to deter this threat, or, failing that, defend its Saudi allies.

On 7th August 1990 the JCS directed that 'three RC-135 BURNING WIND aircraft' be among the first US assets deployed to the Gulf as part of Operation DESERT SHIELD, and the first one arrived at Riyadh AB on 10th August under the command of Captain Brian Janeway. The RC-135Vs and RC-135Ws quickly began continuous aerial surveillance along the borders of Iraq, Kuwait, and the so-called 'Neutral Zone.' Crews were on station for 12 hours at a time except for two brief periods when they left their orbit for aerial refueling. Approximately an hour-and-a-half before the on-station plane ended its shift, the next crew took off to replace them. By the start of DESERT STORM on 17th January 1991, half of the 14 existing RIVET JOINTS had deployed to Riyadh AB. By this time two airplanes were continuously airborne, with a second orbit area added along Iraq's western border with Saudi Arabia near Jordan. Additional RIVET JOINTS flew out of Hellenikon AB at Athens and orbited over Turkey. In conjunction with the Boeing E-3 AWACS airborne radar platform and the Boeing E-8 JointSTARS ground surveillance radar airplane, RC-135s provided real-time SIGINT and COMINT data directly to President George H W Bush and his national security advisors in Washington, DC, as well as to theater commanders in the Gulf. The RC-135 had become the 'Ears of the Storm'.

DESERT STORM was a defining moment in the history of the RC-135. For 30 years RC-135s and their variants routinely flew missions along the periphery of the Soviet Union, its allies, and a variety of nations whose actions and policies interested American decision makers. There were occasional tense encounters with MiGs or other interceptors; sometimes shots were fired but no airplanes were lost or crewmembers injured. Even though RC-135s supported combat operations in Southeast Asia as part of COMBAT APPLE or occasional BURNING PIPE missions, in Grenada as part of URGENT FURY, and in Panama as part of JUST CAUSE, the RC-135's foremost mission was always subsumed by the nickname 'PARPRO' – Peacetime Aerial Reconnaissance Program. The key word was *peacetime*. Although much of the intelligence that RC-135s collected could (and would) be used in war, their primary goal was to gather intelligence to *prevent* war, to preserve peace – the status quo – in a bipolar Cold War world. Armed with accurate knowledge of enemy capabilities and intentions, US civilian policy makers and military leaders could make prudent decisions in both peace and time of crisis. During the

TYPES OF INTELLIGENCE

Although there are many different types of intelligence, these are the primary 'INTs' associated with '135 platforms.

COMINT (COMmunications INTelligence) – functional intelligence processed from voice, visual, and electronic communications, telephone, telegraph, television, facsimile, and satellite sources.

ELINT (ELectronic INTelligence) – technical and intelligence information derived from foreign noncommunications electromagnetic radiations emanating from other than atomic detonations or radioactive sources.

NUDINT (NUclear Detonation INTelligence) – intelligence derived from the collection and analysis of radiation and other effects resulting from radioactive sources.

MASINT (Measurement And Signature INTelligence) – scientific and technical intelligence information obtained by quantitative and qualitative analysis of data (metric, angle, spatial, wavelength, time dependence, modulation, plasma, and hydromagnetic) derived from specific technical sensors for the purpose of identifying any distinctive features associate with the source, emitter, or sender and to facilitate subsequent identification and/or measurement of the same.

PHOTINT (PHOTographic INTelligence) – processed information obtained from all forms of photography, film or electronic, including satellite (currently called **IMINT** for IMagery INTelligence).

SIGINT (SIGnals INTelligence) – intelligence combining COMINT and ELINT.

Definitions are from official US intelligence agency (NSA, CIA, JCS, etc) references, cited in Leo D Carl, *The International Dictionary of Intelligence* (McLean, VA: International Defense Consultant Services, 1990)

New engines, new cockpit avionics, new ELINT and COMINT gear, and new communications and networking architecture have transformed the RIVET JOINT into the ultimate airborne intelligence platform. *Photo courtesy USAF*

decade preceding DESERT STORM, RC-135Vs and RC-135Ws operated routinely around the world and were known ubiquitously by their Operational Order (OpOrd) name of BURNING WIND. Indeed, tail spotters at RAF Mildenhall were always eager to learn that 'the Wind was in town.'

For 30 years the RC-135's ELINT and COMINT capabilities were closely guarded secrets, known largely just to the airplane's crew and the national agencies (usually civilian) that tasked each mission and analyzed each mission's 'take.' To be sure, there were US military commanders who had glimpsed the RC-135's combat potential thanks to its participation in exercises such as RED FLAG and GREEN FLAG. During DESERT STORM, however, military commanders immediately recognized the full value of RC-135s in combat operations. In the post Cold War world, filled with 'contingency operations' in Bosnia or Somalia, full-scale invasions of Afghanistan and Iraq, and seemingly endless 'Operations' in the Middle East, RC-135s are suddenly in demand for abilities that have little to do with their traditional missions, now known as Sensitive Reconnaissance Operations (SRO). RC-135V/Ws are no longer called 'the Wind,' but instead are referred to as 'Rivet Joints' or simply 'RJs'. They still fly peripheral missions in the Baltic, for example, or over former enemies in Eastern Europe as they monitor events in southern Ukraine. There are 17 RIVET JOINTS in the US Air

Force, most of which are deployed to bases at Souda Bay, Crete, or al-Udeid AB, Qatar, supporting operations against terrorists in Syria and Iraq or the Taliban in Afghanistan. Given the 'special relationship' between American and British intelligence agencies, there are also now three RAF RC-135W Airseekers. Even in an age where drones are everywhere, US and allied theater commanders clamor for RIVET JOINTS to meet their battlefield intelligence, surveillance, and reconnaissance (ISR) needs.

It has been more than *half a century* since an OFFICE BOY KC-135A-II assigned to the 4157th SW at Eielson AFB, AK, flew the first COTTON CANDY reconnaissance mission during 1963 in near absolute secrecy. Since then we have learned more about the many different variants of RC-135s and their operational commitments, but we know just as little about their full capabilities. With crewmembers' lives, the lives of US and allied forces and civilians, and the success of each mission at stake, that secrecy is necessary. However desirable it may be to learn the 'big picture,' this book reveals much that was previously classified about early RC-135 operations, but intentionally refrains from exploring too deeply the ongoing missions and capabilities of these airplanes. When the RC-135 is finally retired, perhaps in 2040, it will remain for a new generation of researchers to tell the 'whole story'.

'Visitors'

On 17th November 1970 KC-135T 55-3121 from the 55th SRW at Offutt AFB orbited in international airspace over the Pechora Sea south of Novaya Zemlya, a major Soviet nuclear weapons test site. For decades US and Western strategic reconnaissance aircraft had been routinely intercepted and escorted by Soviet or Red Chinese MiGs, and this COBRA JAW sortie near Vaygach Island was no exception. Two Soviet MiG-17s joined into a tight formation, so close that they were under the KC-135T's engine nacelle. Aggressive intercepts such as this one were commonplace as Soviet pilots sought to 'encourage' the 'intruder' to leave. For the reconnaissance crew these intercepts were gold mines of intelligence data on the MiGs, Sukhois, and Soviet defense procedures. On this occasion, however, the intercept was anything but routine. Without warning the MiG-17s fired their cannons ahead of and parallel to the COBRA JAW's route of flight.

In this photo taken a year after the Pechora Sea Incident with 55-3121, another MiG-17 *Fresco* escorts an RC-135 somewhere off the Soviet coastline. *Photo via Yefim Gordon*

Between August 1946 and July 1960, defense forces from the Soviet Union, People's Republic of China, and the Democratic People's Republic of Korea (DPRK – North Korea) attacked at least 44 US Air Force and Navy reconnaissance planes. Nearly all were fired upon in international airspace (such as the COBRA JAW) or over non-communist territory. Of these 29 were destroyed and over 100 crewmembers killed, considered missing, or taken prisoner. Indeed, the 55th SRW had previously lost RB-50Gs 47-0145 on 29th July 1953 and 47-0133 on 10th September 1956 (both to Soviet MiG-17 *Frescos*), RB-47H 53-4281 on 1st July 1960 (also to a Soviet MiG-17), and RB-47H 53-4290 on 28th April 1965 (which landed but was written off) to North Korean MiG-17s.

Undaunted by the two MiG-17s or their lethal legacy, aircraft commander James W Jones continued the mission, turning back *toward* the Soviet mainland. Russian linguists on the COBRA JAW monitored radio communications between the MiG-17s and their ground controllers, listening anxiously for the next order to the MiG pilots. To the relief of everyone on the COBRA JAW, the Soviets directed the MiG-17s to continue escorting the KC-135T, and the mission proceeded uneventfully.

The consequences, however, in the diplomatic community were significant. As with many earlier aerial incidents, the Soviets protested the 'incursion' of the COBRA JAW, while the United States protested the unwarranted 'attack' on an unarmed airplane in international airspace. The 17th November mission spelled the end of the COBRA JAW program, and 55-3121 moved on to other reconnaissance roles. Peripheral reconnaissance missions continued, however, as did the presence of escorting fighters not only from communist bloc nations but Third World countries such as Libya and even allies, especially in Scandinavia. Indeed, the hallmark of SAC RC-135 sorties during the 'high Cold War' was regular interception by MiGs, reactions which were both exciting and occasionally nerve-wracking.

Each encounter followed a generally peaceful script. As the RC-135 – flying along a carefully plotted 'black line' in international airspace some 20 to 40 miles parallel to the Soviet coast – approached a defense region, the Soviets would launch a Sukhoi Su-15 *Flagon*, a Yakovlev Yak-28 *Firebar*, a MiG-23 *Flogger* or some other interceptor to begin (or continue) escorting the RC-135. Russian linguists aboard the RC-135 would monitor radio communications between the ground controller and MiG pilot, listening for indications that would reveal the character of the intercept: passive and friendly or aggressive and hostile. Once the RC-135 crew visually spotted the MiG, they would broadcast in the clear a 'Harvard' radio message, indicating they were being escorted and were in international airspace. Needless to say, both sides spent a great deal of time looking at (and photographing) one another. RC-135 crews used special HAVE LOOP (later SENSOR LOOP) 35mm cameras to photograph the MiG in detail for later analysis and exploitation at the Foreign Technology Division (FTD) at Wright-Patterson AFB, OH. HAVE LOOP imagery was 'virtually the only opportunity for US intelligence analysts to study enemy fighters fully configured with air-to-air missiles.' On 3rd May 1970, for example, an RC-135C BURNING PIPE mission using HAVE LOOP photographed an Su-15 *Flagon* configured with updated missiles. A little more than a month later, on 10th June, an RC-135C crew took the first photographs of a MiG-19 *Farmer* equipped with AA-2 *Atoll* infrared missile. For the RC-135U COMBAT SENT, intercepts were highly desirable, using its Precision Power Measurement System (PPMS) to assess the emissions from the MiG's radar or other electronics. Mostly, though, the airplanes would fly together with minimal interaction beyond waves, salutes, or the occasional extended middle finger. When the MiG finally turned away, the RC-135 crew broadcast a 'Brother' message in the clear indicating that the escort had departed.

In the event the situation turned hostile there were mechanisms in place to protect the airplane and crew. According to a declassified NSA history, in 1963 the JCS implemented a highly secret 'White Wolf Advisory Warning Program to protect American aircraft flying reconnaissance missions essentially worldwide.' Using ground-based listening stations as well as on-board linguists, flight crews could be warned of impending hostile action, allowing time for the aircraft to egress the area and avoid attack (even with this safety net the North Koreans still shot down a US Navy EC-121 on 15th April 1969). Ground personnel routinely practiced this alerting system to ensure that flight crews could be warned with sufficient time and senior commanders advised of the threat so they could direct a suitable response. During 1971, for example, CINCPAC undertook 12 FORECAST STORM exercises to 'simulate a [White Wolf] Condition One abort of a PARPRO aircraft.'

An intercept provided the ultimate intelligence collection. COMINT recorded the radio conversation between ground controllers and pilots, revealing operational frequencies and procedures. ELINT collected radar and ECM data used by the airplane and ground defense forces. HAVE LOOP showed new modifications, nose numbers, aircraft technical details, and even the metal used in construction based on skin color. A Yak-25M *Flashlight* A shows this to good effect while intercepting an RC-135C. *USAF via Geoff Hays*

Intercepts by Soviet (later Russian) and PRC fighters dwindled after the Cold War, but surged after 2010. Following decades of indifference to these intercepts, the US has suddenly complained that they are highly dangerous. *Photo via Yefim Gordon*

A number of 'flier's tales' show that despite the seriousness of the PARPRO business, there exists a universal sense of humor among pilots of all nations. RC-135 crewmembers are said to have displayed foldouts from magazines such as *Playboy*, prompting the fighters to close to within less than the RC-135's wingspan in order to get a better view. RC-135 crewchiefs put a European driver learner's permit emblem on the fuselage beneath the copilot's window, no doubt producing considerable mirth among the Soviet-bloc pilots at the expense of new and unknowing RC-135 copilots.

Not all encounters with potentially hostile fighters were so routine or innocent, as the reacting fighter attempted to discourage a PARPRO platform from flying in a given area. RC-135s have not been entirely unresponsive to such harassment, as annoying Soviet fighters trailing close behind the RC-135 have been reportedly doused with jet fuel from the fuel dump tube. Soviet fast-jet pilots intent on staying in position with the lumbering RIVET JOINT occasionally failed to notice that the RC-135 was intentionally and insidiously slowing to speeds well below that needed to keep the fighter aloft, with the result being a high altitude stall and hairy recovery on the part of the Soviet pilot.

The warning shots from the Soviet *Frescoes* escorting the COBRA JAW on 17th November may well have been the first directed at a reconnaissance '135, but they were not the last. On 16th September 1980 two *Syrian* pilots flying Libyan MiG-23s intercepted and were ordered to fire at a RIVET JOINT (perhaps 64-14842), which escaped by diving aggressively from 35,000ft (10,668m) to 1,000ft (305m), then dropped even lower to 500ft (152m) at full speed before returning to Hellenikon AB. No missiles were fired. Less than a week later, on 21st September, four Libyan *Floggers* and four Dassault Mirage fighters attempted to surround and 'kidnap' the same RC-135 with the intent of forcing it to land in Libya. This time the RC-135

'Old Timers' chuckle at the modern US characterization of Russian intercepts as dangerous and aggressive. This Cuban MiG-21 *Fishbed* pulls *away* from an RC-135 on a BURNING CIGAR mission. 10-15ft (3-4m) distances were common; today 50ft (15m) provokes hysteria. *USAF via Geoff Hays*

was under radar surveillance by the American aircraft carrier USS *John F Kennedy*, which immediately launched at least five Grumman F-14A Tomcats, all armed and authorized to 'shoot to kill'. This action did not go unnoticed by Libyan ground controllers who promptly recalled their eight interceptors, ending the episode without direct confrontation. The RC-135 landed safely. (The Libyans had been attempting to 'capture' or shoot down US reconnaissance assets for years, beginning with the 21st March 1973 intercept and attack on a C-130B-II).

With the events of *glasnost* and the dissolution of the Soviet Union on 25th December 1991 resulting in the putative end of the Cold War, the number of intercepts decreased significantly. Improved Russian-American relations, the decline in the number of peripheral reconnaissance sorties, constraints on fuel and flying time for former-Soviet interceptors, and a general reduction in the Russian aircraft inventory all lowered the frequency of intercepts to virtually nil. Despite greater US-Russian comity, Western reconnaissance aircraft were not entirely free from risk. On 1st April 2001, in an incident reminiscent of the 13th September 1987 collision between a Soviet Su-27 *Flanker* and a Royal Norwegian Air Force (RNAF) P-3B Orion, a PRC Jian-8 *Finback* collided with a US Navy EP-3E Aries II. The J-8 crashed and the EP-3E landed on Hainan Island. On 3rd March 2003 two North Korean MiG-29 *Fulcrums* and two MiG-23 *Floggers* surprised COBRA BALL RC-135S 61-2663 some 150 miles off the coast of North Korea during a series of missile tests. The RC-135S aborted its mission when one of the MiGs locked onto the COBRA BALL, and future missions were scheduled with US fighter coverage. US officials protested the 'dangerous' incident, saying the MiGs had come within 50ft (15m) of the RC-135S, which landed uneventfully at Kadena AB.

Russian intercepts remained infrequent and certainly uncontentious until 23rd April 2014 when a Russian Su-27 *Flanker* intercepted COMBAT SENT RC-135U 64-14849 in international airspace over the Sea of Okhotsk. US defense officials excoriated the Russians, saying that the *Flanker* conducted a 'reckless intercept' and called it 'one of the most dangerous aerial encounters for a US reconnaissance aircraft since the Cold War' as the *Flanker* crossed some 100ft (30m) in front of the RC-135U. Three months later, on 18th July 2014, a RIVET JOINT operating in international airspace over the Baltic Sea aborted its mission in response to an unspecified threat from a Russian interceptor. As they headed west toward safety, the RC-135 crew requested permission to enter Swedish airspace but this was denied; the RIVET JOINT flew through Swedish airspace anyway, opting for aircrew safety over compliance with international aviation regulations. On 7th April 2015 another Su-27 *Flanker* buzzed an RC-135U over the Baltic Sea in what US officials called 'reckless' and 'unprofessional' behavior, and again on 20th May over the Black Sea. A *Flanker* 'thumped' an RC-135, also over the Black Sea on 25th January 2016, a tactic that uses an aggressive maneuver by the Su-27 to create adverse jet wash to destabilize the RC-135. An Su-27 performed a barrel roll around an RC-135U over the Baltic Sea on 14th April 2016, and again on 29th April, which a US spokesman decried as 'an aggressive maneuver that posed a threat to the safety of the US aircrew in the RC-135U.' The Flanker was some 50ft (15m) away from the RC-135U throughout the maneuver. A People's Republic of China Chengdu J-10 *Firebird* approached a RIVET JOINT RC-135 on 8th June 2016 with 'an unsafe excessive rate of closure,' an 'inappropriate and dangerous act' over the East China Sea.

These recent incidents raise the question of 'what has changed?' since the heyday of Russian intercepts of RC-135s and their Western counterparts. Why – during nearly 25 years of SAC RC-135 operations between 1963 and 1992 – were intercepts as close as 10-20ft (3-6m) considered tolerable (even desirable from an intelligence perspective, especially with the RC-135U), but intercepts of 50-100ft (15-30m) during the 2010s had suddenly become excessively dangerous and unacceptable? US Navy F-14 Tomcats routinely 'thumped' Soviet Tu-16 *Badgers* and Tu-142 *Bears* during the height of the Cold War, but somehow that was acceptable. The risk of collision is a convenient but misleading excuse. In over 70 years and thousands of strategic aerial reconnaissance intercepts there have been only *three* recorded collisions (the RNAF P-3B, the USN EP-3E, and a Soviet Yak-3 that hit a British airliner thought be a 'spyplane' near Berlin in 1948). A more compelling argument might be that the skill level of the aircrew (on both sides) has changed. Given the decreased frequency of intercepts, Russian or PRC fighter pilots have less experience flying in close proximity to large aircraft (despite acquiring aerial refueling skills with comparably sized tanker aircraft), while RC-135 crews have less experience operating with large interceptors 'up close and personal' [the Su-27 *Flanker* and its derivatives are some 73ft (22m) in length, approximately half the length of an RC-135, but still smaller than the 99ft (30m) Tu-128 *Fiddler* that once escorted RC-135s]. The most plausible explanation, however, has nothing to do with airmanship.

The whole point of these aggressive intercepts is to induce the RC-135 to discontinue its mission. Calling the intercepts 'unprofessional' applies a false sense of 'business courtesy' to an inherently dangerous *military* operation designed to achieve a 'win-lose' outcome: the Su-27 wins by making the RC-135 lose when it leaves the area. During the height of the Cold War RC-135s won this battle by staying the course, by continuing their intelligence collection, by taking photos of the interceptor for analysis and exploitation, and by showing the resolve that the airplanes had the legal right to operate freely and unhindered in international airspace. Indeed, by 1950 the global legal consensus – including that of the Soviet Union and communist bloc nations – was that an airplane of any type and from any country could fly without restriction in international airspace *however close* to Soviet airspace, *even if* that airplane was engaged in reconnaissance activities. Attacks on Western reconnaissance aircraft peaked in 1953 with the death of Joseph Stalin and his policies, although there were occasional incidents resulting in the loss of aircraft and lives through the 1960s. The predictability of many reconnaissance flights, especially weather and atmospheric sampling missions, reassured the Soviets because they were routine and were interpreted as non-threatening. As such, they did not warrant an interception that might result in a violent confrontation. The total number of Western peripheral reconnaissance flights of all types increased from dozens, or even a few hundred per year in the late 1940s to perhaps as many as 2,000 flights a year by 1960. The loss of 29 airplanes over the span of 180 months between 1945 and 1960 was, to paraphrase General Curtis LeMay, roughly equivalent to SAC's peacetime training attrition rate for just eight months in 1955, or an average of four per year. For the United States, this marginal loss rate was an acceptable price for the intelligence gained. For the Russians, the flights were at worst an annoyance and generally not worth the international opprobrium should one be attacked and shot down. In short, both the United States and the Soviets had become desensitized to peripheral missions.

RC-135 crewmembers today feel strongly that their flight skills remain unequaled and up to the challenge, and similarly express a keen awareness of and sensitivity to an interceptor's intent, divined through on-board self-protection methods. Whether or not that intent is to attack the RC-135 or merely shoo it away remains classified, although one is hard pressed to believe that the Russians in particular would broadcast in the clear an order for an Su-27 to shoot down an RC-135 in international airspace, let alone intend to do so as a matter of policy. Despite their personal abilities and commitment to 'fly the

mission', however, RC-135 crews conduct operations that reflect a *changed national consensus for risk tolerance.* Rules of engagement for RC-135 missions are defined at the highest levels of the US government. It is there one finds the shift in risk tolerance from the heady days of 'freedom of navigation' sorties that began under President Harry Truman and continued through to President Ronald Reagan, to the absolute avoidance of perilous and provocative sorties under President Barack Obama. As Russia flexes its revanchist muscle, for example, it could easily exploit any event involving the loss – intentional or otherwise – of an Su-27 and an RC-135 as a major international incident that could shift attention away from Russian adventurism in the Ukraine, Syria, the Baltic states, or elsewhere. In so doing, Russian leaders could paint the United States as the threat and aggressor, exploiting long-standing Russian popular beliefs and mitigating Russian domestic problems, just as they did in the 1950s under Stalin. Indeed, US officials parrot the Russian party line saying, 'the unsafe and unprofessional actions of a single [Russian] pilot have the potential to unnecessarily escalate tensions between countries.' With this outcome in mind, US civilian leaders choose not to justify the incremental intelligence benefit of a given RC-135 mission in light of any potential international incident, opting for 'professional' political discretion over military requirements and international legal precedent. Similarly, too many military commanders possess a career-protecting 'not on my watch' mentality. In so doing they both needlessly commit RC-135 crews and airplanes to missions which senior officials are unwilling to support.

BIG SAFARI

For over 60 years the name BIG SAFARI has been synonymous with reconnaissance aircraft. Indeed, every RC-135 program has, in some way, been connected with this extraordinary program. BIG SAFARI traces its origins to the early 1950s when the US Air Force sought to develop aircraft needed for high priority missions. Routine contracting procedures dictated multiple source bids, lengthy evaluation processes, and could not guarantee secrecy. An entirely different, streamlined mechanism was needed to procure the small number of airplanes, leading to a 'sole-source' contract agreement constrained only by the inability to 'manufacture new airplanes.' BIG SAFARI could use any existing airframes, add any necessary equipment or modify the airplanes in any way – anything to get the job done in the short time available, with a limited budget, and in complete secrecy.

BIG SAFARI is neither a place where aircraft modifications are undertaken, nor is it a company. It is an Air Force management program comparable to Lockheed's famous 'Skunk Works' founded by Clarence L 'Kelly' Johnson. Led initially by equally legendary Furman E 'F E' O'Rear, BIG SAFARI's charter is to 'employ the necessary flexibility to respond to high-priority, dynamic operational requirements for programs that involve a limited number of systems that require a rapid response to changes in the operational environment throughout the life of the system.' Tracing the BIG SAFARI history reveals a complex lineage of civilian companies contracted to modify a handful of airplanes, beginning in the early 1950s with Texas Engineering and Manufacturing Company (TEMCO). Corporate mergers, acquisitions, and divestitures led to Ling-TEMCO-Vought (LTV), then to LTV Electrosystems (with a nod to General Dynamics Convair Division), then E-Systems, and, most recently, L-3 Communications. Other entities, such as Lockheed Aircraft Services (LAS) were acquired along the way. Rather than clutter the story of RC-135s with evolving corporate genealogy, this history refers to BIG SAFARI as the organization responsible for aircraft modifications or conversions instead of the actual subsidiary organization unless it is particularly germane to do so.

Training

For decades RC-135 flight crews received their initial qualification through the existing training pipelines. Pilots and navigators joined their KC-135A tanker colleagues at Castle AFB, and the Ravens completed electronic warfare officer training at Mather AFB. However productive this might have been, it was hardly efficient. Pilots destined for RC-135Vs at Offutt AFB, for example, learned to fly in water-injected J57-equipped airplanes rather than the TF33-equipped jets they would fly operationally. They devoted considerable training time to the procedures of tanker air refueling instead of learning the art of receiver air refueling. Although this expanded their understanding of aerial refueling as a whole, the benefit of this broad perspective was typically lost on new copilots occasionally overwhelmed after their transition from the simple T-38 at undergraduate pilot training to the complex KC-135 at Castle. New navigators experienced similar challenges when they began flying RC-135s as 'Nav 2s', cross-checking advanced navigation systems like stellar-inertial Doppler units. Many newly assigned Ravens received their 'real world' training upon arrival at their first assignment at Offutt AFB or Eielson AFB.

Compared with tanker units, RC-135 wings faced challenges with recurring training for fully qualified crewmembers. Whereas a tanker crew could fly any of 15-30 KC-135s on the ramp for a routine training sortie, RC-135 units had far fewer airplanes assigned, not to mention a number deployed operationally. Crews could hardly fly the lone RC-135E on a pilot traffic pattern-only training sortie at Eielson AFB while it was needed on alert at Shemya AFB. The hazards of traffic pattern training were not to be ignored, as fully mission capable reconnaissance KC-135R 59-1465 crashed immediately after takeoff on a training flight from Offutt AFB on 19th July 1967. This costly lesson produced not only the RC-135T but the TC-135B, TC-135S, and TC-135W as well.

The solution to these twin problems was to bring the training 'in house.' Back-end crews continued to train in the mission aircraft whether airborne or on the ground. For front-end crew proficiency reconnaissance units acquired dedicated trainers. These airplanes also doubled as squadron 'hacks', providing deployment capability from the home base to forward operating locations (FOLs) or priority transport of replacement parts to a broken jet somewhere halfway around the world. By 1996 plans were well underway for RIVET JOINT Host Owned Training (HOT), which led to the establishment in 1999 of a dedicated training squadron within the 55th Wing. Currently the 338th Combat Training Squadron (CTS) provides *ab initio* training for all newly assigned pilots, navigators, ravens, and in-flight maintenance personnel after completion of specialized undergraduate pilot training (SUPT), undergraduate combat systems officer training (UCSOT), or basic technical school, respectively. Once fully qualified, they are then assigned to any of the three operational RC-135 squadrons at Offutt AFB based on current or projected manning requirements. The 238th CTS, Nebraska ANG, has an associate role in this process, and provides some of the instructors used in initial and recurring flight training. All RAF RC-135W Airseeker crews are trained at Offutt AFB.

Unlike the AMC pilot training program at Altus AFB, new RC-135 pilots are not dual-seat qualified and instead spend one to two years as mission copilots. This allows sufficient time to master the complex systems knowledge and mission operational procedures prior to upgrading to aircraft commander, sometime around the 800-hour mark. Copilots and navigators assigned to the 45th RS are eligible to transition to the OC-135 and WC-135 at the 500-hour point, as these airplanes do not have the common RC-135 cockpit, instead having the Block 40 PACER CRAG configuration. There are two navigators assigned to each COBRA BALL and OPEN SKIES crew, and one assigned

to each RIVET JOINT, COMBAT SENT, and CONSTANT PHOENIX crew. Although tanker crews carry in-flight publications on a tablet, RC-135 publications and documents include classified material, so reconnaissance crews retain the traditional weighty yet secure flight bags.

C-135B INDIVIDUAL AIRCRAFT

61-2664 From 17th October 1967 through 15th February 1968, this future RC-135S was assigned to the 55th WRS, 9th WRW at McClellan AFB. It does not appear to have been modified in any way to conduct weather or sampling missions, and probably functioned as a transport for AFTAC requirements or, more likely, as a flight-deck proficiency trainer for WC-135B crews.

61-4128 On 7th November 1967 this C-135B was assigned to the 55th WRS, 9th WRW at McClellan AFB. It relocated three days later on 10th November to the 56th WRS at Yokota AB. As with C-135B 61-2664, it appears to have served briefly as both a 'hack' and a flight-deck trainer for WC-135B crews. Less than three months later, on 25th January 1968, it was reassigned to testbed duties with the AFETR.

KC-135A (ARR) INDIVIDUAL AIRCRAFT

58-0124 This KC-135A has an interesting training heritage. It served initially as a standard KC-135A tanker with the 93rd BW at Castle AFB. It is not clear exactly when, but by 1965-66 it had acquired an IFR capability, and served as a receiver air refueling trainer with the 93rd BW. Instructor pilots who flew the KC-135A and KC-135B airborne command posts assigned to Numbered Air Force (NAF) units at Barksdale AFB, Westover AFB, and March AFB completed their initial qualification in this airplane at Castle AFB, then returned to their home units to train remaining pilots. On 6th October 1967 58-0124 was reassigned to the 55th SRW at Offutt AFB, filling the demand for receiver-capable trainer for both the unit's EC-135Cs and the RC-135Cs.

During 1968 the airplane was referred to as the ELF ARROW aircraft, although nothing is known about this. RC-135C 64-14846 was also listed as an ELF ARROW aircraft, implying an ELINT mission. Declassified SAC reconnaissance histories and 55th SRW histories, however, show 58-0124 exclusively as a training aircraft with no reconnaissance mission whatsoever. By 1979 it had been transferred to the 305th AREFW at Grissom AFB.

KC-135E (ARR) INDIVIDUAL AIRCRAFT

59-1514 E-Systems demodified this RIVET QUICK airplane into a KC-135A (ARR) by 4th March 1974, and it was assigned to the 305th AREFW. It was transferred to the 6th SW on 21st March 1975, where it remained until 10th December 1979 when it returned to Grissom AFB. In September 1981 it underwent conversion to the first KC-135E (ARR), returning to Offutt AFB in March 1982. On 31st August 1982, 59-1514 became the primary trainer for 55th SRW flight crews at Offutt AFB who operated turbofan-equipped EC-135s and RC-135s. Plans called for replacing it with RC-135T 55-3121 in July 1985, but when the RC-135T crashed in February 1985 the 55th SRW was forced to continue using KC-135E 59-1514 as a trainer until funds could be made available for the conversion of a replacement. The 22nd April 1988 arrival of TC-135W 62-4129 eliminated the general need for crews from the 38th SRS to use 59-1514, although they continued to fly the airplane on an infrequent basis. In 1997 it was sent to PDM at Hayes in Birmingham, AL, and determined to be suffering from irreparable corrosion and written off on 6th November 1997 and subsequently scrapped (see Appendix III).

NKC-135A INDIVIDUAL AIRCRAFT

55-3129 In 1981 NKC-135A 55-3129 was demodified from winglet testbed duties with NASA and returned to the 4950th TW for routine test duties. From 3rd January through 7th April 1982 it was assigned to the 6th SW at Eielson AFB as a flight-deck trainer during the absence of that unit's RC-135T for re-engining.

RC-135D INDIVIDUAL AIRCRAFT

60-0357 During 1977 this former RC-135D, stripped of its reconnaissance equipment, served as a trainer for the 55th SRW at Offutt AFB.

RC-135T INDIVIDUAL AIRCRAFT

55-3121 During July 1973 BIG SAFARI demodified the RIVET DANDY RC-135T into a flight-deck trainer. The RC-135T received this MDS in May 1971, so reports that the 'T' stood for trainer are incorrect. Most exterior modifications were removed from 55-3121, although there were some exceptions. The airplane retained the hog nose as well as the associated wingtip static booms. Numerous small radomes and dielectric panels remained as inert residue of earlier mission configurations until they were eventually removed during PDM. The windows in the forward fuselage also remained for the balance of the airplane's lifetime. The IFR system was retained but inactivated, and the three-blade LORAN antenna was left in place.

The airplane was assigned to the 376th SW at Kadena AB. In April 1979 the airplane was reassigned to the 305th AREFW at Grissom AFB along with the remainder of the KC-135A (ARR). It lacked an air refueling boom and remained designated an RC-135T, although the IFR system was reactivated. Its stay at Grissom AFB was brief. In December 1979 it was assigned to the 6th SW at Eielson AFB as a flight crew trainer. On 18th January 1982, 55-3121 was flown from Eielson AFB to the BMAC facility for the addition of TF33-PW-102 turbofans, making it more compatible with the turbofan-equipped RC-135S

The RC-135 common pilots' station in use on the RIVET JOINT, COBRA BALL, and COMBAT SENT installed as part of RIVET GLASS. One MFD displays flight information. The other shows battlefield situational awareness. The pilots, who for years were jokingly referred to as 'bus drivers' with little connection to the mission collection, are now a fully integral part of the airplane's operational capability. *USAF photo via Delanie Stafford/Todd Clark*

KC-135A (ARR) 58-0124 served as a trainer for the 55th SRW, seen at Offutt AFB on 27th May 1977. Despite some claims that it may have had a reconnaissance role, official histories describe it only as a trainer. *Photo via Brian Rogers*

After duties in multiple reconnaissance roles, 59-1514 was demodified into a KC-135A (ARR). It became the prototype KC-135E in 1981, and resumed training missions at Offutt AFB. *Photo by Brian Rogers*

By 1973 BIG SAFARI had demodified the RC-135T from its reconnaissance role into a flight deck trainer. Its first assignment was with the 909th AREFS, 376th SW at Kadena AB. This image shows 55-3121 at Osan AB on 25th August 1975. *Photo by Eugene Zorn via Stephen Miller*

The RC-135T was a regular visitor to Offutt AFB for corrosion maintenance or for pilots to use the simulator, and was occasionally accompanied by an RC-135S for a trip to the 'wash rack'. 55-3121 was in this configuration when lost in 1985.
Photo via Bill Strandberg via Jim Rotramel

From 1977 through 1995, 61-2667 served as a trainer for three different aircraft types: E-3s at Tinker AFB, EC-135s at RAF Mildenhall, and RC-135s at Offutt AFB. Despite this, it was only designated a TC-135B for approximately 2 years.
Photo by Horst Jockers via Stephen Miller

The TC-135S wore a 'burning star' tail band from 1986 through 1988, when it was removed. It then gained the traditional black right wing and engines associated with the BURNING STAR mission.
Photo by the author

BMAC replaced the TF33-P-5 engines on the TC-135S with F108s in December 2005. Despite claims to the contrary, 62-4133 was not converted to TC-135W standards nor configured with cheeks.
Photo courtesy USAF

COBRA BALL flown by the 24th SRS aircrews. In its absence, NKC-135A 55-3129 served as a substitute trainer prior to its subsequent conversion into an EC-135P. The RC-135T returned to Eielson AFB on 26th February 1982. Following the change in engines, 55-3121's upper LORAN towel rack antenna was removed. The airplane had a microwave landing system (MLS) installed, the first operational KC-135 variant to be so equipped.

Plans called for the RC-135T to move to Offutt AFB in July 1985 to replace KC-135E (ARR) 59-1514 in its role as a reconnaissance trainer for the 55th SRW. The newly converted TC-135S 62-4133 would take over trainer duties with the 6th SW. The RC-135T crashed, however, on 25th February 1985, near Valdez, AK, while practicing MLS instrument approaches (see Appendix II).

TC-135B INDIVIDUAL AIRCRAFT

61-2667 WC-135B 61-2667 served from 24th March 1977 through 19th December 1984 with the 966th AW&CTS at Tinker AFB as an air refueling receiver trainer for E-3 Sentry crews. It returned to weather duties with the 55th WRS following its replacement at Tinker AFB by two Boeing 707 trainers. It was transferred to the 10th ACCS at RAF Mildenhall on 22nd April 1989 for use as a flight deck trainer much like the TC-135S and TC-135W. It received the STAR CAST modification by 3rd April 1990, reflecting its residual value in the intelligence collection role. Subsequently, it was reassigned to the 24th RS, 55th Wing at Offutt AFB and redesignated a TC-135B in 1993. It was reassigned to the 45th RS on 1st July 1994. In 1995 it was redesignated a WC-135W and resumed its operational duties.

TC-135S INDIVIDUAL AIRCRAFT

62-4133 The 6th SW operated the sole RC-135T (55-3121) to provide initial and recurring training to COBRA BALL flight deck crews without using an RC-135S and subsequently degrading mission coverage capability. The RC-135T was to be reassigned to the 55th SRW in July 1985 in a trainer role, with the 6th SW gaining the newly converted TC-135S as its replacement. The RC-135T crashed, however, on 25th February 1985. The TC-135S was delivered to the 6th SW on 22nd July 1985. Although by outward appearances the TC-135S replaced the RC-135T because it crashed, the TC-135S was intended as the replacement for the RC-135T anyway.

Beginning in early 1985 E-Systems converted the former AFSC EC-135B into the TC-135S. It had TF33-P-5 turbofans and acquired an IFR system. In 1986 it acquired a dark blue tail band with a yellow stylized shooting star, and in 1987 the TC-135S was noted with the nickname *North Star*. In October 1988 it received a black starboard wing and a US flag on the vertical stabilizer, although the colorful tail band was removed. During the 1991 Gulf War, it was pressed into service as a shuttle aircraft, flying personnel and equipment between Offutt AFB and Riyadh AB, making regular stops at RAF Mildenhall. After the 1992 COBRA THAW relocation of the former 24th RS RC-135S, RC-135X and TC-135S from Eielson AFB to Offutt AFB, the TC-135S was assigned to the 55th Wing, eventually receiving F108 engines along with the TC-135Ws. Articles in aviation magazines in the 2010s suggested that having two distinct TC-135 variants for training was a needless and expensive training luxury, raising the specter of retiring the TC-135S. According to these reports, the TC-135S was consequently redesignated as a TC-135W; some articles went further, suggesting that 62-4133 acquired cheeks to provide a common aerodynamic feel for the pilots. If, in fact, this was proposed, it did not take place. By 2016 62-4133 was still designated as a TC-135S, and photos taken as late as 24th October 2016 show it without cheeks.

The TC-135Ws play an important role in initial qualification for pilots and navigators assigned to the RC-135 fleet. *Photo by the author*

The cheeks on TC-135W 62-4129 overlap the crew entry hatch. These are the later E-Systems fairings and are longer than the original Martin cheeks. They began aft of the hatch and have since all been replaced. *Photo by Joe Bruch*

TC-135W INDIVIDUAL AIRCRAFT

62-4127 This C-135B was transferred from the 65th ALS, 15th ABW at Hickam AFB for conversion into a TC-135W on 30th August 2005.

62-4129 After the crash of the RC-135T on 25th February 1985, the 38th SRS was without a dedicated trainer until the availability through commercial sources of two C-137Cs (85-6973 and 85-6974) freed C-135B 62-4129 from its VIP duties with the 89th MAW at Andrews AFB for conversion into the TC-135W beginning in February 1987, with delivery to Offutt on 22nd April 1988. The TC-135Ws have the hog nose and cheeks of its RC-135 sisters but lack the 'antenna farm' seen beneath the fuselage on the RIVET JOINT RC-135s. The cheeks more closely approximate the aerodynamic feel of the RC-135V/W and are not part of any partial reconnaissance capability. In October 1988 the airplane was noted with the name *Greyhound*. Along with other remaining TC-135W it received F108 engines.

TC-135W 62-4129 has had its share of notoriety. In the late 1980s its cargo door opened shortly after takeoff. The crew landed the airplane safely, but for many months afterward received good-natured ribbing in the form of a modified salute that looked like the airplane in flight with the cargo door open! In 1990 it was involved in a landing incident at Offutt AFB, dragging the No.4 engine on the runway. The airplane suffered repairable damage and soon returned to flight status. A more serious incident occurred on 25th February 1993 when, during a pre-flight inspection, the nose gear collapsed, trapping the aircraft commander and crew chief in the nose gear well, where both were critically injured.

In an effort to prevent accidental attacks involving military aircraft, the US and Soviet Union conducted special flights in December 1989 over the Bering Strait and the Mediterranean Sea. These flights were part of the Dangerous Military Activities (DMA) agreement signed in June 1989, and took effect on 1st January 1990. During one flight over the Bering Sea during December 1989, for example, a Tu-95 *Bear* bomber rendezvoused with TC-135W 62-4129. The Tu-95 then proceeded into the US Air Defense Identification Zone (ADIZ) while the TC-135 flew into the Soviet ADIZ. F-15 Eagles intercepted and communicated via radio with the *Bear's* crew, while Su-27 *Flankers* did the same with the TC-135W crew. Neither the Tu-95 nor the TC-135W ever entered the airspace of the other country. In addition to communicating with the interceptors, pilots of the *Bear* and TC-135W were 'able to speak directly to other aircraft or to ground and ship-based controllers'. As a result of this test, both the US and Soviet Union have the means to prevent an incident in an ADIZ, but these procedures have little applicability to intercepts in international airspace.

COMINT AIRCRAFT AND OPERATIONS

KC-135A-II OFFICE BOY

Throughout the 1950s and early 1960s the 55th SRW at Forbes AFB, KS, was SAC's premier strategic reconnaissance unit, flying a variety of RB-50s and RB-47s. It is somewhat surprising, then, that in December 1962 SAC's first dedicated KC-135 reconnaissance version was assigned instead to the 4157th SW at Eielson AFB, AK. Moreover, these three OFFICE BOY KC-135A-IIs were the first C-135s converted into dedicated reconnaissance variants as part of the BIG SAFARI program, beginning more than a half-century of modification and maintenance of the RC-135 fleet by Ling-TEMCO-Vought (LTV) and its successors.

The OFFICE BOY aircraft trace their operational lineage to Cold War COMINT programs undertaken by the Air Force Security Service (AFSS), starting with a lone RB-29A prototype (44-62290). By 1955 this led to the DREAM BOAT RB-50E and RB-50Gs converted under the HAYSTACK program and by 1957 to the SUN VALLEY C-130A-IIs, both part of the Airborne Communication Reconnaissance Platform (ACRP). These airplanes gathered COMINT and initially operated throughout Europe and in the Pacific theater. Neither of these platforms had the necessary range, however, to fly 'over the top' from Alaska to England to collect intelligence from regions through which SAC's bombers would be expected to penetrate Soviet defenses (and which remained largely unexplored despite the massive 1956 RB-47E PHOTINT and RB-47H ELINT HOME RUN overflight program), as well as monitor ongoing developments at the Soviet nuclear test sites on Novaya Zemlya Island. This necessitated the use of jets capable of air refueling, beginning with the RB-47H.

The first known use of COMINT operators on RB-47H missions took place in January 1959 from Thule AB, Greenland, as part of COOL STOOL. This successful initial evaluation led to the 1960 BONUS BABY program to carry COMINT equipment and usually one AFSS linguist or a Morse intercept operator in lieu of the Raven 3. BONUS BABY missions flew in international airspace throughout the Siberian Arctic between Eielson AFB and RAF Brize Norton, and along the Kamchatka Peninsula between Eielson AFB and Yokota AB. SAC assigned linguists to RB-47H missions on an *ad hoc* basis, and the program ended on 15th December 1962 when the RB-47Hs received the QRC-135A(T) automated recording system in the BOX TOP program. All three of these RB-47H efforts demonstrated the value of COMINT collection on Arctic operations as well as self protection

for the 'ferret', and led to the 'Call 100' and OFFICE BOY programs for reconnaissance KC-135s.

During 1961 'Call 100' evaluated potential improvements to the SUN VALLEY C-130A-II platform by taking advantage of enhanced 'collection systems, flight endurance, range and altitude capabilities, and system integration applicable to the KC-135 aircraft.' In September and October 1961 MATS delivered the three C-135As 'Falsies' from the 1611th ATW at McGuire AFB to LTV at Greenville, TX, for conversion into reconnaissance platforms initially identified as 'Call 100 1' through 'Call 100 3'.

The core of the OFFICE BOY SIGINT gear was the G1100 Coherent Automatic Signal Tracking (CAST) system, mounted in cylindrical fairings on the fuselage extending forward from the wing root. The CAST system (not to be confused with the later STAR CAST or CAST GLANCE equipment on WC-135Bs and OC-135Bs) provided a VHF/UHF direction-finding (DF) capability. The system was highly temperamental, and constantly underwent technical changes to mitigate problems and to improve its accuracy and reliability. As with other RC-135 variants, the CAST fairings were often referred to in the press as side-looking airborne radar (SLAR) fairings, a myth which BIG SAFARI and the Air Force did little to dispel in order to obscure their actual purpose. The airplane also had a high-gain VHF receiver installed in the nose, leading to the widely recognized 'hog nose' on the RC-135 fleet. The boom pod was replaced with the radome for the AN/ALA-6 DF receiver. In addition to the reconnaissance related modifications, the OFFICE BOY KC-135A-IIs were the first C-135s of any variant to be configured with an in-flight refueling (IFR) system for receiver air refueling (ARR).

The flight-deck crews for the early RB-50E/G and C-130A-II COMINT platforms lacked the security clearance to know what the system operators (linguists) were actually doing on the mission. Fortunately, the galley and latrine were located between the flight deck and the operators, allowing a curtain (and later a compartment) to provide additional secrecy for the operators. With this in mind, BIG SAFARI planned a hallway along the port side of the KC-135A-II that would allow the front-end crew to reach the galley, latrine, and rest area in the back of the aircraft, conveniently bypassing a closed compartment in which the system operators monitored and recorded a variety of radio and other electronics transmissions. This added considerable weight, complexity, and cost to the conversion program. Giving the flight-deck crew the same security clearance as the operators eliminated the need for this expenditure, so the interior of

By the late 1950s the primary USAF COMINT platform was the SUN VALLEY C-130A-II. These lacked intercontinental range for polar missions. 56-0540 was demodified and then served as a standard C-130 until it crashed on 13th August 1972. *Photo by Stephen Miller*

the OFFICE BOY airplanes remained open, with the Raven and operator consoles along the starboard side of the cargo compartment, a configuration which remains to the present in all RC-135 variants.

Pending delivery of the first OFFICE BOY KC-135A-II, beginning in June 1962 AFSS provided a modest but effective COMINT support capability for SAC RB-47H missions using KC-135A tankers on temporary duty (TDY) to Eielson AFB. Three linguists and an airborne maintenance technician from the 6985th Security Squadron (SS) created a makeshift collection suite inside a 'tent' within a standard KC-135A. This tanker would refuel the RB-47H during its ELINT mission and then establish a figure-eight orbit outside of the 'sensitive area' to monitor Soviet defense communications, providing a rudimentary warning capability for the RB-47H. At least eight such missions were flown, likely more. This basic effort served as the conceptual and practical basis for subsequent COMINT and warning capability on future RC-135s.

This interim ability led to the GARLIC SALT advisory warning program. Beginning in April 1963 BIG SAFARI installed a modest self-protection system in three reconnaissance KC-135Rs: 55-3121, 59-1465, and 59-1514. Using surplus equipment from the SUN VALLEY I C-130A-II COMINT platforms, the positions were manned by two AFSS personnel, later renamed Electronic Security Command (ESC). The airplanes were assigned to the 34th AREFS, 385th SAW at Offutt AFB, where their primary mission was a quick-reaction capability on behalf of the Air Force Technical Applications Center (AFTAC) nuclear detection efforts (described in the KC-135R GARLIC SALT section).

KC-135A-II 60-0357 was the first OFFICE BOY jet delivered to the 4157th SW at Eielson AFB on 19th December 1962, with the two remaining airplanes following thereafter. The operational flight crew included a pilot, copilot, two navigators, and two electronic warfare officers, all assigned directly to the 4157th SW's Reconnaissance Division (DOR). By 1st September 1963 there were six crews, with anywhere from two to four members of each crew holding 'spot'

promotions, reflecting both the importance of the mission and the qualifications of the crewmembers. The remainder of the mission crew was assigned to AFSS in five flights – Able, Baker, Charlie, Dog, and Easy – each made up of 14 operators. An AFSS operator was 'fragged' to SAC for the duration of each mission. All crew members flew with only dog tags, a military ID card, and a 'blood chit' for security should the airplane or crew be 'compromised' during the flight.

The airplanes conducted 'electronic reconnaissance along the periphery of the Sino-Soviet bloc countries' as directed by the COTTON CANDY OpOrd. Early KC-135A-II operations were plagued by frequent aborts, particularly due to problems with the G-1080 navigational system computer and astro tracker. Shortages of spare parts and the awkward logistics pipeline to Alaska further contributed to delays in mission readiness. Once these problems were resolved, the three KC-135A-IIs began fairly steady and productive operations. Air aborts, for example, decreased from 43 in 1964 to 29 in 1965 to just 6 in 1966. The OFFICE BOY aircraft occasionally operated from the 4157th SW's Detachment 1 at Shemya AFB, although this was not an ongoing deployment.

Cheeks covered the Coherent Automatic Tracking System (CAST) on the OFFICE BOY KC-135A-II (later RIVET BRASS RC-135D). Extra plating above cockpit shows initial installation of an ARR system. *Author's collection*

KC-135A-II 60-0357 was the first '135 reconnaissance variant, and was delivered to the 4157th SW at Eielson AFB in 1962. This led to some good-natured ribbing about the 55th SRW being second in the RC-135 community. Many crewdogs flew with both units over their careers. *Author's collection*

By 1963 KC-135A-IIs took part in JIG TIME alert from Eielson AFB, possibly related to Soviet manned space launches. After an alert cycle, crews would fly a COTTON CANDY mission, sometimes to RAF Upper Heyford. *Author's collection*

Beginning in 1963 an OFFICE BOY crew was assigned to JIG TIME alert. This was a quick-reaction posture to ensure that a SIGINT collection platform could be airborne quickly in response to a subject of considerable interest but of unpredictable frequency or brief duration. Speculatively this might have included SIGINT acquired during the reentry of ballistic vehicles at the Kura Test Range at Klyuchi on the Kamchatka Peninsula, but the four-hour flight time from Eielson AFB would have required substantial advance notice of an impending launch. More likely, JIG TIME alert missions were related to monitoring the Soviet space program, which had a more 'generous' warning time. Each crew's alert cycle lasted 48 hours followed by a 'combat crew rest and rehabilitation' (CCRR) period. While on alert the crew planned and briefed an operational COTTON CANDY sortie to be flown after the CCRR period.

The OFFICE BOY KC-135A-IIs flew extensively. From July-December 1963, for example, there were 86 COTTON CANDY sorties, and 120 sorties over the next six months. In September 1963 alone there were 20 OFFICE BOY missions scheduled with 13 completed. During the first half of 1965, the three airplanes flew 133 operational COTTON CANDY sorties for a total of 2,116.7 flying hours, averaging nearly 16 hours per flight. During the second half of 1965 OFFICE BOY KC-135A-IIs flew 129 operational sorties. This was particularly impressive because on 28th July KC-135A-II 60-0357 went to Greenville for upgrade and did not return until 1966, so the two remaining airplanes flew a nearly equal number of sorties completed by three jets earlier in the year. The need for extensive maintenance and upgrade for the three airplanes (typically 135 days out of service) further detracted from their operational capability.

Ongoing changes in national intelligence requirements shifted the geographic focus of the COTTON CANDY sorties accordingly, but the demand for additional sorties reaffirmed the need for more than the three extant OFFICE BOY aircraft, and in 1964 six OFFICE BOY II airplanes were ordered. Events in Southeast Asia exacerbated the shortage of airplanes and resulted in growing tensions between SAC, CINCPAC, and the JCS over who could assign US strategic reconnaissance assets and where they should be prioritized. In a sign of things to come, during February 1965 CINCPAC Admiral Ulysses S Grant Sharp ordered a halt to COTTON CANDY missions along the Kamchatka and Chukotskii Peninsulas (which were in his theater of jurisdiction) and reassigned the missions to Southeast Asia. CINCSAC General John D Ryan objected on the grounds that the airplanes were SAC assets (under his control) and that their primary mission was to gather intelligence on behalf of the SIOP. Shifting them to support what SAC considered as just an 'affray' in a Third World 'domino' conflict was a gross misuse of a critical and severely constrained resource. The JCS agreed with SAC, and in September ordered that the COTTON CANDY sorties along Kamchatka and Chukotskii be resumed but with the proviso that they also support reconnaissance demands in Southeast Asia. With only two airplanes on hand, the need for extra aircraft in the form of the six forthcoming OFFICE BOY IIs had become critical.

In addition to COTTON CANDY missions, KC-135A-IIs participated in special NIGHT LIGHT missions, which 'collected telemetry in the Pacific'. These were dedicated sorties (as opposed to the JIG TIME alert sorties) related to the Soviet manned space effort and were directed by the NSA and the JCS. NIGHT LIGHT is believed to have monitored radio communications between the cosmonauts and ground- and sea-based facilities. Two separate NIGHT LIGHT sorties were flown on 18th and 19th March 1965. The latter mission was of particular interest because the *Voshkod* 2 spacecraft with two astronauts on board landed after 26 orbits during which cosmonaut Alexsei Leonov conducted a 10-minute space walk, the first time anyone had been outside a capsule in space.

RC-135D RIVET BRASS

On 1st January 1965 the three OFFICE BOY KC-135A-IIs were redesignated RIVET BRASS RC-135Ds, although this was not applied until after they completed upgrades at BIG SAFARI. In late 1965, for example, KC-135A-II 60-0357 returned to BIG SAFARI, after which its records show it as an RC-135D. By late 1966 all three KC-135A-IIs had been so modified and redesignated. The RIVET BRASS mission remained the same as the KC-135A-IIs and they flew missions as part of the COTTON CANDY OpOrd. In January 1967 the OpOrd was renamed BURNING CANDY. Regional mission OpOrds included ARCTIC CANDY, BALTIC CANDY, CUBAN CANDY, and MEDITERRANEAN CANDY.

Interestingly, WANDA BELLE RC-135S 59-1491 was a 'phantom' fourth RC-135D. Official SAC documents from 1965 show four RC-135Ds assigned to the 4157th SW – three RIVET BRASS and the WANDA BELLE. This designation does not appear on the aircraft's records, and is presumed to be an internal SAC reference by virtue of its co-location with the three RC-135Ds at Eielson AFB. The airplane's records show it was officially redesignated from JKC-135A to RC-135S on 7th March 1963 as it began upgrade and modification at BIG SAFARI. In January 1965 SAC directed that 59-1491 be designated an RC-135D (almost two years after it officially became an RC-135S), but this errant change never took place. One aberrant MDS change that *did* occur, however, involved RIVET BRASS 60-0362. While at LTV for conversion from a KC-135A-II, on 4th October 1966 it was redesignated (at least administratively) as an RC-135G. This was corrected some three weeks later on 1st November 1966.

As with OFFICE BOY manning, six RIVET BRASS flight crews were assigned to the 4157th SW DOR. Pending the delivery of the LISA ANN RC-135E 62-4137 in 1966, the two crews slated to fly that airplane served as interim adjunct crews for COTTON CANDY RC-135D missions. On 25th March 1967 the 4157th SW was inactivated and its assets absorbed by the 6th SW, and all flight-deck crews assigned to the newly reactivated and redesignated 24th SRS. RC-135Ds conducted SIGINT operations originating at Eielson AFB, and were frequent visitors to the 98th SW's Detachment 1 at RAF Upper Heyford, England, as well as transient operations from Yokota AB and Kadena AB.

The RC-135D configuration was generally similar to its earlier incarnation as a KC-135A-II. It retained the CAST system, the hog nose, the AN/ALA-6 radome, and the IFR system installed while configured as KC-135A-IIs. Small teardrop-shaped fairings were added ahead of each horizontal stabilizer. From 1972 onward RIVET BRASS 3 – RC-135D 60-0362 – had the CAST system removed and had a large steerable antenna mounted in a 200in (508cm) ventral radome between stations 420 and 620 under the forward fuselage. Previously, as the airplane flew past a given emitter or transmitter, it was able to collect data from a signal of interest for only a brief period. Installation of the steerable antenna allowed the moving RIVET BRASS to track the signal for a longer period of time. Subsequent USAF tracking systems used electronic steering to save space and weight.

RIVET BRASS missions routinely monitored targets located in the Arctic from Novaya Zemlya Island in the west along the Siberian coast to the Chukotskii Peninsula at the Bering Sea and then southward along the Kamchatka Peninsula, throughout the Sea of Okhotsk, and on to the East China Sea. Aside from the ubiquitous MiG interception, COTTON CANDY sorties were not immune to danger. During one mission over the Sea of Okhotsk the Soviets fired a SAM at the airplane but to no effect. Beginning in January 1967 RC-135Ds flew SIGINT collections missions off North Korea and China.

In addition to ongoing COTTON CANDY and BURNING CANDY missions focusing on the USSR, RC-135Ds supported combat operations in Southeast Asia. Sorties lasting in excess of 24 hours were not uncommon, departing from Eielson AFB to Vietnam, orbiting as required, and then recovering at Yokota AB. These 'butt

buster' missions ended in May 1967 as the RIVET CARD RC-135Ms began BURNING CANDY missions from Yokota AB. Additional RC-135D operations in Southeast Asia included back up for the RC-135M COMBAT APPLE missions from Kadena AB, beginning in mid 1969. As with any major substitution of mission equipment, the success of these RIVET BRASS deployments was the source of some disagreement. Although filling a need, one crewmember recalls that RC-135Ds 'caused more problems than [they] solved'. Another crewmember disagrees, considering this 'an exaggerated statement'.

Troublesome leaks of all sorts (hydraulic, fuel, water injection, etc) and electronic equipment failures have been attributed to the move from the cold of Alaska to the heat of Okinawa. Given that summer Alaskan temperatures – but not humidity – can approach those at Kadena, these problems were not likely to have been the result of any significant temperature change (not to mention that at FL350 the airplane is cold soaked at -40°F/C no matter where it is). Instead, they were more likely due to the increased humidity and torrential rainfall of the tropics, a problem which beset all RC-135 operations from Kadena AB, not just RC-135Ds. Further, J57 turbojet-powered RC-135Ds lacked the TF33 turbofan-powered RC-135M's range and endurance. This meant that under many conditions the RIVET BRASS could not take off with a full fuel load, necessitating a prompt air refueling just to start the mission. All things

considered, although the RC-135Ds may have suffered due to their somewhat reduced engine performance, they were no more vulnerable to climatic vagaries and the ensuing maintenance problems than were the RC-135Ms.

The final RC-135D BURNING CANDY sortie out of RAF Mildenhall took place on 10th February 1975. There is some official confusion about the date of the final BURNING CANDY missions flown from Eielson AFB, as the 6th SW History shows that it occurred on 13th March 1975 but the SAC Recon History for FY1974 records 21st March 1975. In either case, the RC-135Ds were replaced by the 55th SRW's more advanced RC-135M and RC-135V platforms as part of the new BURNING WIND OpOrd. Replacement of the RIVET BRASS with the RIVET CARD and later the RIVET JOINT was more the result of the natural evolution of RC-135 SIGINT capability than a reflection of the RC-135D's inability to fulfill its mission. Further, the termination of hostilities in Southeast Asia freed the six RC-135Ms from their COMBAT APPLE mission and permitted their use in RIVET CARD global operations. As a consequence, the RC-135Ds were declared 'surplus', demodified into KC-135A(ARR)s and returned to operational status as tankers by 1979. Following the loss of EC-135K 62-3536 on 14th September 1977, two former RC-135Ds (60-0357 and 60-0362) were considered for conversion into a replacement EC-135K, but former FAA KC-135A 59-1518 was chosen instead.

The 1st January 1965 redesignation of US military aircraft changed the KC-135A-II to the RC-135D. At the same time, the program name changed from OFFICE BOY to RIVET BRASS. Externally the airplanes remained the same. *Photo by Richard Vandervord*

RIVET BRASS 3 60-0362 had the CAST system removed and a large steerable antenna under the forward fuselage, barely discernable in this 1974 image taken at Eielson AFB. *Photo by Stephen Miller*

An AN/ALA-6 direction finding antenna was installed where the boom pod was normally located. This became standard on all subsequent RC-135s. *Author's collection*

BIG SAFARI began the conversion of the three C-135A 'falsies' into KC-135A-IIs as part of the Call 100 initiative. In the case of 60-0357, it was Call 100-1, then OFFICE BOY I, and finally RIVET BRASS I.

The KC-135A-IIs and RC-135Ds were equipped with J57 'steam jets,' which proved troublesome in the tropical climate at Kadena AB. All three have since been converted to KC-135R (ARR)s.
Both: Author's collection

C-135A-II/RC-135D INDIVIDUAL AIRCRAFT

60-0356 This airplane arrived at BIG SAFARI on 31st October 1961, as 'Call 100 2' for modification into the OFFICE BOY 2 KC-135A-II, and was delivered to the 4157th SW on 31st January 1963. On 5th March 1966 it returned to BIG SAFARI for a systems upgrade through September 1966, when it was redesignated an RC-135D and delivered to the 4157th SW at Eielson AFB as the RIVET BRASS 2. During June 1969 the airplane deployed briefly to Kadena AB in support of COMBAT APPLE operations. Following the termination of RC-135D BURNING CANDY sorties from Eielson AFB, 60-0356 departed Alaska on 3rd March 1975 for the 376th SW at Kadena AB, although whether it continued in the reconnaissance role while at Kadena is unclear. It was delivered to BIG SAFARI for demodification into a KC-135A(ARR).

60-0357 This airplane was delivered to the BIG SAFARI facility as 'Call 100 1' on 6th October 1961 for conversion into the OFFICE BOY 1 KC-135A-II. It arrived at Eielson AFB on 19th December 1962, making it the first dedicated reconnaissance variant of the KC-135 to be delivered to an operational unit. During late 1965 60-0357 returned to BIG SAFARI and became the first RC-135D. It was delivered to the 4157th SW at Eielson AFB on 18th January 1966 as the RIVET BRASS 1. This airplane was demodified into a KC-135A(ARR) in 1976.

60-0362 Destined for modification into the OFFICE BOY 3 airplane, it was delivered on 6th September 1961 as 'Call 100 3' to the BIG SAFARI facility and reached the 4157th SW on 4th April 1963. In October 1966 it returned to BIG SAFARI for RC-135D upgrade and redesignation. BIG SAFARI converted it into the RC-135D RIVET BRASS 3 from October 1966 through early 1967, when it was assigned to the 4157th SW. This was the first RC-135D to deploy to Kadena AB in support of COMBAT APPLE (doing so from May through June 1969). It was demodified into a KC-135A(ARR) in 1976.

RC-135M RIVET CARD

Buried among the highly visible and immensely popular accounts of MiG killers and LINEBACKER II B-52 raids during the war in Vietnam is the lesser known story of strategic aerial reconnaissance in yet another proxy war between the Soviet Union and the United States. Throughout the Korean War fifteen years earlier, no fewer than eight US Navy and SAC 'ferrets' were shot down. Indeed, the last US loss of the war was arguably 55th SRW RB-50G 47-0145 *Little Red Ass*, shot down on 29th July 1953 in what was likely an ambush in retaliation for the downing two days earlier of a Soviet Ilyushin Il-12 *Coach* carrying Russian generals back from North Korea. The war

in Korea offered two crucial lessons for strategic aerial reconnaissance in combat: (1) a big, lumbering airliner laden with electronics and crewmembers was no match for nimble MiGs; and (2) COMINT was a powerful tool in negating the threat of intercepting MiGs. SAC would apply both of these lessons to the fullest in Vietnam with COMBAT APPLE RC-135M missions.

During 1964 USAF Lieutenant General Gordon A Blake, Director of the National Security Agency (DIRNSA), established the requirement for six follow-on OFFICE BOY II aircraft to meet national collection needs given the heavy demands on the three existing KC-135A-II OFFICE BOY aircraft. These new airplanes were subject to significant budget and basing issues. Original estimates of $3.5 million per aircraft quickly increased to $4.17 million per jet. Nonetheless, final Department of Defense (DoD) approval for the airplanes came in June 1965, and Air Force Logistics Command (AFLC) identified six MAC C-135Bs for conversion into RC-135Ls from March through December 1967. [Effective 13th August 1965, the RC-135L was redesignated RC-135M. However, SAC was not notified of this revision until 8th February 1966 and all SAC references to the OFFICE BOY II aircraft (such as the classified 1965 *Reconnaissance History of SAC*) prior to this date describe them as RC-135Ls. This designation was never used, however, and development and operations of the OFFICE BOY II airplanes took place as RC-135Ms under the RIVET CARD program.]

With the funding issue decided, it remained to resolve the problem of where the new airplanes would be based. Initial planning called for six OFFICE BOY jets based at Eielson AFB (three RC-135Ds and three RC-135Ls) and three based at Yokota AB (three RC-135Ls). This would allow for sustained COTTON CANDY sorties along the northern periphery of the Soviet Union as well as additional sorties in Southeast Asia and along the Chinese and Soviet coastlines. By August 1965, however, Secretary of Defense Robert S McNamara ordered that all six of the new RC-135Ls would be based at Eielson AFB along with the three RC-135Ds. This decision was driven by the ongoing US financial problem known as 'gold flow', where a disproportionate amount of US expenditures were made to foreign countries and hence a corresponding transfer of gold out of the United States, weakening the US economy. Basing the new airplanes in Alaska rather than in Japan would eliminate this thorny economic issue.

Pentagon parochialism interceded, however, as the new DIRNSA, Army Lieutenant General Marshall S Carter, reversed his predecessor's recommendation on the priority of COTTON CANDY and BURNING CANDY missions. Not surprisingly, Carter favored a substantial increase in sorties supporting the growing Army and US Marine ground commitment in Southeast Asia at the expense of ongoing SIOP-related sorties, necessitating a complete revision of the OFFICE BOY basing plan. After an exhaustive series of 'what if' permutations and scenarios, on 29th October 1965 McNamara approved a new (and final) basing plan with all six RC-135Ls at Yokota AB and three RC-135Ds at Eielson AFB. So much for 'gold flow'.

Despite these budget, basing, and designation resolutions in 1965, the first RC-135M had yet to fly. BIG SAFARI converted 62-4135 into the first RC-135M as part of the RIVET CARD program beginning in mid 1965, and the first five aircraft were ready by the end of 1966. They were assigned to Detachment 1, 3rd AD at Yokota AB, beginning with 62-4135 on 23rd May 1967, where they operated in a strategic reconnaissance role as part of the BURNING CANDY OpOrd. Their mission remained SIGINT collection (primarily COMINT with a secondary ELINT capacity) from 'Shanghai to Petropavlovsk' on behalf of national intelligence agencies such as the NSA as well as SAC's ongoing SIOP needs.

The RC-135M airframe was based on the C-135B equipped with TF33-P-5 turbofan engines with thrust reversers. Reconnaissance modifications incorporated ongoing upgrades to existing RC-135D systems as well as new components such as the Litton LN-16A Stellar Inertial Doppler System (SIDS) AN/ASN-59 navigation system that provided 'continuous, automatic, 24-hour, all weather global navigation' to display the RC-135M's 'position, velocity, and altitude.' The complexity of the navigation system proved troublesome, especially with the Stellar Inertial Reference Unit (SIRU), and the airplanes eventually acquired the AN/ASN-121 Inertial Navigation System (INS). The RC-135M received a high-gain VHF receiver in the nose with the hog nose radome, had the IFR system installed, and retained the RC-135D's radome for the AN/ALA-6 receiver in the boom pod, but they did not have the RC-135D's CAST cheeks. Instead, the RC-135Ms had a teardrop fairing located on each side of the fuselage forward of horizontal stabilizer. There were 13 operator positions for the linguists.

As the BIG TEAM RC-135Cs began BURNING PIPE strategic reconnaissance missions in earnest and combat operations in Southeast Asia increased, RC-135Ms were increasingly dedicated to the mission for which they are best remembered – COMBAT APPLE. Created on paper on 20th March 1967, COMBAT APPLE missions were intended to replace QUEEN BEE C-130B-II SILVER DAWN/COMMANDO LANCE operations flown from Da Nang AB in South Vietnam. As originally envisaged, each COMBAT APPLE sortie would fly daily from its planned base at U-Tapao RTNAB to Da Nang AB, pick up AFSS linguists from the 6988th SS, and then depart for its orbit over the Gulf of Tonkin. By 17th February 1967 the increasing number of B-52Ds and KC-135As at U-Tapao RTNAB eliminated that as an option, and SAC was forced to consider other basing possibilities. Da Nang AB and Takhli RTAFB also lacked adequate ramp space and were quickly excluded. Ching Chuan Kang AB (CCK) on Taiwan was eliminated for political reasons. Consequently, on 8th April 1967 Clark AB in the Philippines was selected (almost by default) as the COMBAT APPLE base. In typical military fashion, however, SAC and AFSS 'suddenly' agreed that Kadena AB would be a far better choice, and on 19th June 1967 Air Force Chief of Staff General John P McConnell directed that COMBAT APPLE missions would be conducted from Kadena AB beginning 1st September 1967 with linguists from the newly activated 6990th SS. Beginning 2nd January 1968 front-end crews and airplanes were assigned to the 82nd SRS, 4252nd SW at Kadena AB, and on 1st April 1970 the 376th SW absorbed the assets of the 4252nd SW *in situ*, including the 82nd SRS and its RC-135Ms.

RC-135M 62-4135 under the command of Major Bennie Allen flew the first COMBAT APPLE sortie on 12th September 1967. The crew of 24 included two SAC pilots and two navigators, 13 AFSS operators, four SAC operators, two maintenance technicians, and Lieutenant Colonel (later Major General) Doyle E Larson, the 6990th SS Commander. Mechanical failure prevented the air refueling slipway doors from opening, so the airplane was unable to complete its first planned refueling. It diverted to U-Tapao RTNAB, although it 'achieved roughly 65 per cent of its scheduled orbit time.' Initial sorties took place every third day, and beginning 16th October 1967 COMBAT APPLE sorties were flown daily. This soon increased to two per day (with a spare available) through 1973 when the sortie count dropped to just a daily flight until the end of the program. As RC-135Ms rotated back to the US for PDM or system upgrades, RC-135Ds from the 6th SW at Eielson AFB, and the RIVET DANDY RC-135T 55-3121 and KC-135R 58-0126 from the 55th SRW at Offutt AFB substituted for the absent airplanes.

The debut COMBAT APPLE mission was cut short due to problems with the IFR system. 62-4135, which flew the sortie, undergoes IFR maintenance at Kadena AB to avoid a recurrence. *Photo by Glenn Downer*

A maintenance technician works inside the RC-135M. The interior was cramped with little room to stretch on missions as long as 18-22 hours. 'Ops Tempo' was demanding, but morale was high among both flight and ground crews. *Photo by Glenn Downer*

There remains some confusion about the environmental effects on RC-135Ms in Southeast Asia. One source indicates that tropical torrential rains caused short circuits in the RC-135M thrust reverser system, causing 'the engine to go into reverse' with its associated violent yaw and decay of airspeed. While inadvertent thrust reverser actuation may have occurred, it was unlikely due to any electrical short circuit. The thrust reverser system on the RC-135M was mechanically and pneumatically actuated and operated. The only electrical component of the thrust reverser systems was a 24-volt DC connection which indicated that the forward baffles and aft core reversers had moved into position, turning on the thrust reverser indicator light for that engine on the main instrument panel. Whereas water might short circuit and illuminate the thrust reverser indicator light in the plane's cockpit, it could not actuate the reverser itself. There may indeed have been sudden asymmetries in flight, particularly during takeoff, but these were likely the result of losing an engine (especially a downwind outboard engine) which would have similar results.

During its heyday, a typical COMBAT APPLE sortie lasted 18–22 hours including approximately six hours transit time from Kadena to Vietnam and back. Once on station, the airplane established an orbit over the Gulf of Tonkin. As signals of interest (SOIs) were noted, smaller orbits were established until study of the subject was completed. The airplane then returned to its original orbit, which usually lasted from 12 to 16 hours. The airplanes usually refueled at least once in an orbit just south of the demilitarized zone (DMZ) to allow minimal disruption to their collection effort.

COMBAT APPLE operational tempo was brutal but morale was exceptionally high. Crews occasionally landed from one sortie, completed the required crew rest, and then flew another sortie. Linguists were in particular demand, and all COMBAT APPLE

crewmembers quickly reached and exceeded the monthly limit of 120 flight hours, subsequently waived to 165 hours, sometimes more. In more than a few cases, crewmembers flew sorties without being listed on the crew manifest. A project known as YOGI BEAR sought to reduce this workload though the installation of a 28-track recorder that monitored traffic along the Ho Chi Minh trail and the planned implementation of a data downlink to either Nakhon Phanom RTAFB in Thailand or the Monkey Mountain SIGINT facility near Da Nang for 'real-time exploitation'. The 28-track audio tapes were analysed after landing at Kadena AB, but quickly created a daunting backlog requiring additional linguists to translate. The downlink portion suffered from budget constraints and technical issues, and was not implemented. RC-135Ms continued infrequent BURNING CARD strategic reconnaissance missions around the Asian landmass, so demand for crews and airplanes was considerable. The occasional typhoon also required the evacuation of the airplanes from Kadena AB to Clark AB in the Philippines with the consequent need for crews to live in temporary quarters while continuing their heavy operational demands.

In February 1968 the North Vietnamese changed their General Directorate of Rear Services (GDRS) message system that reported infiltration movements along the Ho Chi Minh Trail. Unaware that their codes had been broken by the end of 1968, the new North Vietnamese messages revealed not only the progress of troops and supplies as they made their way south, but their destination as well. Knowing this enabled US planners to anticipate hostile action at a general time and specific location, as well as undertake more precise interdiction targeting along the trail. New US President Richard M Nixon and his National Security Advisor Henry A Kissinger considered this intelligence – known as the 'Vinh Window' – of crucial importance and directed a robust aerial collection program over Laos and the Ho Chi Minh Trail by C-130B-IIs which were soon replaced by COMBAT APPLES. This meant that on occasion two RC-135Ms were in orbit together (one over Laos and the other over the Gulf of Tonkin). In other cases an RC-135M shared the orbit in the Gulf of Tonkin with a BIG TEAM RC-135C or RIVET DANDY RC-135T and KC-135R delaying while on a BURNING PIPE sortie. Other areas of interest during the war eventually included the Yellow Sea, the East China Sea, and Hainan Island.

EC-135Ls and KC-135A-VIII COMBAT LIGHTNING radio relay airplanes served as an electronic bridge between the RC-135Ms and headquarters or operational units and airplanes. For example, mission specialists aboard a COMBAT APPLE might determine that North Vietnamese defenses were utilizing certain search radar and radio frequencies. These data would then be relayed via COMBAT LIGHTNING to the striking airplane's headquarters (or even directly to US airplanes themselves en route to bomb targets in North Vietnam). Knowing this information, the airplanes' courses could be altered as necessary, threatening radar frequencies jammed more effectively, and weaknesses of the North Vietnamese defenses better exploited (See Table 10-1). COMBAT APPLE sorties also assisted in SAR operations or in the warning of North Vietnamese SAM or MiG activity. The electronic presence of a *Fan Song* radar was a strong indication of potential or actual SAM activity and received the immediate attention of the COMBAT APPLE. Threat warnings were then broadcast to vulnerable airplanes while recordings were made of the SAM's electronic 'fingerprint' for analysis and the development of appropriate jamming equipment.

COMBAT APPLE intelligence contributions were not all electronic. For example, the crew aboard the RC-135M aircraft during Mission F020 flown on 21st December observed heavy antiaircraft artillery fire and 30 to 40 SAM detonations during the 20-minute period between 2030Z and 2052Z, followed by a SAM burst and two large fireballs at 2106Z, and the last SAM detonation at 2105Z. Two

Table 10-1. COMBAT APPLE **Exploitation of North Vietnamese MiG Operations**

• Preflight schedules	• Tactics
• Takeoff and recovery times	• Aircraft characteristics and
• Number active	performance through pilot references
• Pilot billet numbers	to speeds, altitudes, fuel checks,
• Home base and primary and alternate	instrument readings and armament
recovery bases	expenditures
• Alert status	• MiG losses
• Nationality of pilots (North Korean,	• Navigational and recovery procedures
North Vietnamese, etc.)	• IFF usage
• Rotation of aircraft to and from China	• Methods used by analysts to determine
• Pilot-controller relationships	aircraft type
• CAP areas	

[source: 'Damage Assessment of Compromise of Operational Intelligence Broadcast Messages on Board USS *Pueblo* (AEGR-2)', 17th March 1969, TOP SECRET-UMBRA, III-A-I. National Security Archives.]

B-52Ds and a US Navy A-6 were lost. On the following day, 22nd December, the crew of Mission F021 saw 31 SAM launches and detonations as well as almost continual AAA firings in the Hanoi/Haiphong area between 2050Z-2300Z. On 26th December, the RC-135M pilot counted 75 SAM launches between 1530Z and 1550Z, claiming two additional B-52Ds.

RC-135M crews could often detect a MiG's taxi and takeoff (from its radio calls) and could listen to the North Vietnamese ground controller, thus discerning the MiG's vectors and intended targets. Appropriate warnings about the MiG could then be forwarded to waiting Combat Air Patrol (CAP) fighters, often via an orbiting RIVET TOP EC-121K as part of the TEABALL program, and the hunter soon became the prey. Table 10-1 lists specific North Vietnamese MiG capabilities and operations derived from COMBAT APPLE missions. (The Israeli Air Force employed these same tactics with great effect in the 1982 'Peace for Galilee' operation, using 'RC-707s' to monitor Syrian pilot-to-ground communications. The RC-707s then directed Israeli fighters into position to attack the Syrian MiGs even as they became airborne, accounting for, in part, the Israelis' impressive 82-to-0 air-to-air kill ratio during that conflict.)

This significant advisory warning and exploitation capability from COMBAT APPLE suffered a significant setback beginning 23rd January 1968 following the North Korean capture of the USS *Pueblo*. The ship's crew had received some 8,000 highly classified messages about ongoing intelligence efforts in the Pacific, including traffic which 'provided detailed information regarding US capabilities to intercept and exploit North Vietnamese communications associated with air, surface-to-air, and early warning/air surveillance defenses [that were] exploited to provide threat advisory warnings to US aircraft and to develop electronic order of battle.' Some 17 of these many messages directly addressed COMBAT APPLE, and provided detailed summaries of 'mission number, times on station of mission aircraft, general location while on station, significant enemy activity

noted during the mission, observed SAM activity and reports of alerts and warnings,' all revealing a 'reasonably accurate summary of the function of COMBAT APPLE.' Indeed, the 82nd SRS received the 1970 Paul T Cullen Trophy for COMBAT APPLE operations.

The North Koreans promptly passed this information to the Soviet Union, adversely affecting ongoing BURNING CANDY and BURNING PIPE collection capabilities as well as advisory warning, and to the North Vietnamese with similar impact. A 17th March 1969 report by the CIA, DIA, and the combined military intelligence agencies specifically cited the impact of the compromised messages on COMBAT APPLE, and noted that 'COMBAT APPLE mission result summaries and bi-weekly operations reports… [revealed] the depth of US collection programs, the evaluation process of data, and the dissemination and use of final products.' The report concluded, rather optimistically, that the compromise would only result in the 'tightening up' of sources, specifically 'improved security practices, emission control, frequency changes, etc and could cause a loss in timeliness in areas such as advisory warning and other real-time tactical support, but probably would have little effect on long-term collection efforts.' It added 'COMBAT APPLE missions will probably not be affected to a great degree in the future. However, their effectiveness in air and air defense intelligence may be seriously reduced. This in turn would significantly degrade effectiveness of US air operations in Laos and North Vietnam,' reflecting the real contributions made by COMBAT APPLE crews.

Orbiting COMBAT APPLE RC-135s were not immune from pursuit, and US Navy fighters were assigned to Barrier Combat Air Patrol (BARCAP) orbits with the unarmed reconnaissance aircraft. The Navy McDonnell Douglas F-4 Phantoms and Vought F-8 Crusaders soon established a predictable routine for refueling, leaving the COMBAT APPLE unescorted. The North Vietnamese figured this out, and on at least two occasions sent MiG-21s out during this gap in coverage to shoot down the unescorted RC-135M. Neither of these

Opposite page: Crowded bases in Thailand meant that COMBAT APPLE missions operated mostly from Kadena AB. Just to get on station was a three-hour flight, so air refueling was critical to maintain a 12-hour 'watch' followed by another three-hour flight back to Kadena AB. *Photo by Ted Boydston*

This page: Although RC-135Cs on a BURNING PIPE mission occasionally orbited with the COMBAT APPLE, it was RC-135Ms which bore the brunt of continuous missions over both Laos and Gulf of Tonkin. *Photo by Charles Mayer via Stephen Miller*

The COMBAT APPLE warning advisory capability found ready adherents with the Israeli Air Force. RC-707s such as 4X-JYQ contributed to the lop-sided Israeli aerial victory over the Syrian Air Force in the 1982. *Author's collection*

RC-135Ms flew more than just COMBAT APPLE missions, and were equally busy on BURNING CANDY COMINT missions throughout Southeast Asia.
Photo by Charles Mayer via Stephen Miller

was successful. Over time, 'several' MiGs are said to have been lost to these escorts, although a few of these 'MiGs' are now known to have been US drones.

COMBAT APPLE also supported the 21st November 1970 attempted rescue of US prisoners of war at the Son Tay prison camp in North Vietnam. They provided 'MiG warning and monitoring of the Task Group's communications', as well as tracking the North Vietnamese response to the US Navy feint underway near Haiphong. RC-135Ms began night orbits several weeks in advance of the planned mission to 'desensitize' the North Vietnamese to their presence.

In the wake of the 18-29th December 1972 LINEBACKER II bombings of Hanoi and Haiphong, the North Vietnamese returned to the peace table. President Nixon suspended offensive combat operations on 15th January 1973, and on 27th January the 'Paris Peace Accords' were signed, bringing the war to an end for the United States. A week later, on 31st January, CINCPAC Admiral Noel A M Gayler directed that COMBAT APPLE sorties approach no closer than 50nm (92.6km) to North Vietnam. In addition, CINCSAC General John C Meyer suspended the BARCAP requirement. The final COMBAT APPLE mission was flown on 30th April 1975, the same day that North Vietnamese troops captured Saigon, ending nearly three decades of war. In over six years of operations, COMBAT APPLE RC-135Ms (and the occasional RC-135D) flew 3,250 operational sorties with 39,286 orbit hours (averaging 12 hours on station).

After direct US involvement in the war in Southeast Asia ended in 1973, RC-135Ms resumed BURNING CANDY strategic reconnaissance missions from Kadena AB. RC-135Ms later participated in other major operations in Southeast Asia including EAGLE PULL (the evacuation of Phnom Penh from 11-13th April 1975), FREQUENT WIND (the evacuation of Saigon from 29-30th April 1975), and, along with RIVET JOINT RC-135Vs, the 12-15th May 1975 rescue of the SS *Mayaguez* and her crew from their Cambodian pirate captors and Khmer Rouge military forces. Other Southeast Asia PARPRO operations included missions near Hainan Island in the Gulf of Tonkin during the border conflicts between Vietnam and the PRC. RC-135M operations were not restricted to the Pacific theatre. On 14th June 1974, an RC-135M flew the first RIVET CARD mission from Hellenikon AB at Athens, Greece. RC-135M missions from Hellenikon AB increased significantly, and by October 1975 RC-135M 62-4139 flew the 500th sortie from Athens. RC-135Ms monitored the 1974 conflict between Greece and Turkey over Cyprus. An RC-135M was airborne during a routine sortie on 15th

July 1974 when the crisis began and was retasked to follow the rapidly unfolding events. A 20th July RC-135M launched from Hellenikon AB ended up at Torrejon AB, Spain, out of concern for the security of US aircraft at Athens. It returned soon thereafter. By 11th September 1976 all RC-135Ms were reassigned to the 55th SRW at Offutt AFB. Beginning in 1980 BIG SAFARI converted RC-135M 62-4135 into Block III configuration RC-135W RIVET JOINT 9, with the remaining five to follow. The last RC-135M mission from Kadena AB was flown in 62-4139 on 11th November 1984.

The lessons of COMBAT APPLE found direct application nearly two decades later during Operation DESERT STORM. RC-135V/W RIVET JOINTS, operating in conjunction with E-3C AWACS, served in a similar capacity to provide real-time ELINT and COMINT capability. With the advent of improved data link technology, this was passed directly to air and ground forces. Nearly 50 years later, this intelligence can be displayed in the cockpit of each strike aircraft or on the visor of each pilot's helmet, on laptops or tablets held by any soldier on the ground, and on battlefield management displays at regional, theatre, and national command posts. It all began with COMBAT APPLE.

RC-135M INDIVIDUAL AIRCRAFT

62-4131 Transferred to BIG SAFARI on 15th June 1966 for conversion from a C-135B into an RC-135M, and delivered on 5th May 1967. Converted by BIG SAFARI from 29th June 1979 through 9th March 1981 into RC-135W RIVET JOINT 10.

62-4132 This C-135B was transferred to BIG SAFARI on 14th November 1966 for conversion into an RC-135M, and delivered on 25th August 1967. BIG SAFARI converted it into RC-135W RIVET JOINT 13 by 30th November 1984.

62-4134 BIG SAFARI converted this C-135B into an RC-135M from 11th September 1967, and it was delivered on 19th September 1967. It flew the 3,000th COMBAT APPLE mission on 14th January 1973. Modified by BIG SAFARI into RC-135W RIVET JOINT 12 from 7th January 1981 to 16th August 1981.

62-4135 This was the first C-135B converted to RIVET CARD 1 RC-135M beginning in 1966. Delivered to the 55th SRW on 27th April 1967, then to Yokota AB on 23rd May. It flew the first COMBAT APPLE sortie on 12th September 1967 and the 2,000th COMBAT APPLE sortie in 1971. This was also the first RC-135M converted into RC-135W RIVET JOINT 9 from 5th September 1978 through 15th November 1980.

62-4138 Converted into an RC-135M and delivered on 1st November 1967. BIG SAFARI converted it into RC-135W RIVET JOINT 11 from 9th January 1980 through July 1981.

62-4139 This was the last C-135B converted to an RC-135M, delivered on 20th January 1968. It flew the 1,000th COMBAT APPLE sortie on 5th July 1967. This airplane was involved in a takeoff accident in August 1979 at Clark AB in the Philippines, prompting erroneous reports that it had been written off. According to one source, the staff pilot making the takeoff inadvertently pushed up only three throttles to full power, causing the RC-135M to veer abruptly left and head off the runway. The airplane was repaired and resumed operations, although with a slightly twisted fuselage resulting in the airplane flying in a perpetual yaw. This was the last RC-135M to be converted into RC-135W RIVET JOINT 14 on 22nd January 1985, arriving at Offutt AFB in August 1985.

Seen at Offutt AFB in 1981, 62-4132 appears in the final RC-135M configuration with two early SATCOM antennae. Throughout their careers, RC-135Ms were always about COMINT, but that mission changed with they became RIVET JOINTS.
Photo via Brian Rogers

Operations from Kadena AB were always defined in some way by weather. High temperatures often limited takeoff weights, dictating a prompt air refueling. Typhoon evacuations meant relocating to Clark AB.
Photo by Toshiyuki Toda via Stephen Miller

62-4135 had a 'hat trick' of firsts: the first RC-135M conversion, the first COMBAT APPLE mission, and the first RC-135M converted into an RC-135W. In this July 1977 photo it waits to depart Kadena AB. Delayed for some reason, the crew opened the windows and overwing hatch to cool off.
Photo by Toshiyuki Toda via Stephen Miller

62-4139 was the last RC-135M converted into an RC-135W. For a time it was the high-time RC-135, but was surpassed by RC-135W 62-4132, another former RC-135M.
Photo by George Cockle

RC-135T/KC-135R RIVET DANDY

Increasing involvement in the war in Vietnam led to a commensurate demand for more COMINT platforms, especially those assigned to BURNING CANDY missions outside of Southeast Asia. In early 1971 RC-135T 55-3121 had completed a series of specialized ELINT missions and was available; by May 1971 BIG SAFARI modified it into the RIVET DANDY RC-135T. The remaining AFTAC gear was removed and a full COMINT suite from an ACRP C-130 was installed. The airplane had nine AFSS operator positions, a single ELINT position, and an airborne maintenance technician (AMT). SAC histories show that although 55-3121 flew global BURNING CANDY and occasionally COMBAT APPLE missions, it was almost exclusively dedicated to sorties around Cuba as part of the CUBAN CANDY OpOrd, averaging some 20 missions per month.

In July 1973 the COMINT gear was removed from 55-3121 and installed in the RIVET QUICK KC-135R 58-0126, converting it into the second RIVET DANDY airplane. The RC-135T served the remainder of its operational life as a trainer, and eventually crashed on 25th February 1985 (see Appendix II). During January 1976 BIG SAFARI demodified KC-135R 58-0126 into a KC-135A(ARR).

RC-135T/KC-135R INDIVIDUAL AIRCRAFT

55-3121 Converted by June 1971 into the RIVET DANDY RC-135T, assigned to the 55th SRW at Offutt AFB. Flew BURNING CANDY and CUBAN CANDY COMINT missions. Demodified by BIG SAFARI in 1973 as an RC-135T for use as a trainer. Crashed on 25th February 1985 (see Appendix II)

58-0126 BIG SAFARI installed the COMINT gear from RC-135T 55-3121 into this KC-135R and removed the AFTAC equipment by July 1973, converting it into the RIVET DANDY KC-135R. Demodified in January 1976 into a KC-135A(ARR).

ELINT AIRCRAFT AND OPERATIONS

RC-135B/C BIG TEAM

Should America be forced into a nuclear war with the Soviet Union, SAC faced the crucial problem of where its bombers should attack and how they could penetrate Soviet defenses along the way. US military planners knew of few industrial and military facilities other than those in major cities. Locating targets initially with CIA U-2, RAF RB-45, and SAC RB-47 and RB-57 overflights of the USSR (and later with satellites) addressed SAC's top problem in executing its wartime mission, but did little to show how to reach those targets safely. If US bombers were to accomplish their strikes against the USSR, evading Soviet defensive forces would mean the difference between the success and failure of the American war plan.

The first obstacle for SAC planners was to avoid the growing ring of electronic detection and tracking sites around the USSR. Bombers detected by radar sites were easy prey for defensive fighters controlled by those ground-based radars. As early as 1948 the Air Force advocated

'a suitable electronic reconnaissance program' intended to 'determine the exact location, density and effectiveness of early warning defensive nets of radar…. [and] investigate any other types of radio emissions.' This 'electronic reconnaissance should be provided around the perimeter of the USSR and satellite states to a depth of several hundred miles.' Critical areas included 'all of the Russo-European landmass and in the maritime areas of the Far East between Korea and the Bering Strait.' Moreover, US knowledge of Soviet interceptor and defensive fighter bases was 'nonexistent.' Where these bases were located, their operational status, the number and capabilities of interceptors located there, and the specific radar control sites which coordinated their missions were all completely unknown to SAC planners. Ultimately, US bombers entering the Soviet Union would have to penetrate Soviet electronic defenses, meaning they would have to jam or deceive these radars in order to pass safely.

ELINT gathered by a wide variety of US and Western strategic aerial reconnaissance assets, most notably SAC's RB-47H missions flown by the 55th SRW during the 1950s and early 1960s, was essential in developing an electronic order of battle (EOB) for the Soviet Union and its allies. Knowing the operating frequencies of enemy long-range early warning radars meant that US engineers could devise ECM gear specifically designed to jam or blind these radars. ELINT also allowed the development of simulators that could mimic Soviet radars and weapons. SAC bomber crews could thus train in realistic situations and react to specific threats just as they would in time of war. All of these efforts were intended to improve bomber penetration capability and strike effectiveness, adding to the credibility of American deterrence. Although SAC's RB-47s had the requisite range and duration to accomplish peripheral ELINT missions, they suffered from two crucial weaknesses. RB-47s lacked the capacity for more than just a minimal collection suite and three Ravens, and as converted bombers they could be (and often were) mistaken for B-47s carrying bombs rather than recording devices, making them subject to attack. The KC-135 solved both of these problems.

SAC reconnaissance planners were quick to recognize the value in the early OFFICE BOY KC-135A-IIs and the RIVET STAND KC-135Rs as candidates to replace the RB-47 fleet. In lieu of converting existing KC-135As, SAC ordered 10 new RC-135Bs. From 27th May 1964 through 9th February 1965, Boeing delivered ten RC-135Bs to the Glenn L Martin Co, in Baltimore, MD, where they were placed in long term storage pending the installation of reconnaissance equipment under the BIG TEAM conversion program, when they would be redesignated as RC-135Cs. The contract number for this modification was AF33(657)-12648. Although the 10 new jets were hardly a one-for-one replacement of the 30+ RB-47Hs, they were a significant improvement in operational and sensor capability which more than offset their small number. Moreover, the RC-135Cs were planned to enter service by December 1966, approximately the same time as the SR-71, providing SAC with substantial gains in both its overall ELINT and PHOTINT missions.

Beginning in 1962 LTV modified JKC-135A 55-3132 for AFSC to test several 'cheek' configurations, aerodynamic cross-sections, and fuselage locations as part of the evaluation of the XH-1 Electronic Reconnaissance System program, the prototype of the ASD-1 automated ELINT collection system that would be installed on the BIG TEAM RC-135Cs planned conversion by Martin. In late 1963, as part of Project GOLDEN PHEASANT, the airplane flew operational test missions in Europe – implying that it was evaluating more than just external configurations – with 'excellent' results. In

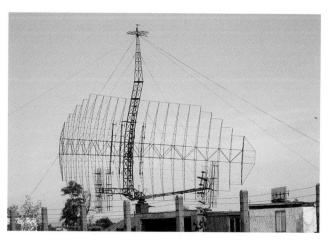

Success of the SIOP depended upon the ability of SAC bombers to penetrate Soviet defenses such as this TALL KING early warning radar. RB-47Hs collected ELINT for a US electronic order of battle. *Author's collection*

64-14841 rolls out on 30th July 1964. The RC-135B was intended to replace the RB-47H on ELINT missions, and there was little interest in SAC to use it for missions that did not support the SIOP such as peripheral COMINT sorties for the NSA. *Photo P37266 courtesy Boeing*

SAC crews flew JKC-135A 55-3132 on reconnaissance deployments as part of GOLDEN PHEASANT to evaluate the new ELINT collection system for the BIG TEAM RC-135Cs. *Photo by Jim Morrow via Stephen Miller*

early 1964 the XH-1 was updated and sent on a second deployment. For operational reasons the airplane was temporarily assigned to the 34th AREFS at Offutt AFB. From 1st April to 30th June 1964, SAC crews – made up of pilots and navigators from the 4157th SW and ravens from the 4157th SW and the 55th SRW – flew 13 sorties from Eielson AFB, Yokota AB, RAF Brize Norton, and Incirlik AB. Again, test results were excellent.

SAC's priorities, however, were not always the same as those elsewhere in the Air Force. In 1965 AFSC downgraded the BIG TEAM development importance from Classification I to IG-II (a substantial drop) and the Precedence Rating from 7 to 36. After the usual parochial wrangling, however, BIG TEAM regained its earlier priority. Production of the BIG TEAM aircraft proceeded with only a few significant problems. Transfer delays of the AN/APR-17 search receiver from retiring RB-47Hs to the RC-135Cs, full integration of ASD-1 collection with SAC's ground-based FINDER (Ferret INtelligence Data EvaluatoR) computer system, and training equipment and systems at Offutt AFB were ongoing issues, ultimately delaying deliveries by approximately 11 months. Original plans called for basing the 10 RC-135Cs at four different locations. Four would be at Offutt AFB, with two each at RAF Mildenhall, Eielson AFB, and Yokota AB. The excessive expense associated with the downloading and analysis of every mission's ELINT collection to a costly FINDER at each of four separate bases coupled with 'gold flow' financial priorities, however, quickly eliminated the four-base plan. All 10 RC-135Cs were located at Offutt AFB. Martin delivered the first airplane (63-9792) to the 55th SRW on 27th January 1967, and the final RC-135C (64-14849) on 29th November 1967. With the exception of 63-9792, it appears the actual MDS change to

RC-135C took place while the RC-135Bs were either in storage at Martin or during their conversion as a result of a bureaucratic directive rather than reaching a milestone.

As part of the BIG TEAM conversion, Martin added the now-famous 'cheeks'. The RC-135C lacked a 'hog nose', having instead a small chin fairing along with a circular radome beneath the forward fuselage. This circular radome caused severe turbulence with resultant cracking of the lower fuselage skin aft of the radome. Consequently, the radome shape was changed to that of a teardrop and its depth decreased which smoothed the airflow and eliminated the cracking problem. A second HF antenna was mounted atop the starboard wingtip. Two of the forward body fuel cells and the upper deck fuel tank were deleted to make room for additional reconnaissance equipment. Boeing delivered the airplanes to Martin with an IFR system installed and a fuel dump tube in lieu of an air refueling boom. The RC-135Cs had TF33-P-9 turbofans without thrust reversers.

Martin revised the flight deck to accommodate a second navigator and the requisite controls for the new navigation equipment. An RC-135C crew originally included a flight crew of three pilots, two navigators, three electronic warfare (EW) officers (the Ravens – EW Director, EW Operator, and EW Specialist), and two Inflight Maintenance Technicians (IMTs) capable of repairing failed equipment during flight, eliminating mission aborts due to equipment problems. For longer sorties, a fourth pilot and a third navigator could be added, but with only one IMT on board. Later in the RC-135C's operational life the crew composition was decreased to an even dozen: two pilots, two navigators, three EWs, one IMT, and four systems operators. These four linguists provided self-protection rather than a dedicated COMINT capability as with the OFFICE BOY

or RIVET CARD aircraft. LTV installed a G-3018 Electronic Reconnaissance Group suite in each RC-135C for this purpose. The large crew number dictated the installation of an additional emergency escape chute in the aft starboard fuselage.

Among the mission equipment installed in the RC-135Cs was a KA-59 camera in the boom operator's compartment. The navigator could take pictures with the KA-59 anytime throughout the sortie, but the image quality was far less than that of U-2s or SR-71s. Mission electronics eventually installed during the RC-135C's lifetime included an AN/ALA-6 pulse analyzer, the AN/APR-17 intercept receiver by Loral, a Sanders AN/ALQ-70 system, and the AIL/Melpar/GTE AN/ASD-1 ELINT system that incorporated an AN/ASR-5 automatic reconnaissance system, an AN/ALD-5 semi-automatic reconnaissance technical analysis system. As part of the COMPASS DANCE program a Watkins-Johnson QRC-259 'fast-sweep' ELINT manual analysis system was installed, but this proved ineffective and was only operational in the RC-135U. Additional equipment was installed under the BURNT ASHES program.

The RC-135C introduced the first operational automated reconnaissance system. Previous platforms (such as those on board ERB-47s and RB-47s) required manual acquisition, tracking, and identification of a signal of interest. The sophisticated equipment aboard the RC-135C eliminated much (but not all) of the tedious and repetitive work demanded by manual operation. For example, the AN/ASR-5 could automatically intercept, locate, identify, and summarily analyze SOIs. The system was programmed to alert the Raven in the event that the signal was unusual or of particular interest. The Raven would then use the AN/ALD-5 system to

determine the signal's special capabilities or characteristics. Finally, the EW Specialist would use the QRC-259 system to conduct a finite and detailed analysis of the SOI, all while the RC-135C remained in close proximity to the signal, allowing for a more thorough and detailed collection. The RC-135C ELINT suite quickly earned the nickname 'Vacuum Cleaner' because of its powerful ability to locate, collect, identify, and record signals from throughout the electromagnetic spectrum. The ALD-5 system, for example, could not only identify an electromagnetic source (perhaps a *Fan Song* radar) but could also recognize anomalies in its signal (perhaps due to a dent in the *Fan Song* radar antenna).

The first RC-135C operational sortie was flown on 5th April 1967, apparently a round-robin BURNING EYES mission flown from Offutt AFB. Less than a month later, a Major Griffin and crew flew the first BURNING SKY global operational sortie on 3rd May with a 22-hour 15-minute flight. On 4th May a Lieutenant Colonel Hailey and crew flew a 12-hour 40-minute sortie as the first BURNING SKY operational sortie launched from a forward operating location. A typical mission might involve a 24-hour (or longer) flight from Offutt AFB, landing at an overseas base. Following a day or two of rest, the crew would then return to Offutt AFB, flying another 24-hour mission. The RC-135Cs initially conducted ELINT missions as part of the BURNING CANDY OpOrd. Beginning 15th February 1968, RC-135C missions were subsumed by the BURNING PIPE OpOrd. Non-operational deployment missions from Offutt AFB to forward operating locations were covered under the 17th June 1969 BUSY PIPELINE OpOrd.

BURNING PIPE sorties from bases in the UK were subject to prior approval by British authorities, including the Prime Minister. Each

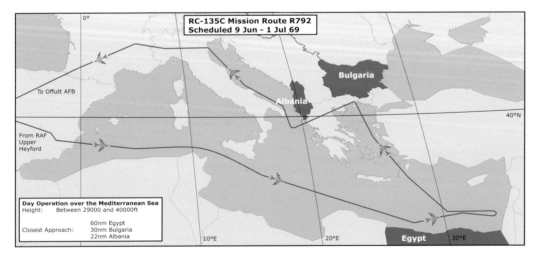

RC-135C missions usually began at Offutt AFB with an 8-10 hour flight to the Baltic or Barents Sea, followed by 8 hours on station, and then a return 8-10 hour trip to Offutt AFB. On occasion the airplane would stop in England for crew rest and then reverse its route back. *Photo by Richard Vandervord*

An actual RC-135C BURNING PIPE mission routing from RAF Upper Heyford through the Mediterranean Sea, the Adriatic Sea, and then back to Offutt AFB.

PLANNED RC-135 MISSIONS TO AND FROM THE UK, AUGUST 1971

Mission routings were carefully planned and strictly followed. Planners developed tracks that would cover known areas as 'repeat' or 'continuous' missions – where an RC-135 flew the same route monthly, weekly, or even daily to establish and update baseline intelligence. What was not operational one day might be 'up and running' another day. The sudden appearance of a signal in an otherwise quiet region could indicate a new deployment or previously undetected radars. Other occasional missions explored areas that had not shown any prior signals of interest in the off chance that something new had been established there. For SAC war planners, knowing the electronic order of battle (EoB) for any region meant the ability to develop a SIOP strike package that would evade the most threatening enemy defenses, as well as be adequately prepared with suitable ECM to suppress those which could not be avoided.

Table 10-2 shows 18 missions planned for August 1971, reflecting the heavy frequency of ELINT missions. A 55th SRW crew would fly a BIG TEAM RC-135C sortie from Offutt AFB to RAF Mildenhall on 3rd August, via the Barents Sea. They returned to Offutt AFB on 6th August with a route through the Baltic Sea and then south along the border with East Germany. These two sorties included roughly 10 hours of transit time and 10-12 hours of time in the 'sensitive area', so crews quickly accrued flying hours. The missions from and to Eielson AFB on 6th August and 16th August could have been either an ELINT BURNING PIPE RC-135C from the 55th SRW or a COMINT BURNING CANDY RC-135D from the 6th SW.

Table 10-2. **Planned RC-135 Missions from the UK, August 1971**

Route	Date	Day/Night	From	To	Area	Closest Point of Approach (nm/km)
B 285	3rd	Day	Offutt AFB	RAF Mildenhall	Barents Sea	52/96 - Soviet Territory
C 221	6th	Day	Eielson AFB	RAF Mildenhall	Barents Sea	53/98 - Soviet Territory
B 162	6th	Day	RAF Mildenhall	Offutt AFB	Baltic Sea & West Germany	11/20 - East Germany 30/56 - Soviet Coast 35/65 - Polish Coast 30/56 - Czechoslovakia
B 141	10th	Day	Offutt AFB	RAF Mildenhall	West Germany	21/39 - East Germany 30/56 - Czechoslovakia
C 231-1	10th	Day	RAF Mildenhall	RAF Mildenhall	Barents Sea	68/126 - Soviet Coast
C 231-2	12th	Day/Night	RAF Mildenhall	RAF Mildenhall	Barents Sea	68/126 - Soviet Coast
B 168	12th	Day	RAF Mildenhall	Offutt AFB	Baltic Sea & West Germany	11/20 - East Germany 32/59 - Soviet Coast 35/65 - Polish Coast 30/56 - Czechoslovakia
C 231-3	14th	Day	RAF Mildenhall	RAF Mildenhall	Barents Sea	68/126 - Soviet Coast
C 241	16th	Day/Night	RAF Mildenhall	Eielson AFB	Barents Sea	53/98 - Soviet Territory
B 157	17th	Day	Offutt AFB	RAF Mildenhall	Baltic Sea & West Germany	11/20 - East Germany 32/59 - Soviet Coast 35/65 - Polish Coast 30/56 - Czechoslovakia
B 162	20th	Day	RAF Mildenhall	Offutt AFB	Baltic Sea & West Germany	11/20 - East Germany 30/56 - Soviet Coast 35/65 - Polish Coast 30/56 - Czechoslovakia
B 284	23rd	Day	Offutt AFB	RAF Mildenhall	Barents Sea	50/93 - Soviet Territory
B 784	26th	Day/Night	Offutt AFB	RAF Mildenhall	Mediterranean Sea	61/113 - Algeria 65/120 - Egypt 28/52 - Bulgaria 30/56 - Czechoslovakia
B 280	27th	Day	Offutt AFB	RAF Mildenhall	Barents Sea	48/89 - Soviet Territory 49/91 - Soviet Coast
B 164	27th	Day	RAF Mildenhall	Offutt AFB	Baltic Sea & West Germany	11/20 - East Germany 30/56 - Soviet Coast 35/65 - Polish Coast 30/56 - Czechoslovakia
B 141	30th	Day/Night	Offutt AFB	RAF Mildenhall	West Germany	21/39 - East Germany 30/56 - Czechoslovakia
B 795	30th	Day	RAF Mildenhall	Offutt AFB	Mediterranean Sea	61/113 - Algeria 60/111 - Soviet Coast 28/52 - Polish Coast 26/48 - Czechoslovakia
B 168	31st	Day	RAF Mildenhall	Offutt AFB	Baltic Sea & West Germany	11/20 - East Germany 32/59 - Soviet Coast 35/65 - Polish Coast 30/56 - Czechoslovakia

month's planned missions were subject to considerable scrutiny, with particular emphasis on the closest point of approach to foreign territory. British approval for these 'Radio Proving Flights' was usually forthcoming, although with occasional limitations. RAF ELINT flights were prohibited from approaching closer than 30nm (56km) to a target territory, although SAC missions routinely flew as close as 20nm (37km). British officials approved these with the proviso that they be reviewed again 24 hours prior to launch. Several routes were far closer to communist territory. Missions along 'the Fence' adjacent to the East Germany border flew as close as 11nm

A distinct advantage of the RC-135C over the RB-47H was its lack of visible armament and basic cargo nature. Should an incident occur, Soviet pilots could not argue that the RC-135C 'fired first.' *Photo by Richard Vandervord*

Throughout their operational lives, several BIG TEAM RC-135Cs were temporarily grounded as redundant. Later efforts attempted to prevent conversion of all nine to RIVET JOINT RC-135Vs as an unnecessary expense. *Author's collection*

Boeing delivered the RC-135Bs to Martin with an IFR system and little else. The airplanes sat idle for months before Martin began their conversion to RC-135Cs. *Photo P37134 courtesy Boeing*

(20km). These were in an internationally recognized airway, however, and were often interspersed with commercial airliners flying between Scandinavia and Italy. All flights, however close they might fly to foreign countries, were reviewed 48 hours prior to scheduled departure. Flights that did not take off within two hours of their planned time or returned with less than 50% completion of the route in the sensitive area were rescheduled for 24 or 48 hours later. Presumably such approval mechanisms were in place for missions from Yokota AB and later Athens, Greece.

In addition to their strategic reconnaissance missions, RC-135Cs were in considerable demand to support combat operations in Vietnam and throughout Southeast Asia, often in conjunction with COMBAT APPLE missions. RC-135Cs were themselves in short supply in Southeast Asia, especially early in their careers, and were occasionally augmented by reconnaissance KC-135Rs. Some RC-135Cs in Southeast Asia were reportedly configured for Project BLUE BIRD and FRESH NEWS, although details of these have not been made public.

In the aftermath of the 1972 spring offensive by North Vietnamese forces, US national intelligence users were keen to identify and locate any new radar sites deployed in North Vietnam or south of the demilitarized zone (DMZ), especially SA-3 Goa SAM sites anywhere in Route Package 6 over North Vietnam. Consequently, the DIA and NSA directed SAC to send an RC-135C to Kadena AB on 17th May 1972 as part of the BUSY PENNY missions. While at Kadena AB, the RC-135C flew two sorties while searching for nine different types of radar transmitters in the Hanoi/Haiphong region, after which it returned to Offutt AFB. On 22nd May 1972, RC-135U 64-14847 deployed from Offutt AFB to Kadena AB to determine what new fire-control systems might be present in Vietnam. It would also gather fine-grain ELINT on Soviet- and Red Chinese-built *Cross Legs*, *Flat Face*, and *Rice Cup* radars known to be operating there. The COMBAT SENT's nose and tail PPMS sensors would also be programmed to collect signals from *Owl Screech* emitters on Soviet naval vessels south of Hainan Island. It flew four sorties between 24th and 30th May, detecting the previously unverified T-8209 radar, an improved version of the *Fan Song* radar. During LINEBACKER II, B-52s proved especially vulnerable to the T-8209 I-band radar, first used with devastating success on 20th December, claiming six B-52s, including four B-52Gs.

RC-135Cs flew an additional seven BUSY PENNY sorties between 6th and 23rd August 1972 in conjunction with RC-135U 63-9792 during its initial RANGE DWELL deployment to Kadena AB. Eight additional BUSY PENNY sorties took place between 6th and 13th January 1973, although the final mission was unsuccessful due to an air abort for equipment malfunction. A week later, on 20th January, intelligence acquired, in part, from the BUSY PENNY missions confirmed the presence of an active SA-3 site just north of Hanoi.

Interestingly, BIG TEAM RC-135Cs participated in BURNING LIGHT task force operations in June 1967 in conjunction with the RIVET STAND KC-135Rs. An RC-135C arrived on 6th June and went on alert the following day. Runway closure at Hickam AFB ended the alert on 23rd June and the joint mission never took place. On 15th August 1968 RC-135C 64-14846 replaced KC-135A (ARR) 58-0124 as the ELF ARROW aircraft at the BURNING LIGHT Task Force. Details about ELF ARROW or the RC-135C's specific mission goals remain classified. KC-135A (ARR) 58-0124 was not configured for reconnaissance, so how it was 'replaced' by an RC-135C is unclear. The RC-135C flew operational missions on 23rd and 24th August and 8th September, collecting ELINT from the disastrous 24th August *Canopus* thermonuclear detonation and the 8th September *Procyon* test which concluded the 1968 French season.

Beginning 6th July 1970, BIG SAFARI modified three of the ten RC-135Cs into RC-135Us as part of the COMBAT SENT program. The first RC-135C delivered to General Dynamics was 64-14847, followed

by 63-9792, and then by 64-14849. In addition, two RC-135Cs were placed in non-operational active (NOA) status, leaving only five RC-135Cs available for BURNING PIPE operations. On 1st December 1972, BIG SAFARI converted the first of the remaining seven RC-135Cs into RC-135Vs. The last RC-135C converted was 64-14841, which was delivered as an RC-135V to the 55th SRW on 19th January 1976. With the deployment of the first few RC-135V RIVET JOINTS, the BURNING PIPE missions came to an end. The final RC-135C deployment returned from RAF Mildenhall on 6th September 1974, and BURNING PIPE operations ended on 1st October 1974.

RC-135B/C INDIVIDUAL AIRCRAFT

63-9792 The Air Force accepted this RC-135B from Boeing on 26th May 1964, and delivered it to Martin the following day for conversion into an RC-135C. It was placed into long-term storage at Martin on 10th July 1964 through 12th March 1966. The conversion was completed by 26th January 1967, and on 27th January it became the first RC-135C delivered, arriving at Offutt AFB. From 17th October 1970 through 28th May 1971, General Dynamics modified it into an RC-135U.

64-14841 Boeing delivered this RC-135B to the Air Force on 1st October 1964. It was then handed over to Martin on 8th October for conversion it into an RC-135C. It was stored from 8th October through 18th June 1966, and the modification was completed on 22nd March 1967. It arrived at Offutt AFB on 22nd March 1967. E-Systems converted the airplane from 1st January 1975 through 19th January 1976 into an RC-135V.

64-14842 Martin converted this RC-135B to an RC-135C from 27th October 1964 through 31st March 1967. The airplane was further converted into an RC-135V from 20th November 1973 through 6th January 1975.

64-14843 Converted from an RC-135B into an RC-135C beginning on 9th November 1964. It was delivered to the 55th SRW on 25th February 1967. From 4th December 1973 through 5th February 1975 E-Systems modified it into an RC-135V.

64-14844 Boeing delivered this RC-135B to Martin on 10th November 1964, for conversion into an RC-135C. It arrived at Offutt AFB on 21st April 1967. The airplane was again modified from 8th January 1974 to 3rd March 1975, into an RC-135V.

64-14845 From 15th December 1964 until 28th April 1967, Martin converted this RC-135B into an RC-135C. E-Systems modified it further into an RC-135V from 1st October 1974 through 21st November 1975.

64-14846 Delivered on 29th December 1964, for conversion into an RC-135C, this airplane arrived at the 55th SRW on 1st June 1967. The airplane was modified into an RC-135V from 22nd January 1974 through 18th December 1975.

64-14847 This RC-135B arrived at Martin for modification into an RC-135C on 26th January 1965. Martin delivered it to Offutt AFB on 1st September 1967. From 6th July 1970 through 18th June 1971, General Dynamics converted the airplane into an RC-135U.

64-14848 Martin converted this RC-135B into an RC-135C from 3rd February 1965 through 26th July 1967. E-Systems converted it from 1st December 1972 until 6th August 1973 into an RC-135V.

64-14849 Boeing delivered this RC-135B to the Martin Company for conversion into an RC-135C on 9th February 1965. It arrived at Offutt AFB on 29th November 1967. General Dynamics converted it into an RC-135U from 19th April 1971 through 17th December 1971. RC-135B 64-14849 was the final '135 produced – although not the last to be delivered to the Air Force – an honor befalling the four RC-135As.

KC-135A ELF ARROW

There is some confusion about any actual reconnaissance role undertaken by KC-135A 58-0124. No records exist that show any specific conversion or installation of intelligence-gathering equipment. Several declassified references associated with the BURNING LIGHT task force mention the 'Christine' tankers, saying 'they were the two previous KC-135Rs (58-0124 and 59-1514), which in former years had been assigned to the 55th SRW for BURNING LIGHT reconnaissance operations.' During 1968 KC-135A 58-0124 was listed as the ELF ARROW mission aircraft, and was replaced by ELF ARROW RC-135C 64-14846, clearly suggesting a reconnaissance role. SAC reconnaissance histories show 58-0124 was only a trainer and never configured for an intelligence role. The aircraft record cards do not show 58-0124 was ever designated as a KC-135R. It is possible that the BURNING LIGHT histories incorrectly assumed that because 58-0124 was indeed a Christine tanker it must have been a reconnaissance platform at some time. The reference to ELF ARROW may relate to the relay aircraft carrying crews and materiel to Hickam AFB from Offutt AFB and back, but this is purely speculative. Nonetheless, 58-0124 remained at Offutt AFB as a flight crew proficiency trainer.

'SPECIAL' ELINT AIRCRAFT AND OPERATIONS

KC-135R/KC-135T BRIAR PATCH/RIVET JAW/COBRA JAW

Traditional ELINT collection focuses on the location of radar sites and the general characteristics of the radar, creating what military planners call the Electronic Order of Battle – EOB. An important but often overlooked ELINT subcategory is 'precision parameter measurements (PPM),' which assesses 'radar signal characteristics to a very high order of accuracy' as well as a radar's operating mechanisms that 'reveal its detection and tracking capabilities.' Precision measurements can then be combined to determine the radar's vulnerability to electronic countermeasures. These measurements include 'precise data on the maximum beam power, the total radiated power, the antenna gain, and variation in gain (side and back lobe distribution) around the antenna.' Effective collection can only be achieved via airborne platforms to avoid ground effects and to take measurements at various angles of elevation. Moreover, the aircraft needs to be stable in all three axes of flight and airspeed to ensure precise collection. Engineers determined that the optimum (in some cases *only*) placement of receiver antennas was on the nose and wingtips of the aircraft. Even this arrangement proved unsuitable in tracking radars that operated in frequencies below 1,000MHz, resulting in the use of 'aerodynamic antenna-carrying vehicles to be towed behind the aircraft.'

Beginning in 1958 the CIA established a program to gather PPM, specifically in response to the Soviet *Bar Lock* early warning radar which had proven so successful in tracking CIA U-2 overflights of the USSR, and which would be equally detrimental to SAC B-47 and B-52 nuclear strike missions. The CIA equipped an unidentified C-119 with rudimentary PPM gear for flights through the Berlin Corridor linking Berlin with West Germany. The results were far from perfect, but showed that a PPM collection capability was feasible and desirable.

By 1962 the CIA placed 'special emphasis' on 'supporting the aircraft reconnaissance program' for specialized ELINT. Particular areas of interest, according to a declassified CIA study for its Deputy Director of Research (DDR) about the 'Office of ELINT', included 'the Soviet early warning net, the SA-2 sites, and the MiG-21 capabilities.' The report continued, saying that 'activities of this nature will increase considerably over the next year.' Initial CIA PPM operations began in the summer of 1963, with FIELD DAY C-97A 53-0106 missions around Cuba and East Germany, and SAC NEW BREED RB-47H 52-4291 missions near Sakhalin Island and throughout the Sea of Japan. The greatest limitation in gathering PPM was the unwillingness of the target radar to 'cooperate' and radiate when the C-97 or RB-47H was in position to observe its performance. Consequently, collection tactics developed where the airplane would fly 'a radial path from the horizon to directly over the radar site,' turning away from denied airspace at the last possible moment. This provided optimum signal coverage, and the provocative flight path usually ensured that the radar would be turned on, however briefly.

By 1966 the limits of the C-97A and RB-47H platforms had become apparent. The C-97A could easily accommodate the

KC-135R 59-1465 was the first BRIAR PATCH, converted in May 1967. It flew ops sorties from RAF Upper Heyford in May and June, but crashed at Offutt AFB on 17th July. This photo, taken at McClellan AFB, caught 59-1465 deploying to England in May.
Photo by Peter B Lewis via René Francillon

BRIAR PATCH 55-3121 KC-135R at RAF Upper Heyford in early 1968. Following a brief stint with the BUSTED JAW NUDINT effort at Hickam AFB, the airplane later acquired the hog nose as part of the RIVET JAW program.
Author's collection

Wearing 'Cobra Hot Wheels' nose art in September 1970, KC-135T 55-3121 operated as part of the COBRA JAW mission (hence the nose art). It retains the blivet and trapeze installed as the replacement KC-135R BRIAR PATCH airplane.
Author's collection

considerable growth in the size, weight, and volume of the collection gear, but lacked the range or air refueling capability to fly long distances (especially along the Arctic coast of the USSR) or loiter for long periods to record the desired signals. The RB-47H had the requisite range and duration aloft, but could not carry any additional equipment or crewmembers. The obvious choice to meet this burgeoning need was the KC-135, and in May 1967 RIVET STAND KC-135A 59-1465 underwent conversion into the BRIAR PATCH fine-grain ELINT configuration. The modification work was undertaken at Lockheed Aircraft Services (LAS) in Ontario, CA. This included the installation of three ELINT operator positions, an AN/ALA-6 DF system, the AN/ALC-101 Long Range Navigation (LORAN) system with its multiple blade antennas, and additional navigation and communication gear. LAS also replaced the air refueling boom with a trapeze-shaped structure that lowered to extend a 1,000ft (305m) wire with a 500 lb (227kg) antenna. This 'blivet' was trailed behind and below the airplane to isolate the antenna from the KC-135A's own electronic signature, ensuring optimum signal collection.

BRIAR PATCH missions took place from late 1967 through early 1968 over the Barents Sea to collect signals from the *Hen House* anti-ballistic missile radar at the Olnegorsk-1 site on the Kola Peninsula and the Skrunda-1 site in Latvia. Although flown on behalf of the CIA, the flight and mission crews were from SAC. The first BRIAR PATCH deployment was to RAF Upper Heyford on 23rd May 1967, where KC-135R 59-1465 flew four operational sorties along Routes U350 and U351 in the Barents Sea under the mission name BONNIE BLUE. Additional sorties in the Barents and Baltic Seas planned for July and August were canceled for 'operational considerations.' The mission gear was removed from the airplane and stored with Detachment 1, 98th SW at RAF Upper Heyford, and 59-1465 returned to Offutt AFB on 20th June. Sadly, it crashed on takeoff at Offutt AFB just three weeks later on 17th July 1967, prompting the hasty conversion of RIVET STAND KC-135R 55-3121 as a replacement BRIAR PATCH airplane. The new airplane flew missions through June 1968, visiting RAF Upper Heyford twice from 28th February to 15th March and from 30th April to 18th May 1968. A reference in the BIG SAFARI history mentions a program known only as 'Zot', undertaken by LAS on behalf of 'other agencies'. 'Zot I' was RB-47H 53-4291, and 'Zot II' was KC-135R 59-1465, both converted by LAS at Ontario, CA. 'Zot III' was 55-3121 which BIG SAFARI converted using the 'components salvaged from the landing accident that damaged' 59-1465.

LAS configured 55-3121 to resume atomic monitoring missions over a two-week period from May-June 1968 as part of the BUSTED JAW program. This was short-lived, as BIG SAFARI further converted the airplane from September 1968 through March 1969 for PPMS missions as the KC-135R RIVET JAW with the addition of a COMINT collection capability. During this time the airplane acquired the hog nose covering side-facing VHF receivers as well as the standard AN/APN-59 radar, a ventral fairing covering a DF antenna, and the FINE CUT surveillance system. Further changes took place on 8th December 1969 when the airplane's MDS was changed to KC-135T and the program name changed to COBRA JAW. ('Cobra' is the first-word code name of programs associated with Air Force Intelligence [AFIN] collection efforts and is not restricted to more visible programs such as COBRA BALL and COBRA DANE associated with foreign ballistic missile intelligence.)

COBRA JAW KC-135T 55-3121 made its first flight on 12th May 1970, and the first operational mission took place on 9th September 1970 over the Baltic Sea. It was during this nine-hour sortie that the airplane sported the famous 'Cobra Hot Wheels' nose art, (from Ford Motor Company's Cobra Hot Wheels pictures and painted by Dave Johnson) earning the unwanted attention of senior US officials after

an intercepting Soviet pilot reported the nose art to his controllers. The COBRA JAW mission on 17th November 1970 was far more stimulating. While orbiting over international waters near Vaygach Island in the Pechora Sea, two Soviet MiG-17 *Fresco* interceptors fired their cannons in a none-too-obvious threat that the KC-135T should leave. Aircraft commander James Jones held firm, and Soviet controllers decided not to escalate the situation any further, directing the MiG-17s to continue their escort duties but not to resume hostile fire. This incident, coupled with the plans to convert the first COMBAT SENT RC-135U, spelled the end of the COBRA JAW mission. KC-135T 55-3121 returned to BIG SAFARI for conversion into the ACRP RIVET DANDY RC-135T.

KC-135R/KC-135T INDIVIDUAL AIRCRAFT

55-3121 Lockheed Aircraft Services at Ontario, CA, modified this RIVET STAND KC-135R into the BRIAR PATCH configuration beginning in July 1967 following the 17th July crash of BRIAR PATCH KC-135R 59-1465. This conversion was undertaken as part of the BIG SAFARI program. It was also assigned to the 55th SRW. During June 1968 it was configured for BUSTED JAW atomic monitoring duties, but resumed its specialized ELINT mission after modification into the lone RIVET JAW by March 1969. On 8th December 1969 it was redesignated a KC-135T and the mission name changed to COBRA JAW. Sometime after November 1970 BIG SAFARI further converted it into the RIVET DANDY RC-135T.

59-1465 Lockheed Aircraft Services at Ontario, CA, modified this RIVET STAND KC-135R into the BRIAR PATCH configuration between 1st and 18th May 1967. This conversion was *not* undertaken as part of the BIG SAFARI program. It was assigned to the 55th SRW. The airplane crashed at Offutt AFB on 17th July 1967 (see Appendix II).

RC-135U COMBAT SENT

With the end of ERB-47H operations in 1967 and the approaching retirement of the RIVET STOCK C-97A in 1970, the Air Force was left with only a single airplane – the COBRA JAW KC-135T 55-3121 – to collect specialized ELINT. Demand for fine-grain ELINT, however, was increasing given the development of new Soviet and Red Chinese radars as well as the evolving capability of radars used by the North Vietnamese in the air war over Southeast Asia. On 17th April 1970 the Air Force approved procurement of a dedicated platform to meet this demand, and the COMBAT SENT was born. BIG SAFARI began conversion of RC-135C 64-14847 on 7th June 1970, the first of three BIG TEAM RC-135Cs modified into RC-135Us. Crew familiarization flights began in April 1971 and the first airplane arrived at the 55th SRW at Offutt AFB on 18th June 1971.

The core of the COMBAT SENT's mission equipment was the next generation of the precision power measurement system (PPMS) installed in RIVET STOCK C-97A 53-0106, manufactured by ITT Gilfillan, 'capable of making very precise measurements of an emitter's maximum power output, transmission pattern and polarisation'. An aluminum fairing was installed on each wingtip to cover the PPMS receivers, and an aft-facing receiver was installed below the tail cone. Additional modifications included the three-phase COMPASS QUICK installation of QRC-501 series equipment. A QRC-259 ELINT analysis system was installed in the RC-135U as part of COMPASS DANCE. The airplanes retained the cheeks acquired as RC-135Cs, and, until 1991, had two large dipole antennas mounted horizontally in tandem above the cheeks. All RC-135Us had TF33-P-9 engines without thrust reversers. Two of the RC-135Us ('847 and '849) had an ASG-21 fire control radar from the B-58 Hustler mounted in a fairing above the rudder on the vertical stabilizer. This had range-only capability and there was no weapon whatsoever installed on the airplane. Concerns about metal fatigue and some system failures led to flutter tests conducted on 63-9792 during late 1970. The vertical stabilizer (with radar) from '847 was temporarily installed on 63-9792 for these tests (flown by crews from Edwards AFB), leading to erroneous reports that all three COMBAT SENT aircraft had the ASG-21 radar installed. Following the tests the tails were all restored to the correct airplanes.

Top: The first COMBAT SENT was 64-14847, seen shortly after arrival in 1971 for evaluation at Offutt AFB. The chin fairing has evolved over time, and remains a trademark of the RC-135U. *Photo via Bill Strandberg*

Left to right: PPMS receivers on the nose, tail, and wingtips of RC-135U 64-14849. The COMBAT SENT carefully positions itself in relation to the transmitter under observation to measure its power output and other technical capabilities. In more than a few cases, the RC-135U 'encourages' the source to emit. *Photos by the author*

Left: The CIA, rather than SAC or DIA, paid for COMBAT SENT 3. When this funding dried up, 63-9792 was converted to the Block II RIVET JOINT.
Author's collection

Bottom: Wearing Olympic rings signifying a possible visit to Athens, RC-135U 64-14849 also shows the COMPASS ERA modification in the boom pod area.
Author's collection

Opposite page:
The chin on the COMBAT SENT functions like a speed brake during air refueling. Inattentive pilots discover how quickly the U-Boat can pitch down.
Photo by Jeffrey Harper

During 1972 COMBAT SENT 1 and 2 were updated to identical configurations incorporating improved systems and replacement of out-of-date equipment. These modifications added 'infrared data collection, digital communications, inertial navigation, and infrared airborne radiation detection' to the RC-135U's mission capabilities. The electronic gear increased the COMBAT SENT's operational weight considerably. On coordinated missions with an RC-135M over the Gulf of Tonkin, for example, planners put the COMBAT SENT at an altitude above the RC-135M. After refueling, the RC-135U struggled to return to this higher altitude, and there were tense moments when the RC-135U was on the verge of losing control. Placing the COMBAT SENT at an orbit altitude below the RC-135M quickly resolved the problem.

COMBAT SENT 3 63-9792 was initially configured differently from the other two RC-135Us as it was funded from a different source agency (believed to be the CIA). By 1975 the funding agency determined that overhead systems (satellites) could achieve the same results as the COMBAT SENT, it ceased funding for 63-9792, and the airplane was shifted to the RIVET JOINT program.

Beginning in 1981 RC-135U 64-14849 received the Sent ELINT Airborne Receiver System (SEARS), which was a significant upgrade over the existing ELINT capability. Improvements to the COMINT suite on board the COMBAT SENT included the G3018 Collection Subsytem. During the mid-1980s RC-135Us 64-14847 and 64-14849 acquired a turret-like structure located in the rear portion of the aft fuselage underbody fairing. This modification is said to be part of a system known as COMPASS ERA, which incorporates infrared thermal imaging, interferometer-spectrometer, and spectral radiometer sensors.

The sizeable 'chin' PPMS fairing on the COMBAT SENT has proven to be the bane of more than a few pilots. The aft portion is an aerodynamic cover and is not pressurized. During the pre-flight walk-around inspection, the aircraft commander (AC) first closes the nose hatch to the pressurized fuselage which is *inside* the 'chin', then closes the door on the fairing. Forgetting to close the inner door first results in an embarrassing moment when the airplane fails to pressurize right after takeoff at a weight often too heavy for an immediate landing to close the errant door. No one knows how many ACs have suffered this fate, and none of those who have are talking. In addition, the flat front of the fairing acts as a speed brake, most noticeably during air refueling. When the center of gravity moves accordingly, the change is just enough for the nose to pitch down abruptly causing an inadvertent disconnect. Proper pitch trim mitigates this problem, and it serves as a good lesson to new copilots.

More recent additions include the Airborne Information Transfer (ABIT) system in a small circular fairing on the top of the vertical stabilizer and Joint Tactical Information Distribution System (JTIDS). These provide timely data sharing for aircrew situational awareness and for other agencies to use in tactical situations. The *Big Safari History* mentions a program known as COBRA CHINE, which installed 'special equipment' that FTD 'acquired' from 'the original manufacturer.' After successful testing on the RC-135U, this 'capability eventually evolved into the EPR-107.' One can only speculate about this given that the US source of the 'special equipment' was FTD! The Advanced Power Measurement System (APMS) has since supplanted the original PPMS, which will itself be replaced by the Primary Sensor Measurement System (PRISM) in the next Baseline update. Current COMBAT SENT configuration is Baseline 5. The earlier TF33-P-9 engines have since been replaced with F108s, improving operational capability such as better takeoff performance and better fuel consumption reducing the need for air refueling.

COMBAT SENT deployments – labeled alphabetically – began in 1972 with Alpha and Bravo, when 64-14847 deployed to RAF Mildenhall in January and 63-9792 went to Eielson AFB that summer. During its trip to Alaska, '9792 was intercepted on 29th June

over the Kara Sea by a Tu-128 *Fiddler*, a beast of an interceptor. Copilot Richard 'Zot' Barazzotto photographed the Tu-128 as it banked away. After the collapse of the Soviet Union, the *Fiddler* pilot, Alex Nirodenko, emigrated to the United States and eventually met Barazzotto. Crews were eager for COMBAT SENT trips, as they invariably got to do something 'interesting.' During 1977 RC-135U 64-14849 flew a coordinated mission with SR-71A 61-7976. The SR-71 departed from Beale AFB while the RC-135U left RAF Mildenhall, and arrived together over the Barents Sea. The presence of the SR-71 no doubt triggered the radars and other emitters which

were of interest to the RC-135U and would otherwise not have been turned on. The same COMBAT SENT and the SR-71 flew another coordinated mission on 16th November, this time over the Baltic Sea. In 1979 an RC-135U collected detailed fine-grain ELINT on the *Back Trap* E-band early warning radar, providing the technical data to develop appropriate ECM, particularly for its low-altitude search capability. The following year an RC-135U collected against the *Square Pair* fire control radar for the SA-5 *Gammon* SAM, as well as the Swiss Super Fledermaus radar. RC-135U 64-14847 is reported to have participated in operations associated with the USSR's 26th

Above: F108 engines improve takeoff performance for the COMBAT SENT, which has the heaviest operational weight of the current RC-135s. They also increase fuel efficiency, reducing (or eliminating) the requirement for air refueling on most missions. *Photo courtesy USAF*

Below and bottom: Coordinated missions between RC-135s and SR-71s were not uncommon, such as the 1977 sortie with 64-14849 and 61-7976. The SR-71 at high altitude provoked Soviet defenses to 'light up' while the RC-135U at medium altitude recorded the signals to update the EOB. *RC-135U photo by Bob Archer, SR-71 photo by Toshiyuki Toda*

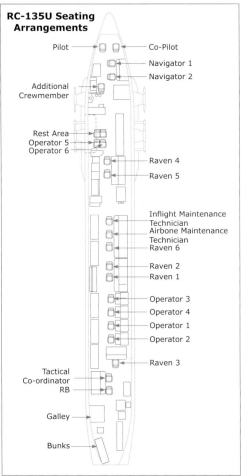

RC-135U Seating Arrangements

Pilot
Co-Pilot
Navigator 1
Navigator 2
Additional Crewmember
Rest Area
Operator 5
Operator 6
Raven 4
Raven 5
Inflight Maintenance Technician
Airbone Maintenance Technician
Raven 6
Raven 2
Raven 1
Operator 3
Operator 4
Operator 1
Operator 2
Raven 3
Tactical Co-ordinator
RB
Galley
Bunks

April 1986 Chernobyl nuclear reactor accident. During May 1990 a COMBAT SENT participated in a US Navy exercise conducting a 'tactical evaluation of Silent Spear and [AEGIS] SPY-1A [radar] satellite vulnerability.' From 1994 RC-135Us reportedly deployed to Kadena AB as part of the DISTANT SENT OpOrd, although details of this are not known. Additional mission tasking for the RC-135U includes HAVE TERRA and HAVE UNION.

In a classic example of reconnaissance lore, Major John 'Box' Elder flew a COMBAT SENT mission that has become the stuff of legend. Unsuccessful in getting the Soviet 'carrier' *Kiev* to turn on any of its new electronic emitters, Elder decided to take a more 'unconventional' approach (pun intended). He established the RC-135U on 'final approach' to the *Kiev*, gear and flaps extended. Ignoring the efforts of the Russians to wave him off, Elder got closer and closer. Suddenly the *Kiev* switched on its radars and the COMBAT SENT got the collection it wanted. The end of the Cold War, however, reduced such encounters to almost nil. Improved US-Russian friendship and reduced Russian operating efforts resulted in fewer intercepts. By the 2010s, however, as tensions increased between the two countries, Russian Su-27 *Flankers* found RC-135Us particularly lucrative 'targets'. On 23rd April 2014 a Russian Su-27 Flanker intercepted RC-135U 64-14849 in international airspace over the Sea of Okhotsk, and nearly a year later another Su-27 *Flanker* buzzed an RC-135U over the Baltic Sea.

Few airplanes are as photogenic with a shark mouth as the RC-135U. Usually acquired while TDY to RAF Mildenhall or Kadena AB, they disappear quickly once the airplane returns to Offutt AFB. *Photo by Joe Bruch*

Bogus serials sometimes appeared on the RC-135Us. This is in fact 64-14847. Why these were used has never been verified. Perhaps the crew chiefs know, but they're not saying! *Photo by Robin Walker via Paul Crickmore*

Taken during a test flight following PDM, this image of 64-14847 represents an intercepting pilot's view of the COMBAT SENT. During the 2010s, Russian Su-27 *Flankers* have proven annoying to the RC-135U. *Photo courtesy USAF*

On several occasions, RC-135Us have been photographed wearing the tail number of a *different* variant of RC-135 or another aircraft type altogether. Most common of these spurious numbers is '64-14848', a number officially allocated to an RC-135V. This particular tail number appeared occasionally on the two RC-135Us, prompting perennial reports of a new RC-135U conversion. On 30th August 1976, for example, RC-135U 64-14847 bore the serial number '64-14850', and on 26th September 1976 it carried '64-14851', both of which were allocated to Hiller H-23F helicopters sold to Uruguay. On 3rd July 1982, this same airplane wore '64-14848', this time while parked next to RC-135V 64-14848! The most recent appearance of this spurious tail number on an RC-135U was on 17th February 1986. Given the absence of any official comment about (or even acknowledgement of) these anomalous markings, their intent remains in the realm of a debate of pure speculation. Several sources refer to 'Combat Pink' as a second name associated with the RC-135U. No official record exists of this program, and it is believed to be the product of an overly imaginative aviation enthusiast who noted a large pink panther painted on the nose of an RC-135U.

RC-135U INDIVIDUAL AIRCRAFT

63-9792 BIG SAFARI converted this RC-135C into an RC-135U beginning 3rd August 1970 as the COMBAT SENT 3. The initial conversion was completed on 28th May 1971, but the airplane was used for fatigue testing at Edwards AFB from 13th-21st July 1971, and other evaluations through the end of the year, when it was delivered to the 55th SRW at Offutt AFB on 9th December 1971. During August 1972 it undertook its initial deployment to Kadena AB on behalf of the CIA, known as RANGE DWELL. While there, it participated with an RC-135C in the second tranche of BUSY PENNY missions (see above). Its final operational deployment (believed to be RANGE WARD to Kadena AB) ended 14th March 1974. From 17th October 1975 through 24th July 1977, BIG SAFARI converted it into the RIVET JOINT 8 RC-135V, serving as the prototype for the Block II prototype, which was incorporated into the RIVET JOINT Block III fleet upgrade. During the late 1970s this airplane wore a skunk beneath the cockpit, ostensibly for 'COMBAT SCENT'.

64-14847 This was the first RC-135C converted into an RC-135U from 7th June 1970 through 28th May 1971 as COMBAT SENT 1. This airplane conducted crew familiarization flights at Offutt AFB in April and May 1971 prior to its official delivery. It deployed to Kadena AB in May 1972, where it participated with an RC-135C in the initial tranche of BUSY PENNY missions (see above). In December 1983 this airplane was photographed at RAF Mildenhall wearing shark's teeth and was named *Jaws II*. In October 1984 it bore the name *Bear Chaser II*, and in late 1986 was known as *Thunder Child*.

64-14849 This was the final RC-135C converted into an RC-135U from 19th April 1971 through 21st December 1971 as COMBAT SENT 2. Among its many missions was BUSY PENNY during the support of the 1972 LINEBACKER II bombing operations against North Vietnam. In June 1984 it was named *Bear Chaser*, and in January 1987 it had the name *Bad News*.

Table 10-3. **RC-135U 64-14849 'Foxtrot Deployment' to Misawa AB, 1973**

Mission No.	Date	Mission No.	Date	Mission No.	Date
GS-B18	3 Sep 73	GS-B21	27 Sep 73	GS-B24	7 Oct 73
GS-B19	21 Sep 73	GS-B22	30 Sep 73	GS-B25	9 Oct 73
GS-B20	22 Sep 73	GS-B23	3 Oct 73	GS-B26	11 Oct 73

MASINT AIRCRAFT AND OPERATIONS

Aside from the cultural and scientific shock of the 4th October 1957 launch of *Sputnik*, the military implications were painfully clear. The Soviet R-7 *Semyorka* rocket that lofted the tiny satellite into orbit was the same SS-6 *Sapwood* ballistic missile that could loft Soviet atom bombs at targets in Europe and America. This new capability changed everything. US reconnaissance flights that previously monitored Soviet bomber bases in Siberia for indications of an impending attack on the United States could detect preparatory signs weeks ahead given the repositioning of additional fuel, aircraft and atomic weapons. Once Soviet Tu-4 *Bull*, Tu-16 *Badger*, and Tu-95 *Bear* bombers were airborne, the Distant Early Warning (DEW) Line would detect them hours ahead of reaching US airspace. Coupled with radar and interceptors located throughout Canada and the northern United States, the DEW line warning allowed plenty of time and opportunity to shoot them down. Intercontinental ballistic missiles (ICBMs), however, radically altered that equation. With as little as 30 minutes' warning, Soviet nuclear warheads could reach SAC bases before any aircraft could take off, preventing a retaliatory strike. With no anti-ballistic missile (ABM) defenses, ICBMs could reach their targets unchallenged.

Building 300-400 *Badgers* and *Bears* required substantial time, heavy industrial and operational infrastructure, new bases, well-trained crews, and lots of rubles. For the same investment, the Soviets could develop thousands of ICBMs. Soviet First Secretary Nikita Khrushchev bragged that the Soviets were pumping out R-7s 'like sausages', indicative of a robust development program, a mature production capability, and a committed shift in national strategy from bombers to rockets.

US analysts and planners knew very little about the Soviet missile program, and even less about the missiles themselves. CIA

U-2 overflights of Tyuratam/Baikonur Cosmodrome cut through some of Khrushchev's bombast and revealed his duplicity. There were fewer than a handful of R-7s, effectively dispelling (among most of the intelligence community) what had become known as the 'Missile Gap.' Alarmist assessments – especially those by SAC analysts – claimed, however, that the Soviets needed only the limited number of missiles shown in U-2 photographs because they were so accurate and powerful. The only way to reconcile this debate was to find out first-hand how well the R-7 actually worked. Without a scientist spy on the inside, the solution was the ultimate aerial 'wiretap.'

For decades scientists and engineers used telemetry to deliver real-time feedback of aircraft and missile performance. From the moment an R-7 ignited its engines and began its ascent, a tiny on-board radio transmitted technical details about speed, pressure, fuel consumption, stability, navigation, and so on. Knowing this enabled Soviet engineers to make appropriate improvements and corrections. Telemetry, as with any other electronic signal, could be intercepted and analyzed by US engineers. The challenge was to be at the right place at the right time. SAC responded with three EB-47E(TT) TELL TWO airplanes (53-2315, 53-2316, and 53-2320) modified first by Boeing and later by Douglas Aircraft to gather TELINT under the CIA-sponsored IRON WORKS program. Based at Incirlik AB in Turkey, one airplane was on alert pending notification of an imminent launch from Tyuratam or the facility at Kapustin Yar. In either case, the TELL TWO would take off and fly to an orbit over the Black Sea or along the Soviet-Iranian border to intercept boost-phase telemetry. Whereas U-2 photos showed how *few* missiles the Soviets had, TELL TWO and U-2 TELINT revealed just how *ineffective* those few missiles were (to be sure, there were other sources of information on Soviet missile tests such as informer Oleg Penkovsky, ground listening posts in Turkey and Alaska, and US Navy aircraft operating from bases in Pakistan).

One example of the value of TELINT is the study of the Soviet *Cosmos* 57 which was launched on 12th February 1965. *Cosmos* 57 was an automated prototype of the *Voskhod* 2 designed to test the operation of its airlock, a critical component of the planned *Voskhod* launch five weeks later for the first space walk by cosmonaut Alexeii Leonov. *Cosmos* 57 was launched at 0730Z, with US TELINT collection beginning 17 minutes later. By comparing this telemetry

with that from previous *Cosmos* and *Voskhod* missions, CIA analysts were able to verify how the airlock worked.

Despite its success in collecting TELINT, the TELL TWO had several significant weaknesses: lack of expandability, limits on operations in crosswinds, and the lack of any real optical collection ability. The EB-47E(TT) had no room for any additional crewmembers or gear, especially the desired (and bulky) optical sensors. The airplane was equally constrained by crosswinds, with 53-2320 lost while attempting to land on 3rd April 1965 at Incirlik AB (not to mention the looming prospect of operations at Shemya AFB with its notorious winds). Most importantly, the TELL TWO had no measurement and signature intelligence (MASINT) capability beyond basic telemetry. A copilot wielding a hand-held camera offered little of intelligence value trying to photograph the missile only briefly and at an unacceptable distance. Advanced spectral, infrared, and ultraviolet cameras that were in use in the burgeoning American space program, however, could observe a missile's exhaust plume and could determine the chemical makeup of the fuel. High-speed optical film could allow for careful study of stage separation or other mechanical functions, as well as ascertain precise external dimensions that would reveal internal structures. In addition, the EB-47E(TT)s were optimized for boost-phase collection only, and could do little to provide intelligence on the reentry phase which could reveal missile accuracy and warhead capability.

Opposite page: RC-135U 64-14849 departs Majors Field at Greenville, TX, for a test flight. Silver band around fuselage and leading back to tail may be aerodynamic tape or other test material.
Photo courtesy USAF

Above: The TELL TWO EB-47E(TT) flew IRON WORKS missions for the CIA to collect boost phase TELINT. The airplane lacked an optical collection capability, and was ill suited for re-entry phase collection from places such as Shemya AFB.
Photo by John Kovacs.

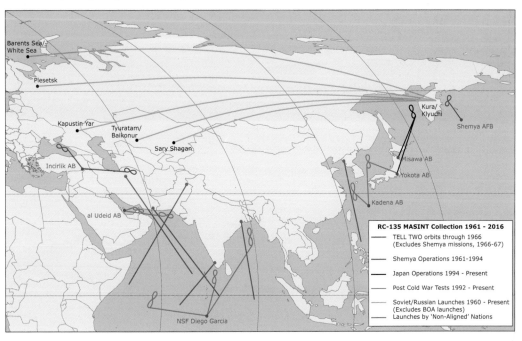

RC-135 MASINT Collection 1961 - 2016
— TELL TWO orbits through 1966 (Excludes Shemya missions, 1966-67)
— Shemya Operations 1961-1994
— Japan Operations 1994 - Present
— Post Cold War Tests 1992 - Present
— Soviet/Russian Launches 1960 - Present (Excludes BOA launches)
— Launches by 'Non-Aligned' Nations

JKC-135A/RC-135S NANCY RAE/WANDA BELLE/RIVET BALL

The first known example of an aerial platform for the optical tracking of missiles was a specially configured Boeing B-29 Superfortress. In 1954 the Servo Corporation of America outfitted one B-29 with equipment designed to detect and analyze a missile given its infrared signature. The success of this effort is not known, but the technical maturity gained provided a sound basis for at least two major follow-on developments that would become the RIVET BALL and the RIVET AMBER. By 1960, modest success with optical sensors developed for the nascent US space program found equal applicability in monitoring foreign missile and rocket tests, and the United States Intelligence Board (USIB) was committed to modify a KC-135 into a 'special collection' platform operating from Shemya AFB with an initial operational capability of no later than 'late 1961'. To meet this requirement, the Air Force transferred KC-135A 59-1491 to the BIG SAFARI program in October 1960. The airplane was only four months old, had fewer than 142 total flight hours, and was given the name NANCY RAE.

Mission equipment primarily included optical sensors mounted on eight platforms that were linked to a manually operated tracking system or could be configured to track reentry vehicles automatically. The manual tracker (a Raven) sat in a small Plexiglas bubble atop the fuselage which covered a gun sight scrounged from a B-50. The airplane had ten large optical windows along the upper starboard fuselage and was not configured with a hog nose. Optical systems included a 70mm (2.75in) visible and infrared (IR) camera, a Ballistic Streak Camera (BSC), an image orthicon, a 70mm (2.75in) multi-image camera, a ballistic spectral camera, a 70mm (2.75in) ultraviolet (UV) spectrograph and UV photometer, a 12-element spectrometer, a 50-element scanner, a radiometer, and a 70mm (2.75in) visible light and IR spectrograph with UV photometer. Clearly, NANCY RAE could finally provide what TELL TWO could only imagine: a robust optical MASINT collection capability. The airplane also had three large dipole antennas on the starboard fuselage capable of intercepting telemetry, and an AN/ALA-6 DF fairing under the forward fuselage. The NANCY RAE retained its original J57-P/F-59W turbojets.

NANCY RAE made its first deployment in 1961 to Hickam AFB, where it was evaluated against US missile tests from Vandenberg AFB to Kwajalein. The airplane also deployed to Dakar IAP in Senegal to support similar tests from Cape Canaveral, FL, over the Atlantic Test Range. Political tensions in Senegal obligated the crew to live inside the airplane, but the evaluation proved successful and the airplane was ready to relocate to Shemya AFB on 31st December 1961. Between 2nd January 1962 and March 1963, AFSC crews from Wright-Patterson AFB flew operational sorties from 'the Rock.' It flew missions under the LITTLE BIT OpOrd. Crews spent 90 days at Shemya AFB, returned home for a week, and then resumed alert at Shemya AFB for another 90 days. On 7th February 1962 the airplane was redesignated a JKC-135A. On 1st March 1963 the airplane was redesignated an RC-135S and transferred from AFSC to SAC and the 4157th SW at Eielson AFB, but it remained functionally assigned to Det 1, 4157th SW at Shemya AFB. Flight-deck crews were assigned to the 4157th SW Reconnaissance Division (DOR). Back-end crews were assigned to one-year remote tours at Shemya AFB, although this ended in 1967 when all crewmembers were assigned to the 24th SRS.

Shemya AFB is located at the western tip of the Aleutian chain at the confluence of the Pacific Ocean and the Bering Sea. The Rock is subject to extreme and unique weather conditions such as simultaneous 65mph (104km/h) winds and dense fog. Severe winds – especially crosswinds – make flight operations there particularly challenging. Shemya AFB was an Army Air Force base during the Second World War, and afterward was a regular fuel stop for trans-Pacific airliners. Its proximity to the Kamchatka Peninsula made it ideal for MASINT operations, and its remote and highly restricted access proved effective in maintaining secrecy (save for the prying eyes and ears of Soviet intelligence trawlers known popularly as 'Cobra Boatskis').

Between July and December 1963, NANCY RAE flew 27 'ops sorties'. It returned to BIG SAFARI from January-February 1964 for system upgrades, 'including all photometric and radiometric systems (PHAROS) and all cameras,' The RC-135S returned to Shemya AFB

This page:
Boeing delivered KC-135A 59-1491 for conversion into a JKC-135A for the ICBM MASINT mission. Known as NANCY RAE, it operated from Shemya AFB but crews were initially from Wright-Patterson AFB.
Photo by Stephen Miller

In 1963 59-1491's MDS changed to RC-135S and the aircraft transferred to SAC. In 1965 the aircraft conversion name changed to WANDA BELLE.
Author's collection

Opposite page:
In preparation for a VIP visit, Kingdon 'King' Hawes and Robert 'Viper' Brown hastily applied this shark mouth to the RIVET BALL.
Author's collection

in March 1964, at which time the OpOrd changed from LITTLE BIT to MUSIC BLUE. The airplane flew 22 missions from Shemya AFB by the middle of 1964. Four JOLLY POLLY AFSS linguist positions were added during a brief visit to BIG SAFARI that June, as well as the traditional hog nose covering the VHF receivers.

In an effort to ensure timely notification of impending Soviet ICBM launches, in April 1964 the NSA created the Defense Special Missile and Astronautics Center (DEFSMAC), providing a 'management arrangement to (a) task and technically control DoD missile and space intelligence collection and processing activities directed against foreign missile and space activities and (b) provide current analysis and reporting of foreign missile and space events.' When DEFSMAC determined that a Soviet missile launch was imminent, it issued an alert to the NANCY RAE crew to take off immediately.

Additional policy decisions in 1964 had equal impact on the RC-135S and its successors. The Air Force planned to retire its TELL TWO TELINT jets in December 1965 despite the increasing demands for TELINT to keep pace with the Soviet missile and space program. SAC expressed concern over the lack of aircraft to accomplish this mission and requested that four MATS C-135Bs, soon to be replaced by C-141s, be given to SAC for conversion to TELL TWO follow-on aircraft. In addition, SAC asked to retain the three EB-47E(TT)s until a follow-on system achieved operational status. RB-57Fs were tested as replacements for the IRON WORKS boost phase, but following the loss of RB-57F 63-13287 on 14th December 1965 over the Black Sea on the first evaluation flight this program was discontinued. Successful continuance of the USAF-required telemetry intercept program depended largely on prompt replacement of the TELL TWOS with properly configured aircraft.

RC-135S operations continued through 1965 without any decision on a replacement for the TELL TWO EB-47E(TT)s. On 16th March 1965 the BIG SAFARI program name changed from NANCY RAE to WANDA BELLE, and by 30th June the airplane had flown 54 MUSIC BLUE sorties for an annual total of 198.8 flying hours. The airplane underwent further upgrades and modifications beginning in late 1965. This left a critical gap in reentry coverage, and during the summer of 1966 one of the two remaining TELL TWOS relocated to Shemya AFB, and that program was renamed HAVE TELL. Crews for the EB-47E(TT)s were assigned to the 338th SRS, 55th SRW activated on 25th March 1967 at Offutt AFB. At the same time the RC-135S back-end crews underwent additional 'training and coordination' with FTD at Wright-Patterson AFB and the NSA. The WANDA BELLE returned from upgrade on 19th December 1966, and resumed operational status on 26th December. On 10th January 1967, 59-1491 was renamed RIVET BALL and the OpOrd name changed to BURNING STAR. The 4157th SW was inactivated on 25th March 1967 and replaced by the 6th SW. The RC-135S flight-deck crews were assigned to the 24th SRS. With the return of the RC-135S, the HAVE TELL program was terminated, the 338th SRS was inactivated on 25th December 1967, and the two EB-47E(TT)s relegated to MASDC.

With the arrival of RC-135E 62-4137 at Shemya AFB, the Rock became a busy place. During the second quarter of 1968, for example, the RIVET BALL flew an average of 17 missions and 70 hours per month. The RIVET BALL also flew missions in conjunction with the RIVET AMBER. Among the notable 'firsts' achieved by the RIVET BALL was the 11th September 1968 mission that collected against an SS-9 Mod 4 ICBM. This was the first time that US assets observed a Soviet missile with multiple reentry vehicles (MRVs). The RC-135S monitored a third test on 4th October, as well as a fourth test in December. Confirmation of a Soviet MRV capability was an important consideration in the strategic policy vis-à-vis the Soviet Union of newly elected President Richard Nixon and his National

Security Advisor Henry Kissinger. As such, the RC-135S and the RC-135E became critical sources of intelligence that informed the evolution of what would come to be known as 'Détente.'

Unfortunately, neither airplane survived the first six months of the new administration. On 12th January 1969, a week before the inauguration, the RIVET BALL hydroplaned on the icy runway at Shemya AFB. Even after shutting down two engines the airplane did not stop, and aircraft commander Major John Achor wisely chose to steer the RC-135S off the runway rather than collide with navigation equipment and stanchions in front of the airplane. Falling into a ravine broke the back of the airplane, but there was no fire or injuries among the crew of 18. On 5th June 1969, the RIVET AMBER disappeared en route from Shemya AFB to Eielson AFB. The US Air Force was now without any aerial MASINT collection capability, and US Navy EA-3Bs from VQ-1 provided a modicum of aerial ELINT capability at the Rock pending a replacement. The Navy also had a substantial collection program in place to collect ship-based ELINT associated with reentry tests in a 'broad ocean area' (BOA was part of the CINCPAC PONY EXPRESS program) as well as off the coast of Kamchatka. Known as IVY GREEN, the effort also collected test debris floating on the surface, derogatorily known as 'TRASHINT'.

RC-135S COBRA BALL

The urgent need to replace the RIVET BALL prompted the search for and conversion of a C-135B (as SAC previously suggested) to meet the operational requirements and the newly imposed safety demands – better brakes and thrust reversers for landings at Shemya AFB. AFSC identified C-135B 61-2663 as a suitable candidate on 26th March 1969. Using parts salvaged from 59-1491 as well as new equipment intended for an imminent upgrade of the destroyed RC-135S, BIG SAFARI began its conversion into the COBRA BALL MINIMUM on 29th April 1969. Externally it looked like the RIVET BALL but with only one optical window in line with the dipole antennas, and 24th October 1969 it was redesignated an RC-135S. Although 6th SRW historical records show that the airplane was assigned on 28th October 1969, the airplane's maintenance records indicate that 61-2663 was still undergoing test and evaluation flights with BIG SAFARI until 11th January 1970. Nonetheless, 61-2663 finally flew 'bare bones' operational missions from Shemya AFB in 1970. AFSC owned eight C-135 ARIA/TRIAs but only seven PMEE sets, so one of the airplanes – in this case C-135B 61-2664 – was declared 'excess' in 1969 and offered to SAC as the second COBRA BALL. The airplane was delivered to the 6th SW in early 1970 as COBRA BALL II, after which RC-135S 61-2663 returned to BIG SAFARI for full modification from the COBRA BALL MINIMUM configuration to the COBRA BALL I. By the end of 1970 there were two fully converted and operational COBRA BALLS at the Rock. Within five years of the loss of the RIVET BALL and RIVET AMBER, the COBRA BALL reaffirmed its value to US intelligence collection. In 1973 alone, the 'RC-135S was on

61-2663 as the RC-135S COBRA BALL MINIMUM. This was the interim configuration to meet tasking requirements while 61-2664 was fully converted. *Author's collection*

The baseline configuration on COBRA BALL II 61-2664. Once '664 was operational, BIG SAFARI fully modified '663 from the COBRA BALL MINIMUM to baseline COBRA BALL I. *Author's collection*

61-2663 was briefly configured with the sliding door over the sensor cavity associated with 'Project 2'. Behind '663 is 61-2664 in the contemporary baseline configuration. *Author's collection*

The COBRA BALL acquired the cheeks associated with the RIVET JOINT, although the RC-135S does not have an AEELS capability. Instead, the fairings cover TELINT antennas. *Photo by Wayne Button*

A brief moment of sunshine illuminates RC-135S 61-2663 as it taxis on Runway 10 at Shemya AFB behind the marker honoring the loss of six crewmen in the 15th March 1981 crash of COBRA BALL II 61-2664.
Photo by Paul Jeanes

station for 200 (88%) of the 227 missions for which DEFSMAC was able to provide alerting data, and critical intelligence was collected on 65 of these sorties.'

The sensor suite on board the COBRA BALL has evolved considerably since the original NANCY RAE configuration. Among the many evolving configurations seen on the RC-135S, 61-2663 was part of 'Project 2', a conceptual precursor to the RC-135X COBRA EYE. A 'large aperture infrared sensor' was installed in a 'big opening in the side of the fuselage, akin to a mini-OAMP' (see below). The sensor was in use for 'a couple of years'. Publicly known equipment on board the COBRA BALL during the late 1980s included a ballistic framing camera system (BFCS) and a medium resolution camera system (MRCS). According to one source, the BFCS imaged 'all the objects of interest in the reentry phase', while the MRCS photographed 'individual reentry vehicles, …determin[ing] the reentry vehicle size. Size estimates [were] used in turn to produce estimates of the explosive yield of the warheads'. On-board TELINT equipment included the Advanced Telemetry System (ATS). More improved systems have since replaced the BFCS and MRCS. This newer gear includes the Real-Time Optical System (RTOS), the Multiple Object Discriminator System (MODS), and the Large Aperture Tracking System (LATS). Later equipment installations may include the TALON LANCE intelligence distribution system. Beginning with the Baseline 5 conversion, the COBRA BALL acquired the famous cheeks associated with the BIG TEAM, RIVET JOINT, and COMBAT SENT. According to official sources, the COBRA BALL is not equipped with AEELS, and despite their common appearance as covers for the AEELS array, the cheeks on the COBRA BALL are hollow fairings over the many TELINT antennas that traditionally adorned the exterior.

The most distinctive feature on the RC-135S is the black starboard wing and engines. This was initially done to reduce glare on the mission optics, although with the newer equipment this anti-glare feature became less important, if not altogether unnecessary. Stenciling on all black areas is red. To preclude obstructing the sensor field of view, the wingtip HF antenna is mounted on the port side rather than the starboard. Beginning with the conversion of 62-4128, the COBRA BALL has been configured with digital sensors allowing collection from either side of the aircraft. The black wing has been retained both out of a sense of tradition and as a clear indicator that the airplane is a national technical means (NTM) verification asset.

COBRA BALL alumni will always remember William Shakespeare's *Julius Caesar's* Soothsayer, who warns Casear to 'beware the ides of March.' On 15th March 1981 RC-135S 61-2664 was on final approach to Runway 10 at Shemya AFB in extremely poor weather. COBRA BALL II was 'low and slow' as it reached the threshold, striking the ground and shearing off the No.3 and No.4 engines. Five crewmembers perished in the accident, and one died later. RC-135S 61-2663 hastily returned from upgrade at BIG SAFARI to Shemya AFB. An interesting story reflects the importance of the COBRA BALL program and the intelligence it provides. Some two weeks after the crash of '664, John Hinkley attempted to assassinate President Ronald Reagan. While recovering, 'one of the few documents he signed in the hospital was a presidential directive to divert funds for a replacement [COBRA BALL] as soon as possible.' SAC and BIG SAFARI wanted the AFSATCOM C-135B 61-2662 because of its similarity to the existing COBRA BALLS, but AFSC offered a C-135A, a wholly unsatisfactory choice given its J57 engines and other shortcomings.

Instead, BIG SAFARI demodified 61-2662 in June 1981 and installed the AFSATCOM gear on C-135A 60-0372. The designation for 61-2662 was changed to RC-135S on 2nd November 1983, and it was delivered to the 6th SW at Eielson AFB on 11th November 1983 as COBRA BALL III.

Bad weather was not the only environmental threat to COBRA BALL operations from Shemya AFB. A 7.6-magnitude earthquake hit the island on 1st February 1975. Although the RC-135S was undamaged, the runway suffered significant cracks rendering it unsuitable for regular operational use. The airplane was granted a one-time waiver on 5th February to take off from the damaged runway at a minimum gross weight prior to returning to Eielson AFB (a second 4.3-magnitude quake struck on 9th February). Degraded missions took place directly from Eielson AFB until the runway was repaired, with Shemya AFB operations resuming on 21st May 1975.

Until 1991 the COBRA BALL was used almost exclusively in strategic reconnaissance operations associated with intercontinental ballistic missiles. The 1991 Gulf War changed this, and the COBRA BALL has since expanded its operational role to include reconnaissance of tactical and theater ballistic missiles (TBMs). With Iraq's combat use of *Scud*, al-Husayn, and al-Hijjara TBMs against Saudi Arabia and Israel, Coalition commanders sought some way to identify the launch sites of these mobile missiles. One proposal was to use the COBRA BALL to spot the TBM early in flight and extrapolate the flight path backward to find the launch position. Although plans were made in January 1991 to deploy one RC-135S and two crews from Eielson AFB to Riyadh AB, these were not carried out. Ten years later the COBRA BALL finally saw combat duty, again in Iraq. The first RC-135S combat mission was on 8th March 2003 in 61-2662 as part of IRAQI FREEDOM. No details of the 3.4-hour mission have been declassified or otherwise made available.

OPERATIONS AT THE ROCK AND AROUND THE WORLD

For over a half century the COBRA BALL and its predecessors have flown peripheral reconnaissance missions in international airspace abeam the Kamchatka peninsula while tracking trajectories and studying Soviet ballistic missiles and reentry vehicles targeted against the Kura test range at Klyuchi, an 'impact site on the Kamchatka Peninsula for missile tests from Plesetsk, Tyuratam, the Barents [Sea], and the White Sea'. Throughout the first three decades, one airplane was typically on 24-hour alert at its forward operating location at Shemya AFB, popularly known as the Rock. Crews ate, slept, and waited in facilities within the COBRA BALL hangar, ensuring a quick response given an indication of an impending Soviet launch.

Most COBRA BALL missions from the Rock followed a common pattern. DEFSMAC would determine that a Soviet missile launch was imminent and alert the COBRA BALL crew to take off immediately. Within 15 minutes the RC-135S would be airborne, often in winds of up to 50 mph and blinding snow. It would then proceed to an orbit area in international airspace east of the Kamchatka Peninsula to await the reentry of the ICBM end-stage booster, bus, and warheads. During a successful 'collection,' sensors recorded telemetry data and measured optical and spectrographic images of reentry objects. The view of these missile components and warheads at the Kura Test Range near Klyuchi, especially at night, was extraordinary – the opening seconds of World War III would be beautiful if not horrific. 'The locals say the warhead flights are spectacular. At first, there's a bright star in the night sky, rapidly approaching the ground. Then a flash so powerful the street's lit like daytime, but doomsday lasts not more than a second. In an instant, the big star separates into several smaller ones. Up to 10 warheads separate from the platform and fly at their own targets. Cooler than any fireworks.'

Sometimes the launches never happened due to unreliable pre-launch intelligence, technical delays, or just the Soviets changing their minds because they knew that the COBRA BALL, among other assets, was on station and ready to observe the reentry. Initially the Soviet launches took place with no warning. As evolving arms agreements stipulated verification procedures, the Soviets were obligated to provide a minimum pre-launch notification, sometimes as little as 30 minutes. Coupled with an average 25-minute ballistic flight time, this left COBRA BALL crews with little less than an hour to get to the airplane, take off, climb to altitude, and fly nearly 400 miles to the collection orbit. The Soviets occasionally had their Cobra Boatski listening for radio transmissions indicating a COBRA BALL launch. This information could then easily be used to delay or postpone the missile launch to avoid collection. Consequently, COBRA BALL missions were typically radio silent.

Initial flight-deck crews assigned to flight operations in the NANCY RAE, LISA ANN, and the occasional OFFICE BOY deployment were all highly experienced instructor pilots and navigators, typically Majors and Lieutenant Colonels, including senior COTTON CANDY crews. Even the copilots were highly experienced, usually arriving with three years of prior flight operations. Upgrade from copilot to aircraft commander took place only after considerable time, typically two years of Shemya AFB experience. By 1965 this restriction had been eased somewhat, and upgrade could take place much sooner. During an unidentified incident in 1966, believed to be a TELL TWO that was nearly lost during a takeoff made by a less-than-experienced pilot, the upgrade criteria was once again increased to require that aircraft commanders be highly experienced instructor pilots. A directive on 3rd November 1966 required that 'only highly experienced first pilots will occupy the left seat during operations at Det 1'. This restriction did not delete the upgrade program, but put restrictions on it and

required higher qualifications on the copilots considered for upgrade. Over time the upgrade restrictions once again eased, contributing to the loss of 61-2664 in 1981. As a result, only the most experienced pilots in SAC were selected for Shemya AFB operations, and copilots could upgrade only en route to their next assignment. Once operations from the Rock ended, copilot upgrade followed the normal mechanism for all RC-135 pilots.

During 1993 Shemya AFB was renamed Colonel William O Eareckson AS, and by 30th August 1994, regular reconnaissance flight operations from the Rock had come to an end. The COBRA BALL air operations facility transferred to caretaker status on 31st March 1995, effectively ending over three decades of regular reconnaissance operations from Shemya AFB.

With the exception of the limited press attention paid to the crash of the two RC-135Ss, COBRA BALL operations continued with little public awareness or interest until 31st August 1983 when a Soviet Sukhoi Su-15 *Flagon* shot down Korean Air Lines Boeing 747-230B HL7442 – flight KE007 – after Soviet military authorities claimed they had identified it as an RC-135. Earlier that evening RC-135S 61-2663 had been airborne in the 'sensitive area' adjacent to Kamchatka but had departed for Shemya AFB. Soviet radar controllers misidentified the westbound Korean 747 as '663 returning to its orbit, setting in motion the final chain of events that resulted in Su-15 pilot Gennadii N Osipovich shooting down the 747 over Sakhalin Island. It is neither possible nor practical to review the arguments associated with the ludicrous claims of the Korean Air Lines 747's role as a 'spy' plane or acting in conjunction with an RC-135. The USSR admitted their mistake in destroying the 747, and released considerable data on this tragic event. Nonetheless, with insinuation came implication, and with it the hue and cry for the termination of RC-135 flights (particularly those by the COBRA BALL) to avoid provoking the Soviet Union into any further such action. Wiser heads prevailed and COBRA BALL operations continued.

Unlike its RC-135 counterparts that flew COTTON CANDY, BURNING WIND, and COMBAT SENT peripheral missions around the USSR, the COBRA BALL seldom encountered Soviet fighters. Given the COBRA BALL's remote orbit area and the distance from the Su-15 *Flagon* base at Anadyr AB or the MiG-25 *Foxbat* (and later MiG-31 *Foxhound*) base at Petropavlovsk AB, intercepts were highly unlikely. After an absence of many years, a MiG-31 *Foxhound* deigned to visit RC-135S 61-2663 on 10th March 1988. Escorts increased throughout the year, with MiG-31 intercepts of 61-2662 on 3rd October and 16th November. The 3rd November mission also included a three-hour escort by a Tu-16 *Badger*. As with many BURNING WIND intercepts, those involving the COBRA BALL were friendly and professional. Some 15 years later, that changed considerably. On 3rd March 2003 two North Korean MiG-29 *Fulcrums* and two MiG-23 *Floggers* surprised COBRA BALL RC-135S 61-2663 some 150 miles off the coast of North Korea during a series of DPRK missile tests. The RC-135S aborted its mission when one of the MiGs locked onto the COBRA BALL, and it landed uneventfully at Kadena AB.

In conjunction with the COBRA DANE land-based radar located at Shemya AFB, and the COBRA JUDY sea-based radar located on board the USNS *Observation Island* and, beginning in 2014, the USNS *Howard O Lorenzen*, the RC-135S has served as a national technical means of verification of Soviet (after 1992 Russian) compliance with the Strategic Arms Limitation Treaty (SALT) and other arms control or elimination treaties. As part of the 1987 US-USSR Intermediate Nuclear Force (INF) treaty, for example, the COBRA BALL was a key component of the verification process for Soviet compliance in destroying their intermediate-range and short-range ballistic missiles. Section III of the elimination protocol allowed missiles to be destroyed by launching them from known test facilities to known

Right: Operations from the Rock were notorious for their bad weather. Blizzards, fog, and severe winds could end abruptly followed by clear, calm skies, only to revert to winds in excess of 75 knots (139km/h). *Photo by Aaron Bowen*

Far right: The runway at Shemya AFB. Upper photo is Runway 28, vulnerable to severe wind shear due to updrafts from the beach on short final. Nizki and Alaid Islands are visible across the short strait, with Attu Island in the far distance. Lower photo is Runway 10. 61-2664 struck the approach lights and the lip of the runway threshold, then veered to the right down an ungraded slope to the right of the runway. *Both photos by the author*

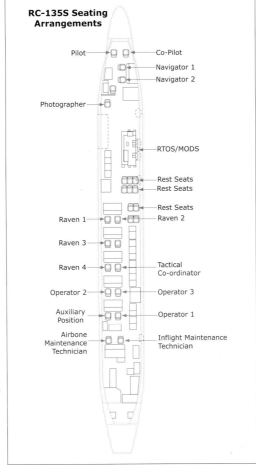

RC-135S Seating Arrangements

- Pilot
- Co-Pilot
- Navigator 1
- Navigator 2
- Photographer
- RTOS/MODS
- Rest Seats
- Rest Seats
- Rest Seats
- Raven 1
- Raven 2
- Raven 3
- Raven 4
- Tactical Co-ordinator
- Operator 2
- Operator 3
- Auxiliary Position
- Operator 1
- Airbone Maintenance Technician
- Inflight Maintenance Technician

Below: Growing demands for the COBRA BALL to meet tasking related to theater ballistic missiles led to the conversion of RC-135X 62-4128 into a third RC-135S. *Photo courtesy USAF*

RC-135S 61-2663 is seen in front of Hangar 7. Facilities at the Rock improved dramatically with funds from SDI. The end of the Cold War eliminated the need for operations from Shemya AFB. *Photo by the author*

Of the five RC-135s that have been lost, four have been from Alaska: RC-135T 55-3121, RC-135E 62-4137, and RC-135S's 59-1491 and 61-2664. A legacy worth honoring. *Photo by Paul Jeanes*

55 years after the NANCY RAE entered service, the COBRA BALL is a far different airplane. Better engines, ability to collect MASINT from either side of the airplane, and real-time data integration enable another 25 years of BURNING STAR operations. *Photo by Ryo Matsuki*

impact sites, with unimpeded observation by any NTM. This process was referred to as 'shoot to destruction.' The COBRA BALL was very active, particularly in monitoring SS-20 *Saber* re-entries. In addition to the usual light show, SS-20 launches were accompanied by a unique phenomenon known as the 'dome of light.' Western intelligence sources suggest this may have served to disable incoming ballistic missiles or mask a Soviet first strike launch from US detection satellites. The Russians know but are not saying.

The end of the Cold War and termination of the SDI program effectively killed the RC-135X COBRA EYE, and its future was in doubt. Concerns about the proliferation of ballistic missiles, especially among actual or potential nuclear nations made a compelling case for an additional RC-135S. Indeed, during 1994 the RC-135S collected against Russia, the People's Republic of China, North Korean, Syria, and India. Beginning in late 1995 BIG SAFARI converted the RC-135X into a third RC-135S. By 2016 the RC-135S

fleet was as busy with global operations as it was 50 years earlier flying from Shemya AFB. Flights from NSF Diego Garcia allowed the COBRA BALL to monitor ballistic missile launches into the Indian Ocean by nuclear rivals India and Pakistan, as 61-2663 did in November 2014. Flights from Australia in 1997 covered launches into the Indian Ocean as well. Flights from al Udeid AB in Qatar monitor missile launches from Iran. Flights from RAF Mildenhall observe Russian SS-N-32 *Bulava* SLBM launches from the Barents Sea, confirming that the COBRA BALL had acquired the operational ability to collect boost-phase intelligence as well as reentry data. Flights from Kadena AB provided ongoing MASINT for Russian missiles, as well as launches of North Korea's (the Democratic People's Republic of Korea – DPRK) fledgling ballistic missile program. The first known flight against the DPRK was 13th September 1988 in 61-2663, which also collected against the last DPRK launch on 7th February 2016.

JKC-135A/RC-135S INDIVIDUAL AIRCRAFT

59-1491 Beginning in October 1960 BIG SAFARI converted this KC-135A into the NANCY RAE. It was assigned to AFSC and deployed operationally to Shemya AFB on 31st December 1961, and on 7th February 1962 was redesignated a JKC-135A. The airplane was transferred to SAC and assigned to the 4157th SW at Eielson AFB on 1st March 1963, the same date it was redesignated an RC-135S. Interestingly, WANDA BELLE RC-135S 59-1491 was a 'phantom' fourth RC-135D. Official SAC documents from 1965 show four RC-135Ds assigned to the 4157th SW – three RIVET BRASS and the WANDA BELLE. This designation does not appear on the aircraft's records, and is presumed to be an internal SAC reference by virtue of its co-location with the three RC-135Ds at Eielson AFB. The airplane's records show it was officially redesignated from JKC-135A to RC-135S on 7th March 1963 as it began upgrade and modification at BIG SAFARI. In January 1965 SAC directed that 59-1491 be designated an RC-135D (almost two years after it officially became an RC-135S), but this errant change never took place. On 13th January 1969 the RIVET BALL failed to stop after landing at Shemya AFB, coming to rest in a ravine. The airplane was written off 10th March 1969 (see Appendix II).

61-2662 Following the loss of RC-135S 61-2664 on 15th March 1981, 61-2662 was selected as the replacement COBRA BALL. C-135B 61-2662 departed Wright-Patterson AFB in June 1981 for conversion by E-Systems into an RC-135S. Its designation was changed to RC-135S on 2nd November 1983, and it was delivered to the 6th SW at Eielson AFB on 11th November 1983. It is the COBRA BALL III, and in 1988 bore the nickname *Island Girl*. Following the 1992 COBRA THAW realignment, the airplane was assigned to the 24th RS, 55th Wing at Offutt AFB, and on 30th June 1994 it was reassigned to the 45th RS, 55th Wing.

61-2663 Following the 13th January 1969 crash of RC-135S 59-1491, this airplane was transferred on 26th March 1969 from AFSC to SAC, and was the first C-135B converted into an RC-135S under the BIG SAFARI conversion program. It arrived at E-Systems on 29th April 1969, and was redesignated an RC-135S on 24th October 1969. It entered service in October 1969 in a 'bare bones' configuration, and was known as the COBRA BALL MINIMUM. During the summer of 1970, the airplane received further equipment upgrades, bringing it to a fully operational configuration as the COBRA BALL I. On 27th October 1978, under the command of Captain Clifford B Carter, 61-2663 led the recovery effort for a downed US Navy P-3 Orion BuNO 159892 some 240nm (445km) west of Shemya AFB. Carter took the RC-135S to just a few hundred feet above the surface under severe storm conditions and spotted the survivors' life rafts, then used the AFSATCOM to relay their location to other rescue forces. When the COBRA BALL ran low on fuel, Clifford climbed to meet a KC-135A strip alert tanker under the command of Captain Frederick S Gersh. Thanks to the actions of the COBRA BALL crew to coordinate the rescue effort, only five of the 15 personnel aboard the P-3 were lost. Beginning in 1987, 61-2663 was nicknamed *No Ka Oi*, which is Hawaiian for 'The Finest'. In 1989 it was renamed *Bering Maiden*. Following the 1992 COBRA THAW realignment, the airplane was assigned to the 24th RS, 55th Wing at Offutt AFB, and on 30th June 1994 it was reassigned to the 45th RS, 55th Wing.

61-2664 As with her sister ship 61-2663, this C-135B was transferred from AFSC to SAC on 16th April 1971 for conversion by E-Systems into an RC-135S under the BIG SAFARI conversion program. The airplane was delivered to the 6th SW on 30th March 1972 as COBRA BALL II. It crashed while attempting to land at Shemya AFB, on 15th March 1981 (see Appendix II). The name COBRA BALL II was temporarily retired in honor of the six crewmen lost in this accident, and 61-2662 became known as the COBRA BALL III. When 62-4128 was converted into an RC-135S it was designated the COBRA BALL II.

62-4128 With the increasing need during the mid-1990s for the mission capability of the RC-135S COBRA BALL, a decision was made in 1995 to convert the stored RC-135X COBRA EYE into an RC-135S. Initially configured with a minimal on-board sensor suite for an early availability, the airplane was eventually equipped with a complete COBRA BALL sensor package. Moreover, its sensors are capable of observation from either side of the airplane, rather than just the starboard side as with the earlier RC-135S platforms. It was delivered to the 45th RS, 55th Wing at Offutt AFB on 8th June 1999.

RC-135E RIVET AMBER

The RC-135E was one of three RC-135 variants dedicated to observing foreign ballistic missile testing to collect MASINT. Following its delivery in 1966 the RC-135E was known operationally as LISA ANN and often flew in conjunction with the WANDA BELLE RC-135S on missions directed by the MUSIC BLUE OpOrd. In January 1967 the operational name for the RC-135E was changed to RIVET AMBER and the OpOrd was renamed BURNING STAR.

The configuration of the RC-135E has been the source of considerable debate and confusion. The airplane had a large laminated fiberglass radome embedded in the starboard side of the forward fuselage to cover its phased-array radar, and some reports incorrectly suggested that this wrapped completely around the fuselage. The RIVET AMBER was the only RC-135 variant equipped with the ubiquitous SLAR. Another source of misunderstanding was the presence of a large pod beneath each wing, spawning reports of an RC-135 with 'sampling pods', an RC-135 with 'SIGINT pods', and even a 'six-engine RC-135',

From 30th September 1963 through 30th March 1966, BIG SAFARI modified the former MAC C-135B into a C-135B-II as part of a 37-

month, \$32 million initiative. This MDS was changed before the airplane was delivered and 62-4137 instead became the sole RC-135E. It was assigned to the 4157th SW at Eielson AFB with flight-deck crews from the wing's Reconnaissance Division. It was deployed to Shemya AFB on 15th September 1966 and became operational the following month. On 25th March 1967 the 4157th SW was inactivated and replaced by the 6th SW. The airplane was reassigned accordingly, with flight-deck crews reassigned to the 24th SRS. Pilot qualification required training at a MATS facility, as SAC's KC-135Bs were equipped with TF33-P-9 engines whereas the RC-135E had TF33-P-5 engines with thrust reversers. Raven training was equally convoluted, as the initial cadre was assigned to Detachment 1, 55th SRW at Offutt AFB (the 55th SRW had yet to relocate from Forbes AFB) and deployed to Shemya AFB.

The RC-135E disappeared over the Bering Sea on 5th June 1969 en route from Shemya AFB to Eielson AFB. Lost presumably due to structural failure of the vertical stabilizer attachment point, no trace of the airplane or the 19 crewmembers on board was ever found. Among those who perished was Staff Sergeant Richard Steen, who was on RC-135S 59-1491 when it slid off the runway five months earlier at Shemya AFB on 13th January 1969 (see Appendix II).

The RC-135E's primary mission equipment was the Hughes Project 863 7.5-megawatt computer-controlled phased-array radar located in the forward fuselage, similar to the radar mounted on the island of the USS *Enterprise* (CVN-65). Efforts to miniaturize the radar to fit into the LISA ANN were frustrating and nearly resulted in its cancelation. The radar was designed to track a 1ft² (0.1m²) object at a distance of 300nm (555km), and track a 10.7ft² (1m²) target at 1,000nm (1,853km). The radar was linked to the airplane's navigation system for precise tracking. The antenna itself was made of metal waveguide material, and was situated behind a 12ft (3m) high by 20ft (6m) long fiberglass panel built by Goodyear Aircraft Co, and incorporated into the body of the fuselage. One official associated with BIG SAFARI has suggested that the fuselage was actually lengthened by an unspecified amount, but this has not been verified. The one-piece laminated fiberglass panel ran from aft of the nose gear well to just aft of the wing root leading edge, covering only the starboard hemisphere of the fuselage, and was designed to withstand basic fuselage bending, pressurization loads, and thermal stresses up to 8gs. 'Strengthened bulkheads and design elements compensating for pressurization and extreme redistribution of load paths' maintained structural integrity. Some reports claim that a thermal blanket could be placed over the antenna to prevent cracking and brittleness while the airplane was on the ground and not heated by either the cabin pressurization system or dissipated energy from the mission equipment, but existence of this blanket has never been corroborated.

The right half of the cargo floor adjacent to the antenna was removed and the affected control cables rearranged. A vertical panel supported the modified floor and allowed for complete normal cabin pressurization above the cargo deck. The BIG SAFARI history reports that bulkheads made from thick lead were installed on each side of the radar compartment to provide the crew with a sizable measure of protection from irradiation by the phased-array radar. Once the radar was in operation, passage from front to back of the airplane was not possible, a source of some concern for the flight deck crew as the latrine was in the back of the airplane. Crew memoirs published in the *Freedom through Vigilance* series, however, contest this: 'contrary to rumors, the radar was not enclosed in lead shielding, and radiation generated by the radar was not a health hazard to the crew,' although external radiation reportedly started a grass fire during ground testing in Texas and 'zapped' a few jackrabbits. Lead weight was added in the aft body as ballast to counteract the weight of the radar and equipment, contributing to the LISA ANN's legacy as the heaviest RC-135.

A large power amplifier provided electricity to the phased-array radar via four power dividers. The amplifier and dividers were so large that installing them first required that they be packed in dry ice for several hours to shrink them in order to fit through the airplane's cargo door. Moving the amplifier itself once inside the airplane necessitated using a 6in (15.2cm) slab of dry ice beneath the device. When the dry ice evaporated, the amplifier was in place to stay, although cocked slightly off center; it was bolted down in just that fashion. The radar compartment also held a phase control unit to direct the radar beam's azimuth. A small circular window on the starboard fuselage aft of the fiberglass antenna covered a telescopic camera, known as a Ballistic Streak Camera (BSC), coupled to the phased-array radar. This camera could be controlled either automatically by the on-board Hughes 863 computer or manually by the system operator and used an 8in (20cm) x 10in (51cm) thick plate glass negative. The phased-array radar located and tracked the vehicles re-entering the atmosphere while the BSC recorded the event.

The considerable power needed to operate the phased-array radar, the BSC, and the extensive computer equipment on the RC-135E exceeded the electrical generating capability of the airplane's four engine-mounted generators. Further, the mission equipment generated tremendous amounts of heat energy – approximately 1 million BTUs (251,000kcal) – which could not only make the interior uncomfortably hot for the crew but could damage the equipment as well. LTV solved these problems by designing and installing an external power generating pod and an external heat exchanger. The starboard pod was a heat exchanger designed to dissipate the considerable heat loads. The port pod contained a modified Lycoming T-55-L5 turbine engine connected to a 350kva generator. Each pod was 37in (93.9cm) in diameter and 127in (322.5cm) in length. Other changes included the deletion of the forward fuselage body fuel tank to allow for the phased-array radar, incorporation of an IFR system, addition of the hog nose, an aft escape chute, and installation of an alternate static system and wingtip static booms.

Program management and modification of the airplane proved highly contentious, with at least two occasions when the project was nearly canceled outright. Most of the structural changes to the airplane were complete by December 1964. Delivery of the Hughes radar, however, slipped repeatedly due to development problems. Initially scheduled for 15th March 1965, Hughes promised it three weeks later on 9th April. It was subsequently delayed even further, adversely affecting the entire production schedule and flight tests. Phase I tests were 'designed to demonstrate the airworthiness of the modified aircraft and provide a functional check of the individual systems,' and were planned to take place over the course of 12 flights between 5th August and 15th September 1965. As of 29th September, however, only six of the 12 flights had taken place; these were finally completed on 14th November. Key problems, aside from the radar, included inadequate air conditioning, hydraulics, and ground power equipment.

At first glance the RIVET AMBER might indeed be mistaken for a 'six-engine' RC-135. The radar system required a cooling pod and an electrical generator pod. *Author's collection*

The civilian engineering staff was essential to keep the system functioning, even after its operational debut. Note the extensive structural work at the junction between the fuselage and the fiberglass antenna panel. *Author's collection*

The small window aft of the radome was for the Ballistic Streak Camera, coupled to the phased-array radar. This collected MASINT. Other sensors gathered TELINT. *Author's collection*

Initial airworthiness flights were delayed pending the arrival of the radar. Vestiges of the MATS markings are still visible on the LISA ANN. *Author's collection*

Phase II testing called for nine flights to evaluate 'the gross performance of the LISA ANN system.' These could not begin until Phase I, already two months late, had ended. The first Phase II test flight took place on 23rd November but was a deemed a failure due to a radar stabilization problem. Moreover, the number of Phase II flights was reduced from nine to five, putting considerable pressure on BIG SAFARI to resolve the LISA ANN's many technical problems before the end of December 1965 when Phase III flights were scheduled to begin. Seven Phase III tests would provide 'operational evaluation by [SAC] with the assistance of AFLC and [BIG SAFARI] contractor personnel' under simulated operational conditions using missiles launched from White Sands, NM. Unfortunately, the system's poor performance during Phase I and II, coupled with dwindling support at senior Air Force levels, led to the elimination of Phase III. SAC asked for (and received) three additional Phase II missions so contractors could check out USAF crews in the radar and other systems, raising the number of test flights from five to eight (including flights from Greenville, TX, on 7th and 11th April 1966).

Tensions were already high between SAC, AFLC, and the BIG SAFARI contractors when Phase III was canceled. LTV reportedly wanted nearly $10,000 a day to keep the airplane at its Greenville facility through mid 1966, amounting to nearly $1.5 million in excess charges. The Air Force decided to 'pull the plug' on the LISA ANN rather than pay these fees. Instead of canceling the program entirely,

SAC and AFLC suggested moving the Phase IV tests from Greenville to Hickam AFB, HI, where there would be no storage fees. The LISA ANN and crews relocated to Hickam AFB by 1st July 1966 as part of Project BUZZ BABY. Missions from Hickam AFB meant that the RC-135E would be tested against US ICBMs launched from Vandenberg AFB, CA, to the Kwajalein Atoll impact site. Data collected by the Hughes radar would then be validated by comparing it to ground-based radar data from Kwajalein. This would also more accurately represent planned operational conditions at Shemya AFB, so test crews assumed an alert posture while awaiting launches from Vandenberg AFB.

The first mission from Hickam AFB defined 'goat rope'. The No.4 engine failed, followed by low oil pressure on the No.3 engine, which was shut down. The airplane flew with a significant yaw until reaching Wake Island, when the No.3 engine was restarted to obviate the need for a dangerous two-engine-out asymmetrical landing (the low oil pressure light was faulty). Replacing the engine delayed the program by several more weeks. The first successful test against an ICBM launched from Vandenberg AFB took place on 25th July 1966 during a marathon 16-hour sortie. The airplane also collected pre-blackout and post-blackout TELINT.

Successful completion of Phase IV tests at Hickam AFB meant that the LISA ANN was ready for its operational evaluation against Soviet ICBMs. Once again, funding issues interfered as LTV asked

for an additional $200,000 a month for test support, and SAC again suggested moving the program, this time to Shemya AFB. The first mission from the Rock took place prior to 7th September 1966 with dismal results. The next six flights, however, all proved highly effective, and SAC declared the airplane fully operational in October 1966. A program that was in danger of cancelation was suddenly the darling of senior defense officials. Secretary of the Air Force Harold Brown wrote in December 1966 that the test flights form Shemya AFB took place during 'an extremely active test period for the Soviets, and as a result excellent data has been collected [*sic*] against five reentry events in the past two weeks' involving SS-7 *Saddlers*, SS-9 *Scarps*, and SS-11 *Segos*. Between September 1966 and April 1967, the LISA ANN RC-135E flew at least 43 operational missions from Shemya AFB.

On 1st May 1967 the RC-135E returned to Greenville for system upgrades, during which time it was renamed from LISA ANN to RIVET AMBER. It departed Greenville for Offutt AFB on 13th June 1968 for equipment checks and flight testing. It was slated to return to Shemya AFB on 15th July, but this slipped to 31st August. Intelligence collected by the RC-135E in May 1969 appeared to validate the belief among hard-line US policy makers that the Soviet SS-9 *Scarp's* three nuclear warheads were multiple independently targetable reentry vehicles (MIRVs). If true, this represented a significant first-strike capability and would be a critical issue in ongoing strategic arms limitation negotiations. In fact, the RIVET AMBER intelligence was at first incorrectly analyzed. Subsequent study correctly showed that it was not MIRV capable and the three warheads were not configured for independent targeting; they were simply multiple reentry vehicles (MRVs). Consequently, the SS-9 was not an extreme threat to US Minuteman silos and hence less of a bargaining chip in the negotiations, much to the dismay of US National Security Advisor Henry Kissinger.

RIVET AMBER flew its last operational sortie on 4th June 1969. While orbiting off the coast of Kamchatka, the airplane experienced 'severe turbulence' and returned to Shemya AFB. It departed the following day for Eielson AFB and disappeared en route. The JCS authorized SAC to replace the RC-135E, but the time and expense involved proved unacceptable, and SAC chose instead to devote its resources to two RC-135S COBRA BALLS following the loss of the RIVET BALL. Interestingly, from 2nd-11th November 1969, two 55th SRW RC-135Cs deployed to Eielson AFB to assist with BURNING STAR operations. They flew 10 missions, but none of them were from Shemya AFB.

RC-135X COBRA EYE

The RC-135X was born of a requirement for an airborne platform dedicated to midcourse optical identification and discrimination of ballistic missile reentry vehicles, and was jointly sponsored by the US Army and Air Force. It collected and recorded 'high-quality spectral data on strategic weapons systems and targets of interest to the US Army Strategic Defense Command' and the Strategic Defense Initiative Organization (SDIO). The airplane was known operationally as COBRA EYE and conducted missions directed by the BURNING VISION OpOrd. The RC-135X was assigned to the 24th SRS, 6th SRW at Eielson AFB (and briefly to the 55th Wing at Offutt AFB from 1992-1993 after the COBRA THAW relocation program), and operated routinely from Shemya AFB observing Soviet ballistic missile tests at the Klyuchi impact site on the Kamchatka Peninsula.

Original specifications for the Optical Aerial Measurement Program (OAMP) aircraft called for the ability to operate at 45,000ft (13,716m) with a payload of 10,000 lb (4,536kg) while deployed to Shemya AFB. The Army, in collaboration with the Massachusetts Institute of Technology's (MIT's) Lincoln Laboratory, initially

recommended a wide-body aircraft – preferably a Boeing 767 – for the OAMP role, similar to the Boeing 767 already in use with the SDIO as the Army's Airborne Optical Adjunct (AOA). The primary sensor onboard the 767 AOA was a long-wave infrared (LWIR) device designed to 'detect and track enemy long-range ballistic missiles', and the Army and Lincoln Lab sought similar capabilities for the COBRA EYE. However, procurement and operating costs for a second 767 were too high and dictated an alternate solution. The availability of an AFSC EC-135B and its flight-deck similarity to the RC-135S (the Air Force flight crews which would fly the RC-135X also flew the RC-135S) made the EC-135B a more economical and practical choice for conversion.

Among the COBRA EYE's mission equipment was a large optical sensor designed 'to observe and record spectral data on the high endoatmospheric characteristics of Soviet reentry vehicles', manufactured by Ball Aerospace Systems. Capabilities of the COBRA EYE sensor included the detection of '... an object's spectra to determine the four dimensions: spatial (location of the object); temporal (temperature of the object) [*sic*]; radiometric (brightness in the infrared); and spectral (color in the infrared). The sensor system's telescope, the first with simultaneous spectral and radiometric measurement capabilities, [took] precise, calibrated measurements in three infrared bands. The sensor [was] a cryogenically cooled system that feature[d] an infrared telescope and focal plane assembly'. Additional sensors on the RC-135X supported other SDIO experiments.

Former AFSC EC-135B 62-4128 arrived on 29th July 1983 at Greenville for demodification, and subsequently underwent wing reskin at BMAC. Actual conversion to the COBRA EYE configuration began in May 1984, with an estimated delivery date of 30th April 1986. The airplane was accorded a 'DX' priority given its importance to the SDIO program, which 'allowed unfettered access to procure equipment.' The sensor reached Greenville in April 1987, and test flights began the same year. Technological delays limited the number of test flights through December 1988 to only six. The RC-135X arrived at Eielson AFB on 16th July 1989, three years after its planned delivery date. A week later it departed to Shemya AFB and assumed alert.

The RC-135X had the hog nose, an alternate static system with wingtip static probes, an IFR system, TF33-P-5 engines, and carried an HF fence-style antenna on the port wingtip. A large sliding door on the starboard side of the fuselage forward of the wing root covered the sensor bay, and, as with the RC-135S, the starboard wing was painted black to reduce glare on the mission optics.

The first operational COBRA EYE mission (call sign *Blind 23*) was on 15th August 1989. During the 7-hour flight, the 'sophisticated computer used to control the COBRA EYE sensor shut down without warning', although the crew was able to restore the computer 'just minutes before the expected event time'. Despite these technical problems, 'the aircraft was perfectly positioned for the event and the first ever data associated with a strategic weapon system was successfully collected'. The COBRA EYE has also been used in conjunction with tests of US ICBMs and SLBMs launched toward Kwajalein. Three days after the first operational flight the RC-135X flew a 14.3-hour mission with three air refuelings to collect data from two Trident D4 SLBMs launched near Midway Island.

The RC-135X's operational future was tied closely to the 1972 Antiballistic Missile (ABM) Treaty. Under at least one interpretation, the COBRA EYE was banned by the treaty. The end of the Cold War and the de-emphasis on SDI projects, however, pre-empted the issue of the COBRA EYE s future. Lacking support amid sweeping budget cuts, the RC-135X was withdrawn from operational use and flown from Offutt AFB to Majors Field at Greenville, TX, on 22nd February

1993. It was placed in long-term storage with its sophisticated sensors removed.

NASA was reportedly interested in replacing its L-300 (C-141) Kuiper Laboratory with a wide-bodied platform, possibly a 747, and the RC-135X could have been used in flight tests of new NASA sensors. By mid-1995, however, the future of the RC-135X was in doubt. According to one plan, it was to be modified for use as a reconnaissance trainer much like the TC-135B, TC-135S, and TC-135W. The need for another COBRA BALL platform, however, proved the most pressing. Beginning in late 1995 the RC-135X underwent conversion into an RC-135S. It was delivered to the 45th RS, 55th Wing at Offutt AFB on 8th June 1999.

Top: After each mission the RC-135E acquired a broom-riding witch symbol. If the crew collected 'an event', a crescent moon was added to signify a successful mission. *Author's collection*

Above: The RIVET AMBER accelerates on Runway 28 en route to another ops sortie from Shemya AFB. The complete disappearance of the RC-135E left a gap among fliers and families that can never be filled. *Photo by Mark Oppenheim via William R Peake*

Above: The sensor on the COBRA EYE is discernable within the compartment covered by a sliding door. Tufts are for airflow research during initial flight tests. *Author's collection*

Below: RC-135X 62-4128 sits outside Hangar 6 at Shemya AFB. White dewar holds liquid nitrogen used to cool the COBRA EYE's IR sensor when not in flight. *Photo by the author*

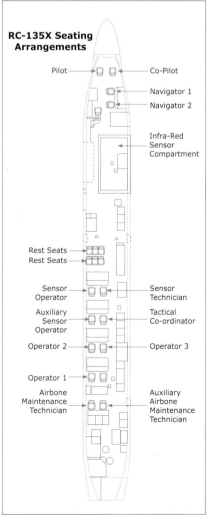

RC-135X Seating Arrangements

Pilot — Co-Pilot

Navigator 1
Navigator 2

Infra-Red Sensor Compartment

Rest Seats
Rest Seats

Sensor Operator — Sensor Technician

Auxiliary Sensor Operator — Tactical Co-ordinator

Operator 2 — Operator 3

Operator 1

Airbone Maintenance Technician — Auxiliary Airbone Maintenance Technician

NUDINT AIRCRAFT AND OPERATIONS

J/KC-135A SPEEDLIGHT-BRAVO, -DELTA and -ECHO

The abrupt Soviet termination on 1st September 1961 of its moratorium on atmospheric nuclear testing prompted the hasty development of an airborne monitoring platform. Although aerial optical and electromagnetic equipment could do little to assess the Soviet tests at Semipalatinsk in Kazakhstan, they would be highly effective tools for tests at Novaya Zemlya in the Barents Sea. There were 18 atmospheric detonations at the two primary test sites there between 10th September and 27th October. With the Soviet announcement on 17th October of a planned test of a 50Mt bomb (first mentioned by Khrushchev in July 1961 as 100Mt), US officials needed some way to monitor the test and they needed it quickly. Given its prior success in other short-notice, high-priority classified conversions, BIG SAFARI was tasked with modifying an existing KC-135 airframe as part of a program named SPEED LIGHT. Despite assertions that SPEED LIGHT was devoted exclusively to the modification of three KC-135s for nuclear monitoring, the program also included the conversion of two C-97s to record television and radio broadcasts from revolutionary Cuba. Indeed, BIG SAFARI delivered SPEED LIGHT-ALPHA C-97G 52-2868 on 23rd July 1961, well before the resumption of Soviet nuclear tests in September. Anecdotally, the name SPEED LIGHT *may* have derived from the need to complete the conversion rapidly, hence the 'speed of light' pun, but this is just speculation. Nonetheless, SPEED LIGHT has become popularly but erroneously associated exclusively with KC-135 nuclear test monitoring.

The first known use of any '135 variant in any strategic reconnaissance capacity was JKC-135A 55-3127 to monitor the Soviet '*Tsar Bomba*' detonation at Novaya Zemlya on 30th October 1961. Hurriedly configured by BIG SAFARI from its existing testbed configuration between 22nd and 27th October 1961, it was 'owned' by Wright-Patterson AFB but flown by SAC crews. JKC-135A 55-3127 was well suited for modification to support the monitoring of the Soviet nuclear tests. It had multiple large, optically ground windows installed from Project SKYSCRAPER, as well as lead curtains and a suitable power supply. BIG SAFARI hastily completed the modification work, even to the extent of using wooden 2x4s to 'shore up' the installation, and SPEED LIGHT-BRAVO was born (the 'Bravo' suffix indicated that it was the second SPEED LIGHT conversion). The 'doghouse' fairing atop the fuselage housed 'three photoelectric sensors...and two EG&G special photo multiplier detectors.' Additional equipment included nine high-speed ciné and photoelectric cameras and a special antenna to collect the electromagnetic pulse (EMP). The airplane departed for RAF Brize Norton on 27th October, and three days later the Soviets detonated

the *Tsar Bomba*, the largest nuclear explosion in history. Hardly a viable nuclear weapon, the device was 26ft (8m) long and dropped from a specially modified Tu-95 *Bear*. The device had been down rated to a 50Mt yield, which proved fortunate. The SPEED LIGHT-BRAVO airplane was close enough to the detonation (by one account 20nm [37km]) that it suffered scorching on the exposed side of the fuselage, and reportedly 'lit up like a Christmas candle.' Had the device detonated with its full yield, 55-3127 would have likely been vaporized. It is difficult to assess the veracity of this claim, as declassified British documents show instead that its orbit area was nearly 200nm (370km) from the test site. Indeed, had 55-3127 been 20nm from the detonation site it would have been inside the 20nm absolute limit to US peripheral reconnaissance flights (if not in Soviet airspace), and almost certainly would have attracted the attention of the MiG-17s at nearby Belushya Guba AB. SPEED LIGHT-BRAVO flew additional missions during the seven additional tests at Novaya Zemlya through 4th November.

The success of 55-3127 in monitoring the Soviet blast raised the desirability of additional aircraft configured to monitor future Soviet detonations as well US nuclear tests in the South Pacific (see Chapter 8). Consequently, BIG SAFARI converted three (and possibly four) KC-135s to fulfill this role. From March-April 1962 BIG SAFARI modified KC-135As 59-1514 and 55-3121 into the SPEED LIGHT-DELTA and SPEED LIGHT-ECHO aircraft, respectively, as well as KC-135A 55-3136 into the DOMINIC U platform. Interestingly, from 1st April through 29th May 1962 BIG SAFARI also converted an unidentified airplane for a program that remains classified. This may have been JKC-135A 55-3131, which was also used to monitor US tests in the South Pacific.

The two new SPEED LIGHT aircraft each had some 19 windows on both sides of the fuselage to allow collection from either side of the airplane. Test equipment included 'eight cameras, a photo-electric system, three panoramic electromagnetic systems, four bhangmeters, and data photo systems for recording the precise chronometer readings.' A closed circuit TV monitored various arrays. The airplanes operated from Hickam AFB. KC-135A 55-3121 participated in each DOMINIC-series test beginning 25th April 1962, and both airplanes flew for each test starting with the 15th June RINCONADA test through the 11th June PAMLICO test. Neither participated in the FISHBOWL series of tests from 2nd-30th October, however, given events on the other side of the world.

Despite the well-documented role of the two SPEED LIGHT airplanes in scientific research associated with the US DOMINIC tests in the South Pacific, they were in fact also used to monitor Soviet tests at Novaya Zemlya. By 12th April 1962 the United States had requested UK approval to conduct nuclear test monitoring flights from RAF Brize Norton as part of 'Operation SPEED LIGHT-DELTA', an operation

Table 10-4. **Reconnaissance Lineage of 55-3121**

From	To	MDS	Program Name	Agency	Location	Tasking
22 Jan 57	29 Apr 57	KC-135A			Renton, WA	Boeing Flight Test Programs
30 Apr 57	6 May 57	KC-135A		AFMC	Wright-Patterson AFB	KC-135 Test Programs
7 May 57	19 Apr 62	JKC-135A		AFMC	Wright-Patterson AFB	KC-135 Test Programs
20 Apr 62	9 May 62	KC-135A			BIG SAFARI	Modification to SPEED LIGHT-ECHO
10 May 62	Apr-63	KC-135A	SPEED LIGHT-ECHO	AFSWC	Hickam AFB	
					RAF Brize Norton	US DOMINIC tests; Soviet tests at Novaya Zemlya
Apr 63	May-63	KC-135R			BIG SAFARI	GARLIC SALT modification with 59-1465 & 59-1514
May-63	Jan 65	KC-135R	RIVET STAND	AFTAC	34th AREFS Offutt AFB	Foreign Nuclear Tests
Jan 65	24 Mar 65	KC-135R			BIG SAFARI	Modification
25 Mar 65	Nov-66	JKC-135A	RIVET STAND	ASD/AFTAC	Wright-Patterson AFB	
					Hickam AFB	ASD Projects/ BURNING LIGHT French Nuclear Tests
Nov-66	4 Jan 67	JKC-135A	RIVET STAND	AFTAC	55th SRW Offutt AFB	
					Hickam AFB	BURNING LIGHT French Nuclear Tests
5 Jan 67	Jul 67	KC-135R	RIVET STAND	AFTAC	55th SRW Offutt AFB	
					Hickam AFB	BURNING LIGHT French Nuclear Tests
Jul 67	Jul-67	KC-135R			BIG SAFARI	Modification to BRIAR PATCH to replace 59-1465
Jul-67	early 68	KC-135R	BRIAR PATCH	CIA	55th SRW Offutt AFB	PPMS ELINT
early 68	Jun-68	KC-135R			BIG SAFARI	Modification to BUSTED JAW
Jun-68	Sep-68	KC-135R	BUSTED JAW	AFTAC	55th SRW Offutt AFB	
					Hickam AFB	BURNING LIGHT French Nuclear Tests
Sep-68	Mar-69	KC-135R			BIG SAFARI	Modification to RIVET JAW
Mar-69	7 Dec 69	KC-135R	RIVET JAW	CIA/AFIN	55th SRW Offutt AFB	PPMS ELINT
8 Dec 69	mid 70	KC-135T	COBRA JAW	CIA/AFIN	BIG SAFARI	MDS and mission redesignation
Aug-70	Nov-70				55th SRW Offutt AFB	PPMS ELINT
Nov-70	May 71	RC-135T			BIG SAFARI	Modification to RIVET DANDY
Jun-71	Jul-73	RC-135T	RIVET DANDY	NSA	55th SRW Offutt AFB	Cuba ACRP
Jul-73	25 Feb 85	RC-135T		SAC	Various	Trainer – Crashed 25 Feb 85, Valdez, Alaska

'very similar to the previous Speedlight operation [in] October/November which caused no Soviet reaction.' The first airplane, KC-135A 59-1514, arrived on 7th May and was quickly established on 15-minute alert. A second, unidentified KC-135A tanker was also on alert to provide refueling as well as 'a cross check on navigation as well as communications.' Once launched, the SPEED LIGHT-DELTA airplane would 'orbit for approximately six hours…with the nearest point of approach to Soviet territory of 195nm (361km).' After landing, both airplanes would be regenerated for future sorties. There were no Soviet tests at Novaya Zemlya however, and 59-1514

Opposite page: JKC-135A 55-3127 was the SPEED LIGHT-BRAVO aircraft, seen here in the same configuration some 18 months after the *Tsar Bomba* test. *Photo by Roger Besecker via Stephen Miller*

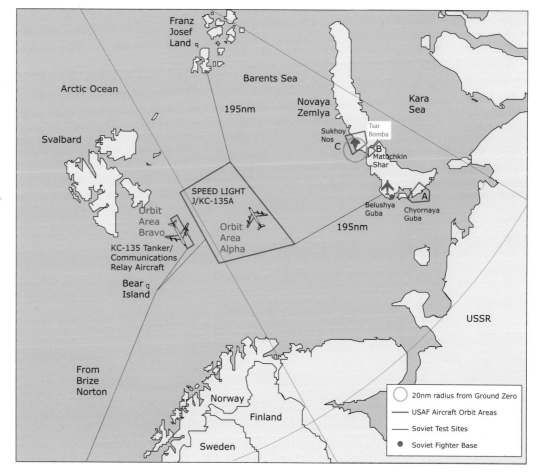

This page: The SPEED LIGHT orbit area was 200nm (370km) from the nearest Soviet territory. Orange ring around detonation site indicates 20nm (37km) distance from blast claimed by crew. KC-135 tanker was for radio relay only, as the SPEED LIGHT aircraft were not originally configured for receiver air refueling.

departed England to participate in the DOMINIC tests along with KC-135 55-3121. In late July, however, the Soviets announced that a 'large area around Novaya Zemlya [would] be dangerous from 5th August to 20th October,' suggesting imminent nuclear tests. By 8th August both 55-3121 and 59-1514 were at RAF Brize Norton and undertook daily missions beginning with the 10th August test at Novaya Zemlya. SAC U-2 sampling missions from RAF Upper Heyford took place as well.

On 20th September American officials requested British permission to conduct the previously unknown 'SPEED LIGHT-HAZEL' mission. No airplane has yet been identified for this role, although the 'HAZEL' suffix suggests that at least three additional airplanes were modified under the SPEED LIGHT program, but this is purely speculative and no documentation survives to support this (one of O'Rear's 'Eight Rules' to guide BIG SAFARI might explain this – 'When no longer needed, documents containing significant details would be destroyed.'). According to declassified British documents for the Prime Minister's consideration, this unidentified airplane – almost certainly a KC-135 given the equipment requirements – 'would approach closer to the actual nuclear dropping zone' and 'obtain high-speed photographs and optical telescopic measurements of the first few microseconds after the detonation when the gamma rays begin to mix with the surrounding air. Such information will provide an accurate measurement of yield and valuable data on the construction of the device ... and will provide a vital yardstick against which all the information collected from other, more distant flights can be measured.' By 16th October the US had canceled its request to fly the SPEED LIGHT-HAZEL mission, and British officials speculated that 'they have managed to collect the information required in other ways.' American planners announced the end of the SPEED LIGHT-DELTA program on 28th October, but the continuance of Soviet testing through the end of November delayed its final termination through the end of 1962.

The story of SPEED LIGHT-BRAVO and the *Tsar Bomba* reflects the limits of oral history in researching the KC-135 and its variants. Two of the pilots who participated were adamant that the airplane was 55-3121, which was still at Wright-Patterson AFB. In fact, 55-3121 did fly a mission to Novaya Zemlya for a Soviet nuclear test on 30th October *1962*, exactly a year after the *Tsar Bomba* mission in 55-3127. Moreover, a senior official associated with the original mission noted that the radioactive 'damage to the aircraft eventually required it to be destroyed, though no long term effects on the crew ever materialized.' In fact, 55-3127 would continue to fly test-bed related missions for another 31 years after its role as the SPEED LIGHT-BRAVO aircraft.

J/KC-135A INDIVIDUAL AIRCRAFT

55-3121 BIG SAFARI converted this KC-135A between 20th April and 9th May 1962 into the SPEED LIGHT-ECHO aircraft. In April 1963 it was further modified into a RIVET STAND KC-135R.

55-3127 This JKC-135A was modified between 22nd-27th October 1961 as the SPEED LIGHT-BRAVO aircraft, it monitored the 30th October *Tsar Bomba* nuclear test. It returned to tesbed duties in early 1962.

59-1514 BIG SAFARI converted this KC-135A between 6th February and 23rd March 1962 into the SPEED LIGHT-DELTA aircraft. In April 1963 it was further modified into a RIVET STAND KC-135R.

KC-135R RIVET STAND/BUSTED JAW/RIVET QUICK

With the August 1963 signing of the Partial Test Ban Treaty (PTBT), the United States, the Soviet Union, and Great Britain agreed to halt all atmospheric, underwater, and outer space nuclear testing. The remaining nuclear power – France – did not sign the accord. US Senate ratification of the treaty was contingent upon its acceptance by the Joint Chiefs of Staff and other critics who worried about Soviet cheating and the ability to detect violations. One solution was the AFSWC EARLY DAY NC-135A program involving three quick-response airborne diagnostic airplanes (see Chapter 8). Pending their lengthy modification, between April and May 1963 BIG SAFARI undertook the configuration of two of the former SPEED LIGHT jets (55-3121 and 59-1514) and a basic KC-135A (59-1465) into the three RIVET STAND reconnaissance KC-135s as part of the GARLIC SALT COMINT program. The modification included installation of the appropriate 'Class A' equipment – wiring, racks, internal components not otherwise easily accessible – and 'Class B' gear that actually performed the mission but could be easily removed for storage, including nuclear detection and recording gear provided by atomic research organizations such as the Denver Research Institute (DRI) and Edgerton, Germeshausen, and Grier (EG&G). The airplanes also received an IFR system. Primary sensors measured and recorded electromagnetic pulses that emanated from nuclear detonations. Secondary sensors photographed the density and the opacity of the nuclear cloud. SAC provided 'front-end' pilots and navigators, AFTAC crews seated in the middle of the airplane operated the sensors, and AFSS crews in the back served to 'get the airplane pointed in the right direction at the right time for the guys in the middle.'

The airplanes were assigned to SAC as the primary operator. Whenever the need arose, the airplanes were tasked to support AFTAC monitoring requirements and the Class B mission equipment stored at McClellan AFB, CA, would be quickly installed. Each airplane also had AFSS personnel on board to provide both self-protection and a basic COMINT capability to exploit voice communications related to the detonation. The EARLY DAY NC-135As received considerable public attention, but the GARLIC SALT KC-135Rs did not, emphasizing their reconnaissance role.

TWO RIVET STAND KC-135Rs (55-3121 and 59-1465) at RAF Upper Heyford in November 1966. Both had a NUDINT mission on behalf of AFTAC, and were configured with the GARLIC SALT COMINT and advisory warning capability. *Author's collection*

There is some confusion about where the airplanes were based as well as their designations. SAC unit histories note that all three were assigned to the 34th AREFS, 385th SAW at Offutt AFB beginning in 1963. However, the BIG SAFARI history indicates that 55-3121 was assigned to the 55th SRW at Forbes AFB, KS, from its delivery in May 1963 until 16th August 1966 when the 55th SRW relocated to Offutt AFB. At the time the 55th SRW operated only RB-47s, so would not have had any qualified KC-135 flight crews. Moreover, the 55th SRW histories for this period make no reference to any KC-135s in the wing, so 55-3121 was almost certainly assigned initially to the 34th AREFS. According to AFSC histories, ASD used 55-3121 for at least two major non-nuclear test programs during 1964 and 1965, and on 25th March 1965 it was redesignated a JKC-135A while based at Wright-Patterson AFB. SAC acquired 55-3121 from ASD on 7th July 1966, although it was not delivered to the 55th SRW at Offutt AFB until November 1966. On 5th January 1967 it was redesignated a reconnaissance KC-135R. This interim assignment with ASD for 55-3121 explains why SAC reconnaissance histories list only two GARLIC SALT airplanes (59-1465 and 59-1514) in service *with SAC* in 1964 through 1966. Although 55-3121 was assigned to ASD during this period, it could still be tasked with its AFTAC mission (flown by SAC and AFSS crews) as long as it was available.

The MDS for the three GARLIC SALT airplanes is equally problematic. The BIG SAFARI history specifically indicates that 55-3121 and 59-1514 were redesignated as KC-135Rs after being reconfigured as RIVET STAND airplanes in 1963, but does not mention 59-1465. SAC reconnaissance histories show 59-1465 and 59-1514 as KC-135Rs throughout 1965, with 55-3121 as a JKC-135A with ASD. The individual airplane record cards from the Air Force Historical Research Agency (AFHRA), however, long considered the 'gold standard' for aircraft data, conflict with both of these sources. AFHRA cards show 55-3121 redesignated from a JKC-135A to a KC-135R on 5th January 1967, and both 59-1465 and -1514 redesignated from KC-135As to KC-135Rs on 30th May 1967. Whatever their historical legacy, the record cards are largely 'reconciliation' documents – often after-the-fact summaries that combined multiple and occasionally incomplete records with bureaucratic decrees detached from reality (such as the 1965 SAC directive that RC-135S 59-1491 be incorrectly designated an RC-135D almost two years after it officially became an RC-135S). Irrespective of what the record cards show, the airplanes were referred to operationally and historically as KC-135Rs well before the 'official' date listed on the cards. Opting for frequency over form, this book refers to them as KC-135Rs beginning in 1963 – *caveat lector*.

After the three GARLIC SALT airplanes first arrived at the 34th AREFS they were assigned to refuel aircraft from the 55th SRW as part of SAC OpOrd 29-64 and 2nd AF OpOrd 60-64. In March 1964, for example, GARLIC SALT 'operational commitments consisted of 19 accomplished sorties and 16 creditable and reliable refuelings' with 55th SRW aircraft. This ambiguity likely results from the GARLIC SALT KC-135Rs having multiple missions and 'owners'. Unless tasked by AFTAC, the airplanes were effectively standard KC-135 tankers (much like KC-135A 55-3136 following its demodification), and their association with the 55th SRW was purely a function of their air refueling role for that unit's RB-47s. The airplanes also served as receiver air refueling trainers – the 34th AREFS histories regularly mention 'successful receiver refueling sorties.' At the time only the three OFFICE BOY KC-135A-IIs in Alaska and the three GARLIC SALT KC-135Rs were capable of receiver air refueling.

Even with the ban on atmospheric detonations, the GARLIC SALT KC-135Rs were busy. There were regular training deployments which began with a stop at McClellan AFB, home base for the AFTAC aerial deployment teams, to reinstall the AFTAC mission equipment prior to flying to overseas bases. During June 1966, for example, KC-135R 59-1465 flew multiple sorties from Offutt AFB to McClellan AFB to Kirtland AFB and then back to McClellan AFB to practice quick response deployment procedures. In November 1966, just three weeks after two underground tests at Novaya Zemlya, KC-135Rs 55-3121 and 59-1465 deployed via McClellan AFB to RAF Upper Heyford (with a weather divert initially to RAF Bentwaters) to practice GARLIC SALT alert procedures and exercise the AFSS components related to the AFTAC mission as part of an unidentified program known as PROUD ELTON III. The following year KC-135R 55-3121 flew 10 practice missions in November and December, and the PROUD ELTON deployments continued as well.

French atmospheric and underground atomic tests continued at the Ekker test site in Algeria between March 1963 and February 1966. It is not known if any of the GARLIC SALT KC-135As operated from Operating Location (OL) OL-36 at Wheelus AB, Libya, to monitor these tests, although declassified documents suggest that they were capable of doing so. The closest they could have approached the test site was at the southern border between Algeria and Libya, in excess of 200nm (370km) from Ekker, which is near the limits of UHF reception for the AFSS component, and well beyond the preferred 80nm (148km) visual range for the optical sensors used by AFTAC. Similarly, the GARLIC SALT airplanes would have been of little value for the first Red Chinese test on 16th November 1964 as the Lop Nor test facility is in northwestern China, thousands of miles beyond any nearest point of approach.

Beginning with the summer of 1966, the GARLIC SALT KC-135As deployed annually to Hickam AFB as part of the BURNING LIGHT aerial task force to monitor French atmospheric atomic tests, relocated from Algeria to the Mururoa Atoll in the Tuamotu Archipelago of French Polynesia earlier in the year. BURNING LIGHT was the airborne portion of a larger nuclear collection effort on behalf of the Defense Nuclear Agency (DNA), the Atomic Energy Commission (AEC), and other US agencies. In addition to collecting technical and operational intelligence related to foreign nuclear weapons development, BURNING LIGHT sought to develop 'a miniaturized, inexpensive, highly sophisticated system for analyzing data from nuclear explosions and to gather information that would improve the US ability to predict the effects of low-altitude nuclear weapons.' The BURNING LIGHT mission is associated with other program names, which may have been 'seasonal' identifiers related to the SAC component in the recurring French summer tests. SAC histories refer to HARD LOOK from FY66 in 1965 through 1967 (there is also a HARD LOOK program during the 1970s that assessed lingering radioactivity from US and British nuclear tests on Christmas Island from 1957-62, but given the disparity in dates it is not clear if these are related). The 1968 tests may have been known as BUSTED JAW, although this was certainly the name of the KC-135Rs used during the tests. There were no tests in 1969. In 1970 the SAC component identifier became NICE DOG. The name changed in 1973 from NICE DOG to HULA HOOP, and again in 1974 from HULA HOOP to DICE GAME. The BURNING LIGHT program ended with the closure of the 1974 tests.

GARLIC SALT operations followed a common pattern. Normally two KC-135Rs were on alert (although in 1973 two NC-135As were used and in 1974 NC-135A 60-0369 provided sole mission coverage). The French tests usually took place early in the morning at Mururoa Atoll some 2,600nm (4,815km) from Hickam AFB. In order to be in place at least an hour prior to the detonation, BURNING LIGHT aircraft were required to launch from Hickam AFB around midnight, fly six hours to the orbit area, remain on station for two to three hours, and then fly six hours back to Hickam AFB for recovery, necessitating a large KC-135A tanker component. During June 1971, for example, SAC deployed seven KC-135As plus the two KC-135Rs in support of two BURNING LIGHT missions. Tanker crews flew sorties as short as two hours (for the first refueling) and as long as 12 hours (for the

refueling immediately prior to the KC-135R entering its orbit area, leaving it with just enough fuel to orbit for about 2.5 hours). As the 11th AREFS history for 1966 recounts, tanker 'missions were all night over-water missions of maximum duration. Maximum fuel off-load was involved. The nature of HARD LOOK was so sensitive that there was no information available concerning its actual purpose. The crews who participated in this mission were not given to disclose any information as to where the refuelings took place, what type of aircraft they supported, or what the supported aircraft were doing.' Not everyone shared the sense of mission importance. Noise abatement regulations at Honolulu IAP (co-located with Hickam AFB) prohibited noisy water injection takeoffs between 2100 and 0700. This meant the mission aircraft and support tankers had to take off with lower fuel loads. Despite entreaties from BURNING LIGHT planners and even JCS requests to Hawai'ian politicians, local

residents and environmental groups succeeded in denying the requested waivers. Paradoxically, this actually increased the overall noise levels as it dictated anywhere from one to three extra KC-135As to provide the necessary fuel.

Once the NSA determined that a French test was imminent, the alert airplanes were launched along with multiple tankers. This was not always easy; the NSA failed to detect plans for the 16th June 1974 *Capricorne* test and the NC-135A did not launch. On 7th July 1974 the NSA believed that a test was scheduled and the NC-135A and tankers were launched. The *Gemeaux* test did indeed take place, but was delayed for some reason until after the NC-135A had departed the test area due to low fuel. In other cases the tests never occurred and the airplanes returned without any meaningful collection.

The missions themselves varied between hours of boredom and considerable excitement. AFSS crews, including French linguists,

From 1962-1969, KC-135R 55-3121 was associated with three NUDINT programs: SPEED LIGHT-ECHO, RIVET STAND, and BUSTED JAW, as well as the CIA's BRIAR PATCH ELINT missions. On 8th December 1969 it became the KC-135T for COBRA JAW ELINT sorties, and in 1971 became the RC-135T for RIVET DANDY COMINT missions. *Author's collection*

RIVET QUICK KC-135R 58-0126 sits behind the Supervisor of Flying (SOF) truck at Offutt AFB. It replaced KC-135R 59-1465 in the NUDINT role, and later replaced RC-135T 55-3121 as the RIVET DANDY aircraft. *Photo HS6214 courtesy Boeing*

RIVET QUICK KC-135R 59-1514 at Hickam AFB during a BURNING LIGHT deployment between 1970 and 1972. *Photo courtesy of Bill Strandberg*

complained of the bitter cold in the back of the airplane during the 14-hour flights. Just prior to detonation, the flight-deck crew put flash curtains in the windows to prevent blindness, but quickly removed them to take photographs of (and avoid flying into) the ensuing mushroom cloud. Much like the BURNING PIPE missions around the Soviet Union, the BURNING LIGHT airplanes had occasional 'visitors'. During 1968 French Dassault Mirage IIIs intercepted and 'escorted' KC-135R 59-1514, and in 1970 intercepted an unspecified KC-135R. French nuclear security failed to extend to all areas, however, and AFSS personnel quickly exploited it. During one test in 1968, AFSS crewmen detected television transmissions. On the next flight (and subsequent sorties) they hooked up a small portable TV and, to their amazement, watched (and recorded) live TV coverage of the French mission control room broadcasting the detonation countdown to participating French forces. *C'est la guerre!*

The 1967 BURNING LIGHT season saw considerable change with the GARLIC SALT mission and fleet. The GARLIC SALT code name appears to have been replaced with ELECTRIC EEL, although GARLIC SALT missions in Europe are still recorded as late as 1968. Crewmembers continued to refer to the airplanes by their earlier name. From 1st-18th May 1967, LAS modified KC-135 59-1465 for the CIA BRIAR PATCH PPM operation. It flew four missions from RAF Upper Heyford through 20th June 1967, when it returned to Offutt AFB. There is no indication that the airplane then deployed to the BURNING LIGHT Task Force for the 27th June or 2nd July French nuclear tests. It crashed on takeoff from Offutt AFB on 17th July 1967 (see Appendix II). Immediately thereafter BIG SAFARI modified 55-3121 as the replacement BRIAR PATCH airplane, although it briefly returned to atomic monitoring duties for the 1968 BUSTED JAW effort. This left KC-135R 59-1514 as the only dedicated GARLIC SALT aircraft. The heavy demand on this lone airplane resulted in BIG SAFARI's conversion of KC-135A 58-0126 from June 1969 through December 1970 into a RIVET QUICK KC-135R, utilizing much of the mission equipment salvaged from KC-135R 59-1465. In addition, KC-135R 59-1514 was updated to RIVET QUICK standards. During 1973 BIG SAFARI removed the AFTAC-related gear from KC-135R 58-0126 and installed the COMINT equipment from RC-135T 55-3121 plus two AFTAC positions, replacing it as the sole RIVET DANDY aircraft. On 4th March 1974, BIG SAFARI demodified KC-135R 59-1514 into a KC-135A(ARR), bringing the KC-135R GARLIC SALT/ELECTRIC EEL mission to a close.

KC-135R INDIVIDUAL AIRCRAFT

55-3121 Between April and May 1963 BIG SAFARI converted the SPEED LIGHT-ECHO KC-135A into a RIVET STAND KC-135R. It incorporated the GARLIC SALT COMINT modification as well as the permanent gear for the AFTAC mission. It also received an IFR capability. Assigned to the 34th AREFS from 1963 through 1964, when it was transferred to ASD and relocated to Wright-Patterson AFB. It continued GARLIC SALT missions as required while with ASD, but was redesignated as a JKC-135A beginning in March 1965. It was reassigned to the 55th SRW in July 1966, but did not arrive there until November 1966. It was again redesignated a KC-135R on 5th January 1967. Beginning in July 1967 BIG SAFARI converted it into BRIAR PATCH KC-135R to replace 59-1465 lost on 17th June 1967. In May 1968 LAS reconfigured 55-3121 for atomic monitoring missions as the BUSTED JAW KC-135R. It deployed to Hickam AFB 29th June through 29th August 1968, and then immediately returned to BIG SAFARI for conversion into the RIVET JAW KC-135R.

58-0126 This KC-135A entered the BIG SAFARI modification program on 24th June 1969 as the first KC-135R RIVET QUICK utilizing the mission suite salvaged from KC-135R 59-1465, and was redesignated a KC-135R on 13th November 1969. The airplane also received an IFR system, and was assigned to the 55th SRW on 6th January 1970. During 1973 it was reconfigured into the second RIVET DANDY airplane using the COMINT gear from RC-135T 55-3121.

59-1465 Between April and May 1963 BIG SAFARI converted this KC-135A into a RIVET STAND KC-135A. This incorporated the GARLIC SALT COMINT modification as well as the permanent gear for the AFTAC mission. It also received an IFR capability. It was assigned to the 34th AREFS beginning in 1963. After conversion by LAS in May 1967 it shifted to the CIA BRIAR PATCH program, and crashed on takeoff from Offutt AFB on 17th July 1967 (see Appendix II).

59-1514 Between April and May 1963 BIG SAFARI converted the SPEED LIGHT-DELTA KC-135A into a RIVET STAND KC-135R. It incorporated the GARLIC SALT COMINT modification, the permanent gear for the AFTAC mission, as well as an IFR capability. Assigned to the 34th AREFS on 17th May 1963. During 1970 BIG SAFARI converted it into the second RIVET QUICK KC-135R. It was fully demodified into a KC-135A(ARR) in 1973.

WC-135B/C/W CONSTANT PHOENIX

The American monopoly on atomic weapons defined the early years of the Cold War, leading to what many Western leaders believed to be a barely sufficient military superiority over Soviet conventional forces. It was just a matter of time, however, until the Soviets developed their own atomic weapons, and the arms race had begun. Although direct detection and monitoring – spies, photographs, and the like – of the Soviet atomic weapons programs was the most desirable evidence of Soviet progress, the only accessible information came from indirect detection and monitoring by long-range aerial weather reconnaissance. These efforts date at least to September 1947, when US Secretary of War Kenneth C Royal announced that overall responsibility for the Long Range Detection Program (LRDP) would be assigned to the Army Air Force. Secretary of the Navy James V Forrestal concurred in this recommendation, and on 16th September 1947 the US Army chief of staff General of the Army Dwight D Eisenhower officially charged the newly constituted 'US Air Force with responsibility for detecting atomic bomb explosions,' creating the CONSTANT PHOENIX aerial sampling program.

By July 1948 USAF Air Weather Service (AWS) airplanes were in operation with special filters to collect radioactive materials from the atmosphere. The first Soviet atomic test – Operation FIRST LIGHTNING – on 29th August 1949 was detected five days later by a WB-29 from the 375th Weather Squadron (WS) flying over the Northern Pacific Ocean. Aerial reconnaissance worked in close coordination with ground-based detection and monitoring facilities to identify and monitor other Soviet tests. For example, on 24th September 1951 an Air Force ground station detected an 'acoustic signal of unusual intensity' near the Soviet test facility at Semipalatinsk. To corroborate the conclusion that the Soviets detonated an atomic device, long-range weather reconnaissance flights were increased over the next few days. On 28th September these flights collected large amounts of radioactive material. Analysis of the collected particles revealed that they could only have come from a high order atomic explosion. US analysts concluded that there was indeed a *bona fide* atomic explosion within the USSR. In fact this was the second Soviet nuclear test, 'Joe 2'. Specially configured SEA FISH B-36s flying from bases in Guam and Washington collected evidence of yet another Soviet detonation on 22nd November 1955. Eventually GIANT FISH B-52s replaced the SEA FISH B-36 samplers, and WB-47s, WC-130s, and WC-135s replaced the WB-29s and WB-50s in these near-daily flights, along with SAC's High Altitude Sampling Program (HASP) U-2 missions as part of the CROWFLIGHT program. These missions, including CONSTANT FISH sorties, were flown over the Pacific Ocean and in the Arctic region at altitudes near 2,500ft (762m). They proved extremely effective and demonstrated '[o]utstanding success in collecting good early [atomic] debris samples.' Sampling is the 'retrieval of microscopic pieces of the bomb itself, which are subjected to radiochemistry to analyze the materials used,' and has since become an essential ingredient in nuclear test ban agreements.

In addition to the critical role of aerial platforms in atmospheric sampling in detecting atomic detonations, the airplanes had a concurrent weather reconnaissance mission as well. Aside from the obvious benefits to international air travel and weather forecasting in general, knowing the weather in detail had real Cold War military implications. Manned bombers, tankers, and missiles of any type engaged in the SIOP were highly vulnerable to the weather. Unpredictable winds could affect the trajectory of a free-fall weapon dropped from high altitude or a warhead re-entering the atmosphere, causing it to miss its target completely. Excessive headwinds could significantly reduce the range of a bomber, causing it to run out of fuel without ever reaching its target. Crosswinds could blow it off course to the degree that it might not be able to find and strike its target. Forecasted good weather at a target might change during the 10+ hour flight from SAC bases to the target. Weather intelligence was therefore nearly as important as data on the targets themselves. Major General Earle E Partridge warned that in any future war with the USSR, the United States would 'be required to forecast the weather in a locality several thousand miles distant from the nearest [US] observation post and provide consistently accurate results. In the face of the weather bureau's inability to forecast the local weather at Washington, I believe there is a great deal of work to be done in this field alone.'

Beginning 22nd April 1965 Hayes International converted ten former MATS C-135Bs as part of Modification 1421 under the PACER DAY program, with the last airplane delivered 21st January 1966. The airplanes were redesignated WC-135Bs and assigned to the CONSTANT PHOENIX sampling program, as well as traditional weather reconnaissance. Modifications to the basic C-135B airframe included an IFR system, although this was not fully implemented until at least 25th June 1966. The airplanes had a fuel dump tube in lieu of an air refueling boom, and the fairing normally occupied on the KC-135 by the boom operator's pod appeared in multiple configurations over time, but most commonly contained the dropsonde pneumatic ejection tube. The airplanes retained TF33-P-5 engines with thrust reversers.

WC-135Bs represented a significant improvement in crew comfort and working conditions. Although missions could be (and often were) longer than those in earlier weather reconnaissance airplanes thanks to air refueling, the WC-135B's large fuselage interior allowed crewmembers to get up and 'stretch' during missions, a difficult task in the WB-47 and impossible in the WB-57 or the U-2. The WC-135B had a crew of seven, including pilot, copilot, navigator, weather officer, flight engineer, and two weather technician/dropsonde operators. Moreover, the mission equipment represented a quantum leap in capability and ease of use.

The Bendix WS 460-L Weather Reconnaissance Suite was developed specifically for the KC-135 airframe, and initial system tests were undertaken aboard the Boeing Dash 80. SAC tanker requirements, however, precluded any KC-135s from undergoing conversion. As C-141As made the MATS C-135B fleet redundant, they – along with WC-130s – became an obvious choice to replace the WB-50s in the sampling role, as well as MAC WB-47Es and SAC RB-47Ks in the weather reconnaissance role. The heart of the WS 460-L was the AN/AMQ-15 Weather Reconnaissance System, designed to provide both global weather and geophysical

reconnaissance in a flying laboratory, as well as the AN/AMQ-25 Meteorological System, an AN/ASN-6 longitude-latitude computer, and the Atmospheric Research Equipment (ARE) System. While airborne the WC-135B could utilize rocketsondes and dropsondes, a variety of probes and sensors, cloud and storm radars, and record and analyze the data collected with several on-board computer systems. In addition, WC-135Bs carried the U-1 foil collection system mounted in a cylindrical fairing above each wing root aft of the overwing hatch for the aerial sampling mission.

The WC-135Bs were active in sampling the French nuclear tests in the South Pacific. In the first such explosion, *Aldébaran* on 2nd July 1966, a WC-135B launched from Lima, Peru, to gather downwind samples. The weather at Lima deteriorated, however, forcing the WC-135 to recover in Tahiti. Another mission from Lima on 11th September 1966 collected samples from the *Bételguese* test which produced excessive fallout over the South Pacific. Other French sampling missions took place from Mendoza, Argentina. The WC-135s were routinely subject to contamination from the tests. For the 24th December 1967 Chinese nuclear test at Lop Nor, for example, the thermonuclear test was uncontained and released large amounts of radiation over Tokyo. At least four WC-135s and two WB-57Fs took samples from the cloud at altitudes of 850mb (5,000ft/1,524m) to well above 100mb (70,000ft/21,336m). Whenever possible after a 'dirty' sampling run, crews would 'find a good rain storm to wash off the aircraft' prior to recovery.

Even when nuclear tests were not expected the WC-135s continued their sampling regimen, collecting baseline data. These missions included a daily flight by 56th WRS crews from Yokota AB to Eielson AFB and from Yokota AB to Ching Chuan Kang AB in Taiwan (or back), as well as a daily flight from McClellan AFB over 90° North, all flown at the 700mb level (10,000ft/3,048m). A sudden spike in the presence of any radioactive material would indicate that a detonation likely occurred, and other AFTAC assets would be activated to determine its location and size. This also had the effect of verifying foreign compliance with the any test bans.

Polar missions, essential for the weather database, were flown, in part, along the 'Ptarmigan Track', the world's oldest weather track (established in 1947). A typical mission would be flown at the 500-millibar pressure altitude (just over 18,000ft – 5,486m), WC-135Bs gathered 'horizontal' data such as wind speed and direction, temperature, latitude, longitude, time, and date. Other observations include air turbulence, icing, and cloud covers. Sensitivities of each observation were acute, with temperature differences of 3° or wind changes of 15kts (27.7km/h) sufficient to require a new series of

Opposite: Several of the WC-135Bs were delivered without the IFR system, but they were all eventually equipped with it. Not only did missions cover long distances, they were often at altitudes that led to excessive fuel consumption. *Photo by Stephen Miller*

Top: WC-135Bs replaced WB-50 and WB-47s in long-range weather missions, as well as medium-altitude atmospheric sampling missions. *Author's collection*

Right: In the wake of the Chernobyl nuclear disaster, WC-135B 61-2672 was among those aircraft that tracked the radioactive plume as it spread across Europe and elsewhere. *Photo by the author*

observations. 'Vertical' data were collected at approximately 450nm (833km) intervals by dropsondes ejected through a pneumatic ejection tube. Dropsondes measured temperature, pressure, and humidity every 500ft (152m) as they descended. At selected intervals (varying between two and 20 minutes), both the 'horizontal' and 'vertical' data were fed into an on-board computer which integrated the data with the other information for storage and eventual broadcast via single-side band radio to military and civilian weather stations worldwide. Other 55th WRS sampling flights 'over the top' began from Eielson AFB. The WC-135B flew at the 700mb level (10,000ft/3,048m) along the 150° West longitude line until reaching 90° North, then proceeded south along the 30° East longitude line. Passing the Norwegian coast the airplane would climb to the 200mb level (39,000ft/11,887m) prior to recovery at RAF Mildenhall.

The weather mission ended following the 6th February 1974 directive that effective 1st July 1974 WC-135Bs would be used only on atmospheric sampling missions. WC-135Bs supported ongoing civilian weather and scientific research long after this date. For example, on 15th January 1979 two WC-135Bs operating from Ascension Island in the Southern Atlantic Ocean 'launched 1,945 dropsondes from heights between 30,000 and 37,000ft [9,144 and 11,277m] in support of the United Nations World Meteorological Organization's attempts to gather information on atmospheric and oceanic phenomena'.

In addition to their atomic sampling mission to assess foreign nuclear capabilities, WC-135Bs served in other military and humanitarian roles. They routinely provided weather reconnaissance for B-52 ARC LIGHT and SR-71 GIANT SCALE missions, as well as recovery of film capsules ejected from KH-8 GAMBIT 3 satellites. In November 1969 a WC-135B conducted a 'sampling' mission of the ejecta from the eruption of the Taal volcano in the Philippines. Two WC-135Bs (61-2666 and 61-2672) provided atmospheric sampling

from RAF Mildenhall during April and May 1986 following the nuclear reactor accident at the Chernobyl facility in the Soviet Union. They collected aerial samples from around the world to determine the extent, amount, and effects of radiation released by the destroyed Soviet reactor. WC-135B 61-2674 also flew sampling missions from a different location. After the 11th March 2011 magnitude 8.9 earthquake and tsunami that severely damaged the Japanese Fukushima Daiichi nuclear power plant, WC-135W 61-2667 conducted flights from Eielson AFB as part of Operation TOMADACHI to measure the level of radioactive atmospheric contamination. During its 6-week deployment to Alaska the aircraft flew more than 51,000nm (94,452km) to collect samples over the Western and Northern Pacific Ocean.

Beginning in 1988 WC-135Bs were modified to carry STAR CAST. This electro-optical system was 'designed to photograph high speed objects in support of several strategic research and development programs', as well as NASA space shuttle tests. On the WC-135B, part of the STAR CAST system replaced the port U-1 foil collector. In addition, a 30in (76.2cm) optical window was installed in the middle of the cargo door at FS480, and a 14in 35.5cm) optical window inserted higher and farther forward on the cargo door at FS460. The

WC-135B 61-2667 flew multiple missions from Eielson AFB to assess the spread of radiation after the 2011 tsunami that damaged the Japanese *Daiichi* nuclear plant. The airplane routinely acquired external contamination, requiring a wash down. *USAF photo*

At least three WC-135Bs (61-2665, 61-2670, and 61-2672) were configured with the STAR CAST optical system, indicated by the circular window in the cargo door. *Photo by Peter Zastrow via Stephen Miller*

first STAR CAST mission was flown on 29th September 1988 during the launch of the Space Shuttle *Discovery*. Orbiting 120nm (222km) east of Cape Canaveral, the WC-135B recorded the launch of the shuttle and the separation of its solid boosters. The WC-135B crew then assisted the Coast Guard in locating and retrieving the boosters.

WC-135B operations were not without hazard, and on at least one occasion a WC-135B was reportedly an unwitting participant in a Soviet laser beam incident. While conducting operations during Soviet ballistic missile test launches into the Pacific Ocean in 1987, the crew of a WC-135 'reported being affected by what appeared to be a laser beam and the copilot was examined for eye damage – this was later found to be inconsequential.' The laser involved is believed to have been part of a ship-based air defense system. WC-135Bs are said to have supported Operations DESERT SHIELD and DESERT STORM, collecting weather data useful in predicting the effects of Iraqi chemical and biological weapons should they have been released into the atmosphere. The WC-135Bs are believed to have operated from RAF Mildenhall, but are not known to have flown missions directly from or into the Gulf combat zone.

WC-135Bs were originally assigned to the 55th WRS (nicknamed '*The Pole Vaulters*') at McClellan AFB and the 56th WRS at Yokota AB, with the airplanes periodically rotating between squadrons. Both squadrons were part of the 9th WRW of the Air Weather Service (along with Boeing WB-47Es and General Dynamics WB-57Fs). The 56th WRS was inactivated on 15th January 1972, and weather operations from Yokota AB were conducted as a 9th WRW operating location (OL) until the wing's disbandment in 1975, when it was replaced by the 41st RW&RW and the OL assigned to it. The 41st RW&RW was inactivated on 31st July 1989 and the 55th WRS was attached directly to Air Rescue Service. Further organizational changes followed the sweeping alterations in the Air Force. On 1st June 1992 the 55th WRS was reassigned directly to AMC, and on 1st January 1993, the 55th WRS was reassigned to the 60th AW. The 55th WRS was finally inactivated on 1st October 1993 and the WC-135Bs transferred to Detachment 1, 24th RS, 55th Wing at Offutt AFB. The 24th RS was inactivated on 30th June 1994, and the airplanes were reassigned on 1st July to the 45th RS, 55th Wing. Call signs for sampling missions are '*Samp*' followed by the last three digits of their tail number.

Throughout their operational lifetime the WC-135B fleet was slowly reduced in number as aircraft were assigned to different roles or retired. During the early 1970s three WC-135Bs (61-2668, 61-2669, and 61-2671) were modified into C-135C VIP transports. Another three (61-2665, 61-2673, and 61-2674) were eventually

relegated to AMARG, two (61-2670 and 61-2672) were slated for conversion to OC-135Bs for the OPEN SKIES program, and one (61-2666) planned for use as the BIG SAFARI NC-135W evaluation platform, leaving only 61-2667 which was then used variously as a sampler, a flight-deck trainer for E-3s and EC-135Hs, and a STAR CAST platform. This final reduction in fleet size was tied to senior Air Force leadership animus and myopia. During the late 1980s, CINCPACAF General Merrill A 'Tony' McPeak sought to restructure the Air Weather Service so that all weather assets were assigned directly to combat wings, but Air Force Chief of Staff General Larry D Welch rejected this plan. Once McPeak became Air Force Chief of Staff in 1990, however, the writing was on the wall, and the elimination of AWS served as a harbinger for the restructuring of the Air Force as a whole. The Soviets had previously announced that it would ratify the Comprehensive Nuclear Test Ban Treaty, and ended all nuclear testing on 24th October 1990. With the dissolution of the Soviet Union on 25th December 1991, McPeak saw no further need for a 'one-trick pony' aircraft which did not have a conventional combat or combat support mission. Rumors abounded that the WC-135 fleet would be grounded or even scrapped, especially because of reportedly severe corrosion problems. The US air sampling fleet appeared doomed. As the final AWS commander noted, 'we were trailblazers for the likes of Strategic Air Command going away, new names for Tactical Air Command, MAC, etc. and consolidated wings among a number of McPeak ideas.' Thanks to the People's Republic of China, however, the WC-135 fleet not only survived but doubled in size.

By the end of September 1993 US intelligence sources detected indicators for an imminent Red Chinese nuclear test at their Lop Nor facility. With no WC-135B flight crews remaining mission ready, the JCS tasked Detachment 2, 645th Materiel Squadron to use its WC-135 testbed and an AFTAC back-end crew. With typical BIG SAFARI speed and effectiveness, 61-2666 was quickly configured and ready for sampling. On 5th October the PRC detonated an 80kt warhead in an underground shaft, and the next day 61-2666 flew 17.5 hours non-stop from Greenville to Kadena AB. During the next two weeks, the airplane flew four DISTANT SCOOP missions averaging 12.5 hours each. It returned to McClellan AFB on 17th October to remove the AFTAC sampling equipment and drop off the samples it had collected, returning to Greenville the following day. The success of this mission demonstrated the importance of the WC-135 and the ill-considered intent to eliminate the program entirely. As part of a 1995 effort to consolidate disparate airframes operating under a variety of technical orders and flight manuals, all former WC-135B airframes not otherwise redesignated were assigned the WC-135W MDS. Concurrently, WC-135B 61-2667 was reassigned to operational status, and former EC-135C 62-3582 was modified into the sole WC-135C. Perhaps disingenuously, McPeak later acknowledged the valuable contribution of the WC-135 to nuclear nonproliferation, saying that 'an airborne sniffer of some kind' was essential to detecting nuclear weapons.

Retention of a WC-135 aerial sampling capability proved far more significant in the post Cold War world than McPeak could have imagined in 1992. Both France and the PRC continued nuclear weapons testing until 1996. Pakistan conducted atomic tests in 1998, as did its longtime adversary India. Most ominously, North Korea has conducted four atomic weapon tests between 2006 and 2016. WC-135W 61-2667 was spotted at Kadena AB on 8th February 2013 in preparation for the North Korean 7kt test on 12th February. When the North Koreans detonated a 10kt nuclear device on 6th January 2016, which they claimed to be a hydrogen bomb, US officials made a highly public show of sending a WC-135 (possibly WC-135C 62-3582) to the area to 'sniff' for traces of any fusion that would confirm it was indeed a hydrogen bomb (it was not). WC-135s also conducted sampling missions to detect possible Iranian production of fissile material that could be or had been 'weaponized' as part of the CONSTANT GULF and IRISH EMERALD programs.

WC-135s now carry a crew of as many as 30 people, including three pilots, two navigators, a deployment commander, a mission commander, as many as three special equipment operators (SEOs), three atmospheric technicians, and up to 18 maintenance personnel who will regenerate the airplane when it lands at foreign bases and repair it as needed.

There are no plans to re-engine the WC-135s as the Boeing conversion line is closed. Instead, a KC-135R from AMARG would be reactivated and configured for sampling. Alternatively, a C-32 or the C-40 might be converted. At present, the WC-135s will remain in service indefinitely.

Three WC-135Bs, including 61-2668, were converted into C-135C VIP transports beginning shortly after this photo was taken at McGuire AFB on 31st May 1972. *Photo by Stephen Miller*

To monitor a 1993 underground nuclear test in the People's Republic of China, the BIG SAFARI testbed WC-135B 61-2666 was hastily modified for the DISTANT SCOOP mission. *Photo courtesy USAF*

WC-135Bs were assigned to McClellan AFB, where AFTAC had a significant presence, and to Yokota AB, an ideal location as the western terminus of sampling flights to monitor nuclear tests in Asia. *Photo by the author*

NC-135W 61-2666 prepares to depart RAF Mildenhall. Other than retaining its TF33-P-5 engines, it is externally identical to the RIVET JOINT, although it does not have an operational capability. It has served in the air sampling role.
Author's collection

ACC inherited all of the aircraft in the 55th SRW, including the WC-135s which it eagerly sought to retire. 61-2670 wears an OF tail code with the ACC serial block and patch on the nose, but with the original *Videmus Omnia* 55th SRW patch.
Photo by Joe Bruch

Lark 21 on final to Runway 21 at Perth, Australia, on 11th September 1989. WC-135s were regular visitors to a number of locations in the Southern Hemisphere to collect baseline atmospheric data.
Photo by David Eyre

WC-135B/C/W INDIVIDUAL AIRCRAFT

61-2665 On 30th March 1966, this C-135B was converted into a WC-135B. It received STAR CAST by November 1988. In 1995 it became a WC-135W and was equipped with hush kits on its TF33 engines to meet Stage 3 noise limitations. Returned to AMARC on 11th September 1996, as AAC0107 due to lack of funding (see Appendix III).

61-2666 This C-135B was converted to a WC-135B 29th September 1965. Assigned in the late 1980s to the E-Systems facility at Greenville as part of Det 2, 55th Wing. It carried the highly unofficial 'MF' tail code (for Majors Field) and was nicknamed *Loose Caboose* in honor of a late Detachment 2 crewmember who had become something of an institution in the reconnaissance community. During May 1995, the single WC-135B used by Detachment 2, 645th MatS, located at the E-Systems facility at Majors Field was redesignated as a WC-135W. The airplane had been used as a test platform for new equipment developed by E-Systems for use in the many RC-135s maintained by the company. In addition, the airplane served as a trainer for the Air Force flight crews assigned to Det 2. As originally configured, it was externally little different from its sister WC-135Bs, distinguishable primarily by small fairings or attachments for equipment under evaluation. In early 1995, E-Systems added cheeks and a hog nose, as well as a complete set of SIGINT antennae, to the airplane. Externally, it is now indistinguishable from the RC-135W except for retaining TF33-P-5 engines. Internally, it has a fundamentally complete reconnaissance suite akin to that in the operational RIVET JOINTs, but its primary role remains the test and evaluation of new advanced systems for all BIG SAFARI efforts. By 1999 it was redesignated the sole NC-135W.

61-2667 This C-135B was redesignated a WC-135B on 16th March 1966. It later served from 24th March 1977, with the 966th AWACTS at Tinker AFB as an air refueling receiver trainer for E-3 Sentry crews. It returned to weather duties with the 55th WRS following its replacement at Tinker AFB on 19th December 1984. It was transferred to the 10th ACCS at RAF Mildenhall on 22nd April 1989 for use as a flight deck trainer. It received STAR CAST by 3rd April 1990. Subsequently, it was reassigned to the 24th RS, 55th Wing at Offutt AFB and redesignated a TC-135B in 1993. It was reassigned to the 45th RS on 1st July 1994. In 1995 it was redesignated a WC-135W.

61-2668 This C-135B was converted on 7th September 1965 to a WC-135B and utilized as such until October 1971. It was demodified and placed in storage at MASDC from 20th July to 1st November 1972 and given the PCN code CA002. It was modified into staff configuration and reactivated as a C-135B on 3rd April 1973. On 6th September 1973 it was further converted into a C-135C. By 1996 it had been scrapped at Tinker AFB (see Appendix III).

61-2669 This C-135B was converted on 7th September 1965 to a WC-135B and so used until January 1972. It was then demodified and relegated to MASDC on 20th July 1972, and given the PCN code CA003. Beginning 8th November 1972 it was modified into staff configuration and reactivated as a C-135B on 21st April 1973. On 11th October 1973 it was redesignated a C-135C. It then became the second SPECKLED TROUT aircraft on 15th October 1976. On 13th January 2006 it was retired and placed on static display at the Air Force Flight Test Center Museum at Edwards AFB.

61-2670 This C-135B was converted on 1st September 1965 to a WC-135B. It was scheduled to receive the STAR CAST system in December 1988. During 1996 it was converted into the third OC-135B assigned to the 45th RS, 55th Wing at Offutt AFB.

61-2671 This C-135B was converted on 21st September 1965 to a WC-135B. During March 1973 it was converted back into a C-135B. On 5th April 1974 it was again converted, this time to staff configuration and designated a C-135C, assigned to Det. 1, 89th MAW at Hickam AFB. It was withdrawn from use on 30th October 1991 due to excessive corrosion, while undergoing PDM at Tinker AFB, and placed on static display there with a 707 vertical stabilizer (see Appendix III).

61-2672 This C-135B was converted on 30th March 1965 into a WC-135B. It received the STAR CAST modification in January 1989. In early 1990 it was noted in a new paint scheme of white fuselage top, vertical stabilizer, engine turbofan nacelles, and nose. During 1994 it began conversion into the second OC-135B, and was redesignated as such in 1996. It remains assigned to the 45th RS, 55th Wing at Offutt AFB.

61-2673 This C-135B was modified on 17th March 1965 into a WC-135B. Noted in 1993 with the nickname *River City Gambler*. It was scheduled for conversion into an OC-135B, but due to extensive corrosion it was instead placed in AMARC on 28th September 1993 as AACA0090 (see Appendix III).

61-2674 This C-135B was modified on 1st September 1965 into a WC-135B. In August 1988 it became the first WC-135B to incorporate the STAR CAST system. Beginning in July 1992 it underwent conversion into the first OC-135B assigned to the 55th Wing at Offutt AFB. It was determined to be unsuitable for future operations and on 21st August 1997 it was relegated to AMARG as AACA0115 (see Appendix III). Reasons for its demise include excessive corrosion and unacceptable levels of residual radiation acquired during the 1986 Chernobyl incident.

62-3582 This EC-135C was demodified in 1999 and converted into a WC-135C. It is assigned to the 45th RS, 55th Wing at Offutt AFB.

Flying WC-135Bs was a highly desirable job, especially for SAC tanker pilots eager to get out of alert duty, see the world, and log as much as 1,000 hours of flying time in a year. *Photo by Richard Vandervord*

62-3582 is the only weather sampler '135 that was not built as such by Boeing. It began life as a KC-135B airborne command post. It was converted from an EC-135C into the sole WC-135C. *Author's collection*

PHOTINT AIRCRAFT AND OPERATIONS

RC-135A PACER SWAN

In 1962 MATS ordered nine RC-135As as part of the PACER SWAN program to replace 14 RB-50F Superfortresses and C-118As assigned to unclassified aerial mapping and geodetic survey duties in non-hostile airspace for DoD and other US Government agencies. The designation 'RC-135A' was introduced in the 1962 edition of DoD Directive 4505.6 *Designation, Redesignation and Naming of Military Aircraft* as a result of the purchase of these nine photo mapping airplanes. This designation has been occasionally and incorrectly applied to the three KC-135A-II OFFICE BOY reconnaissance airplanes.

The RC-135As differed significantly from the balance of MATS's C-135A fleet with over 70 major engineering changes. For example, the RC-135As had an electrically powered wing-flap secondary drive mechanism (whereas the KC-135As had a manually powered wing-flap secondary drive mechanism), and a second air conditioning pack was added to the RC-135A to cool the on-board photo-mapping systems. The RC-135A lacked an IFR system as the intended mission duration did not exceed the airplane's takeoff fuel capacity. The airplanes utilized a fuel dump tube and were never equipped with an air refueling boom.

The RC-135A program ran into problems almost immediately. Additional RC-135A program funds were disapproved in 1963 after the RC-135A was shown to be 27% over budget, and the number of RC-135As on order was reduced to six. A further 20% decrease in 1964 program funding reduced the final number of RC-135As to four. Canceled RC-135A serial numbers include 63-8062 through 63-8066. Production was scheduled for one airplane per month from September through November 1965, with three basic airframes (minus mapping equipment) to be delivered directly to the operational unit and one airplane (including mapping equipment) delivered by February 1966 to Wright-Patterson AFB for testing. Intended initial operational capability (IOC) date was July 1966. Each RC-135A airframe eventually cost $11 million, and each AN/USQ-28 Photo Mapping System cost $24 million.

The RC-135A's first flight was on 28th April 1965, and the first airplane was delivered on 14th September 1965 to the 1371st Mapping and Charting Squadron (MCS), 1370th Photo Mapping

Wing (PMW) at Turner AFB, GA. The 1370th PMW reported to the APCS, which itself answered directly to MATS Headquarters. The first airplane delivered to Turner AFB lacked mapping equipment and was used initially as an aircrew and ground maintenance trainer.

On 1st January 1966 MATS was reorganized into MAC and the APCS was redesignated the Aerospace Audio-Visual Service (AAVS). During August 1967 the 1370th PMW moved to Forbes AFB, KS, and flight testing moved there from Wright-Patterson AFB. Continued problems delayed the IOC to January 1967. Disappointing system and flight test results again deferred the IOC to January 1968, another deadline which would not be met.

On 1st October 1968 the 1370th PMW became the Aerial Cartographic and Geodetic Service (ACGS), with the 1371st MCS RC-135As and crews reassigned to the 1st Aerospace Cartographic and Geodetic Squadron (ACGSq). Category III Test and Evaluation flights were conducted from Forbes AFB from 14th April through 30th June 1969, and RC-135A 63-8058 flew the first operational mapping mission on 15th September 1969. A Category III Follow-on Evaluation was undertaken from 1st November 1969 through 30th April 1970, with operations conducted from Forbes AFB, Brasilia, Brazil, and Santiago, Chile. Only three RC-135As were available, and of these only two were equipped with the AN/USQ-28 mapping system. SAC loaned a KC-135A to ACGS for 30-day intervals every other month during these tests for pilot proficiency. This proficiency trainer may be the source of the occasional reports suggesting the existence of five RC-135As. KC-135As so used were 57-1483 and 57-1514 from Altus AFB, OK, and 56-3639 from Dyess AFB, TX.

Primary purposes of Category III follow-on tests were the development of operational standards for the AN/USQ-28 system, evaluation of the RC-135A and AN/USQ-28 in an operational environment, and determination of the adequacy of the logistical system required to support an aerial survey team in the field. In addition to routine testing, the flights from Santiago would map the border separating Chile and Argentina as part of Project AF 70-14, an effort to help resolve the border dispute between those nations. The first successful flight as part of this project took place on 15th March 1970; the final flight was on 28th April 1970. Flight results were shared with the host nation (a representative from each country flew on each mapping mission), providing a measure of economic

RC-135A 63-8058 underwent test and evaluation flights at Wright-Patterson AFB. This 9th September 1966 image shows nose emblem and red band on the vertical stabilizer. *Photo by Richard Sullivan via Stephen Miller*

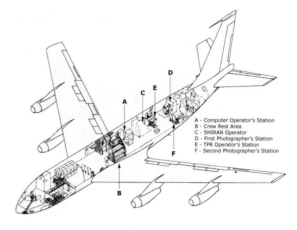

A - Computer Operator's Station
B - Crew Rest Area
C - SHIRAN Operator
D - First Photographer's Station
E - TPR Operator's Station
F - Second Photographer's Station

The crew of the first successful operational flight of the AN/USQ-28 system on 13th September 1969 surrounds Squadron Commander Colonel T P Tatum in front of 63-8058. *Author's collection*

development to these countries as well as the other participating nations – Colombia, Ecuador, and Venezuela.

Results of the follow-on test showed that the RC-135A could deploy efficiently to overseas locations for long periods, although not without some inconveniences. Contaminated fuel made engine starts difficult at best, and the need for 600-plus gallons (2,271 liters) of distilled water for each water-injection augmented takeoff complicated the logistics requirements of remote operations. Existing problems with the S-band high precision ranging (S-band HIRAN, further abbreviated as SHIRAN) system (described below) remained unresolved, notably compromising the RC-135A's mission capability.

Despite progress with individual components, the complete RC-135A system had still not been declared fully operational by November 1970. The program also suffered as a result of growing US commitments in Southeast Asia, which drained funds away from non-combat program development. By May 1971 many considered the RC-135A a program without a future, in part due to the increase in satellite mapping capability and to disillusionment with the program's overall lack of success. As a result, the RC-135A program ended by 1972.

Missions flown as part of the RC-135A system validation included those in South America and a series of flights in February 1971 from Eielson AFB across Alaska and the northern US as part of a project designed to measure snow depth and thus predict springtime melted snow runoff for flood control planning. Mission altitudes were typically between 30,000 and 40,000ft (9,144 and 12,192m) at airspeeds designed for maximum endurance in the project area. Flights usually originated from an airfield in the vicinity of the project area rather than being flown as 'round-robin' sorties from Turner AFB or Forbes AFB. Projected mapping capability was 40,000 miles^2 (103,592km^2) per day.

Flight crews consisted of a pilot, copilot, flight engineer, photo/inertial navigator, (SHIRAN) navigator, computer operator, terrain profile recorder (TPR) operator, and first and second photographers. Not all crewmembers flew on every mission, as the TPR operator, for example, was not needed on a purely photographic mission. Colonel T P Tatum was the first operational commander of the RC-135A squadron.

Heart of the RC-135A mapping system was the Kollman Instrument Corporation AN/USQ-28 Aerial Electro-Photo Mapping System, designed for the following mapping missions:

1. Aerial Electronic Geodetic Survey measured the distance along a course flown between two SHIRAN stations, from which the actual sea level distance between the two sites could be calculated.
2. Electronically Positioned Aerial Photography combined a sophisticated camera mapping system with an airborne inertial navigation system that steered the airplane and recorded its position during each photograph. The tip and tilt of each camera (with respect to the vertical axis of the airplane flight path) was recorded on each film frame. Distances were measured from as many as four SHIRAN stations and were integrated with the high precision navigation system [HIPERNAS (*sic*)] inertial navigation platform. Prior to such flights in the RC-135A, very little HIRAN-controlled photography had been accomplished.
3. Control Point Photography allowed accurate determination of the position of a ground site without requiring any ground surveying.
4. Precision Mapping Photography was a less sophisticated form of Electronically Positioned Aerial Photography, lacking the SHIRAN airplane positioning feature. Nonetheless, landmarks of known position could be used to manually update the airplane's position (already quite accurate given the HIPERNAS positioning) via the navigator's viewfinder.
5. Airborne Terrain Profiling determined the actual profile of terrain overflown by the RC-135A. A barostatic system recorded minute variations in airplane altitude while a narrow beam radar system measured the airplane's actual height above ground.
6. Airborne Geodetic Azimuth Determination was a night-time operation designed to provide an increase in surveyed accuracy of geographical regions not suited to triangulation, such as long narrow chains of islands.

Other projected missions include airborne gravity surveys and weather radar mapping.

Aerial Electronic Geodetic Survey and Precision Mapping Photography were the most common missions undertaken. Airborne Terrain Profiling could be (and often was) combined with any other mission. Electronically Positioned Aerial Photography and Control Point photography had not reached operational status when the RC-135A program ended. Airborne Geodetic Azimuth Determination missions were never declared operational due to lack of equipment.

The RC-135A's navigator's station was redesigned to incorporate both a ground viewfinder and the HIPERNAS, as well as standard KC-135 navigational equipment. The viewfinder looked out of a

Left: The First Photographer's station on the RC-135A controlled both electronic and manual mapping. *Photo P39352 courtesy Boeing*

Below left: The Terrain Profile Recorder followed the contour of terrain below the RC-135A using a radar signal. In the back of this photo is the SHIRAN operator's position. *Photo H30097 courtesy Boeing*

Below right: The RC-135A navigator's station incorporated a viewfinder (lower left) and a rudimentary computer navigation system (lower center). *Photo P39349 courtesy Boeing*

Bottom left: A sliding door was mounted on rails to cover the two KC-6A cameras when not in use. Viewfinder window is immediately aft of the nose radome. *Photo P39952 courtesy Boeing*

Bottom right: The TPR antenna was located within a modified fairing in the boom pod. Essentially a large radar altimeter, it was accurate to within 10ft (3m). *Photo P39354 courtesy Boeing*

window located on the bottom of the forward fuselage just aft of the nose radome and provided a 60° field of view, with limits of 100° forward, 35° aft, and 50° either side of the centerline.

The AN/USQ-28 system used two tandem KC-6A cameras located in the lower fuselage compartment normally occupied by two cells of the forward body fuel tank. The aft camera was the primary mapping camera, and was co-mounted with the HIPERNAS inertial platform. The cameras had a 30in (76.2cm) diameter 2.5in (6.35m) thick optically ground window in the bottom of the fuselage providing 120° of panoramic coverage. An external track-mounted door slid aft to expose the camera window. The camera compartment was pressurized and temperature regulated for optimum camera performance.

Each camera had a 6in (15.2cm) focal length, f/5.0 aperture, color-corrected Geocon IV lens, providing 90° angular coverage on a 9in²

(58cm²) film format. Resolution was sufficient to distinguish 10ft (3m) size objects on the ground from an altitude of 40,000ft (12,192m). The KC-6 development was protracted due to integration problems with the RC-135A, but the camera eventually vindicated itself following installation in the General Dynamics-converted WB-57F.

The Terrain Profile Recorder Antenna was a 44in (111.7cm) stabilized radar dish located in a modified fairing in the boom pod. The TPR had a vertical accuracy of 10ft (3m) from altitudes ranging from 1,500 to 40,000ft (457 to 12,192m).

An Airborne Digital Computer was an integral part of the navigation subsystem which collected and compiled navigational and supporting information for accurate mapping as well as airplane guidance. This computer required a considerable ground warm-up

prior to each flight, and most aborts were due to the failure of this system.

On the underside of the fuselage slightly behind and below the aft wing root was a small structure which provided a point-light source for the Airborne Geodetic Azimuth Determination system using the Sodano method of azimuth measurement. Theodolites at two ground stations tracked the RC-135A as it flew across the line connecting the two stations, with aircraft radio pulses synchronizing the camera exposures of theodolite readings at the stations. From these measurements the azimuth between the stations could then be determined.

Although the RC-135A never achieved fully operational status, it was not necessarily due to the failure of the idea or its execution. The RC-135A was seen as a bridge between existing atmospheric aerial photo mapping technology and the as-yet unrealized use of satellites in photo mapping. Eclipsed financially and operationally by the war in Southeast Asia, the RC-135A lost the aggressive support it needed to overcome its forbidding technological problems such as the limitations of its on-board computer. The RC-135A was the first airplane designed specifically for geodetic survey, and in short, the airplane and its systems were 'too much, too late'.

Following their operational lives as photo-mapping platforms, the four RC-135As were demodified and some were assigned to SAC as Command Support Aircraft (CSAs) – 'demodified tanker/logistics support, cargo carrier, and troop transport aircraft'. All were eventually converted in 1979 under program R-Q6076(1)

by E-Systems into KC-135Ds, and in 1990 received TF33-PW-102 engines, although they were not redesignated as KC-135Es. During 2007 they were retired to AMARC.

RC-135A INDIVIDUAL AIRCRAFT

63-8058 Delivered as an RC-135A to the 1371st MCS, 1370th PMW at Turner AFB, which moved to Forbes AFB in August 1967. On 1st October 1968 the 1371st MCS was redesignated the 1st ACGS. By 1972 the airplane was relegated to SAC for CSA duties with the 55th SRW at Offutt AFB. Eventually it served as a flight-deck trainer loaned to the 132nd AREFS, 101st AREFW, Maine ANG, on 19th July 1978. E-Systems converted it into a KC-135D in 1979, after which it was assigned to the 305th AREFW at Grissom AFB. Retired to AMARC on 19th March 2007 as AACA0152 (see Appendix III).

63-8059 Delivered as an RC-135A to the 1371st MCS, 1370th PMW at Turner AFB, which moved to Forbes AFB in August 1967. On 1st October 1968 the 1371st MCS was redesignated the 1st ACGS. By the end of 1971 it was relegated to SAC for CSA duties with the 55th SRW at Offutt AFB. E-Systems converted it into a KC-135D in 1979, after which it was assigned to the 305th AREFW at Grissom AFB. Retired to AMARC on 14th March 2007 as AACA0151 (see Appendix III).

63-8060 Delivered as an RC-135A to the 1371st MCS, 1370th PMW at Turner AFB, which moved to Forbes AFB in August 1967. On 1st October 1968 the 1371st MCS was redesignated the 1st ACGS. After demodification, 63-8060 became the first '135 stored at AMARC, however briefly, from 29th June through 27th July 1972, and given the PCN CA001. It was then relegated to SAC for CSA duties with the 55th SRW at Offutt AFB. Eventually it served as a flight-deck trainer loaned to the 197th AREFS, 161st AREFG, Arizona ANG on 30th June 1978. E-Systems converted it into a KC-135D in 1979, after which it was assigned to the 305th AREFW at Grissom AFB. Retired to AMARC on 28th March 2007 as AACA0153 (see Appendix III).

63-8061 Delivered as an RC-135A to the 1371st MCS, 1370th PMW at Turner AFB, which moved to Forbes AFB in August 1967. On 1st October 1968 the 1371st MCS was redesignated the 1st ACGS. By the end of 1971 it was relegated to SAC for CSA duties with the 55th SRW at Offutt AFB. E-Systems converted it into a KC-135D in 1979, after which it was assigned to the 305th AREFW at Grissom AFB. Retired to AMARC on 4th April 2007 as AACA0154 (see Appendix III).

Above: The Air Force originally ordered nine RC-135As, but cost overruns and technical problems slashed the final number to just four airplanes. *Photo P39303 courtesy Boeing*

Right: The beginning and the end of '135 deliveries. RC-135A 63-8061 sits next to 55-3118 (by this time an EC-135K) during June 1966. *Photo courtesy Boeing*

OC-135B OPEN SKIES

In the years leading to the height of the Cold War, American fears of an unknown Soviet military capability were considerable. By 1955 the US believed itself to be well behind the Soviet Union in terms of bomber production, with doomsayers and pundits loudly lamenting a fictitious 'bomber gap'. This gap was largely the product of faulty intelligence collection and analysis, and emphasized the need for more accurate sources of intelligence on Soviet capabilities – especially for a surprise attack – than were available. The mid-1950s was also a time of American economic growth. President Eisenhower was committed to this booming prosperity but linked it to a balanced budget. To accomplish this, federal spending (especially defense spending) had to be kept to an absolute minimum. From Ike's perspective, the US could ill afford any unnecessary military expenditure just to keep up with inaccurately assessed Soviet military capability.

For these and other reasons, in 1955 Eisenhower proposed the OPEN SKIES program to the heads of state gathered at the July Geneva Conference. OPEN SKIES would allow each participant to overfly the territory of another and take photographs of military installations and forces, thus reassuring the observing nation with a more realistic appraisal of the other nation's preparedness and thereby minimizing its own defense expenditures. It would also have the added benefit of constraining the growing arms race. Khrushchev viewed Eisenhower's Geneva proposal as legalized espionage, but was not averse to accepting the idea provided the US Congress would allow Soviet planes to overfly American territory. The Soviet Presidium, however, rejected the proposal outright, and Congress never considered the plan. Ike had anticipated this and already planted the seeds of what would become the Lockheed U-2, a platform that would accomplish OPEN SKIES goals for the US without Soviet acquiescence.

In a speech nearly 35 years later on 12th May 1989, US President George H W Bush resurrected Eisenhower's OPEN SKIES proposal. After a series of international conferences, representatives of 25 nations signed the treaty in Helsinki, Finland, on 22nd March 1992, and the US Senate ratified the treaty on 6th August 1993. The OPEN SKIES treaty became effective in 2002 with 34 states participating. Each signatory is required to accept a minimum number of overflights – known as 'quota' flights – per year, with Russia and the United States each obligated to accept up to 42 flights. American operational oversight of the OPEN SKIES mission is through the Defense Threat Reduction Agency (DTRA – in a fit of bureaucratese this would later be redesignated the 'Defense Threat Reduction Agency & USSTRATCOM Center for Combating WMD & Standing Joint Force Headquarters-Elimination').

The goal of the new OPEN SKIES program, much like Eisenhower's, was to 'foster transparency about military activity and reduce the risk of war and miscalculation, especially in Europe.' Given that the airplane is committed exclusively to treaty verification, initial hopes for any collateral intelligence from OPEN SKIES flights were minimal. Many American officials believed that the airplanes would collect little information not otherwise available via more sophisticated and definitive sources such as satellites. Indeed, according to the US On-Site Inspection Agency (OSIA), the real benefits from OPEN SKIES would be 'a more open relationship between participants of the treaty'. Surprisingly, despite their official use as a treaty verification platform, the airplanes offer an unintended Open Source Intelligence (OSINT) component, providing a timely and independent corroboration of other sources, especially in in hot spots such as Ukraine and Crimea. Moreover, the imagery reduces, if not eliminates, denial and duplicity. All data collected on any flight is available in its entirety to any signatory of the treaty – what is collected by one nation is available to all. This makes it extremely difficult for an overflown nation to deny what is clearly observable.

Selecting the OPEN SKIES airplanes was fairly straightforward: the treaty required that they not be previously or currently configured for reconnaissance or intelligence gathering, and that they be large enough to carry not only the observing nation's representatives but a representative from the nation being overflown. Canada and Belgium were among the first nations to conduct OPEN SKIES flights over Russia using C-130s. Other representative aircraft include Sweden's Saab 340B, Great Britain's Hawker Siddeley HS.780 Andover C1(PR), and Turkey's CASA C-235. The former Soviet Union selected several Antonov An-30 *Clank* twin-engine turboprop planes with limited range, capacity, and few passenger comforts. Russia later added at least one Tupolev Tu-154M *Careless*, with two Tupolev Tu-214ONs identified as replacements. (States that do not own a suitably modified OPEN SKIES airplane may use those of any signatory nation. The observation crew would be from the 'borrowing' nation but the flight crew would be from the 'owning' nation.)

For the United States a KC-135 variant was an excellent and economical choice. Early candidates included any of the WC-135Bs and the two TC-135s given their ability to be refueled in flight. The TC-135s were in heavy demand by RC-135 squadrons and the WC-135B sampling mission (apparently not considered a prior reconnaissance mission under the treaty's terms) was on the cusp of elimination, so the WC-135B was chosen by default. The number of airplanes converted (in this case three) was based on the minimum mission requirements to fly 15 sorties per year, increasing to 42 annual sorties at full treaty implementation. The specific WC-135Bs were selected on the basis of their maintenance records, and were designated OC-135Bs ('O' for 'observation'). The 1993 elimination of flight engineers from the OC-135s and WC-135s as a cost-saving measure meant that the MDS should change (owing to tech order demands) to OC-135Ws, but this change did not happen. Pending conversion of the first OC-135B, the US OPEN SKIES program used a modified Convair 580 operated by the Environmental Research Institute of Michigan under contract to OSIA. The first two OPEN SKIES demonstration flights took place over Hungary from 10th-12th July 1992 using the CV580, with 12 observing nations participating.

The Aeronautical Systems Center's 4950th TW Directorate of Aircraft Modification at Wright-Patterson AFB began conversion of the first OC-135B (61-2674) in December 1992. Modifications included the removal of all residual weather gathering and sampling gear, the STAR CAST equipment (but not the STAR CAST window on the port side of the fuselage – interestingly, 61-2674 was the first WC-135B to receive the STAR CAST modification), and the installation of the OPEN SKIES mission equipment. According to the treaty, all mission equipment must be 'off-the shelf', exportable with no technology transfer limitations, and limited to 30cm (11.8in) resolution for wet-film optical cameras and 50cm (19.7in) for synthetic aperture radar (SAR). Phase One modifications included two Chicago Aerial KS-87B oblique-mounted framing cameras on the left and right sides of the fuselage, one KS-87B vertical-mounted framing camera on the aircraft centerline, and a Chicago Aerial KA-91A panoramic camera for wide-area imagery from high altitudes. The airplane also received a Data Annotation/Recording and Mapping System (DARMS) as well as GPS. Additional equipment and interior modifications were surplus from the PACER LINK EC-135 upgrade. These include galleys, tables, latrines, lighting, and seating areas for up to 38 persons. Special film storage areas were installed as well. Additional optical windows were surplus from an unidentified program. These changes were completed by April 1993, with flight tests finished by 30th June 1993. The first OC-135B

Above: 61-2670 visits RAF Fairford along with an An-30 *Clank* (back left). Ventral fairing on the OC-135B is for the synthetic aperture radar. *Photo by Richard Vandervord*

Right: Conversion of the OC-135Bs was undertaken 'in house' at Wright-Patterson AFB. 61-2670 and 61-2672 were modified together during the second phase of the program. *Photo by Dave Brown*

demonstration flight in 61-2674 took place from 4th-12th February 1994 over Germany, and the first joint training mission occurred from 24th-31st August 1994 when American and Ukrainian crews overflew parts of the United States.

Phase Two of the modification process began in March 1994 to meet full operational capability for the program, including the conversion of two additional OC-135Bs. Initially this included 61-2673, but it was relegated to AMARC instead and 61-2670 and 61-2672 chosen instead. The two new OPEN SKIES jets would be configured similarly to 61-2674 but would also have a Goodyear/Loral UPD-8 synthetic aperture radar (SAR) from the McDonnell Douglas RF-4, one infrared line scanner (IRLS), and one video camera (all to be retrofitted to 61-2674 as well). All three airplanes were to be fitted with engine hush kits to meet European noise limits. Total cost for Phase Two was $51 million, with $7 million spent on upgrades to 61-2674, $18 million apiece for full modifications to 61-2670 and 61-2672, and $8 million for the hush kit program, although this was not implemented (the treaty was amended in 2003 so that all OPEN SKIES airplanes are exempt from noise and emission limits). The first demonstration flights for OC-135B 61-2672 took place 5th-17th July 1996 over the Czech Republic. OC-135B 61-2670 had its first demonstration flights on behalf of Slovakia over the United States from 9th-16th March 1997, and on behalf of the United States over Poland from 9th-20th May 1997. Demonstration flights continued until the 2002 implementation of the OPEN SKIES treaty, and the first OC-135B quota flight took place

over Russia from 7th-13th December 2002. By the end of 2013 there were over 1,000 observational flights.

The first OC-135B was assigned to the 55th WRS at McClellan AFB beginning in June 1993. With that unit's inactivation, the airplane was transferred on 1st October 1993, to the 24th RS, 55th Wing at Offutt AFB. On 30th June 1994, the 24th RS was inactivated and replaced by the 45th RS, and the OC-135B reassigned accordingly. For reasons that are ambiguous and somewhat contradictory, 61-2674 was retired to AMARG on 21st August 1997. Some sources suggest that the airplane had extensive corrosion; another claims that it had suffered excessive radiation from its role in monitoring the 1986 Chernobyl disaster. Most likely the US OPEN SKIES budget could simply no longer support a third airplane given that the cost for an OC-135B flight is about $2,500 per hour, with an annual budget for the entire program of only $7 million.

Flight crews from the 45th RS consist of three pilots, two navigators, two sensor maintenance technicians, and eight maintenance personnel (supervisor, two crew chiefs, and one specialist for each of the five specialty areas of communications/navigation, jet engines, electronics, hydraulics, and guidance and control). The flight crews are required to take DTRA training courses to familiarize them with the treaty and its specialized procedures. The DTRA team includes the mission commander, a deputy team chief, and two to four linguist/sensor operators. DTRA crews all have military flying experience, and the linguists are at least 'level-3 Russian speakers'.

A Representative Mission

All OPEN SKIES mission follow a highly choreographed process established by the treaty. Aside from rigorous aircraft and sensor specifications, the treaty stipulates specific entry and exit points for each signatory nation, as well as intermediate bases and a precise timetable for each mission. The following hypothetical US OC-135B quota flight over Russia from west to east demonstrates both the highly structured route and procedures.

A new OPEN SKIES mission is assigned the next sequential number beginning with the first mission flown in 2002. Mission '3456' begins when the United States submits a request for a quota flight 72 hours prior to the desired overflight dates. If the Russians approve the request, the OC-135B must depart from RAF Mildenhall and proceed to Kubinka AB, near Moscow (the western point of entry/exit for Russia). Once the OC-135B reaches Kubinka AB the clock starts and the mission must be completed within 96 hours. Upon arrival a Russian team immediately and thoroughly inspects the OC-135B to ensure that it is in full compliance with the treaty. This may take up to eight hours but must be completed at least four hours prior to the scheduled takeoff time on the observation flight. Should the Russians request a demonstration flight to verify compliance of the sensor equipment, the OC-135B will conduct a local flight near Kubinka AB over a specified target. A demonstration flight adds an additional 24 hours to the 96-hour limit.

The DTRA mission commander then submits the desired flight plan to the Russians at least 24 hours prior to the planned takeoff time. The crew typically is made up of 36 persons, including six Russian personnel plus four observers from other signatory nations. Although the OC-135B is capable of in-flight refueling, there are no tankers available, so it will land at intermediate points for ground refueling and crew rest, if required. Refueling airfields are specified by treaty, and include the primary airfields of Kubinka AB, Ulan-Ude AB, Magadan AP, and Vorkuta AP, as well as other locations such as Khabarovsk AP. The OC-135B must fly the precise route approved by the Russians. Deviations along the flight path are acceptable provided they remain within 27nm (50km) of the planned flight route. Any further deviation requires air traffic control (ATC) approval, and is allowed in the case of inclement weather, aircraft or medical emergencies, or if instructed to do so by ATC. Treaty restrictions also prohibit the OC-135B from overflying the same spot more than once on a single flight. OPEN SKIES mission altitudes vary according to the sensor. For example, the KS-87Bs typically require a height of 3,000 to 6,000ft (9,144-1,828m) above ground level (AGL), whereas the KA-91A panoramic camera best operates at some 20,000ft (6,096m) AGL. Flights at lower altitudes burn more fuel and demand meticulous mission planning and flight plan coordination with ATC to ensure minimum delays, as little interference as possible with civil and military traffic, and adequate fuel reserves necessary to accomplish the mission.

After the final landing at Ulan-Ude AB (the eastern point of entry/exit for Russia) the OPEN SKIES crew has 24 hours to depart Russia for Yokota AB. During this time the films from the flight are developed, and duplicates provided to the Russians. Alternatively, the film may be taken for developing at the Open Skies Media Processing Facility (OSMPF) at Wright-Patterson AFB, although the film must be accompanied by two Russian representatives to monitor its processing there and then act as couriers to return with it.

By early 2016 the OPEN SKIES agreement encountered its first significant threat when a Russian proposal to install digital sensors (with the same resolution as their existing wet-film and radar sensors) on their aircraft for US overflights met with strong American political opposition, despite the fact that similar flights already take place over Europe with US consent. Critics charged that Russian reconnaissance

Table 10-5.

US and Joint US* OPEN SKIES Flights Over Russia and Ukraine, 2002-2013

Year	Flights	Canceled	Year	Flights	Canceled	Year	Flights	Canceled
2002	1		2006	10		2010	13	
2003	7		2007	11		2011	14	2
2004	8		2008	13		2012	14	4
2005	8		2009	13		2013	11	

* Joint US flights are those where another nation also flew on the OC-135B

satellite capability has been so badly degraded over time that the Russian Tu-154 or Tu-214 OPEN SKIES airplane configured with digital sensors would serve as a 'relatively cheap way for Moscow to fill in the important intelligence gaps,' most significantly with 'important infrastructure' such as power grids, hydroelectric facilities, and commercial energy production sites. As the Director of the Defense Intelligence Agency (DIA) US Marine Corps Lieutenant General Vincent R Stewart warned in 2016, OPEN SKIES 'was designed for a different era…I'm very concerned about how it's applied today.' US Navy Admiral Cecil D Haney, Commander of USSTRATCOM, added that the 'vulnerabilities [to US national security and national critical infrastructure] exposed by exploitation of this [digital] data and costs of mitigation are increasingly difficult to characterize.'

These arguments are technically spurious and instead relate to a blend of official American paranoia about the threat of a revanchist Russia, and US retaliation for increasing Russian restrictions on (and cancelations of) OPEN SKIES flights over the Ukraine and Crimea to monitor ongoing conflicts. Despite the treaty's insistence on unfettered territorial access for any flight, Russia imposed excessive limits on flights over certain areas in the vicinity of Moscow and Kaliningrad, as well as over Chechnya, South Ossetia, and Abkhazia, all areas with considerable regional strife and Russian military intervention. Moreover, the treaty guarantees the right of any signatory nation to reject a proposed overflight route, so US complaints may be relevant to the spirit of the OPEN SKIES agreement but not to the letter of the treaty. Finally, US concerns that the Russians would exploit the OPEN SKIES treaty verification process work both ways. If, as senior US officials vigorously assert in public and private forums, the United States and its allies are vulnerable to Russian intelligence benefits derived from legally acceptable photography and imagery collected by Tu-214s, then so, too, are the Russians vulnerable to American and allied exploitation of OPEN SKIES imagery collected by OC-135Bs. Neither side is inclined to ignore vital OSINT which coincidentally happens to be 'caught' in an OPEN SKIES image.

It is difficult to imagine why the proposed digital technology is suddenly a profound threat to US national security when the Russians (or any other nation or even terrorists) can easily purchase similar 'sub 0.5m' resolution imagery available from commercial satellite operators. US funding to upgrade the OC-135B program is virtually non-existent as national technical means such as satellites and other advanced-technology systems earn the lion's share of dollars in the highly classified US intelligence budget. As with many controversial military and intelligence programs, their importance is often based

The OC-135Bs do not sit alert, but are required to be ready in response to a request by DTRA for an OPEN SKIES mission. Crews maintain a quick 'Go Bag' for deployments. *Photo by Brian Rogers*

Each OPEN SKIES mission follows strict guidelines for point of entry, route, and departure. 61-2672 prepares to land at Khabarovsk, Russia, on 12th November 2014. *Photo by Mikhail Glazyrin*

Plans for three OC-135Bs fell afoul of budget cuts and airframe corrosion, as 61-2674 retired to AMARG in 1997. *Photo by Brian Rogers*

less on their technical suitability or operational capability than on their political value or liability.

The future of the OPEN SKIES mission is not altogether clear. There are no plans to re-engine the OC-135s as the Boeing conversion line is closed. Instead, a KC-135R from AMARG would be reactivated and configured for OPEN SKIES. Alternatively, a new platform, perhaps based on the C-32 or the C-40, might be acquired. At present, the OC-135 fleet will remain in service indefinitely.

OC-135B INDIVIDUAL AIRCRAFT

61-2670 This was the third WC-135B converted into an OC-135B. It is assigned to the 45th RS at Offutt AFB.

61-2672 This was the second WC-135B converted into an OC-135B. It is assigned to the 45th RS at Offutt AFB.

61-2674 This was the first WC-135B converted into an OC-135B, and was assigned to the 55th WRS at McClellan AFB. It was transferred on 1st October 1993 to the 24th RS at Offutt AFB, and arrived there on 19th November 1993. It was reassigned to the 45th RS at Offutt AFB on 1st July 1994. It was placed in AMARG on 21st August 1997 as AACA0115 (see Appendix IV).

SIGINT AIRCRAFT AND OPERATIONS

RC-135V/W RIVET JOINT

By 1970 SAC was essentially flying two separate RC-135s for each PARPRO mission. RC-135Ds, RC-135Ms, and the RIVET DANDY KC-135R and RC-135T flew BURNING CANDY COMINT missions, while RC-135Cs and RC-135Us flew BURNING PIPE ELINT and specialized ELINT missions, often along the BURNING CANDY track. At the same time, satellite-based ELINT capabilities had improved sufficiently to reduce the requirement for a fleet of 10 BIG TEAM RC-135Cs. Three of these were earmarked for the COMBAT SENT program, leaving seven to continue BURNING PIPE sorties. Even so, the expensive duplication of mission tasking remained. In an unexpected display of logic, efficiency, and cost effectiveness, SAC and the national intelligence agencies decided to consolidate the COMINT and ELINT missions into a single airplane, although its primary mission would be as an Airborne COMINT Reconnaissance Program (ACRP) replacement for the RIVET VICTOR C-130B-IIs. Indeed, AFSS humorously referred to 'its' new airplane as a 'swept wing C-130'. The combined program was to be called RIVET TEAM to emphasize its dual-role capability, but this name was too similar to the earlier BIG TEAM program, and RIVET JOINT was chosen instead. The RIVET JOINT represented a significant shift in mission tasking for SAC's RC-135 fleet. Previously, SAC, DIA, and CIA had funded the BIG TEAM RC-135Cs in support of a broad range of ELINT collection requirements, especially SAC's SIOP obligations. With the change in mission priority to ACRP at the expense of ELINT, NSA and AFSS became the primary funding sources. This led to considerable interagency tension in terms of tasking priorities.

Beginning in 1972 BIG SAFARI converted seven RC-135Cs and one RC-135U (63-9792) into RIVET JOINT RC-135Vs, and, beginning in 1978, four of the six RC-135Ms into RIVET JOINT RC-135Ws. (Unless otherwise indicated, descriptions of the RC-135W operational capabilities and missions, including those of the RAF RC-135W Airseekers, should be considered identical to those of the RC-135V). RIVET JOINTs provided global COMINT and ELINT reconnaissance as part of the BURNING WIND OpOrd. There was some debate over where the RC-135Vs would be based – Fairchild AFB, Eielson AFB, or Offutt AFB. The optimal choice was for the 55th SRW to remain at Offutt AFB and routinely deploy to such forward operating locations (FOLs) as Kadena AB, RAF Mildenhall, Hellenikon AB, and Eielson AFB. Flight-deck crews were assigned to the 38th SRS and back-end crews were assigned to the 343rd SRS. Post Cold War mission demands resulted in the switch to two squadrons consisting of both 'front enders' and 'back enders' with the 38th RS and 343rd RS, 55th Wing at Offutt AFB. The airplanes are similarly marked, with those assigned to the 38th RS carrying a blue tail band and those assigned to the 343rd marked with a red tail band.

Table 10-6. Typical RIVET JOINT Crew

Front End	Back End
Aircraft Commander (AC)	AEELS Operator (Raven 1)
Copilot (CP)	Tactical Coordinator (Raven 2)
Navigator 1 (Nav1)	Manual ELINT Operator (Raven 3)
	Airborne Mission Supervisor (AMS)
	Airborne Analyst (AA)
	Information Integration Officer (IIO)
	Lead Tactical Operator
	Data Link Operator (DLO)
	Lead Multichannel Operator
	6 Linguists
	Airborne Systems Engineer (ASE3)
	Special Signals Operator 1
	Special Signals Operator 2
	Airborne Systems Engineer (ASE1)
	4 Crew Rest Seats (listen-only)

Configurations

Externally the RIVET JOINT is easily identifiable by its trademark hog nose and cheeks. Although it was not the first RC-135 variant to have either of these features, it was the first to have them both. Addition of the hog nose and cheeks alters the normal airflow around the forward fuselage where various static ports and pitot heads are normally located. Accordingly, wingtip static booms were added to allow for more accurate static pressure readings (such as those used to determine altitude and rate of climb). These booms are often mistaken for HF antennae, which is mounted above the right wingtip.

The hog nose (although some BIG SAFARI personnel refer to this as the 'long nose') extends the fuselage to 133ft 7in (40.7m) and first appeared on the OFFICE BOY KC-135A-II (it later became standard equipment on the remaining SAC RC-135 variants other than the RC-135U). The hog nose contained the standard KC-135 AN/APN-59 navigation radar much farther forward within the radome, along with a high-gain VHF receiver for COMINT. The nose quickly became part of RC-135 heritage, as Kadena AB, for example, earned the nickname 'Hog Heaven', while RAF Mildenhall garnered the nickname 'Hoghenge', Hellenikon AB acquired the name 'Hogcropolis', and Eielson AFB became known as 'The Hog Pole'.

There have been two main 'brands' of cheeks: the original Martin cheeks installed on the BIG TEAM RC-135Cs and retained on the RC-135Us and RC-135Vs, and the later E-Systems cheeks installed initially on the RC-135W. Beginning in the early 1990s, these were retrofitted to the RC-135Us, RC-135Vs, the NC-135W, the TC-135Ws and the RC-135Ss. The Martin cheeks were shorter and did not encroach on the crew entry chute door, as do the longer and shallower E-Systems cheeks. The cheeks are aerodynamic fairings that cover a variety of smaller antennae or receivers. Despite having

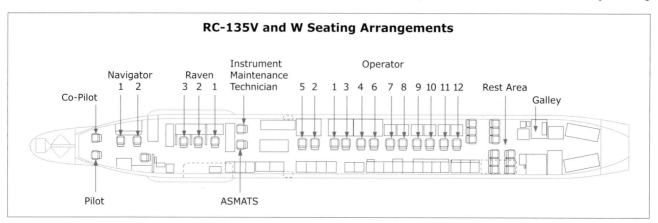

RC-135V and W Seating Arrangements

Co-Pilot · Navigator 1 2 · Raven 3 2 1 · Instrument Maintenance Technician · Operator 5 2 · 1 3 4 6 7 8 9 10 11 12 · Rest Area · Galley

Pilot · ASMATS

been incorrectly identified in the press for many years, they are *absolutely not* side-looking airborne radars – SLARs.

Originally the RC-135Vs had TF33-P-9 engines without thrust reversers and the RC-135Ws had TF33-P-5s with thrust reversers. Beginning in 1986 all RIVET JOINT airplanes were equipped with the TEN HIGH modification, undertaken as part of the HAVE SIREN program. This was an Infrared Countermeasures (IRCM) Self Defense System (ISDS) designed to defeat shoulder-fired heat-seeking missiles, and was also used on other high-value assets including the E-3, C-137, and VC-25A. TEN HIGH was mounted in a cylindrical fairing located on the trailing edge of each engine strut and used only during takeoff and landing, especially at Hellenikon AB at Athens due to terrorist activity there. By 1998 funding had finally been released to re-engine the RC-135 fleet with F108s, and the TEN HIGH equipment was removed.

Internally the RIVET JOINTS have changed considerably as evolving operational requirements and technological changes have redefined both the mission and the means. The first RIVET JOINTS were delivered in the Block I configuration, with 15 COMINT positions plus 3 ELINT Ravens. The Block I modification was not without problems, however. The RIVET CARD RC-135Ms had 43 receiver radios and the RIVET VICTOR C-130B-IIs had 31. AFSS requested 28 radios in the new RIVET JOINT, but AFLC only offered 19. In short, the 'modern' replacement was far less capable than the original. After some bureaucratic wrangling, AFSS got its 28 radios. These provided basic COMINT 'search, interception, analysis, recording, direction-finding, and emitter location capability.' Most importantly, the Block I RIVET JOINT was not about the quantity of receivers as it was about an automated capability to monitor and record each of those radios. Previously AFSS personnel had to tune a radio to a desired frequency, determine if there was relevant radio traffic, then listen (and translate) or record it for future exploitation, not unlike 'surfing' a car radio to find a favorite song. AFSS wanted an automated capability that would reduce a linguist's workload while increasing the volume and quality of the collection, and selected Electromagnetic Systems Laboratory's (ESL) Multiple Position Communications Emitter Locations System (MUCELS – pronounced 'mussels'). These comprise the four large mushroom-shaped antennae located on the bottom of the fuselage forward of the main gear well, and three large blade antennae (and several other smaller antennae) aft of the gear well.

Block I RIVET JOINTS were also the first generation of RC-135s equipped with a fully automated ELINT suite (the BIG TEAM ASD-1 had limited automatic capability). Known as the Automatic ELINT Emitter Locating System (AEELS), the receiver antennae are located in the airplane's cheeks. AEELS was based on satellite ELINT interferometric technology, and by 1974 had been upgraded sufficiently to offer the Ravens 'a real-time modernized manual/automatic emitter location and analysis capability.'

The first Block I RIVET JOINT was RC-135V 64-14848, chosen simply because it happened to be at the BIG SAFARI facility undergoing repairs for a cargo door that opened in flight. Six Block I test flights took place over the United States, with an additional nine flights planned in conjunction with RC-135C operational sorties. Only eight of these latter missions took place, with the final test flight on 25th November 1973. The first operational RIVET JOINT mission took place on 7th January 1974 from RAF Mildenhall, followed by 26 additional missions. Initial results were discouraging, with 129 unique discrepancies identified. SAC ended the operational deployments and returned the airplane to BIG SAFARI for remediation. In its absence, RC-135D 60-0357 was loaned from the 6th SW to the 55th SRW to meet the collection tasking assigned to the 'misbehaving' RIVET JOINT.

The issue, however, was far from 'teething problems' associated with a new platform. Unfortunately, AEELS was a disaster.

The HAVE SIREN IRCM located on the engine strut. Conical section was removed prior to flight, revealing a 'hot' IR source to defeat SA-7 *Strellas*. *Photo by the author*

According to a declassified 1980 SAC study, AEELS 'located accurately only about seven percent of the signals intercepted.' This required that all collections be completely reprocessed by computers at SAC Headquarters. 'By late 1975, AEELS had been installed on a total of four RC-135Vs which were being used on operational missions; however, all four AEELS continued to make the same gross location and [radar] typing errors which had cropped up on the sorties flown with the original unit in early 1974.' The issue became so tendentious that in September 1975 CINCSAC General Dougherty ordered that AEELS be 'fixed once and for all' or he would shelve the program entirely.

The two-stage solution began with a $250,000 software fix, completed in mid-1976, which raised the accuracy of the AEELS locating capability to 65%. It was installed on the seven RC-135Vs in service through 1980. The second stage was an ultimatum to E-Systems: 'demonstrate a near-complete correction of the AEELS

Table 10-7. **RC-135 Status as of 2016**

	Serial	Delivered	Re-engined	Operator
RJ 1	64-14848	6 Aug 73	30 Nov 01	USAF
RJ 2	64-14842	6 Jan 75	31 Aug 01	USAF
RJ 3	64-14843	5 Feb 75	7 Jan 02	USAF
RJ 4	64-14844	3 Mar 75	19 Jun 02	USAF
RJ 5	64-14845	21 Nov 75	20 Feb 03	USAF
RJ 6	64-14846	18 Dec 75	5 Sep 02	USAF
RJ 7	64-14841	19 Jan 76	6 Jun 03	USAF
RJ 8	63-9792	24 Jul 77	17 Dec 99	USAF
RJ 9	62-4135	15 Nov 80	31 Aug 04	USAF
RJ 10	62-4131	9 Mar 81	27 Feb 00	USAF
RJ 11	62-4138	1 Aug 81	n/a	USAF
RJ 12	62-4134	16 Aug 81	16 Aug 00	USAF
RJ 13	62-4132	30 Nov 84	13 Oct 03	USAF
RJ 14	62-4139	22 Jan 85	9 Mar 05	USAF
RJ 15	62-4125	15 Oct 99	23 Feb 04	USAF
RJ 16	62-4130	30 Mar 00	30 Mar 04	USAF
RJ 17	62-4126	15 Nov 06	n/a	USAF
RJ 18	64-14833/ZZ664	18 Oct 13	20 Sep 91	RAF
RJ 19	64-14838/ZZ665	4 Sep 15	10 Mar 93	RAF
RJ 20	64-14830/ZZ666	Jun 2017	16 Apr 91	RAF
CB 1	61-2663	24 Oct 69	n/a	USAF
CB 3	61-2662	2 Nov 83	2 Mar 06	USAF
CB 4	61-4128	8 Jun 99	27 Feb 03	USAF
TC	62-4133	22 Jul 85	1 Dec 05	USAF
TC	62-4127	30 Aug 05	6 Sep 05	USAF
TC	62-4129	22 Apr 88	5 Mar 01	USAF
CS 1	64-14847	28 May 71	26 Jun 02	USAF
CS 2	64-14849	21 Dec 71	n/a	USAF

RJ-RIVET JOINT;   CB-COBRA BALL;   TC-Trainer;   CS-COMBAT SENT;   n/a – not available

The first RIVET JOINT, RC-135V 64-14848, seen during its initial evaluation deployment to RAF Mildenhall in early 1974. Results were not encouraging.
Photo by Richard Vandervord

signal typing and location problems before [SAC] would purchase any additional AEELS for the fleet of 12 programmed RIVET JOINT aircraft.' In short, the conversion of four of the six RC-135M RIVET CARDS to RC-135W RIVET JOINTS was in jeopardy. Known as Improved Automatic ELINT Emitter Location System (IAEELS), this $2.5-million gamble was a one-of-a-kind prototype that would make or break the RIVET JOINT ELINT program. If the IAEELS worked during a planned deployment to Europe with ELINT-heavy routes in the Baltic, Barents, and 'along the fence' with East Germany, then it would be incorporated into the RC-135Ws and retrofitted into the existing RC-135Vs during PDM. Some 17 IAEELS evaluation missions took place from RAF Mildenhall between November 1977 and March 1978. The results reached '90% accuracy', and in mid-1978 the Air Force approved funding for the improved system to be installed in all RIVET JOINT airframes. Nearly six years after the approval to develop RIVET JOINT, and four years after the initial delivery of RC-135V 64-14848, SAC finally had a usable automated ELINT processing capability on the RIVET JOINT. This delay also partly explains why the RC-135Ms were not converted at the same time as the RC-135Cs – SAC refused to spend money on a system that didn't work.

Plans to enhance the RIVET JOINT's automated Airborne SIGINT Recon Platform (ASRP) systems capability led to the Block II configuration, with RC-135V 63-9792 serving as the sole prototype. Only the MUCELS system in the Block I RIVET JOINT was automated, so Block II offered the first truly computerized COMINT capability for AFSS. During the late 1970s, computers capable of fitting into an airplane were the size of refrigerators and cost a fortune. Block II used commercial, off-the-shelf (COTS) equipment like the Hewlett Packard 21 MXE as well as hybrid gear for the Automatic Signals Classification System (AUSCS), and for the upgraded MUCELS system. Money for these programs was always limited given the post-Vietnam, anti-military Congress. In spite of these fiscal constraints, 63-9792 was delivered in July 1977 and began test flights at Offutt AFB. From October 1977 through early 1978 it deployed to RAF Mildenhall for comparative tests with Block I aircraft and participation in Exercise COLD FIRE 78. The evaluations showed mixed results. The automated system collected more signals, but operator expertise meant that manual collections tended to be more 'significant.' Nonetheless, the decision was made to proceed with full-scale implementation across the RIVET JOINT fleet.

In addition to the computerized COMINT enhancements, Block II added global positioning satellite (GPS) capability to the RC-135. The value of GPS in precision navigation became apparent when a RIVET JOINT, participating for the first time in 1989 SAC's bombing and navigation competition overflew each checkpoint with zero positional deviation and within three seconds of its scheduled time, winning the competition (see Appendix V). The precision and accuracy of this equipment was so good that SAC decreed that in future competitions, GPS-equipped airplanes could not use the system because it placed all unequipped airplanes at a significant disadvantage.

In the Spring of 1978, the US Consolidated Cryptological Program endorsed the RIVET JOINT Block III modernization, and NSA director Vice Admiral Bobby Ray Inman approved the procurement of the new system for the remaining RIVET JOINTS. The remaining RC-135Vs were modified from Block I to Block III configuration beginning in 1980. Four of the six RC-135Ms were converted directly to Block III RC-135Ws; 62-4135 was the first Block III conversion of any variant, with its first flight on 20th September 1980, followed by RC-135V 63-9792 on 12th December 1980. Initial Block III calibration flights in conjunction with a Block I RIVET JOINT coincided with the Solidarity movement uprising in Poland. Operational validation of the Block III RIVET JOINT took place during the deployment of 62-4135 to RAF Mildenhall from 5th December 1980 through 9th January 1981. Block III aircraft had three P-band blade antennae added along the ventral fuselage immediately aft of the nose radome, and included SATCOM and colorgraphic map displays for the linguists. Originally, the term Block III had referred only to the final package of fully automated COMINT receivers. By 1980, through the gradual process of association and informal usage, Block III had come to denote an RC-135 that was equipped with both the third-generation COMINT sensors and an AEELS which incorporated all the technological improvements and additional capabilities demonstrated by the IAEELS.

Despite these technical and operational successes, the RIVET JOINT Block III program faced a final obstacle that nearly ended the program: President Jimmy Carter. Carter's FY79 Defense Budget slashed funding for the RIVET JOINT modernization effort by 75%. If allowed to stand, the subsequent FY80 budget would not pay for any new conversions and would fund just the four operational Block III RIVET JOINTS. In reality, this meant that the FY80 budget would result in the cancelation and grounding of the eight unmodified (and hence outdated) Block I RIVET JOINTs in favor of recently upgraded US Navy assets.

Block III supporters appeared *en masse* on Capitol Hill to testify before Congress to save the RIVET JOINT funding. CINCSAC General Richard H Ellis, Air Force Chief of Staff General David C Jones, DIRNSA Vice Admiral Inman, Defense Intelligence Agency (DIA) Director Lieutenant General Eugene F Tighe, and the US Commander-in-Chief, Europe (CINCEUR) General Alexander Haig all championed the need for the full 12 airplanes to be funded. Surprisingly, it was Haig who seemed to carry the day, arguing that without all 12 Block III RIVET JOINTs and the 25 planned Lockheed TR-1s, he could not guarantee that NATO's intelligence needs would be met in the event of war in Europe.

On the opposite side of the argument was the Director of the CIA, Admiral Stansfield M Turner, acting on behalf of President Carter. Turner wanted only eight RC-135V/Ws assigned to the Air Force inventory and just six of the eight aircraft fitted with Block III sensors to meet US PARPRO requirments. The CIA Director's position took on added importance during the FY79 budget hearings because in January 1978 President Carter had placed all nine US intelligence agencies (including NSA and DIA) under the direct budget control of the CIA Director. Congress sided with Turner, and funded only a single Block III conversion for FY79. Efforts to rescue Block III funding for FY80 continued to meet with Carter's insistence that – as Stansfield had already asserted – only eight RIVET JOINTs were needed and only six of these would be Block III configured. Consequently, the FY80 budget included no funding for Block III upgrades, but (fortunately) did provide operational funds for six Block I aircraft for at least one more year.

Ellis tried a new approach for the FY81 budget. He argued that the original plan for 12 RIVET JOINTs did not account for the absence of two airplanes in PDM at any given time, reducing the available operational fleet to only 10 RIVET JOINTs. With this in mind, he called for the total number of RIVET JOINTs to increase to 14 (by modifying the last two RC-135Ms). SAC Brigadier General Monroe Hatch also led a study to determine the actual wartime needs of theater commanders for the RIVET JOINT and reached a surprising conclusion: the US needed 36 RIVET JOINTs to fight a war in Europe. Despite Turner's pontifical assertion that only eight were required for peacetime PARPRO requirements, he failed to account for wartime demands. Secretary of Defense Harold Brown concurred with SAC's argument and began lobbying President Carter and key Congressional leaders in both houses to support funding of 14 Block III RIVET JOINTs, with an eye toward the possible conversion of others in years ahead.

Whether or not SAC's new advocacy approach made a difference in the effort to fund all 14 Block III aircraft will never be known. In

late 1979 Iranian students, operating with the full support of the new fundamentalist regime of Ayatollah Ruhollah Khomeini, seized hostages at the US embassy in Tehran. In December 1979 Soviet forces invaded Afghanistan. War between Vietnam and Cambodia and insurgencies in El Salvador added to these 'surprises' to US security. The Senate quickly saw the value in supporting full Block III funding to mitigate these shortfalls in PARPRO capability, but the House dragged its feet, and it was not until the 1980 elections put Ronald Reagan in office and redistributed the members of the House Intelligence Subcommittee did all 14 Block III RIVET JOINTs finally receive funding.

By 1997 the RIVET JOINT configuration was Block VIC, beginning with RC-135V 64-14842. These aircraft could be distinguished by the addition of antennas along the dorsal fuselage. Internal improvements were substantial, especially among the Raven and linguist positions. There would be no 'Block VII' RIVET JOINTs, however, as the nomenclature changed to 'Baseline 7' instead. Among the significant improvements included in the Baseline 7 jets (beginning with 62-4131 in late 2001) were derivatives of the Link 16 Joint Tactical Information Display System (JTIDS), including Tactical Digital Links (TDL), formerly Tactical Digital Information Links (TADIL). These provided narrowband communications with other tactical airborne assets as well as the Combined Air Operations Center (CAOC), emphasizing the RIVET JOINT's increasing conventional combat support role. The increased electronics created a significant heating problem. To mitigate this, L-3 installed heat exchangers 'against the skin which created 120kW of cooling at 20,000ft (6,096m), lowering the internal air temperature from 80°F to 40°F (27°C to 4.4°C).'

The impressive capabilities of the RIVET JOINT in operations in Bosnia, Afghanistan, Iraq, and elsewhere found strong support among combat commands, and led to a broad range of planned

RC-135V 63-9792 was the sole RIVET JOINT Block II aircraft. Despite mixed results from test flights, the Air Force move ahead with the Block III upgrade. *Photo by Michael Grove via Stephen Miller*

62-4135 was the first RIVET JOINT Block III conversion, and the first RC-135M converted into an RC-135W. *Photo by Joe Bruch*

Top: Each upgrade to the RIVET JOINT seems to add new fairings as well as new capabilities. 62-4138 appears in Baseline 9 configuration.
Photo courtesy USAF

Middle: Interior of the RIVET JOINT. Top left image shows the Raven station opposite the main cargo door (facing starboard). Bottom left image shows the in-flight maintenance technician seats (facing forward). Right image shows operator positions along the length of the fuselage (facing starboard). The crowded conditions have not improved since the early days of OFFICE BOY, COTTON CANDY, and COMBAT APPLE. *All photos USAF*

Bottom: Addition of the FAB-T fairing ahead of the vertical stabilizer emphasizes the ultimate in theater connectivity. For a generation of crewdogs who grew up with the Internet, data transmission is as important, if not more so, than voice.
Photo by the author

enhancements. As of February 2010, the USAF envisaged an RC-135V/W fleet made up of aircraft configured to Baseline 8, 9 and 10 standards over the next five years. Baseline 8 jets incorporated improved collection techniques, 'user friendliness', and system reliability, as well as automated and faster information dissemination capabilities. They were the first to be extensively 'connected' to other airborne and ground-based intelligence, surveillance, and reconnaissance (ISR) and targeting assets. RC-135W 62-4126 was the first Baseline 8 RIVET JOINT. It included the satellite-based Remote Extended Aircraft Position Enabling Reachback (REAPER – also noted as Narrowband Reachback, or NABRE) and Network Centric Collaborative Targeting (NCCT) systems. REAPER facilitates off-board analysis and processing of acquired data, while NCCT creates links that enable previously incompatible multi-intelligence (MINT) sources to work as collaborative teams. Baseline 8 is also able to 'talk' to the U-2S and the ground-based, tri-service Distributed Common Ground System (DCGS) processing and dissemination architecture to connect directly with other ISR airplanes such as the Beechcraft RC-12 Guardrail, Boeing E-8 JointSTARs, and US and allied nation Boeing E-3 AWACS.

By 2004 NCCT translated 'dissimilar sensor data from various ISR platforms into a common language and correlated the multisource data into a refined composite location that is automatically sent to a targeting cell in the CAOC and to DCGS intelligence exploitation sites.' A single RIVET JOINT, for example, might detect a signal of interest (SOI) but be unable to provide a precise location, especially as the RC-135 moves along its flight path. Using multiple, networked NCCT platforms, however, means that a RIVET JOINT, a Guardrail, and a U-2S would all detect the same SOI, and, within seconds, triangulate its precise location and relay that to the CAOC and national targeting agencies. A dedicated Information Integration Officer (IIO) has been added to the 'back end' crew, and serves as a 'real-time gateway between key intelligence nodes, both on and off the battlefield.' The IIO ensures that all tactical ISR platforms work together with an assortment of other mission support functions, like DCGS, Cryptologic Support Groups, and space-based assets.

Additional improvements to the RIVET JOINT include a glass cockpit using two large multifunction displays (MFDs) for each pilot. These display not only flight management and navigation information, but a complete visual representation of the air and ground battlespace using fully integrated intelligence from multiple sources. This gives the pilots exceptional situational awareness and allows them to anticipate positioning the aircraft at the optimal location and altitude to accomplish the task at hand, as well as provides a clear indication of all potential airborne and ground-based threats. At present the RIVET JOINT does not have the digital engine instrument display that is part of the KC-135R Block 45 cockpit, but this may be considered in future upgrades. Other improvements include the Wideband Global Satellite (WGS) communications system that offers an 'exponential leap' in bandwidth to and from the airplane.

Baseline 9 aircraft have a significant computing upgrade, additional liquid cooling to operate more effectively in desert conditions (notably visible in the AEELS cheeks with an air intake and exhaust duct), and improved emergency exits, while Baseline 10 adds further improvements including carbon wheel brakes. Other enhancements include the CONDOR HAWK direction finder (DF) and receiver system. Each airplane is upgraded to the next Baseline during its scheduled 18-month visit to L-3 for PDM, typically every four years or approximately 5,000 flight hours.

Among the latest upgrades to the RIVET JOINT fleet is the FAB-T, a 'second-generation terminal' system capable of passing low-rate data between air and ground assets. The Family of Advanced Beyond Line-of-Sight Terminal can be identified by the large dome-shaped fairing in front of the vertical stabilizer. First tested in 2011 on NC-135W 61-2666, the FAB-T allowed the RIVET JOINT to connect with a MILSTAR satellite and then transmit data and voice communication with a ground facility. Since then, the data transmission rate has increased, allowing a 'more secure communication capability to deliver much higher quantities of actionable intelligence products into the hands of the warfighter.' Cutting through the modern jargon, FAB-T allows the RIVET JOINT to provide intelligence in almost real time to ground units, a significant combat capability. RC-135W 62-4125 was the first operational RIVET JOINT equipped with the FAB-T beginning 2nd March 2012.

Operations

In addition to their traditional BURNING WIND SIGINT role similar to that described for the BURNING CANDY and BURNING PIPE missions, RIVET JOINTS became increasingly dedicated to combat support missions. Indeed, 'some RIVET JOINT veterans wonder if the program might have faded just as SAC did, had the 1991 Gulf War not forced it to change so quickly.' After DESERT STORM some two-thirds of the RIVET JOINT fleet remained in theater to support post-war operations as well as the ensuing wars in Afghanistan and Iraq. By the mid 1990s, 79% of RIVET JOINT missions were 'integrated combat operations in support of joint task for operations in the Middle East and Bosnia,' and only '19% of RC-135 missions involved [traditional PARPRO] reconnaissance operations in the Caribbean, Mediterranean, and the Pacific Rim.' Three additional RC-135Ws were converted from surplus C-135Bs to meet this additional demand, and the UK acquired three RC-135W Airseekers as well. Events in the mid-2010s – the Arab Spring, Russian revanchism in Crimea and Ukraine, and the explosive growth of power projection by the People's Republic of China throughout the Pacific – have shifted RIVET JOINT mission tasking somewhat back toward SRO operations.

The first RIVET JOINT deployment in a tactical SIGINT support role of joint military operations was the 1983 deployment to Cairo-West AB, Egypt, in response to threatened Libyan aggression against Egypt. Beginning 16th February 1983 RC-135V 64-14843 flew from Hellenikon AB to RAF Mildenhall (where it supposedly received a tail-number change), and the following day arrived at Cairo-West AB. Known informally as the 'Allied Camel Expedition', the airplane flew four 8-hour missions along the Egyptian-Libyan border. During the BRIGHT STAR exercise in August 1983, RC-135W 62-4139 deployed to Cairo-West AB. In the wake of Libyan aggression in Chad, the airplane assumed alert at Khartoum IAP, Sudan as part of ARID FARMER. On 12th August it flew a 4.8-hour mission in support of a planned French attack against Libyan forces (which did not take place). The airplane remained on alert but did not fly again until 19th August due to insufficient fuel availability. It finally departed Khartoum IAP on 24th August.

In October 1983 RC-135s supported the US invasion of Grenada as part of Operation URGENT FURY and missions in support of the US peacekeeping efforts in Lebanon. Following the 1985 Palestine Liberation Front (PLF) hijacking of the Italian cruise liner *Achille Lauro* and murder of an American on board, the terrorists involved fled to Egypt and were subsequently allowed to leave on board an EgyptAir Boeing 737 chartered by the Egyptian government. An elaborate US joint-service operation was planned within a matter of hours to intercept the 737 and force it to land at a location where the hijackers could be extradited to the United States for trial. A RIVET JOINT RC-135 participated in this 10th October 1985 operation as an on-scene airborne command post, with orders and essential information relayed via secure data link to the radio-silent intercepting Grumman F-14As. On board the RC-135 were 'Arabic-speaking personnel who were prepared to relay orders to the captain

64-14844 prepares to land at Athens. Aside from the ouzo and steaks in Glyfada, threats to RIVET JOINT crews were real. A car bomb injured several crewdogs following a mission, and operations were eventually moved to Souda Bay on Crete. *Photo by Richard Vandervord*

Nearly a decade before the RIVET JOINT became the standard combat asset for theater commanders, RC-135V 64-14843 deployed to Cairo to monitor Libyan hostility toward Egypt. *Author's collection*

Five RIVET JOINTs, including RC-135W 62-4135, were based at Riyadh AB during DESERT STORM, along with two more at Athens. *Photo by the author*

During DESERT SHIELD and DESERT STORM, RC-135s were at risk of attack by Iraqi air forces, which had successfully downed Iranian F-14 'mini-AWACS'. during the 1980-88 war. Tornado F3 ZE162 escorts 64-14845 on 19th September 1990. *Photo by the author*

Opposite page: Black scimitars indicate DESERT SHIELD missions, red for DESERT STORM. Proposals by Captain Mike Carney to name the airplanes *Kuwaiti Katie*, *Iraqi Jackie*, and *Sweet Saudi Sue* fell on deaf ears. *Photo by the author*

and other crewmembers of the Egyptian plane in the event they did not understand English, or pretended that they did not… The Arabic-speaking personnel also monitored radio conversations between the airliner and Egyptian authorities… [as well as keeping] a close watch on Libyan and Egyptian air bases within close range of the intercept area.' The operation was successful, with the 737 escorted to NAS Sigonella, Sicily. Italian officials, however, refused extradition of the terrorists to the United States. Additional RIVET JOINT operations during the 1980s included EL DORADO CANYON, the 1986 US joint-service strike against Libyan terrorist bases, and JUST CAUSE, the 1989 US invasion of Panama to depose Manuel Noriega.

On 2nd August 1990 Iraqi forces invaded Kuwait. Within a week, US forces began arriving in Saudi Arabia and adjacent countries as part of Operation DESERT SHIELD, intended to protect the Saudi kingdom from Iraqi aggression beyond Kuwait. On 7th August the Joint Chiefs of Staff directed that 'three RC-135 (BURNING WIND) aircraft' deploy to the Gulf 'as soon as possible'. Requests for at least two more RC-135s followed within the next two days. The first RIVET JOINT arrived in-theater on 10th August after departing Hellenikon AB, flying an operational mission en route to its new base at Riyadh Military AB (Old Riyadh), Saudi Arabia. Effective 24th August, deployed RC-135s were assigned to the 1700th RS(P), 1700th SW(P). A fourth airplane arrived at Riyadh AB during the week of 29th August. To bolster the number of RC-135s available during the imminent start of combat operations in DESERT STORM (and aware that a high-value asset such as the RIVET JOINT was liable to at least one combat loss), a fifth RC-135 arrived at Riyadh AB on 9th January 1991, and two more (totalling seven) were in position at the onset of hostilities on 16th January. Continuous 24-hour coverage RC-135 missions (typically lasting 15-plus hours each, and providing surveillance of all of Kuwait and southern Iraq) began on 11th August, and continued through 10th December, when RC-135 coverage dropped to a single 12-hour period. During the ensuing lull, RC-135 crews and aircraft prepared for wartime tempo. On 20th December, 24-hour RC-135 coverage resumed. In conjunction with U-2Rs and TR-1s, RC-135s flew a total of 620 strategic reconnaissance sorties during DESERT SHIELD.

With the outbreak of the war on 16th January, RC-135V and RC-135Ws flew four missions per day in two orbits, one adjacent to Kuwait and one along the western Saudi-Iraqi border. As with the COMBAT APPLE sorties during the war in Southeast Asia, a RIVET JOINT was on station for a 12-hour period before being relieved by a replacement. Including transit time to and from Riyadh AB, missions lasted in excess of 15-18 hours, reminiscent of COMBAT APPLE missions. Whereas these demanding continuous operations were common for programs such as the EC-135 LOOKING GLASS, those for DESERT SHIELD and DESERT STORM were flown in combat and under adverse environmental conditions. During DESERT STORM, RC-135s were chased by Iraqi Mirage F1s and MiG-23 Floggers, were fired upon by SAMs, and suffered minor damage as a consequence of Iraqi Scud missiles during the war. For example, on 25th January, RC-135V 64-14846 suffered moderate damage when a Scud missile exploded over Riyadh AB. Maintenance personnel quickly repaired the damage.

In conjunction with E-3 AWACS, RIVET JOINTs provided 'real-time intelligence coverage' as part of a 'complete theater air picture' distributed through a 'data-sharing network' with EC-130 Airborne Battle Command and Control Centers (ABCCCs), the ground-based Tactical Air Control Center (TACC), and US Navy E-2 Hawkeyes. Such intelligence coverage included monitoring 'the enemy's electronic signals to evaluate how he was reacting to [a coalition] raid's progress'. In addition to the RC-135s at Riyadh AB, at least two RC-135s conducted reconnaissance missions as part of Operation PROVEN FORCE over Turkey, flying from Hellenikon AB. During

DESERT STORM (from 16th January - 28th February), RC-135s flew a total of 197 missions, including 157 combat sorties during the first 42 days. RC-135s also flew 43 PROVEN FORCE missions. In a post-war critique, Congressional inquiries and Air Force tactical analyses reaffirmed the value of RC-135 RIVET JOINT platforms. Although the assessment of US intelligence was considered 'mixed' and the distribution of intelligence found to be 'very poor', intelligence collection – including that by RC-135 RIVET JOINT – was found to be 'generally very good and deserving of praise'.

RIVET JOINT RC-135s subsequently participated in a variety of peace-keeping and contingency operations in the Middle East, Europe, and the Caribbean. The final RIVET JOINT mission from Hellenikon AB took place as part of Operation PROVEN FORCE against the northern no-fly zone in Iraq; they were subsequently deployed to Souda Bay, Crete. As part of Operation SOUTHERN WATCH, intended to prevent Iraqi aircraft from flying into an aerial buffer zone south of the 32nd parallel in southern Iraq, RC-135s watched for hostile aircraft and electronic weapons (such as SAMs or radar-directed anti-aircraft artillery). An RC-135 was involved in the 27th December 1992 F-16C Fighting Falcon shootdown of an Iraqi MiG-25 Foxbat in the Iraqi no-fly zone, the first MiG kill by a USAF F-16 pilot. In response to the civil war in Bosnia, RIVET JOINTS provided regular intelligence on Bosnian Serb troop movements and threat assessments, including the detection of SAM missiles. They also provided aerial threat warning as part of Operation DENY FLIGHT from 1993-1995, and were an essential component of the first NATO combat air operation in the organization's history. An RC-135 was notably unassigned on 2nd June 1995 when a Bosnian Serb SA-6 Gainful shot down US Air Force F-16 pilot Captain Scott O'Grady. The RIVET JOINT arguably could have detected the SA-6's search and tracking radars and issued an appropriate warning. Consequently, RIVET JOINT missions were extended by two hours to provide the necessary coverage given the shortage of airplanes. RIVET JOINTS monitored potential Haitian and Cuban threats in the September 1994 Operation UPHOLD DEMOCRACY against the military regime in Haiti. A month later RC-135s participated in Operation VIGILANT WARRIOR, the US response to a potential Iraqi military operation against Kuwait. Conflict in the Balkans erupted again in 1999, with RC-135s identifying, locating, and tracking Serbian mobile SA-6 Gainfuls, as well as providing search-and-rescue support during Operation ALLIED FORCE. RIVET JOINTS also participated in Operation ODYSSEY DAWN during the Libyan Civil war in 2011.

Flights in the Middle East and Southwest Asia continued from Saudi Arabia. After initial basing in DESERT STORM at Riyadh AB, the RC-135s moved to Prince Sultan AB at al Kharj. In 2003, Saudi Arabia ordered US forces out of the country because of pressure from Muslim extremists, so RIVET JOINTS and other aircraft moved to al Udeid AB, Qatar, and continue to operate from there. Missions

included Operation ENDURING FREEDOM in Afghanistan as part of the 'Global War on Terror', and its post-2013 follow on Operation FREEDOM'S SENTINEL. Counter-terrorism missions in the Horn of Africa took place as well, although it is not clear if the RIVET JOINTS deployed to Camp Lemonier, Djibouti, or if they flew missions directly from al Udeid AB. RC-135V/Ws were instrumental in Operation IRAQI FREEDOM which overthrew Saddam Hussein and his Ba'athist government, and the civil war that followed. Beginning in 2011, US and UK RIVET JOINTS took part in coalition operations in the Syrian civil war. At least one source claims that a RIVET JOINT participated in Operation NEPTUNE'S SPEAR, the 2nd May 2011 mission to capture or kill al Qaeda leader Osama bin Laden. The RC-135 reportedly orbited between Kabul and Jalalabad, Afghanistan, providing advisory warning to the US Navy SEAL team as well as serving as an operational airborne command post in conjunction with an EC-130H and a US Navy E-6B.

Specific details of RIVET JOINT capabilities for these missions remain understandably classified. According to published sources, these include traditional threat warning (both air and ground), support for troops in contact with enemy forces, support for personnel recovery (both search-and-rescue and exfiltration of special forces), and 'cross-cueing' with other ISR assets. Given the traditional role of an RC-135 Raven to track and study signals from SAMs or early warning radars, it is difficult to imagine what a RIVET JOINT Raven would actually do during a mission over Afghanistan, for example, where Taliban forces use little more than cell phones and AK-47s. Not surprisingly, RIVET JOINT capabilities have evolved commensurately with these unsophisticated threats. According to one published source, RIVET JOINTS are actively involved in detecting and defeating roadside improvised explosive devices (IEDs), reflecting just a tiny portion of this new tactical capability. Overall, the RC-135V/W has established itself as the nexus in an American ISR community that, according to one RIVET JOINT commander, 'completely dominates the electromagnetic spectrum.'

What this will mean for the future of the RC-135 fleet is unclear. There are as yet no unclassified plans to replace the RIVET JOINT until at least 2040. During the late 1990s, multiple proposals – ranging

from converted Boeing 767 cargo aircraft, to new-build Boeing 757s, to the Boeing E-10 PAUL REVERE testbed, to fully automated remotely piloted vehicles (RPVs) – raised the potential for an early replacement. Funding was an early barrier. In every crisis situation or during any major combat engagement over the past two decades, the first asset requested by theater commanders was the RIVET JOINT to provide real-time situational awareness. The lack of a four-star ISR 'champion' within the Air Force ranks to advocate for a new airplane, however, meant that any future RIVET JOINT was hostage to the 'fighter mafia' and its commitment to the expensive F-22 and the F-35. The new platform was equally ambiguous. Plans to replace the KC-135 with a KC-767 raised the possibility of an RC-767, but when that tanker proposal was canceled due to a procurement scandal the RC-767 died a sudden death. Ultimately, the crucial obstacle to replacing the RIVET JOINT is the ongoing debate within the civilian and defense ISR community over the future of manned versus unmanned aircraft. A Global Hawk RPV can fly for 22 hours without refueling (even longer if configured for autonomous refueling). Although a RIVET JOINT or other manned aircraft can fly similar long-duration air refueled missions, the weak link becomes crew fatigue. However appealing, Global Hawk lacks the weight and load capacity to carry the necessary sensor suite, fatally compromising the mission. Moreover, there is a bi-directional time lag in the sensor data link, adding needless delay in a time-critical situation. Converting a KC-46 Pegasus into an RC-46 remains an option, but there is no airframe

After 13 years of operations from Riyadh AB and Prince Sultan AB in Saudi Arabia, US forces relocated in 2003 to al-Udeid AB (OL-15) in Qatar.
Photo courtesy USAF

Three generations of the same family have served as RC-135 pilots. With another 25 years of operations ahead, a fourth is not an impossibility. Lieutenant Colonel Golda T Eldridge, Sr (l), First Lieutenant Joshua Eldridge (c), and Lieutenant Colonel Golda T Eldridge, Jr (r). *USAF photo*

availability on the planned Boeing production line to allow for 10-12 new RIVET JOINTs, let alone replacements for the COBRA BALL or COMBAT SENT. Conversion of small commercial airliners or large business jets, such as the RAF's Sentinel R1 based on the Bombardier Global Express, offer the potential for a near-term replacement but with significantly reduced capability.

Until a new RIVET JOINT is delivered, RC-135V/Ws will continue to fly until they are nearly 80 years old. Plans to keep them 'healthy' involve a wing reskin every 5,000 flight hours, as well as replacing critical ribs and spars. However sincere this might be, it is simply a matter of time before some 'unknown unknown' arises. For example, on 30th April 2015 RC-135V 64-14848 experienced an intense fire during takeoff, which was successfully aborted and the crew egressed safely. Investigation revealed that improper sealing of oxygen lines during the airplane's 19th June 2014, PDM with L-3 Communications accelerated a fire of unknown origin at the galley. The airplane was repaired for an estimated $62 million and returned to service, but the incident raised concerns about the extent of any improper repairs across the entire RIVET JOINT fleet, as well as concerns about the age of the fleet. At the time of the fire, 64-14848 had accrued a total of 39,422.9 flight hours, far less than the high-time jet (RC-135W 62-4132) with 56,433 hours. There are simply

no data on which to base airplane longevity in 60+ year old aircraft, and the worst-case scenario is a single unanticipated event that results in the immediate and permanent grounding of the entire '135 fleet.

As RC-135V/W crewdogs are quick to point out, they were the 'first ones in for DESERT STORM and haven't left combat operations in the Middle East and Southwest Asia yet,' leading to a number of operational records. On 11th January 2007, for example, the 763rd Expeditionary Reconnaissance Squadron (ERS), responsible for all in-theater missions, completed 6,000 continuous days of operations, some 16.5 years. By 10th April 2013 the unit had flown 10,000 missions over 2.5 million flight hours, and on 9th August 2015 completed 25 years of RIVET JOINT operations in the Middle East and Southwest Asia. However commendable this accomplishment might be, and whatever the sacrifices made by the crews, maintenance, and support personnel, it is a fundamental indictment of US foreign policy that despite having extraordinarily capable resources like the RIVET JOINT, America has been at war continuously in the Middle East for a quarter of a century with little to show for it. Valuable national intelligence assets like the RC-135 have been used relentlessly. RC-135 crews have been at the center of these operations and have done so safely and with great professionalism. It is no less than a tragedy that they should have to.

Throughout a quarter of a century of continuous RIVET JOINT operations in the Middle East, ground crews have kept the airplanes flying despite the harsh environment, shortage of parts, and brutal 'ops tempo'. *Photo courtesy USAF*

A unique family portrait at al-Udeid AB, shows (clockwise from left) RC-135Vs 63-9792 and 64-14841, RC-135W 62-4132, RC-135S 62-4128, and RC-135U 64-14849. *Photo courtesy USAF*

RC-135W INDIVIDUAL AIRCRAFT

62-4125 E-Systems converted this former C-135B into the RIVET JOINT 15 RC-135W. It was delivered to the 55th Wing on 15th October 1999.

62-4126 This C-135B was the final USAF RC-135W conversion, and was delivered on 15th November 2006 as RIVET JOINT 17.

62-4130 This former C-135B was converted into the RIVET JOINT 16 RC-135W, and delivered to the 55th Wing on 30th March 2000.

62-4131 From 29th June 1979 through 9th March 1981, E-Systems modified this RC-135M into the second RC-135W as RIVET JOINT 10. In January 1985 it was noted with the name *Junk Yard Dog*.

62-4132 The fifth RC-135M converted into an RC-135W by E-Systems, this airplane was delivered to Offutt AFB on 30th November 1984 as RIVET JOINT 13. It was seen in February 1986 with the name *Anticipation*. This RC-135W is reported to have participated in the 1986 EL DORADO CANYON mission.

62-4134 The fourth RC-135M converted by E-Systems into a RC-135W, modified from 7th January 1981 through 16th August 1981 as RIVET JOINT 12. The airplane was noted with the name *Snoopy* in May 1983 and *The Flying W* in September 1985.

62-4135 The first RC-135M converted into an RC-135W by E-Systems from 5th September 1978 through 15th November 1980 as RIVET JOINT 9. It was first seen visiting RAF Mildenhall in December 1980. It has been photographed with five camels painted above the crew chief's name plate. In March 1986 it was named *Rapture*.

62-4138 This was the third RC-135W (RIVET JOINT 11) converted by E-Systems from an RC-135M. It was converted from 9th January 1980 through July 1981. It was named *Smokie* in both November 1984 and May 1985, and *Jungle Assassin* in February 1987.

62-4139 The final RC-135M to be converted by E-Systems into an RC-135W, as RIVET JOINT 14, was delivered to Offutt AFB on 22nd January 1985. It is reported to have participated in EL DORADO CANYON. In January 1986 it was named *Sniper*.

Block VIC cheeks show AEELS High Band (top, front) and AEELS Low Band (bottom, front) receivers. *Photo by Stephen Miller*

62-4126 was the final RIVET JOINT conversion. A replacement is not yet identified, so the RC-135s will continue in service through 2040. *Photo courtesy USAF*

All of the RIVET JOINT RC-135s are maintenance intensive. By 2016, RC-135W 62-4132 was the 'high time' jet with 56,433 flying hours, far more than the 12,000 promised by Boeing in 1964. *Photo by Joe Bruch*

Seen shortly after its conversion to a Block III RC-135W, 62-4134 shows the white over Coroguard paint scheme. Note fiberglass front and back of the cheek, indicating the absence of antennae. *Photo by Bill Sides via Stephen Miller*

Well worn but well loved, 62-4138 gets a tow at RAF Mildenhall on 15th December 1984. The 'Wind' was a regular at 'The Hall,' a venue popular with crews and spotters alike. *Photo by Bob Archer*

Before they received F108 engines, RC-135s at RAF Mildenhall often departed with two tankers on 'over the top' missions to Eielson AFB. *Photo by Richard Vandervord*

63-9792 was a single RC-135B purchased in 1963, whereas the remainder of the RC-135Bs was a bulk buy in 1964. After conversion from an RC-135U, it served as the sole Block II RIVET JOINT. *Photo by Stephen Miller*

Early plans called for basing the new RIVET JOINTS at Fairchild AFB or Eielson AFB, but the practicalities of continuing RC-135 operations at Offutt AFB made it the logical choice. *Photo via William R Peake*

RC-135V 64-14842 was the initial Block VIC RIVET JOINT, effectively the first post-Cold War upgrade. *Photo courtesy USAF*

RC-135V INDIVIDUAL AIRCRAFT

63-9792 E-Systems modified this RC-135U into an RC-135V from 17th October 1975 through 24th July 1977, as RIVET JOINT 8, the final airplane to be converted into an RC-135V. It was delivered to Offutt AFB on 4th August 1977.

64-14841 This was the final RC-135C converted into a RC-135V as RIVET JOINT 7. Although 63-9792 was converted into an RC-135V after 64-14841, the former was converted from an RC-135U while the latter was the last to be converted directly from an RC-135C. It was modified from 1st January 1975 through 19th January 1976. It was noted in August 1985 with the name *Red Eye*.

64-14842 Converted from 20th November 1973 through 6th January 1975, as RIVET JOINT 2, the second RC-135C modified into an RC-135V. This airplane is said to have participated in 1986 in EL DORADO CANYON. In June 1983 it was named *Shot at and Missed*, and in April 1986 it was renamed *Fair Warning*.

64-14843 Converted from 4th December 1973 to 5th February 1975 as RIVET JOINT 3, this former RC-135C was the third RC-135V conversion. In November 1986 it was named *Don't Bet On It!* It was previously noted with a red hog painted on the crew entry door.

64-14844 The fourth RC-135V was converted from an RC-135C from 8th January 1974 through 3rd March 1975, as RIVET JOINT 4. In June 1984 it was named *Nice*, in January 1986 it was known as *Air Assassin*, and by October 1986 was renamed *Problem Child*.

64-14845 This RC-135C was converted into RIVET JOINT 5 from 1st October 1974 through 21st November 1975. In December 1984 it bore the name *Smokey*, and by September 1985 had been renamed *Luna Landa*.

64-14846 RC-135C modified into the sixth RC-135V from 22nd January 1974 through 18th December 1975, as RIVET JOINT 6.

64-14848 The first RC-135C to be converted into an RC-135V, RIVET JOINT 1 was modified from 1st December 1972 through 6th August 1973. This tail number has been seen on an RC-135U.

For decades the RIVET JOINT'S primary subjects of interest were BAR LOCK or FAN SONG radars, and radio communications between regional facilities and headquarters. By 2015, this changed to cell phones and IEDs, and the RJ's sensors changed accordingly.
Photo courtesy USAF

BURNING WIND missions acquired unique nicknames. The author flew RC-135V 64-14843 on a 'Dogger' off Vietnam, refueling in a massive thunderstorm and recovering to Kadena AB in a torrential downpour with no pilot instruments. All in a day's work.
Photo by Joe Bruch

For some recon 'purists,' the only mission that 'counted' was the BURNING WIND. More than a few 55th SRW crewdogs argued that the COBRA BALL missions were never 'Real Recon.' Alaska veterans strongly disagreed.
Photo by Joe Bruch

64-14846 prepares to depart RAF Mildenhall in the summer haze. Missions were long and interspersed with sheer tedium and adrenalin-pumping excitement. There was never a shortage of volunteers to fly the BURNING WIND. *Photo by Bob Archer*

Some 20 years after this image of 64-14848 was taken at RAF Mildenhall prior to an 'ops sortie' (note operational HAVE SIREN), it caught fire during takeoff. Outstanding airmanship prevented an otherwise certain catastrophe, but the RIVET JOINTS are getting old (pun intended). *Photo by Richard Vandervord*

The loss of XV230 over Afghanistan meant that upgrades to the Nimrod MR2 fleet were moot, and the RAF subsequently needed a new ELINT platform. *Photo by Phil Jones*

RC-135W Airseeker

At the July 2006 international airshow at RAE Farnborough, L-3 Communications – the commercial program managers of the USAF RC-135 fleet – announced that BAE Systems would join with the UK's QinetiQ and LogicaCMG as partners with L-3's Integrated Systems (L-3 IS) subsidiary to develop the reconnaissance upgrade to the Royal Air Force's (RAF) fleet of Nimrod R1 aircraft flown by 51 Squadron at RAF Waddington as part of Project HELIX. Just five months earlier L-3 had been selected to lead the 'multi-stage acquisition of an upgraded mission suite for the Nimrod R1 electronic reconnaissance system.' Project HELIX would extend the operation lifetime of the three R1s to at least 2025.

Somewhere over Helmand Province in Southern Afghanistan on 2nd September 2006, RAF Nimrod MR2 XV230 had just completed air refueling from an RAF TriStar while on a routine Intelligence, Surveillance, Target-Acquisition, and Reconnaissance (ISTAR) mission in support of NATO and Afghani ground forces. Suddenly fire warning lights illuminated, smoke appeared in the cabin, and visible flames erupted aft of the starboard engines. After depressurizing the airplane, the crew began an emergency descent into Kandahar AB. Six minutes after the initial warning, the airplane exploded in flight 3,000ft (914m) above ground, killing all 14 crewmembers. Some 14 months later, on 5th November 2007, Nimrod XV235 experienced a similar fire but was able to land safely. The following month the accident report for XV230 – the first Nimrod delivered to the RAF – revealed that a fuel leak came in contact with a hot duct, igniting the fuel and leading to an uncontrollable fire. The report cited a flawed design, poor management in addressing the problem, and a systemic failure of Ministry of Defence (MoD) oversight efforts. The RAF terminated all Nimrod air refueling, and planned fleet-wide corrective modification programs.

These two seemingly unrelated events in 2006, the routine announcement of a business venture and a tragic airplane crash, led to the RAF's highly controversial acquisition of three RC-135W RIVET JOINTS. Initially L-3's remit was only to develop a new ELINT suite to be installed in the R1, but the loss of XV230 raised serious doubts about the suitability of installing a new and costly ELINT suite in the now-suspect Nimrod airframe. Consequently, the collaboration announced at the Farnborough Air Show changed from merely enhancing to completely replacing the Nimrod R1. By July 2008, the original Project HELIX was all but abandoned, and, to many observers, the RIVET JOINT had become the new RAF strategic ELINT platform.

Even before an official announcement that the RC-135W had indeed been selected as the replacement for the Nimrod R1 (which took place on 19th March 2010, with the R1 retirement scheduled for March 2011), the proposal was highly contentious. Proponents argued that the Nimrod R1 'airframe was not quite as good as they thought', and that the RC-135W would improve interoperability with US forces in the air and on the ground. Critics argued that arrival of the first RIVET JOINT – scheduled for delivery in 2014 – would leave a three-year gap in indigenous UK ELINT capability following the R1 retirement. Moreover, the RIVET JOINT was primarily a COMINT platform and would not replicate the full ELINT capability of the Nimrod R1 (a problem solved by the automated, advanced system in the RIVET JOINT versus the ageing, manual system in the R1). In addition, the RC-135W was incompatible with British probe-and-drogue air refueling capability, as with the C-17A. Most importantly, opponents emphasized, replacing the 'ageing and unsafe' Nimrod R1 with an airframe that was already 45 years old and had accrued an average of 22,000 flight hours was an incomprehensibly foolish risk. British safety agencies warned as early as 2009 that given 'the archaic heritage of the [RC-135's] basic design' there was a high 'potential inability to comply with airworthiness regulations... a major program

risk.' With the Airseeker initial acquisition expected to total £634 million ($1 billion), and through-life support costs to add a further £637 million by 2025, the future of the RAF's primary strategic ELINT platform was a risky expenditure of dwindling defense funds and an unpopular choice for 'safety first' advocates who argued instead for new-build Airbus A330s or even converted Boeing 767 freighters.

The RAF undertook two major efforts to mitigate these criticisms. RAF flight crews and senior officers visited the 55th Wing at Offutt AFB, the BIG SAFARI modification facility at Majors Field, and BIG SAFARI headquarters at Wright-Patterson AFB to assess the airframe's safety. They left with a favorable impression, recognizing that the 55th Wing's RC-135s, many approaching or exceeding 50,000 flight hours, were in excellent condition thanks to the intensive maintenance provided by 55th Wing personnel and L-3 Communications in Greenville. The three KC-135Rs slated for conversion to RC-135Ws each had fewer than 25,000 hours, so there was considerable optimism that the RAF fleet had plenty of safe operational life ahead. Beginning in January 2011, four crews from 51 Squadron were assigned for initial training with the 55th Wing at Offutt AFB. Once qualified, they would fly combined operational missions in USAF RIVET JOINTS pending delivery of the first Airseeker in 2014. British crews were afforded 'unprecedented and total access to the highly classified SIGINT systems' on the RC-135W. As the RAF RIVET JOINT would be identically configured to those already in service with the 55th Wing, this provided an exceptional opportunity for crews to be fully mission qualified and highly experienced even before the arrival of their first jet. Indeed, by the time ZZ664 arrived at RAF Waddington in November 2013, RAF crews accrued more than 32,000 RC-135 flying hours over the course of 1,800 sorties.

Conversion of the first aircraft (64-14833) began in January 2011. Modifications to the KC-135R included appropriate reskinning and corrosion elimination procedures, removal of the air refueling boom, installation of an ARR system, and rewiring every system. The airframe then received a complete Baseline 10 RIVET JOINT suite. The airplane, now marked ZZ664, rolled out in March 2013 and began flight tests soon thereafter. It was officially transferred to the RAF at Majors Field on 18th October 2013, well ahead of its scheduled delivery date. The airplane finally reached RAF Waddington on 12th November 2013, still under controversy. As the airplane had yet to receive its airworthiness approval from the British Military Aviation Authority (MAA), it was necessary for American crews to fly the airplane from Texas to England. By April 2014 it had still not flown pending certification by the MAA. With one airplane on the ground, one in modification, and a third identified for conversion, the MAA had yet to announce if the RAF's replacement for the Nimrod R1 was safe to fly.

Training missions in ZZ664 finally began on 23rd May 2014 under a limited Release-to-Service (RTS) from the MAA, and it was tasked almost immediately for its first operational deployment to support British operations in Iraq. On 16th August 2014 the RAF announced that in July the Airseeker saw its combat debut as part of Operation HERRICK and subsequently Operation SHADER, where it provided real-time reconnaissance and intelligence in support of British Tornado GR4s conducting strikes against Islamic State in Iraq and the Levant (ISIL) forces in Iraq. The RIVET JOINT reportedly operated from RAF Akrotiri, Cyprus. As with its US counterpart, the RAF RC-135W provided real-time intelligence to Iraqi Army, Kurdish, and US forces fighting ISIL, as well as humanitarian relief on behalf of refugees in the Sinjar mountains. Despite its successful combat debut, the Airseeker still managed to attract negative press. After its return, the RC-135W was 'out of action for five weeks' pending upgrades and system enhancements. With only one RIVET JOINT on hand, any

L-3 Communications publicity photo shows the Airseeker (a name which has yet to gain widespread popular enthusiasm) prior to its official rollout. Acquisition of the RC-135W was hotly debated. *Photo courtesy of USAF*

extended maintenance period left the RAF without any SIGINT capability.

The second Airseeker ZZ665 (64-14838) incorporated some 60 technical improvements, and eliminated this single-ship vulnerability. ZZ665 arrived on 4th September 2015 at RAF Mildenhall due to runway reconstruction at RAF Waddington. It was quickly deployed operationally from a 'forward base in the Middle East as part of the RAF's 901st Expeditionary Air Wing.' By April 2016, however, ZZ665 was slated to return to Greenville to resolve an unspecified issue that prevents it from 'flying straight' and has grounded the airplane.

The KC-135R scheduled for conversion into the third and final RC-135W Airseeker (64-14830) arrived at Majors Field in July 2014, where it was scheduled to take part in a five-month flight evaluation program. Undertaken concurrently with a USAF RC-135W, this initiative collected information to validate some aspects of the aircraft's flight envelope, augmenting the limited historical flight test data, and enabling 'a full release-to-service clearance' of the RAF RIVET JOINT flight envelope. Once testing was complete, it began the 30-month conversion in January 2015 for delivery in 2017 as ZZ666.

The Airseeker has since acquitted itself as a safe and reliable replacement for the Nimrod R1. On 24th November 2015 an RC-135W logged the type's 100th operational sortie in the fight against ISIL. They are expected to remain in service until 2045.

RC-135W INDIVIDUAL AIRCRAFT

ZZ664 Beginning in January 2011 BIG SAFARI converted KC-135R 64-14833 into RIVET JOINT 18. It was handed over to the RAF on 18th October 2013, and delivered to RAF Waddington on 12th November 2013.

ZZ665 BIG SAFARI converted KC-135R 64-14838 into RIVET JOINT 19. It was delivered to the RAF on 4th September 2015.

ZZ666 BIG SAFARI began conversion of KC-135R 64-14830 into RIVET JOINT 20 in January 2015 following six months of flight testing to determine baseline airframe reliability and safety data. It is scheduled for delivery to the RAF in June 2017.

ZZ664's arrival at RAF Waddington was not without controversy, as the MAA had yet to approve the airplane's airworthiness certificate. *Photo by Bob Archer*

The Airseeker saw its combat debut in July 2014, and two years later acquired special markings in honor of 51 Squadron's Centennial. *Photo by Ryan Dorling*

Pending completion of runway resurfacing at RAF Waddington, Airseekers, including newly delivered ZZ665, operated from RAF Mildenhall. *Photo by Mark Kwiatkowski*

Hard to believe that this 1988 image of KC-135A 64-14830 beginning a water-injected takeoff from Minot AFB shows what will become the third and final RAF RC-135W Airseeker. For many in the RAF, *that* is a serious problem. *Photo by Brian Rogers*

CHAPTER ELEVEN

Beginning of the End

The debate about the future of the manned bomber in the early 1960s was less about the technical specifications of the proposed airplane or the numbers needed to meet operational needs than it was a clash of hubris. On one side was Experience, personified in Air Force Chief of Staff General Curtis Emerson LeMay, who flew the lead bomber in raids over Germany and was responsible for the utter destruction of Japan well before Hiroshima. No one on the planet had a better understanding of bomber operations or the mechanics of nuclear warfare. On the other side was Arrogance, embodied in Secretary of Defense Robert Strange McNamara, wielder of a Harvard MBA degree and champion of the 'Whiz Kids', for whom the theoretical catechism of 'systems analysis' trumped any 'real world' examples. Experience warned that by the 1980s the existing US bomber fleet of late-model B-52s would be both worn out and obsolete. Designed in the late 1940s and early 1950s, the B-52 was essentially Second World War technology and manufacturing. Moreover, Experience argued, if a B-17 or B-29 was obsolete just 5-10 years after it was built in 1944, then surely a B-52H delivered in 1960 would be equally obsolete in 20 years after it was built in 1980, necessitating a replacement. Arrogance disagreed, not only on the relevance of bombers in general, but in the claim that a two-decade old bomber was suited only for the scrap heap. Defending his decision to limit any funding for a new bomber to a tiny exploratory R&D budget, Arrogance told President Lyndon Johnson in 1964 that

'I have not been presented with convincing evidence that this fleet will, from the standpoint of vehicle wear-out, be at the end of its useful service life' by the 1970s or even the 1980s.

Surprisingly, Arrogance was right.

By 2016, some 55 years after delivery of the first B-52H, the BUFF remains in front-line service, flying combat operations around the world. AMSA, the advanced bomber designed to replace the B-52 and which eventually became the B-1B, is still in operation beside the B-52. The FB-111, McNamara's TFX choice to replace the B-58 and the B-52, has long since been retired to the Boneyard. The B-2, the first bomber delivered after the dissolution of SAC, was limited to only 20 operational examples and remains a niche 'silver bullet' next to the B-52's expanding role as the ultimate weapons platform. Plans to build 80-100 Northrop-Grumman B-21 Raiders beginning in 2025 are hostage to Congressional budgetary politics and excessive secrecy (even revealing to the taxpayers how much it costs would compromise the new airplane's advanced capabilities…).

The B-52 is not alone in this Wilderness. The five oldest platforms in US Air Force service in 2016 are the B-52, the C-130, the U-2, the T-38, and the KC-135, designed in the early to mid-1950s. Of these,

Is there a future for manned ISR? Will the next COBRA BALL be a drone? Will there be enough platforms in any future acquisition to meet US reconnaissance requirements, or will the new fleet be too small to make a difference? *Photo courtesy USAF*

newer versions of the C-130 and U-2 are operational, and only the KC-135 has airplanes built prior to 1960 still in service. With its replacement still a year (or more) away in 2016 from initial delivery, let alone operational capability, the future of the KC-135 is mired in debate about its safety and longevity.

A cursory study of the total flight hours of retired KC-135s tells an interesting story about the fleet utilization and its future. The average flight time for each KC-135A assigned in the first tranche of aircraft stored at AMARG (ca 1992-93) is 13,000 hours. With a typical operational span of 35 years this means that each airplane flew approximately 370 hours per year. Average flight time for each KC-135R assigned in the second tranche (ca 2013) is 23,000 hours. Over the span of some 55 years, this equates only to a modest increase to 420 hours per year. Most interesting, however, is a comparison of the two eras. During the two decades between 1993 and 2013, however, the retired KC-135Rs flew an additional 10,000 hours per airplane, averaging 500 hours per year. Several factors account for this annual increase of 130 annual flying hours over that of the prior 35 years: no ground alert, utilization as cargo haulers following the retirement of C-141s, and especially increased 'operational tempo' in contingency operations over Bosnia, Iraq, Afghanistan, Syria, and elsewhere. This substantial increase in annual flight hours comes at a particularly bad time in the airplane's life cycle. Originally designed for 10,000 hours with service life extensions to approximately 27,000 hours via the TCTO 989 Wing Reskin and other efforts, the airplanes are now flying more when there are fewer hours left on the airframe (irrespective of re-engining). As such, the KC-135 is more rapidly approaching its end of useful life at a time when the Air Force should be decreasing its operational demands to preserve the airframe pending its replacement in suitable quantity. With the KC-46 still years away from any meaningful operational capability, this is an increasingly untenable situation. Given an average of 500 hours per year and a remaining service life of 4,000 hours until the fleet hits its design limit, this suggests that by 2023 – not 2040, nearly 20 years early – the KC-135 fleet will have run out of flying time.

Fortunately, this hypothetical calculation overlooks an important consideration. A few airplanes – notably the RC-135s – have flight

In 1964 Curtis LeMay warned that the B-52 fleet would be obsolescent and worn out by 1980 and needed prompt replacement. In this case he was wrong, as both B-52 and KC-135 remain in service some 50 years later. *Author's collection*

time well in excess of the projected 27,000 hour maximum. As of December 2015, for example, RC-135W 62-4132 had 56,433 hours, double that of the retired KC-135R fleet and nearly four times that of the retired KC-135A fleet. The RC-135s are in constant demand and fly long missions from locations ill suited to basic care of an airframe, yet they have easily exceeded their design limits with no end in sight. The secret to their success lies in the extensive, ongoing deep maintenance they receive. Rather than send an RC-135 to PDM at fixed annual cycles of five years (as all '135s did previously), the airplanes enter PDM after a fixed number of flying hours, typically around 5,000, usually around the four-year point. L-3 maintenance personnel pay particular attention to the airplane's backbone and ribs, wing spar and longerons, and the sustainability of spare parts which have not been manufactured in a half century. In addition to any mission upgrades, the airplanes are very nearly taken apart and rebuilt over the course of 18 months.

C-135 FLEET HISTORICAL UTILIZATION

Since introduction into service in 1957, USAF C-135s of all types have accrued a total of 15,369,686 flying hours, with an average of 19,022 hours per airframe. Between 1957 and 2015, total annual flight hours ranged from a maximum of 502,467 in 1968 at the height of the Vietnam War to a minimum of 177,394 in 2000.

A more useful analysis of fleet utilization compares the annual hours flown per aircraft to the total number in the fleet. At its zenith in 1968, the fleet had 763 aircraft in service, with an average annual utilization of 659 hours flown. At its nadir in 2000, the fleet included 560 airplanes of all types and averaged 317 hours per jet, less than half of peak utilization. As fleet size decreased further with the complete retirement of the

KC-135E and the onset of KC-135R retirement, the numbers became more alarming. In 2011, for example, the fleet accrued a seemingly modest 266,860 flying hours, just slightly above the lifetime average annual flight hours of 260,503. Adjusting for the number of airplanes in service, however, in this case 422, results in an average of 632 hours flown per airplane, almost the same as the 1968 maximum.

Despite the appearance of less wear-and-tear on the fleet associated with a lower total annual utilization, the smaller fleet size means the demand on the remaining aircraft is approaching the highest annual flying time in the history of the fleet. Moreover, that maximum took place when the C-135 fleet was only 11 years

old. In 2011 it was 54 years old. In short, each KC-135 and RC-135 in service today, at a time when it should have been duly retired, is tasked with the same level of operational readiness and efficiency as when it was at the height of its service with 45 years of longevity remaining. It is nothing short of a miracle that maintenance personnel and the PDM process have succeeded in keeping the fleet viable under these Draconian conditions.

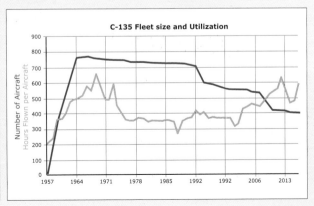

RC-135s are not the only '135s that benefit from this 'enlightened' PDM strategy. The Legacy Tanker Team at the Oklahoma City Air Logistics Center (OCALC) applies similar methods to the entire fleet of KC-135Rs and KC-135Ts. Although normally slated for PDM every five years, each KC-135 is tracked individually to determine if it is ahead of its projected flying hours and needs to enter PDM sooner than planned. During the 130 days each of the average of 68 airplanes is at OCALC in 2015 (a figure that has dropped from a high of 226 days in 2009), they are assessed for their tolerance to age, usage, and the environment. A 40-year-old KC-135 that has flown regularly in a moderate climate might be in better condition than a 30-year-old KC-135 with far more hours acquired in the sandy environment of the Middle East. As of November 2015, the high-time airplane was KC-135R (ARR) 58-0011 with 36,500 hours, and the low-time airplane was KC-135R 61-0290 with 16,000 hours, quite a disparity (58-0011 was previously an airborne command post,

As of 2016 RC-135W 62-4132 is the high-time '135 airframe with over 56,000 hours. It is projected to fly for another 25 years and reach 80,000 hours. *Photo courtesy USAF*

64-14829 is one of approximately 70 KC-135s that pass through PDM at OCALC each year.

Shortly after arrival at PDM each KC-135 is 'depainted' to allow close inspection. Interestingly, this is 64-14830 as it entered PDM prior to conversion into the third RAF RC-135W ZZ666. *USAF photo*

In addition to routine depot maintenance, the aircraft receive qualitative upgrades. 62-3499 received the GATM and MPRS modifications. *USAF photo*

accounting in part for its considerable time). Improvements to the inspection and repair process have benefitted the F108 engine as well, reducing PDM time from 106 to 55 days.

The more than 1,700 men and women who support the KC-135 PDM process with the 76th Maintenance Wing (the largest in the Air Force) are quite passionate about their mission and the airplane. Many of them retired following a 20-year career in the Air Force maintaining the KC-135 or in its logistical pipeline, and have spent another 20 years working at OCALC, establishing a tremendous corporate knowledge about the airplane. They share equal parts of 'what works' with 'what might work' to devise innovative solutions to the problems inherent in maintaining 60-year-old airplanes. With budget cuts and limited maintenance funds, they are often forced to improvise. In some cases, that includes replacing the very material used to make components. As the PDM process becomes increasingly sophisticated, experts are now examining parts of the KC-135 that have not been seen since they were sealed shut at Boeing when it was first built. Using carbon fiber or other advanced materials to fabricate parts not only provides a replacement for something that might not have been manufactured for three decades, but creates a replacement that will last longer and is more sustainable.

There are two tracks for KC-135 PDM, known as the 'staggered line.' Upon arrival each airplane undergoes an initial triage in the 'pre dock' phase, where major components such as engines, flaps, and the vertical stabilizer are removed. The aircraft is stripped of paint and undergoes a visual inspection [including non-destructive inspection (NDI)]. KC-135s that require major structural repairs enter the extended teardown cycle, which averages 82 days, and accounts for approximately 40% of arrivals. KC-135s with lesser problems go to the 'speedy' cycle, which typically lasts 42 days. Arguably the most critical issue in deciding which cycle an airplane enters is the status of the terminal fittings which ensure proper fit of the wings to the fuselage. Each fitting is inside a fuel tank and requires a person to enter the tank, remove the 150 lb (68kg) fitting, and then begin the inspection. Reassembling the airplanes is an equally challenging problem. When built, KC-135 parts were designed to 'slide-rule specifications' and Boeing did not have computerized systems to ensure that each part was precisely made to allow for full interchangeability. Consequently, many KC-135 structural components are unique to each airplane. Mounting holes for the terminal fitting, for example, were originally drilled by hand using a template. Over time, this might introduce a variation of a millimeter or two, a problem seldom encountered in today's computerized design and building process.

Few people appreciate the complexities of the PDM process or the logistical supply effort needed to keep the KC-135 fleet in service.

A maintenance worker inside a fuel cell works on the aft wing spar mount. In some cases, personnel have examined part of KC-135s which were sealed when the airplane was built some 60 years ago. *USAF photo*

The Legacy Tanker Team that makes this happen is understandably reluctant to speculate on any potential delays to the full operational deployment of the KC-46 and retirement of the KC-135 fleet by 2040. One thing is certain, however, and that is commitment to 'keep 'em flying' that pervades the entire PDM process offers the best opportunity to meet the air refueling needs of the US Air Force. Barring any 'unknown unknowns' or unexpected problems, the KC-135s flying today are arguably better and safer than they were when built nearly 60 years ago.

An Airliner's Debt

Out of the 808 KC-135s and variants delivered to the US Air Force, fewer than 50 were assigned to transport duties. As cargo haulers they were minimally effective, providing an interim capability until they could be replaced by the C-141. As passenger transports they were slightly better, but the inadequacies of early jet engines limited their range due to high fuel consumption and dictated the need for long runways at their destination. Following the end of the Cold War, what few transport C-135s remained in service were retired, leaving only the famed SPECKLED TROUT as a joint VIP transport and avionics testbed. With the 2015 termination of this VIP passenger mission, C-135s were finally out of the transport business.

And with good reason. Although C-135s developed military jet transportation, their successes in speed and reliability and their inadequacies in cargo handling and range became defining factors in the next and future generations of military jet transports. Indeed, C-141s, C-5s, C-17s, IL-76s, Kawasaki C-1s, and A400s were specifically designed *not* to look like a C-135. All of today's VIP transports have windows, which were notably absent on airplanes like *Casey 01* and *Trout 99*.

The legacy of transport C-135s, however, transcends their shortcomings. C-135s pioneered jet transport capability – what worked, what did not, and what needed to be done in the future. In this sense they were much like the deHavilland Comet, another pioneer in a world without a successful prior example. Even more significant was their role after their transport days were over. Although a few continued to serve as CSAs and specialized VIP transports, the majority became testbeds and reconnaissance platforms. Supporting the space program and contributing to man's first steps on the moon, conducting basic science experiments that gave us a better understanding of the sun and meteors, and developing the components that would be used on advanced technology aircraft such as the B-2 and satellite communications are all salient examples of how useful these 'airliner wannabes' really were.

Perhaps the ultimate value of the transport C-135s has little to do with them directly, and was instead the benefit they bestowed on their 707 cousins. Bureaucratic fears in 1955 of KC-135s and 707s coproduction were real – Boeing's commercial jet airliner business grew from nothing into the global leader in airliner design and production, thanks in large measure to Air Force funding of manufacturing and assembly processes with dual applicability. Boeing's previous passenger experience was limited to the Boeing 247D (75 were built but it was eclipsed by the Douglas DC-3), the pressurized Boeing 307 (only 10 were built), and the Boeing 377 (56 built but it paled in comparison with sales of Douglas DC-4s and DC-7s, and Lockheed Constellations). Without the largesse of the Air Force, it is debatable if Bill Allen's implicit desire in 1954 to build and sell a jet passenger airplane would have ever been a reality. As it turned out, just over 1,000 Boeing 707s were built, nearly all of which became airliners. By 2016 only two or three civilian 707 remain airworthy, including actor John Travolta's QANTAS Boeing 707-138B. However nostalgic it might be to think of retaining a dedicated VIP C-135 such as the SPECKLED TROUT, its time has finally passed.

With high wings, a T-tail, and clamshell cargo doors, 58th AS Boss Bird C-17A 98-0055 hardly looks like a C-135. The absence of these features accentuated their need, and they have since become standard on cargo airplanes. *Photo by the author*

Modern commercial airliners and business jets now exceed the range and efficiency of C-135 transports, but their lineage is clear. Boeing C-40B 01-0015 *Spar 15*, arriving at Tokyo's Narita IAP is a derivative of the 737, a small twin-jet airliner that descended from the 707. *Photo by Ryo Matsuki*

However cliché, transport variants of the KC-135 have passed the twilight of their career. The cost of maintaining a few four-engine, 50-year old airplanes has become prohibitive, and new generations of fliers lack the nostalgia or even awareness of their legacy. SPECKLED TROUT KC-135E 57-2589 *Trout 99* on 8th September 2006 at Frederic Chopin IAP in Warsaw, Poland. *Photo by Jakub Gornicki*

Gnosis

During the early 1990s the Pentagon agreed to retire nearly all of its testbed fleet, including six KC-135 variants and four other large aircraft. Doing so provided sufficient funding for the conversion of a *single* EC-135C into the second BIG CROW. After 35 years of service, the testbed fleet was gutted to a mere handful of aircraft in the name of budget austerity and priority for the 'warfighter'. By 2016 only the SPECKLED TROUT, the testbed tanker, and the NC-135W reconnaissance testbed remain in service.

Although the Air Force still conducts flight tests with dedicated airplanes, including a secretive NT-43A for 'stealth' research, this overwhelming loss of research capability has been only partly supplanted by civilian aircraft. NASA replaced its KC-135 Weightless Wonder with a former US Navy C-9B. NASA also accommodated some of the shortfall in basic science research aircraft with its DC-8 and the 747SP Stratospheric Observatory for Infrared Astronomy (SOFIA), among other assets. The Zero-G Company provides commercial weightless training in a Boeing 727 at $5,000 per person for 15 parabolas. Individual aircraft and systems manufacturers now fly their own testbeds. A Boeing 757 avionics testbed supported development of the F-22 radar, and the Boeing 737 Avionics Flight Laboratory did the same for Boeing's entry into the Joint Strike Fighter competition. Lockheed-Martin flies its Boeing 737 'CATBird' – the Cooperative Avionics Testbed for F-35 systems development.

Perhaps this is a good thing. Having companies provide their own test platforms eliminates any appearance of favoritism in any competition, especially where the outcome involves potentially billions of dollars. Military officials are also quick to point out that in an age of decreasing budgets and sequestration, money not spent on maintaining a fleet of ageing testbeds can be better spent on other programs considered far more important to an evolving global combat mission. Conversely, when equipment was tested on airplanes assigned to ARDC or AFSC, Air Force engineers and analysts were acutely aware of its successes and failures. Moreover, it condensed the research and development time for large programs by forcing companies to stick to tight schedules to ensure the project was close to being on time and on budget. To be sure, there were real and substantial delays and cost overruns, but there were few *surprises*. Ultimately, however, a fleet of testbed airplanes like the '135 cannot fix the badly broken Pentagon acquisition process. Where once it took three to five years from drawing board to first flight (or even initial delivery), it now takes decades, a process fraught with pork barrel politics and even scandal. One need only consider the process to replace the KC-135 as a prime example. Still, before any B-2 or F-22 ever dropped a bomb in combat, before it ever became operational, before it made its first flight, and even before it came off the drawing board, crucial components had been tested and retested, fixed and improved, validated and moved into production, all thanks to '135 testbeds.

A Real Peace Dividend

EC-135 airborne command posts were the product of the Cold War, emphasizing survivability of the US command and control network following a 'bolt from the blue' surprise attack by Soviet ICBMs. As warning mechanisms increased in scope and capability, fears of an undetected attack waned. Moreover, improvements and redundancies in communication via other sources meant that US leaders would be able to coordinate strategic combat operations despite EMP or organic constraints of aircraft readiness or availability. Ultimately, the value of EC-135 ABNCPs became linked exclusively to the scenario of nuclear war between the United States and the Soviet Union. With the dissolution of the USSR in 1991 and the post-Cold War decline in likelihood of a general war, whether with Russia or the People's Republic of China, the requirement for dedicated airborne command posts has dwindled. This does not mean they are no longer needed, as current alert operations utilizing E-6B TACAMOs attest. Rather, their priority in the US continuity of government and military command and control hierarchy has decreased considerably.

Similarly, the need for EC-135s assigned to theater and battlefield commanders has all but evaporated. Beginning with DESERT STORM, improvements in command, control, communications, and computers (C4) meant that President Bush, Secretary of Defense Dick Cheney, and JCS Chairman General Colin Powell could sit in a conference room in Washington DC and monitor the air and ground battle over Iraq in real time on a large-screen monitor. Today theater commanders no longer need dedicated aerial platforms from which to survey and control battlefields while remaining a safe distance from harm. Nor do they need an EC-135 packed with heavy and bulky communications gear to remain in contact with their constituent forces as they travel the globe. During a flight from CENTCOM Headquarters at MacDill AFB in Florida to al-Udeid AB

Company testbeds such as this Boeing 720 have, in part, replaced the need for dedicated Air Force assets assigned to the R&D mission. *Photo courtesy Boeing*

Long associated with the nuclear warfare mission, the day of airborne command posts is hopefully all but over. Perhaps that is their greatest legacy.
Photo by Richard Vandervord

in Qatar, for example, a commander has access to the latest in voice and data relay, now miniaturized to the size of a tablet. Whether on board a VIP VC-32 equipped with a dedicated communications team or a C-17 carrying a modular airborne command post, theater commanders can travel anywhere in the world with full connectivity.

With this sophistication, however, comes risk. Loss of satellite relay capability, whether from an outright attack to disable the satellite, to EMP from an atmospheric detonation to disrupt transmission, to a random solar coronal mass ejection shutting down 'the grid' can each cripple the ability of these advanced technologies to keep commanders informed and able to issue orders to meet battlefield requirements. Cyberdisruption is equally problematic, as the ability of adversaries to 'hack' into networks and shut them down or insert spurious data (think Stuxnet) can mislead commanders into disastrous decisions. Future changes to the global political dynamic could once again lead to the real possibility of general nuclear war. However unlikely such a confrontation between the US and Russia or China might seem now, a hard-line or irrational leader on either side might be willing to risk nuclear war to achieve some short-term objective such as full sovereignty over the South China Sea. Perhaps even more dangerous is the potential for rogue states such as North Korea to use their fledgling nuclear capability to attack the United States or their allies to preserve the power of their leadership.

In any case, a dedicated airborne command post has little to offer. EC-135s were just as vulnerable to EMP then as they would be today, despite ongoing efforts to 'harden' their voice and data links. Should nuclear weapons be used again, especially if a retaliatory strike takes place, the need for an airborne command post is irrelevant. As one critic of the E-4 AABNCP argued, Americans can find comfort knowing that while they suffer irradiation and starvation during the onset of centuries of nuclear winter following an atomic exchange, their president is airborne plotting retaliation and how to collect income taxes on 15th April to fund the new American government.

Interestingly, there is a future option for an airborne command post based on the model of the Russian Ministry for Emergency Situations. A dedicated civilian aircraft can respond to natural disasters to provide on-scene leadership and communications relay.

A tsunami devastating one of the Hawai'ian Islands or an earthquake causing San Diego to slide into the Pacific Ocean are extreme examples, but an ABNCP orbiting overhead would be crucial for rescue and restorative efforts. Applying defense technologies to humanitarian roles would be the ultimate 'Cold War Peace Dividend'.

The Shape of Things to Come
One question that Air Force officials politely declined to answer during my research for this revised edition was what would replace the RC-135. Whether out of security concerns for future mission capability or proprietary limits associated with an ongoing competition, no one would even hint at what the next generation RC-135 might be. Their reticence to say if the next RIVET JOINT, COBRA BALL, or COMBAT SENT will be an RC-46 or some other airplane goes beyond merely the selection of a suitable replacement aircraft. In September 2016 Boeing proposed a 737 variant instead of a 767 variant for the Air Force's 'boutique fleet' of RC-, OC- and WC-135s (along with the Lockheed EC-130H COMPASS CALL and possibly the E-3). The Air Force has yet to respond as it faces an issue which confronts intelligence, surveillance, and reconnaissance (ISR) across all services and all land, sea, and airborne assets: what will such a platform be?

For decades the central premise of US strategic ISR has been *manned* reconnaissance. At a minimum, this meant a pilot to fly a U-2, for example, along a planned route, switching on cameras at points marked on his map and then turning them off at the next point. It meant pilots and navigators and flight engineers making sure that RB-50s and C-130B-IIs were on course at the right place and time as Ravens and linguists 'in the back' monitored radars and radio conversations. It meant that an RC-135 would launch at a moment's notice and fly to an orbit point awaiting the re-entry of a Soviet ICBM as manually operated on-board sensors would record optical and spectral data.

As the cameras and sensors and recording devices grew increasingly smaller, the size of the airplane decreased in importance. Not willing to waste space, however, intelligence officials added more sensors and operators to the airplanes. Range and endurance remained crucial limits, as the need to fly vast distances or provide continuous orbits became essential mission requirements. Bigger was clearly better.

For many air forces, regional jets meet their SIGINT needs, such as Sentinel R1 ZJ690. They lack the ability to expand, however, to meet future needs. *Author's collection*

Japan's KC-767J may be too much for its needs, but an excess of tanker capability is far better than any shortfall. *Photo by Ryo Matsuki*

Not everyone agreed. Smaller air forces found that although they could not afford large converted airliners as COMINT and ELINT platforms, they could afford smaller converted business jets such as Gulfstream Vs or regional airliners like the Bombardier Global Express. Although these did not have the same robust capabilities as a RIVET JOINT, for example, they provided an entry level SIGINT platform that leveled the battlefield. Other planners discarded the issue of size altogether, opting instead to remove the crew entirely. Whether they were called drones, RPVs, UAVs, or something else, they eliminated what many ISR planners saw as the weakest link. Crewmembers required food and shelter at deployment sites. They required at least eight hours of uninterrupted crew rest prior to each flight, and they were limited by regulation as to how long each flight could be. Most importantly, they were vulnerable to loss or capture should their airplane be forced down, something to which Americans and the West have grown intolerant. Military success must come without loss. Indeed, as early as DESERT STORM Air Force combat crews were told that no mission, no target was worth losing an airplane or its crew.

But can a drone, no matter how big or extensively configured, ever replace a manned aircraft? That question is bitterly debated in the Pentagon and at intelligence agencies around the world. The Air Force wants to retire its venerable U-2 fleet to save money, arguing that improving its sensor suite and installing it on a drone would be far more cost effective, would provided continuous, uninterrupted surveillance without concerns for pilot fatigue or safety, and, should

one crash or be shot down, would avoid the opprobrium of losing an American flier. The solution is merely technical, adapting the relevant to the unmanned platform and then putting a drone pilot in front of a monitor at Creech AFS in Nevada to watch it 'drill holes in the sky'. Satellites would relay the intelligence it gathers to analysts sitting in shirt-sleeve comfort at NSA Headquarters in Ft Meade, MD. A battle staff in a darkened room would look at giant monitors showing the battlefield while directing combat operations from thousands of miles away somewhere in Qatar or Guam. ISR has become a video game.

There are at least two crucial limits to this abdication of human participation in ISR. First of all there are still humans involved, just not at the point of interest. Accident investigation board reports for drone losses reveals a disturbing commonality. Drone pilots staring at a TV screen lose their sense of combat situational awareness and the adrenalin that comes from it. As such, many of the accidents are attributed, at least in part, to inattention on the part of the drone pilot. Given that very few drone pilots are volunteers and have low motivation for this non-flying duty, it is not surprising that they are psychologically detached from the drone. More importantly, despite claims to the contrary, drones are not truly 'real time.' There is a 3-4 second delay due to satellite relay and other technical issues. If an adversary interrupts the data link or hacks into the link, which is inevitable in the history of military innovation and counter-innovation, then the drone is either at risk of being lost or the information it transmits is bogus.

The experience of the past 50 years of operations offers some guidance for what should replace the RC-135. *This is a one-shot deal.* There will not be another time or commitment to procure a new airplane for a half century or more, so make this choice count. *Size matters.* Acquiring smaller aircraft, no matter how many, will never meet the unplanned expansion requirements for the airplane and its mission years into the future. *More is more.* There are 17 RIVET JOINTS, three COBRA BALLS, and two COMBAT SENTS in service in 2016. Given the demands for the RJs alone, buying only six or eight new aircraft will not meet the needs of future operational requirements, especially in light of 25 years of ongoing war in the Middle East and Southwest Asia and any potential two-front obligations in the Pacific Theater. Ask for 40 but accept no fewer than 30. *Everybody pays.* RC-135s no longer serve primarily SAC and the Air Force, so all US military services and intelligence agencies must pony up a share of the acquisition and operating costs. The lessons of funding the SR-71 and replacing the KC-135 should not be forgotten.

Historians are terrible at predicting the past, and are even more unsuccessful when attempting to divine the future. A good option to replace the RC-135 might be a reconnaissance version of the Boeing 787. Capable of carrying a mission suite of 100,000 lb (45,359kg) with a range of some 7,500nm (13,890km), the airplane has the range and endurance to meet any future operational requirement. It would certainly require additional electrical power, and installation of an IFR receptacle would give it unlimited range. Given the challenges Boeing faces in delivering the KC-46, other options might be new Airbus A330s or even the A350. As noted earlier, Boeing has shifted its marketing strategy to the 737 instead of the larger 767, and there has been no inkling of interest in any military variant of the 787. What is certain, though, is that the RC-135s are 55 years old. Despite the attention they receive, they must be replaced if the United States expects their operational capabilities in any future conflicts.

Whither Cassandra?

The future of the KC-135 tanker fleet should not be surprising. Within the next 25 years one of two things will happen: they will all retire, some perhaps 85 years old, an incomprehensible figure in terms of combat aircraft; or they will fall out of the sky, broken, the result of some 'unknown unknown' that permanently grounds the entire fleet, leaving the United States and its allies without the overwhelming majority of their air refueling capability. Air Force planners are obviously hopeful that it will be the former rather than the latter, but hope is a terrible commodity on which to base military capability and national security strategy. That hope is built on the expectation that Boeing will deliver 100 KC-46s with options for another 79 airplanes to allow the KC-135Rs and KC-135Ts to retire gracefully to Arizona and static displays.

Unfortunately, the math simply doesn't add up. In 2009 operational planners determined that – at an absolute minimum – the Air Force needed 520 tankers to meet its existing global aerial refueling requirements. That number was expected to grow to 640 by 2015. Given that there are only some 400 KC-135s available at any time (the remainder is in PDM or serving as 'hangar queens'), plus the 59 KC-10s (minus an equally appropriate number out of service for maintenance), leaving a dramatic shortfall of approximately 180 tankers. After replacing the KC-135 fleet with the guaranteed buy of 100 KC-46s, the shortfall skyrockets to some 550 tankers. Just 100 KC-46s, at the unheard of level of 100% operational readiness, spread out around the globe to support trans-oceanic deployments, contingency operations, projection-of-power missions in the South China Sea, presidential travel support, ongoing refueling training for tanker crews and receivers, and routine maintenance, can never hope to replace the 400 KC-135s which are already overtaxed to meet those

requirements today. Assuming the Air Force exercises all options for a total of 179 KC-46s, the shortfall drops to 400, but that includes all available KC-46s from operational, training, and test units.

No one expected the wars in the Middle East and Southwest Asia to go on for a quarter of a century, with no end in sight. The 'ops tempo' of these missions can only hasten the need to replace the KC-135 as its ages. Nor can the Air Force afford to overlook its manning requirements for the future tanker fleet. During the height of the Cold War, KC-135 crews averaged 25 hours of flying time each month, the remainder of time was spent sitting alert. Current KC-135 crews are limited by regulation to 125 hours per month, an exhausting pace for a combat pilot rather than a 777 captain. Cuts in personnel in exchange for new weapons systems to meet budgetary limitations affect not only fliers but maintenance as well. At this stage of their operational lives the daily wear and tear on KC-135s has an exponential adverse effect on their longevity. The truly amazing work undertaken by the Legacy Tanker Team at OCALC can only do so much during PDM without the daily attention the airplanes need from skilled and experience maintenance personnel. The numbers, again, are just not there. Not enough pilots, not enough navigators or boom operators, not enough wrench turners. Pilots are pulled from the cockpit to fly drones, crew chiefs pulled from the line to provide experienced maintainers for the F-35 as it enters service.

As the first edition of this book went to press in 1997, I argued that the existing Air Force calculus for determining tanker replacement requirements was flawed. The KC-135R, for example, was seen as equivalent to 1.5 KC-135As, meaning that two KC-135Rs could offload the same amount of fuel as three KC-135As. This 'feel good' justification for re-engining the KC-135 fleet missed the critical variable in the refueling equation – the boom-to-receiver ratio. Although two KC-135Rs could indeed offload the same fuel load as three KC-135As, there was one less boom available, hardly a consolation in a fighter drag across the Pacific or over Afghanistan as an F-16, desperately low on fuel, has to wait until his equally thirsty wingmen clear the tanker. Air Force planners disingenuously finessed this issue by extolling the virtues of wingtip air refueling pods, which could not be used by Air Force fighters. But, they argued, these pods would allow US Navy, US Marine, and allied-nation probe-and-drogue fighters to refuel using the pods, eliminating the need for a BDA on the boom, freeing it to meet USAF fighter needs. That same thinking has been applied to the KC-46 and its Wingtip Air Refueling Pods (WARPs). The KC-46 can indeed refuel three airplanes simultaneously, but only one of these can use the boom, leaving *thousands* of planned F-35s, plus F-22s, C-17s, B-2s and B-21s, and no doubt a few remaining B-52s to compete for *no more than 179* air refueling booms worldwide.

This myopia has been driven by the Air Force (indeed, the global defense industry) belief that increasing qualitative technical sophistication offsets any benefits derived from quantitative advantages. The KC-46 is a prime example. Teething problems aside (the KC-135 was no better), its long-term legacy will no doubt show it to be a highly capable refueler, able to exploit its on-board data links to be an effective component of the aerial battlefield, operating in a variety of environmental conditions and operational scenarios around the globe. This capability, however, costs money, funds that are already stretched beyond the breaking point, hostage to budget-busting programs like the F-35 and, no doubt, the B-21. Even the cost of maintaining the KC-135 fleet adds up. Each PDM visit costs $8 million per KC-135. For 400 airplanes that cost translates to $3.2 billion. Multiplying that for a PDM visit every five years through 2045 produces a grand total of $19.2 billion. At nearly $200 million per airplane, that would only buy another 100 KC-46s, still leaving a shortfall of 370 tankers.

One solution to this dilemma lies in the KC-135's own success: simplicity. The KC-135A tanker was never more than that, an amazingly capable one-trick pony. Although it had the added benefit of being able to haul passengers and cargo, it was designed, as Bill Allen had presciently first envisaged in 1954, as a jet-powered tanker. Its 'fly by wire' capability is exactly that – wire pulley cables connecting the pilot to the control surfaces. It is elegant in the strictest sense of the word – superbly capable of aerial refueling without superfluous distraction.

'Tanker equivalent' is a meaningless term when you're low on gas over hostile territory or the Atlantic Ocean. What matters is the boom-to-receiver ratio. *Photo by Jim Benson*

NASA has already demonstrated autonomous aerial refueling using two Global Hawks in its KQ-X Program. Will the US myopic obsession with drones lead to an unmanned tanker? *NASA photo via Dave Lavery*

Technical challenges with the KC-46 boom design and issues with certification of the centerline drogue system and wing air refueling pods highlight this simplicity. During flight tests to refuel C-17s, its 'bow wave effect' generated 'higher-than-expected boom axial loads' and prevented the system from passing fuel. Apologists are quick to point out that this is merely an expected part of program development, and software engineers are working diligently to analyze the data, reprogram the system to accommodate these loads, and get the KC-46 on track for a belated initial delivery. This pre-packaged, public-relations announcement misses the point entirely. KC-135s and KC-10s have been refueling C-17s since its first flight in 1991 – some 15 years – *without* this problem. The difference is in the simplicity of the analog air refueling boom. Digital has strong 'gee whiz' technical appeal, analog gets the job done.

This is hardly a Luddite call to return to the Dark Ages of Aviation. Instead it is the lesson which the KC-135 can teach us about its

The KC-46 will no doubt prove to be a highly capable tanker. In a future world filled with increasing technical complexity, however, will ever it really replace the functional simplicity of the KC-135?
Boeing photo courtesy Mike Lombardi

replacement, a matter of numbers. After adjusting for inflation, the price of a single KC-46 would buy 14 KC-135s and increase the boom-to-receiver ratio by a factor of 10. For half the price of a KC-46 the Air Force could acquire a tanker version of the P-8 Poseidon, for example, doubling the number of air refueling booms in the inventory. Critics might well charge that the 'KC-8' lacks the fuel capacity of a KC-46, an issue obviated by putting an IFR in the airplane. Such armchair debate, while illustrative, still does not resolve the future crisis in aerial refueling. Even 200 'KC-8s' will not meet the demand in 2040 for more than 600 tankers. F-35s and F-22s will sit on the ramp, unable to 'cross the Pond' or engage in sustained combat operations at their designed range limits, all due to tanker shortfall. Deterrence fails, power projection fails, US national security objectives fail, all for want of a nail.

Nor is it simply a matter of inadequate numbers and an excessive affinity for the technological imperative. At a September 2016 airpower conference, AMC Commander General Carlton Everhart effectively dismissed the 15-year-old strategy of replacing the KC-135 with the KC-X, KC-Y, and KC-Z. The KC-46 acquisition will fulfill not only the KC-X program requirements, he said, but also the KC-Y program as well, eliminating the need to buy a replacement for the KC-10. He also discussed a KC-Y 'Plus' program, which he described as a KC-46 'with advanced communication relay systems and other upgrades; possibly lasers that will automatically shoot down incoming missiles.' The KC-Z, planned for 2030-2035, would be even more fantastic. Everhart said the next tanker 'might be a smallish unmanned autonomous vehicle that could penetrate an anti-access, area-denial system along with F-35s and other stealth combat aircraft,' possibly based on stealthy 'blended/hybrid wing designs' under conceptual development. One is hard pressed to imagine an F-35 or B-2 air refueling from a drone in 'full-up' hostile airspace amid Russian and Chinese advanced SAMs and fifth-generation fighters using stealth-negating technology like infrared scanning or just visually spotting the two airplanes flying in a straight

line given the situational awareness limits of the drone tanker pilot. Tankers have always operated in a permissive environment, and it strains credibility to imagine them being considered for use in combat airspace analogous to 'downtown' Hanoi or over an Iranian nuclear facility protected by swarms of 'dumb' first- and second-generation fighters capable of overwhelming stealth out of sheer numbers.

Instead, Air Force planners should consult with the spirit of Curtis LeMay, who would wisely remind them of the experiences of refueling SAC B-52s during the Cold War or PACAF fighters in Southeast Asia. What mattered to any B-52 crew on a CHROME DOME (or heaven forbid a SIOP sortie), what mattered to any F-105 Wild Weasel crew on fumes over the Red River Valley, what mattered to any SR-71 crew exiting airspace over Libya, what mattered to any CORONET pilot low on gas trying to avoid a watery grave crossing the Atlantic Ocean, was that the *tanker was there*. He did not care if the tanker had advanced data relay capability, or if it had lasers and stealth capability, or if it was fuel efficient and ecologically friendly with a reduced carbon footprint, or had the latest software upgrades to integrate it fully into some airspace management system, military or civilian. He only cared that the boom operator could plug in the boom and transfer fuel to keep him alive and dry. *Only four words mattered: 'Contact – you're taking fuel'.* LeMay and Bill Allen understood this. Today's planners and designers have either forgotten or overlooked the real legacy of the KC-135: it was always there when needed. Even after 80 years, 179 of the most advanced tankers ever built will never replace the remaining KC-135s, leaving the United States and its allies without the air refueling capability upon which all other airpower doctrine and tactics are built.

Mission-Design-Series (MDS) List

These tables reflect the evolution and status of individual KC-135s and derivatives. In Table 1 the original Mission-Design-Series (MDS) and block number are shown on the left, followed by the Air Force serial number, Boeing model number, and construction number. Some canceled airplanes were not assigned block or construction numbers, nor were construction numbers always in chronological sequence. The table continues with the roll out date, the first flight date, delivery date (when the airplane officially became the property of the Air Force), and the flyaway date (when the Air Force actually flew the airplane to its first assignment). The next two columns indicate any subsequent MDS changes and the appropriate date. The re-engining date for tanker KC-135Es, KC-135Rs, and KC-135Ts is, by default, the MDS change date, but is certainly different for aircraft such as EC-135K 55-3118 which received new engines 21 years after its MDS change. To avoid needless repetitiveness, when the MDS change date is exclusively the consequence of re-engining then only that date is listed.

In Table I an MDS marked as [KC-135A], [KC-135R], or [KC-135T] indicates a dedicated reconnaissance variant. An MDS marked as (KC-135A), (KC-135E), or (KC-135R) indicates an airplane equipped with an IFR receptacle. Similarly, KC-135s equipped with an IFR receptacle are referred to in the main text as KC-135A(ARR)s, KC-135E(ARR), or KC-135R(ARR)s, unconstrained by the MDS Table's space limitations. Wing schedules routinely listed these airplanes as 'RT-135s' (for Refuelable Tanker). All of these designations are non-standard conventions used only in this book to distinguish these special mission airplanes from standard tanker versions. The final two columns show the re-engining date (if applicable), and the attrition date (see Appendices II and III).

Identifying specific dates for an MDS change, re-engining, or retirement is a fickle process. SAC records, for example, occasionally conflict with the airplane's AFTO Form 781 Weight & Balance Sheet, which is the absolute record for any aircraft. Access to the 781, however, is generally impossible for anyone without a professional requirement to see it. The individual airplane record cards from the Air Force Historical Research Agency (AFHRA) have been long considered the 'gold standard' substitute for aircraft data. Whatever their historical legacy, the record cards are frequently 'reconciliation' documents – after-the-fact summaries that combined multiple and occasionally incomplete records with bureaucratic decrees detached from reality to arrive at a convenient date rather than an absolute record.

There are many reasons why an MDS change might have multiple dates. Classified programs did not always report MDS change dates to the logistics division at SAC Headquarters (SAC/LG) which tracked the airplanes, leading to a 'best estimate' of the date on the record card versus the actual date in the conversion program records. Official histories may list different dates given varying degrees of access to MDS material. Even knowing the date does not necessarily provide any great clarity. An MDS change following modification should be straightforward to identify. Which is it, though, the date the airplane began or finished conversion, the date it arrived at its operational unit after sitting at the depot for a week, or the date someone in an office decided would be the least administrative burden?

Many aircraft have been given an MDS that was unofficial or was simply wrong, most notably among the reconnaissance variants, the testbeds, and the VIP transports. In 1963, for example, SAC directed that KC-135A-II 60-0362 should be redesignated as an RC-135A, completely unaware that this MDS had already been assigned to the nine planned MATS photo-mapping platforms. In 1965 60-0362 was properly redesignated an RC-135D, but the following year – after a significant modification which rendered it substantially different than the other two RC-135Ds – SAC decreed that 60-0362 be designated an RC-135G. Three weeks later SAC officials changed their minds, and the MDS returned to RC-135D.

In other cases the use of Roman numeral suffixes were applied to the basic MDS. The first three reconnaissance '135s were KC-135A-IIs, the COMBAT LIGHTNING radio relay airplanes were KC-135A-VIIIs, and the LISA ANN RC-135E began life as a C-135B-II. These designations were officially applied only to the airplane flight manuals, but soon became synonymous with the airplane MDS. Because of their widespread use within SAC, they are included here for clarity as a 'quasi-official MDS'. Unfortunately, this creates an artificial absence of an MDS change, for example, when a KC-135A-VIII was demodified into a standard KC-135A.

Efforts to track individual airplanes by assigned unit while using the AFHRA record cards are equally problematic. For example, BIG SAFARI modified the SPEED LIGHT-DELTA and SPEED LIGHT-ECHO airplanes in April and May 1962, and they deployed to Hickam AFB and RAF Brize Norton throughout the remainder of 1962 to monitor US and Soviet nuclear tests. The record cards for 59-1514 and 55-3121, however, do not show the conversion and indicate that both airplanes were assigned to the 4042nd SW at K I Sawyer AFB, MI. As much as this book seeks to provide an accurate and definitive reference, the source material is itself ambiguous.

Amid an E-3 AWACS and trainer, an E-6 trainer, and a USAF E-8, a variety of '135s share the desert at AMARG. The EC-135s have been scrapped. Once stripped of their usable parts, the KC-135Es and few remaining KC-135As are sure to follow. *Photo by Martyn Swann*

MDS & Block Number	Serial Number	Boeing Model No.	Const No.	Roll-out Date	First flight Date	Delivered Date	USAF Fly Away	New MDS	New MDS Date	Re-engine Date	Out of Service
KC-135A-01-BN	55-3118	717-100A	17234	18-Jul-56	31-Aug-56	24-Jan-57	Jul-60	EC-135K	21-Jan-61	9-Mar-82	15-Oct-96
	55-3119	717-100A	17235	5-Nov-56	18-Dec-56	27-Feb-57	19-Mar-58	JKC-135A	1-Jul-58		
								NKC-135A	14-May-62		6-Jul-93
	55-3120	717-100A	17236	13-Dec-56	1-Feb-57	11-Mar-57	27-Mar-58	JKC-135A	18 Oct 58		
								KC-135A	27 Oct 67		
								NKC-135A	22 Mar 69		15-Dec-93
KC-135A-02-BN	55-3121	717-100A	17237	22-Jan-57	7-Mar-57	29-Apr-57	30-Apr-57	JKC-135A	7-May-57		
								[KC-135A]	9-May-62		
								[KC-135R]	May 63		
								JKC-135A	Mar 65		
								[KC-135R]	5 Jan 67		
								]KC-135T]	8 Dec 69		
								RC-135T	May-71	1-Mar-82	25-Feb-85
	55-3122	717-100A	17238	8-Feb-57	20-Mar-57	29-Apr-57	30-Apr-57	JKC-135A	17 Feb 58		
								NKC-135A	by 1966		19-Oct-93
	55-3123	717-100A	17239	1-Mar-57	5-Apr-57	18-May-57	18-May-57	JKC-135A	1958		
								NKC-135A	1964		20-May-88
	55-3124	717-100A	17240	13-Mar-57	27-Apr-57	31-May-57	4-Jun-57	JKC-135A	May-58		
								KC-135A	27-Oct-67		
								NKC-135A	10-Mar-69		
								GNKC-135A	7-Mar-91		7-Mar-91
	ntu	717-100A	ntu	25-Jan-57	ntu	ntu	ntu	Static Test			
	55-3125	717-100A	17241	22-Mar-57	10-May-57	31-May-57	4-Jun-57	JKC-135A	9-Nov-57		
								NKC-135A	by 1964		
								EC-135Y	1983	25-Apr-86	4-Feb-99
	55-3126	717-100A	17242	29-Mar-57	17-May-57	25-Jun-57	26-Jun-57				31-Jul-75
KC-135A-03-BN	55-3127	717-100A	17243	4-Apr-57	27-May-57	28-Jun-57	28-Jun-57	JKC-135A	1959		
								KC-135A	21 Feb 68		
								NKC-135A	2-Jul-68		31-Aug-92
	55-3128	717-100A	17244	22-Apr-57	3-Jun-57	27-Jun-57	28-Jun-57	JKC-135A	1958		
								NKC-135A	by 1965		20-May-96
	55-3129	717-100A	17245	30-Apr-57	11-Jun-57	28-Jun-57	28-Jun-57	JKC-135A	28-Jan-60		
								NKC-135A	by 1965		
								NKC-135E		28-Jun-82	
								EC-135P	Jun 84		31-Jan-92
	55-3130	717-100A	17246	7-May-57	28-Jun-57	30-Jul-57	1-Aug-57				15-Dec-92
	55-3131	717-100A	17247	13-May-57	9-Jul-57	31-Jul-57	13-Aug-57	JKC-135A	1-Feb-61		
								KC-135A	27-Oct-67		
								NKC-135A	22 Mar 69		19-Oct-92
	55-3132	717-100A	17248	3-Jun-57	12-Jul-57	30-Jul-57	1-Aug-57	JKC-135A	15-Mar-60		
								NKC-135A	by 1964		
								NKC-135E		31-Jan-91	16-Sep-08
	55-3133	717-100A	17249	14-Jun-57	18-Jul-57	31-Jul-57	5-Aug-57				24-Sep-68
	55-3134	717-100A	17250	25-Jun-57	1-Aug-57	28-Aug-57	28-Aug-57	JKC-135A	1-Oct-59		
								KC-135A	31-Oct-67		
								NKC-135A	10 Mar 69		20-Feb-96
	55-3135	717-100A	17251	8-Jul-57	7-Aug-57	3-Sep-57	4-Sep-57	JKC-135A	11-Jan-65		
								KC-135A	17-Nov-67		
								NKC-135A	10 Mar 69		
								NKC-135E		27-Mar-82	28-Sep-04
KC-135A-04-BN	55-3136	717-100A	17252	18-Jul-57	13-Aug-57	16-Sep-57	18-Sep-57				28-Apr-93
	55-3137	717-100A	17253	24-Jul-57	28-Aug-57	19-Sep-57	19-Sep-57				14-Jul-93
	55-3138	717-100A	17254	1-Aug-57	9-Sep-57	20-Sep-57	24-Sep-57				2-Oct-68
	55-3139	717-100A	17255	8-Aug-57	13-Sep-57	4-Oct-57	8-Oct-57				3-Apr-93
	55-3140	717-100A	17256	19-Aug-57	24-Sep-57	11-Oct-57	16-Oct-57				19-Apr-67
	55-3141	717-100A	17257	25-Aug-57	30-Sep-57	17-Oct-57	21-Oct-57	KC-135E		6-Jan-84	17-Mar-04
	55-3142	717-100A	17258	28-Aug-57	3-Oct-57	23-Oct-57	25-Oct-57				12-Jul-94
	55-3143	717-100A	17259	9-Sep-57	10-Oct-57	28-Oct-57	30-Oct-57	KC-135E		1-Oct-82	7-May-04
	55-3144	717-100A	17260	13-Sep-57	16-Oct-57	11-Nov-57	12-Nov-57	JKC-135A	14-Jun-60		8-Aug-62
	55-3145	717-100A	17261	18-Sep-57	25-Oct-57	16-Dec-57	18-Dec-57	KC-135E		26-Sep-86	28-May-08
	55-3146	717-100A	17262	23-Sep-57	29-Oct-57	25-Nov-57	26-Nov-57	KC-135E		12-Jul-84	5-Jun-07
KC-135A-05-BN	56-3591	717-146	17340	27-Sep-57	31-Oct-57	1-Nov-57	11-Mar-58				28-Jul-93
	56-3592	717-146	17341	3-Oct-57	14-Nov-57	27-Nov-57	6-Dec-57				4-Oct-89
	56-3593	717-146	17342	7-Oct-57	22-Nov-57	28-Dec-57	3-Jan-58	KC-135E		7-Sep-84	13-Jun-07
	56-3594	717-146	17343	14-Oct-57	26-Nov-57	28-Dec-57	3-Jan-58				17-Sep-92
	56-3595	717-146	17344	17-Oct-57	9-Dec-57	31-Dec-57	17-Jan-58				1-Apr-94
	56-3596	717-146	17345	22-Oct-57	9-Dec-57	29-Dec-57	3-Jan-58	JKC-135A	by 1965		
								KC-135A	31-Oct-67		
								NKC-135A	10-Mar-69		25-Jun-95
	56-3597	717-146	17346	29-Oct-57	10-Dec-57	29-Dec-57	10-Jan-58				27-Feb-63
	56-3598	717-146	17347	4-Nov-57	17-Dec-57	29-Dec-57	8-Jan-58				25-Nov-58
	56-3599	717-146	17348	6-Nov-57	18-Dec-57	30-Jan-58	31-Jan-58				27-Jun-58
	56-3600	717-146	17349	11-Nov-57	20-Dec-57	30-Jan-58	31-Jan-58				13-Apr-93
	56-3601	717-146	17350	13-Nov-57	26-Dec-57	31-Jan-58	6-Feb-58				21-Jul-92
	56-3602	717-146	17351	18-Nov-57	30-Dec-57	30-Jan-58	31-Jan-58				25-Mar-69
KC-135A-05-BN	56-3603	717-146	17352	21-Nov-57	31-Dec-57	31-Jan-58	6-Feb-58				21-Jul-92
	56-3604	717-146	17353	25-Nov-57	7-Jan-58	31-Jan-58	6-Feb-58	KC-135E		29-May-84	8-Mar-04
	56-3605	717-146	17354	2-Dec-57	9-Jan-58	30-Jan-58	7-Feb-58				18-Nov-60
	56-3606	717-146	17355	6-Dec-57	17-Jan-58	31-Jan-58	7-Feb-58	KC-135E		1-Feb-84	19-Apr-07
KC-135A-06-BN	56-3607	717-146	17356	10-Dec-57	20-Jan-58	26-Feb-58	4-Mar-58	KC-135E		8-Oct-82	
								GKC-135E	8-Sep-08		8-Sep-08
	56-3608	717-146	17357	13-Dec-57	20-Jan-58	25-Feb-58	27-Feb-58				23-Jul-92
	56-3609	717-146	17358	16-Dec-57	21-Jan-58	27-Feb-58	4-Mar-58	KC-135E		22-Oct-82	30-May-07

MDS & Block Number	Serial Number	Boeing Model No.	Const No.	Roll-out Date	First flight Date	Delivered Date	USAF Fly Away	New MDS	New MDS Date	Re-engine Date	Out of Service
KC-135A-06-BN	56-3610	717-146	17359	20-Dec-57	23-Jan-58	13-Mar-58	16-Mar-58				4-Nov-92
	56-3611	717-146	17360	26-Dec-57	24-Jan-58	25-Feb-58	27-Feb-58	KC-135E		10-Oct-84	21-Dec-06
	56-3612	717-146	17361	30-Dec-57	27-Jan-58	26-Feb-58	9-Mar-58	KC-135E		23-Mar-83	7-May-04
	56-3613	717-146	17362	6-Jan-58	31-Jan-58	20-Feb-58	21-Feb-58				19-Jan-67
	56-3614	717-146	17363	8-Jan-58	4-Feb-58	28-Feb-58	5-Mar-58				7-Jun-93
	56-3615	717-146	17364	16-Jan-58	5-Feb-58	28-Feb-58	5-Mar-58				30-Jul-92
	56-3616	717-146	17365	20-Jan-58	7-Feb-58	27-Feb-58	4-Mar-58				6-Jan-93
	56-3617	717-146	17366	21-Jan-58	11-Feb-58	10-Mar-58	11-Mar-58				3-Mar-93
	56-3618	717-146	17367	22-Jan-58	13-Feb-58	28-Feb-58	6-Mar-58				9-May-62
	56-3619	717-146	17368	23-Jan-58	18-Feb-58	18-Mar-58	20-Mar-58				7-Oct-92
	56-3620	717-146	17369	27-Jan-58	24-Feb-58	6-Mar-58	7-Mar-58				7-Mar-94
	56-3621	717-146	17370	29-Jan-58	18-Feb-58	12-Mar-58	14-Mar-58				23-Jun-94
	56-3622	717-146	17371	31-Jan-58	25-Feb-58	24-Mar-58	25-Mar-58	KC-135E		9-Aug-84	3-May-07
	56-3623	717-146	17372	4-Feb-58	27-Feb-58	13-Mar-58	16-Mar-58	KC-135E		8-Aug-86	
								GKC-135E			n/a
	56-3624	717-146	17373	6-Feb-58	3-Mar-58	27-Mar-58	28-Mar-58				7-Jul-94
	56-3625	717-146	17374	10-Feb-58	6-Mar-58	27-Mar-58	28-Mar-58				5-May-93
	56-3626	717-146	17375	11-Feb-58	10-Mar-58	20-Mar-58	21-Mar-58	KC-135E		3-Aug-83	12-Aug-09
	56-3627	717-146	17376	13-Feb-58	11-Mar-58	2-Apr-58	3-Apr-58				21-Oct-92
	56-3628	717-146	17377	18-Feb-58	14-Mar-58	2-Apr-58	3-Apr-58				3-Feb-60
	56-3629	717-146	17378	19-Feb-58	18-Mar-58	8-Apr-58	9-Apr-58				19-Dec-69
	56-3630	717-146	17379	20-Feb-58	19-Mar-58	8-Apr-58	13-Apr-58	KC-135E		19-Jul-84	23-Sep-09
	56-3631	717-146	17380	24-Feb-58	21-Mar-58	10-Apr-58	11-Apr-58	KC-135E		11-Apr-84	12-Aug-08
KC-135A-07-BN	56-3632	717-146	17381	25-Feb-58	13-Mar-58	25-Mar-58	26-Mar-58				16-Feb-93
	56-3633	717-146	17382	1-Mar-58	28-Mar-58	29-Apr-58	1-May-58				20-Aug-92
	56-3634	717-146	17383	5-Mar-58	31-Mar-58	29-Apr-58	1-May-58				22-Sep-92
	56-3635	717-146	17384	6-Mar-58	3-Apr-58	30-Apr-58	5-May-58				25-Aug-92
	56-3636	717-146	17385	10-Mar-58	4-Apr-58	30-Apr-58	3-May-58				28-Jul-92
	56-3637	717-146	17386	13-Mar-58	8-Apr-58	29-Apr-58	2-May-58				6-Aug-92
	56-3638	717-146	17387	17-Mar-58	9-Apr-58	30-Apr-58	3-May-58	KC-135E		17-Sep-82	6-Sep-07
	56-3639	717-146	17388	19-Mar-58	11-Apr-58	29-Apr-58	29-Apr-58				1-Jul-92
	56-3640	717-146	17389	21-Mar-58	15-Apr-58	13-May-58	14-May-58	KC-135E		18-May-84	9-Aug-07
	56-3641	717-146	17390	24-Mar-58	17-Apr-58	8-May-58	9-May-58	KC-135E		19-Jan-84	27-Feb-08
	56-3642	717-146	17391	26-Mar-58	21-Apr-58	13-May-58	15-May-58				11-Aug-93
	56-3643	717-146	17392	28-Mar-58	24-Apr-58	14-May-58	16-May-58	KC-135E		18-Jan-83	17-Sep-04
	56-3644	717-146	17393	1-Apr-58	28-Apr-58	7-May-58	9-May-58				16-Jul-92
	56-3645	717-146	17394	2-Apr-58	28-Apr-58	8-May-58	12-May-58	KC-135E		15-Aug-90	
								GKC-135E	Dec 11		Dec 11
	56-3646	717-146	17395	4-Apr-58	29-Apr-48	21-May-58	22-May-58				11-Aug-92
	56-3647	717-146	17396	7-Apr-58	30-Apr-58	19-May-58	21-May-58				10-Sep-92
	56-3648	717-146	17397	9-Apr-58	1-May-58	22-May-58	23-May-58	KC-135E		21-Dec-83	7-May-04
	56-3649	717-146	17398	10-Apr-58	2-May-58	19-May-58	23-May-58				16-Jun-93
	56-3650	717-146	17399	14-Apr-58	6-May-58	23-May-58	23-May-58	KC-135E		16-Apr-84	18-Jul-07
	56-3651	717-146	17400	16-Apr-58	8-May-58	2-Jun-58	5-Jun-58				1-Sep-92
	56-3652	717-146	17401	17-Apr-58	13-May-58	26-May-58	29-May-58				9-Aug-93
	56-3653	717-146	17402	23-Apr-58	14-May-58	26-May-58	3-Jun-58				7-Jul-92
	56-3654	717-146	17403	24-Apr-58	16-May-58	18-Jun-58	19-Jun-58	KC-135E		12-Mar-84	25-Feb-04
	56-3655	717-146	17404	25-Apr-58	19-May-58	18-Jun-58	19-Jun-58				30-Jul-68
	56-3656	717-146	17405	29-Apr-58	20-May-58	20-Jun-58	23-Jun-58				13-Nov-92
	56-3657	717-146	17406	30-Apr-58	22-May-58	6-Jun-58	6-Jun-58				25-Jan-62
	56-3658	717-146	17407	2-May-58	26-May-58	5-Jun-58	6-Jun-58	KC-135E		23-Oct-84	Jun 01
KC-135A-08-BN	57-1418	717-148	17489	5-May-58	28-May-58	19-Jun-58	20-Jun-58	KC-135R		18-Apr-91	7-Apr-99
	57-1419	717-148	17490	7-May-58	29-May-58	27-Jun-58	27-Jun-58	KC-135R		26-Feb-91	
	57-1420	717-148	17491	9-May-58	4-Jun-58	20-Jun-58	24-Jun-58				15-Sep-92
	57-1421	717-148	17492	12-May-58	5-Jun-58	18-Jun-58	19-Jun-58	KC-135E		7-Feb-85	2-Jun-09
	57-1422	717-148	17493	13-May-58	9-Jun-58	27-Jun-58	2-Jul-58	KC-135E		6-Aug-86	21-Jan-07
	57-1423	717-148	17494	15-May-58	10-Jun-58	19-Jun-58	20-Jun-58	KC-135R		24-Apr-91	6-Jun-07
	57-1424	717-148	17495	16-May-58	11-Jun-58	25-Jun-58	26-Jun-58				17-May-66
	57-1425	717-148	17496	20-May-58	12-Jun-58	9-Jul-58	9-Jul-58	KC-135E		19-Nov-82	20-May-08
	57-1426	717-148	17497	21-May-58	16-Jun-58	30-Jun-58	3-Jul-58	KC-135E		16-Aug-84	3-Jun-08
	57-1427	717-148	17498	23-May-58	17-Jun-58	8-Jul-58	9-Jul-58	KC-135R		27-Aug-86	
	57-1428	717-148	17499	26-Jun-58	18-Jun-58	15-Jul-58	18-Jul-58	KC-135E		30-Apr-84	
								KC-135R		10-May-96	
	57-1429	717-148	17500	28-May-58	20-Jun-58	14-Jul-58	15-Jul-58	KC-135E		24-Feb-84	May 09
	57-1430	717-148	17501	2-Jun-58	25-Jun-58	15-Jul-58	17-Jul-58	KC-135R		18-Jan-91	
	57-1431	717-148	17502	3-Jun-58	25-Jun-58	15-Jul-58	17-Jul-58	KC-135E		21-Apr-83	
								GKC-135E	Jul 90		Jul 90
	57-1432	717-148	17503	4-Jun-58	27-Jun-58	22-Jul-58	24-Jul-58	KC-135R		9-Feb-93	
	57-1433	717-148	17504	6-Jun-58	1-Jul-58	15-Jul-58	18-Jul-58	KC-135E		26-Aug-82	10-Jun-08
	57-1434	717-148	17505	9-Jun-58	2-Jul-58	28-Jul-58	1-Aug-58	KC-135E		17-Dec-84	16-Apr-08
	57-1435	717-148	17506	11-Jun-58	3-Jul-58	23-Jul-58	24-Jul-58	KC-135E		21-Jan-92	
	57-1436	717-148	17507	12-Jun-58	8-Jul-58	21-Jul-58	25-Jul-58	KC-135E		15-Oct-87	
								KC-135R		21-Aug-96	
	57-1437	717-148	17508	16-Jun-58	9-Jul-58	31-Jul-58	1-Aug-58	KC-135R		12-Apr-91	
	57-1438	717-148	17509	18-Jun-58	11-Jul-58	23-Jul-58	1-Aug-58	KC-135E		8-Jan-85	
								KC-135R			
	57-1439	717-148	17510	19-Jun-58	14-Jul-58	28-Jul-58	31-Jul-58	KC-135R		21-Dec-90	
	57-1440	717-148	17511	20-Jun-58	16-Jul-58	30-Jul-58	31-Jul-58	KC-135R		30-Apr-85	
	57-1441	717-148	17512	24-Jun-58	16-Jul-58	1-Aug-58	26-Aug-58	KC-135E		26-Jan-88	
								KC-135R		14-Jun-05	
	57-1442	717-148	17513	26-Jun-58	18-Jul-58	1-Aug-58	1-Aug-58				16-Jan-65
	57-1443	717-148	17514	27-Jun-58	22-Jul-58	14-Aug-58	15-Aug-58	KC-135E		6-Sep-84	14-Apr-09
	57-1444	717-148	17515	1-Jul-58	24-Jul-58	14-Aug-58	15-Aug-58				18-May-66
	57-1445	717-148	17516	2-Jul-58	24-Jul-58	8-Aug-58	12-Aug-58	KC-135E		14-Sep-84	27-May-09
	57-1446	717-148	17517	7-Jul-58	24-Jul-58	7-Aug-58	8-Aug-58				22-Jun-59
	57-1447	717-148	17518	8-Jul-58	4-Aug-58	29-Aug-58	4-Sep-58	KC-135E		1-Oct-90	9-May-07
	57-1448	717-148	17519	10-Jul-58	4-Aug-58	27-Aug-58	2-Sep-58	KC-135E		3-Apr-84	12-May-09

MDS & Block Number	Serial Number	Boeing Model No.	Const No.	Roll-out Date	First flight Date	Delivered Date	USAF Fly Away	New MDS	New MDS Date	Re-engine Date	Out of Service
KC-135A-08-BN	57-1449	717-148	17520	11-Jul-58	6-Aug-58	15-Aug-58	19-Aug-58				3-Feb-60
	57-1450	717-148	17521	15-Jul-58	6-Aug-58	19-Aug-58	22-Aug-58	KC-135E		9-Jul-84	12-Mar-08
	57-1451	717-148	17522	16-Jul-58	6-Aug-58	22-Aug-58	26-Aug-58	KC-135E		28-Feb-91	
								KC-135R		16-Dec-98	
	57-1452	717-148	17523	17-Jul-58	8-Aug-58	21-Aug-58	26-Aug-58	KC-135E		12-Aug-82	25-Jul-07
	57-1453	717-148	17524	21-Jul-58	12-Aug-58	22-Aug-58	26-Aug-58	KC-135R		10-Jun-92	
	57-1454	717-148	17525	22-Jul-58	12-Aug-58	5-Sep-58	5-Sep-58	KC-135E		2-Jun-89	
	57-1455	717-148	17526	23-Jul-58	14-Aug-58	28-Aug-58	29-Aug-58	KC-135E		10-Sep-82	May 09
	57-1456	717-148	17527	25-Jul-58	19-Aug-58	5-Sep-58	6-Sep-58	KC-135R		26-Jan-90	
	57-1457	717-148	17528	28-Jul-58	19-Aug-58	29-Aug-58	2-Sep-58				3-Feb-60
	57-1458	717-148	17529	30-Jul-58	21-Aug-58	8-Sep-58	10-Sep-58	KC-135E		11-May-83	May 09
	57-1459	717-148	17530	31-Jul-58	21-Aug-58	12-Sep-58	16-Sep-58	KC-135E		15-Aug-91	
								KC-135R		24-May-96	
KC-135A-09-BN	57-1460	717-148	17531	1-Aug-58	26-Aug-58	28-Sep-58	5-Oct-58	KC-135E		11-Jul-84	19-Mar-08
	57-1461	717-148	17532	5-Aug-58	27-Aug-58	11-Sep-58	11-Sep-58	KC-135R		6-Dec-89	
	57-1462	717-148	17533	6-Aug-58	27-Aug-58	15-Sep-58	19-Sep-58	KC-135R		21-Dec-85	
	57-1463	717-148	17534	7-Aug-58	29-Aug-58	28-Sep-58	4-Oct-58	KC-135E		10-May-84	11-Mar-09
	57-1464	717-148	17535	11-Aug-58	2-Sep-58	29-Sep-58	3-Oct-58	KC-135E		6-Mar-84	6-Feb-08
	57-1465	717-148	17536	12-Aug-58	3-Sep-58	29-Sep-58	3-Oct-58	KC-135E		13-Jun-84	1-Apr-09
	57-1466	717-148	17537	14-Aug-58	4-Sep-58	28-Sep-58	3-Oct-58				8-Mar-60
	57-1467	717-148	17538	15-Aug-58	8-Sep-58	22-Sep-58	3-Oct-58				27-Aug-92
	57-1468	717-148	17539	18-Aug-58	5-Sep-58	29-Sep-58	3-Oct-58	KC-135E		4-Feb-85	
								KC-135R		5-Dec-96	
	57-1469	717-148	17540	20-Aug-58	11-Sep-58	30-Sep-58	3-Oct-58	KC-135R		18-Sep-89	
	57-1470	717-148	17541	21-Aug-58	11-Sep-58	30-Sep-58	3-Oct-58	KC-135R		15-Nov-90	10-Dec-93
	57-1471	717-148	17542	22-Aug-58	12-Sep-58	7-Oct-58	9-Oct-58	KC-135E		8-Oct-87	17-Mar-08
	57-1472	717-148	17543	26-Aug-58	16-Sep-58	8-Oct-58	9-Oct-58	KC-135E		8-Dec-89	
	57-1473	717-148	17544	27-Aug-58	17-Sep-58	16-Oct-58	21-Oct-58	KC-135R		7-Aug-85	
	57-1474	717-148	17545	28-Aug-58	19-Sep-58	23-Oct-58	24-Oct-58	KC-135R		6-Dec-91	
	57-1475	717-148	17546	2-Sep-58	22-Sep-58	21-Oct-58	23-Oct-58	KC-135E		21-Dec-82	8-Aug-07
	57-1476	717-148	17547	3-Sep-58	24-Sep-58	14-Oct-58	16-Oct-58				13-Aug-92
	57-1477	717-148	17548	5-Sep-58	25-Sep-58	28-Oct-58	29-Oct-58				18-Aug-92
	57-1478	717-148	17549	8-Sep-58	29-Sep-58	8-Oct-58	12-Oct-58	KC-135E		24-Sep-82	10-Jun-09
	57-1479	717-148	17550	9-Sep-58	3-Oct-58	21-Oct-58	23-Oct-58	KC-135E		18-Jun-86	
								KC-135R		27-Feb-97	
	57-1480	717-148	17551	11-Sep-58	7-Oct-58	27-Oct-58	28-Oct-58	KC-135E		21-Jun-84	20-Feb-08
	57-1481	717-148	17552	12-Sep-58	10-Oct-58	27-Oct-58	29-Oct-58	KC-135E		20-Jun-84	20-Sep-89
	57-1482	717-148	17553	16-Sep-58	16-Oct-58	29-Oct-58	31-Oct-58	KC-135E		30-Aug-84	16-Sep-04
	57-1483	717-148	17554	17-Sep-58	16-Oct-58	28-Oct-58	31-Oct-58	KC-135R		14-Jun-85	
	57-1484	717-148	17555	18-Sep-58	20-Oct-58	31-Oct-58	3-Nov-58	KC-135E		7-Dec-82	27-Jun-07
	57-1485	717-148	17556	22-Sep-58	21-Oct-58	31-Oct-58	2-Nov-58	KC-135E		19-Aug-82	
								GKC-135E	Jul 90		Jul 90
	57-1486	717-148	17557	23-Sep-58	23-Oct-58	10-Nov-58	12-Nov-58	KC-135R		20-Mar-89	
	57-1487	717-148	17558	24-Sep-58	24-Oct-58	7-Nov-58	13-Nov-58	KC-135R		3-Oct-89	
	57-1488	717-148	17559	26-Sep-58	27-Oct-58	12-Nov-58	15-Nov-58	KC-135R		24-Apr-90	
	57-1489	717-148	17560	29-Sep-58	30-Oct-58	10-Nov-58	12-Nov-58				13-Mar-82
	57-1490	717-148	17561	1-Oct-58	30-Oct-58	17-Nov-58	19-Nov-58				29-Sep-92
	57-1491	717-148	17562	2-Oct-58	31-Oct-58	17-Nov-58	19-Nov-58	KC-135E		29-Oct-84	25-Mar-08
	57-1492	717-148	17563	3-Oct-58	31-Oct-58	14-Nov-58	19-Nov-58	KC-135E		18-Dec-87	28-Apr-09
	57-1493	717-148	17564	7-Oct-58	3-Nov-58	21-Nov-58	24-Nov-58	KC-135R		13-Mar-90	
	57-1494	717-148	17565	8-Oct-58	4-Nov-58	19-Nov-58	21-Nov-58	KC-135E		19-Sep-84	13-May-08
	57-1495	717-148	17566	9-Oct-58	6-Jun-58	26-Nov-58	3-Dec-58	KC-135E		5-Nov-82	Jul 10
KC-135A-10-BN	57-1496	717-148	17567	13-Oct-58	7-Nov-58	21-Nov-58	21-Nov-58	KC-135E		20-Jul-82	12-Feb-08
	57-1497	717-148	17568	14-Oct-58	12-Nov-58	21-Nov-58	25-Nov-58	KC-135E		29-May-91	22-Apr-08
	57-1498	717-148	17569	15-Oct-58	8-Nov-58	25-Nov-58	26-Nov-58				21-Jun-63
	57-1499	717-148	17570	17-Oct-58	12-Nov-58	25-Nov-58	26-Nov-58	KC-135R		16-Mar-90	
	57-1500	717-148	17571	20-Oct-58	14-Nov-58	26-Nov-58	3-Dec-58				5-Mar-74
	57-1501	717-148	17572	22-Oct-58	17-Nov-58	4-Dec-58	9-Dec-58	KC-135E		7-Dec-84	
	57-1502	717-148	17573	23-Oct-58	18-Nov-58	8-Dec-58	16-Dec-58	KC-135E		8-Aug-85	
	57-1503	717-148	17574	24-Oct-58	19-Nov-58	4-Dec-58	9-Dec-58	KC-135E		18-Feb-83	
	57-1503							GKC-135E	28-Sep-09		28-Sep-09
	57-1504	717-148	17575	28-Oct-58	21-Nov-58	11-Dec-58	16-Dec-58	KC-135E		3-Apr-86	29-Jul-08
	57-1505	717-148	17576	29-Oct-58	21-Nov-58	22-Dec-58	26-Dec-58	KC-135E		21-Mar-84	1-Apr-08
	57-1506	717-148	17577	31-Oct-58	24-Nov-58	12-Dec-58	16-Dec-58	KC-135R		1-May-90	
	57-1507	717-148	17578	3-Nov-58	24-Nov-58	2-Jan-59	7-Jan-59	KC-135R		26-Jul-84	7-Aug-09
	57-1508	717-148	17579	4-Nov-58	26-Nov-58	12-Dec-58	16-Dec-58	KC-135R		10-Sep-90	
	57-1509	717-148	17580	6-Nov-58	26-Nov-58	23-Dec-58	30-Dec-58	KC-135E		1-Jun-83	20-Jun-07
	57-1510	717-148	17581	7-Nov-58	3-Dec-58	26-Dec-58	5-Jan-59	KC-135E		29-Jul-82	18-Jul-09
	57-1511	717-148	17582	10-Nov-58	3-Dec-58	29-Dec-58	5-Jan-59	KC-135E		7-Jul-86	23-Jun-04
	57-1512	717-148	17583	12-Nov-58	5-Dec-58	7-Jan-59	8-Jan-59	KC-135E		30-Sep-86	
								KC-135R		3-Feb-97	
	57-1513	717-148	17584	13-Nov-58	8-Dec-58	19-Dec-58	27-Dec-58				15-Oct-59
	57-1514	717-148	17585	17-Nov-58	15-Dec-58	22-Dec-58	27-Dec-58	KC-135R		26-Apr-89	
	57-2589	717-148	17725	18-Nov-58	13-Dec-58	16-Jan-59	21-Jan-59	KC-135E		11-Oct-83	Jun 08
	57-2590	717-148	17726	19-Nov-58	15-Dec-58	29-Dec-58	5-Jan-59				3-Sep-92
	57-2591	717-148	17727	21-Nov-58	13-Dec-58	23-Dec-58	30-Dec-58				19-Apr-93
	57-2592	717-148	17728	24-Nov-58	19-Dec-58	15-Jan-59	29-Jan-59				23-Jun-93
	57-2593	717-148	17729	25-Nov-58	19-Dec-58	30-Dec-58	5-Jan-59	KC-135R		17-Oct-91	26-Mar-13
	57-2594	717-148	17730	1-Dec-58	27-Dec-58	13-Jan-59	14-Jan-59	KC-135E		28-Oct-83	
	57-2595	717-148	17731	2-Dec-58	23-Dec-58	15-Jan-59	19-Jan-59	KC-135E		9-Sep-83	30-Jun-09
	57-2596	717-148	17732	4-Dec-58	29-Dec-58	21-Jan-59	23-Jan-59				21-Apr-93
	57-2597	717-148	17733	5-Dec-58	29-Dec-58	13-Jan-59	14-Jan-59	KC-135R		22-May-91	
	57-2598	717-148	17734	8-Aug-58	2-Jan-59	20-Jan-59	22-Jan-59	KC-135E		4-Sep-86	
								KC-135R		2-Apr-97	
	57-2599	717-148	17735	10-Dec-58	2-Jan-59	15-Jan-59	17-Jan-59	KC-135R		17-Oct-90	
	57-2600	717-148	17736	11-Dec-58	6-Jan-59	22-Jan-59	27-Jan-59	KC-135E		18-Feb-86	18-Apr-08
	57-2601	717-148	17737	12-Dec-58	8-Jan-59	28-Jan-59	4-Feb-59	KC-135E		25-Jul-91	14-Apr-08

MDS & Block Number	Serial Number	Boeing Model No.	Const No.	Roll-out Date	First flight Date	Delivered Date	USAF Fly Away	New MDS	New MDS Date	Re-engine Date	Out of Service
KC-135A-10-BN	57-2602	717-148	17738	16-Dec-58	8-Jan-59	27-Jan-59	4-Feb-59	KC-135E		30-Aug-91	4-May-09
	57-2603	717-148	17739	17-Dec-58	12-Jan-59	30-Jan-59	12-Feb-59	KC-135E		15-Jul-86	
								KC-135R		20-Nov-98	
	57-2604	717-148	17740	19-Dec-58	13-Jan-59	29-Jan-59	4-Feb-59	KC-135E		30-Nov-82	26-Aug-08
	57-2605	717-148	17741	22-Dec-58	13-Jan-59	6-Feb-59	10-Feb-59	KC-135R		26-Feb-91	
	57-2606	717-148	17742	26-Dec-58	14-Jan-59	3-Feb-59	4-Feb-59	KC-135E		1-Apr-83	
								KC-135R		28-May-04	
	57-2607	717-148	17743	30-Dec-58	19-Jan-59	6-Feb-59	12-Feb-59	KC-135E		17-Nov-83	22-Feb-07
	57-2608	717-148	17744	31-Dec-58	20-Jan-59	11-Feb-59	12-Feb-59	KC-135E		12-Oct-83	23-Jul-08
	57-2609	717-148	17745	5-Jan-59	21-Jan-59	13-Feb-59	19-Feb-59				20-Jan-93
								KC-135R		20-May-98	
KC-135A-11-BN	58-0001	717-148	17746	6-Jan-59	4-Feb-59	20-Feb-59	25-Feb-59	KC-135R		6-Sep-90	
	58-0002	717-148	17747	8-Jan-59	26-Jan-59	11-Feb-59	17-Feb-59				31-Mar-59
	58-0003	717-148	17748	9-Jan-59	29-Jan-59	10-Feb-59	13-Feb-59	KC-135E		12-Apr-83	11-Jul-07
	58-0004	717-148	17749	13-Jan-59	29-Jan-59	17-Feb-59	19-Feb-59	KC-135R		21-Apr-89	
	58-0005	717-148	17750	14-Jan-59	4-Feb-59	18-Feb-59	20-Feb-59	KC-135E		17-Nov-87	3-Apr-08
	58-0006	717-148	17751	16-Jan-59	4-Feb-59	23-Feb-59	26-Feb-59	KC-135E		15-Oct-82	24-Mar-08
	58-0007	717-148	17752	19-Jan-59	5-Feb-59	20-Feb-59	26-Feb-59	EC-135A	1-Jan-65		
								EC-135P	31-Mar-67		3-Jan-80
	58-0008	717-148	17753	20-Jan-59	11-Feb-59	24-Feb-59	26-Feb-59	KC-135E		10-Feb-84	
								KC-135R		15-Apr-96	10-Jul-13
	58-0009	717-148	17754	22-Jan-59	11-Feb-59	5-Mar-59	9-Mar-59	KC-135R		6-Apr-90	
	58-0010	717-148	17755	23-Jan-59	12-Feb-59	4-Mar-59	9-Mar-59	KC-135R		21-Mar-90	
	58-0011	717-148	17756	27-Jan-59	12-Feb-59	27-Feb-59	3-Mar-59	EC-135A	1-Jan-65		
								EC-135P	31-Mar-67		
								(KC-135A)	28-Jul-76		
								(KC-135R)		27-Apr-90	
	58-0012	717-148	17757	28-Jan-59	13-Feb-59	25-Feb-59	27-Mar-59	KC-135E		6-Jan-83	1-Apr-08
	58-0013	717-148	17758	29-Jan-59	19-Feb-59	10-Mar-59	12-Mar-59	KC-135E		6-May-86	7-Mar-07
	58-0014	717-148	17759	2-Feb-59	19-Feb-59	9-Mar-59	10-Mar-59	KC-135E		21-Oct-87	
	58-0015	717-148	17760	3-Feb-59	20-Feb-59	11-Mar-59	12-Mar-59	KC-135R		26-Mar-91	
	58-0016	717-148	17761	4-Feb-59	20-Feb-59	9-Mar-59	10-Mar-59	KC-135R		1-Feb-91	
	58-0017	717-148	17762	6-Feb-59	25-Feb-59	16-Mar-59	16-Mar-59	KC-135E		30-Apr-84	26-Mar-09
	58-0018	717-148	17763	9-Feb-59	25-Feb-59	4-Mar-59	11-Mar-59	EC-135A	1-Jan-65		
								EC-135P	31-Mar-67		
								(KC-135A)	31-Mar-76		
								(KC-135R)		17-Feb-89	
	58-0019	717-148	17764	10-Feb-59	26-Feb-59	5-Mar-59	10-Mar-59	EC-135A	1-Jan-65		
								EC-135P	31-Mar-67	23-Jun-82	12-Feb-92
	58-0020	717-148	17765	12-Feb-59	27-Feb-59	10-Mar-59	11-Mar-59	KC-135E		14-Jan-86	24-Jul-08
	58-0021	717-148	17766	13-Feb-59	3-Mar-59	19-Mar-59	19-Mar-59	KC-135R		8-Feb-90	
	58-0022	717-148	17767	17-Feb-59	4-Mar-59	19-Mar-59	20-Mar-59	EC-135A	1-Jan-65		
								EC-135P	31-Mar-67	17-May-82	5-Mar-92
	58-0023	717-148	17768	18-Feb-59	5-Mar-59	19-Mar-59	20-Mar-59	KC-135R		8-Mar-90	
	58-0024	717-148	17769	19-Feb-59	10-Mar-59	24-Mar-59	26-Feb-59	KC-135E		20-May-83	12-Feb-08
	58-0025	717-148	17770	23-Feb-59	11-Mar-59	24-Mar-59	26-Feb-59				4-Aug-93
	58-0026	717-148	17771	24-Feb-59	12-Mar-59	3-Apr-59	8-Apr-59				17-Jan-68
	58-0027	717-148	17772	25-Feb-59	13-Mar-59	1-Apr-59	2-Apr-59	KC-135R		5-Jul-90	
	58-0028	717-148	17773	27-Feb-59	17-Mar-59	1-Apr-59	2-Apr-59				7-Apr-93
	58-0029	717-148	17774	2-Mar-59	18-Mar-59	7-Apr-59	8-Apr-59				2-Dec-92
	58-0030	717-148	17775	3-Mar-59	19-Mar-59	8-Apr-59	10-Apr-59	KC-135R		29-Mar-90	
	58-0031	717-148	17776	5-Mar-59	24-Mar-59	15-Apr-59	16-Apr-59				19-Mar-82
	58-0032	717-148	17777	6-Mar-59	24-Mar-59	10-Apr-59	14-Apr-59	KC-135E		12-Aug-83	17-Mar-09
	58-0033	717-148	17778	10-Mar-59	26-Mar-59	22-Apr-59	24-Apr-59				9-Jul-92
	58-0034	717-148	17779	11-Mar-59	27-Mar-59	27-Apr-59	1-May-59	KC-135R		22-Dec-92	
KC-135A-12-BN	58-0035	717-148	17780	12-Mar-59	30-Mar-59	7-Apr-59	9-Apr-59	KC-135R		7-Jun-90	
	58-0036	717-148	17781	16-Mar-59	31-Mar-59	29-Apr-59	1-May-59	KC-135R		15-Oct-92	
	58-0037	717-148	17782	17-Mar-59	3-Apr-59	20-Apr-59	21-Apr-59	KC-135E		4-Dec-87	2-Mar-07
	58-0038	717-148	17783	19-Mar-59	6-Apr-59	28-Apr-59	1-May-59	KC-135R		31-Jan-91	
	58-0039	717-148	17784	20-Mar-59	7-Apr-59	23-Apr-59	1-May-59	KC-135Q	1-Nov-67		3-Jun-71
	58-0040	717-148	17785	23-Mar-59	9-Apr-59	30-Apr-59	7-May-59	KC-135E		16-Sep-83	6-Feb-08
	58-0041	717-148	17786	25-Mar-59	10-Apr-59	4-May-59	6-May-59	KC-135E		18-Aug-86	27-Feb-07
	58-0042	717-148	17787	26-Mar-59	13-Apr-59	4-May-59	7-May-59	KC-135Q	31-Jul-67		
								KC-135T		29-Nov-93	
	58-0043	717-148	17788	27-Mar-59	15-Apr-59	4-May-59	6-May-59	KC-135E		29-Oct-82	28-Apr-08
	58-0044	717-148	17789	31-Mar-59	17-Apr-59	6-May-59	8-May-59	KC-135E		14-Sep-90	6-Feb-08
	58-0045	717-148	17790	1-Apr-59	17-Apr-59	13-May-59	16-May-59	KC-135Q	23-Sep-67		
								KC-135T		21-Feb-95	
	58-0046	717-148	17791	3-Apr-59	20-Apr-59	19-May-59	20-May-59	KC-135Q	31-May-67		
								KC-135T		21-Jul-95	
	58-0047	717-148	17792	6-Apr-59	23-Apr-59	21-May-59	26-May-59	KC-135Q	31-Jul-67		
								KC-135T		11-Jan-94	
	58-0048	717-148	17793	7-Apr-59	29-Apr-59	14-May-59	19-May-59				13-Mar-72
	58-0049	717-148	17794	9-Apr-59	24-Apr-59	15-May-59	20-May-59	KC-135Q	7-Sep-67		
								KC-135T		24-Apr-95	
	58-0050	717-148	17795	9-Apr-59	1-May-59	21-May-59	21-May-59	KC-135Q	31-Jul-67		
								KC-135T		11-Apr-95	
	58-0051	717-148	17796	13-Apr-59	4-May-59	21-May-59	21-May-59	KC-135R		20-Apr-89	
	58-0052	717-148	17797	14-Apr-59	4-May-59	26-May-59	28-May-59	KC-135E		22-May-86	
								KC-135R		6-Jan-97	
	58-0053	717-148	17798	16-Apr-59	5-May-59	4-Jun-59	5-Jun-59	KC-135E		12-Sep-86	15-Apr-04
	58-0054	717-148	17799	17-Apr-59	7-May-59	26-May-59	28-May-59	KC-135Q	8-Nov-67		
								KC-135T		24-May-94	
	58-0055	717-148	17800	21-Apr-59	8-May-59	28-May-59	2-Jun-59	KC-135Q	31-Jul-67		
								KC-135T		28-Feb-95	
	58-0056	717-148	17801	22-Apr-59	12-May-59	28-May-59	3-Jun-59	KC-135R		12-Nov-90	
	58-0057	717-148	17802	24-Apr-59	18-May-59	3-Jun-59	5-Jun-59	KC-135E		8-Nov-83	

MDS & Block Number	Serial Number	Boeing Model No.	Const No.	Roll-out Date	First flight Date	Delivered Date	USAF Fly Away	New MDS	New MDS Date	Re-engine Date	Out of Service
KC-135A-12-BN	58-0057							KC-135R			
	58-0058	717-148	17803	27-Apr-59	18-May-59	9-Jun-59	11-Jun-59	KC-135E		26-Aug-86	
								KC-135R		12-Apr-00	
	58-0059	717-148	17804	29-Apr-59	19-May-59	5-Jun-59	8-Jun-59	KC-135R		3-Nov-89	
	58-0060	717-148	17805	30-Apr-59	20-May-59	18-Jun-59	24-Jun-59	KC-135Q	31-Jul-67		
								KC-135T		3-May-94	
	58-0061	717-148	17806	4-May-59	21-May-59	12-Jun-59	16-Jun-59	KC-135Q	7-Sep-67		
								KC-135T		4-Nov-93	
	58-0062	717-148	17807	5-May-59	22-May-59	12-Jun-59	16-Jun-59	KC-135Q	1-Nov-67		
								KC-135T		6-Jul-94	
	58-0063	717-148	17808	7-May-59	26-May-59	12-Jun-59	16-Jun-59	KC-135R		7-Jan-92	
	58-0064	717-148	17809	8-May-59	27-May-59	23-Jun-59	30-Jun-59	KC-135E		15-Apr-86	23-Aug-04
KC-135A-13-BN	58-0065	717-148	17810	12-May-59	28-May-59	19-Jun-59	24-Jun-59	KC-135Q	12-Sep-67		
								KC-135T		27-Dec-93	
	58-0066	717-148	17811	13-May-59	2-Jun-59	17-Jun-59	19-Jun-59	KC-135R		24-Feb-93	
	58-0067	717-148	17812	15-May-59	5-Jun-59	24-Jun-59	25-Jun-59	KC-135E		26-Sep-83	
	58-0068	717-148	17813	18-May-59	5-Jun-59	30-Jun-59	7-Jul-59	KC-135E		30-Aug-83	15-Apr-08
	58-0069	717-148	17814	20-May-59	9-Jun-59	25-Jun-59	26-Jun-59	KC-135Q	10-Sep-67		
								KC-135T		27-Sep-95	
	58-0070	717-148	17815	21-May-59	10-Jun-59	30-Jun-59	7-Jul-59	GKC-135A	18-Oct-92		18-Oct-92
	58-0071	717-148	17816	25-May-59	11-Jun-59	2-Jul-59	7-Jul-59	KC-135Q	1-Nov-67		
								KC-135T		29-Aug-94	
	58-0072	717-148	17817	26-May-59	15-Jun-59	7-Jul-59	9-Jul-59	KC-135Q	31-Oct-67		
								KC-135T		29-Sep-94	
	58-0073	717-148	17818	28-May-59	18-Jun-59	10-Jul-59	14-Jul-59	KC-135R		8-Mar-90	
	58-0074	717-148	17819	1-Jun-59	17-Jun-59	7-Jul-59	14-Jul-59	KC-135Q	8-Sep-67		
								KC-135T		14-Nov-94	
	58-0075	717-148	17820	3-Jun-59	19-Jun-59	13-Jul-59	14-Jul-59	KC-135R		20-Jun-91	
	58-0076	717-148	17821	5-Jun-59	22-Jun-59	27-Jul-59	29-Jul-59	KC-135R		1-Oct-90	
	58-0077	717-148	17822	8-Jun-59	24-Jun-59	23-Jul-59	24-Jul-59	KC-135Q	1-Nov-67		
								KC-135T		14-Mar-95	
	58-0078	717-148	17823	9-Jun-59	26-Jun-59	14-Jul-59	15-Jul-59	KC-135E		22-Aug-83	15-Jun-09
	58-0079	717-148	17824	11-Jun-59	30-Jun-59	22-Jul-59	28-Jul-59	KC-135R		20-Feb-90	
	58-0080	717-148	17825	12-Jun-59	30-Jun-59	15-Jul-59	17-Jul-59	KC-135E		5-Aug-82	6-May-08
	58-0081	717-148	17826	16-Jun-59	1-Jul-59	15-Jul-59	21-Jul-59				16-Oct-92
	58-0082	717-148	17827	17-Jun-59	6-Jul-59	31-Jul-59	6-Aug-59	KC-135E		12-Mar-86	18-Aug-09
	58-0083	717-148	17828	19-Jun-59	8-Jul-59	22-Jul-59	24-Jul-59	KC-135R		7-Dec-90	
	58-0084	717-148	17829	22-Jun-59	9-Jul-59	30-Jul-59	4-Aug-59	KC-135Q	8-Sep-67		
								KC-135T		13-Sep-95	
	58-0085	717-148	17830	24-Jun-59	14-Jul-59	29-Jul-59	4-Aug-59	KC-135E		24-Mar-86	
								KC-135R		29-Apr-97	
	58-0086	717-148	17831	26-Jun-59	16-Jul-59	7-Aug-59	10-Aug-59	KC-135Q	16-Sep-67		
								KC-135T		19-Jan-95	
	58-0087	717-148	17832	30-Jun-59	21-Jul-59	21-Aug-59	25-Aug-59	KC-135E		16-Jun-83	19-Feb-08
	58-0088	717-148	17833	2-Jul-59	22-Jul-59	21-Aug-59	25-Aug-59	KC-135Q	1-Nov-67		
								KC-135T		14-Apr-94	
	58-0089	717-148	17834	7-Jul-59	27-Jul-59	21-Aug-59	26-Aug-59	KC-135Q	31-Oct-67		
								KC-135T		24-Jan-94	
	58-0090	717-148	17835	9-Jul-59	28-Jul-59	21-Aug-59	27-Aug-59	KC-135E		10-Jun-86	27-Mar-08
	58-0091	717-148	17836	13-Jul-59	29-Jul-59	21-Aug-59	28-Aug-59				18-Aug-93
	58-0092	717-148	17837	15-Jul-59	4-Aug-59	21-Aug-59	26-Aug-59	KC-135R		7-Aug-92	
	58-0093	717-148	17838	20-Jul-59	5-Aug-59	21-Aug-59	26-Aug-59	KC-135R		28-Sep-89	
KC-135A-14-BN	58-0094	717-148	17839	21-Jul-59	7-Aug-59	28-Aug-59	1-Sep-59	KC-135Q	31-Oct-67		
								KC-135T		15-Feb-94	
	58-0095	717-148	17840	23-Jul-59	11-Aug-59	28-Aug-59	1-Sep-59	KC-135Q	1-Aug-67		
	58-0095							KC-135T		13-Dec-94	
	58-0096	717-148	17841	27-Jul-59	17-Aug-59	28-Aug-59	2-Sep-59	KC-135E		18-Jan-85	23-Feb-04
	58-0097	717-148	17842	30-Jul-59	18-Aug-59	31-Aug-59	2-Sep-59				8-Sep-92
	58-0098	717-148	17843	31-Jul-59	19-Aug-59	21-Sep-59	23-Sep-59	KC-135R		15-Jan-86	
	58-0099	717-148	17844	4-Aug-59	20-Aug-59	21-Sep-59	23-Sep-59	KC-135Q	8-Nov-67		
								KC-135T		11-Nov-95	
	58-0100	717-148	17845	7-Aug-59	24-Aug-59	21-Sep-59	23-Sep-59	KC-135R		7-Nov-89	
	58-0101	717-148	17846	10-Aug-59	27-Aug-59	21-Sep-59	25-Sep-59				29-Apr-77
	58-0102	717-148	17847	12-Aug-59	1-Sep-59	21-Sep-59	24-Sep-59	KC-135R		14-Nov-91	
	58-0103	717-148	17848	14-Aug-59	2-Sep-59	21-Sep-59	23-Sep-59	KC-135Q	1-Nov-67		
								KC-135T		8-Nov-95	
	58-0104	717-148	17849	18-Aug-59	8-Sep-59	23-Sep-59	1-Oct-59	KC-135R		15-Jun-90	
	58-0105	717-148	17850	20-Aug-59	9-Sep-59	28-Sep-59	29-Sep-59				23-Aug-93
	58-0106	717-148	17851	24-Aug-59	15-Sep-59	30-Sep-59	2-Oct-59	KC-135R		12-Feb-92	
	58-0107	717-148	17852	27-Aug-59	16-Sep-59	30-Sep-59	6-Oct-59	KC-135E		2-Sep-82	
								KC-135E		8-Jan-04	
	58-0108	717-148	17853	28-Aug-59	17-Sep-59	14-Oct-59	15-Oct-59	KC-135E		14-May-86	30-May-08
	58-0109	717-148	17854	1-Sep-59	21-Sep-59	7-Oct-59	12-Oct-59	KC-135R		22-Aug-89	
	58-0110	717-148	17855	3-Sep-59	23-Sep-59	15-Oct-59	23-Oct-59				27-Sep-93
								KC-135R		30-Jun-97	
	58-0111	717-148	17856	4-Sep-59	24-Sep-59	8-Oct-59	14-Oct-59	KC-135E		10-Feb-83	6-Apr-09
	58-0112	717-148	17857	10-Sep-59	28-Sep-59	15-Oct-59	26-Oct-59	KC-135Q	8-Sep-67		
								KC-135T		1-Feb-95	
	58-0113	717-148	17858	11-Sep-59	30-Sep-59	23-Oct-59	28-Oct-59	KC-135R		30-Jul-92	
	58-0114	717-148	17859	14-Sep-59	2-Oct-59	23-Oct-59	28-Oct-59	KC-135R		6-May-92	29-Apr-13
	58-0115	717-148	17860	18-Sep-59	6-Oct-59	23-Oct-59	4-Nov-59	KC-135E		6-May-83	7-Jul-09
	58-0116	717-148	17861	18-Sep-59	9-Oct-59	30-Oct-59	4-Nov-59	KC-135E		15-Oct-90	12-Sep-07
	58-0117	717-148	17862	24-Sep-59	14-Oct-59	3-Nov-59	4-Nov-59	KC-135Q	9-Sep-67		
								KC-135T		5-Jul-95	
	58-0118	717-148	17863	28-Sep-59	15-Oct-59	4-Nov-59	6-Nov-59	KC-135R		3-Feb-92	
	58-0119	717-148	17864	30-Sep-59	19-Oct-59	13-Nov-59	19-Nov-59	KC-135R		21-Aug-92	
	58-0120	717-148	17865	2-Oct-59	22-Oct-59	10-Nov-59	12-Nov-59	KC-135R		28-Aug-85	

MDS & Block Number	Serial Number	Boeing Model No.	Const No.	Roll-out Date	First flight Date	Delivered Date	USAF Fly Away	New MDS	New MDS Date	Re-engine Date	Out of Service
KC-135A-14-BN	58-0121	717-148	17866	6-Oct-59	27-Oct-59	17-Nov-59	20-Nov-59	KC-135R		26-Jan-93	
	58-0122	717-148	17867	8-Oct-59	28-Oct-59	18-Nov-59	20-Nov-59	KC-135R		8-Jan-91	
	58-0123	717-148	17868	12-Oct-59	30-Oct-59	23-Nov-59	25-Nov-59	KC-135R		12-Feb-91	
	58-0124	717-148	17869	14-Oct-59	4-Nov-59	25-Nov-59	3-Dec-59	(KC-135A) (KC-135R)	n/a	12-May-89	
	58-0125	717-148	17870	16-Oct-59	5-Nov-59	2-Dec-59	8-Dec-59	KC-135Q KC-135T	1-Nov-67	30-Nov-94	
	58-0126	717-148	17871	22-Oct-59	10-Nov-59	7-Dec-59	8-Dec-59	[KC-135R] (KC-135A) (KC-135R)	13 Nov 69 Jan 76	23-Jan-89	
	58-0127	717-148	17872	27-Oct-59	12-Nov-59	2-Dec-59	4-Dec-59				19-Sep-79
	58-0128	717-148	17873	30-Oct-59	17-Nov-59	28-Dec-59	31-Dec-59	KC-135R		2-Jul-91	
	58-0129	717-148	17874	4-Nov-59	25-Nov-59	15-Dec-59	23-Dec-59	KC-135Q KC-135T	8-Sep-67	25-Oct-95	
	58-0130	717-148	17875	9-Nov-59	25-Nov-59	28-Dec-59	31-Dec-59	KC-135R		6-Dec-90	21-May-13
KC-135A-BN	58-0131 to 58-0157	717-148	17876 to 17902	Canceled							
KC-135A-15-BN	59-1443	717-148	17931	12-Nov-59	8-Dec-59	30-Dec-59	5-Jan-60				27-Aug-85
	59-1444	717-148	17932	16-Nov-59	8-Dec-59	30-Dec-59	5-Jan-60	KC-135R		19-Jun-89	
	59-1445	717-148	17933	23-Nov-59	16-Dec-59	7-Jan-60	9-Jan-60	KC-135E		27-Jan-86	14-Jul-09
	59-1446	717-148	17934	25-Nov-59	16-Dec-59	8-Jan-60	14-Jan-60	KC-135R		25-Oct-85	
	59-1447	717-148	17935	2-Dec-59	18-Dec-59	11-Jan-60	14-Jan-60	KC-135E		23-Jul-86	5-Apr-07
	59-1448	717-148	17936	7-Dec-59	28-Dec-59	14-Jan-60	19-Jan-60	KC-135E KC-135R		8-Oct-84 26-Sep-96	
	59-1449	717-148	17937	10-Dec-59	31-Dec-59	19-Jan-60	21-Jan-60				27-Aug-93
	59-1450	717-148	17938	15-Dec-59	14-Jan-60	26-Jan-60	29-Jan-60	KC-135E KC-135R		7-Aug-84 28-Jun-96	
	59-1451	717-148	17939	18-Dec-59	8-Jan-60	21-Jan-60	27-Jan-60	KC-135E		26-Jun-86	27-Aug-08
	59-1452	717-148	17940	23-Dec-59	14-Jan-60	29-Jan-60	1-Feb-60	KC-135E		6-Feb-86	13-Jan-99
	59-1453	717-148	17941	30-Dec-59	19-Jan-60	9-Feb-60	12-Feb-60	KC-135R		5-Sep-85	
	59-1454	717-148	17942	5-Jan-60	22-Jan-60	8-Feb-60	9-Feb-60	KC-135R		9-Jun-00	1-Sep-93
	59-1455	717-148	17943	8-Jan-60	27-Jan-60	11-Feb-60	12-Feb-60	KC-135R		23-Sep-85	
	59-1456	717-148	17944	13-Jan-60	3-Feb-60	16-Feb-60	17-Feb-60	KC-135E		7-Jul-83	26-Feb-08
	59-1457	717-148	17945	18-Jan-60	3-Feb-60	12-Feb-60	16-Feb-60	KC-135E		27-Oct-83	17-Jun-08
	59-1458	717-148	17946	21-Jan-60	11-Feb-60	19-Feb-60	24-Feb-60	KC-135R		31-Jul-85	
	59-1459	717-148	17947	26-Jan-60	11-Feb-60	26-Feb-60	29-Feb-60	KC-135R		7-Jan-86	
	59-1460	717-148	17948	29-Jan-60	16-Feb-60	25-Feb-60	26-Feb-60	KC-135Q KC-135T	9-Sep-67	20-Dec-94	
	59-1461	717-148	17949	3-Feb-60	18-Feb-60	3-Mar-60	14-Mar-60	KC-135R		22-Mar-91	
	59-1462	717-148	17950	8-Feb-60	25-Feb-60	11-Mar-60	1-Apr-60	KC-135Q KC-135T	8-Sep-67	27-Sep-94	
	59-1463	717-148	17951	11-Feb-60	26-Feb-60	11-Mar-60	30-Mar-60	KC-135R		13-Aug-90	
	59-1464	717-148	17952	16-Feb-60	2-Mar-60	11-Mar-60	1-Apr-60	KC-135Q KC-135T	8-Sep-67	20-Jun-95	
	59-1465	717-148	17953	19-Feb-60	8-Mar-60	28-Mar-60	31-Mar-60	[KC-135A] [KC-135R]	May 63 30-May-67		17-Jul-67
	59-1466	717-148	17954	24-Feb-60	11-Mar-60	31-Mar-60	1-Apr-60	KC-135R		6-May-85	
	59-1467	717-148	17955	29-Feb-60	16-Mar-60	29-Mar-60	1-Apr-60	KC-135Q KC-135T	8-Sep-67	9-Feb-94	
	59-1468	717-148	17956	2-Mar-60	18-Mar-60	8-Apr-60	12-Apr-60	KC-135Q KC-135T	8-Sep-67	16-Jun-94	
	59-1469	717-148	17957	8-Mar-60	23-Mar-60	8-Apr-60	14-Apr-60	KC-135R		11-Sep-90	
	59-1470	717-148	17958	11-Mar-60	28-Mar-60	15-Apr-60	15-Apr-60	KC-135Q KC-135T	9-Sep-67	4-Nov-94	
	59-1471	717-148	17959	16-Mar-60	31-Mar-60	18-Apr-60	21-Apr-60	KC-135Q KC-135T	8-Sep-67	22-May-95	
	59-1472	717-148	17960	22-Mar-60	7-Apr-60	15-Apr-60	19-Apr-60	KC-135R		7-May-90	
KC-135A-16-BN	59-1473	717-148	17961	21-Mar-60	4-Apr-60	22-Apr-60	27-Apr-60	KC-135E		12-Nov-82	6-Mar-08
	59-1474	717-148	17962	24-Mar-60	13-Apr-60	28-Apr-60	3-May-60	KC-135Q KC-135T	8-Sep-67	8-May-95	
	59-1475	717-148	17963	29-Mar-60	18-Apr-60	4-May-60	6-May-60	KC-135R		13-Jan-89	
	59-1476	717-148	17964	1-Apr-60	21-Apr-60	10-May-60	11-May-60	KC-135R		5-Jun-90	
	59-1477	717-148	17965	6-Apr-60	25-Apr-60	18-May-60	19-May-60	KC-135E		2-Jun-86	25-Jun-08
	59-1478	717-148	17966	11-Apr-60	26-Apr-60	18-May-60	19-May-60	KC-135R		30-Apr-86	
	59-1479	717-148	17967	14-Apr-60	29-Apr-60	17-May-60	19-May-60	KC-135E		28-Feb-83	24-Apr-07
	59-1480	717-148	17968	19-Apr-60	4-May-60	18-May-60	18-May-60	KC-135Q KC-135T	31-Jul-67	22-Nov-95	
	59-1481	717-148	17969	22-Apr-60	10-May-60	20-May-60	1-Jun-60	KC-135A			Oct-95
	59-1482	717-148	17970	27-Apr-60	13-May-60	2-Jun-60	3-Jun-60	KC-135R		13-May-85	
	59-1483	717-148	17971	2-May-60	18-May-60	1-Jun-60	3-Jun-60	KC-135R		14-Jun-89	
	59-1484	717-148	17972	5-May-60	20-May-60	8-Jun-60	10-Jun-60	KC-135E		11-Mar-83	21-Jul-09
	59-1485	717-148	17973	10-May-60	25-May-60	13-Jun-60	14-Jun-60	KC-135E		19-Oct-83	20-Apr-09
	59-1486	717-148	17974	13-May-60	31-May-60	8-Jun-60	10-Jun-60	KC-135R		7-Jun-93	
	59-1487	717-148	17975	18-May-60	6-Jun-60	17-Jun-60	22-Jun-60	KC-135E		25-Jul-83	26-Oct-06
	59-1488	717-148	17976	23-May-60	8-Jun-60	24-Jun-60	25-Jun-60	KC-135R		13-Mar-92	
	59-1489	717-148	17977	26-May-60	13-Jun-60	23-Jun-60	24-Jun-60	KC-135E		8-Feb-83	10-Mar-08
	59-1490	717-148	17978	1-Jun-60	17-Jun-60	1-Jul-60	1-Jul-60	KC-135Q KC-135T	8-Sep-67	22-Dec-95	
	59-1491	717-148	17979	6-Jun-60	21-Jun-60	5-Jul-60	6-Jul-60	JKC-135A RC-135S	7-Feb-62 1-Mar-63		13-Jan-69
	59-1492	717-148	17980	9-Jun-60	24-Jun-60	13-Jul-60	14-Jul-60	KC-135R		16-Oct-90	
	59-1493	717-148	17981	14-Jun-60	29-Jun-60	13-Jul-60	15-Jul-60	KC-135E		12-Jan-88	6-Mar-08
	59-1494	717-148	17982	17-Jun-60	6-Jul-60	14-Jul-60	22-Jul-60	KC-135E		26-Oct-84	11-Jan-90
	59-1495	717-148	17983	22-Jun-60	12-Jul-60	25-Jul-60	26-Jul-60	KC-135R		8-Apr-86	

MDS & Block Number	Serial Number	Boeing Model No.	Const No.	Roll-out Date	First flight Date	Delivered Date	USAF Fly Away	New MDS	New MDS Date	Re-engine Date	Out of Service
KC-135A-16-BN	59-1496	717-148	17984	27-Jun-60	14-Jul-60	25-Jul-60	26-Jul-60	KC-135E		1-Apr-91	23-May-07
	59-1497	717-148	17985	30-Jun-60	19-Jul-60	3-Aug-60	4-Aug-60	KC-135E		8-Jul-83	May 09
	59-1498	717-148	17986	6-Jul-60	22-Jul-60	2-Aug-60	5-Aug-60	KC-135R		2-Aug-89	
	59-1499	717-148	17987	11-Jul-60	27-Jul-60	10-Aug-60	11-Aug-60	KC-135E		11-Jun-84	
								KC-135R		24-May-96	
	59-1500	717-148	17988	14-Jul-60	29-Jul-60	10-Aug-60	11-Aug-60	KC-135R		11-May-93	
	59-1501	717-148	17989	19-Jul-60	3-Aug-60	12-Aug-60	17-Aug-60	KC-135R		11-Mar-92	
	59-1502	717-148	17990	22-Jul-60	8-Aug-60	19-Aug-60	22-Aug-60	KC-135R		12-Jun-92	
KC-135A-17-BN	59-1503	717-148	17991	27-Jul-60	11-Aug-60	24-Aug-60	26-Aug-60	KC-135E		30-Oct-87	3-Mar-08
	59-1504	717-148	17992	1-Aug-60	17-Aug-60	2-Sep-60	9-Sep-60	KC-135Q	31-Oct-67		
								KC-135T		6-Jun-95	
	59-1505	717-148	17993	4-Aug-60	19-Aug-60	7-Sep-60	8-Sep-60	KC-135E		23-Aug-84	
								KC-135R		19-Apr-96	
	59-1506	717-148	17994	9-Aug-60	24-Aug-60	9-Sep-60	14-Sep-60	KC-135E		2-Aug-83	
								KC-135R		8-Oct-02	
	59-1507	717-148	17995	12-Aug-60	1-Sep-60	13-Sep-60	15-Sep-60	KC-135R		26-Aug-92	
	59-1508	717-148	17996	17-Aug-60	8-Sep-60	19-Sep-60	20-Sep-60	KC-135R		9-Oct-92	
	59-1509	717-148	17997	22-Aug-60	13-Sep-60	21-Sep-60	23-Sep-60	KC-135E		31-Oct-84	
								KC-135R		28-Oct-96	
	59-1510	717-148	17998	25-Aug-60	15-Sep-60	23-Sep-60	23-Sep-60	KC-135Q	31-Jul-67		
								KC-135T		17-Aug-94	
	59-1511	717-148	17999	30-Aug-60	20-Sep-60	3-Oct-60	5-Oct-60	KC-135R		1-Dec-86	
	59-1512	717-148	18000	2-Sep-60	23-Sep-60	3-Oct-60	4-Oct-60	KC-135Q	8-Sep-67		
								KC-135T		28-Mar-95	
	59-1513	717-148	18001	8-Sep-60	28-Sep-60	10-Oct-60	11-Oct-60	KC-135Q	1-Nov-67		
								KC-135T		21-Mar-94	
	59-1514	717-148	18002	13-Sep-60	4-Oct-60	18-Oct-60	20-Oct-60	[KC-135A]	23 Mar 62		
								[KC-135R]	May 63		
								(KC-135A)	4-Mar-74		
								(KC-135E)		30-Jan-82	6-Nov-97
	59-1515	717-148	18003	16-Sep-60	7-Oct-60	17-Oct-60	20-Oct-60	KC-135R		30-Jul-85	
	59-1516	717-148	18004	21-Sep-60	12-Oct-60	26-Oct-60	28-Oct-60	KC-135E		3-Nov-87	
								KC-135R		12-Jun-96	
	59-1517	717-148	18005	26-Sep-60	13-Oct-60	25-Oct-60	28-Oct-60	KC-135E		4-Nov-85	
	59-1518	717-148	18006	29-Sep-60	14-Oct-60	19-Oct-60	20-Oct-60	EC-135K	Nov 79	24-Apr-82	
	59-1518							C-135K	96		10-Mar-03
	59-1519	717-148	18007	4-Oct-60	25-Oct-60	3-Nov-60	8-Nov-60	KC-135E		14-Dec-82	
	59-1520	717-148	18008	7-Oct-60	27-Oct-60	3-Nov-60	7-Nov-60	KC-135Q	8-Sep-67		
								KC-135T		1-Aug-95	
	59-1521	717-148	18009	17-Oct-60	4-Nov-60	17-Nov-60	17-Nov-60	KC-135R		27-Mar-87	
	59-1522	717-148	18010	12-Oct-60	1-Nov-60	14-Nov-60	14-Nov-60	KC-135R		30-Sep-92	
	59-1523	717-148	18011	20-Oct-60	11-Nov-60	21-Nov-60	22-Nov-60	KC-135Q	1-Nov-67		
								KC-135T		3-Jun-94	
KC-135A-18-BN	60-0313	717-148	18088	2-Nov-60	22-Nov-60	29-Nov-60	1-Dec-60	KC-135R		23-Dec-87	
	60-0314	717-148	18089	28-Oct-60	22-Nov-60	30-Nov-60	9-Dec-60	KC-135R		23-May-89	
	60-0315	717-148	18090	30-Nov-60	20-Dec-60	29-Dec-60	30-Dec-60	KC-135R		11-Aug-89	
	60-0316	717-148	18091	7-Nov-60	29-Nov-60	7-Dec-60	12-Dec-60	KC-135E		18-Mar-91	
								KC-135R		5-Feb-02	
	60-0317	717-148	18092	10-Nov-60	5-Dec-60	16-Dec-60	20-Dec-60				11-Oct-88
	60-0318	717-148	18093	15-Nov-60	12-Dec-60	19-Dec-60	20-Dec-60	KC-135R		14-Aug-92	
	60-0319	717-148	18094	18-Nov-60	13-Dec-60	21-Dec-60	22-Dec-60	KC-135R		29-Jun-92	20-Jun-12
	60-0320	717-148	18095	23-Nov-60	20-Dec-60	28-Dec-60	30-Dec-60	KC-135R		21-Oct-91	
	60-0321	717-148	18096	28-Dec-60	18-Jan-61	25-Jan-61	27-Jan-61	KC-135R		14-Sep-85	18-Apr-13
	60-0322	717-148	18097	5-Dec-60	10-Jan-61	18-Jan-61	20-Jan-61	KC-135R		30-Sep-86	
	60-0323	717-148	18098	8-Dec-60	6-Jan-61	13-Jan-61	16-Jan-61	KC-135R		27-Jun-89	
	60-0324	717-148	18099	13-Dec-60	6-Jan-61	12-Jan-61	13-Jan-61	KC-135R		15-Mar-91	
	60-0325	717-148	18100	16-Dec-60	12-Jan-61	18-Jan-61	1-Feb-61				22-Sep-93
								KC-135R		19-Apr-98	
	60-0326	717-148	18101	21-Dec-60	16-Jan-61	31-Jan-61	2-Feb-61				2-Sep-93
								KC-135R		1-Nov-97	
	60-0327	717-148	18102	24-Jan-61	16-Feb-61	28-Feb-61	3-Mar-61	KC-135E		14-May-91	24-Apr-08
	60-0328	717-148	18103	3-Jan-61	24-Jan-61	2-Feb-61	3-Feb-61	KC-135R		10-Dec-91	
	60-0329	717-148	18104	6-Jan-61	26-Jan-61	6-Feb-61	8-Feb-61	KC-135R		10-Mar-86	
	60-0330	717-148	18105	11-Jan-61	2-Feb-61	9-Feb-61	15-Feb-61				13-Feb-87
	60-0331	717-148	18106	16-Jan-61	7-Feb-61	27-Feb-61	3-Mar-61	KC-135R		30-Mar-89	
	60-0332	717-148	18107	19-Jan-61	8-Feb-61	28-Feb-61	2-Mar-61	KC-135R		28-Apr-92	
	60-0333	717-148	18108	17-Feb-61	13-Mar-61	22-Mar-61	23-Mar-61	KC-135R		11-Aug-89	
	60-0334	717-148	18109	27-Jan-61	22-Feb-61	3-Mar-61	6-Mar-61	KC-135R		19-Sep-89	
	60-0335	717-148	18110	1-Feb-61	22-Feb-61	14-Mar-61	15-Mar-61	KC-135Q	30-Jul-67		
								KC-135T		11-Aug-94	
	60-0336	717-148	18111	6-Feb-61	28-Feb-61	9-Mar-61	10-Mar-61	KC-135Q	30-Jul-67		
								KC-135T		14-Jul-94	
	60-0337	717-148	18112	9-Feb-61	1-Mar-61	13-Mar-61	14-Mar-61	KC-135Q	30-Jul-67		
								KC-135T		21-Mar-94	
	60-0338	717-148	18113	14-Feb-61	3-Mar-61	16-Mar-61	17-Mar-61	KC-135Q	30-Jul-67		8-Feb-80
	60-0339	717-148	18114	17-Feb-61	8-Mar-61	3-Apr-61	4-Apr-61	KC-135Q	30-Jul-67		
								KC-135T		20-May-94	
	60-0340	717-148	18115	22-Feb-61	14-Mar-61	3-Apr-61	4-Apr-61				8-Jul-64
	60-0341	717-148	18116	27-Feb-61	17-Mar-61	3-Apr-61	5-Apr-61	KC-135R		26-Jun-87	
	60-0342	717-148	18117	2-Mar-61	22-Mar-61	4-Apr-61	6-Apr-61	KC-135Q	30-Jul-67		
								KC-135T		15-Aug-95	
KC-135A-19-BN	60-0343	717-148	18118	7-Mar-61	27-Mar-61	12-Apr-61	13-Apr-61	KC-135Q	30-Jul-67		
								KC-135T		18-Nov-93	
	60-0344	717-148	18119	10-Mar-61	31-Mar-61	18-Apr-61	18-Apr-61	KC-135Q	30-Jul-67		
								KC-135T		20-Oct-94	
	60-0345	717-148	18120	15-Mar-61	7-Apr-61	9-May-61	12-May-61	KC-135Q	30-Jul-67		

MDS & Block Number	Serial Number	Boeing Model No.	Const No.	Roll-out Date	First flight Date	Delivered Date	USAF Fly Away	New MDS	New MDS Date	Re-engine Date	Out of Service
KC-135A-19-BN	60-0345							KC-135T		8-Dec-95	
	60-0346	717-148	18121	20-Mar-61	11-Apr-61	3-May-61	5-May-61	KC-135Q	30-Jul-67		
								KC-135T		26-Jul-94	
	60-0347	717-148	18122	23-Mar-61	24-Apr-61	4-May-61	8-May-61	KC-135R		27-Feb-86	
	60-0348	717-148	18123	28-Mar-61	19-Apr-61	2-May-61	3-May-61	KC-135R		4-Mar-92	
	60-0349	717-148	18124	23-Jun-61	17-Jul-61	11-Sep-61	11-Sep-61	KC-135R		5-Jul-91	
	60-0350	717-148	18125	5-Apr-61	26-Apr-61	15-May-61	15-May-61	KC-135R		4-Oct-91	
	60-0351	717-148	18126	10-Apr-61	28-Apr-61	12-May-61	12-May-61	KC-135R		8-Aug-91	
	60-0352	717-148	18127	13-Apr-61	3-May-61	1-Jun-61	1-Jun-61				10-Sep-62
	60-0353	717-148	18128	18-Apr-61	8-May-61	1-Jun-61	5-Jun-61	KC-135R		9-May-86	
	60-0354	717-148	18129	21-Apr-61	11-May-61	1-Jun-61	5-Jun-61				7-Dec-75
	60-0355	717-148	18130	26-Apr-61	16-May-61	6-Jun-61	7-Jun-61	KC-135R		8-Apr-93	
	60-0356	717-148	18131	1-May-61	19-May-61	2-Jun-61	9-Jun-61	C-135A	9-Jun-61		
								KC-135A-II	31-Jan-63		
								RC-135D	Sep 66		
								(KC-135A)	4-Jan-78		
								(KC-135R)		5-Jan-89	
	60-0357	717-148	18132	4-May-61	24-May-61	6-Jun-61	9-Jun-61	C-135A	9-Jun-61		
								KC-135A-II	19-Dec-62		
								RC-135D	18-Jan-66		
								(KC-135A)	76		
								(KC-135R)		5-Jul-88	
	60-0358	717-148	18133	9-May-61	29-May-61	3-Jul-61	6-Jul-61	KC-135R		19-Dec-91	
	60-0359	717-148	18134	12-May-61	2-Jun-61	3-Jul-61	10-Jul-61	KC-135R		14-Jul-86	
	60-0360	717-148	18135	17-May-61	7-Jun-61	10-Jul-61	11-Jul-61	KC-135R		23-Mar-89	
	60-0361	717-148	18136	22-May-61	12-Jun-61	5-Jul-61	11-Jul-61				13-Mar-87
	60-0362	717-148	18137	25-May-61	14-Jun-61	5-Jul-61	5-Jul-61	C-135A	5-Jul-61		
								KC-135A-II	4-Apr-63		
								RC-135G	4-Oct-66		
								RC-135D	1 Nov 66		
								(KC-135A)	76		
								(KC-135R)		27-May-88	
	60-0363	717-148	18138	31-May-61	20-Jun-61	3-Aug-61	3-Aug-61	KC-135R		24-Sep-91	
	60-0364	717-148	18139	5-Jun-61	22-Jun-61	3-Aug-61	3-Aug-61	KC-135R		23-Aug-88	
	60-0365	717-148	18140	29-Jun-61	19-Jul-61	3-Oct-61	6-Oct-61	KC-135R		20-Jan-86	
	60-0366	717-148	18141	13-Jun-61	30-Jun-61	3-Aug-61	3-Aug-61	KC-135R		8-May-89	
	60-0367	717-148	18142	16-Jun-61	6-Jul-61	1-Sep-61	5-Sep-61	KC-135R		4-Oct-85	
	60-0368	717-148	18143	21-Jun-61	13-Jul-61	7-Sep-61	8-Sep-61				6-Feb-76
C-135A-01-BN	60-0369	717-157	18144	14-Jun-61	23-Jun-61	6-Oct-61	6-Oct-61	NC-135A	3 Jun 64		
								GNC-135A			9-Jun-76
	60-0370	717-157	18145	3-Jul-61	20-Jul-61	11-Aug-61	12-Aug-61	NC-135A	3 Jun 64		30-Jun-76
	60-0371	717-157	18146	18-Jul-61	9-Aug-61	23-Aug-61	23-Aug-61	NC-135A	3 Jun 64		12-Aug-94
	60-0372	717-157	18147	1-Aug-61	24-Aug-61	31-Aug-61	31-Aug-61	EC-135N	29 Apr 66		
								C-135N	79		
								C-135E		24-May-82	28-Sep-05
	60-0373	717-157	18148	14-Aug-61	5-Sep-61	15-Sep-61	15-Sep-61				25-Jun-65
	60-0374	717-157	18149	24-Aug-61	15-Sep-61	22-Sep-61	25-Sep-61	EC-135N	16 Apr 66		
								EC-135E		10-Apr-82	3-Nov-00
	60-0375	717-157	18150	7-Sep-61	22-Sep-61	28-Sep-61	28-Sep-61	EC-135N	16 Apr 66		
								C-135N	76		
								C-135E		3-May-82	18-Apr-01
	60-0376	717-157	18151	13-Sep-61	11-Oct-61	27-Oct-61	30-Oct-61	JC-135A	23-Jun-65		
								C-135A	31-Oct-67		
								C-135E		17-Apr-82	21-Jun-01
	60-0377	717-157	18152	22-Sep-61	12-Oct-61	31-Oct-61	1-Nov-61				15-Dec-95
	60-0378	717-157	18153	28-Sep-61	17-Oct-61	1-Nov-61	3-Nov-61	C-135A	31-Aug-77		23-Jul-94
KC-135A-BN	60-0379 to 60-0408	717-148 717-148	n/a n/a	Canceled							
KC-135A-19-BN	61-0261	717-148	18168	10-Jul-61	31-Jul-61	6-Oct-61	10-Oct-61	EC-135L	25-Sep-67		29-May-92
	61-0262	717-148	18169	13-Jul-61	2-Aug-61	23-Jan-62	26-Jan-62	EC-135A	1-Jan-65		30-Mar-92
	61-0263	717-148	18170	18-Jul-61	8-Aug-61	15-Oct-61	18-Oct-61	EC-135L	13-Dec-67		5-May-92
	61-0264	717-148	18171	21-Jul-61	16-Aug-61	8-Nov-61	8-Nov-61	KC-135R		18-Jul-89	
	61-0265	717-148	18172	31-Jul-61	25-Aug-61	15-Nov-61	16-Nov-61				4-Jan-65
	61-0266	717-148	18173	3-Aug-61	29-Aug-61	17-Nov-61	21-Nov-61	KC-135R		24-Oct-91	
	61-0267	717-148	18174	16-Aug-61	8-Sep-61	27-Nov-61	27-Nov-61	KC-135R		27-Nov-91	
	61-0268	717-148	18175	21-Aug-61	14-Sep-61	28-Nov-61	30-Nov-61	KC-135A-VIII	n/a		
								KC-135A	n/a		
								KC-135E		4-Sep-90	18-Mar-08
	61-0269	717-148	18176	5-Sep-61	26-Sep-61	8-Dec-61	8-Dec-61	EC-135L	21-Dec-67		29-Jun-92
	61-0270	717-148	18177	12-Sep-61	29-Sep-61	18-Dec-61	20-Dec-61	KC-135A-VIII	n/a		
								KC-135A	n/a		
								KC-135E		12-Jun-90	17-Sep-08
	61-0271	717-148	18178	15-Sep-61	20-Oct-61	20-Dec-61	21-Dec-61	KC-135A-VIII	n/a		
								KC-135A	n/a		
								KC-135E		26-Apr-90	21-May-07
	61-0272	717-148	18179	2-Oct-61	24-Oct-61	28-Dec-61	9-Jan-62	KC-135R		21-Jul-87	
	61-0273	717-148	18180	10-Oct-61	1-Nov-61	28-Dec-61	29-Dec-61				17-Jan-66
	61-0274	717-148	18181	19-Oct-61	17-Nov-61	4-Jan-62	8-Jan-62	EC-135H	Feb 68	16-Mar-82	
								EC-135P	23-May-88		27-Feb-92
	61-0275	717-148	18182	27-Oct-61	22-Nov-61	11-Jan-62	12-Jan-62	KC-135R		23-May-89	
	61-0276	717-148	18183	6-Nov-61	1-Dec-61	16-Jan-62	19-Jan-62	KC-135R		30-Jul-85	
	61-0277	717-148	18184	13-Nov-61	12-Dec-61	16-Jan-62	19-Jan-62	KC-135R		3-Sep-87	
KC-135A-20-BN	61-0278	717-148	18185	20-Nov-61	21-Dec-61	1-Feb-62	2-Feb-62	EC-135A	1-Jan-65		18-Sep-92
	61-0279	717-148	18186	27-Nov-61	26-Dec-61	1-Feb-62	6-Feb-62	EC-135L	27-Oct-65		22-May-92

MDS & Block Number	Serial Number	Boeing Model No.	Const No.	Roll-out Date	First flight Date	Delivered Date	USAF Fly Away	New MDS	New MDS Date	Re-engine Date	Out of Service
KC-135A-20-BN	61-0280	717-148	18187	3-Dec-61	29-Dec-61	2-Feb-62	8-Feb-62	KC-135A-VIII	n/a		
								KC-135A	n/a		
								KC-135E		22-May-90	
								KC-135R		7-Aug-98	
	61-0281	717-148	18188	7-Dec-61	4-Jan-62	8-Feb-62	12-Feb-62	EC-135L	30-Jun-66		
								KC-135A	1-May-70		
								EC-135L	6-Jan-71		
								KC-135A	14-Sep-71		
								KC-135E		15-Feb-91	25-Aug-09
	61-0282	717-148	18189	12-Dec-61	9-Jan-62	12-Feb-62	13-Feb-62	EC-135A	16-Nov-64		
								EC-135H	67	15-Jun-82	
								GEC-135H	15-Nov-91		15-Nov-91
	61-0283	717-148	18190	14-Dec-61	10-Jan-62	1-Mar-62	2-Mar-62	EC-135L	16-Aug-65		6-May-92
	61-0284	717-148	18191	18-Dec-61	16-Jan-62	1-Mar-62	5-Mar-62	KC-135R		30-Jul-91	
	61-0285	717-148	18192	21-Dec-61	18-Jan-62	12-Mar-62	12-Mar-62	EC-135A	16-Nov-64		
								EC-135H	5-Oct-66	6-Apr-82	9-Mar-92
	61-0286	717-148	18193	27-Dec-61	23-Jan-62	6-Mar-62	9-Mar-62	EC-135H	2-Mar-68	10-May-82	
								GEC-135H	22-Jan-92		22-Jan-92
	61-0287	717-148	18194	2-Jan-62	29-Jan-62	12-Mar-62	28-Mar-62	EC-135A	1-Jan-65		10-Feb-92
	61-0288	717-148	18195	5-Jan-62	31-Jan-62	2-Apr-62	4-Apr-62	EC-135L	9-Jan-68		
								KC-135A	1-May-70		
								EC-135L	5-Jan-71		
								KC-135A	14-Sep-71		
								KC-135R		29-Jun-92	
	61-0289	717-148	18196	12-Jan-62	9-Feb-62	11-Apr-62	11-Apr-62	EC-135A	1-Jan-65		8-Jun-92
	61-0290	717-148	18197	16-Jan-62	12-Feb-62	9-Apr-62	11-Apr-62	KC-135R		21-Jan-88	
	61-0291	717-148	18198	19-Jan-62	13-Feb-62	13-Apr-62	20-Apr-62	EC-135H	10-Oct-66	8-Jun-82	30-May-91
	61-0292	717-148	18199	27-Jan-62	19-Feb-62	19-Mar-62	23-Mar-62	KC-135R		12-Jan-87	
	61-0293	717-148	18200	3-Feb-62	23-Feb-62	4-May-62	7-May-62	EC-135A	1-Jan-65		
								(KC-135A)	10-Jan-75		
								(KC-135R)		29-Jun-84	
	61-0294	717-148	18201	9-Feb-62	5-Mar-62	18-Jun-62	19-Jun-62	KC-135R		10-Feb-87	
	61-0295	717-148	18202	20-Feb-62	12-Mar-62	4-May-62	7-May-62	KC-135R		12-Oct-87	
	61-0296	717-148	18203	1-Mar-62	28-Mar-62	4-May-62	7-May-62				26-Sep-76
	61-0297	717-148	18204	13-Mar-62	9-Apr-62	9-May-62	11-May-62	EC-135A	1-Jan-65		2-Jun-92
	61-0298	717-148	18205	22-May-62	19-Apr-62	15-May-62	16-May-62	KC-135R		18-Nov-84	
	61-0299	717-148	18206	3-Apr-62	30-Apr-62	9-May-62	9-May-62	KC-135R		22-Jan-88	
	61-0300	717-148	18207	12-Apr-62	8-May-62	5-Jun-62	8-Jun-62	KC-135R		16-Apr-90	
	61-0301	717-148	18208	25-Apr-62	29-May-62	8-Jun-62	8-Jun-62				22-Oct-68
	61-0302	717-148	18209	3-May-62	1-Jun-62	13-Jun-62	14-Jun-62	EC-135L	11-Dec-67		
								KC-135A	20-May-70		
								KC-135R		15-May-90	27-Jun-13
KC-135A-21-BN	61-0303	717-148	18210	17-May-63	8-Jun-62	2-Jul-62	2-Jul-62	KC-135A-VIII	n/a		
								KC-135A	n/a		
								KC-135E		1-Jun-90	13-May-08
	61-0304	717-148	18211	28-May-62	15-Jun-62	28-Jun-62	29-Jun-62	KC-135R		27-Nov-84	4-Nov-13
	61-0305	717-148	18212	6-Jun-62	21-Jun-62	13-Jul-62	16-Jul-62	KC-135R		10-May-88	
	61-0306	717-148	18213	8-Jun-62	26-Jun-62	10-Jul-62	12-Jul-62	KC-135R		12-Feb-85	6-Jun-13
	61-0307	717-148	18214	14-Jun-62	3-Jul-62	18-Jul-62	18-Jul-62	KC-135R		21-Sep-84	
	61-0308	717-148	18215	16-Jun-62	10-Jul-62	19-Jul-62	23-Jul-62	KC-135R		26-Mar-85	
	61-0309	717-148	18216	22-Jun-62	12-Jul-62	20-Jul-62	23-Jul-62	KC-135R		29-Mar-85	
	61-0310	717-148	18217	26-Jun-62	18-Jul-62	25-Jul-62	28-Jul-62	KC-135R		19-Oct-84	
	61-0311	717-148	18218	2-Jul-62	31-Jul-62	6-Aug-62	8-Aug-62	KC-135R		22-Apr-85	
	61-0312	717-148	18219	7-Jul-62	6-Aug-62	9-Aug-62	14-Aug-62	KC-135R		27-Jun-85	21-Feb-13
	61-0313	717-148	18220	17-Jul-62	10-Aug-62	17-Aug-62	20-Aug-62	KC-135R		28-Jan-85	
	61-0314	717-148	18221	20-Jul-62	16-Aug-62	27-Aug-62	27-Aug-62	KC-135R		8-Feb-86	
	61-0315	717-148	18222	25-Jul-62	22-Aug-62	29-Aug-62	29-Aug-62	KC-135R		7-Nov-84	
	61-0316	717-148	18223	31-Jul-62	22-Aug-62	30-Aug-62	5-Sep-62				19-Mar-85
	61-0317	717-148	18224	2-Aug-62	28-Aug-62	4-Sep-62	5-Sep-62	KC-135R		19-Mar-85	
	61-0318	717-148	18225	9-Aug-62	31-Aug-62	12-Sep-62	12-Sep-62	KC-135R		20-Dec-84	
	61-0319	717-148	18226	10-Aug-62	6-Sep-62	6-Sep-62	6-Sep-62				28-Aug-63
	61-0320	717-148	18227	13-Aug-62	12-Sep-62	18-Sep-62	19-Sep-62	KC-135R		2-Jul-91	
	61-0321	717-148	18228	20-Aug-62	14-Sep-62	21-Sep-62	21-Sep-62	KC-135A-VIII	n/a		
								KC-135A	n/a		
								KC-135R		31-Jul-90	
	61-0322	717-148	18229	23-Aug-62	17-Sep-62	24-Sep-62	25-Sep-62				28-Aug-63
	61-0323	717-148	18230	24-Aug-62	20-Sep-62	25-Sep-62	25-Sep-62	KC-135R		18-Jan-90	
	61-0324	717-148	18231	28-Aug-62	25-Sep-62	28-Sep-62	3-Oct-62	KC-135R		15-Jan-85	
	61-0325	717-148	18232	28-Aug-62	27-Sep-62	4-Oct-62	5-Oct-62				29-Sep-93
								KC-135R		20-Dec-99	
C-135A-02-BN	61-0326	717-157	18233	11-Oct-61	3-Nov-61	16-Nov-61	17-Nov-61	EC-135N	11 Feb 67		
								EC-135E		14-Nov-84	1-Jun-98
	61-0327	717-157	18234	16-Oct-61	13-Nov-61	29-Nov-61	29-Nov-61	EC-135N	7 Sep 66		
								C-135N	85		
	61-0327							EC-135N		28-Feb-86	Feb 03
	61-0328	717-157	18235	24-Oct-61	14-Nov-61	1-Dec-61	6-Dec-61	EC-135N	8 Sep 67		6-May-81
	61-0329	717-157	18236	1-Nov-61	1-Dec-61	11-Dec-61	12-Dec-61	EC-135N	1 Sep 67		
								EC-135E		2-Dec-83	Jun 96
	61-0330	717-157	18237	9-Nov-61	14-Dec-61	2-Jan-62	3-Jan-62	EC-135N	9 Sep 66		
								EC-135E		20-Mar-82	
C-135B-01-BN	61-0331	717-158	18238	4-Dec-61	20-Dec-61	31-Jan-62	9-Oct-62				13-Jun-71
	61-0332	717-158	18239	9-Jan-62	2-Feb-62	2-Feb-62	27-Apr-62				11-May-64
C-135B-02-BN	61-2662	717-158	18292	25-Jan-62	15-Feb-62	28-Feb-62	1-Mar-62	RC-135S	2-Nov-83	2-Mar-06	
	61-2663	717-158	18333	31-Jan-62	26-Feb-62	23-Mar-62	24-Mar-62	RC-135S	24-Oct-69	n/a	
	61-2664	717-158	18340	8-Feb-62	9-Mar-62	28-Mar-62	28-Mar-62	RC-135S	30 Mar 72		15-Mar-81

MDS & Block Number	Serial Number	Boeing Model No.	Const No.	Roll-out Date	First flight Date	Delivered Date	USAF Fly Away	New MDS	New MDS Date	Re-engine Date	Out of Service
C-135B-02-BN	61-2665	717-158	18341	13-Feb-62	16-Mar-62	29-Mar-62	29-Mar-62	WC-135B WC-135W	30-Mar-66 95		11-Sep-96
C-135B-03-BN	61-2666	717-158	18342	15-Feb-62	21-Mar-62	30-Mar-62	30-Mar-62	WC-135B WC-135W NC-135W	29-Sep-65 May 95 99		
	61-2667	717-158	18343	22-Feb-62	22-Mar-62	20-Apr-62	20-Apr-62	WC-135B TC-135B WC-135W	16-Mar-66 93 95		
	61-2668	717-158	18344	27-Feb-62	29-Mar-62	20-Apr-62	20-Apr-62	WC-135B C-135B C-135C	7-Sep-65 3 Apr 73 6 Sep 73		96
	61-2669	717-158	18345	7-Mar-62	11-Apr-62	24-Apr-62	25-Apr-62	WC-135B C-135B C-135C	7-Sep-65 21-Apr-73 11-Oct-73		13-Jan-06
	61-2670	717-158	18346	9-Mar-62	18-Apr-62	25-Apr-62	26-Apr-62	WC-135B OC-135B	1-Sep-65 96		
	61-2671	717-158	18347	15-Mar-62	25-Apr-62	27-Apr-62	28-Apr-62	WC-135B C-135B C-135C	21-Sep-65 Mar 73 5 Apr 74		30-Oct-91
	61-2672	717-158	18348	20-Mar-62	27-Apr-62	30-Apr-62	30-Apr-62	WC-135B OC-135B	30-Mar-65 96		
	61-2673	717-158	18349	27-Mar-62	7-May-62	16-May-62	16-May-62	WC-135B	17-Mar-65		28-Sep-93
	61-2674	717-158	18350	29-Mar-62	11-May-62	18-May-62	18-May-62	WC-135B OC-135B	1-Sep-65 94		21-Aug-97
KC-135A-22-BN	62-3497	717-148	18480	31-Aug-62	28-Sep-62	8-Oct-62	8-Oct-62	KC-135R KC-135RG	n/a	1-Sep-96	15-Jul-93
	62-3498	717-148	18481	4-Sep-62	5-Oct-62	12-Oct-62	12-Oct-62	KC-135R		24-Feb-92	
	62-3499	717-148	18482	7-Sep-62	8-Oct-62	12-Oct-62	15-Oct-62	KC-135R		1-Apr-86	
	62-3500	717-148	18483	13-Sep-62	12-Oct-62	18-Oct-62	19-Oct-62	KC-135R		16-Apr-87	
	62-3501	717-148	18484	14-Sep-62	15-Oct-62	22-Oct-62	22-Oct-62				7-Jul-93
	62-3502	717-148	18485	21-Sep-62	17-Oct-62	25-Oct-62	25-Oct-62	KC-135R		2-Dec-92	
	62-3503	717-148	18486	24-Sep-62	19-Oct-62	25-Oct-62	25-Oct-62	KC-135R		26-Feb-92	
	62-3504	717-148	18487	28-Sep-62	24-Oct-62	27-Oct-62	27-Oct-62	KC-135R		19-Jun-86	4-Nov-13
	62-3505	717-148	18488	28-Sep-62	26-Oct-62	29-Oct-62	29-Oct-62	KC-135R		22-Aug-91	
	62-3506	717-148	18489	3-Oct-62	27-Oct-62	30-Oct-62	30-Oct-62	KC-135R		26-Jan-87	
	62-3507	717-148	18490	5-Oct-62	1-Nov-62	6-Nov-62	7-Nov-62	KC-135R		21-Apr-87	
	62-3508	717-148	18491	9-Oct-62	5-Nov-62	12-Nov-62	14-Nov-62	KC-135R		2-Jul-87	
	62-3509	717-148	18492	12-Oct-62	7-Nov-62	13-Nov-62	13-Nov-62	KC-135R		29-Jan-92	
	62-3510	717-148	18493	16-Oct-62	12-Nov-62	15-Nov-62	16-Nov-62	KC-135R		14-Aug-87	
	62-3511	717-148	18494	19-Oct-62	14-Nov-62	19-Nov-62	19-Nov-62	KC-135R		9-Jun-87	
	62-3512	717-148	18495	23-Oct-62	20-Nov-62	5-Dec-62	5-Dec-62	KC-135R		26-Nov-91	
	62-3513	717-148	18496	26-Oct-62	21-Nov-62	6-Dec-62	7-Dec-62	KC-135R		10-Nov-88	
	62-3514	717-148	18497	30-Oct-62	28-Nov-62	3-Dec-62	4-Dec-62	KC-135R		26-Aug-88	
	62-3515	717-148	18498	2-Nov-62	3-Dec-62	11-Dec-62	12-Dec-62	KC-135R		1-Aug-88	
	62-3516	717-148	18499	6-Nov-62	7-Dec-62	12-Dec-62	13-Dec-62	KC-135R		20-Jul-88	
	62-3517	717-148	18500	9-Nov-62	12-Dec-62	18-Dec-62	20-Dec-62	KC-135R		18-Dec-92	
	62-3518	717-148	18501	13-Nov-62	13-Dec-62	19-Dec-62	20-Dec-62	KC-135R		30-May-91	
	62-3519	717-148	18502	16-Nov-62	20-Dec-62	26-Dec-62	27-Dec-62	KC-135R		8-Dec-87	
KC-135A-23-BN	62-3520	717-148	18503	20-Nov-62	20-Dec-62	4-Jan-63	7-Jan-63	KC-135R		10-Sep-91	10-Dec-13
	62-3521	717-148	18504	27-Nov-62	27-Dec-62	4-Jan-63	15-Jan-63	KC-135R		22-Aug-90	
	62-3522	717-148	18505	29-Nov-62	2-Jan-63	7-Jan-63	8-Jan-63				4-Mar-77
	62-3523	717-148	18506	4-Dec-62	10-Jan-63	17-Jan-63	18-Jan-63	KC-135R		5-Mar-86	
	62-3524	717-148	18507	6-Dec-62	9-Jan-63	15-Jan-63	16-Jan-63	KC-135R		8-May-91	
	62-3525	717-148	18508	11-Dec-62	10-Jan-63	17-Jan-63	17-Jan-63	KC-135R KC-135RG	n/a	2-Jun-97	24-Aug-93
	62-3526	717-148	18509	13-Dec-62	2-Jan-63	18-Jan-63	21-Jan-63	KC-135R		10-Feb-92	
	62-3527	717-148	18510	18-Dec-62	17-Jan-63	18-Jan-63	18-Jan-63	KC-135E		31-Jul-91	26-Feb-08
	62-3528	717-148	18511	20-Dec-62	22-Jan-63	1-Feb-63	4-Feb-63	KC-135R		28-Aug-93	
	62-3529	717-148	18512	27-Dec-62	25-Jan-63	5-Feb-63	6-Feb-63	KC-135R		18-Oct-92	
	62-3530	717-148	18513	2-Jan-63	30-Jan-63	7-Feb-63	8-Feb-63	KC-135R		3-Jul-86	
	62-3531	717-148	18514	4-Jan-63	5-Feb-63	8-Feb-63	11-Feb-63	KC-135R		10-Aug-87	
	62-3532	717-148	18515	8-Jan-63	11-Feb-63	26-Feb-63	27-Feb-63				5-Aug-93
	62-3533	717-148	18516	13-Jan-63	12-Feb-63	26-Feb-63	28-Feb-63	KC-135R		8-Jul-85	
	62-3534	717-148	18517	15-Jan-63	14-Jan-63	26-Feb-63	28-Feb-63	KC-135R		8-Aug-86	
	62-3535	717-148	18518	18-Jan-63	20-Feb-63	28-Feb-63	4-Mar-63	KC-135A			6-Apr-70
	62-3536	717-148	18519	22-Jan-63	27-Feb-63	28-Feb-63	11-Mar-63	EC-135K	May 70		14-Sep-77
	62-3537	717-148	18520	25-Jan-63	26-Feb-63	6-Mar-63	8-Mar-63	KC-135R		21-Mar-88	
	62-3538	717-148	18521	30-Jan-63	28-Feb-63	12-Mar-63	12-Mar-63	KC-135R		31-Jul-92	
	62-3539	717-148	18522	1-Feb-63	4-Mar-63	8-Mar-63	9-Mar-63	KC-135R		27-Jan-98	1-Apr-94
	62-3540	717-148	18523	5-Feb-63	7-Mar-63	21-Mar-63	25-Mar-63	KC-135R		24-Oct-85	
	62-3541	717-148	18524	8-Feb-63	11-Mar-63	13-Mar-63	15-Mar-63	KC-135R		7-Sep-89	
	62-3542	717-148	18525	12-Feb-63	13-Mar-63	18-Mar-63	20-Mar-63	KC-135R		26-May-88	
	62-3543	717-148	18526	15-Feb-63	20-Mar-63	26-Mar-63	27-Mar-63	KC-135R		5-Nov-86	
	62-3544	717-148	18527	19-Feb-63	20-Mar-63	2-Apr-63	5-Apr-63	KC-135R		7-May-91	
	62-3545	717-148	18528	22-Feb-63	22-Mar-63	10-Apr-63	12-Apr-63	KC-135R		22-Feb-89	
	62-3546	717-148	18529	26-Feb-63	27-Mar-63	26-Apr-63	29-Apr-63	KC-135R		10-Aug-87	14-May-13
	62-3547	717-148	18530	1-Mar-63	25-Apr-63	9-May-63	10-May-63	KC-135R		12-Jan-88	
	62-3548	717-148	18531	5-Mar-63	30-Apr-63	22-May-63	23-May-63	KC-135R		6-Sep-88	14-Mar-13
	62-3549	717-148	18532	8-Mar-63	9-May-63	22-May-63	24-May-63	KC-135R		6-Jun-88	
KC-135A-24-BN	62-3550	717-148	18533	12-Mar-63	21-May-63	3-Jun-63	4-Jun-63	KC-135R		9-Oct-86	
	62-3551	717-148	18534	15-Mar-63	22-Apr-63	30-Apr-63	1-May-63	KC-135R		23-Aug-90	
	62-3552	717-148	18535	19-Mar-63	11-Apr-63	26-Apr-63	26-Apr-63	KC-135R		11-Aug-86	

MDS & Block Number	Serial Number	Boeing Model No.	Const No.	Roll-out Date	First flight Date	Delivered Date	USAF Fly Away	New MDS	New MDS Date	Re-engine Date	Out of Service
KC-135A-24-BN	62-3553	717-148	18536	22-Mar-63	12-Apr-63	23-Apr-63	23-Apr-63	KC-135R		15-Mar-88	
	62-3554	717-148	18537	26-Mar-63	16-Apr-63	26-Apr-63	28-Apr-63	KC-135R		24-Sep-86	
	62-3555	717-148	18538	29-Mar-63	19-Apr-63	29-Apr-63	30-Apr-63				20-Sep-93
	62-3556	717-148	18539	2-Apr-63	24-Apr-63	6-May-63	6-May-63	KC-135R		31-Jul-87	
	62-3557	717-148	18540	5-Apr-63	2-May-63	9-May-63	10-May-63	KC-135R		18-Jul-86	
	62-3558	717-148	18541	9-Apr-63	6-May-63	16-May-63	17-May-63	KC-135R		16-May-91	
	62-3559	717-148	18542	11-Apr-63	8-May-63	23-May-63	23-May-63	KC-135R		23-Jan-92	
	62-3560	717-148	18543	16-Apr-63	14-May-63	27-May-63	27-May-63				16-Jun-94
	62-3561	717-148	18544	19-Apr-63	17-May-63	3-Jun-63	4-Jun-63	KC-135R		15-May-87	
	62-3562	717-148	18545	23-Apr-63	22-May-63	3-Jun-63	4-Jun-63	KC-135R		18-Jun-93	
	62-3563	717-148	18546	26-Apr-63	27-May-63	7-Jun-63	10-Jun-63				18-Mar-94
								KC-135R		19-Aug-97	
	62-3564	717-148	18547	30-Apr-63	3-Jun-63	19-Jun-63	21-Jun-63	KC-135R		16-Dec-85	
	62-3565	717-148	18548	3-May-63	4-Jun-63	11-Jun-63	13-Jun-63	KC-135R		11-Dec-87	
	62-3566	717-148	18549	7-May-63	6-Jun-63	18-Jun-63	19-Jun-63	KC-135E		11-Jun-91	
	62-3567	717-148	18550	9-May-63	11-Jun-63	17-Jun-63	18-Jun-63				13-Sep-93
								KC-135R		25-Feb-98	
	62-3568	717-148	18551	14-May-63	13-Jun-63	1-Jul-63	2-Jul-63	KC-135R		6-May-87	
	62-3569	717-148	18552	17-May-63	18-Jun-63	1-Jul-63	2-Jul-63	KC-135R		16-May-86	
	62-3570	717-148	18553	21-May-63	20-Jun-63	1-Jul-63	1-Jul-63	EC-135G	14-Feb-66		23 Jun 92
	62-3571	717-148	18554	24-May-63	24-Jun-63	11-Jul-63	11-Jul-63	KC-135R		21-Apr-88	
	62-3572	717-148	18555	28-May-63	26-Jun-63	12-Jul-63	12-Jul-63	KC-135R		20-Sep-90	
	62-3573	717-148	18556	31-May-63	1-Jul-63	17-Jul-63	17-Jul-63	KC-135R		29-Oct-87	
	62-3574	717-148	18557	5-Jun-63	5-Jul-63	12-Jul-63	12-Jul-63	KC-135R		5-Dec-97	
								KC-135RG	n/a		
	62-3575	717-148	18558	10-Jun-63	9-Jul-63	17-Jul-63	17-Jul-63	KC-135R		19-Oct-88	
	62-3576	717-148	18559	12-Jun-63	12-Jul-63	7-Aug-63	8-Aug-63	KC-135R		5-Sep-91	
	62-3577	717-148	18560	14-Jun-63	16-Jul-63	1-Aug-63	5-Aug-63	KC-135R		23-Oct-87	
	62-3578	717-148	18561	17-Jun-63	18-Jul-63	8-Aug-63	8-Aug-63	KC-135R		31-Mar-92	
	62-3579	717-148	18562	20-Jun-63	24-Jul-63	2-Aug-63	7-Aug-63	EC-135A	2-Sep-64		
								EC-135G	31-Dec-64		16-Jun-92
	62-3580	717-148	18563	24-Jun-63	25-Jul-63	13-Aug-63	16-Aug-63	KC-135R		11-Mar-91	
KC-135B-01-BN	62-3581	717-166	18564	9-Jan-64	14-Feb-64	28-Feb-64	29-Sep-64	EC-135C	1-Jan-65		10-Feb-99
	62-3582	717-166	18565	19-Feb-64	21-May-64	5-Jun-64	16-Sep-64	EC-135C	1-Jan-65		
								WC-135C	99		
	62-3583	717-166	18566	1-Apr-64	15-Jun-64	21-Jul-64	21-Jul-64	EC-135C	1-Jan-65		26-May-92
	62-3584	717-166	18567	20-Apr-64	4-Jun-64	29-Jun-64	2-Jul-64	EC-135C	1-Jan-65		
								EC-135J	Feb 80		29-May-92
	62-3585	717-166	18568	7-May-64	8-Jul-64	24-Jul-64	24-Jul-64	EC-135C			2-Jun-98
C-135B-04-BN	62-4125	717-158	18465	5-Apr-62	16-May-62	28-May-62	28-May-62	VC-135B	15 Dec 68		
								C-135B	27-Mar-77		
								RC-135W	15-Oct-99	23-Feb-04	
	62-4126	717-158	18466	10-Apr-62	18-May-62	28-May-62	29-May-62	VC-135B	15 Dec 68		
								C-135B	28-Jul-78		
								RC-135W	15 Nov 06	n/a	
	62-4127	717-158	18467	17-Apr-62	25-May-62	29-May-62	31-May-62	VC-135B	15-Dec-68		
								C-135B	28-Jul-78		
								TC-135W	30 Aug 05	6-Sep-05	
	62-4128	717-158	18468	19-Apr-62	25-May-62	31-May-62	1-Jun-62	RC-135X	16-Jul-89		
								RC-135S	8-Jun-99	27-Feb-03	
	62-4129	717-158	18469	27-Apr-62	4-Jun-62	8-Jun-62	9-Jun-62	VC-135B	15 Dec 68		
								C-135B	1 Jul 77		
								TC-135W	22-Apr-88	5-Mar-01	
	62-4130	717-158	18470	2-May-62	6-Jun-62	15-Jun-62	15-Jun-62	VC-135B	8 Dec 68		
								C-135B	20 Jul 77		
								RC-135W	30-Mar-00	30-Mar-04	
	62-4131	717-158	18471	8-May-62	8-Jun-62	19-Jun-62	22-Jun-62	RC-135L	ntu		
								RC-135M	5-May-67		
								RC-135W	9-Mar-81	27-Feb-00	
	62-4132	717-158	18472	10-May-62	12-Jun-62	27-Jun-62	28-Jun-62	RC-135L	ntu		
								RC-135M	25-Aug-67		
								RC-135W	30-Nov-84	13-Oct-03	
	62-4133	717-158	18473	21-May-62	14-Jun-62	29-Jun-62	29-Jun-62	EC-135B	7 Nov 78		
								TC-135S	22 Jul 85	1-Dec-05	
	62-4134	717-158	18474	23-May-62	19-Jun-62	29-Jun-62	3-Jul-62	RC-135L	ntu		
								RC-135M	19-Sep-67		
								RC-135W	16-Aug-81	16-Aug-00	
	62-4135	717-158	18475	1-Jun-62	21-Jun-62	29-Jun-62	3-Jul-62	RC-135L	ntu		
								RC-135M	27-Apr-67		
								RC-135W	15-Nov-80	31-Aug-04	
	62-4136	717-158	18476	12-Jun-62	3-Jul-62	13-Jul-62	16-Jul-62				23-Oct-62
	62-4137	717-158	18477	20-Jun-62	18-Jul-62	24-Jul-62	27-Jul-62	C-135B-II	30-Sep-63		
								RC-135E	30-Mar-66		5-Jun-69
	62-4138	717-158	18478	29-Jun-62	1-Aug-62	8-Aug-88	15-Aug-62	RC-135L	ntu		
								RC-135M	1-Nov-67		
								RC-135W	1 Aug 81	n/a	
	62-4139	717-158	18479	12-Jul-62	17-Aug-62	29-Aug-62	29-Aug-62	RC-135L	ntu		
								RC-135M	20-Jan-68		
								RC-135W	22-Jan-85	9-Mar-05	
KC-135A-24-BN	63-7976	717-148	18593	27-Jun-63	29-Jul-63	20-Aug-63	20-Aug-63	KC-135R		8-Mar-88	
	63-7977	717-148	18594	3-Jul-63	1-Aug-63	16-Aug-63	19-Aug-63	KC-135R		30-Oct-86	
	63-7978	717-148	18595	9-Jul-63	7-Aug-63	21-Aug-63	22-Aug-63	KC-135R		20-Jul-88	
	63-7979	717-148	18596	11-Jul-63	12-Aug-63	9-Sep-63	10-Sep-63	KC-135R		1-Oct-87	
	63-7980	717-148	18597	16-Jul-63	15-Aug-63	10-Sep-63	10-Sep-63	KC-135R		25-Jul-88	
KC-135A-25-BN	63-7981	717-148	18598	18-Jul-63	19-Aug-63	9-Sep-63	10-Sep-63	KC-135R		6-Nov-87	

MDS & Block Number	Serial Number	Boeing Model No.	Const No.	Roll-out Date	First flight Date	Delivered Date	USAF Fly Away	New MDS	New MDS Date	Re-engine Date	Out of Service
KC-135A-25-BN	63-7982	717-148	18599	22-Jul-63	21-Aug-63	10-Sep-63	10-Sep-63	KC-135R		19-Nov-91	
	63-7983	717-148	18600	25-Jul-63	26-Aug-63	16-Sep-63	17-Sep-63				17-Jun-86
	63-7984	717-148	18601	30-Jul-63	28-Aug-63	17-Sep-63	18-Sep-63	KC-135R		30-Jan-87	
	63-7985	717-148	18602	1-Aug-63	3-Sep-63	18-Sep-63	18-Sep-63	KC-135R		16-Nov-88	
	63-7986	717-148	18603	6-Aug-63	5-Sep-63	13-Sep-63	14-Sep-63				15-Sep-93
	63-7987	717-148	18604	8-Aug-63	10-Sep-63	2-Oct-63	3-Oct-63	KC-135R		8-Sep-92	
	63-7988	717-148	18605	13-Aug-63	12-Sep-63	3-Oct-63	4-Oct-63	KC-135R		8-Nov-90	
	63-7989	717-148	18606	15-Aug-63	17-Sep-63	4-Oct-63	9-Oct-63				8-Mar-73
	63-7990	717-148	18607	20-Aug-63	19-Sep-63	2-Oct-63	9-Oct-63				31-Jan-89
	63-7991	717-148	18608	22-Aug-63	24-Sep-63	10-Oct-63	10-Oct-63	KC-135R		29-Jan-86	
	63-7992	717-148	18609	27-Aug-63	26-Sep-63	8-Oct-63	8-Oct-63	KC-135R		20-Oct-89	
	63-7993	717-148	18610	29-Aug-63	1-Oct-63	16-Oct-63	17-Oct-63	KC-135R		26-Feb-87	
	63-7994	717-148	18611	4-Sep-63	3-Oct-63	17-Oct-63	18-Oct-63	EC-135G	3-May-66		11-Sep-92
	63-7995	717-148	18612	6-Sep-63	8-Oct-63	4-Nov-63	4-Nov-63	KC-135R		25-Apr-86	
	63-7996	717-148	18613	11-Sep-63	10-Oct-63	5-Nov-63	6-Nov-63	KC-135R		15-Apr-88	
	63-7997	717-148	18614	13-Sep-63	15-Oct-63	4-Nov-63	5-Nov-63	KC-135R		4-Jun-85	
	63-7998	717-148	18615	18-Sep-63	18-Oct-63	22-Nov-63	26-Nov-63	KC-135A			10-Dec-04
	63-7999	717-148	18616	20-Sep-63	22-Oct-63	13-Nov-63	13-Nov-63	KC-135R		22-May-85	
	63-8000	717-148	18617	25-Sep-63	25-Oct-63	27-Nov-63	27-Nov-63	KC-135R		24-Mar-93	
	63-8001	717-148	18618	27-Sep-63	29-Oct-63	18-Nov-63	18-Nov-63	EC-135G	6-Jun-66		18-May-92
	63-8002	717-148	18619	3-Oct-63	31-Oct-63	27-Nov-63	27-Nov-63	KC-135R		18-Mar-86	
	63-8003	717-148	18620	7-Oct-63	5-Nov-63	6-Dec-63	9-Dec-63	KC-135R		4-Apr-88	
	63-8004	717-148	18621	9-Oct-63	8-Nov-63	9-Dec-63	13-Dec-63	KC-135R		26-Sep-90	
	63-8005	717-148	18622	11-Oct-63	12-Nov-63	9-Dec-63	9-Dec-63				11-Jul-94
	63-8006	717-148	18623	18-Oct-63	15-Nov-63	17-Dec-63	17-Dec-63	KC-135R		12-Nov-87	
	63-8007	717-148	18624	23-Oct-63	20-Nov-63	13-Dec-62	13-Dec-62	KC-135R		12-Jan-90	
	63-8008	717-148	18625	29-Oct-63	27-Nov-63	19-Dec-63	19-Dec-63	KC-135R		3-Jun-86	
	63-8009	717-148	18626	31-Oct-63	6-Dec-63	19-Dec-63	20-Dec-63				26-Jul-93
								KC-135R		25-May-99	
	63-8010	717-148	18627	6-Nov-63	11-Dec-63	27-Dec-63	30-Dec-63				15-Sep-93
	63-8011	717-148	18628	11-Nov-63	16-Dec-63	27-Jan-64	28-Jan-64	KC-135R		6-Apr-90	
	63-8012	717-148	18629	15-Nov-63	19-Dec-63	9-Jan-64	10-Jan-64	KC-135R		30-Jul-93	
	63-8013	717-148	18630	15-Nov-63	31-Dec-63	8-Jan-64	8-Jan-64	KC-135R		12-Dec-90	
	63-8014	717-148	18631	25-Nov-63	6-Jan-64	21-Jan-64	22-Jan-64	KC-135R		20-Nov-92	
	63-8015	717-148	18632	2-Dec-63	10-Jan-64	17-Jan-64	20-Jan-64	KC-135R		26-Jun-89	
KC-135A-26-BN	63-8016	717-148	18633	10-Dec-63	16-Jan-64	27-Jan-64	28-Jan-64				12-May-94
								KC-135R		by Dec 00	
	63-8017	717-148	18634	16-Dec-63	20-Jan-64	7-Feb-64	10-Feb-64	KC-135R		3-Apr-92	
	63-8018	717-148	18635	18-Dec-63	23-Jan-64	12-Feb-64	13-Feb-64	KC-135R		13-May-92	
	63-8019	717-148	18636	15-Dec-63	28-Jan-64	14-Feb-64	14-Feb-64	KC-135R		4-May-93	
	63-8020	717-148	18637	3-Jan-64	5-Feb-64	20-Feb-64	25-Feb-64	KC-135R		3-Jul-86	
	63-8021	717-148	18638	8-Jan-64	13-Feb-64	24-Feb-64	25-Feb-64	KC-135R		17-Jun-88	
	63-8022	717-148	18639	10-Jan-64	17-Feb-64	26-Feb-64	26-Feb-64	KC-135R		13-Apr-92	
	63-8023	717-148	18640	16-Jan-64	21-Feb-64	2-Mar-64	3-Mar-64	KC-135R		7-Dec-88	
	63-8024	717-148	18641	27-Jan-64	27-Feb-64	11-Mar-64	11-Mar-64	KC-135R		2-Apr-87	
	63-8025	717-148	18642	28-Jan-64	4-Mar-64	19-Mar-64	19-Mar-64	KC-135R		26-Aug-87	
	63-8026	717-148	18643	3-Feb-64	9-Mar-64	17-Mar-64	18-Mar-64	KC-135R		18-May-93	
	63-8027	717-148	18644	6-Feb-64	12-Mar-64	19-Mar-64	19-Mar-64	KC-135R		28-May-92	
	63-8028	717-148	18645	13-Feb-64	19-Mar-64	27-Mar-64	31-Mar-64	KC-135R		22-Jun-88	
	63-8029	717-148	18646	19-Feb-64	24-Mar-64	6-Apr-64	7-Apr-64	KC-135R		13-Aug-90	
	63-8030	717-148	18647	24-Feb-64	30-Mar-64	13-Apr-64	15-Apr-64	KC-135R		24-Feb-88	
	63-8031	717-148	18648	27-Feb-64	1-Apr-64	9-Apr-64	9-Apr-64	KC-135R		26-May-92	
	63-8032	717-148	18649	3-Mar-64	8-Apr-64	16-Apr-64	17-Apr-64	KC-135R		17-Feb-87	
	63-8033	717-148	18650	10-Mar-64	13-Apr-64	23-Apr-64	23-Apr-64	KC-135R		27-Sep-88	
	63-8034	717-148	18651	17-Mar-64	16-Apr-64	28-Apr-64	28-Apr-64	KC-135R		9-Apr-93	
	63-8035	717-148	18652	19-Mar-64	20-Apr-64	4-May-64	6-May-64	KC-135R		15-Apr-92	
	63-8036	717-148	18653	27-Mar-64	27-Apr-64	13-May-64	15-May-64	KC-135R		11-Dec-86	
	63-8037	717-148	18654	3-Apr-64	4-May-64	19-May-64	20-May-64	KC-135R		8-Aug-88	5-Mar-13
	63-8038	717-148	18655	7-Apr-64	6-May-64	19-May-64	20-May-64	KC-135R		18-Feb-88	
	63-8039	717-148	18656	20-Apr-64	19-May-64	25-May-64	28-May-64	KC-135R		5-May-88	
	63-8040	717-148	18657	23-Apr-64	21-May-64	25-May-64	28-May-64	KC-135R		3-Jun-87	
	63-8041	717-148	18658	28-Apr-64	27-May-64	4-Jun-64	8-Jun-64	KC-135R		11-Mar-87	
	63-8042	717-148	18659	1-May-64	2-Jun-64	11-Jun-64	12-Jun-64	KC-135R			3-Jun-65
	63-8043	717-148	18660	11-May-64	10-Jun-64	16-Jun-64	22-Jun-64	KC-135R		26-Sep-92	
	63-8044	717-148	18661	14-May-64	15-Jun-64	22-Jun-64	26-Jun-64	KC-135R		16-Jul-93	
	63-8045	717-148	18662	19-May-64	18-Jun-64	25-Jun-64	26-Jun-64	KC-135R		19-Aug-93	
KC-135B-01-BN	63-8046	717-166	18663	25-Jun-64	22-Jul-64	13-Aug-64	13-Aug-64	EC-135C	1-Jan-65		21-Oct-98
	63-8047	717-166	18664	11-Jun-64	6-Aug-64	26-Aug-64	26-Aug-64	EC-135C	1-Jan-65		12-Oct-93
	63-8048	717-166	18665	29-Jun-64	14-Aug-64	14-Sep-64	30-Sep-64	EC-135C	1-Jan-65		26-Feb-99
	63-8049	717-166	18666	16-Jul-64	28-Aug-64	5-Oct-64	23-Oct-64	EC-135C	1-Jan-65		29-Jan-92
	63-8050	717-166	18667	3-Aug-64	15-Sep-64	23-Sep-64	30-Sep-64	EC-135C	1-Jan-65		
								NKC-135B	by 93		16-Sep-08
	63-8051	717-166	18668	19-Aug-64	5-Oct-64	12-Nov-64	13-Nov-64	EC-135C	1-Jan-65		10-Jul-92
	63-8052	717-166	18669	4-Sep-64	20-Oct-64	30-Oct-64	30-Oct-64	EC-135C	1-Jan-65		16-Jan-98
	63-8053	717-166	18701	23-Sep-64	4-Nov-64	30-Nov-64	8-Dec-64	EC-135C	1-Jan-65		2-Sep-97
	63-8054	717-166	18702	9-Oct-64	23-Nov-64	9-Dec-64	29-Dec-64	EC-135C	1-Jan-65		28-Oct-98
	63-8055	717-166	18703	27-Oct-64	23-Nov-64	6-Jan-65	20-Jan-65	EC-135C	1-Jan-65		
								EC-135J	21-Sep-66		4-Oct-93
	63-8056	717-166	18704	13-Nov-64	16-Feb-65	25-Feb-65	2-Mar-65	EC-135C	1-Jan-65		
								EC-135J	31-May-67		24-Mar-92
	63-8057	717-166	18705	3-Dec-64	16-Feb-65	25-Feb-65	4-Mar-65	EC-135C	1-Jan-65		
								EC-135J	31-May-67		31-Mar-92
	63-8058	739-700	18670	1-Apr-65	27-Apr-65	29-Dec-65	14-Jun-66	KC-135D	79	13-Jul-90	19-Mar-07
	63-8059	739-700	18671	21-Apr-65	19-May-65	15-Sep-65	15-Sep-65	KC-135D	79	31-Jul-90	14-Mar-07
	63-8060	739-700	18672	11-Jun-65	15-Jul-65	14-Sep-65	15-Sep-65	KC-135D	79	21-Jun-90	28-Mar-07
	63-8061	739-700	18673	12-Jul-65	8-Aug-65	1-Oct-65	2-Jun-66	KC-135D	79	27-Jul-90	4-Apr-07

MDS & Block Number	Serial Number	Boeing Model No.	Const No.	Roll-out Date	First flight Date	Delivered Date	USAF Fly Away	New MDS	New MDS Date	Re-engine Date	Out of Service
RC-135A-BN	63-8062 to 63-8066	739-700 739-700	18674 to 18678	Canceled							
C-135F-01-BN	63-8470	717-165	18679	5-Nov-63	26-Nov-63	11-Dec-64	12-Dec-64	C-135FR		15-Aug-86	
	63-8471	717-165	18680	9-Dec-63	17-Jan-64	27-Jan-64	3-Feb-64	C-135FR		3-Feb-86	
	63-8472	717-165	18681	31-Dec-63	31-Jan-64	3-Mar-64	4-Mar-64	C-135FR		18-Sep-87	
	63-8473	717-165	18682	21-Jan-64	26-Feb-64	6-Apr-64	8-Apr-64				1 Jul 72
	63-8474	717-165	18683	11-Feb-64	16-Mar-64	4-May-64	6-May-64	C-135FR		22-Oct-86	
	63-8475	717-165	18684	5-Mar-64	6-Apr-64	2-Jun-64	3-Jun-64	C-135FR		8-Jan-87	
KC-135A-26-BN	63-8871	717-148	18719	22-May-64	19-Jun-64	26-Jun-64	30-Jun-64	KC-135R		19-Dec-88	
	63-8872	717-148	18720	2-Jun-64	30-Jun-64	10-Jul-64	14-Jul-64	KC-135R		20-Sep-89	
	63-8873	717-148	18721	5-Jun-64	7-Jul-64	14-Jul-64	16-Jul-64	KC-135R		9-Nov-92	
	63-8874	717-148	18722	10-Jul-64	10-Jul-64	23-Jul-64	28-Jul-64	KC-135R		18-Mar-92	
	63-8875	717-148	18723	16-Jun-64	15-Jul-64	16-Jul-64		KC-135R		15-Aug-91	
	63-8876	717-148	18724	23-Jun-64	22-Jul-64	29-Jul-64	6-Aug-64	KC-135R		25-Oct-90	
	63-8877	717-148	18725	26-Jun-64	23-Jul-64	29-Jul-64	29-Jul-64	KC-135R		28-Jan-93	3-May-13
	63-8878	717-148	18726	1-Jul-64	27-Jul-64	31-Jul-64	11-Aug-64	KC-135R		27-Aug-91	
	63-8879	717-148	18727	7-Jul-64	31-Jul-64	11-Aug-64	21-Aug-64	KC-135R		2-Feb-93	
	63-8880	717-148	18728	16-Jul-64	11-Aug-64	20-Aug-64	4-Sep-64	KC-135R		22-Dec-88	
	63-8881	717-148	18729	21-Jul-64	14-Aug-64	25-Aug-64	6-Sep-64	KC-135A-VIII KC-135A KC-135R	n/a n/a	24-Sep-93 27-Sep-93	
	63-8882	717-148	18730	21-Jul-64	18-Aug-64	26-Aug-64	11-Sep-64				26-Feb-65
	63-8883	717-148	18731	27-Jul-64	21-Aug-64	28-Aug-64	15-Sep-64	KC-135R		20-Mar-89	
	63-8884	717-148	18732	5-Aug-64	26-Aug-64	28-Aug-64	1-Sep-64	KC-135R		15-Dec-89	
	63-8885	717-148	18733	10-Aug-64	4-Sep-64	16-Sep-64	18-Sep-64	KC-135R		20-Oct-93	
	63-8886	717-148	18734	14-Aug-64	9-Sep-64	18-Sep-64	21-Sep-64	KC-135R		21-Jun-90	23-Sep-06
	63-8887	717-148	18735	19-Aug-64	16-Sep-64	23-Sep-64	24-Sep-64	KC-135R		11-May-93	
	63-8888	717-148	18736	25-Aug-64	21-Sep-64	29-Sep-64	29-Sep-64	KC-135R		9-Aug-93	
RC-135B-01-BN	63-9792	739-445B	18706	15-Apr-64	18-May-64	27-May-64	27-May-64	RC-135C RC-135U RC-135V	27-Jan-67 28-May-71 24-Jul-77	17-Dec-99	
C-135F-02-BN	63-12735	717-165	18695	25-Mar-64	23-Apr-64	6-Jul-64	8-Jul-64	C-135FR		27-Sep-85	
	63-12736	717-165	18696	10-Apr-64	13-May-64	21-Jul-64	22-Jul-64	C-135FR		6-Aug-85	
	63-12737	717-165	18697	6-May-64	9-Jun-64	4-Aug-64	5-Aug-64	C-135FR		5-Apr-88	
	63-12738	717-165	18698	27-May-64	29-Jun-64	17-Aug-64	19-Aug-64	C-135FR		30-Jan-88	
	63-12739	717-165	18699	18-Jun-64	21-Jul-64	4-Sep-64	9-Sep-64	C-135FR		23-Nov-85	
	63-12740	717-165	18700	10-Jul-64	7-Aug-64	21-Sep-64	28-Sep-64	C-135FR		21-Nov-87	
KC-135A-27-BN	64-14828	717-148	18768	3-Sep-64	29-Sep-64	8-Oct-64	13-Oct-64	KC-135R		13-Jan-89	
	64-14829	717-148	18769	9-Sep-64	6-Oct-64	15-Oct-64	16-Oct-64	KC-135R		29-May-90	
	64-14830	717-148	18770	15-Sep-64	12-Oct-64	20-Oct-64	22-Oct-64	KC-135R RC-135W	Jul 17	16-Apr-91	
	64-14831	717-148	18771	24-Sep-64	21-Oct-64	23-Oct-64	30-Oct-64	KC-135R		13-May-91	
	64-14832	717-148	18772	29-Sep-64	26-Oct-64	28-Oct-64	30-Oct-64	KC-135R		16-Feb-89	
	64-14833	717-148	18773	5-Oct-64	29-Oct-64	6-Nov-64	9-Nov-64	KC-135R RC-135W	18-Oct-13	20-Sep-91	
	64-14834	717-148	18774	16-Oct-64	11-Nov-64	19-Nov-64	20-Nov-64	KC-135R		7-Feb-91	
	64-14835	717-148	18775	22-Oct-64	16-Nov-64	25-Nov-64	1-Dec-64	KC-135R		16-May-90	
	64-14836	717-148	18776	28-Oct-64	23-Nov-64	30-Nov-64	2-Dec-64	KC-135R		13-Sep-93	
	64-14837	717-148	18777	11-Nov-64	4-Dec-64	14-Dec-64	16-Dec-64	KC-135R		6-Oct-93	
	64-14838	717-148	18778	17-Nov-64	11-Dec-64	22-Dec-64	22-Dec-64	KC-135R RC-135W	4-Sep-15	10-Mar-93	
	64-14839	717-148	18779	30-Nov-64	23-Dec-64	30-Dec-64	6-Jan-65	KC-135R		20-Jul-93	
	64-14840	717-148	18780	7-Dec-64	31-Dec-64	31-Dec-64	12-Jan-65	KC-135R		26-Apr-91	
RC-135B-01-BN	64-14841	739-445B	18781	30-Jul-64	2-Sep-64	1-Oct-64	1-Oct-64	RC-135C RC-135V	31-Jan-66 19-Jan-76	6-Jun-03	
	64-14842	739-445B	18782	28-Aug-64	24-Sep-64	12-Oct-64	26-Oct-64	RC-135C RC-135V	31-Jan-66 6-Jan-75	31-Aug-01	
	64-14843	739-445B	18783	18-Sep-64	14-Oct-64	2-Nov-64	9-Nov-64	RC-135C RC-135V	31-Jan-66 5-Feb-75	7-Jan-02	
	64-14844	739-445B	18784	9-Oct-64	6-Nov-64	13-Nov-64	14-Nov-64	RC-135C RC-135V	28-Feb-66 3-Mar-75	19-Jun-02	
	64-14845	739-445B	18785	4-Nov-64	2-Dec-64	11-Dec-64	15-Dec-64	RC-135C RC-135V	21-Sep-65 21-Nov-75	20-Feb-03	
	64-14846	739-445B	18786	24-Nov-64	17-Dec-64	23-Dec-64	29-Dec-64	RC-135C RC-135V	31-Jan-66 18-Dec-75	5-Sep-02	
	64-14847	739-445B	18787	15-Dec-64	14-Jan-65	20-Jan-65	25-Jan-65	RC-135C RC-135U	21-Sep-65 28-May-71	26-Jun-02	
	64-14848	739-445B	18788	22-Dec-64	21-Jan-65	26-Jan-65	3-Feb-65	RC-135C RC-135V	31-Jan-66 6-Aug-73	30-Nov-01	
	64-14849	739-445B	18789	30-Dec-64	27-Jan-65	9-Feb-65	9-Feb-65	RC-135C RC-135U	31-Jan-66 21-Dec-71	n/a	

Note: Abbreviations used in the table: n/a – not available; ntu – not taken up.

KC-135E Donor Aircraft

This table shows the donor Boeing 707s and 720s for each of the JT3D conversions in sequence. A variety of print and World Wide Web sources are searchable by construction number for more details about the history of these donor aircraft and their disposition.

Modification Number	New MDS	Serial Number	Donor Aircraft	C/n Number
1	KC-135E	59-1514	707-123B	19337
2	RC-135T	55-3121	707-123B	18885
3	EC-135K	55-3118	707-123B	18882
4	EC-135H	61-0274	707-123B	19344
5	EC-135E	61-0330	707-123B	19326
6	NKC-135E	55-3135	707-123B	19342
7	EC-135H	61-0285	707-123B	19325
8	EC-135E	60-0374	707-123B	19332
9	C-135E	60-0376	707-123B	19329
10	EC-135K	59-1518	707-123B	19328
11	C-135E	60-0375	707-123B	19187
12	EC-135H	61-0286	707-123B	19330
13	EC-135P	58-0022	707-123B	19341
14	C-135E	60-0372	707-123B	19340
15	EC-135H	61-0291	707-123B	19334
16	EC-135H	61-0282	707-123B	19331
17	EC-135P	58-0019	707-123B	19343
18	EC-135P	55-3129	707-123B	19327
19	KC-135E	57-1496	707-131B	18394
20	KC-135E	57-1510	707-131B	18396
21	KC-135E	58-0080	707-131B	18392
22	KC-135E	57-1452	707-131B	18389
23	KC-135E	57-1485	707-131B	18391
24	KC-135E	57-1433	707-131B	18403
25	KC-135E	58-0107	707-131B	18385
26	KC-135E	57-1455	707-131B	19220
27	KC-135E	56-3638	707-131B	19219
28	KC-135E	57-1478	707-131B	19223
29	KC-135E	55-3143	707-131B	19436
30	KC-135E	56-3607	707-131B	20057
31	KC-135E	58-0006	707-131B	18988
32	KC-135E	56-3609	707-131B	19216
33	KC-135E	58-0043	707-131B	20056
34	KC-135E	57-1495	707-131B	18402
35	KC-135E	57-1473	707-131B	18397
36	KC-135E	57-1425	707-131B	18387
37	KC-135E	57-2604	707-131B	18759
38	KC-135E	57-1484	707-131B	19221
39	KC-135E	59-1519	707-131B	18400
40	KC-135E	57-1475	707-131B	18989
41	KC-135E	58-0012	707-131B	19222
42	KC-135E	56-3643	707-131B	18386
43	KC-135E	59-1489	707-131B	18401
44	KC-135E	58-0111	707-131B	19218
45	KC-135E	57-1503	707-131B	18761
46	KC-135E	59-1479	707-131B	19217
47	KC-135E	59-1484	707-131B	18986
48	KC-135E	56-3512	707-131B	18761
49	KC-135E	57-2606	707-131B	18393
50	KC-135E	58-0003	707-131B	18404
51	KC-135E	57-1431	707-131B	19215
52	KC-135E	58-0115	707-131B	18388
53	KC-135E	57-1458	707-131B	18390
54	KC-135E	58-0024	707-131B	18762
55	KC-135E	57-1509	707-131B	18758
56	KC-135E	58-0087	707-131B	19568
57	KC-135E	57-1480	707-131B	19569
58	KC-135E	59-1456	707-123B	18884
59	KC-135E	59-1497	707-123B	19188
60	KC-135E	59-1487	707-123B	19324
61	KC-135E	59-1506	707-123B	18883
62	KC-135E	56-3626	720-047B	19438
63	KC-135E	58-0032	720-047B	19413
64	KC-135E	58-0078	720-047B	19028
65	KC-135E	58-0068	720-047B	19207
66	KC-135E	57-2595	720-047B	19414
67	KC-135E	58-0040	707-123B	17646
68	KC-135E	56-0067	707-123B	19333
69	KC-135E	59-1485	707-123B	19336
70	KC-135E	57-2589	720-047B	19523
71	KC-135E	57-2608	707-123B	19338
72	KC-135E	59-1457	707-123B	17636
73	KC-135E	57-2594	707-123B	17640
74	KC-135E	58-0057	720-023B	18022
75	KC-135E	57-2607	707-138B	17700
76	EC-135E	61-0329	720-051B	18382
77	KC-135E	56-3648	720-051B	18383
78	KC-135E	55-3141	720-058B	18425
79	KC-135E	56-3641	707-123B	17652
80	KC-135E	56-3606	720-030B	18059
81	KC-135E	56-0008	707-123B	17651
82	KC-135E	57-1429	720-051B	18381
83	KC-135E	57-1464	707-331B	18980
84	KC-135E	56-3654	707-331B	18982
85	KC-135E	57-1505	707-331B	18405
86	KC-135E	57-1448	707-331B	18984
87	KC-135E	56-3631	707-131B	18764
88	KC-135E	58-0013	707-131B	18916
89	KC-135E	58-0017	707-331B	20061
90	KC-135E	57-1428	707-331B	18408
91	KC-135E	57-1463	707-331B	18406
92	KC-135E	56-3640	707-331B	18913
93	KC-135E	56-3604	707-331B	18981
94	KC-135E	59-1499	707-331B	18918
95	KC-135E	57-1465	707-331B	18983
96	KC-135E	57-1481	707-331B	20058
97	KC-135E	57-1450	707-331B	18979
98	KC-135E	57-1460	707-321B	19697
99	KC-135E	55-3146	707-321B	20019
100	KC-135E	56-3630	707-321B	20020
101	KC-135E	57-1507	707-321B	19698
102	KC-135E	57-1450	707-321B	19699
103	KC-135E	56-3622	707-331B	18409
104	KC-135E	57-1426	707-331B	20059
105	KC-135E	59-1505	707-331B	19224
106	KC-135E	57-1482	707-331B	19227
107	KC-135E	56-3593	707-321B	20024
108	KC-135E	57-1445	707-321B	18840
109	KC-135E	57-1494	707-331B	19226
110	KC-135E	59-1448	707-331B	18407
111	KC-135E	56-3611	707-331B	18914
112	KC-135E	57-1443	707-331B	18915
113	KC-135E	56-3658	707-331B	19225
114	KC-135E	59-1494	707-323C	19383
115	KC-135E	59-1509	707-323C	19237
116	KC-135E	57-1491	707-331B	20064
117	EC-135E	61-0326	707-331B	20067
118	KC-135E	57-1501	707-331C	18756
119	KC-135E	57-1434	707-321B	19275
120	KC-135E	57-1438	720-023B	18037
121	KC-135E	58-0096	720-059B	18831
122	KC-135E	57-1468	707-331C	19567
123	KC-135E	57-1421	720-040B	18380
124	KC-135E	58-0020	707-123B	19185
125	KC-135E	59-1445	707-123B	19186
126	KC-135E	59-1452	707-123B	19323
127	KC-135E	57-2600	707-123B	19339
128	EC-135N	61-0327	720-023B	18033
129	KC-135E	58-0082	707-321B	20026
130	KC-135E	58-0085	720-030B	18251
131	KC-135E	57-1504	707-321B	20027
132	KC-135E	58-0064	707-331B	20066
133	EC-135Y	55-3125	720-023B	18016
134	KC-135E	58-0041	707-331B	20065
135	KC-135E	58-0108	720-024B	18419
136	KC-135E	58-0052	707-323C	20089
137	KC-135E	59-1451	720-024B	18418
138	KC-135E	58-0090	707-338C	18954
139	KC-135E	57-1479	707-351C	19034
140	KC-135E	59-1477	707-321B	18836
141	KC-135E	57-1511	707-321B	18834
142	KC-135E	57-2598	720-023B	18014
143	KC-135E	59-1447	707-321B	18842
144	KC-135E	55-3145	707-321B	19693
145	KC-135E	56-3623	707-139B	17903
146	KC-135E	58-0013	707-338C	18953
147	KC-135E	58-0058	707-323G	18691
148	KC-135E	57-2603	707-323C	16690
149	KC-135E	58-0053	707-321B	18833
150	KC-135E	57-1422	707-321B	18336
151	KC-135E	57-1512	707-331B	20062
152	KC-135E	57-1471	707-324C	19351
153	KC-135E	57-1436	720-051B	18422
154	KC-135E	58-0014	707-138B	18068
155	KC-135E	59-1503	720-051B	18792
156	KC-135E	59-1516	707-328B	18686
157	KC-135E	58-0005	707-123B	17645
158	KC-135E	58-0037	707-368B	19810
159	KC-135E	57-1492	720-051B	18421
160	KC-135E	57-1493	707-336B	20456
161	KC-135E	57-1441	707-123B	17639
162	KC-135E	61-0271	707-321C	20018
163	KC-135E	61-0280	720-060B	18455
164	KC-135E	61-0303	720-024B	18417
165	KC-135E	61-0270	720-047B	18063
166	KC-135D	63-8060	707-331B	18985
167	KC-135D	63-8058	707-358B	19502
168	KC-135D	63-0061	707-358B	20097
169	KC-135D	63-8059	707-337B	19247
170	KC-135E	56-3645	707-337B	18873
171	KC-135E	61-0268	707-358B	19004
172	KC-135E	58-0044	707-321B	18339
173	KC-135E	57-1447	707-337B	18708
174	KC-135E	58-0116	720-051B	18688
175	KC-135E	61-0281	707-321B	18832
176	NKC-135E	55-3132	707-123B	17631
177	KC-135E	57-1451	707-323C	19383
178	KC-135E	60-0316	707-384B	20036
179	KC-135E	59-1496	707-323B	20179
180	KC-135E	57-1423	707-351C	19163
181	KC-135E	60-0327	707-123B	17635
182	KC-135E	57-1497	720-047B	18829
183	KC-135E	62-3566	707-334B	19133
184	KC-135E	57-2601	707-321B	19266
185	KC-135E	62-3527	707-321B	18837
186	KC-135E	57-1459	707-330B	19315
187	KC-135E	57-2602	707-384B	20035

KC-135As with Arizona and Utah ANG both suffered from poor engine performance with J57 'water wagons' due to high pressure altitude and temperature. Converting them to KC-135Es proved successful. *Photo via Brian Rogers*

Attrition

Sometimes it began with a phone call. Other times it started with a glance out the window, seeing the Wing Commander and the chaplain walking somberly to the front door. In a few cases it happened in real time, watching a tragedy unfold with a feeling of utter helplessness, that nothing can be done to stop it. Losing an airplane is never an easy experience. Losing a life is unimaginable.

For people who fly or work around airplanes, they have a soul, a personality. As with ships, they are all female – the 'old gal.' There is often a deeply personal connection between flier and airplane. One jet always brings you home, another always tries to kill you, or so it seems. For a crew chief, the jet is his (or her) baby, just borrowed by the crew for today's mission. '664' is not just a serial number, it is an old friend, a partner, a life memory. Most importantly, there are the people, the husbands and fathers, wives and mothers, sons and daughters, who choose to devote their lives to the proposition that flying is important, flying is a patriotic duty, flying is fun. These are the people willing to risk their lives to accomplish something much bigger than themselves, who share that passion indirectly with their families and friends, knowing that there is always the real possibility they won't come home.

During the first forty years of the KC-135's operational lifetime, 74 airplanes were destroyed (averaging nearly two a year), claiming hundreds of lives. The first of these was 'Cocoa', the third airplane in a flight of four seeking to establish a new speed record from New York to London. The crash killed nine crewmembers (including a general) and six newspaper reporters (including a retired general) because of an improper flap setting. Bad weather in 1964 led to the deaths of 78 passengers and crew plus an American in a taxi on the ground when a MATS C-135B crashed short of the runway in the Philippines. In 1965, 84 persons, including 72 US Marines on their way to Vietnam and 12 crewmen – the greatest loss of life in a '135 crash – perished when a MATS C-135A struck a mountain at night while flying an instrument departure repeatedly criticized as beyond the C-135's climb capability. The sole RC-135E disappeared in 1969 over the Bering Sea en route from Shemya AFB to Eielson AFB. No trace of the airplane or 19 crewmen aboard was ever found, just cryptic radio transmissions suggesting structural break up likely due to (but never proven) failure of the vertical stabilizer attachment point. It wasn't only military personnel or the press who lost their lives in KC-135 accidents. On a bright but bitterly cold January morning in 1965 a KC-135 crashed after takeoff into a poor neighborhood of Wichita, KS, killing seven crewmen and 23 civilians on the ground (including six children, a baby, and an unborn child).

The lessons from these tragedies appear today as impersonal Warnings, Cautions, and Notes throughout the pages of the Dash One flight manual. A few accidents are regular fodder for Hangar Flying meetings and simulator sessions. By and large, however, the 'corporate knowledge' of these accidents from the first 40 years of service is increasingly forgotten as 'old heads' retire, and remain unlearned as yet another generation of tanker crewdogs takes their place.

Since the publication of the first edition of this book in 1997, only four additional KC-135s have been destroyed – one of which was a depot maintenance error – and just seven lives lost over the span of 20 years. Many of the contributing factors to the early accidents are long gone: underpowered engines and the vagaries of water injection, lack of crew experience in flying high-performance heavy jets in a world populated by piston-powered transports and tankers, or operations in instrument meteorological conditions (IMC) for which adequate flight and navigation aids had yet to be developed. With these changes came an increased and justifiable sense of reliability and safety. There is a concurrent challenge, however, that reliance on technological solutions to inherent aviation risks may well lead to new problems and accidents. As this edition goes to press in 2017, the last loss of a KC-135 was the result of improper response to Dutch Roll, a basic aviation skill passed over in the evolving emphasis on computerized flight management systems and simulator-only training to cut costs. It is no joke to say that radical changes in cockpit technology have shifted the focus of aviation away from airmanship (measured in total flying time) to data entry skills (measured in words per minute). Pilots have ceased to be stick-and-rudder fliers and instead have become flight system managers, a problem endemic to commercial aviation as well.

This appendix includes a detailed summary of each loss in serial number sequence. Table A2-1 provides a brief summary by date to facilitate researching a specific loss. In addition to those airplanes which have been removed from service, a number have been involved in notable incidents. There are too many to list them in their entirety, but a few are recounted in Table A2-2.

As much as this listing appears to emphasize the loss of airplanes, I have chosen to list only a few historically significant names of those who were in or perished in the accidents that follow. In more than a few cases some of them bear responsibility for the incident, and mentioning them here serves little positive purpose. In other cases families need no reminder of the details surrounding the loss of a loved one. Indeed, the words I wrote in 1997 are just as true today as they were nearly 20 years ago:

'It is the recognition that flying is often done at the limit of an aircraft's or crewmember's capabilities, whether intentionally or not, that leads to a deep appreciation for the risks inherent in flying these airplanes. In remembering the loss of these airplanes, we are remembering the loss of the people on board, what they stood for, and what they were willing to sacrifice in order to achieve it.'

Too many have been my friends.

Key
Serial MDS
Home Unit
Incident Date, Location, and Total Hours (where known)

Table A2-1. **Attrition by Date**

Date	Serial	MDS	Attrition Location	Summary
27-Jun-58	56-3599	KC-135A	Westover AFB, MA	Improper climb procedures during heavyweight takeoff
25-Nov-58	56-3598	KC-135A	Loring AFB, ME	Loss of control following engine failure during a touch-and-go
31-Mar-59	58-0002	KC-135A	Near Belton, TX	In-flight break up due to severe thunderstorm penetration
22-Jun-59	57-1446	KC-135A	Walker AFB, NM	Ground explosion and fire during routine maintenance
15-Oct-59	57-1513	KC-135A	Near Hardinsburg, KY	Collided during air refueling with B-52F 57-0036
3-Feb-60	56-3628	KC-135A	Walker AFB, NM	Loss of control during crosswind takeoff
3-Feb-60	57-1449	KC-135A	Walker AFB, NM	Struck by KC-135A 56-3628 following loss of control takeoff
3-Feb-60	57-1457	KC-135A	Walker AFB, NM	Struck by KC-135A 56-3628 following loss of control takeoff
8-Mar-60	57-1466	KC-135A	Carswell AFB, TX	Landed short due to improper instrument landing procedures
18-Nov-60	56-3605	KC-135A	Loring AFB, ME	Landed nose gear first, rupturing forward body fuel tank
25-Jan-62	56-3657	KC-135A	Altus AFB, OK	Starter failure during maintenance led to ground explosion and fire
9-May-62	56-3618	KC-135A	Loring AFB, ME	Engine failure during heavyweight takeoff
8-Aug-62	55-3144	JKC-135A	Concord, MA	Crashed during approach to Hanscom AFB, cause unknown
10-Sep-62	60-0352	KC-135A	Mount Kit Carson, WA	Struck a mountain during instrument approach
23-Oct-62	62-4136	C-135B	Guantanamo Bay, Cuba	Stalled and crashed on final approach
27-Feb-63	56-3597	KC-135A	Eielson AFB, AK	Engine failure during heavyweight takeoff
21-Jun-63	57-1498	KC-135A	Near Westover AFB, MA	Descended below minimum safe altitude on instrument approach
28-Aug-63	61-0319	KC-135A	Atlantic Ocean	Collided with KC-135A 61-0322 in clouds 500 nm NE of Homestead AFB, FL
28-Aug-63	61-0322	KC-135A	Atlantic Ocean	Collided with KC-135A 61-0319 in clouds 500 nm NE of Homestead AFB, FL
11-May-64	61-0332	C-135B	Clark AB, Philippines	Struck a TACAN antenna during final approach in bad weather
8-Jul-64	60-0340	KC-135A	Death Valley, CA	Collided during air refueling with F-105D 61-0091
4-Jan-65	61-0265	KC-135A	Loring AFB, ME	In-flight break up during departure due to severe turbulence
16-Jan-65	57-1442	KC-135A	Wichita, KS	Loss of control during takeoff led to crash in a civilian neighborhood
28-Feb-65	63-8882	KC-135A	Atlantic Ocean	Collided during air refueling with B-47E 52-0171 410 nm SSE Harmon AB, NF
3-Jun-65	63-8042	KC-135A	Walker AFB, NM	Crashed during visual final approach in sudden nightime sandstorm
25-Jun-65	60-0373	C-135A	Near MCAS El Toro, CA	Struck a mountain during instrument departure that exceeded C-135 performance
17-Jan-66	61-0273	KC-135A	Palomares, Spain	Collided during air refueling with B-52G 58-0256
17-May-66	57-1424	KC-135A	Amarillo AFB, TX	Loss of control during final approach
18-May-66	57-1444	KC-135A	Kadena AB, Okinawa	Improper heavyweight takeoff procedures
19-Jan-67	56-3613	KC-135A	Shadow Mountain, WA	Struck a mountain during instrument approach
19-Apr-67	55-3140	KC-135A	Wake Island	Maintenance error led to ground explosion and fire
17-Jul-67	59-1465	KC-135R	Offutt AFB, NE	Overrotated on takeoff and stalled
17-Jan-68	58-0026	KC-135A	Minot AFB, ND	Overrotated on takeoff in snowstorm and stalled
30-Jul-68	56-3655	KC-135A	Near Mount Lassen, CA	Improper control led to loss of the vertical stabilizer
24-Sep-68	55-3133	KC-135A	Wake Island	Improper configuration during 3-engine approach
2-Oct-68	55-3138	KC-135A	U-Tapao RTNAB, Thailand	Struck runway lights following engine failure on takeoff
22-Oct-68	61-0301	KC-135A	Taiwan	Descended below minimum safe altitude on instrument approach
13-Jan-69	59-1491	RC-135S	Shemya AFB, AK	Airplane failed to slow after landing on icy runway
25-Mar-69	56-3602	KC-135A	Loring AFB, ME	Loss of control on icy runway following aborted takeoff
5-Jun-69	62-4137	RC-135E	Bering Sea	In-flight break up likely due to structural failure of the vertical stabilizer
19-Dec-69	56-3629	KC-135A	Near Taiwan	Loss of control due to severe turbulence during climbout
3-Jun-71	58-0039	KC-135Q	North of Torrejon AB, Spain	Struck a hill during instrument approach, may have been hit by lightning
13-Jun-71	61-0331	C-135B	Pacific Ocean	Structural failure 700 nm SSW Honolulu, HI
13-Mar-72	58-0048	KC-135A	Carswell AFB, TX	Improper visual approach procedures led to loss of control and impact
1-Jul-72	63-8473	C-135F	French Polynesia	Engine failure during heavyweight takeoff during French nuclear test
8-Mar-73	63-7989	KC-135A	Lockbourne AFB, OH	Struck by KC-135A 63-7980 during night practice alert on unlit ramp
5-Mar-74	57-1500	KC-135A	McConnell AFB, KS	Improper control during takeoff
7-Dec-75	60-0354	KC-135A	Near Eielson AFB, AK	Loss of control after takeoff due to severe hypothermia
6-Feb-76	60-0368	KC-135A	Near Torrejon AB, Spain	Struck a mountain during instrument approach
26-Sep-76	61-0296	KC-135A	Near Alpena, MI	Controlled flight into terrain during approach to Wurtsmith AFB
4-Mar-77	62-3522	KC-135A	Griffiss AFB, NY	Engine disintegration during ground maintenance
29-Apr-77	58-0101	KC-135A	Beale AFB, CA	Struck cattle that had wandered onto the runway in the darkness
14-Sep-77	62-3536	EC-135K	Near Kirtland AFB, NM	Struck high terrain during instrument departure
19-Sep-79	58-0127	KC-135A	Castle AFB, CA	Improper student response to simulated loss of engine
3-Jan-80	58-0007	EC-135P	Langley AFB, VA	Burned on the ground due to electrical short in water injection heater
8-Feb-80	60-0338	KC-135Q	Plattsburgh AFB, NY	Fire and explosion during ground refueling
15-Mar-81	61-2664	RC-135S	Shemya AFB, AK	Struck an embankment during final approach in bad weather
6-May-81	61-0328	EC-135N	Walkersville, MD	Structural failure caused by unrecoverable nose-down autpilot disconnect
13-Mar-82	57-1489	KC-135A	Near Luke AFB, AZ	Struck in instrument conditions by a small private airplane
19-Mar-82	58-0031	KC-135A	Greenwood, IL	Exploded during descent to landing due to overheated body tank fuel pump
19-Mar-85	61-0316	KC-135A	Cairo West AB, Egypt	APU caught fire during ground refueling
27-Aug-85	59-1443	KC-135A	Beale AFB, CA	Stalled during improper recovery following engine fire after runway impact
25-Oct-85	55-3121	RC-135T	Near Valdez, AK	Struck a mountain during missed approach
17-Jun-86	63-7983	KC-135A	Howard AB, Panama	Struck a ridge during go-around following hard landing
13-Feb-87	60-0330	KC-135A	Altus AFB, OK	Exploded during landing due to overheated aft body tank fuel pump
13-Mar-87	60-0361	KC-135A	Fairchild AFB, WA	Lost control after encountering B-52 wake turbulence during practice display
11-Oct-88	60-0317	KC-135A	Wurtsmith AFB, MI	Loss of control during crosswind landing
31-Jan-89	63-7990	KC-135A	Dyess AFB, TX	Water injection failure during heavyweight crosswind takeoff
20-Sep-89	57-1481	KC-135E	Eielson AFB, AK	Ground explosion due to overheated aft body fuel pump
4-Oct-89	56-3592	KC-135A	Near Perth-Andover, NB	Overheated aft body fuel tank pump caused explosion
11-Jan-90	59-1494	KC-135E	Pease AFB, NH	Fire of unknown origin during ground maintenance
29-May-92	62-3584	EC-135J	Pope AFB, NC	Ran off the runway following long and fast landing with tailwind
10-Dec-93	57-1470	KC-135R	General Mitchell Field, WI	Ground explosion due to overheated body tank fuel pump
2-Sep-97	63-8053	EC-135C	Pope AFB, NC	Hard landing led to nose gear collapse and runway departure
13-Jan-99	59-1452	KC-135E	Geilenkirchen, Germany	Runaway trim motor cause abrupt pitch up and stall during approach
7-Apr-99	57-1418	KC-135R	Tinker AFB, OK	Overpressurized during ground maintenance test and fuselage destroyed
23-Sep-06	63-8886	KC-135R	Bishkek-Manas IAP, Kyrgyzstan	Struck while waiting on runway by Russian Tu-154 cleared for takeoff
3-May-13	63-8877	KC-135R	Near Chaldovar, Kyrgyzstan	Structural failure from improper response to Dutch roll

55-3121 RC-135T
6th SW, 24th SRS, Eielson AFB, AK
25th February 1985, near Valdez, AK, TH: 15,072.0

After flying two practice Microwave Landing System (MLS) approaches to the airport at Valdez, the RC-135T crew commenced their third approach some 4nm (6.4km) north of the prescribed MLS inbound course. The airplane, call sign *Mary 24*, descended along this parallel course until passing beneath radar coverage at 7,100ft (2,164m) MSL, thereafter striking a mountain top during the missed approach. Weather at the time was extremely poor (the airport was closed due to bad weather) and may have contributed to crew disorientation. In addition, the MLS approach to Valdez used by the RC-135T crew was certified for use by only short take-off and landing (STOL) aircraft, specifically the de Havilland Dash 7, and required a glide slope and missed approach significantly steeper and more demanding than those usable by the RC-135T. Despite intensive searches (including flights by SR-71s), the wreck was not found until 2nd August 1985. Investigators finally reached the crash site two weeks later to recover the Select crew of three. The airplane was written off on 1st March 1985.

55-3133 KC-135A
509th BW, Pease AFB, NH
24th September 1968, Wake Island, TH: 6,681.2

This KC-135A, on temporary duty with the 4258th SW, diverted to Wake Island because of an in-flight engine failure and shutdown. To expedite the descent from cruise altitude down to sea level, the crew extended the speed brakes. Perhaps because of the confusion associated with the diversion and the planned three-engine approach and landing, the crew neglected to retract the speed brakes and the airplane developed an excessive sink rate on final approach. The pilot attempted a missed approach, but the airplane struck the ground gear-up short of the runway. The impact separated the tail section from the fuselage. Eleven of the 52 passengers were killed, several of whom were seated behind the aft hatch. This accident resulted in the addition of a well-known Warning to the Dash One prohibiting the seating of passengers behind this hatch. The airplane was written off on 2nd December 1968.

55-3138 KC-135A
93rd BW, Castle AFB, CA
2nd October 1968, U-Tapao RTNAB, Thailand, TH: 6,999.6

This KC-135A was TDY to the 4258th SW. The No.4 engine failed after the airplane was committed to takeoff. Asymmetric thrust and the plane's heavyweight caused one nose gear tire to fail followed by the other. The airplane finally became airborne just prior to the end of the runway, but struck reinforced concrete and steel light stanchions 1,800ft (548m) beyond the end of the runway and crashed, killing the crew of four. The airplane was written off on 16th November 1968.

Clockwise from top left:
KC-135A 55-3133 seen at Castle AFB in 1957.
Photo courtesy Boeing

KC-135A 55-3140 *Aroostook Queen* arrives at Loring AFB in 1957. *Photo courtesy Boeing*

KC-135A 55-3144 at Castle AFB in 1957.
Photo courtesy Boeing

KC-135A 56-3592 seen in September 1989.
Photo by Philippe Colin via Stephen Miller

55-3140 KC-135A
93rd BW, Castle AFB, CA
19th April 1967, Wake Island TH: 6,550.0

During servicing of the right main landing gear strut with compressed air to correct a severe hydraulic leak, the high-pressure air cart was left unattended, allowing the strut to over-inflate and explode. This caused the wing tanks to rupture, releasing fuel which then ignited. The airplane burned beyond repair and was cannibalized for parts and then scrapped.

55-3144 JKC-135A
93rd BW, Castle AFB, CA
8th August 1962, Concord, MA

This airplane was on temporary loan to Wright-Patterson AFB as a nuclear weapons test aircraft dedicated to the AFCRL at Hanscom Field, MA. While on a flight after returning from Operation DOMINIC in the South Pacific, it crashed fully configured for landing and 8° nose down in rough terrain during approach to Hanscom Field. All three crewmen aboard, the two pilots and an enlisted man, were killed. Cause of the crash remains unknown. In a heroic and noble act, the Reverend Edmund Higgins of St Bernard's Roman Catholic Church in Concord, MA, entered the wreckage as the flames subsided and administered Last Rites to the crew.

56-3592 KC-135A
42nd BW, Loring AFB, ME
4th October 1989, near Perth-Andover, New Brunswick, Canada

This KC-135A exploded while on approach to Loring AFB, killing the crew of four. A hydraulically driven aft body tank fuel pump was operating without fuel in the tank (used to cool the pump), overheated, and caused fuel vapor in the tank to explode. This accident spurred a temporary fleet-wide grounding, as two weeks earlier KC-135E 57-1481 exploded on the ground in a similar fashion. Even earlier, KC-135As 58-0031 and 60-0330 were lost to the same cause, as was KC-135R 57-1470 some four years later. The Air Force circumvented the problem by keeping 3,000 lb (1,360kg) of fuel in each body tank to cover and cool the pumps.

56-3597 KC-135A
93rd BW, Castle AFB, CA
27th February 1963, Eielson AFB, AK

Immediately after take-off to refuel a CHROME DOME airborne alert mission, 56-3597 lost an engine, inducing an asymmetric thrust condition from which recovery proved impossible. It crashed into the base gate. In addition to claiming the airplane's eight crew and passengers, the accident took the life of a pedestrian and the gate guard, for whom the facility is now named the 'Roy L. Hursey Gate'. The airplane was written off on 28th February 1963.

56-3598 KC-135A
42nd BW, 42nd AREFS, Loring AFB, ME
25th November 1958, Loring AFB, ME, TH: 150 (approx.)

During a touch-and-go landing in moderate crosswind, the downwind No.4 engine failed due to a faulty fuel control unit (a fleetwide problem at the time). The airplane became airborne in an extremely nose high/right wing low attitude. The right wing struck the ground, and the airplane cartwheeled and crashed near the wreckage of B-47B 51-2199 from the 321st BW at Pinecastle AFB, FL, which had crashed three days earlier on 22nd November. Two of the seven KC-135 crewmembers survived.

56-3599 KC-135A
4050th AREFW, 99th AREFS, Westover AFB, MA
27th June 1958, Westover AFB, MA, TH: 80 (approx.)

This was the third airplane in a four-ship flight (designated 'Top Sail-Cocoa') attempting to set a new round trip trans-Atlantic speed record (see Appendix V). Gross weight and temperature dictated a 40° flaps take-off (a procedure no longer in use). Once airborne the crew failed to retract the flaps to 30° as required, causing the airplane to sink and strike trees. This was the first KC-135 to crash. Among the 15 fatalities were seven crewmembers, including Brigadier General Donald W Saunders, the 57th Air Division commander (who made the takeoff and for whom the Saunders Trophy is named), Lieutenant Colonel George M Broutsas, the 99th AREFS commander, and eight journalists and NAA observers.

56-3602 KC-135A
42nd BW, 42nd AREFS, Loring AFB, ME
25th March 1969, Loring AFB, ME, TH: 3,712.0

After losing left-side water injection causing reduced power on engines Nos.1 and 2, the pilot aborted the take-off above the abort speed (S$_1$). Because of the snow and ice covering the runway, the airplane was unable to stop within the confines of the runway, slid off the end and down an embankment, breaking the fuselage into two sections. The crew egressed safely. The airplane was unrepairable and cannibalized for parts and scrapped. It was written off on 11th April 1969.

KC-135A 56-3629 departs an unidentified UK base. *Author's collection*

KC-135R 57-1418 at Meridian AP on 15th August 1995.
Photo by Don Logan

56-3605 KC-135A
42nd BW, 42nd AREFS, Loring AFB, ME
18th November 1960, Loring AFB, ME

Pitch response during the approach was 'mushy', and in the landing flare the airplane failed to respond to pilot pitch and trim commands altogether. Consequently, the airplane struck the runway nose gear first and with an excessive sink rate, driving the nose gear into the forward body fuel tank. The airplane bounced and settled back to the runway. Sparks ignited the fuel, destroying the plane. One crewmember among the 17 crew and passengers was fatally injured.

56-3613 KC-135A
92nd SAW, Fairchild AFB, WA
19th January 1967, Shadow Mountain, WA, TH: 4,300.1

During an instrument approach for a landing at Fairchild AFB, the airplane struck Shadow Mountain at an elevation of 4,340ft (1,322m) and was totally destroyed. It is possible that the pilot may have suffered a heart attack or otherwise became incapacitated, distracting the remainder of the crew from safely flying the airplane during a critical phase of flight.

56-3618 KC-135A
42nd BW, 42nd AREFS, Loring AFB, ME
9th May 1962, Loring AFB, ME

The No.2 engine failed after abort speed (S$_1$) during a heavyweight, water-injected take-off. The aircraft yawed to the left and became airborne but continued to lose airspeed. The 25-second flight ended when the left wing struck the ground 1,500ft (457m) from the end of the runway, and the airplane skidded to a stop and was destroyed. The crew of four and two passengers were killed.

56-3628 KC-135A
6th BW, 6th AREFS, Walker AFB, NM
3rd February 1960, Walker AFB, NM

Take-off conditions for this flight included extremely gusty crosswinds 70° from the runway heading at 27-34kts (50-63km/h). The 6th BW commander had directed that an instructor pilot (IP) accompany all training flights under these conditions, and that the IP be in one of the pilot's seats. Instead, the IP on 56-3628 sat in the IP/jump seat, inaccessible to a set of flight controls. The pilot making the take-off was unable to maintain directional control and rotated 5-10 KIAS (9-18km/h) early, forcing the airplane into the air in an unflyable condition. It settled onto the dirt beside the runway where two engines were torn from the wing, and then skidded onto the mass parking area, destroying two parked KC-135As (57-1449 and 57-1457). The airplane came to rest in a hangar. Eight people were killed, including the entire flight crew.

56-3629 KC-135A
93rd BW, Castle AFB, CA
19th December 1969, near Taiwan, TH: 6,794.5

This was the third airplane in a three-ship cell departure from Ching Chuan Kang AB, Taiwan, while on temporary duty with the 4220th AREFS, 4252nd SW. The flight encountered severe low-level turbulence during climbout, from which 56-3629 was apparently unable to recover. Aircraft wreckage was spotted after the accident but the airplane and crew of four were never found.

56-3655 KC-135A
93rd BW, Castle AFB, CA
30th July 1968, near Mount Lassen, CA, TH: 6,089.0

The airplane was on an initial training flight for a new crew. While performing a practice emergency descent from FL390 to FL230, the pilot (who had a total of 6,000 flying hours, but only eight in the KC-135) made a series of extremely sharp, un-coordinated, and aggressive descending turns. The vertical stabilizer separated from the aircraft, which then departed controlled flight and crashed into the foothills of Mt Lassen. All nine on board were killed. Written off on 20th August 1968. This accident sparked efforts by OCAMA to address long-standing weaknesses in the vertical stabilizer as part of the PACER FIN program.

56-3657 KC-135A
11th BW, 96th AREFS, Altus AFB, OK
25th January 1962, Altus AFB, OK

Maintenance personnel attempted to start the No.4 engine after its fuel-air starter was replaced. The starter did not disengage at its prescribed limit, and disintegrated due to excessive RPM. The explosion damaged the wing fuel tanks, and the leaking fuel ignited immediately. Despite fire fighting efforts, the airplane was completely destroyed.

KC-135A 57-1449 was on this spot when struck by 56-3628. *USAF photo, author's collection*

57-1418 KC-135R
153rd ARS, 186th ARW, Key Field, MS
7th April 1999, Tinker AFB, OK

The airplane was undergoing a ground pressurization check following PDM. However, the pressurization outflow valves which had been properly capped shut during the PDM were never reopened. The technician completing the pressurization test also reportedly used an uncalibrated homemade pressure gauge (which read incorrectly), and the fuselage exploded due to excessive pressurization.

57-1424 KC-135A
461st BW, 909th AREFS, Amarillo AFB, TX
17th May 1966, Amarillo AFB, TX, TH: 3,482.1

This airplane, known as *Miss Amarillo*, struck the ground 961ft (293m) short of the runway during an oscillating, unstable approach to landing. The right wing struck first, followed by the left wingtip, No.1 engine, and boom. The airplane burst into flames, departed the runway, broke apart, and exploded, killing the crew of four and one passenger.

57-1442 KC-135A
70th BW, 902nd AREFS, Clinton-Sherman AFB, OK
16th January 1965, Wichita, KS

Following a heavyweight takeoff after a B-52 at McConnell AFB, KS, the crew of *Raggy 42* reported lateral control problems. Shortly thereafter the airplane crashed into a poor neighborhood along North Piatt Street in Wichita, killing the crew of seven and 23 residents, including children. A rumor began that the airplane had become entangled in an F-105 Thunderchief drag chute accidentally left on the runway and blown onto the KC-135 by the departing B-52, binding one of the tanker's ailerons and thus accounting for the lateral control problems. Moreover, there were claims that parachute cord of the type used in drag chutes was found ingested into the aft compressor section of one engine, possibly complicating the airplane's control problem by causing asymmetric thrust.

Investigators found no evidence, however, of a drag chute. A Boeing test pilot in a B-52 behind the mishap airplane who watched it throughout its takeoff roll and subsequent loss denied seeing any drag chute or other debris. The investigation board concluded that the primary cause of the crash was a 'rudder control system malfunction producing roll, yaw, and nose left skid of such magnitude as to compromise control of the aircraft and preclude proper interpretation and corrective action by the pilots in the short time available.' The board noted that although there was a 'reduction of thrust during at least a portion of the flight, [it was] firmly established that all four engines were operating at high power on impact.' The decrease in thrust most likely came as the crew unsuccessfully attempted to regain control through differential thrust. This is believed to be the first accident in which a crewmember attempted to bail out. The boom operator was found apart from the wreckage with a tattered parachute, which may account for the reports of parachute cords entangled with the wreck.

57-1444 KC-135A
484th BW, 919th AREFS, Turner AFB, GA
18th May 1966, Kadena AB, Okinawa, TH: 3,387.2

This tanker, on temporary duty with the 4220th AREFS, 4252th SW, was ferrying an engine for a reconnaissance variant KC-135 from Kadena AB to Eielson AFB. During a heavyweight take-off on a wet runway, the airplane rotated prematurely and became airborne. It failed to sustain adequate airspeed, settled back to the runway, eventually became airborne again, and finally crashed 450 ft (137 m) beyond the end of the runway. The crew of five, eight passengers, and one civilian on the ground were killed. Written off 19th May 1966.

57-1446 KC-135A
6th BW, 6th AREFS, Walker AFB, NM
22nd June 1959, Walker AFB, NM

During routine maintenance of the wing fuel tanks, a spark from static electricity discharge detonated fuel vapor. The explosion released more fuel which promptly ignited and set fire to the aircraft. The fire destroyed the airplane and hangar; there were no fatalities. Cause of the accident was determined to be an improperly grounded air blower cart.

57-1449 KC-135A
6th BW, 6th AREFS, Walker AFB, NM
3rd February 1960, Walker AFB, NM

This airplane was destroyed on the ground when KC-135A 56-3628 lost control during a crosswind take-off, departed the runway, and crashed into the KC-135 and B-52 mass parking area. Also destroyed in the crash were KC-135A 57-1457 and a maintenance hangar.

57-1457 KC-135A
6th BW, 6th AREFS, Walker AFB, NM
3rd February 1960, Walker AFB, NM

This airplane was destroyed on the ground when KC-135A 56-3628 lost control during a crosswind take-off, departed the runway, and crashed into the KC-135 and B-52 mass parking area. Also destroyed in the crash were KC-135A 57-1449 and a maintenance hangar.

57-1466 KC-135A
7th BW, 7th AREFS, Carswell AFB, TX
8th March 1960, Carswell AFB, TX

During a second instrument landing attempt under poor weather conditions and with extremely low fuel reserves, the airplane was consistently below the glide slope. The pilot mistook a lighted area on the ground for the runway and, ignoring ground control approach (GCA) recommendations, dropped farther below the glideslope to land. The airplane struck the ground almost a mile from the end of the runway, bounced back into the air, and finally crashed 1,000ft (304m) from the end of the runway. The crew survived the accident.

57-1470 KC-135R
128th ARG, 126th AREFS, General Mitchell Field, Milwaukee IAP, WI
10th December 1993, General Mitchell Field, Milwaukee IAP, WI

This KC-135R exploded during routine ground maintenance for minor electrical and avionics discrepancies. The explosion was probably as a consequence of an overheated body tank fuel pump, an accident similar to the loss of KC-135As 56-3592, 58-0031, 60-0330, and KC-135E 57-1481. This Wisconsin ANG airplane was the first KC-135R lost or destroyed. Six maintenance personnel were killed in the explosion and ensuing fire. The wreckage of the airplane was moved to Volk Field, WI, for use as a range decoy and target.

KC-135R 57-1470 at RAF Mildenhall on 20th June 1991 prior to transfer to the Wisconsin ANG. *Photo by Bob Archer*

57-1481 KC-135E
176th CompG, 168th AREFS, Eielson AFB, AK
20th September 1989, Eielson AFB, AK

While shutting down engines following a training flight, the airplane exploded in the vicinity of the aft fuselage. Additional explosions and fire completely destroyed the airplane. Five crewmembers escaped, although two boom operators, believed to be in the aft fuselage when it exploded, were killed. This Alaska ANG airplane was the first KC-135E lost. Cause of the explosion was an overheated aft body fuel pump, similar to that responsible for the loss of KC-135As 56-3592, 58-0031, 60-0330, and KC-135R 57-1470.

57-1489 KC-135A
161st AREFG, 197th AREFS, Phoenix (Sky Harbor) IAP, AZ
13th March 1982, near Luke AFB, AZ, TH: 10,650.6

While flying in instrument conditions a Grumman-American AA-1 Yankee struck this KC-135A of the Arizona ANG. The small airplane hit immediately forward of the empennage, causing the entire tail section to separate from the KC-135A, which rolled to the left, nosed over, and crashed. Both civilians in the Grumman were killed, as was the crew of four in the KC-135A, including Lieutenant Colonel James N Floor, the 197th AREFS commander.

57-1498 KC-135A
499th AREFW, Westover AFB, MA
21st June 1963, six miles north of Westover AFB, MA

After a normal refueling mission the airplane began an instrument approach in heavy rain. The aircraft descended below published minimum approach altitude and struck a 790ft (240m) hill approximately six miles north of Westover AFB. Three of the four crewmembers survived. Written off on 24th June 1963.

KC-135A 57-1489 at Phoenix-Sky Harbor IAP on 29th December 1980. *Photo by Nelson Hare via Stephen Miller*

KC-135A 57-1498 at Andrews AFB in September 1962. *Photo by Robert Mikesh via Stephen Miller*

KC-135A 58-0031 at Chicago O'Hare IAP. *Photo by William R Peake*

57-1500 KC-135A
384th AREFW, McConnell AFB, KS
5th March 1974, McConnell AFB, KS TH: 7,434.4

Immediately after take-off on an ORI refueling support mission, the airplane's No.1 engine was perceived to have failed and the instructor pilot (in the copilot's position) retarded its throttle. Cockpit confusion between the IP and the student aircraft commander (making the take-off in the pilot's position) resulted in overcontrol of the airplane. The No.1 throttle was then advanced to full thrust, but the airplane still departed controlled flight, crashing 23 seconds after take-off. Two of the seven crewmembers were killed. Written off on 21st March 1974.

57-1513 KC-135A
4228th SW, 901st AREFS, Columbus AFB, MS
15th October 1959, between Hardinsburg and Leitchfield, KY

The KC-135A was No.2 in a two-ship cell formation scheduled to refuel several 4228th SW B-52Fs. Soon after air refueling started at approximately 7:50 pm, the tanker and its receiver collided, destroying both airplanes. The B-52F (57-0036) carried unarmed nuclear weapons, all of which were recovered; one was damaged but released no contamination.

58-0002 KC-135A
4130th SW, 910th AREFS, Bergstrom AFB, TX
31st March 1959, near Belton, TX, TH: 50 (approx.)

This KC-135A encountered severe thunderstorms (possibly even a tornado) four minutes after completing a navigation leg during a routine training flight. Two engines separated from the airplane, one striking the tail section. The airplane also may have been struck by lightning, causing it to explode as it descended, crashing ten miles southwest of Belton, killing the crew of four. Interestingly, 58-0002 was delivered on 17th February 1959, and had only some 50 hours total time when it crashed, making it the 'youngest' KC-135 of any variant ever lost. It was written off on 1st April 1959.

58-0007 EC-135P
1st TFW, 6th ACCS, Langley AFB, VA
3rd January 1980, Langley AFB, VA, TH: 16,896.6

An electrical short in the water injection tank heater wiring while the airplane was on the ground caused an insidious fire that was not discovered until it had already caused significant damage. Dense smoke hampered fire-fighting efforts and the fuselage was completely burned. The wings, engines, landing gear, and empennage were salvaged.

58-0026 KC-135A
22nd BW, March AFB, CA
17th January 1968, Minot AFB, ND, TH: 4,996.8

During take-off in a snowstorm the pilot over rotated the airplane causing it to stall and crash. All 13 on board were killed, including Major General Charles M Eisenhart, the 15th Air Force Vice Commander, who made the takeoff. The existing flight director had a tendency to fail without any warning indication, and may have misled the pilot. IMC at takeoff compromised the ability of either pilot to crosscheck the outside horizon visually to recognize the over rotation. This accident is believed to have prompted the installation of the Collins FD-109 flight director and rotation/go around (RGA) system, especially after a similar loss of KC-135R 59-1465 on 17th July 1967. The airplane was written off on 1st February 1968.

58-0031 KC-135A
126th AREFW, Chicago (O'Hare) IAP, IL
19th March 1982, Greenwood, IL, TH: 9,249.5

The airplane departed K I Sawyer AFB, MI, for Chicago's O'Hare IAP with 23 AFRES passengers on board, previously stranded when their C-130A broke down at K I Sawyer AFB. At 13,700ft (4,175m) during the descent into Chicago *Happy 33* exploded, killing all 27 persons on board. Original cause of the accident was undetermined, but is now believed to have been due to an overheated aft body fuel pump exploding fuel vapors, as in KC-135As 56-3592 and 60-0330, KC-135E 57-1481, and KC-135R 57-1470.

58-0039 KC-135Q
306th BW, 306th AREFS, McCoy AFB, FL
3rd June 1971, north of Torrejon AB, Spain, TH: 5,406.1

The second in a flight of two KC-135Qs TDY to the 98th SW, this airplane was cleared for an instrument approach to Torrejon AB. The lead tanker reported light to moderate rain and turbulence during the approach. After

KC-135E 59-1452 at Rhein Main AB, 29th May 1989.
Photo by Manfred Faber

Final remains of RC-135S 59-1491 at Shemya AFB. Note ARR receptacle has been removed for use in another airplane. *Jim Moseley collection*

commencing its approach, 58-0039 struck a hill and was completely destroyed. Some sources suggest that lightning struck the left wingtip, causing the No.1 wing fuel tank to explode.

58-0048 KC-135A
7th BW, 7th AREFS, Carswell AFB, TX
13th March 1972, Carswell AFB, TX

During a practice visual approach and landing, the airplane remained higher than normal throughout the pattern. It then began a steep, idle power descending turn and final approach. The right wingtip struck the ground, the airplane then cartwheeled, crashed and exploded, killing all five crewmembers on board. The airplane was written off on 14th March 1972. This accident prompted the Dash One Warning prohibiting steep, idle power approaches.

58-0101 KC-135A
93rd BW, Castle AFB, CA
29th April 1977, Beale AFB, CA, TH: 7,821.5

During a night touch-and-go landing the airplane struck a herd of cattle that had wandered onto the runway. The nose and left main landing gear were sheared off and forced into the fuselage, spilling fuel which promptly ignited. After departing the runway, the airplane stopped and the entire crew egressed safely. The same cannot be said about the cattle. The airplane was written off on 24th May 1977.

58-0127 KC-135A
93rd BW, Castle AFB, CA
19th September 1979, Castle AFB, CA, TH: 8,046.9

After a student training mission, the airplane returned to Castle AFB for landing practice. During one touch-and-go landing the instructor simulated the loss of an outboard engine. The student pilot responded abruptly with incorrect opposite control responses causing the airplane to drag the left wing and crash. All five crewmembers were killed.

59-1443 KC-135A
93rd BW, Castle AFB, CA
27th August 1985, Beale AFB, CA, TH: 9,936.7

Because of a pronounced wing rock during a student copilot landing, the No.1 engine struck the runway. The engine failed and caught fire. After recovering the aircraft, the instructor pilot attempted to reverse course and land in the opposite direction on Beale's single runway. In so doing he climbed too steeply in the turn, reached an altitude of approximately 250ft (76m), stalled, and crashed. All seven crewmembers were killed. This was the first KC-135 loss involving the fatality of a female crewmember, in this case two, the student aircraft commander (not at the controls at the time of the accident) and the student boom operator. Since then, two other female crewmembers have perished in accidents on 20th September 1989 (a boom operator) and on 3rd May 2013 (the copilot).

59-1452 KC-135E
116th ARS, 141st ARW, Fairchild AFB, WA
13th January 1999, Geilenkirchen AP, Germany

During final approach following an operational refueling mission the crew of *Esso 77* initiated a go-around. As the power increased the nose of the airplane pitched up abruptly to a near vertical attitude, causing an immediate stall and crash. Investigators determined that the trim was 7.5 units nose up, likely the result of a runaway stabilizer trim. Cause of the trim motor malfunction remains unknown. All four crewmembers perished in the crash.

59-1465 KC-135R
55th SRW, 38th SRS, Offutt AFB, NE
17th July 1967, Offutt AFB, NE, TH: 4,107.4

The pilot overrotated this reconnaissance KC-135R on initial take-off, placing the airplane in a nose-high attitude from which recovery was impossible. The airplane stalled and began a series of Dutch Rolls which continued until impact. Four crewmembers survived; one did not. The airplane was written off on 19th July 1967.

59-1491 RC-135S
6th SW, 24th SRS, Eielson AFB, AK
13th January 1969, Shemya AFB, AK

After the runway at Shemya AFB had been deiced, the RIVET BALL RC-135S attempted to land under severe runway conditions. Unbeknown to the crew, the melted ice on the runway began to refreeze prior to landing, which made the necessary stopping distance greater than the available runway length. After a normal touchdown, the RIVET BALL failed to slow despite normal braking procedures (the airplane was configured with J57 engines without thrust reversers). Even after emergency shutdown of the two inboard engines, the airplane did not slow appreciably. To avoid running off the departure end of the runway and striking approach light poles, the pilot steered the airplane off the right side of the runway. The RIVET BALL broke in half near the wing root. There was no fire, and the entire crew egressed safely. The airplane was cannibalized. Written off on 10th March 1969.

59-1494 KC-135E
157th AREFG, 133rd AREFS, Pease AFB, NH
11th January 1990, Pease AFB, NH

After routine servicing of the gaseous oxygen system, a fire of unknown origin erupted and quickly spread out of control. Despite fire-fighting efforts, there were several explosions, the fuselage was gutted by fire, and the airplane was damaged beyond economical repair.

60-0317 KC-135A
379th BW, 920th AREFS, Wurtsmith AFB, MI
11th October 1988, Wurtsmith AFB, MI

After a steep final approach in a severe crosswind, a hard landing and a bounce, the airplane veered sharply off the left side of the runway and broke up. After stopping it began to burn and eventually exploded. All ten passengers were able to escape, although the crew of six perished in the accident.

KC-135E 59-1494 at Pease AFB in 1987. *Author's collection*

60-0330 KC-135A
340th AREFW, Altus AFB, OK
13th February 1987, Altus AFB, OK, TH: 10,305.6

Immediately after touchdown an explosion occurred in the aft fuselage. The airplane stopped on the runway as the fire and ensuing explosions consumed the fuselage. The crew egressed the airplane but failed to shut down the engines or set the brakes before doing so, allowing the airplane to roll off the runway onto soft ground, where it burned to destruction. Cause of the explosion was originally attributed to frayed wiring in the vicinity of the aft fuel tank, but in light of the loss of KC-135As 56-3592 and 58-0031, KC-135E 57-1581, and KC-135R 57-1470, the cause for 60-0330's demise may also have been overheated fuel pumps exploding in a body fuel tank.

60-0338 KC-135Q
380th BW, Plattsburgh AFB, NY
8th February 1980, Plattsburgh AFB, NY, TH: 8,015.3

Despite fire fighting efforts, this airplane burned on the ramp after catching fire during ground refueling operations. Although damaged beyond economic repair for operational use, the airplane was disassembled and its fuselage and wings moved by trailer truck to the RADC at Griffiss AFB. It was superficially repaired and is used as a ground testbed (upright, unlike the other 'upside down air force' platforms at RADC) for antenna placement. The right wing has since been donated to an operational KC-135, and been replaced with a 707 wing.

60-0340 KC-135A
462nd SAW, 43rd AREFS, Larson AFB, WA
8th July 1964, Death Valley, CA

This is the only mid-air collision between a KC-135 and a fighter aircraft in which both the fighter and the tanker were lost. F-105D 61-0091 of the 355th TFW at McConnell AFB (*Tar 86*) struck the tanker during air refueling, sending them both out of control. The tanker (*Shag 21*) crashed some 65 miles (104km) north of George AFB, CA. The tanker crew of four and the 'Thud' pilot were killed.

60-0352 KC-135A
28th BW, 28th AREFS, Ellsworth AFB, SD
10th September 1962, Mount Kit Carson, WA, TH: 303 (approx.)

Pending runway closure for repaving and repairs at Ellsworth AFB, *Mourn 79* deployed to Fairchild AFB. After beginning the final descent in instrument conditions around 1045L, the airplane struck Mt Kit Carson 900ft (275m) below the ridgeline. Investigation revealed that there were two separate approaches, one *around* the mountains at 4,500ft (1,372m) and another *over* the mountains at 8,000ft (2,438m). Moreover, the two approaches were on opposite sides of the same page. Sadly, the crew was using the wrong chart. As one newspaper account noted, 'The crew was using the map for the route that would take them around the mountains; they were on the path that took them over the mountains. High enough to pass safely around the mountains, they were too low to clear them.' In addition, maintenance records showed the radar had failed in nine of the plane's 11 previous flights, so they may not have had radar to warn them of the impending terrain. The crash claimed the lives of the crew of four and 40-some passengers.

Top left: KC-135A 60-0330 at Altus AFB on 9th July 1986. *Author photo*

Top right: KC-135A 60-0338 moves from Plattsburgh AFB to the Rome Test Facility. *Jim Moseley collection*

Right: Crash sequence for KC-135A 60-0361 on 13th March 1987.

60-0354 KC-135A
380th BW, Plattsburgh AFB, NY
7th December 1975, near Eielson AFB, AK, TH: 6,594.4

Following extensive ground delays while awaiting the last-minute repair of an RC-135 in cell formation with this tanker on temporary duty with the 6th SW, the flight was cleared to launch. Weather was severe with extremely cold temperatures in excess of −40°F. After take-off the crew reported that the landing gear would not retract and requested a right turn. The pilot then began the right turn while simultaneously reducing power and retracting the flaps. The airplane descended onto the frozen Tanana River and struck an island. The crew of four, who were all killed, likely suffered from severe hypothermia as a consequence of their extended delay prior to takeoff in an unheated airplane in bitter cold, which degraded their flight skills and judgement, and contributed to the crash. The airplane was written off on 10th December 1975.

60-0361 KC-135A
92nd BW, Fairchild AFB, WA
13th March 1987, Fairchild AFB, WA, TH: 10,956.0

Fairchild AFB has been the site of two highly controversial crashes related to aerial demonstrations. The most visible of these was B-52H 61-0026 (*Czar 52*) on 24th June 1994 (which was filmed and posted on the World Wide Web), attributed to a 'rogue pilot' coupled with lack of appropriate command oversight. The first of the Fairchild AFB air show losses, however, became a case study for not treating heavy jet aircraft as equivalents of nimble fighters.

The 'Thunderhawks' were SAC's answer to the Thunderbirds, designed to show off the impressive aerial capabilities of SAC's bomber and tanker force as well as build *esprit de corps* within SAC. Despite these lofty goals, SAC's heavy jets earned their salaries flying straight-and-level: B-52s dropped bombs and KC-135s refueled other airplanes in generally 'vanilla' flight parameters. Although B-52s were used in low-level bombing and their crews trained for this environment, KC-135 crews had little experience with 'gas in the grass'.

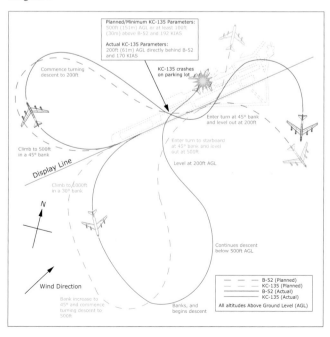

Initial efforts to demonstrate the KC-135's mission began in November 1986 at McConnell AFB with the re-engined KC-135R, showcasing its impressive rate of climb and decreased noise footprint. The star of the envisaged 'Thunderhawk' show, however, would be the B-52, and Fairchild AFB's strong reputation made it the appropriate choice in December 1986 for the bomber crew. Distance between McConnell AFB and Fairchild AFB proved unworkable for regular practice sessions, so SAC decided that a Fairchild AFB KC-135A would be the other half of the 'Thunderhawk' duo, but that it would be used only to demonstrate simulated aerial refueling and would not participate in 'integrated maneuvers' with the B-52H. Several flight evaluations were held as senior SAC commanders observed and tweaked the planned demonstration. The first of these evaluations, held at Offutt on 23rd January 1987, expanded the role of the KC-135 in conjunction with the B-52H beyond simulated aerial refueling. This was achieved through the addition of the 'snake' maneuver, in which the KC-135A would follow the B-52H while rolling left to right to left to show the bottom then the top of the airplanes. The new profile was demonstrated to senior SAC leadership on 3rd March and approved.

On Friday, 13th March 1987, exactly one month after Altus AFB KC-135A 60-0330 exploded and burned while landing, the 'Thunderhawks' flew their planned final practice mission. KC-135A 60-0361 took off first, followed by the B-52H, and began a climbing separation maneuver for timing so that the B-52H would lead the flight during the 'snake' maneuver. This would place the KC-135A some 30 seconds behind the B-52H (which was at 200ft [61m] above the runway) and at 500ft (151m) above ground level (AGL) or at least 100ft (30m) above the B-52H. The KC-135A would then execute a 45° bank to the left at 170 KIAS followed by an immediate 45° bank to the right and another 45° bank to the left and then egress the flight demonstration airspace over the crowd line until the simulated aerial refueling. SAC regulations forbade bank angles in excess of 30°, but there was nothing inherently unsafe about a 45° bank under controlled conditions. Indeed, simulator results showed that the 'snake' maneuver could safely be performed at either 300ft (91m) or 500ft (151m) AGL. However, winds aloft changed the planned ground track. While descending and at decreased thrust the KC-135A entered the jet wash of the B-52, abruptly increasing the bank angle from 45° to nearly 90°. In addition to losing all lift from the wings, the two engines on the left wing began a series of compressor stalls. The KC-135A crew was able to level the wings, but with reduced power and at extremely low altitude could not recover and crashed into an open area adjacent to hangars and squadron buildings. Tragically, the airplane skidded through a fence onto a car driven by a 'Thunderhawk' crewman who was not flying that day. Seven crewmembers perished.

Investigators determined that for some unknown reason the KC-135A was at only 200ft (61m) AGL when it encountered the B-52 jet wash. Had it been at the specified higher altitude of 500ft (151m) AGL (or at least 100ft [30m] above the B-52, placing it at a minimum of 300ft [91m]) the jet wash would have passed safely underneath it and the additional height would have added a safety margin to any upset recovery. Moreover, the minimum airspeed should have been the calculated stall speed of 148 KIAS in a 45° bank plus the SAC-mandated 30% safety margin of 44 KIAS, totaling 192 KIAS, not the 170 KIAS used in the show. The crash prompted a Congressional investigation by the Government Accountability Office (GAO), which determined that a lack of clear, *written* directives and command oversight at all levels and stages of the program's development contributed to the accident. As a consequence of this accident, all future heavy aircraft displays would be straight-and-level passes parallel to the crowd line and at a minimum of 500ft (151m) AGL.

60-0368 KC-135A
410th BW, 46th AREFS, K I Sawyer AFB, MI
6th February 1976, near Torrejon AB, Spain, TH: 5,481.9

After a normal air refueling mission launched from RAF Mildenhall, this KC-135A TDY to the 98th SW began its penetration and approach into Torrejon AB. No problems were reported from the aircraft. Shortly after being told to contact Torrejon's radar approach control the airplane struck a mountain, killing all seven aboard.

60-0373 C-135A
1611th ATW, McGuire AFB, NJ
25th June 1965, near MCAS El Toro, CA

At 1 minute, 14 seconds after takeoff at 0144 hours and in light rain and heavy fog, this C-135A struck Loma Ridge 200ft (60m) below the peak, 3.2 miles (5.1km) from the runway. The airplane did not follow the prescribed departure flight path, which required a left turn within two miles after takeoff.

Official cause of the accident was determined to be the excessive climb rate required to fly the departure with adequate obstacle clearance, a rate beyond the C-135A's performance capability. Previously, MATS C-135 pilots had issued a hazard report for MCAS El Toro because the departure requirements exceeded the C-135's operational limits and were incompatible with its take-off and climb procedures. The crew of 12 and the 72 US Marines en route to Vietnam via Okinawa were killed.

61-0265 KC-135A
42nd BW, 42nd AREFS, Loring AFB, ME
4th January 1965, Loring AFB, ME, TH: 1,353.0

Following a normal take-off, this KC-135A encountered turbulence of such magnitude as to induce severe wing rock accompanied by lateral stress sufficient to shear off the Nos. 3 and 4 engines. The airplane crashed just over 2 miles (3.7km) from the runway's departure end. All four crewmembers were killed.

61-0273 KC-135A
340th BW, 910th AREFS, Bergstrom AFB, TX
17th January 1966, over Palomares, Spain, TH: 1,947.0

During a CHROME DOME airborne nuclear alert aerial refueling, B-52G 58-0256, *Tea 16,* collided with KC-135A *Troubadour 14* causing both airplanes to crash. All four tanker crewmembers and three from the B-52 were killed. Three of the four B28 nuclear weapons in the B-52 were recovered soon after the accident; the fourth was recovered from the Mediterranean Sea on 7th April 1966 following an extensive bi-national multi-service recovery effort. (The incident took place a month after the world premier of the James Bond film *Thunderball*, in which evildoers hijack an RAF Avro Vulcan to steal its nuclear bombs after ditching it in the Caribbean Sea near Nassau. Although there was no relationship between the two events, the search for the missing B-52 bombs conflated the public perception of the tragedy with the movie.)

61-0296 KC-135A
410th BW, 46th AREFS, K I Sawyer AFB, MI
26th September 1976, 12 miles (19km) SW of Alpena, MI, TH: 6,109.7

This KC-135A was carrying a group of 'First Team' officers from four SAC bases to Offutt AFB. En route to Wurtsmith AFB the airplane developed a cabin pressurization problem which dictated a lower cruise altitude. The crew, likely distracted by this issue, failed to maintain situational awareness and struck high terrain during their approach into Wurtsmith AFB, killing all 15 on board. The airplane was written off on 1st October 1976.

61-0301 KC-135A
99th BW, 99th AREFS, Westover AFB, MA
22nd October 1968, 47 miles (75km) from Ching Chuan Kang AB, Taiwan

During a night approach over mountainous terrain, the airplane descended below the safe approach altitude, striking the ground 1,000ft (304m) below the top of a 7,300ft (2,225m) mountain. The flight crew of four from the 901st AREFS, 454th BW, Columbus AFB, and the two crew chiefs from the 99th BW were killed. The plane was written off on 20th November 1968.

61-0316 KC-135A
2nd BW, 71st AREFS, Barksdale AFB, LA
19th March 1985, Cairo IAP, Egypt, TH: 10,235.0

The auxiliary power unit (APU) caught fire during ground refueling. As the airplane had a modified VIP interior for use by the 8th Air Force Commander, the fire spread rapidly, completely consuming the airplane's plush interior. The fire occurred at Cairo IAP, and the wreckage was moved a week later to Cairo-East AB for salvage or scrap.

C-135A 60-0373 at McGuire AFB in 1963. *Author's collection*

61-0319 KC-135A
19th BW, 407th AREFS, Homestead AFB, FL
28th August 1963, 500 miles (804km) northeast of Homestead AFB

This was one of two tankers on a Reflex support mission. After air refueling the receivers saw this and the other tanker (61-0322) enter a deck of cirrus clouds and disappear, probably colliding with one another. A 10-square-mile (19-square-km) debris field was located 300nm (556km) SW of Bermuda and 500nm (840km) NE of Homestead AFB, FL. Two days after the disappearance, searchers found additional wreckage some 400nm (741km) E of Fort Pierce, FL. This second field, 160nm (296km) west of the first site, raised questions about the initial assumption that the two airplanes collided and then both immediately crashed, suggesting that one airplane crashed at the collision site while the other airplane attempted to limp back to Florida but eventually crashed at the second location. Written off on 29th August 1963.

EC-135N 61-0328 at McClellan AFB. *Photo by Peter B Lewis via René J Francillon*

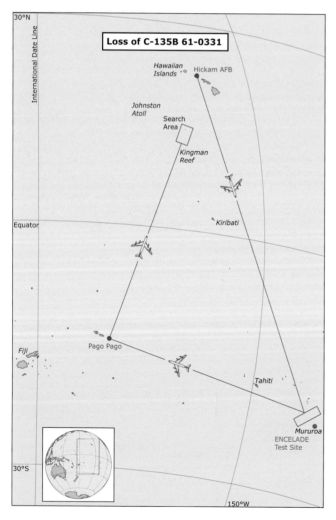

Final routing of C-135B 61-0331.

61-0322 KC-135A
19th BW, 407th AREFS, Homestead AFB, FL
28th August 1963, 500 miles (804km) northeast of Homestead AFB

This was one of two tankers on a Reflex support mission. After air refueling the receivers saw this and the other tanker (61-0319) enter a deck of cirrus clouds and disappear, probably colliding with one another. A 10-square-mile (19-square-km) debris field was located 300nm (556km) SW of Bermuda and 500nm (840km) NE of Homestead AFB, FL. Two days after the disappearance, searchers found additional wreckage some 400nm (741km) E of Fort Pierce, FL. This second field, 160nm (296km) west of the first site, raised questions about the initial assumption that the two airplanes collided and then both immediately crashed, suggesting that one airplane crashed at the collision site while the other airplane attempted to limp back to Florida but eventually crashed at the second location. Written off on 29th August 1963.

61-0328 EC-135N
4950th TW, 4952nd TS, Wright-Patterson AFB, OH
6th May 1981, near Walkersville, MD, TH: 13,471.2

This flight was a scheduled ARIA training mission and incentive flight for two crew spouses and wing staff. Some 45 minutes into the mission *Agar 23* began an uncontrolled dive from FL290 (approximately 29,000ft/8,839m). At 1,300ft (396m) AGL the airplane experienced an internal explosion before crashing into wooded terrain, killing all 21 people on board.

Investigation reported that at the time of the departure from controlled flight, the Instructor Pilot (IP) was in the right seat and his wife occupied the left seat. The aircraft pitch trim was full nose down from an undetermined cause. When the nose down trim exceeded the ability of the autopilot to maintain attitude, the autopilot disconnected and the airplane nose dropped abruptly. This induced a microgravity environment which caused all four engine-driven electrical generators to drop off line, leaving the airplane without any electrical power to quickly correct the nose-down trim condition. The IP would have to use his left hand to turn the manual trim wheel on the opposite side of the aisle control stand while simultaneously using both hands to pull back on the yoke to arrest the dive. Simulator studies showed that corrective action applied within eight seconds of the upset would prevent the crash; after eight seconds the airplane was unrecoverable.

Investigators were unable to determine why the trim was full nose down or explain why the IP was unable to recover the airplane within eight seconds. Speculation that the wife in the left seat pushed the trim switch on the front of the yoke instead of the interphone switch on the back might account for the misadjusted trim condition. The delay in IP response has been unofficially attributed to the possibility that personnel standing in the cockpit may have fallen forward into the throttle quadrant (firewalling the engines) or impeding the IP's recovery efforts. The accident report was unequivocal, however, in stating that the presence of the spouses and non-crew personnel in the cockpit contributed to or caused the accident.

In a 29th May 1995 investigative report published in *Time*, Pulitzer-Prize winning reporter Mark Thompson found evidence of doctored and falsified Air Force Accident Investigation Boards (AIB), intended to avoid litigation or subsequent inquiries over malfeasance or knowing acceptance of substandard equipment. Thompson claimed that the AIB report for the crash of 61-0328 was intentionally falsified, as the IP was reportedly in the *jump* seat and two the spouses occupied *both* pilot seats. Several 'old timers' from the 4950th TW echo this highly controversial conclusion.

61-0331 C-135B
4950th TW, 4952nd TS, Wright-Patterson AFB, OH
13th June 1971, 700 miles (1,126km) SSW of Honolulu, HI, TH: 11,062.0

The airplane was returning from Pago Pago, American Samoa, to Hickam AFB, HI, the day after monitoring the 12th June 1971 *Encelade* atmospheric nuclear test at the French *Centre d'Experimentation du Pacifique* (CEP) on Mururoa Atoll in the South Pacific. The crew issued normal position reports until approximately 3¼ hours into the flight, when the final position report was abruptly broken off and there were no further transmissions. A search began when the airplane failed to reach Hickam AFB by its scheduled 1500L arrival time. Rescue efforts focused some 200 miles (370km) north of Palmyra Island (approximately 10°31' N, 161°59' W) based on an emergency beacon and scattered wreckage in the area, but no trace of the crew was ever found. All 24 crewmembers were lost, including 12 military personnel and 12 civilian sensor operators and manufacturer's technical representatives. No official cause of the crash has been determined, but a court found LTV liable due to insufficient testing of modifications made to the airframe – including a dorsal radome and multiple fuselage windows – less than a week prior to

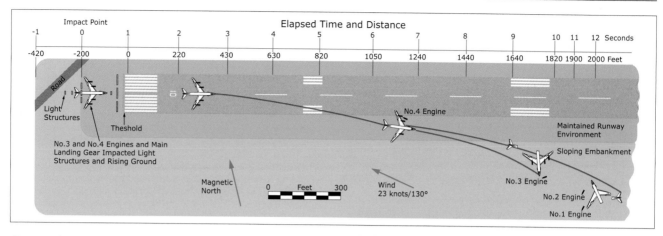

Elapsed Time and Distance

Above: Crash sequence for RC-135S 61-2664 at Shemya AFB.

Right: The last picture of RC-135S 61-2664, taken on 15th March 1981 *en route* from Eielson AFB to the 'area', from whence it returned for its fateful landing at Shemya AFB. *Photo by Paul Jeanes*

Bottom: EC-135J 62-3584 at Hickam AFB. *Author's collection*

its deployment. Indeed, the crash occurred only 38.2 flight hours after the modification work was completed in Texas, which included transit time to Hickam AFB and the operational mission the preceding day.

61-0332 C-135B
1501st ATW, 44th ATS, Travis AFB, CA
11th May 1964, Clark AB, Republic of the Philippines

After descending below the instrument approach glidepath in heavy rain showers with low visibility, the pilot attempted to complete a visual approach. The plane struck a 42ft (12.8m) tall TACAN antenna 0.25nm (0.4km) short of the runway and plunged into the ground nose first. Five crewmembers survived; the remaining 78 on board were killed in the crash or died afterwards. An American in a taxi struck by the crashing airplane was also killed.

61-2664 RC-135S
6th SW, 24th SRS, Eielson AFB, AK
15th March 1981, Shemya AFB, AK, TH: 18,638.9

At 2245 Bering Standard Time (BST), *Exult 66* struck the embankment at the approach end of runway 10 at Shemya AFB while landing under extremely severe conditions, including gusty crosswinds, low visibility, and blowing snow. Six crewmembers were killed. Although the bad weather was a contributing factor, cause of the accident was reportedly an inadequately trained and underqualified aircraft commander under pressure to land the airplane at Shemya AFB. As a result, SAC increased the qualifications necessary for Shemya-certified aircraft commanders from 1,000 hours (for former COBRA BALL copilots) to 2,500 hours plus standing as an instructor pilot. Apparently an earlier incident in 1966 had a similar effect, also increasing the number of hours required for RC-135 copilots to upgrade. The airplane was written off on 16th March 1981.

62-3522 KC-135A
416th BW, 41st AREFS, Griffiss AFB, NY
4th March 1977, Griffiss AFB, NY, TH: 6,423.4

During a ground engine maintenance run, one of the No.2 engine turbine stages disintegrated, causing the engine to explode. Fragments and debris penetrated the airplane's skin, dumping fuel onto the fire. The empennage and right wing survived the blaze. The airplane was written off 10th March 1977.

62-3536 EC-135K
19th AF, 8th TDCS, Seymour Johnson AFB, NC
14th September 1977, near Kirtland AFB, NM, TH: 7,307.1

This airplane was a backup airborne command post for a Readiness Command joint task force exercise. After an extended crew duty day and considerable delays on the ground at Kirtland AFB en route to Nellis AFB, NV, the exhausted flight crew failed to account for steep terrain along their intended climbout path, which they struck at approximately 11:48pm. The airplane was written off the following day.

62-3584 EC-135J
55th Wing, 2nd ACCS, Offutt AFB, NE
29th May 1992, Pope AFB, NC

This EC-135J was returning to Pope AFB after a mission in support of the US Army. The EC-135 reportedly landed on the non-optimum runway (i.e., with a tailwind), which was also wet from a recent rainshower. The airplane touched down far beyond the normal landing zone (2,000-3,000ft – 609-914m from the approach end) and well above landing speed. When braking by the aircraft commander failed to stop the airplane, the copilot applied his brakes which locked the wheels and blew out several tires. The airplane ran off the end of the runway, crossed a road, sheared off the landing gear, stopped, and broke up. There was no fire or explosion, and the crew egressed safely. This airplane was intended for storage in AMARC.

On 5th June 1970 the 6th SW HQ building at Eielson AFB was renamed 'Amber Hall' in memory of 62-4137's crew. *USAF photo, author's collection*

62-4136 C-135B
1611th ATW, McGuire AFB, NJ
23rd October 1962, NAS Leeward Point, Guantanamo Bay, Cuba, TH: c.150

This new C-135B was heavily loaded with ammunition for the US military build up during the Cuban Missile Crisis. The airplane stalled and crashed on final approach 1,000ft (304m) short of the runway. The seven crewmembers were lost, their memory eclipsed by the global events that precipitated their deaths.

62-4137 RC-135E
6th SW, 24th SRS, Eielson AFB, AK
5th June 1969, the Bering Sea, TH: 3,350.7

RIVET AMBER flew its last operational sortie on 4th June 1969. While orbiting off the coast of Kamchatka, the airplane experienced 'severe turbulence' and returned to Shemya AFB. According to a 21st September 2002 report, examination of the airplane after landing revealed 'extensive skin damage to the tail section, to include the vertical stabilizer and areas close to the long wire High Frequency (HF) antenna tail mounts.' A careful study of the S-band radome revealed no damage. The airplane was directed to return to Eielson AFB the next day for further inspection, although maintenance personnel at Shemya AFB objected, considering the three-hour flight too dangerous given the extent of the tail damage.

On 5th June the RC-135E and crew of 19 – *Irene 92* – departed for Eielson AFB. Its last reported position was approximately 250nm (402km) east of Shemya AFB. Some 45 minutes later at 1736Z a USAFSS systems operator on board another RC-135 flying an operational mission near Provideniya, USSR, overheard a Mayday broadcast on HF reporting severe vibration and that the airplane was descending to a lower altitude. A second radio transmission was unintelligible other than the call sign '*Irene 92*'. A third transmission directed the crew to 'go on oxygen' but was likely meant to be via intercom rather than over the radio. HF tones continued to be heard until 1822Z, approximately 46 minutes after the initial Mayday call, after which all contact was lost. No trace of the airplane, debris, or the emergency locator transmitter (ELT) has ever been found, and there are no records of any other radio transmissions on any frequencies. The exhaustive search effort ended after three weeks, and the airplane was written off on 20th June 1969.

Speculation about the loss centers on structural damage to the vertical stabilizer's attachment point. The crashes of Boeing 707-436 G-APFE on 5th March 1966 and KC-135A 56-3655 on 30th July 1968 both involved high side loads on the vertical stabilizer (the former from severe turbulence and the latter from improper rudder inputs), and suggested a pattern of fatigue-related problems that likely affected the RC-135E as well. This crucial issue

prompted the 1968 fleet-wide PACER FIN modification for all '135s. Significantly, the RIVET AMBER did not have this modification. Inspections of the attachment point on 62-4137 on 10th August 1968 (in compliance with TCTO 772, the preliminary inspection of C-135B attachment points) revealed no signs of fatigue. At this point the airplane had some 2,960 total flight hours, which required that the PACER FIN modification be completed within the next 500-1,200 hours and was planned for September 1970. After this inspection in August 1968 the RC-135E flew 50 additional missions and approximately 390 hours over the next nine months before it disappeared.

Other possible causes are fire or structural failure associated with one of the external pods, particularly the electrical generator. Another widely held belief is that the laminated fiberglass radome panel failed, causing cabin depressurization. Both of these would account for the reported vibrations and the need for the crew to go on oxygen. As the airplane flew for 46 minutes after the initial Mayday call, it almost certainly did not experience an explosive decompression and in-flight break up that radome failure would have produced, nor was any debris consistent from such a break up ever found. A fire might well have incapacitated the crew, and the airplane flew uncontrolled to a location far from where any search effort took place (it is possible that Soviet HF tracking stations may have detected further transmissions or could more accurately place the airplane's track given the final HF tones, but no evidence suggests that they did).

Sadly, the loss of the RIVET AMBER spawned its share of ludicrous conspiracy theories, many of which are little different from those associated with the 8th March 2014 disappearance of Malaysian Airlines Boeing 777-200ER 9M-MRO, which also left no trace. One RC-135E fiction is that the Soviets – distraught that 62-4137 had collected incontrovertible evidence of their clandestine effort to MIRV their ICBMs – shot down the airplane from a submarine and then collected the debris.

63-7983 KC-135A
305th AREFW, Grissom AFB, IN
17th June 1986, nr Rodman Naval Station, Republic of Panama, TH: 8,041.1

During a night landing at Howard AB, Republic of Panama, the airplane struck the runway and sheared off the No.3 engine, setting the right wing on fire. The airplane became airborne again but subsequently failed to clear a ridge near Rodman Naval Station, where it crashed. All four crew were killed.

63-7989 KC-135A
301st AREFW, 32nd AREFS, Lockbourne AFB, OH
8th March 1973, Lockbourne AFB, OH, TH: 4,933.1

Standard SAC procedure during 1973 to initiate an ORI/BUY NONE exercise was to issue a 'Green Dot 15' fast reaction message to establish a 'Posture 8' for the aircraft on alert. During a Posture 8 exercise, the crews would respond to their aircraft, start engines, free-flow taxi to the designated runway, simulate a takeoff using minimum-interval takeoff (MITO) intervals, then taxi back to the alert area and shut down engines. On the night of 8th March the 301st AREFW was given a Posture 8 message in support of the ORI for the 509th BW. As the airplanes began to taxi on the unlit ramp, the left wingtip of KC-135A 63-7980 struck the forward fuselage of KC-135A 63-7989. Fire erupted and 63-7989 was damaged beyond economical repair, and three crewmembers were killed. Salvaged parts were used to repair 63-7980, which later became the KC-135R SPECKLED TROUT. Written off on 7th September 1973. As a result of this incident, SAC temporarily restricted alert ground force operations to starting engines and reporting ready when polled by the command post.

63-7990 KC-135A
410th BW, K. I. Sawyer AFB, MI
31st January 1989, Dyess AFB, TX

This KC-135A crashed at 1210 CST during take-off from Dyess AFB. It had arrived there earlier from K I Sawyer AFB and was en route to Hickam AFB. The water injection system failed during a heavyweight take-off in gusty crosswinds. Improper pilot recovery technique caused the airplane to stall and crash. All 19 on board were killed.

63-8042 KC-135A
6th SAW, 6th AREFS, Walker AFB, NM
3rd June 1965, Walker AFB, NM

During a series of touch-and-go landings, visibility was suddenly obscured by blowing dust and sand. The pilot flying the airplane may have become disoriented and descended below the instrument approach glide path. The airplane crashed shortly before 11:00 pm, 1nm (1.9km) short of the end of the runway, killing the crew of five.

KC-135A 63-7983 at Lockbourne AFB in the 1970s. *Author's collection*

KC-135A 63-7990 at RAF Mildenhall in 1979. *Author's collection*

EC-135C 63-8053 at Offutt AFB in November 1993. *Photo by Joe Bruch*

63-8053 EC-135C
7th ACCS, 55th Wing, Offutt AFB, NE
2nd September 1997, Pope AFB, NC

After a hard landing at Pope AFB, the nose gear collapsed on this EC-135C which then departed the runway. There were no fatalities among the eleven crewmembers. As the airplane was due for retirement by the end of the year, plans were made to scrap it in place rather than repair it.

63-8473 C-135F
1st July 1972, Hao AB, French Polynesia

The sole French C-135F lost, this airplane lost an engine during take-off due to water contamination while heavily loaded with fuel and crashed immediately afterward. All six crewmembers were lost. It departed Hao AB, the forward operating location for the *Centre d'Experimentation du Pacifique*, from which France conducted its later atmospheric nuclear tests. The C-135F was likely on a weather reconnaissance mission associated with the *Titania* 4kt TN-60 warhead test.

63-8877 KC-135R
22nd ARW, McConnell AFB, KS
3rd May 2013, Near Chaldovar, Kyrgyzstan

During initial departure on a combat refueling mission *Shell 77* began a subtle yawing that developed into increasingly significant Dutch Roll. Approximately 11 minutes after takeoff, the aft fuselage broke off and the vertical and both horizontal stabilizers separated due to excessive lateral forces and the airplane experienced structural breakup. The crash killed the crew of three from Fairchild AFB. Investigation revealed a failed component of the rudder power control unit (PCU). This prevented the series yaw damper (SYD) from eliminating the resulting 'rudder hunting' oscillating yaw. The crew failed to turn off the malfunctioning SYD, repeatedly tried to use the autopilot to control the oscillations, and manually overcontrolled aileron and rudder inputs, causing the condition to worsen. According to the report, 'The cumulative effects of the malfunctioning SYD, coupled with autopilot use and rudder movements during the unrecognized Dutch Roll, generated Dutch Roll forces that exceeded the aircraft's design structural limits.' Investigators found that there was insufficient training in identifying and correcting Dutch Roll, that the Dash One guidance for handling 'rudder hunting' was unclear and confusing, and that the crew's overall inexperience led to the loss of an otherwise recoverable aircraft.

A significant part of the unofficial post-crash critique focused on the removal of parachutes and deactivation of the forward hatch emergency egress bar and spoiler from all KC-135s as a cost and weight saving measure (a harness was retained in each airplane for use by the Boom Operator to check hatches in flight). Critics argued that not having the parachutes, especially in a combat zone, devalued lives of crewmembers in lieu of savings. Air refueling operations over Afghanistan, including low-level refueling of fighters and special operations missions, changed the tanker threat equation. Parachutes were available, if not frequently worn, during initial missions of Operation ENDURING FREEDOM beginning 7th October 2001 and Operation IRAQI FREEDOM beginning 20th March 2003. By 2008, however, the absence of any aerial threat and any known SAM threat from Taliban forces (and a similar assessment of the Iraqi threat) justified the decision to remove the 'unnecessary' parachutes from the KC-135 fleet.

The debate over the wisdom of this decision should not mask the realities of their benefit. In the case of *Shell 77* – a catastrophic in-flight break up – there would simply have been no time to unstrap from their crew seats, find and don a parachute (which were not routinely worn) and then bail out. The argument that the airplane was in a combat environment without parachutes misses the point that this incident was completely unrelated to combat, could have happened anywhere in the world, and was the result not of hostile action

but improper crew response to a minor malfunction. For the crew of *Shell 77*, the absence of parachutes was irrelevant to their tragic loss.

63-8882 KC-135A
397th BW, 71st AREFS, Dow AFB, ME
26th February 1965, 410 miles (659km) SSE of Harmon AB, Newfoundland

This KC-135A was part of a cell scheduled to refuel three Boeing B-47s returning from a three-week alert deployment to Torrejon AB, Spain. The second B-47 approached the air refueling boom and, while maneuvering into the contact position, failed to maintain adequate separation from the tanker. B-47E 52-0171 struck the KC-135A, and both airplanes and all eight crewmembers aboard them were lost. 52-0171 was the second B-47E lost in an air refueling collision with a KC-135A, as B-47E 52-0051 crashed after colliding with KC-135A 60-0342 (which landed safely) from the 43rd AREFS, 4170th SW, Larson AFB, WA, over Yellowstone National Park, WY, on 3rd May 1962.

63-8886 KC-135R
92nd ARW, Fairchild AFB, WA
26th September 2006, Bishkek-Minas IAP, Kyrgyzstan

The airplane landed normally at 2003L following a combat refueling mission. The Kyrgyz tower controller directed the crew to exit the runway at taxiway Golf, which was normally usable only in daylight hours. The crew stopped the airplane at the intersection of the runway and taxiway, awaiting further guidance from the US ground liaison controller and a 'follow me' truck. Unaware that the KC-135R was partially blocking the runway, the tower controller cleared Altyn Air Tupolev Tu-154M *Careless* (EX-85718) for takeoff. In the darkness the Russian pilot did not clearly see the stopped tanker, and the Tu-154 – used for both commercial flights and Kyrgyz presidential support – struck the KC-135R. The KC-135R's left wing and No.1 engine were destroyed. The Tu-154 lost six feet of the right wing but continued the takeoff, landed safely and eventually re-entered service. There were no injuries among the three tanker crewmembers or the Tu-154 crew and 52 passengers.

KC-135R 63-8877 on 13th October 2006 at MCAS Miramar. *Photo by Matthew Lyons*

KC-135R 63-8886 at Minot AFB on 7th August 1996. *Photo by Brian Rogers*

SIGNIFICANT INCIDENTS

Every day there are hundreds of air refueling contacts between KC-135s and receivers all over the world. During wartime this number is profoundly higher. Surprisingly, no KC-135s have been lost in mid-air collisions during combat air refueling. Indeed, only four KC-135s have been destroyed – along with their receivers – during peacetime air refueling operations. Two of these involved B-52s carrying nuclear weapons, one was a B-47 during a trans-Atlantic deployment, and one was an F-105 during training. Nonetheless, '135s have been involved in a several mid-air collisions resulting in the loss of the receiver, as well as other incidents causing significant damage (see Table A2-2). Several of these events have led researchers to claim incorrectly that the '135 was lost as well.

Table A2-1. **Selected Significant Incidents**

Date	Serial	MDS	Attrition Location	Summary
12 Nov 57	53-5540	NT-33A	Near Edwards AFB, CA	Collided with JKC-135A 55-3125, killing NT-33 pilot; 55-3125 landed safely
2 Jan 61	58-0056	KC-135A	Offutt AFB, NE	The KC-135 skidded on an the icy runway while taxiing
1 Mar 62	56-6677	U-2F	Near Edwards AFB, CA	During refueling trials the U-2F entered the KC-135A jet wash and broke up
3 May 63	52-0051	B-47E	Yellowstone, WY	Mid-air collision with KC-135A 60-0342 (landed safely) during air refueling
13 Jan 70	63-7619	F-4C	Anderson AB, Guam	KC-135A 58-0020 struck the F-4C on the runway during KC-135A takeoff roll
17 Jun 70	61-7970	SR-71A	East of El Paso, NM	SR-71A collided with KC-135Q 59-1474 during air refueling
9 Feb 74	60-3506	T-39A	Near Colorado Springs, CO	Collided with NC-135 'celestial observation' aircraft (which landed safely)
17 Aug 76	64-7430	F-4C	AR-603 60nm NW Luke AFB, AZ	Mid-air collision with KC-135A 58-0079 (landed safely at Edwards) during A/R
Aug 79	62-4139	RC-135M	Clark AB, Philippines	Improper throttle management on takeoff caused the airplane to veer into the mud
17 Sep 82	76-1604	E-3A	ELF One, Saudi Arabia	Collision with E-3, both recovered; KC-135A landed with Nos. 3 and 4 engines inop
6 Feb 91	58-0013	KC-135E	Jeddah IAP, Saudi Arabia	Turbulence tore off Nos. 1 and 2 engines; aircraft landed safely

Above: KC-135A 58-0056 slid off the icy runway at Offutt AFB while turning around on 2nd January 1961. *USAF, author's collection*

Right: Unable to stop as F-4C 63-7619 pulled onto the runway, the No.4 engine on KC-135A 58-0020 struck the F-4 and began to drag it along the runway. Despite being fully laden with fuel, fire crews prevented all but moderate damage to the tanker's right wing, which was replaced. *Photo by George Flynn*

Below: During air refueling on 17th August 1976, F-4C 64-7430 collided with KC-135A 58-0079's tail section and ripped off the air refueling boom. The tanker landed safely at Edwards AFB, CA, and the F-4 crew ejected safely. *Photo courtesy Bill Strandberg*

Right: During a typhoon evacuation from Kadena AB to Clark AB in August 1979, RC-135M 62-4139 ended up in the mud next to the runway. Damage was minimal, but the airplane reportedly still flies slightly 'crooked'. *Photo by Ken Hopkins courtesy Larry Tart*

Retirements

Officially it has been called many things – MASDC, AMARC, AMARG, DM, and the 309th Aerospace Maintenance and Regeneration Group. Unofficially, it is known around the world simply as 'the Boneyard,' the place where military airplanes are stored, picked apart, or scrapped. After nearly 60 years in service, it is not surprising that a substantial number of KC-135s and variants should spend their final days baking in the dry Arizona heat, their parts cannibalized to keep others flying, before finally being melted down into the next generation of beer can.

The Boneyard (a name disliked by many of the professionals who take justifiable pride in their work there) was established at Davis-Monthan Airfield after the Second World War to store or scrap surplus Army Air Force airplanes. On 1st February 1965 it became known as the Military Storage and Disposition Center (MASDC). By 1st October 1985 it was renamed as the Aerospace Maintenance and Regeneration Center (AMARC), finally becoming the Aerospace Maintenance and Regeneration Group (AMARG) on 2nd May 2007. For the sake of consistency, all references in this book use the AMARG designation, although nearly half of the '135 residents were relegated to AMARC (and five to MASDC).

Aircraft assigned to MASDC were given a 5-digit Processing Control Number (PCN), sometimes referred unofficially as a 'storage code' (see Table A3-1). This was a 2-letter identifier based on the airplane type (for the KC-135 it was CA) followed by the sequential arrival number from 001 to 999; for example, RC-135A 63-8060 was given the PCN CA001. Following MADSC's redesignation as AMARC, the PCN changed to 8-digits; for example, EC-135H 61-0291 was assigned PCN AACA0007. In September 2010 the PCN numbering system was replaced by a four-digit asset number, and in September 2013 this changed to a six-digit number with the addition

of thousands of line items of tooling. Aircraft now are labeled with simply the MDS and tail number (e.g., 'KC-135R 623504') in lieu of the PCN.

Airplanes may have multiple PCNs, one for each time period it was stored at AMARG. The assigned entry date ('Date In') is when the airplane was officially processed into the system. In some cases, the date listed may differ from when the airplane arrived. For example, several airplanes arrived at AMARG after duty hours on one day and were not accessioned until the following day. In other cases, AMARG records show the *projected* date of arrival. When the airplane *actually* arrived is properly recorded only on the individual aircraft records which are not part of the AMARG system. The assigned departure date ('Date Out') is when the airplane either departed for further duty or when it was listed as scrapped or written off.

In addition to being stored or scrapped at AMARG, at least two dozen airplanes have been pressed into ground use or flyable storage pending sale and delivery to other nations (see Table A3-2). Ground trainers provide hands-on experience for fledgling 'wrench turners' undergoing initial training. Others serve as battle damage repair (BDR) airframes, allowing maintenance personnel the opportunity to practice repairing large jets that need repair under combat or 'bare bones' conditions. Still others are training aids for flight stewards or other aircrew. Four were used in destructive testing, described in Chapter 7.

Most visibly, nearly three dozen of the 820 KC-135 airframes have been or are displayed to the public in museums, displays, or as 'gate guards' (See Table A3-3) Interestingly, these are all in the United States and notably exclude Great Britain and Japan, which have for so long played host to '135 units. As of 2015 other KC-135 operators such as Chile, France, Singapore, and Turkey have not retired any of their modest fleets to provide any display aircraft.

Table A3-1. **AMARG Retirements**

PCN Code	MDS	Serial	Last Unit	Last Base	Date In	Date Out	Total Hrs	Comments
CA001	RC-135A	63-8060	AEGSR	Forbes AFB, KS	29-Jun-72	27-Jul-72		Returned to Service
CA002	C-135B	61-2668	55th WRS	McClellan AFB, CA	20-Jul-72	1-Nov-72		Returned to Service
CA003	WC-135B	61-2669	56th WRS	McClellan AFB, CA	20-Jul-72	8-Nov-72		Returned to Service
CA004	KC-135A	55-3126	1st CW	Andrews AFB, MD	31-Jul-75	5-Jan-78		Scrapped
CA005	NC-135A	60-0370	4949th TW	Kirtland AFB, NM	30-Jun-76	20-May-96	6,354.2	Scrapped
CA006	367-80	N70700	Boeing	Boeing Field, WA	17-Feb-76	7-May-90		To Boeing for restoration; to Smithsonian/Udvar-Hazy
AACA0007	EC-135H	61-0291	10th ACCS	RAF Mildenhall, UK	30-May-91	4-Dec-95	16,533.0	Scrapped; corrosion studies
AACA0008	EC-135P	55-3129	6th ACCS, 1st FW	Langley AFB, VA	31-Jan-92	11-May-16	7,665.7	Scrapped
AACA0009	EC-135P	58-0019	6th ACCS, 1st FW	Langley AFB, VA	12-Feb-92	25-Nov-13	23,598.3	Scrapped
AACA0010	EC-135P	61-0274	6th ACCS, 1st FW	Langley AFB, VA	27-Feb-92	20-Jun-16	15,808.7	Scrapped
AACA0011	EC-135P	58-0022	6th ACCS, 1st FW	Langley AFB, VA	5-Mar-92	21-Nov-13	23,353.2	Scrapped
AACA0012	EC-135H	61-0285	6th ACCS, 1st FW	Langley AFB, VA	9-Mar-92	5-Nov-13	17,082.3	Scrapped
AACA0013	EC-135J	63-8056	9th ACCS, 15th ABW	Hickam AFB, HI	24-Mar-92	14-Nov-13	13,022.5	Scrapped
AACA0014	EC-135J	63-8057	9th ACCS, 15th ABW	Hickam AFB, HI	31-Mar-92	20-Apr-93	13,692.4	To Pima Air Museum
AACA0015	EC-135L	61-0263	70th ARS, 305th ARW	Grissom AFB, IN	5-May-92	3-Dec-13	10,895.1	Scrapped
AACA0016	EC-135L	61-0283	70th ARS, 305th ARW	Grissom AFB, IN	6-May-92	20-Nov-13	12,971.4	Scrapped
AACA0017	EC-135G	63-8001	4th ACCS, 28th Wg	Ellsworth AFB, SD	18-May-92	5-Dec-13	11,485.9	Scrapped
AACA0018	EC-135L	61-0279	70th ARS, 305th ARW	Grissom AFB, IN	22-May-92	16-Jun-16	11,301.3	Scrapped
AACA0019	EC-135C	62-3583	2nd ACCS, 55th Wg	Offutt AFB, NE	26-May-92	6-Nov-13	27,849.2	Scrapped
AACA0020	EC-135L	61-0261	70th ARS, 305th ARW	Grissom AFB, IN	29-May-92	9-Dec-13	11,000.3	Scrapped
AACA0021	EC-135A	61-0297	4th ACCS, 28th Wg	Ellsworth AFB, SD	2-Jun-92	16-Jun-16	14,524.0	Scrapped
AACA0022	EC-135A	61-0289	4th ACCS, 28th Wg	Ellsworth AFB, SD	8-Jun-92	21-Jun-16	13,085.3	Scrapped
AACA0023	EC-135G	62-3579	4th ACCS, 28th Wg	Ellsworth AFB, SD	16-Jun-92	31-Oct-13	12,701.9	Scrapped
AACA0024	EC-135G	62-3570	4th ACCS, 28th Wg	Ellsworth AFB, SD	23-Jun-92	3-Feb-10	12,515.4	Scrapped
AACA0025	KC-135A	56-3653	7th ARS, 19th ARW	Robins AFB, GA	7-Jul-92	11-May-16	11,730.7	Scrapped
AACA0026	KC-135A	58-0033	7th ARS, 19th ARW	Robins AFB, GA	9-Jul-92	29-Apr-09	15,680.7	Scrapped
AACA0027	EC-135C	63-8051	4th ACCS, 28th Wg	Ellsworth AFB, SD	10-Jul-92	1-Aug-16	19,634.9	Scrapped
AACA0028	KC-135A	56-3644	46th ARS, 305th ARW	McGuire AFB, NJ	16-Jul-92		12,318.0	
AACA0029	KC-135A	56-3603	917th ARS, 96th Wg	Dyess AFB, TX	21-Jul-92	4-Aug-09	14,273.9	Scrapped
AACA0030	KC-135A	56-3608	93rd ARS, 398th OG	Fairchild AFB, WA	23-Jul-92		12,555.3	

PCN Code	MDS	Serial	Last Unit	Last Base	Date In	Date Out	Total Hrs	Comments
AACA0031	KC-135A	56-3636	71st ARS, 2nd Wg	Barksdale AFB, LA	28-Jul-92	29-Apr-09	12,061.4	Scrapped
AACA0032	KC-135A	56-3615	71st ARS, 2nd Wg	Barksdale AFB, LA	30-Jul-92	23-Jun-16	11,225.6	Scrapped
AACA0033	KC-135A	56-3637	46th ARS, 305th ARW	McGuire AFB, NJ	6-Aug-92		15,105.0	
AACA0034	KC-135A	56-3646	917th ARS, 96th Wg	Dyess AFB, TX	11-Aug-92		10,807.4	
AACA0035	KC-135A	57-1476	920th ARS, 305th ARW	McGuire AFB, NJ	13-Aug-92		12,431.6	
AACA0036	KC-135A	57-1477	93rd ARS, 398th OG	Fairchild AFB, WA	18-Aug-92		11,979.0	
AACA0037	KC-135A	56-3633	920th ARS, 305th ARW	McGuire AFB, NJ	20-Aug-92		11,746.8	
AACA0038	KC-135A	56-3635	917th ARS, 96th Wg	Dyess AFB, TX	25-Aug-92		15,035.4	
AACA0039	KC-135A	57-1467	920th ARS, 305th ARW	McGuire AFB, NJ	27-Aug-92	28-Oct-13	14,105.6	Scrapped
AACA0040	NKC-135A	55-3127	4950th TW	Wright-Patterson AFB, OH	31-Aug-92		11,355.8	
AACA0041	KC-135A	56-3651	906th ARS, 43rd ARW	Scott AFB, IL	1-Sep-92	22-Jun-16	12,578.1	Scrapped
AACA0042	KC-135A	57-2590	93rd ARS, 398th OG	Fairchild AFB, WA	3-Sep-92	7-Oct-09	13,761.0	Scrapped
AACA0043	KC-135A	58-0097	7th ARS, 19th ARW	Robins AFB, GA	8-Sep-92		14,284.1	
AACA0044	KC-135A	56-3647	93rd ARS, 398th OG	Fairchild AFB, WA	10-Sep-92		11,561.1	
AACA0045	EC-135G	63-7994	4th ACCS, 28th Wg	Ellsworth AFB, SD	11-Sep-92	29-Oct-13	12,019.9	Scrapped
AACA0046	KC-135A	57-1420	93rd ARS, 398th OG	Fairchild AFB, WA	15-Sep-92		12,639.8	
AACA0047	KC-135A	56-3594	93rd ARS, 398th OG	Fairchild AFB, WA	17-Sep-92	24-Jun-16	15,331.5	Scrapped
AACA0048	EC-135A	61-0278	4th ACCS, 28th Wg	Ellsworth AFB, SD	18-Sep-92	22-Jun-16	13,049.0	Scrapped
AACA0049	KC-135A	56-3634	920th ARS, 305th ARW	McGuire AFB, NJ	22-Sep-92		15,448.6	
AACA0050	KC-135A	57-1490	93rd ARS, 398th OG	Fairchild AFB, WA	29-Sep-92	24-Jun-16	14,841.1	Scrapped
AACA0051	KC-135A	56-3619	46th ARS, 305th ARW	McGuire AFB, NJ	7-Oct-92	1-Aug-16	11,198.9	Scrapped
AACA0052	KC-135A	58-0081	71st ARS, 2nd Wg	Barksdale AFB, LA	16-Oct-92		19,850.5	
AACA0053	NKC-135A	55-3131	4950th TW	Wright-Patterson AFB, OH	19-Oct-92	2-Sep-10	13,296.9	Scrapped
AACA0054	KC-135A	56-3627	71st ARS, 2nd Wg	Barksdale AFB, LA	21-Oct-92		13,682.1	
AACA0055	KC-135A	56-3610	7th ARS, 19th ARW	Robins AFB, GA	4-Nov-92		11,565.9	
AACA0056	KC-135A	58-0029	7th ARS, 19th ARW	Robins AFB, GA	2-Dec-92		13,262.0	
AACA0057	KC-135A	57-2609	917th ARS, 96th Wg	Dyess AFB, TX	20-Jan-93	27-Mar-97	12,740.5	Converted to KC-135R for Turkey; returned as AACA0121
AACA0058	KC-135A	58-0028	46th ARS, 305th ARW	McGuire AFB, NJ	7-Apr-93	21-Jun-16	12,165.2	Scrapped
AACA0059	KC-135A	56-3600	93rd ARS, 398th OG	Fairchild AFB, WA	13-Apr-93		12,809.9	
AACA0060	KC-135A	57-2591	46th ARS, 305th ARW	McGuire AFB, NJ	19-Apr-93		13,733.0	
AACA0061	KC-135A	57-2596	906th ARS, 43rd ARW	Scott AFB, IL	21-Apr-93		13,139.4	
AACA0062	KC-135A	55-3136	917th ARS, 96th Wg	Dyess AFB, TX	28-Apr-93		14,062.3	
AACA0063	KC-135A	56-3625	917th ARS, 96th Wg	Dyess AFB, TX	5-May-93	7-Oct-09	11,881.3	Scrapped
AACA0064	KC-135A	56-3614	46th ARS, 305th ARW	McGuire AFB, NJ	7-Jun-93	17-Jun-16	12,458.3	Scrapped
AACA0065	KC-135A	56-3649	93rd ARS, 398th OG	Fairchild AFB, WA	16-Jun-93		12,865.3	
AACA0066	KC-135A	57-2592	906th ARS, 43rd ARW	Scott AFB, IL	23-Jun-93		12,292.9	
AACA0067	NKC-135A	55-3119	55th Wg	Offutt AFB, NE	6-Jun-93		17,206.4	
AACA0068	KC-135A	62-3501	93rd ARS, 398th OG	Fairchild AFB, WA	7-Jul-93		11,444.2	
AACA0069	KC-135A	62-3574	46th ARS, 305th ARW	McGuire AFB, NJ	12-Jul-93	1-Jul-96		To PDM for France. Returned as AACA0112
AACA0070	KC-135A	55-3137	906th ARS, 43rd ARW	Scott AFB, IL	14-Jul-93		17,405.2	
AACA0071	KC-135A	62-3497	906th ARS, 43rd ARW	Scott AFB, IL	15-Jul-93	19-Jan-96		To PDM for France. Returned as AACA0108
AACA0072	KC-135A	56-3601	93rd ARS, 398th OG	Fairchild AFB, WA	21-Jul-92		16,603.6	
AACA0073	KC-135A	63-8009	46th ARS, 305th ARW	McGuire AFB, NJ	26-Jul-93	24-Jul-97	11,882.4	To Singapore as KC-135R 750
AACA0074	KC-135A	56-3591	906th ARS, 43rd ARW	Scott AFB, IL	28-Jul-93	1-Aug-16	11,143.3	Scrapped
AACA0075	KC-135A	58-0025	93rd ARS, 398th OG	Fairchild AFB, WA	4-Aug-93		13,839.5	
AACA0076	KC-135A	62-3532	917th ARS, 96th Wg	Dyess AFB, TX	5-Aug-93	1-Aug-16	10,325.2	Scrapped
AACA0077	KC-135A	56-3652	906th ARS, 43rd ARW	Scott AFB, IL	9-Aug-93		17,367.5	
AACA0078	KC-135A	56-3642	906th ARS, 43rd ARW	Scott AFB, IL	11-Aug-93		13,350.5	
AACA0079	KC-135A	58-0091	906th ARS, 43rd ARW	Scott AFB, IL	18-Aug-93	21-Jun-16	11,874.9	Scrapped
AACA0080	KC-135A	58-0105	906th ARS, 43rd ARW	Scott AFB, IL	23-Aug-93		11,821.1	
AACA0081	KC-135A	62-3525	906th ARS, 43rd ARW	Scott AFB, IL	24-Aug-93	19-Sep-95		To PDM for France. Returned as AACA0105
AACA0082	KC-135A	59-1449	46th ARS, 305th ARW	McGuire AFB, NJ	27-Aug-93		12,559.6	
AACA0083	KC-135A	59-1454	906th ARS, 43rd ARW	Scott AFB, IL	1-Sep-93	19-Jun-98	12,475.6	To Singapore as KC-135R 752
AACA0084	KC-135A	60-0326	917th ARS, 96th Wg	Dyess AFB, TX	2-Sep-93	17-May-96		Converted to KC-135R for Turkey. Returned as AACA0116
AACA0085	KC-135A	62-3567	46th ARS, 305th ARW	McGuire AFB, NJ	13-Sep-93	9-Aug-96		To PDM for Turkey. Returned as AACA0111
AACA0086	KC-135A	63-7986	906th ARS, 43rd ARW	Scott AFB, IL	15-Sep-93		12,765.9	
AACA0087	KC-135A	62-3555	46th ARS, 305th ARW	McGuire AFB, NJ	20-Sep-93		12,283.9	
AACA0088	KC-135A	60-0325	93rd ARS, 398th OG	Fairchild AFB, WA	22-Sep-93	7-Aug-96		Converted to KC-135R for Turkey. Returned as AACA0120
AACA0089	KC-135A	58-0110	46th ARS, 305th ARW	McGuire AFB, NJ	27-Sep-93	28-Feb-96		To PDM for Turkey. Returned as AACA0109
AACA0090	WC-135B	61-2673	56th WRS	McClellan AFB, CA	28-Sep-93	25-Oct-13	26,581.6	Scrapped
AACA0091	KC-135A	61-0325	93rd ARS, 398th OG	Fairchild AFB, WA	29-Sep-93	12-Dec-97	10,745.5	To Singapore as KC-135R 751
AACA0092	EC-135J	63-8055	2nd ACCS, 55th Wg	Offutt AFB, NE	4-Oct-93	17-Oct-13	13,933.1	Scrapped
AACA0093	EC-135C	63-8047	2nd ACCS, 55th Wg	Offutt AFB, NE	12-Oct-93	1-Aug-16	21,666.9	Scrapped
AACA0094	NKC-135A	55-3122	4950th TW	Wright-Patterson AFB, OH	19-Oct-93		9,390.9	
AACA0095	NKC-135A	55-3120	4950th TW	Wright-Patterson AFB, OH	15-Dec-93		12,134.2	
AACA0096	KC-135A	56-3620	71st ARS, 2nd BW	Barksdale AFB, LA	7-Mar-94		14,297.7	
AACA0097	KC-135A	62-3563	917th ARS, 96th Wg	Dyess AFB, TX	18-Mar-94	26-Mar-96	12,043.9	To PDM for Turkey. Returned as AACA0110
AACA0098	KC-135A	62-3539	917th ARS, 96th Wg	Dyess AFB, TX	1-Apr-94	13-Jun-96		Converted to KC-135R for Turkey. Returned as AACA0118
AACA0099	KC-135A	63-8016	93rd ARS, 398th OG	Fairchild AFB, WA	12-May-94	6-Nov-98	13,443.4	To Singapore as KC-135R 753
AACA0100	KC-135A	63-7998	917th ARS, 96th Wg	Dyess AFB, TX	23-May-94	4-Nov-94		To NASA as KC-135A N931NA
AACA0101	KC-135A	62-3560	93rd ARS, 398th OG	Fairchild AFB, WA	16-Jun-94		10,940.1	
AACA0102	KC-135A	56-3621	93rd ARS, 398th OG	Fairchild AFB, WA	23-Jun-94		12,815.8	
AACA0103	KC-135A	56-3624	93rd ARS, 398th OG	Fairchild AFB, WA	7-Jul-94	23-Sep-97	11,149.5	To Altus AFB, OK
AACA0104	KC-135A	55-3142	93rd ARS, 398th OG	Fairchild AFB, WA	12-Jul-94		17,368.0	
AACA0105	KC-135A	62-3525	GRV02.91	BA Istres-LeTube	15-May-96	19-Feb-97		Converted to KC-135R, to France as KC-135RG 525/93-CN
AACA0106	NKC-135A	55-3128	412th TW	Edwards AFB, CA	20-May-96			
AACA0107	WC-135W	61-2665	55th Wg	Offutt AFB, NE	11-Sep-96			
AACA0108	KC-135A	62-3497	GRV02.91	BA Istres-LeTube	19-Sep-96	21-May-97		Converted to KC-135R, then to France as KC-135RG 497/93-CM
AACA0109	KC-135A	58-0110			28-Oct-96	18-Mar-97		Converted to KC-135R. Returned as AACA0113 interim for Turkey
AACA0110	KC-135A	62-3563			8-Nov-96	22-Apr-97		Converted to KC-135R. Returned as AACA0114 interim for Turkey
AACA0111	KC-135A	62-3567			29-Apr-97	22-Oct-97		Converted to KC-135R. Returned as AACA0119 interim for Turkey

PCN Code	MDS	Serial	Last Unit	Last Base	Date In	Date Out	Total Hrs	Comments
AACA0112	KC-135A	62-3574	GRV02.91	BA Istres-LeTube	5-May-97	15-Aug-97		Converted to KC-135RG then delivered to France as 574/93-CP
AACA0113	KC-135R	58-0110	101 Filo	Incirlik AB	1-Jul-97	11-Dec-97		Stored pending delivery to Turkey as KC-135R 80110
AACA0114	KC-135R	62-3563	101 Filo	Incirlik AB	19-Aug-97	15-Dec-97		Stored pending delivery to Turkey as KC-135R 23563
AACA0115	OC-135B	61-2674	55th Wg	Offutt AFB, NE	21-Aug-97			
AACA0116	KC-135R	60-0326	101 Filo	Incirlik AB	3-Nov-97	17-Dec-97		Stored pending delivery to Turkey as KC-135R 00326
AACA0117	EC-135C	63-8052	7th ACCS, 55th Wg	Offutt AFB, NE	16-Jan-98	1-Aug-16		Scrapped
AACA0118	KC-135R	62-3539	101 Filo	Incirlik AB	27-Jan-98	15-Mar-98		To Turkey as 23539
AACA0119	KC-135R	62-3567	101 Filo	Incirlik AB	25-Feb-98	21-Apr-98		To Turkey as KC-135R 23567
AACA0120	KC-135R	60-0325	101 Filo	Incirlik AB	20-Apr-98	20-Jun-98		To Turkey as KC-135R 00325
AACA0121	KC-135R	57-2609	101 Filo	Incirlik AB	21-May-98	17-Jul-98		To Turkey as KC-135R 72609
AACA0122	EC-135E	61-0326	412th TW	Edwards AFB, CA	1-Jun-98	27-Jun-16		Scrapped
AACA0123	EC-135C	62-3585	7th ACCS, 55th Wg	Offutt AFB, NE	2-Jun-98	21-Sep-16		Scrapped
AACA0124	EC-135C	63-8046	7th ACCS, 55th Wg	Offutt AFB, NE	21-Oct-98	1-Aug-16		Scrapped
AACA0125	EC-135C	63-8054	7th ACCS, 55th Wg	Offutt AFB, NE	28-Oct-98	20-Sep-16		Scrapped
AACA0126	EC-135Y	55-3125	6th ARW	MacDill AFB, FL	4-Feb-99	12-Sep-13		Scrapped
AACA0127	EC-135C	62-3581	7th ACCS, 55th Wg	Offutt AFB, NE	10-Feb-99	8-Aug-16		Scrapped
AACA0128	EC-135C	63-8048	7th ACCS, 55th Wg	Offutt AFB, NE	26-Feb-99	4-Aug-16		Scrapped
AACA0129	C-135E	60-0375	452nd FTS, 412th TW	Edwards AFB, CA	18-Apr-01	12-Sep-13		Scrapped
AACA0130	C-135E	60-0376	65th AS, 15th ABW	Hickam AFB, HI	21-Jun-01	11-May-16		Scrapped
AACA0131	EC-135K	59-1518	65th AS, 15th ABW	Hickam AFB, HI	10-Mar-03	21-Sep-16		Scrapped
AACA0132	KC-135E	58-0096	314th ARS, 940th ARW	Beale AFB, CA	23-Feb-04		18,613.4	
AACA0133	KC-135E	56-3654	132nd ARS, 101 ARW	Bangor ANGB, ME	25-Feb-04		18,539.7	
AACA0134	KC-135E	56-3604	108th ARS, 126th ARW	Scott AFB, IL	8-Mar-04		15,931.6	
AACA0135	KC-135E	55-3141	174th ARS, 185th ARW	Sioux City ANGB, IA	17-Mar-04		16,680.7	
AACA0136	KC-135E	58-0053	314th ARS, 940th ARW	Beale AFB, CA	15-Apr-04		18,468.4	
AACA0137	KC-135E	55-3143	197th ARS, 161st ARW	Sky Harbor IAP, AZ	7-May-04	4-Jun-16	17,002.0	McFarland R&D, Wichita, KS
AACA0138	KC-135E	56-3648	171st ARW	Pittsburgh IAP, PA	7-May-04		17,063.5	
AACA0139	KC-135E	56-3612	171st ARW	Pittsburgh IAP, PA	7-May-04	9-Aug-16	16,776.7	Scrapped
AACA0140	KC-135E	57-1511	314th ARS, 940th ARW	Beale AFB, CA	23-Jun-04		19,077.0	
AACA0141	KC-135E	58-0064	314th ARS, 940th ARW	Beale AFB, CA	23-Aug-04		17,948.0	
AACA0142	KC-135E	57-1482	108th ARS, 126th ARW	Scott AFB, IL	16-Sep-04		18,071.3	
AACA0143	KC-135E	56-3643	151st ARS, 134th ARW	McGhee Tyson AP, TN	17-Sep-04		17,005.0	
AACA0144	NKC-135E	55-3135	412th TW	Edwards AFB, CA	28-Sep-04		17,380.8	
AACA0145	C-135E	60-0372	452nd FTS, 412th TW	Edwards AFB, CA	28-Sep-05	13-Mar-13	13,994.8	Scrapped
AACA0146	KC-135E	57-1422	314th ARS, 940th ARW	Beale AFB, CA	21-Jan-07		21,936.5	
AACA0147	KC-135E	57-2607	117th ARS, 190th ARW	Forbes ANGB, KS	22-Feb-07		18,188.7	
AACA0148	KC-135E	58-0041	314th ARS, 940th ARW	Beale AFB, CA	27-Feb-07		20,597.6	
AACA0149	KC-135E	58-0037	117th ARS, 190th ARW	Forbes ANGB, KS	2-Mar-07		16,628.1	
AACA0150	KC-135E	58-0013	117th ARS, 190th ARW	Forbes ANGB, KS	7-Mar-07		17,499.5	
AACA0151	KC-135D	63-8059	117th ARS, 190th ARW	Forbes ANGB, KS	14-Mar-07		14,371.6	
AACA0152	KC-135D	63-8058	117th ARS, 190th ARW	Forbes ANGB, KS	19-Mar-07		14,032.9	
AACA0153	KC-135D	63-8060	117th ARS, 190th ARW	Forbes ANGB, KS	28-Mar-07		14,669.7	
AACA0154	KC-135D	63-8061	117th ARS, 190th ARW	Forbes ANGB, KS	4-Apr-07		13,340.2	
AACA0155	KC-135E	59-1447	314th ARS, 940th ARW	Beale AFB, CA	5-Apr-07		18,188.0	
AACA0156	KC-135E	56-3606	132nd ARS, 101 ARW	Bangor ANGB, ME	19-Apr-07		16,942.8	
AACA0157	KC-135E	59-1479	151st ARS, 134th ARW	McGhee Tyson AP, TN	24-Apr-07		18,665.5	
AACA0158	KC-135E	56-3622	132nd ARS, 101 ARW	Bangor ANGB, ME	3-May-07		16,421.3	
AACA0159	KC-135E	57-1447	174th ARS, 185th ARW	Sioux City ANGB, IA	9-May-07		16,643.5	
AACA0160	KC-135E	61-0271	63rd ARS, 927th ARW	MacDill AFB, FL	21-May-07		23,910.3	
AACA0161	KC-135E	59-1496	171st ARW	Pittsburgh IAP, PA	23-May-07		16,720.6	
AACA0162	KC-135E	56-3609	151st ARS, 134th ARW	McGhee Tyson AP, TN	30-May-07		17,417.1	
AACA0163	KC-135E	55-3146	141st ARS, 108th ARW	McGuire AFB, NJ	5-Jun-07		18,123.7	
AACA0164	KC-135E	57-1423	171st ARW	Pittsburgh IAP, PA	6-Jun-07		20,401.7	
AACA0165	KC-135E	57-1509	171st ARW	Pittsburgh IAP, PA	20-Jun-07		17,583.0	
AACA0166	KC-135E	56-3593	141st ARS, 108th ARW	McGuire AFB, NJ	13-Jun-07		16,543.7	
AACA0167	KC-135E	58-0003	108th ARS, 126th ARW	Scott AFB, IL	11-Jul-07		18,302.1	
AACA0168	KC-135E	56-3650	174th ARS, 185th ARW	Sioux City ANGB, IA	18-Jul-07			
AACA0169	KC-135E	57-1452	197th ARS, 161st ARW	Sky Harbor IAP, AZ	25-Jul-07		17,804.7	
AACA0170	KC-135E	56-3640	132nd ARS, 101 ARW	Bangor ANGB, ME	9-Aug-07		17,629.9	
AACA0171	KC-135E	57-1475	197th ARS, 161st ARW	Sky Harbor IAP, AZ	8-Aug-07		20,770.8	
AACA0172	KC-135E	57-1484	197th ARS, 161st ARW	Sky Harbor IAP, AZ	27-Jun-07		18,008.9	
AACA0173	KC-135E	58-0116	197th ARS, 161st ARW	Sky Harbor IAP, AZ	12-Sep-07		17,087.0	
AACA0174	KC-135E	56-3638	197th ARS, 161st ARW	Sky Harbor IAP, AZ	6-Sep-07		17,389.6	
AACA0175	KC-135E	58-0044	141st ARS, 108th ARW	McGuire AFB, NJ	6-Feb-08		17,467.0	
AACA0176	KC-135E	58-0040	150th ARS, 108th ARW	McGuire AFB, NJ	6-Feb-08		18,528.4	
AACA0177	KC-135E	57-1464	141st ARS, 108th ARW	McGuire AFB, NJ	6-Feb-08		18,520.7	
AACA0178	KC-135E	58-0024	108th ARS, 126th ARW	Scott AFB, IL	12-Feb-08		17,678.1	
AACA0179	KC-135E	57-1496	132nd ARS, 101 ARW	Bangor ANGB, ME	12-Feb-08		19,229.3	
AACA0180	KC-135E	62-3527	141st ARS, 108th ARW	McGuire AFB, NJ	26-Feb-08		15,930.7	
AACA0181	KC-135E	57-1480	108th ARS, 126th ARW	Scott AFB, IL	20-Feb-08		18,740.1	
AACA0182	KC-135E	58-0087	150th ARS, 108th ARW	McGuire AFB, NJ	19-Feb-08		18,125.5	
AACA0183	KC-135E	61-0268	314th ARS, 940th ARW	Beale AFB, CA	18-Mar-08		21,961.6	
AACA0184	KC-135E	59-1456	141st ARS, 108th ARW	McGuire AFB, NJ	26-Feb-08		17,345.2	
AACA0185	KC-135E	59-1503	141st ARS, 108th ARW	McGuire AFB, NJ	3-Mar-08		15,663.9	
AACA0186	KC-135E	59-1493	132nd ARS, 101 ARW	Bangor ANGB, ME	6-Mar-08		17,149.7	
AACA0187	KC-135E	59-1473	191st ARS, 151st ARW	Salt Lake City IAP, UT	6-Mar-08		17,495.9	
AACA0188	KC-135E	59-1489	108th ARS, 126th ARW	Scott AFB, IL	10-Mar-08		18,220.3	
AACA0189	KC-135E	56-3641	117th ARS, 190th ARW	Forbes ANGB, KS	27-Feb-08		18,170.8	
AACA0190	KC-135E	58-0043	132nd ARS, 101 ARW	Bangor ANGB, ME	28-Apr-08		18,455.7	
AACA0191	KC-135E	57-1450	132nd ARS, 101 ARW	Bangor ANGB, ME	12-Mar-08		18,898.7	
AACA0192	KC-135E	57-1460	117th ARS, 190th ARW	Forbes ANGB, KS	19-Mar-08		17,509.0	
AACA0193	KC-135E	58-0006	108th ARS, 126th ARW	Scott AFB, IL	24-Mar-08		21,810.1	
AACA0194	KC-135E	57-1471	132nd ARS, 101 ARW	Bangor ANGB, ME	17-Mar-08		18,074.5	
AACA0195	KC-135E	57-1491	132nd ARS, 101 ARW	Bangor ANGB, ME	25-Mar-08		19,007.2	
AACA0196	KC-135E	58-0012	191st ARS, 151st ARW	Salt Lake City IAP, UT	1-Apr-08		17,821.7	
AACA0197	KC-135E	55-3145	117th ARS, 190th ARW	Forbes ANGB, KS	28-May-08		18,551.2	
AACA0198	KC-135E	57-2601	133rd ARS, 157th OG	Pease ANGB, NH	14-Apr-08		18,011.1	
AACA0199	KC-135E	57-2600	174th ARS, 185th ARW	Sioux City ANGB, IA	18-Apr-08		17,356.2	
AACA0200	KC-135E	58-0068	108th ARS, 126th ARW	Scott AFB, IL	15-Apr-08		17,859.7	

PCN Code	MDS	Serial	Last Unit	Last Base	Date In	Date Out	Total Hrs	Comments
AACA0201	KC-135E	57-1434	174th ARS, 185th ARW	Sioux City ANGB, IA	16-Apr-08		19,471.5	
AACA0202	KC-135E	57-1497	108th ARS, 126th ARW	Scott AFB, IL	22-Apr-08		16,973.5	
AACA0203	KC-135E	60-0327	191st ARS, 151st ARW	Salt Lake City IAP, UT	24-Apr-08		15,356.1	
AACA0204	KC-135E	61-0303	77th ARS, 916th ARW	Seymour Johnson AFB, NC	13-May-08		22,007.4	
AACA0205	KC-135E	57-1505	132nd ARS, 101 ARW	Bangor ANGB, ME	1-Apr-08	26-Oct-10	19,817.9	Disassembled at AMARG for fatigue inspection
AACA0206	KC-135E	58-0080	174th ARS, 185th ARW	Sioux City ANGB, IA	6-May-08		18,431.2	
AACA0207	KC-135E	57-2608	137th ARW	Will Rogers ANGB, OK	23-Jul-08		18,980.4	
AACA0208	KC-135E	57-1494	108th ARS, 126th ARW	Scott AFB, IL	13-May-08		18,693.5	
AACA0209	KC-135E	57-1465	151st ARS, 134th ARW	McGhee Tyson AP, TN	1-Apr-08	29-Jun-12		Aircraft disassembled for engineering study
AACA0210	KC-135E	57-1433	151st ARS, 134th ARW	McGhee Tyson AP, TN	10-Jun-08		18,931.6	
AACA0211	KC-135E	57-2604	137th ARW	Will Rogers ANGB, OK	26-Aug-08		17,507.7	
AACA0212	KC-135E	61-0270	63rd ARS, 927th ARW	MacDill AFB, FL	17-Sep-08		23,259.9	
AACA0213	KC-135E	57-1426	117th ARS, 190th ARW	Forbes ANGB, KS	3-Jun-08		18,461.8	
AACA0214	KC-135E	56-3631	117th ARS, 190th ARW	Forbes ANGB, KS	12-Aug-08		15,469.6	
AACA0215	KC-135E	58-0020	174th ARS, 185th ARW	Sioux City ANGB, IA	24-Jul-08		17,365.2	
AACA0216	KC-135E	57-1425	151st ARS, 134th ARW	McGhee Tyson AP, TN	20-May-08		19,565.0	
AACA0217	KC-135E	59-1477	314th ARS, 940th ARW	Beale AFB, CA	25-Jun-08		16,420.0	
AACA0218	KC-135E	57-1504	314th ARS, 940th ARW	Beale AFB, CA	29-Jul-08		17,046.1	
AACA0219	KC-135E	59-1451	314th ARS, 940th ARW	Beale AFB, CA	27-Aug-08		16,788.5	
AACA0220	KC-135E	58-0108	314th ARS, 940th ARW	Beale AFB, CA	30-May-08		17,581.0	
AACA0221	KC-135E	58-0090	314th ARS, 940th ARW	Beale AFB, CA	27-Mar-08		17,667.2	
AACA0222	KC-135E	58-0005	117th ARS, 190th ARW	Forbes ANGB, KS	3-Apr-08		17,272.3	
AACA0223	KC-135E	59-1457	117th ARS, 190th ARW	Forbes ANGB, KS	17-Jun-08		17,551.6	
AACA0224	NKC-135E	55-3132	452nd FTS, 412th TW	Kirtland AFB, NM	16-Sep-08		11,060.1	
AACA0225	NKC-135B	63-8050	452nd FTS, 412th TW	Kirtland AFB, NM	16-Sep-08		30,627.2	
AACA0226	KC-135E	57-1463	117th ARS, 190th ARW	Forbes ANGB, KS	11-Mar-09		21,703.5	
AACA0227	KC-135E	59-1485	150th ARS, 108th ARW	McGuire AFB, NJ	20-Apr-09			
AACA0228	KC-135E	58-0017	132nd ARS, 101 ARW	Bangor ANGB, ME	26-Mar-09		17,701.8	
AACA0229	KC-135E	58-0111	141st ARS, 108th ARW	McGuire AFB, NJ	6-Apr-09		18,854.2	
AACA0230	KC-135E	57-1443	132nd ARS, 101 ARW	Bangor ANGB, ME	14-Apr-09		19,888.7	
AACA0231	KC-135E	58-0032	150th ARS, 108th ARW	McGuire AFB, NJ	17-Mar-09		18,869.3	
AACA0232	KC-135E	57-1492	151st ARS, 134th ARW	McGhee Tyson AP, TN	28-Apr-09			
AACA0233	KC-135E	57-2602	150th ARS, 108th ARW	McGuire AFB, NJ	4-May-09			
AACA0234	KC-135E	57-1448	132nd ARS, 101 ARW	Bangor ANGB, ME	12-May-09		17,396.9	
AACA0235	KC-135E	57-1445	141st ARS, 108th ARW	McGuire AFB, NJ	27-May-09		18,005.2	
AACA0236	KC-135E	58-0078	141st ARS, 108th ARW	McGuire AFB, NJ	15-Jun-09		19,782.6	
AACA0237	KC-135E	57-2595	117th ARS, 190th ARW	Forbes ANGB, KS	30-Jun-09		18,480.0	
AACA0238	KC-135E	57-1478	133rd ARS, 157th OG	Pease ANGB, NH	10-Jun-09		18,284.2	
AACA0239	KC-135E	57-1421	174th ARS, 185th ARW	Sioux City ANGB, IA	2-Jun-09		18,925.5	
AACA0240	KC-135E	58-0115	137th ARW	Will Rogers ANGB, OK	7-Jul-09		17,260.8	
AACA0241	KC-135E	59-1445	137th ARW	Will Rogers ANGB, OK	14-Jul-09		16,415.0	
AACA0242	KC-135E	59-1484	137th ARW	Will Rogers ANGB, OK	21-Jul-09		20,987.7	
AACA0243	KC-135E	61-0281	117th ARS, 190th ARW	Forbes ANGB, KS	25-Aug-09		17,209.7	
AACA0244	KC-135E	56-3626	137th ARW	Will Rogers ANGB, OK	12-Aug-09		17,494.7	
AACA0245	NKC-135A	56-3596	FEWSG	Waco/TSTI AP, TX	1-Aug-09			ex AN6G0001
AACA0246	NKC-135A	55-3134	FEWSG	Waco/TSTI AP, TX	1-Aug-09			ex ANG60002
AACA0247	KC-135E	58-0082	137th ARW	Will Rogers ANGB, OK	18-Aug-09		16,797.9	
AACA0248	KC-135E	56-3630	132nd ARS, 101 ARW	Bangor ANGB, ME	23-Sep-09		15,259.7	
5612	KC-135R	60-0319	22nd ARW	McConnell AFB, KS	20-Jun-12	18-Nov-14	23,734.1	CAStLE
7799	KC-135R	57-2593	166th ARS, 121st ARW	Rickenbacker IAP, OH	26-Mar-13		22,656.7	
7810	KC-135R	58-0008	133rd ARS, 157th OG	Pease ANGB, NH	10-Jul-13		22,942.3	
7807	KC-135R	58-0114	191st ARS, 151st ARW	Salt Lake City IAP, UT	29-Apr-13		22,808.1	
7809	KC-135R	58-0130	126th ARS, 128th ARW	General Mitchell ANGB, WI	21-May-13		25,129.8	
7806	KC-135R	60-0321	336th ARS, 452nd OG	March JARB, CA	18-Apr-13		23,355.3	
7811	KC-135R	61-0302	203rd ARS, 154th Wg	Hickam AFB, HI	27-Jun-13		23,501.6	
7814	KC-135R	61-0304	92nd ARW	Fairchild AFB, WA	4-Nov-13		22,523.1	
7815	KC-135R	61-0306	351st ARS, 100th OG	RAF Mildenhall, UK	6-Jun-13			
7794	KC-135R	61-0312	54th ARS, 97th AMW	Altus AFB, OK	21-Feb-13		22,304.1	
7812	KC-135R	62-3504	151st ARS, 134th ARW	McGhee Tyson AP, TN	4-Nov-13		20,324.9	
7813	KC-135R	62-3520	133rd ARS, 157th OG	Pease ANGB, NH	10-Dec-13		24,599.6	
7808	KC-135R	62-3546	203rd ARS, 154th Wg	Hickam AFB, HI	14-May-13		23,857.7	
7798	KC-135R	62-3548	909th ARS, 18 Wg	Kadena AB, Japan	14-Mar-13		21,840.5	
7800	KC-135R	63-8037	22nd ARW	McConnell AFB, KS	5-Mar-13		21,977.3	
389595	KC-135R	63-8877	22nd ARW	McConnell AFB, KS	7-Apr-14			Parts from destroyed aircraft
AN6G0001	NKC-135A	56-3596	FEWSG	Waco/TSTI AP, TX	25-Jun-95	1-Aug-09		to AACA0245
AN6G0002	NKC-135A	55-3134	FEWSG	Waco/TSTI AP, TX	20-Feb-96	1-Aug-09		to AACA0246

Above: A sad misplacement of a significant airplane. 55-3118 on display as a KC-135A at McConnell AFB. Once converted to an EC-135K in January 1961 following initial testing, it never carried a boom or served as a tanker for the next 35 years, nor did it ever have any association with McConnell AFB.
USAF photo

Table A3-2. **Withdrawn from Service**

Serial	MDS	Date In	Location	Comments
55-3124	GNKC-135A	7-Mar-91	Sheppard AFB, TX	Ground Trainer
56-3607	GKC-135E	8-Sep-08	Sheppard AFB, TX	Medical Readiness Training Flight
56-3616	KC-135A	6-Jan-93	NATC Patuxent River, MD	Explosive Testing
56-3617	KC-135A	3-Mar-93	NATC Patuxent River, MD	Explosive Testing
56-3623	GKC-135E	n/a	Sheppard AFB, TX	Medical Readiness Training Flight
56-3632	KC-135A	16-Feb-93	NATC Patuxent River, MD	Explosive Testing
56-3645	GKC-135E	Dec 11	Sheppard AFB, TX	Medical Readiness Training Flight
56-3656	KC-135A	13-Nov-92	NATC Patuxent River, MD	Explosive Testing
57-1431	GKC-135E	Jul 90	Sheppard AFB, TX	Ground Trainer
57-1485	GKC-135E	Jul 90	Sheppard AFB, TX	Ground Trainer
57-1503	GKC-135E	28-Sep-09	Sheppard AFB, TX	Ground Trainer
58-0070	GKC-135A	18-Oct-92	Sheppard AFB, TX	Training Aid
60-0369	GNC-135A	9-Jun-76	Chanute AFB, IL	Ground Trainer – Scrapped October 1991
60-0378	C-135A	23-Jul-94	Tinker AFB, OK	BDR
61-0282	GEC-135H	15-Nov-91	Sheppard AFB, TX	Ground Trainer; last noted 2008
61-0286	GEC-135H	22-Jan-92	Sheppard AFB, TX	Ground Trainer; last noted 2006
61-0329	EC-135E	Jun-96	Tinker AFB, OK	Training Aid / BDR
61-0330	EC-135E	n/a	Kirtland AFB, NM	Last noted 2007
61-2668	C-135C	96	Tinker AFB, OK	Scrapped
62-3535	KC-135A	6-Apr-70	BMAC, Wichita, KS	Cyclic test to destruction 1 May 1970
63-8010	KC-135A	15-Sep-93	MidAmerica AP, IL	Training airframe

Table A3-3. **Static Display**

Serial	MDS	Date	Total Hrs	Location	Comments
55-3118	EC-135K	15-Oct-96		McConnell AFB Air Park, Wichita, KS	Configured as a KC-135A
55-3123	NKC-135A	20-May-88	6550.0	National Museum of the US Air Force, Dayton, OH	
55-3130	KC-135A	15-Dec-92		March Field Museum, Riverside, CA	
55-3139	KC-135A	3-Apr-93		Castle Air Museum, Merced, CA	
56-3595	KC-135A	1-Apr-94		Barksdale Global Power Museum, Barksdale AFB, LA	
56-3611	KC-135E	21-Dec-06		Scott Field Heritage Air Park, Scott AFB, IL	At main gate
56-3639	KC-135A	1-Jul-92		Linear Air Park, Dyess AFB, TX	
56-3658	KC-135E	Jun 01		Kansas Aviation Museum, Wichita, KS	
57-1429	KC-135E	May 09		Museum of the Kansas National Guard, Topeka, KS	
57-1455	KC-135E	May 09		Portsmouth, NH	
57-1458	KC-135E	May 09		Eielson AFB Heritage Park, Eielson AFB, AK	
57-1495	KC-135E	Jul 10		Lincoln, NE	
57-1507	KC-135E	7-Aug-09		Air Mobility Command Museum, Dover AFB, DE	
57-1510	KC-135E	18-Jul-09		Hill Aerospace Museum, Hill AFB, UT	
57-2589	KC-135E	Jun 08		Medina Annex, Lackland AFB, TX	
58-0070	KC-135A	15-Oct-92		Altus AFB, OK	As 56-3617
59-1481	KC-135A	Oct-95		Johnson Space Center, Houston, TX	NASA N930
59-1487	KC-135E	26-Oct-06		Scott Field Heritage Air Park, Scott AFB, IL	At 126th ARW facility
59-1497	KC-135E	May 09		McGuire AFB, NJ	
60-0371	NC-135A	12-Aug-94		Kirtland AFB	Last noted 2000
60-0374	EC-135E	3-Nov-00		National Museum of the US Air Force, Dayton, OH	
60-0377	C-135A	15-Dec-95		Air Force Flight Test Center Museum, Edwards AFB, CA	
61-0262	EC-135A	30-Mar-92		South Dakota Air & Space Museum, Ellsworth AFB, SD	
61-0269	EC-135L	29-Jun-92		Grissom Air Museum, Grissom AFB, IN	
61-0287	EC-135A	10-Feb-92	13000.0	Gate Guard, Offutt AFB, NE	
61-0327	EC-135N	Feb 03		Museum of Aviation, Warner Robins, GA	Up for disposal
61-2669	C-135C	13-Jan-06		Air Force Flight Test Center Museum, Edwards AFB, CA	
61-2671	C-135C	30-Oct-91		Charles B. Hall Air Park, Tinker AFB, OK	With 707 vertical stabilizer
63-7998	KC-135A	10-Dec-04	13605.0	Pima Air & Space Museum, Tucson, AZ	NASA N931NA
63-8005	KC-135A	11-Jul-94		Grand Forks Air Park, Grand Forks AFB, ND	
63-8049	EC-135C	29-Jan-92		Strategic Air & Space Museum Ashland, NE	
63-8057	EC-135J	31-Mar-92	13692.4	Pima Air & Space Museum, Tucson, AZ	

Opposite page:
By 21st September 2016 EC-135K 59-1518 had been scrapped, concurrent with all of the remaining EC-135s, to be hauled away and converted into 'beer cans.' Despite their historical significance, there are neither the funds nor the official interest in preserving these airplanes.
Photo by Barry Fryer

APPENDIX IV
SAC Tail Markings

SAC tail markings were based on unit assignment, either 8th AF or 15th AF. Aircraft assigned to 8th AF initially had geometric tail markings, although these later changed to more specialized designs (except for the 305th AREFW). Those units assigned to 15th AF had specialized designs from the onset.

8th Air Force

19th Air Division
Diamonds

7th BW Carswell AFB

Initial: Yellow and black diamonds.
Photo via Brian Rogers

Later: Fort Worth city flag with black band on top, white band and steer head in middle, and dark green band on bottom. *Photo by Brian Rogers*

340th AREFW Altus AFB

Initial: Light blue and silver diamonds.
Photo by Brian Rogers

Later: Blue map of Oklahoma with Conestoga wagon in center. *Photo by Brian Rogers*

384th AREFW McConnell AFB

Initial: Light blue and insignia blue diamonds.
Photo via Brian Rogers

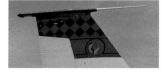

Later: A variety of 'Keeper of the Plains' or 'McConnell' bands, some while retaining the original blue diamonds (as seen here). *Photo by Brian Rogers*

8th Air Force

40th Air Division
Vertical stripes

379th BW Wurtsmith AFB

Initial: Yellow and red vertical stripes.
Photo via Brian Rogers

Later: Corvette blue stripe with '379BMW' and a gold eagle outline in blue. *Photo by Brian Rogers*

410th BW K I Sawyer AFB

Initial: Red and white vertical stripes.
Photo by Brian Rogers

Later: Rainbow with 'K I Sawyer'. Early version had curved rainbow, later version had straight rainbow with black bird in center. *Photo by Brian Rogers*

416th BW Griffiss AFB

Initial: Yellow and blue vertical stripes.
Photo via Brian Rogers

Later: Statue of Liberty on white disc with 'Griffiss' and black band. *Photo by Brian Rogers*

8th Air Force   *42nd Air Division – Checkerboards*

2nd BW Barskdale AFB

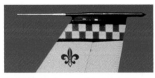

Initial: Yellow and green small checkerboard, some with black bands at top and bottom. Some also carried the black fleur-de-lis. *Photo by Brian Rogers*

Later: 'Barksdale' in black Old English Script with fleur-de-lis. *Photo by Brian Rogers*

19th AREFW Robins AFB

Initial: Yellow and dark blue large checkerboard. Some appeared with black knight's head to reflect the 19th 'Black Knights' nickname *Photo by Brian Rogers*

Later: White band with blue Georgia map and silver sword, retaining the black knight head.
Photo by Brian Rogers

97th BW Blytheville AFB

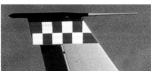

Initial: Red and white large checkerboard.
Photo by Bob Archer

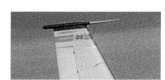

Later: Light blue band with orange trim and orange flaming arrow. *Photo by author*

305th AREFW Grissom AFB

Initial: Black and white large checkerboard with black trim. *Photo by Brian Rogers*

Later: Black and white large checkerboard with black trim, with 'Pacesetter' emblem. *Photo by Brian Rogers*

8th Air Force

*45th Air Division
Diagonal stripes*

42nd BW Loring AFB

Initial: Yellow and blue diagonal stripes.
Photo by Brian Rogers

Later: 'Loring' in green or red with black moose holding bomb in matching color.
Photo by Brian Rogers

380th BW Plattsburgh AFB

Initial: Green and white diagonal stripes.
Photo via Brian Rogers

Later: Plattsburgh' in script on a white stripe with apple. *Photo by Brian Rogers*

509th BW Pease AFB

Initial: Red and insignia blue diagonal stripes.
Photo by Brian Rogers

Later: White band with red Pegasus.
Photo by Brian Rogers

15th Air Force

5th BW Minot AFB

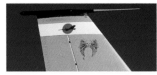

White band with black tanker over red disc ('the sun never sets...'). Black winged skull added later.
Photo by Brian Rogers

6th SRW Eielson AFB

Dark blue band with yellow star and trim. Appeared only on TC-135S 62-4133. *Photo by author*

9th SRW Beale AFB

Four black Maltese crosses on yellow band with black trim. *Photo by Bob Archer*

22nd AREFW March AFB

White and green diamonds with black mission bell on yellow disc. *Photo by Brian Rogers*

28th BW Ellsworth AFB

Initial: Yellow and blue undulating band.
Photo by Brian Rogers

Later: 'Ellsworth' with Mt Rushmore in blue on white band with yellow (top) and blue (bottom) trim.
Photo by Brian Rogers

92nd BW Fairchild AFB

Initial: Insignia blue band with 'Fairchild' in script and stars in either white or dark blue. Crown was too similar to trademark of Hallmark Greeting Card company which insisted it be removed. *Photo by Bob Archer*

Later: 'Fairchild' in white on Seattle Seahawks football team logo inspired by Native American *Kwakwaka'wakw* tribal mask (neither of which objected to any potential trademark infringement).
Photo by Brian Rogers

93rd BW Castle AFB

Black band with white rook chess piece.
Photo by Brian Rogers

96th BW Dyess AFB

Texas state flag with golden steer head.
Photo via Brian Rogers

301st AREFW Malmstrom AFB

'Malmstrom' in white with insignia blue sky, white mountain tops, and dark brown earth, superimposed with white bison skull drawn by Western artist Charles M Russell. *Photo by Brian Rogers*

319th BW Grand Forks AFB

Blue and orange 'snowflake' with orange and blue bands. *Photo by Brian Rogers*

320th BW Mather AFB

Black and white tiny checkerboard with yellow map of California and brown bear. *Photo by Brian Rogers*

379th SW Kadena AB

Cropped image missing

'Kadena' in red on white band with black trim following a white disc with 'torii' gate.
Photo by Brian Rogers

APPENDIX V

Records and Special Achievements

In an age where world records are made by aircraft flying around the world non-stop and unrefueled, by aircraft flying to the edge of space, and by aircraft streaking across the United States in nearly an hour, it may be surprising that KC-135s have set comparable records. When it first entered service the KC-135 was faster than all types but supersonic jets, and given the KC-135's fuel capacity, was a natural candidate for long distance speed records. The KC-135 could also carry heavier cargo aloft than could extant piston-powered transports, and, when empty of cargo and equipped with high-bypass turbofan engines, could reach altitudes faster than even some smaller aircraft, including a few fighters.

To the proponents of record setting flights, they accomplish many goals. Foremost among these is their effect on national pride, in the past accentuated by the Cold War rivalry between the US and the Soviet Union. In a classic variation of 'whose dad has the most credit cards', American and Soviet airmen boasted of which aircraft could fly the farthest, the fastest, and the highest. When US aircraft held the records, it was testimony to the superiority of American aerospace know-how and military skill. When the Soviets held the record, it was a gauntlet to be picked up, a challenge with not only national pride at stake but with national security in the balance as well. If Soviet aircraft outperformed those of the US, then Soviet military superiority loomed ominously over American security. If US types flew circles around their Soviet counterparts, then Americans could rest easier in their daily Cold War struggle (although that made the *Russians* worry a bit more…).

To critics of record setting flights, they were little more than 'fly boy grandstanding'. Excessive and unnecessary risks were taken. The first KC-135 to crash did so while taking off on a trans-Atlantic speed run, killing all aboard including a SAC general, a retired general, and civilian newsmen. To others, record flights were public relations gimmicks and the rewards incommensurate with the risk. After

members of one crew received the Distinguished Flying Cross or the Air Medal for their record setting flight, the Air Force Chief of Staff received a letter from a bitter parent saying that his son, killed at his waist gun station defending his B-17 Flying Fortress from attacking fighters while on a bombing raid over Nazi Germany, was denied a decoration for his heroism. If Distinguished Flying Crosses and Air Medals were doled out for mundane events such as flying an aircraft from New York to Argentina, the parent continued, then it rendered meaningless the efforts of those who received such decorations for valor, often at the expense of their lives.

Despite the merit in some of the criticism, record setting flights have been an integral part of the history of civil and military aviation. They demonstrate the limits of man, his machines, and his weapons, and send a clear signal of what they are capable of doing if need be, perhaps causing a potential adversary to think twice before provoking their use. To show the performance of military aircraft in peacetime may preclude demonstrating their performance in wartime. If record setting flights act in some small way as deterrents to warfare, then neither apologist nor critic has properly recognised their ultimate value.

Above: KC-135A 55-3122 took part in one of 26 air refuelings for the RF-101Cs of Operation SUN RUN on 27th November 1957, in this case, Lieutenant Gustav B Klatt in *Sun Run 3.* With slower KC-97s, these records would not have been possible. *Author's collection*

Opposite, left: A movie camera and an Argentine guard watch as KC-135A 55-3126 taxis to parking at the end of the LONG LEGS flight to Buenos Aires. *USAF Photo, Author's collection*

Opposite, right: A happy Curtis LeMay, cigar in hand, brags about the capability of the KC-135 as an exemplar of US strategic airpower. *Photo courtesy Boeing*

SPECIFIC AIRCRAFT RECORDS

KC-135A 55-3126 Operation LONG LEGS   11-13th November 1957
Flown by Air Force Vice Chief of Staff General Curtis LeMay, this aircraft set
two world records as part of Operation LONG LEGS, America's contribution to
Argentina's Annual Aeronautics Week. On the southbound unrefueled flight on
11-12th November, LeMay and crew established a world record non-stop
distance (including the addition of nearly 1,000 miles – 1,609km – induced by
flying around the 'hump' of Brazil) of 6,322.85 miles (10,175km) from Westover
AFB to Ezeiza Airport at Buenos Aires, Argentina. The flight lasted 13 hours,
two minutes, 51 seconds. During the northbound unrefueled flight on 13th
November, LeMay and crew set a speed record over a recognised course from
Buenos Aires to Washington DC, averaging 471.45mph (758.7km/h) over a
distance of 5,204 miles (8,374km) in a total time of eleven hours, three minutes,
57.38 seconds. This record remains unbroken. For this round-trip flight, hailed
as a 'critical test of the new jet Stratotanker in its utility role as a jet speed high
altitude global transport,' General LeMay was awarded the Harmon Trophy.
LeMay and three other crewmembers, including Captains Charles L Gandy
(pilot, who was also the Phase II Test and Evaluation project pilot), Captain
Howard Dries and Lieutenant L E Carter (navigators), received the
Distinguished Flying Cross. The 18 others in the crew received the Air Medal.

LONG LEGS captured America's attention in late 1957 as a major national
event. A little over a month earlier, on 4th October, the USSR orbited *Sputnik*,
the world's first artificial satellite. Pundits around the world announced the
death of air power and the pre-eminence of ballistic missiles and satellite
weapons. Bombers were dead, and with their demise came the end of the
American strategic deterrent. The US was, in the eyes of the doomsayers, now
horribly vulnerable to Soviet strategic missile power. LeMay responded to
these critics as he always had, with actions rather than words. By 2nd
November the flight had been approved by the Air Staff, including a waiver
to the Air Force regulation which required 'that aircraft be in the operational
inventory for a period of six months prior to record attempts'. Another waiver
came from the Civil Aviation Authority (CAA) to enable the jet-powered
KC-135A to land at Washington's National Airport rather than the originally
planned landing site at Baltimore. Yet another waiver came in approving the
proposed 269,000 lb (122,018kg) gross weight for the mission, heavier than
the 250,000 lb (113,400kg) limit then in use by the Air Force.

The flight did what it was intended to do. The Stratotanker's circuitous
route from Westover AFB to Buenos Aires covered a distance in excess of
that from New York to Moscow, sending a clear message to the Kremlin: the
Soviet Union *talked* about satellites and ballistic missiles as the strategic
weapons of the future, but the United States *showed* that current operational
manned aircraft were fully capable of accomplishing their strategic mission.
Americans of all walks of life responded enthusiastically to the flight. One
housewife wrote that LONG LEGS 'was like [Jimmy] Doolittle over Tokyo'.
Another was so impressed by LeMay and 55-3126 that she sent a telegram
reading 'Congratulations to you and KC-135. Have taken up cigar chewing'.
Boeing President Bill Allen, anxious to sell more aircraft, added 'We are
grateful to you and your crew for your able demonstration of the capabilities
of the [KC-135]'. The Nashville *Banner* newspaper concluded that LONG LEGS
'should reassure any who might have gotten their thinking out of focus in the
blowing propaganda wind about the significance of *Sputnik.*'

As another part of Operation LONG LEGS, seven KC-135As from the 93rd
BW at Castle AFB, operating from Homestead AFB, FL, refueled six 42nd
BW B-52s that flew non-stop from Homestead AFB to Buenos Aires and back

to Plattsburgh AFB on 16-17th November. This epic flight required three
aerial refuelings, two by KC-97s and one by KC-135As. Participating 93rd
BW KC-135As were 55-3127, 55-3128, 55-3129, 55-3130, 55-3131 (spare),
55-3132, 55-3138, and 55-3141. (Earlier, on 13th November, three TAC B-66s
flew nonstop with air refueling by TAC KB-50s from the west coast of the
US to the Philippines. Again, the message was clear: American strategic and
tactical bombing capacity was global and was ready for immediate use).

KC-135A (55-3126)   11th July 1958
This KC-135A set an unofficial record of eleven hours, eight minutes in a
non-stop flight from Andrews AFB to Hickam AFB. Secretary of Defense
Neil McElroy was on board the flight, which later carried McElroy to observe
a US H-bomb test in the South Pacific.

KC-135A 55-3126   13th September 1958
General LeMay established an unofficial speed record in this aircraft while
returning from Yokota AB to Andrews AFB. The KC-135A flew 7,100 miles
(11,426km) unrefueled in 12 hours, 28 minutes for an average speed of
570mph (917km/h). The time was not recognised as a record because the
flight was not made under contest timing rules. Interestingly, the aircraft
landed on 13th September at 0724 Eastern time, 32 minutes 'on the clock'
before it took off on 13th September at 0756 Japanese time. Other
crewmembers included Majors Lawrence J Tacker and Ernest Campbell,
Captain Edward Schickling, and Lieutenant Meredith Sutton.

LeMay set other unofficial records or 'notable firsts' in 55-3126 on other
occasions, most well publicized. For example, on 27th March 1958 he flew
some 6,000 miles (9,655km) non-stop from Castle AFB to Ohakea Airfield,
New Zealand, in 15 hours. On his 3rd April return from the Pacific, he flew
non-stop from Hickam AFB to Andrews AFB. In June 1958 LeMay took his
KC-135 to NATO Headquarters. These flights were heady accomplishments
in the days of 'island hopping' and slow piston-powered airliners, and
underscored not only US military air power but the future of jet air travel.

KC-135A 56-3601 Operation JET STREAM   7-8th April 1958
This KC-135A, assigned to the 93rd AREFS, 93rd BW at Castle AFB and
commanded by Brigadier General William E Eubank, Jr, 93rd BW
Commander, established two Class C Group 1 (aircraft with jet engines or
mixed powerplants) world records. The first of these was distance in a straight
line without refueling of 10,229.3 miles (16,462.5km) from Tokyo to Lajes
Field, the Azores (in 18 hours, 48 minutes); the second was speed of
492.262mph 795.4km/h) in 13 hours, 45 minutes, 46.5 seconds, on the Tokyo
to Washington, DC, portion of the flight (LeMay previously established the
existing category distance record in Operation LONG LEGS).

As planned, the JET STREAM mission was scheduled to fly 11,487 miles
(18,486km) non-stop from Tokyo to Madrid, Spain, and in so doing break the
absolute non-stop unrefueled distance record held since 1946 by the *Truculent
Turtle*, a US Navy Lockheed P2V-1 Neptune (BuNO 89082) that flew 11,236
miles (18,082km) from Perth, Australia, to Columbus, OH. According to an
Air Force spokesman, however, 'capricious jet stream winds failed to give
the plane the necessary "power push" to carry it' to Madrid. Eubank and crew
held out hope that they could reach Torrejon AB, near Madrid, until some two
hours prior to landing at Lajes, when Eubank radioed that they lacked the fuel
to go on and would land in the Azores.

Meanwhile, back at Yokota AB, a second unidentified KC-135A (named
The Kiwi) under the command of Major Jack N Fancher, took off on 13th

KC-135A 56-3601 from the 416th BW at Griffiss AFB during a TDY to Carswell AFB.
Photo by Brian Rogers

Major Vernon Hamann (kneeling) and Major David Craw (right of sign) celebrate the twin records set on 17th April 1962 in 61-2666. Hamann's crew from McGuire AFB set the speed record, and Craw's crew from Travis set the payload-to-height record.
Photo P29458 courtesy Boeing

April to try again for the record. In an effort to reduce drag, the air refueling boom had been removed. As before, the lack of favorable tail winds cut the mission short. Carrying fuel for 10,000 miles (16,093km), the KC-135 needed the wintertime jet stream winds, often well in excess of 100kts (185km/h), to push it the extra 1,500 miles (2,413km). Some 660 miles (1,062km) out over the Atlantic Ocean, Fancher and crew 'called it quits' and turned around, landing at 0735 on 13th April at Westover AFB.

Four months later, aided by the winter jet stream, LeMay set an unofficial speed record (in KC-135A 55-3126) on the Tokyo–Washington DC route of 12 hours, 28 minutes, 75 minutes better than Eubank's flight. Other crewmembers on board JET STREAM included Lieutenant Colonel Kenneth R Rea and Major Cecil Wells (co-pilots), Captains George Henriet and James S A O'Shea (navigators), and Master Sergeant James W Bridges and Sergeant Clifton E Pfleger (boom operators). Bertrand Rhind of the National Aeronautics Association (NAA) was the observer. Still, the *Truculent Turtle's* record remained unbeaten until 10-11th January 1962, when B-52H 60-0040 from the 4136th SW at Minot AFB flew 12,532 miles (20,167km) unrefueled from Kadena AB to Torrejon AB in Operation PERSIAN RUG.

KC-135A (serial unknown)   13th June 1958
An unidentified KC-135A from the 99th AREFS, 4050th AREFW at Westover AFB, claimed a record for the fastest flight between Los Angeles and New York. It did so in three hours, 42 minutes, 45 seconds, just beating the previous record of three hours, 44 minutes established in 1955 by a Northrop F-89 Scorpion.

KC-135A 56-3613   17th September 1958
Captain Charles E Gibbs (aircraft commander), 1st Lieutenant Dale E Shartzer (co-pilot), 1st Lieutenant Cornelius A Hayes (navigator), and Technical Sergeant Fred H Quinn (boom operator), Colonel Don E Hillman (92nd BW Commander and air commander during the flight), and two NAA observers – F A W Stiefler and Ted Carpenter – flew this 92nd AREFS, 92nd BW, KC-135A from Fairchild AFB to establish four Class C Group 1 world records. The aircraft, named *Queen of the Inland Empire*, was the first KC-135A delivered to the 92nd BW. It flew five continuous round trips over a course from Spokane to Hoquiam, WA. Payload for the KC-135's record-setting flight was 22,046 lb (exactly 10,000kg) of lawn fertiliser. Among his many distinguished career accomplishments, Colonel Hillman flew the first SAC B-47B overflight of the USSR on 15th October 1952.

Records on this flight include: (1) Distance in a closed circuit without refueling 3,125.56 statute miles (5,026.9km); (2) speed over a 1,242 mile (2,000km) closed circuit with 2,204.6, 4,409.2, 11,023.0, and 22,046.0 lb (10,000, 2,000, 5,000 and 10,000kg) payloads 589.278mph (948.354km/h); (3) speed over a 3,106 mile (5,000km) closed circuit 587.136mph (944.907km/h); and (4) speed over a 3,106 mile (5,000km) closed circuit with 2,204.6, 4,409.2, 11,023.0, and 22,046.0 lb (10,000, 2,000, 5,000 and 10,000kg) payloads 587.136mph (944.907km/h).

KC-135A 56-3630 Operation TOP SAIL   27th and 29th June 1958
Four KC-135As from the 99th AREFS, 4050th AREFW at Westover AFB, attempted to set world speed records for New York to London flights as part of Operation TOP SAIL, originally called SURE THING. The first aircraft, known as TOP SAIL-ALPHA and commanded by Major Burl B Davenport, set records of New York to London of five hours, 29 minutes, 14.64 seconds for an average speed of 630.223mph (1,014.248km/h), and London to New York of five hours, 53 minutes, 12.77 seconds at an average speed of 587.457mph

(945.423km/h). The aircraft departed Westover AFB, passed over the 'entry gate' above New York City's Idlewild IAP, flew to the 'exit gate' over London, and landed at RAF Brize Norton. The westbound flight reversed this route, landing at Floyd Bennett Naval Air Station, New York. Additional crewmembers on the flight included Lieutenant James J Jones (co-pilot), Lieutenant Eugene A Miller (navigator), and Staff Sergeant William M Minchew (boom operator), Colonel Harry R Burrell (air commander) plus ten observers and passengers.

The second aircraft (TOP SAIL-BRAVO KC-135A 56-3637) provided support and back up for the record-setting aircraft. The crew under the command of Major Quentin W Raaz, included 1st Lieutenant Frank Kemahele (co-pilot), Captain Cecil B Smith, Jr (navigator), and Technical Sergeant Jimmy H. Ruiz (boom operator). This aircraft returned to Westover AFB on 29th June.

The third KC-135A (TOP SAIL-COCOA KC-135A 56-3599) crashed on take-off from Westover AFB, killing all 15 on board. Among these were Lieutenant Colonel George M Broutsas, 99th AREFS Commander, and Brigadier General Donald W Saunders, 57th Air Division Commander, after whom the Saunders Trophy is named. The last aircraft (TOP SAIL-DELTA, serial number unknown) did not take-off. News of this tragedy was not passed to the preceding two TOP SAIL aircraft until after they had landed in England.

KC-135R 58-0001   19th December 1992
A KC-135R assigned to the 11th AREFS, 97th AMW at Altus AFB set a record for Class C-1.P (220,458 to 330,687 lb – 100,000 to 150,000kg) aircraft for non-stop, unrefueled flight from Kadena AB to McGuire AFB while returning from the Pacific Tanker Task Force. The flight covered 10,151 miles (16,336km) in 17 hours, 31 minutes, but still did not beat the *Truculent Turtle's* distance record set in 1946 and challenged by two KC-135s in 1958. The KC-135R's flight crew included Captains Jeff Kennedy (instructor pilot), Robert Kilgore (aircraft commander), and Mark Hostetter (instructor navigator), 1st Lieutenant John Isakson (pilot), 2nd Lieutenant Robert Fischer (navigator), Senior Master Sergeant Daniel Deloy and Master Sergeant Temur Ablay (instructor boom operators) and crew chiefs Sergeant Steven Rowland, Senior Airman Andrew Haynes, and Airman First Class Jason Houk. Raymond Lutz was the NAA observer.

C-135B 61-2666 Operation SWIFT LIFT   17th April 1962

To demonstrate the newly acquired jet-transport capability of the C-135B and its impact on MATS' operational effectiveness, as well as 'contribute to public confidence in the Armed Forces', MATS planned two flights to topple seven existing world records and establish three new ones. Nicknamed Operation SWIFT LIFT, the two flights enabled a top crew from both Travis AFB (WESTAF) and McGuire AFB (EASTAF) to set the records. The 1501st ATW at Travis AFB provided two aircraft – 61-2664 and 61-2666 – for the attempts, which were conducted at Edwards AFB. During a trial run 61-2664 suffered 'stringer and skin damage', eliminating it from the record setting efforts.

C-135B 61-2666 made two flights on 17th April. The first of these established a payload-to-height record of 66,139 lb (30,000kg) taken to 47,171ft (14,378m), as well as records for the 33,068, 44,091 and 55,114 lb (15,000, 20,000, and 25,000kg) categories. The 44th ATS, 1501st ATW crew, under the command of Major David W Craw, included Captain Max L Richardson (co-pilot), Senior Master Sergeant Patrick F Murtha (flight engineer), and Technical Sergeant Robert J Sutton (loadmaster, who did not fly on the record-setting sortie).

The second flight set a record for carrying a 66,137 lb (30,000kg) payload around a 1,243 mile (2,000km) closed circuit at an average speed of 615.59mph (991.01km/h). This flight also set records for 11,022, 22,045, 33,068, 44,091 and 55,114 lb (5,000, 10,000, 15,000, 20,000, and 25,000kg) payload classes. Crew for this flight was Major Vernon W Hamann (aircraft commander), Captain Donald R Bachelder (co-pilot), Technical Sergeant Dean W Wilson (flight engineer), and Technical Sergeant Victor Fredlund (loadmaster) from the 18th ATS, 1611th ATW at McGuire AFB. Both aircraft commanders received the Distinguished Flying Cross; the remaining crewmembers received the Air Medal.

C-135C 61-2669   3-4th October 1985

Lieutenant Colonel Royce Grones and Major Robyn Read set a record for speed over a recognised course from Tokyo to Beijing of four hours, ten minutes, averaging 318.55mph (512.64km/h). They also set a record for speed over a recognised course for the portion of their flight from Yokota AB to Beijing of four hours, averaging 318.63mph (512.77km/h).

KC-135R 62-3554   16th November 1988

This KC-135R set time-to-climb records to five different altitudes in four different groups (dependent upon aircraft weight). One aircraft from the 19th AREFW at Robins AFB was used for all four record flights. KC-135R 62-3554 was named *Cherokee Rose* in honour of the Georgia state flower. All four flights took place at Robins AFB (with 19th AREFW KC-135R 62-3530 as the back up for the record attempts).

The KC-135R's engines were uprated to their full design thrust of 24,000 lb (106.7kN) per engine for the attempt, and Boeing provided flight planning technical data for the higher thrust settings. The results were impressive: on its last of four flights, for example, the aircraft was airborne five seconds after brake release, it climbed out at 325 KIAS (until reaching and then maintaining Mach 0.78) and 27° nose up, was cleared by air traffic control for an unrestricted climb to the block altitude of FL450B510, and used only 4,000 lb (1,814kg) of fuel for the 24-minute flight to FL499, performance unimagined in the mid-1950s for the KC-135A 'water wagons'. In addition to the NAA

Table A5-1. **KC-135R 62-3554** *Cherokee Rose* **Time-to-Climb Records**

Class	Altitude		Time (in minutes)
C-1.M	3,000m	(9,843ft)	1:39.22
99,206 to 132,275 lb	6,000m	(19,685ft)	2:56.97
(45,000 to 60,000kg)	9,000m	(29,528ft)	4:23.51
	12,000m	(39,370ft)	5:50.94
	15,000m	(49,213ft)	8:15.20
C-1.N	3,000m	(9,843ft)	1:42.52
132,275 to 176,366 lb	6,000m	(19,685ft)	2:58.21
(60,000 to 80,000kg)	9,000m	(29,528ft)	4:29.28
	12,000m	(39,370ft)	5:43.71
C-1.O	3,000m	(9,843ft)	2:12.10
176,366 to 220,458 lb	6,000m	(19,685ft)	3:46.41
(80,000 to 100,000kg)	9,000m	(29,528ft)	5:40.33
	12,000m	(39,370ft)	7:49.19
C-1.P	3,000m	(9,843ft)	2:48.34
220,458 to 330,687 lb	6,000m	(19,685ft)	n/a
(100,000 to 150,000kg)	9,000m	(29,528ft)	7:13.62
	12,000m	(39,370ft)	10:14.80

Cherokee Rose nose art on KC-135R 62-3554 was painted by Ruth Glisson, wife of Captain David Glisson, aircraft commander on one of the record-setting flights. *Photo by Bruce Radebaugh*

representative, Lieutenant Colonel Ira S Paul, III, from the 19th AREFW was aboard each flight as the safety observer.

Class C-1.M (99,206 to 132,275 lb – 45,000 to 60,000kg): Captain David Glisson (aircraft commander), 1st Lieutenant Scott Neumann (pilot), Captain Marc Moss (navigator) and Staff Sergeant Randy Seip (boom operator) from the 19th AREFW demolished records set in 1981 by a Soviet Yak-42 *Clobber*.

Class C-1.N (132,275 to 176,366 lb – 60,000 to 80,000kg): Major Stan Yarbough (aircraft commander), 1st Lieutenant Don Colbacchini (pilot), 1st Lieutenant Dave Wesinand (navigator), and Staff Sergeant Dave Passey (boom operator) from the 340th AREFW at Altus AFB.

Class C-1.O (176,366 to 220,458 lb – 80,000 to 100,000kg): Captain Robert Locke (aircraft commander), Captain Steve Wabrowetz (pilot), Captain Mike Cloyd (navigator), and Staff Sergeant Jim Hackworth (boom operator) from the 319th BW from Grand Forks AFB.

Class C-1.P (220,458 to 330,687 lb – 100,000 to 150,000kg): Major Rod Bell (aircraft commander), Captain Jim Melancon (pilot), Captain Julie Keck (navigator), and Master Sergeant Stan Sears (boom operator) from the 384th BW at McConnell AFB.

KC-135A (serial unknown)   24th September 1958

This KC-135A was assigned to the 99th AREFS, 4050th AREFW at Westover AFB, and was crewed by Captain William H Howell (aircraft commander), Lieutenant James E Freel (co-pilot), an unidentified navigator, boom operator and an observer. They established a world weight-lifting record by lifting a payload of 78,089.5 lb (35,421kg) of nails, concrete blocks, and steel plate to an altitude of 6,561ft (2,000m). The previous record (44,214 lb – 20,055kg) was set on 6th September 1958, by a Soviet Tu-104A *Camel*.

C-135A (serial not known)   11th January 1962

During exercise LONG THRUST II, a MATS C-135A flew non-stop from Fort Lewis, WA, to Rhine-Main AB, West Germany, a distance of 5,100 miles, (8,207km) in ten hours, ten minutes to set unofficial time and distance records. On board were 73 members of the 4th Infantry Division. Captain Harold L Neff commanded the flight, along with crewmembers Captain Veryl I Coulter (first pilot), Major George C Schwessinger (second pilot), Captain Spencer L Nichols and 1st Lieutenant John T Steves (navigators), Staff Sergeant James H Biggie (flight engineer), and Airman First Class Hugh F Carey (loadmaster).

C-135B (serial unknown)   1st May 1962

The first C-135B medical evacuation (medevac) flight from Yokota AB to Travis AFB set a new 'jet air ambulance' record of 5,148 miles (8,284km) in nine hours, seven minutes. The aircraft carried 38 military patients, including 16 on litters. C-135B flights saved 27 hours flying time between the Orient and US hospitals for American military personnel and their dependent patients. Although this first flight was non-stop, subsequent flights landed en route at Hickam AFB to discharge or pick up patients from Hawaiian hospitals. In addition to the passengers, the C-135B carried senior Air Force, Army, and Navy surgeons general. The flight was commanded by Major General Glen R Birchard, WESTAF commander, assisted by first pilot Lieutenant Colonel William L Brinson, squadron commander of the 44th ATS, 1501st ATW at Travis AFB.

C-135B (serial unknown)   **October 1962**

Returning from Operation NEW TAPE, the deployment of Swedish United Nations peacekeeping troops to the Congo, a C-135B set an unofficial record for its 6,900 mile (11,104km) non-stop flight from Leopoldville, Republic of Congo, to McGuire AFB in 12 hours, 54 minutes. The aircraft carried no cargo or troops. Lieutenant Colonel Wallace G Matthews, commander of the 40th ATS, 1611th ATW at McGuire AFB was the aircraft commander. His crew included Captain Gary Weitzel (first pilot), 1st Lieutenant Anthony J Burshnick (second pilot), Captain Seymour Freidman and 2nd Lieutenant David C Nelson (navigators), Master Sergeant Walter E Stewart (flight engineer), and Staff Sergeant Robert E Briles and Technical Sergeant Charles S Smith (loadmasters).

C-135B (serial unknown)   **20th-21st February 1963**

MATS added an unofficial record for the 'longest non-stop flight ever made by a transport aircraft' when a C-135B flew from Clark AB in the Philippines to McGuire AFB, a distance of 9,868 miles (15,880km) in 15 hours, 22 minutes.25 Although this distance was less than that set in Operation JET STREAM, that record was made in a 'jet tanker' rather than a 'transport aircraft', a subtle distinction lost on more than a few observers. The C-135B benefitted from tail winds as high as 228mph (366km/h), allowing it to overfly its normal stopping point at Travis AFB. MATS officials 'hailed the flight as evidence of US ability to swiftly airlift [sic] troops or defense materials anytime, anyplace'.

The aircraft, assigned to the 1611th ATW at McGuire AFB, was under the command of Captain Joseph A Yovin. Other crewmembers included Captain Robert L Lapenta (first pilot), 1st Lieutenant Robert S Cheney, Jr (second pilot), 1st Lieutenant Paul Mankowich and 1st Lieutenant Thomas W Connell (navigators), Technical Sergeant James W Tobias and Technical Sergeant Henry W Harrison (flight engineers), Technical Sergeant Donald W Smith (loadmaster), and Staff Sergeant Howard R Lau (flight traffic specialist).

NAMED AWARDS FOR UNITS AND CREWS

The Cullen Trophy

The Paul T. Cullen Trophy, which was inactive from 1957 through 1970, is in memory of a leading photo-reconnaissance authority killed in a 1951 crash of a Douglas C-124 Globemaster II. The award is presented to the unit that contributes the most to the Air Force's PHOTINT and SIGINT efforts. Units awarded the Cullen trophy operated or supported RC-135s or KC-135Qs as part of Lockheed SR-71 missions.

1991 9th Wing, Beale AFB, CA – KC-135Q support for U-2Rs
1990 Awarded to a unit which did not operate or support RC-135s or SR-71/KC-135Qs
1989 Awarded to a unit which did not operate or support RC-135s or SR-71/KC-135Qs
1988 55th SRW, Offutt AFB, NE – RC-135
1987 9th SRW, Beale AFB, CA – SR-71/KC-135Q
1986 9th SRW, Beale AFB, CA – SR-71/KC-135Q
1985 9th SRW, Beale AFB, CA – SR-71/KC-135Q
1984 55th SRW, Offutt AFB, NE – RC-135
1983 6th SW, Eielson AFB, AK – RC-135
1982 306th SW, RAF Mildenhall, England – SR-71/KC-135Q and RC-135 support
1981 922nd SS, Hellenikon AB, Greece – RC-135 support
1980 9th SRW, Beale AFB, CA – SR-71/KC-135Q
1979 55th SRW, Offutt AFB, NE – RC-135
1978 6th SW, Eielson AFB, AK – RC-135
1977 9th SRW, Beale AFB, CA – SR-71/KC-135Q
1976 306th SW, Ramstein AB, FRG – SR-71/ KC-135Q and RC-135 support
1975 55th SRW, Offutt AFB, NE – RC-135
1974 9th SRW, Beale AFB, CA – SR-71/KC-135Q
1973 6th SW, Eielson AFB, AK – RC-135
1972 Awarded to a unit which did not operate or support RC-135s or SR-71/KC-135Qs
1971 55th SRW, Offutt AFB, NE – RC-135
1970 82nd SRS, 376th SW, Kadena AB, Okinawa – RC-135

The Holloway Trophy

The Bruce K Holloway Trophy is named after a former CINCSAC. Prior to 1976 it was known as the 'Navigation Trophy'. After 1976 it was awarded to the tanker unit that compiled the most points during the navigation phase of SAC's PROUD SHIELD competition (formerly known as 'Bomb Comp').

1991 Competition not held due to DESERT STORM
1990 Competition not held due to DESERT SHIELD
1989 91st AREFS, 301st AREFW, Malmstrom AFB, MT – KC-135R
1988 42nd BW, Loring AFB, ME – KC-135A
1987 ANG 'White Team' (191st AREFS, 151st AREFG, Utah ANG, Salt Lake City IAP, UT, and 197th AREFS, 161st AREFG, Arizona ANG, Phoenix IAP, AZ) – KC-135E
1986 7th AREFS, 7th BW, Carswell AFB, TX – KC-135A
1985 336th AREFS, 452nd AREFW (AFRES), March AFB, CA – KC-135E
1984 9th SRW, Beale AFB, CA – KC-135Q
1983 336th AREFS, 452nd AREFW (AREFS), March AFB, CA – KC-135E
1982 509th AREFS, 509th BW, Pease AFB, NH – KC-135A
1981 92nd BW, Fairchild AFB, WA – KC-135A
1980 305th AREFW, Grissom AFB, IN – KC-135A, KC-135D, EC-135G and EC-135L
1979 133rd AREFS, 157th AREFG, (New Hampshire ANG) Pease AFB, NH – KC-135A
1978 924th AREFS, 93rd BW, Castle AFB, CA – KC-135A
1977 380th BW, Plattsburgh AFB, NY – KC-135A

The Hoyt Award

The Air Force Association's Brigadier General Ross G. Hoyt Award is an annual award presented to the unit which executed the Air Force's most meritorious air refueling mission of the year. (Only awards given to KC-135 units are listed)

2015 The crew of *Elite 60*, 350th and 384th ARS, 22nd ARW, McConnell AFB, KS
2012 The crew of *Blue 32*, 351st ARS, 22nd ARW, McConnell AFB, KS
2001 The crew of *Cacti 02*, 349th ARS, 22nd ARW, McConnell AFB, KS
1998 The crew of *Mazda 85*, 911th ARS, 319th ARW, Grand Forks AFB, ND
1997 A crew from the 909th ARS, 18th Wing, Kadena AB, Japan
1996 A crew from the 384th ARS, 22nd ARW, McConnell AFB, KS
1995 A crew from the 905th ARS, 319th ARW, Grand Forks AFB, ND
1994 A crew from the 380th OG, Plattsburgh AFB, NY

The Mackay Trophy

The Mackay Trophy is the oldest aerial achievement award intended exclusively for members of the United States Air Force. It was established in 1912 by Clarence H Mackay, a wealthy industrialist, philanthropist, communications pioneer, and aviation enthusiast. In 1922 the National Aeronautic Association began sponsoring the award, which is awarded annually for the 'most meritorious flight of the year' by an Air Force person, persons, or organisation, with preference given to individuals.

1967 – A 902nd AREFS, 70th BW, Clinton-Sherman AFB KC-135A crew commanded by Major John H Casteel (including Captain Dean L Hoar, [co-pilot] Captain Richard L. Trail [navigator], and Master Sergeant Nathan C Campbell, boom operator) was the first KC-135 crew to receive the Mackay Trophy. Their drogue-equipped KC-135A 60-0329 refueled two USAF F-104 Starfighters and six Navy aircraft during the sortie. At one point the KC-135A refueled a Navy Douglas KA-3 Skywarrior tanker that was simultaneously refueling a Navy Vought F-8 Crusader fighter. This was the first recorded case of a triple refueling involving a KC-135 in a combat situation. From May 1972-May 1974, Major Casteel served as the aircraft commander on *Casey 01* 57-2589 for CINCSAC General John C Meyer.

KC-135A 60-0329 from the first Mackay Trophy flight visits Offutt AFB in May 1981. *Photo via Brian Rogers*

1983 – On 5th September 1983, KC-135A 62-3503 from the 42nd BW at Loring AFB participated in a CRESTED CAP I F-4E trans-Atlantic deployment. One of the Phantoms suffered reduced power in one engine and diverted to Gander International Airport, Newfoundland, Canada, a distance of over 500 miles (804km). Accompanied by the KC-135A, the F-4E soon had to shut down the bad engine and reduce power on the remaining engine, causing the F-4E to lose nearly 20,000ft (6,096m) of altitude and considerable airspeed. Through four air refuelings, the KC-135A gave the F-4E enough fuel to get it to Gander, despite descending to altitudes as low as 2,000ft (609m) above the ocean. At times the KC-135 actually towed the F-4E with the air refueling boom, a difficult and dangerous procedure. For meritorious action, crew E-115, commanded by Captain Robert J Goodman (including Capt Michael R Clover, copilot; 1st Lieutenant Karol R Wojcikoski, navigator; and Staff Sergeant Douglas D Simmons, boom operator), was awarded the 1983 Mackay Trophy.

1985 – KC-135A 61-0266 from the 97th BW at Blytheville AFB was unable to lower its nose landing gear. Following numerous unsuccessful attempts to extend the nose gear, the tanker reverse air refueled from an EC-135 flown by a crew assigned to the 1st Combat Evaluation Group (1CEVG) based at Barksdale AFB. Fuel onload for the KC-135 was limited to approximately 8,000 lb (3,628.7kg) at a time due to centre-of-gravity restrictions, requiring an air refueling nearly every 20 minutes. The EC-135 was relieved by a KC-10, which itself ran low on fuel. The 97th BW strip alert KC-135A launched to refuel the KC-10, which continued to reverse refuel the emergency KC-135. After nearly 13 hours airborne and with no success in lowering the stuck nose gear, the crew completed a nose gear up landing with minimal damage to the aircraft. For his superior performance, aircraft commander Lieutenant Colonel David E Faught was named the recipient of the 1985 Mackay Trophy. Faught and pilot Captain Robert M Sauers were nominated for the Distinguished Flying Cross, while the other crewmembers (Captains Stephen Wolborsky, Walter Price, and Russell S Cochran, 1st Lieutenant Darrell J Pratt, and Master Sergeants Larry B Burrus and Jay Wilson), as well as the crew of the strip alert tanker, received the Air Medal.

KC-135 Tanker Support
for Other Mackay Trophy Recipients
Thanks to the jet-powered KC-135 tanker, meritorious flights which garnered the Mackay trophy increasingly benefitted from aerial refueling to achieve longer distances or duration as part of power projection missions, combat sorties, or international logistics.

1961 – On 26th May 1961, en route from Carswell AFB to the Paris Airshow, 43rd BW B-58A 59-2451 *The Firefly* established the New York-to-Paris speed record and the Washington DC-to-Paris speed record (beating an unofficial record set by a Boeing 707).

1962 – On 5th March 1962, 43rd BW B-58A 59-2458 *Cowtown Hustler* established three transcontinental speed records for Los Angeles-to-New York, New York-to-Los Angeles, and round trip. Operation HEAT RISE, which also won the 1962 Bendix Trophy, required three in-flight refuelings from KC-135As.

1965 – YF-12A 60-6936 set three world absolute and Class records for speed during three separate flights on 1st March 1965. The fastest of these was over 15nm/25km straight course at 2,070.102 mph (3,352 kph).

1969 – The 49th TFW received the Mackay Trophy for its deployment of 72 F-4D Phantom IIs from Spangdahlem AB, West Germany, to Holloman AFB, NM, without a single abort. KC-135As provided 504 successful air-to-air refuelings on the 5,000nm (8,046km) trip.

1971 – On 26th April 1971, SR-71A 61-7968 completed a 10.5-hour flight, covering 15,000nm (27,780km) at speeds over Mach 3 and altitudes above 80,000ft (24,384m). The flight required five refuelings by KC-135Qs. The SR-71 crew of Lieutenant Colonel Tom Estes and Major Dewain Vick also received the 1972 Harmon International Trophy for the flight. Far from being a publicity stunt, this flight validated the ability of the SR-71A to fly long-duration operation missions, culminating in the first of nine GIANT REACH combat reconnaissance missions over the Middle East, lasting up to 11 hours and requiring six aerial refuelings apiece.

Left: KC-135A 62-3503 from the second Mackay Trophy flight at Carswell AFB on 17th March 1987. Photo by Brian Rogers

Right: KC-135A 61-0266 from the third Mackay Trophy flight at Offutt AFB. Photo by George Cockle

1977 – During June 1977 a C-5A Galaxy crew commanded by Captain David M Sprinkel airlifted a 40-ton superconducting electromagnet and 45 short tons of support equipment from Chicago's O'Hare International Airport to Moscow's Shermetyevo Airport. The magnet was used in a joint Soviet-American energy research program. The flight was the C-5A's longest to date with so large and heavy a payload. The crew was composed of officers and airmen from MAC's 436th MAW and 512th MAW (Reserve Associate) at Dover Air Force Base, DE.

1978 – A C-5A transported a 130,000 lb (58,967kg) outsize cargo load and passengers to Zaire in support of efforts to defeat rebel forces trying to topple the legitimate government of Zaire. Lieutenant Colonel Robert F Schultz and Captain Todd H Hohberger were in command of the 438th MAW C-5.

1980 – In the third such flight conducted by a SAC aircraft, two B-52Hs from the 644th BS, 410th BW, K I Sawyer AFB, Michigan, flew non-stop around the world on 12-14th March 1980 in 42.5 hours. The objective of the flight was to locate and photograph elements of the Soviet Navy in the Arabian Gulf. Each B-52H refueled five times taking on 600,000 lb (272,160kg) of fuel from nine KC-135As.

1995 – Two B-1Bs from the 9th BS, 7th BW at Dyess AFB flew non-stop around the world while dropping practice weapons on target ranges in three different continents (see Sidebar CORONET BAT).

1996 – During September 1996 two B-52Hs from the 96th BS, 2nd BW at Barksdale AFB, operating as *Duke 01* and *Duke 02* from Andersen AB, Guam, fired conventional air-launched cruise missiles (CALCMs) against Iraqi forces threatening Kurdish civilians. This mission – Operation DESERT STRIKE – marked the combat debut of the B-52H.

1997 – MC-130H *Whisk 05,* flown by a crew from the 7th SOS, overcame hostile gunfire, three heavyweight air refuelings, and over 13 hours flying 3,179nm (5,888km) to insert a European survey and assessment team and extract 56 people from the carnage and wanton violence in Brazzaville, Republic of Congo, achieving this goal while on the ground for less than 23 minutes.

2003 – The crew of C-17A *Vijay 10* from the 7th AS, 62nd AW at McChord AFB, WA, led Operation NORTHERN DELAY, the largest formation airdrop since World War II. On 26th March 2003, as part of Operation IRAQI FREEDOM, 15 C-17As completed the safe and successful airdrop of 990 paratroopers and 20 heavy platforms into Bashur Airfield, effectively establishing a second front in Iraq.

2007 – *Panther 11* flight, a four ship of F-16CJ's from the 13th Expeditionary Fighter Squadron, 332nd Expeditionary Operations Group, 332nd Air Expeditionary Wing, Balad Air Base, Iraq, conducted a 10.9-hour mission to strike 16 high-value targets within the Tora Bora region of Afghanistan the night of 12th-13th August 2007. After covertly transiting the airspace of six foreign nations, the F-16CJs had a two-minute time-on-target window over 2,100nm (3,889km) from their home base. In the first combat employment of GBU-38 airburst munitions, the flight successfully destroyed 15 entrenched enemy fighting positions clearing the way for ground forces to raid a high-level Taliban meeting. Approaching a dangerously low fuel state, *Panther 11* flight coordinated for supplemental fuel from a residual tanker allowing for the safe return of four F-16CJs to Balad Air Base.

2008 – While flying in support of Operation ENDURING FREEDOM on 13th July 2008, B-1B *Bone 23* (assigned to the 37th Expeditionary Bomb Squadron, 379th Air Expeditionary Wing, al Udeid AB, Qatar) was tasked to support troops in contact at Vehicle Patrol Base Wanat in Afghanistan. Faced with a critical fuel situation, the crew coordinated to move their tanker closer providing more time on station. Within thirty minutes, *Bone 23* accomplished three bomb runs decisively slowing the enemy attack, allowing coalition forces to regroup.

CORONET BAT

Curtis LeMay first flew KC-135A 55-3126 to Buenos Aires in November 1957 to demonstrate the operational capability of American airpower in the face of Soviet ICBM potential. For most observers, however, LONG LEGS was a publicity flight. Some 15 years later, Americans had become jaded by multiple moon-walking missions, the quagmire in Vietnam, and the self-destruction of a president. There was little public interest in notable aviation accomplishments. Military fliers, however, understood the practical applications of record-setting flights and pursued them without expectation of public accolades. In March 1980, for example, two B-52Hs from K I Sawyer AFB, MI, flew around the world non-stop, loitering over the Gulf of Arabia to monitor Soviet naval developments there. Hardly a grandstanding stunt, the flight showed that even without basing rights in a newly anti-American Iran, the United States could still keep tabs on the Soviet presence in the oil rich Straits of Hormuz. Strategic airpower trumped local weakness.

During Operation DESERT STORM, SAC's newest bomber, the B-1B Lancer sat idle as it remained on SIOP alert and suffered from engine problems. With the end of the Cold War and the rise in conventional regional conflicts, it was essential to demonstrate that the B-1 had the

B-1B 85-0047 *Hellion* **at Rhein-Main AB on 21st June 1994.** *Photo by Peter Zastrow*

B-1B 85-0082 *Global Power* **at Edwards AFB on 26th October 2002.** *Photo by Craig Kaston via Stephen Miller*

Table A5-2 CORONET BAT **Air Refueling 2nd-3rd June 1995**

A/R	Time	ARCT (Z)	A/R Block	Tankers	Onload (1,000 lb)
1	Night	0953	18B22	5 KC-135Rs HURON 11-15 OH ANG and 91st ARS, Malmstrom AFB	BAT 01 - 68+102=170 BAT 02 - 68+102=170 BAT 03 - 102+34+34=170
2	Day	1511	18B23	5 KC-135Rs QUID 71-75 92nd ARW TDY to RAF Mildenhall forward deployed to NAS Rota, Spain	BAT 01 - 68+102=170 BAT 02 - 68+102=170 BAT 03 - 102+34+34=170
3	Night	2031	18B22	3 KC-10s BASS 31-33 Deployed to al Dhafra	BAT 01 - 200 BAT 02 - 200
4	Day	0328	15B17	3 KC-10s HURON 41-43 Deployed to Kadena AB Travis AFB Active March AFB Reserve March AFB	BAT 01 - 150+50=200 BAT 02 - 150+50=200
5	Day	0719	15B19	4 KC-135Rs HURON 51-54 Kadena AB	BAT 01 - 100+100=200 BAT 02 - 100+100=200
6	Night	1318	18B22	5 KC-135Rs CHENA 61-64 168th ARS, AK ANG	BAT 01 - 75+75=150 BAT 02 - 75+75=150
				Aircraft Fuel Onload Totals	BAT 01 - 1,090 BAT 02 - 1,090 BAT 03 - 340
				Grand Total Onloaded	**2,520**

same global combat reach with conventional weapons as the B-52. What better way than to repeat the success of a globe-circling mission, replete with practice weapon drops at target ranges on three continents.

During the 2nd-3rd June 1995 CORONET BAT mission, two 9th BS, 7th BW B-1Bs (*Bat 01* 85-0047 *Hellion*, and *Bat 02* 85-0082 *Global Power*) under the command of Lieutenant Colonel Doug Raaberg and Captain Chris Stewart, respectively, flew non-stop from Dyess AFB, TX, to the Pachino Range at Sicily, then onward to the Tori Shima Range south of Japan, and finally to the Utah Test and Training

Range (UTTR) in the United States before landing again at Dyess AFB 36 hours, 13 minutes after takeoff. The B-1s flew the entire route at 0.92 Mach using 100% Military Power, a day-and-a-half of continuous maximum non-afterburner performance. To do so required six aerial refuelings, with each airplane receiving on average 200,000 lb (90,718kg) of fuel during each refueling. Coordinating six different refueling tracks involving 25 tankers from 12 different active duty, ANG, and AFRES units around the world was critical, as failure to 'get the gas' meant the end of the mission (or worse). The first two refuelings also

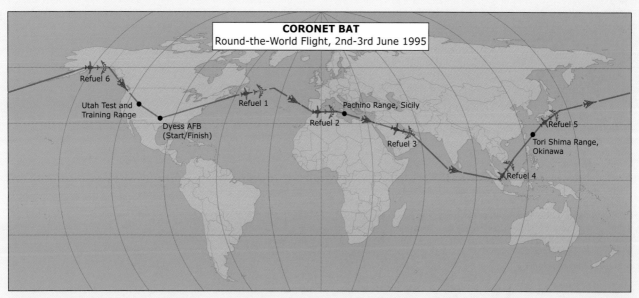

CORONET BAT
Round-the-World Flight, 2nd-3rd June 1995

included an airborne spare B-1, complicating tanker sequencing and fuel onloads. The second air refueling over the Western Mediterranean Sea demonstrated the many challenges of any multi-aircraft refueling, made even more difficult by the operational and timing demands of the round-the-world mission.

Each B-1B planned to arrive at GOLFO, the Air Refueling Initial Point (ARIP), with a minimum of 83,000 lb (37,648kg) of fuel. Should the receiver be unable to complete the air refueling, there were three designated divert bases, with each listed by initial magnetic heading (MH), distance in nautical miles, time en route at 0.72M, and the amount of fuel required to reach the divert airfield. Mission timing was critical in order to set the speed record. The B-1s could not slow down to meet planned ARIP times, nor could they orbit at the ARIP to wait for their tankers. Moreover, the B-1s would fly from the ARIP to the tanker at 570 KIAS, far faster than the normal speed of 310 KIAS, complicating the tanker turn range/offset calculations. During the second air refueling, each B-1B was scheduled to receive a total of 170,000 lb (77,111kg) of fuel from multiple KC-135Rs. The airborne spare, *Bat 03*, had the greatest challenge as it took on 102,000 lb (46,266kg) during its first contact, making it quite heavy and sluggish during the two subsequent contacts. The B-1 crews were unaugmented, which meant a basic crew of two pilots and an offensive and defensive systems operator, so fatigue became a critical issue as the mission progressed, especially for the final refueling above Alaska.

Over the course of the 36-hour mission, the B-1s took on some 2.5 million pounds (1.13 million kilograms) of fuel, hit all of their designated targets (within 15ft/4.6m at Pachino) and set three world records in the C1.Q (330,000-440,000 lb or 149,685-199,581kg) Class. At every refueling, the tankers were on time, ready to offload to the

B-1s with no delay. As one of the B-1 pilots noted, 'The tanker units just couldn't have done any better and they were an extremely important part of our success.' Aside from setting these records, the mission provided the B-1 unit and crews the opportunity to learn significant lessons in airspace management, tanker coordination, diplomatic clearances, fuel planning, weapons employment, and foreign range procedures.

Most importantly, CORONET BAT offered two crucial lessons. First, the mission's success by means of advanced global communications made it appear straightforward, even simple, despite being highly complex and vulnerable

to even minor interruptions. This demonstrates just how lucky earlier round-the-world flights – beginning with the aptly named *Lucky Lady II* in 1949 – were to be successful. Second, the lessons of CORONET BAT were soon applied to 509th BW B-2 global airpower projection missions. Indeed, as the B-2 prepared for non-stop combat missions from Whiteman AFB, MO, to Iraq as part of Operation IRAQI FREEDOM, the 509th BW commander was Brigadier General Raaberg, whose personal experience as *Bat 01* pilot and mission commander contributed directly to the success of those and future B-2 missions. Through it all, KC-135s and KC-10s made it look easy.

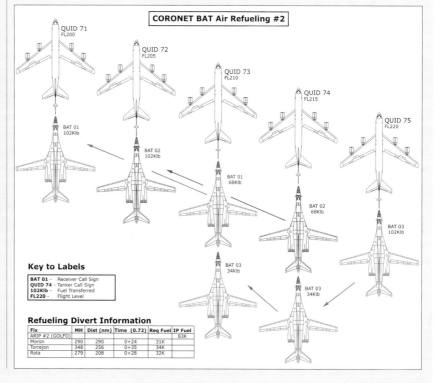

CORONET BAT Air Refueling #2

Key to Labels

BAT 01 -	Receiver Call Sign
QUID 74 -	Tanker Call Sign
102Klb -	Fuel Transferred
FL220 -	Flight Level

Refueling Divert Information

Fix	MH	Dist (nm)	Time (0.72)	Req Fuel	IP Fuel
ARIP #2 (GOLFO)					83K
Moron	290	290	0+24	31K	
Torrejon	348	256	0+35	34K	
Rota	279	208	0+28	32K	

2009 – Operating as *Ironhand 41* flight, Captains Gregory R. Balzhiser and David A. Kroontje conducted four flawless attacks during an eight-hour night mission, flying over 500 miles in enemy-controlled terrain. Their F-16Cs destroyed three Islamic State in Iraq and the Levant (ISIL) blockades, multiple armored vehicles, one observation post, and killed ISIL fighters who were firing upon trapped Yazidi civilians who had fled to Mount Sinjar. *Ironhand 41*'s battle management caused the cessation of ISIL indirect fires on civilians, ended ISIL freedom of movement around Mount Sinjar, facilitated the evacuation corridor by reducing pressure on Peshmerga ground forces, and ultimately saved the lives of 40,000 civilians including women, children, elderly, and the infirm.

2010 – Two F-15Es, call signs *Dude 01 and Dude 02* and flown by Lieutenant Colonel Donald D. Cornwell, Lieutenant Colonel Dylan T. Wells, Captain Leigh P. Larkin, and First Lieutenant Nicholas R. Tsougas, were tasked to support a Combined Joint Special Operations Task Force team surrounded by over 100 enemy fighters in the town of Bala Morgab, Afghanistan, on 6th April 2010. With weather below rescue force launch minimums, *Dude* flight used Terrain Following Radar to execute five 'Show of Force' passes in a valley surrounded by high terrain. When hostilities escalated, the Strike Eagles employed six Joint Direct Attack Munitions (JDAMs), helping kill over 80 Taliban fighters who occupied reinforced positions within the town. Their efforts helped save the lives of approximately 30 coalition troops with no civilian causalities.

The John C Meyer Trophy
Established in 1976 and named after a former CINCSAC. The Meyer Trophy was originally awarded to the 'best F/FB-111A unit in low altitude bombing' during 'Bomb Comp'. Beginning in 1992, the award was reassigned to honor an outstanding air refueling unit.
1993 9th Wing, Beale AFB, CA – KC-135Q
1992 132nd AREFS, 101st AREFW, Maine ANG, Bangor IAP, MA – KC-135E

The O'Malley Award
The Air Force Association General Jerome F. 'Jerry' O'Malley Award is given annually to a USAF reconnaissance crew or unit. It is named in honor of the former CINCTAC who flew the first SR-71 mission over North Vietnam.
2016 Crew of *Python 71*, 55th Wing, Offutt AFB, NE – RC-135 RIVET JOINT
2015 Crew of *Elite 72*, 55th Wing, Offutt AFB, NE – RC-135 RIVET JOINT
2014 Awarded to a unit or crew which did not operate RC-135s
2013 Crews of *Ronin 03* and *Ronin 04*, 45th RS, 55th Wing, Offutt AFB, NE, operating from Kadena AB, Japan – RC-135S COBRA BALL
2012 Crew of *Olive 22*, 55th Wing, Offutt AFB, NE, operating from Souda Bay, Crete – RC-135 RIVET JOINT
2011 Awarded to a unit or crew which did not operate RC-135s
2010 Crew of *Tora 62*, 55th Wing, Offutt AFB, NE, operating from Kadena AB, Japan – RC-135 RIVET JOINT
2009 Crew of *Python 75*, 55th Wing, Offutt AFB, NE – RC-135 RIVET JOINT
2008 Crew of *Python 76*, 55th Wing, Offutt AFB, NE – RC-135 RIVET JOINT
2007 Crew of *Crowe 45*, 55th Wing, Offutt AFB, NE – RC-135 RIVET JOINT
2006 Crew of *Guss 01*, 55th Wing, Offutt AFB, NE – RC-135 RIVET JOINT
2005 Awarded to a unit or crew which did not operate RC-135s
2004 Crew of *Isaac 41*, 55th Wing, Offutt AFB, NE – RC-135 RIVET JOINT
2003 Crew of *Kobie 35*, 55th Wing, Offutt AFB, NE – RC-135 RIVET JOINT
2002 Crew of *Easy 67*, 55th Wing, Offutt AFB, NE – RC-135 RIVET JOINT
2001 Awarded to a unit or crew which did not operate RC-135s
2000 RIVET JOINT crew, 55th Wing, Offutt AFB, NE – RC-135
1999 RIVET JOINT crew, 55th Wing, Offutt AFB, NE – RC-135
1998 RIVET JOINT crew, 55th Wing, Offutt AFB, NE – RC-135
1997 COBRA BALL crew S-01/S-101, 45th RS, 55th Wing, Offutt AFB, NE – RC-135S
1996 COBRA BALL crew, 45th RS, 55th Wing, Offutt AFB, NE – RC-135S
1995 COBRA BALL crew, 45th RS, 55th Wing, Offutt AFB, NE – RC-135S
1994 RIVET JOINT crew, 55th Wing, Offutt AFB, NE – RC-135
1993 RIVET JOINT crew, 55th Wing, Offutt AFB, NE – RC-135
1992 Awarded to a unit or crew which did not operate RC-135s
1991 Awarded to a unit or crew which did not operate RC-135s
1990 COBRA EYE crew S-02/R-18, 24th SRS, 6th SRW, Eielson AFB, AK – RC-135X
1989 Awarded to a unit or crew which did not operate RC-135s
1988 Awarded to a unit or crew which did not operate RC-135s
1987 Awarded to a unit or crew which did not operate RC-135s
1986 Awarded to a unit or crew which did not operate RC-135s
1985 Awarded to a unit or crew which did not operate RC-135s

The Saunders Trophy
First presented in 1960, the Donald W Saunders award is given to the best air refueling squadron participating in SAC's 'Proud Shield' competition. The award honors the 57th Air Division commander killed during the 1958 TOP SAIL transatlantic speed record attempt. From 1963 through 1966 and in 1969, tanker squadrons did not participate in a formal competition. Award of the trophy in these years was based upon the unit's performance in the preceding year.
1993 305th AREFW, Grissom AFB, IN – KC-135R
1992 Recipient not identified
1991 Competition not held due to DESERT STORM
1990 Competition not held due to DESERT SHIELD
1989 384th AREFS, 384th BW, McConnell AFB, KS – KC-135R
1988 42nd BW, Loring AFB, ME – KC-135A
1987 314th AREFS, 940th AREFG (AFRES), Mather AFB, CA – KC-135E
1986 92nd BW, Fairchild AFB, WA – KC-135A
1985 336th AREFS, 452nd AREFW (AFRES), March AFB, CA – KC-135E
1984 380th BW, Plattsburgh AFB, NY – KC-135A
1983 117th AREFS, 190th AREFG (Kansas ANG), Topeka, KS – KC-135E
1982 509th AREFS, 509th BW, Pease AFB, NH – KC-135A
1981 920th AREFS, 379th BW, Wurtsmith AFB, MI – KC-135A
1980 384th AREFW, McConnell AFB, KS – KC-135A
1979 380th BW, Plattsburgh AFB, NY – KC-135A
1978 28th AREFS, 28th BW, Ellsworth AFB, SD – KC-135A
1977 384th AREFW, McConnell AFB, KS – KC-135A
1976 92nd BW, Fairchild AFB, WA – KC-135A
1975 Not awarded
1974 911th AREFS, 68th BW, Seymour Johnson AFB, NC – KC-135A
1973 Not awarded
1972 Not awarded
1971 11th AREFS (19th AD), Altus AFB, OK – KC-135A
1970 11th AREFS (19th AD), Altus AFB, OK – KC-135A
1969 919th AFRES, 306th BW, McCoy AFB, FL – KC-135A
1968 Not awarded
1967 Not awarded
1966 906th AREFS, 450th BW, Minot AFB, ND – KC-135A
1965 922nd AREFS, 17th BW, Wright-Patterson AFB, OH – KC-135A
1964 42nd AREFS, 42nd BW, Loring AFB, ME – KC-135A
1963 46th AREFS, 410th BW, K I Sawyer AFB, MI – KC-135A
1962 Not awarded
1961 915th AREFS, 72nd BW, Ramey AB, PR – KC-135A
1960 Awarded to a unit which did not operate KC-135s

The Schilling Award
The Air Force Association David C Schilling award is given annually for the most outstanding contribution to the nation's defense in the field of manned flight in the atmosphere or space. (Only awards given to '135 units are listed)
2013 93rd ARS, Fairchild AFB, WA – KC-135R/T
2008 906th ARS, Grand Forks AFB, ND – KC-135R
1982 24th SRS, Eielson AFB, AK – RC-135S

The Senter Award
Established in 1956 in honor of Major General William O Senter, Commander, Air Weather Service, 1950-1954. Presented yearly to the Weather Reconnaissance Squadron (WRS) with the highest overall effectiveness rating. (Only awards given to WC-135 units are listed)
1970 55th WRS, 9th WRW, McClellan AFB, CA
1969 56th WRS, 9th WRW, Yokota AB, Japan
1966 56th WRS, 9th WRW, Yokota AB, Japan

The Spaatz Trophy
In appreciation of SAC's tanker support of TAC's fighters, TAC created the General Carl 'Tooey' Spaatz Award on 4th September 1975. The award honors a pioneer in aerial refueling and the first Air Force Chief of Staff, and was presented to the best air refueling unit in SAC, later AMC.
2015 349th ARS, 22nd ARW, McConnell AFB, KS – KC-135R
2014 349th ARS, 22nd ARW, McConnell AFB, KS – KC-135R
2013 351st ARS, 100th ARW, RAF Mildenhall, UK – KC-135R
2012 351st ARS, 100th ARW, RAF Mildenhall, UK – KC-135R
2011 384th ARS, 22nd ARW, McConnell AFB, KS – KC-135R
2010 349th ARS, 22nd ARW, McConnell AFB, KS – KC-135R

2009 911th ARS, 6th OG, Seymour Johnson AFB, NC – KC-135R/T
2008 349th ARS, 22nd ARW, McConnell AFB, KS – KC-135R
2007 912th ARS, 319th ARW, Grand Forks, ND – KC-135R
2006 384th ARS, 22nd ARW, McConnell AFB, KS – KC-135R
2005 Awarded to a unit which did not operate KC-135s
2004 906th ARS, 319th ARW, Grand Forks, ND – KC-135R
2003 384th ARS, 22nd ARW, McConnell AFB, KS – KC-135R
2002 Awarded to a unit which did not operate KC-135s
2001 Awarded to a unit which did not operate KC-135s
2000 99th ARS, 19th ARW, Robins AFB, GA – KC-135R
1999 99th ARS, 19th ARW, Robins AFB, GA – KC-135R
1998 99th ARS, 19th ARW, Robins AFB, GA – KC-135R
1997 319th ARW, Grand Forks, ND – KC-135R
1996 911th ARS, 319th ARW, Grand Forks, ND – KC-135R
1995 911th ARS, 319th ARW, Grand Forks, ND – KC-135R
1994 384th ARS, 22nd ARW, McConnell AFB, KS – KC-135R
1993 9th ARS, 22nd ARW, March AFB – KC-135A
1992 Not awarded
1991 133rd AREFS, 157th AREFG, New Hampshire ANG, Pease AFB, NH – KC-135E
1990 91st AREFS, 301st AREFW, Malmstrom AFB, MT – KC-135R
1989 Awarded to a unit which did not operate KC-135s
1988 909th AREFS, 376th SW, Kadena AB, Okinawa – KC-135A, KC-135Q
1987 Awarded to a unit which did not operate KC-135s
1986 43rd AREFS, 92nd BW, Fairchild AFB, WA – KC-135A
1985 906th AREFS, 5th BW, Minot AFB, ND – KC-135A
1984 906th AREFS, 5th BW, Minot AFB, ND – KC-135A
1983 407th AREFS, 42nd BW, Loring AFB, ME – KC-135A
1982 46th AREFS, 410th BW, K I Sawyer AFB, MI – KC-135A
1981 305th AREFS, 305th AREFW, Grissom AFB, IN – KC-135A, KC-135D
1980 336th AREFS, 452nd AREFW, (AFRES) March AFB, CA – KC-135A
1979 916th AREFS, 307th AREFG, Travis AFB, CA – KC-135A
1978 912th AREFS, 19th BW, Robins AFB, GA – KC-135A
1977 306th SW, Ramstein AB, FRG – KC-135A
1976 41st AREFS, 416th BW, Griffiss AFB, NY – KC-135A
1975 22nd AREFS, 22nd BW, March AFB, CA – KC-135A, and 11thAREFS, 19th AD, Altus AFB, OK – KC-135A
(The Spaatz Trophy was awarded twice in 1975: First to the 11th AREFS for its performance during January-June 1975, and then to the 22nd AREFS for its performance during July-December 1975)

The Kolligian Trophy

The Koren Kolligian Trophy, established in 1958, recognizes outstanding feats of airmanship by aircrew members who by extraordinary skill, exceptional alertness, ingenuity or proficiency, averted accidents or minimized the seriousness of the accidents in terms of injury, loss of life, aircraft damage or property damage.

1970 – Major Henry M. Dyches, Jr, for his outstanding feat of airmanship while flying a WC-135B at Yokota AB, Japan, 7th July 1969. During takeoff roll, a mechanical failure caused the flight controls to bind so that, at rotation speed, the aircraft could not be rotated to takeoff attitude. With the use of only elevator trim control, a successful takeoff was accomplished at the runway overrun. By expertly utilizing available trim, differential spoilers, and throttle control, Major Dyches executed a successful emergency landing in minimum weather conditions, averting a major catastrophe that would have taken the lives of many civilians residing near the airfield.

The Yates Award

This award was established in 1956 in honor of Major General Donald N. Yates, Commander, Air Weather Service, 1945-1950. Given yearly to the AWS reconnaissance aircrew with the most consistent record of excellence in the performance of weather reconnaissance flights. (Only awards given to WC-135 crew are listed)

1971 Captain Edgar A. Gideons, 55th WRS, 9th WRW, McClellan AFB, CA
1970 Captain John W. Pavone, 55th WRS, 9th WRW, McClellan AFB, CA
1969 Captain Lawrence B. Dillehay, 56th WRS, 9th WRW, Yokota AB, Japan
1968 Major Charles A. Erni, 55th WRS, 9th WRW, McClellan AFB, CA

BOMBING AND NAVIGATION COMPETITION AWARDS

In addition to the Holloway and Saunders Trophies, other awards have been presented to Boeing KC-135 units and crews participating in 'Bomb Comp'. Following the 1st June 1992 absorption of most KC-135 tanker units into AMC, some former SAC competitions and awards were incorporated into 'Airlift Rodeo'.

Best Tanker Crew – Navigation and Air Refueling
1961 Crew J-20, 911th AREFS, 4241st SW, Seymour Johnson AFB, NC – KC-135A

Best KC-135 Unit
1961 915th AREFS, 72nd BW, Ramey AFB, PR – KC-135A
1960 96th AREFS, 11th BW, Altus AFB, OK – KC-135A
1959 917th AREFS, 95th BW, Biggs AFB, TX – KC-135A

Best KC-135 Crew in 'Airlift Rodeo'
1993 305th AREFS, 305th AREFW, Grissom AFB, IN – KC-135R

Best KC-135 Crew
1991 Competition not held due to DESERT STORM
1990 Competition not held due to DESERT SHIELD
1989 Crew R-019, 38th SRS, 55th SRW, Offutt AFB, NE – RC-135
1988 Crew IT-05, 93rd AREFS, 93rd BW, Castle AFB, CA – KC-135
1987 Crew R-015, 336th AREFS, 452nd AREFW (AFRES) March AFB, CA – KC-135E
1986 Crew S-152, 92nd BW, Fairchild AFB, WA – KC-135A
1985 Crew S-102, 92nd BW, Fairchild AFB, WA – KC-135A
1984 Crew E-118, 906th AREFS, 5th BW, Minot AFB, ND – KC-135A
1983 Crew E-125, 9th SRW, Beale AFB, CA – KC-135Q
1982 Crew S-121, 509th AREFS, 509th BW, Pease AFB, NH – KC-135A
1981 Crew S-101, 904th AREFS, 320th BW, Mather AFB, CA – KC-135A
1980 Crew E-108, 384th AREFW, McConnell AFB, KS – KC-135A
1979 Crew S-152, 380th BW, Plattsburgh AFB, NY – KC-135A
1978 Crew R-113, 924th AREFS, 93rd BW, Castle AFB, CA – KC-135A
1977 Crew E-108, 384th AREFW, McConnell AFB, KS – KC-135A
1976 Crew R-162, 92nd BW, Fairchild AFB, WA – KC-135A

Best KC-135 Crew—Single Mission
1974 Crew E-113, 911th AREFS, 68th BW, Seymour Johnson AFB, NC KC-135A

Best Tanker Wing in 'Airlift Rodeo'
1993 305th AREFW, Grissom AFB, IN – KC-135R

Best KC-135 Navigation in 'Airlift Rodeo'
1993 917th AREFS, 96th Wing, Dyess AFB, TX – KC-135A

Best KC-135 Aerial Refueling Crew in 'Airlift Rodeo'
1993 305th AREFS, 305th AREFW, Grissom AFB, IN – KC-135R

Perhaps the most unusual 'record' for a KC-135 is that of Mark Kirisch. On 1st July 2011, Kirisch pulled 97th AMW KC-135R 62-3584 at an air show at Battle Creek AP, MI. The airplane weighed in at 140,000 lb (63,503kg) compared to Kirisch's 310 lb (22 stone/141kg). *USAF photo*

Glossary

AABNCP	Advanced Airborne Command Post	ALL	Airborne Laser Laboratory		Bomb damage assessment
AAF	Army Air Force	ALOTS	Airborne Lightweight Optical Tracking System	BDR	Battle damage repair
AACS	Airborne Astrographic Camera System			BFCS	Ballistic Framing Camera System
AARB	Advanced Air Refueling Boom	ALS	Airlift Squadron	BG	Bombardment Group
AARD	Autonomous Airborne Refueling Demonstration	ALTB	Airborne Laser Test Bed	BMAC	Boeing Military Airplane Company
		AMARC	Aerospace Maintenance and Regeneration Center	BMEWS	Ballistic Missile Early Warning System
AAS	Advanced Avionics System	AMARG	Aerospace Maintenance and Regeneration Group		
AAVS	Aerospace Audio Visual Service			BOA	Broad Ocean Area
AB	Air Base	AMC	Air Materiel Command or Air Mobility Command	BSC	Ballistic Streak Camera
ABCCC	Airborne Battlefield Command, Control and Communications			BuNO	Bureau of Naval Operations
		AMRAAM	Advanced Medium Range Air-to-Air Missile	BW	Bombardment Wing
ABIT	Airborne Imagery Transmission			CAA	Civil Aeronautics Administration
ABL	Airborne laser	AMPSS	Advanced Manned Precision Strike System	CALCM	Conventional air-launched cruise missile
ABW	Air Base Wing				
a/c	Aircraft	AMSA	Advanced Manned Strategic Aircraft	CAOC	Combined Air Operations Center
AC	Aircraft commander or alternating current	ANG	Air National Guard	CAP	Combat air patrol
		ANGB	Air National Guard Base	CASF	Composite Air Strike Force
ACC	Air Combat Command	ANP	Aircraft Nuclear Propulsion	CAST	Coherent Automatic Signal Tracking
ACDS	Acoustic Crack Detection System	AOA	Airborne Optical Adjunct	CAStLE	Center for Aircraft Structural Life Extension
ACE	Accelerated Co-pilot Enrichment or Aviation Career Enhancement	AP	Airport		
		APCS	Air Photographic and Charting Service	CBO	Congressional Budget Office
ACW	Airborne Control Wing	APMS	Advanced Power Measurement System	CCK	Ching Chuan Kang AB, Taiwan
ACCS	Airborne Command and Control Squadron	APS	Atmospheric Properties Study	CENTAF	Central Command Air Force
		APU	Auxiliary power unit	CENTAUX	Central Auxiliary Command Post
ACCW	Airborne Command and Control Wing	ARCP	Air refueling control point	CENTCOM	Central Command
ACGS	Aerospace Cartographic and Geodetic Service	ARCT	Air refueling control time	CEP	*Centre d'Experimentation du Pacifique* or
		ARDC	Air Research and Development Command		Circular error probable
ACGSq	Aerospace Cartographic and Geodetic Squadron			CIA	Central Intelligence Agency
		ARE	Atmospheric Research Equipment	CIAP	Climatic Impact Assessment Program
ACM	Advanced Cruise Missile	AREFG	Air Refueling Group	CID	Controlled Impact Demonstration
ACP	Airborne command post	AREFS	Air Refueling Squadron	CINC	Commander-in-Chief
ACRP	Airborne Communication Reconnaissance Platform	AREFW	Air Refueling Wing	CINCEUR	Commander-in-Chief, European Command
		ARG	Air Refueling Group		
AD	Air Division	ARIA	Apollo Range Instrumented Aircraft later	CINCLANT	Commander-in-Chief, Atlantic Command
ADA	Airborne data automation				
ADC	Air Defense Command		Advanced Range Instrumented Aircraft	CINCPAC	Commander-in-Chief, Pacific Command
ADCS	Air Deployment Control Squadron	ARIS	Apollo Range Instrumented Ship	CINCPACAF	Commander-in-Chief, Pacific Air Force
ADI	Attitude direction indicator	ARIP	Air refueling initial point		
ADIZ	Air Defense Identification Zone	ARPA	Advanced Research Projects Agency	CINCSAC	Commander-in-Chief, Strategic Air Command
AEAO	Airborne Emergency Action Officer	ARR	Air refueling receiver		
AEC	Atomic Energy Commission	ARS	Air Refueling Squadron	CINCTAC	Commander in Chief, Tactical Air Command
AEELS	Automatic ELINT Emitter Locating System	ART	Air refuelable tanker		
		ARW	Air Refueling Wing	CMMCA	Cruise Missile Mission Control Aircraft
AF	Air Force	AS	Airlift Squadron		
AFA	Air Force Academy	AS&CS	Airborne Surveillance and Control System	CNS	Communications, Navigation, and Surveillance
AFAIB	Air Force Accident Investigation Board				
		ASARA	Airborne Sensor and Atmospheric Research Aircraft	CNS/ATM	Communications, Navigation, and Surveillance for Air Traffic Management
AFAL	Air Force Avionics Laboratory				
AFB	Air Force Base	ASC	Aeronautical Systems Center		
AFCRL	Air Force Cambridge Research Laboratory	ASD	Aeronautical Systems Division	CNTBT	Comprehensive Nuclear Test Ban Treaty
		ASDC	Army Strategic Defense Command		
AFCS	Air Force Communications Service	ASEAN	Association of Southeast Asian Nations	COD	Carrier on-board delivery
AFETR	Air Force Eastern Test Range			COIL	Chemical Oxygen Iodine Laser
AFFS	Air Force Security Service	ASIP	Aircraft Structural Integrity Program	CombW	Combat Wing
AFTAC	Air Force Technical Applications Center	ASRP	Aerospace Radio Propagation or Airborne SIGINT Reconnaissance Platform	COMINT	Communications intelligence
				COMMACC	Commander, Air Combat Command
AFFTC	Air Force Flight Test Center			CompG	Composite Group
AFGL	Air Force Geophysics Laboratory	ATB	Advanced Technology Bomber	CompW	Composite Wing
AFHRA	Air Force Historical Research Agency	ATCA	Advanced Tanker/Cargo Aircraft	CONUS	Continental United States
AFIN	Air Force Intelligence	ATF	Advanced Technology Fighter	CoTAM	*Commandement du Transport Aérienne Militaire*
AFMC	Air Force Materiel Command	ATG	Air Transport Group		
AFRC	Air Force Reserve Command	ATS	Air Transport Squadron or Advanced Telemetry System	COTS	Commercial, off-the-shelf
AFRES	Air Force Reserve			CP	Co-pilot
AFS	Air Force Station	ATTF	Alaskan Tanker Task Force	CRAG	Compass Radar And GPS
AFSATCOM	Air Force Satellite Communications	ATW	Air Transport Wing	CSA	Command Support Aircraft
AFSC	Air Force Systems Command	AUSCS	Automatic Signals Classification System	CSD	Constant speed drive
AFSS	Air Force Security Service			CSS	Contrail Suppression System
AFSWC	Air Force Special Weapons Center	AUXCP	Auxiliary Command Post	CSW	Command Support Wing
AFTAC	Air Force Technical Applications Center	AW	Airlift Wing	CTAS	Chrysler Technologies Airborne Systems
		AW&CTS	Airborne Warning & Control Training Squadron		
AFTB	Avionics Flight Test Bed			CTTC	Chanute Technical Training Center
AFWAL	Air Force Wright Aeronautical Laboratory	AW&CW	Airborne Warning and Control Wing	CVR	Cockpit voice recorder
		AWACS	Airborne Warning and Control System	CW	Composite Wing
AFWTR	Air Force Western Test Range	AWS	Air Weather Service	DARMS	Data Annotation/Recording and Mapping System
AIO	Airborne Ionospheric Observatory	BA	*Base Aérienne*		
ALCC	Airborne Launch Control Center	BARCAP	Barrier Combat Air Patrol	DARPA	Defense Advanced Research Projects Agency
ALCS	Airborne Launch Control System	BAS	Bomb Alarm System		
ALCM	Air-launched cruise missile	BDA	Boom drogue adapter or		
ALD	Airlift Division				

DASA	Defense Atomic Support Agency	FOL	Forward operating location	ISIL	Islamic State in Iraq and the Levant
DC	Direct current	FRG	Federal Republic of Germany	ISR	Intelligence, surveillance, and
DCGS	Distributed Common Ground System	FRI	Flight Refuelling, Inc.		reconnaissance
DEFSMAC	Defense Special Missile &	FRL	Flight Refuelling, Ltd.	ISTAR	Intelligence, Surveillance, Target-
	Astronautics Center	FS	Fuselage Station or		Acquisition, and
Det	Detachment		Federal Standard		Reconnaissance
DEW	Distant Early Warning	FSA/CAS	Fuel Savings Advisory/Cockpit	IUS	Inertial Upper Stage
DFRC	Dryden Flight Research Center		Avionics System	JCS	Joint Chiefs of Staff
DIA	Defense Intelligence Agency	FSO	Flight systems operator	JDAM	Joint Direct Attack Munitions
DIRNSA	Director of the National Security	FSTA	Future Strategic Tanker Aircraft	JSC	Johnson Space Center
	Agency	FTD	Foreign Technology Division	JTF	Joint Task Force
DMA	Dangerous Military Activities	FTRG	Fleet Tactical Readiness Group	JTF-8	Joint Task Force 8
DMCCC	Deputy Missile Combat Crew	FTS	Flight Test Squadron	JTIDS	Joint Tactical Information Distribution
	Commander	FMS	Foreign military sales		System
DME	Distance measuring equipment	FVB	Fleet Viability Board	KIAS	Knots indicated airspeed
DMSP	Defense Meteorological Satellite	FW	Fighter Wing	kph	Kilometers per hour
	Program	FY	Fiscal Year	kt	kiloton
DNA	Defense Nuclear Agency	GAO	Government Accountability Office	KVA	Kilovolt-ampere
DNS	Doppler navigation system	GATMS	Global Air Traffic Management	LAAR	Low Altitude Air Refueling
DoA	Department of Agriculture		System	LACE	Laser Airborne Communication
DoD	Department of Defense	GBS	Global Broadcast Satellite		Experiment
DoE	Department of Energy	GDRS	General Directorate of Rear Services	LAIRCM	Large Aircraft Infrared
DoT	Department of Transportation	GEANS	Gimballed Electrostatic Aircraft		Countermeasures
DRI	Denver Research Institute		(Navigation) System	LAMP	Low-Altitude Manned Penetrator
DTRA	Defense Threat Reduction Agency	GFAE	Government-furnished aircraft	LANL	Los Alamos National Laboratory
DUSC	Deep Underground Support Center		equipment	LaRC	Langley Research Center
EADS	European Aeronautic Defense and	gpm	Gallons per minute	LAS	Lockheed Aircraft Systems
	Space Company	GPS	Global positioning satellite	LASL	Los Alamos Scientific Laboratory
EAM	Emergency Action Message	GRV	*Groupe de Ravaitaillement en Vol*	LASERCOM	Laser communications
EART	Emergency Air Refueling Tanker	GTTF	Goose Tanker Task Force	LATS	Large Aperture Tracking System
EARS	Expeditionary Air Refueling Squadron	GWOT	Global War on Terror	LCC	Launch control centers
EASTAF	Eastern Transport Air Force	HALO	High Altitude Learjet Observatory	LF	Low frequency
EASTAUX	East Auxiliary Airborne Command	HARDS	High Altitude Radiation Detection	LIDAR	Light detection and ranging
	Post		System	LLNL	Lawrence Livermore National
EB	*Escadre de Bombardment*	HASP	High Altitude Sampling Program		Laboratory
ECM	Electronic countermeasures	HAWK	Homing All-the-Way Killer	LORAN	Long Range Aid to Navigation
ECP	Engineering change proposal	HAT	Heavy aircraft training	LRC	Langley Research Center
EDA	Excess Defense Articles	HDU	Hose drum unit	LRDP	Long Range Detection Program
EFAS	Engine Failure Assist System	HEL	High energy laser	LRL	Lawrence Radiation Laboratory
EGPWS	Enhanced ground proximity warning	HF	High frequency	LTV	Ling-TEMCO-Vought Company
	system	HIPERNAS	High Precision Navigational System	LWIR	Long-wave infrared
EGT	Exhaust Gas Temperature	HIRAN	High Precision Ranging	MAA	Military Aviation Authority
EHF	Extra-high frequency	HOT	Host Owned Training	MAC	Military Airlift Command
EIR	Expanded Interim [Strut] Repairs	HQ	Headquarters	MAD	Magnetic anomaly detection
ELINT	Electronic Intelligence	HSFS	High Speed Flight Station	MAG	Military Airlift Group
ELT	Emergency locator transmitter	HSI	Horizontal situation indicator	MANPAD	Man-portable air defense missile
EMP	Electromagnetic pulse	HST	Hydrostatic Test fuselage	MAO	Major Attack Option
EPR	Exhaust pressure ratio	HTTF	Howard Tanker Task Force	MAS	Military Airlift Squadron
ERCS	Emergency Rocket Communication	HUMINT	Human intelligence	MASDC	Military Aircraft Storage and Disposal
	System	IAEELS	Improved Automatic ELINT Emitter		Center
ERS	Expeditionary Reconnaissance		Location System	MASINT	Measurement and Signature
	Squadron	IAI	Israel Aircraft Industries		Intelligence
ERSA	Extended Range Strike Aircraft	IAP	International Airport	MATS	Military Air Transport Service or
ERV	*Escadre de Ravaitaillement en Vol*	IARS	Improved Aerial Refueling System		Midcourse Acquisition and Tracking
	[wing] or	IAS	Indicated airspeed		System
	Escadron de Ravaitaillement en Vol	IBO	Instructor boom operator	MatS	Materiel Squadron
	[squadron]	ICAO	International Civil Aviation	MAW	Military Airlift Wing
ESD	Electronic Systems Division		Organization	mb	Millibar
ESTS	*Escadron des soutiens techniques*	ICBM	Intercontinental Ballistic Missile	MCAS	Marine Corps Air Station
	spécialisés	ICNIA	Integrated Communication Navigation	MCCC	Missile Combat Crew Commander
ESI	Electrospace Systems, Inc.		Identification Avionics	MCS	Mapping and Charting Squadron
ESL	Electromagnetic Systems Laboratory	IDG	Integrated drive generator	MCT	Mission Control Team
ETTF	European Tanker Task Force	IED	Improvised explosive device (IED)	MDA	Missile Defense Agency
EVA	Extravehicular activity	IFF	Identification, Friend or Foe	MDS	Mission-Design-Series
EW	Electronic warfare	IFR	Instrument flight rules or	MFD	Multifunction display
EWO	Electronic warfare officer or		In-flight refueling	MHz	Megahertz
	Emergency War Order	IIO	Information integration officer	MIDAUXCP	Mid Auxiliary Command Post
EWP	Emergency War Plan	ILS	Instrument landing system	MIRV	Multiple independently targetable
FAA	Federal Aviation Administration	IMC	Instrument meteorological conditions		reentry vehicle
FAB-T	Family of Advanced Beyond Line-of-	IMINT	Imagery Intelligence	MIT	Massachusetts Institute of Technology
	Sight Terminal	IMT	In-flight maintenance technician	MITO	Minimum-interval takeoff
FACh	*Fuerza Aérea de Chile*	IN	Instructor navigator	MLS	Microwave landing system
FAS	*Force Aérienne Stratégique*	INI	Integrated NAV/SAT Inertial	MoD	Ministry of Defence
FBW	Fighter Bomber Wing		Navigation	MODS	Multiple Object Discriminator System
FDR	Flight data recorder	INF	Intermediate Nuclear Force	MPRS	Multi-point refueling system
FEAF	Far East Air Force	INMARSAT	International Maritime Satellite	MRCS	Medium Resolution Camera System
FEW	Fighter Escort Wing	INS	Inertial Navigation System	MRTT	Multirole Tanker Transport
FEWSG	Fleet Electronic Warfare and Support	IOC	Initial operational capability	MRV	Multiple reentry vehicle
	Group	IP	Instructor pilot	MSBLS	Microwave Scanning Beam Landing
FINDER	Ferret Intelligence Data Evaluator	IR	Infrared		System
FISTA	Flying Infrared Signatures and	IRBM	Intermediate Range Ballistic Missile	MSEWG	Multi-Service Electronic Warfare
	Technology Aircraft	IRCM	Infrared countermeasures (IRCM)		Support Group
FL	Flight level	IRLS	Infrared line scanner	MSTS	Multisource tactical system
FLEP	Fatigue Life Extension Program	IRST	Infrared search-while-tracking	MTBF	Mean time between failure
FLTS	Flight Test Squadron	IS	Intelligence Squadron	MUCELS	Multiple Position Communications
FMS	Flight management system	ISAF	International Security Assistance Force		Emitter Locations System

n/a	Not available
N-ABLE	Non-Proliferation Airborne Laser Experiment
NAA	National Aeronautics Association
NABRE	Narrowband Reachback
NACA	National Advisory Committee for Aeronautics
NAF	Numbered Air Force
NALS	Natural alternative landing sites
NAS	Naval Air Station
NASA	National Aeronautics and Space Administration
NATC	Naval Air Test Center
NATO	North Atlantic Treaty Organization
NCA	National Command Authority
NCAR	National Center for Atmospheric Research
NCCT	Network Centric Collaborative Targeting
NDAA	National Defense Authorization Act
NDB	Non-directional beacon
NDI	Non-destructive testing
NEACP	National Emergency Airborne Command Post
NG	*Nouvelle Génération*
NKAWTG	Nobody Kicks Ass Without Tanker Gas
NMCC	National Military Command Center
NNTRP	National Nuclear Test Readiness Program
NOA	Non-operational aircraft
NRO	National Reconnaissance Office
NS	Naval Station
NSA	National Security Agency
NTM	National technical means
ntu	Not taken up
NUDINT	Nuclear Detonation Intelligence
OAMP	Optical Aerial Measurement Program
OCALC	Oklahoma City Air Logistics Center
OCAMA	Oklahoma City Air Materiel Area
OF	Operational Flight
OMEW	Office of Missile Electronic Warfare
OMS	Organizational Maintenance Squadron
OpOrd	Operational order
OpsG	Operations Group
OPTINT	Optical intelligence
ORI	Operational Readiness Inspection
OS	Operational Squadron
OSD-AT&L	Office of the Undersecretary of Defense – Acquisitions, Technology & Logistics
OSIA	On-Site Inspection Agency
OSINT	Open Source Intelligence
OSMPF	Open Skies Media Processing Facility
OT&E	Operational Test and Evaluation
OTH-B	Over-the-horizon–Backscatter
(P)	Provisional or Proposed
PACAF	Pacific Air Force
PACCS	Post Attack Command and Control System
PARPRO	Peacetime Aerial Reconnaissance Program
PAS	Primary Alerting System
PCA	Polar Cap Absorption
PCN	Processing Control Number
PDI	Pilot director indicator
PDM	Programmed depot maintenance
PHAROS	Photometric and radiometric systems
PHOTINT	Photo Intelligence
PIFAX	Pilot Control Factors
PINS	Palletized Inertial Navigation System
PLF	Palestine Liberation Front
PLO	Palestine Liberation Organization
PMD	Program Management Directive
PMEE	Prime Mission Electronic Equipment
PMS	Photo Mapping Squadron
PMW	Photo Mapping Wing
PPMS	Precision Power Measurement System
PRC	People's Republic of China
PRISM	Primary Sensor Measurement System
psi	Pounds per square inch
PTBT	Partial Test Ban Treaty
PTTF	Pacific Tanker Task Force
QEC	Quick Engine Change
QRC	Quick Reaction Capability
RAAF	Royal Australian Air Force

RADC	Rome Air Development Center
RAE	Royal Aircraft Establishment
RAF	Royal Air Force
RAMP	Radiation Monitoring Program
RCAF	Royal Canadian Air Force
RDJTF	Rapid Deployment Joint Task Force
REAPER	Remote Extended Aircraft Position Enabling Reachback
RF	Radio frequency
RGA	Rotation/Go-Around
RINT	Radiation Intelligence
ROBE	Roll-on Beyond Line of Sight Enhancement
RPV	Remotely piloted vehicle
RS	Reconnaissance Squadron
RSAF	Royal Saudi Air Force or Republic of Singapore Air Force
RTAFB	Royal Thai Air Force Base
RTNAB	Royal Thai Navy Air Base
RTOS	Real-Time Optical System
RTS	Release-to-Service
RV	Re-entry vehicle
RVSM	Reduced vertical separation minima
RW	Reconnaissance Wing
RW&RW	Rescue Weather and Refueling Wing
SA	Saudi Arabia
SAC	Strategic Air Command
SACCS	SAC Control System
SACEUR	Supreme Allied Commander, Europe
SAD	Strategic Aerospace Division
SALT	Strategic Arms Limitation Treaty
SAM	Surface-to-air missile or Special Air Mission
SAO	Selective Attack Option
SAR	Search and Rescue or Synthetic Aperture Radar
SATCOM	Satellite communications
SAW	Strategic Aerospace Wing
SCA	Shuttle Carrier Aircraft
SCACS	Strategic Command Airborne Control System
SDI	Strategic Defense Initiative
SDIO	Strategic Defense Initiative Organization
SEA	Southeast Asia
SEAGA	Selective Employment of Air/Ground Alert
SEARS	Sent ELINT Airborne Receiver System
SECC	Secure Enduring Command Center
SELM	Simulated Electronic Launch-Minuteman
SEMR	Standard Electronics Module Radar
SEX	Solar EXpedition or Solar Eclipse eXpedtion
SF	Support Flight
SGLS	Space Ground Link Subsystem
SHIRAN	S-band high precision ranging
SHF	Super high frequency
SIDS	Stellar Inertial Doppler System
SIGINT	Signals Intelligence
SIOP	Single Integrated Operations Plan
SIRU	Stellar Inertial Reference Unit
SITREP	Situation report
SLAB	Subsonic Low-Altitude Bomber
SLAR	Side-looking airborne radar
SLBM	Sea-launched ballistic missile
SLFCS	Survivable Low Frequency Communications System
SMD	Strategic Missile Division
SMS	Strategic Missile Squadron
SMW	Strategic Missile Wing
SNL	Sandia National Laboratory
SOF	Supervisor of Flying
SOFIA	Stratospheric Observatory for Infrared Astronomy
SOR	Specific Operational Requirement
SPF	Strategic Projection Force
SRF	Strategic Reserve Force
SRO	Sensitive Reconnaissance Operations
SRS	Strategic Reconnaissance Squadron
SRW	Strategic Reconnaissance Wing
SS	Strategic Squadron or Support Squadron
STAR	Scattered-Light Test Airborne Receiver
STDN	Shuttle Tracking Data Net
STOL	Short take-off and landing

STRATCOM	Strategic Command
STRC	Strategic Training Range Complex
STRICOM	Strike Command
STTF	Spanish Tanker Task Force
SUPT	Specialized Undergraduate Pilot Training
SW	Strategic Wing
SWC	Strategic Warfare Center
SYD	Series yaw damper
TAC	Tactical Air Command
TACAN	Tactical aerial navigation
TACC	Tactical Air Control Center
TADIL	Tactical Digital Information Links
TAW	Tactical Airlift Wing
TBM	Theater ballistic missile
TCTO	Time compliant technical order
TDCS	Tactical Deployment Control Squadron
TDL	Tactical digital links
TDY	Temporary duty
TELINT	Telemetry Intelligence
TEMCO	Texas Engineering and Manufacturing Company
TENCAP	Tactical Exploitation of National Capabilities
TESTS	Test Squadron
TFW	Tactical Fighter Wing
TG	Test Group or Tactical Group
THK	*Türk Hava Kuvvetleri* (Turkish Air Force)
TMF	Tail-mounted floodlight
ToA	Time of arrival
TOOS/TASP	Temporary Overmanning of the Operations Staff/Temporary Augmentee Support Program
TPR	Terrain profile recorder
TPS	Test Pilot School
TRAACE	Transport Advanced Avionics and Cockpit Enhancement
TRACALS	Traffic Control and Landing System
TRAP	Terminal Radiation Program
TRIA	Telemetry Range Instrumented Aircraft
TS	Test Squadron
TTF	Tanker Task Force
TW	Test Wing
TWA	Trailing wire antenna
UAV	Unmanned Aerial Vehicle
UCSOT	Undergraduate Combat Systems Officer Training
UHF	Ultra high frequency
UK	United Kingdom
UN	United Nations
US	United States
USAF	United States Air Force
USAFE	United States Air Force, Europe
USCINCEUR	US Commander-in-Chief, Europe
USCINCLANT	US Commander-in-Chief, Atlantic
USCINCPAC	US Commander-in-Chief, Pacific
USIB	United States Intelligence Board
USSR	Union of Soviet Socialist Republics
UTTR	Utah Test and Training Range
VHF	Very high frequency
VIC	Variable Instruction Computer
VIP	Very important person or Very important passenger
VLF	Very low frequency
VMC	Visual meteorological conditions
VOR	Very high frequency omni-directional radio
VFR	Visual flight rules
WADC	Wright Air Development Center
WADD	Wright Aeronautical Development Division
WARP	Wingtip air refueling pod
WESTAF	Western Transport Air Force
WESTAUX	Western Auxiliary Command Post
wfu	Withdrawn from use
Wg	Wing
WGS	Wideband Global Satellite
WMD	Weapons of mass destruction
w/o	Written off
WRS	Weather Reconnaissance Squadron
WRW	Weather Reconnaissance Wing

Index